W9-CUA-715

FOURTH EDITION

Programming iOS 7

Matt Neuburg

Beijing · Cambridge · Farnham · Köln · Sebastopol · Tokyo

Programming iOS 7, Fourth Edition

by Matt Neuburg

Published by O'Reilly Media, Inc., 1005 Gravenstein Highway North, Sebastopol, CA 95472.

O'Reilly books may be purchased for educational, business, or sales promotional use. Online editions are also available for most titles (*http://my.safaribooksonline.com*). For more information, contact our corporate/institutional sales department: (800) 998-9938 or *corporate@oreilly.com*.

Editor: Rachel Roumeliotis
Production Editor: Kristen Brown
Proofreader: O'Reilly Production Services
Indexer: Matt Neuburg

Cover Designer: Randy Comer
Interior Designer: David Futato
Illustrator: Matt Neuburg

May 2011:   First Edition

March 2012:   Second Edition

March 2013:   Third Edition

December 2013:   Fourth Edition

Revision History for the Fourth Edition:

2013-12-09:   First release

See *http://oreilly.com/catalog/errata.csp?isbn=9781449372347* for release details.

ISBN: 978-1-449-37234-7

[LSI]

Table of Contents

Part I.   Views

Part II. Interface

Part III.   Some Frameworks

Part IV.   Final Topics

Preface

Aut lego vel scribo; doceo scrutorve sophian.

—Sedulius Scottus

This book, now in its fourth edition, has grown in size to encompass the growth in its subject, until it can grow no more. The previous editions — *Programming iOS 4* (May 2011), *Programming iOS 5* (March 2012), and *Programming iOS 6* (March 2013) — were approximately 800 pp., 950 pp., and 1150 pp. in length, respectively, not because I had more to say each time, but because Apple, as it added features to iOS 4 to make iOS 5, and to iOS 5 to make iOS 6, had given me more to describe.

Now iOS 7 has come along with even more new features, and drastic action was needed. Accordingly, the book has been ripped violently but neatly in two — neatly, because there was already a perfectly natural place to do the ripping, namely right after the end of what used to be Part III (Chapter 13). There are now *two* books:

- A new book, *iOS 7 Programming Fundamentals*, comprising chapters 1–13 of the earlier books.
- This book, *Programming iOS 7*, comprising chapters 14–40 of the earlier books.

The truth is that this is a division I had wanted to make even before *Programming iOS 4* was published — indeed, before it was even conceived of. My original proposal to O'Reilly Media, back in early 2010, had been for a book to be called *Fundamentals of Cocoa Programming*, intended to cover very much the same material as *iOS 7 Programming Fundamentals* covers now. But the proposal was accepted only on condition that it be extended to cover much more of Cocoa Touch (iOS) programming; so I complied and set to work on this longer project, and later, despite my impassioned pleas in the autumn of 2010, I was unable to persuade the publisher to break up the lengthy manuscript into two: by that time, all the king's horses and all the king's men could no longer crack Humpty Dumpty apart.

The new situation, therefore, is just what I always wanted in the first place — but not quite, because what I most desired was a single book in two volumes. My idea was that the books would have the same title, distinguished as Volume I and Volume II, with successive numbering of pages and chapters: if Volume I ended, say, with Chapter 13 and page 400, then Volume II would start with Chapter 14 and page 401. To this delightfully Victorian extreme, I'm sorry to say, O'Reilly Media were implacably opposed.

Thus, *Programming iOS 7*, though it starts with its own Chapter 1 and page 1, nevertheless still picks up exactly where *iOS 7 Programming Fundamentals* leaves off. They complement and supplement one another. Those who desire a complete grounding in the knowledge needed to begin writing iOS apps with a solid and rigorous understanding of what they are doing and where they are heading will, I hope, obtain both books. At the same time, the two-book architecture should, I believe, render the size and scope of each book individually more acceptable and attractive to more readers.

Those who feel that they know already all there is to know about C, Objective-C, Xcode, and the linguistic and architectural basis of the Cocoa framework, or who are content to pick up such underpinnings as they go along, need no longer (as some in the past have done) complain that the book is occupied with 13 preliminary chapters before the reader starts really writing any significant iOS code, because those 13 chapters have now been abstracted into a separate volume, *iOS 7 Programming Fundamentals*, and this book, *Programming iOS 7*, now begins, like Homer's *Iliad*, in the middle of the story, with the reader jumping with all four feet into views and view controllers, and with a knowledge of the language and the Xcode IDE already presupposed. And if such a reader subsequently changes his or her mind and decides that a thorough grounding in those underpinnings might in fact be desirable, *iOS 7 Programming Fundamentals* will still be available and awaiting study.

Moreover, the existence of *iOS 7 Programming Fundamentals* means that I, as author and teacher, can make the same assumption in this edition about you, as reader and student, that I made in previous editions — namely, that you have a command of the material in that book. If you find yourself mystified by terminology or concepts used in *this* book, then it might be wise to stop reading it and take up *iOS 7 Programming Fundamentals* first! In it, I explain such things as:

- The Objective-C language, starting with C and building up to the object-oriented concepts and mechanics of classes and instances in Objective-C itself.

- Xcode, the world in which all iOS programming ultimately takes place, including what an Xcode project is and how it is transformed into an app, and how to work comfortably and nimbly with Xcode to consult the documentation and to write, navigate, and debug code, as well as how to bring your app through the subsequent stages of running on a device and submission to the App Store. There is also a very important chapter on nibs and the nib editor (Interface Builder), including outlets and actions as well as the mechanics of nib loading. (However, some additional important nib-related topics, such as autolayout constraints and storyboard segues, are discussed in *this* book.)

- The Cocoa Touch framework, which provides important foundational classes and adds linguistic and architectural devices such as categories, protocols, delegation, and notifications, as well as the pervasive responsibilities of memory management, plus key–value coding and key–value observing.

With those basics having been laid down in *iOS 7 Programming Fundamentals*, this book, *Programming iOS 7*, assumes that you already know Objective-C and how to work with Xcode to edit code and nibs, make properties and outlets and actions, and so forth, and proceeds to explain the constituents of practical iOS app construction:

- Part I describes *views*, the fundamental units of an iOS app's interface. Views are what the user can see and touch in an iOS app. To make something appear before the user's eyes, you need a view. To let the user interact with your app, you need a view. This part of the book explains how views are created, arranged, drawn, layered, animated, and touched.

- Part II starts by discussing *view controllers*. Perhaps the most remarkable and important feature of iOS programming, view controllers enable views to come and go coherently within the interface, thus allowing a single-windowed app running on what may be a tiny screen to contain multiple screens of material. This part of the book talks about all the ways in which view controllers can be manipulated in order to make their views appear. It also describes *every kind of view* provided by the Cocoa framework — the built-in "widgets" with which you'll construct an app's interface.

- Part III surveys many of the secondary *frameworks* provided by iOS. These are clumps of code, sometimes with built-in interface, that are not part of your app by default, but are there for the asking if you need them, allowing you to work with such things as sound, video, user libraries, mail, maps, and the device's sensors.

- Part IV wraps up the book with some miscellaneous but important topics: files, networking, threading, and how to implement Undo and Redo.

- Appendix A summarizes the most important lifetime event messages sent to your app delegate.

Someone who has read this book (and who, it goes without saying, is conversant with the material in *iOS 7 Programming Fundamentals*) will, I believe, be capable of writing a real-life iOS app, and to do so with a clear understanding of what he or she is doing and where the app is going as it grows and develops. The book itself doesn't show how to write any particularly interesting iOS apps (though it is backed by dozens of example projects that you can download from my GitHub site, *http://github.com/mattneub/ Programming-iOS-Book-Examples*), but it does constantly use my own real apps and real programming situations to illustrate and motivate its explanations.

Just as important, this book is intended to prepare you for your own further explorations. In the case of some topics, especially in Part III and Part IV, I guide you past the initial barrier of no knowledge into an understanding of the topic, its concepts, its capabilities, and its documentation, along with some code examples; but the topic itself may be so huge that there is room only to introduce it here. Your feet, nevertheless, will now be set firmly on the path, and you will know enough that you can now proceed further down that path on your own whenever the need or interest arises.

Indeed, there is *always* more to learn about iOS. iOS is vast! It is all too easy to find areas of iOS that have had to be ruled outside the scope of this book. In Part IV, for example, I peek at Core Data, and demonstrate its use in code, but a true study of Core Data would require an entire book of its own (and such books exist); so, having opened the door, I quickly close it again, lest this book suddenly double in size. By the same token, many areas of iOS are not treated at all in this book:

OpenGL
> An open source C library for drawing, including 3D drawing, that takes full advantage of graphics hardware. This is often the most efficient way to draw, especially when animation is involved. iOS incorporates a simplified version of OpenGL called OpenGL ES. See Apple's *OpenGL Programming Guide for iOS*. Open GL interface configuration, texture loading, shading, and calculation are simplified by the GLKit framework; see the *GLKit Framework Reference*.

Sprite Kit
> New in iOS 7, Sprite Kit provides a built-in framework for designing 2D animated games.

Accelerate
> Certain computation-intensive processes will benefit from the vector-based Accelerate framework. See the *vDSP Programming Guide*.

Game Kit
> The Game Kit framework covers three areas that can enhance your user's game experience: Wireless or Bluetooth communication directly between devices (peer-to-peer); voice communication across an existing network connection; and Game Center, which facilitates these and many other aspects of interplayer communication, such as posting and viewing high scores and setting up combinations of players who wish to compete. See the *Game Kit Programming Guide*.

Advertising
> The iAD framework lets your free app attempt to make money by displaying advertisements provided by Apple. See the *iAD Programming Guide*.

Newsstand
> Your app may represent a subscription to something like a newspaper or magazine. See the *Newsstand Kit Framework Reference*.

Printing
> See the "Printing" chapter of the *Drawing and Printing Guide for iOS*.

Security

This book does not discuss security topics such as keychains, certificates, and encryption. See the *Security Overview* and the Security framework.

Accessibility

VoiceOver assists visually impaired users by describing the interface aloud. To participate, views must be configured to describe themselves usefully. Built-in views already do this to a large extent, and you can extend this functionality. See the *Accessibility Programming Guide for iOS.*

Telephone

The Core Telephony framework lets your app get information about a particular cellular carrier and call.

Pass Kit

The Pass Kit framework allows creation of downloadable passes to go into the user's Passbook app. See the *Passbook Programming Guide.*

External accessories

The user can attach an external accessory to the device, either directly via USB or wirelessly via Bluetooth. Your app can communicate with such an accessory. See *External Accessory Programming Topics.*

Versions

This book is geared to iOS 7 and Xcode 5. In general, only very minimal attention is given to earlier versions of iOS and Xcode. It is not my intention to embrace in this book any detailed knowledge about earlier versions of the software, which is, after all, readily and compendiously available in my earlier books. There are, nevertheless, a few words of advice about backward compatibility, and now and then I will call out a particularly noteworthy change from earlier versions.

(For example, it has been hard to refrain from pointing out the confusion caused by the changes in how the status bar works, or in the meaning of `tintColor`, or the nightmarish way in which your perfectly viable iOS 6 project, when recompiled against iOS 7, will try to resize and reposition its views incorrectly, underlapping the navigation bar.)

Xcode 5 no longer offers the user, creating a new app project from one of the project templates, an option as to whether or not to use Automatic Reference Counting (ARC), the compiler-based manual memory management technology that has made life so much easier for iOS programmers in recent years. ARC is simply turned on by default. Therefore, this book assumes from the outset that you are using ARC.

Xcode also no longer provides a template-based option as to whether or not to use a storyboard. All projects (except the Empty Application template) come with a main storyboard, and there is no option to use a main *.xib* file instead. Taking my cue from this, I have adapted my teaching style to assume that storyboards are primary and that you'll usually be using one. (I do also assume that you know how to make and work with a *.xib* file when you need one, as this is explained in *iOS 7 Programming Fundamentals.*)

I have also embraced, often without much fanfare, the various other iOS 7 and Xcode 5 innovations. Apple has clearly set out, with this generation of their software, to make iOS programming easier and more pleasant than ever; and by and large they have succeeded. For example, modules and autolinking have made it much simpler than in the past to work with additional frameworks, and I simply assume as a matter of course that you will be using them; thus, when telling you what to do in order to employ a certain framework, I give simply the relevant `@import` command. Similarly, in discussing drawing and images in Chapter 2, I naturally steer you toward the use of asset catalogs.

Acknowledgments

My thanks go first and foremost to the people at O'Reilly Media who have made writing a book so delightfully easy: Rachel Roumeliotis, Sarah Schneider, Kristen Brown, and Adam Witwer come particularly to mind. And let's not forget my first and long-standing editor, Brian Jepson, who had nothing whatever to do with this edition, but whose influence is present throughout.

As in the past, I have been greatly aided by some fantastic software, whose excellences I have appreciated at every moment of the process of writing this book. I should like to mention, in particular:

- git (*http://git-scm.com*)
- SourceTree (*http://www.sourcetreeapp.com*)
- TextMate (*http://macromates.com*)
- AsciiDoc (*http://www.methods.co.nz/asciidoc*)
- BBEdit (*http://barebones.com/products/bbedit/*)
- Snapz Pro X (*http://www.ambrosiasw.com*)
- GraphicConverter (*http://www.lemkesoft.com*)
- OmniGraffle (*http://www.omnigroup.com*)

The book was typed and edited entirely on my faithful Unicomp Model M keyboard (*http://pckeyboard.com*), without which I could never have done so much writing over so long a period so painlessly. For more about my physical work environment, see *http://matt.neuburg.usesthis.com*.

From the Programming iOS 4 Preface

A programming framework has a kind of personality, an overall flavor that provides an insight into the goals and mindset of those who created it. When I first encountered Cocoa Touch, my assessment of its personality was: "Wow, the people who wrote this are really clever!" On the one hand, the number of built-in interface widgets was severely and deliberately limited; on the other hand, the power and flexibility of some of those widgets, especially such things as UITableView, was greatly enhanced over their OS X counterparts. Even more important, Apple created a particularly brilliant way (UIView-Controller) to help the programmer make entire blocks of interface come and go and supplant one another in a controlled, hierarchical manner, thus allowing that tiny iPhone display to unfold virtually into multiple interface worlds within a single app without the user becoming lost or confused.

The popularity of the iPhone, with its largely free or very inexpensive apps, and the subsequent popularity of the iPad, have brought and will continue to bring into the fold many new programmers who see programming for these devices as worthwhile and doable, even though they may not have felt the same way about OS X. Apple's own annual WWDC developer conventions have reflected this trend, with their emphasis shifted from OS X to iOS instruction.

The widespread eagerness to program iOS, however, though delightful on the one hand, has also fostered a certain tendency to try to run without first learning to walk. iOS gives the programmer mighty powers that can seem as limitless as imagination itself, but it also has fundamentals. I often see questions online from programmers who are evidently deep into the creation of some interesting app, but who are stymied in a way that reveals quite clearly that they are unfamiliar with the basics of the very world in which they are so happily cavorting.

It is this state of affairs that has motivated me to write this book, which is intended to ground the reader in the fundamentals of iOS. I love Cocoa and have long wished to write about it, but it is iOS and its popularity that has given me a proximate excuse to do so. Here I have attempted to marshal and expound, in what I hope is a pedagogically helpful and instructive yet ruthlessly Euclidean and logical order, the principles and elements on which sound iOS programming rests. My hope, as with my previous books, is that you will both read this book cover to cover (learning something new often enough to keep you turning the pages) and keep it by you as a handy reference.

This book is not intended to disparage Apple's own documentation and example projects. They are wonderful resources and have become more wonderful as time goes on. I have depended heavily on them in the preparation of this book. But I also find that they don't fulfill the same function as a reasoned, ordered presentation of the facts. The online documentation must make assumptions as to how much you already know; it can't guarantee that you'll approach it in a given order. And online documentation is more suitable to reference than to instruction. A fully written example, no matter how well commented, is difficult to follow; it demonstrates, but it does not teach.

A book, on the other hand, has numbered chapters and sequential pages; I can assume you know views before you know view controllers for the simple reason that Part I precedes Part II. And along with facts, I also bring to the table a degree of experience, which I try to communicate to you. Throughout this book you'll find me referring to "common beginner mistakes"; in most cases, these are mistakes that I have made myself, in addition to seeing others make them. I try to tell you what the pitfalls are because I assume that, in the course of things, you will otherwise fall into them just as naturally as I did as I was learning. You'll also see me construct many examples piece by piece or extract and explain just one tiny portion of a larger app. It is not a massive finished program that teaches programming, but an exposition of the thought process that developed that program. It is this thought process, more than anything else, that I hope you will gain from reading this book.

Conventions Used in This Book

The following typographical conventions are used in this book:

Italic
: Indicates new terms, URLs, email addresses, filenames, and file extensions.

`Constant width`
: Used for program listings, as well as within paragraphs to refer to program elements such as variable or function names, databases, data types, environment variables, statements, and keywords.

`Constant width bold`
: Shows commands or other text that should be typed literally by the user.

`Constant width italic`
: Shows text that should be replaced with user-supplied values or by values determined by context.

 This icon signifies a tip, suggestion, or general note.

 This icon indicates a warning or caution.

Using Code Examples

Supplemental material (code examples, exercises, etc.) is available for download at *https://github.com/mattneub/Programming-iOS-Book-Examples*.

This book is here to help you get your job done. In general, if example code is offered with this book, you may use it in your programs and documentation. You do not need to contact us for permission unless you're reproducing a significant portion of the code. For example, writing a program that uses several chunks of code from this book does not require permission. Selling or distributing a CD-ROM of examples from O'Reilly books does require permission. Answering a question by citing this book and quoting example code does not require permission. Incorporating a significant amount of example code from this book into your product's documentation does require permission.

We appreciate, but do not require, attribution. An attribution usually includes the title, author, publisher, and ISBN. For example: *"Programming iOS 7* by Matt Neuburg (O'Reilly). Copyright 2014 Matt Neuburg, 978-1-449-37234-7."

If you feel your use of code examples falls outside fair use or the permission given above, feel free to contact us at *permissions@oreilly.com*.

Safari® Books Online

 *Safari Books Online* is an on-demand digital library that delivers expert content in both book and video form from the world's leading authors in technology and business.

Technology professionals, software developers, web designers, and business and creative professionals use Safari Books Online as their primary resource for research, problem solving, learning, and certification training.

Safari Books Online offers a range of product mixes and pricing programs for organizations, government agencies, and individuals. Subscribers have access to thousands of books, training videos, and prepublication manuscripts in one fully searchable database from publishers like O'Reilly Media, Prentice Hall Professional, Addison-Wesley Professional, Microsoft Press, Sams, Que, Peachpit Press, Focal Press, Cisco Press, John Wiley & Sons, Syngress, Morgan Kaufmann, IBM Redbooks, Packt, Adobe Press, FT Press, Apress, Manning, New Riders, McGraw-Hill, Jones & Bartlett, Course Technology, and dozens more. For more information about Safari Books Online, please visit us online.

How to Contact Us

Please address comments and questions concerning this book to the publisher:

O'Reilly Media, Inc.
1005 Gravenstein Highway North
Sebastopol, CA 95472
800-998-9938 (in the United States or Canada)
707-829-0515 (international or local)
707-829-0104 (fax)

We have a web page for this book, where we list errata, examples, and any additional information. You can access this page at *http://oreil.ly/programmingiOS7_4e*.

To comment or ask technical questions about this book, send email to *bookquestions@oreilly.com*.

For more information about our books, courses, conferences, and news, see our website at *http://www.oreilly.com*.

Find us on Facebook: *http://facebook.com/oreilly*

Follow us on Twitter: *http://twitter.com/oreillymedia*

Watch us on YouTube: *http://www.youtube.com/oreillymedia*

PART I

Views

The things that appear in your app's interface are, ultimately, *views*. A view is a unit of your app that knows how to draw itself. A view also knows how to sense that the user has touched it. Views are what your user sees on the screen, and what your user interacts with by touching the screen. Thus, views are the primary constituent of an app's visible, touchable manifestation. They *are* your app's interface. So it's going to be crucial to know how views work.

- Chapter 1 discusses views in their most general aspect — their hierarchy, visibility, and position, including an explanation of autolayout.

- Chapter 2 is about drawing. A view knows how to draw itself; this chapter explains how to tell a view what you want it to draw, from displaying an existing image to constructing a drawing in code.

- Chapter 3 explains about layers. The drawing power of a view comes ultimately from its layer. To put it another way, a layer is effectively the aspect of a view that knows how to draw — with even more power.

- Chapter 4 tells about animation. An iOS app's interface isn't generally static; it's lively. Much of that liveliness comes from animation. iOS gives you great power to animate your interface with remarkable ease; that power, it turns out, resides ultimately in layers.

- Chapter 5 is about touches. A view knows how to sense that the user is touching it. This chapter explains the iOS view-based mechanisms for sensing and responding to touches, with details on how touches are routed to the appropriate view and how you can customize that routing.

CHAPTER 1

Views

A *view* (an object whose class is UIView or a subclass of UIView) knows how to draw itself into a rectangular area of the interface. Your app has a visible interface thanks to views. Creating and configuring a view can be extremely simple: "Set it and forget it." For example, you can drag an interface widget, such as a UIButton, into a view in the nib editor; when the app runs, the button appears, and works properly. But you can also manipulate views in powerful ways, in real time. Your code can do some or all of the view's drawing of itself (Chapter 2); it can make the view appear and disappear, move, resize itself, and display many other physical changes, possibly with animation (Chapter 4).

A view is also a responder (UIView is a subclass of UIResponder). This means that a view is subject to user interactions, such as taps and swipes. Thus, views are the basis not only of the interface that the user sees, but also of the interface that the user touches (Chapter 5). Organizing your views so that the correct view reacts to a given touch allows you to allocate your code neatly and efficiently.

The *view hierarchy* is the chief mode of view organization. A view can have subviews; a subview has exactly one immediate superview. Thus there is a tree of views. This hierarchy allows views to come and go together. If a view is removed from the interface, its subviews are removed; if a view is hidden (made invisible), its subviews are hidden; if a view is moved, its subviews move with it; and other changes in a view are likewise shared with its subviews. The view hierarchy is also the basis of, though it is not identical to, the responder chain.

A view may come from a nib, or you can create it in code. On balance, neither approach is to be preferred over the other; it depends on your needs and inclinations and on the overall architecture of your app.

The Window

The top of the view hierarchy is the app's window. It is an instance of UIWindow (or your own subclass thereof), which is a UIView subclass. Your app should have *exactly one main window*. It is created at launch time and is never destroyed or replaced. It occupies the entire screen and forms the background to, and is the ultimate superview of, all your other visible views. Other views are visible by virtue of being subviews, at some depth, of your app's window.

> If your app can display views on an external screen, you'll create an additional UIWindow to contain those views; but in this chapter I'll behave as if there were just one screen, the device's own screen, and just one window. I repeat: if there is just one screen, your app should create just one UIWindow. You may encounter online tutorials that advise explicit creation of a second UIWindow as a way of making content appear in front of the app's main interface; *such statements are wrong* and should be disregarded. To make content appear in front of the interface, add a view, not another entire window.

The window must fill the device's screen. Therefore, its size and position must be identical to the size and position of the screen. This is done by setting the window's frame to the screen's bounds as the window is instantiated (and I'll explain later in this chapter what "frame" and "bounds" are):

```
UIWindow* w = [[UIWindow alloc] initWithFrame:[[UIScreen mainScreen] bounds]];
```

The window must persist for the lifetime of the app. To make this happen, the app delegate class has been given a window property with a strong retain policy. As the app launches, UIApplicationMain (called in the main function in *main.m*) instantiates the app delegate class and retains the resulting instance. This is the app delegate instance; it is never released, so it persists for the lifetime of the app. The window instance is assigned to the app delegate instance's window property; therefore it, too, persists for the lifetime of the app.

You will typically not put any view content manually and directly inside your main window. Instead, you'll obtain a view controller and assign it to the main window's root-ViewController property. This causes the view controller's main view (its view) to be made the one and only immediate subview of your main window — the main window's *root view*. All other views in your main window will be subviews of the root view. Thus, the root view is the highest object in the view hierarchy that the user will usually see. There might be just a chance, under certain circumstances, that the user will catch a glimpse of the window, behind the root view; for this reason, you may want to assign the main window a reasonable `backgroundColor`. But this seems unlikely, and in general you'll have no reason to change anything about the window itself.

Your app's interface is not visible until the window, which contains it, is made the app's key window. This is done by calling the UIWindow instance method `makeKeyAnd-Visible`.

All of the configuration that I've just described is trivial to perform, because the Xcode app templates implement all of it for you:

App with a main storyboard

If your app has a main storyboard, as specified by its *Info.plist* key "Main storyboard file base name" (`UIMainStoryboardFile`) — the default for most Xcode 5 app templates, except the Empty Application template — then `UIApplicationMain` instantiates UIWindow with the correct frame and assigns that instance to the app delegate's `window` property. It also instantiates the storyboard's initial view controller and assigns that instance to the window's `rootViewController` property. All of that happens *before* the app delegate's `application:didFinishLaunchingWith-Options:` is called (Appendix A).

Finally, `UIApplicationMain` calls `makeKeyAndVisible` to display your app's interface. This in turn automatically causes the root view controller to obtain its main view (typically by loading it from a nib), which the window adds as its own root view. That happens *after* `application:didFinishLaunchingWithOptions:` is called.

App without a main storyboard

If your app has no main storyboard, then creation and configuration of the window must be done in some other way. Typically, it is done in code. You can see this in a project generated from the Empty Application template, where all the configuration I've just described is performed explicitly, in code, in `application:didFinish-LaunchingWithOptions:`, like this:

```
self.window =
    [[UIWindow alloc] initWithFrame:[[UIScreen mainScreen] bounds]];
// Override point for customization after application launch.
self.window.backgroundColor = [UIColor whiteColor];
[self.window makeKeyAndVisible];
```

It is extremely improbable that you would ever need to subclass UIWindow. If, however, you wanted to create a UIWindow subclass and make an instance of that subclass your app's main window, then *how* you proceed depends on how the window is instantiated in the first place:

App with a main storyboard

As the app launches, after `UIApplicationMain` has instantiated the app delegate, it asks the app delegate instance for the value of its `window` property. If that value is nil, `UIApplicationMain` instantiates UIWindow and assigns that instance to the app delegate's `window` property. If that value is *not* nil, `UIApplicationMain` leaves it alone and uses it as the app's main window. Therefore, the way to instantiate a UIWindow subclass and use that instance as your app's main window is to implement the getter for the app delegate's `window` property in such a way as to generate the UIWindow subclass instance *exactly once* (that is, instantiate the UIWindow subclass only if you haven't already done so), like this:

```
- (UIWindow*) window {
    UIWindow* w = self->_window;
    if (!w) {
        w = [[MyWindow alloc] initWithFrame:
                [[UIScreen mainScreen] bounds]];
        self->_window = w;
    }
    return w;
}
```

App without a main storyboard

You're already instantiating UIWindow and assigning that instance to the app delegate's `self.window`, in code. So instantiate your UIWindow subclass instead.

Once the app is running, there are various ways to refer to the window:

- If a UIView is in the interface, it automatically has a reference to the window through its own `window` property.

  You can also use a UIView's `window` property as a way of asking whether it is ultimately embedded in the window; if it isn't, its `window` property is nil. A UIView whose `window` property is nil cannot be visible to the user.

- The app delegate instance maintains a reference to the window through its `window` property. You can get a reference to the app delegate from elsewhere through the shared application's `delegate` property, and through it you can refer to the window:

    ```
    UIWindow* w = [[[UIApplication sharedApplication] delegate] window];
    ```

- The shared application maintains a reference to the window through its `keyWindow` property:

    ```
    UIWindow* w = [[UIApplication sharedApplication] keyWindow];
    ```

  That reference, however, is slightly volatile, because the system can create temporary windows and interpose them as the application's key window. For example, while a UIAlertView is showing (Chapter 13), it is the application's `keyWindow`.

Experimenting With Views

In the course of this and subsequent chapters, you may want to experiment with views in a project of your own. Since view controllers aren't formally explained until Chapter 6, I'll just outline two simple approaches.

One way is to start your project with the Single View Application template. It gives you a main storyboard containing one scene with one view controller instance which itself contains its own main view; when the app runs, that view controller will become the app's main window's `rootViewController`, and its main view will become the window's root view. You can drag a view from the Object library into the main view as a subview, and it will be instantiated in the interface when the app runs. Alternatively, you can create views and add them to the interface in code; the simplest place to do this, for now, is the view controller's `viewDidLoad` method, which has a reference to the view controller's main view as `self.view`. For example:

```
- (void)viewDidLoad {
    [super viewDidLoad];
    UIView* mainview = self.view;
    UIView* v = [[UIView alloc] initWithFrame:CGRectMake(100,100,50,50)];
    v.backgroundColor = [UIColor redColor]; // small red square
    [mainview addSubview: v]; // add it to main view
}
```

Alternatively, you can start your project with the Empty Application template. It has no *.xib* or *.storyboard* file, so your views will have to be created entirely in code. The Empty Application template does not supply any view controllers, and does not assign any view controller to the window's `rootViewController` property. This situation causes the runtime to complain when the application is launched: "Application windows are expected to have a root view controller at the end of application launch." A simple solution is to put your code in the app delegate's `application:didFinishLaunching-WithOptions:`, creating a minimal root view controller and accessing its main view through its `view` property. For example:

```
- (BOOL)application:(UIApplication *)application
        didFinishLaunchingWithOptions:(NSDictionary *)launchOptions {
    // (template code:)
    self.window =
        [[UIWindow alloc] initWithFrame:[[UIScreen mainScreen] bounds]];
    // Override point for customization after application launch.
    // (your code:)
    self.window.rootViewController = [UIViewController new];
    UIView* mainview = self.window.rootViewController.view;
    UIView* v = [[UIView alloc] initWithFrame:CGRectMake(100,100,50,50)];
    v.backgroundColor = [UIColor redColor]; // small red square
    [mainview addSubview: v]; // add it to the main view
    // (template code:)
```

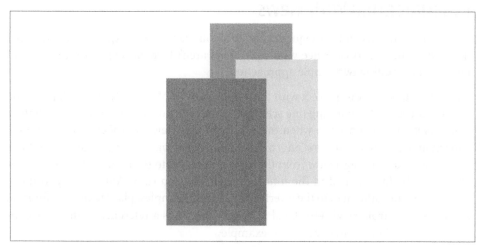

Figure 1-1. Overlapping views

```
    self.window.backgroundColor = [UIColor whiteColor];
    [self.window makeKeyAndVisible];
    return YES;
}
```

Subview and Superview

Once upon a time, and not so very long ago, a view owned precisely its rectangular area. No part of any view that was not a subview of this view could appear inside it, because when this view redrew its rectangle, it would erase the overlapping portion of the other view. No part of any subview of this view could appear outside it, because the view took responsibility for its own rectangle and no more.

Those rules, however, were gradually relaxed, and starting in OS X 10.5, Apple introduced an entirely new architecture for view drawing that lifted those restrictions completely. iOS view drawing is based on this revised architecture. In iOS, some or all of a subview can appear outside its superview, and a view can overlap another view and can be drawn partially or totally in front of it without being its subview.

For example, Figure 1-1 shows three overlapping views. All three views have a background color, so each is completely represented by a colored rectangle. You have no way of knowing, from this visual representation, exactly how the views are related within the view hierarchy. In actual fact, the view in the middle (horizontally) is a sibling view of the view on the left (they are both direct subviews of the root view), and the view on the right is a subview of the middle view.

When views are created in the nib, you can examine the view hierarchy in the nib editor's document outline to learn their actual relationship (Figure 1-2). When views are created

Figure 1-2. A view hierarchy as displayed in the nib editor

in code, you know their hierarchical relationship because you created that hierarchy. But the visible interface doesn't tell you, because view overlapping is so flexible.

> To see an outline of a view's subview hierarchy at runtime while paused in the debugger, use the debugger console to send the `recursiveDescription` command to that view; for example, `po [someView recursiveDescription]`.

Nevertheless, a view's position within the view hierarchy is extremely significant. For one thing, the view hierarchy dictates the *order* in which views are drawn. Sibling subviews of the same superview have a definite order: one is drawn before the other, so if they overlap, it will appear to be behind its sibling. Similarly, a superview is drawn before its subviews, so if they overlap it, it will appear to be behind them.

You can see this illustrated in Figure 1-1. The view on the right is a subview of the view in the middle and is drawn on top of it. The view on the left is a sibling of the view in the middle, but it is a later sibling, so it is drawn on top of the view in the middle and on top of the view on the right. The view on the left *cannot* appear behind the view on the right but in front of the view in the middle, because those two views are subview and superview and are drawn together — both are drawn either before or after the view on the left, depending on the ordering of the siblings.

This layering order can be governed in the nib editor by arranging the views in the document outline. (If you click in the canvas, you may be able to use the menu items of the Editor → Arrange menu instead — Send to Front, Send to Back, Send Forward, Send Backward.) In code, there are methods for arranging the sibling order of views, which we'll come to in a moment.

Here are some other effects of the view hierarchy:

- If a view is removed from or moved within its superview, its subviews go with it.
- A view's degree of transparency is inherited by its subviews.
- A view can optionally limit the drawing of its subviews so that any parts of them outside the view are not shown. This is called *clipping* and is set with the view's `clipsToBounds` property.

- A superview *owns* its subviews, in the memory-management sense, much as an NSArray owns its elements; it retains them and is responsible for releasing a subview when that subview ceases to be its subview (it is removed from the collection of this view's subviews) or when it itself goes out of existence.

- If a view's size is changed, its subviews can be resized automatically (and I'll have much more to say about that later in this chapter).

A UIView has a `superview` property (a UIView) and a `subviews` property (an NSArray of UIViews, in back-to-front order), allowing you to trace the view hierarchy in code. There is also a method `isDescendantOfView:` letting you check whether one view is a subview of another at any depth. If you need a reference to a particular view, you will probably arrange this beforehand as an instance variable, perhaps through an outlet. Alternatively, a view can have a numeric tag (its `tag` property), and can then be referred to by sending any view higher up the view hierarchy the `viewWithTag:` message. Seeing that all tags of interest are unique within their region of the hierarchy is up to you.

Manipulating the view hierarchy in code is easy. This is part of what gives iOS apps their dynamic quality, and it compensates for the fact that there is basically just a single window. It is perfectly reasonable for your code to rip an entire hierarchy of views out of the superview and substitute another! You can do this directly; you can combine it with animation (Chapter 4); you can govern it through view controllers (Chapter 6).

The method `addSubview:` makes one view a subview of another; `removeFrom-Superview` takes a subview out of its superview's view hierarchy. In both cases, if the superview is part of the visible interface, the subview will appear or disappear; and of course this view may itself have subviews that accompany it. Just remember that re-moving a subview from its superview releases it; if you intend to reuse that subview later on, you will wish to retain it first. This is often taken care of through a property with a retain policy.

Events inform a view of these dynamic changes. To respond to these events requires subclassing. Then you'll be able to override any of these methods:

- `didAddSubview:` and `willRemoveSubview:`
- `didMoveToSuperview` and `willMoveToSuperview:`
- `didMoveToWindow` and `willMoveToWindow:`

When `addSubview:` is called, the view is placed last among its superview's subviews; thus it is drawn last, meaning that it appears frontmost. A view's subviews are indexed, starting at 0, which is rearmost. There are additional methods for inserting a subview at a given index, or below (behind) or above (in front of) a specific view; for swapping two sibling views by index; and for moving a subview all the way to the front or back among its siblings:

- insertSubview:atIndex:

- insertSubview:belowSubview:, insertSubview:aboveSubview:

- exchangeSubviewAtIndex:withSubviewAtIndex:

- bringSubviewToFront:, sendSubviewToBack:

Oddly, there is no command for removing all of a view's subviews at once. However, a view's subviews array is an immutable copy of the internal list of subviews, so it is legal to cycle through it and remove each subview one at a time:

```
for (UIView* v in view.subviews)
    [v removeFromSuperview];
```

Here's an alternative way to do that:

```
[view.subviews makeObjectsPerformSelector:@selector(removeFromSuperview)];
```

Visibility and Opacity

A view can be made invisible by setting its hidden property to YES, and visible again by setting it to NO. This takes it (and its subviews, of course) out of the visible interface without the overhead of actually removing it from the view hierarchy. A hidden view does not (normally) receive touch events, so to the user it really is as if the view weren't there. But it is there, so it can still be manipulated in code.

A view can be assigned a background color through its backgroundColor property. A color is a UIColor; this is not a difficult class to use, and I'm not going to go into details. A view whose background color is nil (the default) has a transparent background. It is perfectly reasonable for a view to have a transparent background and to do no additional drawing of its own, just so that it can act as a convenient superview to other views, making them behave together.

A view can be made partially or completely transparent through its alpha property: 1.0 means opaque, 0.0 means transparent, and a value may be anywhere between them, inclusive. This affects subviews: if a superview has an alpha of 0.5, none of its subviews can have an *apparent* opacity of more than 0.5, because whatever alpha value they have will be drawn relative to 0.5. (Just to make matters more complicated, colors have an alpha value as well. So, for example, a view can have an alpha of 1.0 but still have a transparent background because its backgroundColor has an alpha less than 1.0.) A view that is completely transparent (or very close to it) is like a view whose hidden is YES: it is invisible, along with its subviews, and cannot (normally) be touched.

A view's alpha property value affects both the apparent transparency of its background color and the apparent transparency of its contents. For example, if a view displays an image and has a background color and its `alpha` is less than 1, the background color will seep through the image (and whatever is behind the view will seep through both).

A view's `opaque` property, on the other hand, is a horse of a different color; changing it has no effect on the view's appearance. Rather, this property is a hint to the drawing system. If a view completely fills its bounds with ultimately opaque material and its `alpha` is 1.0, so that the view has no effective transparency, then it can be drawn more efficiently (with less drag on performance) if you inform the drawing system of this fact by setting its `opaque` to YES. Otherwise, you should set its `opaque` to NO. The `opaque` value is *not* changed for you when you set a view's `backgroundColor` or `alpha`! Setting it correctly is entirely up to you; the default, perhaps surprisingly, is YES.

Frame

A view's `frame` property, a CGRect, is the position of its rectangle within its superview, *in the superview's coordinate system.* By default, the superview's coordinate system will have the origin at its top left, with the x-coordinate growing positively rightward and the y-coordinate growing positively downward.

Setting a view's frame to a different CGRect value repositions the view, or resizes it, or both. If the view is visible, this change will be visibly reflected in the interface. On the other hand, you can also set a view's frame when the view is not visible — for example, when you create the view in code. In that case, the frame describes where the view *will* be positioned within its superview when it is given a superview. UIView's designated initializer is `initWithFrame:`, and you'll often assign a frame this way, especially because the default frame might otherwise be `{{0,0},{0,0}}`, which is rarely what you want.

 Forgetting to assign a view a frame when creating it in code, and then wondering why it isn't appearing when added to a superview, is a common beginner mistake. A view with a zero-size frame is effectively invisible. If a view has a standard size that you want it to adopt, especially in relation to its contents (like a UIButton in relation to its title), an alternative is to send it the `sizeToFit` message.

We are now in a position to generate programmatically the interface displayed in Figure 1-1:

```
UIView* v1 = [[UIView alloc] initWithFrame:CGRectMake(113, 111, 132, 194)];
v1.backgroundColor = [UIColor colorWithRed:1 green:.4 blue:1 alpha:1];
UIView* v2 = [[UIView alloc] initWithFrame:CGRectMake(41, 56, 132, 194)];
v2.backgroundColor = [UIColor colorWithRed:.5 green:1 blue:0 alpha:1];
UIView* v3 = [[UIView alloc] initWithFrame:CGRectMake(43, 197, 160, 230)];
```

Figure 1-3. A subview inset from its superview

```
v3.backgroundColor = [UIColor colorWithRed:1 green:0 blue:0 alpha:1];
[mainview addSubview: v1];
[v1 addSubview: v2];
[mainview addSubview: v3];
```

In that code, we determined the layering order of v1 and v3 (the middle and left views, which are siblings) by the order in which we inserted them into the view hierarchy with addSubview:.

Bounds and Center

Suppose we have a superview and a subview, and the subview is to appear inset by 10 points, as in Figure 1-3. The utility function CGRectInset makes it easy to derive one rectangle as an inset from another, so we'll use it to determine the subview's frame. But *what* rectangle should this be inset from? Not the superview's frame; the frame represents a view's position within *its* superview, and in that superview's coordinates. What we're after is a CGRect describing our superview's rectangle in its *own* coordinates, because those are the coordinates in which the subview's frame is to be expressed. The CGRect that describes a view's rectangle in its own coordinates is the view's bounds property.

So, the code to generate Figure 1-3 looks like this:

```
UIView* v1 = [[UIView alloc] initWithFrame:CGRectMake(113, 111, 132, 194)];
v1.backgroundColor = [UIColor colorWithRed:1 green:.4 blue:1 alpha:1];
UIView* v2 = [[UIView alloc] initWithFrame:CGRectInset(v1.bounds, 10, 10)];
v2.backgroundColor = [UIColor colorWithRed:.5 green:1 blue:0 alpha:1];
[mainview addSubview: v1];
[v1 addSubview: v2];
```

You'll very often use a view's bounds in this way. When you need coordinates for drawing inside a view, whether drawing manually or placing a subview, you'll often refer to the view's bounds.

Figure 1-4. A subview exactly covering its superview

Interesting things happen when you set a view's bounds. If you change a view's bounds *size*, you change its *frame*. The change in the view's frame takes place around its *center*, which remains unchanged. So, for example:

```
UIView* v1 = [[UIView alloc] initWithFrame:CGRectMake(113, 111, 132, 194)];
v1.backgroundColor = [UIColor colorWithRed:1 green:.4 blue:1 alpha:1];
UIView* v2 = [[UIView alloc] initWithFrame:CGRectInset(v1.bounds, 10, 10)];
v2.backgroundColor = [UIColor colorWithRed:.5 green:1 blue:0 alpha:1];
[mainview addSubview: v1];
[v1 addSubview: v2];
CGRect r = v2.bounds;
r.size.height += 20;
r.size.width += 20;
v2.bounds = r;
```

What appears is a single rectangle; the subview completely and exactly covers its superview, its frame being the same as the superview's bounds. The call to CGRectInset started with the superview's bounds and shaved 10 points off the left, right, top, and bottom to set the subview's frame (Figure 1-3). But then we added 20 points to the subview's bounds height and width, and thus added 20 points to the subview's frame height and width as well (Figure 1-4). The center didn't move, so we effectively put the 10 points back onto the left, right, top, and bottom of the subview's frame.

When you create a UIView, its bounds coordinate system's {0,0} point is at its top left. If you change a view's bounds *origin*, you move the *origin of its internal coordinate system*. Because a subview is positioned in its superview with respect to its superview's coordinate system, a change in the bounds origin of the superview will change the apparent position of a subview. To illustrate, we start once again with our subview inset evenly within its superview, and then change the bounds origin of the superview:

```
UIView* v1 = [[UIView alloc] initWithFrame:CGRectMake(113, 111, 132, 194)];
v1.backgroundColor = [UIColor colorWithRed:1 green:.4 blue:1 alpha:1];
UIView* v2 = [[UIView alloc] initWithFrame:CGRectInset(v1.bounds, 10, 10)];
v2.backgroundColor = [UIColor colorWithRed:.5 green:1 blue:0 alpha:1];
[mainview addSubview: v1];
```

Figure 1-5. The superview's bounds origin has been shifted

```
[v1 addSubview: v2];
CGRect r = v1.bounds;
r.origin.x += 10;
r.origin.y += 10;
v1.bounds = r;
```

Nothing happens to the superview's size or position. But the subview has moved up and to the left so that it is flush with its superview's top-left corner (Figure 1-5). Basically, what we've done is to say to the superview, "Instead of calling the point at your upper left {0,0}, call that point {10,10}." Because the subview's frame origin is itself at {10,10}, the subview now touches the superview's top-left corner. The effect of changing a view's bounds origin may seem directionally backward — we increased the superview's origin in the positive direction, but the subview moved in the negative direction — but think of it this way: a view's bounds origin point coincides with its frame's top left.

We have seen that changing a view's bounds size affects its frame size. The converse is also true: changing a view's frame size affects its bounds size. What is *not* affected by changing a view's bounds size is the view's center. This property, like the frame property, represents the view's position within its superview, in the superview's coordinates, but it is the position of the bounds center, the point derived from the bounds like this:

```
CGPoint c = CGPointMake(CGRectGetMidX(theView.bounds),
                        CGRectGetMidY(theView.bounds));
```

A view's center is thus a single point establishing the positional relationship between a view's bounds and its superview's bounds. Changing a view's bounds does not change its center; changing a view's center does not change its bounds.

Thus, a view's bounds and center are orthogonal (independent), and describe (among other things) both the view's size and its position within its superview. The view's frame is therefore superfluous! In fact, the frame property is merely a convenient expression of the center and bounds values. In most cases, this won't matter to you; you'll use the `frame` property anyway. When you first create a view from scratch, the designated initializer is `initWithFrame:`. You can change the frame, and the bounds size and center will change to match. You can change the bounds size or the center, and the frame will change to match. Nevertheless, the proper and most reliable way to position and size a view within its superview is to use its bounds and center, not its frame; there are some situations in which the frame is meaningless (or will at least behave very oddly), but the bounds and center will always work.

We have seen that every view has its own coordinate system, expressed by its bounds, and that a view's coordinate system has a clear relationship to its superview's coordinate system, expressed by its `center`. This is true of every view in a window, so it is possible to convert between the coordinates of any two views in the same window. Convenience methods are supplied to perform this conversion both for a CGPoint and for a CGRect:

- `convertPoint:fromView:`, `convertPoint:toView:`
- `convertRect:fromView:`, `convertRect:toView:`

If the second parameter is nil, it is taken to be the window.

For example, if v2 is a subview of v1, then to center v2 within v1 you could say:

```
v2.center = [v1 convertPoint:v1.center fromView:v1.superview];
```

 When setting a view's position by setting its center, if the height or width of the view is not an integer (or, on a single-resolution screen, not an even integer), the view can end up *misaligned*: its point values in one or both dimensions are located between the screen pixels. This can cause the view to be displayed incorrectly; for example, if the view contains text, the text may be blurry. You can detect this situation in the Simulator by checking Debug → Color Misaligned Images. A simple solution is to set the view's frame, after positioning it, to the CGRect-Integral of its frame.

Transform

A view's `transform` property alters how the view is drawn — it may, for example, change the view's perceived size and orientation — without affecting its bounds and center. A transformed view continues to behave correctly: a rotated button, for example, is still a button, and can be tapped in its apparent location and orientation.

A transform value is a CGAffineTransform, which is a struct representing six of the nine values of a 3×3 transformation matrix (the other three values are constants, so there's no point representing them in the struct). You may have forgotten your high-school linear algebra, so you may not recall what a transformation matrix is. For the details, which are quite simple really, see the "Transforms" chapter of Apple's *Quartz 2D Programming Guide*, especially the section called "The Math Behind the Matrices." But you don't really need to know those details, because convenience functions, whose names start with CGAffineTransformMake..., are provided for creating three of the basic types of transform: rotation, scaling, and translation (i.e., changing the view's apparent position). A fourth basic transform type, skewing or shearing, has no convenience function.

By default, a view's transformation matrix is CGAffineTransformIdentity, the identity transform. It has no visible effect, so you're unaware of it. Any transform that you do apply takes place around the view's center, which is held constant.

Here's some code to illustrate use of a transform:

```
UIView* v1 = [[UIView alloc] initWithFrame:CGRectMake(113, 111, 132, 194)];
v1.backgroundColor = [UIColor colorWithRed:1 green:.4 blue:1 alpha:1];
UIView* v2 = [[UIView alloc] initWithFrame:CGRectInset(v1.bounds, 10, 10)];
v2.backgroundColor = [UIColor colorWithRed:.5 green:1 blue:0 alpha:1];
[mainview addSubview: v1];
[v1 addSubview: v2];
v1.transform = CGAffineTransformMakeRotation(45 * M_PI/180.0);
```

The transform property of the view v1 is set to a rotation transform. The result (Figure 1-6) is that the view appears to be rocked 45 degrees clockwise. (I think in degrees, but Core Graphics thinks in radians, so my code has to convert.) Observe that the view's center property is unaffected, so that the rotation seems to have occurred

Figure 1-6. A rotation transform

around the view's center. Moreover, the view's bounds property is unaffected; the internal coordinate system is unchanged, so the subview is drawn in the same place relative to its superview. The view's frame, however, is now useless, as no mere rectangle can describe the region of the superview apparently occupied by the view; the frame's actual value, roughly {{63.7416, 92.7416}, {230.517, 230.517}}, describes the minimal bounding rectangle surrounding the view's apparent position. The rule is that if a view's transform is not the identity transform, you should not set its frame; also, automatic resizing of a subview, discussed later in this chapter, requires that the superview's transform be the identity transform.

Suppose, instead of CGAffineTransformMakeRotation, we call CGAffineTransform-MakeScale, like this:

```
v1.transform = CGAffineTransformMakeScale(1.8, 1);
```

The bounds property of the view v1 is still unaffected, so the subview is still drawn in the same place relative to its superview; this means that the two views seem to have stretched horizontally together (Figure 1-7). No bounds or centers were harmed by the application of this transform!

Transformation matrices can be chained. There are convenience functions for applying one transform to another. Their names do *not* contain "Make." These functions are not commutative; that is, order matters. If you start with a transform that translates a view to the right and then apply a rotation of 45 degrees, the rotated view appears to the right of its original position; on the other hand, if you start with a transform that rotates a view 45 degrees and then apply a translation to the right, the meaning of "right" has changed, so the rotated view appears 45 degrees down from its original position. To demonstrate the difference, I'll start with a subview that exactly overlaps its superview:

Figure 1-7. A scale transform

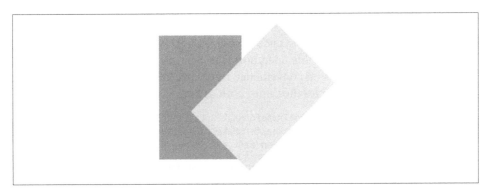

Figure 1-8. Translation, then rotation

```
UIView* v1 = [[UIView alloc] initWithFrame:CGRectMake(20, 111, 132, 194)];
v1.backgroundColor = [UIColor colorWithRed:1 green:.4 blue:1 alpha:1];
UIView* v2 = [[UIView alloc] initWithFrame:v1.bounds];
v2.backgroundColor = [UIColor colorWithRed:.5 green:1 blue:0 alpha:1];
[mainview addSubview: v1];
[v1 addSubview: v2];
```

Then I'll apply two successive transforms to the subview, leaving the superview to show where the subview was originally. In this example, I translate and then rotate (Figure 1-8):

```
v2.transform = CGAffineTransformMakeTranslation(100, 0);
v2.transform = CGAffineTransformRotate(v2.transform, 45 * M_PI/180.0);
```

In this example, I rotate and then translate (Figure 1-9):

```
v2.transform = CGAffineTransformMakeRotation(45 * M_PI/180.0);
v2.transform = CGAffineTransformTranslate(v2.transform, 100, 0);
```

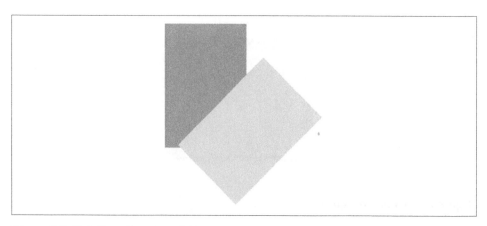

Figure 1-9. Rotation, then translation

The function `CGAffineTransformConcat` concatenates two transform matrices using matrix multiplication. Again, this operation is not commutative. The order is the *opposite* of the order when using convenience functions for applying one transform to another. For example, this gives the same result as Figure 1-9:

```
CGAffineTransform r = CGAffineTransformMakeRotation(45 * M_PI/180.0);
CGAffineTransform t = CGAffineTransformMakeTranslation(100, 0);
v2.transform = CGAffineTransformConcat(t,r); // not r,t
```

To remove a transform from a combination of transforms, apply its inverse. A convenience function lets you obtain the inverse of a given affine transform. Again, order matters. In this example, I rotate the subview and shift it to its "right," and then remove the rotation (Figure 1-10):

```
CGAffineTransform r = CGAffineTransformMakeRotation(45 * M_PI/180.0);
CGAffineTransform t = CGAffineTransformMakeTranslation(100, 0);
v2.transform = CGAffineTransformConcat(t,r);
v2.transform =
    CGAffineTransformConcat(CGAffineTransformInvert(r), v2.transform);
```

Finally, as there are no convenience methods for creating a skew (shear) transform, I'll illustrate by creating one manually, without further explanation (Figure 1-11):

```
v1.transform = CGAffineTransformMake(1, 0, -0.2, 1, 0, 0);
```

Transforms are useful particularly as temporary visual indicators. For example, you might call attention to a view by applying a transform that scales it up slightly, and then applying the identity transform to restore it to its original size, and animating those changes (Chapter 4).

The `transform` property lies at the heart of an iOS app's ability to rotate its interface. The window's frame and bounds, as I've already said, are invariant, locked to the screen;

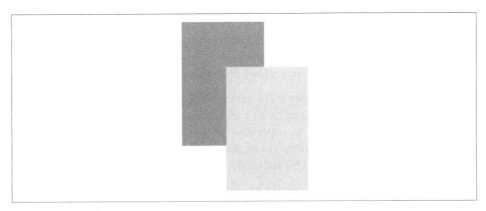

Figure 1-10. Rotation, then translation, then inversion of the rotation

Figure 1-11. Skew (shear)

but the root view's frame and bounds are not. Suppose the user rotates the device 90 degrees and the app interface is to rotate to compensate. How is this done? A 90-degree rotation transform is applied to the root view, so that its {0,0} point moves to what the user now sees as the top left of the view. The root view's subviews have their frame in the root view's bounds coordinate system, so they are effectively rotated.

In addition, the root view's bounds height and width are effectively swapped, so that its dimensions still fit the window in spite of the rotation transform: the long dimension becomes the short dimension, and *vice versa*. This raises concerns about the *position* of the root view's subviews. Consider, for example, a subview of the root view, located at the bottom right of the screen when the device is in portrait orientation. If the root view's bounds width and bounds height are effectively swapped, then that poor old subview will now be outside the bounds height, and therefore off the screen — unless something further is done. That's the subject of the next section.

Layout

We have seen that a subview moves when its superview's bounds *origin* is changed. But what happens to a subview when its superview's bounds *size* is changed? (And remember, this includes changing the superview's frame size.)

Of its own accord, nothing happens. The subview's bounds and center haven't changed, and the superview's bounds origin hasn't moved, so the subview stays in the same position relative to the top left of its superview. In real life, however, that often won't be what you want. You'll want subviews to be resized and repositioned when their superview's bounds size is changed. This is called *layout*.

The need for layout is obvious in a context such as OS X, where the user can freely resize a window, potentially disturbing your interface. For example, you'd want an OK button near the lower-right corner to stay in the lower-right corner as the window grows, while a text field at the top of the window should stay at the top of the window, but perhaps should widen as the window widens.

There are no user-resizable windows on an iOS device, but still, a superview might be resized dynamically. For example, your app might respond to the user rotating the device 90 degrees by applying a rotation transform to a view and swapping its bounds width and height values, to match the new orientation of the screen. An iPhone app might launch on two different sizes of screen: the screen of the iPhone 5 and later is taller than that of the iPhone 4S and before. A view instantiated from a nib, such as a view controller's main view or a table view cell, might be resized to fit into the interface into which it is placed.

 New in Xcode 5, you can test your nib-based interface's basic layout behavior under different conditions without running the app. While in the nib editor, open an assistant pane and switch its Tracking menu (the first component in its jump bar, Control-4) to Preview. Buttons at the lower right let you toggle between "iOS 7.0 and Later" vs. "iOS 6.1 and Earlier", between portrait and landscape orientation, and between the taller and shorter iPhone screen. See also Chapter 6.

Layout is performed in three primary ways:

Manual layout

The superview is sent the `layoutSubviews` message whenever it is resized; so, to lay out subviews manually, provide your own subclass and override `layoutSubviews`. Clearly this could turn out to be a lot of work, but it means you can do anything you like.

Autoresizing

> Autoresizing is the pre-iOS 6 way of performing layout automatically. A subview will respond to its superview's being resized, in accordance with the rules prescribed by the subview's `autoresizingMask` property value.

Autolayout

> Autolayout, introduced in iOS 6 (and incompatible with earlier systems), depends on the *constraints* of views. A constraint (an instance of NSLayoutConstraint) is a full-fledged object with numeric values; it is much more sophisticated, descriptive, and powerful than the `autoresizingMask`. Many constraints can apply to a view, and they can describe a relationship between *any* two views (not just a subview and its superview). Autolayout is implemented behind the scenes in `layoutSubviews`; in effect, constraints allow you to write sophisticated `layoutSubviews` functionality without code.

Your layout strategy can involve any combination of these. The need for manual layout is rare, but it's there if you need it. Autoresizing is used automatically unless you deliberately turn it off by setting a superview's `autoresizesSubviews` property to NO, or unless a view uses autolayout instead. Autolayout is an opt-in technology, and can be used for whatever areas of your interface you find appropriate; a view that uses autolayout can live side by side with a view that uses autoresizing.

One of the chief places where you opt in to autolayout is the nib file, and in Xcode 5 all new *.storyboard* and *.xib* files do opt in — they have autolayout turned on, by default. To see this, select the file in the Project navigator, show the File inspector, and examine the "Use Auto Layout" checkbox. On the other hand, a view that your code creates and adds to the interface, by default, uses autoresizing, not autolayout.

> If a nib's "Use Auto Layout" is checked, do not load it on any system earlier than iOS 6. If you do, your app will crash, because you're using a class, NSLayoutConstraint, that doesn't exist before iOS 6.

Autoresizing

Autoresizing is a matter of conceptually assigning a subview "springs and struts." A spring can stretch; a strut can't. Springs and struts can be assigned internally or externally, horizontally or vertically. Thus you can specify (using internal springs and struts) whether and how the view can be resized, and (using external springs and struts) whether and how the view can be repositioned. For example:

- Imagine a subview that is centered in its superview and is to stay centered, but is to resize itself as the superview is resized. It would have struts externally and springs internally.

- Imagine a subview that is centered in its superview and is to stay centered, and is *not* to resize itself as the superview is resized. It would have springs externally and struts internally.

- Imagine an OK button that is to stay in the lower right of its superview. It would have struts internally, struts externally to its right and bottom, and springs externally to its top and left.

- Imagine a text field that is to stay at the top of its superview. It is to widen as the superview widens. It would have struts externally; internally it would have a vertical strut and a horizontal spring.

To experiment with autoresizing in the nib editor, you'll need to ensure that autolayout is turned off for the *.storyboard* or *.xib* file you're editing. To do so, select that file in the Project navigator and show the File inspector: uncheck "Use Auto Layout."

When editing a nib file with autolayout turned off, you can assign a view springs and struts in the Size inspector (Autosizing). A solid line externally represents a strut; a solid line internally represents a spring. A helpful animation shows you the effect on your view's position as its superview is resized.

In code, a combination of springs and struts is set through a view's `autoresizing-Mask` property. It's a bitmask, so you use bitwise-or to combine options. The options, with names that start with `UIViewAutoresizingFlexible...`, represent springs; whatever isn't specified is a strut. The default is `UIViewAutoresizingNone`, apparently meaning all struts — but of course it can't really be *all* struts, because if the superview is resized, *something* needs to change; in reality, `UIViewAutoresizingNone` is the same as `UIViewAutoresizingFlexibleRightMargin` together with `UIViewAutoresizing-FlexibleBottomMargin`.

 In debugging, when you log a UIView to the console, its `autoresizing-Mask` is reported using the word "autoresize" and a list of the springs. The margins are LM, RM, TM, and BM; the internal dimensions are W and H. For example, `autoresize = W+BM` means that what's flexible is the width and the bottom margin.

To demonstrate autoresizing, I'll start with a view and two subviews, one stretched across the top, the other confined to the lower right (Figure 1-12):

```
UIView* v1 = [[UIView alloc] initWithFrame:CGRectMake(100, 111, 132, 194)];
v1.backgroundColor = [UIColor colorWithRed:1 green:.4 blue:1 alpha:1];
UIView* v2 = [[UIView alloc] initWithFrame:CGRectMake(0, 0, 132, 10)];
v2.backgroundColor = [UIColor colorWithRed:.5 green:1 blue:0 alpha:1];
UIView* v3 = [[UIView alloc] initWithFrame:CGRectMake(v1.bounds.size.width-20,
                                                      v1.bounds.size.height-20,
```

Figure 1-12. Before autoresizing

Figure 1-13. After autoresizing

```
                                                    20, 20)];
v3.backgroundColor = [UIColor colorWithRed:1 green:0 blue:0 alpha:1];
[mainview addSubview: v1];
[v1 addSubview: v2];
[v1 addSubview: v3];
```

To that example, I'll add code applying springs and struts to the two subviews to make them behave like the text field and the OK button I was hypothesizing earlier:

```
v2.autoresizingMask = UIViewAutoresizingFlexibleWidth;
v3.autoresizingMask = UIViewAutoresizingFlexibleTopMargin |
                      UIViewAutoresizingFlexibleLeftMargin;
```

Now I'll resize the superview, thus bringing autoresizing into play; as you can see (Figure 1-13), the subviews remain pinned in their correct relative positions:

```
CGRect r = v1.bounds;
r.size.width += 40;
r.size.height -= 50;
v1.bounds = r;
```

That example shows exactly what autoresizing is about, but it's a little artificial; in real life, the superview is more likely to be resized, not because you resize it in code, but because of automatic behavior, such as compensatory rotation of the interface when the device is rotated. To see this, you might modify the previous example to pin the size of v1 to the size of the root view, and then run the app and rotate the device. Thus you might initially configure v1 like this:

```
v1.frame = mainview.bounds;
v1.autoresizingMask = UIViewAutoresizingFlexibleHeight |
                      UIViewAutoresizingFlexibleWidth;
```

Now run the app and rotate the device (in the Simulator, repeatedly choose Hardware → Rotate Left). The view v1 now fills the screen as the interface rotates, and its subviews stay pinned in their correct relative position.

Autoresizing is effective but simple — sometimes too simple. The only relationship it describes is between a subview and its superview; it can't help you do such things as space a row of views evenly across the screen relative to one another. Before autolayout, the way to achieve more sophisticated goals of that sort was to combine autoresizing with manual layout in layoutSubviews. Autoresizing happens before layout-Subviews is called, so your layoutSubviews code is free to come marching in and tidy up whatever autoresizing didn't get quite right.

Autoresizing for subviews can be turned off at the superview level: to do so, set the superview's autoresizesSubviews property to NO.

Autolayout

Autolayout is an opt-in technology, at the level of each individual view. If no views in the interface opt in to autolayout, layout for the entire interface behaves as in iOS 5 and before. A view may opt in to autolayout in any of three ways:

- Your code adds an autolayout constraint to a view. The views involved in this constraint use autolayout.
- Your app loads a nib for which "Use Auto Layout" is checked. *Every* view instantiated from that nib uses autolayout.
- A view in the interface, which would be an instance of a custom UIView subclass of yours, returns YES from the class method `requiresConstraintBasedLayout`. That view uses autolayout.

The reason for this third approach to opting in to autolayout is that you might need autolayout to be switched on in order to add autolayout constraints in code. A common place to create constraints in code is in a view's `updateConstraints` implementation (discussed later in this chapter). However, if autolayout isn't switched on, `updateConstraints` won't be called. So `requiresConstraintBasedLayout` provides a way of switching it on.

One sibling view can use autolayout while another sibling view does not, and a superview can use autolayout while one or indeed all of its subviews do not. However, autolayout is implemented through the superview chain, so if a view uses autolayout, then automatically so do all its superviews; and if (as will almost certainly be the case) one of those views is the main view of a view controller, that view controller also uses autolayout, and receives autolayout-related events that it would not have received otherwise.

 You can't turn off autolayout for just part of a nib. Either all views instantiated from a nib use autolayout or they all use autoresizing. To generate different parts of your interface from nibs, one part with autoresizing, another part with autolayout, separate those parts into different nibs (different *.storyboard* or *.xib* files) and then load and combine them at runtime.

Constraints

An autolayout constraint, or simply *constraint*, is an NSLayoutConstraint instance, and describes either the absolute width or height of a view or a relationship between an attribute of one view and an attribute of another view. In the latter case, the attributes don't have to be the same attribute, and the two views don't have to be siblings (subviews of the same superview) or parent and child (superview and subview) — the only requirement is that they share a common ancestor (a superview at some height up the view hierarchy).

Here are the chief properties of an NSLayoutConstraint:

`firstItem`, `firstAttribute`, `secondItem`, `secondAttribute`
: The two views and their respective attributes involved in this constraint. If the constraint is describing a view's absolute height or width, the second view will be nil and the second attribute will be `NSLayoutAttributeNotAnAttribute` (which you'll probably write as 0). Additional attribute types are:

  - `NSLayoutAttributeLeft`, `NSLayoutAttributeRight`
  - `NSLayoutAttributeTop`, `NSLayoutAttributeBottom`
  - `NSLayoutAttributeLeading`, `NSLayoutAttributeTrailing`
  - `NSLayoutAttributeWidth`, `NSLayoutAttributeHeight`
  - `NSLayoutAttributeCenterX`, `NSLayoutAttributeCenterY`
  - `NSLayoutAttributeBaseline`

  The meanings of the attributes are intuitively obvious, except that you might wonder what "leading" and "trailing" mean: they are the international equivalent of "left" and "right", automatically reversing their meaning on systems whose language is written right-to-left (making it easy, say, to align the beginnings of several labels of different lengths, irrespective of localization).

`multiplier`, `constant`
: These numbers will be applied to the second attribute's value to determine the first attribute's value. The `multiplier` is multiplied by the second attribute's value; the `constant` is added to that product. The first attribute is set to the result. (The name *constant* is a very poor choice, as this value isn't constant; have the Apple folks never heard the term *addend*?) Basically, you're writing an equation of the form $a_1 = ma_2 + c$, where a_1 and a_2 are the two attributes, and m and c are the multiplier and the constant. Thus, in the degenerate case where the first attribute's value is to equal the second attribute's value, the multiplier will be 1 and the constant will be 0. If the second attribute is 0 because you're describing a view's width or height absolutely, the multiplier will be 1 and the constant will be the width or height value.

`relation`
: How the two attribute values are to be related to one another, as modified by the `multiplier` and the `constant`. This is the operator that goes in the spot where I put the equal sign in the equation in the preceding paragraph. It might be an equal sign (`NSLayoutRelationEqual`, which you'll probably write as 0), but inequalities are also permitted (`NSLayoutRelationLessThanOrEqual`, `NSLayoutRelationGreater-ThanOrEqual`).

`priority`

> Priority values range from 1000 (required) down to 1, and certain standard behaviors have standard priorities. Constraints can have different priorities, determining the order in which they are applied. Constraints are permitted to conflict with one another provided they have different priorities.

A constraint belongs to a view. A view can have many constraints: a UIView has a `constraints` property, along with these instance methods:

- `addConstraint:`, `addConstraints:`
- `removeConstraint:`, `removeConstraints:`

The question then is *which* view a given constraint should belong to. The answer is: the *closest superview* of both views involved in a constraint. Thus, for example, if the constraint dictates a view's absolute width, it belongs to that view; if it aligns the tops of two sibling views, it belongs to their superview; if it sets the top of a view in relation to the top of its superview, it belongs to the superview. (The runtime may permit you to cheat and add a constraint at too high a level.) Adding a constraint that refers to a view outside the subview hierarchy of the view to which you add it will cause a crash (with a helpful error message).

Both views involved in a constraint must be present in the view hierarchy before the constraint can be added.

NSLayoutConstraint properties are read-only, except for `priority` and `constant`. In Chapter 4, it will turn out that changing a constraint's `constant` in real time is a good way to animate a view. If you want to change anything else about an existing constraint, you must remove the constraint and add a new one.

Autoresizing constraints

The mechanism whereby individual views can opt in to autolayout can suddenly involve other views in autolayout, even though those other views were not using autolayout previously. Therefore, there needs to be a way, when such a view becomes involved in autolayout, to determine that view's position and layout through constraints in the same way they were previously being determined through its frame and its `autoresizing-Mask`. The runtime takes care of this for you: it translates the view's frame and `autoresizingMask` settings into constraints. The result is a set of implicit constraints, of class NSAutoresizingMaskLayoutConstraint, affecting this view (though they may be attached to its superview). Thanks to these implicit constraints, the layout dictated by the view's `autoresizingMask` continues to work, even though the view is no longer obeying its `autoresizingMask` but rather is using autolayout and constraints.

For example, suppose I have a UILabel whose frame is {{20,20},{42,22}}, and whose autoresizingMask is UIViewAutoresizingNone. If this label were suddenly to come under autolayout, then its superview would acquire four implicit constraints setting its width and height at 42 and 22 and its center X and center Y at 41 and 31.

This conversion is performed only if the view in question has its translates-AutoresizingMaskIntoConstraints property set to YES. That is, in fact, the default if the view came into existence either in code or by instantiation from a nib where "Use Auto Layout" is not checked. The assumption is that if a view came into existence in either of those ways, you want its frame and autoresizingMask to act as its constraints if it becomes involved in autolayout.

That's a sensible rule, but it means that if you intend to apply any explicit constraints of your own to such a view, you'll probably want to remember to turn off this automatic behavior by setting the view's translatesAutoresizingMaskIntoConstraints property to NO. If you don't, you're going to end up with both implicit constraints and explicit constraints affecting this view, and it's unlikely that you would want that. Typically, that sort of situation will result in a conflict between constraints, as I'll explain a little later; indeed, what usually happens to me is that I *don't* remember to set the view's translates-AutoresizingMaskIntoConstraints property to NO, and am reminded to do so only when I *do* get a conflict between constraints.

Creating constraints in code

We are now ready to write some code involving constraints! I'll generate the same views and subviews and layout behavior as in Figure 1-12 and Figure 1-13, but using constraints. Observe that I don't bother to assign the subviews explicit frames, because constraints will take care of positioning them, and that I remember (for once) to set their translatesAutoresizingMaskIntoConstraints properties to NO:

```
UIView* v1 = [[UIView alloc] initWithFrame:CGRectMake(100, 111, 132, 194)];
v1.backgroundColor = [UIColor colorWithRed:1 green:.4 blue:1 alpha:1];
UIView* v2 = [UIView new];
v2.backgroundColor = [UIColor colorWithRed:.5 green:1 blue:0 alpha:1];
UIView* v3 = [UIView new];
v3.backgroundColor = [UIColor colorWithRed:1 green:0 blue:0 alpha:1];
[mainview addSubview: v1];
[v1 addSubview: v2];
[v1 addSubview: v3];
v2.translatesAutoresizingMaskIntoConstraints = NO;
v3.translatesAutoresizingMaskIntoConstraints = NO;
[v1 addConstraint:
 [NSLayoutConstraint
  constraintWithItem:v2 attribute:NSLayoutAttributeLeft
  relatedBy:0
  toItem:v1 attribute:NSLayoutAttributeLeft
  multiplier:1 constant:0]];
```

```
[v1 addConstraint:
 [NSLayoutConstraint
  constraintWithItem:v2 attribute:NSLayoutAttributeRight
  relatedBy:0
  toItem:v1 attribute:NSLayoutAttributeRight
  multiplier:1 constant:0]];
[v1 addConstraint:
 [NSLayoutConstraint
  constraintWithItem:v2 attribute:NSLayoutAttributeTop
  relatedBy:0
  toItem:v1 attribute:NSLayoutAttributeTop
  multiplier:1 constant:0]];
[v2 addConstraint:
 [NSLayoutConstraint
  constraintWithItem:v2 attribute:NSLayoutAttributeHeight
  relatedBy:0
  toItem:nil attribute:0
  multiplier:1 constant:10]];
[v3 addConstraint:
 [NSLayoutConstraint
  constraintWithItem:v3 attribute:NSLayoutAttributeWidth
  relatedBy:0
  toItem:nil attribute:0
  multiplier:1 constant:20]];
[v3 addConstraint:
 [NSLayoutConstraint
  constraintWithItem:v3 attribute:NSLayoutAttributeHeight
  relatedBy:0
  toItem:nil attribute:0
  multiplier:1 constant:20]];
[v1 addConstraint:
 [NSLayoutConstraint
  constraintWithItem:v3 attribute:NSLayoutAttributeRight
  relatedBy:0
  toItem:v1 attribute:NSLayoutAttributeRight
  multiplier:1 constant:0]];
[v1 addConstraint:
 [NSLayoutConstraint
  constraintWithItem:v3 attribute:NSLayoutAttributeBottom
  relatedBy:0
  toItem:v1 attribute:NSLayoutAttributeBottom
  multiplier:1 constant:0]];
```

Now, I know what you're thinking. You're thinking: "What are you, nuts? That is a
boatload of code!" (Except that you probably used another four-letter word instead of
"boat".) But that's something of an illusion. I'd argue that what we're doing here is actually
simpler than the code with which we created Figure 1-12 using explicit frames and
autoresizing.

After all, we merely create eight constraints in eight simple commands. (I've broken
each command into multiple lines, but that's just a matter of formatting.) They're

verbose, but they are the same command repeated with different parameters, so creating them is just a matter of copy-and-paste. Moreover, our eight constraints determine the *position, size, and layout behavior* of our two subviews, so we're getting a lot of bang for our buck.

Even more telling, constraints are a far clearer expression of what's supposed to happen than setting a frame and `autoresizingMask`. The position of our subviews is described once and for all, both as they will initially appear and as they will appear if their superview is resized. And it is described meaningfully; we don't have to use arbitrary math. Recall what we had to say before:

```
v3 = [[UIView alloc] initWithFrame:CGRectMake(v1.bounds.size.width-20,
                                              v1.bounds.size.height-20,
                                              20, 20)];
```

That business of subtracting the view's height and width from its superview's bounds height and width in order to position the view is confusing and error-prone. With constraints, we can speak the truth directly; our constraints say, plainly and simply, "v3 is 20 points wide and 20 points high and flush with the bottom-right corner of v1".

In addition, of course, constraints can express things that autoresizing can't. For example, instead of applying an absolute height to v2, we could require that its height be exactly one-tenth of v1's height, regardless of how v1 is resized. To do that without constraints, you'd have to implement `layoutSubviews` and enforce it manually, in code.

 Once you are using explicit constraints to position and size a view, *do not set its frame* (or bounds and center) subsequently; use constraints alone. Otherwise, when `layoutSubviews` is called, the view will jump back to where its constraints position it. (The exception is that you *may* set a view's frame if you are *in* `layoutSubviews`, as I'll explain later.)

Visual format

If you find constraint-creation code too verbose, it may be possible to condense it somewhat. Instead of creating each constraint individually, it is sometimes possible to describe multiple constraints simultaneously through a sort of text-based shorthand, called a *visual format*. The shorthand is best understood by example:

```
@"V:|[v2(10)]"
```

In that expression, `V:` means that the vertical dimension is under discussion; the alternative is `H:`, which is also the default (so it is permitted to specify no dimension). A view's name appears in square brackets, and a pipe (|) signifies the superview, so here we're portraying v2's top edge as butting up against its superview's top edge. Numeric dimensions appear in parentheses, and a numeric dimension accompanying a view's name sets that dimension of that view, so here we're also setting v2's height to 10.

To use a visual format, you have to provide a dictionary mapping the string name of each view mentioned to the actual view. For example, the dictionary accompanying the preceding expression might be @{@"v2":v2}. We can form this dictionary automatically with a macro, NSDictionaryOfVariableBindings, which takes a list of variable names. So here's another way of expressing of the preceding code example, using the visual format shorthand throughout:

```
UIView* v1 = [[UIView alloc] initWithFrame:CGRectMake(100, 111, 132, 194)];
v1.backgroundColor = [UIColor colorWithRed:1 green:.4 blue:1 alpha:1];
UIView* v2 = [UIView new];
v2.backgroundColor = [UIColor colorWithRed:.5 green:1 blue:0 alpha:1];
UIView* v3 = [UIView new];
v3.backgroundColor = [UIColor colorWithRed:1 green:0 blue:0 alpha:1];
[mainview addSubview: v1];
[v1 addSubview: v2];
[v1 addSubview: v3];
v2.translatesAutoresizingMaskIntoConstraints = NO;
v3.translatesAutoresizingMaskIntoConstraints = NO;
NSDictionary *vs = NSDictionaryOfVariableBindings(v2,v3);
[v1 addConstraints:
 [NSLayoutConstraint
  constraintsWithVisualFormat:@"H:|[v2]|"
  options:0 metrics:nil views:vs]];
[v1 addConstraints:
 [NSLayoutConstraint
  constraintsWithVisualFormat:@"V:|[v2(10)]"
  options:0 metrics:nil views:vs]];
[v1 addConstraints:
 [NSLayoutConstraint
  constraintsWithVisualFormat:@"H:[v3(20)]|"
  options:0 metrics:nil views:vs]];
[v1 addConstraints:
 [NSLayoutConstraint
  constraintsWithVisualFormat:@"V:[v3(20)]|"
  options:0 metrics:nil views:vs]];
```

That example creates the same constraints as the previous example, but in four commands instead of eight.

The visual format syntax shows itself to best advantage when multiple views are laid out in relation to one another along the same dimension; in that situation, you get a lot of bang for your buck (many constraints generated by one visual format string). The syntax, however, is somewhat limited in what constraints it can express (you can't even use it to center things); it conceals the number and exact nature of the constraints that it produces; and personally I find it easier to make a mistake with the visual format syntax than with the complete expression of each constraint. Still, you'll want to become familiar with the visual format syntax, not least because console messages describing a constraint sometimes use it.

Here are some further things to know when generating constraints with the visual format syntax:

- The `metrics:` parameter is a dictionary of NSNumber values. This lets you use a name in the visual format string where a numeric value needs to go.

- The `options:` parameter is a bitmask letting you do things like add alignments. The alignments you specify are applied to all the views mentioned in the visual format string.

- To specify the distance between two successive views, use hyphens surrounding the numeric value, like this: `@"[v1]-20-[v2]"`. The numeric value may optionally be surrounded by parentheses. A single hyphen means that a default distance should be used.

- A numeric value in parentheses may be preceded by an equality or inequality operator, and may be followed by an at sign with a priority. Multiple numeric values, separated by comma, may appear in parentheses together. For example: `@"[v1(>=20@400,<=30)]"`.

For formal details of the visual format syntax, see the "Visual Format Syntax" chapter of Apple's *Auto Layout Guide*.

Mistakes with constraints

You can (and will) make two major kinds of mistake with constraints:

Conflict
> You can apply constraints that can't be satisfied simultaneously. This will be reported in the console (at great length). Only required constraints (priority 1000) can contribute to a conflict, as the runtime is free to ignore lower-priority constraints that it can't satisfy. For example, to the previous code, append this line:

```
[v1 addConstraints:
 [NSLayoutConstraint
  constraintsWithVisualFormat:@"V:[v3(10)]|"
  options:0 metrics:nil views:vs]];
```

> The height of v3 can't be both 10 (as here) and 20 (as in the preceding line). The runtime reports the conflict, and tells you which constraints are causing it.

Underdetermination (ambiguity)
> A view uses autolayout, but you haven't supplied sufficient information to determine its size and position. This is a far more insidious problem, because nothing bad may seem to happen, so you might not discover it until much later. If you're lucky, the view will at least fail to appear, or will appear in an undesirable place,

alerting you to the problem. For example, in the last line of the previous code, we set the height of v3 to 20; suppose we remove that specification:

```
[v1 addConstraints:
 [NSLayoutConstraint
  constraintsWithVisualFormat:@"V:[v3]|"
  options:0 metrics:nil views:vs]];
```

Fortunately, v3 fails to appear in the interface, so we know we've made a mistake.

To help you analyze ambiguity, log a view's hasAmbiguousLayout property (a BOOL); be sure to remove that call before submitting your app to the App Store. I find it useful to set up a category on NSLayoutConstraint with a method that lets me check a view and all its subviews at any depth for ambiguity:

```
@implementation NSLayoutConstraint (Ambiguity)
+ (void) reportAmbiguity:(UIView*) v {
    if (nil == v)
        v = [[UIApplication sharedApplication] keyWindow];
    for (UIView* vv in v.subviews) {
        NSLog(@"%@ %d", vv, vv.hasAmbiguousLayout);
        if (vv.subviews.count)
            [self reportAmbiguity:vv];
    }
}
@end
```

Alternatively, pause the running app and ask the debugger for the key window's _autolayoutTrace; ambiguously laid out views are clearly marked:

```
(lldb) po [[UIWindow keyWindow] _autolayoutTrace]
(id) $1 = 0x074a41a0
*<UIWindow:0x749b890>
|   *<UIView:0x749ccb0>
|   |   *<UIView:0x749c280>
|   |   |   *<UIView:0x749c790>
|   |   |   *<UIView:0x749c930> - AMBIGUOUS LAYOUT
```

To get a full list of the constraints responsible for positioning a particular view within its superview, log the results of calling the UIView instance methods constraints-AffectingLayoutForAxis:; again, be sure to remove that call before finalizing your app. These constraints do not necessarily belong to this view (and the output doesn't tell you what view they do belong to). Your choices of axis are UILayoutConstraint-AxisHorizontal and UILayoutConstraintAxisVertical, but you are more likely to write these as 0 and 1, and if you are paused in the debugger and talking to it through the console, you'll have to. If a view doesn't participate in autolayout, the result will be an empty array. Again, a category method can come in handy:

```
@implementation NSLayoutConstraint (Listing)
+ (void) listConstraints:(UIView*) v {
    if (nil == v)
        v = [[UIApplication sharedApplication] keyWindow];
    for (UIView* vv in v.subviews) {
        NSArray* arr1 = [vv constraintsAffectingLayoutForAxis:0];
        NSArray* arr2 = [vv constraintsAffectingLayoutForAxis:1];
        NSLog(@"%@\nH: %@\nV:%@", vv, arr1, arr2);
        if (vv.subviews.count)
            [self listConstraints:vv];
    }
}
@end
```

Given the notions of conflict and ambiguity, we can understand what priorities are for. Imagine that all constraints have been placed in boxes, where each box is a priority value, in descending order. The first box (1000) contains all the required constraints, so all required constraints are obeyed first. (If they conflict, that's bad, and a report appears in the log; meanwhile, the system implicitly lowers the priority of one of the conflicting constraints, so that it doesn't have to obey it and can continue with layout by satisfying the remaining required constraints.) If there still isn't enough information to perform unambiguous layout given the required priorities alone, we pull the constraints out of the next box and try to obey them. If we can, consistently with what we've already done, fine; if we can't, or if ambiguity remains, we look in the *next* box — and so on. For a box after the first, we don't care about obeying exactly the constraints it contains; if an ambiguity remains, we can use a lower-priority constraint value to give us something to aim at, resolving the ambiguity, without fully obeying the lower-priority constraint's desires. For example, an inequality is an ambiguity, because an infinite number of values will satisfy it; a lower-priority equality can tell us what value to prefer, resolving the ambiguity, but there's no conflict even if we can't fully achieve that preferred value.

Intrinsic content size

Some built-in interface objects, when using autolayout, have an inherent size in one or both dimensions, so they are not ambiguously laid out even if no explicit NSLayout-Constraint dictates their size. Rather, the inherent size is used to generate constraints implicitly, of class NSContentSizeLayoutConstraint. For example, a button has a standard height, and its width is determined by its title. This inherent size is the object's *intrinsic content size.*

 In iOS 7, a user can be permitted to change the size of text throughout the interface (see Chapter 10). If your views, such as buttons and labels, can respond to such a change, their intrinsic size can change as well. You will want to configure your autolayout constraints so that your interface responds to such changes gracefully.

The tendency of an interface object to size itself to its intrinsic content size must not be allowed to conflict with its tendency to obey explicit constraints. Assigning a UILabel an explicit, absolute width constraint should not cause a conflict with its intrinsic content size; and we wouldn't want a UILabel with a lot of text to be compelled by its intrinsic content size to extend outside of its superview. Therefore these tendencies have a lowered priority, and come into force only if no constraint of a higher priority prevents them. Methods allow you to access these priorities:

contentHuggingPriorityForAxis:
> A view's resistance to growing larger than its intrinsic size in this dimension. In effect, there is an inequality constraint saying that the view's size in this dimension should be less than or equal to its intrinsic size. The default priority is 250 (also known as UILayoutPriorityDefaultLow).

contentCompressionResistancePriorityForAxis:
> A view's resistance to shrinking smaller than its intrinsic size in this dimension. In effect, there is an inequality constraint saying that the view's size in this dimension should be greater than or equal to its intrinsic size. The default priority is 750 (also known as UILayoutPriorityDefaultHigh).

(The dimensions are UILayoutConstraintAxisHorizontal and UILayoutConstraintAxisVertical.)

Those methods are getters; there are corresponding setters. Situations where you would need to change the priorities of these tendencies are few, but they do exist. For example, here are the visual formats configuring two adjacent labels pinned to the superview and to one another:

```
@"V:|-[_lab1]"
@"V:|-[_lab2]"
@"H:|-20-[_lab1]"
@"H:[_lab2]-20-|"
@"H:[_lab1]-(>=20)-[_lab2]"
```

There may be no ambiguity initially, but as the superview becomes narrower or the text of the labels becomes longer, an ambiguity arises: which label should be truncated? To dictate the answer, it suffices to raise the compression resistance priority of one of the labels by a single point:

```
[self.lab1 setContentCompressionResistancePriority:751
    forAxis:UILayoutConstraintAxisHorizontal];
```

Alternatively, you may want to lower the priority of some other constraint, to allow intrinsic content size to predominate. An example that Apple gives is a label to the left of a centered button and not permitted to overlap with it. As the text of the label becomes longer, at first, the label grows leftward. But the label should not stretch leftward past the left side of its superview, so it has an inequality constraint pinning its left at a guaranteed minimum distance from the superview's left. When it hits that limit, the label's text should not then be truncated if it doesn't have to be, so the priority with which the button is horizontally centered is set lower than the label's compression resistance priority; in effect, the label is able to force the button to move to the right:

```
self.button.translatesAutoresizingMaskIntoConstraints = NO;
self.label.translatesAutoresizingMaskIntoConstraints = NO;
NSDictionary* d = NSDictionaryOfVariableBindings(_button,_label);
[self.view addConstraints:
 [NSLayoutConstraint
  constraintsWithVisualFormat:@"V:[_button]-(112)-|"
  options:0 metrics:nil views:d]];
[self.view addConstraints:
 [NSLayoutConstraint
  constraintsWithVisualFormat:@"H:|-(>=10)-[_label]-[_button]-(>=10)-|"
  options:NSLayoutFormatAlignAllBaseline metrics:nil views:d]];
NSLayoutConstraint* con =
[NSLayoutConstraint
 constraintWithItem:_button attribute:NSLayoutAttributeCenterX
 relatedBy:0
 toItem:self.view attribute:NSLayoutAttributeCenterX
 multiplier:1 constant:0];
con.priority = 700; // try commenting this out to see the difference
[self.view addConstraint:con];
```

You can supply an intrinsic size in your own custom UIView subclass by implementing `intrinsicContentSize`. Obviously you should do this only if your view's size depends on its contents. If you need the runtime to call `intrinsicContentSize` again, because that size has changed and the view needs to be laid out afresh, send your view the `invalidateIntrinsicContentSize` message.

By the same token, you may want to be able to align your custom UIView with another view by their baselines. If your view's baseline is its own bottom, there's nothing to do; but it may be that your view has content that gives a different meaning to the notion of a baseline. To dictate where your custom view's baseline should be, you do not provide a numeric value. Rather, your custom view must contain a subview whose bottom will function as the baseline, and you return that subview in your UIView subclass's `view-ForBaselineLayout`.

 The intrinsic size of a UILabel has some additional complications connected with its text wrapping behavior. I'll discuss the matter in detail in Chapter 10.

Constraints in the Nib

In a *.xib* or *.storyboard* file where "Use Auto Layout" is checked, a vast array of tools springs to life in the nib editor to help you create constraints that will be instantiated from the nib along with the views.

The nib editor would like to help prevent you from ending up with conflicting or ambiguous constraints. In Xcode 4.5, the nib editor did this by making it impossible for conflicting or ambiguous constraints to exist in the nib, even for a moment. This, however, turned out to be too much help. Developers were surprised and confused when their app turned out to be full of constraints they hadn't asked for, and editing the nib so as to dictate the constraints you wanted, instead of the constraints the nib editor wanted, was often difficult or impossible. In Xcode 5, therefore, the nib editor is much more relaxed about conflicting and ambiguous constraints, and gives you full power to edit constraints as you please, but of course the cost of such increased power is increased complexity.

The Xcode 5 nib editor *doesn't generate any constraints* unless you ask it to. However, it doesn't want the app to run with ambiguous layout, because then you might not see any views at all; you wouldn't be able to test your app until you'd fully worked out all the constraints throughout the interface. Therefore, if your views lack needed constraints, the nib supplies them implicitly behind the scenes so that they are present at runtime:

No constraints
> If a view is affected by no constraints at all, it is given constraints tagged in the debugger as "IB auto generated at build time for view with fixed frame."

Ambiguous constraints
> If a view is affected by some constraints but not enough to disambiguate fully, it is given additional constraints tagged in the debugger as "IB auto generated at build time for view with ambiguity."

The Xcode 5 nib editor also *doesn't change any constraints* unless you ask it to. If you create constraints and then move or resize a view affected by those constraints, the constraints are *not* automatically changed. This means that the constraints no longer match the way the view is portrayed; if the constraints were to position the view, they wouldn't put it where you've put it. The nib editor will alert you to this situation (a Misplaced Views issue), and can readily resolve it for you, but it won't do so unless you explicitly ask it to.

Creating a constraint

The Xcode 5 nib editor provides two primary ways to create a constraint:

- Control-drag from one view to another. A HUD appears, listing constraints that you can create (Figure 1-14). Either view can be in the canvas or in the document outline. To create an internal width or height constraint, control-drag from a view to itself! When you control-drag within the canvas, the direction of the drag is used to winnow the options presented in the HUD; for example, if you control-drag horizontally within a view in the canvas, the HUD lists Width but not Height.

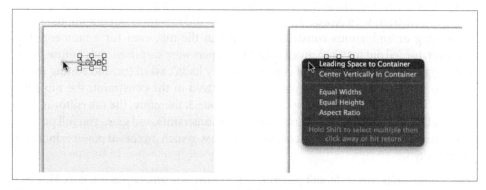

Figure 1-14. Creating a constraint by control-dragging

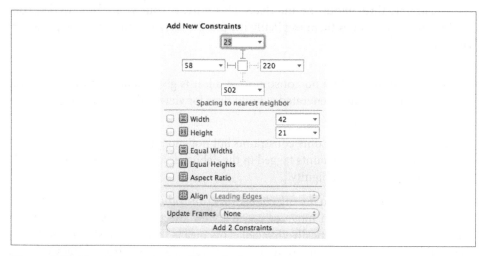

Figure 1-15. Creating constraints from the layout bar

- Choose from the Editor → Align or Editor → Pin hierarchical menus, or click the first or second buttons in the four-button cartouche (the layout bar) at the lower right of the canvas.

The buttons in the layout bar are very powerful! They present little popover dialogs where you can choose multiple constraints to create (possibly for multiple views, if that's what you've selected beforehand) and provide them with numeric values (Figure 1-15). Constraints are not actually added until you click Add Constraints at the bottom. Before clicking Add Constraints, think about the Update Frames pop-up menu; if you don't update frames, the views may end up being drawn in the canvas differently from how the constraints describe them (a Misplaced Views issue).

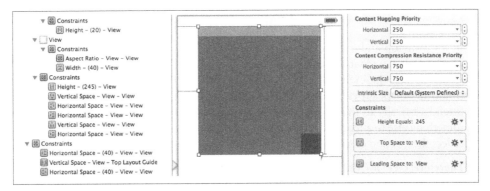

Figure 1-16. A view's constraints displayed in the nib

Viewing and editing constraints

Constraints in the nib are full-fledged objects. They can be selected, edited, and deleted. Moreover, you can create an outlet to a constraint (and there are reasons why you might want to do so).

Constraints in the nib are visible in three places (Figure 1-16):

In the document outline
> Constraints are listed in a special category, "Constraints", under the view to which they belong. (You'll have a much easier time distinguishing these constraints if you give your views meaningful labels!)

In the canvas
> Constraints appear graphically as dimension lines when you select a view that they affect.

In the Size inspector
> When a view affected by constraints is selected, the Size inspector displays those constraints.

When you select a constraint in the document outline or the canvas, you can view and edit its values in the Attributes inspector. Alternatively, for simple editing of a constraint's constant, relation, and priority, double-click the constraint in the canvas to summon a little popover dialog.

When you're viewing a view's constraints in the Size inspector, you can't edit those constraints in the Attributes inspector — you're in the Size inspector instead! However, the gear menu at the right of a constraint lets you choose Select and Edit, which switches to the Attributes inspector for that constraint.

The Size inspector also provides access to a view's content hugging and content compression resistance priority settings. Beneath these, there's an Intrinsic Size pop-up

Top and Bottom Layout Guides

In iOS, the top and bottom of the interface are often occupied by a bar (status bar, navigation bar, toolbar, tab bar — see Chapter 12). Your layout will typically occupy the region *between* these bars. On iOS 6 and before, this was trivial, because a view controller would automatically resize its view to fit into that region. But in iOS 7, a root view can extend vertically to the edges of the screen *behind* those bars. Therefore, you need something else to anchor your constraints to — something that will move vertically to reflect the location of the bars.

Therefore, UIViewController in iOS supplies and maintains two invisible views, the *top layout guide* and the *bottom layout guide*, which it injects as subviews into the view hierarchy of its root view. Your vertical constraints will usually not be between a subview and the top or bottom of the root view, but between a subview and the bottom of the top layout guide, or a subview and the top of the bottom layout guide.

You can access these guides programmatically through the UIViewController properties topLayoutGuide and bottomLayoutGuide. For example:

```
UIView* tlg = (id)self.topLayoutGuide;
NSDictionary* d = NSDictionaryOfVariableBindings(v, tlg);
[self.view addConstraints:
  [NSLayoutConstraint constraintsWithVisualFormat:@"V:[tlg][v(10)]"
     options:0 metrics:nil views:d]];
```

In the nib editor, the guides are listed in the document outline and elsewhere, and an attempt to create a vertical constraint to the root view by Control-dragging will automatically use a guide rather than the top or bottom of the root view.

menu. The idea here is that your custom view might have an intrinsic size, but the nib editor doesn't know this, so it will report an ambiguity when you fail to provide (say) a width constraint that you know isn't actually needed; choose Placeholder to supply an intrinsic size and relieve the nib editor's worries (and to prevent the missing constraints from being generated automatically at runtime).

There is also a Placeholder checkbox in the Attributes inspector when you've selected a constraint. If you check this checkbox, the constraint you're editing won't be instantiated when the nib is loaded: in effect, it will be removed at runtime. It will *not* be replaced by an automatically generated constraint; you are deliberately generating ambiguous layout when the views and constraints are instantiated from the nib.

A typical reason for doing this is that your code will be adding another constraint that will make up for the loss of this one. You don't want to omit the constraint from the nib, because then the nib editor will complain of ambiguity and will automatically generate a constraint to make up for it. The reason for the Placeholder checkbox is that, without it, not only would you have to add the new constraint in code, but also you'd have to remove the existing constraint in code after it is instantiated from the nib. That is rather elaborate to configure; you have to make an outlet in order to access the existing constraint after the nib loads, which seems wasteful considering that you're immediately going to delete that outlet's destination object. (In Xcode 4.5 and 4.6, where there was no Placeholder checkbox, that was exactly what you had to do.)

Problems with constraints

If a view is affected by any constraints, the Xcode 5 nib editor will happily permit them to be ambiguous or conflicting, but it will also call the situation to your attention:

Issue navigator
> At build time, the Issue navigator will display Ambiguous Layout and Unsupported Configuration entries, as appropriate.

Canvas
> Constraints drawn in the canvas when you select a view that they affect use color coding to express their status:

> *Conflicting constraints*
> > Drawn in red.

> *Insufficient constraints*
> > Drawn in orange. These are ambiguous constraints: they don't conflict, but they aren't sufficient to describe a view completely.

> *Satisfactory constraints*
> > Drawn in blue.

Document outline
> If there are layout issues, the document outline displays a right arrow in a red or orange circle. Click it to see a detailed list of the issues (Figure 1-17). Hover the mouse over a title to see an Info button which you can click to learn more about the nature of this issue. The icons at the right are buttons: click one for a list of things the nib editor is offering to do to fix the issue for you. The chief issues are:

> *Conflicting Constraints*
> > A conflict between constraints.

> *Missing Constraints*
> > Ambiguous layout.

> *Misplaced Views*
> > If you manually change the frame of a view that is affected by constraints (including its intrinsic size), then the nib editor canvas may be displaying that view differently from how it would really appear if the current constraints were obeyed. A Misplaced Views situation is also reflected in the canvas:

Figure 1-17. Layout issues in the document outline

- The constraints in the canvas display the numeric *difference* between their values and the view's frame. They are drawn in orange even if they are not insufficient.

- A dotted outline in the canvas may show where the view would be drawn if the existing constraints were obeyed.

A hierarchical menu, Editor → Resolve Auto Layout Issues (also available from the third button in the layout bar at the bottom right of the canvas), proposes five large-scale moves involving *all* the constraints affecting selected views or all views:

Update Frames

Changes the way the view is drawn in the canvas, to show how it would really appear in the running app under the constraints as they stand. Be careful: if constraints are ambiguous, *this can cause a view to disappear.*

Alternatively, if you have resized a view with intrinsic size constraints, such as a button or a label, and you want it to resume the size it would have according to those intrinsic size constraints, select the view and choose Editor → Size to Fit Content.

Update Constraints

Choose this menu item to change numerically all the existing constraints affecting a view to match the way the canvas is currently drawing the view's frame.

Add Missing Constraints

Create new constraints so that the view has sufficient constraints to describe its frame unambiguously. The added constraints correspond to the way the canvas is currently drawing the view's frame.

Not everything that this command does may be what you ultimately want; you should regard it as a starting point. For example, the nib editor doesn't know whether you think a certain view's width should be determined by an internal width constraint or by pinning it to the left and right of its superview; and it may generate alignment constraints with other views that you never intended.

Reset to Suggested Constraints
This is as if you chose Clear Constraints followed by Add Missing Constraints: it removes all constraints affecting the view, and replaces them with a complete set of automatically generated constraints describing the way the canvas is currently drawing the view's frame.

Clear Constraints
Removes all constraints affecting the view.

Order of Layout Events

When the moment comes to lay out a view, the following events take place:

1. The view and its subviews are sent `updateConstraints`, starting at the *bottom* of the hierarchy (the deepest subview) and working up to the top (the view itself, possibly the root view). This event may be omitted for a view if its constraints have not changed, but it will certainly be called for the view at the top of the hierarchy.

   You can override `updateConstraints` in a UIView subclass. You might do this, for example, if your subclass is capable of altering its own constraints and you need a signal that now is the time to do so. You must call `super` or the app will crash (with a helpful error message).

   You should never call `updateConstraints` directly. To trigger an immediate call to `updateConstraints`, send a view the `updateConstraintsIfNeeded` message. But `updateConstraints` may still not be sent unless constraints have changed or the view is at the top of the hierarchy. To force `updateConstraints` to be sent to a view, send it the `setNeedsUpdateConstraints` message.

2. The view and its subviews are sent `layoutSubviews`, starting at the *top* of the hierarchy (the view itself, possibly the root view) and working down to the bottom (the deepest subview).

   You can override `layoutSubviews` in a subclass in order to take a hand in the layout process. If you're not using autolayout, `layoutSubviews` does nothing by default; `layoutSubviews` is your opportunity to perform manual layout after autoresizing has taken place. If you are using autolayout, you must call `super` or the app will crash (with a helpful error message).

You should never call `layoutSubviews` directly; to trigger an immediate call to `layoutSubviews`, send a view the `layoutIfNeeded` message (which may cause layout of the entire view tree, not only below but also above this view), or send `setNeedsLayout` to trigger a call to `layoutSubviews` later on, after your code finishes running, when layout would normally take place.

When you're using autolayout, what happens in `layoutSubviews`? The runtime examines all the constraints affecting this view's subviews, works out values for their frames, and assigns those views those frames. In other words, `layoutSubviews` performs manual layout! The constraints are merely instructions attached to the views; `layoutSubviews` reads them and responds accordingly, setting frames in the good old-fashioned way. (Thus, `layoutSubviews` is a place where it is legal — and indeed necessary — to set the frame of a view governed by explicit constraints.)

Knowing this, you might override `layoutSubviews` when you're using autolayout, in order to tweak the outcome. First you call `super`, causing all the subviews to adopt their new frames. Then you examine those frames. If you don't like the outcome, you can change the situation, removing subviews, adding or removing constraints, and so on — and then you call `super` again, to get a new layout outcome.

Unless you explicitly demand immediate layout, layout isn't performed until your code finishes running (and then only if needed). Moreover, ambiguous layout isn't ambiguous until layout actually takes place. Thus, for example, it's perfectly reasonable to cause an ambiguous layout temporarily, provided you resolve the ambiguity before `layoutSubviews` is called. On the other hand, a conflicting constraint conflicts the instant it is added.

It is also possible to *simulate* layout of a view in accordance with its constraints and those of its subviews. This is useful for discovering ahead of time what a view's size would be if layout were performed at this moment. Send the view the `systemLayoutSizeFittingSize:` message. The system will attempt to reach or at least approach the size you specify, at a very low priority; mostly likely you'll specify either `UILayoutFittingCompressedSize` or `UILayoutFittingExpandedSize`, depending on whether what you're after is the smallest or largest size the view can legally attain. I'll show an example in Chapter 8.

Autolayout and View Transforms

Suppose I apply to a view a transform that grows it slightly:

```
v.transform = CGAffineTransformMakeScale(1.2,1.2);
```

I expect the view to expand in both dimensions, with all four sides moving away from the center. Under autolayout, that might not be what I see at all. The view might grow down and right, while its left and top hold steady. The view might not grow at all in one or both dimensions. It all depends on the view's constraints.

The fact is that autolayout does not play well with view transforms. There are two reasons for this:

- Applying a transform to a view triggers layout immediately.
- When layout is triggered, `layoutSubviews` applies constraints to a view by setting its frame.

Thus, when you apply a transform to a view that uses autolayout, autolayout can come along and change the view's frame in such a way as to thwart the transform. This seems like a bug. There is no reason why a transform should cause layout to be triggered, and setting a view's frame is exactly what you're *not* supposed to do when a view has a nonidentity transform.

This problem is not easy to solve. I have three suggestions, none of them entirely satisfactory:

- Plan your constraints in advance. If you're going to be applying a transform to a view, set up that view's constraints so that they affect its center, not its frame.
- Set up a host view and a subview. The host view is positioned by constraints, in whatever way you like: it is also invisible. Now take the subview out of the influence of autolayout altogether: remove any constraints that affect it, and set its `translatesAutoresizingMaskIntoConstraints` to YES.
- Use a layer transform (Chapter 3) instead of a view transform, since applying a layer transform doesn't trigger layout.

CHAPTER 2

Drawing

Many UIView subclasses, such as a UIButton or a UILabel, know how to draw themselves; sooner or later, though, you're going to want to do some drawing of your own. You can draw an image in code, and then display it in your interface in a class that knows how to show an image, such as a UIImageView or a UIButton. A pure UIView is all about drawing, and it leaves that drawing largely up to you; your code determines what the view draws, and hence what it looks like in your interface.

This chapter discusses the mechanics of drawing. Don't be afraid to write drawing code of your own! It isn't difficult, and it's often the best way to make your app look the way you want it to.

(For how to draw text, see Chapter 12.)

UIImage and UIImageView

The basic general UIKit image class is UIImage. UIImage can read a file from disk, so if an image does not need to be created dynamically, but has already been created before your app runs, then drawing may be as simple as providing an image file as a resource in your app's bundle. The system knows how to work with many standard image file types, such as TIFF, JPEG, GIF, and PNG; when an image file is to be included in your app bundle, iOS has a special affinity for PNG files, and you should prefer them whenever possible. You can also obtain image data in some other way, such as by downloading it, and transform this into a UIImage. Conversely, you can draw your own image for display in your interface or for saving to disk (image file output is discussed in Chapter 23).

In the very simplest case, an image file in your app's bundle can be obtained through the UIImage class method `imageNamed:`. Now that there are asset catalogs, this method looks in two places for the image:

Top level of app bundle

We look at the top level the app's bundle for an image file with the supplied name. The name is case-sensitive and should include the file extension; if the supplied name doesn't include a file extension, *.png* is assumed, but I never take advantage of this feature.

Asset catalog

We look in the asset catalog for an image set with the supplied name. If the supplied name has a file extension, it is stripped off; this allows old code to keep working after an image is moved into an asset catalog. This search takes priority: if a matching image set is found in an asset catalog, it is used, and the top level of the app bundle is not searched.

A nice thing about `imageNamed:` is that memory management is handled for you: the image data may be cached in memory, and if you ask for the same image by calling `imageNamed:` again later, the cached data may be supplied immediately. Alternatively, you can read an image file from anywhere in your app's bundle directly and without caching, using the class method `imageWithContentsOfFile:` or the instance method `initWithContentsOfFile:`, both of which expect a pathname string; you can get a reference to your app's bundle with [`NSBundle mainBundle`], and NSBundle then provides instance methods for getting the pathname of a file within the bundle, such as `pathForResource:ofType:`.

Methods that specify a resource in the app bundle, such as `imageNamed:` and `pathForResource:ofType:`, respond to suffixes in the name of an actual resource file. On a device with a double-resolution screen, when an image is obtained by name from the app bundle, a file with the same name extended by `@2x`, if there is one, will be used automatically, with the resulting UIImage marked as double-resolution by assigning it a `scale` property value of 2. In this way, your app can contain both a single-resolution and a double-resolution version of an image file; on the double-resolution display device, the double-resolution version of the image is used, and is drawn at the same size as the single-resolution image. Thus, on the double-resolution screen, your code continues to work without change, but your images look sharper.

Similarly, a file with the same name extended by `~ipad` will automatically be used if the app is running on an iPad. You can use this in a universal app to supply different images automatically depending on whether the app runs on an iPhone or iPod touch, on the one hand, or on an iPad, on the other. (This is true not just for images but for *any* resource obtained by name from the bundle. See Apple's *Resource Programming Guide*.)

One of the great benefits of an asset catalog, though, is that you can forget all about those name suffix conventions. An asset catalog knows when to use an alternate image within an image set, not from its name, but from its place in the catalog. Put the single- and double-resolution alternatives into the slots marked "1x" and "2x" respectively. For a distinct iPad version of an image, switch the Devices pop-up menu in the image set's Attributes inspector from Universal to Device Specific and check the boxes for the cases you want to distinguish; separate slots for those device types will appear in the asset catalog.

 iOS 7 doesn't run on any single-resolution iPhone-sized devices, so an iPhone-only app doesn't need any single-resolution image variants. But iOS 7 does run on both single-resolution and double-resolution iPads.

Many built-in Cocoa interface objects will accept a UIImage as part of how they draw themselves; for example, a UIButton can display an image, and a UINavigationBar or a UITabBar can have a background image. I'll discuss those in Chapter 12. But when you simply want an image to appear in your interface, you'll probably hand it to a UIImage-View, which has the most knowledge and flexibility with regard to displaying images and is intended for this purpose.

When you configure an interface object's image in the nib editor, you're instructing that interface object to call `imageNamed:` to fetch its image, and everything about how `image-Named:` conducts the search for the image will be true of how the interface object finds its image at runtime. The nib editor supplies some shortcuts in this regard: the Attributes inspector of an interface object that can have an image will have a pop-up menu listing known images in your project, and such images are also listed in the Media library (Command-Option-Control-4). Media library images can often be dragged onto an interface object in the canvas to assign them, and if you drag a Media library image into a plain view, it is transformed into a UIImageView displaying that image.

A UIImageView can actually have *two* images, one assigned to its `image` property and the other assigned to its `highlightedImage` property; the value of the UIImageView's `highlighted` property dictates which of the two is displayed at any given moment. A UIImageView does not automatically highlight itself merely because the user taps it, the way a button does. However, there are certain situations where a UIImageView will respond to the highlighting of its surroundings; for example, within a table view cell, a UIImageView will show its highlighted image when the cell is highlighted. You can, of course, also use the notion of UIImageView highlighting yourself however you like.

A UIImageView is a UIView, so it can have a background color in addition to its image, it can have an alpha (transparency) value, and so forth (see Chapter 1). A UIImageView without a background color is invisible except for its image, so the image simply appears in the interface, without the user being aware that it resides in a rectangular host. An image may have areas that are transparent, and a UIImageView will respect this; thus an image of any shape can appear. A UIImageView without an image and without a background color is invisible, so you could start with an empty UIImageView in the

Figure 2-1. Mars appears in my interface

place where you will later need an image and subsequently assign the image in code. You can assign a new image to substitute one image for another.

How a UIImageView draws its image depends upon the setting of its `contentMode` property. (The `contentMode` property is inherited from UIView; I'll discuss its more general purpose later in this chapter.) For example, `UIViewContentModeScaleToFill` means the image's width and height are set to the width and height of the view, thus filling the view completely even if this alters the image's aspect ratio; `UIViewContentModeCenter` means the image is drawn centered in the view without altering its size. The best way to get a feel for the meanings of the various `contentMode` settings is to assign a UIImageView a small image in a nib and then, in the Attributes inspector, change the Mode pop-up menu, and see where and how the image draws itself.

You should also pay attention to a UIImageView's `clipsToBounds` property; if it is NO, its image, even if it is larger than the image view and even if it is not scaled down by the `contentMode`, may be displayed in its entirety, extending beyond the image view itself.

When creating a UIImageView in code, you can take advantage of a convenience initializer, `initWithImage:` (or `initWithImage:highlightedImage:`). The default `contentMode` is `UIViewContentModeScaleToFill`, but the image is not initially scaled; rather, the view itself is sized to match the image. You will still probably need to position the UIImageView correctly in its superview. In this example, I'll put a picture of the planet Mars in the center of the app's interface (Figure 2-1):

```
UIImageView* iv =
    [[UIImageView alloc] initWithImage:[UIImage imageNamed:@"Mars"]];
[mainview addSubview: iv];
iv.center = CGPointMake(CGRectGetMidX(iv.superview.bounds),
                        CGRectGetMidY(iv.superview.bounds));
iv.frame = CGRectIntegral(iv.frame);
```

What happens to the size of an existing UIImageView when you assign an image to it depends on whether the image view is using autolayout. If it isn't, or if its size is constrained absolutely, the image view's size doesn't change. But under autolayout, the size of the new image becomes the image view's new `intrinsicContentSize`, so the image view will adopt the image's size unless other constraints prevent. (If a UIImageView is assigned both an `image` and a `highlightedImage`, and if they are of different sizes, the view's `intrinsicContentSize` adopts the size of the `image`.)

Resizable Images

A UIImage can be transformed into a *resizable image,* by sending it the `resizableImage-WithCapInsets:resizingMode:` message. The `capInsets:` argument is a UIEdgeInsets, a struct consisting of four floats representing inset values starting at the top and proceeding counterclockwise — top, left, bottom, right. They represent distances inward from the edges of the image. In a context larger than the image, a resizable image can behave in one of two ways, depending on the `resizingMode:` value:

`UIImageResizingModeTile`
> The interior rectangle of the inset area is tiled (repeated) in the interior; each edge is formed by tiling the corresponding edge rectangle outside the inset area. The four corner rectangles outside the inset area are drawn unchanged.

`UIImageResizingModeStretch`
> The interior rectangle of the inset area is stretched *once* to fill the interior; each edge is formed by stretching the corresponding edge rectangle outside the inset area *once.* The four corner rectangles outside the inset area are drawn unchanged.

Certain places in the interface require a resizable image; for example, a custom image that serves as the track of a slider or progress view (Chapter 12) must be resizable, so that it can fill a space of any length. And there can frequently be other situations where you want to fill a background by tiling or stretching an existing image.

In these examples, assume that `self.iv` is a UIImageView with absolute height and width (so that it won't adopt the size of its image) and with a `contentMode` of `UIView-ContentModeScaleToFill` (so that the image will exhibit resizing behavior). First, I'll illustrate tiling an entire image (Figure 2-2); note that the `capInsets:` is `UIEdgeInsets-Zero`:

```
UIImage* mars = [UIImage imageNamed:@"Mars"];
UIImage* marsTiled =
    [mars resizableImageWithCapInsets: UIEdgeInsetsZero
                        resizingMode: UIImageResizingModeTile];
self.iv.image = marsTiled;
```

Now we'll tile the interior of the image, changing the `capInsets:` argument from the previous code (Figure 2-3):

```
UIImage* marsTiled = [mars resizableImageWithCapInsets:
                    UIEdgeInsetsMake(mars.size.height/4.0,
                            mars.size.width/4.0,
                            mars.size.height/4.0,
                            mars.size.width/4.0)
                resizingMode: UIImageResizingModeTile];
```

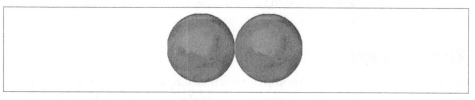

Figure 2-2. Tiling the entire image of Mars

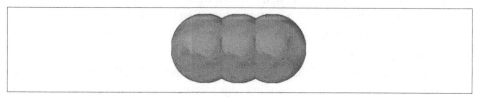

Figure 2-3. Tiling the interior of Mars

Figure 2-4. Stretching the interior of Mars

Next, I'll illustrate stretching. We'll start by changing just the `resizingMode:` from the previous code (Figure 2-4):

```
UIImage* marsTiled = [mars resizableImageWithCapInsets:
                        UIEdgeInsetsMake(mars.size.height/4.0,
                                         mars.size.width/4.0,
                                         mars.size.height/4.0,
                                         mars.size.width/4.0)
                        resizingMode: UIImageResizingModeStretch];
```

A common stretching strategy is to make almost half the original image serve as a cap inset, leaving just a pixel or two in the center to fill the entire interior of the resulting image (Figure 2-5):

```
UIImage* marsTiled = [mars resizableImageWithCapInsets:
                        UIEdgeInsetsMake(mars.size.height/2.0 - 1,
                                         mars.size.width/2.0 - 1,
                                         mars.size.height/2.0 - 1,
                                         mars.size.width/2.0 - 1)
                        resizingMode: UIImageResizingModeStretch];
```

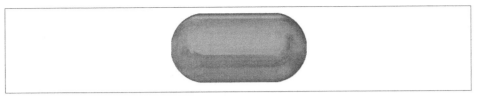

Figure 2-5. Stretching a few pixels at the interior of Mars

Figure 2-6. Mars, stretched and clipped

You should also experiment with different scaling `contentMode` settings. In the preceding example, if the image view's `contentMode` is `UIViewContentModeScaleAspect-Fill`, and if the image view's `clipsToBounds` is YES, we get a sort of gradient effect, because the top and bottom of the stretched image are outside the image view and aren't drawn (Figure 2-6).

New in Xcode 5, you can configure a resizable image without code, in the project itself. This is a feature of asset catalogs, and another great reason to use them. It is often the case that a particular image will be used in your app chiefly as a resizable image, and always with the same `capInsets:` and `resizingMode:`, so it makes sense to configure this image once rather than having to repeat the same code. And even if an image is configured in the asset catalog to be resizable, it can appear in your interface as a normal image as well — for example, if you use it to initialize an image view, or assign it to an image view under autolayout, or if the image view doesn't scale its image (it has a `content-Mode` of `UIViewContentModeCenter` or larger).

To configure an image in an asset catalog as a resizable image, select the image and, in the Slicing section of the Attributes inspector, change the Slices pop-up menu to Horizontal, Vertical, or Horizontal and Vertical. You can specify the `resizingMode` with another pop-up menu. You can work numerically, or click Show Slicing at the lower right of the canvas and work graphically. The graphical editor is zoomable, so zoom in to work comfortably.

The reason this feature is called Slicing and not Resizing is that it can do more than `resizableImageWithCapInsets:resizingMode:` can do: it lets you specify the end caps *separately* from the tiled or stretched region, with the rest of the image being sliced out. The meaning of your settings is intuitively clear from the graphical slicing editor. In

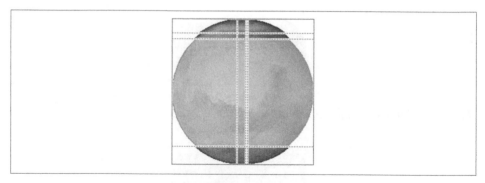

Figure 2-7. Mars, sliced in the asset catalog

Figure 2-8. Mars, sliced and stretched

Figure 2-7, for example, the dark areas at the top left, top right, bottom left, and bottom right will be drawn as is. The narrow bands will be stretched, and the small rectangle at the top center will be stretched to fill most of the interior. But the rest of the image, the large central area covered by a sort of gauze curtain, will be omitted entirely. The result is shown in Figure 2-8.

 Don't use image slicing in an asset catalog if your deployment target isn't 7.0 or higher.

Image Rendering Mode

Several places in an iOS app's interface automatically treat an image as a *transparency mask*, also known as a *template*. This means that the image color values are ignored, and only the transparency (alpha) values of each pixel matter. The image shown on the screen is formed by combining the image's transparency values with a single tint color. Such, for example, is the behavior of a tab bar item's image.

New in iOS 7, the way an image will be treated is a property of the image, its rendering-Mode. This property is read-only; to change it, make from an existing image a new image with a different rendering mode, by calling imageWithRenderingMode:. The rendering mode values are:

Figure 2-9. Transparency mask icons in the Settings app

Figure 2-10. One image in two rendering modes

- `UIImageRenderingModeAutomatic`
- `UIImageRenderingModeAlwaysOriginal`
- `UIImageRenderingModeAlwaysTemplate`

The default is `UIImageRenderingModeAutomatic`, which results in the old behavior: such an image is drawn normally everywhere except in certain limited contexts, where it is used as a transparency mask.

With the `renderingMode` property, you can force an image to be drawn normally, even in a context that would usually treat it as a transparency mask. You can also do the opposite: you can force an image to be treated as a transparency mask, even in a context that would otherwise treat it normally. Apple wants iOS 7 apps to adopt more of a transparency mask look throughout the interface; some of the icons in the Settings app, for example, appear to be transparency masks (Figure 2-9).

To accompany this feature, iOS 7 gives every UIView a `tintColor`, which will be used to tint any template images it contains. Moreover, this `tintColor` by default is inherited down the view hierarchy, and indeed throughout the entire app, starting with the UI-Window (Chapter 1). Thus, assigning your app's main window a tint color is probably one of the few changes you'll make to the window; otherwise, your app adopts the system's blue tint color. (Alternatively, if you're using a main storyboard, set the tint color in its File inspector.) Individual views can be assigned their own tint color, which is inherited by their subviews. Figure 2-10 shows two buttons displaying the same background image, one in normal rendering mode, the other in template rendering mode, in an app whose window tint color is red. (I'll say more about template images and the `tintColor` in Chapter 12.)

Graphics Contexts

UIImageView draws an image for you and takes care of all the details; in many cases, it will be all you'll need. Eventually, though, you may want to create some drawing yourself, directly, in code. To do so, you will always need a *graphics context*.

A graphics context is basically a place you can draw. Conversely, you can't draw in code unless you've got a graphics context. There are several ways in which you might obtain a graphics context; in this chapter I will concentrate on two, which have proven in my experience to be far and away the most common:

You create an image context
> The function `UIGraphicsBeginImageContextWithOptions` creates a graphics context suitable for use as an image. You then draw into this context to generate the image. When you've done that, you call `UIGraphicsGetImageFromCurrentImage-Context` to turn the context into a UIImage, and then `UIGraphicsEndImage-Context` to dismiss the context. Now you have a UIImage that you can display in your interface or draw into some other graphics context or save as a file.

Cocoa hands you a graphics context
> You subclass UIView and implement `drawRect:`. At the time your `drawRect:` implementation is called, Cocoa has already created a graphics context and is asking you to draw into it, right now; whatever you draw is what the UIView will display. (A slight variant of this situation is that you subclass a CALayer and implement `drawInContext:`, or make some object the delegate of a layer and implement `draw-Layer:inContext:`; layers are discussed in Chapter 3.)

Moreover, at any given moment there either is or is not a *current graphics context*:

- `UIGraphicsBeginImageContextWithOptions` not only creates an image context, it also makes that context the current graphics context.
- When `drawRect:` is called, the UIView's drawing context is already the current graphics context.
- Callbacks with a `context:` argument have *not* made any context the current graphics context; rather, that argument is a reference to a graphics context.

What beginners find most confusing about drawing is that there are two separate sets of tools with which you can draw, and they take different attitudes toward the context in which they will draw:

UIKit
> Various Objective-C classes know how to draw themselves; these include UIImage, NSString (for drawing text), UIBezierPath (for drawing shapes), and UIColor. Some

of these classes provide convenience methods with limited abilities; others are extremely powerful. In many cases, UIKit will be all you'll need.

With UIKit, you can draw *only into the current context*. So if you're in a `UIGraphics-BeginImageContextWithOptions` or `drawRect:` situation, you can use the UIKit convenience methods directly; there is a current context and it's the one you want to draw into. If you've been handed a `context:` argument, on the other hand, then if you want to use the UIKit convenience methods, you'll have to make that context the current context; you do this by calling `UIGraphicsPushContext` (and be sure to restore things with `UIGraphicsPopContext` later).

Core Graphics
This is the full drawing API. Core Graphics, often referred to as Quartz, or Quartz 2D, is the drawing system that underlies all iOS drawing — UIKit drawing is built on top of it — so it is low-level and consists of C functions. There are a lot of them! This chapter will familiarize you with the fundamentals; for complete information, you'll want to study Apple's *Quartz 2D Programming Guide*.

With Core Graphics, you must *specify a graphics context* (a CGContextRef) to draw into, explicitly, in every function call. If you've been handed a `context:` argument, then that's probably the graphics context you want to draw into. But in a `UIGraphics-BeginImageContextWithOptions` or `drawRect:` situation, you have no reference to a context; to use Core Graphics, you need to get such a reference. Since the context you want to draw into is the current graphics context, you call `UIGraphicsGet-CurrentContext` to get the needed reference.

So we have two sets of tools and three ways in which a context might be supplied; that makes six ways of drawing. To clarify, I'll now demonstrate all six of them! Without worrying just yet about the actual drawing commands, focus your attention on how the context is specified and on whether we're using UIKit or Core Graphics. First, I'll draw a blue circle by implementing a UIView subclass's `drawRect:`, using UIKit to draw into the current context, which Cocoa has already prepared for me:

```
- (void) drawRect: (CGRect) rect {
    UIBezierPath* p =
        [UIBezierPath bezierPathWithOvalInRect:CGRectMake(0,0,100,100)];
    [[UIColor blueColor] setFill];
    [p fill];
}
```

Now I'll do the same thing with Core Graphics; this will require that I first get a reference to the current context:

```
- (void) drawRect: (CGRect) rect {
    CGContextRef con = UIGraphicsGetCurrentContext();
    CGContextAddEllipseInRect(con, CGRectMake(0,0,100,100));
    CGContextSetFillColorWithColor(con, [UIColor blueColor].CGColor);
    CGContextFillPath(con);
}
```

Next, I'll implement a UIView subclass's drawLayer:inContext:. In this case, we're handed a reference to a context, but it isn't the current context. So I have to make it the current context in order to use UIKit:

```
- (void)drawLayer:(CALayer*)lay inContext:(CGContextRef)con {
    UIGraphicsPushContext(con);
    UIBezierPath* p =
        [UIBezierPath bezierPathWithOvalInRect:CGRectMake(0,0,100,100)];
    [[UIColor blueColor] setFill];
    [p fill];
    UIGraphicsPopContext();
}
```

To use Core Graphics in drawLayer:inContext:, I simply keep referring to the context I was handed:

```
- (void)drawLayer:(CALayer*)lay inContext:(CGContextRef)con {
    CGContextAddEllipseInRect(con, CGRectMake(0,0,100,100));
    CGContextSetFillColorWithColor(con, [UIColor blueColor].CGColor);
    CGContextFillPath(con);
}
```

Finally, for the sake of completeness, let's make a UIImage of a blue circle. We can do this at any time (we don't need to wait for some particular method to be called) and in any class (we don't need to be in a UIView subclass). The resulting UIImage (here called im) is suitable anywhere you would use a UIImage. For instance, you could hand it over to a visible UIImageView as its image, thus causing the image to appear onscreen. Or you could save it as a file. Or, as I'll explain in the next section, you could use it in another drawing.

First, I'll draw my image using UIKit:

```
UIGraphicsBeginImageContextWithOptions(CGSizeMake(100,100), NO, 0);
UIBezierPath* p =
    [UIBezierPath bezierPathWithOvalInRect:CGRectMake(0,0,100,100)];
[[UIColor blueColor] setFill];
[p fill];
UIImage* im = UIGraphicsGetImageFromCurrentImageContext();
UIGraphicsEndImageContext();
// im is the blue circle image, do something with it here ...
```

Here's the same thing using Core Graphics:

Figure 2-11. Two images of Mars combined side by side

```
UIGraphicsBeginImageContextWithOptions(CGSizeMake(100,100), NO, 0);
CGContextRef con = UIGraphicsGetCurrentContext();
CGContextAddEllipseInRect(con, CGRectMake(0,0,100,100));
CGContextSetFillColorWithColor(con, [UIColor blueColor].CGColor);
CGContextFillPath(con);
UIImage* im = UIGraphicsGetImageFromCurrentImageContext();
UIGraphicsEndImageContext();
// im is the blue circle image, do something with it here ...
```

You may be wondering about the arguments to `UIGraphicsBeginImageContextWith-Options`. The first argument is obviously the size of the image to be created. The second argument declares whether the image should be opaque; if I had passed YES instead of NO here, my image would have a black background, which I don't want. The third argument specifies the image scale, corresponding to the UIImage `scale` property I discussed earlier; by passing `0`, I'm telling the system to set the scale for me in accordance with the main screen resolution, so my image will look good on both single-resolution and double-resolution devices.

You don't have to use UIKit or Core Graphics exclusively; on the contrary, you can intermingle UIKit calls and Core Graphics calls to operate on the same graphics context. They merely represent two different ways of telling a graphics context what to do.

UIImage Drawing

A UIImage provides methods for drawing itself into the current context. We know how to obtain a UIImage, and we know how to obtain an image context and make it the current context, so we can experiment with these methods. Here, I'll make a UIImage consisting of two pictures of Mars side by side (Figure 2-11):

```
UIImage* mars = [UIImage imageNamed:@"Mars"];
CGSize sz = mars.size;
UIGraphicsBeginImageContextWithOptions(
    CGSizeMake(sz.width*2, sz.height), NO, 0);
[mars drawAtPoint:CGPointMake(0,0)];
[mars drawAtPoint:CGPointMake(sz.width,0)];
UIImage* im = UIGraphicsGetImageFromCurrentImageContext();
UIGraphicsEndImageContext();
```

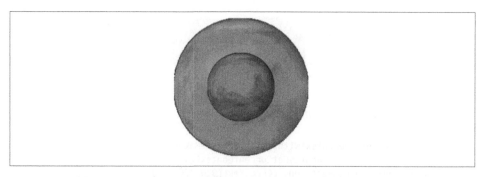

Figure 2-12. Two images of Mars in different sizes, composited

Observe that image scaling works perfectly in that example. If we have a single/double-resolution pair for our original Mars image, the correct one for the current device is used, and is assigned the correct `scale` value. Our call to `UIGraphicsBeginImage-ContextWithOptions` has a third argument of `0`, so the image context that we are drawing into also has the correct `scale`. And the image that results from calling `UIGraphicsGet-ImageFromCurrentImageContext` has the correct `scale` as well. Thus, this same code produces an image that looks correct on the current device, whatever its screen resolution may be.

Additional UIImage methods let you scale an image into a desired rectangle as you draw, and specify the compositing (blend) mode whereby the image should combine with whatever is already present. To illustrate, I'll create an image showing Mars centered in another image of Mars that's twice as large, using the Multiply blend mode (Figure 2-12):

```
UIImage* mars = [UIImage imageNamed:@"Mars"];
CGSize sz = mars.size;
UIGraphicsBeginImageContextWithOptions(
    CGSizeMake(sz.width*2, sz.height*2), NO, 0);
[mars drawInRect:CGRectMake(0,0,sz.width*2,sz.height*2)];
[mars drawInRect:CGRectMake(sz.width/2.0, sz.height/2.0, sz.width, sz.height)
    blendMode:kCGBlendModeMultiply alpha:1.0];
UIImage* im = UIGraphicsGetImageFromCurrentImageContext();
UIGraphicsEndImageContext();
```

There is no UIImage drawing method for specifying the source rectangle — that is, for specifying that you want to extract a smaller region of the original image. You can work around this by specifying a smaller graphics context and positioning the image drawing so that the desired region falls into it. For example, to obtain an image of the right half of Mars, you'd make a graphics context half the width of the `mars` image, and then draw `mars` shifted left, so that only its right half intersects the graphics context. There is no harm in doing this, and it's a perfectly standard strategy; the left half of `mars` simply isn't drawn (Figure 2-13):

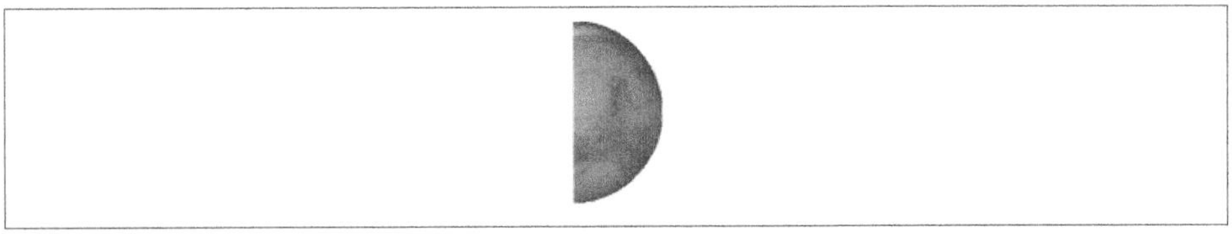

Figure 2-13. Half the original image of Mars

```
UIImage* mars = [UIImage imageNamed:@"Mars"];
CGSize sz = mars.size;
UIGraphicsBeginImageContextWithOptions(
    CGSizeMake(sz.width/2.0, sz.height), NO, 0);
[mars drawAtPoint:CGPointMake(-sz.width/2.0, 0)];
UIImage* im = UIGraphicsGetImageFromCurrentImageContext();
UIGraphicsEndImageContext();
```

CGImage Drawing

The Core Graphics version of UIImage is CGImage (actually a CGImageRef). They are easily converted to one another: a UIImage has a `CGImage` property that accesses its Quartz image data, and you can make a UIImage from a CGImage using `imageWith-CGImage:` or `initWithCGImage:` (in real life, you are likely to use their more configurable siblings, `imageWithCGImage:scale:orientation:` and `initWithCGImage:scale:orientation:`).

A CGImage lets you create a new image directly from a rectangular region of the original image, which you can't do with UIImage. (A CGImage has other powers a UIImage doesn't have; for example, you can apply an image mask to a CGImage.) I'll demonstrate by splitting the image of Mars in half and drawing the two halves separately (Figure 2-14). Observe that we are now operating in the CFTypeRef world and must take care to manage memory manually:

```
UIImage* mars = [UIImage imageNamed:@"Mars"];
// extract each half as a CGImage
CGSize sz = mars.size;
CGImageRef marsLeft = CGImageCreateWithImageInRect([mars CGImage],
                    CGRectMake(0,0,sz.width/2.0,sz.height));
CGImageRef marsRight = CGImageCreateWithImageInRect([mars CGImage],
                    CGRectMake(sz.width/2.0,0,sz.width/2.0,sz.height));
// draw each CGImage into an image context
UIGraphicsBeginImageContextWithOptions(
    CGSizeMake(sz.width*1.5, sz.height), NO, 0);
CGContextRef con = UIGraphicsGetCurrentContext();
CGContextDrawImage(con,
                    CGRectMake(0,0,sz.width/2.0,sz.height), marsLeft);
CGContextDrawImage(con,
```

Figure 2-14. Image of Mars split in half (and flipped)

```
                    CGRectMake(sz.width,0,sz.width/2.0,sz.height), marsRight);
    UIImage* im = UIGraphicsGetImageFromCurrentImageContext();
    UIGraphicsEndImageContext();
    CGImageRelease(marsLeft); CGImageRelease(marsRight);
```

But there's a problem with that example: the drawing is upside-down! It isn't rotated; it's mirrored top to bottom, or, to use the technical term, *flipped*. This phenomenon can arise when you create a CGImage and then draw it with `CGContextDrawImage`, and is due to a mismatch in the native coordinate systems of the source and target contexts.

There are various ways of compensating for this mismatch between the coordinate systems. One is to draw the CGImage into an intermediate UIImage and extract *another* CGImage from that. Example 2-1 presents a utility function for doing this.

Example 2-1. Utility for flipping an image drawing

```
CGImageRef flip (CGImageRef im) {
    CGSize sz = CGSizeMake(CGImageGetWidth(im), CGImageGetHeight(im));
    UIGraphicsBeginImageContextWithOptions(sz, NO, 0);
    CGContextDrawImage(UIGraphicsGetCurrentContext(),
                    CGRectMake(0, 0, sz.width, sz.height), im);
    CGImageRef result = [UIGraphicsGetImageFromCurrentImageContext() CGImage];
    UIGraphicsEndImageContext();
    return result;
}
```

Armed with the utility function from Example 2-1, we can fix our calls to `CGContext-DrawImage` in the previous example so that they draw the halves of Mars the right way up:

```
    CGContextDrawImage(con, CGRectMake(0,0,sz.width/2.0,sz.height),
                    flip(marsLeft));
    CGContextDrawImage(con, CGRectMake(sz.width,0,sz.width/2.0,sz.height),
                    flip(marsRight));
```

However, we've *still* got a problem: on a double-resolution device, if there is a double-resolution variant of our image file, the drawing comes out all wrong. The reason is that we are obtaining our initial Mars image using `imageNamed:`, which returns a UIImage that compensates for the doubled size of a double-resolution image by setting its own `scale` property to match. But a CGImage doesn't have a `scale` property, and knows nothing of the fact that the image dimensions are doubled! Therefore, on a double-resolution device, the CGImage that we extract from our Mars UIImage by calling [mars CGImage] is twice as large (in each dimension) as mars.size, and all our calculations after that are wrong.

So, in extracting a desired piece of the CGImage, we must either multiply all appropriate values by the scale or express ourselves in terms of the CGImage's dimensions. Here's a version of our original code that draws correctly on either a single-resolution or a double-resolution device, and compensates for flipping:

```
UIImage* mars = [UIImage imageNamed:@"Mars"];
CGSize sz = mars.size;
// Derive CGImage and use its dimensions to extract its halves
CGImageRef marsCG = [mars CGImage];
CGSize szCG = CGSizeMake(CGImageGetWidth(marsCG), CGImageGetHeight(marsCG));
CGImageRef marsLeft =
    CGImageCreateWithImageInRect(
        marsCG, CGRectMake(0,0,szCG.width/2.0,szCG.height));
CGImageRef marsRight =
    CGImageCreateWithImageInRect(
        marsCG, CGRectMake(szCG.width/2.0,0,szCG.width/2.0,szCG.height));
UIGraphicsBeginImageContextWithOptions(
    CGSizeMake(sz.width*1.5, sz.height), NO, 0);
// The rest is as before, calling flip() to compensate for flipping
CGContextRef con = UIGraphicsGetCurrentContext();
CGContextDrawImage(con, CGRectMake(0,0,sz.width/2.0,sz.height),
                   flip(marsLeft));
CGContextDrawImage(con, CGRectMake(sz.width,0,sz.width/2.0,sz.height),
                   flip(marsRight));
UIImage* im = UIGraphicsGetImageFromCurrentImageContext();
UIGraphicsEndImageContext();
CGImageRelease(marsLeft); CGImageRelease(marsRight);
```

Another solution is wrap a CGImage in a UIImage and draw the UIImage instead of the CGImage. The UIImage can be formed in such a way as to compensate for scale: call imageWithCGImage:scale:orientation: as you form the UIImage from the CGImage. Moreover, by drawing a UIImage instead of a CGImage, we avoid the flipping problem! So here's an approach that deals with both flipping and scale (without calling the flip utility):

```
UIImage* mars = [UIImage imageNamed:@"Mars"];
CGSize sz = mars.size;
// Derive CGImage and use its dimensions to extract its halves
CGImageRef marsCG = [mars CGImage];
CGSize szCG = CGSizeMake(CGImageGetWidth(marsCG), CGImageGetHeight(marsCG));
CGImageRef marsLeft =
    CGImageCreateWithImageInRect(
        marsCG, CGRectMake(0,0,szCG.width/2.0,szCG.height));
CGImageRef marsRight =
    CGImageCreateWithImageInRect(
```

```
        marsCG, CGRectMake(szCG.width/2.0,0,szCG.width/2.0,szCG.height));
    UIGraphicsBeginImageContextWithOptions(
        CGSizeMake(sz.width*1.5, sz.height), NO, 0);
    [[UIImage imageWithCGImage:marsLeft
                      scale:mars.scale
                 orientation:UIImageOrientationUp]
     drawAtPoint:CGPointMake(0,0)];
    [[UIImage imageWithCGImage:marsRight
                      scale:mars.scale
                 orientation:UIImageOrientationUp]
     drawAtPoint:CGPointMake(sz.width,0)];
    UIImage* im = UIGraphicsGetImageFromCurrentImageContext();
    UIGraphicsEndImageContext();
    CGImageRelease(marsLeft); CGImageRelease(marsRight);
```

Yet another solution to flipping is to apply a transform to the graphics context before drawing the CGImage, effectively flipping the context's internal coordinate system. This is elegant, but can be confusing if there are other transforms in play. I'll talk more about graphics context transforms later in this chapter.

Snapshots

An entire view — anything from a single button to your whole interface, complete with its contained hierarchy of views — can be drawn into the current graphics context by calling the UIView instance method `drawViewHierarchyInRect:afterScreen-Updates:`. This method is new in iOS 7 (and is much faster than the CALayer method `renderInContext:`, which it effectively replaces). The result is a *snapshot* of the original view: it looks like the original view, but it's basically just a bitmap image of it, a lightweight visual duplicate. Snapshots are useful because of the dynamic nature of the iOS interface. For example, you might place a snapshot of a view in your interface in front of the real view to hide what's happening, or use it during an animation to present the illusion of a view moving when in fact it's just a snapshot.

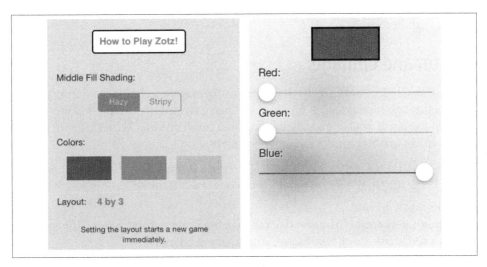

Figure 2-15. A view seems blurred by an occluding view

Figure 2-15 shows how a snapshot is used in one of my apps. The user can tap any of three color swatches to edit that color. When the color-editing interface appears, I want the user to have the impression that it is just temporary, with the original interface still lurking behind it. So the color-editing interface shows the original interface behind it. But the original interface mustn't be too distracting, so it's blurred. In reality, what's blurred is a snapshot of the original interface.

Here's how the snapshot in Figure 2-15 is created:

```
UIGraphicsBeginImageContextWithOptions(vc1.view.frame.size, YES, 0);
[vc1.view drawViewHierarchyInRect: vc1.view.frame afterScreenUpdates:NO];
UIImage* im = UIGraphicsGetImageFromCurrentImageContext();
UIGraphicsEndImageContext();
```

The image im is then blurred, and the blurred image is made the image of a UIImageView inserted behind the color-editing interface. How to achieve a blur effect is another question. I might have used a CIFilter (the subject of the next section), but it's too slow; instead, I used a UIImage category distributed by Apple as part of the Blurring and Tinting an Image sample code.

An even faster way to obtain a snapshot of a view is to use the UIView (or UIScreen) instance method snapshotViewAfterScreenUpdates:. The result is a UIView, not a UIImage; it's rather like a UIImageView that knows how to draw only one image, namely the snapshot. Such a snapshot view will typically be used as is, but you can enlarge its bounds and the snapshot image will stretch. If you want the stretched snapshot to behave like a resizable image, call resizableSnapshotViewFromRect:afterScreen-

`Updates:withCapInsets:` instead. It is perfectly reasonable to make a snapshot view from a snapshot view.

CIFilter and CIImage

The "CI" in CIFilter and CIImage stands for Core Image, a technology for transforming images through mathematical filters. Core Image started life on the desktop (OS X); some of the filters available on the desktop aren't available in iOS (perhaps are they are too intensive mathematically for a mobile device).

A filter is a CIFilter. The available filters (there are about 120 of them, with nearly two dozen being new in iOS 7) fall naturally into several categories:

Patterns and gradients
> These filters create CIImages that can then be combined with other CIImages, such as a single color, a checkerboard, stripes, or a gradient.

Compositing
> These filters combine one image with another, using compositing blend modes familiar from image processing programs such as Photoshop.

Color
> These filters adjust or otherwise modify the colors of an image. Thus you can alter an image's saturation, hue, brightness, contrast, gamma and white point, exposure, shadows and highlights, and so on.

Geometric
> These filters perform basic geometric transformations on an image, such as scaling, rotation, and cropping.

Transformation
> These filters distort, blur, or stylize an image. Relatively few of them are available on iOS.

Transition
> These filters provide a frame of a transition between one image and another; by asking for frames in sequence, you can animate the transition (I'll demonstrate in Chapter 4).

Special purpose
> These filters perform highly specialized operations such as face detection and generation of QR codes.

The basic use of a CIFilter is quite simple; it essentially works as if a filter were a kind of dictionary consisting of keys and values. You create the filter with `filterWith-Name:`, supplying the string name of a filter; to learn what these names are, consult Apple's *Core Image Filter Reference*, or call the CIFilter class method `filterNamesIn-`

`Categories:` with a nil argument. Each filter has a small number of keys and values that determine its behavior. You can learn about these keys entirely in code, but typically you'll consult the documentation. For each key that you're interested in, you supply a key–value pair, either by calling `setValue:forKey:` or by supplying the keys and values as you specify the filter name by calling `filterWithName:keysAndValues:`. In supplying values, a number must be wrapped up as an NSNumber, and there are a few supporting classes such as CIVector (like CGPoint and CGRect combined) and CIColor, whose use is easy to grasp.

A CIFilter's keys include any image or images on which the filter is to operate; such an image must be a CIImage. You can obtain a CIImage as the output of a filter; thus filters can be chained together. But what about the *first* filter in the chain? Where will its CIImage come from? You can obtain a CIImage from a CGImage with `initWith-CGImage:`, and you can obtain a CGImage from a UIImage as its `CGImage` property.

 Do not attempt, as a shortcut, to obtain a CIImage directly from a UIImage by calling the UIImage instance method `CIImage`. This method does *not* transform a UIImage into a CIImage! It merely points to the CIImage that already backs the UIImage, and your images are not backed by a CIImage, but rather by a CGImage. I'll explain where a CIImage-backed UIImage comes from in just a moment.

As you build a chain of filters, nothing actually happens. The only calculation-intensive move comes at the very end, when you transform the final CIImage in the chain into a bitmap drawing. There are two ways to do this:

- Create a CIContext (by calling `contextWithOptions:`) and then call `create-CGImage:fromRect:`, handing it the final CIImage as the first argument. The only mildly tricky thing here is that a CIImage doesn't have a frame or bounds; it has an extent. You will often use this as the second argument to `createCGImage:from-Rect:`. The final output CGImage is ready for any purpose, such as for display in your app, for transformation into a UIImage, or for use in further drawing.

- Create a UIImage directly from the final CIImage by calling one of these methods:
  — `imageWithCIImage:`
  — `initWithCIImage:`
  — `imageWithCIImage:scale:orientation:`
  — `initWithCIImage:scale:orientation:`

You must then *draw the UIImage* into some graphics context. That last step is essential; the CIImage is not transformed into a bitmap until you do it. Thus, a UIImage generated from `imageWithCIImage:` is *not* suitable for display directly in a

UIImageView; it contains no drawing of its own. It is useful for drawing, not for display.

To illustrate, I'll start with an ordinary photo of myself (it's true I'm wearing a motorcycle helmet, but it's still ordinary) and create a circular vignette effect (Figure 2-16). We derive from the image of me (moi) a CGImage and from there a CIImage (moi2). We use a CIFilter to form a radial gradient between the default colors of white and black. Then we use a second CIFilter that treats the radial gradient as a mask for blending between the photo of me and a default clear background: where the radial gradient is white (everything inside the gradient's inner radius) we see just me, and where the radial gradient is black (everything outside the gradient's outer radius) we see just the clear color, with a gradation in between, so that the image fades away in the circular band between the gradient's radii. From the last CIImage output by this CIFilter chain, we form a CGImage (moi3), which we transform into a UIImage (moi4):

```
UIImage* moi = [UIImage imageNamed:@"Moi"];
CIImage* moi2 = [[CIImage alloc] initWithCGImage:moi.CGImage];
CGRect moiextent = moi2.extent;
// first filter
CIFilter* grad = [CIFilter filterWithName:@"CIRadialGradient"];
CIVector* center = [CIVector vectorWithX:moiextent.size.width/2.0
                                        Y:moiextent.size.height/2.0];
[grad setValue:center forKey:@"inputCenter"];
[grad setValue:@85 forKey:@"inputRadius0"];
[grad setValue:@100 forKey:@"inputRadius1"];
CIImage *gradimage = [grad valueForKey: @"outputImage"];
// second filter
CIFilter* blend = [CIFilter filterWithName:@"CIBlendWithMask"];
[blend setValue:moi2 forKey:@"inputImage"];
[blend setValue:gradimage forKey:@"inputMaskImage"];
// extract a bitmap
CGImageRef moi3 =
    [[CIContext contextWithOptions:nil]
      createCGImage:blend.outputImage
      fromRect:moiextent];
UIImage* moi4 = [UIImage imageWithCGImage:moi3];
CGImageRelease(moi3);
```

Instead of generating a CGImage from the last CIImage in the chain and transforming that into a UIImage, we could capture that CIImage as a UIImage directly — but then we must draw with it in order to generate the bitmap output of the filter chain. For example, we could draw it into an image context:

```
UIGraphicsBeginImageContextWithOptions(moiextent.size, NO, 0);
[[UIImage imageWithCIImage:blend.outputImage] drawInRect:moiextent];
UIImage* moi4 = UIGraphicsGetImageFromCurrentImageContext();
UIGraphicsEndImageContext();
```

Figure 2-16. A photo of me, vignetted

A filter chain can be encapsulated into a single custom filter by subclassing CIFilter. Your subclass just needs to implement `outputImage` (and possibly other methods such as `setDefaults`), with private properties to make it key–value coding compliant for any input keys. Here's our vignette filter as a simple CIFilter subclass, where the only input key is the input image:

```
@interface MyVignetteFilter ()
@property (nonatomic, strong) CIImage* inputImage;
@end
@implementation MyVignetteFilter
-(CIImage *)outputImage {
    CGRect inextent = self.inputImage.extent;
    CIFilter* grad = [CIFilter filterWithName:@"CIRadialGradient"];
    CIVector* center = [CIVector vectorWithX:inextent.size.width/2.0
                                           Y:inextent.size.height/2.0];
    [grad setValue:center forKey:@"inputCenter"];
    [grad setValue:@85 forKey:@"inputRadius0"];
    [grad setValue:@100 forKey:@"inputRadius1"];
    CIImage *gradimage = [grad valueForKey: @"outputImage"];

    CIFilter* blend = [CIFilter filterWithName:@"CIBlendWithMask"];
    [blend setValue:self.inputImage forKey:@"inputImage"];
    [blend setValue:gradimage forKey:@"inputMaskImage"];
    return blend.outputImage;
}
@end
```

And here's how to use our CIFilter subclass and display its output:

```
CIFilter* vig = [MyVignetteFilter new];
CIImage* im =
    [CIImage imageWithCGImage:[UIImage imageNamed:@"Moi"].CGImage];
[vig setValue:im forKey:@"inputImage"];
CIImage* outim = vig.outputImage;
UIGraphicsBeginImageContextWithOptions(outim.extent.size, NO, 0);
```

```
[[UIImage imageWithCIImage:outim] drawInRect:outim.extent];
UIImage* result = UIGraphicsGetImageFromCurrentImageContext();
UIGraphicsEndImageContext();
self.iv.image = result;
```

Drawing a UIView

The examples of drawing so far in this chapter have mostly produced UIImage objects, chiefly by calling `UIGraphicsBeginImageContextWithOptions` to obtain a graphics context, suitable for display by a UIImageView or any other interface object that knows how to display an image. But, as I've already explained, a UIView provides a graphics context; whatever you draw into that graphics context will appear in that view. The technique here is to subclass UIView and implement the subclass's `drawRect:` method. At the time that `drawRect:` is called, the current graphics context has already been set to the view's own graphics context. You can use Core Graphics functions or UIKit convenience methods to draw into that context.

So, for example, let's say we have a UIView subclass called MyView. You would then instantiate this class and get the instance into the view hierarchy. One way to do this would be to drag a UIView into a view in the nib editor and set its class to MyView in the Identity inspector; another would be to create the MyView instance and put it into the interface in code. The result is that, from time to time, MyView's `drawRect:` will be called. This is your subclass, so you get to write the code that runs at that moment. Whatever you draw will appear inside the MyView instance. There will usually be no need to call `super`, since UIView's own implementation of `drawRect:` does nothing.

 You should *never* call `drawRect:` yourself! If a view needs updating and you want its `drawRect:` called, send the view the `setNeeds-Display` message. This will cause `drawRect:` to be called at the next proper moment. Also, don't override `drawRect:` unless you are assured that this is legal. For example, it is not legal to override `drawRect:` in a subclass of UIImageView; you cannot combine your drawing with that of the UIImageView.

The need to draw in real time, on demand, surprises some beginners, who worry that drawing may be a time-consuming operation. This can indeed be a reasonable consideration, and where the same drawing will be used in many places in your interface, it may well make sense to draw a UIImage instead, once, and then reuse that UIImage. In general, however, you should not optimize prematurely. The code for a drawing operation may appear verbose and yet be extremely fast. Moreover, the iOS drawing system is efficient; it doesn't call `drawRect:` unless it has to (or is told to, through a call to `set-NeedsDisplay`), and once a view has drawn itself, the result is cached so that the cached drawing can be reused instead of repeating the drawing operation from scratch. (Apple refers to this cached drawing as the view's *bitmap backing store*.) You can readily satisfy yourself of this fact with some caveman debugging, logging in your `drawRect:` implementation; you may be amazed to discover that your code is called only once in the entire lifetime of the app! In fact, moving code to `drawRect:` is commonly a way to *increase* efficiency. This is because it is more efficient for the drawing engine to render directly onto the screen than for it to render offscreen and then copy those pixels onto the screen.

Where drawing is extensive and can be compartmentalized into sections, you may be able to gain some additional efficiency by paying attention to the `rect` parameter passed into `drawRect:`. It designates the region of the view's bounds that needs refreshing. Normally, this is the view's entire bounds; but if you call `setNeedsDisplayInRect:`, it will be the CGRect that you passed in as argument. You could respond by drawing only what goes into those bounds; but even if you don't, your drawing will be clipped to those bounds, so, while you may not spend less time drawing, the system will draw more efficiently.

When creating a custom UIView subclass instance in code, you may be surprised and annoyed to find that the view has a black background:

```
MyView* mv = [[MyView alloc] initWithFrame:CGRectMake(20,20,150,100)];
[self.view addSubview: mv]; // appears as a black rectangle
```

This can be frustrating if what you expected and wanted was a transparent background, and it's a source of considerable confusion among beginners. The black background arises when two things are true:

- The view's `backgroundColor` is nil.
- The view's `opaque` is YES.

Unfortunately, when creating a UIView in code, both those things *are* true by default! So if you don't want the black background, you must do something about one or the other of them (or both). If a view isn't going to be opaque, its `opaque` should be set to NO anyway, so that's probably the cleanest solution:

```
MyView* mv = [[MyView alloc] initWithFrame:CGRectMake(20,20,150,100)];
[self.view addSubview: mv];
mv.opaque = NO;
```

Alternatively, this being your own UIView subclass, you could implement its `initWithFrame:` (the designated initializer) to have the view set its *own* `opaque` to NO:

```
- (id)initWithFrame:(CGRect)frame {
    self = [super initWithFrame:frame];
    if (self) {
        self.opaque = NO;
    }
    return self;
}
```

With a UIView created in the nib, on the other hand, the black background problem doesn't arise. This is because such a UIView's `backgroundColor` is not nil. The nib assigns it *some* actual background color, even if that color is [`UIColor clearColor`].

Of course, if a view fills its rectangle with opaque drawing or has an opaque background color, you can leave `opaque` set to YES and gain some drawing efficiency (see Chapter 1).

Graphics Context Settings

As you draw in a graphics context, the drawing obeys the context's current settings. Thus, the procedure is always to configure the context's settings first, and then draw. For example, to draw a red line followed by a blue line, you would first set the context's line color to red, and then draw the first line; then you'd set the context's line color to blue, and then draw the second line. To the eye, it appears that the redness and blueness are properties of the individual lines, but in fact, at the time you draw each line, line color is a feature of the entire graphics context. This is true regardless of whether you use UIKit methods or Core Graphics functions.

A graphics context thus has, at every moment, a *state*, which is the sum total of all its settings; the way a piece of drawing looks is the result of what the graphics context's state was at the moment that piece of drawing was performed. To help you manipulate entire states, the graphics context provides a *stack* for holding states. Every time you call `CGContextSaveGState`, the context pushes the entire current state onto the stack; every time you call `CGContextRestoreGState`, the context retrieves the state from the top of the stack (the state that was most recently pushed) and sets itself to that state.

Thus, a common pattern is: call `CGContextSaveGState`; manipulate the context's settings, thus changing its state; draw; call `CGContextRestoreGState` to restore the state and the settings to what they were before you manipulated them. You do not have to do this before *every* manipulation of a context's settings, however, because settings don't necessarily conflict with one another or with past settings. You can set the context's line color to red and then later to blue without any difficulty. But in certain situations you do want your manipulation of settings to be undoable, and I'll point out several such situations later in this chapter.

Many of the settings that constitute a graphics context's state, and that determine the behavior and appearance of drawing performed at that moment, are similar to those of any drawing application. Here are some of them, along with some of the commands that determine them. I list Core Graphics functions, followed by some UIKit convenience methods that call them:

Line thickness and dash style
CGContextSetLineWidth, CGContextSetLineDash (and UIBezierPath lineWidth, setLineDash:count:phase:)

Line end-cap style and join style
CGContextSetLineCap, CGContextSetLineJoin, CGContextSetMiterLimit (and UIBezierPath lineCapStyle, lineJoinStyle, miterLimit)

Line color or pattern
CGContextSetRGBStrokeColor, CGContextSetGrayStrokeColor, CGContextSetStrokeColorWithColor, CGContextSetStrokePattern (and UIColor setStroke)

Fill color or pattern
CGContextSetRGBFillColor, CGContextSetGrayFillColor, CGContextSetFillColorWithColor, CGContextSetFillPattern (and UIColor setFill)

Shadow
CGContextSetShadow, CGContextSetShadowWithColor

Overall transparency and compositing
CGContextSetAlpha, CGContextSetBlendMode

Anti-aliasing
CGContextSetShouldAntialias

Additional settings include:

Clipping area
Drawing outside the clipping area is not physically drawn.

Transform (or "CTM," for "current transform matrix")
Changes how points that you specify in subsequent drawing commands are mapped onto the physical space of the canvas.

Many of these settings will be illustrated by examples later in this chapter.

Paths and Shapes

By issuing a series of instructions for moving an imaginary pen, you trace out a *path*. Such a path does *not* constitute drawing! First you provide a path; *then* you draw. Drawing can mean stroking the path or filling the path, or both. Again, this should be a familiar notion from certain drawing applications.

A path is constructed by tracing it out from point to point. Think of the drawing system as holding a pen. Then you must first tell that pen where to position itself, setting the current point; after that, you issue a series of commands telling it how to trace out each subsequent piece of the path. Each additional piece of the path starts at the current point; its end becomes the new current point.

Here are some path-drawing commands you're likely to give:

Position the current point
CGContextMoveToPoint

Trace a line
CGContextAddLineToPoint, CGContextAddLines

Trace a rectangle
CGContextAddRect, CGContextAddRects

Trace an ellipse or circle
CGContextAddEllipseInRect

Trace an arc
CGContextAddArcToPoint, CGContextAddArc

Trace a Bezier curve with one or two control points
CGContextAddQuadCurveToPoint, CGContextAddCurveToPoint

Close the current path
CGContextClosePath. This appends a line from the last point of the path to the first point. There's no need to do this if you're about to fill the path, since it's done for you.

Stroke or fill the current path
CGContextStrokePath, CGContextFillPath, CGContextEOFillPath, CGContext-DrawPath. Stroking or filling the current path *clears the path*. Use CGContextDraw-Path if you want both to fill and to stroke the path in a single command, because if you merely stroke it first with CGContextStrokePath, the path is cleared and you can no longer fill it. There are also a lot of convenience functions that create a path and stroke or fill it all in a single move:

- CGContextStrokeLineSegments
- CGContextStrokeRect
- CGContextStrokeRectWithWidth
- CGContextFillRect
- CGContextFillRects
- CGContextStrokeEllipseInRect
- CGContextFillEllipseInRect

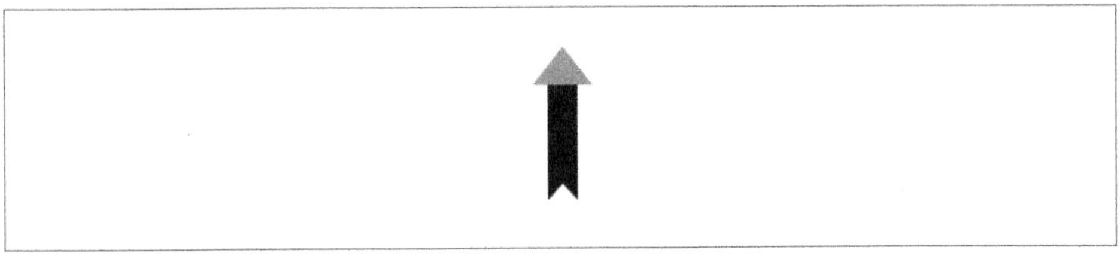

Figure 2-17. A simple path drawing

A path can be compound, meaning that it consists of multiple independent pieces. For example, a single path might consist of two separate closed shapes: a rectangle and a circle. When you call CGContextMoveToPoint in the middle of constructing a path (that is, after tracing out a path and without clearing it by filling, stroking, or calling CGContextBeginPath), you pick up the imaginary pen and move it to a new location without tracing a segment, thus preparing to start an independent piece of the same path. If you're worried, as you begin to trace out a path, that there might be an existing path and that your new path might be seen as a compound part of that existing path, you can call CGContextBeginPath to specify that this is a different path; many of Apple's examples do this, but in practice I usually do not find it necessary.

To illustrate the typical use of path-drawing commands, I'll generate the up-pointing arrow shown in Figure 2-17. This might not be the best way to create the arrow, and I'm deliberately avoiding use of the convenience functions, but it's clear and shows a nice basic variety of typical commands:

```
// obtain the current graphics context
CGContextRef con = UIGraphicsGetCurrentContext();
// draw a black (by default) vertical line, the shaft of the arrow
CGContextMoveToPoint(con, 100, 100);
CGContextAddLineToPoint(con, 100, 19);
CGContextSetLineWidth(con, 20);
CGContextStrokePath(con);
// draw a red triangle, the point of the arrow
CGContextSetFillColorWithColor(con, [[UIColor redColor] CGColor]);
CGContextMoveToPoint(con, 80, 25);
CGContextAddLineToPoint(con, 100, 0);
CGContextAddLineToPoint(con, 120, 25);
CGContextFillPath(con);
// snip a triangle out of the shaft by drawing in Clear blend mode
CGContextMoveToPoint(con, 90, 101);
CGContextAddLineToPoint(con, 100, 90);
CGContextAddLineToPoint(con, 110, 101);
CGContextSetBlendMode(con, kCGBlendModeClear);
CGContextFillPath(con);
```

If a path needs to be reused or shared, you can encapsulate it as a CGPath, which is actually a CGPathRef. You can either create a new CGMutablePathRef and construct the path using various CGPath functions that parallel the CGContext path-construction functions, or you can copy the graphics context's current path using `CGContextCopy-Path`. There are also a number of CGPath functions for creating a path based on simple geometry or based on an existing path:

- `CGPathCreateWithRect`
- `CGPathCreateWithEllipseInRect`
- `CGPathCreateCopyByStrokingPath`
- `CGPathCreateCopyByDashingPath`
- `CGPathCreateCopyByTransformingPath`

The UIKit class UIBezierPath wraps CGPath; it, too, provides methods parallel to the CGContext path-construction functions, such as:

- `moveToPoint:`
- `addLineToPoint:`
- `bezierPathWithRect:`
- `bezierPathWithOvalInRect:`
- `addArcWithCenter:radius:startAngle:endAngle:clockwise:`
- `addQuadCurveToPoint:controlPoint:`
- `addCurveToPoint:controlPoint1:controlPoint2:`
- `closePath`

Also, UIBezierPath offers one extremely useful convenience method, `bezierPathWith-RoundedRect:cornerRadius:` — drawing a rectangle with rounded corners using only Core Graphics functions is rather tedious.

When you call the UIBezierPath instance method `fill` or `stroke` (or `fillWithBlend-Mode:alpha:` or `strokeWithBlendMode:alpha:`), the current graphics context is saved, the wrapped CGPath path is made the current graphics context's path and stroked or filled, and the current graphics context is restored.

Thus, using UIBezierPath together with UIColor, we could rewrite our arrow-drawing routine entirely with UIKit methods:

```
// shaft of the arrow
UIBezierPath* p = [UIBezierPath bezierPath];
[p moveToPoint:CGPointMake(100,100)];
[p addLineToPoint:CGPointMake(100, 19)];
```

```
[p setLineWidth:20];
[p stroke];
// point of the arrow
[[UIColor redColor] set];
[p removeAllPoints];
[p moveToPoint:CGPointMake(80,25)];
[p addLineToPoint:CGPointMake(100, 0)];
[p addLineToPoint:CGPointMake(120, 25)];
[p fill];
// snip out triangle in the tail
[p removeAllPoints];
[p moveToPoint:CGPointMake(90,101)];
[p addLineToPoint:CGPointMake(100, 90)];
[p addLineToPoint:CGPointMake(110, 101)];
[p fillWithBlendMode:kCGBlendModeClear alpha:1.0];
```

There's no savings of code here over calling Core Graphics functions. UIBezierPath is particularly useful when you want to capture a CGPath and pass it around as an object; an example appears in Chapter 21.

Clipping

Another use of a path is to mask out areas, protecting them from future drawing. This is called *clipping*. By default, a graphics context's clipping region is the entire graphics context: you can draw anywhere within the context.

The clipping area is a feature of the context as a whole, and any new clipping area is applied by intersecting it with the existing clipping area; so if you apply your own clipping region, the way to remove it from the graphics context later is to plan ahead and wrap things with calls to CGContextSaveGState and CGContextRestoreGState.

To illustrate, I'll rewrite the code that generated our original arrow (Figure 2-17) to use clipping instead of a blend mode to "punch out" the triangular notch in the tail of the arrow. This is a little tricky, because what we want to clip to is not the region inside the triangle but the region outside it. To express this, we'll use a compound path consisting of more than one closed area — the triangle, and the drawing area as a whole (which we can obtain with CGContextGetClipBoundingBox).

Both when filling a compound path and when using it to express a clipping region, the system follows one of two rules:

Winding rule

The fill or clipping area is denoted by an alternation in the direction (clockwise or counterclockwise) of the path demarcating each region.

Even-odd rule (EO)

The fill or clipping area is denoted by a simple count of the paths demarcating each region.

Our situation is extremely simple, so it's easier to use the even-odd rule. So we set up the clipping area using CGContextEOClip and then draw the arrow:

```
// obtain the current graphics context
CGContextRef con = UIGraphicsGetCurrentContext();
// punch triangular hole in context clipping region
CGContextMoveToPoint(con, 90, 100);
CGContextAddLineToPoint(con, 100, 90);
CGContextAddLineToPoint(con, 110, 100);
CGContextClosePath(con);
CGContextAddRect(con, CGContextGetClipBoundingBox(con));
CGContextEOClip(con);
// draw the vertical line
CGContextMoveToPoint(con, 100, 100);
CGContextAddLineToPoint(con, 100, 19);
CGContextSetLineWidth(con, 20);
CGContextStrokePath(con);
// draw the red triangle, the point of the arrow
CGContextSetFillColorWithColor(con, [[UIColor redColor] CGColor]);
CGContextMoveToPoint(con, 80, 25);
CGContextAddLineToPoint(con, 100, 0);
CGContextAddLineToPoint(con, 120, 25);
CGContextFillPath(con);
```

The UIBezierPath clipping commands are usesEvenOddFillRule and addClip.

Gradients

Gradients can range from the simple to the complex. A simple gradient (which is all I'll describe here) is determined by a color at one endpoint along with a color at the other endpoint, plus (optionally) colors at intermediate points; the gradient is then painted either linearly between two points in the context or radially between two circles in the context.

You can't use a gradient as a path's fill color, but you can restrict a gradient to a path's shape by clipping, which amounts to the same thing.

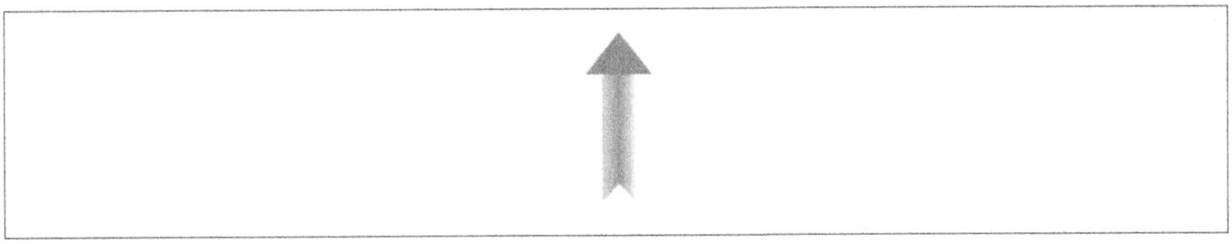

Figure 2-18. Drawing with a gradient

To illustrate, I'll redraw our arrow, using a linear gradient as the "shaft" of the arrow (Figure 2-18):

```
// obtain the current graphics context
CGContextRef con = UIGraphicsGetCurrentContext();
CGContextSaveGState(con);
// punch triangular hole in context clipping region
CGContextMoveToPoint(con, 90, 100);
CGContextAddLineToPoint(con, 100, 90);
CGContextAddLineToPoint(con, 110, 100);
CGContextClosePath(con);
CGContextAddRect(con, CGContextGetClipBoundingBox(con));
CGContextEOClip(con);
// draw the vertical line, add its shape to the clipping region
CGContextMoveToPoint(con, 100, 100);
CGContextAddLineToPoint(con, 100, 19);
CGContextSetLineWidth(con, 20);
CGContextReplacePathWithStrokedPath(con);
CGContextClip(con);
// draw the gradient
CGFloat locs[3] = { 0.0, 0.5, 1.0 };
CGFloat colors[12] = {
    0.3,0.3,0.3,0.8, // starting color, transparent gray
    0.0,0.0,0.0,1.0, // intermediate color, black
    0.3,0.3,0.3,0.8 // ending color, transparent gray
};
CGColorSpaceRef sp = CGColorSpaceCreateDeviceGray();
CGGradientRef grad =
    CGGradientCreateWithColorComponents (sp, colors, locs, 3);
CGContextDrawLinearGradient (
    con, grad, CGPointMake(89,0), CGPointMake(111,0), 0);
CGColorSpaceRelease(sp);
CGGradientRelease(grad);
CGContextRestoreGState(con); // done clipping
// draw the red triangle, the point of the arrow
CGContextSetFillColorWithColor(con, [[UIColor redColor] CGColor]);
CGContextMoveToPoint(con, 80, 25);
CGContextAddLineToPoint(con, 100, 0);
CGContextAddLineToPoint(con, 120, 25);
CGContextFillPath(con);
```

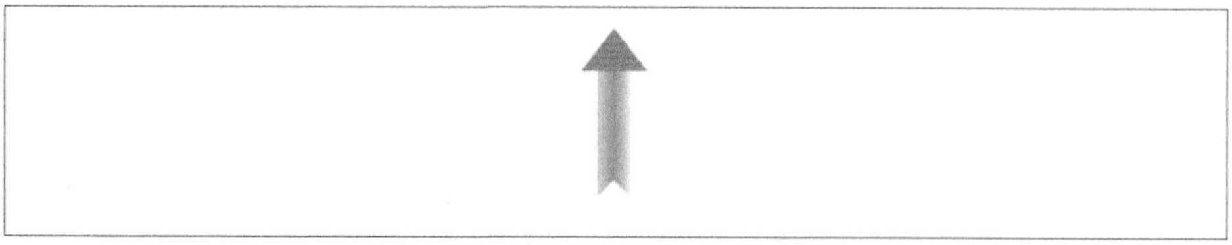

Figure 2-19. A patterned fill

The call to `CGContextReplacePathWithStrokedPath` pretends to stroke the current path, using the current line width and other line-related context state settings, but then creates a new path representing the outside of that stroked path. Thus, instead of a thick line we have a rectangular region that we can use as the clip region.

We then create the gradient and paint it. The procedure is verbose but simple; everything is boilerplate. We describe the gradient as a set of locations on the continuum between one endpoint (0.0) and the other endpoint (1.0), along with the colors corresponding to each location; in this case, I want the gradient to be lighter at the edges and darker in the middle, so I use three locations, with the dark one at 0.5. We must also supply a color space in order to create the gradient. Finally, we create the gradient, paint it into place, and release the color space and the gradient.

Colors and Patterns

A color is a CGColor (actually a CGColorRef). CGColor is not difficult to work with, and can be converted to and from a UIColor through UIColor's `colorWithCGColor:` and `CGColor` methods.

A pattern, on the other hand, is a CGPattern (actually a CGPatternRef). You can create a pattern and stroke or fill with it. The process is rather elaborate. As an extremely simple example, I'll replace the red triangular arrowhead with a red-and-blue striped triangle (Figure 2-19). To do so, remove this line:

```
CGContextSetFillColorWithColor(con, [[UIColor redColor] CGColor]);
```

In its place, put the following:

```
CGColorSpaceRef sp2 = CGColorSpaceCreatePattern(nil);
CGContextSetFillColorSpace (con, sp2);
CGColorSpaceRelease (sp2);
CGPatternCallbacks callback = {
    0, drawStripes, nil
};
CGAffineTransform tr = CGAffineTransformIdentity;
CGPatternRef patt = CGPatternCreate(nil,
                    CGRectMake(0,0,4,4),
                    tr,
```

```
                    4, 4,
                    kCGPatternTilingConstantSpacingMinimalDistortion,
                    true,
                    &callback);
    CGFloat alph = 1.0;
    CGContextSetFillPattern(con, patt, &alph);
    CGPatternRelease(patt);
```

That code is verbose, but it is almost entirely boilerplate. To understand it, it almost helps to read it backward. What we're leading up to is the call to `CGContextSetFill-Pattern`; instead of setting a fill color, we're setting a fill pattern, to be used the next time we fill a path (in this case, the triangular arrowhead). The third parameter to `CGContextSetFillPattern` is a pointer to a CGFloat, so we have to set up the CGFloat itself beforehand. The second parameter to `CGContextSetFillPattern` is a CGPattern-Ref, so we have to create that CGPatternRef beforehand (and release it afterward).

So now let's talk about the call to `CGPatternCreate`. A pattern is a drawing in a rectangular "cell"; we have to state both the size of the cell (the second argument) and the spacing between origin points of cells (the fourth and fifth arguments). In this case, the cell is 4×4, and every cell exactly touches its neighbors both horizontally and vertically. We have to supply a transform to be applied to the cell (the third argument); in this case, we're not doing anything with this transform, so we supply the identity transform. We supply a tiling rule (the sixth argument). We have to state whether this is a color pattern or a stencil pattern; it's a color pattern, so the seventh argument is `true`. And we have to supply a pointer to a callback function that actually draws the pattern into its cell (the eighth argument).

Except that that's *not* what we have to supply as the eighth argument. To make matters more complicated, what we actually have to supply here is a pointer to a CGPattern-Callbacks struct. This struct consists of the number 0 and pointers to *two* functions, one called to draw the pattern into its cell, the other called when the pattern is released. We're not specifying the second function, however; it is for memory management, and we don't need it in this simple example.

We have almost worked our way backward to the start of the code. It turns out that before you can call `CGContextSetFillPattern` with a colored pattern, you have to set the context's fill color space to a pattern color space. If you neglect to do this, you'll get an error when you call `CGContextSetFillPattern`. So we create the color space, set it as the context's fill color space, and release it.

But we are *still* not finished, because I haven't shown you the function that actually draws the pattern cell! This is the function whose address is taken as `drawStripes` in our code. Here it is:

```
void drawStripes (void *info, CGContextRef con) {
    // assume 4 x 4 cell
    CGContextSetFillColorWithColor(con, [[UIColor redColor] CGColor]);
    CGContextFillRect(con, CGRectMake(0,0,4,4));
    CGContextSetFillColorWithColor(con, [[UIColor blueColor] CGColor]);
    CGContextFillRect(con, CGRectMake(0,0,4,2));
}
```

As you can see, the actual pattern-drawing code is very simple. The only tricky issue is that the call to CGPatternCreate must be in agreement with the pattern-drawing function as to the size of a cell, or the pattern won't come out the way you expect. We know in this case that the cell is 4×4. So we fill it with red, and then fill its lower half with blue. When these cells are tiled touching each other horizontally and vertically, we get the stripes that you see in Figure 2-19.

Note, finally, that the code as presented has left the graphics context in an undesirable state, with its fill color space set to a pattern color space. This would cause trouble if we were later to try to set the fill color to a normal color. The solution, as usual, is to wrap the code in calls to CGContextSaveGState and CGContextRestoreGState.

You may have observed in Figure 2-19 that the stripes do not fit neatly inside the triangle of the arrowhead: the bottommost stripe is something like half a blue stripe. This is because a pattern is positioned not with respect to the shape you are filling (or stroking), but with respect to the graphics context as a whole. We could shift the pattern position by calling CGContextSetPatternPhase before drawing.

For such a simple pattern, it would have been easier to take advantage of UIColor's colorWithPatternImage:, which takes a UIImage:

```
UIGraphicsBeginImageContextWithOptions(CGSizeMake(4,4), NO, 0);
drawStripes(nil, UIGraphicsGetCurrentContext());
UIImage* stripes = UIGraphicsGetImageFromCurrentImageContext();
UIGraphicsEndImageContext();
UIColor* stripesPattern = [UIColor colorWithPatternImage:stripes];
[stripesPattern setFill];
UIBezierPath* p = [UIBezierPath bezierPath];
[p moveToPoint:CGPointMake(80,25)];
[p addLineToPoint:CGPointMake(100,0)];
[p addLineToPoint:CGPointMake(120,25)];
[p fill];
```

Graphics Context Transforms

Just as a UIView can have a transform, so can a graphics context. However, applying a transform to a graphics context has no effect on the drawing that's already in it; it affects only the drawing that takes place after it is applied, altering the way the coordinates you provide are mapped onto the graphics context's area. A graphics context's transform is called its CTM, for "current transform matrix."

It is quite usual to take full advantage of a graphics context's CTM to save yourself from performing even simple calculations. You can multiply the current transform by any CGAffineTransform using CGContextConcatCTM; there are also convenience functions for applying a translate, scale, or rotate transform to the current transform.

The base transform for a graphics context is already set for you when you obtain the context; this is how the system is able to map context drawing coordinates onto screen coordinates. Whatever transforms you apply are applied to the current transform, so the base transform remains in effect and drawing continues to work. You can return to the base transform after applying your own transforms by wrapping your code in calls to CGContextSaveGState and CGContextRestoreGState.

For example, we have hitherto been drawing our upward-pointing arrow with code that knows how to place that arrow at only one location: the top left of its rectangle is hard-coded at {80,0}. This is silly. It makes the code hard to understand, as well as inflexible and difficult to reuse. Surely the sensible thing would be to draw the arrow at {0,0}, by subtracting 80 from all the x-values in our existing code. Now it is easy to draw the arrow at *any* position, simply by applying a translate transform beforehand, mapping {0,0} to the desired top-left corner of the arrow. So, to draw it at {80,0}, we would say:

```
CGContextTranslateCTM(con, 80, 0);
// now draw the arrow at (0,0)
```

A rotate transform is particularly useful, allowing you to draw in a rotated orientation without any nasty trigonometry. However, it's a bit tricky because the point around which the rotation takes place is the origin. This is rarely what you want, so you have to apply a translate transform first, to map the origin to the point around which you really want to rotate. But then, after rotating, in order to figure out where to draw you will probably have to reverse your translate transform.

To illustrate, here's code to draw our arrow repeatedly at several angles, pivoting around the end of its tail (Figure 2-20). Since the arrow will be drawn multiple times, I'll start by encapsulating the drawing of the arrow as a UIImage. This is not merely to reduce repetition and make drawing more efficient; it's also because we want the entire arrow to pivot, including the pattern stripes, and this is the simplest way to achieve that:

```
- (UIImage*) arrowImage {
    UIGraphicsBeginImageContextWithOptions(CGSizeMake(40,100), NO, 0.0);
    // obtain the current graphics context
    CGContextRef con = UIGraphicsGetCurrentContext();
    // draw the arrow into the image context
    // draw it at (0,0)! adjust all x-values by subtracting 80
    // ... actual code omitted ...
    UIImage* im = UIGraphicsGetImageFromCurrentImageContext();
    UIGraphicsEndImageContext();
    return im;
}
```

Figure 2-20. Drawing rotated with a CTM

We produce the arrow image once and store it somewhere — I'll use an instance variable accessed as `self.arrow`. In our `drawRect:` implementation, we draw the arrow image multiple times:

```
- (void)drawRect:(CGRect)rect {
    CGContextRef con = UIGraphicsGetCurrentContext();
    [self.arrow drawAtPoint:CGPointMake(0,0)];
    for (int i=0; i<3; i++) {
        CGContextTranslateCTM(con, 20, 100);
        CGContextRotateCTM(con, 30 * M_PI/180.0);
        CGContextTranslateCTM(con, -20, -100);
        [self.arrow drawAtPoint:CGPointMake(0,0)];
    }
}
```

A transform is also one more solution for the "flip" problem we encountered earlier with `CGContextDrawImage`. Instead of reversing the drawing, we can reverse the context into which we draw it. Essentially, we apply a "flip" transform to the context's coordinate system. You move the context's top downward, and then reverse the direction of the y-coordinate by applying a scale transform whose y-multiplier is `-1`:

```
CGContextTranslateCTM(con, 0, theHeight);
CGContextScaleCTM(con, 1.0, -1.0);
```

How far down you move the context's top (`theHeight`) depends on how you intend to draw the image.

Shadows

To add a shadow to a drawing, give the context a shadow value before drawing. The shadow position is expressed as a CGSize, where the positive direction for both values indicates down and to the right. The blur value is an open-ended positive number; Apple doesn't explain how the scale works, but experimentation shows that 12 is nice and blurry, 99 is so blurry as to be shapeless, and higher values become problematic.

Figure 2-21 shows the result of the same code that generated Figure 2-20, except that before we start drawing the arrow repeatedly, we give the context a shadow:

Figure 2-21. Drawing with a shadow

```
con = UIGraphicsGetCurrentContext();
CGContextSetShadow(con, CGSizeMake(7, 7), 12);
[self.arrow drawAtPoint:CGPointMake(0,0)]; // ... and so on
```

However, there's a subtle cosmetic problem with this approach. It may not be evident from Figure 2-21, but we are adding a shadow each time we draw. Thus the arrows are able to cast shadows on one another. What we want, however, is for all the arrows to cast a single shadow collectively. The way to achieve this is with a *transparency layer*; this is basically a subcontext that accumulates all drawing and then adds the shadow. Our code for drawing the shadowed arrows now looks like this:

```
CGContextRef con = UIGraphicsGetCurrentContext();
CGContextSetShadow(con, CGSizeMake(7, 7), 12);
CGContextBeginTransparencyLayer(con, nil);
[self.arrow drawAtPoint:CGPointMake(0,0)];
for (int i=0; i<3; i++) {
    CGContextTranslateCTM(con, 20, 100);
    CGContextRotateCTM(con, 30 * M_PI/180.0);
    CGContextTranslateCTM(con, -20, -100);
    [self.arrow drawAtPoint:CGPointMake(0,0)];
}
CGContextEndTransparencyLayer(con);
```

Erasing

The function CGContextClearRect erases all existing drawing in a rectangle; combined with clipping, it can erase an area of any shape. The result can "punch a hole" through all existing drawing.

The behavior of CGContextClearRect depends on whether the context is transparent or opaque. This is particularly obvious and intuitive when drawing into an image context. If the image context is transparent — the second argument to UIGraphicsBegin-ImageContextWithOptions is NO — CGContextClearRect erases to transparent; otherwise it erases to black.

When drawing directly into a view (as with drawRect: or drawLayer:inContext:), if the view's background color is nil or a color with even a tiny bit of transparency, the

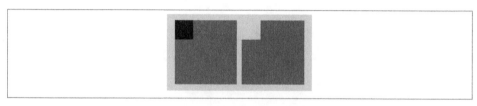

Figure 2-22. The very strange behavior of CGContextClearRect

result of CGContextClearRect will appear to be transparent, punching a hole right through the view including its background color; if the background color is completely opaque, the result of CGContextClearRect will be black. This is because the view's background color determines whether the view's graphics context is transparent or opaque; thus, this is essentially the same behavior that I described in the preceding paragraph.

Figure 2-22 illustrates; the blue square on the left has been partly cut away to black, while the blue square on the right has been partly cut away to transparency. Yet these are instances of the same UIView subclass, drawn with exactly the same code! The difference between the views is that the backgroundColor of the first view is solid red with an alpha of 1, while the backgroundColor of the second view is solid red with an alpha of 0.99. This difference is utterly imperceptible to the eye (not to mention that the red color never appears, as it is covered with a blue fill), but it completely changes the effect of CGContextClearRect. The UIView subclass's drawRect: looks like this:

```
CGContextRef con = UIGraphicsGetCurrentContext();
CGContextSetFillColorWithColor(con, [UIColor blueColor].CGColor);
CGContextFillRect(con, rect);
CGContextClearRect(con, CGRectMake(0,0,30,30));
```

Points and Pixels

A point is a dimensionless location described by an x-coordinate and a y-coordinate. When you draw in a graphics context, you specify the points at which to draw, and this works regardless of the device's resolution, because Core Graphics maps your drawing nicely onto the physical output using the base CTM and anti-aliasing. Therefore, throughout this chapter I've concerned myself with graphics context points, disregarding their relationship to screen pixels.

However, pixels do exist. A pixel is a physical, integral, dimensioned unit of display in the real world. Whole-numbered points effectively lie between pixels, and this can matter if you're fussy, especially on a single-resolution device. For example, if a vertical path with whole-number coordinates is stroked with a line width of 1, half the line falls on each side of the path, and the drawn line on the screen of a single-resolution device will seem to be 2 pixels wide (because the device can't illuminate half a pixel).

You will sometimes encounter advice suggesting that if this effect is objectionable, you should try shifting the line's position by 0.5, to center it in its pixels. This advice may appear to work, but it makes some simpleminded assumptions. A more sophisticated approach is to obtain the UIView's contentScaleFactor property. This value will be either 1.0 or 2.0, so you can divide by it to convert from pixels to points. Consider also that the most accurate way to draw a vertical or horizontal line is not to stroke a path but to fill a rectangle. So this UIView subclass code will draw a perfect 1-pixel-wide vertical line on any device:

```
CGContextFillRect(con, CGRectMake(100,0,1.0/self.contentScaleFactor,100));
```

Content Mode

A view that draws something within itself, as opposed to merely having a background color and subviews (as in the previous chapter), has *content*. This means that its content-Mode property becomes important whenever the view is resized. As I mentioned earlier, the drawing system will avoid asking a view to redraw itself from scratch if possible; instead, it will use the cached result of the previous drawing operation (the bitmap backing store). So, if the view is resized, the system may simply stretch or shrink or reposition the cached drawing, if your contentMode setting instructs it to do so.

It's a little tricky to illustrate this point when the view's content is coming from draw-Rect:, because I have to arrange for the view to obtain its content (from drawRect:) and then cause it to be resized without also causing it to be redrawn (that is, without drawRect: being called *again*). Here's how I'll do that. As the app starts up, I'll create an instance of a UIView subclass that knows how to draw our arrow. Then I'll use delayed performance to resize the instance after the window has shown and the interface has been initially displayed:

```
void (^resize) (void) = ^{
    CGRect f = mv.bounds; // mv is the MyView instance
    f.size.height *= 2;
    mv.bounds = f;
};
dispatch_time_t popTime = dispatch_time(DISPATCH_TIME_NOW, NSEC_PER_SEC);
dispatch_after(popTime, dispatch_get_main_queue(), resize);
```

We double the height of the view without causing drawRect: to be called. The result is that the view's drawing appears at double its correct height. For example, if our view's drawRect: code is the same as the code that generated Figure 2-18, we get Figure 2-23.

Sooner or later, however, drawRect: will be called, and the drawing will be refreshed in accordance with our code. Our code doesn't say to draw the arrow at a height that is relative to the height of the view's bounds; it draws the arrow at a fixed height. Thus, the arrow will snap back to its original size.

Figure 2-23. Automatic stretching of content

A view's `contentMode` property should therefore usually be in agreement with how the view draws itself. Our `drawRect:` code dictates the size and position of the arrow relative to the view's bounds origin, its top left; so we could set its `contentMode` to `UIViewContent-ModeTopLeft`. Alternatively, we could set it to `UIViewContentModeRedraw`; this will cause automatic scaling of the cached content to be turned off — instead, when the view is resized, its `setNeedsDisplay` method will be called, ultimately triggering `drawRect:` to redraw the content.

CHAPTER 3

Layers

The tale told in Chapter 1 and Chapter 2 of how a UIView works and how it draws itself is only half the story. A UIView has a partner called its *layer*, a CALayer. A UIView does not actually draw itself onto the screen; it draws itself into its layer, and it is the layer that is portrayed on the screen. As I've already mentioned, a view is not redrawn frequently; instead, its drawing is cached, and the cached version of the drawing (the bitmap backing store) is used where possible. The cached version is, in fact, the layer. What I spoke of in Chapter 2 as the view's graphics context is actually the layer's graphics context.

This might seem like a mere implementation detail, but layers are important and interesting. To understand layers is to understand views more deeply; layers extend the power of views. In particular:

Layers have properties that affect drawing.
> Layers have drawing-related properties beyond those of a UIView. Because a layer is the recipient and presenter of a view's drawing, you can modify how a view is drawn on the screen by accessing the layer's properties. In other words, by reaching down to the level of its layer, you can make a view do things you can't do through UIView methods alone.

Layers can be combined within a single view.
> A UIView's partner layer can contain additional layers. Since the purpose of layers is to draw, portraying visible material on the screen, this allows a UIView's drawing to be composited of multiple distinct pieces. This can make drawing easier, with the constituents of a drawing being treated as objects.

Layers are the basis of animation.
> Animation allows you to add clarity, emphasis, and just plain coolness to your interface. Layers are made to be animated; the "CA" in "CALayer" stands for "Core Animation". Animation is the subject of Chapter 4.

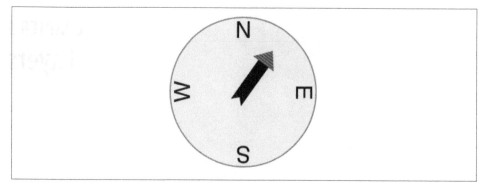

Figure 3-1. A compass, composed of layers

For example, suppose we want to add a compass indicator to our app's interface. Figure 3-1 portrays a simple version of such a compass. It takes advantage of the arrow that we figured out how to draw in Chapter 2; the arrow is drawn into a layer of its own. The other parts of the compass are layers too: the circle is a layer, and each of the cardinal point letters is a layer. The drawing is thus easy to composite in code (and later in this chapter, that's exactly what we'll do); even more intriguing, the pieces can be repositioned and animated separately, so it's easy to rotate the arrow without moving the circle (and in Chapter 4, that's exactly what we'll do).

The documentation discusses layers chiefly in connection with animation (in particular, in the *Core Animation Programming Guide*). This categorization gives the impression that layers are of interest only if you intend to animate. That's misleading. Layers are the basis of animation, but they are also the basis of view drawing, and are useful and important even if you don't use them for animation.

View and Layer

A UIView instance has an accompanying CALayer instance, accessible as the view's layer property. This layer has a special status: it is partnered with this view to embody all of the view's drawing. The layer has no corresponding view property, but the view is the layer's delegate. The documentation sometimes speaks of this layer as the view's "underlying layer."

By default, when a UIView is instantiated, its layer is an instance of CALayer. But if you subclass UIView and you want your subclass's underlying layer to be an instance of a CALayer subclass (built-in or your own), implement the UIView subclass's layerClass class method to return that CALayer subclass.

That, for example, is how the compass in Figure 3-1 is created. We have a UIView subclass, CompassView, and a CALayer subclass, CompassLayer. CompassView contains these lines:

```
+ (Class) layerClass {
    return [CompassLayer class];
}
```

Thus, when CompassView is instantiated, its underlying layer is a CompassLayer. In this example, there is no drawing in CompassView; its job is to give CompassLayer a place in the visible interface, because a layer cannot appear without a view.

Because every view has an underlying layer, there is a tight integration between the two. The layer portrays all the view's drawing; if the view draws, it does so by contributing to the layer's drawing. The view is the layer's delegate. And the view's properties are often merely a convenience for accessing the layer's properties. For example, when you set the view's backgroundColor, you are really setting the layer's backgroundColor, and if you set the layer's backgroundColor directly, the view's backgroundColor is set to match. Similarly, the view's frame is really the layer's frame and *vice versa*.

A CALayer's delegate property is settable, but you must never set the delegate property of a UIView's underlying layer. To do so would be to break the integration between them, thereby causing drawing to stop working correctly. A UIView *must* be the delegate of its underlying layer; moreover, it must *not* be the delegate of any *other* layer. *Don't do anything to mess this up.*

The view draws into its layer, and the layer caches that drawing; the layer can then be manipulated, changing the view's appearance, without necessarily asking the view to redraw itself. This is a source of great efficiency in the drawing system. It also explains such phenomena as the content stretching that we encountered in the last section of Chapter 2: when the view's bounds size changes, the drawing system, by default, simply stretches or repositions the cached layer image, until such time as the view is told to draw freshly (drawRect:), replacing the layer's content.

OS X Programmer Alert
On OS X, NSView existed long before CALayer was introduced, so today a view might have no layer, or, if it does have a layer, it might relate to it in various ways. You may be accustomed to terms like *layer-backed view* or *layer-hosting view*. On iOS, layers were incorporated from the outset: every UIView has an underlying layer and relates to it in the same way (layer-backed).

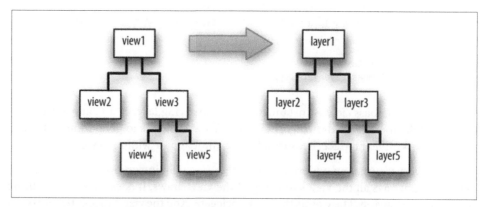

Figure 3-2. A hierarchy of views and the hierarchy of layers underlying it

Layers and Sublayers

A layer can have sublayers, and a layer has at most one superlayer. Thus there is a tree of layers. This is similar and parallel to the tree of views (Chapter 1). In fact, so tight is the integration between a view and its underlying layer that these hierarchies are effectively the same hierarchy. Given a view and its underlying layer, that layer's superlayer is the view's superview's underlying layer, and that layer has as sublayers all the underlying layers of all the view's subviews. Indeed, because the layers are how the views actually get drawn, one might say that the view hierarchy really *is* a layer hierarchy (Figure 3-2).

At the same time, the layer hierarchy can go beyond the view hierarchy. A view has exactly one underlying layer, but a layer can have sublayers that are not the underlying layers of any view. So the hierarchy of layers that underlie views exactly matches the hierarchy of views (Figure 3-2), but the total layer tree may be a superset of that hierarchy. In Figure 3-3, we see the same view-and-layer hierarchy as in Figure 3-2, but two of the layers have additional sublayers that are theirs alone (that is, sublayers that are not any view's underlying layers).

From a visual standpoint, there may be nothing to distinguish a hierarchy of views from a hierarchy of layers. For example, in Chapter 1 we drew three overlapping rectangles using a hierarchy of views (Figure 1-1). This code gives exactly the same visible display by manipulating layers (Figure 3-4):

```
CALayer* lay1 = [CALayer new];
lay1.frame = CGRectMake(113, 111, 132, 194);
lay1.backgroundColor =
    [[UIColor colorWithRed:1 green:.4 blue:1 alpha:1] CGColor];
[mainview.layer addSublayer:lay1];
CALayer* lay2 = [CALayer new];
lay2.backgroundColor =
```

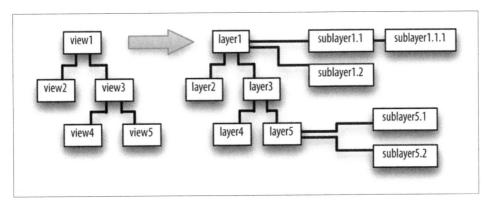

Figure 3-3. Layers that have sublayers of their own

Figure 3-4. Overlapping layers

```
    [[UIColor colorWithRed:.5 green:1 blue:0 alpha:1] CGColor];
lay2.frame = CGRectMake(41, 56, 132, 194);
[lay1 addSublayer:lay2];
CALayer* lay3 = [CALayer new];
lay3.backgroundColor =
    [[UIColor colorWithRed:1 green:0 blue:0 alpha:1] CGColor];
lay3.frame = CGRectMake(43, 197, 160, 230);
[mainview.layer addSublayer:lay3];
```

A view's subview's underlying layer is a sublayer of that view's underlaying layer, just like any *other* sublayers of that view's underlying layer. Therefore, it can positioned anywhere among them in the drawing order. The fact that a view can be interspersed among the sublayers of its superview's underlying layer is surprising to beginners. For

Figure 3-5. Overlapping layers and a view

example, let's construct Figure 3-4 again, but between adding lay2 and lay3 to the interface, we'll add a subview:

```
// ...
[lay1 addSublayer:lay2];
UIImageView* iv =
    [[UIImageView alloc] initWithImage:[UIImage imageNamed:@"smiley"]];
CGRect r = iv.frame;
r.origin = CGPointMake(180,180);
iv.frame = r;
[mainview addSubview:iv];
CALayer* lay3 = [CALayer new];
// ...
```

The result is Figure 3-5. The smiley face was added to the interface before the red (left) rectangle, so it appears behind that rectangle. The smiley face is a *view*, whereas the rectangle is just a *layer*; so they are not siblings as views, since the rectangle is not a view. But the smiley face is both a view and its layer, and as layers the smiley face and the rectangle *are* siblings, since they have the same superlayer; thus, either one can be made to appear in front of the other.

Whether a layer displays regions of its sublayers that lie outside that layer's own bounds depends upon the value of its masksToBounds property. This is parallel to a view's clips-ToBounds property, and indeed, for a layer that is its view's underlying layer, they are the same thing. In Figure 3-4 and Figure 3-5, the layers all have clipsToBounds set to NO (the default); that's why the right layer is visible beyond the bounds of the middle layer, which is its superlayer.

Like a UIView, a CALayer has a hidden property that can be set to take it and its sublayers out of the visible interface without actually removing it from its superlayer.

Manipulating the Layer Hierarchy

Layers come with a full set of methods for reading and manipulating the layer hierarchy, parallel to the methods for reading and manipulating the view hierarchy. A layer has a superlayer property and a sublayers property, and these methods:

- addSublayer:
- insertSublayer:atIndex:
- insertSublayer:below:, insertSublayer:above:
- replaceSublayer:with:
- removeFromSuperlayer

Unlike a view's subviews property, a layer's sublayers property is writable; thus, you can give a layer multiple sublayers in a single move, by assigning to its sublayers property. To remove all of a layer's sublayers, set its sublayers property to nil.

Although a layer's sublayers have an order, reflected in the sublayers order and regulated with the methods I've just mentioned, this is not necessarily the same as their back-to-front drawing order. By default, it is, but a layer also has a zPosition property, a CGFloat, and this also determines drawing order. The rule is that all sublayers with the same zPosition are drawn in the order they are listed among their sublayers siblings, but lower zPosition siblings are drawn before higher zPosition siblings. (The default zPosition is 0.)

Sometimes, the zPosition property is a more convenient way of dictating drawing order than sibling order is. For example, if layers represent playing cards laid out in a solitaire game, it will likely be a lot easier and more flexible to determine how the cards overlap by setting their zPosition than by rearranging their sibling order. Moreover, a subview's layer is itself just a layer, so you can rearrange the drawing order of subviews by setting the zPosition of their underlying layers. In our code constructing Figure 3-5, if we assign the image view's underlying layer a zPosition of 1, it is drawn in front of the red (left) rectangle:

```
[mainview addSubview:iv];
iv.layer.zPosition = 1;
```

Methods are also provided for converting between the coordinate systems of layers within the same layer hierarchy:

- convertPoint:fromLayer:, convertPoint:toLayer:
- convertRect:fromLayer:, convertRect:toLayer:

Positioning a Sublayer

Layer coordinate systems and positioning are similar to those of views. A layer's own internal coordinate system is expressed by its bounds, just like a view; its size is its bounds size, and its bounds origin is the internal coordinate at its top left.

However, a sublayer's position within its superlayer is not described by its center, like a view; a layer does not have a center. Instead, a sublayer's position within its superlayer is defined by a combination of two properties, its position and its anchorPoint. Think of the sublayer as pinned to its superlayer; then you have to say both where the pin passes through the sublayer and where it passes through the superlayer. (I didn't make up that analogy, but it's pretty apt.)

position
    A point expressed in the superlayer's coordinate system.

anchorPoint
    Where the position point is located, with respect to the layer's own bounds. It is a pair of floating-point numbers (a CGPoint) describing a fraction (or multiple) of the layer's own bounds width and bounds height. Thus, for example, {0,0} is the top left of the layer's bounds, and {1,1} is the bottom right of the layer's bounds.

If the anchorPoint is {0.5,0.5} (the default), the position property works like a view's center property. A view's center is thus a special case of a layer's position. This is quite typical of the relationship between view properties and layer properties; the view properties are often a simpler, more convenient, and less powerful version of the layer properties.

A layer's position and anchorPoint are orthogonal (independent); changing one does not change the other. Therefore, changing either of them without changing the other changes where the layer is drawn within its superlayer.

For example, in Figure 3-1, the most important point in the circle is its center; all the other objects need to be positioned with respect to it. Therefore they all have the same position: the center of the circle. But they differ in their anchorPoint. For example, the arrow's anchorPoint is {0.5,0.8}, the middle of the shaft, near the end. On the other hand, the anchorPoint of a cardinal point letter is more like {0.5,3}, well outside the letter's bounds, so as to place the letter near the edge of the circle.

A layer's frame is a purely derived property. When you get the frame, it is calculated from the bounds size along with the position and anchorPoint. When you set the frame, you set the bounds size and position. In general, you should regard the frame as a convenient façade and no more. Nevertheless, it is convenient! For example, to position a sublayer so that it exactly overlaps its superlayer, you can just set the sublayer's frame to the superlayer's bounds.

A layer created in code (as opposed to a view's underlying layer) has a `frame` and `bounds` of `{{0,0},{0,0}}` and will not be visible on the screen even when you add it to a superlayer that is on the screen. Be sure to give your layer a nonzero width and height if you want to be able to see it. Creating a layer and adding it to a superlayer and then wondering why it isn't appearing in the interface is a common beginner error.

CAScrollLayer

If you're going to be moving a layer's bounds origin as a way of repositioning its sublayers *en masse*, you might like to make the layer a CAScrollLayer, a CALayer subclass that provides convenience methods for this sort of thing. (Despite the name, a CAScrollLayer provides no scrolling interface; the user can't scroll it by dragging, for example.) By default, a CAScrollLayer's `masksToBounds` property is YES; thus, the CAScrollLayer acts like a window through which you see can only what is within its bounds. (You can set its `masksToBounds` to NO, but this would be an odd thing to do, as it somewhat defeats the purpose.)

To move the CAScrollLayer's bounds, you can talk either to it or to a sublayer (at any depth):

Talking to the CAScrollLayer
  `scrollToPoint:`
      Changes the CAScrollLayer's bounds origin to that point.

  `scrollToRect:`
      Changes the CAScrollLayer's bounds origin minimally so that the given portion of the bounds rect is visible.

Talking to a sublayer
  `scrollPoint:`
      Changes the CAScrollLayer's bounds origin so that the given point *of the sublayer* is at the top left of the CAScrollLayer.

  `scrollRectToVisible:`
      Changes the CAScrollLayer's bounds origin so that the given rect *of the sublayer's bounds* is within the CAScrollLayer's bounds area. You can also ask the sublayer for its `visibleRect`, the part of this sublayer now within the CAScrollLayer's bounds.

Layout of Sublayers

The view hierarchy is actually a layer hierarchy (Figure 3-2). The positioning of a view within its superview is actually the positioning of its layer within its superlayer (the superview's layer). A view can be repositioned and resized automatically in accordance with its `autoresizingMask` or through autolayout based on its constraints. Thus, there is automatic layout for layers *if they are the underlying layers of views*. Otherwise, there is *no* automatic layout for layers. The only option for layout of sublayers that are not the underlying layers of views is manual layout that you perform in code.

OS X Programmer Alert
On OS X, layers have extensive automatic layout support, including both constraints and custom layout managers. But iOS lacks all of this.

When a layer needs layout, either because its bounds have changed or because you called `setNeedsLayout`, you can respond in either of two ways:

- The layer's `layoutSublayers` method is called; to respond, override `layout-Sublayers` in your CALayer subclass.

- Alternatively, implement `layoutSublayersOfLayer:` in the layer's delegate. (Remember, if the layer is a view's underlying layer, the view is its delegate.)

To do effective manual layout of sublayers, you'll probably need a way to identify or refer to the sublayers. There is no layer equivalent of `viewWithTag:`, so such identification and reference is entirely up to you. Key–value coding can be helpful here; layers implement key–value coding in a special way, discussed at the end of this chapter.

For a view's underlying layer, `layoutSublayers` or `layoutSublayersOfLayer:` is called after the view's `layoutSubviews`. Under autolayout, you must call `super` or else autolayout will break. Moreover, these methods may be called more than once during the course of autolayout; if you're looking for an automatically generated signal that it's time to do manual layout of sublayers (because the device has been rotated, for example), the view's `layoutSubviews` might be a better choice.

Drawing in a Layer

A view draws into its underlying layer if its `drawRect:` is implemented (Chapter 2). Now let's talk about how draw into *other* layers.

The simplest way to make something appear in a layer is through its `contents` property. This is parallel to the `image` in a UIImageView (Chapter 2). It is expected to be a CGImageRef (or nil, signifying no image). A CGImageRef is not an object type, but the `contents` property is typed as an `id`; in order to quiet the compiler, you'll have to typecast your CGImageRef to an `id` as you assign it.

So, for example, here's how we might modify the code that generated Figure 3-5 in such a way as to generate the smiley face as a layer rather than a view:

```
CALayer* lay4 = [CALayer new];
UIImage* im = [UIImage imageNamed:@"smiley"];
CGRect r = lay4.frame;
r.origin = CGPointMake(180,180);
r.size = im.size;
lay4.frame = r;
lay4.contents = (id)im.CGImage;
[mainview.layer addSublayer:lay4];
```

 Setting a layer's contents to a UIImage, rather than a CGImage, will fail silently — the image doesn't appear, but there is no error either. This is absolutely maddening, and I wish I had a nickel for every time I've done it and then wasted hours figuring out why my layer isn't appearing.

There are also four methods that can be implemented to provide or draw a layer's content on demand, similar to a UIView's drawRect:. A layer is very conservative about calling these methods (and you must not call any of them directly). When a layer *does* call these methods, I will say that the layer *redisplays itself*. Here is how a layer can be caused to redisplay itself:

- If the layer's needsDisplayOnBoundsChange property is NO (the default), then the only way to cause the layer to redisplay itself is by calling setNeedsDisplay (or setNeedsDisplayInRect:). Even this might not cause the layer to redisplay itself right away; if that's crucial, then you will also call displayIfNeeded.

- If the layer's needsDisplayOnBoundsChange property is YES, then the layer will also redisplay itself when the layer's bounds change (rather like a UIView's UIViewContentModeRedraw).

Here are the four methods that can be called when a layer redisplays itself; pick one to implement (don't try to combine them, you'll just confuse things):

display *in a subclass*

> Your CALayer subclass can override display. There's no graphics context at this point, so display is pretty much limited to setting the contents image.

displayLayer: *in the delegate*

> You can set the CALayer's delegate property and implement displayLayer: in the delegate. As with display, there's no graphics context, so you'll just be setting the contents image.

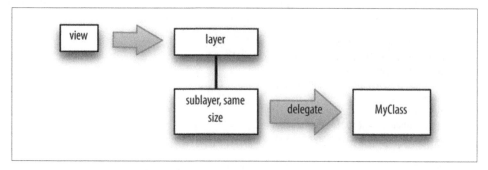

Figure 3-6. A view and a layer delegate that draws into it

drawInContext: *in a subclass*

Your CALayer subclass can override drawInContext:. The parameter is a graphics context into which you can draw directly; it is *not* automatically made the current context.

drawLayer:inContext: *in the delegate*

You can set the CALayer's delegate property and implement drawLayer:in-Context:. The second parameter is a graphics context into which you can draw directly; it is *not* automatically made the current context.

Remember, you must not set the delegate property of a view's underlying layer! The view is its delegate and must remain its delegate. A useful architecture for drawing into a layer through a delegate of your choosing is to treat a view as a *layer-hosting* view: the view and its underlying layer do nothing except to serve as a host to a sublayer of the view's underlying layer, which is where the drawing occurs (Figure 3-6).

Assigning a layer a contents image and drawing directly into the layer are, in effect, mutually exclusive. So:

- If a layer's contents is assigned an image, this image is shown immediately and replaces whatever drawing may have been displayed in the layer.

- If a layer redisplays itself and drawInContext: or drawLayer:inContext: draws into the layer, the drawing replaces whatever image may have been displayed in the layer.

- If a layer redisplays itself and none of the four methods provides any content, the layer will be empty.

A layer has a scale, its contentsScale, which maps point distances in the layer's graphics context to pixel distances on the device. A layer that's managed by Cocoa, if it has contents, will adjust its contentsScale automatically as needed; for example, if a UI-View implements drawRect:, then on a device with a double-resolution screen its underlying layer is assigned a `contentsScale` of 2. A layer that you are creating and managing yourself, however, has no such automatic behavior; it's up to you, if you plan to draw into the layer, to set its `contentsScale` appropriately. Content drawn into a layer with a `contentsScale` of 1 may appear pixellated or fuzzy on a double-resolution screen. And when you're starting with a UIImage and assigning its CGImage as a layer's `contents`, if there's a mismatch between the UIImage's `scale` and the layer's `contentsScale`, then the image may be displayed at the wrong size.

Three layer properties strongly affect what the layer displays, in ways that can be baffling to beginners: its `backgroundColor` property, its `opaque` property, and its `opacity` property. Here's what you need to know:

- Think of the `backgroundColor` as separate from the layer's own drawing, and as painted *behind* the layer's own drawing. It is equivalent to a view's `backgroundColor` (and if this layer is a view's underlying layer, it *is* the view's `backgroundColor`). Changing the `backgroundColor` takes effect immediately.

- The `opaque` property determines whether the layer's *graphics context is opaque.* An opaque graphics context is black; you can draw on top of that blackness, but the blackness is still there. A non-opaque graphics context is clear; where no drawing is, it is completely transparent. Changing the `opaque` property has no effect until the layer redisplays itself. A view's underlying layer's `opaque` property is independent of the view's `opaque` property; they are unrelated and do entirely different things.

- The `opacity` property affects the overall apparent transparency of the layer. It is equivalent to a view's `alpha` (and if this layer is a view's underlying layer, it *is* the view's `alpha`). It affects the apparent transparency of the layer's sublayers as well. It affects the apparent transparency of the background color and the apparent transparency of the layer's content separately (just as with a view's `alpha`). Changing the `opacity` property takes effect immediately.

 If a layer is the underlying layer of a view that implements `drawRect:`, then setting the view's `backgroundColor` changes the layer's `opaque` — setting it to YES if the new background color is opaque (alpha component of 1), to NO otherwise. This is the reason behind the strange behavior of `CGContextClearRect` described in Chapter 2.

Also, when drawing directly into a *layer*, the behavior of `CGContextClearRect` differs from what was described in Chapter 2 for drawing into a *view*: instead of punching a hole through the background color, it effectively paints with the layer's background color. (This can have curious side effects.)

I regard all this as deeply weird.

Automatically Redisplaying a View's Underlying Layer

A layer is not told automatically to redisplay itself (unless its bounds are resized when needsDisplayOnBoundsChange is YES), but a view is. For example, a view is told to redraw itself when it first appears; basically, it is sent setNeedsDisplay, much as if you had sent it explicitly. When a view is sent setNeedsDisplay, the view's underlying layer is also sent setNeedsDisplay — unless the view has no drawRect: implementation (because in that case, it is assumed that the view never needs redrawing). So, if you're drawing a view entirely by drawing to its underlying layer directly, and if you want the underlying layer to be redisplayed automatically when the view is told to redraw itself, you should implement drawRect:, even if it does nothing. (This technique has no effect on sublayers of the underlying layer.)

Content Resizing and Positioning

A layer's content is stored (cached) as a bitmap which is then treated like an image and drawn in relation to the layer's bounds in accordance with various layer properties:

- If the content came from setting the layer's contents property to an image, the cached content is that image; its size is the point size of the CGImage we started with.

- If the content came from drawing directly into the layer's graphics context (drawIn-Context:, drawLayer:inContext:), the cached content is the layer's entire graphics context; its size is the point size of the layer itself at the time the drawing was performed.

The layer properties in question cause the cached content to be resized, repositioned, cropped, and so on, as it is displayed. The properties are:

contentsGravity
    This property, a string, is parallel to a UIView's contentMode property, and describes how the content should be positioned or stretched in relation to the bounds. For example, kCAGravityCenter means the content is centered in the bounds without resizing; kCAGravityResize (the default) means the content is sized to fit the bounds, even if this means distorting its aspect; and so forth.

    For historical reasons, the terms "bottom" and "top" in the names of the contentsGravity settings have the opposite of their expected meanings.

contentsRect

A CGRect expressing the proportion of the content that is to be displayed. The default is {{0,0},{1,1}}, meaning the entire content is displayed. The specified part of the content is sized and positioned in relation to the bounds in accordance with the contentsGravity. Thus, for example, by setting the contentsRect, you can scale up part of the content to fill the bounds, or slide part of a larger image into view without redrawing or changing the contents image.

You can also use the contentsRect to scale down the content, by specifying a larger contentsRect such as {{-.5, -.5}, {1.5, 1.5}}; but any content pixels that touch the edge of the contentsRect will then be extended outward to the edge of the layer (to prevent this, make sure that the outermost pixels of the content are all empty).

contentsCenter

A CGRect, structured like contentsRect, expressing the central region of nine rectangular regions of the contentsRect that are variously allowed to stretch if the contentsGravity calls for stretching. The central region (the actual value of the contentsCenter) stretches in both directions. Of the other eight regions (inferred from the value you provide), the four corner regions don't stretch, and the four side regions stretch in one direction. (This should remind you of how a resizable image stretches! See Chapter 2.)

If a layer's content comes from drawing directly into its graphics context, then the layer's contentsGravity, of itself, has no effect, because the size of the graphics context, by definition, fits the size of the layer exactly; there is nothing to stretch or reposition. But the contentsGravity *will* have an effect on such a layer if its contentsRect is not {{0,0},{1,1}}, because now we're specifying a rectangle of some *other* size; the contentsGravity describes how to fit that rectangle into the layer.

Again, if a layer's content comes from drawing directly into its graphics context, then when the layer is resized, if the layer is asked to display itself again, the drawing is performed again, and once more the layer's content fits the size of the layer exactly. But if the layer's bounds are resized when needsDisplayOnBoundsChange is NO, then the layer does *not* redisplay itself, so its cached content no longer fits the layer, and the contentsGravity matters.

By a judicious combination of settings, you can get the layer to perform some clever drawing for you that might be difficult to perform directly. For example, Figure 3-7 shows the result of the following settings:

```
arrow.needsDisplayOnBoundsChange = NO;
arrow.contentsCenter = CGRectMake(0.0, 0.4, 1.0, 0.6);
arrow.contentsGravity = kCAGravityResizeAspect;
arrow.bounds = CGRectInset(arrow.bounds, -20, -20);
```

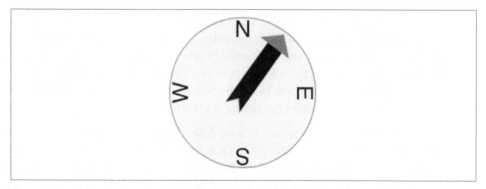

Figure 3-7. One way of resizing the compass arrow

Because needsDisplayOnBoundsChange is NO, the content is not redisplayed when the arrow's bounds are increased; instead, the cached content is used. The contents-Gravity setting tells us to resize proportionally; therefore, the arrow is both longer and wider than in Figure 3-1, but not in such a way as to distort its proportions. However, notice that although the triangular arrowhead is wider, it is not longer; the increase in length is due entirely to the stretching of the arrow's shaft. That's because the contents-Center region is within the shaft.

A layer's masksToBounds property has the same effect on its content that it has on its sublayers. If it is NO, the whole content is displayed, even if that content (after taking account of the contentsGravity and contentsRect) is larger then the layer. If it is YES, only the part of the content within the layer's bounds will be displayed.

The value of a layer's bounds origin does not affect where its content is drawn. It affects only where its sublayers are drawn.

Layers that Draw Themselves

A few built-in CALayer subclasses provide some basic but extremely helpful self-drawing ability:

CATextLayer

A CATextLayer has a string property, which can be an NSString or NSAttributed-String, along with other text formatting properties; it draws its string. The default text color, the foregroundColor property, is white, which is unlikely to be what you want. The text is different from the contents and is mutually exclusive with it: either the contents image or the text will be drawn, but not both, so in general you

Figure 3-8. A gradient drawn behind the compass

should not give a CATextLayer any contents image. In Figure 3-1 and Figure 3-7, the cardinal point letters are CATextLayer instances.

CAShapeLayer

A CAShapeLayer has a `path` property, which is a CGPath. It fills or strokes this path, or both, depending on its `fillColor` and `strokeColor` values, and displays the result; the default is a `fillColor` of black and no `strokeColor`. A CAShapeLayer may also have `contents`; the shape is displayed on top of the contents image, but there is no property permitting you to specify a compositing mode. In Figure 3-1 and Figure 3-7, the background circle is a CAShapeLayer instance, stroked with gray and filled with a lighter, slightly transparent gray.

CAGradientLayer

A CAGradientLayer covers its background with a simple linear gradient; thus, it's an easy way to draw a gradient in your interface (and if you need something more elaborate you can always draw with Core Graphics instead). The gradient is defined much as in the Core Graphics gradient example in Chapter 2, an array of locations and an array of corresponding colors (except that these are NSArrays, not C arrays), along with a start and end point. To clip the gradient's shape, you can add a mask to the CAGradientLayer (masks are discussed later in this chapter). A CAGradient-Layer's `contents` are not displayed.

The `colors` array requires CGColors, not UIColors. But CGColorRef is not an object type, whereas NSArray expects objects, so to quiet the compiler you'll need to typecast each color to `id`.

Figure 3-8 shows our compass drawn with an extra CAGradientLayer behind it.

Transforms

The way a layer is drawn on the screen can be modified though a transform. This is not surprising, because a view can have a transform (see Chapter 1), and a view is drawn on the screen by its layer. But a layer's transform is more powerful than a view's transform; you can use it to accomplish things that you can't accomplish with a view's transform alone.

In the simplest case, when a transform is two-dimensional, you can use a layer's affine-Transform. The value is a CGAffineTransform, familiar from Chapter 1 and Chapter 2. The transform is applied around the anchorPoint. (Thus, the anchorPoint has a second purpose that I didn't tell you about when discussing it earlier.)

You now know everything needed to understand the code that generated Figure 3-8, so here it is. In this code, self is the CompassLayer; it does no drawing of its own, but merely assembles and configures its sublayers. The four cardinal point letters are each drawn by a CATextLayer and placed using a transform. They are drawn at the same coordinates, but they have different rotation transforms; even though the CATextLayers are small (just 40 by 40) and appear near the perimeter of the circle, they are anchored, and so their rotation is centered, at the center of the circle. To generate the arrow, we make ourselves the arrow layer's delegate and call setNeedsDisplay; this causes draw-Layer:inContext: to be called in CompassLayer (that code is just the same code we developed for drawing the arrow in Chapter 2, and is not repeated here). The arrow layer is positioned by an anchorPoint pinning its tail to the center of the circle, and rotated around that pin by a transform:

```
// the gradient
CAGradientLayer* g = [CAGradientLayer new];
g.contentsScale = [UIScreen mainScreen].scale;
g.frame = self.bounds;
g.colors = @[(id)[UIColor blackColor].CGColor,
             (id)[UIColor redColor].CGColor];
g.locations = @[@0.0f,
                @1.0f];
[self addSublayer:g];
// the circle
CAShapeLayer* circle = [CAShapeLayer new];
circle.contentsScale = [UIScreen mainScreen].scale;
circle.lineWidth = 2.0;
circle.fillColor =
    [UIColor colorWithRed:0.9 green:0.95 blue:0.93 alpha:0.9].CGColor;
circle.strokeColor = [UIColor grayColor].CGColor;
CGMutablePathRef p = CGPathCreateMutable();
CGPathAddEllipseInRect(p, nil, CGRectInset(self.bounds, 3, 3));
circle.path = p;
[self addSublayer:circle];
circle.bounds = self.bounds;
circle.position = CGPointMake(CGRectGetMidX(self.bounds),
```

```
                        CGRectGetMidY(self.bounds));
// the four cardinal points
NSArray* pts = @[@"N", @"E", @"S", @"W"];
for (int i = 0; i < 4; i++) {
    CATextLayer* t = [CATextLayer new];
    t.contentsScale = [UIScreen mainScreen].scale;
    t.string = pts[i];
    t.bounds = CGRectMake(0,0,40,40);
    t.position = CGPointMake(CGRectGetMidX(circle.bounds),
                             CGRectGetMidY(circle.bounds));
    CGFloat vert = CGRectGetMidY(circle.bounds) / CGRectGetHeight(t.bounds);
    t.anchorPoint = CGPointMake(0.5, vert);
    t.alignmentMode = kCAAlignmentCenter;
    t.foregroundColor = [UIColor blackColor].CGColor;
    t.affineTransform = CGAffineTransformMakeRotation(i*M_PI/2.0);
    [circle addSublayer:t];
}
// the arrow
CALayer* arrow = [CALayer new];
arrow.contentsScale = [UIScreen mainScreen].scale;
arrow.bounds = CGRectMake(0, 0, 40, 100);
arrow.position = CGPointMake(CGRectGetMidX(self.bounds),
                             CGRectGetMidY(self.bounds));
arrow.anchorPoint = CGPointMake(0.5, 0.8);
arrow.delegate = self;
arrow.affineTransform = CGAffineTransformMakeRotation(M_PI/5.0);
[self addSublayer:arrow];
[arrow setNeedsDisplay];
```

A full-fledged layer transform, the value of the transform property, takes place in three-dimensional space; its description includes a z-axis, perpendicular to both the x-axis and y-axis. (By default, the positive z-axis points out of the screen, toward the viewer's face.) Layers do not magically give you realistic three-dimensional rendering — for that you would use OpenGL, which is beyond the scope of this discussion. Layers are two-dimensional objects, and they are designed for speed and simplicity. Nevertheless, they do operate in three dimensions, quite sufficiently to give a cartoonish but effective sense of reality, especially when performing an animation. We've all seen the screen image flip like turning over a piece of paper to reveal what's on the back; that's a rotation in three dimensions.

A three-dimensional transform takes place around a three-dimensional extension of the anchorPoint, whose z-component is supplied by the anchorPointZ property. Thus, in the reduced default case where anchorPointZ is 0, the anchorPoint is sufficient, as we've already seen in using CGAffineTransform.

The transform itself is described mathematically by a struct called a CATransform3D. The *Core Animation Function Reference* lists the functions for working with these transforms. They are a lot like the CGAffineTransform functions, except they've got a third dimension. For example, here's the declaration of the function for making a 2D scale transform:

```
CGAffineTransform CGAffineTransformMakeScale (
    CGFloat sx,
    CGFloat sy
);
```

And here's the declaration of the function for making a 3D scale transform:

```
CATransform3D CATransform3DMakeScale (
    CGFloat sx,
    CGFloat sy,
    CGFloat sz
);
```

The rotation 3D transform is a little more complicated. In addition to the angle, you also have to supply three coordinates describing the vector around which the rotation takes place. Perhaps you've forgotten from your high-school math what a vector is, or perhaps trying to visualize three dimensions boggles your mind, so think of it this way.

Pretend for purposes of discussion that the anchor point is the origin, {0,0,0}. Now imagine an arrow emanating from the anchor point; its other end, the pointy end, is described by the three coordinates you provide. Now imagine a plane that intersects the anchor point, perpendicular to the arrow. That is the plane in which the rotation will take place; a positive angle is a clockwise rotation, as seen from the side of the plane with the arrow (Figure 3-9). In effect, the three coordinates you supply describe, relative to the anchor point, where your eye would have to be to see this rotation as an old-fashioned two-dimensional rotation.

A vector, however, specifies a direction, not a point. Thus it makes no difference on what scale you give the coordinates: {1,1,1} means the same thing as {10,10,10}. If the three values are {0,0,1}, with all other things being equal, the case is collapsed to a simple CGAffineTransform, because the rotational plane is the screen. On the other hand, if the three values are {0,0,-1}, it's a backward CGAffineTransform, so that a positive angle looks counterclockwise (because we are looking at the "back side" of the rotational plane).

A layer can itself be rotated in such a way that its "back" is showing. For example, the following rotation flips a layer around its y-axis:

```
someLayer.transform = CATransform3DMakeRotation(M_PI, 0, 1, 0);
```

By default, the layer is considered double-sided, so when it is flipped to show its "back," what's drawn is an appropriately reversed version of the content of the layer (along with its sublayers, which by default are still drawn in front of the layer, but reversed and positioned in accordance with the layer's transformed coordinate system). But if the layer's doubleSided property is NO, then when it is flipped to show its "back," the layer disappears (along with its sublayers); its "back" is transparent and empty.

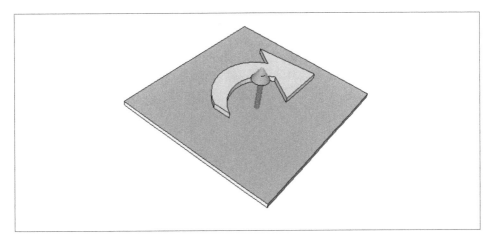

Figure 3-9. An anchor point plus a vector defines a rotation plane

Depth

There are two ways to place layers at different nominal depths with respect to their siblings. One is through the z-component of their `position`, which is the `zPosition` property. (Thus the `zPosition`, too, has a second purpose that I didn't tell you about earlier.) The other is to apply a transform that translates the layer's position in the z-direction. These two values, the z-component of a layer's position and the z-component of its translation transform, are related; in some sense, the `zPosition` is a shorthand for a translation transform in the z-direction. (If you provide both a `zPosition` and a z-direction translation, you can rapidly confuse yourself.)

In the real world, changing an object's `zPosition` would make it appear larger or smaller, as it is positioned closer or further away; but this, by default, is not the case in the world of layer drawing. There is no attempt to portray perspective; the layer planes are drawn at their actual size and flattened onto one another, with no illusion of distance. (This is called *orthographic projection*, and is the way blueprints are often drawn to display an object from one side.)

However, there's a widely used trick for introducing a quality of perspective into the way layers are drawn: make them sublayers of a layer whose `sublayerTransform` property maps all points onto a "distant" plane. (This is probably just about the only thing the `sublayerTransform` property is ever used for.) Combined with orthographic projection, the effect is to apply one-point perspective to the drawing, so that things do get perceptibly smaller in the negative z-direction.

For example, let's try applying a sort of "page-turn" rotation to our compass: we'll anchor it at its right side and then rotate it around the y-axis. Here, the sublayer we're rotating

Figure 3-10. A disappointing page-turn rotation

Figure 3-11. A dramatic page-turn rotation

(accessed through a property, rotationLayer) is the gradient layer, and the circle and arrow are its sublayers so that they rotate with it:

```
self.rotationLayer.anchorPoint = CGPointMake(1,0.5);
self.rotationLayer.position =
    CGPointMake(CGRectGetMaxX(self.bounds), CGRectGetMidY(self.bounds));
self.rotationLayer.transform = CATransform3DMakeRotation(M_PI/4.0, 0, 1, 0);
```

The results are disappointing (Figure 3-10); the compass looks more squashed than rotated. Now, however, we'll also apply the distance-mapping transform. The superlayer here is self:

```
CATransform3D transform = CATransform3DIdentity;
transform.m34 = -1.0/1000.0;
self.sublayerTransform = transform;
```

The results (shown in Figure 3-11) are better, and you can experiment with values to replace 1000.0; for example, 500.0 gives an even more exaggerated effect. Also, the zPosition of the rotationLayer will now affect how large it is.

Another way to draw layers with depth is to use CATransformLayer. This CALayer subclass doesn't do any drawing of its own; it is intended solely as a host for other layers. It has the remarkable feature that you can apply a transform to it and it will maintain the depth relationships among its own sublayers. For example:

```
// lay1 is a layer, f is a CGRect
CALayer* lay2 = [CALayer layer];
lay2.frame = f;
lay2.backgroundColor = [UIColor blueColor].CGColor;
[lay1 addSublayer:lay2];
CALayer* lay3 = [CALayer layer];
lay3.frame = CGRectOffset(f, 20, 30);
lay3.backgroundColor = [UIColor greenColor].CGColor;
lay3.zPosition = 10;
[lay1 addSublayer:lay3];
lay1.transform = CATransform3DMakeRotation(M_PI, 0, 1, 0);
```

In that code, the superlayer lay1 has two sublayers, lay2 and lay3. The sublayers are added in that order, so lay3 is drawn in front of lay2. Then lay1 is flipped like a page being turned by setting its transform. If lay1 is a normal CALayer, the sublayer drawing order doesn't change; lay3 is *still* drawn in front of lay2, even after the transform is applied. But if lay1 is a CATransformLayer, lay3 is drawn *behind* lay2 after the transform; they are both sublayers of lay1, so their depth relationship is maintained.

Figure 3-12 shows our page-turn rotation yet again, still with the sublayerTransform applied to self, but this time the only sublayer of self is a CATransformLayer:

```
CATransform3D transform = CATransform3DIdentity;
transform.m34 = -1.0/1000.0;
self.sublayerTransform = transform;
CATransformLayer* master = [CATransformLayer layer];
master.frame = self.bounds;
[self addSublayer: master];
self.rotationLayer = master;
```

The CATransformLayer, to which the page-turn transform is applied, holds the gradient layer, the circle layer, and the arrow layer. Those three layers are at different depths (using different zPosition settings), and I've tried to emphasize the arrow's separation from the circle by adding a shadow (discussed in the next section):

```
circle.zPosition = 10;
arrow.shadowOpacity = 1.0;
arrow.shadowRadius = 10;
arrow.zPosition = 20;
```

Figure 3-12. Page-turn rotation applied to a CATransformLayer

You can see from its apparent offset that the circle layer floats in front of the gradient layer, but I wish you could see this page-turn as an animation, which makes the circle jump right out from the gradient as the rotation proceeds.

Even more remarkable, I've added a little white peg sticking through the arrow and running into the circle! It is a CAShapeLayer, rotated to be perpendicular to the CATransformLayer (I'll explain the rotation code later in this chapter):

```
CAShapeLayer* peg = [CAShapeLayer new];
peg.contentsScale = [UIScreen mainScreen].scale;
peg.bounds = CGRectMake(0,0,3.5,50);
CGMutablePathRef p2 = CGPathCreateMutable();
CGPathAddRect(p2, nil, peg.bounds);
peg.path = p2;
CGPathRelease(p2);
peg.fillColor =
    [UIColor colorWithRed:1.0 green:0.95 blue:1.0 alpha:0.95].CGColor;
peg.anchorPoint = CGPointMake(0.5,0.5);
peg.position =
    CGPointMake(CGRectGetMidX(master.bounds), CGRectGetMidY(master.bounds));
[master addSublayer: peg];
[peg setValue:@(M_PI/2) forKeyPath:@"transform.rotation.x"];
[peg setValue:@(M_PI/2) forKeyPath:@"transform.rotation.z"];
peg.zPosition = 15;
```

In that code, the peg runs straight out of the circle toward the viewer, so it is seen end-on, and because a layer has no thickness, it is invisible. But as the CATransformLayer pivots forward in our page-turn rotation, the peg maintains its orientation relative to the circle, and comes into view. In effect, the drawing portrays a 3D model constructed entirely out of layers.

There is, I think, a slight additional gain in realism if the same `sublayerTransform` is applied also to the CATransformLayer, but I have not done so here.

Shadows, Borders, and Masks

A CALayer has many additional properties that affect details of how it is drawn. Since these drawing details can be applied to a UIView's underlying layer, they are effectively view features as well.

A CALayer can have a shadow, defined by its `shadowColor`, `shadowOpacity`, `shadowRadius`, and `shadowOffset` properties. To make the layer draw a shadow, set the `shadowOpacity` to a nonzero value. The shadow is normally based on the shape of the layer's nontransparent region, but deriving this shape can be calculation-intensive (so much so that in early versions of iOS, layer shadows weren't implemented). You can vastly improve performance by defining the shape yourself and assigning this shape as a CGPath to the `shadowPath` property.

A CALayer can have a border (`borderWidth`, `borderColor`); the `borderWidth` is drawn inward from the bounds, potentially covering some of the content unless you compensate.

A CALayer can be bounded by a rounded rectangle, by giving it a `cornerRadius` greater than zero. If the layer has a border, the border has rounded corners too. If the layer has a `backgroundColor`, that background is clipped to the shape of the rounded rectangle. If the layer's `masksToBounds` is YES, the layer's content and its sublayers are clipped by the rounded corners.

A CALayer can have a `mask`. This is itself a layer, whose content must be provided somehow. The transparency of the mask's content in a particular spot becomes (all other things being equal) the transparency of the layer at that spot. The hues in the mask's colors are irrelevant; only transparency matters. To position the mask, pretend it's a sublayer.

For example, Figure 3-13 shows our arrow layer, with the gray circle layer behind it, and a mask applied to the arrow layer. The mask is silly, but it illustrates very well how masks work: it's an ellipse, with an opaque fill and a thick, semitransparent stroke. Here's the code that generates and applies the mask:

```
CAShapeLayer* mask = [CAShapeLayer new];
mask.frame = arrow.bounds;
CGMutablePathRef p2 = CGPathCreateMutable();
CGPathAddEllipseInRect(p2, nil, CGRectInset(mask.bounds, 10, 10));
mask.strokeColor = [UIColor colorWithWhite:0.0 alpha:0.5].CGColor;
mask.lineWidth = 20;
mask.path = p2;
arrow.mask = mask;
CGPathRelease(p2);
```

Figure 3-13. A layer with a mask

Using a mask, we can do manually and in a more general way what the cornerRadius and masksToBounds properties do. For example, here's a utility method that generates a CALayer suitable for use as a rounded rectangle mask:

```
- (CALayer*) maskOfSize:(CGSize)sz roundingCorners:(CGFloat)rad {
    CGRect r = (CGRect){CGPointZero, sz};
    UIGraphicsBeginImageContextWithOptions(r.size, NO, 0);
    CGContextRef con = UIGraphicsGetCurrentContext();
    CGContextSetFillColorWithColor(
        con,[UIColor colorWithWhite:0 alpha:0].CGColor);
    CGContextFillRect(con, r);
    CGContextSetFillColorWithColor(
        con,[UIColor colorWithWhite:0 alpha:1].CGColor);
    UIBezierPath* p =
        [UIBezierPath bezierPathWithRoundedRect:r cornerRadius:rad];
    [p fill];
    UIImage* im = UIGraphicsGetImageFromCurrentImageContext();
    UIGraphicsEndImageContext();
    CALayer* mask = [CALayer layer];
    mask.frame = r;
    mask.contents = (id)im.CGImage;
    return mask;
}
```

The CALayer returned from that method can be placed as a mask anywhere in a layer by adjusting its frame origin and assigning it as the layer's mask. The result is that all of that layer's content drawing and its sublayers (and, if this layer is a view's underlying layer, the view's subviews) are clipped to the rounded rectangle shape; everything outside that shape is not drawn. That's just one example of the sort of thing you can do with a mask. A mask can have values between opaque and transparent, and it can be any shape. And the transparent region doesn't have to be on the outside of the mask; you can use a mask that's opaque on the outside and transparent on the inside to punch a hole in a layer (or a view).

Layer Efficiency

By now, you're probably envisioning all sorts of compositing fun, with layers masking sublayers and laid semitransparently over other layers. There's nothing wrong with that, but when an iOS device is asked to shift its drawing from place to place, the movement may stutter because the device lacks the necessary computing power to composite repeatedly and rapidly. This sort of issue is likely to emerge particularly when your code performs an animation (Chapter 4) or when the user is able to animate drawing through touch, as when scrolling a table view (Chapter 8). You may be able to detect these problems by eye, and you can quantify them on a device by using the Core Animation template in Instruments, which shows the frame rate achieved during animation. Also, both the Core Animation template and the Simulator's Debug menu let you summon colored overlays that provide clues as to possible sources of inefficient drawing which can lead to such problems.

In general, opaque drawing is most efficient. (Nonopaque drawing is what Instruments marks in red as "blended layers.") If a layer will always be shown over a background consisting of a single color, you can give the layer its own background of that same color; when additional layer content is supplied, the visual effect will be the same as if that additional layer content were composited over a transparent background. For example, instead of an image masked to a rounded rectangle (with a layer's cornerRadius or mask property), you could use Core Graphics to clip the drawing of that image into the graphics context of a layer whose background color is the same as that of the destination in front of which the drawing will be shown. Here's an example from a view's drawRect: in one of my own apps:

```
// clip to rounded rect
CGRect r = CGRectInset(rect, 1, 1);
[[UIBezierPath bezierPathWithRoundedRect:r cornerRadius:6] addClip];
// draw image
UIImage* im = [UIImage imageNamed: @"linen.jpg"];
// simulate UIViewContentModeScaleAspectFill
// make widths the same, image height will be too tall
CGFloat scale = im.size.width/rect.size.width;
CGFloat y = (im.size.height/scale - rect.size.height) / 2.0;
CGRect r2 = CGRectMake(0,-y,im.size.width/scale, im.size.height/scale);
r2 = CGRectIntegral(r2); // looks a whole lot better if we do this
[im drawInRect:r2];
```

Another way to gain some efficiency is by "freezing" the entirety of the layer's drawing as a bitmap. In effect, you're drawing everything in the layer to a secondary cache and using the cache to draw to the screen. Copying from a cache is less efficient than drawing directly to the screen, but this inefficiency may be more than compensated for, if there's a deep or complex layer tree, by not having to composite that tree every time we render. To do this, set the layer's shouldRasterize to YES and its rasterizationScale to some sensible value (probably [UIScreen mainScreen].scale). You can always turn rasterization off again by setting shouldRasterize to NO, so it's easy to rasterize just before some massive or sluggish rearrangement of the screen and then unrasterize afterward. (In addition, you can get some cool "out of focus" effects by setting the rasterizationScale to around 0.3.)

In addition, there's a layer property `drawsAsynchronously`. The default is NO. If set to YES, the layer's graphics context accumulates drawing commands and obeys them later on a background thread. Thus, your drawing commands run very quickly, because they are not in fact being obeyed at the time you issue them. I haven't had occasion to use this, but presumably there could be situations where it keeps your app responsive when drawing would otherwise be time-consuming.

Layers and Key–Value Coding

All of a layer's properties are accessible through key–value coding by way of keys with the same name as the property. Thus, to apply a mask to a layer, instead of saying this:

```
layer.mask = mask;
```

we could have said:

```
[layer setValue: mask forKey: @"mask"];
```

In addition, CATransform3D and CGAffineTransform values can be expressed through key–value coding and key paths. For example, instead of writing this:

```
self.rotationLayer.transform = CATransform3DMakeRotation(M_PI/4.0, 0, 1, 0);
```

we can write this:

```
[self.rotationLayer setValue:[NSNumber numberWithFloat:M_PI/4.0]
                  forKeyPath:@"transform.rotation.y"];
```

This notation is possible because CATransform3D is key–value coding compliant for a repertoire of keys and key paths. These are not properties, however; a CATransform3D doesn't have a `rotation` property. It doesn't have *any* properties, because it isn't even an object. You cannot say:

```
self.rotationLayer.transform.rotation.y = //... No, sorry
```

The transform key paths you'll use most often are:

- `rotation.x`, `rotation.y`, `rotation.z`
- `rotation` (same as `rotation.z`)
- `scale.x`, `scale.y`, `scale.z`
- `translation.x`, `translation.y`, `translation.z`
- `translation` (two-dimensional, a CGSize)

The Quartz Core framework also injects KVC compliance into CGPoint, CGSize, and CGRect, allowing you to use keys and key paths matching their struct component names. For a complete list of KVC compliant classes related to CALayer, along with the keys and key paths they implement, plus rules for how to wrap nonobject values as objects, see "Core Animation Extensions to Key-Value Coding" in Apple's *Core Animation Programming Guide.*

Moreover, you can treat a CALayer as a kind of NSDictionary, and get and set the value for *any* key. This means you can attach arbitrary information to an individual layer instance and retrieve it later. For example, earlier I mentioned that to apply manual layout to a layer's sublayers, you will need a way of identifying those sublayers. This feature could provide a way of doing that. For example:

```
[myLayer1 setValue:@"Manny" forKey:@"name"];
[myLayer2 setValue:@"Moe" forKey:@"name"];
```

A layer doesn't have a `name` property; the `@"name"` key is something I'm attaching to these layers arbitrarily. Now I can identify these layers later by getting the value of their respective `@"name"` keys.

Also, CALayer has a `defaultValueForKey:` class method; to implement it, you'll need to subclass and override. In the case of keys whose value you want to provide a default for, return that value; otherwise, return the value that comes from calling `super`. Thus, even if a value for a particular key has never been explicitly provided, it can have a non-nil value.

The truth is that this feature, though delightful (and I often wish that all classes behaved like this), is not put there for your convenience and enjoyment. It's there to serve as the basis for animation, which is the subject of the next chapter.

CHAPTER 4
Animation

Animation is the visible change of an attribute over time. The changing attribute might be positional: something moves or changes size. But other kinds of attribute can animate as well. For example, a view's background color might change from red to green, not instantly, but perceptibly fading from one to the other. Or a view might change from opaque to transparent, not instantly, but perceptibly fading away.

Without help, most of us would find animation beyond our reach. There are just too many complications — complications of calculation, of timing, of screen refresh, of threading, and many more. Fortunately, help is provided. You don't perform an animation yourself; you describe it, you order it, and it is performed for you. You get *animation on demand*.

Asking for an animation can be as simple as setting a property value; under some circumstances, a single line of code will result in animation:

```
myLayer.backgroundColor = [UIColor redColor].CGColor; // animate to red
```

And this is no coincidence. Apple wants to facilitate your use of animation. Animation is crucial to the character of the iOS interface. It isn't just cool and fun; it clarifies that something is changing or responding. For example, one of my first apps was based on an OS X game in which the user clicks cards to select them. In the OS X version, a card was highlighted to show it was selected, and the computer would beep to indicate a click on an ineligible card. On iOS, these indications were insufficient: the highlighting felt weak, and you can't use a sound warning in an environment where the user might have the volume turned off or be listening to music. So in the iOS version, animation is the indicator for card selection (a selected card waggles eagerly) and for tapping on an ineligible card (the whole interface shudders, as if to shrug off the tap).

(If you're looking to create a complete constantly running animated world, as for certain types of game, look into Sprite Kit, which is new in iOS 7. This book doesn't discuss

Sprite Kit, but an understanding of the concepts in this chapter will prepare you very well for Sprite Kit.)

 The Simulator's Debug → Toggle Slow Animations menu item helps you inspect animations by making them run more slowly.

Drawing, Animation, and Threading

When you change a visible view property, even *without* animation, that change does *not* visibly take place there and then. Rather, the system records that this is a change you would like to make, and marks the view as needing to be redrawn. You can change many visible view properties, but these changes merely constitute an accumulated set of instructions. Later, when all your code has run to completion and the system has, as it were, a free moment, then it redraws all views that need redrawing, applying their new visible property features. Let's call this the *redraw moment*. (I'll explain what the redraw moment really is later in this chapter.)

You can see that this is true simply by changing some visible aspect of a view and changing it back again, in the same code: on the screen, nothing happens. For example, suppose a view's background color is green. Suppose your code changes it to red, and then later changes it back to green:

```
// view starts out green
view.backgroundColor = [UIColor redColor];
// ... time-consuming code goes here ...
view.backgroundColor = [UIColor greenColor];
// code ends, redraw moment arrives
```

The system accumulates all the desired changes until the redraw moment happens, and the redraw moment doesn't happen until after your code has finished, so when the redraw moment does happen, the last accumulated change in the view's color is to green — which is its color already. Thus, no matter how much time-consuming code lies between the change from green to red and the change from red to green, the user won't see any color change at all.

That's why you don't order a view to be redrawn; rather, you tell it that it *needs* redrawing — setNeedsDisplay — at the next redraw moment. It's also why I used delayed performance in the contentMode example in Chapter 2: by calling dispatch_after, I allowed the redraw moment a chance to happen, thus giving the view some content, *before* resizing the view. This use of delayed performance to let a redraw moment happen is quite common; later in this chapter I'll suggest another way of accomplishing the same goal.

Similarly, when you ask for an animation to be performed, the animation doesn't start happening on the screen until the next redraw moment. (You can force an animation to be performed immediately, but this is unusual.)

Now let's talk about the mechanism by which animation is performed. It's all a kind of ingenious illusion. Think of the animation as a kind of movie, a cartoon, interposed between the user and the "real" screen. While the animation lasts, this movie is superimposed onto the screen. When the animation is finished, the movie is removed, revealing the state of the "real" screen behind it. The user is unaware of all this, because (if you've done things correctly) at the time that it starts, the movie's first frame looks just like the state of the "real" screen at that moment, and at the time that it ends, the movie's last frame looks just like the state of the "real" screen at *that* moment.

So, when you reposition a view from position 1 to position 2 with animation, you can envision a typical sequence of events like this:

1. The view is set to position 2, but there has been no redraw moment, so it is still portrayed at position 1.
2. The rest of your code runs to completion.
3. The redraw moment arrives. If there were no animation, the view would now suddenly be portrayed at position 2. But there *is* an animation, and it (the "animation movie") starts with the view portrayed at position 1, so that is still what the user sees.
4. The animation proceeds, portraying the view at intermediate positions between position 1 and position 2. The documentation describes the animation as now *in-flight*.
5. The animation ends, portraying the view ending up at position 2.
6. The "animation movie" is removed, revealing the view indeed at position 2.

Realizing that the "animation movie" is different from what happens to the *real* view is key to configuring an animation correctly. A frequent complaint of beginners is that a position animation is performed as expected, but then, at the end, the view "jumps" to some other position. This happens because you set up the animation but failed to move the view to match its final position in the "animation movie"; the "jump" happens because, when the "movie" is whipped away at the end of the animation, the real situation that's revealed doesn't match the last frame of the "movie".

Animation takes place on an independent thread. You don't have to worry about the details (thank heavens, because multithreading is generally rather tricky and complicated), but you can't ignore it either. Your code runs independently of and possibly simultaneously with the animation — that's what multithreading means — so communication between the animation and your code can require some planning.

Presentation Layer

There isn't really an "animation movie" in front of the screen — though the effect is much the same. In reality, it is not a layer itself that is portrayed on the screen; it's a derived layer called the *presentation layer*. Thus, when you animate the change of a view's position or a layer's position from position 1 to position 2, its nominal position changes immediately; meanwhile, the presentation layer's position remains unchanged until the redraw moment, and then changes over time, and because that's what's actually drawn on the screen, that's what the user sees.

A layer's presentation layer can be accessed through its `presentationLayer` property (and the layer itself is the presentation layer's `modelLayer`). It is typed as an `id`, so in order to work with it as a layer, you will probably want to typecast it to a `CALayer*`. Accessing the `presentationLayer` is not a common thing to do, but it might come in handy if your code needs to learn the current state of an in-flight animation.

Arranging for your code to be notified when an animation ends is a common need. Most of the animation APIs provide a way to set up such a notification. One use of an "animation ended" notification might be to chain animations together: one animation ends and then another begins, in sequence. Another use is to perform some sort of cleanup. A very frequent kind of cleanup has to do with handling of touches: while an animation is in-flight, if your code is not running, the interface by default is responsive to the user's touches, which might cause all kinds of havoc as your views try to respond while the animation is still happening and the screen presentation doesn't match reality. To take care of this, it's common practice to turn off your app's responsiveness to touches as you set up an animation and then turn it back on when you're notified that the animation is over; locking down all the relevant situations so that this toggling of the app's responsiveness is performed coherently can be challenging.

Since your code can run even after you've set up an animation, or might start running while an animation is in-flight, you need to be careful about setting up conflicting animations. Multiple animations can be set up (and performed) simultaneously, but trying to animate or change a property that's already in the middle of being animated is an incoherency that can kill the animation there and then. You may sometimes do this intentionally as a way of interrupting an animation, but just as often you'll want to take care not to let your animations step on each other's feet.

Outside forces can interrupt your animations as well. The user might click the Home button to send your app to the background, or a phone call might come in while an animation is in-flight. The system deals coherently with this situation by simply canceling all in-flight animations when an app is backgrounded; you've already arranged *before* the animation for your views to assume the final states they will have *after* the animation, so no harm is done — when your app resumes, everything is in that final state you arranged beforehand. But if you wanted your app to appear to pick up an animation in the middle, where it left off, that would require some canny coding on your part.

UIImageView and UIImage Animation

UIImageView provides a form of animation so simple as to be scarcely deserving of the name; still, sometimes it might be all you need. You supply the UIImageView with an array of UIImages, as the value of its `animationImages` or `highlightedAnimation-Images` property. This array represents the "frames" of a simple cartoon; when you send the `startAnimating` message, the images are displayed in turn, at a frame rate determined by the `animationDuration` property, repeating as many times as specified by the `animationRepeatCount` property (the default is 0, meaning to repeat forever, or until the `stopAnimating` message is received). Before and after the animation, the image view continues displaying its `image` (or `highlightedImage`).

For example, suppose we want an image of Mars to appear out of nowhere and flash three times on the screen. This might seem to require some sort of NSTimer-based solution, but it's far simpler to use an animating UIImageView:

```
UIImage* mars = [UIImage imageNamed: @"Mars"];
UIGraphicsBeginImageContextWithOptions(mars.size, NO, 0);
UIImage* empty = UIGraphicsGetImageFromCurrentImageContext();
UIGraphicsEndImageContext();
NSArray* arr = @[mars, empty, mars, empty, mars];
UIImageView* iv = [[UIImageView alloc] initWithImage:empty];
CGRect r = iv.frame;
r.origin = CGPointMake(100,100);
iv.frame = r;
[self.view addSubview: iv];
iv.animationImages = arr;
iv.animationDuration = 2;
iv.animationRepeatCount = 1;
[iv startAnimating];
```

You can combine UIImageView animation with other kinds of animation. For example, you could flash the image of Mars while at the same time sliding the UIImageView rightward, using view animation as described in the next section.

In addition, UIImage supplies a parallel form of animation: an image can itself be an *animated image*. Just as with UIImageView, this really means that you've multiple images that form a sequence serving as the "frames" of a simple cartoon. You can designate an image as an animated image with one of these UIImage class methods:

`animatedImageWithImages:duration:`
As with UIImageView's `animationImages`, you supply an array of UIImages. You also supply the duration for the whole animation.

`animatedImageNamed:duration:`
You supply the name of a single image file, as with `imageNamed:`, with no file extension. The runtime appends `@"0"` (or, if that fails, `@"1"`) to the name you supply and makes *that* image file the first image in the animation sequence. Then it increments the appended number, gathering images and adding them to the sequence (until there are no more, or we reach `@"1024"`).

`animatedResizableImageNamed:capInsets:resizingMode:duration:`
Combines an animated image with a resizable image (Chapter 2).

You do not tell an animated image to start animating, nor are you able to tell it how long you want the animation to repeat. Rather, an animated image is *always animating*, repeating its sequence once every `duration` seconds, so long as it appears in your interface; to control the animation, add the image to your interface or remove it from the interface, possibly exchanging it for a similar image that isn't animated. Moreover, an animated image can appear in the interface *anywhere a UIImage can appear* as a property of some interface object.

In this example, I construct a sequence of red circles of different sizes, in code, and build an animated image which I then display in a UIButton:

```
NSMutableArray* arr = [NSMutableArray array];
float w = 18;
for (int i = 0; i < 6; i++) {
    UIGraphicsBeginImageContextWithOptions(CGSizeMake(w,w), NO, 0);
    CGContextRef con = UIGraphicsGetCurrentContext();
    CGContextSetFillColorWithColor(con, [UIColor redColor].CGColor);
    CGContextAddEllipseInRect(con, CGRectMake(0+i,0+i,w-i*2,w-i*2));
    CGContextFillPath(con);
    UIImage* im = UIGraphicsGetImageFromCurrentImageContext();
    UIGraphicsEndImageContext();
    [arr addObject:im];
}
UIImage* im = [UIImage animatedImageWithImages:arr duration:0.5];
// assume self.b is a button in the interface
[self.b setImage:im forState:UIControlStateNormal];
```

View Animation

Animation is ultimately layer animation. However, for a limited range of properties, you can animate a UIView directly: these are its `alpha`, `backgroundColor`, `bounds`, `center`, `frame`, and `transform`. You can also animate a UIView's change of contents. This list of animatable features, despite its brevity, will often prove quite sufficient. (If it doesn't, you can drop down to a lower level and animate a layer, as described later in this chapter.)

Block-Based View Animation

The syntax for animating a UIView involves calling a UIView class method and expressing the desired animation in an Objective-C block. For example, suppose we have a UIView `self.v` in the interface, with a yellow background color, and we want to animate that view's change of background color to red. This will do it:

```
[UIView animateWithDuration:0.4 animations:^{
    self.v.backgroundColor = [UIColor redColor];
}];
```

Due to considerations of space, the older view animation methods `beginAnimations:context:` and `commitAnimations`, along with the other methods and constants to be used in conjunction with them, are not discussed in this edition of the book. In any case their use is "discouraged", according to Apple.

Any animatable change made within an `animations:` block will be animated, so we can animate a change both to the view's color and to its position simultaneously:

```
[UIView animateWithDuration:0.4 animations:^{
    self.v.backgroundColor = [UIColor redColor];
    CGPoint p = self.v.center;
    p.y -= 100;
    self.v.center = p;
}];
```

We can also animate changes to multiple views within the same `animations:` block. For example, suppose we want to make one view dissolve into another. We start with the second view present in the view hierarchy, but with an `alpha` of 0, so that it is invisible. Then we animate the change of the first view's `alpha` to 0 and the second view's `alpha` to 1.

In that case, we might like to place the second view in the view hierarchy just before the animation starts (invisibly, because its `alpha` starts at 0) and remove the first view just after the animation ends (invisibly, because its `alpha` ends at 0). An additional parameter, `completion:`, lets us specify what should happen after the animation ends:

```
UIView* v2 = // ... create and configure new view
v2.alpha = 0;
[self.v.superview addSubview:v2];
[UIView animateWithDuration:0.4 animations:^{
    self.v.alpha = 0;
    v2.alpha = 1;
} completion:^(BOOL finished) {
    [self.v removeFromSuperview];
}];
```

Code that isn't about animatable view properties can appear in an `animations:` block with no problem, but we must be careful to keep any changes to animatable properties that we do *not* want animated out of the `animations:` block. In that example, in setting `v2.alpha` to 0, I just want to set it right now, instantly; I don't want that change to be animated. So I've put that line before `animations:` block.

Sometimes, though, that's not so easy; perhaps, within the `animations:` block, we must call a method that might perform animatable changes. New in iOS 7, the `performWithoutAnimation:` method solves the problem; it goes inside an `animations:` block, but whatever happens in *its* block is *not* animated. In this rather artificial example, the view jumps to its new position and then slowly turns red:

```
[UIView animateWithDuration:0.4 animations:^{
    self.v.backgroundColor = [UIColor redColor];
    [UIView performWithoutAnimation:^{
        CGPoint p = self.v.center;
        p.y -= 100;
        self.v.center = p;
    }];
}];
```

The material inside an `animations:` block (but not inside a `performWithoutAnimation:` block) *orders* the animation — that is, it gives instructions for what the animation will be when the redraw moment comes. If you change an animatable view property as part of the animation, you should not change that property again afterward; the results can be confusing. For example, try to guess what this code does:

```
[UIView animateWithDuration:2 animations:^{
    CGPoint p = self.v.center;
    p.y = 100;
    self.v.center = p;
    CGPoint p2 = self.v.center;
    p2.y = 300;
    self.v.center = p2;
}];
```

The result is not two successive animations. What we have here is just one animation containing conflicting orders: animate so that the view's center y value becomes 100, and animate so that the view's center y value becomes 300. The second order causes the animation described by the first order to be cancelled; the change described by the first animation is performed *without* animation. Therefore, when the animation runs, the view *jumps* so that its center y value is 100, and then *animates* down 200 points.

Even a change *after* the animation block can have confusing effects. Try to guess what this code does:

```
[UIView animateWithDuration:2 animations:^{
    CGPoint p = self.v.center;
    p.y = 100;
    self.v.center = p;
}];
CGPoint p2 = self.v.center;
p2.y = 300;
self.v.center = p2;
```

The view animates *from where it already is* to where its center y value becomes 300! The code inside the animations: block might as well never have happened. The code that follows the animations: block behaves as if it were *inside* the animations: block; it has become part of the animation — in fact, it has become the animation! It's exactly the same as if that code had said this:

```
[UIView animateWithDuration:2 animations:^{
    CGPoint p2 = self.v.center;
    p2.y = 300;
    self.v.center = p2;
}];
```

These are edge cases, and you should avoid them. The moral is, after you've ordered an animatable view property to be animated inside an animations: block, *don't change that view property's value again* until after the animation is over.

View Animation Options

For the maximum in flexibility and power, call the UIView class method animateWith-Duration:delay:options:animations:completion:. (The two methods I've already described are merely reduced versions of this method.) The parameters are:

duration
> The duration of the animation: how long it takes (in seconds) to run from start to finish. You can also think of this as the animation's speed. Obviously, if two views are told to move different distances in the same time, the one that must move further must move faster.

delay
> The delay before the animation starts. The default is no delay.

options
> A bitmask combining additional options (using the bitwise-or operator).

animations
> The block containing view property changes to be animated.

completion
> The block to run when the animation ends (or nil). It takes one BOOL parameter indicating whether the animation ran to completion. The block is called, with a

parameter indicating YES, even if nothing in the `animations:` block triggers any animations. It's fine for this block to order a further animation, thus chaining animations.

Here are some of the chief `options:` values you might wish to use:

Animation curve

An animation curve describes how the animation changes speed during its course. The term "ease" means that there is a gradual acceleration or deceleration between the animation's central speed and the zero speed at its start or end. Specify one at most; `UIViewAnimationOptionCurveEaseInOut` is the default. Your choices are:

* `UIViewAnimationOptionCurveEaseInOut`

* `UIViewAnimationOptionCurveEaseIn`

* `UIViewAnimationOptionCurveEaseOut`

* `UIViewAnimationOptionCurveLinear` (constant speed throughout)

`UIViewAnimationOptionRepeat`

If included, the animation will repeat indefinitely. There is no way to specify a certain number of repetitions; you either repeat forever or not at all. This feels like an oversight (a serious oversight); I'll suggest a workaround in a moment.

`UIViewAnimationOptionAutoreverse`

If included, the animation will run from start to finish (in the given duration time), and will then run from finish to start (also in the given duration time). The documentation's claim that you can autoreverse only if you also repeat is incorrect; you can use either or both (or neither).

When using `UIViewAnimationOptionAutoreverse`, you will want to clean up at the end so that the view is back in its original position when the animation is over. To see what I mean, consider this code:

```
NSUInteger opts = UIViewAnimationOptionAutoreverse;
[UIView animateWithDuration:1 delay:0 options:opts animations:^{
    CGPoint p = self.v.center;
    p.x += 100;
    self.v.center = p;
} completion:nil];
```

The view animates 100 points to the right and then animates 100 points back to its original position — and then jumps 100 points to the right again. The reason is that the last actual value we assigned to the view's center x is 100 points to the right, so when the animation is over and the "animation movie" is whipped away, the view is revealed still sitting 100 points to the right. The solution is to move the view back to its original position in the `completion:` handler:

```
    CGPoint pOrig = self.v.center;
    NSUInteger opts = UIViewAnimationOptionAutoreverse;
    [UIView animateWithDuration:1 delay:0 options:opts animations:^{
        CGPoint p = self.v.center;
        p.x += 100;
        self.v.center = p;
    } completion:^(BOOL finished) {
        self.v.center = pOrig;
    }];
```

Working around the inability to specify a finite number of repetitions is not easy. Here's one approach using recursion to chain animations:

```
- (void) animate: (int) count {
    CGPoint pOrig = self.v.center;
    NSUInteger opts = UIViewAnimationOptionAutoreverse;
    [UIView animateWithDuration:1 delay:0 options:opts animations:^{
        CGPoint p = self.v.center;
        p.x += 100;
        self.v.center = p;
    } completion:^(BOOL finished) {
        self.v.center = pOrig;
        if (count)
            [self animate:count-1];
    }];
}
```

If we call the `animate:` method with an argument of 2, our animation takes place three times and stops. There is always a danger, with recursion, of filling up the stack and running out of memory, but I think we're safe if we start with a small count value.

There are also some options saying what should happen if another animation is already ordered or in-flight:

`UIViewAnimationOptionBeginFromCurrentState`
If this animation animates a property already being animated by an animation that is previously ordered or in-flight, then instead of canceling the previous animation (completing the requested change instantly), this animation will use the presentation layer to decide where to start, and, if possible, will "blend" its animation with the previous animation.

`UIViewAnimationOptionOverrideInheritedDuration`
Prevents inheriting the duration from a surrounding or in-flight animation (the default is to inherit it).

`UIViewAnimationOptionOverrideInheritedCurve`
Prevents inheriting the animation curve from a surrounding or in-flight animation (the default is to inherit it).

To illustrate `UIViewAnimationOptionBeginFromCurrentState`, consider the following:

```
[UIView animateWithDuration:1 animations:^{
    CGPoint p = self.v.center;
    p.x += 100;
    self.v.center = p;
}];
NSUInteger opts = 0;
[UIView animateWithDuration:1 delay:0 options:opts animations:^{
    CGPoint p = self.v.center;
    p.x = 0;
    self.v.center = p;
} completion:nil];
```

The result is that the view *jumps* 100 points rightward, and then animates leftward. That's because the second animation caused the first animation to be thrown away; the move 100 points rightward was performed instantly, instead of being animated. But if we set opts to UIViewAnimationOptionBeginFromCurrentState, the result is that the view animates leftward from its current position, with *no jump*.

Even more interesting is what happens when we change x to y in the second animation. If opts is 0, the view jumps to the right and then animates upward. If opts is UIView-AnimationOptionBeginFromCurrentState, then the two animations are combined: the view animates *diagonally* (right by 100 points, and up to where its center y is 0).

An option such as UIViewAnimationOptionOverrideInheritedDuration comes into play when animations: blocks are nested, like this:

```
[UIView animateWithDuration:2 animations:^{
    CGPoint p = self.v.center;
    p.x += 100;
    self.v.center = p;
    NSUInteger opts = 0;
    [UIView animateWithDuration:0.5 delay:0 options:opts animations:^{
        self.v.backgroundColor = [UIColor blackColor];
    } completion:nil];
}];
```

If opts is 0, the color animation takes the same time as the center animation; it inherits the duration value of the surrounding animations: block. But if opts is UIView-AnimationOptionOverrideInheritedDuration, each animation has its own duration.

Canceling an in-flight animation at the UIView level is a tricky problem (as opposed to doing it at the CALayer level, where it's pretty easy). The technique I use is to order another animation that brings the animated view immediately to its final state. But the second animation must not assign the animated property exactly the same value that the first animation assigned it, or nothing will happen; we need to generate a *conflict* between the two animations.

In this example, presume that cancel is executed while the animation started in animate is in-flight. Our goal in cancel is to bring the animate animation to its completion immediately. So in `cancel` we order a very slightly different, conflicting animation and then use the `completion:` handler to assign the view property its true final value:

```
-(void) animate {
    CGPoint p = self.v.center;
    p.x += 100;
    self.pFinal = p;
    [UIView animateWithDuration:4 animations:^{
        self.v.center = p;
    }];
}
-(void) cancel {
    [UIView animateWithDuration:0 animations:^{
        CGPoint p = self.pFinal;
        p.x += 1;
        self.v.center = p;
    } completion:^(BOOL finished) {
        CGPoint p = self.pFinal;
        self.v.center = p;
    }];
}
```

We can use the same trick to stop a repeating animation. In this example, `animate` launches a repeating, autoreversing animation of our view's center. To stop the animation, `cancel` sets the view back to its original position:

```
-(void) animate {
    CGPoint p = self.v.center;
    self.pOrig = p;
    p.x += 100;
    NSUInteger opts = UIViewAnimationOptionAutoreverse |
    UIViewAnimationOptionRepeat;
    [UIView animateWithDuration:1 delay:0 options:opts animations:^{
        self.v.center = p;
    } completion: nil];
}
-(void) cancel {
    [UIView animateWithDuration:0 animations:^{
        self.v.center = self.pOrig;
    }];
}
```

If you prefer `cancel` to behave a bit less abruptly, gliding quickly into position rather than jumping, give the animation a longer duration and specify `UIViewAnimation-OptionBeginFromCurrentState`:

```
-(void) cancel {
    NSUInteger opts = UIViewAnimationOptionBeginFromCurrentState;
    [UIView animateWithDuration:0.1 delay:0 options:opts animations:^{
        self.v.center = self.pOrig;
    } completion:nil];
}
```

Springing View Animation

New in iOS 7, there's a built-in animation curve that causes a positional animation to behave as if it were being snapped into place by a spring. To use it, call `animateWith-Duration:delay:usingSpring....` For example:

```
[UIView animateWithDuration:0.8 delay:0
    usingSpringWithDamping:0.7 initialSpringVelocity:0
                  options:0 animations:^{
    CGPoint p = self.v.center;
    p.y += 100;
    self.v.center = p;
} completion:nil];
```

The `damping:` and `initialSpringVelocity:` parameters modify the behavior of the animation curve. If the damping is less than 1, there's a waggle as the animated view assumes its final position; this waggle becomes quite pronounced at values less than about `0.7`, and at values like `0.3` there are several waggles before the view settles into place.

The initial spring velocity seems to govern the tendency of the view to overshoot its final position on its first approach. Depending on the duration and damping amount, it may need to be quite large to make an appreciable difference; try setting it to `20` in the preceding example. You can have a lot of fun with smaller damping values and larger spring velocity values.

The `options:` values are the same as in the previous section. You might like to experiment with different animation curves; I think `UIViewAnimationOptionCurveEaseIn` looks nice, starting slowly from a stationary position and using the imaginary spring alone to snap into the final position.

Keyframe View Animation

New in iOS 7, a view animation can be ordered as a set of keyframes. (Previously, this was possible only at the CALayer level, as I'll describe later in this chapter.) This means that you specify stages in the animation and those stages are joined together for you. You call `animateKeyframesWithDuration:...;` it has an `animations:` block, and inside that block you call `addKeyframe...` multiple times to specify each stage. Each keyframe's start time and duration is between 0 and 1, relative to the animation as a whole.

For example, here I'll waggle a view back and forth horizontally while moving it down the screen vertically:

```
__block CGPoint p = self.v.center;
[UIView animateKeyframesWithDuration:4 delay:0 options:0 animations:^{
    [UIView addKeyframeWithRelativeStartTime:0 relativeDuration:.25
                            animations:^{
        p.x += 100;
```

```
        p.y += 50;
        self.v.center = p;
    }];
    [UIView addKeyframeWithRelativeStartTime:.25 relativeDuration:.25
                               animations:^{
        p.x -= 100;
        p.y += 50;
        self.v.center = p;
    }];
    [UIView addKeyframeWithRelativeStartTime:.5 relativeDuration:.25
                               animations:^{
        p.x += 100;
        p.y += 50;
        self.v.center = p;
    }];
    [UIView addKeyframeWithRelativeStartTime:.75 relativeDuration:.25
                               animations:^{
        p.x -= 100;
        p.y += 50;
        self.v.center = p;
    }];
}];
```

In that code, there are four keyframes, evenly spaced: each is .25 in duration (one-fourth of the whole animation) and each starts .25 later than the previous one. In each keyframe, the view's center x value increases and decreases by 100, alternately, while its center y value keeps increasing by 50.

The path and timing depends upon options whose names begin with UIViewKeyframe-AnimationOptionCalculationMode. The default, if the options: argument is 0, is Linear. In our example, this means that the path followed by the view is a sharp zig-zag, the view seeming to bounce off invisible walls at the right and left. But if the calculation mode is Cubic, our view describes a smooth S-curve, starting at the view's initial position and ending at the last keyframe point, and passing through the three other keyframe points like the maxima and minima of a sine wave.

In that example, because my keyframes are perfectly even, I could achieve the same effects by using the calculation modes Paced (same effect as Linear) and CubicPaced (same effect as Cubic). These two Paced options simply ignore the relative start time and relative duration values of the keyframes; you might as well pass 0 for all of them. Instead, they divide up the times and durations evenly, exactly as my code has done.

Finally, Discrete calculation mode means that the changed animatable properties don't animate: the animation jumps to each keyframe.

The outer animations: block can contain other changes to animatable view properties, as long as they don't conflict with the keyframe animations:; these are animated over the total duration. For example:

```
[UIView animateKeyframesWithDuration:4 delay:0 options:0 animations:^{
    self.v.alpha = 0;
    // ... and the rest as before ...
```

The result is that as the view zigzags back and forth down the screen, it also gradually fades away.

It is also legal to supply an animation curve as part of the `options:` argument. (The documentation fails to make this clear.) For example:

```
NSUInteger opts =
    UIViewKeyframeAnimationOptionCalculationModeLinear |
    UIViewAnimationOptionCurveLinear;
[UIView animateKeyframesWithDuration:4 delay:0 options:opts animations:^{
```

That's two different senses of "Linear". The first means that the path described by the moving view is a sequence of straight lines. The second means that the moving view's speed along that path is steady.

Transitions

A transition is an animation that emphasizes a view's change of content. Transitions are ordered using one of two methods:

- `transitionWithView:duration:options:animations:completion:`
- `transitionFromView:toView:duration:options:completion:`

The transition animation types are expressed as part of the `options:` bitmask:

- `UIViewAnimationOptionTransitionFlipFromLeft`
- `UIViewAnimationOptionTransitionFlipFromRight`
- `UIViewAnimationOptionTransitionCurlUp`
- `UIViewAnimationOptionTransitionCurlDown`
- `UIViewAnimationOptionTransitionCrossDissolve`
- `UIViewAnimationOptionTransitionFlipFromBottom`
- `UIViewAnimationOptionTransitionFlipFromTop`

Be careful not to confuse these with the older transition options `UIView-AnimationTransitionFlipFromLeft` and so forth.

In this example, a UIImageView containing an image of Mars flips over as its image changes to a smiley face; it looks as if the image view were two-sided, with Mars on one side and the smiley face on the other:

```
[UIView transitionWithView:self.iv duration:0.8
        options:UIViewAnimationOptionTransitionFlipFromLeft animations:^{
    self.iv.image = [UIImage imageNamed:@"Smiley"];
} completion:nil];
```

In that example, I've put the content change inside the `animations:` block. That's conventional but misleading; the truth is that if all that's changing is the content, *nothing* needs to go into the `animations:` block. The change of content can be anywhere, before or even after this entire line of code. It's the flip that's being animated. You might use the `animations:` block here to order additional animations, such a change in a view's center.

You can do the same sort of thing with a custom view that does its own drawing. Imagine that I have a UIView subclass, MyView, that draws either a rectangle or an ellipse depending on the value of its BOOL `reverse` property:

```
- (void)drawRect:(CGRect)rect {
    CGRect f = CGRectInset(self.bounds, 10, 10);
    CGContextRef con = UIGraphicsGetCurrentContext();
    if (self.reverse)
        CGContextStrokeEllipseInRect(con, f);
    else
        CGContextStrokeRect(con, f);
}
```

This code flips a MyView instance while changing its drawing from a rectangle to an ellipse or *vice versa*:

```
self.v.reverse = !self.v.reverse;
[UIView transitionWithView:self.v duration:1
        options:UIViewAnimationOptionTransitionFlipFromLeft animations:^{
    [self.v setNeedsDisplay];
} completion:nil];
```

During a transition, by default, the view's appearance changes directly to its final appearance; in effect, a snapshot of the view's final appearance has been taken beforehand. If that isn't what you want, use `UIViewAnimationOptionAllowAnimatedContent` in the `options` bitmask.

In this example, `outer` is the view to be animated using a transition, and `inner` is a subview of outer that currently occupies part of its width. In the course of the transition, we increase the width of `inner` to occupy the entire width of `outer`:

```
[UIView transitionWithView:self.outer duration:1
        options:opts animations:^{
    CGRect f = self.inner.frame;
    f.size.width = self.outer.frame.size.width;
    f.origin.x = 0;
    self.inner.frame = f;
} completion:nil];
```

If opts is UIViewAnimationOptionTransitionFlipFromLeft, we see outer flip over to the same appearance it had before, and then the change in inner happens in a jump. But if opts also includes UIViewAnimationOptionAllowAnimatedContent, then inner is seen expanding gradually as the flip animation is completing.

transitionFromView:toView:duration:options:completion: names two views; the first is replaced by the second, while their superview undergoes the transition animation. There are two possible configurations, depending on the options you provide:

Remove one subview, add the other
> If UIViewAnimationOptionShowHideTransitionViews is *not* one of the options, then the second subview is not in the view hierarchy when we start; the transition removes the first subview from its superview and adds the second subview to that same superview.

Hide one subview, show the other
> If UIViewAnimationOptionShowHideTransitionViews *is* one of the options, then both subviews are in the view hierarchy when we start; the hidden of the first is NO, the hidden of the second is YES, and the transition reverses these values.

In this example, a label lab is already in the interface. The animation causes the superview of lab to flip over, while at the same time a different label, lab2, is substituted for it:

```
UILabel* lab2 = [[UILabel alloc] initWithFrame:self.lab.frame];
lab2.text = @"Howdy";
[lab2 sizeToFit];
[UIView transitionFromView:self.lab toView:lab2 duration:0.8
    options:UIViewAnimationOptionTransitionFlipFromLeft
    completion:nil];
```

It's up to you to make sure beforehand that the second view (toView:) has the desired position, so that it will appear in the right place in its superview.

Implicit Layer Animation

If a layer is already present in the interface and is not a view's underlying layer, animating it can be as simple as setting a property. A change in what the documentation calls an *animatable property* is automatically interpreted as a request to animate that change. In other words, animation of layer property changes is the default! Multiple property changes are considered part of the same animation. This mechanism is called *implicit animation.*

 You cannot use implicit animation on a UIView's underlying layer. You can animate a UIView's underlying layer directly, but you must use explicit layer animation (discussed later in this chapter).

For example, in Chapter 3 we constructed a compass out of layers. The compass itself is a CompassView that does no drawing of its own; its underlying layer is a Compass-Layer that also does no drawing, serving only as a superlayer for the layers that constitute the drawing. None of the layers that constitute the actual drawing is the underlying layer of a view, so a property change to any of them, once they are established in the interface, is animated automatically.

So, presume that we have a reference to the arrow layer (`arrow`). If we rotate the arrow by changing its `transform` property, that rotation is animated:

```
// the next line is an implicit animation
arrow.transform = CATransform3DRotate(arrow.transform, M_PI/4.0, 0, 0, 1);
```

CALayer properties listed in the documentation as animatable in this way are `anchorPoint` and `anchorPointZ`, `backgroundColor`, `borderColor`, `borderWidth`, `bounds`, `contents`, `contentsCenter`, `contentsRect`, `cornerRadius`, `doubleSided`, `hidden`, `masksToBounds`, `opacity`, `position` and `zPosition`, `rasterizationScale` and `shouldRasterize`, `shadowColor`, `shadowOffset`, `shadowOpacity`, `shadowRadius`, and `sublayerTransform` and `transform` (but *not* `affineTransform`!). In addition, a CAShapeLayer's `path`, `fillColor`, `strokeColor`, `lineWidth`, `lineDashPhase`, and `miterLimit` are animatable; so are a CATextLayer's `fontSize` and `foregroundColor`, and a CAGradientLayer's `colors`, `locations`, and `endPoint`. (See Chapter 3 for discussion of those properties.)

Basically, a property is animatable because there's some sensible way to interpolate the intermediate values between one value and another. The nature of the animation attached to each property is therefore just what you would intuitively expect. When you change a layer's `hidden` property, it fades out of view (or into view). When you change a layer's `contents`, the old contents are dissolved into the new contents. And so forth.

 A layer's `frame` is *not* an animatable property! To animate the changing of a layer's frame, you'll change other properties such as its `bounds` and `position`. Trying to animate a layer's frame is a common beginner error.

Implicit layer animation doesn't affect a layer as it is being created, configured, and added to the interface. Implicit animation comes into play when you change an animatable property of a layer that is *already* present in the interface.

Animation Transactions

Implicit animation operates with respect to a *transaction* (a CATransaction), which groups animation requests into a single animation. Every animation request takes place in the context of a transaction. You can make this explicit by wrapping your animation requests in calls to the CATransaction class methods `begin` and `commit`; the result is a *transaction block*. Additionally, there is an *implicit transaction* surrounding all your code, and you can operate on this implicit transaction without any `begin` and `commit`.

To modify the characteristics of an implicit animation, you modify the transaction that surrounds it. Typically, you'll use these CATransaction class methods:

setAnimationDuration:
> The duration of the animation.

setAnimationTimingFunction:
> A CAMediaTimingFunction; timing functions are discussed in the next section.

setCompletionBlock:
> A block to be called when the animation ends. The block takes no parameters. The block is called even if no animation is triggered during this transaction.

By nesting transaction blocks, you can apply different animation characteristics to different elements of an animation. But you can also use transaction commands outside of any transaction block to modify the implicit transaction. So, in our previous example, we could slow down the animation of the arrow like this:

```
[CATransaction setAnimationDuration:0.8];
arrow.transform = CATransform3DRotate(arrow.transform, M_PI/4.0, 0, 0, 1);
```

Another useful feature of animation transactions is to turn implicit animation *off*. It's important to be able to do this, because implicit animation is the default, and can be unwanted (and a performance drag). To do so, call the CATransaction class method `setDisableActions:` with argument YES. There are other ways to turn off implicit animation (discussed later in this chapter), but this is the simplest.

`setCompletionBlock:` is an extraordinarily useful and probably underutilized tool. The transaction's completion block signals the end, not only of the implicit layer property animations you yourself have ordered as part of this transaction, but of *all* animations ordered during this transaction, including Cocoa's own animations. For example, consider what happens when you explicitly dismiss a popover with animation:

```
[myPopoverController dismissPopoverAnimated: YES];
```

Transactions and the Redraw Moment

The "redraw moment" that I've spoken of in connection with drawing, layout, layer property settings, and animation is actually the end of the current transaction (usually the implicit transaction). You set a view's background color; the displayed color of the background is changed when the transaction ends. You call setNeedsDisplay; drawRect: is called when the transaction ends. You call setNeedsLayout; layout happens when the transaction ends. You order an animation; the animation starts when the transaction ends.

Your code runs within an implicit transaction. Your code comes to an end, and the transaction commits itself. It is then, as part of the transaction commit procedure, that the screen is updated: first layout, then drawing, then obedience to layer property changes, then the start of any animations. The transaction then continues on a background thread while any animations are performed, and finally calls its completion block, if any, when the animations are over.

There's no completion block, and this isn't your animation, so how can you learn when the animation is over and the popover is well and truly gone? A transaction completion block solves the problem.

CATransaction implements KVC to allow you to set and retrieve a value for an arbitrary key, similar to CALayer. An example appears later in this chapter.

 An explicit transaction block that orders an animation to a layer, if the block is *not preceded by any other changes to the layer*, can cause animation to begin immediately when the CATransaction class method commit is called, without waiting for the redraw moment, while your code continues running. In my experience, this can cause trouble (animation delegate messages cannot arrive, and the presentation layer can't be queried properly) and should be avoided.

Media Timing Functions

The CATransaction class method setAnimationTimingFunction: takes as its parameter a media timing function (CAMediaTimingFunction). This class is the general expression of the animation curves we have already met (ease-in-out, ease-in, ease-out, and linear), and you can use it with those very same predefined curves, by calling the CAMediaTimingFunction class method functionWithName: with one of these parameters:

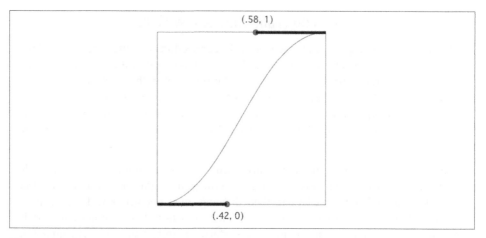

Figure 4-1. An ease-in-out Bézier curve

- kCAMediaTimingFunctionLinear
- kCAMediaTimingFunctionEaseIn
- kCAMediaTimingFunctionEaseOut
- kCAMediaTimingFunctionEaseInEaseOut
- kCAMediaTimingFunctionDefault

A media timing function is a Bézier curve defined by two points. The curve graphs the fraction of the animation's time that has elapsed (the x-axis) against the fraction of the animation's change that has occurred (the y-axis); its endpoints are therefore at {0,0} and {1,1}, because at the beginning of the animation there has been no elapsed time and no change, and at the end of the animation all the time has elapsed and all the change has occurred.

The curve's defining points are its endpoints, and each endpoint needs only one Bézier control point to define the tangent to the curve. And because the curve's endpoints are known, defining the two control points is sufficient to describe the entire curve. And because a point is a pair of floating-point values, a media timing function can be expressed as four floating-point values. That is, in fact, how it is expressed.

So, for example, the ease-in-out timing function is expressed as the four values 0.42, 0.0, 0.58, 1.0. That defines a Bézier curve with one endpoint at {0,0}, whose control point is {0.42,0}, and the other endpoint at {1,1}, whose control point is {0.58,1} (Figure 4-1).

To define your own media timing function, supply the coordinates of the two control points by calling functionWithControlPoints:::: or initWithControlPoints::::;

this is one of those rare cases where the parameters of an Objective-C method have no name. (It helps to design the curve in a standard drawing program first so that you can visualize how the placement of the control points shapes the curve.) For example, here's a media timing function that starts out quite slowly and then whips quickly into place after about two-thirds of the time has elapsed. I call this the "clunk" timing function, and it looks great with the compass arrow:

```
CAMediaTimingFunction* clunk =
    [CAMediaTimingFunction functionWithControlPoints:.9 :.1 :.7 :.9];
[CATransaction setAnimationTimingFunction: clunk];
arrow.transform = CATransform3DRotate(arrow.transform, M_PI/4.0, 0, 0, 1);
```

Core Animation

Core Animation is the fundamental underlying iOS animation technology. View animation and implicit layer animation are merely convenient façades for Core Animation. Core Animation is *explicit layer animation*, and revolves primarily around the CAAnimation class and its subclasses, which allow you to create far more elaborate specifications of an animation than anything we've encountered so far.

You may never program at the level of Core Animation, but you should read this section anyway, if only to learn how animation really works and to get a sense of its mighty powers. In particular, Core Animation:

- Works even on a view's underlying layer. Thus, Core Animation is the *only* way to apply full-on layer property animation to a view.
- Provides fine control over the intermediate values and timing of an animation.
- Allows animations to be grouped into complex combinations.
- Adds transition animation effects that aren't available otherwise, such as new content "pushing" the previous content out of a layer.

 Animating a view's underlying layer with Core Animation is layer animation, not view animation — so you don't get any automatic layout of that view's subviews. This can be a reason for preferring view animation.

CABasicAnimation and Its Inheritance

The simplest way to animate a property with Core Animation is with a CABasicAnimation object. CABasicAnimation derives much of its power through its inheritance, so I'll describe that inheritance along with CABasicAnimation itself. You will readily see that all the property animation features we have met so far are embodied in a CABasicAnimation instance.

CAAnimation

CAAnimation is an abstract class, meaning that you'll only ever use a subclass of it. Some of CAAnimation's powers come from its implementation of the CAMediaTiming protocol.

`animation`
A class method, a convenient way of creating an animation object.

`delegate`
The delegate messages are `animationDidStart:` and `animationDidStop:` `finished:`.

A CAAnimation instance *retains its delegate*; this is very unusual behavior and can cause trouble if you're not conscious of it (I'm speaking from experience). Alternatively, don't set a delegate; to make your code run after the animation ends, call the CATransaction class method `setCompletionBlock:` before configuring the animation.

`duration, timingFunction`
The length of the animation, and its timing function (a CAMediaTimingFunction). A duration of `0` (the default) means `.25` seconds unless overridden by the transaction.

`autoreverses, repeatCount, repeatDuration, cumulative`
The first two are familiar from UIView animation. The `repeatDuration` property is a different way to govern repetition, specifying how long the repetition should continue rather than how many repetitions should occur; don't specify both a `repeatCount` and a `repeatDuration`. If `cumulative` is YES, a repeating animation starts each repetition where the previous repetition ended (rather than jumping back to the start value).

`beginTime`
The delay before the animation starts. To delay an animation with respect to now, call `CACurrentMediaTime` and add the desired delay in seconds. The delay does not eat into the animation's duration.

`timeOffset`
A shift in the animation's overall timing; looked at another way, specifies the starting frame of the "animation movie," which is treated as a loop. For example, an animation with a duration of 8 and a time offset of 4 plays its second half followed by its first half.

CAAnimation, along with all its subclasses, implements KVC to allow you to set and retrieve a value for an arbitrary key, similar to CALayer (Chapter 3) and CATransaction.

CAPropertyAnimation

CAPropertyAnimation is a subclass of CAAnimation. It too is abstract, and adds the following:

keyPath

The all-important string specifying the CALayer key that is to be animated. Recall from Chapter 3 that CALayer properties are accessible through KVC keys; now we are using those keys! A CAPropertyAnimation convenience class method animationWithKeyPath: creates the instance and assigns it a keyPath.

additive

If YES, the values supplied by the animation are added to the current presentation layer value.

valueFunction

Converts a simple scalar value that you supply into a transform.

 There is no animatable CALayer key called @"frame" — because frame is not an animatable layer property. (And the same for affineTransform.)

CABasicAnimation

CABasicAnimation is a subclass (not abstract!) of CAPropertyAnimation. It adds the following:

fromValue, toValue

The starting and ending values for the animation. These values must be objects, so numbers and structs will have to be wrapped accordingly, using NSNumber and NSValue. If neither fromValue nor toValue is provided, the former and current values of the property are used. If just one of fromValue or toValue is provided, the other uses the current value of the property.

byValue

Expresses one of the endpoint values as a *difference* from the other rather than in absolute terms. So you would supply a byValue instead of a fromValue or instead of a toValue, and the actual fromValue or toValue would be calculated for you by subtraction or addition with respect to the other value. If you supply *only* a byValue, the fromValue is the property's current value.

Using a CABasicAnimation

Having constructed and configured a CABasicAnimation, the way you order it to be performed is to *add it to a layer*. This is done with the CALayer instance method add-

Animation:forKey:. (I'll discuss the purpose of the forKey: parameter later; it's fine to ignore it and use nil, as I do in the examples that follow.)

However, there's a slight twist. A CAAnimation is *merely* an animation; all it does is describe the hoops that the presentation layer is to jump through, the "animation movie" that is to be presented. It has no effect on the layer *itself*. Thus, if you naively create a CABasicAnimation and add it to a layer with addAnimation:forKey:, the animation happens and then the "animation movie" is whipped away to reveal the layer sitting there in exactly the same state as before. It is up to *you* to change the layer to match what the animation will ultimately portray.

This requirement may seem odd, but keep in mind that we are now in a much more fundamental, flexible world than the automatic, convenient worlds of view animation and implicit layer animation. Using explicit animation is more work, but you get more power. The converse, as we shall see, is that you *don't* have to change the layer if it *doesn't* change as a result of the animation.

To assure good results, start by taking a plodding, formulaic approach to the use of CABasicAnimation, like this:

1. Capture the start and end values for the layer property you're going to change, because you're likely to need these values in what follows.

2. Change the layer property to its end value, first calling setDisableActions: if necessary to prevent implicit animation.

3. Construct the explicit animation, using the start and end values you captured earlier, and with its keyPath corresponding to the layer property you just changed.

4. Add the explicit animation to the layer.

Here's how you'd use this approach to animate our compass arrow rotation:

```
// capture the start and end values
CATransform3D startValue = arrow.transform;
CATransform3D endValue =
    CATransform3DRotate(startValue, M_PI/4.0, 0, 0, 1);
// change the layer, without implicit animation
[CATransaction setDisableActions:YES];
arrow.transform = endValue;
// construct the explicit animation
CABasicAnimation* anim =
    [CABasicAnimation animationWithKeyPath:@"transform"];
anim.duration = 0.8;
CAMediaTimingFunction* clunk =
    [CAMediaTimingFunction functionWithControlPoints:.9 :.1 :.7 :.9];
anim.timingFunction = clunk;
```

```
anim.fromValue = [NSValue valueWithCATransform3D:startValue];
anim.toValue = [NSValue valueWithCATransform3D:endValue];
// ask for the explicit animation
[arrow addAnimation:anim forKey:nil];
```

Once you know the full form, you will find that in many cases it can be condensed. For example, when fromValue and toValue are not set, the former and current values of the property are used automatically. (This magic is possible because the presentation layer still has the former value of the property, while the layer itself has the new value.) Thus, in this case there was no need to set them, and so there was no need to capture the start and end values beforehand either. Here's the condensed version:

```
[CATransaction setDisableActions:YES];
arrow.transform =
    CATransform3DRotate(arrow.transform, M_PI/4.0, 0, 0, 1);
CABasicAnimation* anim =
    [CABasicAnimation animationWithKeyPath:@"transform"];
anim.duration = 0.8;
CAMediaTimingFunction* clunk =
    [CAMediaTimingFunction functionWithControlPoints:.9 :.1 :.7 :.9];
anim.timingFunction = clunk;
[arrow addAnimation:anim forKey:nil];
```

As I mentioned earlier, you will omit changing the layer if it doesn't change as a result of the animation. For example, let's make the compass arrow appear to vibrate rapidly, without ultimately changing its current orientation. To do this, we'll waggle it back and forth, using a repeated animation, between slightly clockwise from its current position and slightly counterclockwise from its current position. The "animation movie" neither starts nor stops at the current position of the arrow, but for this animation it doesn't matter, because it all happens so quickly as to appear perfectly natural:

```
// capture the start and end values
CATransform3D nowValue = arrow.transform;
CATransform3D startValue =
    CATransform3DRotate(nowValue, M_PI/40.0, 0, 0, 1);
CATransform3D endValue =
    CATransform3DRotate(nowValue, -M_PI/40.0, 0, 0, 1);
// construct the explicit animation
CABasicAnimation* anim =
    [CABasicAnimation animationWithKeyPath:@"transform"];
anim.duration = 0.05;
anim.timingFunction =
    [CAMediaTimingFunction functionWithName:kCAMediaTimingFunctionLinear];
anim.repeatCount = 3;
anim.autoreverses = YES;
anim.fromValue = [NSValue valueWithCATransform3D:startValue];
anim.toValue = [NSValue valueWithCATransform3D:endValue];
// ask for the explicit animation
[arrow addAnimation:anim forKey:nil];
```

That code, too, can be shortened considerably from its full form. We can eliminate the need to calculate the new rotation values based on the arrow's current transform by setting our animation's `additive` property to YES; this means that the animation's property values are added to the existing property value for us, so that they are relative, not absolute. For a transform, "added" means "matrix-multiplied," so we can describe the waggle without any dependence on the arrow's current rotation. Moreover, because our rotation is so simple (around a cardinal axis), we can take advantage of CAProperty-Animation's `valueFunction`; the animation's property values can then be simple scalars (in this case, angles), because the `valueFunction` tells the animation to interpret these as rotations around the z-axis:

```
CABasicAnimation* anim =
    [CABasicAnimation animationWithKeyPath:@"transform"];
anim.duration = 0.05;
anim.timingFunction =
    [CAMediaTimingFunction functionWithName:kCAMediaTimingFunctionLinear];
anim.repeatCount = 3;
anim.autoreverses = YES;
anim.additive = YES;
anim.valueFunction =
    [CAValueFunction functionWithName:kCAValueFunctionRotateZ];
anim.fromValue = @(M_PI/40);
anim.toValue = @(-M_PI/40);
[arrow addAnimation:anim forKey:nil];
```

 Instead of using a `valueFunction`, we could have set the animation's key path to `@"transform.rotation.z"` to achieve the same effect. However, Apple advises against this, as it can result in mathematical trouble when there is more than one rotation.

Remember that there is no `@"frame"` key. To animate a layer's frame, if both its `position` and bounds are to change, you must animate both. Recall this earlier example from a view animation's `animations:` block, where `outer` is the superview of `inner`, and `inner` expands to fill the width of `outer`:

```
CGRect f = self.inner.frame;
f.size.width = self.outer.frame.size.width;
f.origin.x = 0;
self.inner.frame = f;
```

Here's how to do that with Core Animation:

```
CABasicAnimation* anim1 =
    [CABasicAnimation animationWithKeyPath:@"bounds"];
CGRect f = self.inner.layer.bounds;
f.size.width = self.outer.layer.bounds.size.width;
self.inner.layer.bounds = f;
[self.inner.layer addAnimation: anim1 forKey: nil];
```

```
CABasicAnimation* anim2 =
    [CABasicAnimation animationWithKeyPath:@"position"];
CGPoint p = self.inner.layer.position;
p.x = CGRectGetMidX(self.outer.layer.bounds);
self.inner.layer.position = p;
[self.inner.layer addAnimation:anim2 forKey: nil];
```

Keyframe Animation

Keyframe animation (CAKeyframeAnimation) is an alternative to basic animation (CABasicAnimation); they are both subclasses of CAPropertyAnimation and they are used in identical ways. The difference is that a keyframe animation, in addition to specifying a starting and ending value, also specifies multiple values through which the animation should pass on the way, the stages (*frames*) of the animation. This can be as simple as setting the animation's `values` property (an NSArray).

Here's a more sophisticated version of our animation for waggling the compass arrow: the animation includes both the start and end states, and the degree of waggle gets progressively smaller:

```
NSMutableArray* values = [NSMutableArray array];
[values addObject: @0.0f];
int direction = 1;
for (int i = 20; i < 60; i += 5, direction *= -1) { // alternate directions
    [values addObject: @(direction*M_PI/(float)i)];
}
[values addObject: @0.0f];
CAKeyframeAnimation* anim =
    [CAKeyframeAnimation animationWithKeyPath:@"transform"];
anim.values = values;
anim.additive = YES;
anim.valueFunction =
    [CAValueFunction functionWithName: kCAValueFunctionRotateZ];
[arrow addAnimation:anim forKey:nil];
```

Here are some CAKeyframeAnimation properties:

values
: The array of values the animation is to adopt, including the starting and ending value.

timingFunctions
: An array of timing functions, one for each stage of the animation (so that this array will be one element shorter than the `values` array).

keyTimes
: An array of times to accompany the array of values, defining when each value should be reached. The times start at 0 and are expressed as increasing fractions of 1, ending at 1.

`calculationMode`

Describes how the `values` are treated to create *all* the values through which the animation must pass.

- The default is `kCAAnimationLinear`, a simple straight-line interpolation from value to value.
- `kCAAnimationCubic` constructs a single smooth curve passing through all the values (and additional advanced properties, `tensionValues`, `continuity-Values`, and `biasValues`, allow you to refine the curve).
- `kCAAnimationPaced` and `kCAAnimationCubicPaced` means the timing functions and key times are ignored, and the velocity is made constant through the whole animation.
- `kCAAnimationDiscrete` means no interpolation: we jump directly to each value at the corresponding key time.

`path`

When you're animating a property whose values are pairs of floats (CGPoints), this is an alternative way of describing the values; instead of a `values` array, which must be interpolated to arrive at the intermediate values along the way, you supply the entire interpolation as a single CGPathRef. The points used to draw the path are the keyframe values, so you can still apply timing functions and key times. If you're animating a position, the `rotationMode` property lets you ask the animated object to rotate so as to remain perpendicular to the path.

In this example, the `values` array is a sequence of five images to be presented successively and repeatedly in a layer's `contents`, like the frames in a movie; the effect is similar to UIImageView and UIImage animation, discussed earlier in this chapter:

```
CAKeyframeAnimation* anim =
    [CAKeyframeAnimation animationWithKeyPath:@"contents"];
anim.values = self.images;
anim.keyTimes = @[@0,@0.25,@0.5,@0.75,@1];
anim.calculationMode = kCAAnimationDiscrete;
anim.duration = 1.5;
anim.repeatCount = HUGE_VALF;
[self.sprite addAnimation:anim forKey:nil];
```

Making a Property Animatable

So far, we've been animating built-in animatable properties. If you define your own property on a CALayer subclass, you can make that property animatable through a CAPropertyAnimation (a CABasicAnimation or a CAKeyframeAnimation). For example, here we animate the increase and decrease in a CALayer subclass property called `thickness`:

```
CALayer* lay = self.v.layer;
CABasicAnimation* ba =
    [CABasicAnimation animationWithKeyPath:@"thickness"];
ba.toValue = [NSNumber numberWithFloat: 10.0];
ba.autoreverses = YES;
[lay addAnimation:ba forKey:nil];
```

To make our layer responsive to such a command, it needs a thickness property declared @dynamic (so that Core Animation can create its accessors), and it must return YES from the class method needsDisplayForKey:, where the key is the string name of the property:

```
@interface MyLayer ()
@property CGFloat thickness;
@end
@implementation MyLayer
@dynamic thickness;
+ (BOOL) needsDisplayForKey:(NSString *)key {
    if ([key isEqualToString: @"thickness"])
        return YES;
    return [super needsDisplayForKey:key];
}
// ...
@end
```

Returning YES from needsDisplayForKey: causes this layer to be redisplayed repeatedly as the thickness property changes. So if we want to *see* the animation, this layer also needs to draw itself in some way that depends on the thickness property. Here, I'll implement the layer's drawInContext: to make thickness the thickness of the black border around a red rectangle:

```
- (void) drawInContext:(CGContextRef)con {
    CGRect r = CGRectInset(self.bounds, 20, 20);
    CGContextSetFillColorWithColor(con, [UIColor redColor].CGColor);
    CGContextFillRect(con, r);
    CGContextSetLineWidth(con, self.thickness);
    CGContextStrokeRect(con, r);
}
```

At every step of the animation, drawInContext: is called, and because the thickness value differs at each step, it appears animated.

Grouped Animations

A grouped animation (CAAnimationGroup) combines multiple animations into one, by means of its animations property (an NSArray of animations). By delaying and timing the various component animations, complex effects can be achieved.

A CAAnimationGroup is itself an animation; it is a CAAnimation subclass, so it has a duration and other animation features. Think of the CAAnimationGroup as the parent and its `animations` as its children. Then *the children inherit default values from their parent*. Thus, for example, if you don't set a child's duration explicitly, it will inherit the parent's duration. Also, make sure the parent's duration is sufficient to include all parts of the child animations that you want displayed.

Let's use a grouped animation to construct a sequence where the compass arrow rotates and then waggles. This requires very little modification of code we've already written. We express the first animation in its full form, with explicit `fromValue` and `toValue`. We postpone the second animation using its `beginTime` property; notice that we express this in relative terms, as a number of seconds into the parent's duration, not with respect to `CACurrentMediaTime`. Finally, we set the overall parent duration to the sum of the child durations, so that it can embrace both of them:

```
// capture current value, set final value
CGFloat rot = M_PI/4.0;
[CATransaction setDisableActions:YES];
CGFloat current =
    [[arrow valueForKeyPath:@"transform.rotation.z"] floatValue];
[arrow setValue: @(current + rot)
      forKeyPath:@"transform.rotation.z"];
// first animation (rotate and clunk)
CABasicAnimation* anim1 =
    [CABasicAnimation animationWithKeyPath:@"transform"];
anim1.duration = 0.8;
CAMediaTimingFunction* clunk =
    [CAMediaTimingFunction functionWithControlPoints:.9 :.1 :.7 :.9];
anim1.timingFunction = clunk;
anim1.fromValue = @(current);
anim1.toValue = @(current + rot);
anim1.valueFunction =
    [CAValueFunction functionWithName:kCAValueFunctionRotateZ];
// second animation (waggle)
NSMutableArray* values = [NSMutableArray array];
[values addObject: @0.0f];
int direction = 1;
for (int i = 20; i < 60; i += 5, direction *= -1) { // alternate directions
    [values addObject: @(direction*M_PI/(float)i)];
}
[values addObject: @0.0f];
CAKeyframeAnimation* anim2 =
    [CAKeyframeAnimation animationWithKeyPath:@"transform"];
anim2.values = values;
anim2.duration = 0.25;
anim2.beginTime = anim1.duration;
anim2.additive = YES;
anim2.valueFunction =
    [CAValueFunction functionWithName:kCAValueFunctionRotateZ];
// group
```

Figure 4-2. A boat and the course she'll sail

```
CAAnimationGroup* group = [CAAnimationGroup animation];
group.animations = @[anim1, anim2];
group.duration = anim1.duration + anim2.duration;
[arrow addAnimation:group forKey:nil];
```

In that example, I grouped two animations that animated the same property sequentially. Now let's go to the other extreme and group some animations that animate different properties simultaneously. I have a small view (`self.v`), located near the top-right corner of the screen, whose layer contents are a picture of a sailboat facing to the left. I'll "sail" the boat in a curving path, both down the screen and left and right across the screen, like an extended letter "S" (Figure 4-2). Each time the boat comes to a vertex of the curve, changing direction across the screen, I'll turn the boat picture so that it faces the way it's about to move. At the same time, I'll constantly rock the boat, so that it always appears to be pitching a little on the waves.

Here's the first animation, the movement of the boat along its curving path. It illustrates the use of a CAKeyframeAnimation with a CGPath; the `calculationMode` of `kCAAnimationPaced` ensures an even speed over the whole path. We don't set an explicit duration because we want to adopt the duration of the group:

```
CGFloat h = 200;
CGFloat v = 75;
CGMutablePathRef path = CGPathCreateMutable();
int leftright = 1;
CGPoint next = self.v.layer.position;
CGPoint pos;
CGPathMoveToPoint(path, nil, next.x, next.y);
for (int i = 0; i < 4; i++) {
    pos = next;
```

```
    leftright *= -1;
    next = CGPointMake(pos.x+h*leftright, pos.y+v);
    CGPathAddCurveToPoint(path, nil, pos.x, pos.y+30, next.x, next.y-30,
                          next.x, next.y);
}
CAKeyframeAnimation* anim1 =
    [CAKeyframeAnimation animationWithKeyPath:@"position"];
anim1.path = path;
anim1.calculationMode = kCAAnimationPaced;
```

Here's the second animation, the reversal of the direction the boat is facing. This is simply a rotation around the y-axis. It's another CAKeyframeAnimation, but we make no attempt at visually animating this reversal: the calculationMode is kCAAnimation-Discrete, so that the boat image reversal is a sudden change, as in our earlier "sprite" example. There is one less value than the number of points in our first animation's path, and the first animation has an even speed, so the reversals take place at each curve apex with no further effort on our part. (If the pacing were more complicated, we could give both the first and the second animation identical keyTimes arrays, to coordinate them.) Once again, we don't set an explicit duration:

```
NSArray* revs = @[@0.0f,
                  @M_PI,
                  @0.0f,
                  @M_PI];
CAKeyframeAnimation* anim2 =
    [CAKeyframeAnimation animationWithKeyPath:@"transform"];
anim2.values = revs;
anim2.valueFunction =
    [CAValueFunction functionWithName:kCAValueFunctionRotateY];
anim2.calculationMode = kCAAnimationDiscrete;
```

Here's the third animation, the rocking of the boat. It has a short duration, and repeats indefinitely (by giving its repeatCount an immense value):

```
NSArray* pitches = @[@0.0f,
                     @(M_PI/60.0),
                     @0.0f,
                     @(-M_PI/60.0),
                     @0.0f];
CAKeyframeAnimation* anim3 =
    [CAKeyframeAnimation animationWithKeyPath:@"transform"];
anim3.values = pitches;
anim3.repeatCount = HUGE_VALF;
anim3.duration = 0.5;
anim3.additive = YES;
anim3.valueFunction =
    [CAValueFunction functionWithName:kCAValueFunctionRotateZ];
```

Finally, we combine the three animations, assigning the group an explicit duration that will be adopted by the first two animations. As we hand the animation over to the layer displaying the boat, we also change the layer's position to match the final position from the first animation, so that the boat won't jump back to its original position afterward:

```
CAAnimationGroup* group = [CAAnimationGroup animation];
group.animations = @[anim1, anim2, anim3];
group.duration = 8;
[self.v.layer addAnimation:group forKey:nil];
[CATransaction setDisableActions:YES];
self.v.layer.position = next;
```

Here are some further CAAnimation properties (from the CAMediaTiming protocol) that come into play especially when animations are grouped:

speed

The ratio between a child's timescale and the parent's timescale. For example, if a parent and child have the same duration, but the child's speed is 1.5, its animation runs one-and-a-half times as fast as the parent.

fillMode

Suppose the child animation begins after the parent animation, or ends before the parent animation, or both. What should happen to the appearance of the property being animated, outside the child animation's boundaries? The answer depends on the child's fillMode:

- kCAFillModeRemoved means the child animation is removed, revealing the layer property at its actual current value whenever the child is not running.
- kCAFillModeForwards means the final presentation layer value of the child animation remains afterward.
- kCAFillModeBackwards means the initial presentation layer value of the child animation appears right from the start.
- kCAFillModeBoth combines the previous two.

 CALayer adopts the CAMediaTiming protocol. Thus, a layer can have a speed. This will affect any animation attached to it. A CALayer with a speed of 2 will play a 10-second animation in 5 seconds. A layer can also have a timeOffset; changing a layer's timeOffset effectively changes what "frame" of its animation is displayed.

Transitions

A layer transition is an animation involving two "copies" of a single layer, in which the second "copy" appears to replace the first. It is described by an instance of CATransition (a CAAnimation subclass), which has these chief properties describing the animation:

type

Your choices are:

- kCATransitionFade

- kCATransitionMoveIn

- kCATransitionPush

- kCATransitionReveal

subtype

If the type is not kCATransitionFade, your choices are:

- kCATransitionFromRight

- kCATransitionFromLeft

- kCATransitionFromTop

- kCATransitionFromBottom

 For historical reasons, the terms "bottom" and "top" in the names of the subtype settings have the opposite of their expected meanings.

To understand a layer transition, first implement one without changing anything else about the layer:

```
CATransition* t = [CATransition animation];
t.type = kCATransitionPush;
t.subtype = kCATransitionFromBottom;
[layer addAnimation: t forKey: nil];
```

The entire layer exits moving down from its original place, and another copy of the very same layer enters moving down from above. If, at the same time, we change something about the layer's contents, then the old contents will appear to exit downward while the new contents appear to enter from above.

A common device is to have the layer that is to be transitioned live inside a superlayer that is exactly the same size and whose masksToBounds is YES. This confines the visible transition to the bounds of the layer itself. Otherwise, the entering and exiting versions of the layer are visible outside the layer.

In this example, we change the sublayer's contents image, while transitioning it with a push transition from the bottom (meaning from the top), from an image of Mars to a smiley face; with the sublayer masked by its superlayer, it looks as if the smiley face

Figure 4-3. A push transition

pushes Mars down out of the frame (which I've emphasized in Figure 4-3 by giving the superlayer a border as well):

```
CATransition* t = [CATransition animation];
t.type = kCATransitionPush;
t.subtype = kCATransitionFromBottom;
t.duration = 2;
[CATransaction setDisableActions:YES];
lay.contents = (id)[UIImage imageNamed: @"Smiley"].CGImage;
[lay addAnimation: t forKey: nil];
```

A transition on a superlayer can happen simultaneously with animation of a sublayer. The animation will be seen to occur on the second "copy" of the layer as it moves into position. This is analogous to what we achieved earlier with the UIViewAnimation-OptionAllowAnimatedContent option using block-based view animation.

Animations List

The method that asks for an explicit animation to happen is CALayer's add-Animation:forKey:. To understand how this method actually works (and what the "key" is), you need to know about a layer's *animations list*.

An animation is an object (a CAAnimation) that modifies how a layer is drawn. It does this merely by being attached to the layer; the layer's drawing mechanism does the rest. A layer maintains a list of animations that are currently in force. To add an animation to this list, you call addAnimation:forKey:. When the time comes to draw itself, the layer looks through its animations list and draws itself in accordance with any animations it finds there. (The list of things the layer must do in order to draw itself is sometimes referred to by the documentation as the *render tree*.)

The animations list is maintained in a curious way. The list is not exactly a dictionary, but it behaves somewhat like a dictionary. An animation has a key — the forKey: parameter in addAnimation:forKey:. If an animation with a certain key is added to the list, and an animation with that key is already in the list, the one that is already in the list is removed. Thus a rule is maintained that *only one animation with a given key* can be in the list at a time (the *exclusivity rule*). This explains why sometimes ordering an animation can cancel an animation already ordered or in-flight: the two animations had the same key, so the first one was removed. It is also possible to add an animation with *no key* (the key is nil); it is then *not* subject to the exclusivity rule (that is, there can be more than one animation in the list with no key). The order in which animations were added to the list is the order in which they are applied.

The `forKey:` parameter in `addAnimation:forKey:` is thus *not a property name*. It *could* be a property name, but it can be any arbitrary value. Its purpose is to enforce the exclusivity rule. It does *not* have any meaning with regard to what property a CAPropertyAnimation animates; that is the job of the animation's `keyPath`. (Apple's use of the term "key" in `addAnimation:forKey:` is thus unfortunate and misleading; I wish they had named this method `addAnimation:withIdentifier:` or something like that.)

 Actually, there *is* a relationship between the "key" in `add-Animation:forKey:` and a CAPropertyAnimation's `keyPath` — if a CAPropertyAnimation's `keyPath` is nil at the time that it is added to a layer with `addAnimation:forKey:`, *that `keyPath` is set to the `forKey:` value*. Thus, you can *misuse* the `forKey:` parameter in `add-Animation:forKey:` as a way of specifying what `keyPath` an animation animates. (This fact is not documented, so far as I know, but it's easily verified experimentally, and it should remain reliably true, as implicit animation crucially depends on it.) I have seen many prominent but misleading examples that use this technique, apparently in the mistaken belief that the "key" in `addAnimation:forKey:` is the way you are *supposed* to specify what property to animate. *This is wrong.* Set the CAPropertyAnimation's `keyPath` explicitly (as do all my examples); that's what it's for.

You can use the exclusivity rule to your own advantage, to keep your code from stepping on its own feet. Some code of yours might add an animation to the list using a certain key; then later, some other code might come along and correct this, removing that animation and replacing it with another. By using the same key, the second code is easily able to override the first: "You may have been given some other animation with this key, but throw it away; play this one instead."

In some cases, the key you supply is ignored and a different key is substituted. In particular, the key with which a CATransition is added to the list is always `kCATransition` (which happens to be `@"transition"`); thus there can be only one transition animation in the list.

You can think of an animation in a layer's animations list as being the "animation movie" I spoke of at the start of this chapter. As long as an animation is in the list, the movie is present, either waiting to be played or actually playing. An animation that has finished playing is, in general, pointless; the animation should now be removed from the list.

Therefore, an animation has a removedOnCompletion property, which defaults to YES: when the "movie" is over, the animation removes itself from the list.

You can, if desired, set removedOnCompletion to NO. However, even the presence in the list of an animation that has already played might make no difference to the layer's appearance, because an animation's fillMode is kCAFillModeRemoved, which removes the animation from the layer's drawing when the movie is over. Thus, it can usually do no harm to leave an animation in the list after it has played, but it's not a great idea either, because this is just one more thing for the drawing system to worry about. Typically, you'll leave removedOnCompletion set at YES.

 You may encounter examples that set removedOnCompletion to NO and set the animation's fillMode to kCAFillModeForwards or kCAFill- ModeBoth, as a way of causing the layer to keep the appearance of the last frame of the "animation movie" even after the animation is over, and preventing a property from apparently jumping back to its initial value when the animation ends. *This is wrong.* The correct approach, as I have explained, is to change the property value to match the final frame of the animation. The proper use of kCAFillMode- Forwards is in connection with a child animation within a grouped animation.

You can't access the entire animations list directly. You can access the key names of the animations in the list, with animationKeys; and you can obtain or remove an animation with a certain key, with animationForKey: and removeAnimationForKey:; but animations with a nil key are inaccessible. You can, however, remove all animations, including animations with a nil key, using removeAllAnimations. When your app is suspended, removeAllAnimations is called on all layers for you; that is why it is possible to suspend an app coherently in the middle of an animation.

If an animation is in-flight when you remove it from the animations list manually, by calling removeAllAnimations or removeAnimationForKey:, it will stop; however, that doesn't happen until the next redraw moment. You might be able to work around this, if you need an animation to be removed immediately, by wrapping the remove... call in an explicit transaction block.

Actions

For the sake of completeness, I will now explain how implicit animation really works — that is, how implicit animation is turned into explicit animation behind the scenes. The basis of implicit animation is the *action mechanism.*

What an Action Is

An *action* is an object that adopts the CAAction protocol. This means simply that it implements `runActionForKey:object:arguments:`. The action object could do *anything* in response to this message. The notion of an action is completely general. However, in real life, the only class that adopts the CAAction protocol is CAAnimation.

You would never send `runActionForKey:object:arguments:` to an animation directly. Rather, this message is sent to an animation for you, as the basis of implicit animation. The `key` is the property that you set, and the `object` is the layer whose property you set.

What an animation does when it receives `runActionForKey:object:arguments:` is to assume that the second parameter, the `object:`, is a layer, and to add itself to that layer's animations list. Thus, for an animation, receiving the `runActionForKey:object:arguments:` message is like being told: "Play yourself!"

This is where the rule comes into play, which I mentioned earlier, that if an animation's `keyPath` is nil, the key by which the animation is assigned to a layer's animations list is used as the `keyPath`. When an animation is sent `runActionForKey:object:arguments:`, it responds by calling `[object addAnimation:self forKey:key]`, where the key is the name of the property that was set. The animation's key-Path for an implicit layer animation is in fact usually nil, *so this call also sets the animation's keyPath to the same key!* That is how the property that you set ends up being the property that is animated.

Action Search

When you set a property of a layer and trigger an implicit animation, you are actually triggering the *action search*. This basically means that the layer searches for an *action object* to which it can send the `runActionForKey:object:arguments:` message; because that action object will be an animation, and because it will respond to this message by adding itself to the layer's animations list, this is the same as saying that the layer searches for an animation to play itself with respect to the layer. The procedure by which the layer searches for this animation is quite elaborate.

The search for an action object begins because you do something that causes the layer to be sent the `actionForKey:` message. Let us presume that what you do is to change the value of an animatable property. (Other things can cause the `actionForKey:` message to be sent, as I'll show later.) The action mechanism then treats the name of the property as a key, and the layer receives `actionForKey:` with that key — and the action search begins.

At each stage of the action search, the following rules are obeyed regarding what is returned from that stage of the search:

An action object

If an action object (an animation) is produced, that is the end of the search. The action mechanism sends that animation the `runActionForKey:object:arguments:` message; the animation responds by adding itself to the layer's animations list.

`[NSNull null]`

If `[NSNull null]` is produced, that is the end of the search. There will be no implicit animation; `[NSNull null]` means, "Do nothing and stop searching."

nil

If nil is produced, the search continues to the next stage.

The action search proceeds by stages, as follows:

1. The layer's `actionForKey:` might terminate the search before it even starts. For example, the layer will do this if it is the underlying layer of a view, or if a property is set to the same value it already has. In such a case, there should be no implicit animation, so the whole mechanism is nipped in the bud. (This stage is special in that a returned value of nil ends the search and no animation takes place.)

2. If the layer has a delegate that implements `actionForLayer:forKey:`, that message is sent to the delegate, with this layer as the layer and the property name as the key. If an animation or `[NSNull null]` is returned, the search ends.

3. The layer has a property called `actions`, which is a dictionary. If there is an entry in this dictionary with the given key, that value is used, and the search ends.

4. The layer has a property called `style`, which is a dictionary. If there is an entry in this dictionary with the key `actions`, it is assumed to be a dictionary; if this `actions` dictionary has an entry with the given key, that value is used, and the search ends. Otherwise, if there is an entry in the `style` dictionary called `style`, the same search is performed within it, and so on recursively until either an `actions` entry with the given key is found (the search ends) or there are no more `style` entries (the search continues).

   (If the `style` dictionary sounds profoundly weird, that's because it is profoundly weird. It is actually a special case of a larger, separate mechanism, which is also profoundly weird, having to do not with actions, but with a CALayer's implementation of KVC. When you call `valueForKey:` on a layer, if the key is undefined by the layer itself, the `style` dictionary is consulted. I have never written or seen code that uses this mechanism for anything, and I'll say no more about it.)

5. The layer's class is sent `defaultActionForKey:`, with the property name as the key. If an animation or `[NSNull null]` is returned, the search ends.

6. If the search reaches this last stage, a default animation is supplied, as appropriate. For a property animation, this is a plain vanilla CABasicAnimation.

Both the delegate's `actionForLayer:forKey:` and the subclass's `defaultActionForKey:` are declared as returning an `id<CAAction>`. To return [NSNull null], therefore, you'll need to typecast it to `id<CAAction>` to quiet the compiler; you're lying (NSNull does not adopt the CAAction protocol), but it doesn't matter.

Hooking Into the Action Search

You can affect the action search at various stages to modify what happens when the search is triggered. Perhaps the most common real-life case is to turn off implicit animation for some particular property. This is done by returning nil from `actionForKey:` itself, in a CALayer subclass; this suppresses the action search altogether. Here's the code from a CALayer subclass that doesn't animate its `position` property (but does animate its other properties normally):

```
-(id<CAAction>)actionForKey:(NSString *)event {
    if ([event isEqualToString:@"position"])
        return nil;
    return [super actionForKey:event];
}
```

For more flexibility, we can take advantage of the fact that a CALayer acts like a dictionary (allowing us to set an arbitrary key's value) — we'll embed a switch in our CALayer subclass that we can use to turn implicit `position` animation on and off at will:

```
-(id<CAAction>)actionForKey:(NSString *)event {
    if ([event isEqualToString:@"position"] &&
            [self valueForKey:@"suppressPositionAnimation"])
        return nil;
    return [super actionForKey:event];
}
```

To turn off implicit `position` animation for an instance of this layer, we set its `@"suppressPositionAnimation"` key to a non-nil value:

```
[layer setValue:@YES forKey:@"suppressPositionAnimation"];
```

Assuming now that the action search is permitted, you could cause some stage of the search to produce an animation of your own; that animation will then be used. Assuming that the search is triggered by setting an animatable layer property, you would then be affecting how implicit animation behaves.

You will probably want your animation to be fairly minimal. You may have no way of knowing the former and current values of the property that is being changed, so it would then be pointless (and very strange) to set a CABasicAnimation's `fromValue` or `toValue`. Moreover, although animation properties that you don't set can be set through

CATransaction, in the usual manner for implicit property animation, animation properties that you *do* set can *not* be overridden through CATransaction. For example, if you set the duration of the animation that you produce at some stage of the action search, a call to CATransaction's `setAnimationDuration:` cannot change it.

Let's say we want a certain layer's duration for an implicit `position` animation to be 5 seconds. We can achieve this with a minimally configured animation, like this:

```
CABasicAnimation* ba = [CABasicAnimation animation];
ba.duration = 5;
```

The idea now is to situate this animation, `ba`, where it will be produced by the action search when implicit animation is triggered on the `position` property of our layer. We could, for instance, put it into the layer's `actions` dictionary:

```
layer.actions = @{@"position": ba};
```

The result is that when we set that layer's `position`, if an implicit animation results, its duration is 5 seconds, even if we try to change it through CATransaction:

```
[CATransaction setAnimationDuration:1];
layer.position = CGPointMake(100,100); // animation takes 5 seconds
```

Using the layer's `actions` dictionary to set default animations is a somewhat inflexible way to hook into the action search, however. It has the disadvantage in general that you must write your animation beforehand. By contrast, if you set the layer's delegate to an instance that responds to `actionForLayer:forKey:`, your code runs at the time the animation is needed, and you have access to the layer that is to be animated. So you can create the animation on the fly, possibly modifying it in response to current circumstances.

Moreover, CATransaction (like CALayer) implements KVC to allow you to set and retrieve the value of arbitrary keys. We can take advantage of this fact to pass additional information from the code that sets the property value, and triggers the action search, to the code that supplies the action (because they both run within the same transaction).

In this example, we use the layer delegate to change the default `position` animation so that the path, instead of being a straight line, has a slight waggle. To do this, the delegate constructs a keyframe animation. The animation depends on the old `position` value and the new `position` value; the delegate can get the former direct from the layer, but the latter must be handed to the delegate somehow. Here, a CATransaction key `@"newP"` is used to communicate this information. When we set the layer's `position`, we put its future value where the delegate can retrieve it, like this:

```
CGPoint newP = CGPointMake(300,300);
[CATransaction setValue: [NSValue valueWithCGPoint: newP] forKey: @"newP"];
layer.position = newP;
```

The delegate is called by the action search and constructs the animation:

```
- (id < CAAction >)actionForLayer:(CALayer *)layer forKey:(NSString *)key {
    if ([key isEqualToString: @"position"]) {
        CGPoint oldP = layer.position;
        CGPoint newP = [[CATransaction valueForKey: @"newP"] CGPointValue];
        CGFloat d = sqrt(pow(oldP.x - newP.x, 2) + pow(oldP.y - newP.y, 2));
        CGFloat r = d/3.0;
        CGFloat theta = atan2(newP.y - oldP.y, newP.x - oldP.x);
        CGFloat wag = 10*M_PI/180.0;
        CGPoint p1 = CGPointMake(oldP.x + r*cos(theta+wag),
                                 oldP.y + r*sin(theta+wag));
        CGPoint p2 = CGPointMake(oldP.x + r*2*cos(theta-wag),
                                 oldP.y + r*2*sin(theta-wag));
        CAKeyframeAnimation* anim = [CAKeyframeAnimation animation];
        anim.values = @[
                        [NSValue valueWithCGPoint:oldP],
                        [NSValue valueWithCGPoint:p1],
                        [NSValue valueWithCGPoint:p2],
                        [NSValue valueWithCGPoint:newP]
                        ];
        anim.calculationMode = kCAAnimationCubic;
        return anim;
    }
    return nil;
}
```

Finally, I'll demonstrate overriding defaultActionForKey:. This code would go into a
CALayer subclass; setting this layer's contents will now automatically trigger a push
transition from the left:

```
+ (id < CAAction >)defaultActionForKey:(NSString *)aKey {
    if ([aKey isEqualToString:@"contents"]) {
        CATransition* tr = [CATransition animation];
        tr.type = kCATransitionPush;
        tr.subtype = kCATransitionFromLeft;
        return tr;
    }
    return [super defaultActionForKey: aKey];
}
```

Nonproperty Actions

Changing a property is not the only way to trigger a search for an action; an action
search is also triggered when a layer is added to a superlayer (key kCAOnOrderIn) and
when a layer's sublayers are changed by adding or removing a sublayer (key
@"sublayers").

These triggers and their keys are incorrectly described in Apple's documentation (and headers).

In this example, we use our layer's delegate so that when our layer is added to a superlayer, it will "pop" into view. We implement this by fading the layer quickly in from an opacity of 0 and at the same time scaling the layer's transform to make it momentarily appear a little larger:

```
- (id < CAAction >)actionForLayer:(CALayer *)lay forKey:(NSString *)key {
    if ([key isEqualToString:kCAOnOrderIn]) {
        CABasicAnimation* anim1 =
            [CABasicAnimation animationWithKeyPath:@"opacity"];
        anim1.fromValue = @0.0f;
        anim1.toValue = @(lay.opacity);
        CABasicAnimation* anim2 =
            [CABasicAnimation animationWithKeyPath:@"transform"];
        anim2.toValue =
            [NSValue valueWithCATransform3D:
                CATransform3DScale(lay.transform, 1.1, 1.1, 1.0)];
        anim2.autoreverses = YES;
        anim2.duration = 0.1;
        CAAnimationGroup* group = [CAAnimationGroup animation];
        group.animations = @[anim1, anim2];
        group.duration = 0.2;
        return group;
    }
}
```

The documentation says that when a layer is removed from a superlayer, an action is sought under the key kCAOnOrderOut. This is true but useless, because by the time the action is sought, the layer has already been removed from the superlayer, so returning an animation has no visible effect. Similarly, an animation returned as an action when a layer's hidden is set to YES is never played. A possible workaround is to trigger the animation via the opacity property, perhaps in conjunction with a CATransaction key functioning as a switch, and remove the layer afterward:

```
[CATransaction setCompletionBlock: ^{
    [layer removeFromSuperlayer];
}];
[CATransaction setValue:@YES forKey:@"byebye"];
layer.opacity = 0;
```

Now the delegate's actionForLayer:forKey: can test for the incoming key @"opacity" and the CATransaction key @"byebye", and return the animation appropriate to removal from the superlayer. Here's a possible implementation:

```
if ([key isEqualToString:@"opacity"]) {
    if ([CATransaction valueForKey:@"byebye"]) {
        CABasicAnimation* anim1 =
            [CABasicAnimation animationWithKeyPath:@"opacity"];
        anim1.fromValue = @(layer.opacity);
        anim1.toValue = @0.0f;
        CABasicAnimation* anim2 =
            [CABasicAnimation animationWithKeyPath:@"transform"];
```

```
    anim2.toValue =
        [NSValue valueWithCATransform3D:
            CATransform3DScale(layer.transform, 0.1, 0.1, 1.0)];
    CAAnimationGroup* group = [CAAnimationGroup animation];
    group.animations = @[anim1, anim2];
    group.duration = 0.2;
    return group;
    }
}
```

Emitter Layers

Emitter layers (CAEmitterLayer) are, to some extent, on a par with animated images: once you've set up an emitter layer, it just sits there animating all by itself. The nature of this animation is rather narrow: an emitter layer emits particles, which are CAEmitterCell instances. However, by clever setting of the properties of an emitter layer and its emitter cells, you can achieve some astonishing effects. Moreover, the animation is itself animatable using Core Animation.

Here are some useful basic properties of a CAEmitterCell:

contents, contentsRect
> These are modeled after the eponymous CALayer properties, although CAEmitter-Layer is not a CALayer subclass; so, respectively, an image (a CGImageRef) and a CGRect specifying a region of that image. They define the image that a cell will portray.

birthrate, lifetime
> How many cells per second should be emitted, and how many seconds each cell should live before vanishing, respectively.

velocity
> The speed at which a cell moves. The unit of measurement is not documented; perhaps it's points per second.

emissionLatitude, emissionLongitude
> The angle at which the cell is emitted from the emitter, as a variation from the perpendicular. Longitude is an angle within the plane; latitude is an angle out of the plane.

So, here's code to create a very elementary emitter cell:

```
// make a gray circle image
UIGraphicsBeginImageContextWithOptions(CGSizeMake(10,10), NO, 1);
CGContextRef con = UIGraphicsGetCurrentContext();
CGContextAddEllipseInRect(con, CGRectMake(0,0,10,10));
CGContextSetFillColorWithColor(con, [UIColor grayColor].CGColor);
CGContextFillPath(con);
UIImage* im = UIGraphicsGetImageFromCurrentImageContext();
```

```
UIGraphicsEndImageContext();
// make a cell with that image
CAEmitterCell* cell = [CAEmitterCell emitterCell];
cell.birthRate = 5;
cell.lifetime = 1;
cell.velocity = 100;
cell.contents = (id)im.CGImage;
```

(In the first line, we deliberately don't double the scale on a double-resolution screen, because a CAEmitterLayer has no contentsScale, like a CALayer; we're going to derive a CGImage from this image, and we don't want its size doubled.)

The result is that little gray circles should be emitted slowly and steadily, five per second, each one vanishing in one second. Now we need an emitter layer from which these circles are to be emitted. Here are some basic CAEmitterLayer properties (beyond those it inherits from CALayer); these define an imaginary object, an emitter, that will be producing the emitter cells:

emitterPosition
> The point at which the emitter should located, in superlayer coordinates. You can optionally add a third dimension to this point, emitterZPosition.

emitterSize
> The size of the emitter.

emitterShape
> The shape of the emitter. The dimensions of the shape depend on the emitter's size; the cuboid shape depends also on a third size dimension, emitterDepth. Your choices are:

> - kCAEmitterLayerPoint
> - kCAEmitterLayerLine
> - kCAEmitterLayerRectangle
> - kCAEmitterLayerCuboid
> - kCAEmitterLayerCircle
> - kCAEmitterLayerSphere

emitterMode
> The region of the shape from which cells should be emitted. Your choices are:

> - kCAEmitterLayerPoints
> - kCAEmitterLayerOutline
> - kCAEmitterLayerSurface
> - kCAEmitterLayerVolume

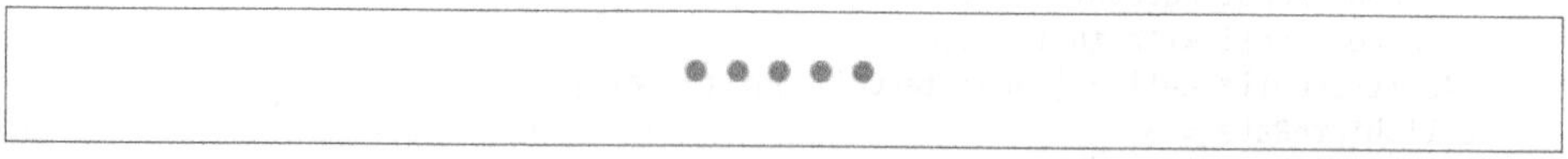

Figure 4-4. A really boring emitter layer

Let's start with the simplest possible case, a single point emitter:

```
CAEmitterLayer* emit = [CAEmitterLayer new];
emit.emitterPosition = CGPointMake(30,100);
emit.emitterShape = kCAEmitterLayerPoint;
emit.emitterMode = kCAEmitterLayerPoints;
```

We tell the emitter what types of cell to emit by assigning those cells to its `emitter-Cells` property (an array of CAEmitterCell). We then add the emitter to our interface, and presto, it starts emitting:

```
emit.emitterCells = @[cell];
[self.view.layer addSublayer:emit];
```

The result is a constant stream of gray circles emitted from the point {30,100}, each circle marching steadily to the right and vanishing after one second (Figure 4-4).

Now that we've succeeded in creating a boring emitter layer, we can start to vary some parameters. The `emissionRange` defines a cone in which cells will be emitted; if we increase the `birthRate` and widen the `emissionRange`, we get something that looks like a stream shooting from a water hose:

```
cell.birthRate = 100;
cell.lifetime = 1.5;
cell.velocity = 100;
cell.emissionRange = M_PI/5.0;
```

In addition, as the cell moves, it can be made to accelerate (or decelerate) in each dimension, using its `xAcceleration`, `yAcceleration`, and `zAcceleration` properties. Here, we turn the stream into a falling cascade, like a waterfall coming from the left:

```
cell.xAcceleration = -40;
cell.yAcceleration = 200;
```

All aspects of cell behavior can be made to vary randomly, using the following CAEmitterCell properties:

`lifetimeRange, velocityRange`
> How much the lifetime and velocity values are allowed to vary randomly for different cells.

scale

scaleRange, scaleSpeed

> The scale alters the size of the cell; the range and speed determine how far and how rapidly this size alteration is allowed to change over the lifetime of each cell.

color

redRange, greenRange, blueRange, alphaRange

redSpeed, greenSpeed, blueSpeed, alphaSpeed

> The color is painted in accordance with the opacity of the cell's contents image; it combines with the image's color, so if we want the color stated here to appear in full purity, our contents image should use only white. The range and speed determine how far and how rapidly each color component is to change.

spin, spinRange

> The spin is a rotational speed (in radians per second); its range determines how far this speed is allowed to change over the lifetime of each cell.

Here we add some variation so that the circles behave a little more independently of one another. Some live longer than others, some come out of the emitter faster than others. And they all start out a shade of blue, but change to a shade of green about half-way through the stream (Figure 4-5):

```
cell.lifetimeRange = .4;
cell.velocityRange = 20;
cell.scaleRange = .2;
cell.scaleSpeed = .2;
cell.color = [UIColor blueColor].CGColor;
cell.greenRange = .5;
cell.greenSpeed = .75;
```

Once the emitter layer is in place and animating, you can change its parameters and the parameters of its emitter cells through key–value coding on the emitter layer. You can access the emitter cells through the emitter layer's @"emitterCells" key path; to specify a cell type, use its name property (which you'll have to have assigned earlier) as the next piece of the key path. For example, suppose we've set cell.name to @"circle"; now we'll change the cell's greenSpeed so that each cell changes from blue to green much earlier in its lifetime:

```
[emit setValue:@3.0f
    forKeyPath:@"emitterCells.circle.greenSpeed"];
```

The significance of this is that such changes can themselves be animated! Here, we'll attach to the emitter layer a repeating animation that causes our cell's greenSpeed to move back and forth between two values. The result is that the stream varies, over time, between being mostly blue and mostly green:

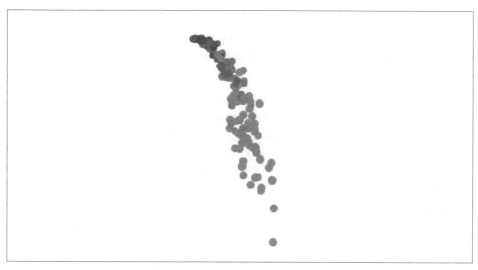

Figure 4-5. An emitter layer that makes a sort of waterfall

```
NSString* key = @"emitterCells.circle.greenSpeed";
CABasicAnimation* ba = [CABasicAnimation animationWithKeyPath:key];
ba.fromValue = @-1.0f;
ba.toValue = @3.0f;
ba.duration = 4;
ba.autoreverses = YES;
ba.repeatCount = HUGE_VALF;
[emit addAnimation:ba forKey:nil];
```

A CAEmitterCell can itself function as an emitter — that is, it can have cells of its own. Both CAEmitterLayer and CAEmitterCell conform to the CAMediaTiming protocol, and their beginTime and duration properties can be used to govern their times of operation, much as in a grouped animation. For example, this code causes our existing waterfall to spray tiny droplets in the region of the "nozzle" (the emitter):

```
CAEmitterCell* cell2 = [CAEmitterCell emitterCell];
cell.emitterCells = @[cell2];
cell2.contents = (id)im.CGImage;
cell2.emissionRange = M_PI;
cell2.birthRate = 200;
cell2.lifetime = 0.4;
cell2.velocity = 200;
cell2.scale = 0.2;
cell2.beginTime = .04;
cell2.duration = .2;
```

But if we change the beginTime to be larger (hence later), the tiny droplets happen near the bottom of the cascade. We must also increase the duration, or stop setting it

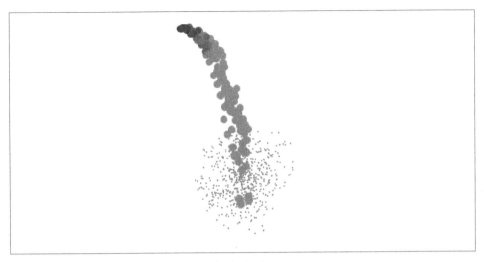

Figure 4-6. The waterfall makes a kind of splash

altogether, since if the `duration` is less than the `beginTime`, no emission takes place at all (Figure 4-6):

```
cell2.beginTime = .7;
cell2.duration = .8;
```

We can also alter the picture by changing the behavior of the emitter itself. This change turns the emitter into a line, so that our cascade becomes broader:

```
emit.emitterPosition = CGPointMake(100,25);
emit.emitterSize = CGSizeMake(100,100);
emit.emitterShape = kCAEmitterLayerLine;
emit.emitterMode = kCAEmitterLayerOutline;
cell.emissionLongitude = 3*M_PI/4;
```

There's more to know about emitter layers and emitter cells, but at this point you know enough to understand Apple's sample code simulating such things as fire and smoke and pyrotechnics, and you can explore further on your own.

CIFilter Transitions

Core Image filters (Chapter 2) include transitions. You supply two images and a frame time between 0 and 1; the filter supplies the corresponding frame of a one-second animation transitioning from the first image to the second. For example, Figure 4-7 shows the frame at frame time .75 for a starburst transition from a solid red image to a photo of me. (You don't see the photo of me, because this transition, by default, "explodes" the first image to white first, and then quickly fades to the second image.)

Figure 4-7. Midway through a starburst transition

Animating a Core Image transition filter is up to you. Thus we need a way of rapidly calling the same method repeatedly; in that method, we'll request and draw each frame of the transition. This could be a job for an NSTimer, but an even better way is to use a *display link* (CADisplayLink), a form of timer that's highly efficient, especially when repeated drawing is involved, because it is linked directly to the refreshing of the display (hence the name). The display refresh rate is typically about one-sixtieth of a second; the actual value is given as the display link's duration, and will undergo slight fluctuations. Like a timer, the display link calls a designated method of ours every time it fires. We can slow the rate of calls by an integral amount by setting the display link's frame-Interval; for example, a display link with a frameInterval of 2 will call us about every one-thirtieth of a second. We can learn the exact time when the display link last fired by querying its timestamp.

In this example, I'll display the animation in a view's layer. We start by initializing and storing ahead of time, in instance variables, everything we'll need later to obtain an output image for a given frame of the transition: the CIFilter, the image's extent, and the CIContext used for rendering. We also have instance variables _frame and _timestamp, which we initialize as well:

```
UIImage* moi = [UIImage imageNamed:@"moi"];
CIImage* moi2 = [[CIImage alloc] initWithCGImage:moi.CGImage];
self->_moiextent = moi2.extent;
CIFilter* col = [CIFilter filterWithName:@"CIConstantColorGenerator"];
CIColor* cicol = [[CIColor alloc] initWithColor:[UIColor redColor]];
[col setValue:cicol forKey:@"inputColor"];
CIImage* colorimage = [col valueForKey: @"outputImage"];
CIFilter* tran = [CIFilter filterWithName:@"CIFlashTransition"];
[tran setValue:colorimage forKey:@"inputImage"];
[tran setValue:moi2 forKey:@"inputTargetImage"];
CIVector* center =
    [CIVector vectorWithX:self->_moiextent.size.width/2.0
                        Y:self->_moiextent.size.height/2.0];
```

```
[tran setValue:center forKey:@"inputCenter"];
self->_con = [CIContext contextWithOptions:nil];
self->_tran = tran;
self->_timestamp = 0.0;
```

We create the display link, setting it to call into our `nextFrame:` method, and set it going by adding it to the run loop, which retains it:

```
CADisplayLink* link =
    [CADisplayLink displayLinkWithTarget:self
        selector:@selector(nextFrame:)];
[link addToRunLoop:[NSRunLoop mainRunLoop] forMode:NSDefaultRunLoopMode];
```

Our `nextFrame:` method is called with the display link as parameter (`sender`). We store the initial `timestamp` in an instance variable, and use the difference between that and each successive `timestamp` value to calculate our desired frame. We ask the filter for the corresponding image and display it. When the frame value exceeds 1, the animation is over and we invalidate the display link (just like a repeating timer), which releases it from the run loop:

```
if (self->_timestamp < 0.01) { // pick up and store first timestamp
    self->_timestamp = sender.timestamp;
    self->_frame = 0.0;
} else { // calculate frame
    self->_frame = sender.timestamp - self->_timestamp;
}
sender.paused = YES; // defend against frame loss
// get frame image and show it
[_tran setValue:@(self->_frame) forKey:@"inputTime"];
CGImageRef moi = [self->_con createCGImage:_tran.outputImage
                               fromRect:_moiextent];
[CATransaction setDisableActions:YES];
self.v.layer.contents = (__bridge id)moi;
CGImageRelease(moi);
// check for done, clean up
if (_frame > 1.0) {
    [sender invalidate];
}
sender.paused = NO;
```

I have surrounded the time-consuming calculation and drawing of the image with calls to the display link's `paused` property, in case the calculation time exceeds the time between screen refreshes; perhaps this isn't necessary, but it can't hurt. Our animation occupies one second; changing that value is merely a matter of multiplying by a scale value when we set our `_frame` instance variable. If you experiment with this code, run on the device, as display links do not work well in the Simulator.

UIKit Dynamics

A suite of classes, *UIKit dynamics*, supplies a convenient API for animating views in a manner reminiscent of real-world physical behavior. For example, views can be subjected to gravity, collisions, and momentary forces, with effects that would otherwise be difficult to achieve.

UIKit dynamics should not be treated as a game engine. It is deliberately quite cartoony and simple, treating views as rectangular blocks and animating only their position (center) and rotation transform within a flat two-dimensional space. Nor is it intended for extended use. Like other ways of achieving animation, it is a way of momentarily emphasizing or clarifying functional transformations of your interface.

Implementing UIKit dynamics involves configuring a "stack" of three things:

A dynamic animator

A dynamic animator, a UIDynamicAnimator instance, is the ruler of the physics world you are creating. It has a reference view, which is the superview of the views to be animated, and which defines the coordinate system of its world. Retaining the animator is up to you; a strong property will do. It's fine for an animator to sit empty until you need it; an animator whose world is empty (or at rest) is not running, and occupies no processor time.

A behavior

A UIDynamicBehavior is a rule describing how a view should behave. You'll typically use a built-in subclass, such as UIGravityBehavior or UICollisionBehavior. You configure the behavior and add it to the animator; an animator has methods and properties for managing its behaviors, such as addBehavior:, behaviors, removeBehavior:, and removeAllBehaviors. A behavior's configuration can be changed, and behaviors can be added to and removed from an animator, even while an animation is in progress.

An item

An item is any object that implements the UIDynamicItem protocol. A UIView is such an object! You add a UIView (one that's a subview of your animator's reference view) to a behavior (one that belongs to that animator) — and at that moment, the view comes under the influence of that behavior. If this behavior is one that causes motion, and if no other behaviors prevent, the view will now move (the animator is running).

Some behaviors can accept multiple items, and have methods and properties such as addItem:, items, and removeItem:. Others can have just one or two items and must be initialized with these from the outset.

That's sufficient to get started, so let's try it! I'll start by creating my animator and storing it in a property:

```
self.anim = [[UIDynamicAnimator alloc] initWithReferenceView:self.view];
```

Now I'll cause an existing subview of self.view (a UIImageView, self.iv) to drop off the screen, under the influence of gravity. I create a UIGravityBehavior, add it to the animator, and add self.iv to it:

```
UIGravityBehavior* grav = [UIGravityBehavior new];
[self.anim addBehavior:grav];
[grav addItem:self.iv];
```

As a result, self.iv comes under the influence of gravity and is now animated downward off the screen. (A UIGravityBehavior object has properties configuring the strength and direction of gravity, but I've left them here at their defaults.)

An immediate concern is that our view falls forever. This is a waste of memory and processing power. If we no longer need the view after it has left the screen, we should take it out of the influence of UIKit dynamics by removing it from any behaviors to which it belongs (and we can also remove it from its superview). One way to do this is by removing from the animator any behaviors that are no longer needed. In our simple example, where the animator's entire world contains just this one item, it will be sufficient to call removeAllBehaviors.

But how will we know when the view is off the screen? A UIDynamicBehavior can have an action block, which is called repeatedly as the animator drives the animation. I'll use this block to check whether self.iv is still within the bounds of the reference view, by calling the animator's itemsInRect: method:

```
grav.action = ^{
    NSArray* items = [self.anim itemsInRect:self.view.bounds];
    if (NSNotFound == [items indexOfObject:self.iv]) {
        [self.anim removeAllBehaviors];
        [self.iv removeFromSuperview];
    }
};
```

 If a dynamic behavior's action block refers to the dynamic behavior itself, there's a danger of a retain cycle, because the behavior retains the block which refers to the behavior. Express yourself in some other way (perhaps attaching the block to some other behavior), or use the weak–strong dance to break the retain cycle in the block.

Let's add some further behaviors. If falling straight down is too boring, we can add a UIPushBehavior to create a slight rightward impulse to be applied to the view as it begins to fall:

```
UIPushBehavior* push =
    [[UIPushBehavior alloc] initWithItems:@[self.iv]
        mode:UIPushBehaviorModeInstantaneous];
push.pushDirection = CGVectorMake(2, 0);
[self.anim addBehavior:push];
```

The view now falls in a parabola to the right.

Next, let's add a UICollisionBehavior to make our view strike the "floor" of the screen:

```
UICollisionBehavior* coll = [UICollisionBehavior new];
coll.collisionMode = UICollisionBehaviorModeBoundaries;
[coll addBoundaryWithIdentifier:@"floor"
    fromPoint:CGPointMake(0,self.view.bounds.size.height)
    toPoint:CGPointMake(self.view.bounds.size.width,
                        self.view.bounds.size.height)];
[self.anim addBehavior:coll];
[coll addItem:self.iv];
```

The view now falls in a parabola onto the floor of the screen, bounces a tiny bit, and comes to rest. It would be nice if the view bounced a bit more. Characteristics internal to a dynamic item's physics, such as bounciness (`elasticity`), are configured by assigning it to a UIDynamicItemBehavior:

```
UIDynamicItemBehavior* bounce = [UIDynamicItemBehavior new];
bounce.elasticity = 0.4;
[self.anim addBehavior:bounce];
[bounce addItem:self.iv];
```

Our view now bounces higher; nevertheless, when it hits the floor, it stops moving to the right, so it ends up at rest on the floor. I'd prefer that, after it bounces, it should start spinning to the right, so that it eventually leaves the screen. A UICollisionBehavior has a delegate to which it sends messages when a collision occurs. I'll make `self` the collision behavior's delegate, and when the delegate message arrives, I'll add rotational velocity to the existing dynamic item behavior bounce, so that our view starts spinning clockwise:

```
-(void)collisionBehavior:(UICollisionBehavior *)behavior
        beganContactForItem:(id<UIDynamicItem>)item
        withBoundaryIdentifier:(id<NSCopying>)identifier
        atPoint:(CGPoint)p {
    for (UIDynamicBehavior* b in self.anim.behaviors) {
        if ([b isKindOfClass: [UIDynamicItemBehavior class]]) {
            UIDynamicItemBehavior* bounce = (UIDynamicItemBehavior*) b;
            CGFloat v = [bounce angularVelocityForItem:self.iv];
            if (v <= 0.1) // do this just once
                [bounce addAngularVelocity:30 forItem:self.iv];
            break;
        }
    }
}
```

The view now falls in a parabola to the right, strikes the floor, spins clockwise, and bounces off the floor and out the right side of the screen!

We have now developed a complex behavior by a combination of several built-in UI-DynamicBehavior subclass instances. For neatness, clarity, maintainability, and reusability, it might make sense to express that combination as a single custom UIDynamicBehavior subclass. Let's call it MyDropBounceAndRollBehavior. Now we can apply this behavior to our view, self.iv, very simply:

```
[self.anim addBehavior:
    [[MyDropBounceAndRollBehavior alloc] initWithView:self.iv]];
```

All the work is now done by the MyDropBounceAndRollBehavior instance. This instance has received a reference to the view to be animated, and it may reasonably assume that its superview is the dynamic animator's reference view (if not, we could provide the reference view as another parameter to the initializer). A UIDynamicBehavior receives a reference to its dynamic animator just before being added to it, by implementing willMoveToAnimator:, and can refer to it subsequently as self.dynamicAnimator. To incorporate actual behaviors into itself, our custom UIDynamicBehavior subclass creates and configures them, and calls addChildBehavior:; it can refer to the array of its child behaviors as self.childBehaviors. When our custom behavior is added to or removed from the dynamic animator, the effect is the same as if its child behaviors themselves were added or removed.

Here is our UIDynamicAnimator subclass. Assume that the initializer has stored the incoming view to be animated in a property v. Observe that, as I warned earlier, we must take care in the action block not to cause a retain cycle:

```
-(void)willMoveToAnimator:(UIDynamicAnimator *)anim {
    if (!anim)
        return;
    UIView* sup = self.v.superview;
    // the gravity child
    UIGravityBehavior* grav = [UIGravityBehavior new];
    __weak MyDropBounceAndRollBehavior* wself = self;
    grav.action = ^{
        MyDropBounceAndRollBehavior* sself = wself;
        if (sself) {
            NSArray* items = [anim itemsInRect:sup.bounds];
            if (NSNotFound == [items indexOfObject:sself.v]) {
                [anim removeBehavior:sself];
                [sself.v removeFromSuperview];
            }
        }
    };
    [self addChildBehavior:grav];
    [grav addItem:self.v];
    // the push child
    UIPushBehavior* push =
```

```
                [[UIPushBehavior alloc] initWithItems:@[self.v]
                    mode:UIPushBehaviorModeInstantaneous];
        push.pushDirection = CGVectorMake(2, 0);
        [self addChildBehavior:push];
        // the collision child
        UICollisionBehavior* coll = [UICollisionBehavior new];
        coll.collisionMode = UICollisionBehaviorModeBoundaries;
        coll.collisionDelegate = self;
        [coll addBoundaryWithIdentifier:@"floor"
                        fromPoint:CGPointMake(0,sup.bounds.size.height)
                          toPoint:CGPointMake(sup.bounds.size.width,
                                              sup.bounds.size.height)];
        [self addChildBehavior:coll];
        [coll addItem:self.v];
        // the bounce child
        UIDynamicItemBehavior* bounce = [UIDynamicItemBehavior new];
        bounce.elasticity = 0.4;
        [self addChildBehavior:bounce];
        [bounce addItem:self.v];
    }
    -(void)collisionBehavior:(UICollisionBehavior *)behavior
            beganContactForItem:(id<UIDynamicItem>)item
            withBoundaryIdentifier:(id<NSCopying>)identifier
            atPoint:(CGPoint)p {
        for (UIDynamicBehavior* b in self.childBehaviors) {
            if ([b isKindOfClass: [UIDynamicItemBehavior class]]) {
                UIDynamicItemBehavior* bounce = (UIDynamicItemBehavior*) b;
                CGFloat v = [bounce angularVelocityForItem:item];
                if (v <= 0.1) {
                    [bounce addAngularVelocity:30 forItem:item];
                }
                break;
            }
        }
    }
```

Here are some further UIDynamicAnimator methods and properties:

delegate

> The delegate (UIDynamicAnimatorDelegate) is sent messages dynamicAnimator-DidPause: and dynamicAnimatorWillResume:. The animator is paused when it has nothing to do: it has no dynamic items, or all its dynamic items are at rest.

running

> If YES, the animator is not paused; some dynamic item is being animated.

elapsedTime

> The total time during which this animator has been running since it first started running. The elapsedTime does not increase while the animator is paused, nor is it reset. You might use this in a delegate method or action method to decide that the animation is over.

`updateItemUsingCurrentState:`

Once a dynamic item has come under the influence of the animator, the animator is responsible for positioning that dynamic item. If your code subsequently manually changes the dynamic item's position or other relevant attributes, call this method so that the animator can take account of those changes.

Here is some more about the various built-in UIDynamicBehavior subclasses:

UIGravityBehavior

Imposes an acceleration on its dynamic items. By default, this acceleration is downward with a magnitude of 1 (arbitrarily defined as 1000 points per second per second).

UIPushBehavior

Applies a force either instantaneously or continuously (`mode`), the latter constituting an acceleration. How this force affects an object depends in part upon the object's "mass", which is based on its size combined with its `density` (the latter can be set through a UIDynamicItemBehavior); thus, by default, a smaller view is easier to push. The effect of a push behavior can be toggled with the `active` property; an instantaneous push is repeated each time the `active` property is set to YES.

In addition to a direction and a magnitude, a push may be given an offset from the center of an item. This will apply an additional angular acceleration. Thus, I could have started `self.iv` spinning clockwise by means of its initial push, like this:

```
[push setTargetOffsetFromCenter:UIOffsetMake(0, -200) forItem:self.iv];
```

UICollisionBehavior

Watches for collisions either amongst items belonging to this same behavior or between an item and a boundary (`mode`). One collision behavior can have many boundaries. A boundary may be described as a line between two points or as a UIBezierPath, or you can turn the reference view's bounds into boundaries (`setTranslatesReferenceBoundsIntoBoundaryWithInsets:`). Boundaries that you create can have an identifier. The `collisionDelegate` (UICollisionBehaviorDelegate) is called when a collision begins and again when it ends.

How a given collision affects the item(s) involved depends on the physical characteristics of the item(s), which may be configured through a UIDynamicItemBehavior.

UISnapBehavior

Causes one item to snap to one point as if pulled by a spring. Its `damping` describes how much the item should oscillate as its settles into that point. This is a very simple behavior: the snap occurs once, immediately (when the behavior is added to the animator), and there's no notification when it's over.

UIAttachmentBehavior

Attaches an item by a bar or a spring to another item (`initWithItem:attachedTo-Item:`) or to a point in the reference view (`initWithItem:attachedToAnchor:`). The attachment point is, by default, the item's center; to change that, initialize with `initWithItem:offsetFromCenter:attachedToItem:offsetFromCenter:` or `init-WithItem:offsetFromCenter:attachedToAnchor:`.

The physics of the attaching medium is governed by the behavior's `length`, `frequency`, and `damping`. They are set for you when you initialize the behavior, but you can modify them, and the `anchorPoint` (if attachment is to an anchor), over the behavior's lifetime.

As the other item or the `anchorPoint` moves, this item moves with it, in accordance with the physics of the attaching medium. An `anchorPoint` is particularly useful for implementing a draggable view within an animator world, as I'll demonstrate in the next chapter.

UIDynamicItemBehavior

Endows its items with internal physical characteristics such as `density` (changes the impulse-resisting mass in relation to size), `elasticity` (bounce on collision), `friction`, and `resistance` (tendency to come to rest unless forces are actively applied), as well as injecting linear velocity or angular velocity.

Motion Effects

New in iOS 7, a view can respond in real time to the way the user tilts the device. Typically, the view's response will be to shift its position slightly. This is used, for example, in various parts of the interface, to give a sense of the interface's being layered. When a UIAlertView is present, if the user tilts the device, the UIAlertView shifts its position; the effect is subtle, but sufficient to suggest subconsciously that the UIAlertView is floating slightly in front of everything else on the screen.

Your own views can behave in the same way. A view will respond to shifts in the position of the device if it has one or more motion effects (UIMotionEffect). Motion effects are added to a view with `addMotionEffect:`, listed with `motionEffects`, and removed with `removeMotionEffect:`.

The UIMotionEffect class is abstract: its job is to be subclassed. The chief subclass provided is UIInterpolatingMotionEffect. Every UIInterpolatingMotionEffect has a single key path, which uses key–value coding to specify the property it affects. It also has a type, specifying which axis of the device's tilting (horizontal tilt or vertical tilt) is to affect this property. Finally, it has a maximum and minimum relative value, the furthest distance that the affected property of the view is to be permitted to wander from its actual value as the user tilts the device. Related motion effects should be combined into a UIMotionEffectGroup (a UIMotionEffect subclass), and the group added to the view.

So, for example:

```
UIInterpolatingMotionEffect* m1 =
    [[UIInterpolatingMotionEffect alloc] initWithKeyPath:@"center.x"
    type:UIInterpolatingMotionEffectTypeTiltAlongHorizontalAxis];
m1.maximumRelativeValue = @10.0;
m1.minimumRelativeValue = @-10.0;
UIInterpolatingMotionEffect* m2 =
    [[UIInterpolatingMotionEffect alloc] initWithKeyPath:@"center.y"
    type:UIInterpolatingMotionEffectTypeTiltAlongVerticalAxis];
m2.maximumRelativeValue = @10.0;
m2.minimumRelativeValue = @-10.0;
UIMotionEffectGroup* g = [UIMotionEffectGroup new];
g.motionEffects = @[m1,m2];
[self.mars addMotionEffect:g];
```

You can write your own UIMotionEffect subclass by implementing a single method, `keyPathsAndRelativeValuesForViewerOffset:`, but this will rarely be necessary.

 The user can turn off motion effects in the Settings app (under General → Accessibility → Reduce Motion).

Animation and Autolayout

The interplay between animation and autolayout can be tricky. As part of an animation, you may be changing a view's frame (or bounds, or center). You're really not supposed to do that when you're using autolayout. As a result, an animation may not work correctly. Or, it may appear to work perfectly, because no layout has happened; however, it is entirely possible that layout *will* happen, and that it will be accompanied by undesirable effects.

As I explained in Chapter 1, when layout takes place under autolayout, what matters are a view's constraints. If the constraints affecting a view don't resolve to the size and position that the view has at the moment of layout, the view will jump as the constraints are obeyed. This is almost certainly not what you want.

To persuade yourself that this can be a problem, just animate a view's position and then ask for immediate layout by calling `layoutIfNeeded`, like this:

```
CGPoint p = self.v.center;
p.x += 100;
[UIView animateWithDuration:1 animations:^{
    self.v.center = p;
} completion:^(BOOL b){
    [self.v layoutIfNeeded]; // this is what will happen at layout time
}];
```

If we're using autolayout, the view slides to the right and then jumps back to the left. This is bad. It's up to us to keep the constraints synchronized with the reality, so that when layout comes along in the natural course of things, our views don't jump into undesirable states.

One option is to revise the violated constraints to match the new reality. If we've planned far ahead, we may have armed ourselves in advance with a reference to those constraints; in that case, our code can now remove and replace them — or, if the only thing that needs changing is the constant value of a constraint, we can change that value in place (recall that the constant is the *only* writable property of an existing constraint). Otherwise, discovering what constraints are now violated, and getting a reference to them, is not at all easy.

An alternative approach, in the case where the only thing that needs changing is a constraint's constant, is this: instead of animating the view's position and then compensating by changing the constant value of the constraint that positions it, *animate the change in the constant value in the first place*. To do so, we set the constraint's constant to its new value, and animate the act of layout. Again, this assumes that we have a reference to the constraint in question.

For example, if we are animating a view 100 points rightward, and if we have a reference to the constraint whose constant positions that view horizontally, we would say this:

```
// con is the constraint
con.constant += 100;
[UIView animateWithDuration:1 animations:^{
    [self.v layoutIfNeeded];
}];
```

Another issue has to do with view transforms. As I said at the end of Chapter 1, applying a view transform triggers layout immediately, and constraints then take a hand in positioning the view. Thus an animation involving a view transform will likely misbehave under autolayout.

For example, you would expect a simple autoreversing animation that waggles a view, or scales it up and back down, to work under autolayout (after all, we're not ultimately changing anything's frame). But, alas, that's not true. Even this simple "throb" animation can break under autolayout — instead of simply throbbing, the view may also jump momentarily to a different position:

```
[UIView animateWithDuration:0.3 delay:0
        options:UIViewAnimationOptionAutoreverse animations:^{
    self.v.transform = CGAffineTransformMakeScale(1.1, 1.1);
} completion:^(BOOL finished) {
    self.v.transform = CGAffineTransformIdentity;
}];
```

One solution in this case is to use Core Animation instead; this works because applying a layer transform, unlike a view transform, does not trigger layout:

```
CABasicAnimation* ba =
    [CABasicAnimation animationWithKeyPath:@"transform"];
ba.autoreverses = YES;
ba.duration = 0.3;
ba.toValue =
    [NSValue valueWithCATransform3D:CATransform3DMakeScale(1.1, 1.1, 1)];
[self.v.layer addAnimation:ba forKey:nil];
```

Another possibility is to use a snapshot of the original view (Chapter 1). Add the snapshot temporarily to the interface — without using autolayout, and perhaps hiding the original view — and animate the snapshot:

```
UIView* snap = [self.v snapshotViewAfterScreenUpdates:YES];
snap.frame = self.v.frame;
[self.v.superview addSubview:snap];
self.v.hidden = YES;
[UIView animateWithDuration:0.3 delay:0
        options:UIViewAnimationOptionAutoreverse animations:^{
    snap.transform = CGAffineTransformMakeScale(1.1, 1.1);
} completion:^(BOOL finished) {
    snap.transform = CGAffineTransformIdentity;
    self.v.hidden = NO;
    [snap removeFromSuperview];
}];
```

However, if the nature of the animation is such that the real view ultimately needs to be shifted to a new permanent position, then its constraints will still have to be revised.

Another useful trick is to take advantage of the fact that the "animation movie" masks the reality. In this example from one of my apps, I apparently shrink a view (english) down to nothingness:

```
CABasicAnimation* ba = [CABasicAnimation animationWithKeyPath:@"opacity"];
self.english.layer.opacity = 0;
ba.duration = 0.2;
[self.english.layer addAnimation:ba forKey:nil];
CABasicAnimation* ba2 = [CABasicAnimation animationWithKeyPath:@"bounds"];
ba2.duration = 0.2;
ba2.toValue = [NSValue valueWithCGRect:self.english.layer.bounds];
[self.english.layer addAnimation:ba2 forKey:nil];
```

This doesn't break under autolayout, because I never did anything to violate any existing constraints: I never changed the view's bounds! I did, however, make it invisible, changing its opacity to 0. The "animation movie", on the other hand, *portrays* the view as shrinking to nothingness, and also as fading away; and by the time the "animation movie" is ripped away, the view is invisible, so the user doesn't see that it's actually still at its full size.

Yet another possibility, as I suggested at the end of Chapter 1, is to combine an invisible "host view" that is positioned in relation to the surrounding interface by autolayout with a subview that is *not* positioned in relation to its superview by autolayout — and can thus be animated however you like without violating any constraints.

The need for such elaborate tactics is most unfortunate. Autolayout was introduced into iOS 6 with a seeming disregard for its fundamental incompatibility with animation. That incompatibility is a serious flaw in iOS, and Apple, far from acknowledging and grappling with it, has studiously glossed over it.

CHAPTER 5

Touches

[Winifred the Woebegone illustrates hit-testing:]
Hey nonny nonny, is it you? — Hey nonny nonny
nonny no! — Hey nonny nonny, is it you? — *Hey*
nonny nonny nonny no!

—Marshall Barer, *Once Upon a Mattress*

A *touch* is an instance of the user putting a finger on the screen. The system and the hardware, working together, know *when* a finger contacts the screen and *where* it is. A finger is fat, but its location is cleverly reduced to a single appropriate point.

A UIView, by virtue of being a UIResponder, is the visible locus of touches. There are other UIResponder subclasses, but none of them is visible on the screen. What the user sees are views; what the user is touching are views. (The user actually sees layers, but a layer is not a UIResponder and is not involved with touches.)

It would make sense, therefore, if every touch were reported directly to the view in which it occurred. However, what the system "sees" is not particular views but an app as a whole. So a touch is represented as an object (a UITouch instance) which is bundled up in an envelope (a UIEvent) which the system delivers to your app. It is then up to your app to deliver the envelope to an appropriate UIView. In the vast majority of cases, this will happen automatically the way you expect, and you will respond to a touch by way of the view in which the touch occurred.

In fact, usually you won't concern yourself with UIEvents and UITouches at all. Most built-in interface views deal with these low-level touch reports themselves, and notify your code at a higher level — you hear about functionality and intention rather than raw touches. When a UIButton emits an action message to report a control event such as Touch Up Inside, it has already performed a reduction of a complex sequence of touches ("the user put a finger down inside me and then, possibly with some dragging hither and yon, raised it when it was still reasonably close to me"). A UITextField reports touches on the keyboard as changes in its own text. A UITableView reports that the user selected a cell. A UIScrollView, when dragged, reports that it scrolled; when pinched outward, it reports that it zoomed.

Nevertheless, it is useful to know how to respond to touches directly, so that you can implement your own touchable views, and so that you understand what Cocoa's built-in views are actually doing. This chapter discusses touch detection and response by views (and other UIResponders) at their lowest level, along with a slightly higher-level mechanism, gesture recognizers, that categorizes touches into gesture types for you; then it deconstructs the touch-delivery architecture by which touches are reported to your views in the first place.

Touch Events and Views

Imagine a screen that the user is not touching at all: the screen is "finger-free." Now the user touches the screen with one or more fingers. From that moment until the time the screen is once again finger-free, all touches and finger movements together constitute what Apple calls a single *multitouch sequence*.

The system reports to your app, during a given multitouch sequence, every change in finger configuration, so that your app can figure out what the user is doing. Every such report is a UIEvent. In fact, every report having to do with the same multitouch sequence is *the same UIEvent instance*, arriving repeatedly, each time there's a change in finger configuration.

Every UIEvent reporting a change in the user's finger configuration contains one or more UITouch objects. Each UITouch object corresponds to a single finger; conversely, every finger touching the screen is represented in the UIEvent by a UITouch object. Once a UITouch instance has been created to represent a finger that has touched the screen, *the same UITouch instance* is used to represent that finger throughout this multitouch sequence until the finger leaves the screen.

Now, it might sound as if the system has to bombard the app with huge numbers of reports constantly during a multitouch sequence. But that's not really true. The system needs to report only *changes* in the finger configuration. For a given UITouch object (representing, remember, a specific finger), only four things can happen. These are called *touch phases*, and are described by a UITouch instance's `phase` property:

UITouchPhaseBegan
: The finger touched the screen for the first time; this UITouch instance has just been created. This is always the first phase, and arrives only once.

UITouchPhaseMoved
: The finger moved upon the screen.

`UITouchPhaseStationary`

> The finger remained on the screen without moving. Why is it necessary to report this? Well, remember, once a UITouch instance has been created, it must be present every time the UIEvent arrives. So if the UIEvent arrives because something *else* happened (e.g., a new finger touched the screen), we must report what *this* finger has been doing, even if it has been doing nothing.

`UITouchPhaseEnded`

> The finger left the screen. Like `UITouchPhaseBegan`, this phase arrives only once. The UITouch instance will now be destroyed and will no longer appear in UIEvents for this multitouch sequence.

Those four phases are sufficient to describe everything that a finger can do. Actually, there is one more possible phase:

`UITouchPhaseCancelled`

> The system has aborted this multitouch sequence because something interrupted it. What might interrupt a multitouch sequence? There are many possibilities. Perhaps the user clicked the Home button or the screen lock button in the middle of the sequence. A local notification alert may have appeared (Chapter 13); on an iPhone, a call might have come in. And as we shall see, a gesture recognizer recognizing its gesture may also trigger touch cancellation. The point is, if you're dealing with touches yourself, you cannot afford to ignore touch cancellation; they are your opportunity to get things into a coherent state when the sequence is interrupted.

When a UITouch first appears (`UITouchPhaseBegan`), your app works out which UIView it is associated with. (I'll give full details, later in this chapter, as to how it does that.) This view is then set as the touch's `view` property; from then on, this UITouch is *always* associated with this view. In other words, *a touch's view is that touch's view forever* (until that finger leaves the screen).

The same UIEvent containing the same UITouches can be sent to multiple views. Accordingly, a UIEvent is distributed to *all the views of all the UITouches it contains*. Conversely, if a view is sent a UIEvent, it's because that UIEvent contains at least one UITouch whose `view` is this view.

If every UITouch in a UIEvent associated with a certain UIView has the phase `UITouchPhaseStationary`, that UIEvent is *not* sent to that UIView. There's no point, because as far as that view is concerned, nothing happened.

Receiving Touches

A UIResponder, and therefore a UIView, has four methods corresponding to the four UITouch phases that require UIEvent delivery. A UIEvent is delivered to a view by calling one or more of these four methods (the *touches... methods*):

`touchesBegan:withEvent:`

A finger touched the screen, creating a UITouch.

`touchesMoved:withEvent:`

A finger previously reported to this view with `touchesBegan:withEvent:` has moved.

`touchesEnded:withEvent:`

A finger previously reported to this view with `touchesBegan:withEvent:` has left the screen.

`touchesCancelled:withEvent:`

We are bailing out on a finger previously reported to this view with `touches-Began:withEvent:`.

The parameters of these methods are:

The relevant touches

These are the event's touches whose phase corresponds to the name of the method and (normally) whose view is this view. They arrive as an NSSet. If there is only one touch in the set, or if any touch in the set will do, you can retrieve it with `any-Object` (an NSSet doesn't implement `lastObject` because a set is unordered).

The event

This is the UIEvent instance. It contains its touches as an NSSet, which you can retrieve with the `allTouches` message. This means *all* the event's touches, including but not necessarily limited to those in the first parameter; there might be touches in a different phase or intended for some other view. You can call `touchesFor-View:` or `touchesForWindow:` to ask for the set of touches associated with a particular view or window.

A UITouch has some useful methods and properties:

`locationInView:, previousLocationInView:`

The current and previous location of this touch with respect to the coordinate system of a given view. The view you'll be interested in will often be `self` or `self.superview`; supply nil to get the location with respect to the window. The previous location will be of interest only if the phase is `UITouchPhaseMoved`.

`timestamp`

When the touch last changed. A touch is timestamped when it is created (`UITouch-PhaseBegan`) and each time it moves (`UITouchPhaseMoved`). There can be a delay between the occurrence of a physical touch and the delivery of the corresponding UITouch, so to learn about the timing of touches, consult the timestamp, not the clock.

tapCount

If two touches are in roughly the same place in quick succession, and the first one is brief, the second one may be characterized as a repeat of the first. They are different touch objects, but the second will be assigned a tapCount one larger than the previous one. The default is 1, so if (for example) a touch's tapCount is 3, then this is the third tap in quick succession in roughly the same spot.

view

The view with which this touch is associated.

Here are some additional UIEvent properties:

type

This will be UIEventTypeTouches. There are other event types, but you're not going to receive any of them this way.

timestamp

When the event occurred.

So, when we say that a certain view *is receiving a touch*, that is a shorthand expression meaning that it is being sent a UIEvent containing this UITouch, over and over, by calling one of its touches... methods, corresponding to the phase this touch is in, from the time the touch is created until the time it is destroyed.

Restricting Touches

Touch events can be turned off entirely at the application level with UIApplication's beginIgnoringInteractionEvents. It is quite common to do this during animations and other lengthy operations during which responding to a touch could cause undesirable results. This call should be balanced by endIgnoringInteractionEvents. Pairs can be nested, in which case interactivity won't be restored until the outermost endIgnoringInteractionEvents has been reached.

A number of UIView properties also restrict the delivery of touches to particular views:

userInteractionEnabled

If set to NO, this view (along with its subviews) is excluded from receiving touches. Touches on this view or one of its subviews "fall through" to a view behind it.

alpha

If set to 0.0 (or extremely close to it), this view (along with its subviews) is excluded from receiving touches. Touches on this view or one of its subviews "fall through" to a view behind it.

`hidden`

> If set to YES, this view (along with its subviews) is excluded from receiving touches. This makes sense, since from the user's standpoint, the view and its subviews are not even present.

`multipleTouchEnabled`

> If set to NO, this view never receives more than one touch simultaneously; once it receives a touch, it doesn't receive any other touches until that first touch has ended.

`exclusiveTouch`

> This is the only one of these properties that can't be set in the nib editor. An `exclusiveTouch` view receives a touch only if no other views in the same window have touches associated with them; once an `exclusiveTouch` view has received a touch, then while that touch exists no other view in the same window receives any touches.

Interpreting Touches

Thanks to gesture recognizers (discussed later in this chapter), in most cases you won't have to interpret touches at all; you'll let a gesture recognizer do most of that work. Even so, it is beneficial to be conversant with the nature of touch interpretation; this will help you interact with a gesture recognizer, write your own gesture recognizer, or subclass an existing one. Furthermore, not every touch sequence can be codified through a gesture recognizer; sometimes, directly interpreting touches is the best approach.

To figure out what's going on as touches are received by a view, your code must essentially function as a kind of state machine. You'll receive various `touches...` method calls, and your response will partly depend upon what happened previously, so you'll have to record somehow, such as in instance variables, the information that you'll need in order to decide what to do when the next `touches...` method is called. Such an architecture can make writing and maintaining touch-analysis code quite tricky. Moreover, although you can distinguish a particular UITouch or UIEvent object over time by keeping a reference to it, you mustn't retain that reference; it doesn't belong to you.

To illustrate the business of interpreting touches, we'll start with a view that can be dragged with the user's finger. For simplicity, I'll assume that this view receives only a single touch at a time. (This assumption is easy to enforce by setting the view's `multipleTouchEnabled` to NO, which is the default.)

The trick to making a view follow the user's finger is to realize that a view is positioned by its `center`, which is in superview coordinates, but the user's finger might not be at the center of the view. So at every stage of the drag we must change the view's center by the change in the user's finger position in superview coordinates:

```
- (void) touchesMoved:(NSSet *)touches withEvent:(UIEvent *)event {
    UITouch* t = touches.anyObject;
    CGPoint loc = [t locationInView: self.superview];
    CGPoint oldP = [t previousLocationInView: self.superview];
    CGFloat deltaX = loc.x - oldP.x;
    CGFloat deltaY = loc.y - oldP.y;
    CGPoint c = self.center;
    c.x += deltaX;
    c.y += deltaY;
    self.center = c;
}
```

Next, let's add a restriction that the view can be dragged only vertically or horizontally. All we have to do is hold one coordinate steady; but which coordinate? Everything seems to depend on what the user does initially. So we'll do a one-time test the first time we receive touchesMoved:withEvent:. Now we're maintaining two BOOL state variables, _decided and _horiz:

```
- (void) touchesBegan:(NSSet *)touches withEvent:(UIEvent *)event {
    self->_decided = NO;
}
- (void) touchesMoved:(NSSet *)touches withEvent:(UIEvent *)event {
    UITouch* t = touches.anyObject;
    if (!self->_decided) {
        self->_decided = YES;
        CGPoint then = [t previousLocationInView: self];
        CGPoint now = [t locationInView: self];
        CGFloat deltaX = fabs(then.x - now.x);
        CGFloat deltaY = fabs(then.y - now.y);
        self->_horiz = (deltaX >= deltaY);
    }
    CGPoint loc =
        [t locationInView: self.superview];
    CGPoint oldP =
        [t previousLocationInView: self.superview];
    CGFloat deltaX = loc.x - oldP.x;
    CGFloat deltaY = loc.y - oldP.y;
    CGPoint c = self.center;
    if (self->_horiz)
        c.x += deltaX;
    else
        c.y += deltaY;
    self.center = c;
}
```

Look at how things are trending. We are maintaining multiple state variables, which we are managing across multiple methods, and we are subdividing a touches... method implementation into tests depending on the state of our state machine. Our state machine is very simple, but already our code is becoming difficult to read and to maintain — and things will only become more messy as we try to make our view's behavior more sophisticated.

Another area in which manual touch handling can rapidly prove overwhelming is when it comes to distinguishing between different gestures that the user is to be permitted to perform on a view. Imagine, for example, a view that distinguishes between a finger tapping briefly and a finger remaining down for a longer time. We can't know how long a tap is until it's over, so one approach might be to wait until then before deciding:

```
- (void) touchesBegan:(NSSet *)touches withEvent:(UIEvent *)event {
    self->_time = [(UITouch*)touches.anyObject timestamp];
}
- (void) touchesEnded:(NSSet *)touches withEvent:(UIEvent *)event {
    NSTimeInterval diff = event.timestamp - self->_time;
    if (diff < 0.4)
        NSLog(@"short");
    else
        NSLog(@"long");
}
```

On the other hand, one might argue that if a tap hasn't ended after some set time (here, 0.4 seconds), we know that it is long, and so we could begin responding to it without waiting for it to end. The problem is that we don't automatically get an event after 0.4 seconds. So we'll create one, using delayed performance:

```
- (void) touchesBegan:(NSSet *)touches withEvent:(UIEvent *)event {
    self->_time = [(UITouch*)touches.anyObject timestamp];
    [self performSelector:@selector(touchWasLong)
        withObject:nil afterDelay:0.4];
}
- (void) touchesEnded:(NSSet *)touches withEvent:(UIEvent *)event {
    NSTimeInterval diff = event.timestamp - self->_time;
    if (diff < 0.4)
        NSLog(@"short");
}
- (void) touchWasLong {
    NSLog(@"long");
}
```

But there's a bug. If the tap is short, we report that it was short, but we *also* report that it was long. That's because the delayed call to touchWasLong arrives anyway. We could use some sort of boolean flag to tell us when to ignore that call, but there's a better way: NSObject has a class method that lets us cancel any pending delayed performance calls:

```
- (void) touchesBegan:(NSSet *)touches withEvent:(UIEvent *)event {
    self->_time = [(UITouch*)touches.anyObject timestamp];
    [self performSelector:@selector(touchWasLong)
            withObject:nil afterDelay:0.4];
}
- (void) touchesEnded:(NSSet *)touches withEvent:(UIEvent *)event {
    NSTimeInterval diff = event.timestamp - self->_time;
    if (diff < 0.4) {
        NSLog(@"short");
        [NSObject cancelPreviousPerformRequestsWithTarget:self
```

```
                selector:@selector(touchWasLong) object:nil];
        }
    }
    - (void) touchWasLong {
        NSLog(@"long");
    }
```

Here's another use of the same technique. We'll distinguish between a single tap and a double tap. The UITouch tapCount property already makes this distinction, but that, by itself, is not enough to help us react differently to the two. What we must do, having received a tap whose tapCount is 1, is to delay responding to it long enough to give a second tap a chance to arrive. This is unfortunate, because it means that if the user intends a single tap, some time will elapse before anything happens in response to it; however, there's nothing we can easily do about that.

Distributing our various tasks correctly is a bit tricky. We *know* when we have a double tap as early as touchesBegan:withEvent:, so that's when we cancel our delayed response to a single tap, but we *respond* to the double tap in touchesEnded:withEvent:. We don't start our delayed response to a single tap until touchesEnded:withEvent:, because what matters is the time between the taps as a whole, not between the starts of the taps. This code is adapted from Apple's own example:

```
    - (void) touchesBegan:(NSSet *)touches withEvent:(UIEvent *)event {
        int ct = [(UITouch*)touches.anyObject tapCount];
        if (ct == 2) {
            [NSObject cancelPreviousPerformRequestsWithTarget:self
                selector:@selector(singleTap) object:nil];
        }
    }
    - (void) touchesEnded:(NSSet *)touches withEvent:(UIEvent *)event {
        int ct = [(UITouch*)touches.anyObject tapCount];
        if (ct == 1)
            [self performSelector:@selector(singleTap)
                withObject:nil afterDelay:0.3];
        if (ct == 2)
            NSLog(@"double tap");
    }
    - (void) singleTap {
        NSLog(@"single tap");
    }
```

Now let's consider combining our detection for a single or double tap with our earlier code for dragging a view horizontally or vertically. This is to be a view that can detect four kinds of gesture: a single tap, a double tap, a horizontal drag, and a vertical drag. We must include the code for all possibilities and make sure they don't interfere with each other. The result is rather horrifying — a forced join between two already complicated sets of code, along with an additional pair of state variables to track the decision between the tap gestures on the one hand and the drag gestures on the other:

```objc
- (void) touchesBegan:(NSSet *)touches withEvent:(UIEvent *)event {
    // be undecided
    self->_decidedTapOrDrag = NO;
    // prepare for a tap
    int ct = [(UITouch*)touches.anyObject tapCount];
    if (ct == 2) {
        [NSObject cancelPreviousPerformRequestsWithTarget:self
                                        selector:@selector(singleTap)
                                          object:nil];
        self->_decidedTapOrDrag = YES;
        self->_drag = NO;
        return;
    }
    // prepare for a drag
    self->_decidedDirection = NO;
}
- (void) touchesMoved:(NSSet *)touches withEvent:(UIEvent *)event {
    UITouch* t = touches.anyObject;
    if (self->_decidedTapOrDrag && !self->_drag)
        return;
    self->_decidedTapOrDrag = YES;
    self->_drag = YES;
    if (!self->_decidedDirection) {
        self->_decidedDirection = YES;
        CGPoint then = [t previousLocationInView: self];
        CGPoint now = [t locationInView: self];
        CGFloat deltaX = fabs(then.x - now.x);
        CGFloat deltaY = fabs(then.y - now.y);
        self->_horiz = (deltaX >= deltaY);
    }
    CGPoint loc = [t locationInView: self.superview];
    CGPoint oldP = [t previousLocationInView: self.superview];
    CGFloat deltaX = loc.x - oldP.x;
    CGFloat deltaY = loc.y - oldP.y;
    CGPoint c = self.center;
    if (self->_horiz)
        c.x += deltaX;
    else
        c.y += deltaY;
    self.center = c;
}
- (void) touchesEnded:(NSSet *)touches withEvent:(UIEvent *)event {
    if (!self->_decidedTapOrDrag || !self->_drag) {
        // end for a tap
        int ct = [(UITouch*)touches.anyObject tapCount];
        if (ct == 1)
            [self performSelector:@selector(singleTap)
                withObject:nilafterDelay:0.3];
        if (ct == 2)
            NSLog(@"double tap");
        return;
    }
```

```
    }
- (void) singleTap {
    NSLog(@"single tap");
}
```

That code seems to work, but it's hard to say whether it covers all possibilities coherently; it's barely legible and the logic borders on the mysterious. This is the kind of situation for which gesture recognizers were devised.

Gesture Recognizers

Writing and maintaining a state machine that interprets touches across a combination of three or four `touches...` methods is hard enough when a view confines itself to expecting only one kind of gesture, such as dragging. It becomes even more involved when a view wants to accept and respond differently to different kinds of gesture. Furthermore, many types of gesture are conventional and standard; it seems insane to require developers to implement independently the elements that constitute what is, in effect, a universal vocabulary.

The solution is gesture recognizers, which standardize common gestures and allow the code for different gestures to be separated and encapsulated into different objects.

Gesture Recognizer Classes

A *gesture recognizer* (a subclass of UIGestureRecognizer) is an object whose job is to detect that a multitouch sequence equates to *one particular type of gesture*. It is attached to a UIView, which has for this purpose methods `addGestureRecognizer:` and `removeGestureRecognizer:`, and a `gestureRecognizers` property. A UIGestureRecognizer implements the four `touches...` handlers, but it is not a responder (a UIResponder), so it does not participate in the responder chain.

If a new touch is going to be delivered to a view, it is also associated with and delivered to that view's gesture recognizers if it has any, and that view's superview's gesture recognizers if it has any, and so on up the view hierarchy. Thus, the place of a gesture recognizer in the view hierarchy matters, even though it isn't part of the responder chain.

UITouch and UIEvent provide complementary ways of learning how touches and gesture recognizers are associated. UITouch's `gestureRecognizers` lists the gesture recognizers that are currently handling this touch. UIEvent's `touchesForGestureRecognizer:` lists the touches that are currently being handled by a particular gesture recognizer.

Each gesture recognizer maintains its own state as touch events arrive, building up evidence as to what kind of gesture this is. When one of them decides that it has recognized *its own particular type of gesture*, it emits either a single message (to indicate, for example, that a finger has tapped) or a series of messages (to indicate, for example, that a finger is moving); the distinction here is between a *discrete* and a *continuous* gesture.

What message a gesture recognizer emits, and to what object it sends it, is set through a target–action dispatch table attached to the gesture recognizer; a gesture recognizer is rather like a UIControl in this regard. Indeed, one might say that a gesture recognizer simplifies the touch handling of *any* view to be like that of a control. The difference is that one control may report several different control events, whereas each gesture recognizer reports only one gesture type, with different gestures being reported by different gesture recognizers.

This architecture implies that it is unnecessary to subclass UIView merely in order to implement touch analysis.

UIGestureRecognizer itself is abstract, providing methods and properties to its subclasses. Among these are:

initWithTarget:action:
> The designated initializer. Each message emitted by a UIGestureRecognizer is a matter of sending the action message to the target. Further target–action pairs may be added with addTarget:action: and removed with removeTarget:action:.

> Two forms of action: selector are possible: either there is no parameter, or there is a single parameter which will be the gesture recognizer. Most commonly, you'll use the second form, so that the target can identify and query the gesture recognizer; moreover, using the second form also gives the target a reference to the view, through the gesture recognizer's view property.

locationOfTouch:inView:
> The touch is specified by an index number. The numberOfTouches property provides a count of current touches; the touches themselves are inaccessible by way of the gesture recognizer.

enabled
> A convenient way to turn a gesture recognizer off without having to remove it from its view.

state, view
> I'll discuss state later on. The view is the view to which this gesture recognizer is attached.

Built-in UIGestureRecognizer subclasses are provided for six common gesture types: tap, pinch (inward or outward), pan (drag), swipe, rotate, and long press. Each embodies properties and methods likely to be needed for each type of gesture, either in order to configure the gesture recognizer beforehand or in order to query it as to the state of an ongoing gesture:

UITapGestureRecognizer (discrete)
  Configuration: `numberOfTapsRequired`, `numberOfTouchesRequired` ("touches" means simultaneous fingers).

UIPinchGestureRecognizer (continuous)
  Two fingers moving toward or away from each other. State: `scale`, `velocity`.

UIRotationGestureRecognizer (continuous)
  Two fingers moving round a common center. State: `rotation`, `velocity`.

UISwipeGestureRecognizer (discrete)
  A straight-line movement in one of the four cardinal directions. Configuration: `direction` (meaning permitted directions, a bitmask), `numberOfTouchesRequired`.

UIPanGestureRecognizer (continuous)
  Dragging. Configuration: `minimumNumberOfTouches`, `maximumNumberOfTouches`. State: `translationInView:`, `setTranslation:inView:`, and `velocityInView:`; the coordinate system of the specified view is used.

  UIScreenEdgePanGestureRecognizer
    A UIPanGestureRecognizer subclass, new in iOS 7. It recognizes a pan gesture that starts at an edge of the screen. It adds a configuration property, `edges`, a UIRectEdge; despite the name (and the documentation), this must be set to a single edge.

UILongPressGestureRecognizer (continuous)
  Configuration: `numberOfTapsRequired`, `numberOfTouchesRequired`, `minimum-PressDuration`, `allowableMovement`. The `numberOfTapsRequired` is the count of taps *before* the tap that stays down; so it can be 0 (the default). The `allowable-Movement` setting lets you compensate for the fact that the user's finger is unlikely to remain steady during an extended press; thus we need to provide some limit before deciding that this gesture is, say, a drag, and not a long press after all. On the other hand, once the long press is recognized, the finger is permitted to drag.

UIGestureRecognizer also provides a `locationInView:` method. This is a single point, even if there are multiple touches. The subclasses implement this variously. For example, for UIPanGestureRecognizer, the location is where the touch is if there's a single touch, but it's a sort of midpoint ("centroid") if there are multiple touches.

We already know enough to implement, using a gesture recognizer, a view that responds to a single tap, or a view that responds to a double tap. We don't yet know quite enough to implement a view that lets itself be dragged around, or a view that can respond to more than one gesture; we'll come to that. Meanwhile, here's code that implements a view (v) that responds to a single tap:

```
UITapGestureRecognizer* t =
    [[UITapGestureRecognizer alloc]
        initWithTarget:self
        action:@selector(singleTap)];
[v addGestureRecognizer:t];
// ...
- (void) singleTap {
    NSLog(@"single");
}
```

And here's code that implements a view (v) that responds to a double tap:

```
UITapGestureRecognizer* t =
    [[UITapGestureRecognizer alloc]
        initWithTarget:self
        action:@selector(doubleTap)];
t.numberOfTapsRequired = 2;
[v addGestureRecognizer:t];
// ...
- (void) doubleTap {
    NSLog(@"double");
}
```

For a continuous gesture like dragging, we need to know both when the gesture is in progress and when the gesture ends. This brings us to the subject of a gesture recognizer's state.

A gesture recognizer implements a notion of *states* (the state property); it passes through these states in a definite progression. The gesture recognizer remains in the Possible state until it can make a decision one way or the other as to whether this is in fact the correct gesture. The documentation neatly lays out the possible progressions:

Wrong gesture
Possible → Failed. No action message is sent.

Discrete gesture (like a tap), recognized
Possible → Ended. One action message is sent, when the state changes to Ended.

Continuous gesture (like a drag), recognized
Possible → Began → Changed (repeatedly) → Ended. Action messages are sent once for Began, as many times as necessary for Changed, and once for Ended.

Continuous gesture, recognized but later cancelled
Possible → Began → Changed (repeatedly) → Cancelled. Action messages are sent once for Began, as many times as necessary for Changed, and once for Cancelled.

The actual state names are UIGestureRecognizerStatePossible and so forth. The name UIGestureRecognizerStateRecognized is actually a synonym for the Ended state; I find this unnecessary and confusing and I'll ignore it in my discussion.

The same action message arrives at the same target every time, so the handler must differentiate by asking about the gesture recognizer's state. To illustrate, we will implement, using a gesture recognizer, a view (v) that lets itself be dragged around in any direction by a single finger. Our maintenance of state is greatly simplified, because a UIPanGestureRecognizer maintains a delta (translation) for us. This delta, available using translationInView:, is reckoned from the touch's initial position. So we need to store our center only once:

```
UIPanGestureRecognizer* p =
    [[UIPanGestureRecognizer alloc]
        initWithTarget:self
        action:@selector(dragging:)];
[v addGestureRecognizer:p];
// ...
- (void) dragging: (UIPanGestureRecognizer*) p {
    UIView* vv = p.view;
    if (p.state == UIGestureRecognizerStateBegan)
        self->_origC = vv.center;
    CGPoint delta = [p translationInView: vv.superview];
    CGPoint c = self->_origC;
    c.x += delta.x; c.y += delta.y;
    vv.center = c;
}
```

Actually, it's possible to write that code without maintaining any state at all, because we are allowed to reset the UIPanGestureRecognizer's delta, using setTranslation:in-View:. So:

```
- (void) dragging: (UIPanGestureRecognizer*) p {
    UIView* vv = p.view;
    if (p.state == UIGestureRecognizerStateBegan ||
            p.state == UIGestureRecognizerStateChanged) {
        CGPoint delta = [p translationInView: vv.superview];
        CGPoint c = vv.center;
        c.x += delta.x; c.y += delta.y;
        vv.center = c;
        [p setTranslation: CGPointZero inView: vv.superview];
    }
}
```

A pan gesture recognizer can be used also to make a view draggable under the influence of a UIDynamicAnimator (Chapter 4). The strategy here is that the view is attached to one or more anchor points through a UIAttachmentBehavior; as the user drags, we move the anchor point(s), and the view follows. In this example, I set up the whole UIKit dynamics "stack" of objects as the gesture begins, anchoring the view at the point where the touch is; then I move the anchor point to stay with the touch. Instance variables anim and att store the UIDynamicAnimator and the UIAttachmentBehavior, respectively; self.view is our view's superview, and is the animator's reference view:

```
- (void) dragging: (UIPanGestureRecognizer*) g {
    if (g.state == UIGestureRecognizerStateBegan) {
        self.anim =
            [[UIDynamicAnimator alloc] initWithReferenceView:self.view];
        CGPoint loc = [g locationOfTouch:0 inView:g.view];
        CGPoint cen =
            CGPointMake(CGRectGetMidX(g.view.bounds),
                        CGRectGetMidY(g.view.bounds));
        UIOffset off = UIOffsetMake(loc.x-cen.x, loc.y-cen.y);
        CGPoint anchor = [g locationOfTouch:0 inView:self.view];
        UIAttachmentBehavior* att =
            [[UIAttachmentBehavior alloc] initWithItem:g.view
                offsetFromCenter:off attachedToAnchor:anchor];
        [self.anim addBehavior:att];
        self.att = att;
    }
    else if (g.state == UIGestureRecognizerStateChanged) {
        self.att.anchorPoint = [g locationOfTouch:0 inView:self.view];
    }
    else {
        self.anim = nil;
    }
}
```

The outcome is that the view both moves and rotates in response to dragging, like a plate being pulled about on a table by a single finger. Another implementation, suggested in a WWDC 2013 video, is to attach the view by springs to four anchor points at some distance outside its corners and move all four anchor points; the view then jiggles while being dragged.

Gesture Recognizer Conflicts

The question naturally arises of what happens when multiple gesture recognizers are in play. This isn't a matter merely of multiple recognizers attached to a single view, because, as I have said, if a view is touched, not only its own gesture recognizers but any gesture recognizers attached to views further up the view hierarchy are also in play, simultaneously. I like to think of a view as surrounded by a *swarm* of gesture recognizers — its own, and those of its superview, and so on. (In reality, it is a touch that has a swarm of gesture recognizers; that's why a UITouch has a gestureRecognizers property, in the plural.)

The superview gesture recognizer swarm comes as a surprise to beginners, but it makes sense, because without it, certain gestures would be impossible. Imagine, for example, a pair of views on each of which the user can tap individually, but which the user can also touch simultaneously (one finger on each view) and rotate together around their mutual centroid. Neither view can detect the rotation *qua* rotation, because neither view receives both touches; only the superview can detect it, so the fact that the views themselves respond to touches must not prevent the superview's gesture recognizer from operating.

In general, once a gesture recognizer succeeds in recognizing its gesture, any *other* gesture recognizers associated with its touches are *forced into the Failed state*, and whatever touches were associated with those gesture recognizers are no longer sent to them; in effect, the first gesture recognizer in a swarm that recognizes its gesture owns the gesture, and those touches, from then on.

In many cases, this "first past the post" behavior, on its own, will correctly eliminate conflicts. If it doesn't, you can modify it.

For example, we can add *both* our UITapGestureRecognizer for a single tap *and* our UIPanGestureRecognizer to a view and everything will just work; "first past the post" is exactly the desired behavior. What happens, though, if we also add the UITapGesture-Recognizer for a double tap? Dragging works, and single tap works; double tap works too, but without preventing the single tap from working. So, on a double tap, both the single tap action handler and the double tap action handler are called.

If that isn't what we want, we don't have to use delayed performance, as we did earlier. Instead, we can create a *dependency* between one gesture recognizer and another, telling the first to suspend judgement until the second has decided whether this is its gesture. We can do this by sending the first gesture recognizer the `requireGesture-RecognizerToFail:` message. (This message is rather badly named; it doesn't mean "force this other recognizer to fail", but rather, "you can't succeed unless this other recognizer has failed.")

So our view v is now configured as follows:

```
UITapGestureRecognizer* t2 = [[UITapGestureRecognizer alloc]
                              initWithTarget:self
                              action:@selector(doubleTap)];
t2.numberOfTapsRequired = 2;
[v addGestureRecognizer:t2];
UITapGestureRecognizer* t1 = [[UITapGestureRecognizer alloc]
                              initWithTarget:self
                              action:@selector(singleTap)];
[t1 requireGestureRecognizerToFail:t2];
[v addGestureRecognizer:t1];
UIPanGestureRecognizer* p = [[UIPanGestureRecognizer alloc]
                             initWithTarget:self
                             action:@selector(dragging:)];
[v addGestureRecognizer:p];
```

Apple would prefer, if you're going to have a view respond both to a single tap and to a double tap, that you *not* make the former wait upon the latter (because this delays your response after the single tap). Rather, they would like you to arrange things so that it doesn't matter that you respond to a single tap that is the first tap of a double tap. This isn't always feasible, of course; Apple's own Mobile Safari is a clear counterexample.

Another conflict that can arise is between a gesture recognizer and a view that already knows how respond to the same gesture, such as a UIControl. This problem pops up particularly when the gesture recognizer belongs to the UIControl's superview. The UIControl's mere presence does not "block" the superview's gesture recognizer from recognizing a gesture on the UIControl, even if it is a UIControl that responds autonomously to touches. For example, your window's root view might have a UITapGesture-Recognizer attached to it (perhaps because you want to be able to recognize taps on the background), but there is also a UIButton within it. How is that gesture recognizer to ignore a tap on the button?

The UIView instance method `gestureRecognizerShouldBegin:` solves the problem. It is called automatically; to modify its behavior, use a custom UIView subclass and override it. Its parameter is a gesture recognizer belonging to this view or to a view further up the view hierarchy. That gesture recognizer has recognized its gesture as taking place in this view; but by returning NO, the view can tell the gesture recognizer to bow out and do nothing, not sending any action messages, and permitting this view to respond to the touch as if the gesture recognizer weren't there.

Thus, for example, a UIButton could return NO for a single tap UITapGesture-Recognizer; a single tap on the button would then trigger the button's action message, not the gesture recognizer's action message. And in fact a UIButton, by default, *does* return NO for a single tap UITapGestureRecognizer whose view is not the UIButton itself. (If the gesture recognizer is for some gesture other than a tap, then the problem never arises, because a tap on the button won't cause the gesture recognizer to recognize in the first place.) Other built-in controls may also implement `gestureRecognizer-ShouldBegin:` in such a way as to prevent accidental interaction with a gesture recognizer; the documentation says that a UISlider implements it in such a way that a UISwipeGestureRecognizer won't prevent the user from sliding the "thumb," and there may be other cases that aren't documented explicitly. Naturally, you can take advantage of this feature in your own UIView subclasses.

Another way of resolving possible gesture recognizer conflicts is through the gesture recognizer's delegate, or with a gesture recognizer subclass. I'll discuss these in a moment.

Subclassing Gesture Recognizers

To subclass UIGestureRecognizer or a built-in gesture recognizer subclass, you must do the following things:

- At the start of the implementation file, import `<UIKit/UIGestureRecognizer-Subclass.h>`. This file contains a category on UIGestureRecognizer that allows you to set the gesture recognizer's state (which is otherwise read-only), along with declarations for the methods you may need to override.

- Override any `touches...` methods you need to (as if the gesture recognizer were a UIResponder); if you're subclassing a built-in gesture recognizer subclass, you will almost certainly call `super` so as to take advantage of the built-in behavior. In overriding a `touches...` method, you need to think like a gesture recognizer. As these methods are called, a gesture recognizer is setting its state; you must interact with that process.

To illustrate, we will subclass UIPanGestureRecognizer so as to implement a view that can be moved only horizontally or vertically. Our strategy will be to make *two* UIPan-GestureRecognizer subclasses — one that allows only horizontal movement, and another that allows only vertical movement. They will make their recognition decisions in a mutually exclusive manner, so we can attach an instance of each to our view. This separates the decision-making logic in a gorgeously encapsulated object-oriented manner — a far cry from the spaghetti code we wrote earlier to do this same task.

I will show only the code for the horizontal drag gesture recognizer, because the vertical recognizer is symmetrically identical. We maintain just one instance variable, `_origLoc`, which we will use once to determine whether the user's initial movement is horizontal. We override `touchesBegan:withEvent:` to set our instance variable with the first touch's location:

```
- (void) touchesBegan:(NSSet *)touches withEvent:(UIEvent *)event {
    self->_origLoc =
        [(UITouch*)touches.anyObject locationInView:self.view.superview];
    [super touchesBegan: touches withEvent: event];
}
```

We then override `touchesMoved:withEvent:`; all the recognition logic is here. This method will be called for the first time with the state still at Possible. At that moment, we look to see if the user's movement is more horizontal than vertical. If it isn't, we set the state to Failed. But if it is, we just step back and let the superclass do its thing:

```
- (void) touchesMoved:(NSSet *)touches withEvent:(UIEvent *)event {
    if (self.state == UIGestureRecognizerStatePossible) {
        CGPoint loc =
            [(UITouch*)touches.anyObject locationInView:self.view.superview];
        CGFloat deltaX = fabs(loc.x - self->_origLoc.x);
```

```
        CGFloat deltaY = fabs(loc.y - self->_origLoc.y);
        if (deltaY >= deltaX)
            self.state = UIGestureRecognizerStateFailed;
    }
    [super touchesMoved: touches withEvent:event];
}
```

We now have a view that moves only if the user's initial gesture is horizontal. But that isn't the entirety of what we want; we want a view that, itself, moves horizontally only. To implement this, we'll simply lie to our client about where the user's finger is, by overriding translationInView::

```
- (CGPoint)translationInView:(UIView *)v {
    CGPoint proposedTranslation = [super translationInView:v];
    proposedTranslation.y = 0;
    return proposedTranslation;
}
```

That example was simple, because we subclassed a fully functional built-in UIGesture-Recognizer subclass. If you were to write your own UIGestureRecognizer subclass entirely from scratch, there would be more work to do:

- You should definitely implement all four touches... handlers. Their job, at a minimum, is to advance the gesture recognizer through the canonical progression of its states. When the first touch arrives at a gesture recognizer, its state will be Possible; you never explicitly set the recognizer's state to Possible yourself. As soon as you know this can't be our gesture, you set the state to Failed (Apple says that a gesture recognizer should "fail early, fail often"). If the gesture gets past all the failure tests, you set the state instead either to Ended (for a discrete gesture) or to Began (for a continuous gesture); if Began, then you might set it to Changed, and ultimately you must set it to Ended. Action messages will be sent automatically at the appropriate moments.

- You should probably implement reset. This is called after you reach the end of the progression of states to notify you that the gesture recognizer's state is about to be set back to Possible; it is your chance to return your state machine to its starting configuration (resetting instance variables, for example).

Keep in mind that your gesture recognizer might stop receiving touches without notice. Just because it gets a touchesBegan:withEvent: call for a particular touch doesn't mean it will ever get touchesEnded:withEvent: for that touch. If your gesture recognizer fails to recognize its gesture, either because it declares failure or because it is still in the Possible state when another gesture recognizer recognizes, it won't get any more touches... calls for any of the touches that were being sent to it. This is why reset is so important; it's the one reliable signal that it's time to clean up and get ready to receive the beginning of another possible gesture.

Gesture Recognizer Delegate

A gesture recognizer can have a delegate (UIGestureRecognizerDelegate), which can perform two types of task.

These delegate methods can *block a gesture recognizer's operation*:

gestureRecognizerShouldBegin:
> Sent to the delegate before the gesture recognizer passes out of the Possible state; return NO to force the gesture recognizer to proceed to the Failed state. (This happens *after* gestureRecognizerShouldBegin: has been sent to the view in which the touch took place. That view must not have returned NO, or we wouldn't have reached this stage.)

gestureRecognizer:shouldReceiveTouch:
> Sent to the delegate before a touch is sent to the gesture recognizer's touches-Began:... method; return NO to prevent that touch from ever being sent to the gesture recognizer.

These delegate methods can *mediate gesture recognition conflict*:

gestureRecognizer:shouldRecognizeSimultaneouslyWithGestureRecognizer:
> Sent when a gesture recognizer recognizes its gesture, if this will force the failure of another gesture recognizer, to the delegates of *both* gesture recognizers. Return YES to prevent that failure, thus allowing both gesture recognizers to operate simultaneously. For example, a view could respond to both a two-fingered pinch and a two-fingered pan, the one applying a scale transform, the other changing the view's center.

gestureRecognizer:shouldRequireFailureOfGestureRecognizer:
gestureRecognizer:shouldBeRequiredToFailByGestureRecognizer:
> New in iOS 7, these messages are sent very early in the life of a gesture, when all gesture recognizers in a view's swarm are still in the Possible state, to the delegates of *all* of them, pairing the gesture recognizer whose delegate this is with every other gesture recognizer in the swarm. Return YES to prioritize between a pair, saying that one gesture recognizer cannot succeed until another has first failed. In essence, these delegate methods turn the decision made once and permanently in require-GestureRecognizerToFail: into a live decision that can be made freshly every time a gesture occurs.

As an example, we will use delegate messages to combine a UILongPressGesture-Recognizer and a UIPanGestureRecognizer, as follows: the user must perform a tap-and-a-half (tap and hold) to "get the view's attention," which we will indicate by a pulsing animation on the view; then (and only then) the user can drag the view.

The UILongPressGestureRecognizer's handler will take care of starting and stopping the animation (and the UIPanGestureRecognizer's handler will take care of the drag, as shown earlier in this chapter):

```
- (void) longPress: (UILongPressGestureRecognizer*) lp {
    if (lp.state == UIGestureRecognizerStateBegan) {
        CABasicAnimation* anim =
            [CABasicAnimation animationWithKeyPath: @"transform"];
        anim.toValue =
            [NSValue valueWithCATransform3D:
                CATransform3DMakeScale(1.1, 1.1, 1)];
        anim.fromValue =
            [NSValue valueWithCATransform3D:CATransform3DIdentity];
        anim.repeatCount = HUGE_VALF;
        anim.autoreverses = YES;
        [lp.view.layer addAnimation:anim forKey:nil];
    }
    if (lp.state == UIGestureRecognizerStateEnded ||
            lp.state == UIGestureRecognizerStateCancelled) {
        [lp.view.layer removeAllAnimations];
    }
}
```

As we created our gesture recognizers, we kept a reference to the UILongPressGesture-Recognizer (longPresser), and we made ourself the UIPanGestureRecognizer's delegate. So we will receive delegate messages. If the UIPanGestureRecognizer tries to declare success while the UILongPressGestureRecognizer's state is Failed or still at Possible, we prevent it. If the UILongPressGestureRecognizer succeeds, we permit the UIPanGestureRecognizer to operate as well:

```
- (BOOL) gestureRecognizerShouldBegin: (UIGestureRecognizer*) g {
    if (self.longPresser.state == UIGestureRecognizerStatePossible ||
            self.longPresser.state == UIGestureRecognizerStateFailed)
        return NO;
    return YES;
}
- (BOOL)gestureRecognizer: (UIGestureRecognizer*) g1
        shouldRecognizeSimultaneouslyWithGestureRecognizer:
            (UIGestureRecognizer*) g2 {
    return YES;
}
```

The result is that the view can be dragged only while it is pulsing; in effect, what we've done is to compensate, using delegate methods, for the fact that UIGestureRecognizer has no requireGestureRecognizerToSucceed: method.

If you are subclassing a gesture recognizer class, you can incorporate delegate-like behavior into the subclass, by overriding the following methods:

- `canPreventGestureRecognizer:`
- `canBePreventedByGestureRecognizer:`
- `shouldRequireFailureOfGestureRecognizer:`
- `shouldBeRequiredToFailByGestureRecognizer:`

The "Prevent" methods are similar to the delegate `shouldBegin:` method, and the "Fail" methods are similar to the delegate "Fail" methods. In this way, you can mediate gesture recognizer conflict at the class level. The built-in gesture recognizer subclasses already do this; that is why, for example, a single tap UITapGestureRecognizer does not, by recognizing its gesture, cause the failure of a double tap UITapGestureRecognizer.

You can also, in a gesture recognizer subclass, send `ignoreTouch:forEvent:` directly to a gesture recognizer (typically, to `self`). This has the same effect as the delegate method `gestureRecognizer:shouldReceiveTouch:` returning NO, blocking all future delivery of that touch to the gesture recognizer. For example, if you're in the middle of an already recognized gesture and a new touch arrives, you might well elect to ignore it.

Gesture Recognizers in the Nib

Instead of instantiating a gesture recognizer in code, you can create and configure it in a *.xib* or *.storyboard* file. In the nib editor, drag a gesture recognizer from the Object library into a view; the gesture recognizer becomes a top-level nib object, and the view's `gestureRecognizers` outlet is connected to the gesture recognizer. (You can add more than one gesture recognizer to a view in the nib: the view's `gestureRecognizers` property is an array, and its `gestureRecognizers` outlet is an outlet collection.) The gesture recognizer's properties are configurable in the Attributes inspector, and the gesture recognizer has a `delegate` outlet. The gesture recognizer is a full-fledged nib object, so you can make an outlet to it.

To configure a gesture recognizer's target–action pair in the nib, treat it like a UIControl's control event. The action method's signature should return IBAction, and it should take a single parameter, which will be a reference to the gesture recognizer. You will then be able to form the Sent Action connection in the usual way.

 A gesture recognizer can have multiple target–action pairs, but only one target–action pair can be configured for a gesture recognizer using the nib editor.

A view retains its gesture recognizers, so there will usually be no need for additional memory management on a gesture recognizer instantiated from a nib.

Touch Delivery

Here's the full standard procedure by which a touch is delivered to views and gesture recognizers:

- Whenever a new touch appears, the application uses hit-testing (see the next section) to determine the view that was touched, and that will be permanently associated with this touch. This view is called, appropriately, the *hit-test view*. The logic of ignoring a view (denying it the ability to become the hit-test view) in response to its userInteractionEnabled, hidden, and alpha is implemented at this stage.

- Each time the touch situation changes, the application calls its own sendEvent:, which in turn calls the window's sendEvent:. The window delivers each of an event's touches by calling the appropriate touches... method(s), as follows:

  - As a touch first appears, the logic of obedience to multipleTouchEnabled and exclusiveTouch is considered. If permitted by that logic (which I'll discuss in detail later):

    - The touch is delivered to the hit-test view's swarm of gesture recognizers.

    - The touch is delivered to the hit-test view itself.

  - If a gesture is recognized by a gesture recognizer, then for any touch associated with this gesture recognizer:

    - touchesCancelled:forEvent: is sent to the touch's view, and the touch is no longer delivered to its view.

    - If that touch was associated with any other gesture recognizer, that gesture recognizer is forced to fail.

  - If a gesture recognizer fails, either because it declares failure or because it is forced to fail, its touches are no longer delivered to it, but (except as already specified) they continue to be delivered to their view.

  - If a touch would be delivered to a view, but that view does not respond to the appropriate touches... method, a responder further up the responder chain is sought that does respond to it, and the touch is delivered there.

The rest of this chapter discusses the details. As you'll see, nearly every bit of that standard procedure can be customized to some extent.

Hit-Testing

Hit-testing is the determination of what view the user touched. View hit-testing uses the UIView instance method hitTest:withEvent:, which returns either a view (the hit-test view) or nil. The idea is to find the frontmost view containing the touch point. This method uses an elegant recursive algorithm, as follows:

1. A view's `hitTest:withEvent:` first calls the same method on its own subviews, if it has any, because a subview is considered to be in front of its superview. The subviews are queried in reverse order, because that's front-to-back order (Chapter 1): thus, if two sibling views overlap, the one in front reports the hit first.

2. If, as a view hit-tests its subviews, any of those subviews responds by returning a view, it stops querying its subviews and immediately returns the view that was returned to it. Thus, the very first view to declare itself the hit-test view immediately percolates all the way to the top of the call chain and *is* the hit-test view.

3. If, on the other hand, a view has no subviews, or if all of its subviews return nil (indicating that neither they nor their subviews was hit), then the view calls `pointInside:withEvent:` on itself. If this call reveals that the touch was inside this view, the view returns itself, declaring itself the hit-test view; otherwise it returns nil.

   No problem arises if a view has a transform, because `pointInside:withEvent:` takes the transform into account. That's why a rotated button continues to work correctly.

It is also up to `hitTest:withEvent:` to implement the logic of touch restrictions exclusive to a view. If a view's `userInteractionEnabled` is NO, or its `hidden` is YES, or its `alpha` is close to `0.0`, it returns nil without hit-testing any of its subviews and without calling `pointInside:withEvent:`. Thus these restrictions do not, of themselves, exclude a view from being hit-tested; on the contrary, they operate precisely by modifying a view's hit-test result.

However, hit-testing knows nothing about `multipleTouchEnabled` (which involves multiple touches) or `exclusiveTouch` (which involves multiple views). The logic of obedience to these properties is implemented at a later stage of the story.

You can use hit-testing yourself at any moment where it might prove useful. In calling `hitTest:withEvent:`, supply a point *in the coordinates of the view to which the message is sent*. The second parameter can be nil if you have no event.

For example, suppose we have a UIView with two UIImageView subviews. We want to detect a tap in either UIImageView, but we want to handle this at the level of the UIView. We can attach a UITapGestureRecognizer to the UIView, but how will we know which subview, if any, the tap was in?

First, verify that `userInteractionEnabled` is YES for both UIImageViews. UIImage-View is one of the few built-in view classes where this is NO by default, and a view whose `userInteractionEnabled` is NO won't normally be the result of a call to `hitTest:with-Event:`. Then, when our gesture recognizer's action handler is called, we can use hit-testing to determine where the tap was:

```
// g is the gesture recognizer
CGPoint p = [g locationOfTouch:0 inView:g.view];
UIView* v = [g.view hitTest:p withEvent:nil];
if (v && [v isKindOfClass:[UIImageView class]]) { // ...
```

You can also override `hitTest:withEvent:` in a view subclass, to alter its results during touch delivery, thus customizing the touch delivery mechanism. I call this *hit-test munging*. Hit-test munging can be used selectively as a way of turning user interaction on or off in an area of the interface. In this way, some unusual effects can be produced.

An important use of hit-test munging is to permit the touching of parts of subviews outside the bounds of their superview. If a view's `clipsToBounds` is NO, a paradox arises: the user can *see* the regions of its subviews that are outside its bounds, but can't *touch* them. This can be confusing and seems wrong. The solution is for the view to override `hitTest:withEvent:` as follows:

```
-(UIView *)hitTest:(CGPoint)point withEvent:(UIEvent *)event {
    UIView* result = [super hitTest:point withEvent:event];
    if (result)
        return result;
    for (UIView* sub in [self.subviews reverseObjectEnumerator]) {
        CGPoint pt = [self convertPoint:point toView:sub];
        result = [sub hitTest:pt withEvent:event];
        if (result)
            return result;
    }
    return nil;
}
```

Hit-testing for layers

There is also hit-testing for layers. It doesn't happen automatically, as part of `sendEvent:` or anything else; it's up to you. It's just a convenient way of finding out which layer would receive a touch at a point, if layers received touches. To hit-test layers, call `hitTest:` on a layer, with a point *in superlayer coordinates*.

Keep in mind, though, that layers do *not* receive touches. A touch is reported to a view, not a layer. A layer, except insofar as it is a view's underlying layer and gets touch reporting because of its view, is completely untouchable; from the point of view of touches and touch reporting, it's as if the layer weren't on the screen at all. No matter where a layer may appear to be, a touch falls through the layer, to whatever view is behind it.

In the case of the layer that is a view's underlying layer, you don't need hit-testing. It is the view's drawing; where it appears is where the view is. So a touch in that layer is equivalent to a touch in its view. Indeed, one might say (and it is often said) that this is what views are actually for: to provide layers with touchability.

The only layers on which you'd need special hit-testing, then, would presumably be layers that are not themselves any view's underlying layer, because those are the only ones you don't find out about by normal view hit-testing. However, all layers, including a layer that is its view's underlying layer, are part of the layer hierarchy, and can participate in layer hit-testing. So the most comprehensive way to hit-test layers is to start with the topmost layer, the window's layer. In this example, we subclass UIWindow and override its `hitTest:withEvent:` so as to get layer hit-testing every time there is view hit-testing:

```
- (UIView*) hitTest:(CGPoint)point withEvent:(UIEvent *)event {
    CALayer* lay = [self.layer hitTest:point];
    // ... possibly do something with that information ...
    return [super hitTest:point withEvent:event];
}
```

In that example, the view hit-test point works as the layer hit-test point; window bounds are screen bounds (Chapter 1). But usually you'll have to convert to superlayer coordinates. In this next example, we return to the CompassView developed in Chapter 3, in which all the parts of the compass are layers; we want to know whether the user tapped on the arrow layer. For simplicity, we've given the CompassView a UITapGesture-Recognizer, and this is its action handler, in the CompassView itself. We convert to our superview's coordinates, because these are also our layer's superlayer coordinates:

```
// self is the CompassView
CGPoint p = [t locationOfTouch: 0 inView: self.superview];
CALayer* hitLayer = [self.layer hitTest:p];
if (hitLayer == ((CompassLayer*)self.layer).arrow) // ...
```

Layer hit-testing works by calling `containsPoint:`. However, `containsPoint:` takes a point in the layer's coordinates, so to hand it a point that arrives through `hitTest:` you must first convert from superlayer coordinates:

```
BOOL hit =
    [lay containsPoint: [lay convertPoint:point fromLayer:lay.superlayer]];
```

Layer hit-testing knows nothing of the restrictions on touch delivery; it just reports on every sublayer, even one whose view (for example) has `userInteractionEnabled` set to NO.

 The documentation warns that `hitTest:` must not be called on a CATransformLayer.

Hit-testing for drawings

The preceding example (letting the user tap on the compass arrow) worked, but we might complain that it is reporting a hit on the arrow even if the hit misses the *drawing* of the arrow. That's true for view hit-testing as well. A hit is reported if we are within the view or layer as a whole; hit-testing knows nothing of drawing, transparent areas, and so forth.

If you know how the region is drawn and can reproduce the edge of that drawing as a CGPath, you can test whether a point is inside it with `CGPathContainsPoint`. So, for a layer, you could override `hitTest` along these lines:

```
- (CALayer*) hitTest:(CGPoint)p {
    CGPoint pt = [self convertPoint:p fromLayer:self.superlayer];
    CGMutablePathRef path = CGPathCreateMutable();
    // ... draw path here ...
    CALayer* result =
        CGPathContainsPoint(path, nil, pt, true) ? self : nil;
    CGPathRelease(path);
    return result;
}
```

Alternatively, it might be the case that if a pixel of the drawing is transparent, it's outside the drawn region, so that it suffices to detect whether the pixel tapped is transparent. Unfortunately, there's no way to ask a drawing (or a view, or a layer) for the color of a pixel; you have to make a bitmap and copy the drawing into it, and then ask the bitmap for the color of a pixel. If you can reproduce the content as an image, and all you care about is transparency, you can make a one-pixel alpha-only bitmap, draw the image in such a way that the pixel you want to test is the pixel drawn into the bitmap, and examine the transparency of the resulting pixel:

```
// assume im is a UIImage, point is the CGPoint to test
unsigned char pixel[1] = {0};
CGContextRef context =
    CGBitmapContextCreate(pixel, 1, 1, 8, 1, nil,
                          (CGBitmapInfo)kCGImageAlphaOnly);
UIGraphicsPushContext(context);
[im drawAtPoint:CGPointMake(-point.x, -point.y)];
UIGraphicsPopContext();
CGContextRelease(context);
CGFloat alpha = pixel[0]/255.0;
BOOL transparent = alpha < 0.01;
```

However, there may not be a one-to-one relationship between the pixels of the underlying drawing and the points of the drawing as portrayed on the screen — because the drawing is stretched, for example. In many cases, the CALayer method `renderIn-Context:` can be helpful here. This method allows you to copy a layer's actual drawing into a context of your choice. If that context is, say, an image context created with `UIGraphicsBeginImageContextWithOptions`, you can now use the resulting image as `im` in the code above:

```
UIGraphicsBeginImageContextWithOptions(self.bounds.size, NO, 0);
CALayer* lay = // ... the layer whose content we're interested in
[lay renderInContext:UIGraphicsGetCurrentContext()];
UIImage* im = UIGraphicsGetImageFromCurrentImageContext();
UIGraphicsEndImageContext(); // ... and the rest is as before
```

Hit-testing during animation

The simplest solution to the problem of touch during animation is to disallow it entirely. By default, view animation turns off touchability of a view while it's being animated (though you can prevent that with `UIViewAnimationOptionAllowUserInteraction` in the `options:` argument), and you can temporarily turn off touchability altogether with UIApplication's `beginIgnoringInteractionEvents`, as I mentioned earlier in this chapter.

If user interaction is allowed during an animation that moves a view from one place to another, then if the user taps on the animated view, the tap might mysteriously fail because the view in the model layer is elsewhere; conversely, the user might accidentally tap where the view actually is in the model layer, and the tap will hit the animated view even though it appears to be elsewhere. If the position of a view or layer is being animated and you want the user to be able to tap on it, therefore, you'll need to hit-test the presentation layer.

In this simple example, we have a superview containing a subview. To allow the user to tap on the subview even when it is being animated, we implement hit-test munging in the superview:

```
- (UIView*) hitTest:(CGPoint)point withEvent:(UIEvent *)event {
    // v is the animated subview
    CALayer* lay = [v.layer presentationLayer];
    CALayer* hitLayer = [lay hitTest: point];
    if (hitLayer == lay)
        return v;
    UIView* hitView = [super hitTest:point withEvent:event];
    if (hitView == v)
        return self;
    return hitView;
}
```

If the user taps outside the presentation layer, we cannot simply call `super`, because the user might tap at the spot to which the subview has in reality already moved (behind the "animation movie"), in which case `super` will report that it hit the subview. So if `super` does report this, we return `self` (assuming that we are what's behind the animated subview at its new location).

However, as Apple puts it in the WWDC 2011 videos, the animated view "swallows the touch." For example, suppose the view in motion is a button. Although our hit-test munging makes it possible for the user to tap the button as it is being animated, and although the user sees the button highlight in response, the button's action message is not sent in response to this highlighting if the animation is in-flight when the tap takes place. This behavior seems unfortunate, but it's generally possible to work around it (for instance, with a gesture recognizer).

Initial Touch Event Delivery

When the touch situation changes, an event containing all touches is handed to the UIApplication instance by calling its sendEvent:, and the UIApplication in turn hands it to the relevant UIWindow by calling *its* sendEvent:. The UIWindow then performs the complicated logic of examining, for every touch, the hit-test view and its superviews and their gesture recognizers and deciding which of them should be sent a touches... message, and does so.

These are delicate and crucial maneuvers, and you wouldn't want to lame your application by interfering with them. Nevertheless, you can override sendEvent: in a subclass, and this is just about the only reason you might have for subclassing UIApplication; if you do, remember to change the third argument in the call to UIApplication-Main in your *main.m* file to the string name of your UIApplication subclass, so that your subclass is used to generate the app's singleton UIApplication instance. Subclassing UI-Window is discussed in Chapter 1.

It is unlikely, however, that you will need to resort to such measures. A typical case before the advent of gesture recognizers was that you needed to detect touches directed to an object of some built-in interface class in a way that subclassing it wouldn't permit. For example, you want to know when the user swipes a UIWebView; you're not allowed to subclass UIWebView, and in any case it eats the touch. The solution used to be to subclass UIWindow and override sendEvent:; you would then work out whether this was a swipe on the UIWebView and respond accordingly, or else call super. Now, however, you can attach a UISwipeGestureRecognizer to the UIWebView.

Gesture Recognizer and View

When a touch first appears and is delivered to a gesture recognizer, it is also delivered to its hit-test view, the same touches... method being called on both. Later, if a gesture recognizer in a view's swarm recognizes its gesture, that view is sent touches-Cancelled:withEvent: for any touches that went to that gesture recognizer and were hit-tested to that view, and subsequently the view no longer receives those touches.

This comes as a surprise to beginners, but it is the most reasonable approach, as it means that touch interpretation by a view isn't jettisoned just because gesture recognizers are in the picture. Later on in the multitouch sequence, if all the gesture recognizers in a view's swarm declare failure to recognize their gesture, that view's internal touch interpretation just proceeds as if gesture recognizers had never been invented.

Moreover, touches and gestures are two different things; sometimes you want to respond to both. In one of my apps, where the user can tap cards, each card has a single tap gesture recognizer and a double tap gesture recognizer, but it also responds directly to touchesBegan:withEvent: by reducing its own opacity (and restores its opacity on `touchesEnded:withEvent:` and `touchesCancelled:withEvent:`). The result is that user always sees feedback when touching a card, *instantly*, regardless of what the gesture turns out to be.

This behavior can be changed by setting a gesture recognizer's `cancelsTouchesIn-View` property to NO. If this is the case for every gesture recognizer in a view's swarm, the view will receive touch events more or less as if no gesture recognizers were in the picture.

If a gesture recognizer happens to be ignoring a touch (because, for example, it was told to do so by `ignoreTouch:forEvent:`), then `touchesCancelled:withEvent:` *won't* be sent to the view for that touch when that gesture recognizer recognizes its gesture. Thus, a gesture recognizer's ignoring a touch is the same as simply letting it fall through to the view, as if the gesture recognizer weren't there.

Gesture recognizers can also *delay* the delivery of touches to a view, and by default they do. The UIGestureRecognizer property `delaysTouchesEnded` is YES by default, meaning that when a touch reaches `UITouchPhaseEnded` and the gesture recognizer's `touches-Ended:withEvent:` is called, if the gesture recognizer is still allowing touches to be delivered to the view because its state is still Possible, it doesn't deliver this touch until it has resolved the gesture. When it does, either it will recognize the gesture, in which case the view will have `touchesCancelled:withEvent:` called instead (as already explained), or it will declare failure and *now* the view will have `touchesEnded:with-Event:` called.

The reason for this behavior is most obvious with a gesture where multiple taps are required. The first tap ends, but this is insufficient for the gesture recognizer to declare success or failure, so it withholds that touch from the view. In this way, the gesture recognizer gets the proper priority. In particular, if there is a second tap, the gesture recognizer should succeed and send `touchesCancelled:withEvent:` to the view — but it can't do that if the view has already been sent `touchesEnded:withEvent:`.

It is also possible to delay the entire suite of `touches...` methods from being called on a view, by setting a gesture recognizer's `delaysTouchesBegan` property to YES. Again, this delay would be until the gesture recognizer can resolve the gesture: either it will recognize it, in which case the view will have `touchesCancelled:withEvent:` called, or it will declare failure, in which case the view will receive `touchesBegan:withEvent:` plus any further `touches...` calls that were withheld — except that it will receive *at most* one `touchesMoved:withEvent:` call, the last one, because if a lot of these were withheld, to queue them all up and send them all at once now would be simply insane.

It is unlikely that you'll change a gesture recognizer's `delaysTouchesBegan` property to YES, however. You might do so, for example, if you have an elaborate touch analysis within a view that simply cannot operate simultaneously with a gesture recognizer, but this is improbable, and the latency involved may look strange to your user.

When touches are delayed and then delivered, what's delivered is the original touch with the original event, which still have their original timestamps. Because of the delay, these timestamps may differ significantly from now. For this reason (and many others), Apple warns that touch analysis that is concerned with timing should always look at the timestamp, not the clock.

Touch Exclusion Logic

It is up to the UIWindow's sendEvent: to implement the logic of multipleTouch-Enabled and exclusiveTouch.

If a new touch is hit-tested to a view whose multipleTouchEnabled is NO and which already has an existing touch hit-tested to it, then sendEvent: never delivers the new touch to that view. However, that touch *is* delivered to the view's swarm of gesture recognizers.

Similarly, if there's an exclusiveTouch view in the window, then sendEvent: must decide whether a particular touch should be delivered, in accordance with the meaning of exclusiveTouch, which I described earlier. If a touch is not delivered to a view because of exclusiveTouch restrictions, it is *not* delivered to its swarm of gesture recognizers either.

> The logic of touch delivery to gesture recognizers in response to exclusiveTouch has changed in a confusing and possibly buggy way from system to system, but I believe I'm describing it correctly for the current system. The statement in Apple's SimpleGestureRecognizers sample code that "Recognizers ignore the exclusive touch setting for views" probably dates back to an earlier implementation; it appears to be flat-out false at this point.

Gesture Recognition Logic

When a gesture recognizer recognizes its gesture, everything changes. As we've already seen, the touches for this gesture recognizer are sent to their hit-test views as a touches-Cancelled:forEvent: message, and then no longer arrive at those views (unless the gesture recognizer's cancelsTouchesInView is NO). Moreover, all other gesture recognizers pending with regard to these touches are made to fail, and then are no longer sent the touches they were receiving either.

If the very same event would cause more than one gesture recognizer to recognize, there's an algorithm for picking the one that will succeed and make the others fail: a gesture recognizer lower down the view hierarchy (closer to the hit-test view) prevails over one higher up the hierarchy, and a gesture recognizer more recently added to its view prevails over one less recently added.

There are various means for modifying this "first past the post" behavior:

Dependency order

Certain methods institute a dependency order, causing a gesture recognizer to be put on hold when it tries to transition from the Possible state to the Began (continuous) or Ended (discrete) state; only if a certain other gesture recognizer fails is this one permitted to perform that transition. Apple says that in a dependency like this, the gesture recognizer that fails first is not sent reset (and won't receive any touches) until the second finishes its state sequence and is sent reset, so that they resume recognizing together. The methods are:

- requireGestureRecognizerToFail: (sent to a gesture recognizer)
- shouldRequireFailureOfGestureRecognizer: (overridden in a subclass)
- shouldBeRequiredToFailByGestureRecognizer: (overridden in a subclass)
- gestureRecognizer:shouldRequireFailureOfGestureRecognizer: (implemented by the delegate)
- gestureRecognizer:shouldBeRequiredToFailByGestureRecognizer: (implemented by the delegate)

The first of those methods sets up a permanent relationship between two gesture recognizers, and cannot be undone; but the others are sent every time a gesture starts in a view whose swarm includes both gesture recognizers, and applies only on this occasion.

The delegate methods work together as follows. For each pair of gesture recognizers in the hit-test view's swarm, the members of that pair are arranged in a fixed order (as I've already described). The first of the pair is sent shouldRequire and then shouldBeRequired, and then the second of the pair is sent shouldRequire and then shouldBeRequired, and then if any of those four methods returns YES, the relationship between that pair is settled; the sequence stops (and we proceed to the next pair).

Success into failure

Certain methods, by returning NO, turn success into failure; at the moment when the gesture recognizer is about to declare that it recognizes its gesture, transitioning from the Possible state to the Began (continuous) or Ended (discrete) state, it is forced to fail instead:

- UIView's gestureRecognizerShouldBegin:
- The delegate's gestureRecognizerShouldBegin:

Simultaneous recognition

A gesture recognizer succeeds, but some other gesture recognizer is *not* forced to fail, in accordance with these methods:

- `gestureRecognizer:shouldRecognizeSimultaneouslyWithGesture-Recognizer:` (implemented by the delegate)
- `canPreventGestureRecognizer:` (overridden in a subclass)
- `canBePreventedByGestureRecognizer:` (overridden in a subclass)

In the subclass methods, "prevent" means "by succeeding, you force failure upon this other," and "be prevented" means "by succeeding, this other forces failure on you." They work together as follows. `canPreventGestureRecognizer:` is called first; if it returns NO, that's the end of the story for that gesture recognizer, and `canPreventGestureRecognizer:` is called on the other gesture recognizer. But if `canPreventGestureRecognizer:` returns YES when it is first called, the other gesture recognizer is sent `canBePreventedByGestureRecognizer:`. If it returns YES, that's the end of the story; if it returns NO, the process starts over the other way around, sending `canPreventGestureRecognizer:` to the second gesture recognizer, and so forth. In this way, conflicting answers are resolved without the device exploding: prevention is regarded as exceptional (even though it is in fact the norm) and will happen only if it is acquiesced to by everyone involved.

Touches and the Responder Chain

A UIView is a responder, and participates in the responder chain. In particular, if a touch is to be delivered to a UIView (because, for example, it's the hit-test view) and that view doesn't implement the relevant `touches...` method, a walk up the responder chain is performed, looking for a responder that *does* implement it; if such a responder is found, the touch is delivered to that responder. Moreover, the default implementation of the `touches...` methods — the behavior that you get if you call `super` — is to perform the same walk up the responder chain, starting with the next responder in the chain.

The relationship between touch delivery and the responder chain can be useful, but you must be careful not to allow it to develop into an incoherency. For example, if `touches-Began:withEvent:` is implemented in a superview but not in a subview, then a touch to the subview will result in the superview's `touchesBegan:withEvent:` being called, with the first parameter (the touches) containing a touch whose `view` is the subview. But most UIView implementations of the `touches...` methods rely upon the assumption that the first parameter consists of all and only touches whose `view` is `self`; built-in UIView subclasses certainly assume this.

Again, if touchesBegan:withEvent: is implemented in both a superview and a subview, and you call super in the subview's implementation, passing along the same arguments that came in, then the same touch delivered to the subview will trigger both the subview's touchesBegan:withEvent: and the superview's touchesBegan:withEvent: (and once again the first parameter to the superview's touchesBegan:withEvent: will contain a touch whose view is the subview).

The solution is to behave rationally, as follows:

- If all the responders in the affected part of the responder chain are instances of your own subclass of UIView itself or of your own subclass of UIViewController, you will generally want to follow the simplest possible rule: implement *all* the touches... events together in one class, so that touches arrive at an instance either because it was the hit-test view or because it is up the responder chain from the hit-test view, and do *not* call super in any of them. In this way, "the buck stops here" — the touch handling for this object or for objects below it in the responder chain is bottlenecked into one well-defined place.
- If you subclass a built-in UIView subclass and you override its touch handling, you don't have to override every single touches... event, but you *do* need to call super so that the built-in touch handling can occur.
- Don't allow touches to arrive from lower down the responder chain at an instance of a built-in UIView subclass that implements built-in touch handling, because such a class is completely unprepared for the first parameter of a touches... method containing a touch not intended for itself. Judicious use of userInteraction-Enabled or hit-test munging can be a big help here.

  I'm not saying, however, that you have to block all touches from percolating up the responder chain; it's normal for unhandled touches to arrive at the UIWindow or UIApplication, for example, because these classes do not (by default) do any touch handling — so those touches will remain unhandled and will percolate right off the end of the responder chain, which is perfectly fine.
- Never call a touches... method directly (except to call super).

 Apple's documentation has some discussion of a technique called *event forwarding* where you *do* call touches... methods directly. But you are far less likely to need this now that gesture recognizers exist, and it can be extremely tricky and even downright dangerous to implement, so I won't give an example, and I suggest that you not use it.

PART II

Interface

This part of the book is about view controllers, and about all the various kinds of view provided by the Cocoa framework — the built-in "widgets" with which you'll construct an app's interface.

- Chapter 6 is about view controllers, the fundamental iOS mechanism for allowing an entire interface to be replaced by another. Every app you write will have its interface managed by at least one view controller.
- Chapter 7 is about scroll views, the iOS mechanism for letting the user scroll and zoom the interface.
- Chapter 8 explains table views, a type of scroll view that lets the user navigate through any amount of data, along with collection views, a generalization of table views.
- Chapter 9 is about two forms of interface unique to, and characteristic of, the iPad — popovers and split views.
- Chapter 10 describes several ways of presenting text (including styled text) in an app's interface — labels, text fields, text views, and text drawn directly.
- Chapter 11 discusses web views. A web view is an easy-to-use interface widget backed by the power of a full-fledged web browser.
- Chapter 12 describes all the remaining built-in iOS (UIKit) interface widgets.
- Chapter 13 is about the forms of modal dialog that can appear in front of an app's interface.

CHAPTER 6
View Controllers

An iOS app's interface is dynamic, and with good reason. On the desktop, an application's windows can be big, and there can be more than one of them, so there's room for lots of interface. With iOS, everything needs to fit on a single display consisting of a single window, which in the case of the iPhone is almost forbiddingly tiny. The iOS solution is to introduce, at will, completely new interface — a new view, possibly with an elaborate hierarchy of subviews — replacing or covering the previous interface.

For this to work, regions of interface material — often the entire contents of the screen — must come and go in an agile fashion that is understandable to the user. There will typically be a logical, structural, and functional relationship between the view that was present and the view that replaces or covers it, and this relationship will need to be maintained behind the scenes, in your code, as well as being indicated to the user: multiple views may be pure alternatives or siblings of one another, or one view may be a temporary replacement for another, or views may be like successive pages of a book. Animation is often used to emphasize and clarify these relationships as one view is superseded by another. Navigational interface and a vivid, suggestive gestural vocabulary give the user an ability to control what's seen and an understanding of the possible options: a tab bar whose buttons summon alternate views, a back button or a swipe gesture for returning to a previously visited view, a tap on an interface element to dive deeper into a conceptual world, a Done or Cancel button to escape from a settings screen, and so forth.

In iOS, this management of the dynamic interface is performed through view controllers. A *view controller* is an instance of UIViewController. Actually, a view controller is most likely to be an instance of a UIViewController subclass; the UIViewController class is designed to be subclassed, and you are very unlikely to use a plain vanilla UIViewController object without subclassing it. You might write your own UIViewController subclass; you might use a built-in UIViewController subclass such as

UINavigationController or UITabBarController; or you might subclass a built-in UIViewController subclass such as UITableViewController (Chapter 8).

A view controller manages a single view (which can, of course, have subviews); its `view` property points to the view it manages. This is the view controller's *main view*, or simply its view. A view controller's main view has no explicit pointer to the view controller that manages it, but a view controller is a UIResponder and is in the responder chain just above its view, so it is the view's `nextResponder`.

View Controller Responsibilities

A view controller's most important responsibility is its view. A view controller must have a view (it is useless without one). If that view is to be useful, it must somehow *get into the interface*, and hence onto the screen; a view controller is usually responsible for seeing to that, too, but typically *not* the view controller whose view this is; rather, it will be some view controller whose view is *already* in the interface. In most cases, this will be taken care of automatically for you by a built-in mechanism (I'll talk more about this in the next section), but you can participate in the process, and for some view controllers you may have to do the work yourself. The reverse is also true: a view that comes may also eventually go, and the view controller responsible for putting a view into the interface will also be responsible for removing it.

A view controller will also typically provide *animation* of the interface as a view comes or goes. Built-in view controller subclasses and built-in ways of summoning or removing a view controller and its view come with built-in animations. We are all familiar, for example, with tapping something to make new interface slide in from the right, and then tapping a back button to make that interface slide back out to the right. In cases where you are responsible for getting a view controller's view onto the screen, you are also responsible for providing the animation. And, new in iOS 7, you can take complete charge of the animation even for built-in view controllers.

View controllers, working together, can *save and restore state* automatically. This feature, introduced in iOS 6, helps you ensure that if your app is terminated in the background and subsequently relaunched, it will quickly resume displaying the same interface that was showing when the user last saw it.

The most powerful view controller is the *root view controller*. This is the view controller managing the view that sits at the top of the view hierarchy, as the one and only direct subview of the main window, acting as the superview for all other interface (the *root view*). I described in Chapter 1 how this view controller attains its lofty position: it is assigned to the window's `rootViewController` property. The window then takes that view controller's main view, gives it the correct frame (resizing it if necessary), and makes it its own subview.

An app without a root view controller, while theoretically possible, is strongly discouraged by a warning from the runtime ("Applications are expected to have a root view controller at the end of application launch"). I don't consider such an option in this book.

The root view controller is responsible for *rotation* of the interface. The user can rotate the device, and you might like the interface to rotate in response, to compensate. As I explained in Chapter 1, the window is effectively pinned to the physical display (window bounds are screen bounds and do not change), but a view can be given a transform so that its top moves to the current top of the display. The root view controller can respond to device rotation by applying this transform to the root view.

The root view controller also bears ultimate responsibility for manipulation of the *status bar*. The status bar is actually a secondary window belonging to the runtime, but the runtime consults the root view controller as to whether the status bar should be present and, if so, whether its text should be light or dark. (This view controller responsibility is new in iOS 7.)

Your participation in all these view controller responsibilities depends upon your customization of a view controller, through properties and methods provided for this purpose. View controllers do many things automatically, but the options that specify the details are up to you. The root view controller rotates the interface in response to the user's rotation of the device; but should it do so on this particular occasion? A certain transition between views of built-in view controllers may come with a choice of built-in animations; which one would you like? (Or, in iOS 7, do you prefer to supply your own animation?) Similarly, some view controllers add navigation interface to their views; how should that interface look? You'll determine all of this, and more, through your customization of view controllers.

View Controller Hierarchy

As I said in the previous section, there is always one root view controller, along with its view, the root view. There may also be other view controllers, each of which has its own main view. Such view controllers are *subordinate* to the root view controller. In iOS, there are two subordination relationships between view controllers:

Parentage (containment)
    A view controller can *contain* another view controller. The containing view controller is the *parent* of the contained view controller; the contained view controller is a *child* of the containing view controller. This containment relationship of the view controllers is reflected in their views: the child view controller's view is a *subview* of the parent view controller's view. ("Subview" here means "subview at some depth.")

Figure 6-1. The TidBITS News app

Replacement of one view with another often involves a parent view controller managing its children and their views. The parent view controller is responsible for getting a child view controller's view into the interface, by making it a subview of its own view, and (if necessary) for removing it later.

A familiar example is the navigation interface: the user taps something and new interface slides in from the right, replacing the current interface. Figure 6-1 shows the TidBITS News app displaying a typical iPhone interface, consisting of a list of story headlines and summaries. This interface is managed by a parent view controller (a UINavigationController) with a child view controller whose view is the list of headlines and summaries. If the user taps an entry in the list, the whole list will slide away to the left and the text of that story will slide in from the right; the parent view controller has added a new child view controller, and has manipulated the views of its two children to bring about this animated change of the interface. The parent view controller itself, meanwhile, stays put — and so does its own view. (In this example, the UINavigationController is the root view controller, and its view is the root view.)

Presentation (modal views)

A view controller can *present* another view controller. The first view controller is the *presenting* view controller (not the parent) of the second; the second view controller is the *presented* view controller (not a child) of the first. The second view controller's view replaces or covers the first view controller's view.

The name for this mechanism and relationship between view controllers has changed over time. In iOS 4 and before, the presented view controller was called a *modal view controller*, and its view was a *modal view*; there is an analogy here to the desktop, where a window is modal if it sits in front of, and denies the user access to, the rest of the interface until it is explicitly dismissed. The terms *presented view controller* and *presented view* are more recent and more general, but the term "modal" still appears in the documentation and in the API.

A presented view controller's view does indeed sometimes look rather like a desktop modal view; for example, it might have a button such as Done or Save for dismissing the view, the implication being that this is a place where the user must make a decision and can do nothing else until the decision is made. However, as I'll explain later, that isn't the only use of a presented view controller.

There is thus a *hierarchy of view controllers*. In a properly constructed iOS app, there should be exactly one root view controller, and it is the *only* nonsubordinate view controller — it has neither a parent view controller nor a presenting view controller. Any other view controller, if its view is to appear in the interface, must be a child view controller (of some parent view controller) or a presented view controller (of some presenting view controller).

At the same time, at any given moment, the actual views of the interface form a hierarchy dictated by and parallel to some portion of the view controller hierarchy. Every view visible in the interface owes its presence to a view controller's view: either it *is* a view controller's view, or it's a subview of a view controller's view.

The place of a view controller's view in the view hierarchy will most often be *automatic*. You might never need to put a UIViewController's view into the view hierarchy manually. You'll manipulate view controllers; their hierarchy and their built-in functionality will construct and manage the view hierarchy for you.

For example, in Figure 6-1, we see two interface elements:

- The navigation bar, containing the TidBITS logo.
- The list of stories, which is actually a UITableView.

I will describe how all of this comes to appear on the screen through the view controller hierarchy and the view hierarchy (Figure 6-2):

- The app's root view controller is a UINavigationController; the UINavigationController's view, which is never seen in isolation, is the window's sole immediate subview (the root view). The navigation bar is a subview of that view.

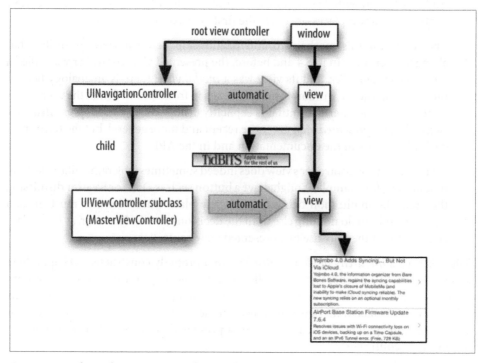

Figure 6-2. The TidBITS News app's initial view controller and view hierarchy

- The UINavigationController contains a second UIViewController — a parent–child relationship. The child is a custom UIViewController subclass; *its* view is what occupies the rest of the window, as another subview of the UINavigationController's view. That view is the UITableView. This architecture means that when the user taps a story listing in the UITableView, the whole table will slide out, to be replaced by the view of a different UIViewController, while the navigation bar stays.

In Figure 6-2, notice the word "automatic" in the two large right-pointing arrows associating a view controller with its view. This is intended to tell you how the view controller's view became part of the view hierarchy. The UINavigationController's view became the window's subview automatically, by virtue of the UINavigationController being the window's rootViewController. The custom UIViewController's view became the UINavigationController's view's second subview automatically, by virtue of the UIViewController being the UINavigationController's child.

Sometimes, you'll write your own parent view controller class. In that case, *you* will be doing the kind of work that the UINavigationController was doing in that example, so you will need to put a child view controller's view into the interface *manually*, as a subview (at some depth) of the parent view controller's view.

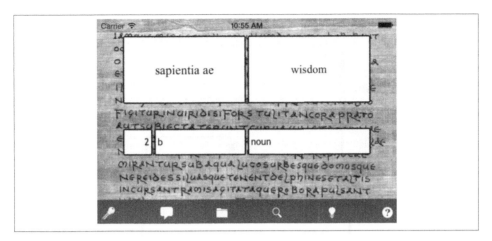

Figure 6-3. A Latin flashcard app

I'll illustrate with another app of mine (Figure 6-3). The interface displays a flashcard containing information about a Latin word, along with a toolbar (the dark area at the bottom) where the user can tap an icon to choose additional functionality.

Again, I will describe how the interface shown in Figure 6-3 comes to appear on the screen through the view controller hierarchy and the view hierarchy (Figure 6-4). The app actually contains over a thousand of these Latin words, and I want the user to be able to navigate between flashcards to see the next or previous word; there is an excellent built-in view controller for this purpose, the UIPageViewController. However, that's just for the card; the toolbar at the bottom stays there, so it can't be inside the UIPageViewController's view. Therefore:

- The app's root view controller is my own UIViewController subclass, which I call RootViewController; its view contains the toolbar, and is also to contain the UIPageViewController's view. My RootViewController's view becomes the window's subview (the root view) automatically, by virtue of the RootViewController's being the window's `rootViewController`.

- In order for the UIPageViewController's view to appear in the interface, since it is not the root view controller, it *must* be some view controller's child. There is only one possible parent — my RootViewController. It must function as a custom parent view controller, with the UIPageViewController as its child. So I have made that happen, and I have therefore also had to put the UIPageViewController's view *manually* into my RootViewController's view.

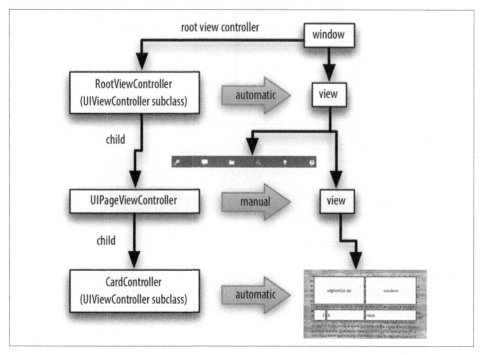

Figure 6-4. The Latin flashcard app's initial view controller and view hierarchy

- I hand the UIPageViewController an instance of my CardController class (another UIViewController subclass) as its child, and the UIPageViewController displays the CardController's view automatically.

Finally, here's an example of a presented view controller. My Latin flashcard app has a second mode, where the user is drilled on a subset of the cards in random order; the interface looks very much like the first mode's interface (Figure 6-5), but it behaves completely differently.

To implement this, I have another UIViewController subclass, DrillViewController; it is structured very much like RootViewController. When the user is in drill mode, a DrillViewController is being *presented* by the RootViewController, meaning that the DrillViewController's interface takes over the screen automatically: the DrillView-Controller's view, with its whole subview hierarchy, replaces the RootViewController's view and *its* whole subview hierarchy (Figure 6-6). The RootViewController and its hierarchy of child view controllers remains in place, but the corresponding view hierarchy is not in the interface; it will be returned to the interface automatically when we leave drill mode (because the presented DrillViewController is dismissed), and the situation will look like Figure 6-4 once again.

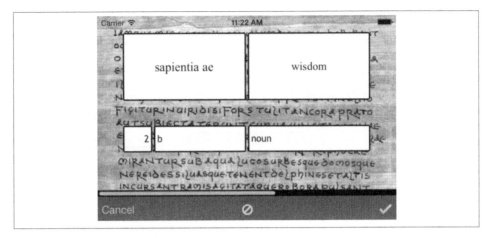

Figure 6-5. The Latin flashcard app, in drill mode

For any app that you write, you should be able to construct a diagram showing the hierarchy of view controllers and charting how each view controller's view fits into the view hierarchy. The diagram should be similar to mine! The view hierarchy should run neatly parallel with the view controller hierarchy; there should be no crossed wires or orphan views. And every view controller's view should be placed automatically into the view hierarchy, unless you have written your own parent view controller.

 Do *not* put a view controller's view into the interface manually, unless one of the following is the case:

- The view controller is the child of your custom parent view controller. There is a complicated parent–child dance you have to do. See "Container View Controllers" on page 315.
- You're doing a custom transition animation. See "Custom Transition Animations" on page 290.

View Controller Creation

A view controller is an instance like any other instance, and it is created like any other instance — by instantiating its class. You might perform this instantiation in code; in that case, you will of course have to initialize the instance properly as you create it. Here's an example from one of my own apps:

```
LessonListController* llc =
    [[LessonListController alloc] initWithTerms: self.data];
UINavigationController* nav =
    [[UINavigationController alloc] initWithRootViewController:llc];
```

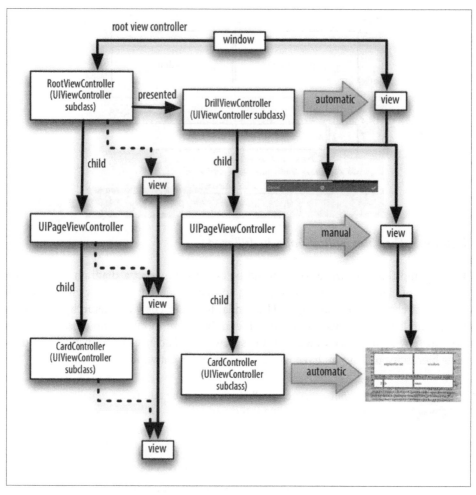

Figure 6-6. The Latin flashcard app's drill mode view controller and view hierarchy

In that example, LessonListController is my own UIViewController subclass, so I have called its designated initializer, which I myself have defined; UINavigationController is a built-in UIViewController subclass, and I have used one of its convenience initializers.

Alternatively, a view controller instance might come into existence through the loading of a nib. To make it possible to get a view controller into the nib in the first place, view controllers are included among the object types available through the Object library in the nib editor.

It is legal, though in practice not common, for a *.xib* file to contain a view controller. A *.storyboard* file, on the other hand, is chock full of view controllers; view controllers are the basis of a storyboard's structure, with each scene consisting of one top-level view controller object. A view controller in a storyboard will go into a nib file in the built app, and that nib file will be loaded when the view controller instance is needed.

A nib file that comes from a storyboard is typically loaded automatically. If the nib file contains a view controller, this will happen under two primary circumstances:

- This nib file contains the storyboard's *initial view controller*, and the app is currently launching.
- This nib file contains a view controller that is the *destination of a segue*, and that segue is being performed.

Nevertheless, despite this automatic behavior of the storyboard mechanism, a view controller in a storyboard is an ordinary nib object and, if it is to be used in the running app, will be instantiated through the loading of the nib just like any other nib object. I'll give full details on how a view controller is instantiated from a storyboard later in this chapter.

Once a view controller comes into existence, it must be retained so that it will persist. This will happen automatically when the view controller is assigned a place in the view controller hierarchy that I described in the previous section. A view controller assigned as a window's `rootViewController` is retained by the window. A view controller assigned as another view controller's child is retained by that other view controller (the parent). A presented view controller is retained by the presenting view controller. The parent view controller or presenting view controller then takes ownership, and will release the other view controller in good order when it is no longer needed.

Here's an example, from one of my apps, of view controllers being instantiated and then being retained by being placed into the view controller hierarchy:

```
LessonListController* llc =
    [[LessonListController alloc] initWithTerms: self.data];
UINavigationController* nav =
    [[UINavigationController alloc] initWithRootViewController:llc];
[self presentViewController:nav animated:YES completion:nil];
```

That's the same code I showed a moment ago, extended by one line. It comes from a view controller class called RootViewController. In the first line, I instantiate Lesson-ListController. In the second line, I instantiate UINavigationController, and I assign the LessonListController instance to the UINavigationController instance as its child; the UINavigationController retains and takes ownership of the LessonListController instance. In the third line, I present the UINavigationController instance on `self`, a RootViewController instance; the RootViewController instance is the presenting view controller, and it retains and takes ownership of the UINavigationController instance. The RootViewController instance itself is the window's `rootViewController`, and so the view controller hierarchy is safely established.

View controllers can be used in other ways, and you must take care to perform correct memory management in those situations as well. For example, passing a view controller as the argument to UIPopoverController's `initWithContentViewController:` causes the UIPopoverController instance to retain the view controller instance, but there is then the problem of who will retain the UIPopoverController — this will cause much gnashing of teeth in Chapter 9.

All of this sounds straightforward, but it is worth dwelling on, because things can go wrong. It is quite possible, if things are mismanaged, for a view controller's view to get into the interface while the view controller itself is allowed to go out of existence. *This must not be permitted.* If it does, at the very least the view will apparently misbehave, failing to perform its intended functionality, because that functionality is embodied by the view controller, which no longer exists. (I've made this mistake, so I speak from experience here.) If you instantiate a view controller in code, you should immediately ask yourself who will be retaining this view controller.

If a view controller is instantiated automatically from a storyboard, on the other hand, it will be retained automatically. That isn't magic, however; it's done in exactly the same ways I just listed — by assigning it as the window's `rootViewController`, or by making it another view controller's child view controller or presented view controller.

How a View Controller Gets Its View

Initially, when it first comes into existence, a view controller has no view. A view controller is a small, lightweight object; a view is a relatively heavyweight object, involving interface elements that occupy memory. Therefore, a view controller postpones obtaining its view until it has to do so, namely, when it is asked for the value of its `view` property. At that moment, if its `view` property is nil, the view controller sets about obtaining its view. (We say that a view controller loads its view *lazily*.) Typically, this happens because it is time to put the view controller's view into the interface.

In working with a newly instantiated view controller, be careful not to refer to its `view` property if you don't need to, since this will trigger the view controller's obtaining its view prematurely. To learn whether a view controller has a view without causing it to load its view, call `isViewLoaded`. (As usual, I speak from experience here. I once made the mistake of mentioning a UIViewController's `view` in its `awakeFromNib` and caused the view to be loaded twice.)

As soon as a view controller has its view, its `viewDidLoad` method is called. If this view controller is an instance of your own UIViewController subclass, `viewDidLoad` is your opportunity to modify the contents of this view — to populate it with subviews, to tweak the subviews it already has, and so forth — as well as to perform other initializations of the view controller consonant with its acquisition of a view. The `view` property is now pointing to the view, so it is safe to refer to `self.view`. Bear in mind, however, that the view may not yet be part of the interface! In fact, it almost certainly is not; self.view.window will be nil. Thus, for example, you cannot rely on the *dimensions* of the view at this point to be the dimensions that the view will assume when it becomes visible in the interface. Performing certain customizations prematurely in viewDid-Load is a common beginner mistake. I'll have more to say about this later in the chapter.

Before viewDidLoad will be called, however, the view controller must obtain its view. The question of where and how the view controller will get its view is often crucial. In some cases, to be sure, you won't care about this; in particular, when a view controller is an instance of a built-in UIViewController subclass such as UINavigationController or UITabBarController, its view is out of your hands — you might never even have cause to refer to it over the entire course of your app's lifetime — and you simply trust that the view controller will somehow generate its view. But when the view controller is of your own subclass of UIViewController, and when you yourself will design or modify its view, it becomes essential to understand the process whereby a view controller gets its view.

This process is not difficult to understand, but it is rather elaborate, because there are multiple possibilities. Most important, this process is *not magic*. Yet it quite possibly causes more confusion to beginners than any other matter connected with iOS programming. Therefore, I will explain it in detail. The more you know about the details of how a view controller gets its view, the deeper and clearer will be your understanding of the entire workings of your app, its view controllers, its *storyboard* and *xib* files, and so on.

The alternatives are as follows:

- The view may be created in the view controller's own code, manually.
- The view may be created as an empty generic view, automatically.
- The view may be created in its own separate nib.
- The view may be created in a nib, which is the same nib from which the view controller itself is instantiated.

Manual View

To supply a UIViewController's view manually, in code, implement its loadView method. Your job here is to obtain an instance of UIView (or a subclass of UIView) and *assign it to self.view*. You must *not* call super (for reasons that I'll make clear later on).

 Do not confuse loadView with viewDidLoad. Yes, I've made this mistake myself. I confess! loadView creates the view; viewDidLoad is called afterward.

Let's try it. Start with a project made (with Use Core Data *unchecked*, of course) from the Empty Application project template (not the Single View Application template; our purpose here is to generate the entire interface in code, ourselves):

1. We need a UIViewController subclass, so choose File → New → File; specify an iOS Cocoa Touch Objective-C class. Click Next.

2. Name the class RootViewController, and specify that it is to be a UIViewController subclass. *Uncheck* the XIB checkbox. Click Next.

3. Confirm that we're saving into the appropriate folder and group, and that these files will be part of the app target. Click Create.

We now have a RootViewController class, and we proceed to edit its code. In *Root-ViewController.m*, we'll implement `loadView`. To convince ourselves that the example is working correctly, we'll give the view an identifiable color, and we'll put some interface inside it, namely a "Hello, World" label:

```
- (void) loadView {
    UIView* v = [UIView new];
    v.backgroundColor = [UIColor greenColor];
    self.view = v;
    UILabel* label = [UILabel new];
    [v addSubview:label];
    label.text = @"Hello, World!";
    label.autoresizingMask = (
                            UIViewAutoresizingFlexibleTopMargin |
                            UIViewAutoresizingFlexibleLeftMargin |
                            UIViewAutoresizingFlexibleBottomMargin |
                            UIViewAutoresizingFlexibleRightMargin
                            );
    [label sizeToFit];
    label.center = CGPointMake(CGRectGetMidX(v.bounds),
                            CGRectGetMidY(v.bounds));
    label.frame = CGRectIntegral(label.frame);
}
```

We have not yet given a RootViewController instance a place in our view controller hierarchy — in fact, we have no RootViewController instance (and no view controller hierarchy). Let's make one. To do so, we turn to *AppDelegate.m*. (It's a little frustrating having to set things up in two different places before our labors can bear any visible fruit, but such is life.)

In *AppDelegate.m*, add the line `#import "RootViewController.h"` at the start, so that our code can speak of the RootViewController class. Then modify the implementation of `application:didFinishLaunchingWithOptions:` (Appendix A) to create a Root-ViewController instance and make it the window's `rootViewController`. Observe that we must do this *after* our `window` property actually has a UIWindow as its value! That's why the template's comment, "Override point for customization after application launch," comes *after* the line that creates the UIWindow:

```
self.window = [[UIWindow alloc] initWithFrame:[[UIScreen mainScreen] bounds]];
// Override point for customization after application launch.
RootViewController* theRVC = [RootViewController new];
self.window.rootViewController = theRVC;
// ... and the rest is as in the template
```

Build and run the app. Sure enough, there's our green background and our "Hello, world" label!

We have proved that we can create a view controller and get its view into the interface. But perhaps you're not persuaded that the view controller is *managing* that view in an interesting way. To prove this, let's rotate our interface. While our app is running in the simulator, choose Hardware → Rotate Left or Hardware → Rotate Right. Observe that both the app, as indicated by the orientation of the status bar, and the view, as indicated by the orientation of the "Hello, World" label, automatically rotate to compensate; that's the work of the view controller. We were careful to give the label an appropriate `autoresizingMask`, to keep it centered in the view even when the view's bounds are changed to fit the rotated window.

When we created our view controller's view (`self.view`), we never gave it a reasonable frame. This is because we are relying on someone else to frame the view appropriately. In this case, the "someone else" is the window, which responds to having its `rootView-Controller` property set to a view controller by framing the view controller's view appropriately as the root view before putting it into the window as a subview. In general, it is the responsibility of whoever puts a view controller's view into the interface to give the view the correct frame — and this will never be the view controller itself. Indeed, the size of a view controller's view may be changed as it is placed into the interface, and you must keep in mind, as you design your view controller's view and its subviews, the possibility that this will happen.

Generic Automatic View

We should distinguish between creating a view and populating it. The preceding example fails to draw this distinction. The lines that create our RootViewController's view are merely these:

```
UIView* v = [UIView new];
self.view = v;
```

Everything else configures and populates the view, turning it green and putting a label in it. A more appropriate place to populate a view controller's view is in its `viewDid-Load` implementation, which, as I've already mentioned, is called after the view exists (so that it can be referred to as `self.view`). We could therefore rewrite the preceding example like this:

```
- (void) loadView {
    UIView* v = [UIView new];
    self.view = v;
}
- (void)viewDidLoad {
    [super viewDidLoad];
    UIView* v = self.view;
    v.backgroundColor = [UIColor greenColor];
    UILabel* label = [UILabel new];
    [v addSubview:label];
    label.text = @"Hello, World!";
    label.autoresizingMask = (
                              UIViewAutoresizingFlexibleTopMargin |
                              UIViewAutoresizingFlexibleLeftMargin |
                              UIViewAutoresizingFlexibleBottomMargin |
                              UIViewAutoresizingFlexibleRightMargin
                              );
    [label sizeToFit];
    label.center = CGPointMake(CGRectGetMidX(v.bounds),
                               CGRectGetMidY(v.bounds));
    label.frame = CGRectIntegral(label.frame);
}
```

But if we're going to do that, we can go even further and remove our implementation of loadView altogether! If you don't implement loadView, and if no view is supplied in any other way, then UIViewController's implementation of loadView will do exactly what we are already doing in code: it creates a generic UIView object and assigns it to self.view. If we needed our view controller's view to be a particular UIView subclass, that wouldn't be acceptable; but in this case, our view controller's view *is* a generic UIView object, so it *is* acceptable. Comment out or delete the entire loadView implementation from the preceding code, and build and run the app; our example still works!

View in a Separate Nib

A view controller's view can be supplied from a nib file. This approach gives you the convenience of configuring and populating the view by designing it graphically in the nib editor interface.

When the nib loads, the view controller instance will already have been created, and it will serve as the nib's owner. The view controller has a view property; the view controller's representative in the nib has a view outlet, which must point to the view object in the nib. Thus, when the nib loads, the view controller obtains its view through the nib-loading mechanism.

I'll illustrate by modifying the preceding example to use a *.xib* file. (I'll deal later with the use of a *.storyboard* file; knowing first how the process works for a *.xib* file will greatly enhance your understanding of how it works for a *.storyboard* file.)

In a *.xib* file, the owner's representative is the File's Owner proxy object. Therefore, a *.xib* file that is to serve as the source of a view controller's view must be a *.xib* file in which the following two things are true:

- The File's Owner class must be set to a UIViewController subclass (depending on the class of the view controller whose view this will be).
- The File's Owner proxy now has a `view` outlet, corresponding to a UIViewController's `view` property. This outlet must be connected to the view.

Let's try it. We begin with the example we've already developed, with our RootViewController class. Delete the implementation of `loadView` and `viewDidLoad` from *RootViewController.m*, because we want the view to come from a nib and we're going to populate it in the nib. Then:

1. Choose File → New → File and specify an iOS User Interface View document. This will be a *.xib* file containing a UIView object. Click Next.
2. In the Device Family pop-up menu, choose iPhone. Click Next.
3. Name the file *MyNib* (or *MyNib.xib*). Confirm the appropriate folder and group, and make very sure that the file will be part of the app target. Click Create.
4. Edit *MyNib.xib*. Prepare it in the way I described a moment ago:
   a. Set the File's Owner class to RootViewController (in the Identity inspector).
   b. Connect the File's Owner `view` outlet to the View object.
5. Design the view. To make it clear that this is not the same view we were creating previously, perhaps you should give the view a red background color (in the Attributes inspector). Drag a UILabel into the middle of the view and give it some text, such as "Hello, World!"

We have designed the nib, but we have done nothing as yet to associate this nib with our RootViewController instance. To do so, we must once again return to *AppDelegate.m*, where we create our RootViewController instance:

```
RootViewController* theRVC = [RootViewController new];
self.window.rootViewController = theRVC;
```

We need to modify this code so that our RootViewController instance, `theRVC`, is aware of this nib file, *MyNib.xib*, as its own nib file. That way, when `theRVC` needs to acquire its view, it will load that nib file with itself as owner, thus ending up with the correct view as its own `view` property. A UIViewController has a `nibName` property for this purpose. However, we are not allowed to set its `nibName` directly (it is read-only). Instead, as we instantiate the view controller, we must use the designated initializer, `initWithNibName:bundle:`, like this:

```
RootViewController* theRVC =
    [[RootViewController alloc] initWithNibName:@"MyNib" bundle:nil];
self.window.rootViewController = theRVC;
```

(The nil argument to the `bundle:` parameter specifies the main bundle, which is almost always what you want.)

To prove that this works, build and run. The red background appears! Our view is loading from the nib.

Now I'm going to show you a shortcut based on the name of the nib. It turns out that if the nib name passed to `initWithNibName:bundle:` is nil, a nib will be sought automatically *with the same name as the view controller's class*. Moreover, UIViewController's `init` calls `initWithNibName:bundle:`, passing nil for both arguments. This means, in effect, that we can return to using `new` (or `init`) to initialize the view controller, provided that the nib file has a name that matches the name of the view controller class.

Let's try it. Rename *MyNib.xib* to *RootViewController.xib*, and change the code that instantiates and initializes our RootViewController back to what it was before, like this:

```
RootViewController* theRVC = [RootViewController new];
self.window.rootViewController = theRVC;
```

Build and run. The project still works!

There's an additional aspect to this shortcut based on the name of the nib. It seems ridiculous that we should end up with a nib that has "Controller" in its name merely because our view controller, as is so often the case, has "Controller" in *its* name. A nib, after all, is not a controller. It turns out that the runtime, in looking for a view controller's corresponding nib, will in fact try stripping "Controller" off the end of the view controller class's name. (This feature is undocumented, but it works reliably and I can't believe it would ever be retracted.) Thus, we can name our nib file *RootView.xib* instead of *RootViewController.xib*, and it will *still* be properly associated with our RootViewController instance when we initialize that instance using `init` (or `new`).

When you create the files for a UIViewController subclass, the Xcode dialog has a XIB checkbox (which we unchecked earlier) offering to create an eponymous *.xib* file at the same time. If you accept that option, the nib is created with the File's Owner's class already set to the view controller's class and with its `view` outlet already hooked up to the view. This automatically created *.xib* file does *not* have "Controller" stripped off the end of its name; you can rename it manually later (I generally do) if the default name bothers you.

Another convention involving the nib name has to do with the rules for loading resources by name generally. I mentioned in Chapter 2 that when an image file is sought by calling `imageNamed:` or `pathForResource:ofType:`, an image file with the specified name but extended by the suffix `~ipad` will be used, if there is one, when the app runs on an iPad. The same rule applies to nib files. So, for example, a nib file named

RootViewController~ipad.xib will be loaded on an iPad when a nib named @"RootView-Controller" is sought, regardless of whether it is specified explicitly (as the first argument to initWithNibName:bundle:) or implicitly (because the view controller class is RootViewController, and the first argument to initWithNibName:bundle: is nil). This principle can greatly simplify your life when you're writing a universal app.

Finally, let's be specific about the place of this way of obtaining a view controller's view among the other of ways of obtaining it:

1. When the view controller first decides that it needs its view, loadView is *always* called.

2. If we override loadView, we supply and set the view in code, and we do *not* call super. Therefore the process of seeking a view comes to an end.

3. If we *don't* override loadView, UIViewController's built-in default implementation of loadView is used. It is this default implementation of loadView that loads the view controller's associated nib (the one specified by its nibName, or, if that's nil, the one whose name matches the name of the view controller's class).

   That, indeed, is why, if we do override loadView, we must *not* call super — that would cause us to get *both* behaviors!

4. If the previous steps all fail — we don't override loadView, and there is no associated nib — UIViewController's default implementation of loadView proceeds to create a generic UIView as discussed in the previous section.

 It follows from what I've just said if a view controller's view is to come from a nib, you should *not* implement loadView. Once again, I've made this mistake. The results were not pretty.

Nib-Instantiated View Controller

As I mentioned earlier, a view controller can be a nib object, to be instantiated through the loading of the nib. In the nib editor, the Object library contains a View Controller (UIViewController) as well as several built-in UIViewController subclasses. Any of these can be dragged into the nib. This is the standard way of creating a scene in a *.storyboard* file; it can also be used with a *.xib* file, but this is rarely done.

When a view controller has been instantiated from a nib, and when it comes eventually to obtain its view, all the ways I've already described whereby a view controller can obtain its view still apply.

If you'd like to try it, start over with a new project from the Empty Application template, and give it a *.xib* file containing a view controller, as follows:

1. Choose File → New → File and ask for an iOS User Interface Empty document. Press Next.

2. Set the device family to iPhone. Press Next.

3. Name the new file *Main.xib*, make sure it's being saved into the right place and that it is part of the app target, and click Create.

4. Edit *Main.xib*. Drag a plain vanilla View Controller object into the canvas.

In *AppDelegate.m*, we must now arrange to load *Main.xib* and extract the view controller instance created from the nib object we just put into the nib, making that view controller our app's root view controller. Here's one very simple way to do that:

```
NSArray* arr =
    [[UINib nibWithNibName:@"Main" bundle:nil]
        instantiateWithOwner:nil options:nil];
self.window.rootViewController = arr[0];
```

You can now proceed, if you like, to experiment with various ways of helping this view controller get its view. At the moment it is a plain UIViewController instance. Let's make it a class of our own:

1. Give the project a RootViewController class (a UIViewController subclass).

2. In *Main.xib*, select the view controller object and use its Identity inspector to set its class to RootViewController.

Now you can implement `loadView` in RootViewController, or implement `viewDid-Load` but not `loadView`. Alternatively, you can add another nib called *RootView-Controller.xib* (or *RootView.xib*) and configure it properly, and sure enough, the view controller instantiated from *Main.xib* will find that nib, load it, and get its view from it. There is also a way to specify *in the nib editor* the name of the nib that this view controller should use to find its nib: select the view controller in its nib, and enter the name of the view's nib in the NIB Name field in its Attributes inspector. (This is the equivalent of specifying a nib name when you call `initWithNibName:bundle:`).

When a nib contains a view controller, there is *an additional way* for it to obtain its view: provide the view *in the same nib* as the view controller. In fact, using the nib editor we can design the interface *in the view controller itself*. You've probably noticed that the view controller, as portrayed in the canvas in the nib editor, is represented by a rectangle the size of an iPhone screen, even though a view controller is not a view. This is intended to accommodate the view controller's view!

Let's try it:

1. If you've been experimenting with the code in *RootViewController.m*, remove any implementation of `loadView` or `viewDidLoad` from it.

2. In *Main.xib*, find the plain vanilla View object in the Object library and drag it *into the view controller object* in the canvas. This view object automatically becomes this view controller's view, and is drawn inside it in the canvas. Thus, you can now add further interface objects to this view.

Build and run. The interface you designed inside the view object inside the view controller object in *Main.xib* appears in the running app. (This way of supplying a view controller's view takes priority over looking for the view in another nib, so if you also created a *RootViewController.xib* or *RootView.xib* as the source of this view controller's view, it is ignored.)

 Like any other nib object, when a view controller is instantiated from a nib, its designated initializer in *your* code (initWithNib-Name:bundle:) is *not* called. If your UIViewController subclass code needs access to the view controller instance very early in its lifetime, it can override initWithCoder: or awakeFromNib.

Storyboard-Instantiated View Controller

If you've ever used a storyboard, it will not have escaped your attention that what we constructed in *Main.xib*, in the previous section — a view controller directly containing its view — looks a lot like a scene in a storyboard. That's because, by default, this *is* the structure of a scene in a storyboard.

Each scene in a *.storyboard* file is rather like a *.xib* file containing a view controller nib object. Each scene's view controller is instantiated only when needed; the underlying mechanism is that each scene's view controller (or the view controllers of multiple scenes with a parent–child relationship) is stored in a nib file in the built app, inside the *.storyboardc* bundle, and this nib file is loaded on demand and the view controller is instantiated from it, as we did in the previous section.

Moreover, by default, the view controller in a scene in a *.storyboard* file comes equipped with a view, which appears inside it in the canvas. You design the view and its subviews in the nib editor. When the app is built, each view controller's view goes into *a separate nib file*, inside the *.storyboardc* bundle, and the view controller, once instantiated, loads its view from that nib file lazily, exactly as we did earlier.

In this way, a storyboard embodies the very same mechanisms we've already explored through *.xib* files. Even though a storyboard may appear, in the nib editor, to contain many view controllers and their main views, each view controller and each main view is loaded from its own nib in the running app, on demand, when needed, just as if we had configured the project with multiple *.xib* files. Thus a storyboard combines the memory management advantages of *.xib* files, which are not loaded until they're needed, and can be loaded multiple times to give additional instances of the same nib objects, with the convenience of your being able to see and edit a lot of your app's interface simultaneously in one place.

Furthermore, you don't *have* to use the default scene structure in a storyboard. The default is that a view controller in a storyboard contains its view — *but you can delete it*. If you do, then that view controller will obtain its view in any of the *other* ways we've already discussed: by an implementation of loadView in the code of that view controller class, or by loading a nib file that comes from a *.xib* with the same name as this view controller's class, or even (if all of that fails) by creating a generic UIView.

(However, there's no way in a *.storyboard* file to specify as the source of a view controller's view a *.xib* file with a different name from the view controller's class. The nib editor lacks the NIB Name field in a view controller's Attributes inspector when you're working in a storyboard.)

The Xcode 5 app templates (with the exception of the Empty Application template) start with a single main storyboard called *Main.storyboard*, which is designated the app's main storyboard by the *Info.plist* key "Main storyboard file base name" (UIMain-StoryboardFile). Therefore, as the app launches, UIApplicationMain gets a reference to this storyboard (by calling storyboardWithName:bundle:), instantiates its initial view controller (by calling instantiateInitialViewController), and makes that instance the window's rootViewController. If you edit the storyboard to contain segues, then when one of those segues is performed — which can be configured to happen automatically in response to the user tapping an interface object — the destination view controller is automatically instantiated. In this way it is perfectly possible for a single storyboard to be the source of every view controller that your app will ever instantiate, and for all of that instantiation to take place automatically.

That's convenient for beginners, but it can also be restrictive. You might have a feeling that your app *must* have a main storyboard, and that every view controller *must* be instantiated from it automatically. That's not the case. It is possible to use storyboards in a much more agile, intentional way, much as one would use *.xib* files. For example, your app can have multiple storyboards. Why might that be useful? Well, since autolayout is configured at the file level — either an entire *.storyboard* file uses autolayout or none of it does — multiple storyboards constitute a very good way to use autolayout selectively in only certain areas of your interface. Or you might use an ancillary storyboard as a source of just one view controller, a more convenient and memory-efficient way to do what we did with a view controller in a *.xib* file earlier.

I'll summarize the ways in which a view controller can be instantiated from a storyboard. You can get a reference to a storyboard either by calling the UIStoryboard class method storyboardWithName:bundle: or through the storyboard property of a view controller that has already been instantiated from that storyboard. With a storyboard instance in hand, a view controller can be instantiated from that storyboard in one of four ways:

- At most one view controller in the storyboard is designated the storyboard's *initial view controller*. To instantiate that view controller, call `instantiateInitialViewController`. The instance is returned.

- A view controller in a storyboard can be assigned an arbitrary string identifier; this is its Storyboard ID in the Identity inspector. To instantiate that view controller, call `instantiateViewControllerWithIdentifier:`. The instance is returned.

- A parent view controller in a storyboard may have immediate children, such as a UINavigationController and its initial child view controller. The nib editor will show a *relationship* connection between them. When the parent is instantiated (the source of the relationship), the initial children (the destination of the relationship) are instantiated automatically.

- A view controller in a storyboard may be (or contain) the source of a *segue* whose destination is a *future* child view controller or a *future* presented view controller. When the segue is triggered and performed, it instantiates the new view controller.

I'll go into much greater detail about storyboards and segues later in this chapter.

View Resizing and the Status Bar

As I've already mentioned, a view controller's main view may be resized as it is placed into the interface, in order to fit into that interface correctly. You will want to design your main view so as to accommodate such resizing. The same view may end up at different sizes under different circumstances:

- An app's interface may be rotated to compensate for device rotation, effectively swapping its height and width measurements. (I'll discuss rotation in detail in the next section.)

- An iPhone app may run on a device with either of two screen heights — 480 points or 568 points.

- Some built-in parent view controllers may resize a child view controller's main view differently depending on what other views are present. In particular:

  — A navigation controller (UINavigationController) may resize a child view controller's view differently depending on whether it (the navigation controller) is also displaying a navigation bar at the top or a toolbar at the bottom (or both).

  — A tab bar controller (UITabBarController) may resize a child view controller's view to accommodate the tab bar at the bottom.

- An app may be capable of running on multiple systems; the rules for how main views are automatically resized are different in iOS 7 than in iOS 6 and before.

In the nib editor, the size at which a view controller's main view is shown may not be the size it will end up at when the app runs and the view is placed into the interface. On the other hand, the nib editor gives you tools to simulate a variety of specific sizes that your view may assume:

- The Attributes inspector contains five Simulated Metrics pop-up menus letting you set the view's display size to match the taller or shorter iPhone screen, the rotation of the app, and the presence of top bars and bottom bars. In a *.storyboard* file, this is the Attributes inspector for a view controller; in a *.xib* file, it appears also for a top-level view (since this might be intended as a view controller's main view).

- New in Xcode 5, when you summon an assistant pane, if the main editor pane is the nib editor, you can switch the assistant pane to Preview mode (through the Tracking menu, the first component in the assistant pane's jump bar, Control-4). Buttons at the lower right let you toggle between "iOS 7.0 and Later" vs. "iOS 6.1 and Earlier", between portrait and landscape orientation, and between the taller and shorter iPhone screen.

These, however, are merely ways of experimenting with *possible* ultimate sizes that your view *may* assume. The size at which a view controller's main view is portrayed in the nib has *no effect on the size it will assume at runtime*. The only way to discover the view's true size at runtime is to run the app.

In iOS 7, the rules have changed, in comparison to earlier systems, for how a view controller's view is resized to fit the screen as a whole (when, for example, it is the root view controller's view) or to fit into a navigation controller's view or a tab bar controller's view:

The status bar is transparent

The iOS 7 status bar is transparent, so that the region of a view behind it is visible through it. The root view, and any other fullscreen view such as a presented view controller's view, occupies the *entire window*, including the status bar area, the top 20 pixels of the view being visible behind the transparent status bar. You'll want to design your view so that its top doesn't contain any interface objects that will be overlapped by the status bar.

(In iOS 6 and before, the status bar was usually opaque, and a view was usually sized smaller than the screen, so that the status bar would not overlap it, by setting its frame to [UIScreen mainScreen].applicationFrame. Alternatively, a view controller's view could be fullscreen, and this was desirable in cases where the status bar was translucent or hidden, but you had to take explicit steps to achieve this result, such as setting the view controller's wantsFullScreenLayout to YES. In iOS 7, wantsFullScreenLayout is deprecated, and *all* apps are fullscreen apps.)

Top and bottom bars may be underlapped

In iOS 7, top and bottom bars (navigation bar, tab bar, toolbar) can be translucent. When they are, the main view displayed within the view of a navigation controller or tab bar controller, by default, is extended behind the translucent bar, underlapping it. (In iOS 6, this *never* happened; the top of the view was the bottom of the top bar, and bottom of the view was the top of the bottom bar.)

You can change this behavior for your UIViewController whose parent is a navigation controller or tab bar controller using two UIViewController properties:

edgesForExtendedLayout

A UIRectEdge. The default is UIRectEdgeAll, meaning that this view controller's view will underlap a translucent top bar or a translucent bottom bar. The other extreme is UIRectEdgeNone, meaning that this view controller's view won't underlap top and bottom bars, just as on iOS 6 and before. Other possibilities are UIRectEdgeTop (underlap top bars only) and UIRectEdgeBottom (underlap bottom bars only).

Note that edgesForExtendedLayout has *nothing to do with the status bar*. On iOS 7, the status bar is transparent, all apps are fullscreen apps, and that's that; you can't change this behavior.

extendedLayoutIncludesOpaqueBars

If YES, then if edgesForExtendedLayout permits underlapping of bars, those bars will be underlapped *even if they are opaque*. The default is NO, meaning that only translucent bars are underlapped.

 It is possible to set these two extendedLayout properties using the three Extend Edges checkboxes in a view controller's Attributes inspector. However, if there are already subviews in this view controller's main view, changing the checkboxes may cause those subviews to be repositioned unpredictably. I recommend changing these properties in code instead; a view controller's viewDidLoad is a good place.

If you're using autolayout, a view controller can help you position subviews within its main view in a way that compensates for changes in the size of the view. The view controller supplies two properties, its topLayoutGuide and its bottomLayoutGuide, to which you can form constraints. Typically, you'll pin a view by its top to the topLayoutGuide, or you'll pin a view by its bottom to the bottomLayoutGuide. The position of these guide objects moves automatically at runtime to reflect the view's environment:

`topLayoutGuide`

The `topLayoutGuide` is positioned as follows:

- If there is a status bar and no top bar, the `topLayoutGuide` is positioned at the bottom of the status bar.
- If there is a top bar, the `topLayoutGuide` is positioned at the bottom of the top bar.
- If there is no top bar and no status bar, the `topLayoutGuide` is positioned at the top of the view.

`bottomLayoutGuide`

The `bottomLayoutGuide` is positioned as follows:

- If there is a bottom bar, the `bottomLayoutGuide` is positioned at the top of the bottom bar.
- If there is no bottom bar, the `bottomLayoutGuide` is positioned at the bottom of the view.

Thus, by pinning your subviews to the guides, you can achieve consistent results, regardless of whether or not the main view underlaps a bar (and regardless of whether or not the status bar is present).

You can create constraints involving the `topLayoutGuide` and the `bottomLayoutGuide` in the nib editor or in code:

- In the nib editor, if a view controller is a nib object (not a proxy object), it has Top Layout Guide and Bottom Layout Guide objects in the document outline, and you can control-drag to form constraints to them. In fact, if a view is the main view inside a view controller in the nib, you can't form a constraint between a subview and the top or bottom of the main view; you *must* form that constraint to the Top Layout Guide or the Bottom Layout Guide.
- In code, cast the view controller's `topLayoutGuide` or `bottomLayoutGuide` to a UI-View and use that UIView as you form a constraint, as I demonstrated in "Top and Bottom Layout Guides" on page 42.

A layout guide's distance from the corresponding edge of the view controller's main view is reported by its `length` property. Note that `viewDidLoad` is too early to obtain a meaningful value; the earliest coherent opportunity is probably `viewWillLayoutSubviews` (see on rotation and layout events, in the next section).

The job of determining the look of the status bar is also vested, by default, in view controllers — in the root view controller in the first instance. A view controller can override these methods:

Consistent Layout Across Systems

This book concentrates on iOS 7 and isn't concerned with backward compatibility, but the changes in how views are resized is the cause of much confusion. So here are some hints on how to lay out the subviews of a view controller's main view so as to achieve consistent results between iOS 6 and iOS 7.

If you're using autolayout and creating constraints in the nib editor, pin the top of a subview to the top layout guide (and possibly the bottom of a subview to the bottom layout guide) and lay everything else out in relation to those. If you create these constraints in the nib, they will work on iOS 6, even though iOS 6 has no top layout guide or bottom layout guide: on iOS 6, the guides are expressed as views with zero height at the top and bottom of the main view, so the outcome is the same as if you had pinned your subviews to the top or bottom of the main view — which, given the way the main view is resized on iOS 6, gives exactly the same result as the guides will give in iOS 7.

If you're using autolayout and creating constraints in code, use conditional code to pin to a layout guide in iOS 7 and to the top or bottom of the main view in iOS 6.

If you're not using autolayout and you're laying out subviews in the nib editor, use the iOS 6/7 Deltas settings to compensate for the difference in the resizing behavior of the earlier and later systems. Typically, this will mean setting a ΔY of -20, as I suggested in Chapter 1, to compensate for the fact that iOS 7 adds 20 pixels of height to the main view in order to underlap the status bar.

If you're not using autolayout and you're laying out subviews in code, you'll have to use conditional code to perform that same compensation.

Also, if you're not using autolayout, you can use conditional code on iOS 7 to set your view controller's `edgesForExtendedLayout` to `UIRectEdgeNone`, to make the resizing behavior of the view controller's view inside a navigation controller or tab bar controller's view the same on iOS 7 as on iOS 6 — namely, the view doesn't underlap top bars and bottom bars. (If you do this, though, you sacrifice the cool look of your view underlapping a transparent bar.)

`preferredStatusBarStyle`
> Your choices are `UIStatusBarStyleDefault` and `UIStatusBarStyleLight‐Content`, meaning dark text and light text, respectively. Use light text for legibility if the view content underlapping the status bar is dark.

`prefersStatusBarHidden`
> Return YES to make the status bar invisible.

`childViewControllerForStatusBarStyle`
`childViewControllerForStatusBarHidden`

> Used to delegate the decision on the status bar style or visibility to a child view controller's `preferredStatusBarStyle` or `prefersStatusBarHidden` instead of this view controller. For example, a navigation controller implements these methods to allow your view controller to decide the status bar style and visibility when its view becomes visible in the navigation controller's view.

You never call any of those methods yourself; they are called automatically when the view controller situation changes. If you want them to be called immediately, because they are not being called when you need them to be, or because the situation has changed and a call to one of them would now give a different answer, call the view controller instance method `setNeedsStatusBarAppearanceUpdate` on your view controller. If this call is inside an animation block, the animation of the change in the look of the status bar will have the specified duration, thus matching the other animations that are also taking place. The character of the animation from a visible to an invisible status bar (and *vice versa*) is set by your view controller's implementation of `preferredStatusBar-UpdateAnimation`; you can return one of these values:

- `UIStatusBarAnimationNone`
- `UIStatusBarAnimationFade`
- `UIStatusBarAnimationSlide`

This entire view controller–based mechanism for determining the look of the status bar is new in iOS 7. Previously, the status bar was controlled by calls to various UIApplication methods. If your app is to be backward-compatible with iOS 6 or before, you may want to opt out of the new mechanism and use the old UIApplication calls instead. To do so, set the *Info.plist* key "View controller–based status bar appearance" (`UIViewController-BasedStatusBarAppearance`) to NO. In that case, you can also hide the status bar initially by setting the *Info.plist* key "Status bar is initially hidden" (`UIStatusBarHidden`) to YES.

 When you toggle the visibility of the status bar, the top layout guide will move up or down by 20 points. If your main view has subviews with constraints to the top layout guide, those subviews will move. If this happens when the main view is visible, the user will *see* the subviews move (as a jump). This is probably not what you want.

The resizing of the view as it is placed into the interface takes place *after* `viewDidLoad`. For this reason, you should not use `viewDidLoad` to make any changes whose validity depends upon the final dimensions of the view. A better location for such changes is `viewWillAppear:` or `viewDidAppear:`; even better, perhaps (because they have to do with layout) are `viewWillLayoutSubviews` and `viewDidLayoutSubviews`. However, `viewDidLoad` has the advantage of being called only once during the lifetime of a view controller; the others can be called any number of times, so if you need to perform one-time initializations in any of them, use a BOOL instance variable flag to ensure that your code runs only the first time:

```
-(void) viewWillLayoutSubviews {
    if (!self.didSetup) {
        self.didSetup = YES;
        // ... perform one-time setup here ...
    }
}
```

 If you have older app code in which you were manually setting the frame of a view controller's view, in code, to `[[UIScreen mainScreen] applicationFrame]` in iOS 6 or before, do *not* do that in iOS 7. Delete that line, or use conditional code. In iOS 7, allow the runtime to resize your view controller's view automatically.

Rotation

A major part of a view controller's job is to know how to rotate the view. The user will experience this as rotation of the app itself: the top of the app shifts so that it is oriented against a different side of the device's display. There are two complementary uses for rotation:

Compensatory rotation
> The app rotates to compensate for the orientation of the device, so that the app appears right way up with respect to how the user is holding the device. The challenge of compensatory rotation stems, quite simply, from the fact that the screen is not square. This means that if the app rotates 90 degrees, the interface no longer fits the screen, and must be changed to compensate.

Forced rotation
> The app rotates when a particular view appears in the interface, or when the app launches, to indicate that the user needs to rotate the device in order to view the app the right way up. This is typically because the interface has been specifically designed, in the face of the fact that the screen is not square, to appear in one particular mode (portrait or landscape).

In the case of the iPhone, no law says that your app has to perform compensatory rotation. Most of my iPhone apps do not do so; indeed, I have no compunction about doing just the opposite, forcing the user to rotate the device differently depending on what view is being displayed. The iPhone is small and easily reoriented with a twist of the user's wrist, and it has a natural right way up, especially because it's a phone. (The iPod touch isn't a phone, but the same argument works by analogy.) On the other hand, Apple would prefer iPad apps to rotate to at least two opposed orientations (such as landscape with the button on the right and landscape with the button on the left), and preferably to all four possible orientations, so that the user isn't restricted in how the device is held.

It's fairly trivial to let your app rotate to two opposed orientations, because once the app is set up to work in one of them, it can work with no change in the other. But allowing a single interface to rotate between two orientations that are 90 degrees apart is trickier, because its dimensions must change — roughly speaking, its height and width are swapped — and this may require a change of layout and might even call for more substantial alterations, such as removal or addition of part of the interface. A good example is the behavior of Apple's Mail app on the iPad: in landscape mode, the master pane and the detail pane appear side by side, but in portrait mode, the master pane is removed and must be summoned as a temporary overlay on top of the detail pane.

In iOS 7 (and iOS 6), an app is free, by default, to perform compensatory rotation in response to the user's rotation of the device. For an iPhone app, this means that the app can appear with its top at the top of the device or either of the two sides of the device; having the app's top appear at the bottom of the device (because the device is held upside-down) is generally frowned on. For an iPad app, this means that the app can assume any orientation.

If this isn't what you want, it is up to you to prevent it, as follows:

- The app itself, in its *Info.plist*, may declare once and for all every orientation the interface will ever be permitted to assume. It does this under the "Supported interface orientations" key, `UISupportedInterfaceOrientations` (supplemented, for a universal app, by "Supported interface orientations (iPad)", `UISupportedInterface-Orientations~ipad`). You don't usually have to meddle directly with the *Info.plist* file, though; these keys are set through checkboxes when you edit the app target, in the General tab.

- The app delegate may implement `application:supportedInterface-OrientationsForWindow:`, returning a bitmask listing every orientation the interface is permitted to assume. This list *overrides* the *Info.plist* settings. Thus, the app delegate can do dynamically what the *Info.plist* can do only statically. `application:supportedInterfaceOrientationsForWindow:` is called at least once every time the device rotates.

- A view controller may implement `supportedInterfaceOrientations`, returning a bitmask listing a set of orientations that *intersects* the set of orientations permitted by the app or the app delegate. The resulting intersection will then be the set of permitted orientations. The resulting intersection must not be empty; if it is, your app will crash. `supportedInterfaceOrientations` is called at least once every time the device rotates.

The view controller has a second way to interfere with the app's permitted orientations: it can implement `shouldAutorotate`. This method returns a BOOL, and the default is YES. `shouldAutorotate` is called at least once every time the device rotates; if it returns NO, the interface will not rotate to compensate at this moment. This can be a simpler way than `supportedInterfaceOrientations` to veto the app's rotation. If `shouldAutorotate` is implemented and returns NO, `supportedInterfaceOrientations` is not called.

Only the view controller at the top of the visible view controller hierarchy is consulted — that is, the root view controller, or a view controller presented fullscreen by the root view controller. Built-in view controllers do not consult their children in response. Thus, if your view controller is, say, a child view controller of a UINavigationController, it has no say in how the app rotates. (This was a major change from iOS 5 to iOS 6, and is still the cause of much confusion, not to mention gnashing of teeth.)

A UIViewController class method `attemptRotationToDeviceOrientation` prompts the runtime to do immediately what it would do if the user were to rotate the device, namely to walk the three levels I've just described and, if the results permit rotation of the interface to match the current device orientation, to rotate the interface. This would be useful if, say, your view controller had returned NO from `shouldAutorotate`, so that the interface does not match the current device orientation, but is now for some reason prepared to return YES and wants to be asked again, immediately.

The bitmask you return from `application:supportedInterfaceOrientationsFor-Window:` or `supportedInterfaceOrientations` may be one of these values, or multiple values combined with bitwise-or:

- `UIInterfaceOrientationMaskPortrait`
- `UIInterfaceOrientationMaskLandscapeLeft`
- `UIInterfaceOrientationMaskLandscapeRight`
- `UIInterfaceOrientationMaskPortraitUpsideDown`
- `UIInterfaceOrientationMaskLandscape` (a convenient combination of `Left` and `Right`)
- `UIInterfaceOrientationMaskAll` (a convenient combination of `Portrait`, `UpsideDown`, `Left`, and `Right`)
- `UIInterfaceOrientationMaskAllButUpsideDown` (a convenient combination of `Portrait`, `Left`, and `Right`)

What Rotates?

We say that your app rotates, and you'll think of it as rotating, but what really rotates is the status bar's position. When the device rotates, a `UIDeviceOrientationDidChange-Notification` is emitted by the UIDevice, and if the app's interface is to rotate to match, the UIApplication instance is sent the `setStatusBarOrientation:animated:` message. A transform is applied so that the window's root view appears "right way up," and in a 90-degree rotation, the window's root view has its width and height dimensions swapped. Moreover, this is all accompanied by animation, so it really looks to the user as if the app is rotating. But the window *itself* doesn't budge; it remains pinned to the screen (window bounds are screen bounds). It is taller than it is wide, and its top is at the top of the device (away from the home button). As for the root view, its *bounds* are wider than tall in a landscape orientation, but its *frame* remains taller than wide (though you really shouldn't be referring to the root view's frame in this situation, because it has a transform applied; see Chapter 1).

If your code needs to know the current orientation of the device, it can ask the device, by calling [`UIDevice currentDevice`].`orientation`. Possible results are `UIDevice-OrientationUnknown`, `UIDeviceOrientationPortrait`, and so on. Convenience macros `UIDeviceOrientationIsPortrait` and `UIDeviceOrientationIsLandscape` let you test a given orientation for whether it falls into that category. By the time you get a rotation-related query event, the device's orientation has already changed.

The current orientation of the interface is available as a view controller's `interface-Orientation` property. Never ask for this value if the device's `orientation` is `UIDevice-OrientationUnknown`.

 The interface orientation *mask* values (`UIInterfaceOrientation-Mask...`) that you return from `application:supportedInterface-OrientationsForWindow:` or `supportedInterfaceOrientations` are not the same as the device orientation values used by UIDevice to report the current device orientation, or the interface orientation values used by UIViewController to report the current interface orientation. Do *not* return a device orientation or interface orientation value where an interface orientation *mask* value is expected!

Rotation and Layout Events

The resizing of your view controller's view when the app rotates 90 degrees is even more dramatic than the resizing that took place when it was inserted into the interface to begin with (discussed in the previous section). The view doesn't merely become taller or shorter in height; rather, its height and width bounds dimensions are effectively swapped. You will want to implement layout (Chapter 1) that can adapt to such a change. Autoresizing or autolayout can change the size and position of your view's subviews in response to the change in bounds size.

In some cases, however, this won't be sufficient; you may have to perform manual layout, perhaps even adding or removing views entirely. For example, as I've already mentioned, Apple's Mail app on the iPad eliminates the entire master view (the list of messages) when the app assumes a portrait orientation. The question is then when to perform this manual layout. I will demonstrate two possible approaches.

Your UIViewController subclass can override any of the following methods (which are called in the order shown) to be alerted in connection with interface rotation:

willRotateToInterfaceOrientation:duration:
> The first parameter is the new orientation; self.interfaceOrientation is the old orientation, and the view's bounds are the old bounds.

willAnimateRotationToInterfaceOrientation:duration:
> The first parameter is the new orientation; self.interfaceOrientation is the new orientation, and the view's bounds are the new bounds. The call is wrapped by an animation block, so changes to animatable view properties are animated.

didRotateFromInterfaceOrientation:
> The parameter is the old orientation; self.interfaceOrientation is the new orientation, and the view's bounds are the new bounds.

You might take advantage of these events to perform manual layout in response to interface rotation. Imagine, for example, that our app displays a black rectangle at the left side of the screen if the device is in landscape orientation, but not if the device is in portrait orientation. We could implement that as follows:

```
- (UIView*) blackRect { // property getter
    if (!self->_blackRect) {
        if (UIInterfaceOrientationIsPortrait(self.interfaceOrientation))
            return nil;
        CGRect f = self.view.bounds;
        f.size.width /= 3.0;
        f.origin.x = -f.size.width;
        UIView* br = [[UIView alloc] initWithFrame:f];
        br.backgroundColor = [UIColor blackColor];
        self.blackRect = br;
    }
    return self->_blackRect;
}
-(void)willAnimateRotationToInterfaceOrientation:(UIInterfaceOrientation)io
                                        duration:(NSTimeInterval)duration {
    UIView* v = self.blackRect;
    if (UIInterfaceOrientationIsLandscape(io)) {
        if (!v.superview) {
```

```
                [self.view addSubview:v];
                CGRect f = v.frame;
                f.origin.x = 0;
                v.frame = f;
            }
        } else {
            if (v.superview) {
                CGRect f = v.frame;
                f.origin.x -= f.size.width;
                v.frame = f;
            }
        }
    }
}
- (void) didRotateFromInterfaceOrientation:(UIInterfaceOrientation)io {
    if (UIInterfaceOrientationIsPortrait(self.interfaceOrientation))
        [self.blackRect removeFromSuperview];
}
```

We have a UIView property, blackRect, to retain the black rectangle; we implement its
getter to create the black rectangle if it hasn't been created already, but only if we are in
landscape orientation, since otherwise we cannot set the rectangle's dimensions
properly. The implementation of willAnimateRotationToInterfaceOrientation:
duration: slides the black rectangle in from the left as part of the rotation animation
if we have ended up in a landscape orientation, but only if it isn't in the interface already;
after all, the user might rotate the device 180 degrees, from one landscape orientation
to the other. Similarly, it slides the black rectangle out to the left if we have ended up in
a portrait orientation, but only if it *is* in the interface already. Finally, didRotateFrom-
InterfaceOrientation:, called after the rotation animation is over, makes sure the
rectangle is removed from its superview if we have ended up in a portrait orientation.

However, there's another way that I think is better. Recall from Chapter 1 that when a
view's bounds change, it is asked to update its constraints (if necessary) with a call to
updateConstraints, and then to perform layout with a call to layoutSubviews. It turns
out that if this is a view controller's view, the view controller is notified just before the
view's constraints are updated, with updateViewConstraints; it is also notified before
and after view layout, with viewWillLayoutSubviews and viewDidLayoutSubviews.
Here's the full sequence during rotation:

- willRotateToInterfaceOrientation:duration:
- updateViewConstraints (and you must call super!)
- updateConstraints (to the view)
- viewWillLayoutSubviews
- layoutSubviews (to the view)
- viewDidLayoutSubviews

- `willAnimateRotationToInterfaceOrientation:duration:`

- `didRotateFromInterfaceOrientation:`

These UIViewController events allow your view controller to participate in its view's layout, without your having to subclass UIView so as to implement `update-Constraints` and `layoutSubviews` directly. Our problem is a layout problem, so it seems more elegant to implement it through layout events.

Here's a two-part solution involving constraints. I won't bother to remove the black rectangle from the interface; I'll add it once and for all as I configure the view initially, and just slide it onscreen and offscreen as needed. In `viewDidLoad`, then, we add the black rectangle to our interface, and then we prepare two sets of constraints, one describing the black rectangle's position onscreen (within our `view` bounds) and one describing its position offscreen (to the left of our `view` bounds):

```
-(void)viewDidLoad {
    UIView* br = [UIView new];
    br.translatesAutoresizingMaskIntoConstraints = NO;
    br.backgroundColor = [UIColor blackColor];
    [self.view addSubview:br];
    // b.r. is pinned to top and bottom of superview
    [self.view addConstraints:
     [NSLayoutConstraint
      constraintsWithVisualFormat:@"V:|[br]|"
      options:0 metrics:nil views:@{@"br":br}]];
    // b.r. is 1/3 the width of superview
    [self.view addConstraint:
     [NSLayoutConstraint
      constraintWithItem:br attribute:NSLayoutAttributeWidth
      relatedBy:0
      toItem:self.view attribute:NSLayoutAttributeWidth
      multiplier:1.0/3.0 constant:0]];
    // onscreen, b.r.'s left is pinned to superview's left
    NSArray* marrOn =
     [NSLayoutConstraint
      constraintsWithVisualFormat:@"H:|[br]"
      options:0 metrics:nil views:@{@"br":br}];
    // offscreen, b.r.'s right is pinned to superview's left
    NSArray* marrOff = @[
     [NSLayoutConstraint
      constraintWithItem:br attribute:NSLayoutAttributeRight
      relatedBy:NSLayoutRelationEqual
      toItem:self.view attribute:NSLayoutAttributeLeft
      multiplier:1 constant:0]
     ];
    // store constraints in instance variables
    self.blackRectConstraintsOnscreen = marrOn;
    self.blackRectConstraintsOffscreen = marrOff;
}
```

That's a lot of preparation, but the payoff is that responding to a request for layout is simple and clear; we simply swap in the constraints appropriate to the new interface orientation (`self.interfaceOrientation` at layout time):

```
-(void)updateViewConstraints {
    [self.view removeConstraints:self.blackRectConstraintsOnscreen];
    [self.view removeConstraints:self.blackRectConstraintsOffscreen];
    if (UIInterfaceOrientationIsLandscape(self.interfaceOrientation))
        [self.view addConstraints:self.blackRectConstraintsOnscreen];
    else
        [self.view addConstraints:self.blackRectConstraintsOffscreen];
    [super updateViewConstraints];
}
```

Moreover, the movement of the black rectangle is animated as the interface rotates, because *any* constraint-based layout performed as the interface rotates is animated.

Initial Orientation

The basic way to dictate your app's initial orientation, as the user will see it when launching, is to use your app's *Info.plist* settings. The reason is that the system can consult those settings during launch, before any of your code runs:

On the iPhone

The app will launch, preferentially, into the *first* orientation listed in the *Info.plist* in the "Supported interface orientations" array (`UISupportedInterface-Orientations`). In Xcode, edit the *Info.plist*; the editor lets you drag the elements of the array to reorder them.

If the root view controller limits the supported interface orientations, you should arrange the order of the "Supported interface orientations" entries to agree with it. For example, suppose your app as a whole supports portrait, landscape left, and landscape right, but your initial root view controller supports only landscape left and landscape right. Then you should put "Landscape (right home button)" and "Landscape (left home button)" before "Portrait" in the *Info.plist* "Supported interface orientations" array. Otherwise, if "Portrait" comes first, the app will try to launch into portrait orientation, only to discover, as your code finally starts running and your root view controller's `supportedInterfaceOrientations` is called, that this was wrong.

On the iPad

iPad apps are supposed to be more or less orientation-agnostic, so the order of orientations listed in the *Info.plist* in the "Supported interface orientations" array (`UISupportedInterfaceOrientations`) or "Supported interface orientations (iPad)" (`UISupportedInterfaceOrientations~ipad`) is ignored. Instead, the app will launch into whatever permitted orientation is closest to the device's current orientation.

Nevertheless, *all apps launch into portrait mode initially*. This is because the window goes only one way, with its top at the top of the device (away from the home button) — window bounds are screen bounds (see "What Rotates?" on page 254). If the app's initial visible orientation is not portrait, then there must be an initial rotation to that initial visible orientation, even if the user never sees it. Thus, an app whose initial orientation is landscape mode *must be configured to rotate from portrait to landscape* even if it doesn't support rotation after that.

A common beginner mistake, in this situation, is to try to work with the interface dimensions in your code *too soon*, before the rotation has taken place, in viewDidLoad. At the time viewDidLoad is called, the view controller has loaded its view — there is now something called self.view — but this view has not yet been put into the interface. It has not yet been resized to fit the interface (as I described in the previous section), and if the app needs to rotate on launch, that rotation has not yet taken place. If you try to work with the view's dimensions in viewDidLoad in an app that launches into a non-portrait orientation, it will appear that the width and height values of your interface bounds are the reverse of what you expect.

For example, let's say that our iPhone app's *Info.plist* has its "Supported interface orientations" ordered with "Landscape (right home button)" first, and our root view controller's viewDidLoad code places a small black square at the top center of the interface, like this:

```
- (void) viewDidLoad {
    [super viewDidLoad];
    UIView* square =
        [[UIView alloc] initWithFrame:CGRectMake(0,0,10,10)];
    square.backgroundColor = [UIColor blackColor];
    square.center =
        CGPointMake(CGRectGetMidX(self.view.bounds),5); // top center?
    [self.view addSubview:square];
}
```

The app launches into landscape orientation; the user must hold the device with the home button at the right to see it correctly. That's good. But where's the little black square? *Not* at the top center of the screen! The square appears at the top of the screen, but only about a third of the way across. The trouble is that in determining the x-coordinate of the square's center we examined the view's bounds too soon, at a time when the view's x-dimension (its width dimension) was still its shorter dimension.

So when *is* it safe to work with our view's initial dimensions? In iOS 5 and before, a possible solution was to override one of the rotation events discussed in the previous section, such as didRotateFromInterfaceOrientation:, and complete the configuration of your view there. In iOS 6 and iOS 7, however, that won't work, because *rotation events are not sent* in conjunction with the initial rotation of your app's interface.

The earliest event we receive at launch time after `self.view` has assumed its initial size in the interface is `viewWillLayoutSubviews`. This seems a perfectly appropriate place to configure our additional subview, since layout is exactly what we're doing. This event can be received multiple times over the lifetime of the view controller, but we want to perform our initial configuration only once, so we'll use a BOOL instance variable as a flag:

```
- (void) viewWillLayoutSubviews {
    if (!self->_viewInitializationDone) {
        self->_viewInitializationDone = YES;
        UIView* square =
            [[UIView alloc] initWithFrame:CGRectMake(0,0,10,10)];
        square.backgroundColor = [UIColor blackColor];
        square.center = CGPointMake(CGRectGetMidX(self.view.bounds),5);
        [self.view addSubview:square];
    }
}
```

The best solution of all, I think, is to use autolayout if at all possible, positioning our black square through constraints instead of its frame. The beauty of constraints is that you describe your layout conceptually rather than numerically; those concepts continue to apply through any future rotation. We don't need a BOOL instance variable, and we can even put our code back into `viewDidLoad`, because our constraints will continue to position the subview correctly whenever the view assumes its ultimate size:

```
- (void) viewDidLoad {
    [super viewDidLoad];
    UIView* square = [UIView new];
    square.backgroundColor = [UIColor blackColor];
    [self.view addSubview:square];
    square.translatesAutoresizingMaskIntoConstraints = NO;
    CGFloat side = 10;
    [square addConstraint:
     [NSLayoutConstraint
      constraintWithItem:square attribute:NSLayoutAttributeWidth
      relatedBy:0
      toItem:nil attribute:0
      multiplier:1 constant:side]];
    [self.view addConstraints:
     [NSLayoutConstraint
      constraintsWithVisualFormat:@"V:|[square(side)]"
      options:0 metrics:@{@"side":@(side)}
      views:@{@"square":square}]];
    [self.view addConstraint:
     [NSLayoutConstraint
      constraintWithItem:square attribute:NSLayoutAttributeCenterX
      relatedBy:0
      toItem:self.view attribute:NSLayoutAttributeCenterX
      multiplier:1 constant:0]];
}
```

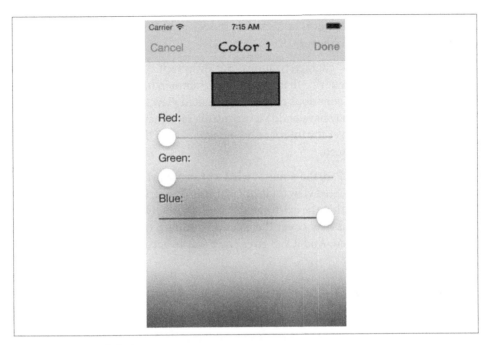

Figure 6-7. A modal view

Presented View Controller

Back when the only iOS device was an iPhone, a presented view controller was called a *modal view controller*. The root view controller remained in place, but its view was taken out of the interface and the modal view controller's view was used instead. Thus, this was the simplest way to replace the entire interface with a different interface.

You can see why this configuration was characterized as "modal". The presented view controller's view has, in a sense, blocked access to the "real" view, the root view controller's view. The user is thus forced to work in the presented view controller's view, until that view is "dismissed" and the "real" view is visible again. These notions are analogous to a modal dialog in a desktop application, where the user can't do anything else but work in the dialog as long as it is present. A presented view controller's view often reinforces this analogy with obvious dismissal buttons with titles like Save, Done, or Cancel.

The color picker view in my own Zotz! app is a good example (Figure 6-7); this is an interface that says, "You are now configuring a color, and that's all you can do; change the color or cancel, or you'll be stuck here forever." The user can't get out of this view without tapping Cancel or Done, and the view that the user was previously using is visible as a blur behind this view, waiting for the user to return to it.

Figure 6-5, from my Latin flashcard app, is another example of a presented view. It has a Cancel button, and the user is in a special "mode", performing a drill exercise rather than scrolling through flashcards.

Nevertheless, the "modal" characterization is not always apt. A presented view controller might be no more than a device that you, the programmer, have used to alter the interface; the user needn't be conscious of this. A presented view controller's view may have a complex interface; it may have child view controllers; it may present yet *another* view controller; it may take over the interface *permanently*, with the user *never* returning to the interface that it replaced.

With the coming of the iPad, the range of what a presented view controller's view could do was extended. A presented view on the iPad, instead of replacing the entire interface, can replace a *subview* within the existing interface. Alternatively, a presented view controller's view on the iPad may cover the existing interface only *partially*; the existing interface is never removed. And iOS 7 gives you a way to accomplish the same thing on the iPhone.

Presenting a View

To make a view controller present another view controller, you send the first view controller presentViewController:animated:completion:, handing it the second view controller, which you will probably instantiate for this very purpose. (The first view controller is very typically self.) We now have two view controllers that stand in the relationship of presentingViewController and presentedViewController, and the latter is retained. The presented view controller's view effectively replaces (or covers) the presenting view controller's view in the interface.

This state of affairs persists until the presenting view controller is sent dismissViewControllerAnimated:completion:. The presented view controller's view is then removed from the interface, and the presented view controller is released; it will thereupon typically go out of existence, together with its view, its child view controllers and *their* views, and so on.

As the view of the presented view controller appears, and again when it is dismissed, there's an option for animation as the transition takes place (the animated: argument). The completion: parameter, which can be nil, lets you supply a block of code to be run after the transition (including the animation) has occurred. I'll talk later about how to determine the nature of the animation.

The presenting view controller (the presented view controller's presentingViewController) is not necessarily the view controller to which you sent presentViewController:animated:completion:. It will help if we distinguish *three* roles that view controllers can play in presenting a view controller:

Presented view controller

The view controller specified as the first argument to `presentView-Controller:animated:completion:`.

Original presenter

The view controller to which `presentViewController:animated:completion:` was sent. Apple sometimes refers to this view controller as the *source*; "original presenter" is my own term.

The presented view controller is set as the original presenter's `presentedViewController`.

Presenting view controller

The presented view controller's `presentingViewController`. This is the view controller whose view is replaced or covered by the presented view controller's view. By default, it is *the view controller whose view is the entire interface* — namely, either the root view controller or an already existing presented view controller. It might not be the same as the original presenter.

The presented view controller is set as the presenting view controller's `presentedViewController`. Thus, the presented view controller might be the `presentedViewController` of two different view controllers.

The receiver of `dismissViewControllerAnimated:completion:` may be *any* of those three objects; the runtime will use the linkages between them to transmit the necessary messages up the chain on your behalf to the `presentingViewController`.

A view controller can have at most one `presentedViewController`. If you send `presentViewController:animated:completion:` to a view controller whose `presentedViewController` isn't nil, nothing will happen (and you'll get a warning from the runtime). However, a presented view controller can itself present a view controller, so there can be a chain of presented view controllers.

Conversely, you can test for a nil `presentedViewController` or `presentingViewController` to learn whether view presentation is occurring. For example, a view controller whose `presentingViewController` is nil is not a presented view controller at this moment.

Let's make one view controller present another. We could do this simply by connecting one view controller to another in a storyboard with a modal segue, but I don't want you to do that: a modal segue calls `presentViewController:animated:completion:` for you, whereas I want you to call it yourself.

So start with an iPhone project made from the Single View Application template. This contains one view controller class, called ViewController. Our first move must be to add a second view controller class, an instance of which will function as the presented view controller:

1. Choose File → New → File and make a new iOS Cocoa Touch Objective-C class. Click Next.

2. Name the class SecondViewController, make sure it is a subclass of UIViewController, and check the XIB checkbox so that we can design this view controller's view quickly and easily in a nib. Click Next.

3. Confirm the folder, group, and app target membership, and click Create.

4. Edit *SecondViewController.xib*, and do something there to make the view distinctive, so that you'll recognize it when it appears; for example, give it a red background color.

5. We need a way to trigger the presentation of SecondViewController. Edit *Main.storyboard* and add a button to the ViewController's view's interface. Connect that button to an action method in *ViewController.m*; let's call it doPresent:.

6. Import "SecondViewController.h" at the top of *ViewController.m*, so that we can speak of SecondViewController, and write the code for doPresent:, as follows:

```
- (IBAction)doPresent:(id)sender {
    [self presentViewController:[SecondViewController new]
                    animated:YES completion:nil];
}
```

Run the project. In ViewController's view, tap the button. SecondViewController's view slides into place over ViewController's view.

In our lust for instant gratification, we have neglected to provide a way to dismiss the presented view controller. If you'd like to do that, put a button into SecondViewController's view and connect it to an action method in *SecondViewController.m*:

```
- (IBAction)doDismiss:(id)sender {
    [self.presentingViewController
        dismissViewControllerAnimated:YES completion:nil];
}
```

Run the project. You can now alternate between ViewController's view and SecondViewController's view.

Communication With a Presented View Controller

In real life, it is quite probable that both presentation and dismissal will be a little more involved; in particular, it is likely that the original presenter will have additional information to impart to the presented view controller as the latter is created and presented, and that the presented view controller will want to pass information back to the original presenter as it is dismissed. Knowing how to arrange this exchange of information is very important.

Passing information from the original presenter to the presented view controller is usually easy, because the original presenter typically has a reference to the presented view controller before the latter's view appears in the interface. For example, suppose the presented view controller has a public `data` property. Then the original presenter can easily set this property:

```
SecondViewController* svc = [SecondViewController new];
svc.data = @"This is very important data!";
[self presentViewController: svc
                animated: YES completion:nil];
```

Indeed, if you're calling `presentViewController:animated:completion:` explicitly like this, you might even give SecondViewController a designated initializer that accepts the required data. In my Latin vocabulary app, the transition that engenders Figure 6-6 looks like this:

```
DrillViewController* dvc =
    [[DrillViewController alloc] initWithData:drillTerms];
[self presentViewController:dvc animated:YES completion:nil];
```

I've given DrillViewController a designated initializer `initWithData:` precisely so that whoever creates it can pass it the data it will need to do its job while it exists.

Passing information back from the presented view controller to the original presenter is a more interesting problem. The presented view controller will need to know who the original presenter is, but it doesn't automatically have a reference to it (the original presenter, remember, is not necessarily the same as the `presentingViewController`). Moreover, the presented view controller will need to know the signature of some method implemented by the original presenter, so that it can call that method and hand over the information — and this needs to work regardless of the original presenter's class.

The standard solution is to use delegation. The presented view controller defines a protocol declaring a method that the presented view controller wants to call before it is dismissed. The original presenter conforms to this protocol, and hands the presented view controller a reference to itself as it creates and configures the presented view controller; we can call this the presented view controller's *delegate*. The delegate reference is declared as an `id` adopting the presented view controller's protocol, so the presented view controller now not only has the required reference to the original presenter, but it also knows the signature of a method that the original presenter implements.

Let's modify our example to embody this architecture. First, modify SecondView-Controller to look like this:

```
// SecondViewController.h:
@protocol SecondViewControllerDelegate
- (void) dismissWithData: (id) data;
@end
@interface SecondViewController : UIViewController
@property (nonatomic, weak) id <SecondViewControllerDelegate> delegate;
@property (nonatomic, strong) id data;
@end


// SecondViewController.m:
- (IBAction)doDismiss:(id)sender {
    [self.delegate dismissWithData: @"Even more important data!"];
}
```

ViewController will need to declare itself as adopting SecondViewControllerDelegate; I like to do this in a class extension in the implementation file (*ViewController.m*):

```
@interface ViewController () <SecondViewControllerDelegate>
@end
```

ViewController could then present and dismiss SecondViewController like this:

```
- (IBAction)doPresent:(id)sender {
    SecondViewController* svc = [SecondViewController new];
    svc.data = @"This is very important data!";
    svc.delegate = self;
    [self presentViewController: svc
                      animated: YES completion:nil];
}
- (void) dismissWithData:(id)data {
    // do something with the data here
    [self dismissViewControllerAnimated:YES completion:nil];
}
```

In that example, the original presenter is sent the data and told to dismiss the presented view controller, in a single method. It might be wiser to separate these two functionalities. Here, I'll rename dismissWithData: as acceptData:, and its job is just to receive the data; ViewController will no longer dismiss SecondViewController. Rather, Second-ViewController will dismiss itself, and will then hear about that dismissal in a lifetime event, viewWillDisappear:, which calls acceptData: to ensure that the data is handed across. There is more than one reason why viewWillDisappear: might be called; we can test that this is the moment of our own dismissal by calling isBeingDismissed. Here is what SecondViewController looks like now:

```
// SecondViewController.h:
@protocol SecondViewControllerDelegate
- (void) acceptData: (id) data;
@end
@interface SecondViewController : UIViewController
@property (nonatomic, weak) id <SecondViewControllerDelegate> delegate;
@property (nonatomic, strong) id data;
@end
```

```
// SecondViewController.m:
- (IBAction)doDismiss:(id)sender {
    [self.presentingViewController
        dismissViewControllerAnimated:YES completion:nil];
}
- (void) viewWillDisappear:(BOOL)animated {
    [super viewWillDisappear: animated];
    if ([self isBeingDismissed])
        [self.delegate acceptData: @"Even more important data!"];
}
```

Configuring this architecture involves considerable work, and I know from experience that there is a strong temptation to be lazy and avoid it. It may indeed be possible to get by with a simplified solution; for example, SecondViewController could post a notification for which ViewController has supposedly registered. Nevertheless, delegation is the most reliable way for a presented view controller to communicate back to its original presenter.

Presented View Animation

When a view is presented and later when it is dismissed, an animation can be performed, according to whether the animated: parameter of the corresponding method is YES.

There are several built-in animation styles, whose names preserve the legacy "modal" designation:

UIModalTransitionStyleCoverVertical *(the default)*
> The presented view slides up from the bottom to cover the presenting view on presentation and down to reveal the presenting view on dismissal. "Bottom" is defined differently depending on the orientation of the device and the orientations the view controllers support.

UIModalTransitionStyleFlipHorizontal
> The view flips on the vertical axis as if the two views were the front and back of a piece of paper. The "vertical axis" is the device's long axis, regardless of the app's orientation.
>
> This animation style provides one of those rare occasions where the user may glimpse the window behind the transitioning views. You may want to set the window's background color appropriately.

UIModalTransitionStyleCrossDissolve
> The views remain stationary, and one fades into the other.

`UIModalTransitionStylePartialCurl`

> The first view curls up like a page in a notepad to expose most of the second view, but remains covering the top-left region of the second view. Thus there must not be any important interface in that region, as the user will not be able to see it.
>
> If the user clicks on the curl, `dismissViewControllerAnimated:completion:` is called on the original presenter. That's convenient, but make sure it doesn't disrupt communication between your view controllers; this is another reason for factoring out any final handing back of information from the presented view controller into its `viewWillDisappear:`, as I did in the previous section.

You do not pass the animation style as a parameter when presenting or dismissing a view controller; rather, it is attached beforehand to a view controller as its `modalTransitionStyle` property. (It is legal, but not common, for the `modalTransitionStyle` value to differ at the time of dismissal from its value at the time of presentation. Reversing on dismissal with the same animation style that was used on presentation is a subtle cue to the user that we're returning to a previous state.) The view controller that should have this `modalTransitionStyle` property set will generally be the *presented view controller* (I'll talk about the exception to this rule later). There are three typical ways in which this happens:

- The original presenter sets the presented view controller's `modalTransitionStyle` property.
- The presented view controller sets its own `modalTransitionStyle` property early in its lifetime; for example, it might override `initWithNibName:bundle:`.
- The presented view controller is instantiated from a nib; there's a Transition Style pop-up menu in the nib editor.

New in iOS 7, you can supply your own animation instead of using one of the built-in modal transition styles. Moreover, if you do this, you are able, for the first time in iOS history, to have the presented view controller's view cover the original presenter's view only partially, even on the iPhone. I'll discuss this topic later in the chapter.

Presentation Styles

On the iPad, additional options for how the presented view controller's view should cover the screen, and for what view controller should be the presenting view controller, are expressed through the presented view controller's `modalPresentationStyle` property. Your choices (which display more legacy "modal" names) are:

`UIModalPresentationFullScreen`

> The default. As on the iPhone, the presenting view controller is the root view controller or a fullscreen presented view controller, and its view — meaning the entire

interface — is replaced. (This is the only mode in which `UIModalTransitionStyle-PartialCurl` is legal.)

`UIModalPresentationPageSheet`
> Similar to `UIModalPresentationFullScreen`, but in a landscape orientation, the presented view has the width of the portrait-oriented screen, so the presenting view controller's view remains partially visible behind the presented view controller's view, dimmed so that the user can't interact with it.

`UIModalPresentationFormSheet`
> Similar to `UIModalPresentationPageSheet`, but the presented view controller's view is smaller, allowing the user to see more of the presenting view controller's view behind it. As the name implies, this is intended to allow the user to fill out a form (Apple describes this as "gathering structured information from the user").

`UIModalPresentationCurrentContext`
> The presenting view controller is *not* necessarily the root view controller or a full-screen presented view controller; it can be any view controller, such as a child view controller or a popover's view controller. The presented view controller's view replaces the presenting view controller's view, both of which may occupy only a portion of the screen.

When the presented view controller's `modalPresentationStyle` is `UIModalPresentationCurrentContext`, a decision has to be made by the runtime as to what view controller should be the presenting view controller. This will determine what view will be replaced by the presented view controller's view. The decision involves another UIViewController property, `definesPresentationContext` (a BOOL), and possibly still *another* UIViewController property, `providesPresentationContextTransitionStyle`. Here's how the decision operates:

1. Starting with the original presenter (the view controller to which `presentViewController:animated:completion:` was sent), we walk up the chain of parent view controllers, looking for one whose `definesPresentationContext` property is YES. If we find one, that's the one; it will be the `presentingViewController`, and its view will be replaced by the presented view controller's view.

   (If we *don't* find one, things work as if the presented view controller's `modalPresentationStyle` had been `UIModalPresentationFullScreen`.)

2. If, during the search just described, we find a view controller whose `definesPresentationContext` property is YES, we also look to see if that view controller's `providesPresentationContextTransitionStyle` property is *also* YES. If so, that view controller's `modalTransitionStyle` is used for this transition animation, instead of using the presented view controller's `modalTransitionStyle`.

To illustrate, I need a parent–child view controller arrangement to work with. This chapter hasn't yet discussed any parent view controllers in detail, but the simplest is UITabBarController, which I discuss in the next section, and it's easy to create a working app with a UITabBarController-based interface, so that's the example I'll use.

Start with a universal version of the Tabbed Application project template. As in the previous example, I want us to create and present the presented view controller manually, rather than letting the storyboard do it automatically; so make a new view controller class with an accompanying *.xib* file, to use as a presented view controller — call it ExtraViewController. In *ExtraViewController.xib*, give the view a distinctive background color, so you'll recognize it when it appears.

In the iPad storyboard, put a button in the First View Controller view, and connect it to an action method in *FirstViewController.m* that summons the new view controller as a presented view controller:

```
- (IBAction)doPresent:(id)sender {
    UIViewController* vc = [ExtraViewController new];
    [self presentViewController:vc animated:YES completion:nil];
}
```

(You'll also need to import "ExtraViewController.h" at the top of that file, obviously.) Run the project in the iPad Simulator, and tap the button. Observe that the presented view controller's view occupies the *entire* interface, covering even the tab bar; it replaces the root view.

Now change the code to look like this:

```
- (IBAction)doPresent:(id)sender {
    UIViewController* vc = [ExtraViewController new];
    self.definesPresentationContext = YES;
    vc.modalPresentationStyle = UIModalPresentationCurrentContext;
    [self presentViewController:vc animated:YES completion:nil];
}
```

Run the project in the iPad Simulator, and tap the button. The presented view controller's view replaces only the first view controller's view; the tab bar remains, and you can switch back and forth between the tab bar's first and second views (while the first view remains covered by the presented view). That's because the presented view controller's modalPresentationStyle is UIModalPresentationCurrentContext, and the original presenter's definesPresentationContext is YES. Thus the search for a context stops in FirstViewController (the original presenter), which thus also becomes the presenting view controller — and the presented view replaces FirstViewController's view instead of the root view.

We can also override the presented view controller's transition animation through the modalTransitionStyle property of the presenting view controller:

```
- (IBAction)doPresent:(id)sender {
    UIViewController* vc = [ExtraViewController new];
    self.definesPresentationContext = YES;
    self.providesPresentationContextTransitionStyle = YES;
    self.modalTransitionStyle = UIModalTransitionStyleFlipHorizontal;
    vc.modalPresentationStyle = UIModalPresentationCurrentContext;
    vc.modalTransitionStyle = UIModalTransitionStyleCoverVertical;
    [self presentViewController:vc animated:YES completion:nil];
}
```

The transition uses the flip horizontal animation belonging to the presenting view controller, rather than the cover vertical animation of the presented view controller.

It's helpful to experiment with the above code, commenting out individual lines to see what effect they have on the overall result. Note too that all the properties discussed in this section can be set by way of the nib editor.

Finally, put the same button with the same action in the iPhone storyboard, and observe that none of this works; the UIModalPresentationCurrentContext, and all that follows from it, is an iPad-only feature.

There is, however, one more presentation style (other than UIModalPresentationFull-Screen) that works on the iPhone — UIModalPresentationCustom. Its use has to do with custom transition animations, which I'll discuss later in this chapter.

When a view controller is presented, and its presentation style is *not* UIModal-PresentationFullScreen, a question arises of whether its status bar methods (prefers-StatusBarHidden and preferredStatusBarStyle) should be consulted. By default, the answer is no, because this view controller is not becoming the top-level view controller, supplanting the root view controller. To make the answer be yes, set this view controller's modalPresentationCapturesStatusBarAppearance to YES.

Rotation of a Presented View

When the presenting view controller is the top-level view controller — the root view controller, or a fullscreen presented view controller — the presented view controller becomes the new top-level view controller. This means that its supportedInterface-Orientations is consulted and honored. If these supportedInterfaceOrientations do not intersect with the app's current orientation, the app's orientation will be *forced to rotate* as the presented view appears — and the same thing will be true in reverse when the presented view controller is dismissed. This is a perfectly reasonable thing to do, especially on the iPhone, where the user can easily rotate the device to compensate for the new orientation of the interface.

In iOS 6 and iOS 7, a presented view controller is the *only* officially sanctioned way to force the interface to rotate. In iOS 5 and before, the interface could be forced to rotate by other kinds of view controller transition, such as pushing a view controller onto a navigation controller's stack, but this is no longer the case; attempts to circumvent this change and restore the iOS 5 behavior are generally futile (and unnecessary).

For example, in my Latin flashcard app (Figure 6-3), the individual flashcards are viewed only in landscape orientation. But there is also an option to display a list (a UITableView) of all vocabulary, which is permitted to assume portrait orientation only. Therefore the interface rotates when the vocabulary list appears (to portrait orientation), and again when it disappears (back to landscape orientation); the user is expected to respond by rotating the device. Here's how this is achieved:

- The app as a whole, as dictated by its *Info.plist*, supports three orientations, in this order: "Landscape (right home button)," "Landscape (left home button)," and "Portrait" — the set of all orientations the app will *ever* be permitted to assume.
- The RootViewController class implements supportedInterfaceOrientations to return UIInterfaceOrientationMaskLandscape.
- The AllTermsListController class, whose view contains the total vocabulary list, implements supportedInterfaceOrientations to return UIInterfaceOrientationMaskPortrait — and an AllTermsListController instance is used only as a presented view controller.

In addition, a presented view controller whose supportedInterfaceOrientations: is a mask permitting multiple possible orientations is able to specify which of those orientations it would like to appear in *initially*. To do so, override preferredInterfaceOrientationForPresentation; this method is called before supportedInterfaceOrientations:, and should return a single interface orientation (*not* a mask). For example:

```
-(UIInterfaceOrientation)preferredInterfaceOrientationForPresentation {
    return UIInterfaceOrientationPortrait;
}
-(NSUInteger)supportedInterfaceOrientations {
    return UIInterfaceOrientationMaskAll;
}
```

That says, "When I am summoned initially as a presented view controller, the app should be rotated to portrait orientation. After that, while my view is being presented, the app can rotate to compensate for any orientation of the device."

The presented view controller's supportedInterfaceOrientations (preceded by its preferredInterfaceOrientationForPresentation if implemented) is consulted when the presented view controller is first summoned. Subsequently, both the presenting and presented view controllers' supportedInterfaceOrientations are called on each rotation of the device, and the presenting view controller's supportedInterfaceOrientations is called when the presented view controller is dismissed. Both view controllers may get layout events both when the presented view controller is summoned and when it is dismissed.

Presenting a View in Response to Rotation

An interesting alternative to performing complex layout on rotation, as in "Rotation and Layout Events" on page 254, might be to summon a presented view controller instead. We detect the rotation of the device directly. If the device passes into a landscape orientation, we present a view controller whose view is suited to landscape orientation; if the device passes out of landscape orientation, we dismiss that view controller.

Call the two view controllers ViewController and SecondViewController. SecondViewController is landscape-only:

```
-(NSUInteger)supportedInterfaceOrientations {
    return UIInterfaceOrientationMaskLandscape;
}
```

ViewController sets itself up to receive notifications when the device orientation changes. When such a notification arrives, it presents or dismisses SecondViewController as appropriate:

```
- (void) viewDidLoad {
    [super viewDidLoad];
    [[UIDevice currentDevice] beginGeneratingDeviceOrientationNotifications];
    [[NSNotificationCenter defaultCenter]
        addObserver:self selector:@selector(screenRotated:)
        name:UIDeviceOrientationDidChangeNotification object:nil];
}
- (void)screenRotated:(NSNotification *)n {
    UIDeviceOrientation r = [UIDevice currentDevice].orientation;
    if (UIDeviceOrientationIsLandscape(r) & !self.presentedViewController) {
        UIViewController* vc = [SecondViewController new];
        vc.modalTransitionStyle = UIModalTransitionStyleCrossDissolve;
        [self presentViewController:vc animated:YES completion:nil];
    } else if (UIDeviceOrientationPortrait == rot) {
        [self dismissViewControllerAnimated:YES completion:nil];
    }
}
```

This works, but it lacks the animated rotation of the status bar as we transition from portrait to landscape or from landscape to portrait. Adding the status bar rotation is tricky, because setStatusBarOrientation:animated:, the UIApplication instance method we want to call, doesn't actually perform any animation unless `supported-InterfaceOrientations` returns 0 — which the documentation says is forbidden. Nevertheless, I'll demonstrate a way to do it.

In SecondViewController, `supportedInterfaceOrientations` now allows the interface to rotate automatically if the user switches from one landscape orientation to the other, but returns 0 if we're rotating back to portrait:

```
-(NSUInteger)supportedInterfaceOrientations {
    if ([UIDevice currentDevice].orientation == UIDeviceOrientationPortrait)
        return 0;
    return UIInterfaceOrientationMaskLandscape;
}
```

And here's ViewController:

```
-(NSUInteger)supportedInterfaceOrientations {
    return 0;
}
- (void) viewDidLoad {
    [super viewDidLoad];
    [[UIDevice currentDevice] beginGeneratingDeviceOrientationNotifications];
    [[NSNotificationCenter defaultCenter]
        addObserver:self selector:@selector(screenRotated:)
        name:UIDeviceOrientationDidChangeNotification object:nil];
}
- (void)screenRotated:(NSNotification *)n {
    UIDeviceOrientation r = [UIDevice currentDevice].orientation;
    UIInterfaceOrientation r2 = (UIInterfaceOrientation)r;
    if (UIDeviceOrientationIsLandscape(r) & !self.presentedViewController) {
        [[UIApplication sharedApplication]
            setStatusBarOrientation:r2 animated:YES];
        UIViewController* vc = [SecondViewController new];
        vc.modalTransitionStyle = UIModalTransitionStyleCrossDissolve;
        [self presentViewController:vc animated:YES completion:nil];
    } else if (UIDeviceOrientationPortrait == r) {
        [[UIApplication sharedApplication]
            setStatusBarOrientation:r2 animated:YES];
        [self dismissViewControllerAnimated:YES completion:nil];
    }
}
```

Tab Bar Controllers

A *tab bar* (UITabBar, see also Chapter 12) is a horizontal bar containing items. Each item is a UITabBarItem; it displays, by default, an image and a title. At all times, exactly one of these items is selected (highlighted); when the user taps an item, it becomes the selected item.

If there are too many items to fit on a tab bar, the excess items are automatically subsumed into a final More item. When the user taps the More item, a list of the excess items appears, and the user can select one; the user can also be permitted to edit the tab bar, determining which items appear in the tab bar itself and which ones spill over into the More list.

A tab bar is an independent interface object, but it is most commonly used in conjunction with a *tab bar controller* (UITabBarController, a subclass of UIViewController) to form a tab bar interface. The tab bar controller displays the tab bar at the bottom of its own view. From the user's standpoint, the tab bar items correspond to views; when the user selects a tab bar item, the corresponding view appears. The user is thus employing the tab bar to choose an entire area of your app's functionality. In reality, the UITabBarController is a parent view controller; you give it child view controllers, which the tab bar controller then contains, and the views summoned by tapping the tab bar items are the views of those child view controllers.

Familiar examples of a tab bar interface on the iPhone are Apple's Clock app, which has four tab bar items, and Apple's Music app, which has four tab bar items plus a More item that reveals a list of five more.

You can get a reference to the tab bar controller's tab bar through its `tabBar` property. In general, you won't need this. When using a tab bar interface by way of a UITabBarController, you do not interact (as a programmer) with the tab bar itself; you don't create it or set its delegate. You provide the UITabBarController with children, and it does the rest; when the UITabBarController's view is displayed, there's the tab bar along with the view of the selected item. You can, however, customize the *look* of the tab bar (see Chapter 12 for details).

As discussed earlier in this chapter, your app's automatic rotation in response to user rotation of the device depends on the interplay between the app (represented by the *Info.plist* and the app delegate) and the top-level view controller. If a UITabBarController is the top-level view controller, it will help determine your app's automatic rotation, through its implementation of `supportedInterfaceOrientations`. By default, a UITabBarController does not implement `supportedInterfaceOrientations`, so your interface will be free to rotate to any orientation permitted by the app as a whole.

In iOS 6, the only way around this was to subclass UITabBarController for the sole purpose of implementing `supportedInterfaceOrientations`, like this:

```
@implementation MyTabBarController : UITabBarController
-(NSUInteger)supportedInterfaceOrientations {
    return UIInterfaceOrientationMaskPortrait;
}
@end
```

It seems silly, however, to be compelled to subclass UITabBarController merely to take control of its rotation behavior, and in iOS 7 there's a better way: you can govern the tab bar controller's rotation behavior in its delegate instead, by implementing `tabBar-ControllerSupportedInterfaceOrientations:`. In this example, the tab bar controller's first child view controller makes itself the tab bar controller's delegate, and prevents the app from rotating:

```
-(void)viewDidLoad {
    [super viewDidLoad];
    self.tabBarController.delegate = self;
}
-(NSUInteger)tabBarControllerSupportedInterfaceOrientations:
        (UITabBarController *) tabBarController {
    return UIInterfaceOrientationMaskPortrait;
}
```

Another tab bar controller delegate method that's new in iOS 7, `tabBarController-PreferredInterfaceOrientationForPresentation:`, comes into play when the tab bar controller is a presented view controller. It dictates the orientation to which the app will rotate when the tab bar controller's view *initially* appears as a presented view.

Tab Bar Items

For each view controller you assign as a tab bar controller's child, you're going to need a *tab bar item*, which will appear as its representative in the tab bar. This tab bar item will be your child view controller's `tabBarItem`. A tab bar item is a UITabBarItem; this is a subclass of UIBarItem, an abstract class that provides some of its most important properties, such as `title`, `image`, and `enabled`.

There are two ways to make a tab bar item:

By borrowing it from the system
> Instantiate UITabBarItem using `initWithTabBarSystemItem:tag:`, and assign the instance to your child view controller's `tabBarItem`. Consult the documentation for the list of available system items. Unfortunately, you can't customize a system tab bar item's title; you must accept the title the system hands you. (You can't work around this restriction by somehow copying a system tab bar item's image.)

By making your own
> Instantiate UITabBarItem using `initWithTitle:image:tag:` and assign the instance to your child view controller's `tabBarItem`. Alternatively, use the view controller's existing `tabBarItem` and set its `image` and `title`. Instead of setting the `title` of the `tabBarItem`, you can set the `title` property of the view controller itself; setting a view controller's `title` automatically sets the `title` of its current `tabBarItem` (unless the tab bar item is a system tab bar item), but the converse is not true.

New in iOS 7, you can add a separate selectedImage (possibly by initializing with initWithTitle:image:selectedImage:). The selectedImage will be displayed in place of the normal image when this tab bar item is selected in the tab bar.

The image (and selectedImage) for a tab bar item should be a 30×30 PNG; if it is larger, it will be scaled down as needed. By default, it will be treated as a transparency mask (a template): the hue of its pixels will be ignored, and the transparency of its pixels will be combined with the tab bar's tintColor, which may be inherited from higher up the view hierarchy. However, new in iOS 7, you can instead display the image as is, and not as a transparency mask. Send your image the imageWithRenderingMode: message, with an argument of UIImageRenderingModeAlwaysOriginal (see Chapter 2), and use the resulting image in your tab bar item.

(The finishedSelectedImage and finishedUnselectedImage of iOS 5 and 6 are thus no longer necessary, and are deprecated in iOS 7.)

You can also give a tab bar item a badge (see the documentation on the badgeValue property). Other ways in which you can customize the look of a tab bar item are discussed in Chapter 12. For example, you can control the font and style of the title, or you can give it an empty title and offset the image.

Configuring a Tab Bar Controller

As I've already said, you configure a tab bar controller by handing it the view controllers that will be its children. To do so, collect those view controllers into an array and set the UITabBarController's viewControllers property to that array. The view controllers in the array are now the tab bar controller's child view controllers; the tab bar controller is the parentViewController of the view controllers in the array. The tab bar controller is also the tabBarController of the view controllers in the array and of all their children; thus a child view controller at any depth can learn that it is contained by a tab bar controller and can get a reference to that tab bar controller. The tab bar controller retains the array, and the array retains the child view controllers.

Here's a simple example excerpted from the app delegate's application:didFinishLaunchingWithOptions: of one of my apps, in which I construct and display a tab bar interface in code:

```
UITabBarController* tbc = [UITabBarController new];
UIViewController* b = [GameBoardController new];
UIViewController* s = [SettingsController new]
UINavigationController* n =
    [[UINavigationController alloc] initWithRootViewController:s];
tbc.viewControllers = @[b, n];
self.window.rootViewController = tbc;
```

The tab bar controller's tab bar will automatically display the `tabBarItem` of each child view controller. The order of the tab bar items is the order of the view controllers in the tab bar controller's `viewControllers` array. Thus, a child view controller will probably want to configure its `tabBarItem` property early in its lifetime, so that the `tabBarItem` is ready by the time the view controller is handed as a child to the tab bar controller. Observe that `viewDidLoad` is not early enough, because the view controllers (other than the initially selected view controller) have no view when the tab bar controller initially appears. Thus it is common to override `initWithNibName:bundle:` (or `initWith-Coder:` or `awakeFromNib`, if appropriate) for this purpose. For example, in the same app as the previous code:

```
// GameBoardController.m:
- (id) initWithNibName:(NSString *)nib bundle:(NSBundle *)bundle {
    self = [super initWithNibName:nib bundle:bundle];
    // we will be embedded in a tab view, configure
    if (self) {
        UIImage* im = [UIImage imageNamed:@"game.png"];
        self.tabBarItem.image = im;
        self.title = @"Game";
    }
    return self;
}
```

If you change the tab bar controller's view controllers array later in its lifetime and you want the corresponding change in the tab bar's display of its items to be animated, call `setViewControllers:animated:`.

Initially, by default, the first child view controller's tab bar item is selected and its view is displayed. To tell the tab bar controller which tab bar item should be selected, you can couch your choice in terms of the contained view controller (`selectedView-Controller`) or by index number in the array (`selectedIndex`). The same properties also tell you what view controller's view the user has displayed by tapping in the tab bar.

New in iOS 7, you can supply an animation when a tab bar controller's selected tab item changes and one child view controller's view is replaced by another. I'll discuss this topic later in the chapter.

You can also set the UITabBarController's delegate; the delegate should adopt the UITabBarControllerDelegate protocol. The delegate gets messages allowing it to prevent a given tab bar item from being selected, and notifying it when a tab bar item is selected and when the user is customizing the tab bar from the More item.

If the tab bar contains few enough items that it doesn't need a More item, there won't be one and the tab bar won't be user-customizable. If there *is* a More item, you can exclude some tab bar items from being customizable by setting the `customizableView-Controllers` property to an array that lacks them; setting this property to nil means that the user can see the More list but can't rearrange the items. Setting the `view-

Controllers property sets the `customizableViewControllers` property to the same value, so if you're going to set the `customizableViewControllers` property, do it *after* setting the `viewControllers` property. The `moreNavigationController` property can be compared with the `selectedViewController` property to learn whether the user is currently viewing the More list; apart from this, the More interface is mostly out of your control, but I'll discuss some sneaky ways of customizing it in Chapter 12.

(If you allow the user to rearrange items, you would presumably want to save the new arrangement and restore it the next time the app runs. You might use NSUserDefaults for this; you could also take advantage of the built-in automatic state saving and restoration facilities, discussed later in this chapter.)

You can also configure a UITabBarController in a *.storyboard* or *.xib* file. The UITabBarController's contained view controllers can be set directly — in a storyboard, there will be a "view controllers" relationship between the tab bar controller and each of its children — and the contained view controllers will be instantiated together with the tab bar controller. Moreover, each contained view controller has a Tab Bar Item; you can select this and set many aspects of the `tabBarItem` directly in the nib, such as its system item or its title, image (but not its selected image), and tag, directly in the nib. (If a view controller in a nib *doesn't* have a Tab Bar Item and you want to configure this view controller for use in a tab bar interface, drag a Tab Bar Item from the Object library onto the view controller.)

To start a project with a main storyboard that has a UITabBarController as its root view controller, begin with the Tabbed Application template.

 See the discussion earlier in this chapter of how a view controller's view is resized to fit the interface. You will want to prepare your view for this resizing. In iOS 7, a tab bar controller's child controller's view by default will underlap the tab bar if the tab bar is translucent.

Navigation Controllers

A *navigation bar* (UINavigationBar, see also Chapter 12) is a horizontal bar displaying a center title and a right button. When the user taps the right button, the navigation bar animates, sliding its interface out to the left and replacing it with a new interface that enters from the right. The new interface displays a back button at the left side, and a new center title — and possibly a new right button. The user can tap the back button to go back to the first interface, which slides in from the left; or, if there's a right button in the second interface, the user can tap it to go further forward to a third interface, which slides in from the right.

The successive interfaces of a navigation bar thus behave like a stack. In fact, a navigation bar does represent an actual stack — an internal stack of *navigation items* (UINavigationItem). It starts out with one navigation item: the *root* or *bottom item* of the stack. Since there is just one navigation item, this is also the *top item* of the stack (the navigation bar's topItem). It is the top item whose interface is always reflected in the navigation bar. When the user taps a right button, a new navigation item is pushed onto the stack; it becomes the top item, and its interface is seen. When the user taps a back button, the top item is popped off the stack, and what was previously the next item beneath it in the stack — the *back item* (the navigation bar's backItem) — becomes the top item, and its interface is seen.

The state of the stack is thus reflected in the navigation bar's interface. The navigation bar's center title comes automatically from the top item, and its back button comes from the back item. (See Chapter 12 for a complete description.) Thus, the title tells the user what item is current, and the left side is a button telling the user what item we would return to if the user were to tap that button. The animations reinforce this notion of directionality, giving the user a sense of position within a chain of items.

A navigation bar is an independent interface object, but it is most commonly used in conjunction with a *navigation controller* (UINavigationController, a subclass of UIViewController) to form a navigation interface. Just as there is a stack of navigation items in the navigation bar, there is a stack of view controllers in the navigation controller. These view controllers are the navigation controller's children, and each navigation item belongs to a view controller — it is a view controller's navigationItem.

The navigation controller performs automatic coordination of the navigation bar and the overall interface. Whenever a view controller comes to the top of the navigation controller's stack, its view is displayed in the interface. At the same time, its navigation-Item is automatically pushed onto the top of the navigation bar's stack — and thus is automatically displayed in the navigation bar. Moreover, the animation in the navigation bar is reinforced by animation of the interface as a whole: by default, a view controller's view slides into the main interface from the left or right just as its navigation item slides into the navigation bar from the left or right. (New in iOS 7, the animation of the view controller's view can be changed; I'll discuss that later in the chapter.)

Your code can control the overall navigation, so in real life, the user may well navigate to the right, not by tapping the right button in the navigation bar, but by tapping something inside the main interface, such as a listing in a table view. (Figure 6-1 is a navigation interface that works this way.) In this situation, your code is deciding in real time what the next view should be; typically, you won't even create the next view controller until the user asks to navigate to it. The navigation interface thus becomes a *master–detail interface*.

Conversely, you might put a view controller inside a navigation controller just to get the convenience of the navigation bar, with its title and buttons, even when no actual push-and-pop navigation is going to take place.

You can get a reference to the navigation controller's navigation bar through its navigationBar property. In general, you won't need this. When using a navigation interface by way of a UINavigationController, you do not interact (as a programmer) with the navigation bar itself; you don't create it or set its delegate. You provide the UINavigationController with children, and it does the rest, handing each child view controller's navigationItem to the navigation bar for display and showing the child view controller's view each time navigation occurs. You can, however, customize the *look* of the navigation bar (see Chapter 12 for details).

A navigation interface may also optionally display a toolbar at the bottom. A toolbar (UIToolbar) is a horizontal view displaying a row of items, any of which the user can tap. Typically, the tapped item may highlight momentarily, but it is not selected; it represents the initiation of an action, like a button. You can get a reference to a UINavigationController's toolbar through its toolbar property. The look of the toolbar can be customized (Chapter 12). In a navigation interface, however, the *contents* of the toolbar are determined automatically by the view controller that is currently the top item in the stack: they are its toolbarItems.

A UIToolbar can also be used independently, and often is. It then typically appears at the bottom on an iPhone — Figure 6-3 has a toolbar at the bottom — but often appears at the top on an iPad, where it plays something of the role that the menu bar plays on the desktop. When a toolbar is displayed by a navigation controller, though, it always appears at the bottom.

A familiar example of a navigation interface is Apple's Settings app on the iPhone. The Mail app on the iPhone is a navigation interface that includes a toolbar.

As discussed earlier in this chapter, your app's automatic rotation in response to user rotation of the device depends on the interplay between the app (represented by the *Info.plist* and the app delegate) and the top-level view controller. If a UINavigation-Controller is the top-level view controller, it will help determine your app's automatic rotation, through its implementation of supportedInterfaceOrientations. By default, a UINavigationController does not implement supportedInterface-Orientations, so your interface will be free to rotate to any orientation permitted by the app as a whole.

In iOS 6, the only way around this was to subclass UINavigationController for the sole purpose of implementing supportedInterfaceOrientations, like this:

```
@implementation MyNavigationController : UINavigationController
-(NSUInteger)supportedInterfaceOrientations {
    return UIInterfaceOrientationMaskPortrait;
}
@end
```

It seems silly, however, to be compelled to subclass UINavigationController merely to take control of its rotation behavior, and in iOS 7 there's a better way: you can govern the navigation controller's rotation in its delegate instead, by implementing `navigationControllerSupportedInterfaceOrientations:`.

Another navigation controller delegate method that's new in iOS 7, `navigationControllerPreferredInterfaceOrientationForPresentation:`, comes into play when a navigation controller is a presented view controller. It dictates the orientation to which the app will rotate when the navigation controller's view *initially* appears as a presented view.

Bar Button Items

The buttons in a UIToolbar or a UINavigationBar are bar button items — UIBarButtonItem, a subclass of UIBarItem. A bar button item comes in one of two broadly different flavors:

Basic bar button item
> The bar button item behaves like a simple button.

Custom view
> The bar button item has no inherent behavior, but has (and displays) a `customView`.

UIBarItem is not a UIView subclass. A basic bar button item is button-like, but it has no frame, no UIView touch handling, and so forth. A UIBarButtonItem's `customView`, however, *is* a UIView — indeed, it can be *any* kind of UIView. Thus, a bar button item with a `customView` can display any sort of view in a toolbar or navigation bar, and that view can implement touch handling however it likes.

Let's start with the basic bar button item (no custom view). A bar button item, like a tab bar item, inherits from UIBarItem the `title`, `image`, and `enabled` properties. The title text color, by default, comes from the bar button item's `tintColor`, which may be inherited from the bar itself or from higher up the view hierarchy. Assigning an image removes the title. The image should usually be quite small; Apple recommends 22×22. By default, the image will be treated as a transparency mask (a template): the hue of its pixels will be ignored, and the transparency of its pixels will be combined with the bar button item's `tintColor`. However, new in iOS 7, you can instead display the image as is, and not as a transparency mask. Send your image the `imageWithRenderingMode:` message, with an argument of `UIImageRenderingModeAlwaysOriginal` (see Chapter 2), and use the resulting image in your bar button item.

A basic bar button item has a `style` property; this will usually be `UIBarButtonItem-StylePlain`. The alternative, `UIBarButtonItemStyleDone`, causes the title to be bold. You can further refine the title font and style. In addition, a bar button item can have a background image; this will typically be a small, resizable image, and can be used to provide a border. Full details appear in Chapter 12.

 A bar button item looks quite different in iOS 7 from iOS 6 and before. In iOS 6, a bar button item could display both an image and a title (in a toolbar), and there was usually a border around the item (though this could be prevented in a toolbar by using `UIBarButton-ItemStylePlain`). In iOS 7, the bar button item never draws its own border, and the `UIBarButtonItemStyleBordered` style is irrelevant. And the use and effect of the `tintColor` is completely changed in iOS 7. Adapting your iOS 6 app to look good when compiled for iOS 7 can be quite a chore.

A bar button item also has `target` and `action` properties. These contribute to its button-like behavior: tapping a bar button item can trigger an action method elsewhere.

There are three ways to make a bar button item:

By borrowing it from the system
> Instantiate UIBarButtonItem using `initWithBarButtonSystemItem:target:action:`. Consult the documentation for the list of available system items; they are not the same as for a tab bar item. You can't assign a title or change the image. (But you can change the tint color or assign a background image.)

By making your own basic bar button item
> Instantiate UIBarButtonItem using `initWithTitle:style:target:action:` or `initWithImage:style:target:action:`.
>
> An additional method, `initWithImage:landscapeImagePhone:style:target:action:`, lets you supply two images, one for portrait orientation, the other for landscape orientation; this is because by default, the bar's height might change when the interface is rotated.

By making a custom view bar button item
> Instantiate UIBarButtonItem using `initWithCustomView:`, supplying a UIView that the bar button item is to display. The bar button item has no action and target; the UIView itself must somehow implement button behavior if that's what you want. For example, the `customView` might be a UISegmentedButton, but then it is the UISegmentedButton's target and action that give it button behavior.

Bar button items in a toolbar are horizontally positioned automatically by the system. You can provide hints to help with this positioning. If you know that you'll be changing

Figure 6-8. A segmented control in the center of a navigation bar

an item's title dynamically, you'll probably want its width to accommodate the longest possible title right from the start; to arrange that, set the `possibleTitles` property to an NSSet of strings that includes the longest title. Alternatively, you can supply an absolute `width`. Also, you can incorporate spacers into the toolbar; these are created with `initWithBarButtonSystemItem:target:action:`, but they have no visible appearance, and cannot be tapped. The `UIBarButtonSystemItemFlexibleSpace` is the one most frequently used; place these between the visible items to distribute the visible items equally across the width of the toolbar. There is also a `UIBarButtonSystemItemFixed-Space` whose `width` lets you insert a space of defined size.

Navigation Items and Toolbar Items

What appears in a navigation bar (UINavigationBar) depends upon the navigation items (UINavigationItem) in its stack. In a navigation interface, the navigation controller will manage the navigation bar's stack for you, but you must still configure each navigation item by setting properties of the `navigationItem` of each child view controller. The UINavigationItem properties are as follows (see also Chapter 12):

`title` *or* `titleView`

Determines what is to appear in the center of the navigation bar when this navigation item is at the top of the stack.

The `title` is a string. Setting the view controller's `title` property sets the `title` of the `navigationItem` automatically, and is usually the best approach.

The `titleView` can be any kind of UIView; if set, it will be displayed instead of the `title`. The `titleView` can implement further UIView functionality; for example, it can be tappable. Even if you are using a `titleView`, you should still give your view controller a `title`, as it will be needed for the back button when a view controller is pushed onto the stack on top of this one.

Figure 6-1 shows the TidBITS News master view, with the navigation bar displaying a `titleView` which is a (tappable) image view; the master view's `title` is therefore not displayed. In the TidBITS News detail view controller's navigation bar (Figure 6-8), the `titleView` is a segmented control providing a Previous and Next button, and the back button displays the master view controller's `title`.

prompt
>   An optional string to appear centered above everything else in the navigation bar. The navigation bar's height will be increased to accommodate it.

`rightBarButtonItem` *or* `rightBarButtonItems`
>   A bar button item or, respectively, an array of bar button items to appear at the right side of the navigation bar; the first item in the array will be rightmost.

>   In Figure 6-8, the text size button is a right bar button item; it has nothing to do with navigation, but is placed here merely because space is at a premium on the small iPhone screen.

`backBarButtonItem`
>   When a view controller is pushed on top of this view controller, the navigation bar will display at its left a button pointing to the left, whose title is this view controller's `title`. That button is *this* view controller's navigation item's `backBarButtonItem`. That's right: the back button displayed in the navigation bar belongs, not to the top item (the `navigationItem` of the current view controller), but to the back item (the `navigationItem` of the view controller that is one level down in the stack). In Figure 6-8, the back button in the detail view is the master view controller's default back button, displaying its `title`.

>   The vast majority of the time, the default behavior is the behavior you'll want, and you'll leave the back button alone. If you wish, though, you can customize the back button by setting a view controller's `navigationItem.backBarButtonItem` so that it contains an image, or a title differing from the view controller's `title`. The best technique is to provide a new UIBarButtonItem whose target and action are nil; the runtime will add a correct target and action, so as to create a working back button:

```
UIBarButtonItem* b =
    [[UIBarButtonItem alloc] initWithTitle:@"Go Back"
        style:UIBarButtonItemStylePlain target:nil action:nil];
self.navigationItem.backBarButtonItem = b;
```

>   A BOOL property, `hidesBackButton`, allows the top navigation item to suppress display of the back item's back bar button item. Obviously, if you set this to YES, you'll probably ensure some other means of letting the user navigate back.

>   In iOS 7, the visible indication that the back button *is* a back button is a left-pointing chevron (the *back indicator*) that's separate from the button itself. (This contrasts with iOS 6 and before, where the button itself had a left-pointing shape.) This chevron can also be customized, but it's a feature of the navigation bar, not the bar button item: set the navigation bar's `backIndicatorImage` and `backIndicator-TransitionMask` (I'll give an example in Chapter 12). Alternatively, if the back button is assigned a background image, the back indicator is removed; it is up to the background image to point left, if desired.

`leftBarButtonItem` *or* `leftBarButtonItems`

A bar button item or, respectively, an array of bar button items to appear at the left side of the navigation bar; the first item in the array will be leftmost. The `leftItems-SupplementBackButton` property, if set to YES, allows both the back button and one or more left bar button items to appear.

A view controller's navigation item can have its properties set at any time while being displayed in the navigation bar. This (and not direct manipulation of the navigation bar) is the way to change the navigation bar's contents dynamically. For example, in one of my apps, the `titleView` is a progress view (UIProgressView, Chapter 12) that needs updating every second, and the right bar button should be either the system Play button or the system Pause button, depending on whether music from the library is playing, paused, or stopped. So I have a timer that periodically checks the state of the music player:

```
// change the progress view
if (self->_nowPlayingItem) {
    MPMediaItem* item = self->_nowPlayingItem;
    NSTimeInterval current = self.mp.currentPlaybackTime;
    NSTimeInterval total =
        [[item valueForProperty:MPMediaItemPropertyPlaybackDuration]
            doubleValue];
    self.prog.progress = current / total;
} else {
    self.prog.progress = 0;
}
// change the bar button
int whichButton = -1;
if ([self.mp playbackState] == MPMusicPlaybackStatePlaying)
    whichButton = UIBarButtonSystemItemPause;
else if ([self.mp playbackState] == MPMusicPlaybackStatePaused ||
        [self.mp playbackState] == MPMusicPlaybackStateStopped)
    whichButton = UIBarButtonSystemItemPlay;
if (whichButton == -1)
    self.navigationItem.rightBarButtonItem = nil;
else {
    UIBarButtonItem* bb =
        [[UIBarButtonItem alloc]
            initWithBarButtonSystemItem:whichButton
            target:self action:@selector(doPlayPause:)];
    self.navigationItem.rightBarButtonItem = bb;
}
```

Each view controller to be pushed onto the navigation controller's stack is responsible for supplying the items to appear in the navigation interface's toolbar, if there is one. To configure this, set the view controller's `toolbarItems` property to an array of UIBar-ButtonItem instances. You can change the toolbar items even while the view controller's view and current `toolbarItems` are showing, optionally with animation, by sending `setToolbarItems:animated:` to the view controller.

A view controller has the power to specify that its ancestor's bottom bar (a navigation controller's toolbar, or a tab bar controller's tab bar) should be hidden as this view controller is pushed onto a navigation controller's stack. To do so, set the view controller's hidesBottomBarWhenPushed property to YES. The trick is that you must do this very early, before the view loads; the view controller's initializer is a good place. The bottom bar remains hidden from the time this view controller is pushed to the time it is popped, even if other view controllers are pushed and popped on top of it in the meantime. For more flexibility, you can send setToolbarHidden:animated: to the UINavigation-Controller at any time.

Configuring a Navigation Controller

You configure a navigation controller by manipulating its stack of view controllers. This stack is the navigation controller's viewControllers array property, though, as I'll explain in a moment, you will rarely need to manipulate that property directly.

The view controllers in a navigation controller's viewControllers array are the navigation controller's child view controllers; the navigation controller is the parentView-Controller of the view controllers in the array. The navigation controller is also the navigationController of the view controllers in the array and of all their children; thus a child view controller at any depth can learn that it is contained by a navigation controller and can get a reference to that navigation controller. The navigation controller retains the array, and the array retains the child view controllers.

The normal way to manipulate a navigation controller's stack is by pushing or popping one view controller at a time. When the navigation controller is instantiated, it is usually initialized with initWithRootViewController:; this is a convenience method that assigns the navigation controller a single initial child view controller, the root view controller that goes at the bottom of the stack:

```
FirstViewController* fvc = [FirstViewController new];
UINavigationController* nav =
    [[UINavigationController alloc] initWithRootViewController:fvc];
self.window.rootViewController = nav;
```

Instead of initWithRootViewController:, you might choose to create the navigation controller with initWithNavigationBarClass:toolbarClass:, in which case you'll have to set its root view controller in a subsequent line of code. The reason for wanting to set the navigation bar and toolbar class has to do with customization of the appearance of the navigation bar and toolbar; sometimes you'll create, say, a UIToolbar subclass for no other reason than to mark this kind of toolbar as needing a certain appearance. I'll explain about that in Chapter 12.

You can also set the UINavigationController's delegate; the delegate should adopt the UINavigationControllerDelegate protocol. The delegate receives messages before and after a child view controller's view is shown.

A navigation controller will typically appear on the screen initially containing just its root view controller, and displaying its root view controller's view. There will be no back button, because there is no back item; there is nowhere to go back to. Subsequently, when the user asks to navigate to a new view, you obtain the next view controller (typically by creating it) and push it onto the stack by calling pushView-Controller:animated: on the navigation controller. The navigation controller performs the animation, and displays the new view controller's view:

```
// FirstViewController.m:
SecondViewController* svc = [SecondViewController new];
[self.navigationController pushViewController:svc animated:YES];
```

Typically, that's all there is to it! There is usually no need to worry about going back; when the user taps the back button to navigate back, the runtime will call popView-ControllerAnimated: for you. When a view controller is popped from the stack, the viewControllers array removes and releases the view controller, which is usually permitted to go out of existence at that point.

New in iOS 7, the user can alternatively go back by dragging a pushed view controller's view from the left edge of the screen. This too is a way of calling popViewController-Animated:, with the difference that the animation is interactive. (Interactive view controller transition animation is the subject of the next section.) The UINavigation-Controller uses a UIScreenEdgePanGestureRecognizer to detect and track the user's gesture. You can obtain a reference to this gesture recognizer as the navigation controller's interactivePopGestureRecognizer; thus you can disable the gesture recognizer and prevent this way of going back, or you can mediate between your own gesture recognizers and this one (see Chapter 5).

You can manipulate the stack more directly if you wish. You can call popViewController-Animated: yourself; to pop multiple items so as to leave a particular view controller at the top of the stack, call popToViewController:animated:, or to pop all the items down to the root view controller, call popToRootViewControllerAnimated:. All of these methods return the popped view controller (or view controllers, as an array), in case you want to do something with them.

To set the entire stack at once, call setViewControllers:animated:. You can access the stack through the viewControllers property. Manipulating the stack directly is the only way, for instance, to delete or insert a view controller in the middle of the stack.

The view controller at the top of the stack is the topViewController; the view controller whose view is displayed is the visibleViewController. Those will normally be the same view controller, but they needn't be, as the topViewController might present a view controller, in which case the presented view controller will be the visibleView-Controller. Other view controllers can be accessed through the viewControllers array by index number. The root view controller is at index 0; if the array's count is c, the back view controller (the one whose navigationItem.backBarButtonItem is currently displayed in the navigation bar) is at index c-2.

The topViewController may need to communicate with the next view controller as the latter is pushed onto the stack, or with the back view controller as it itself is popped off the stack. The problem is parallel to that of communication between an original presenter and a presented view controller, which I discussed earlier in this chapter.

The navigation controller's navigation bar will automatically display the navigation-Item of the topViewController (and the back button of the navigationItem of the back view controller). Thus, a child view controller will probably want to configure its navigationItem early in its lifetime, so that the navigationItem is ready by the time the view controller is handed as a child to the navigation controller. Apple warns (in the UIViewController class reference, under navigationItem) that loadView and viewDid-Load are not appropriate places to do this, because the circumstances under which the view is needed are not related to the circumstances under which the navigation item is needed; however, Apple's own code examples, including the Master–Detail Application template, violate this warning. It is probably best to override initWithNib-Name:bundle: (or initWithCoder: or awakeFromNib, if appropriate) for this purpose.

A navigation controller's navigation bar is accessible as its navigationBar, and can be hidden and shown with setNavigationBarHidden:animated:. (It is possible, though not common, to maintain and manipulate a navigation stack through a navigation controller whose navigation bar never appears.) Its toolbar is accessible as its toolbar, and can be hidden and shown with setToolbarHidden:animated:.

You can also configure a UINavigationController or any view controller that is to serve in a navigation interface in a *.storyboard* or *.xib* file. In the Attributes inspector, use a navigation controller's Bar Visibility checkboxes to determine the presence of the navigation bar and toolbar. The navigation bar and toolbar are themselves subviews of the navigation controller, and you can configure them with the Attributes inspector as well. A navigation controller's root view controller can be specified; in a storyboard, there will be a "root view controller" relationship between the navigation controller and its root view controller.

A view controller in a *.storyboard* or *.xib* file has a Navigation Item where you can specify its title, its prompt, and the text of its back button. (If a view controller in a nib *doesn't* have a Navigation Item and you want to configure this view controller for use in a navigation interface, drag a Navigation Item from the Object library onto the view controller.) You can drag Bar Button Items into a view controller's navigation bar in the canvas to set the left button and right button of its navigationItem. Moreover, the

Navigation Item has outlets, one of which permits you to set its `titleView`. (However, you can't assign a navigation item multiple `rightBarButtonItems` or `leftBarButton-Items` in the nib editor.) Similarly, you can give a view controller Bar Button Items that will appear in the toolbar.

To start an iPhone project with a main storyboard that has a UINavigationController as its root view controller, begin with the Master–Detail Application template. Alternatively, start with the Single View Application template, remove the existing view controller from the storyboard, and add a Navigation Controller in its place. Unfortunately, the nib editor assumes that the navigation controller's root view controller should be a UITableViewController; if that's not the case, here's a better way: select the existing view controller and choose Editor → Embed In → Navigation Controller. A view controller to be subsequently pushed onto the navigation stack can be configured in the storyboard as the destination of a push segue; I'll talk more about that later in the chapter.

 See the discussion earlier in this chapter of how a view controller's view is resized to fit the interface. You will want to prepare your view for this resizing. In iOS 7, a navigation controller's child controller's view by default will underlap a navigation bar or toolbar if the bar is translucent; if it underlaps a navigation bar, it will also underlap the status bar. If the view does not underlap a bar and you hide or show that bar dynamically, the view will be resized then and there. If you show or hide the status bar dynamically, the navigation bar's height will expand or contract accordingly; this too may cause the view's size to change. Showing or hiding the navigation bar or status bar will cause your view controller's `topLayoutGuide` to move; showing or hiding the toolbar will cause your view controller's `bottomLayoutGuide` to move.

Custom Transition Animations

New in iOS 7, you can supply your own custom transition animation for a tab bar controller as its selected view controller changes, for a navigation controller as its child view controller is pushed or popped, or for a presented view controller as it is presented or dismissed.

Given the extensive animation resources of iOS 7 (see Chapter 4), this is an excellent chance for you to provide your app with variety, interest, and distinctiveness. The view of a child view controller pushed onto a navigation controller's stack needn't arrive sliding from the right; it can expand by zooming from the middle of the screen, drop from above and fall into place with a bounce, snap into place like a spring, or whatever else you can dream up.

In your custom transition animation, you have control of both the outgoing view controller's view and the incoming view controller's view. Moreover, you are free to add further temporary views during the course of the animation. For example, as the outgoing view departs and the incoming view arrives, a third view can move across from the outgoing view to the incoming view. This might be a way for you to suggest or emphasize the significance of the transition that is now taking place. In a master–detail navigation interface, for instance, where the master view is a list of story titles, when the user taps a title and the detail view arrives to reveal the full story, the tapped title might simultaneously fly from its place within the list to its new place at the top of the full story, to clarify that these are the same story.

As you contemplate what might be possible and how it might be achieved, don't forget about view snapshotting (see Chapter 2). This is exactly why snapshotting was invented for iOS 7. Instead of moving a view, which could upset the arrangement of things, you can take a snapshot of that view and move the snapshot.

In addition, a custom animation can be interactively gesture-driven (similar to the way a navigation controller's view can be popped, in iOS 7, by dragging from the left edge of the screen). The user does not merely tap and cause an animation to take place; the user performs an extended gesture and gradually summons the new view to supersede the old one. The user can thus participate in the progress of the transition.

Noninteractive Custom Transition Animation

Let's start with the simpler case, where the custom animation is not interactive. Configuring your custom animation requires three steps:

1. The view controller in charge of the transition must have a delegate.

2. As the transition begins, the delegate will be asked for an *animation controller*. This can be any object adopting the UIViewControllerAnimatedTransitioning protocol. Return nil to specify that the default animation (if any) should be used.

3. The animation controller will be sent two messages:

   transitionDuration:
   > The duration of the custom animation.

   animateTransition:
   > The animation controller should perform the animation.

The implementation of animateTransition: works, in general, as follows:

- The parameter is an object supplied by the runtime, adopting the UIViewControllerContextTransitioning protocol, called the *transition context*. The transition context points to a view, the *container view*, where all the action is to take place. Typically, the outgoing view controller's view is in the container view.

- By querying the transition context, you can obtain the outgoing and incoming view controllers and their views. You can also learn the initial frame of the outgoing view controller's view and the ultimate frame of the incoming view controller's view.

- Having gathered this information, your job is to put the incoming view controller's view into the container view and animate it in such a way as to end up at its correct ultimate position.

- When the animation ends, you must call the transition context's `complete-Transition:` to tell it that the animation is over. The outgoing view is then typically removed automatically.

To illustrate, I'll start by animating the transition between two child view controllers of a tab bar controller. The most obvious custom animation is that the new view controller's view should slide in from the side while the old view controller's view should slide out the other side. The direction of the slide should depend on whether the index of the new view controller is greater or less than that of the old view controller.

The first step is to configure a delegate for the tab bar controller. Let's assume that the tab bar controller is our app's root view controller. For simplicity, I'll set its delegate in the app delegate's `application:didFinishLaunchingWithOptions:`, and I'll make that delegate be the app delegate itself:

```
UITabBarController* tbc = (UITabBarController*)self.window.rootViewController;
tbc.delegate = self;
```

The result is that when the user taps a tab bar item to change view controllers, the corresponding delegate method is called, asking for an animation controller. This is what that delegate method looks like for a tab bar controller:

```
- (id<UIViewControllerAnimatedTransitioning>)
        tabBarController:
            (UITabBarController *)tabBarController
        animationControllerForTransitionFromViewController:
            (UIViewController *)fromVC
        toViewController:
            (UIViewController *)toVC {
    return self;
}
```

There is no particular reason why the animation controller should be `self`; indeed, the animation code can be rather elaborate, and it might make for cleaner code to move it off into a class of its own. The animation controller can be any object implementing the UIViewControllerAnimatedTransitioning protocol, and thus may be extremely light-weight; it can be a simple NSObject.

There is also no reason why the animation controller should be the same object every time this method is called. We are provided with plenty of information about what's about to happen: we know the tab bar controller and both child view controllers. Thus we could readily decide in real time to provide a different animation controller under different circumstances, or we could return nil to use the default transition (which, for a tab bar controller, means no animation).

One way or another, then, here we are in the animation controller. Our first job is to reveal in advance the duration of our animation:

```
-(NSTimeInterval)transitionDuration:
        (id<UIViewControllerContextTransitioning>)transitionContext {
    return 0.4;
}
```

Again, the value returned needn't be the same every time this method is called. The transition context has arrived as parameter, and we could query it to identify the two view controllers involved and make a decision based on that. But make sure that the value you return here is indeed the duration of the animation you'll perform in animate-Transition:.

Finally, we come to animateTransition: itself:

```
-(void)animateTransition:
        (id<UIViewControllerContextTransitioning>)transitionContext {
    // ...
}
```

There are certain standard tasks to perform in animateTransition:, so its structure will be roughly the same in every case:

1. Query the transition context (the transitionContext parameter) to get the view controllers, the frames of their views, and the container view.

2. Put the second view controller's view into the container view.

3. Perform the animation, ending with completeTransition:.

First, query the transition context. This code is practically boilerplate for any custom view controller transition animation:

```
UIViewController* vc1 =
    [transitionContext viewControllerForKey:
        UITransitionContextFromViewControllerKey];
UIViewController* vc2 =
    [transitionContext viewControllerForKey:
        UITransitionContextToViewControllerKey];
UIView* con = [transitionContext containerView];
CGRect r1start = [transitionContext initialFrameForViewController:vc1];
CGRect r2end = [transitionContext finalFrameForViewController:vc2];
UIView* v1 = vc1.view;
UIView* v2 = vc2.view;
```

We have the view controllers and their views, and the initial frame of the outgoing view and the destination frame of the incoming view. Now, for our intended animation, we want to calculate the converse, the final frame of the outgoing view and the initial frame of the incoming view. We are sliding the views sideways, so those frames should be positioned sideways from the initial frame of the outgoing view and the final frame of the incoming view. *Which* side they go on depends upon the relative place of these view controllers among the children of the tab bar controller — is this to be a leftward slide or a rightward slide? Since the animation controller is the app delegate, we can get a reference to the tab bar controller the same way we did before:

```
UITabBarController* tbc = (UITabBarController*)self.window.rootViewController;
int ix1 = [tbc.viewControllers indexOfObject:vc1];
int ix2 = [tbc.viewControllers indexOfObject:vc2];
int dir = ix1 < ix2 ? 1 : -1;
CGRect r = r1start;
r.origin.x -= r.size.width * dir;
CGRect r1end = r;
r = r2end;
r.origin.x += r.size.width * dir;
CGRect r2start = r;
```

We now put the second view controller's view into the container view at its initial frame, and perform the animation. We must not forget to call `completeTransition:` after the animation ends:

```
v2.frame = r2start;
[con addSubview:v2];
[UIView animateWithDuration:0.4 animations:^{
    v1.frame = r1end;
    v2.frame = r2end;
} completion:^(BOOL finished) {
    [transitionContext completeTransition:YES];
}];
```

A custom transition for a navigation controller is similar to a custom transition for a tab bar controller, so I don't need to give a separate example. The only slight difference lies in the name of the navigation controller delegate method that will be called to discover whether there's a custom transition animation:

- `navigationController:animationControllerForOperation:fromView-Controller:toViewController:`

The `operation:` parameter allows you to distinguish a push from a pop.

Interactive Custom Transition Animation

With an interactive custom transition animation, the idea is that we track something the user is doing, typically using a gesture recognizer (see Chapter 5), and perform the "frames" of the transition in response. There are two ways to write an interactive custom transition animation. We're going to need an *interactive controller*, namely an object that conforms to the UIViewControllerInteractiveTransitioning protocol. The two ways of writing the code correspond to the two ways of supplying this object:

Create a UIPercentDrivenInteractiveTransition object

We supply a UIPercentDrivenInteractiveTransition object (let's call this the *percent driver*). This percent driver object performs the frames of the animation for us by calling our `animateTransition:` and "freezing" the animation block. All we have to do is track the interaction and call the percent driver's `updateInteractive-Transition:`, telling it how far the interaction has proceeded; the percent driver updates the interface, performing our animation partially to match the extent of the gesture. At the end of the gesture, we decide whether to finish or cancel the transition; accordingly, we call the percent driver's `finishInteractive-Transition` or `cancelInteractiveTransition`. Finally, we call the transition context's `completeTransition:`

Adopt UIViewControllerInteractiveTransitioning

We supply our own object with our own code. This object, conforming to the UI-ViewControllerInteractiveTransitioning protocol, will need to respond to `start-InteractiveTransition:`, whose parameter will be the `transitionContext` object supplied by the system, adopting the UIViewControllerContextTransitioning protocol. Once we are told that the transition has started, we will set up the initial conditions for the animation and then constantly track the interaction, changing the interface and calling the transition context's `updateInteractiveTransition:`. When the interaction ends, we decide whether to finish or cancel the transition; accordingly, we animate into the final or initial conditions, and call the transition context's `finishInteractiveTransition` or `cancelInteractiveTransition`. Finally, we call the transition context's `completeTransition:`.

As an example, I'll describe how to make an interactive version of the tab bar controller transition animation that we've just developed. We'll attach a UIScreenEdgePanGestureRecognizer to the interface so that the user can drag the tab bar controller's adjacent view controller in from the right or from the left.

Since we have already written a noninteractive version of our transition animation, using the percent driver is going to be the simpler approach, because it lets us keep our existing `animateTransition:` code. So let's do that first. The steps build upon those of a noninteractive transition animation; in fact, all the code we've already written can be left more or less as is (which is one of the main reasons for using a percent driver):

1. The view controller in charge of the transition must have a delegate.

2. We observe that the user is interacting in a way that should trigger a change of view controller. We respond by triggering that change.

3. As the transition begins, the delegate will be asked for an animation controller, as before. We return an object adopting the UIViewControllerAnimatedTransitioning protocol, as before.

4. The delegate is also asked for an *interactive controller*. (This happened before, but we didn't supply one, which is why our transition animation wasn't interactive.) We have elected to use a UIPercentDrivenInteractiveTransition object. So we return that object.

5. The animation controller is sent the same two messages as before:

    `transitionDuration:`
    The duration of the custom animation.

    `animateTransition:`
    The animation controller should perform the animation. But the animation will not in fact take place at this moment; its "frames" will be produced as the interaction proceeds.

6. We continue tracking the interaction, calling our percent driver's `update-InteractiveTransition:` to tell it how far the interaction has proceeded. The percent driver performs that much of our animation for us.

7. Sooner or later the interaction will end. At this point, we must decide whether to declare the transition completed or cancelled. The usual approach is to say that if the user performed more than half the full interactive gesture, that constitutes completion; otherwise, it constitutes cancellation. We call the percent driver's `finishInteractiveTransition` or `cancelInteractiveTransition` accordingly. The percent driver either completes the animation or (if we cancelled) *reverses the animation*.

8. The animation is now completed, and its completion block is called. We call `completeTransition:`, with the argument stating whether the transition was finished or cancelled.

Now I'll write the code performing the additional steps. To track the user's gesture, I'll put a pair of UIScreenEdgePanGestureRecognizers into the interface, and keep references to them so they can be identified later. The gesture recognizers are attached to the tab view controller's view (`tbc.view`), as this will remain constant while the views of its view controllers are sliding across the screen:

```
UIScreenEdgePanGestureRecognizer* sep =
    [[UIScreenEdgePanGestureRecognizer alloc]
        initWithTarget:self action:@selector(pan:)];
sep.edges = UIRectEdgeRight;
[tbc.view addGestureRecognizer:sep];
sep.delegate = self;
self.rightEdger = sep;
sep =
```

```
        [[UIScreenEdgePanGestureRecognizer alloc]
            initWithTarget:self action:@selector(pan:)];
    sep.edges = UIRectEdgeLeft;
    [tbc.view addGestureRecognizer:sep];
    sep.delegate = self;
    self.leftEdger = sep;
```

The delegate of the two gesture recognizers prevents the pan gesture from operating
unless there is another child of the tab view controller available on that side of the current
child:

```
-(BOOL)gestureRecognizerShouldBegin:(UIScreenEdgePanGestureRecognizer *)g {
    UITabBarController* tbc =
        (UITabBarController*)self.window.rootViewController;
    BOOL result = NO;
    if (g == self.rightEdger)
        result = (tbc.selectedIndex < tbc.viewControllers.count - 1);
    else
        result = (tbc.selectedIndex > 0);
    return result;
}
```

So much for preparation. If the gesture recognizer action handler pan: is called, we now
know that this means our interactive transition animation is to take place. I'll break
down the discussion to examine each of the gesture recognizer's stages separately:

```
- (void) pan: (UIScreenEdgePanGestureRecognizer *) g {
    UIView* v = g.view;
    if (g.state == UIGestureRecognizerStateBegan) {
        self.inter = [UIPercentDrivenInteractiveTransition new];
        UITabBarController* tbc =
            (UITabBarController*)self.window.rootViewController;
        if (g == self.rightEdger)
            tbc.selectedIndex = tbc.selectedIndex + 1;
        else
            tbc.selectedIndex = tbc.selectedIndex - 1;
    }
    // ... more to come ...
}
```

As the gesture begins, we create the UIPercentDrivenInteractiveTransition object and
store it in an instance variable (self.inter). We then set the tab bar controller's
selectedIndex. This triggers the animation! As before, the runtime turns to the tab bar
controller's delegate to see whether there is a transition animation; as before, we make
ourselves the animation controller:

```
- (id<UIViewControllerAnimatedTransitioning>)
        tabBarController:
            (UITabBarController *)tabBarController
        animationControllerForTransitionFromViewController:
            (UIViewController *)fromVC
```

```
        toViewController:
            (UIViewController *)toVC {
    return self;
}
```

The runtime now asks if there is also an interactive controller. There wasn't one in our previous example, but now there is — the percent driver:

```
-(id<UIViewControllerInteractiveTransitioning>)
    tabBarController:
        (UITabBarController *)tabBarController
    interactionControllerForAnimationController:
        (id<UIViewControllerAnimatedTransitioning>)animationController {
    return self.inter;
}
```

The runtime now calls our percent driver's startInteractiveTransition:, handing it a reference to the transition context. This is where the magic happens. The percent driver immediately turns around and calls our animateTransition: method. Yet the animation does not happen! The percent driver has "frozen" the animation described in the animation block. Our job now is to keep calling the percent driver, telling it what "frame" of the animation to display at every moment; the percent driver will move the views to correspond to that "frame" of the animation as the interaction proceeds, and will call the transition context on our behalf.

(I suppose you're wondering how this magic is performed. The percent driver takes advantage of the fact that a CALayer conforms to the CAMediaTiming protocol, as I mentioned in Chapter 4. It asks the transition context for the container view, obtains that view's layer, and sets the layer's speed to 0. This freezes the animation. Then, as we call the percent driver's updateInteractiveTransition:, it adjusts that layer's time-Offset accordingly, thus displaying a different "frame" of the animation.)

We are now back in the gesture recognizer's action handler, as the gesture proceeds; we keep sending updateInteractiveTransition: to the percent driver:

```
- (void) pan: (UIScreenEdgePanGestureRecognizer *) g {
    UIView* v = g.view;
    // ...
    else if (g.state == UIGestureRecognizerStateChanged) {
        CGPoint delta = [g translationInView: v];
        CGFloat percent = fabs(delta.x/v.bounds.size.width);
        [self.inter updateInteractiveTransition:percent];
    }
    // ...
}
```

When the gesture ends, we decide whether this counts as finishing or canceling, and we report to the percent driver accordingly:

```
- (void) pan: (UIScreenEdgePanGestureRecognizer *) g {
    UIView* v = g.view;
    // ...
    else if (g.state == UIGestureRecognizerStateEnded) {
        CGPoint delta = [g translationInView: v];
        CGFloat percent = fabs(delta.x/v.bounds.size.width);
        if (percent > 0.5)
            [self.inter finishInteractiveTransition];
        else
            [self.inter cancelInteractiveTransition];
    }
    // ...
}
```

If we call `finishInteractiveTransition`, the percent driver plays the rest of the animation forward to completion. If we call `cancelInteractiveTransition`, the percent driver plays the animation backward to its beginning!

Finally, we find ourselves back inside `animateTransition:`, in the animation `completion:` handler. This is the only place where a change is needed in our previously existing code. As I've just said, the transition can complete in one of two ways. We must still call `completeTransition:` ourselves, but we must tell the transition context which way things turned out, so that the transition context can restore the previous state of things if the transition was cancelled. Luckily, the transition context already knows whether the transition was cancelled. So we ask it:

```
BOOL cancelled = [transitionContext transitionWasCancelled];
[transitionContext completeTransition:!cancelled];
```

The amazing thing is that, with only a tiny bit of further modification (not shown), the very same code will now serve us both for an interactive and a noninteractive version of the transition animation. That is the point of using a percent driver.

If we *don't* use a percent driver, then the entire interactive transition animation is up to us. We ourselves must repeatedly reposition the views at every stage of the gesture, and when the gesture ends, we ourselves must animate them either into their final position or back into their initial position. We will no longer need an `animateTransition:` method (it must be present, to satisfy the protocol requirements, but it can be empty); all the logic of initializing, positioning, and finalizing the moving views must be effectively deconstructed and folded into the various stages of our gesture recognizer action handler. There is no percent driver; at every stage, we must keep talking to the transition context itself.

The resulting code is verbose, and can be difficult to express in a compact or object-oriented way. However, it is more powerful, more flexible, and possibly more reliable than using a percent driver. I'll just sketch the structure. We have our gesture recognizer(s) as before. When the gesture begins, the `UIGestureRecognizerStateBegan` section of the action handler triggers the transition as before. The delegate is asked for an animation controller and an interaction controller; the interaction controller is now not a percent driver, but some object that we will supply — let's say it's self:

```
-(id<UIViewControllerInteractiveTransitioning>)
    tabBarController:
        (UITabBarController *)tabBarController
    interactionControllerForAnimationController:
        (id<UIViewControllerAnimatedTransitioning>)animationController {
    return self;
}
```

The result is that, in our role as adopter of the UIViewControllerInteractiveTransitioning protocol, our startInteractiveTransition: is called; here, we set up the initial conditions of the transition, putting the view controllers' views into place, and storing a reference to the transitionContext in an instance variable where our gesture recognizer action handler can access it:

```
-(void)startInteractiveTransition:
        (id<UIViewControllerContextTransitioning>)transitionContext {
    // store transition context so the gesture recognizer can get at it
    self.context = transitionContext;
    // ... set up initial conditions ...
    // ... store any additional instance variables ...
}
```

Now our gesture recognizer action handler is called again, repeatedly, at the UIGesture-RecognizerStateChanged stage. We keep repositioning our views (not animating them) in accordance with the progress of the interactive gesture. At the same time, we keep informing the transition context of that progress:

```
else if (g.state == UIGestureRecognizerStateChanged) {
    // calculate progress
    CGPoint delta = [g translationInView: v];
    CGFloat percent = fabs(delta.x/v.bounds.size.width);
    // ... put views into position corresponding to current "frame" ...
    // ... and finally, notify the transition context
    v1.frame = // whatever
    v2.frame = // whatever
    [self.context updateInteractiveTransition:percent];
}
```

Finally, our gesture recognizer action handler is called one last time, at the UIGesture-RecognizerStateEnded stage. We now animate our views the rest of the way, or else back to the start, and call either finishInteractiveTransition or cancelInteractive-Transition followed by completeTransition: with the appropriate argument:

```
if (percent > 0.5) {
    [UIView animateWithDuration:0.2 animations:^{
        v1.frame = r1end;
        v2.frame = r2end;
    } completion:^(BOOL finished) {
```

```
        [transitionContext finishInteractiveTransition];
        [transitionContext completeTransition:YES];
    }];
}
else {
    [UIView animateWithDuration:0.2 animations:^{
        v1.frame = r1start;
        v2.frame = r2start;
    } completion:^(BOOL finished) {
        [transitionContext cancelInteractiveTransition];
        [transitionContext completeTransition:NO];
    }];
}
```

Why must we call updateInteractiveTransition: throughout the progress of the interactive gesture? For a tab bar controller's transition, this call has little or no significance. But in the case, say, of a navigation controller, the animation has a component separate from what you're doing — the change in the appearance of the navigation bar (as the old title departs and the new title arrives, and so forth). The transition context needs to coordinate that animation with the interactive gesture and with your animation. So you need to keep telling it where things are in the course of the interaction.

Custom Presented View Controller Transition

A new iOS 7 view controller property, transitioningDelegate, allows you to set a delegate (on the *presented* view controller) that will be asked for an animation controller and an interactive controller separately for both the presentation and the dismissal:

- animationControllerForPresentedController:presenting-
  Controller:sourceController:
- interactionControllerForPresentation:
- animationControllerForDismissedController:
- interactionControllerForDismissal:

If you return the same object as the animation controller for both presentation and dismissal, your implementation of animateTransition: will need to distinguish which is happening. During presentation, the "from" view controller's view is the old interface, and the "to" view controller is the presented view controller. But during dismissal, it's the other way round: the "from" view controller is the presented view controller.

A presented view controller transition has a problem that a tab bar controller or navigation controller transition doesn't have — there's no existing view to serve as the container view. Therefore, as the transition begins, the runtime has to pull some serious hanky-panky (that's a technical programming term): it creates an extra container view and inserts it into the view hierarchy, and removes it after the transition is over.

When the modal presentation style is UIModalPresentationFullScreen or UIModal-PresentationCurrentContext, the effect from your point of view is similar to a tab bar controller or navigation controller animation. By the time you have a transition context, the runtime has already ripped the "from" view out of its superview, created the container view, put it into the "from" view's old superview, and put the "from" view into the container view. You put the "to" view into the container view and do the animation, and afterward the runtime rips the "to" view out of the container view, puts it into the container view's superview, removes the "from" view from the interface, and throws away the container view.

Other modal presentation styles, however, leave both view controllers' views in place: the presented view controller's view appears only partially covering the already existing view. You may have to make allowance for the special conditions of this arrangement.

Let's consider, for example, the iPad's UIModalPresentationFormSheet presentation style. The presented view controller's view appears smaller than the screen, leaving the presenting view controller's view in place, visible only "through a glass darkly". That darkness is in fact due to an extra view, a "dimming view"; in front of the dimming view is a "drop shadow view", and the presented view controller's view is inside that. Moreover, at the time the custom animation begins, neither view is in the transition context's containerView; both are already in their final places in the real interface.

This is a complicated arrangement, and we mustn't do anything to upset it. Nevertheless, I am quite willing to pluck the presented view controller's view from its place in the interface, stick it into the containerView, animate it, and return it to its original place. Let's say, for instance, that we want the presented view controller's view to appear to grow from the center of the screen. I pull the second view (v2) out of its superview, preserve its frame, animate it, restore its frame, and put it back in its old superview. The transition context has nothing useful to say about v2's frame relative to the container-View, so I copy its superview's frame:

```
-(void)animateTransition:
    (id<UIViewControllerContextTransitioning>)transitionContext {
    UIViewController* vc2 =
        [transitionContext viewControllerForKey:
            UITransitionContextToViewControllerKey];
    UIView* con = [transitionContext containerView];
    UIView* v2 = vc2.view;
    UIView* drop = v2.superview;
    CGRect oldv2frame = v2.frame;
    [con addSubview: v2];
    v2.frame = drop.frame;
    v2.transform = CGAffineTransformMakeScale(0.1, 0.1);
    [UIView animateWithDuration:0.4 animations:^{
        v2.transform = CGAffineTransformIdentity;
    } completion:^(BOOL finished) {
        [drop addSubview: v2];
```

```
            v2.frame = oldv2frame;
            [transitionContext completeTransition:YES];
        }];
    }
```

If that seems extreme, we might prefer to leave v2 in place and animate a snapshot instead. But it is not easy to do this, because at the time animateTransition: is called, v2 has not been rendered; there is nothing to take a snapshot of. I don't know any way to force v2 to be rendered immediately, short of calling its layer's renderInContext:. So I do that, rendering it into an image context, and end up animating an image view:

```
-(void)animateTransition:
        (id<UIViewControllerContextTransitioning>)transitionContext {
    UIViewController* vc2 =
        [transitionContext viewControllerForKey:
            UITransitionContextToViewControllerKey];
    UIView* con = [transitionContext containerView];
    UIView* v2 = vc2.view;
    // force rendering and snapshot now
    UIGraphicsBeginImageContextWithOptions(v2.bounds.size, YES, 0);
    [v2.layer renderInContext:UIGraphicsGetCurrentContext()];
    UIImage* im = UIGraphicsGetImageFromCurrentImageContext();
    UIGraphicsEndImageContext();
    UIView* snap = [[UIImageView alloc] initWithImage:im];
    snap.frame = v2.superview.frame;
    snap.transform = CGAffineTransformMakeScale(0.1, 0.1);
    [con addSubview: snap];
    // animate the snapshot
    [UIView animateWithDuration:0.4 animations:^{
        snap.transform = CGAffineTransformIdentity;
    } completion:^(BOOL finished) {
        [transitionContext completeTransition:YES];
    }];
}
```

When the modal presentation style is UIModalPresentationCustom (new in iOS 7), the runtime leaves the final position of the presented view controller's view *entirely up to you* — possibly only partially covering the existing view, *even on an iPhone*. This is possible because the transition context's container view is *not* taken away when the presentation transition ends; it remains in place until after the dismissal transition. Therefore, you can also put extra views into the container view, and they will stay there together with the presented view controller's view.

To illustrate, I'll write a presented view controller that imitates a UIAlertView — a small view that floats over the existing interface, which is behind a darkened glass. This is something that developers have longed for since the earliest days of iOS. A UIAlertView is convenient and small, but you can't (legally) customize its content very much. A presented view controller's view, on the other hand, is completely up to you. In the past, a presented view controller's view on the iPhone had to cover the entire screen. Now that restriction is lifted.

Our view controller, then, has a small view — let's say about 260×150 — and we aren't going to resize it. We will cause this view to shrink into place in the middle of the screen when it is presented, and to shrink further when it is dismissed, just as an alert view does. While our view is present, the surrounding screen behind it will be darkened slightly.

Our view controller's `modalPresentationStyle` is `UIModalPresentationCustom`, and its `transitioningDelegate` is `self`. When the transitioning delegate methods are called, the view controller returns `self` as the animation controller. When `animate-Transition:` is called, we start by gathering up the relevant information from the transition context, as usual:

```
UIViewController* vc1 =
    [transitionContext
        viewControllerForKey:UITransitionContextFromViewControllerKey];
UIViewController* vc2 =
    [transitionContext
        viewControllerForKey:UITransitionContextToViewControllerKey];
UIView* con = [transitionContext containerView];
UIView* v1 = vc1.view;
UIView* v2 = vc2.view;
```

We can distinguish presentation from dismissal easily: if this is presentation, the "to" view controller's view is our own view:

```
if (v2 == self.view) {
    // ... presentation ...
}
```

The "to" view is not yet in the `containerView`. The "from" view, on the other hand, *is* in the `containerView`, where it will remain until after dismissal. We start by adding a shadow view that fills the container view, covering the "to" view and creating the "through a glass darkly" effect:

```
UIView* shadow = [[UIView alloc] initWithFrame:con.bounds];
shadow.backgroundColor = [UIColor colorWithWhite:0.4 alpha:0.2];
shadow.alpha = 0;
shadow.tag = 987;
[con addSubview: shadow];
```

Now we position the incoming view in the center of the container view, in front of the shadow view. We must be careful in our treatment of this view, because of the possibility that the interface will be rotated. If the interface has already been rotated when presentation occurs, the incoming view has a transform; we mustn't accidentally remove that transform. If the interface is rotated while our view is present, our view mustn't be resized as its superview's bounds dimensions are swapped; I'll use an autoresizing mask to ensure that:

```
v2.center =
    CGPointMake(CGRectGetMidX(con.bounds), CGRectGetMidY(con.bounds));
v2.autoresizingMask =
    UIViewAutoresizingFlexibleTopMargin |
    UIViewAutoresizingFlexibleBottomMargin |
    UIViewAutoresizingFlexibleRightMargin |
    UIViewAutoresizingFlexibleLeftMargin;
CGAffineTransform scale = CGAffineTransformMakeScale(1.6,1.6);
v2.transform = CGAffineTransformConcat(scale, v2.transform);
v2.alpha = 0;
[con addSubview: v2];
```

Both the shadow view and our view are initially invisible. We animate them into visibility, shrinking our view's scale transform to its proper size at the same time. As we do so, we set the existing view's `tintAdjustmentMode` to its dimmed appearance, just as a UIAlertView does, to add to the sense that the user can work only within our view (see Chapter 12 for more about the `tintAdjustmentMode`):

```
v1.tintAdjustmentMode = UIViewTintAdjustmentModeDimmed;
[UIView animateWithDuration:0.25 animations:^{
    v2.alpha = 1;
    v2.transform =
        CGAffineTransformConcat(CGAffineTransformInvert(scale), v2.transform);
    shadow.alpha = 1;
} completion:^(BOOL finished) {
    [transitionContext completeTransition:YES];
}];
```

At dismissal time, both views and our extra shadow view are still in the container-View. We animate away the shadow view — we cleverly gave it a tag earlier so as to be able to identify it now — while at the same time we animate away the presented view (the "from" view); at the end, we restore the tint color of the background view (the "to" view):

```
} else {
    UIView* shadow = [con viewWithTag:987];
    [UIView animateWithDuration:0.25 animations:^{
        shadow.alpha = 0;
        v1.transform = CGAffineTransformScale(v1.transform,0.5,0.5);
        v1.alpha = 0;
    } completion:^(BOOL finished) {
        v2.tintAdjustmentMode = UIViewTintAdjustmentModeAutomatic;
        [transitionContext completeTransition:YES];
    }];
}
```

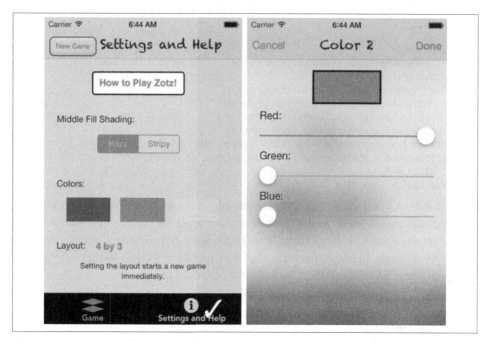

Figure 6-9. A view and a presented view that covers it

I'll conclude by describing an elaborate real-life presentation animation from one of my own apps. Figure 6-9 shows the existing view and the presented view. The presented view appears to cover the existing view, which is visible through it in a blurred way.

The modal presentation style of the second view controller is `UIModalPresentation-Custom`. The second view rises from the bottom of the screen, in imitation of a `UIModal-TransitionStyleCoverVertical` animation. At the same time, the color swatch that was tapped in the first view, which summons the presented view controller, rises to become the color swatch in the second view; this serves as an almost subconscious indication that the user is editing this swatch.

We thus have to manage three things simultaneously: the blurred background, the rising presented view, and the moving swatch.

To create the blurred background, the first view is snapshotted into an image context:

```
[vc1.view drawViewHierarchyInRect: v1.bounds afterScreenUpdates: NO];
```

The image is then blurred and put into a UIImageView. This image view cannot simply be the background of the second view, because the second view is going to rise from the bottom of the screen: we don't want the blurred image to rise with it, as this would break the illusion that the second view itself is blurring the first view behind it. So the image view is a separate view placed into the container view, with a `contentMode` of `UIView-`

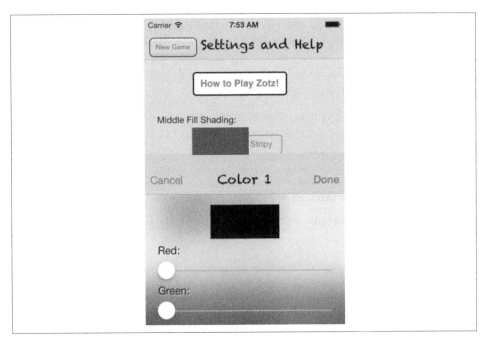

Figure 6-10. An elaborate transition animation

ContentModeBottom and an initial height of zero. The second view, meanwhile, has a transparent background. As the second view rises from the bottom of the screen, we simultaneously increase the height of the image view behind it, also from the bottom of the screen! Thus the blur is stationary behind the second view.

Figure 6-10 is a freeze frame in the middle of the animation, as the second view rises from the bottom of the screen; as you can see, the part of the first view that's behind the second view appears blurred, but the part of the first view that isn't yet covered by the second view is still sharp.

At the same time, in Figure 6-10, the blue swatch, which the user tapped, is rising from its place in the first view to its place in the second view. It is currently higher than the black rectangle in the second view that it will eventually occupy, but they are both heading toward the same spot, and will meet there precisely at the end of the animation. The swatch is not really moving from one view to the other; what the user sees during the transition is actually just a snapshot view, taken by snapshotting the colored rectangle that the user originally tapped:

```
UIView* swatch = [self.tappedColor snapshotViewAfterScreenUpdates:NO];
```

The swatch in the second view has been hidden; when the transition ends, the snapshot of the swatch will be removed and the swatch in the second view will be made visible.

The really tricky part is getting the initial and final frame of the snapshot view and translating those into `containerView` coordinates. The solution is to start by putting the "to" view into its *final* position and then *requesting immediate layout*:

```
v2.frame = v1.bounds;
[con addSubview: v2];
[con layoutIfNeeded];
```

This causes everything in v2 to assume its ultimate position, and now we can work out the initial and final frames of the moving swatch snapshot view:

```
CGRect r1 = self.tappedColor.frame;
r1 = [self.tappedColor.superview convertRect:r1 toView:vc1.view];
CGRect r2 = cpc.swatch.frame;
r2 = [vc2.view convertRect:r2 fromView:cpc.swatch.superview];
```

Then and only then do we move v2 to its position below the bottom of the screen, ready to begin the animation.

Transition Coordinator

While a view controller is involved in a transition, its `transitionCoordinator` property is set by the runtime to an object implementing the UIViewControllerTransitionCoordinator protocol. This object, the *transition coordinator*, is a kind of wrapper around the transition context, and also adopts the UIViewControllerTransitionCoordinatorContext protocol, just like the transition context. Thus, in effect, view controllers can find out about the transition they are involved in.

Unfortunately, exactly *when* the transition coordinator is available seems to differ depending on the type of transition. Take, for example, an interactive transition instigated through a pan gesture from the right edge of the screen, such as I described earlier. If the view controllers involved in this transition are children of a UINavigationController, then the transition coordinator is available in the second view controller's `viewWillAppear:`; but if their parent is a UITabBarController, it isn't. I regard this inconsistency as a bug. You'll have to experiment for your particular situation.

One use of the transition coordinator is to ascertain whether we are in an interactive transition and, if so, whether it has been cancelled. It may well be that what your view controller wants to do will differ in this situation. You can send the transition coordinator the `notifyWhenInteractionEndsUsingBlock:` message to run a block at the moment the user abandons the interactive gesture and the transition is about to be either completed or cancelled. Here's code from a view controller that might be pushed interactively onto a UINavigationController:

```
-(void)viewWillAppear:(BOOL)animated {
    [super viewWillAppear:animated];
    id<UIViewControllerTransitionCoordinator> tc = self.transitionCoordinator;
    if (tc && [tc initiallyInteractive]) {
        [tc notifyWhenInteractionEndsUsingBlock:
          ^(id<UIViewControllerTransitionCoordinatorContext> context) {
            if ([context isCancelled]) {
                // ...
            }
        }];
    }
}
```

If the view controller's parent is a UITabBarController, it can ask whether its view is disappearing because an interactive gesture was abandoned and the transition was cancelled, like this:

```
- (void) viewWillDisappear:(BOOL)animated {
    [super viewWillDisappear:animated];
    id<UIViewControllerTransitionCoordinator> tc = self.transitionCoordinator;
    if (tc && [tc initiallyInteractive] && [tc isCancelled]) {
        // ...
    }
}
```

You can also use the transition coordinator to be notified when the transition ends. This works *even if this is not a custom transition*; for example, you can run code in response to the default push transition ending. Call the transition coordinator's animate-AlongsideTransition:completion: with a completion: block. This code is from the top view controller of a UINavigationController as another view controller is pushed on top of it:

```
-(void)viewWillDisappear:(BOOL)animated {
    [super viewWillDisappear:animated];
    id<UIViewControllerTransitionCoordinator> tc = self.transitionCoordinator;
    if (tc) {
        [tc animateAlongsideTransition:nil completion:
          ^(id<UIViewControllerTransitionCoordinatorContext> context) {
            // ...
        }];
    }
}
```

Another use of animateAlongsideTransition:completion: is, as the name suggests, to supply an additional animation. This works even if the transition is interactive. If the view affected by this additional animation is outside the transition context's container view, call animateAlongsideTransitionInView:animation:completion: instead. (But this secondary animation is not reliable; sometimes, the affected view property is changed immediately, without animation.)

Page View Controller

A page view controller (UIPageViewController) displays a view controller's view. The user, by a gesture, can navigate in one direction or the other to see the next or the previous view controller's view, successively — like turning the pages of a book.

To create a UIPageViewController, initialize it with `initWithTransition-Style:navigationOrientation:options:`. Here's what the parameters mean:

`transitionStyle:`
> The animation style during navigation. Your choices are:
>
> * `UIPageViewControllerTransitionStylePageCurl`
> * `UIPageViewControllerTransitionStyleScroll` (sliding)

`navigationOrientation:`
> The direction of navigation. Your choices are:
>
> * `UIPageViewControllerNavigationOrientationHorizontal`
> * `UIPageViewControllerNavigationOrientationVertical`

`options:`
> A dictionary. Possible keys are:
>
> `UIPageViewControllerOptionSpineLocationKey`
> > If you're using the page curl transition, this is the position of the pivot line around which those page curl transitions rotate. The value is an NSNumber wrapping one of the following:
> >
> > * `UIPageViewControllerSpineLocationMin` (left or top)
> > * `UIPageViewControllerSpineLocationMid` (middle; two pages are shown at once)
> > * `UIPageViewControllerSpineLocationMax` (right or bottom)
>
> `UIPageViewControllerOptionInterPageSpacingKey`
> > If you're using the scroll transition, this is the spacing between successive pages, visible as a gap during the transition. The value is an NSNumber wrapping a float.

You then assign the page view controller a `dataSource`, which should conform to the UIPageViewControllerDataSource protocol, and configure the page view controller's initial content by handing it its initial child view controller(s). You do that by calling `setViewControllers:direction:animated:completion:`. Here's what the parameters mean:

`viewControllers:`

> An array of one view controller, unless you're using the page curl transition and the `Mid` spine location, in which case it's an array of two view controllers.

`direction:`

> The animation direction. This probably won't matter when you're assigning the page view controller its initial content, as you are not likely to want any animation. Possible values are:
>
> - `UIPageViewControllerNavigationDirectionForward`
> - `UIPageViewControllerNavigationDirectionBackward`

`animated:, completion:`

> A BOOL and a completion handler.

Here's a minimal example. First I need to explain where my pages come from. I've got a UIViewController subclass called Pep and a data model consisting of an array (`self.pep`) of the names of the Pep Boys, along with eponymous image files in my app bundle portraying each Pep Boy. I initialize a Pep object by calling `initWithPep-Boy:nib:bundle:`, supplying the name of a Pep Boy from the array; Pep's `viewDid-Load` then fetches the corresponding image and assigns it as the image of a UIImageView within its own view:

```
self.pic.image = [UIImage imageNamed: self.boy];
```

Thus, each page in the page view controller portrays an image of a named Pep Boy. Here's how I create the page view controller:

```
// make a page view controller
UIPageViewController* pvc =
    [[UIPageViewController alloc]
        initWithTransitionStyle:
            UIPageViewControllerTransitionStylePageCurl
        navigationOrientation:
            UIPageViewControllerNavigationOrientationHorizontal
        options: nil];
// give it an initial page
Pep* page = [[Pep alloc] initWithPepBoy:self.pep[0] nib:nil bundle:nil];
[pvc setViewControllers: @[page]
            direction: UIPageViewControllerNavigationDirectionForward
             animated: NO completion: nil];
// give it a data source
pvc.dataSource = self;
```

As for the page view controller's view, the page view controller is a UIViewController, and its view must get into the interface by standard means. You can make the page view controller the window's `rootViewController`, you can make it a presented view controller, or you can make it a child view controller of a tab bar controller or a navigation controller. If you want the page view controller's view to be a subview of some other view controller's view, you must turn that other view controller into a custom container view controller (as I'll describe in the next section). At the same time, you must retain the page view controller itself; that will happen in the natural course of things if you get its view into the interface correctly.

We now have a page view controller's view in our interface, itself containing and displaying the view of a Pep view controller that is its child. We have three pages, because we have three Pep Boys and their images — but only potentially. Just as with a navigation controller, you don't supply (or even create) a page until the moment comes to navigate to it. When that happens, one of these data source methods will be called:

- `pageViewController:viewControllerAfterViewController:`
- `pageViewController:viewControllerBeforeViewController:`

The job of those methods is to return the requested successive view controller. You'll need a strategy for doing that; the strategy you devise will depend on how your model maintains the data.

My data is an array of unique strings, so all I have to do is find the previous name or the next name in the array. Here's one of my data source methods:

```
-(UIViewController *)pageViewController:(UIPageViewController *)pvc
        viewControllerAfterViewController:(UIViewController *)viewController {
    NSString* boy = [(Pep*)viewController boy]; // string name of this Pep Boy
    NSUInteger ix = [self.pep indexOfObject:boy]; // find it in the data model
    ix++;
    if (ix >= [self.pep count])
        return nil; // there is no next page
    return [[Pep alloc] initWithPepBoy: self.pep[ix] nib: nil bundle: nil];
}
```

You can also, at any time, call `setViewControllers:...` to change programmatically what page is being displayed, possibly with animation. I do that in my Latin flashcard app during drill mode (Figure 6-5), to advance to the next term in the current drill:

```
[self.terms shuffle];
Term* whichTerm = self.terms[0];
CardController* cdc = [[CardController alloc] initWithTerm:whichTerm];
[self.pvc setViewControllers:@[cdc]
                   direction:UIPageViewControllerNavigationDirectionForward
                    animated:YES completion:nil];
```

If you refer, in the `completion` block of `setViewControllers:...`, to the page view controller to which the message was sent, ARC will warn of a possible retain cycle. I don't know why there would be a retain cycle, but I take no chances: I do the weak–strong dance to prevent it.

A page view controller with the scroll transition style has a long-standing bug that you might need to watch out for. In order to be ready with the next or previous page as the user starts to scroll, the page view controller caches the next or previous view controller in the sequence. If you navigate manually with `setViewControllers:...` to a view controller that isn't the next or previous in the sequence, and if `animated:` is YES, this cache is not refreshed; if the user now navigates with a scroll gesture, the wrong view controller is shown. I have developed a gut-wrenchingly horrible workaround: in the `completion:` handler, perform the same navigation again without animation. This requires doing the weak–strong dance and using delayed performance:

```
__weak UIPageViewController* pvcw = pvc;
[pvc setViewControllers:@[page]
    direction:UIPageViewControllerNavigationDirectionForward
    animated:YES completion:^(BOOL finished) {
        UIPageViewController* pvcs = pvcw;
        if (!pvcs) return;
        dispatch_async(dispatch_get_main_queue(), ^{
            [pvcs setViewControllers:@[page]
                direction:UIPageViewControllerNavigationDirectionForward
                animated:NO completion:nil];
        });
    }];
```

If you're using the scroll style, the page view controller will optionally display a page indicator (a UIPageControl, see Chapter 12). The user can look at this to get a sense of what page we're on, and can tap to the left or right of it to navigate. To get the page indicator, you must implement two more data source methods; they are consulted in response to `setViewControllers:...`. We called that method initially to configure the page view controller, and if we never call it again, these data source methods won't be called again either, as the page view controller can keep track of the current index on its own. Here's my implementation for the Pep Boy example:

```
-(NSInteger)presentationCountForPageViewController:(UIPageViewController*)pvc {
    return [self.pep count];
}
-(NSInteger)presentationIndexForPageViewController:(UIPageViewController*)pvc {
    Pep* page = [pvc viewControllers][0];
    NSString* boy = page.boy;
    return [self.pep indexOfObject:boy];
}
```

In iOS 7, the page view controller's page indicator by default has white dots and a clear background, so it is invisible in front of a white background. Moreover, there is no direct access to it. Use the appearance proxy (Chapter 12) to customize it. For example:

```
UIPageControl* proxy =
    [UIPageControl appearanceWhenContainedIn:
        [UIPageViewController class], nil];
[proxy setPageIndicatorTintColor:
    [[UIColor redColor] colorWithAlphaComponent:0.6]];
[proxy setCurrentPageIndicatorTintColor:[UIColor redColor]];
[proxy setBackgroundColor:[UIColor yellowColor]];
```

It is also possible to assign a page view controller a delegate, which adopts the UIPage-ViewControllerDelegate protocol. You get an event when the user starts turning the page and when the user finishes turning the page, and you get a chance to change the spine location dynamically in response to a change in device orientation. As with a tab bar controller's delegate or a navigation controller's delegate, a page view controller's delegate in iOS 7 also gets messages allowing it to specify the page view controller's rotation policy, so that you don't have to subclass UIPageViewController solely for that purpose.

If you've assigned the page view controller the page curl transition, the user can ask for navigation by tapping at either edge of the view or by dragging across the view. These gestures are detected through two gesture recognizers, which you can access through the page view controller's `gestureRecognizers` property. The documentation suggests that you might change where the user can tap or drag by attaching them to a different view, and other customizations are possible as well. In this code, I change the page view controller's behavior so that the user must double tap to request navigation:

```
for (UIGestureRecognizer* g in pvc.gestureRecognizers)
    if ([g isKindOfClass: [UITapGestureRecognizer class]])
        ((UITapGestureRecognizer*)g).numberOfTapsRequired = 2;
```

Of course you are also free to add to the user's stock of gestures for requesting navigation. You can supply any controls or gesture recognizers that make sense for your app, and respond by calling `setViewControllers:...`. For example, if you're using the scroll transition style, there's no tap gesture recognizer, so the user can't tap at either edge of the page view controller's view to request navigation. Let's change that. I've added invisible views at either edge of my Pep view controller's view, with tap gesture recognizers attached. When the user taps, the tap gesture recognizer fires, and the action handler posts a notification whose `object` is the tap gesture recognizer. I receive this notification and use the tap gesture recognizer's view's `tag` to learn which view it is; I then navigate accordingly (n is the notification, pvc is the page view controller):

```
UIGestureRecognizer* g = n.object;
int which = g.view.tag;
UIViewController* vc =
    which == 0 ?
        [self pageViewController:pvc
            viewControllerBeforeViewController:pvc.viewControllers[0]] :
        [self pageViewController:pvc
            viewControllerAfterViewController:pvc.viewControllers[0]];
```

```
    if (!vc) return;
    UIPageViewControllerNavigationDirection dir =
        which == 0 ?
        UIPageViewControllerNavigationDirectionReverse :
        UIPageViewControllerNavigationDirectionForward;
    [pvc setViewControllers:@[vc] direction:dir animated:YES completion:nil];
```

One further bit of configuration, if you're using the page curl transition, is performed through the doubleSided property. If it is YES, the next page occupies the back of the previous page. The default is NO, unless the spine is in the middle, in which case it's YES and can't be changed. Your only option here, therefore, is to set it to YES when the spine isn't in the middle, and in that case the back of each page would be a sort of throwaway page, glimpsed by the user during the page curl animation.

A page view controller in a storyboard lets you configure its transition style, navigation orientation, and spine location. It also has delegate and data source outlets, though you're not allowed to connect them to other view controllers (you can't draw an outlet from one scene to another in a storyboard). It has no child view controller relationship, so you can't set the page view controller's initial child view controller in the storyboard; you'll have to complete the page view controller's initial configuration in code.

Container View Controllers

UITabBarController, UINavigationController, and UIPageViewController are built-in *parent view controllers*: you hand them a child view controller and they put that child view controller's view into the interface for you, inside their own view. What if you want your own view controller to do the same thing?

In iOS 3 and 4, that was illegal; the only way a view controller's view could get into the interface was if a built-in parent view controller put it there. You could put a view into the interface, of course — but not a view controller's view. Naturally, developers ignored this restriction, and got themselves into all kinds of difficulties. In iOS 5, Apple relented, and created a coherent way for you to create your own parent view controllers, which can legally manage child view controllers and put their views into the interface. A custom parent view controller of this sort is called a *container view controller*.

Your view controller has a childViewControllers array. You must not, however, just wantonly populate this array however you like. A child view controller needs to receive certain events as it becomes a child view controller, as it ceases to be a child view controller, and as its view is added to and removed from the interface. Therefore, to act as a parent view controller, your UIViewController subclass must fulfill certain responsibilities:

Adding a child

When a view controller is to *become your view controller's child*, your view controller must do these things, in this order:

1. Send addChildViewController: to itself, with the child as argument. The child is automatically added to your childViewControllers array and is retained.

2. Get the child view controller's view into the interface (as a subview of your view controller's view), if that's what adding a child view controller means.

3. Send didMoveToParentViewController: to the child with your view controller as its argument.

Removing a child

When a view controller is to *cease being your view controller's child*, your view controller must do these things, in this order:

1. Send willMoveToParentViewController: to the child with a nil argument.

2. Remove the child view controller's view from your interface.

3. Send removeFromParentViewController to the child. The child is automatically removed from your childViewControllers array and is released.

This is a clumsy and rather confusing dance. The underlying reason for it is that a child view controller must always receive willMoveToParentViewController: followed by didMoveToParentViewController: (and your own child view controllers can take advantage of these events however you like). But it turns out that addChildView-Controller: sends willMoveToParentViewController: for you, and that removeFrom-ParentViewController sends didMoveToParentViewController: for you; so in each case you must send manually the *other* message, the one that adding or removing a child view controller *doesn't* send for you — and of course you must send it so that everything happens in the correct order, as dictated by the rules I just listed.

I'll illustrate two versions of the dance. First, we'll simply obtain a new child view controller and put its view into the interface, where no child view controller's view was previously:

```
UIViewController* vc = // whatever; this the initial child view controller
[self addChildViewController:vc]; // "will" is called for us
[self.view addSubview: vc.view];
// when we call "add", we must call "did" afterward
[vc didMoveToParentViewController:self];
vc.view.frame = // whatever, or use constraints
```

This could very well be all you need to do. For example, consider Figure 6-3 and Figure 6-4. My view controller's view contains a UIPageViewController's view *as one of its subviews*. The only to achieve this legally and coherently is for my view controller — in this case, it's the app's root view controller — to act as the UIPageViewController's parent view controller. Here's the actual code as the root view controller configures its interface:

```
// create the page view controller
UIPageViewController* pvc =
 [[UIPageViewController alloc]
  initWithTransitionStyle:UIPageViewControllerTransitionStylePageCurl
  navigationOrientation:UIPageViewControllerNavigationOrientationHorizontal
  options: @{UIPageViewControllerOptionSpineLocationKey:
             @(UIPageViewControllerSpineLocationMin)}
 ];
pvc.delegate = self;
pvc.dataSource = self;
// add its view to the interface
[self addChildViewController:pvc];
[self.view addSubview:pvc.view];
[pvc didMoveToParentViewController:self];
// configure the view
pvc.view.translatesAutoresizingMaskIntoConstraints = NO;
[self.view addConstraints:
 [NSLayoutConstraint
  constraintsWithVisualFormat:@"|[pvc]|"
  options:0 metrics:nil views:@{@"pvc":pvc.view}]];
[self.view addConstraints:
 [NSLayoutConstraint
  constraintsWithVisualFormat:@"V:|[pvc]|"
  options:0 metrics:nil views:@{@"pvc":pvc.view}]];
```

(A storyboard makes it simpler to configure a custom container view controller's initial child view controller and its view, as I'll explain in the next section.)

The next question is how to replace one child view controller's view in the interface with another (comparable to how UITabBarController behaves when a different tab bar item is selected). The simplest, most convenient way is for the parent view controller to send itself this message:

- `transitionFromViewController:toViewController:duration:options:` `animations:completion:`

That method manages the stages in good order, adding one child view controller's view to the interface before the transition and removing the other child view controller's view from the interface after the transition, and seeing to it that the child view controllers receive lifetime events (such as `viewWillAppear:`) at the right moment. Here's what the last three arguments are for:

`options:`
A bitmask comprising the same possible options that apply to any block-based view transition (see "Transitions" on page 136; these are the options whose names start with `UIViewAnimationOption...`).

animations:

A block that may be used for additional view animations, besides the transition animation specified in the `options:` argument. Alternatively, if none of the built-in transition animations is suitable, you can animate the views yourself here; they are both in the interface during this block.

completion:

This block will be important if the transition is part of removing or adding a child view controller. At the time `transitionFromViewController:...` is called, both view controllers involved must be children of the parent view controller; so if you're going to remove one of the view controllers as a child, you'll do it in the `completion:` block. Similarly, if you owe a new child view controller a `didMoveToParentView-Controller:` call, you'll use the `completion:` block to fulfill that debt.

Here's an example. To keep things simple, suppose that our view controller has just one child view controller at a time, and displays the view of that child view controller within its own view. So let's say that when our view controller is handed a new child view controller, it substitutes that new child view controller for the old child view controller and replaces the old child view controller's view with the new child view controller's view. Here's code that does that correctly; the two view controllers are called `fromvc` and `tovc`:

```
// we have already been handed the new view controller
// set up the new view controller's view's frame
tovc.view.frame = // ... whatever
// must have both as children before we can transition between them
[self addChildViewController:tovc]; // "will" is called for us
// when we call "remove", we must call "will" (with nil) beforehand
[fromvc willMoveToParentViewController:nil];
[self transitionFromViewController:fromvc
    toViewController:tovc
    duration:0.4
    options:UIViewAnimationOptionTransitionFlipFromLeft
    animations:nil
    completion:^(BOOL done){
        // we called "add"; we must call "did" afterward
        [tovc didMoveToParentViewController:self];
        [fromvc removeFromParentViewController];
        // "did" is called for us
    }];
```

If we're using constraints to position the new child view controller's view, where will we set up those constraints? Before `transitionFromViewController:...` is too soon, as the new child view controller's view is not yet in the interface. The `completion:` block is too late: if the view is added with no constraints, it will have no initial size or position, so the animation will be performed and then the view will suddenly seem to pop into existence as we provide its constraints. The `animations:` block turns out to be a very good place:

```
tovc.view.translatesAutoresizingMaskIntoConstraints = NO;
// must have both as children before we can transition between them
[self addChildViewController:tovc]; // "will" called for us
// when we call remove, we must call "will" (with nil) beforehand
[fromvc willMoveToParentViewController:nil];
[self transitionFromViewController:fromvc
    toViewController:tovc
    duration:0.4
    options:UIViewAnimationOptionTransitionFlipFromLeft
    animations:^{
      [self.panel addConstraints:
       [NSLayoutConstraint
        constraintsWithVisualFormat:@"H:|[v]|"
        options:0 metrics:nil views:@{@"v":tovc.view}]];
      [self.panel addConstraints:
       [NSLayoutConstraint
        constraintsWithVisualFormat:@"V:|[v]|"
        options:0 metrics:nil views:@{@"v":tovc.view}]];
    }
    completion:^(BOOL done){
        // when we call add, we must call "did" afterward
        [tovc didMoveToParentViewController:self];
        [fromvc removeFromParentViewController];
        // "did" is called for us
    }];
```

As I mentioned earlier, if the built-in transition animations are unsuitable, you can set the `options:` argument to `UIViewAnimationOptionTransitionNone` and provide your own animation in the `animations:` block, at which time both views are in the interface:

```
[self addChildViewController:tovc];
[fromvc willMoveToParentViewController:nil];
tovc.view.transform = CGAffineTransformMakeScale(0.1,0.1);
[self transitionFromViewController:fromvc
    toViewController:tovc
    duration:0.4
    options:UIViewAnimationOptionTransitionNone
    animations:^{
        tovc.view.transform = CGAffineTransformIdentity;
    }
    completion:^(BOOL done){
        [tovc didMoveToParentViewController:self];
        [fromvc removeFromParentViewController];
    }];
```

If your parent view controller is going to be consulted about the status bar (whether it should be shown or hidden, and if shown, whether its text should be light or dark), it can elect to defer the decision to one of its children, by implementing these methods:

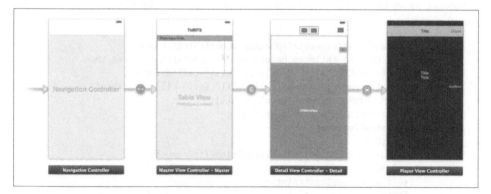

Figure 6-11. The storyboard of an actual app

- `childViewControllerForStatusBarStyle`
- `childViewControllerForStatusBarHidden`

Storyboards

Throughout this chapter, I've been describing how to create a view controller and present it or make it another view controller's child *manually*, entirely in code. But if you're using a storyboard, you will often (or always) allow the storyboard to do those things for you *automatically*. A storyboard can be helpful and convenient in this regard, though not, perhaps, for the reasons one might expect. It doesn't necessarily reduce the amount of code you'll have to write; indeed, in some cases using a storyboard may compel you to write more code, and in a less readable and maintainable way, than if you were creating your view controllers manually. But a storyboard does clarify the relationships between your view controllers over the course of your app's lifetime. Instead of having to hunt around in each of your classes to see which class creates which view controller and when, you can view and manage the chain of view controller creation graphically in the nib editor (Figure 6-11).

A storyboard, as I've already explained, is basically a collection of view controller nibs (scenes) and view nibs. Each view controller is instantiated from its own nib, as needed, and will then obtain its view, as needed — typically from a view nib that you've configured by editing the view controller's view, within the view controller itself, in the same storyboard. I described this process in detail, and listed the ways in which a view controller in a storyboard can be instantiated, in "Storyboard-Instantiated View Controller" on page 243. One of those ways is manual (calling `instantiateViewController-WithIdentifier:`); the other three are, or can be, automatic:

Initial view controller

If your app has a main storyboard, as specified by its *Info.plist*, that storyboard's initial view controller will be instantiated and assigned as the window's rootViewController automatically as the app launches. To specify that a view controller is a storyboard's initial view controller, check the "Is Initial View Controller" checkbox in its Attributes inspector. This will cause any existing initial view controller to lose its initial view controller status. The initial view controller is distinguished graphically in the canvas by an arrow pointing to it from the left. If a view controller is added to an empty canvas, it is made the initial view controller automatically.

Relationship

Two built-in parent view controllers can specify their children directly in the storyboard, setting their viewControllers array:

- UITabBarController can specify many children.
- UINavigationController can specify its single initial child (its root view controller).

To add a view controller as a viewControllers child to a parent view controller, Control-drag from the parent view controller to the child view controller; in the little HUD that appears, choose "view controllers" for a UITabBarController, or "root view controller" for a UINavigationController. The result is a *relationship* whose source is the parent and whose destination is the child. The destination view controller will be instantiated automatically when the source view controller is instantiated, and will be assigned into its viewControllers array, thus making it a child and retaining it.

Segue

A segue configures a *future* situation, when the segue will be *triggered*. At that time, one view controller that already exists will cause the instantiation of another, bringing the latter into existence. The two chief types of segue are:

Push

The future view controller will be pushed onto the stack of the navigation controller of which the existing view controller is already a child.

Modal

The future view controller will be a presented view controller (and the existing view controller will be its original presenter).

Unlike a relationship, a segue does not have to emanate from a view controller; it can emanate from certain kinds of gesture recognizer, or from an appropriate view (such as a button or a table view cell) in the first view controller's view. This is a graphical shorthand signifying that the segue should be triggered, bringing the second view controller into existence, when a tap or other gesture occurs.

To create a segue, Control-drag from the view in the first view controller, or from the first view controller itself, to the second view controller. In the little HUD that appears, choose the type of segue you want.

(The arrows to the left of the four view controllers in Figure 6-11 are, sequentially, the initial view controller indicator, a relationship, a push segue, and a modal segue.)

Segues

A segue is a full-fledged object, an instance of UIStoryboardSegue (or your custom subclass thereof). In a storyboard, however, it is not a nib object, in the sense that it is not instantiated by the loading of a nib, and it cannot be pointed to by an outlet. Rather, it will be instantiated when the segue is triggered, at which time its designated initializer will be called, namely initWithIdentifier:source:destination:. It can, however, be configured in the nib editor, through the Attributes inspector.

A segue's source and destination are the two view controllers between which it runs. The segue is directional, so the source and destination are clearly distinguished. The source view controller is the one that will exist at the time the segue is triggered; the destination view controller is the one that the segue itself will be responsible for instantiating.

A segue's identifier is a string. You can set this string for a segue in a storyboard through its Attributes inspector; this can be useful when you want to trigger the segue manually in code (you'll specify it by means of its identifier), or when you have code that can receive a segue as parameter and you need to distinguish which segue this is.

In the case of a push segue, the identifier is the only thing you can customize in the Attributes inspector. The segue is going to call pushViewController:animated: for you, and you can't change anything about that.

In the case of a modal segue, the Attributes inspector lets you specify a Transition; if this is not Default, you're telling the segue to assign the destination view controller this transition style (animation), which may be different from (and will therefore override) the modalTransitionStyle that the destination view controller already has. This is effectively the same as the code I showed earlier, where a view controller creates another view controller and sets its modalTransitionStyle before presenting it:

```
UIViewController* vc = [ExtraViewController new];
vc.modalTransitionStyle = UIModalTransitionStyleCoverVertical;
[self presentViewController:vc animated:YES completion:nil];
```

A modal segue's Attributes inspector also has an Animates checkbox. This is effectively the same as the second argument in presentViewController:animated:completion:.

If neither of these behaviors is what you want, you can configure the segue as a Custom segue. The Attributes inspector lets you specify a custom class, which must be a

UIStoryboardSegue subclass. In that subclass, you must override `perform`, which will be called after the segue is triggered and instantiated. Your `perform` implementation can access the segue's `identifier`, `sourceViewController`, and `destinationView-Controller` properties. The `destinationViewController` has already been instantiated, but that's all; doing something with this view controller so as to make it a child view controller or presented view controller, retaining it and causing its view to appear in the interface, is entirely up to your code.

You do not, however, need a custom segue just in order to implement a custom transition animation in iOS 7. A built-in segue is calling `pushViewController:animated:` or `presentViewController:animated:completion:` just as you would do in code, so if the relevant view controller has a delegate which returns an animation controller, your custom transition animation will be performed as usual. Remember, though, to configure the view controller early enough; `viewDidLoad` will not do as a place for a view controller to assign itself, say, a `transitioningDelegate`. This view controller is being instantiated from a nib, so `awakeFromNib` or `initWithCoder:` is appropriate.

Now let's talk about how a segue will be triggered:

- If a segue emanates from a gesture recognizer or from a tappable view, it will be triggered automatically when the tap or other gesture occurs.

  The source view controller can prevent this; if you don't want this segue triggered on this occasion, implement `shouldPerformSegueWithIdentifier:sender:` and return NO.

- If a segue emanates from a view controller as a whole, then triggering it is up to your code. To do so, send `performSegueWithIdentifier:sender:` to the source view controller.

  (In this case, `shouldPerformSegueWithIdentifier:sender:` will not be called.)

When a segue is triggered, the destination view controller is instantiated automatically. This is nice in the sense that automatic behavior is convenient, but how are you going to communicate between the source view controller and the destination view controller? This, you'll remember, was the subject of an earlier section of this chapter ("Communication With a Presented View Controller" on page 264), where I used this code as an example:

```
SecondViewController* svc = [SecondViewController new];
svc.data = @"This is very important data!";
[self presentViewController: svc
               animated:YES completion:nil];
```

In that code, the first view controller created the second view controller, and therefore had an opportunity of passing along some data to it before presenting it. With a push segue, however, the second view controller is instantiated for you, and the segue itself is going to call `presentViewController:animated:completion:`. So when and how will you be able to set `svc.data`?

The answer is that, after the segue has instantiated the second view controller but before it is performed, the source view controller is sent `prepareForSegue:sender:`. (For a custom segue, this happens before the segue's own `perform` is called.) This is the moment when the source view controller and the destination view controller meet; the source view controller can thus perform configurations on the destination view controller, hand it data, and so forth. The source view controller can work out which segue is being triggered by examining the segue's `identifier` and `destinationViewController` properties, and the `sender` is the interface object that was tapped to trigger the segue (or, if `performSegueWithIdentifier:sender:` was called in code, whatever object was supplied as the `sender:` argument).

This solves the communication problem, though in a clumsy way; `prepareFor-Segue:sender:` feels like a blunt instrument. The `destinationViewController` arrives typed as a generic `id`, and it is up to your code to know its actual type, cast it, and configure it. Moreover, if more than one segue emanates from a view controller, they are all bottlenecked through the same `prepareForSegue:sender:` implementation, which thus devolves into an ugly collection of conditions to distinguish them.

Container Views

You can configure a UITabViewController's child view controllers or a UINavigation-Controller's root view controller in a storyboard, because these are built-in parent view controllers and the nib editor understands how they work. But if you write your own custom container view controller, the nib editor doesn't even know that your view controller *is* a container view controller. Nevertheless, if you're able to conform to some basic assumptions that the nib editor makes, you can perform some initial parent–child configuration of your container view controller in a storyboard.

Those assumptions are:

- Your parent view controller will have one initial child view controller.
- You want the child view controller's view placed somewhere in the parent view controller's view when the child view controller is instantiated.

Those are reasonable assumptions, and you can work around them if they don't quite give the desired effect. For example, if your parent view controller is to have additional children, you can always add them later; and if the child view controller's view is not to be initially visible in the parent view controller's view, you can always hide it.

To configure your parent view controller in a storyboard, locate the Container View object in the Object library and drag it into the parent view controller's view in the canvas. The result is a view, together with a segue from it to an additional child view controller. You can then assign the child view controller its correct class in its Identity inspector.

The segue here is an *embed* segue. When it is triggered, the destination view controller is instantiated and made the source view controller's child, and its view is placed exactly inside the container view as its subview. Thus, the container view is not only a way of generating the embed segue, but also a way of specifying where you want the child view controller's view to go. The entire child-addition dance is performed correctly and automatically for you: `addChildViewController:` is called, the child's view is put into the interface, and `didMoveToParentViewController` is called.

By default, an embed segue is triggered automatically, and the child view controller is instantiated, when the parent view controller is instantiated. If that isn't what you want, override `shouldPerformSegueWithIdentifier:sender:` in the parent view controller to return NO for this segue, and call `performSegueWithIdentifier:sender:` later when you do want the child view controller instantiated.

Since this is a segue, the parent view controller is sent `prepareForSegue:sender:` before the child's view loads. At this time, the child has not yet been added to the parent's `child-ViewControllers` array. If you allow the segue to be triggered when the parent view controller is instantiated, then by the time the parent's `viewDidLoad` is called, the child has been added to the parent's `childViewControllers`, and the child's view is inside the parent's view.

Subsequently replacing one child view controller's view with another in the interface will require that you call `transitionFromViewController:...` just as you would have done if a storyboard weren't involved (as I described earlier in this chapter). Still, you can configure this through a storyboard by using a custom segue and a UIStoryboard-Segue subclass.

Unwind Segues

Storyboards and segues would appear to be useful only half the time, because segues are asymmetrical. There is a push segue but no pop segue. There is a modal segue that says `presentViewController:animated:completion:` but no modal segue that says `dismissViewControllerAnimated:completion:`.

In a nutshell, you can't use push and modal segues to mean "go back". A segue's destination is a *class*; triggering the segue instantiates that class. But when dismissing a presented view controller or popping a pushed view controller, we don't need any *new* view controller instances. We want to return, somehow, to an *existing instance* of a view controller.

A common mistake among beginners is to make a modal segue from view controller A to view controller B, and then try to express the notion "go back" by making *another* modal segue from view controller B to view controller A. The result, of course, is not presentation and subsequent dismissal, but presentation piled on presentation, one view controller instantiated on top of another on top of another. *Do not construct a cycle of segues.* (Unfortunately, the nib editor doesn't alert you to this mistake.)

Thus, when storyboards were introduced in iOS 5, the way to call `popViewController-Animated:` was to call it, in code (or let a back button call it for you), just as if there were no such thing as a storyboard. The way to call `dismissViewController-Animated:completion:` was to call it, in code, just as if there were no such thing as a storyboard.

To deal with this shortcoming, iOS 6 introduced the *unwind segue*. An unwind segue *does* let you express the notion "go back" in a storyboard. It works in an ingenious and rather elaborate way. It has to, because (as I've just shown) it can't possibly work like a normal segue! There are two chief problems to be solved: exactly what does "go back" *mean*, and exactly where should we "go back" *to*?

The answer to both questions depends upon the notion of a *view controller chain*. This is similar to, though not quite the same as, the view controller hierarchy; it refers to the chain of view controller instantiations, making each new view controller instance a child view controller or a presented view controller, that got us to the current view controller situation. To "go back" means to walk this chain in reverse: every view controller has either a `parentViewController` or a `presentingViewController`, so the next view controller up the chain is that view controller.

(Observe that this chain is well-defined even if it takes us out of the storyboard. The app's entire view controller hierarchy might not come from a single storyboard, and some parts of it might not come from a storyboard at all. Even so, there is a well-defined chain and it still leads all the way back up to the root view controller.)

Before you can create an unwind segue, you implement an *unwind method* in the class of any view controller represented in the storyboard. This should be a method returning an IBAction (as a hint to the storyboard editor) and taking a single parameter, a UIStoryboardSegue.

Once you've done that, you can create an unwind segue. Doing so involves the use of the Exit proxy object that appears in every scene of a storyboard. Control-drag from the view controller you want to go back *from*, connecting it to the Exit proxy object *in the same scene*. A little HUD appears, listing all the unwind methods known to this storyboard (similar to how action methods are listed in the HUD when you connect a button to its target). Click the name of the unwind method you want. You have now made an unwind segue, bound to that unwind method.

Even so, the name of the unwind method to which the unwind segue is bound is *only a name*. The unwind segue's source view controller is the view controller that contains it. But its destination view controller is unknown; it will not be determined until the app runs and the segue is triggered.

At runtime, when the unwind segue is triggered, the runtime conducts a search among the existing view controllers for a destination view controller. Put simply, the first view controller it finds that *implements the unwind method* will be the destination view controller. (I'll describe the actual details of this search in a moment.)

Once the destination view controller is found, the following steps are performed:

1. The source view controller's `shouldPerformSegueWithIdentifier:sender:` is called. It can stop the whole process dead at this point by returning NO.

2. The source view controller's `prepareForSegue:identifier:` is called. The two view controllers are now in contact (because the other view controller is the segue's `destinationViewController`). This is an opportunity for the source view controller to hand information to the destination view controller before being destroyed.

3. *The destination view controller's unwind method is called.* Its parameter is the segue; this segue can be identified through its `identifier` property. The two view controllers are now in contact *again* (because the other view controller is the segue's `sourceViewController`). It is perfectly reasonable, however, for the unwind method body to be empty; the unwind method's real purpose is to mark this view controller as the destination view controller.

4. The segue is performed, *destroying* the source controller and any intervening view controllers up to (but not including) the destination view controller, in good order.

Now I'll go back and explain in detail how the destination view controller is found and used to construct the actual segue. This is partly out of sheer interest (it's a devilishly clever procedure), and partly in case you need to customize the process.

When an unwind segue is triggered, the runtime starts walking back along the view controller chain from the source view controller instance toward the root view controller, asking each view controller for the destination view controller, by calling `viewControllerForUnwindSegueAction:fromViewController:withSender:`. There are two possible responses:

- If a view controller returns nil, the runtime will proceed to the next view controller up the chain.

- If a view controller returns a view controller (which may be itself), the search ends: the destination view controller has been found.

The default UIViewController implementation of `viewControllerForUnwindSegue-Action:...` is for a view controller to send itself `canPerformUnwindSegueAction:from-ViewController:withSender:`. Thus:

- If `canPerformUnwindSegueAction:...` returns NO, `viewControllerForUnwind-SegueAction:...` returns nil, and the search continues.
- If `canPerformUnwindSegueAction:...` returns YES, `viewControllerForUnwind-SegueAction:...` returns `self`, and the search ends here.

The default implementation of `canPerformUnwindSegueAction:...`, in turn, is for a view controller to send itself `respondsToSelector:` for the unwind method! Thus, the *normal outcome* is that if a view controller implements the unwind method, it will end up as the destination view controller, and otherwise, the search will continue on up the chain. You can, however, override `canPerformUnwindSegueAction:...` to return NO, to force the runtime search to continue on up the view controller chain past this view controller.

What I have said so far does not explain how a push is reversible. After all, the next view controller up the chain from a pushed view controller is the UINavigationController itself; nevertheless, a push can unwind by popping, which means that we end up at one of the pushed view controller's siblings, further down the navigation stack, as the unwind segue's destination view controller. How is that possible?

The answer is that UINavigationController implements `viewControllerForUnwind-SegueAction:...` differently from UIViewController. It doesn't consider itself as a possible destination. Instead, it *consults its children*, starting at the top of the stack and polling them in reverse order, looking for the first one that returns YES from `canPerform-UnwindSegueAction:...`; if it finds one, it returns it (and otherwise it returns nil). By default, `canPerformUnwindSegueAction:...` returns NO if the `fromView-Controller:` is `self`, so if a pushed view controller is the source view controller of an unwind segue, this constitutes an attempt to find a view controller to pop to.

Your own custom container view controller class, too, can override `viewControllerFor-UnwindSegueAction:fromViewController:withSender:` to intervene in the process of choosing a destination view controller. The unwind method will be called on the destination view controller that you return, so do not return a view controller that doesn't implement the unwind method, as you'll be setting the app up to crash.

Presume that the search is now over, and the runtime has found a destination view controller. The segue is now constructed by sending `segueForUnwindingToView-Controller:fromViewController:identifier:` to the destination view controller —

or, if the destination view controller has a parent, to the parent. That view controller then returns a segue whose `perform` method is tailor-made for the current situation, dictating the entire "go back" sequence that will release the source view controller and all intervening view controllers in good order, and performing an appropriate transition animation.

This segue's `identifier` is the identifier, if any, that you specified in the storyboard; its `sourceViewController` is the source view controller from the storyboard (the `fromView-Controller:`); and its `destinationViewController` is the destination view controller we have at last settled on (the `toViewController:`).

Your view controller, typically a custom container view controller, can override `segue-ForUnwindingToViewController:fromViewController:identifier:`. The simplest implementation is to call the UIStoryboardSegue class method `segueWith-Identifier:source:destination:performHandler:`, which lets you create on the fly a segue complete with a `perform` implementation supplied as a block.

For example, consider this chain: a navigation controller, its root view controller, a pushed view controller, and a presented view controller. By default, if we unwind directly from the presented view controller to the root view controller, we get only the reverse of the presented view controller's original animation. That's not very clear to the user, since in fact we're going back two steps. To improve things, our UINavigationController subclass can substitute a segue that performs two successive animations:

```
-(UIStoryboardSegue*)segueForUnwindingToViewController:
        (UIViewController *)toViewController
      fromViewController:(UIViewController *)fromViewController
      identifier:(NSString *)identifier {
    return [UIStoryboardSegue segueWithIdentifier:identifier
        source:fromViewController
        destination:toViewController performHandler:^{
            [fromViewController.presentingViewController
                dismissViewControllerAnimated:YES completion:^{
                [self popToViewController:toViewController animated:YES];
            }];
        }];
}
```

View Controller Lifetime Events

As views come and go, driven by view controllers and the actions of the user, events arrive that give your view controller the opportunity to respond to the various stages of its own existence and the management of its view. By overriding these methods, your UIViewController subclass can perform appropriate tasks at appropriate moments. Here's a list:

`viewDidLoad`

> The view controller has obtained its view. See the discussion earlier in this chapter of how a view controller gets its view.

`willRotateToInterfaceOrientation:duration:`
`willAnimateRotationToInterfaceOrientation:duration:`
`didRotateFromInterfaceOrientation:`

> The view controller is undergoing rotation. See the discussion of rotation earlier in this chapter. When an app launches into an orientation other than portrait, these events are not sent even though rotation takes place.

`updateViewConstraints`
`viewWillLayoutSubviews`
`viewDidLayoutSubviews`

> The view is receiving `updateConstraints` and `layoutSubviews` events. See Chapter 1, and the discussion of rotation earlier in this chapter. Your implementation of `updateViewConstraints` must call `super`.

`willMoveToParentViewController:`
`didMoveToParentViewController:`

> The view controller is being added or removed as a child of another view controller. See the discussion of container view controllers earlier in this chapter.

`viewWillAppear:`
`viewDidAppear:`
`viewWillDisappear:`
`viewDidDisappear:`

> The view is being added to or removed from the interface. This includes being supplanted by another view controller's view or being restored by the removal of another view controller's view. A view that has appeared (or has not yet disappeared) is in the window; it is part of your app's active view hierarchy. A view that has disappeared (or has not yet appeared) is not in the window; its `window` is nil. *You must call super* in your override of any of these four methods; if you forget to do so, things may go wrong in subtle ways.

> To distinguish more precisely *why* your view is appearing or disappearing, call any of these methods on `self`:
>
> - `isBeingPresented`
> - `isBeingDismissed`
> - `isMovingToParentViewController`
> - `isMovingFromParentViewController`

A good way to get a sense for when these events are useful is to track the sequence in which they normally occur. Take, for example, a UIViewController being pushed onto the stack of a navigation controller. It receives, in this order, the following messages:

- `willMoveToParentViewController:`
- `viewWillAppear:`
- `updateViewConstraints`
- `viewWillLayoutSubviews`
- `viewDidLayoutSubviews`
- `viewDidAppear:`
- `didMoveToParentViewController:`

When this same UIViewController is popped off the stack of the navigation controller, it receives, in this order, the following messages:

- `willMoveToParentViewController:` (with argument nil)
- `viewWillDisappear:`
- `viewDidDisappear:`
- `didMoveToParentViewController:` (with argument nil)

Disappearance, as I mentioned a moment ago, can happen because another view controller's view supplants this view controller's view. For example, consider a UIViewController functioning as the top (and visible) view controller of a navigation controller. When another view controller is pushed on top of it, the first view controller gets these messages:

- `viewWillDisappear:`
- `viewDidDisappear:`

The converse is also true. For example, when a view controller is popped from a navigation controller, the view controller that was below it in the stack (the back view controller) receives these events:

- `viewWillAppear:`
- `updateViewConstraints`
- `viewWillLayoutSubviews`
- `viewDidLayoutSubviews`
- `viewDidAppear:`

Incoherencies in View Controller Events

Unfortunately, the exact sequence of events and the number of times they will be called for any given view controller transition situation sometimes seems nondeterministic or incoherent. For example:

- Sometimes `didMoveToParentViewController:` arrives without a corresponding `willMoveToParentViewController:`.

- Sometimes `didMoveToParentViewController:` arrives even though this view controller was previously the child of this parent and remains the child of this parent.

- Sometimes the layout events (`updateViewConstraints`, `viewWillLayout-Subviews`, `viewDidLayoutSubviews`) arrive more than once for the same view controller for the same transition.

- Sometimes `updateViewConstraints` arrives needlessly, as when the view controller's view is about to leave the interface and the view controller is about to be destroyed.

- Sometimes `viewWillAppear:` or `viewWillDisappear:` arrives without the corresponding `viewDidAppear:` or `viewDidDisappear:`. For example, if an interactive transition animation begins and is cancelled, the cancelled view controller receives `viewWillAppear:` at the start, *without* `viewDidAppear:`, and receives `viewWill-Disappear:` and `viewDidDisappear:` at the end.

The best advice I can offer is that you should try to structure your code in such a way that incoherencies of this sort don't matter.

Appear and Disappear Events

The `appear`/`disappear` methods are particularly appropriate for making sure that a view reflects the model or some form of saved state whenever it appears. Changes to the interface performed in `viewDidAppear:` or `viewWillDisappear:` may be visible to the user as they occur! If that's not what you want, use the other member of the pair. For example, in a certain view containing a long scrollable text, I want the scroll position to be the same when the user returns to this view as it was when the user left it, so I save the scroll position in `viewWillDisappear:` and restore it in `viewWillAppear:` (not `view-DidAppear:`, where the user might see the scroll position jump).

Similarly, they are useful when something must be true exactly while a view is visible. For example, a timer that must be running while a view is visible can be started in its `viewDidAppear:` and stopped in its `viewWillDisappear:`. (This architecture also allows you to avoid the retain cycle that could result if you waited to invalidate the timer in a `dealloc` that might never arrive.)

A view does not disappear if a presented view controller's view merely covers it rather than supplanting it. For example, a view controller that presents another view controller using the UIModalPresentationFormSheet presentation style gets no lifetime events during presentation and dismissal.

Similarly, a view does not disappear merely because the app is backgrounded and suspended. Once suspended, your app might be killed. So you cannot rely on viewWill-Disappear: and viewDidDisappear: alone for saving data that the app will need the next time it launches. If you are to cover every case, you may need to ensure that your data-saving code also runs in response to an application lifetime event such as applicationWillResignActive: or applicationDidEnterBackground: (and see Appendix A for a discussion of the application lifetime events).

Manual Event Forwarding to a Child View Controller

A custom container (parent) view controller, as I explained earlier, must effectively send willMoveToParentViewController: and didMoveToParentViewController: to its children manually. But other lifetime events, such as the appear events and rotation events, are normally passed along automatically. However, you can take charge of calling these events manually, by implementing these methods:

shouldAutomaticallyForwardRotationMethods
> If you override this method to return NO, you are responsible for calling these methods on your view controller's children:
>
> - willRotateToInterfaceOrientation:duration:
> - willAnimateRotationToInterfaceOrientation:duration:
> - didRotateFromInterfaceOrientation:
>
> I have no idea how common it is to take charge of sending these events manually; I've never done it.

shouldAutomaticallyForwardAppearanceMethods
> If you override this method to return YES, you are responsible for seeing that these methods on your view controller's children are called:
>
> - viewWillAppear:
> - viewDidAppear:
> - viewWillDisappear:
> - viewDidDisappear:
>
> In iOS 6 and iOS 7, however, you do *not* do this by calling these methods directly. The reason is that you have no access to the correct moment for sending them. Instead, you call these two methods on your child view controller:

- `beginAppearanceTransition:animated:`; the first parameter is a BOOL saying whether this view controller's view is about to appear (YES) or disappear (NO)

- `endAppearanceTransition`

There are two main occasions on which your custom container controller must forward `appear` events to a child. First, what happens when your custom container controller's own view itself appears or disappears? If it has a child view controller's view within its own view, it must implement and forward all four `appear` events to that child. You'll need an implementation along these lines, for each of the four `appear` events:

```
- (void) viewWillAppear:(BOOL)animated {
    [super viewWillAppear:animated];
    UIViewController* child = // child whose view might be in our interface;
    if (child.isViewLoaded && child.view.superview)
        [child beginAppearanceTransition:YES animated:YES];
}
- (void) viewDidAppear:(BOOL)animated {
    [super viewDidAppear:animated];
    UIViewController* child = // child whose view might be in our interface;
    if (child.isViewLoaded && child.view.superview)
        [child endAppearanceTransition];
}
```

(The implementations for `viewDidAppear:` and `viewDidDisappear:` are similar, except that the first argument for `beginAppearanceTransition:` is NO.)

Second, what happens when you swap one view controller's child for another in your interface? You must *not* call the UIViewController method `transitionFromView-Controller:toViewController:...`! It takes charge of sending the `appear` calls to the children itself, and it isn't going to do so correctly in this situation. Instead, you must perform the transition animation directly. A minimal correct implementation might involve the UIView method `transitionFromView:toView:...`. Here, you can and should call `beginAppearanceTransition:` and `endAppearanceTransition` yourself.

Here's an example of a parent view controller swapping one child view controller and its view for another, while taking charge of notifying the child view controllers of the appearance and disappearance of their views. I've put asterisks to call attention to the additional method calls that forward the `appear` events to the children:

```
[self addChildViewController:tovc];
[fromvc willMoveToParentViewController:nil];
[fromvc beginAppearanceTransition:NO animated:YES]; // *
[tovc beginAppearanceTransition:YES animated:YES]; // *
[UIView transitionFromView:fromvc.view
    toView:tovc.view
    duration:0.4
    options:UIViewAnimationOptionTransitionFlipFromLeft
```

```
completion:^(BOOL finished) {
    [tovc endAppearanceTransition]; // *
    [fromvc endAppearanceTransition]; // *
    [tovc didMoveToParentViewController:self];
    [fromvc removeFromParentViewController];
}];
```

View Controller Memory Management

Memory is at a premium on a mobile device. Thus you want to minimize your app's use of memory — especially when the memory-hogging objects you're retaining are not needed at this moment. Because a view controller is the basis of so much of your application's architecture, it is likely to be a place where you'll concern yourself with releasing unneeded memory.

The object of releasing memory, in the multitasking world, is partly altruistic and partly selfish. You want to keep your memory usage as low as possible so that other apps can be launched and the user can switch between suspended apps. You also want to prevent your own app from being terminated! If your app is backgrounded and suspended while using a lot of memory, it may be terminated in the background when memory runs short. If your app uses an inordinate amount of memory while in the foreground, it may be summarily killed before the user's very eyes.

One of your view controller's most memory-intensive objects is its view. Fortunately, the iOS runtime manages a view controller's view's memory for you. If a view controller has never received viewDidAppear:, or if it has received viewDidDisappear: without subsequently receiving viewWillAppear:, its view is not in the interface, and can be temporarily dispensed with. In such a situation, if memory is getting tight, then even though the view controller itself persists, the runtime may release its view's backing store (the cached bitmap representing the view's drawn contents). The view will then be redrawn when and if it is to be shown again later.

In addition, if memory runs low, your view controller may be sent didReceiveMemory-Warning (preceded by a call to the app delegate's applicationDidReceiveMemory-Warning:, together with a UIApplicationDidReceiveMemoryWarningNotification posted to any registered objects). You are invited to respond by releasing any data that you can do without. Do not release data that you can't readily and quickly recreate! The documentation advises that you should call super.

If you're going to release data in didReceiveMemoryWarning, you must concern yourself with how you're going to get it back. A simple and reliable mechanism is *lazy loading* — a getter that reconstructs or fetches the data if it is nil.

In this example, we have a property myBigData which might be a big piece of data. In didReceiveMemoryWarning we write myBigData out as a file to disk (Chapter 23) and release it from memory. We have also overridden the synthesized accessors for `myBig-Data` to implement lazy loading: if we try to get `myBigData` and it's nil, we attempt to fetch it from disk — and if we succeed, we delete it from disk (to prevent stale data):

```
@interface ViewController ()
@property (strong) NSData* myBigDataAlias;
@property (nonatomic, strong) NSData* myBigData;
@end
@implementation ViewController
@synthesize myBigDataAlias = _myBigData;
- (void) setMyBigData: (NSData*) data {
    self.myBigDataAlias = data;
}
- (NSData*) myBigData { // lazy loading
    if (!self.myBigDataAlias) {
        NSFileManager* fm = [NSFileManager new];
        NSString* f =
            [NSTemporaryDirectory()
                stringByAppendingPathComponent:@"myBigData"];
        if ([fm fileExistsAtPath:f]) {
            self.myBigDataAlias = [NSData dataWithContentsOfFile:f];
            NSError* err = nil;
            BOOL ok = [fm removeItemAtPath:f error:&err];
            NSAssert(ok, @"Couldn't remove temp file");
        }
    }
    return self.myBigDataAlias;
}
- (void)saveAndReleaseMyBigData {
    if (self.myBigData) {
        NSString* f =
            [NSTemporaryDirectory()
                stringByAppendingPathComponent:@"myBigData"];
        [self.myBigData writeToFile:f atomically:NO];
        self.myBigData = nil;
    }
}
- (void)didReceiveMemoryWarning {
    [super didReceiveMemoryWarning];
    [self saveAndReleaseMyBigData];
}
@end
```

To test low-memory circumstances artificially, run your app in the Simulator and choose Hardware → Simulate Memory Warning. I don't believe this has any actual effect on memory, but a memory warning of sufficient severity is sent to your app, so you can see the results of triggering your low-memory response code, including the app delegate's `applicationDidReceiveMemoryWarning:` and your view controller's `didReceive-MemoryWarning`.

On the device, the equivalent is to call an undocumented method:

```
[[UIApplication sharedApplication]
    performSelector:@selector(_performMemoryWarning)];
```

(Be sure to remove this code when it is no longer needed for testing, as the App Store won't accept it.)

You will also wish to concern yourself with releasing memory when your app is about to be suspended. If your app has been backgrounded and suspended and the system later discovers it is running short of memory, it will go hunting through the suspended apps, looking for memory hogs that it can kill in order to free up that memory. If the system decides that your suspended app is a memory hog, it isn't politely going to wake your app and send it a memory warning; it's just going to terminate your app in its sleep. The time to be concerned about releasing memory, therefore, is *before* the app is suspended. You'll probably want your view controller to be registered with the shared application to receive `UIApplicationDidEnterBackgroundNotification`. The arrival of this notification is an opportunity to release any easily restored memory-hogging objects, such as `myBigData` in the previous example:

```
-(void)backgrounding:(NSNotification*)n {
    // got UIApplicationDidEnterBackgroundNotification
    [self saveAndReleaseMyBigData];
}
```

Testing how your app's memory behaves in the background isn't easy. In a WWDC 2011 video, an interesting technique is demonstrated. The app is run under Instruments on the device, using the virtual memory instrument, and is then backgrounded by pressing the Home button, thus revealing how much memory it voluntarily relinquishes at that time. Then a special memory-hogging app is launched on the device: its interface loads and displays a very large image in a UIImageView. Even though your app is backgrounded and suspended, the virtual memory instrument continues to track its memory usage, and you can see whether further memory is reclaimed under pressure from the demands of the memory-hogging app in the foreground.

State Restoration

In the multitasking world, when the user leaves your app and then later returns to it, one of two things might have happened in the meantime:

Your app was suspended
> Your app was suspended in the background, and remained suspended while the user did something else. When the user returns to your app, the system simply unfreezes your app, and there it is, looking just as it did when the user left it.

Your app was terminated
> Your app was suspended in the background, and then, as the user worked with other apps, a moment came where the system decided it needed the resources (such as

memory) being held by your suspended app. Therefore it terminated your app. When the user returns to your app, the app launches from scratch.

For most apps, a general goal should be to make those two situations more or less indistinguishable to the user. The user, after all, doesn't know the difference between those two things, so why should the app behave differently some of the time? It should *always* feel to the user as if the app is being resumed from where it left off the last time it was in the foreground, even if in fact the app was terminated while suspended in the background. Otherwise, as the WWDC 2013 video on this topic puts it, the user will feel that the app has mysteriously and annoyingly "lost my place."

This goal is *state restoration*. Your app has a state at every moment: some view controller's view is occupying the screen, and views within it are displaying certain values (for example, a certain switch is set to On, or a certain table view is scrolled to a certain position). The idea of state restoration is to save that information when the app goes into the background, and use it to make all those things true again if the app is subsequently launched from scratch.

iOS provides a general solution to the problem of state restoration (introduced originally in iOS 6). This solution is centered around view controllers, which makes sense, since view controllers are the heart of the problem. What is the user's "place" in the app, which we don't want to "lose"? It's the chain of view controllers that got us to where we were when the app was backgrounded, along with the configuration of each one. The goal of state restoration must therefore be to reconstruct all existing view controllers, initializing each one into the state it previously had.

Note that state, in this sense, is neither user defaults nor data. If something is a preference, make it a preference and store it in NSUserDefaults. If something is data (for example, the underlying model on which your app's functionality is based), keep it in a file (Chapter 23). Don't misuse the state saving and restoration mechanism for such things. The reason for this is not only conceptual; it's also because *saved state can be lost*. You don't want to commit anything to the state restoration mechanism if it would be a disaster to have lost it the next time the app launches.

For example, suppose the user kills your app outright by double-clicking the Home button to show the app switcher interface and flicking your app's snapshot upward; the system will throw away its state. Similarly, if your app crashes, the system will throw away its state. In both cases, the system assumes that something went wrong, and doesn't want to launch your app into what might be a troublesome saved state. Instead, your app will launch cleanly, from the beginning. There's no problem for the user, barring a mild inconvenience — as long as the only thing that gets thrown away is state.

How to Test State Restoration

To test whether your app is saving and restoring state as you expect:

1. Run the app as usual, in the Simulator or on a device.

2. At some point, in the Simulator or on the device, click the Home button. This causes the app to be suspended in good order, and state is saved.

3. Now, back in Xcode, stop the running project (Product → Stop).

4. Run the project again. If there is saved state, it is restored.

(To test the app's behavior from a truly cold start, delete it from the Simulator or device. You might need to do this after changing something about the underlying save-and-restore model.)

Apple also provides a number of debugging tools (find them at *http://develop er.apple.com/downloads*):

restorationArchiveTool
> A command-line tool for reading a saved state archive in textual format. The archive is in a folder called Saved Application State in your app's sandboxed Library. See Chapter 23 for more about the app's sandbox, and how to copy it to your computer from a device.

StateRestorationDebugLogging.mobileconfig
> A configuration profile. When installed on a device (through the iPhone Configuration Utility, or by emailing it to yourself and opening it on the device), it causes the console to dump information as state saving and restoration proceeds.

StateRestorationDeveloperMode.mobileconfig
> A configuration profile. When installed on a device, it prevents the state archive from being jettisoned after unexpected termination of the app (a crash, or manual termination through the app switcher interface). This can allow you to test state restoration a bit more conveniently.

Participating in State Restoration

Built-in state restoration operates more or less automatically. All you have to do is tell the system that you want to participate in it. To do so, you take three basic steps:

Implement app delegate methods
> The app delegate must implement application:shouldSaveApplicationState: and application:shouldRestoreApplicationState: to return YES. (Naturally, your code can instead return NO to prevent state from being saved or restored on some particular occasion.)

Implement application:willFinishLaunchingWithOptions:
> Although it is very early, application:didFinishLaunchingWithOptions: is too late for state restoration. Your app needs its basic interface *before* state restoration begins. The solution is to use a different app delegate method, application:will-

`FinishLaunchingWithOptions:`. Typically, you can just change "did" to "will" in the name of this method, keeping your existing code unchanged.

Provide restoration IDs

Both UIViewController and UIView have a `restorationIdentifier` property, which is a string. Setting this string to a non-nil value is your signal to the system that you want this view controller (or view) to participate in state restoration. If a view controller's `restorationIdentifier` is nil, neither it nor any subsequent view controllers down the chain — neither its children nor its presented view controller, if any — will be saved or restored. (A nice feature of this architecture is that it lets you participate *partially* in state restoration, omitting some view controllers by not assigning them a restoration identifier.)

You can set the `restorationIdentifier` manually, in code; typically you'll do that early in a view controller's lifetime. If a view controller or view is instantiated from a nib, you'll want to set the restoration identifier in the nib editor; the Identity inspector has a Restoration ID field for this purpose. (If you're using a storyboard, it's a good idea, in general, to make a view controller's restoration ID in the storyboard the same as its storyboard ID, the string used to identify the view controller in a call to `instantiateViewControllerWithIdentifier:`; in fact, it's such a good idea that the storyboard editor provides a checkbox, "Use Storyboard ID," that makes the one value automatically the same as the other.)

In the case of a simple storyboard-based app, where each needed view controller instance can be reconstructed directly from the storyboard, those steps alone can be sufficient to bring state restoration to life, operating correctly at the view controller level. Let's test it. Start with a storyboard-based app with the following architecture (Figure 6-12):

- A navigation controller.
- Its root view controller, connected by a relationship from the navigation controller. Call its class RootViewController.
  — A presented view controller, connected by a modal segue from a Present button in the root view controller's view. Call its class PresentedViewController. Its view contains a Pop button.
- A second view controller, connected by a push segue from a Push bar button item in the root view controller's navigation item. Call its class SecondViewController.
  — The very same presented view controller (PresentedViewController), also connected by a modal segue from a Present button in the second view controller's view.

This storyboard-based app runs perfectly with just about no code at all; all we need is an empty implementation of an unwind method in RootViewController and Second-

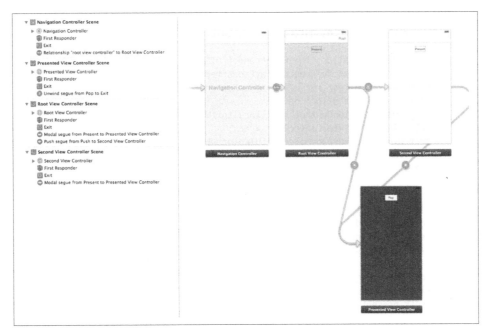

Figure 6-12. Architecture of an app for testing state restoration

ViewController so that we can create an unwind segue from the PresentedViewController Pop button.

We will now make this app implement state restoration:

1. Change the name of `application:didFinishLaunchingWithOptions:` in the app delegate to `application:willFinishLaunchingWithOptions:`.

2. Implement `application:shouldSaveApplicationState:` and `application:shouldRestoreApplicationState:` to return YES.

3. Give all four view controller instances in the storyboard restoration IDs: let's call them `@"nav"`, `@"root"`, `@"second"`, and `@"presented"`.

That's all! The app now saves and restores state.

Restoration ID, Identifier Path, and Restoration Class

Having everything done for us by the storyboard reveals nothing about what's really happening. To learn more, let's rewrite the example without a storyboard. Throw away the storyboard (and delete the Main Storyboard entry from the *Info.plist*) and implement the same architecture using code alone:

```
// AppDelegate.m:
- (BOOL)application:(UIApplication *)application
       didFinishLaunchingWithOptions:(NSDictionary *)launchOptions {
    self.window =
        [[UIWindow alloc] initWithFrame:[[UIScreen mainScreen] bounds]];
    // Override point for customization after application launch.
    RootViewController* rvc = [RootViewController new];
    UINavigationController* nav =
        [[UINavigationController alloc] initWithRootViewController:rvc];
    self.window.rootViewController = nav;
    self.window.backgroundColor = [UIColor whiteColor];
    [self.window makeKeyAndVisible];
    return YES;
}

// RootViewController.m:
-(void)viewDidLoad {
    [super viewDidLoad];
    // ... color view background, create buttons ...
}
-(void)doPresent:(id)sender {
    PresentedViewController* pvc = [PresentedViewController new];
    [self presentViewController:pvc animated:YES completion:nil];
}
-(void)doPush:(id)sender {
    SecondViewController* svc = [SecondViewController new];
    [self.navigationController pushViewController:svc animated:YES];
}

// SecondViewController.m:
-(void)viewDidLoad {
    [super viewDidLoad];
    // ... color view background, create button ...
}
-(void)doPresent:(id)sender {
    PresentedViewController* pvc = [PresentedViewController new];
    [self presentViewController:pvc animated:YES completion:nil];
}

// PresentedViewController.m:
-(void)viewDidLoad {
    [super viewDidLoad];
    // ... color view background, create button ...
}
-(void)doDismiss:(id)sender {
    [self dismissViewControllerAnimated:YES completion:nil];
}
```

That's a working app. Now let's start adding state restoration, just as before:

1. Change the name of application:didFinishLaunchingWithOptions: in the app
   delegate to application:willFinishLaunchingWithOptions:.

2. Implement `application:shouldSaveApplicationState:` and `application:shouldRestoreApplicationState:` to return YES.

3. Give all four view controller instances restoration IDs: let's call them `@"nav"`, `@"root"`, `@"second"`, and `@"presented"`. We'll have to do this in code. We're creating each view controller instance manually, so we may as well assign its `restorationIdentifier` in the next line, like this:

```
RootViewController* rvc = [RootViewController new];
rvc.restorationIdentifier = @"root";
UINavigationController* nav =
    [[UINavigationController alloc] initWithRootViewController:rvc];
nav.restorationIdentifier = @"nav";
```

And so on.

Run the app. We are *not* getting state restoration. Why not?

The reason is that the `restorationIdentifier` alone is not sufficient to tell the state restoration mechanism what to do as the app launches. The restoration mechanism knows the chain of view controller *classes* that needs to be generated, but it is up to us to generate the *instances* of those classes. (Our storyboard-based example didn't exhibit this problem, because the storyboard itself was the source of the instances.) To do that, we need to know about the *identifier path* and the *restoration class*.

The `restorationIdentifier` serves as a guide during restoration as to what view controller is needed at each point in the view controller hierarchy. Any particular view controller instance, given its position in the view controller hierarchy, is uniquely identified by the sequence of `restorationIdentifier` values of *all* the view controllers (including itself) in the chain that leads to it. Those `restorationIdentifier` values, taken together and in sequence, constitute the *identifier path* for any given view controller instance.

Each identifier path is, in fact, merely an array of strings. In effect, the identifier paths are like a trail of breadcrumbs that you left behind as you created each view controller while the app was running, and that will now be used to identify each view controller *again* as the app launches.

For example, if we launch the app and press the Push button and then the Present button, then all four view controllers have been instantiated; those instances are identified as:

- `@[@"nav"]`
- `@[@"nav", @"root"]`
- `@[@"nav", @"second"]`

- `@[@"nav", @"presented"]` (because the navigation controller is the actual presenting view controller)

Observe that a view controller's identifier path is not the full story of how we got here. It's just an identifier! The state-saving mechanism also saves a relational tree of identifiers. For example, if the app is suspended in the current situation, then the state-saving mechanism will record that the root view controller has two children and a presented view controller, along with their identifiers.

Now consider what the state restoration mechanism needs to do when the app has been suspended and killed, and comes back to life, from the situation I just described. We need to restore four view controllers; we know their identifiers and mutual relationships. State restoration doesn't start until *after* `application:willFinishLaunchingWithOptions:`. So when the state restoration mechanism starts examining the situation, it discovers that the `@[@"nav"]` and `@[@"nav", @"root"]` view controller instances have already been created! However, the view controller instances for `@[@"nav", @"second"]` and `@[@"nav", @"presented"]` must also be created now. The state restoration mechanism doesn't know how to do that — so it's going to ask your code for the instances.

But *what* code should it ask? One way of specifying this is for you to provide a *restoration class* for each view controller instance that is *not* restored in `application:willFinishLaunchingWithOptions:`. Here's how you do that:

1. Give the view controller a `restorationClass`. Typically, this will be the view controller's own class, or the class of the view controller responsible for creating this view controller instance.

2. Implement the class method `viewControllerWithRestorationIdentifierPath:coder:` on the class named by each view controller's `restorationClass` property, returning a view controller instance as specified by the identifier path. Very often, `viewControllerWithRestorationIdentifierPath:coder:` will itself instantiate the view controller and return it.

3. Specify formally that each class named as a `restorationClass` implements the UIViewControllerRestoration protocol.

Let's make our PresentedViewController and SecondViewController instances restorable. I'll start with PresentedViewController. Our app can have *two* PresentedViewController instances (though not simultaneously) — the one created by RootViewController, and the one created by SecondViewController. Let's start with the one created by RootViewController.

Since RootViewController creates and configures a PresentedViewController instance, it can reasonably act also as the restoration class for that instance. In its implementation of `viewControllerWithRestorationIdentifierPath:coder:`, RootViewController should then create and configure a PresentedViewController instance *exactly* as it was doing before we added state restoration to our app — except for putting it into the view controller hierarchy! The state restoration mechanism itself, remember, is responsible for assembling the view controller hierarchy; our job is merely to supply any needed view controller instances.

So RootViewController now must adopt UIViewControllerRestoration, and will contain this code:

```
+ (UIViewController*) viewControllerWithRestorationIdentifierPath:
            (NSArray*)ip
        coder: (NSCoder*)coder {
    UIViewController* vc = nil;
    if ([[ip lastObject] isEqualToString:@"presented"]) {
        PresentedViewController* pvc = [PresentedViewController new];
        pvc.restorationIdentifier = @"presented";
        pvc.restorationClass = [self class];
        vc = pvc;
    }
    return vc;
}
-(void)doPresent:(id)sender {
    PresentedViewController* pvc = [PresentedViewController new];
    pvc.restorationIdentifier = @"presented";
    pvc.restorationClass = [self class];
    [self presentViewController:pvc animated:YES completion:nil];
}
```

You can see what I mean when I say that the restoration class must do exactly what it was doing before state restoration was added. Clearly this situation has led to some annoying code duplication, so let's factor out the common code. In doing so, we must bear in mind that doPresent: is an instance method, whereas `viewControllerWith-RestorationIdentifierPath:coder:` is a class method; our factored-out code must therefore be a class method, so that they can both call it:

```
+ (UIViewController*) makePresentedViewController {
    PresentedViewController* pvc = [PresentedViewController new];
    pvc.restorationIdentifier = @"presented";
    pvc.restorationClass = [self class];
    return pvc;
}
+ (UIViewController*) viewControllerWithRestorationIdentifierPath:
            (NSArray*)ip
        coder:(NSCoder*)coder {
    UIViewController* vc = nil;
    if ([[ip lastObject] isEqualToString:@"presented"]) {
        vc = [self makePresentedViewController];
    }
    return vc;
}
```

```
-(void)doPresent:(id)sender {
    UIViewController* pvc = [[self class] makePresentedViewController];
    [self presentViewController:pvc animated:YES completion:nil];
}
```

Continuing in the same vein, we expand RootViewController still further to make it also the restoration class for SecondViewController:

```
+ (UIViewController*) makePresentedViewController {
    PresentedViewController* pvc = [PresentedViewController new];
    pvc.restorationIdentifier = @"presented";
    pvc.restorationClass = [self class];
    return pvc;
}
+ (UIViewController*) makeSecondViewController {
    SecondViewController* svc = [SecondViewController new];
    svc.restorationIdentifier = @"second";
    svc.restorationClass = [self class];
    return svc;
}
+ (UIViewController*) viewControllerWithRestorationIdentifierPath:
            (NSArray*)ip
        coder:(NSCoder*)coder {
    UIViewController* vc = nil;
    if ([[ip lastObject] isEqualToString:@"presented"]) {
        vc = [self makePresentedViewController];
    }
    else if ([[ip lastObject] isEqualToString:@"second"]) {
        vc = [self makeSecondViewController];
    }
    return vc;
}
-(void)doPresent:(id)sender {
    UIViewController* pvc = [[self class] makePresentedViewController];
    [self presentViewController:pvc animated:YES completion:nil];
}
-(void)doPush:(id)sender {
    UIViewController* svc = [[self class] makeSecondViewController];
    [self.navigationController pushViewController:svc animated:YES];
}
```

Finally, SecondViewController can make itself the restoration class for the Presented-ViewController instance that it creates. (I won't bother showing the code, which just repeats what we've already done for RootViewController.) There's no conflict in the notion that both RootViewController and SecondViewController can fulfill this role, as we're talking about two different PresentedViewController instances.

The structure of our viewControllerWithRestorationIdentifierPath:coder: is typical. We test the identifier path — usually, it's sufficient to examine its last element — and return the corresponding view controller; ultimately, we are also prepared to return nil, in case we are called with an identifier path we can't interpret.

`viewControllerWithRestorationIdentifierPath:coder:` can also return nil deliberately, to tell the restoration mechanism, "Go no further; don't restore the view controller you're asking for here, or any view controller further down the same path."

I said earlier that the state restoration mechanism can ask your code for needed instances in two ways. The second way is that you implement your app delegate's `application:viewControllerWithRestorationIdentifierPath:coder:`. If you do, it will be called for *every* view controller that doesn't have a restoration class. This works in a storyboard-based app, and thus is a chance for you to intervene and prevent the restoration of a particular view controller on a particular occasion (by returning nil).

If you do implement this method, be prepared to receive identifier paths for existing view controllers! For example, if we were to implement `application:viewController-WithRestorationIdentifierPath:coder:` in the example app I've been describing, it would be called for `@[@"nav"]` and for `@[@"nav", @"root"]`, because those view controllers have no restoration class. But we needn't, and we mustn't, create a new view controller; those view controller instances have already been created (in `application:willFinishLaunchingWithOptions:`), and we must return pointers to those instances.

Here's an implementation of `application:viewControllerWithRestoration-IdentifierPath:coder:` that works correctly with the storyboard-based version of our example app. For the two view controllers that have already been created, it returns pointers to them. For the other two, it instantiates them from the storyboard by treating their restoration IDs as their storyboard IDs (I told you it was a good idea for these to be the same!). The result is that there is no result: state restoration just keeps working as it did before. The point, however, is that we could now, on some occasion, return nil instead, in order to prevent restoration of a particular view controller:

```
-(UIViewController *)application:(UIApplication *)app
        viewControllerWithRestorationIdentifierPath:(NSArray *)ip
        coder:(NSCoder *)coder {
    if ([[ip lastObject] isEqualToString:@"nav"]) {
        return self.window.rootViewController;
    }
    if ([[ip lastObject] isEqualToString:@"root"]) {
        return [(UINavigationController*)self.window.rootViewController
                viewControllers][0];
    }
    UIStoryboard* board =
        [coder decodeObjectForKey:
            UIStateRestorationViewControllerStoryboardKey];
    return [board instantiateViewControllerWithIdentifier:[ip lastObject]];
}
```

Restoring View Controller State

The very simple example of four view controllers that I've been using in the preceding couple of sections (diagrammed in Figure 6-12) is *so* simple that it ignores half the problem. The truth is that when the state restoration mechanism creates a view controller and places it into the view controller hierarchy, the work of restoration is only half done.

A newly restored view controller probably won't yet have the data and instance variable values it was holding at the time the app was terminated. The history of the creation and configuration of this view controller are *not* repeated during restoration. If the view controller comes from a storyboard, then any settings in its Attributes inspector are obeyed, but the segue that generated the view controller in the first place is never run, so the previous view controller's prepareForSegue:sender: is never called, and the previous view controller never gets to hand this view controller any data. If the view controller is created by calling viewControllerWithRestorationIdentifier-Path:coder:, it may have been given some initial configuration, but this very likely falls short of the full state that the view controller was holding when the app was terminated. Any additional communication between one view controller and another to hand it data will be missing from the process. Indeed, since the history of the app during its previous run is not repeated, there will be no data to hand over in the first place.

It is up to each view controller, therefore, to *restore its own state* when it itself is restored. And in order to do that, it must previously *save its own state* when the app is backgrounded. The state saving and restoration mechanism provides a way of helping your view controllers do this, through the use of a *coder* (an NSCoder object). Think of this coder as a box in which the view controller is invited to place its valuables for safekeeping, and from which it can retrieve them later. Each of these valuables needs to be identified, so it is tagged with a key (an arbitrary string) when it is placed into the box, and is then later retrieved by using the same key, much as in a dictionary.

Anyone who has anything to save at the time it is handed a coder can do so by sending the coder an appropriate encode message with a key, such as encodeFloat:forKey: or encodeObject:forKey:. If an object's class doesn't adopt the NSCoding protocol, you may have to archive it to an NSData object before you can encode it. However, views and view controllers can be handled by the coder directly, because they are treated as references. Whatever was saved in the coder can later be extracted by sending the coder the reverse operation using the same key, such as decodeFloatForKey: or decodeObject-ForKey:.

The keys do not have to be unique across the entire app; they only need to be unique for a particular view controller. Each object that is handed a coder is handed *its own personal coder*. It is handed this coder at state saving time, and it is handed the same coder (that is, a coder with the same archived objects and keys) at state restoration time.

Here's the sequence of events involving coders:

When state is saved
When it's time to save state (as the app is about to be backgrounded), the state saving mechanism provides coders as follows:

1. The app delegate is sent `application:shouldSaveApplicationState:`. The coder is the second parameter.

2. The app delegate is sent `application:willEncodeRestorableStateWith-Coder:`. This is the same coder as in the previous step, because this is the same object (the app delegate).

3. Each view controller down the chain, starting at the root view controller, is sent `encodeRestorableStateWithCoder:` if it implements it. The implementation should call `super`. Each view controller gets its own coder.

When state is restored
When the app is launched, if state is to be restored, the state restoration mechanism provides coders as follows:

1. The app delegate is sent `application:shouldRestoreApplicationState:`. The coder (the one belonging to the app delegate) is the second parameter.

2. As each view controller down the chain is to be created, either the app delegate's `application:viewControllerWithRestorationIdentifierPath:coder:` (if implemented) or the restoration class's `viewControllerWithRestoration-IdentifierPath:coder:` (if the view controller has a restoration class) is called. The coder is the one appropriate to the view controller that's to be created.

3. Each view controller down the chain, starting at the root view controller, is sent `decodeRestorableStateWithCoder:` if it implements it. The implementation should call `super`. The coder is the one appropriate to this view controller.

4. The app delegate is sent `application:didDecodeRestorableStateWith-Coder:`. The coder is the same one sent to `application:shouldRestore-ApplicationState:` (the one belonging to the app delegate).

The *UIStateRestoration.h* header file describes five built-in keys that are available from every coder during restoration:

`UIStateRestorationViewControllerStoryboardKey`
A reference to the storyboard from which this view controller came, if any. (I took advantage of this key in the example at the end of preceding section.)

`UIApplicationStateRestorationBundleVersionKey`
Your *Info.plist* `CFBundleVersion` string when state saving happened.

`UIApplicationStateRestorationUserInterfaceIdiomKey`

An NSNumber wrapping either `UIUserInterfaceIdiomPhone` or `UIUser-InterfaceIdiomPad`, telling what kind of device we were running on when state saving happened.

`UIApplicationStateRestorationTimestampKey`

An NSDate telling when state saving happened.

`UIApplicationStateRestorationSystemVersionKey`

A NSString telling the system version from when state saving happened.

One purpose of these keys is to allow your app to opt out of state restoration, wholly or in part, because the archive is too old, was saved on the wrong kind of device (and presumably migrated to this one by backup and restore), and so forth.

A typical implementation of `encodeRestorableStateWithCoder:` and `decode-RestorableStateWithCoder:` will concern itself with instance variables and interface views. `decodeRestorableStateWithCoder:` is guaranteed to be called *after* `viewDid-Load`, so you know that `viewDidLoad` won't overwrite any direct changes to the interface performed in `decodeRestorableStateWithCoder:`.

Here's an example from the TidBITS News app. Note that `decodeRestorableStateWith-Coder:` uses nil tests, and that it updates the interface directly:

```
-(void)encodeRestorableStateWithCoder:(NSCoder *)coder {
    if (self.parsedData)
        [coder encodeObject: self.parsedData forKey:@"parsedData"];
    [coder encodeObject: self.refreshControl.attributedTitle.string
            forKey: @"lastPubDate"];
    [super encodeRestorableStateWithCoder:coder];
}
-(void)decodeRestorableStateWithCoder:(NSCoder *)coder {
    NSData* parsedData = [coder decodeObjectForKey:@"parsedData"];
    if (parsedData)
        self.parsedData = parsedData;
    NSString* s = [coder decodeObjectForKey:@"lastPubDate"];
    if (s)
        [self setRefreshControlTitle:s];
    [super decodeRestorableStateWithCoder:coder];
}
```

As a more complete demonstration, I'll add state saving and restoration to my earlier UIPageViewController example, the one that displays a Pep Boy on each page. The project has no storyboard. There are just two classes, the app delegate and the Pep view controller. The app delegate creates a UIPageViewController and makes it the window's root view controller, and makes itself the page view controller's data source. The page view controller's data source creates and supplies an appropriate Pep instance whenever a page is needed for the page view controller, along these lines:

```
Pep* page = [[Pep alloc] initWithPepBoy:self.pep[ix] nib: nil bundle: nil];
```

The challenge is to restore the Pep object displayed in the page view controller as the app launches. One solution involves recognizing that a Pep object is completely configured once created, and it is created just by handing it the name of a Pep Boy in its designated initializer, which becomes its boy property. Thus it happens that we can mediate between a Pep object and a mere string, so all we really need to save and restore is that string.

All the additional work, therefore, can be performed in the app delegate. As usual, we change "did" to "will" so that we are now implementing application:willFinish-LaunchingWithOptions:, and we implement application:shouldSaveApplication-State: and application:shouldRestoreApplicationState: to return YES. Now we save and restore the current Pep Boy name in the app delegate's encode and decode methods:

```
-(void)application:(UIApplication *)application
        willEncodeRestorableStateWithCoder:(NSCoder *)coder {
    UIPageViewController* pvc =
        (UIPageViewController*)self.window.rootViewController;
    NSString* boy = [(Pep*)pvc.viewControllers[0] boy];
    [coder encodeObject:boy forKey:@"boy"];
}
-(void)application:(UIApplication *)application
        didDecodeRestorableStateWithCoder:(NSCoder *)coder {
    NSString* boy = [coder decodeObjectForKey:@"boy"];
    if (boy) {
        UIPageViewController* pvc =
            (UIPageViewController*)self.window.rootViewController;
        Pep* pep = [[Pep alloc] initWithPepBoy:boy nib:nil bundle:nil];
        [pvc setViewControllers:@[pep]
            direction:UIPageViewControllerNavigationDirectionForward
            animated:NO completion:nil];
    }
}
```

A second solution, which is more realistic, assumes that we want our Pep view controller class to be capable of saving and restoration. This means that every view controller down the chain from the root view controller to our Pep view controller must have a restoration identifier. In our simple app, there's just one such view controller, the UIPage-ViewController; the app delegate can assign it a restoration ID when it creates it:

```
UIPageViewController* pvc =
    [[UIPageViewController alloc]
        initWithTransitionStyle:
            UIPageViewControllerTransitionStyleScroll
        navigationOrientation:
            UIPageViewControllerNavigationOrientationHorizontal
        options:nil];
pvc.restorationIdentifier = @"pvc";
```

The app delegate is also the data source, and thus ends up creating Pep objects many times. To prevent duplication of code, we'll have a Pep object assign itself a restoration ID in its own designated initializer. The Pep object will also need a restoration class; as I mentioned earlier, this can perfectly well be the Pep class itself, and that seems most appropriate here:

```
- (id) initWithPepBoy: (NSString*) inputboy
                  nib: (NSString*) nib bundle: (NSBundle*) bundle {
    self = [self initWithNibName:nib bundle:bundle];
    if (self) {
        self->_boy = [inputboy copy];
        self.restorationIdentifier = @"pep";
        self.restorationClass = [self class];
    }
    return self;
}
```

Let's be clever and efficient. The most important state that a Pep object needs to save is its boy string. The coder in which that boy value is saved will come back to us in Pep's `viewControllerWithRestorationIdentifierPath:coder:`, so we can use it to create the new Pep object by calling the designated initializer, thus avoiding code duplication:

```
-(void)encodeRestorableStateWithCoder:(NSCoder *)coder {
    [coder encodeObject:self->_boy forKey:@"boy"];
}
+(UIViewController *)viewControllerWithRestorationIdentifierPath:(NSArray*)ip
        coder:(NSCoder *)coder {
    NSString* boy = [coder decodeObjectForKey:@"boy"];
    return [[Pep alloc] initWithPepBoy: boy nib: nil bundle: nil];
}
```

Now comes a surprise. We run the app and test it, and we find that we're not getting saving and restoration of our Pep object. It isn't being archived. Its `encodeRestorableStateWithCoder:` isn't even being called. The reason is that the state saving mechanism doesn't work automatically for a UIPageViewController and its children (or for a custom container view controller and *its* children, for that matter). It is up to us to see to it that the current Pep object is archived.

To do so, we can archive and unarchive the current Pep object in an implementation of `encodeRestorableStateWithCoder:` and `decodeRestorableStateWithCoder:` that *is* being called. For our app, that would have to be in the app delegate. The code we've written so far has all been necessary to make the current Pep object archivable and restorable; now the app delegate will make sure that it *is* archived and restored:

```
-(void)application:(UIApplication *)application
        willEncodeRestorableStateWithCoder:(NSCoder *)coder {
    UIPageViewController* pvc =
        (UIPageViewController*)self.window.rootViewController;
    Pep* pep = (Pep*)pvc.viewControllers[0];
    [coder encodeObject:pep forKey:@"pep"];
```

```
    }
    -(void)application:(UIApplication *)application
            didDecodeRestorableStateWithCoder:(NSCoder *)coder {
        Pep* pep = [coder decodeObjectForKey:@"pep"];
        if (pep) {
            UIPageViewController* pvc =
                (UIPageViewController*)self.window.rootViewController;
            [pvc setViewControllers:@[pep]
                direction:UIPageViewControllerNavigationDirectionForward
                animated:NO completion:nil];
        }
    }
```

This solution may seem rather heavyweight, but it isn't. We're not really archiving an entire Pep instance; it's just a reference. The actual Pep instance is the one created by `viewControllerWithRestorationIdentifierPath:coder:`.

Restoration Order of Operations

When you implement state saving and restoration for a view controller, the view controller ends up with two different ways of being configured. One way involves the lifetime events I discussed earlier in this chapter ("View Controller Lifetime Events" on page 329). The other involves the events I've been discussing in this section. You want your view controller to be correctly configured no matter whether this view controller is undergoing state restoration or not.

Before state saving and restoration, you were probably configuring your view controller, at least in part, in `viewWillAppear:` and `viewDidAppear:`. With state saving and restoration added to the picture, you may also be receiving `decodeRestorableStateWith-Coder:`. If you configure your view controller here, will you be overriding what happens in `viewWillAppear:` and `viewDidAppear:`, or will they come along later and override what you do in `decodeRestorableStateWithCoder:`?

The unfortunate fact is that you don't know. For `viewWillAppear:` and `viewDid-Appear:`, in particular, the only thing you *do* know during state restoration is that you'll get both of them for the top view controller (the one whose view actually appears). You don't know *when* they will arrive; it might be before or after `decodeRestorableState-WithCoder:`. For other view controllers, you don't even know *whether* `viewDid-Appear:` will arrive: it might well *never* arrive, even if `viewWillAppear:` arrives.

In iOS 6, this indeterminacy made adoption of state saving and restoration difficult and frustrating. In iOS 7, a new UIViewController event is available, `applicationFinished-RestoringState`. If you implement this method, it will be called if and only if we're doing state restoration, at a time when all view controllers have already been sent `decode-RestorableStateWithCoder:`.

Thus, the known order of events during state restoration is like this:

- application:shouldRestoreApplicationState:
- application:viewControllerWithRestorationIdentifierPath:coder:
- viewControllerWithRestorationIdentifierPath:coder:, in order down the chain
- viewDidLoad, in order down the chain; possibly interleaved with the foregoing
- decodeRestorableStateWithCoder:, in order down the chain
- application:didDecodeRestorableStateWithCoder:
- applicationFinishedRestoringState, in order down the chain

You still don't know when viewWillAppear: and viewDidAppear: will arrive, or whether viewDidAppear: will arrive at all. But in applicationFinishedRestoringState you can reliably finish configuring your view controller and your interface.

Here's an example from one of my own apps. My configureView method relies on self.detailItem. If state restoration is not happening, then detailItem was set by another view controller, and viewWillAppear: will call configureView based on it; if state restoration *is* happening, then detailItem was set by decodeRestorableStateWithCoder:, and applicationFinishedRestoringState will call configureView based on it:

```
-(void)decodeRestorableStateWithCoder:(NSCoder *)coder {
    FPItem* detailItem = [coder decodeObjectForKey:@"detailItem"];
    if (detailItem)
        self->_detailItem = detailItem;
    [super decodeRestorableStateWithCoder:coder];
}
-(void)applicationFinishedRestoringState {
    [self configureView];
}
- (void) viewWillAppear:(BOOL)animated {
    [super viewWillAppear:animated];
    [self configureView];
}
- (void)configureView {
    if (self.detailItem) {
        // ...
    }
}
```

The worst that can happen is that configureView will be called twice in quick succession with the same detailItem. If I don't like that, I can prevent it — but not by trying to mediate between viewWillAppear: and applicationFinishedRestoringState! That's a hopeless task; their order is undefined and unreliable. Instead, configureView can use another instance variable as a flag. For example:

```
if (self.detailItem == self.lastDetailItem)
    return; // pointless to configure interface again
self.lastDetailItem = self.detailItem;
// ... configure ...
```

 If your app has additional state restoration work to do on a background thread (Chapter 25), the documentation says you should call
UIApplication's extendStateRestoration as you begin and complete-
StateRestoration when you've finished. The idea is that if you *don't*
call completeStateRestoration, the system can assume that something has gone very wrong (like, your app has crashed) and will throw
away the saved state information, which may be faulty.

Restoration of Other Objects

A view will participate in automatic saving and restoration of state if its view controller
does, and if it itself has a restoration identifier. Some built-in UIView subclasses have
built-in restoration abilities. For example, a scroll view that participates in state saving
and restoration will automatically return to the point to which it was scrolled previously.
You should consult the documentation on each UIView subclass to see whether it participates usefully in state saving and restoration, and I'll mention a few significant cases
when we come to discuss those views in later chapters.

New in iOS 7, an arbitrary object can be made to participate in automatic saving and
restoration of state. There are three requirements for such an object:

- The object's class must adopt the UIStateRestoring protocol. This declares three
  optional methods:
  — encodeRestorableStateWithCoder:
  — decodeRestorableStateWithCoder:
  — applicationFinishedRestoringState
- When the object is created, someone must register it with the runtime by calling
  this UIApplication class method:
  — registerObjectForStateRestoration:restorationIdentifier:
- Some other object that participates in saving and restoration, such as a view controller, must make the archive aware of this object by storing it in the archive (typically in encodeRestorableStateWithCoder:).

So, for example, here's an NSObject subclass Thing that participates in saving and
restoration:

```
// Thing.h:
@interface Thing : NSObject <UIStateRestoring>
@end

// Thing.m:
@implementation Thing
-(void)encodeRestorableStateWithCoder:(NSCoder *)coder {
    // ...
}
-(void)decodeRestorableStateWithCoder:(NSCoder *)coder {
    // ...
}
-(void)applicationFinishedRestoringState {
    // ...
}
@end
```

Here's a view controller with a Thing instance variable:

```
+(Thing*)makeThing {
    Thing* thing = [Thing new];
    [UIApplication registerObjectForStateRestoration:thing
        restorationIdentifier:@"thing"];
    return thing;
}
-(void)awakeFromNib {
    [super awakeFromNib];
    self.thing = [[self class] makeThing];
}
-(void)encodeRestorableStateWithCoder:(NSCoder *)coder {
    [super encodeRestorableStateWithCoder:coder];
    [coder encodeObject:self.thing forKey:@"mything"];
}
```

That last line is crucial; it introduces our Thing object to the archive and brings its UIStateRestoring methods to life.

There is an objectRestorationClass property of the restorable object, and an object-WithRestorationIdentifierPath:coder: method that the designated class must implement. But our object is restorable even without an objectRestorationClass! I presume that this is because registerObjectForStateRestoration:restoration-Identifier: sufficiently identifies this object to the runtime. If you do want to assign an objectRestorationClass, you'll have to redeclare the property, as it is read-only by default:

```
@property (strong, nonatomic)
    Class<UIObjectRestoration> objectRestorationClass;
```

As the declaration shows, the class in question must adopt the UIObjectRestoration protocol; its objectWithRestorationIdentifierPath:coder: will then be called, and can return the restorable object, by creating it or pointing to it. Alternatively, it can return nil to prevent restoration.

Another optional property of the restorable object is `restorationParent`. Again, if you want to assign to it, you'll have to redeclare it, as it is read-only by default:

```
@property (strong, nonatomic) id<UIStateRestoring> restorationParent;
```

The parent must adopt the UIStateRestoring protocol, as the declaration shows. The purpose of the parent is to give the restorable object an identifier path. For example, if we have a chain of view controllers with a path `@[@"nav", @"second"]`, then if that last view controller is the `restorationParent` of our Thing object, the Thing object's identifier path in `objectWithRestorationIdentifierPath:coder:` will be `@[@"nav", @"second", @"thing"]`, rather than simply `@[@"thing"]`. This is useful if we are worried that `@[@"thing"]` alone will not uniquely identify this object.

Snapshot Suppression

When your app is backgrounded, the system takes a snapshot of your interface. It is used in the app switcher interface, and as a launch image when your app is resumed. But what happens if your app is killed in the background and relaunched?

If your app isn't participating in state restoration, then its default launch image is used. This makes sense, because your app is starting from scratch. But if your app *is* participating in state restoration, then the snapshot is used as a launch image. This makes sense, too, because the interface that was showing when the app was backgrounded is presumably the very interface your state restoration process is about to restore.

However, you might decide, while saving state, that there is reason not to use the system's snapshot when relaunching. (Perhaps there is something in your interface that it would be inappropriate to display when the app is subsequently launched.) In that case, you can call the UIApplication instance method `ignoreSnapshotOnNextApplication-Launch`. When the app launches with state restoration, the user will see your app's default launch image, followed by a change to the restored interface. They may not match, but at least there is a nice cross-dissolve between them.

By the same token, if the view controller whose view was showing at state saving time is not restorable (it has no restoration ID), then if the app is killed in the background and subsequently launches with state restoration, the restoration mechanism knows that the snapshot taken at background time doesn't match the interface we're about to restore to, so the user will initially see your app's default launch image.

CHAPTER 7

Scroll Views

A scroll view (UIScrollView) is a view whose content is larger than its bounds. To reveal a desired area, the user can scroll the content by dragging or flicking, or you can reposition the content in code.

A scroll view isn't magic; it takes advantage of ordinary UIView features (Chapter 1). The content is simply the scroll view's subviews. When the scroll view scrolls, what's really changing is the scroll view's own bounds origin; the subviews are positioned with respect to the bounds origin, so they move with it. The scroll view's `clipsToBounds` is usually YES, so any content positioned within the scroll view's bounds width and height is visible and any content positioned outside them is not.

In addition, a scroll view brings to the table some nontrivial abilities:

- It knows how to shift its bounds origin in response to the user's gestures.
- It provides scroll indicators whose size and position give the user a clue as to the content's size and position.
- It can optionally enforce paging, whereby the user can view only integral portions of the content.
- It supports zooming, so that the user can resize the content with a pinch gesture.
- It provides a plethora of delegate methods, so that your code knows exactly how the user is scrolling and zooming.

A scroll view's subviews, like those of any view, are positioned with respect to its bounds origin; to scroll is to change the bounds origin. The scroll view thus knows how far it should be allowed to slide its subviews downward and rightward — the limit is reached when the scroll view's bounds origin is {0,0}. What the scroll view needs to know is how far it should be allowed to slide its subviews upward and leftward. That is the scroll view's *content size* — its `contentSize` property.

The scroll view uses its `contentSize`, in combination with its own bounds size, to set the limits on how large its bounds origin can become. It may also be helpful to think of the scroll view's scrollable *content* as the rectangle defined by {CGPointZero, content-Size}; this is the rectangle that the user can inspect by scrolling. In effect, therefore, the `contentSize` is how large the scrollable content is.

If a dimension of the `contentSize` isn't larger than the same dimension of the scroll view's own bounds, the content won't be scrollable in that dimension: there is nothing to scroll, as the entire scrollable content is already showing. The `contentSize` is {0,0} by default, meaning that the scroll view isn't scrollable.

You can set the `contentSize` directly, in code. If you're using autolayout (Chapter 1), the `contentSize` is calculated for you based on the constraints of the scroll view's subviews.

Creating a Scroll View in Code

To illustrate, I'll start by creating a scroll view, providing it with subviews, and making those subviews viewable by scrolling, entirely in code. In the first instance, let's not use autolayout. Our project is based on the Single View Application template, with a single view controller class, ViewController, and with the storyboard's "Use Auto Layout" unchecked. In the ViewController's `viewDidLoad`, I'll create the scroll view to fill the main view, and populate it with 30 UILabels whose text contains a sequential number so that we can see where we are when we scroll:

```
UIScrollView* sv = [[UIScrollView alloc] initWithFrame: self.view.bounds];
sv.autoresizingMask = UIViewAutoresizingFlexibleWidth |
                      UIViewAutoresizingFlexibleHeight;
[self.view addSubview:sv];
sv.backgroundColor = [UIColor whiteColor];
CGFloat y = 10;
for (int i=0; i<30; i++) {
    UILabel* lab = [UILabel new];
    lab.text = [NSString stringWithFormat:@"This is label %d", i+1];
    [lab sizeToFit];
    CGRect f = lab.frame;
    f.origin = CGPointMake(10,y);
    lab.frame = f;
    [sv addSubview:lab];
    y += lab.bounds.size.height + 10;
}
CGSize sz = sv.bounds.size;
sz.height = y;
sv.contentSize = sz;
```

The crucial move is the last line, where we tell the scroll view how large its content is to be. If we omit this step, the scroll view won't be scrollable; the window will appear to consist of a static column of labels.

There is no rule about the order in which you perform the two operations of setting the contentSize and populating the scroll view with subviews. In that example, we set the contentSize afterward because it is more convenient to track the heights of the subviews as we add them than to calculate their total height in advance. Similarly, you can alter a scroll view's content (subviews) or contentSize, or both, dynamically as the app runs.

Any direct subviews of the scroll view may need to have their autoresizing set appropriately in case the scroll view is resized, as would happen, for instance, if our app performs compensatory rotation. To see this, add these lines to the preceding example, inside the for loop:

```
f.size.width = self.view.bounds.size.width - 20;
lab.frame = f;
lab.backgroundColor = [UIColor redColor]; // make label bounds visible
lab.autoresizingMask = UIViewAutoresizingFlexibleWidth;
```

Run the app, and rotate the device or the Simulator. The labels are wider in portrait orientation because the scroll view itself is wider.

This, however, has nothing to do with the contentSize! The contentSize does not change just because the scroll view's bounds change; if you want the contentSize to change in response to rotation, you will need to change it manually, in code. Conversely, resizing the contentSize has no effect on the size of the scroll view's subviews; it merely determines the scrolling limit.

With autolayout, things are different. The difficult thing to understand — and it is certainly counterintuitive — is that a constraint between a scroll view and a direct subview of that scroll view is *not* a way of positioning the subview relative to the scroll view (as it would be if the superview were an ordinary UIView). Instead, it's a way of describing the scroll view's contentSize.

To see this, let's rewrite the preceding example to use autolayout. If the only change is that the storyboard's "Use Auto Layout" is checked, the example continues to work, because the scroll view and its subviews all have their translatesAutoresizingMask-IntoConstraints set to YES by default; all constraints are implicit, as if we weren't using autolayout at all. But what if the scroll view and its subviews have their translates-AutoresizingMaskIntoConstraints set to NO, and we're giving them explicit constraints? Let's try it:

```
UIScrollView* sv = [UIScrollView new];
sv.backgroundColor = [UIColor whiteColor];
sv.translatesAutoresizingMaskIntoConstraints = NO;
[self.view addSubview:sv];
[self.view addConstraints:
 [NSLayoutConstraint constraintsWithVisualFormat:@"H:|[sv]|"
                                         options:0 metrics:nil
                                           views:@{@"sv":sv}]];
[self.view addConstraints:
 [NSLayoutConstraint constraintsWithVisualFormat:@"V:|[sv]|"
                                         options:0 metrics:nil
                                           views:@{@"sv":sv}]];
UILabel* previousLab = nil;
for (int i=0; i<30; i++) {
    UILabel* lab = [UILabel new];
    lab.translatesAutoresizingMaskIntoConstraints = NO;
    lab.text = [NSString stringWithFormat:@"This is label %d", i+1];
    [sv addSubview:lab];
    [sv addConstraints:
     [NSLayoutConstraint constraintsWithVisualFormat:@"H:|-(10)-[lab]"
                                             options:0 metrics:nil
                                               views:@{@"lab":lab}]];
    if (!previousLab) { // first one, pin to top
        [sv addConstraints:
         [NSLayoutConstraint constraintsWithVisualFormat:@"V:|-(10)-[lab]"
                                                 options:0 metrics:nil
                                                   views:@{@"lab":lab}]];
    } else { // all others, pin to previous
        [sv addConstraints:
         [NSLayoutConstraint
          constraintsWithVisualFormat:@"V:[prev]-(10)-[lab]"
          options:0 metrics:nil
          views:@{@"lab":lab, @"prev":previousLab}]];
    }
    previousLab = lab;
}
```

The labels are correctly positioned relative to one another, but the scroll view isn't scrollable. Moreover, setting the contentSize manually doesn't help. The solution is to add one more constraint, showing the scroll view what the height of its contentSize should be:

```
// pin last label to bottom, dictating content size height
[sv addConstraints:
 [NSLayoutConstraint constraintsWithVisualFormat:@"V:[lab]-(10)-|"
                                         options:0 metrics:nil
                                           views:@{@"lab":previousLab}]];
```

The constraints of the scroll view's subviews now describe the contentSize height: the top label is pinned to the top of the scroll view, the next one is pinned to the one above it, and so on — *and the bottom one is pinned to the bottom of the scroll view.*

Consequently, the runtime calculates the `contentSize` height from the inside out, as it were, as the sum of all the vertical constraints (including the intrinsic heights of the labels), and the scroll view is vertically scrollable to show all the labels.

Using a Content View

Instead of putting all of our scroll view's content directly inside the scroll view as its immediate subviews, we can provide a generic UIView as the sole immediate subview of the scroll view; everything else inside the scroll view is to be a subview of this generic UIView, which we may term the *content view*. This is a commonly used arrangement.

Under autolayout, we then have two choices for setting the scroll view's `contentSize`:

- Set the content view's `translatesAutoresizingMaskIntoConstraints` to YES, and set the scroll view's `contentSize` manually to the size of the generic content view.

- Set the content view's `translatesAutoresizingMaskIntoConstraints` to NO, set its size with width and height constraints, and pin its edges to its superview (the scroll view).

A convenient consequence of this arrangement is that it works independently of whether the content view's own subviews are positioned explicitly by their frames or using constraints. There are thus four possible combinations.

I'll illustrate by rewriting the previous example to use a content view. All four possible combinations start the same way:

```
UIScrollView* sv = [UIScrollView new];
sv.backgroundColor = [UIColor whiteColor];
sv.translatesAutoresizingMaskIntoConstraints = NO;
[self.view addSubview:sv];
[self.view addConstraints:
 [NSLayoutConstraint constraintsWithVisualFormat:@"H:|[sv]|"
                                         options:0 metrics:nil
                                           views:@{@"sv":sv}]];
[self.view addConstraints:
 [NSLayoutConstraint constraintsWithVisualFormat:@"V:|[sv]|"
                                         options:0 metrics:nil
                                           views:@{@"sv":sv}]];
UIView* v = [UIView new]; // content view
[sv addSubview: v];
```

The first combination is that no constraints are used. It's just like the first example in the previous section, except that the labels are added to the content view, not to the scroll view:

```
CGFloat y = 10;
for (int i=0; i<30; i++) {
    UILabel* lab = [UILabel new];
    lab.text = [NSString stringWithFormat:@"This is label %d", i+1];
    [lab sizeToFit];
    CGRect f = lab.frame;
    f.origin = CGPointMake(10,y);
    lab.frame = f;
    [v addSubview:lab]; // add to content view, not scroll view
    y += lab.bounds.size.height + 10;
}
// set content view frame and content size explicitly
v.frame = CGRectMake(0,0,0,y);
sv.contentSize = v.frame.size;
```

The second combination is that the content view uses explicit constraints, but its sub-views don't. It's just like the preceding code, except that we set the content view's constraints rather than the scroll view's content size:

```
CGFloat y = 10;
for (int i=0; i<30; i++) {
    // ... same as before, create labels, keep incrementing y
}
// configure the content view using constraints
v.translatesAutoresizingMaskIntoConstraints = NO;
[sv addConstraints:
 [NSLayoutConstraint constraintsWithVisualFormat:@"V:|[v(y)]|"
   options:0 metrics:@{@"y":@(y)} views:@{@"v":v}]];
[sv addConstraints:
 [NSLayoutConstraint constraintsWithVisualFormat:@"H:|[v(0)]|"
   options:0 metrics:nil views:@{@"v":v}]];
```

The third combination is that explicit constraints are used throughout. This is just like the second example in the previous section (except that the labels are added to the content view) combined with the preceding code, setting the content view's constraints:

```
UILabel* previousLab = nil;
for (int i=0; i<30; i++) {
    UILabel* lab = [UILabel new];
    lab.translatesAutoresizingMaskIntoConstraints = NO;
    lab.text = [NSString stringWithFormat:@"This is label %d", i+1];
    [v addSubview:lab];
    [v addConstraints:
     [NSLayoutConstraint constraintsWithVisualFormat:@"H:|-(10)-[lab]"
                                            options:0 metrics:nil
                                              views:@{@"lab":lab}]];
    if (!previousLab) { // first one, pin to top
        [v addConstraints:
         [NSLayoutConstraint constraintsWithVisualFormat:@"V:|-(10)-[lab]"
                                                options:0 metrics:nil
                                                  views:@{@"lab":lab}]];
    } else { // all others, pin to previous
        [v addConstraints:
```

```
        [NSLayoutConstraint
          constraintsWithVisualFormat:@"V:[prev]-(10)-[lab]"
          options:0 metrics:nil
          views:@{@"lab":lab, @"prev":previousLab}]];
    }
    previousLab = lab;
}
// last one, pin to bottom, this dictates content view height
[v addConstraints:
 [NSLayoutConstraint constraintsWithVisualFormat:@"V:[lab]-(10)-|"
                                 options:0 metrics:nil
                                   views:@{@"lab":previousLab}]];
// configure the content view using constraints
v.translatesAutoresizingMaskIntoConstraints = NO;
[sv addConstraints:
 [NSLayoutConstraint constraintsWithVisualFormat:@"V:|[v]|"
   options:0 metrics:nil views:@{@"v":v}]];
[sv addConstraints:
 [NSLayoutConstraint constraintsWithVisualFormat:@"H:|[v(0)]|"
   options:0 metrics:nil views:@{@"v":v}]];
```

The fourth combination is a curious hybrid: the content view's subviews are positioned using constraints, but we set the content view's frame and the scroll view's content size explicitly. There is no y to track as we position the subviews, so how can we find out the final content size height? Fortunately, `systemLayoutSizeFittingSize:` tells us:

```
UILabel* previousLab = nil;
// ... same as before, add subviews and constraints to content view ...
// autolayout helps us learn the consequences of those constraints
CGSize minsz = [v systemLayoutSizeFittingSize:UILayoutFittingCompressedSize];
// set content view frame and content size explicitly
v.frame = CGRectMake(0,0,0,minsz.height);
sv.contentSize = v.frame.size;
```

Scroll View in a Nib

A UIScrollView is available in the nib editor in the Object library, so you can drag it into a view in the canvas and give it subviews. Alternatively, you can wrap existing views in the canvas in a UIScrollView as an afterthought: select the views and choose Editor → Embed In → Scroll View. The scroll view can't be scrolled in the nib editor, so to design its subviews, you make the scroll view large enough to accommodate them; if this makes the scroll view too large, you can resize the actual scroll view instance when the nib loads. If the scroll view is inside the view controller's main view, you may have to make *that* view too large, in order to see and work with the full scroll view and its contents (Figure 7-1). Set the view controller's Size pop-up menu in the Simulated Metrics section of its Attributes inspector to Freeform; now you can change the main view's size, and the view controller's size in the canvas will change with it.

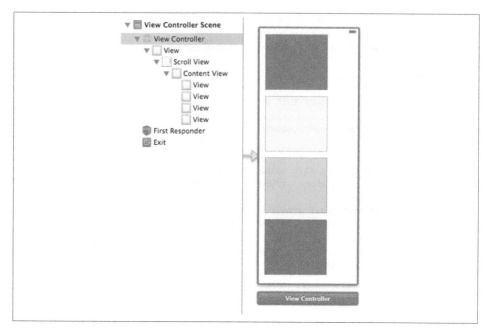

Figure 7-1. A scroll view in the nib editor

If you're not using autolayout, judicious use of autoresizing settings in the nib editor can be a big help here. In Figure 7-1, the scroll view is the main view's subview; the scroll view's edges are pinned (struts) to its superview, and its width and height are flexible (springs). Thus, when the app runs and the main view is resized (as I discussed in Chapter 6), the scroll view will be resized too, to fit the main view. The content view, on the other hand, must not be resized, so its width and height are not flexible (they are struts, not springs), and only its top and left edges are pinned to its superview (struts).

But although everything is correctly sized at runtime, the scroll view doesn't scroll. That's because we have failed to set the scroll view's contentSize. Unfortunately, the nib editor provides no way to do that! Thus, we'll have to do it in code. This, in fact, is why I'm using a content view. The content view is the correct size in the nib, and it won't be resized through autoresizing, so at runtime, when the nib loads, its size will be the desired contentSize. I have an outlet to the scroll view, and I set its contentSize to the content view's size in viewDidLayoutSubviews. I don't need an outlet to the content view, because it is known to be the scroll view's first subview:

```
-(void)viewDidLayoutSubviews {
    if (!_didSetup) {
        _didSetup = YES;
        self.sv.contentSize = ((UIView*)self.sv.subviews[0]).bounds.size;
    }
}
```

If you *are* using autolayout, constraints take care of everything; there is no need for any code to set the scroll view's `contentSize`. The scroll view's edges are pinned to those of its superview, the main view. The content view's edges are pinned to those of *its* superview, the scroll view. The content view's size will dictate the scroll view's `contentSize` automatically. The only question now is how you'd like to dictate the content view's size.

You have two choices, roughly corresponding to the second and third combinations in the preceding section: you can set the content view's width and height constraints explicitly, or you can let the content view's width and height be completely determined by the constraints of its subviews. Do whichever feels suitable.

In Xcode 4, configuring a scroll view's content view under autolayout could be tricky, sometimes requiring a content view constraint's `constant` to be changed at runtime. You won't need to do that with Xcode 5. Indeed, the Xcode 5 nib editor is extremely helpful: it understands this aspect of scroll view configuration, and will alert you with a warning (about the "scrollable content size") until you've provided enough constraints to determine unambiguously the scroll view's `contentSize`.

Scrolling

For the most part, the purpose of a scroll view will be to let the user scroll. A number of properties affect the user experience with regard to scrolling:

scrollEnabled
> If NO, the user can't scroll, but you can still scroll in code (as explained later in this section). You could put a UIScrollView to various creative purposes other than letting the user scroll; for example, scrolling in code to a different region of the content might be a way of replacing one piece of interface by another, possibly with animation.

scrollsToTop
> If YES (the default), and assuming scrolling is enabled, the user can tap on the status bar as a way of making the scroll view scroll its content to the top (that is, the content moves all the way down). You can also override this setting dynamically through the scroll view's delegate, discussed later in this chapter.

bounces
> If YES (the default), then when the user scrolls to a limit of the content, it is possible to scroll somewhat further (possibly revealing the scroll view's `backgroundColor` behind the content, if a subview was covering it); the content then snaps back into place when the user releases it. Otherwise, the user experiences the limit as a sudden inability to scroll further in that direction.

`alwaysBounceVertical, alwaysBounceHorizontal`

> If YES, and assuming that `bounces` is YES, then even if the `contentSize` in the given dimension isn't larger than the scroll view (so that no scrolling is actually possible in that dimension), the user can nevertheless scroll somewhat and the content then snaps back into place when the user releases it; otherwise, the user experiences a simple inability to scroll in that dimension.

`directionalLockEnabled`

> If YES, and if scrolling is possible in both dimensions (even if only because the appropriate `alwaysBounce...` is YES), then the user, having begun to scroll in one dimension, can't scroll in the other dimension without ending the gesture and starting over. In other words, the user is constrained to scroll vertically or horizontally but not both at once.

`decelerationRate`

> The rate at which scrolling is damped out, and the content comes to a stop, after a flick gesture. As convenient examples, standard constants are provided:
>
> - `UIScrollViewDecelerationRateNormal` (0.998)
>
> - `UIScrollViewDecelerationRateFast` (0.99)
>
> Lower values mean faster damping; experimentation suggests that values lower than 0.5 are viable but barely distinguishable from one another. You can also effectively override this value dynamically through the scroll view's delegate, discussed later in this chapter.

`showsHorizontalScrollIndicator, showsVerticalScrollIndicator`

> The scroll indicators are bars that appear only while the user is scrolling in a scrollable dimension (where the content is larger than the scroll view), and serve to indicate both the size of the content in that dimension relative to the scroll view and where the user is within it. The default is YES for both.
>
> Because the user cannot see the scroll indicators except when actively scrolling, there is normally no indication that the view is scrollable. I regard this as somewhat unfortunate, because it makes the possibility of scrolling less discoverable; I'd prefer an option to make the scroll indicators constantly visible. Apple suggests that you call `flashScrollIndicators` when the scroll view appears, to make the scroll indicators visible momentarily.

 The scroll indicators are subviews of the scroll view (they are actually UIImageViews). Do not assume that the subviews you add to a UIScrollView are its only subviews!

`indicatorStyle`
> The way the scroll indicators are drawn. Your choices are:
>
> - `UIScrollViewIndicatorStyleDefault` (black with a white border)
> - `UIScrollViewIndicatorStyleBlack` (black)
> - `UIScrollViewIndicatorStyleWhite` (white)

You can scroll in code even if the user can't scroll. The content simply moves to the position you specify, with no bouncing and no exposure of the scroll indicators. You can specify the new position in two ways:

`contentOffset`
> The point (CGPoint) of the content that is located at the scroll view's top left (effectively the same thing as the scroll view's bounds origin). You can get this property to learn the current scroll position, and set it to change the current scroll position. The values normally go up from 0 until the limit dictated by the `contentSize` and the scroll view's own bounds is reached.
>
> To set the `contentOffset` with animation, call `setContentOffset:animated:`. The animation does not cause the scroll indicators to appear; it just slides the content to the desired position.
>
> If a scroll view participates in state restoration (Chapter 6), its `contentOffset` is saved and restored, so when the app is relaunched, the scroll view will reappear scrolled to the same position as before.

`scrollRectToVisible:animated:`
> Adjusts the content so that the specified CGRect of the content is within the scroll view's bounds. This is less precise than setting the `contentOffset`, because you're not saying exactly what the resulting scroll position will be, but sometimes guaranteeing the visibility of a certain portion of the content is exactly what you're after.

If you call a method to scroll with animation and you need to know when the animation ends, implement `scrollViewDidEndScrollingAnimation:` in the scroll view's delegate.

Finally, these properties affect the scroll view's structural dimensions:

`contentInset`
> A UIEdgeInsets struct (four CGFloats in the order `top`, `left`, `bottom`, `right`) specifying margin space around the content.
>
> If a scroll view participates in state restoration (Chapter 6), its `contentInset` is saved and restored.

`scrollIndicatorInsets`
> A UIEdgeInsets struct specifying a shift in the position of the scroll indicators.

A typical use for the `contentInset` would be that your scroll view underlaps an interface element, such as a status bar, navigation bar, or toolbar, and you want your content to be visible even when scrolled to its limit.

A good example is the app with 30 labels that we created at the start of this chapter. The scroll view occupies the entirety of the view controller's main view. But in iOS 7, all apps are fullscreen apps, so the scroll view underlaps the status bar. This means that at launch time, and whenever the scroll view's content is scrolled all the way down, the first label, which is as far down as it can go, is partly hidden by the text of the status bar. We can prevent this by setting the scroll view's `contentInset`:

```
sv.contentInset = UIEdgeInsetsMake(20, 0, 0, 0);
```

When changing the `contentInset`, you will probably want to change the `scroll-IndicatorInsets` to match. Consider again the scroll view whose `contentInset` we have just set. When scrolled all the way down, it now has a nice gap between the bottom of the status bar and the top of the first label; but the top of the scroll indicator is still up behind the status bar. We can prevent this by setting the `scrollIndicatorInsets` to the same value as the `contentInset`:

```
sv.contentInset = UIEdgeInsetsMake(20, 0, 0, 0);
sv.scrollIndicatorInsets = sv.contentInset;
```

In iOS 7, the `contentInset` and `scrollIndicatorInsets` are of increased importance because top bars and bottom bars are likely to be translucent. When they are, the runtime would like to make your view underlap them. With a scroll view, this looks cool, because the scroll view's contents are visible in a blurry way through the translucent bar; but the `contentInset` and `scrollIndicatorInsets` need to be adjusted so that the scrolling limits stay between the top bar and the bottom bar. Moreover, the height of the bars can change, depending on such factors as how the interface is rotated.

Therefore, if a scroll view is going to underlap top and bottom bars, it would be nice, instead of hard-coding the top inset of 20 as in the preceding code, to make the scroll view's inset respond to its environment. A layout event seems the best place for such a response, and we can use the view controller's `topLayoutGuide` and `bottomLayout-Guide` to help us:

```
- (void) viewWillLayoutSubviews {
    if (self.sv) {
        CGFloat top = self.topLayoutGuide.length;
        CGFloat bot = self.bottomLayoutGuide.length;
        self.sv.contentInset = UIEdgeInsetsMake(top, 0, bot, 0);
        self.sv.scrollIndicatorInsets = self.sv.contentInset;
    }
}
```

Even better, if our view controller's main view contains one primary scroll view, and if it contains it sufficiently early — in the nib, for example — then if our view controller's automaticallyAdjustsScrollViewInsets property (new in iOS 7) is YES, the runtime will adjust our scroll view's contentInset and scrollIndicatorInsets with no code on our part. This property won't help us in the examples earlier in this chapter where we create the scroll view in code. But if the scroll view is created from the nib, as in Figure 7-1, this property applies and works. Moreover, a value of YES is the default. In the nib editor, you can change it with the Adjust Scroll View Insets checkbox in the Attributes inspector. Be sure to set this property to NO if you want to take charge of adjusting a scroll view's contentInset and scrollIndicatorInsets yourself.

Paging

If its pagingEnabled property is YES, the scroll view doesn't let the user scroll freely; instead, the content is considered to consist of sections. The user can scroll only in such a way as to move to a different section. The size of a section is set automatically to be equal to the size of the scroll view's bounds. The sections are the scroll view's *pages*.

When the user stops dragging, a paging scroll view gently snaps automatically to the nearest whole page. For example, let's say that the scroll view scrolls only horizontally, and that its subviews are image views showing photos, sized to match the scroll view's bounds. If the user drags horizontally to the left to a point where *less* than half of the next photo to the right is visible, and raises the dragging finger, the paging scroll view snaps its content back to the right until the entire first photo is visible again. If the user drags horizontally to the left to a point where *more* than half of the next photo to the right is visible, and raises the dragging finger, the paging scroll view snaps its content further to the left until the entire second photo is visible.

The usual arrangement is that a paging scroll view is at least as large, or nearly as large, in its scrollable dimension, as the screen. A moment's thought will reveal that, under this arrangement, it is impossible for the user to move the content more than a single page in any direction with a single gesture. The reason is that the size of the page is the size of the scroll view's bounds. Thus the user will run out of surface area to drag on before being able to move the content the distance of a page and a half, which is what would be needed to make the scroll view snap to a page not adjacent to the page we started on.

Sometimes, indeed, the paging scroll view will be slightly *larger* than the window in its scrollable dimension. This allows each page's content to fill the scroll view while also providing gaps between the pages, visible when the user starts to scroll. The user is still able to move from page to page, because it is still readily possible to drag more than half a new page into view (and the scroll view will then snap the rest of the way when the user raises the dragging finger).

When the user raises the dragging finger, the scroll view's action in adjusting its content is considered to be *decelerating*, and the scroll view's delegate (discussed in more detail later in this chapter) will receive `scrollViewWillBeginDecelerating:`, followed by `scrollViewDidEndDecelerating:` when the scroll view's content has stopped moving and a full page is showing. I do not believe it is possible for the scroll view *not* to emit these messages after a drag in a paging scroll view. Thus they can be used to detect efficiently that the page may have changed.

You can take advantage of this, for example, to coordinate a paging scroll view with a UIPageControl (Chapter 12). In this example, a page control (`pager`) is updated whenever the user causes a horizontally scrollable scroll view (`sv`) to display a different page:

```
-(void)scrollViewDidEndDecelerating:(UIScrollView *)scrollView {
    CGFloat x = self.sv.contentOffset.x;
    CGFloat w = self.sv.bounds.size.width;
    self.pager.currentPage = x/w;
}
```

Conversely, we can scroll the scroll view to a new page manually when the user taps the page control; in this case we have to calculate the page boundaries ourselves:

```
- (IBAction) userDidPage: (id) sender {
    NSInteger p = self.pager.currentPage;
    CGFloat w = self.sv.bounds.size.width;
    [self.sv setContentOffset:CGPointMake(p*w,0) animated:YES];
}
```

A useful interface is a paging scroll view where you supply pages dynamically as the user scrolls. In this way, you can display a huge number of pages without having to put them all into the scroll view at once. A scrolling UIPageViewController (Chapter 6) provides exactly that interface. Its `UIPageViewControllerOptionInterPageSpacing-Key` even provides the gap between pages that I mentioned earlier. Prior to iOS 5, before UIPageViewController was introduced, I was using a paging scroll view that did the same thing. If you're curious about the technique I was using, watch the Advanced Scroll View Techniques video from WWDC 2011, which describes something very similar, calling it "infinite scrolling."

A compromise between a UIPageViewController and a completely preconfigured paging scroll view is a scroll view whose `contentSize` can accommodate all pages, but whose actual pages are supplied lazily. The only pages that have to be present at all times are the page visible to the user and the two pages adjacent to it on either side (so that there is no delay in displaying a new page's content when the user starts to scroll). This approach is exemplified by Apple's PageControl sample code.

There are times when a scroll view, even one requiring a good deal of dynamic configuration, is better than a scrolling UIPageViewController, because the scroll view provides full information to its delegate about the user's scrolling activity (as described later in this chapter). For example, if you wanted to respond to the user's dragging one area of the interface by programmatically scrolling another area of the interface in a coordinated fashion, you might want what the user is dragging to be a scroll view, because it tells you what the user is up to at every moment.

Tiling

Suppose we have some finite but really big content that we want to display in a scroll view, such as a very large image that the user can inspect, piecemeal, by scrolling. To hold the entire image in memory may be onerous or impossible.

Tiling is one solution to this kind of problem. It takes advantage of the insight that there's really no need to hold the entire image in memory; all we need at any given moment is the part of the image visible to the user right now. Mentally, divide the content rectangle into a matrix of rectangles; these rectangles are the tiles. In reality, divide the huge image into corresponding rectangles. Then whenever the user scrolls, we look to see whether part of any empty tile has become visible, and if so, we supply its content. At the same time, we can release the content of all tiles that are completely offscreen. Thus, at any given moment, only the tiles that are showing have content. There is some latency associated with this approach (the user scrolls, then any empty newly visible tiles are filled in), but we will have to live with that.

There is actually a built-in CALayer subclass for helping us implement tiling — CATiledLayer. Its `tileSize` property sets the dimensions of a tile. Its `drawLayer:in-Context:` is called when content for an empty tile is needed; calling `CGContextGetClipBoundingBox` on the context reveals the location of the desired tile, and now we can supply that tile's content.

The usual approach is to implement `drawRect:` in a UIView that hosts the CATiledLayer. Here, the CATiledLayer is the view's underlying layer; therefore the view is the CATiledLayer's delegate. This means that when the CATiledLayer's `drawLayer:inContext:` is called, the host view's `drawRect:` is called, and the `drawRect:` parameter is the same as the result of calling `CGContextGetClipBoundingBox` — namely, it's the rect of the tile we are to draw.

The `tileSize` may need to be adjusted for the screen resolution. On a double-resolution device, the CATiledLayer's `contentsScale` will be doubled, and the tiles will be half the size that we ask for. If that isn't acceptable, we can double the `tileSize` dimensions.

To illustrate, we'll use some tiles already created for us as part of Apple's own Photo-Scroller sample code. In particular, I'll use a few of the "CuriousFrog_500" images. These all have names of the form *CuriousFrog_500_x_y.png*, where *x* and *y* are integers corresponding to the picture's position within the matrix. The images are 256×256 pixels, except for the ones on the extreme right and bottom edges of the matrix, which are shorter in one dimension, but I won't be using those in this example; I've selected a square matrix of 9 square images.

We will give our scroll view (sv) one subview, a TiledView, a UIView subclass that exists purely to give our CATiledLayer a place to live. TILESIZE is defined as 256, to match the image dimensions:

```
-(void)viewDidLoad {
    CGRect f = CGRectMake(0,0,3*TILESIZE,3*TILESIZE);
    TiledView* content = [[TiledView alloc] initWithFrame:f];
    float tsz = TILESIZE * content.layer.contentsScale;
    [(CATiledLayer*)content.layer setTileSize: CGSizeMake(tsz, tsz)];
    [self.sv addSubview:content];
    [self.sv setContentSize: f.size];
}
```

Here's the code for TiledView. As Apple's sample code points out, we must fetch images with imageWithContentsOfFile: in order to avoid the automatic caching behavior of imageNamed: — after all, we're going to all this trouble exactly to avoid using more memory than we have to:

```
+ (Class) layerClass {
    return [CATiledLayer class];
}
-(void)drawRect:(CGRect)r {
    CGRect tile = r;
    int x = tile.origin.x/TILESIZE;
    int y = tile.origin.y/TILESIZE;
    NSString *tileName =
        [NSString stringWithFormat:@"CuriousFrog_500_%d_%d", x+3, y];
    NSString *path =
        [[NSBundle mainBundle] pathForResource:tileName ofType:@"png"];
    UIImage *image = [UIImage imageWithContentsOfFile:path];
    [image drawAtPoint:CGPointMake(x*TILESIZE,y*TILESIZE)];
}
```

There is no special call for invalidating an offscreen tile. You can call setNeeds-Display or setNeedsDisplayInRect: on the TiledView, but this doesn't erase offscreen tiles. You're just supposed to trust that the CATiledLayer will eventually clear offscreen tiles if needed to conserve memory.

 There's an iOS 7 bug that causes a CATiledLayer to unload previously loaded tiles when there's a low memory situation, and then when the user scrolls, no drawRect: is sent and the tiles are not reloaded. This results in a partially blank CATiledLayer, and makes CATiled-Layer somewhat useless until the bug is fixed.

CATiledLayer has a class method fadeDuration that dictates the duration of the animation that fades a new tile into view. You can create a CATiledLayer subclass and override this method to return a value different from the default (0.25), but this is probably not worth doing, as the default value is a good one. Returning a smaller value won't make tiles appear faster; it just replaces the nice fade-in with an annoying flash.

Zooming

To implement zooming of a scroll view's content, you set the scroll view's `minimumZoomScale` and `maximumZoomScale` so that at least one of them isn't 1 (the default). You also implement `viewForZoomingInScrollView:` in the scroll view's delegate to tell the scroll view which of its subviews is to be the scalable view. The scroll view then zooms by applying a scale transform (Chapter 1) to this subview. The amount of that transform is the scroll view's `zoomScale` property. Typically, you'll want the scroll view's entire content to be scalable, so you'll have one direct subview of the scroll view that acts as the scalable view, and anything else inside the scroll view will be a subview of the scalable view, so as to be scaled together with it. This is another reason for arranging your scroll view's subviews inside a single content view, as I suggested earlier.

To illustrate, we can start with any of the four content view–based versions of our scroll view containing 30 labels. I called the content view v. Now we add these lines:

```
v.tag = 999;
sv.minimumZoomScale = 1.0;
sv.maximumZoomScale = 2.0;
sv.delegate = self;
```

We have assigned a tag to the view that is to be scaled, so that we can refer to it later. We have set the scale limits for the scroll view. And we have made ourselves the scroll view's delegate. Now all we have to do is implement `viewForZoomingInScrollView:` to return the scalable view:

```
- (UIView *)viewForZoomingInScrollView:(UIScrollView *)scrollView {
    return [scrollView viewWithTag:999];
}
```

One more thing from those examples needs fixing. Earlier, I gave the content view and the `contentSize` a zero width; that was sufficient to prevent the scroll view from scrolling horizontally, which was all that mattered. However, these widths now also affect how the content behaves as the user zooms it. This particular example, I think, looks good while zooming if the content view width is a bit wider than the widest label. (Implementing that is left as an exercise for the reader.)

The scroll view now responds to pinch gestures by scaling appropriately! The user can actually scale considerably beyond the limits we set in both directions; in that case, when the gesture ends, the scale snaps back to the limit value. If we wish to confine scaling strictly to our defined limits, we can set the scroll view's `bouncesZoom` to NO; when the user reaches a limit, scaling will simply stop.

The actual amount of zoom is reflected as the scroll view's current zoomScale. If a scroll view participates in state restoration, its zoomScale is saved and restored, so when the app is relaunched, the scroll view will reappear zoomed by the same amount as before.

 The scroll view zooms by applying a scale transform to the scalable view; therefore *the frame of the scalable view is scaled as well*. More-over, the scroll view is concerned to make scrolling continue to work correctly: the limits as the user scrolls should continue to match the limits of the content, and commands like scrollRectTo-Visible:animated: should continue to work the same way for the same values. Therefore, the scroll view *automatically scales its own contentSize* to match the current zoomScale.

If the minimumZoomScale is less than 1, then when the scalable view becomes smaller than the scroll view, it is pinned to the scroll view's top left. If you don't like this, you can change it by subclassing UIScrollView and overriding layoutSubviews, or by implementing the scroll view delegate method scrollViewDidZoom:. Here's a simple example (drawn from a WWDC 2010 video) demonstrating an override of layout-Subviews that keeps the scalable view centered in either dimension whenever it is smaller than the scroll view in that dimension:

```
-(void)layoutSubviews {
    [super layoutSubviews];
    UIView* v = [self.delegate viewForZoomingInScrollView:self];
    CGFloat svw = self.bounds.size.width;
    CGFloat svh = self.bounds.size.height;
    CGFloat vw = v.frame.size.width;
    CGFloat vh = v.frame.size.height;
    CGRect f = v.frame;
    if (vw < svw)
        f.origin.x = (svw - vw) / 2.0;
    else
        f.origin.x = 0;
    if (vh < svh)
        f.origin.y = (svh - vh) / 2.0;
    else
        f.origin.y = 0;
    v.frame = f;
}
```

Zooming Programmatically

To zoom programmatically, you have two choices:

`setZoomScale:animated:`

> Zooms in terms of scale value. The `contentOffset` is automatically adjusted to keep the current center centered and the content occupying the entire scroll view.

`zoomToRect:animated:`

> Zooms so that the given rectangle of the content occupies as much as possible of the scroll view's bounds. The `contentOffset` is automatically adjusted to keep the content occupying the entire scroll view.

In this example, I implement double tapping as a zoom gesture. In my action handler for the double-tap UITapGestureRecognizer attached to the scalable view, a double tap means to zoom to maximum scale, minimum scale, or actual size, depending on the current scale value:

```
- (void) tapped: (UIGestureRecognizer*) tap {
    UIView* v = tap.view;
    UIScrollView* sv = (UIScrollView*)v.superview;
    if (sv.zoomScale < 1)
        [sv setZoomScale:1 animated:YES];
    else if (sv.zoomScale < sv.maximumZoomScale)
        [sv setZoomScale:sv.maximumZoomScale animated:YES];
    else
        [sv setZoomScale:sv.minimumZoomScale animated:YES];
}
```

Zooming with Detail

By default, when a scroll view zooms, it merely applies a scale transform to the scaled view. The scaled view's drawing is cached beforehand into its layer, so when we zoom in, the bits of the resulting bitmap are drawn larger. This means that a zoomed-in scroll view's content may be fuzzy (pixellated). In some cases this might be acceptable, but in others you might like the content to be redrawn more sharply at its new size.

(On a double-resolution device, this might not be such an issue. For example, if the user is allowed to zoom only up to double scale, you can draw at double scale right from the start; the results will look good at single scale, because the screen has double resolution, as well as at double scale, because that's the scale you drew at.)

One solution is to take advantage of a CATiledLayer feature that I didn't mention earlier. It turns out that CATiledLayer is aware not only of scrolling but also of scaling: you can configure it to ask for tiles to be drawn when the layer is scaled to a new order of magnitude. When your drawing routine is called, the graphics context itself has already been scaled appropriately by a transform.

In the case of an image into which the user is to be permitted to zoom deeply, you would be forearmed with multiple tile sets constituting the image, each set having double the tile size of the previous set (as in Apple's PhotoScroller example). In other cases, you may not need tiles at all; you'll just draw again, at the new resolution.

Besides its `tileSize`, you'll need to set two additional CATiledLayer properties:

`levelsOfDetail`
> The number of different resolutions at which you want to redraw, where each level has twice the resolution of the previous level. So, for example, with two levels of detail we can ask to redraw when zooming to double size (2x) and when zooming back to single size (1x).

`levelsOfDetailBias`
> The number of levels of detail that are *larger* than single size (1x). For example, if `levelsOfDetail` is 2, then if we want to redraw when zooming to 2x and when zooming back to 1x, the `levelsOfDetailBias` is 1, because one of those levels is larger than 1x; if we were to leave `levelsOfDetailBias` at 0 (the default), we would be saying we want to redraw when zooming to 0.5x and back to 1x — we have two levels of detail but neither is larger than 1x, so one must be smaller than 1x.

The CATiledLayer will ask for a redraw at a higher resolution as soon as the view's size becomes larger than the previous resolution. In other words, if there are two levels of detail with a bias of 1, the layer will be redrawn at 2x as soon as it is zoomed even a little bit larger than 1x. This is an excellent approach, because although a level of detail would look blurry if scaled up, it looks pretty good scaled down.

For example, let's say I have a TiledView that hosts a CATiledLayer, in which I intend to draw an image. I haven't broken the image into tiles, because the maximum size at which the user can view it isn't prohibitively large; the original image is 838×958, and can be held in memory easily. Rather, I'm using a CATiledLayer in order to take advantage of its ability to change resolutions automatically. The image will be displayed initially at 208×238, and if the user never zooms in to view it larger, we can save memory by drawing a quarter-size version of the image.

The CATiledLayer is configured as follows:

```
CGFloat scale = lay.contentsScale;
lay.tileSize = CGSizeMake(208*scale,238*scale);
lay.levelsOfDetail = 3;
lay.levelsOfDetailBias = 2;
```

The `tileSize` has been adjusted for screen resolution, so the result is as follows:

- As originally displayed at 208×238, there is one tile and we can draw our image at quarter size.
- If the user zooms in, to show the image larger than its originally displayed size, there will be 4 tiles and we can draw our image at half size.

- If the user zooms in still further, to show the image larger than double its originally displayed size (416×476), there will be 16 tiles and we can draw our image at full size, which will continue to look good as the user zooms all the way in to the full size of the original image.

We do not, however, need to draw each tile individually. Each time we're called upon to draw a tile, we'll draw the entire image into the TiledView's bounds; whatever falls outside the requested tile will be clipped out and won't be drawn.

Here's my TiledView's `drawRect:` implementation. I have a UIImage property `current-Image`, initialized to nil, and an NSValue property `currentSize`, initialized to an NSValue wrapping `CGSizeZero`. Each time `drawRect:` is called, I compare the tile size (the incoming `rect` parameter's size) to `currentSize`. If it's different, I know that we've changed by one level of detail and we need a new version of `currentImage`, so I create the new version of `currentImage` at a scale appropriate to this level of detail. Finally, I draw `currentImage` into the TiledView's bounds:

```
- (void)drawRect:(CGRect)rect {
    CGSize oldSize = self.currentSize.CGSizeValue;
    if (!CGSizeEqualToSize(oldSize, rect.size)) {
        // make a new current size
        self.currentSize = [NSValue valueWithCGSize:rect.size];
        // make a new current image
        CATiledLayer* lay = (CATiledLayer*) self.layer;
        CGAffineTransform tr =
            CGContextGetCTM(UIGraphicsGetCurrentContext());
        CGFloat sc = tr.a/lay.contentsScale; // tr.a is our scale transform
        CGFloat scale = sc/4.0;
        NSString* path =
            [[NSBundle mainBundle]
                pathForResource:@"earthFromSaturn" ofType:@"png"];
        UIImage* im = [[UIImage alloc] initWithContentsOfFile:path];
        CGSize sz =
            CGSizeMake(im.size.width * scale, im.size.height * scale);
        UIGraphicsBeginImageContextWithOptions(sz, YES, 1);
        [im drawInRect:CGRectMake(0,0,sz.width,sz.height)];
        self.currentImage = UIGraphicsGetImageFromCurrentImageContext();
        UIGraphicsEndImageContext();
    }
    [self.currentImage drawInRect:self.bounds];
}
```

An alternative and much simpler approach (from a WWDC 2011 video) is to make yourself the scroll view's delegate so that you get an event when the zoom ends, and then change the scalable view's `contentScaleFactor` to match the current zoom scale, compensating for the double-resolution screen at the same time:

```
- (void)scrollViewDidEndZooming:(UIScrollView *)scrollView
                        withView:(UIView *)view
                         atScale:(float)scale {
    view.contentScaleFactor = scale * [UIScreen mainScreen].scale;
}
```

In response, the scalable view's `drawRect:` will be called, and its `rect` parameter will be the CGRect to draw into. Thus, the view may appear fuzzy for a while as the user zooms in, but when the user stops zooming, the view is redrawn sharply.

That approach comes with a caveat, however: you mustn't overdo it. If the zoom scale, screen resolution, and scalable view size are high, you will be asking for a very large graphics context to be maintained in memory, which could cause your app to run low on memory or even to be abruptly terminated by the system.

For more about displaying a large image in a zoomable scroll view, see Apple's Large Image Downsizing example.

Scroll View Delegate

The scroll view's delegate (adopting the UIScrollViewDelegate protocol) receives lots of messages that can help you track, in great detail, exactly what the scroll view is up to:

`scrollViewDidScroll:`
> If you scroll in code without animation, you will receive this message *once* afterward. If the user drags or flicks, or uses the scroll-to-top feature, or if you scroll in code with animation, you will receive this message *repeatedly* throughout the scroll, including during the time the scroll view is decelerating after the user's finger has lifted; there are other delegate messages that tell you, in those cases, when the scroll has finally ended.

`scrollViewDidEndScrollingAnimation:`
> If you scroll in code with animation, you will receive this message afterward, when the animation ends.

`scrollViewWillBeginDragging:`
`scrollViewWillEndDragging:withVelocity:targetContentOffset:`
`scrollViewDidEndDragging:willDecelerate:`
> If the user scrolls by dragging or flicking, you will receive these messages at the start and end of the user's finger movement. If the user brings the scroll view to a stop before lifting the finger, `willDecelerate` is NO and the scroll is over. If the user lets go of the scroll view while the finger is moving, or when paging is turned on, `willDecelerate` is YES and we proceed to the delegate messages reporting deceleration.

> The purpose of `scrollViewWillEndDragging:...` is to let you customize the outcome of the content's deceleration. The third argument is a pointer to a CGPoint;

you can use it to set a different CGPoint, specifying the `contentOffset` value the scroll view should have when the deceleration is over.

`scrollViewWillBeginDecelerating:`
`scrollViewDidEndDecelerating:`
> Sent once each after `scrollViewDidEndDragging:willDecelerate:` arrives with a value of YES. When `scrollViewDidEndDecelerating:` arrives, the scroll is over.

`scrollViewShouldScrollToTop:`
`scrollViewDidScrollToTop:`
> These have to do with the feature where the user can tap the status bar to scroll the scroll view's content to its top. You won't get either of them if `scrollsToTop` is NO, because the scroll-to-top feature is turned off in that case. The first lets you prevent the user from scrolling to the top on this occasion even if `scrollsToTop` is YES. The second tells you that the user has employed this feature and the scroll is over.

In addition, the scroll view has read-only properties reporting its state:

`tracking`
> The user has touched the scroll view, but the scroll view hasn't decided whether this is a scroll or some kind of tap.

`dragging`
> The user is dragging to scroll.

`decelerating`
> The user has scrolled and has lifted the finger, and the scroll is continuing.

So, if you wanted to do something after a scroll ends completely regardless of how the scroll was performed, you'd need to implement multiple delegate methods:

- `scrollViewDidEndDragging:willDecelerate:` in case the user drags and stops (`willDecelerate` is NO).
- `scrollViewDidEndDecelerating:` in case the user drags and the scroll continues afterward.
- `scrollViewDidScrollToTop:` in case the user uses the scroll-to-top feature.
- `scrollViewDidEndScrollingAnimation:` in case you scroll with animation.

(You don't need a delegate method to tell you when the scroll is over after you scroll in code without animation: it's over immediately, so if you have work to do after the scroll ends, you can do it in the next line of code.)

There are also three delegate messages that report zooming:

`scrollViewWillBeginZooming:withView:`

If the user zooms or you zoom in code, you will receive this message as the zoom begins.

`scrollViewDidZoom:`

If you zoom in code, even with animation, you will receive this message *once*. If the user zooms, you will receive this message *repeatedly* as the zoom proceeds. (You will probably also receive `scrollViewDidScroll:`, possibly many times, as the zoom proceeds.)

`scrollViewDidEndZooming:withView:atScale:`

If the user zooms or you zoom in code, you will receive this message after the last `scrollViewDidZoom:`.

In addition, the scroll view has read-only properties reporting its state during a zoom:

`zooming`

The scroll view is zooming. It is possible for `dragging` to be true at the same time.

`zoomBouncing`

The scroll view is returning automatically from having been zoomed outside its minimum or maximum limit. As far as I can tell, you'll get only one `scrollView-DidZoom:` while the scroll view is in this state.

Scroll View Touches

Improvements in UIScrollView's internal implementation have eliminated most of the worry once associated with scroll view touches. A scroll view will interpret a drag or a pinch as a command to scroll or zoom, and any other gesture will fall through to the subviews; thus buttons and similar interface objects inside a scroll view work just fine.

You can even put a scroll view inside a scroll view, and this can be quite a useful thing to do, in contexts where you might not think of it at first. Apple's PhotoScroller example, based on principles discussed in a delightful WWDC 2010 video, is an app where a single photo fills the screen: you can page-scroll from one photo to the next, and you can zoom into the current photo with a pinch gesture. This is implemented as a scroll view inside a scroll view: the outer scroll view is for paging between images, and the inner scroll view contains the current image and is for zooming (and for scrolling to different parts of the zoomed-in image).

A WWDC 2013 video discusses the iOS 7 lock screen in terms of scroll views. The lock screen itself is a horizontal paging scroll view; you scroll rightward to see the other page, containing the passcode screen or the springboard. Notifications in the lock screen are listed in a vertical scroll view, and the individual notifications are themselves horizontal scroll views.

Gesture recognizers (Chapter 5) have also greatly simplified the task of adding custom gestures to a scroll view. For instance, some older code in Apple's documentation, showing how to implement a double tap to zoom in and a two-finger tap to zoom out, uses old-fashioned touch handling, but this is no longer necessary. Simply attach to your scroll view's scalable subview any gesture recognizers for these sorts of gesture, and they will mediate automatically among the possibilities.

In the past, making something inside a scroll view draggable required setting the scroll view's `canCancelContentTouches` property to NO. (The reason for the name is that the scroll view, when it realizes that a gesture is a drag or pinch gesture, normally sends `touchesCancelled:forEvent:` to a subview tracking touches, so that the scroll view and not the subview will be affected.) However, unless you're implementing old-fashioned direct touch handling, you probably won't have to concern yourself with this. Regardless of how `canCancelContentTouches` is set, a draggable control, such as a UI-Slider, remains draggable inside a scroll view.

Here's an example of a draggable object inside a scroll view implemented through a gesture recognizer. Suppose we have an image of a map, larger than the screen, and we want the user to be able to scroll it in the normal way to see any part of the map, but we also want the user to be able to drag a flag into a new location on the map. We'll put the map image in an image view and wrap the image view in a scroll view, with the scroll view's `contentSize` the same as the map image view's size. The flag is a small image view; it's another subview of the scroll view, and it has a UIPanGestureRecognizer. The gesture recognizer's action handler allows the flag to be dragged, as described in Chapter 5:

```
- (void) dragging: (UIPanGestureRecognizer*) p {
    UIView* v = p.view;
    if (p.state == UIGestureRecognizerStateBegan ||
            p.state == UIGestureRecognizerStateChanged) {
        CGPoint delta = [p translationInView: v.superview];
        CGPoint c = v.center;
        c.x += delta.x; c.y += delta.y;
        v.center = c;
        [p setTranslation: CGPointZero inView: v.superview];
    }
}
```

The user can now drag the map or the flag (Figure 7-2). Dragging the map brings the flag along with it, but dragging the flag doesn't move the map. The state of the scroll view's `canCancelContentTouches` is irrelevant, because the flag view isn't tracking the touches manually.

An interesting addition to that example would be to implement autoscrolling, meaning that the scroll view scrolls itself when the user drags the flag close to its edge. This, too, is greatly simplified by gesture recognizers; in fact, we can add autoscrolling code directly to the `dragging:` action handler:

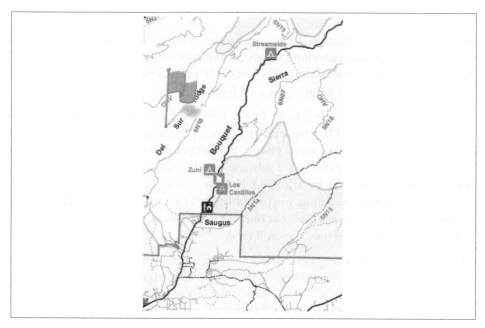

Figure 7-2. A scrollable map with a draggable flag

```
- (void) dragging: (UIPanGestureRecognizer*) p {
    UIView* v = p.view;
    if (p.state == UIGestureRecognizerStateBegan ||
            p.state == UIGestureRecognizerStateChanged) {
        CGPoint delta = [p translationInView: v.superview];
        CGPoint c = v.center;
        c.x += delta.x; c.y += delta.y;
        v.center = c;
        [p setTranslation: CGPointZero inView: v.superview];
    }
    // autoscroll
    if (p.state == UIGestureRecognizerStateChanged) {
        UIScrollView* sv = self.sv;
        CGPoint loc = [p locationInView: sv];
        CGRect f = sv.bounds;
        CGPoint off = sv.contentOffset;
        CGSize sz = sv.contentSize;
        CGPoint c = v.center;
        // to the right
        if (loc.x > CGRectGetMaxX(f) - 30) {
            CGFloat margin = sz.width - CGRectGetMaxX(sv.bounds);
            if (margin > 6) {
                off.x += 5;
                sv.contentOffset = off;
                c.x += 5;
                v.center = c;
```

```
                [self keepDragging:p];
            }
        }
        // to the left
        if (loc.x < f.origin.x + 30) {
            CGFloat margin = off.x;
            if (margin > 6) {
                // ... omitted ...
            }
        }
        // to the bottom
        if (loc.y > CGRectGetMaxY(f) - 30) {
            CGFloat margin = sz.height - CGRectGetMaxY(sv.bounds);
            if (margin > 6) {
                // ... omitted ...
            }
        }
        // to the top
        if (loc.y < f.origin.y + 30) {
            CGFloat margin = off.y;
            if (margin > 6) {
                // ... omitted ...
            }
        }
    }
}
- (void) keepDragging: (UIPanGestureRecognizer*) p {
    float delay = 0.1;
    dispatch_time_t popTime =
        dispatch_time(DISPATCH_TIME_NOW, delay * NSEC_PER_SEC);
    dispatch_after(popTime, dispatch_get_main_queue(), ^{
        [self dragging: p];
    });
}
```

The delay in keepDragging:, combined with the change in offset, determines the speed of autoscrolling. The material marked as omitted in the second, third, and fourth cases is obviously parallel to the first case, and is left as an exercise for the reader.

A scroll view's touch handling is itself based on gesture recognizers attached to the scroll view, and these are available to your code through the scroll view's panGesture-Recognizer and pinchGestureRecognizer properties. This means that if you want to customize a scroll view's touch handling, it's easy to add more gesture recognizers and have them interact with those already attached to the scroll view.

To illustrate, I'll build on the previous example. Suppose we want the flag to start out offscreen, and we'd like the user to be able to summon it with a rightward swipe. We can attach a UISwipeGestureRecognizer to our scroll view, but it will never recognize its gesture because the scroll view's own pan gesture recognizer will recognize first. But we have access to the scroll view's pan gesture recognizer, so we can compel it to yield to our swipe gesture recognizer by sending it `requireGestureRecognizerToFail::`

```
[self.sv.panGestureRecognizer requireGestureRecognizerToFail:self.swipe];
```

The UISwipeGestureRecognizer will recognize a rightward swipe. In my implementation of its action handler, we position the flag, which has been waiting invisibly offscreen, just off to the top left of the scroll view's visible content, and animate it onto the screen:

```
- (IBAction) swiped: (UISwipeGestureRecognizer*) g {
    UIScrollView* sv = self.sv;
    CGPoint p = sv.contentOffset;
    CGRect f = self.flag.frame;
    f.origin = p;
    f.origin.x -= self.flag.bounds.size.width;
    self.flag.frame = f;
    self.flag.hidden = NO;
    [UIView animateWithDuration:0.25 animations:^{
        CGRect f = self.flag.frame;
        f.origin.x = p.x;
        self.flag.frame = f;
        // thanks for the flag, now stop operating altogether
        g.enabled = NO;
    }];
}
```

Floating Scroll View Subviews

A scroll view's subview will appear to "float" over the scroll view if it remains stationary while the rest of the scroll view's content is being scrolled.

Before autolayout, this sort of thing was rather tricky to arrange; you had to use a delegate event to respond to every change in the scroll view's bounds origin by shifting the "floating" view's position to compensate, so as to appear to remain fixed.

With autolayout, however, all you have to do is set up constraints pinning the subview to something *outside* the scroll view. Here's an example:

```
UIImageView* iv = [[UIImageView alloc]
                    initWithImage:[UIImage imageNamed:@"smiley.png"]];
iv.translatesAutoresizingMaskIntoConstraints = NO;
[sv addSubview:iv];
UIView* sup = sv.superview;
[sup addConstraint:
 [NSLayoutConstraint
   constraintWithItem:iv attribute:NSLayoutAttributeRight
   relatedBy:0
   toItem:sup attribute:NSLayoutAttributeRight
   multiplier:1 constant:-5]];
[sup addConstraint:
 [NSLayoutConstraint
```

```
constraintWithItem:iv attribute:NSLayoutAttributeTop
relatedBy:0
toItem:sup attribute:NSLayoutAttributeTop
multiplier:1 constant:30]];
```

Scroll View Performance

At several points in earlier chapters I've mentioned performance problems and ways to increase drawing efficiency. Nowhere are you so likely to need these as in connection with a scroll view. As a scroll view scrolls, views must be drawn very rapidly as they appear on the screen. If the view-drawing system can't keep up with the speed of the scroll, the scrolling will visibly stutter.

Performance testing and optimization is a big subject, so I can't tell you exactly what to do if you encounter stuttering while scrolling. But certain general suggestions (mostly extracted from a really great WWDC 2010 video) should come in handy:

- Everything that can be opaque should be opaque: don't force the drawing system to composite transparency, and remember to tell it that an opaque view or layer *is* opaque by setting its `opaque` property to YES. If you really must composite transparency, keep the size of the nonopaque regions to a minimum; for example, if a large layer is transparent at its edges, break it into five layers — the large central layer, which is opaque, and the four edges, which are not.

- If you're drawing shadows, don't make the drawing system calculate the shadow shape for a layer: supply a `shadowPath`, or use Core Graphics to create the shadow with a drawing. Similarly, avoid making the drawing system composite the shadow as a transparency against another layer; for example, if the background layer is white, your opaque drawing can itself include a shadow already drawn on a white background.

- Don't make the drawing system scale images for you; supply the images at the target size for the correct resolution.

- In a pinch, you can just eliminate massive swatches of the rendering operation by setting a layer's `shouldRasterize` to YES. You could, for example, do this when scrolling starts and then set it back to NO when scrolling ends.

Apple's documentation also says that setting a view's `clearsContextBeforeDrawing` to NO may make a difference. I can't confirm or deny this; it may be true, but I haven't encountered a case that positively proves it.

Xcode provides tools that will help you detect inefficiencies in the drawing system. In the Simulator, the Debug menu shows you blended layers (where transparency is being composited) and images that are being copied, misaligned, or rendered offscreen. On the device, the Core Animation module of Instruments provides the same functionality, plus it tracks the frame rate for you, allowing you to scroll and measure performance objectively where it really counts.

CHAPTER 8

Table Views and Collection Views

I'm gonna ask you the three big questions. — Go ahead. — Who made you? — You did. — Who owns the biggest piece of you? — You do. — What would happen if I dropped you? — I'd go right down the drain.

—Dialogue by Garson Kanin and Ruth Gordon,
Pat and Mike

A table view (UITableView) is a vertically scrolling UIScrollView (Chapter 7) containing a single column of rectangular cells (UITableViewCell, a UIView subclass). It is a keystone of Apple's strategy for making the small iPhone screen useful and powerful, and has three main purposes:

Presentation of information

The cells typically contain text, which the user can read. The cells are usually quite small, in order to maximize the quantity appearing on the screen at once, so this text is often condensed, truncated, or simplified.

Selection

A table view can provide the user with a column of choices. The user chooses by tapping a cell, which selects the cell; the app responds appropriately to that choice.

Navigation

The appropriate response to the user's choosing a cell is often navigation to another interface. This might be done, for example, through a presented view controller or a navigation interface (Chapter 6). An extremely common configuration is a *master–detail interface*, where the master view is a table view within a navigation interface: the user taps a table view cell to navigate to the details about that cell. This is one reason why truncation of text in a table view cell is acceptable: the detail view contains the full information.

In addition to its column of cells, a table view can be extended by a number of other features that make it even more useful and flexible:

- A table can display a header view at the top and a footer view at the bottom.
- The cells can be clumped into sections. Each section can have a header and footer, and these remain visible as long as the section itself occupies the screen, giving the user a clue as to where we are within the table. Moreover, a section index can be provided, in the form of an overlay column of abbreviated section titles, which the user can tap or drag to jump to the start of a section, thus making a long table tractable.
- A table can have a grouped format. This is often used for presenting small numbers of related cells.
- Tables can be editable: the user can be permitted to insert, delete, and reorder cells.

Figure 8-1 illustrates four variations of the table view:

- Apple's Music app lists song titles and artists for a given album in truncated form in a table view within a navigation interface which is itself within a tab bar interface; tapping an album in a table of album titles summons the list of songs within that album, and tapping a song in that list plays it.
- Apple's Settings app uses table view cells in a grouped format with a header, within a navigation interface, to display a switch and a list of Bluetooth devices; tapping a device name searches for it, while tapping the detail (info) button navigates to reveal more information about it.
- My Latin vocabulary app lists Latin words and their definitions in alphabetical order, divided into sections by first letter, with section headers and a section index.
- Apple's Music app allows a custom playlist to be edited, with interface for deleting and rearranging cells.

Table view cells, too, can be extremely flexible. Some basic cell formats are provided, such as a text label along with a small image view, but you are free to design your own cell as you would any other view. There are also some standard interface items that are commonly used in a cell, such as a checkmark to indicate selection or a right-pointing chevron to indicate that tapping the cell navigates to a detail view.

It would be difficult to overestimate the importance of table views. An iOS app without a table view somewhere in its interface would be a rare thing, especially on the small iPhone screen. I've written apps consisting almost entirely of table views. Indeed, it is not uncommon to use a table view even in situations that have nothing particularly table-like about them, simply because it is so convenient.

Figure 8-1. Four table view variations

Figure 8-2. A grouped table view as an interface for choosing options

For example, in one of my apps I want the user to be able to choose between three levels of difficulty and two sets of images. In a desktop application I'd probably use radio buttons; but there are no radio buttons among the standard iOS interface objects. Instead, I use a grouped table view so small that it doesn't even scroll. This gives me section headers, tappable cells, and a checkmark indicating the current choice (Figure 8-2).

There is a UIViewController subclass, UITableViewController, dedicated to the presentation of a table view. You never really *need* to use a UITableViewController; it's a convenience, but it doesn't do anything that you couldn't do yourself by other means. Here's some of what using a UITableViewController gives you:

- UITableViewController's `initWithStyle:` creates the table view with a plain or grouped format.

- The view controller is automatically made the table view's delegate and data source, unless you specify otherwise.

- The table view is made the view controller's `tableView`. It is also, of course, the view controller's `view`, but the `tableView` property is typed as a UITableView, so you can send table view messages to it without typecasting.

Table View Cells

Beginners may be surprised to learn that a table view's structure and contents are generally not configured in advance. Rather, you supply the table view with a data source and a delegate (which will often be the same object), and the table view turns to these in real time, as the app runs, whenever it needs a piece of information about its structure and contents.

This architecture is part of a brilliant strategy to conserve resources. Imagine a long table consisting of thousands of rows. It must appear, therefore, to consist of thousands of cells as the user scrolls. But a cell is a UIView and is memory-intensive; to maintain thousands of cells internally would put a terrible strain on memory. Therefore, the table typically maintains only as many cells as are showing simultaneously at any one moment (about ten, let's say). As the user scrolls to reveal new cells, those cells are created on the spot; meanwhile, the cells that have been scrolled out of view are permitted to die.

This sounds ingenious but a bit wasteful, and possibly time-consuming. Wouldn't it be even cleverer if, instead of letting a cell die as it is scrolled *out* of view, it were whisked around to the other side and used again as one of the cells being scrolled *into* view? Yes, and in fact that's exactly what you're supposed to do. You do it by assigning each cell a *reuse identifier*.

As cells with a given reuse identifier are scrolled out of view, the table view maintains a bunch of them in a pile. As cells are scrolled into view, you ask the table view for a cell from that pile, specifying it by means of the reuse identifier. The table view hands an old used cell back to you, and now you can configure it as the cell that is about to be scrolled into view. Cells are thus *reused* to minimize not only the number of actual cells in existence at any one moment, but the number of actual cells *ever created*. A table of 1000 rows might very well never need to create more than a dozen cells over the entire lifetime of the app.

Your code must be prepared, on demand, to supply the table with pieces of requested data. Of these, the most important is the cell to be slotted into a given position. A position in the table is specified by means of an index path (NSIndexPath), a class used here to combine a section number with a row number, and is often referred to simply as a *row* of the table. Your data source object may at any moment be sent the message `table-View:cellForRowAtIndexPath:`, and must respond by returning the UITableViewCell to be displayed at that row of the table. And you must return it *fast*: the user is scrolling *now*, so the table needs the next cell *now*.

In this section, I'll discuss *what* you're going to be supplying — the table view cell. After that, I'll talk about *how* you supply it.

Built-In Cell Styles

The simplest way to obtain a table view cell is to start with one of the four built-in table view cell styles. To create a cell using a built-in style, call `initWithStyle:reuse-Identifier:`. The `reuseIdentifier:` is what allows cells previously assigned to rows that are no longer showing to be reused for cells that are; it will usually be the same for all cells in a table. Your choices of cell style are:

`UITableViewCellStyleDefault`
> The cell has a UILabel (its `textLabel`), with an optional UIImageView (its `image-View`) at the left. If there is no image, the label occupies the entire width of the cell.

`UITableViewCellStyleValue1`
> The cell has two UILabels (its `textLabel` and its `detailTextLabel`), side by side, with an optional UIImageView (its `imageView`) at the left. The first label is left-aligned; the second label is right-aligned. If the first label's text is too long, the second label won't appear.

`UITableViewCellStyleValue2`
> The cell has two UILabels (its `textLabel` and its `detailTextLabel`), side by side. No UIImageView will appear. The first label is right-aligned; the second label is left-aligned. The label sizes are fixed, and the text of either will be truncated if it's too long.

`UITableViewCellStyleSubtitle`
> The cell has two UILabels (its `textLabel` and its `detailTextLabel`), one above the other, with an optional UIImageView (its `imageView`) at the left.

To experiment with the built-in cell styles, do this:

1. Make a new iPhone project from the Empty Application project template.
2. Choose File → New → File and ask for a Cocoa Touch Objective-C class.
3. Make it a UITableViewController subclass called RootViewController. The XIB checkbox should be checked; Xcode will create a *.xib* file containing a table view, correctly hooked to our RootViewController class.

Hello there! 1

Hello there! 2

Hello there! 3

Hello there! 4

Figure 8-3. The world's simplest table

4. Make sure you're saving into the correct folder and group, and that the app target is checked. Click Create.

To get our table view into the interface, import "RootViewController.h" into *App-Delegate.m*, and add this line to AppDelegate's `application:didFinishLaunchingWith-Options:` at the override point:

```
self.window.rootViewController = [RootViewController new];
```

Now modify the RootViewController class (which comes with a lot of templated code), as in Example 8-1. Run the app to see the world's simplest table (Figure 8-3).

Example 8-1. The world's simplest table

```
- (NSInteger)numberOfSectionsInTableView:(UITableView *)tableView {
    return 1; ❶
}
- (NSInteger)tableView:(UITableView *)tableView
        numberOfRowsInSection:(NSInteger)section {
    return 20; ❷
}
- (UITableViewCell *)tableView:(UITableView *)tableView
        cellForRowAtIndexPath:(NSIndexPath *)indexPath {
    static NSString *CellIdentifier = @"Cell";
    UITableViewCell *cell =
        [tableView dequeueReusableCellWithIdentifier:CellIdentifier];
    if (cell == nil) {
        cell =
            [[UITableViewCell alloc] initWithStyle:UITableViewCellStyleDefault
                                   reuseIdentifier:CellIdentifier]; ❸
        cell.textLabel.textColor = [UIColor redColor]; ❹
    }
    cell.textLabel.text =
        [NSString stringWithFormat:@"Hello there! %d", indexPath.row]; ❺
    return cell;
}
```

The key parts of the code are:

❶   Our table will have one section.

❷   Our table will consist of 20 rows. Having multiple rows will give us a sense of how our cell looks when placed next to other cells.

❸   This is where you specify the built-in table view cell style you want to experiment with.

❹   At this point in the code you can modify characteristics of the cell (`cell`) that are to be the same for *every* cell of the table. For the moment, I've symbolized this by assuming that every cell's text is to be the same color.

❺   We now have the cell to be used for *this* row of the table, so at this point in the code you can modify characteristics of the cell (`cell`) that are unique to this row. I've symbolized this by appending successive numbers to the text of each row. Of course, that's completely unrealistic; but that's just because we're only beginners. In real life the different cells would reflect meaningful data. I'll talk about that later in this chapter.

Now you can experiment with your cell's appearance by tweaking the code and running the app. Feel free to try different built-in cell styles in the place where we are now specifying `UITableViewCellStyleDefault`.

The flexibility of each built-in style is based mostly on the flexibility of UILabels. Not everything can be customized, because after you return the cell some further configuration takes place, which may override your settings. For example, the size and position of the cell's subviews are not up to you. (I'll explain, a little later, how to get around that.) But you get a remarkable degree of freedom. Here are a few basic UILabel properties for you to play with now (by customizing `cell.textLabel`), and I'll talk much more about UILabels in Chapter 10:

`text`
> The string shown in the label.

`textColor`, `highlightedTextColor`
> The color of the text. The `highlightedTextColor` applies when the cell is highlighted or selected (tap on a cell to select it).
>
> In earlier versions of iOS, if you didn't set the `highlightedTextColor`, the label would choose its own variant of the `textColor` when the cell was highlighted or selected. In iOS 7, that's no longer the case; the `textColor` is used unless you set the `highlightedTextColor` explicitly.

`textAlignment`
> How the text is aligned; some possible choices are `NSTextAlignmentLeft`, `NSText-AlignmentCenter`, and `NSTextAlignmentRight`.

`numberOfLines`

The maximum number of lines of text to appear in the label. Text that is long but permitted to wrap, or that contains explicit linefeed characters, can appear completely in the label if the label is tall enough and the number of permitted lines is sufficient. 0 means there's no maximum.

`font`

The label's font. You could reduce the font size as a way of fitting more text into the label. A font name includes its style. For example:

```
cell.textLabel.font = [UIFont fontWithName:@"Helvetica-Bold" size:12.0];
```

`shadowColor`, `shadowOffset`

The text shadow. Adding a little shadow can increase clarity and emphasis for large text.

You can also assign the image view (`cell.imageView`) an image. The frame of the image view can't be changed, but you can inset its apparent size by supplying a smaller image and setting the image view's `contentMode` to `UIViewContentModeCenter`. It's probably a good idea in any case, for performance reasons, to supply images at their drawn size and resolution rather than making the drawing system scale them for you (see the last section of Chapter 7). For example:

```
CGFloat side = 30;
UIImage* im = [UIImage imageNamed:@"smiley"];
UIGraphicsBeginImageContextWithOptions(CGSizeMake(side,side), YES, 0);
[im drawInRect:CGRectMake(0,0,side,side)];
UIImage* im2 = UIGraphicsGetImageFromCurrentImageContext();
UIGraphicsEndImageContext();
cell.imageView.image = im2;
cell.imageView.contentMode = UIViewContentModeCenter;
```

The cell itself also has some properties you can play with:

`accessoryType`

A built-in type of accessory view, which appears at the cell's right end. For example:

```
cell.accessoryType = UITableViewCellAccessoryDisclosureIndicator;
```

`accessoryView`

Your own UIView, which appears at the cell's right end (overriding the `accessory-Type`). For example:

```
UIButton* b = [UIButton buttonWithType:UIButtonTypeSystem];
[b setTitle:@"Tap Me" forState:UIControlStateNormal];
[b sizeToFit];
// ... also assign button a target and action ...
cell.accessoryView = b;
```

`indentationLevel`, `indentationWidth`

These properties give the cell a left margin, useful for suggesting a hierarchy among cells. You can also set a cell's indentation level in real time, with respect to the table row into which it is slotted, by implementing the delegate's `table-View:indentationLevelForRowAtIndexPath:` method.

`separatorInset`

A new iOS 7 feature. Only the left and right insets matter. The default is a left inset of 15, though if you don't set it explicitly, the built-in table view cell styles may shift it. This property affects both the drawing of the separator between cells and the indentation of content of the built-in cell styles.

`selectionStyle`

How the background looks when the cell is selected. The default, new in iOS 7, is solid gray (`UITableViewCellSelectionStyleDefault`), or you can choose `UITable-ViewCellSelectionStyleNone`.

(The blue and gray gradient backgrounds designated by `UITableViewCell-SelectionStyleBlue` and `UITableViewCellSelectionStyleGray` in iOS 6 and before are now abandoned, and are treated as equivalent to `UITableViewCell-SelectionStyleDefault`.)

`backgroundColor`
`backgroundView`
`selectedBackgroundView`

What's behind everything else drawn in the cell. The `selectedBackgroundView` is drawn in front of the `backgroundView` (if any) when the cell is selected, and will appear instead of whatever the `selectionStyle` dictates. The `backgroundColor` is behind the `backgroundView`. (Thus, if both the `selectedBackgroundView` and the `backgroundView` have some transparency, both of them and the `background-Color` can appear composited together when the cell is selected.)

There is no need to set the frame of the `backgroundView` and `selectedBackground-View`; they will be resized automatically to fit the cell.

`multipleSelectionBackgroundView`

If defined (not nil), and if the table's `allowsMultipleSelection` (or, if editing, `allowsMultipleSelectionDuringEditing`) is YES, used instead of the `selected-BackgroundView` when the cell is selected.

In this example, we set the cell's `backgroundView` to display an image with some transparency at the outside edges, so that the `backgroundColor` shows behind it, and we set the `selectedBackgroundView` to an almost transparent blue rectangle, to darken that image when the cell is selected (Figure 8-4):

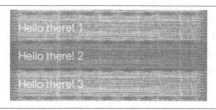

Figure 8-4. A cell with an image background

```
cell.textLabel.textColor = [UIColor whiteColor];
UIImageView* v = [UIImageView new]; // no need to set frame
v.contentMode = UIViewContentModeScaleToFill;
v.image = [UIImage imageNamed:@"linen.png"];
cell.backgroundView = v;
UIView* v2 = [UIView new]; // no need to set frame
v2.backgroundColor = [[UIColor blueColor] colorWithAlphaComponent:0.2];
cell.selectedBackgroundView = v2;
cell.backgroundColor = [UIColor redColor];
```

If those features are to be true of every cell ever displayed in the table, then that code should go in the spot numbered 4 in Example 8-1; there's no need to waste time doing the same thing all over again when an existing cell is reused.

Finally, here are a few properties of the table view itself worth playing with:

rowHeight

> The height of a cell. A taller cell may accommodate more information. You can also change this value in the nib editor; the table view's row height appears in the Size inspector. The cell's subviews have their autoresizing set so as to compensate correctly. You can also set a cell's height in real time by implementing the delegate's tableView:heightForRowAtIndexPath: method; thus a table's cells may differ from one another in height (more about that later in this chapter).

separatorStyle
separatorColor
separatorInset

> These can also be set in the nib. The table's separatorInset is adopted by individual cells that don't have their own explicit separatorInset. Separator styles are:

> - UITableViewCellSeparatorStyleNone
> - UITableViewCellSeparatorStyleSingleLine.

> (The former UITableViewCellSeparatorStyleSingleLineEtched style is abandoned in iOS 7, and equates to None.)

`backgroundColor`, `backgroundView`

What's behind all the cells of the table; this may be seen if the cells have transparency, or if the user scrolls the cells beyond their limit. The `backgroundView` is drawn on top of the `backgroundColor`.

`tableHeaderView`, `tableFooterView`

Views to be shown before the first row and after the last row, respectively (as part of the table's scrolling content). Their background color is, by default, the background color of the table, but you can change that. You dictate their heights; their widths will be dynamically resized to fit the table. The user can, if you like, interact with these views (and their subviews); for example, a view can be (or can contain) a UIButton.

You can alter a table header or footer view dynamically during the lifetime of the app; if you change its height, you must set the corresponding table view property afresh to notify the table view of what has happened.

Registering a Cell Class

In `tableView:cellForRowAtIndexPath:`, there are actually two possible ways to obtain a reusable cell:

- `dequeueReusableCellWithIdentifier:`
- `dequeueReusableCellWithIdentifier:forIndexPath:`

If you use the second method, which was introduced in iOS 6, you pass along as the second argument the same `indexPath:` value that you already received. I prefer the second method, and will use it from now on. It has three advantages:

The result is never nil

Unlike `dequeueReusableCellWithIdentifier:`, the value returned by `dequeueReusableCellWithIdentifier:forIndexPath:` is never nil. If there is a free reusable cell with the given identifier, it is returned. If there isn't, a new one is created for you. Step 3 of Example 8-1 can thus be eliminated.

The row height is known earlier

Unlike `dequeueReusableCellWithIdentifier:`, the cell returned by `dequeueReusableCellWithIdentifier:forIndexPath:` has its final bounds. That's possible because you've passed the index path as an argument, so the runtime knows this cell's ultimate destination within the table, and has already consulted the table's `rowHeight` or the delegate's `tableView:heightForRowAtIndexPath:`. This makes laying out the cell's contents much easier.

The identifier is consistent

A danger with dequeueReusableCellWithIdentifier: is that you may accidentally pass an incorrect reuse identifier, or nil, and end up not reusing cells. With dequeueReusableCellWithIdentifier:forIndexPath:, that can't happen.

Before you call dequeueReusableCellWithIdentifier:forIndexPath: for the first time, you must *register* with the table itself. You do this by calling registerClass:forCellReuseIdentifier:. This associates a class (which must be UITableViewCell or a subclass thereof) with a string identifier. That's how dequeueReusableCellWithIdentifier:forIndexPath: knows what class to instantiate when it creates a new cell for you: you pass an identifier, and you've already told the table what class it signifies. The only cell types you can obtain are those for which you've registered in this way; if you pass a bad identifier, the app will crash (with a helpful log message).

This is a very elegant mechanism. It also raises some new questions:

When should I call registerClass:forCellReuseIdentifier:?

Call it early, before the table view starts generating cells. viewDidLoad is a good place:

```
- (void)viewDidLoad {
    [super viewDidLoad];
    [self.tableView registerClass:[UITableViewCell class]
        forCellReuseIdentifier:@"Cell"];
}
```

How do I specify a built-in table view cell style?

We are no longer calling initWithStyle:reuseIdentifier:, so where do we make our choice of built-in cell style? The default cell style is UITableViewCellStyleDefault, so if that's what you wanted, the problem is solved. Otherwise, subclass UITableViewCell and override initWithStyle:reuseIdentifier: to substitute the cell style you're after (passing along the reuse identifier you were handed).

For example, let's call our UITableViewCell subclass MyCell. So we now specify [MyCell class] in our call to registerClass:forCellReuseIdentifier:. MyCell's initializer looks like this:

```
- (id)initWithStyle:(UITableViewCellStyle)style
        reuseIdentifier:(NSString *)reuseIdentifier {
    self = [super initWithStyle:UITableViewCellStyleSubtitle // or whatever
                reuseIdentifier:reuseIdentifier];
    if (self) {
        // ...
    }
    return self;
}
```

How do I know whether the returned cell is new or reused?

It's important to know this, because there needs to be a way distinguish between step 4 of Example 8-1 (configurations to apply *once and for all* to a new cell) and step 5 (configurations that differ for each row). It's up to you, when performing one-time configuration on a cell, to give that cell some distinguishing mark that you can look for later to determine whether a cell requires one-time configuration.

For example, if every cell is to have a green background, there is no point giving *every* cell returned by dequeueReusableCellWithIdentifier:forIndexPath: a green background; the reused cells already have one. Now, however, no cell is nil, and we are never instantiating the cell ourselves. So how will we know which ones need to be given a green background? It's easy: they are the ones *without* a green background:

```
- (UITableViewCell *)tableView:(UITableView *)tableView
        cellForRowAtIndexPath:(NSIndexPath *)indexPath {
    UITableViewCell *cell =
        [tableView dequeueReusableCellWithIdentifier:@"Cell"
            forIndexPath:indexPath];
    if (![cell.backgroundColor isEqual:[UIColor greenColor]]) {
        // do one-time configurations
        cell.textLabel.textColor = [UIColor redColor];
        cell.backgroundColor = [UIColor greenColor];
    }
    // do individual cell configurations
    cell.textLabel.text =
        [NSString stringWithFormat:@"Hello there! %d", indexPath.row];
    return cell;
}
```

Cell class registration with registerClass:forCellReuseIdentifier: is also consistent with ways of generating a cell when you *don't* want one of the four built-in table view cell styles, or when you want to design the cell with the nib editor, as I'll now proceed to explain.

Custom Cells

The built-in cell styles give the beginner a leg up in getting started with table views, but there is nothing sacred about them, and soon you'll probably want to transcend them, putting yourself in charge of how a table's cells look and what subviews they contain. The thing to remember is that the cell has a contentView property, which is one of its subviews; things like the accessoryView are outside the contentView. All *your* customizations must be confined to subviews of the contentView; this allows the cell to continue working correctly.

There are four possible approaches:

- Start with a built-in cell style, but supply a UITableViewCell subclass and override `layoutSubviews` to alter the frames of the built-in subviews.

- In `tableView:cellForRowAtIndexPath:`, add subviews to each cell's `contentView` as the cell is created. This approach can be combined with the previous one, or you can ignore the built-in subviews and use your own exclusively. As long as the built-in subviews for a particular built-in cell style are not referenced, they are never created or inserted into the cell, so you don't need to remove them if you don't want to use them.

- Design the cell in a nib, and load that nib in `tableView:cellForRowAtIndexPath:` each time a cell needs to be created.

- Design the cell in a storyboard.

I'll illustrate each approach.

Overriding a cell's subview layout

You can't directly change the frame of a built-in cell style subview in `tableView:cellForRowAtIndexPath:`, because after your changes, the cell's `layoutSubviews` comes along and overrides them. The workaround is to override the cell's `layoutSubviews`! This is a straightforward solution if your main objection to a built-in style is the frame of an existing subview.

To illustrate, let's modify a `UITableViewCellStyleDefault` cell so that the image is at the right end instead of the left end (Figure 8-5). We'll make a UITableViewCell subclass, MyCell, remembering to register MyCell with the table view, so that `dequeueReusableCellWithIdentifier:forIndexPath:` produces a MyCell instance; here is MyCell's `layoutSubviews`:

```
- (void) layoutSubviews {
    [super layoutSubviews];
    CGRect cvb = self.contentView.bounds;
    CGRect imf = self.imageView.frame;
    imf.origin.x = cvb.size.width - imf.size.width - 15;
    self.imageView.frame = imf;
    CGRect tf = self.textLabel.frame;
    tf.origin.x = 15;
    self.textLabel.frame = tf;
}
```

In using this technique, I find it easier to move the subviews using their frame, rather than with constraints. Otherwise, the runtime (which still thinks it owns these subviews) tries to fight us.

| The author of this book, who would rather be out dirt biking | |

Figure 8-5. A cell with its label and image view swapped

Adding subviews in code

Instead of modifying the existing default subviews, you can add completely new views to each UITableViewCell's content view. This has some great advantages over the preceding technique. We won't be fighting the runtime, so we can make our changes in `tableView:cellForRowAtIndexPath:`, and we can assign a frame or constraints. Here are some things to keep in mind:

- The new views must be added when we instantiate a new cell, but not when we reuse a cell (because a reused cell already has them).

- We must never send `addSubview:` to the cell itself — only to its `contentView` (or some subview thereof).

- We should assign the new views an appropriate `autoresizingMask` or constraints, because the cell's content view might be resized.

- Each new view should be assigned a tag so that it can be referred to elsewhere.

I'll rewrite the previous example (Figure 8-5) to use this technique. We are no longer using a UITableViewCell subclass; the registered cell class is UITableViewCell itself. If this is a new cell, we add the subviews and assign them tags. If this is a reused cell, we don't add the subviews (the cell already has them), and we use the tags to refer to the subviews:

```
- (UITableViewCell *)tableView:(UITableView *)tableView
        cellForRowAtIndexPath:(NSIndexPath *)indexPath
{
    UITableViewCell *cell =
        [tableView dequeueReusableCellWithIdentifier:@"Cell"
            forIndexPath:indexPath];
    if (![cell viewWithTag:1]) {
        UIImageView* iv = [UIImageView new];
        iv.tag = 1;
        [cell.contentView addSubview:iv];
        UILabel* lab = [UILabel new];
        lab.tag = 2;
        [cell.contentView addSubview:lab];
        // position using constraints
        NSDictionary* d = NSDictionaryOfVariableBindings(iv, lab);
        iv.translatesAutoresizingMaskIntoConstraints = NO;
        lab.translatesAutoresizingMaskIntoConstraints = NO;
        // image view is vertically centered
```

```
            [cell.contentView addConstraint:
             [NSLayoutConstraint
              constraintWithItem:iv attribute:NSLayoutAttributeCenterY
              relatedBy:0
              toItem:cell.contentView attribute:NSLayoutAttributeCenterY
              multiplier:1 constant:0]];
            // it's a square
            [cell.contentView addConstraint:
             [NSLayoutConstraint
              constraintWithItem:iv attribute:NSLayoutAttributeWidth
              relatedBy:0
              toItem:iv attribute:NSLayoutAttributeHeight
              multiplier:1 constant:0]];
            // label has height pinned to superview
            [cell.contentView addConstraints:
             [NSLayoutConstraint
              constraintsWithVisualFormat:@"V:|[lab]|"
              options:0 metrics:nil views:d]];
            // horizontal margins
            [cell.contentView addConstraints:
             [NSLayoutConstraint
              constraintsWithVisualFormat:@"H:|-15-[lab]-15-[iv]-15-|"
              options:0 metrics:nil views:d]];
        }
        UILabel* lab = (UILabel*)[cell.contentView viewWithTag: 2];
        UIImageView* iv = (UIImageView*)[cell.contentView viewWithTag: 1];
        // ...
        return cell;
    }
```

Using our own cell subviews instead of the built-in cell style subviews has some clear advantages; we no longer have to perform an elaborate dance to escape from the restrictions imposed by the runtime. Still, the verbosity of this code is somewhat overwhelming. We can avoid this by designing the cell in a nib.

Designing a cell in a nib

In designing a cell in a nib, we start by creating a *.xib* file that will consist, in effect, solely of this one cell. In Xcode, create a new iOS User Interface View *.xib* file for iPhone. Let's call it *MyCell.xib*. In the nib editor, delete the existing View and replace it with a Table View Cell from the Object library.

The cell's design window shows a standard-sized cell; you can resize it as desired, but the actual size of the cell in the interface will be dictated by the table view's width and its rowHeight (or the delegate's response to tableView:heightForRowAtIndexPath:). The cell already has a contentView, and any subviews you add will be inside that; do not subvert that arrangement.

You can choose a built-in table view cell style in the Style pop-up menu of the Attributes inspector, and this gives you the default subviews, locked in their standard positions;

for example, if you choose Basic, the textLabel appears, and if you specify an image, the imageView appears. If you set the Style pop-up menu to Custom, you start with a blank slate. Let's do that.

We'll implement, from scratch, the same subviews we've already implemented in the preceding two examples: a UILabel on the left side of the cell, and a UIImageView on the right side. Just as when adding subviews in code, we should set each subview's autoresizing behavior or constraints, and *give each subview a tag*, so that later, in table-View:cellForRowAtIndexPath:, we'll be able to refer to the label and the image view using viewWithTag:, exactly as in the previous example:

```
UILabel* lab = (UILabel*)[cell viewWithTag: 2];
UIImageView* iv = (UIImageView*)[cell viewWithTag: 1];
// ...
return cell;
```

The only remaining question is how to load the cell from the nib. This the Really Cool Part. When we register with the table view, which we're currently doing in viewDid-Load, instead of calling registerClass:forCellReuseIdentifier:, we call register-Nib:forCellReuseIdentifier:. To specify the nib, call UINib's class method nibWith-NibName:bundle:, like this:

```
[self.tableView registerNib:[UINib nibWithNibName:@"MyCell" bundle:nil]
        forCellReuseIdentifier:@"Cell"];
```

That's all there is to it! In tableView:cellForRowAtIndexPath:, when we call dequeue-ReusableCellWithIdentifier:forIndexPath:, if the table has no free reusable cell already in existence, the nib will automatically be loaded and the cell will be instantiated from it and returned to us.

You may wonder how that's possible, when we haven't specified a File's Owner class or added an outlet from the File's Owner to the cell in the nib. The answer is that the nib conforms to a specific format. The UINib instance method instantiateWith-Owner:options: can load a nib with a nil owner; regardless, it returns an NSArray of the nib's instantiated top-level objects. A nib registered with the table view is expected to have exactly one top-level object, and that top-level object is expected to be a UITableViewCell; that being so, the cell can easily be extracted from the resulting NSArray, as it is the array's only element. Our nib meets those expectations!

The advantages of this approach should be immediately obvious. The subviews can now be designed in the nib, and code that was creating *and configuring* each subview can be deleted. For example, suppose we previously had this code:

```
if (![cell viewWithTag:1]) {
    UIImageView* iv = [UIImageView new];
    iv.tag = 1;
    [cell.contentView addSubview:iv];
    UILabel* lab = [UILabel new];
```

```
        lab.tag = 2;
        [cell.contentView addSubview:lab];
        // ...
        lab.font = [UIFont fontWithName:@"Helvetica-Bold" size:16];
        lab.lineBreakMode = NSLineBreakByWordWrapping;
        lab.numberOfLines = 2;
    }
```

All of that can now be eliminated, including setting the label's font, lineBreakMode, and numberOfLines; those configurations are to be applied to the label in *every* cell, so they can be performed in the nib instead.

 The nib *must* conform to the format I've described: it must have exactly one top-level object, a UITableViewCell. This means that some configurations are difficult or impossible in the nib. Consider, for example, the cell's backgroundView. The cell in the nib has a background-View outlet, but if we drag a view into the canvas and hook that outlet to it, our app will crash when the nib loads (because there are now two top-level nib objects). The simplest workaround is to add the backgroundView in code.

In tableView:cellForRowAtIndexPath:, we are still referring to the cell's subviews by way of viewWithTag:. There's nothing wrong with that, but perhaps you'd prefer to use names. Now that we're designing the cell in a nib, that's easy. Provide a UITableViewCell subclass with outlet properties, and configure the nib file accordingly:

1. Create the files for a UITableViewCell subclass; let's call it MyCell. In *MyCell.h*, declare two outlet properties:

    ```
    @property (nonatomic, weak) IBOutlet UILabel* theLabel;
    @property (nonatomic, weak) IBOutlet UIImageView* theImageView;
    ```

2. Edit the table view cell nib *MyCell.xib*. Change the class of the cell to MyCell, and link up the outlets from the cell to the respective subviews.

The result is that in our implementation of tableView:cellForRowAtIndexPath:, once we've typed the cell as a MyCell (which will require importing "MyCell.h"), the compiler will let us use the property names to access the subviews:

```
MyCell* cell =
    [tableView dequeueReusableCellWithIdentifier:@"Cell"
        forIndexPath:indexPath];
UILabel* lab = cell.theLabel;
UIImageView* iv = cell.theImageView;
```

Designing a cell in a storyboard

When your table view comes from a storyboard, it is open to you to employ any of the ways of obtaining and designing its cells that I've already described. There is also an additional option, available only if you're using a UITableViewController subclass — that is, there needs to be a UITableViewController scene in the storyboard. In that case, you can have the table view obtain the cells from the storyboard itself, and you can also *design* the cell directly in the table view in the storyboard.

To experiment with this way of obtaining and designing a cell, start with an iPhone project based on the Single View Application template:

1. In the storyboard, delete the View Controller scene. In the project, delete the View Controller class files.

2. In the project, create files for a UITableViewController subclass called RootView-Controller, *without* a corresponding *.xib* file.

3. In the storyboard, drag a Table View Controller into the empty canvas, and set its class to RootViewController.

4. Now comes the Interesting Part. The table view controller in the storyboard comes with a table view. In the storyboard, select that table view, and, in the Attributes inspector, set the Content pop-up menu to Dynamic Prototypes, and set the number of Prototype Cells to 1 (these are the defaults).

The table view now contains a single table view cell with a content view. You can do in this cell exactly what we were doing before when designing a table view cell in a *.xib* file.

So, let's do that. I like being able to refer to my custom cell subviews with property names. Our procedure is just like what we did in the previous example:

1. In the project, create the files for a UITableViewCell subclass; let's call it MyCell. In *MyCell.h*, declare two outlet properties:

   ```
   @property (nonatomic, weak) IBOutlet UILabel* theLabel;
   @property (nonatomic, weak) IBOutlet UIImageView* theImageView;
   ```

2. In the storyboard, select the prototype cell and change its class to MyCell.

3. Drag a label and an image view into the prototype cell, position and configure them as desired, and hook up the cell's outlets to them appropriately.

There is one question I have not yet answered: How will your code tell the table view to get its cells from the storyboard? Clearly, *not* by calling `registerClass:forCellReuse-Identifier:`, and *not* by calling `registerNib:forCellReuseIdentifier:`; each of those would do something perfectly valid, but not the thing we want done in this case. The answer is that you *don't register anything with the table view at all!* Instead, when you call dequeueReusableCellWithIdentifier:forIndexPath:, you supply an identifier that matches the prototype cell's identifier in the storyboard.

So, return once more to the storyboard:

1. Select the prototype cell.

2. In the Attributes inspector, enter Cell in the Identifier field. (This is an NSString, so capitalization counts.)

Now RootViewController's tableView:cellForRowAtIndexPath: works exactly as it did in the previous example:

```
MyCell* cell =
    [tableView dequeueReusableCellWithIdentifier:@"Cell"
        forIndexPath:indexPath];
UILabel* lab = cell.theLabel;
UIImageView* iv = cell.theImageView;
```

If you call dequeueReusableCellWithIdentifier:forIndexPath: with an identifier that you have *not* registered with the table view and that *doesn't* match the identifier of a prototype cell in the storyboard, your app will crash (with a helpful message in the console).

Table View Data

The structure and content of the actual data portrayed in a table view comes from the data source, an object pointed to by the table view's dataSource property and adopting the UITableViewDataSource protocol. The data source is thus the heart and soul of the table. What surprises beginners is that the data source operates not by *setting* the table view's structure and content, but by *responding on demand*. The data source, *qua* data source, consists of a set of methods that the table view will call when it needs information. This architecture has important consequences for how you write your code, which can be summarized by these simple guidelines:

Be ready
> Your data source cannot know *when* or *how often* any of these methods will be called, so it must be prepared to answer *any question at any time.*

Be fast
> The table view is asking for data in real time; the user is probably scrolling through the table *right now*. So you mustn't gum up the works; you must be ready to supply responses just as fast as you possibly can. (If you can't supply a piece of data fast enough, you may have to skip it, supply a placeholder, and insert the data into the table later. This may involve you in threading issues that I don't want to get into here. I'll give an example in Chapter 24.)

Be consistent

There are multiple data source methods, and you cannot know *which* one will be called at a given moment. So you must make sure your responses are mutually consistent at *any* moment. For example, a common beginner error is forgetting to take into account, in your data source methods, the possibility that the data might not yet be ready.

This may sound daunting, but you'll be fine as long as you maintain an unswerving adherence to the principles of model–view–controller. How and when you accumulate the actual data, and how that data is structured, is a *model* concern. Acting as a data source is a *controller* concern. So you can acquire and arrange your data whenever and however you like, just so long as when the table view actually turns to you and asks what to do, you can lay your hands on the relevant data rapidly and consistently. You'll want to design the model in such a way that the controller can access any desired piece of data more or less instantly.

Another source of confusion for beginners is that methods are rather oddly distributed between the data source and the delegate, an object pointed to by the table view's delegate property and adopting the UITableViewDelegate protocol; in some cases, one may seem to be doing the job of the other. This is not usually a cause of any real difficulty, because the object serving as data source will probably also be the object serving as delegate. Nevertheless, it is rather inconvenient when you're consulting the documentation; you'll probably want to keep the data source and delegate documentation pages open simultaneously as you work.

 If a table view's contents are known beforehand, you can alternatively design the entire table, *including the contents of individual cells*, in a storyboard. I'll give an example later in this chapter.

The Three Big Questions

Like Katherine Hepburn in *Pat and Mike*, the basis of your success (as a data source) is your ability, at any time, to answer the Three Big Questions. The questions the table view will ask you are a little different from the questions Mike asks Pat, but the principle is the same: know the answers, and be able to recite them at any moment. Here they are:

How many sections does this table have?

The table will call numberOfSectionsInTableView:; respond with an integer. In theory you can sometimes omit this method, as the default response is 1, which is often correct. However, I never omit it; for one thing, returning 0 is a good way to say that the table has no data, and will prevent the table view from asking any other questions.

How many rows does this section have?

The table will call `tableView:numberOfRowsInSection:`. The table supplies a section number — the first section is numbered 0 — and you respond with an integer. In a table with only one section, of course, there is probably no need to examine the incoming section number.

What cell goes in this row of this section?

The table will call `tableView:cellForRowAtIndexPath:`. The index path is expressed as an NSIndexPath; this is a sophisticated and powerful class, but you don't actually have to know anything about it, because UITableView provides a category on it that adds two read-only properties — `section` and `row`. Using these, you extract the requested section number and row number, and return a fully configured UITableViewCell, ready for display in the table view. The first row of a section is numbered 0. I have already explained how to obtain the cell in the first place, by calling `tableView:dequeueReusableCellWithIdentifier:`.

I have nothing particular to say about precisely how you're going to fulfill these obligations. It all depends on your data model and what your table is trying to portray. The important thing is to remember that you're going to be receiving an NSIndexPath specifying a section and a row, and you need to be able to lay your hands on the data corresponding to that slot *now* and configure the cell *now*. So construct your model, and your algorithm for consulting it in the Three Big Questions, and your way of configuring the cell, in accordance with that necessity.

For example, suppose our table is to list the names of the Pep Boys. Our data model might be an NSArray of string names (`self.pep`). Our table has only one section. So our code might look like this:

```
- (NSInteger)numberOfSectionsInTableView:(UITableView *)tableView {
    if (!self.pep) // data not ready?
        return 0;
    return 1;
}
- (NSInteger)tableView:(UITableView *)tableView
        numberOfRowsInSection:(NSInteger)section {
    return [self.pep count];
}
- (UITableViewCell *)tableView:(UITableView *)tableView
        cellForRowAtIndexPath:(NSIndexPath *)indexPath {
    MyCell *cell =
        [tableView dequeueReusableCellWithIdentifier:@"Cell"
            forIndexPath:indexPath];
    cell.theLabel.text = (self.pep)[indexPath.row];
    return cell;
}
```

At this point you may be feeling some exasperation. You want to object: "But that's trivial!" Exactly so! Your access to the data model *should* be trivial. That's the sign of a data model that's well designed for access by your table view's data source. Your implementation of `tableView:cellForRowAtIndexPath:` might have some interesting work to do in order to configure the *form* of the cell, but accessing the actual *data* should be simple and boring.

For example, consider Figure 6-1. The actual code that fetches the data is trivial:

```
FPItem* item = self.parsedData.items[indexPath.row];
NSString* title = item.title;
NSString* blurb = item.blurbOfItem;
```

That's all there is to it. And the reason why that's all there is to it is that I've structured the data model to be ready for access in exactly this way. (To be sure, there then follow about thirty lines of code elaborately — but very quickly — *formatting* the layout of the text within the cell.)

Reusing Cells

Another important goal of `tableView:cellForRowAtIndexPath:` should be to conserve resources by reusing cells. As I've already explained, once a cell's row is no longer visible on the screen, that cell can be slotted into a row that *is* visible — with its portrayed data appropriately modified, of course! — so that only a few more than the number of simultaneously visible cells will ever need to be instantiated.

A table view is ready to implement this strategy for you; all you have to do is call `dequeue-ReusableCellWithIdentifier:forIndexPath:`. For any given identifier, you'll be handed either a newly minted cell or a reused cell that previously appeared in the table view but is now no longer needed because it has scrolled out of view.

The table view can maintain more than one cache of reusable cells; this could be useful if your table view contains more than one type of cell (where the meaning of the concept "type of cell" is pretty much up to you). This is why you must *name* each cache, by attaching an identifier string to any cell that can be reused. All the examples in this chapter (and in this book, and in fact in every UITableView I've ever created) use just one cache and just one identifier, but there can be more than one. If you're using a storyboard as a source of cells, there would then need to be more than one prototype cell.

To prove to yourself the efficiency of the cell-caching architecture, do something to differentiate newly instantiated cells from reused cells, and count the newly instantiated cells, like this:

```
- (NSInteger)numberOfSectionsInTableView:(UITableView *)tableView {
    return 1;
}
- (NSInteger)tableView:(UITableView *)tableView
        numberOfRowsInSection:(NSInteger)section {
    return 1000;
```

```
    }
- (UITableViewCell *)tableView:(UITableView *)tableView
        cellForRowAtIndexPath:(NSIndexPath *)indexPath {
    MyCell *cell =
        [tableView dequeueReusableCellWithIdentifier:@"Cell"
            forIndexPath:indexPath];
    UILabel* lab = cell.theLabel;
    lab.text = [NSString stringWithFormat:@"This is row %d of section %d",
                indexPath.row, indexPath.section];
    if (lab.tag != 999) {
        lab.tag = 999;
        NSLog(@"%@", @"New cell");
    }
    return cell;
}
```

When we run this code and scroll through the table, every cell is numbered correctly, so there appear to be 1000 cells. But the log messages show that only about a dozen distinct cells are ever actually created.

Be certain that *your* table view code passes that test, and that you are truly reusing cells! Fortunately, one of the benefits of calling dequeueReusableCellWithIdentifier:for-IndexPath: is that it forces you to use a valid reuse identifier. Still, I've seen beginners obtain a cell in some other way, or even call dequeueReusableCellWithIdentifier:for-IndexPath: without understanding what it really does, only to instantiate a fresh cell manually in the next line. Don't do that.

When your tableView:cellForRowAtIndexPath: implementation configures *individual* cells (stage 5 in Example 8-1), the cell might be new or reused; at this point in your code, you don't know or care which. Therefore, you should always configure *everything* about the cell that might need configuring. If you fail to do this, and if the cell is reused, you might be surprised when some aspect of the cell is left over from its previous use; similarly, if you fail to do this, and if the cell is new, you might be surprised when some aspect of the cell isn't configured at all.

As usual, I learned that lesson the hard way. In the TidBITS News app, there is a little loudspeaker icon that should appear in a given cell in the master view's table view only if there is a recording associated with this article. So I initially wrote this code:

```
if (item.enclosures && [item.enclosures count])
    cell.speaker.hidden = NO;
```

That turned out to be a mistake, because the cell might be reused, and therefore *always* had a visible loudspeaker icon if, in a previous usage, that cell had *ever* had a visible loudspeaker icon! The solution was to rewrite the logic to cover all possibilities completely, like this:

```
cell.speaker.hidden = !(item.enclosures && [item.enclosures count]);
```

You do get a sort of second bite of the cherry: there's a delegate method, `tableView:will-DisplayCell:forRowAtIndexPath:`, that is called for every cell just before it appears in the table. This is absolutely the last minute to configure a cell. But don't misuse this method. You're functioning as the delegate here, not the data source; you may set the final details of the cell's appearance, but you shouldn't be consulting the data model at this point.

An additional delegate method (introduced in iOS 6) is `tableView:didEndDisplaying-Cell:forRowAtIndexPath:`. This tells you that the cell no longer appears in the interface and has become free for reuse. You could take advantage of this to tear down any resource-heavy customization of the cell — I'll give an example in Chapter 24 — or simply to prepare it somehow for subsequent future reuse.

Table View Sections

Your table data can be expressed as divided into sections. You might clump your data into sections for various reasons (and doubtless there are other reasons beyond these):

- You want to supply section headers (or footers, or both). This can clarify the presentation of your data by dividing the rows into groups and by giving the user a sense, at every moment, of where we are within the table (because the current section header and footer are always visible). Also, a section header or footer can contain custom views, so it's a place where you might put additional information, or even functional interface, such as a button the user can tap.

- You want to make navigation of the table easier by supplying an index down the right side. You can't have an index without sections.

- You want to facilitate programmatic rearrangement of the table. For example, it's very easy to hide or move an entire section at once, possibly with animation.

Don't confuse the section headers and footers with the header and footer of the table as a whole. The latter are view properties of the table view itself and are set through its properties `tableHeaderView` and `tableFooterView`, discussed earlier in this chapter. The table header appears only when the table is scrolled all the way down; the table footer appears only when the table is scrolled all the way up.

A section header or footer, on the other hand, appears before or after its section, but (in a nongrouped table) it also detaches itself while the user scrolls the table, positioning itself at the top or bottom of the table view and floating over the scrolled rows, so that the user always knows what section is currently being viewed.

The number of sections is determined by your reply to `numberOfSectionsInTable-View:`. For each section, the table view will consult your data source and delegate to learn whether this section has a header or a footer, or both, or neither (the default).

The UITableViewHeaderFooterView class (introduced in iOS 6) is a UIView subclass intended specifically for use as the view of a header or footer; much like a table view cell, it is reusable. It has the following properties:

textLabel
 Label (UILabel) for displaying the text of the header or footer.

detailTextLabel
 This label, if you set its text, appears only in a grouped style table.

contentView
 A subview, the size of the header or footer. You can add subviews to this. If you do, you probably should not use the built-in textLabel; the textLabel is not inside the contentView and in a sense doesn't belong to you.

backgroundView
 Any view you want to assign. The contentView is in front of the backgroundView. The contentView has a clear background by default, so the backgroundView shows through. An opaque contentView.backgroundColor, on the other hand, would completely obscure the backgroundView. In iOS 7, the header or footer view has a default backgroundView whose backgroundColor is derived (in some annoyingly unspecified way) from the table's backgroundColor.

backgroundColor
 You're not supposed to set the header or footer's backgroundColor; instead, set the backgroundColor of its contentView, or assign a new backgroundView and configure it as you like.

tintColor
 In iOS 7, this property appears to be meaningless. (This is a change from iOS 6, where the tintColor affected the color of the background of the view. It also feels like a bug; the tintColor should now affect the color of subviews, such a UIButton's title, but, as of this writing, it doesn't.)

You can supply a header or footer in two ways:

Header or footer title string
 You implement the data source method tableView:titleForHeaderInSection: or tableView:titleForFooterInSection: (or both). Return nil to indicate that the given section has no header (or footer). The header or footer view itself is a UITableViewHeaderFooterView, and is reused automatically: there will be only as many as needed for simultaneous display on the screen. The string you supply becomes the view's textLabel.text; however, in a grouped style table the string's capitalization may be changed. To avoid that, use the second way of supplying the header or footer.

Header or footer view

You implement the delegate method `tableView:viewForHeaderInSection:` or `tableView:viewForFooterInSection:` (or both). The view you supply is used as the entire header or footer and is automatically resized to the table's width and the section header or footer height (I'll discuss how the height is determined in a moment).

You are not required to return a UITableViewHeaderFooterView, but you will probably want to, in order to take advantage of reusability. To do so, the procedure is much like making a cell reusable. You register beforehand with the table view by calling `registerClass:forHeaderFooterViewReuseIdentifier:`. To supply the reusable view, send the table view `dequeueReusableHeaderFooterViewWithIdentifier:`; the result will be either a newly instantiated view or a reused view.

You can then configure this view as desired. For example, you can set its `text-Label.text`, or you can give its `contentView` custom subviews. In the latter case, be sure to set proper autoresizing or constraints, so that the subviews will be positioned and sized appropriately when the view itself is resized.

The documentation lists a second way of registering a header or footer view for reuse — `registerNib:forHeaderFooterViewReuse-Identifier:`. But the nib editor's Object library doesn't include a UI-TableViewHeaderFooterView! This makes `registerNib:forHeader-FooterViewReuseIdentifier:` pretty much useless, because there's no way to configure the view correctly in the nib.

In addition, two pairs of delegate methods permit you to perform final configurations on your header or footer views:

`tableView:willDisplayHeaderView:forSection:`
`tableView:willDisplayFooterView:forSection:`

You can perform further configuration here, if desired. A useful possibility is to generate the default UITableViewHeaderFooterView by implementing `title-For...` and then tweak its form slightly here. These delegate methods are matched by `tableView:didEndDisplayingHeaderView:forSection:` and `tableView:did-EndDisplayingFooterView:forSection:`.

`tableView:heightForHeaderInSection:`
`tableView:heightForFooterInSection:`

The runtime resizes your header or footer before displaying it. Its width will be the table view's width; its height will be the table view's `sectionHeaderHeight` and `sectionFooterHeight` unless you implement one of these methods to say otherwise.

It is possible to implement *both* `viewFor...` and `titleFor....` In that case, `view-For...` is called first, and if it returns a UITableViewHeaderFooterView, `titleFor...` will set its `textLabel.text`. If you implement both methods and you want `height-For...` to return the height as set by the table view based on `titleFor...`, return `UITableViewAutomaticDimension`.

Some lovely effects can be created by making use of the fact that a header or footer view will be further forward than the table's cells. For example, a header with transparency shows the cells as they scroll behind it; a header with a shadow casts that shadow on the adjacent cell.

Now let's talk about where the header or footer view's data will come from. Clearly, a table that is to have section headers or footers (or both) may require some advance planning in the formation of its data model. Just as with a cell, a section title must be readily available so that it can be supplied quickly in real time. A structure that I commonly use is a pair of parallel arrays: an array of strings containing the section names, and an array of subarrays containing the data for each section.

For example, suppose we intend to display the names of all 50 U.S. states in alphabetical order as the rows of a table view, and that we wish to divide the table into sections according to the first letter of each state's name. I'll prepare the data model by walking through the alphabetized list of state names, creating a new section name and a new subarray when I encounter a new first letter:

```
NSString* s =
    [NSString stringWithContentsOfFile:
        [[NSBundle mainBundle] pathForResource:@"states" ofType:@"txt"]
            encoding:NSUTF8StringEncoding error:nil];
NSArray* states = [s componentsSeparatedByString:@"\n"];
self.sectionNames = [NSMutableArray array];
self.sectionData = [NSMutableArray array];
NSString* previous = @"";
for (NSString* aState in states) {
    // get the first letter
    NSString* c = [aState substringToIndex:1];
    // only add a letter to sectionNames when it's a different letter
    if (![c isEqualToString: previous]) {
        previous = c;
        [self.sectionNames addObject: [c uppercaseString]];
        // and in that case, also add a new subarray to our array of subarrays
        NSMutableArray* oneSection = [NSMutableArray array];
        [self.sectionData addObject: oneSection];
    }
    [[self.sectionData lastObject] addObject: aState];
}
```

The value of this preparatory dance is evident when we are bombarded with questions from the table view about cells and headers; supplying the answers is trivial:

```
- (NSInteger)numberOfSectionsInTableView:(UITableView *)tableView {
    return [self.sectionNames count];
}
- (NSInteger)tableView:(UITableView *)tableView
        numberOfRowsInSection:(NSInteger)section {
    return [(self.sectionData)[section] count];
}
- (UITableViewCell *)tableView:(UITableView *)tableView
        cellForRowAtIndexPath:(NSIndexPath *)indexPath {
    UITableViewCell *cell =
        [tableView dequeueReusableCellWithIdentifier:@"Cell"
                                        forIndexPath:indexPath];
    NSString* s = self.sectionData[indexPath.section][indexPath.row];
    cell.textLabel.text = s;
    return cell;
}
- (NSString *)tableView:(UITableView *)tableView
        titleForHeaderInSection:(NSInteger)section {
    return self.sectionNames[section];
}
```

Let's modify that example to illustrate customization of a header view. I've already registered my header identifier in viewDidLoad:

```
[self.tableView registerClass:[UITableViewHeaderFooterView class]
    forHeaderFooterViewReuseIdentifier:@"Header"];
```

Now, instead of tableView:titleForHeaderInSection:, I'll implement tableView:viewForHeaderInSection:. For completely new views, I'll place my own label and an image view inside the contentView and give them their basic configuration; then I'll perform individual configuration on all views, new or reused (very much like tableView:cellForRowAtIndexPath:):

```
- (UIView *)tableView:(UITableView *)tableView
        viewForHeaderInSection:(NSInteger)section {
    UITableViewHeaderFooterView* h =
        [tableView dequeueReusableHeaderFooterViewWithIdentifier:@"Header"];
    if (![h.tintColor isEqual: [UIColor redColor]]) {
        h.tintColor = [UIColor redColor];
        h.backgroundView = [UIView new];
        h.backgroundView.backgroundColor = [UIColor blackColor];
        UILabel* lab = [UILabel new];
        lab.tag = 1;
        lab.font = [UIFont fontWithName:@"Georgia-Bold" size:22];
        lab.textColor = [UIColor greenColor];
        lab.backgroundColor = [UIColor clearColor];
        [h.contentView addSubview:lab];
        UIImageView* v = [UIImageView new];
        v.tag = 2;
        v.backgroundColor = [UIColor blackColor];
        v.image = [UIImage imageNamed:@"us_flag_small.gif"];
        [h.contentView addSubview:v];
```

```
      lab.translatesAutoresizingMaskIntoConstraints = NO;
      v.translatesAutoresizingMaskIntoConstraints = NO;
      [h.contentView addConstraints:
       [NSLayoutConstraint
        constraintsWithVisualFormat:@"H:|-5-[lab(25)]-10-[v(40)]"
         options:0 metrics:nil views:@{@"v":v, @"lab":lab}]];
      [h.contentView addConstraints:
       [NSLayoutConstraint
        constraintsWithVisualFormat:@"V:|[v]|"
         options:0 metrics:nil views:@{@"v":v}]];
      [h.contentView addConstraints:
       [NSLayoutConstraint
        constraintsWithVisualFormat:@"V:|[lab]|"
         options:0 metrics:nil views:@{@"lab":lab}]];
    }
    UILabel* lab = (UILabel*)[h.contentView viewWithTag:1];
    lab.text = self.sectionNames[section];
    return h;
}
```

Section Index

If your table view has the plain style, you can add an index down the right side of the table, where the user can tap or drag to jump to the start of a section — helpful for navigating long tables. To generate the index, implement the data source method `sectionIndexTitlesForTableView:`, returning an NSArray of string titles to appear as entries in the index. This works even if there are no section headers. The index will appear only if the number of rows exceeds the table view's `sectionIndexMinimum-DisplayRowCount` property value; the default is 0, so the index is always displayed by default. You will want the index entries to be short — preferably just one character — because they will be partially obscuring the right edge of the table; plus, each cell's content view will shrink to compensate, so you're sacrificing some cell real estate.

For our list of state names, that's trivial, as it should be:

```
- (NSArray *)sectionIndexTitlesForTableView:(UITableView *)tableView {
    return self.sectionNames;
}
```

You can modify three properties that affect the index's appearance:

`sectionIndexColor`
 The index text color.

`sectionIndexBackgroundColor`
 The index background color (new in iOS 7). I advise giving the index some background color, even if it is `clearColor`, because otherwise the index distorts the colors of what's behind it in a distracting way.

`sectionIndexTrackingBackgroundColor`
> The index background color while the user's finger is sliding over it. By default, it's the same as the `sectionIndexBackgroundColor`.

Normally, there will be a one-to-one correspondence between the index entries and the sections; when the user taps an index entry, the table jumps to the start of the corresponding section. However, under certain circumstances you may want to customize this correspondence.

For example, suppose there are 100 sections, but there isn't room to display 100 index entries comfortably on the iPhone. The index will automatically curtail itself, omitting some index entries and inserting bullets to suggest the omission, but you might prefer to take charge of the situation.

To do so, supply a shorter index, and implement the data source method `tableView:sectionForSectionIndexTitle:atIndex:`, returning the number of the section to jump to. You are told both the title and the index number of the section index listing that the user chose, so you can use whichever is convenient.

Apple's documentation elaborates heavily on the details of implementing the model behind a table with an index and suggests that you rely on a class called UILocalizedIndexedCollation. This class is effectively a way of generating an ordered list of letters of the alphabet, with methods for helping to sort an array of strings and separate it into sections. This might be useful if you need your app to be localized, because the notion of the alphabet and its order changes automatically depending on the user's preferred language.

Unfortunately, you can't readily use a UILocalizedIndexCollation to implement your own sort order. For example, UILocalizedIndexCollation was of no use to me in writing my Greek and Latin vocabulary apps, in which the Greek words must be sorted, sectioned, and indexed according to the Greek alphabet, and the Latin words use a reduced version of the English alphabet (no initial J, K, or V through Z). Thus I've never actually bothered to use UILocalizedIndexedCollation.

Refreshing Table View Data

The table view has no direct connection to the underlying data. If you want the table view display to change because the underlying data have changed, you have to cause the table view to refresh itself; basically, you're requesting that the Big Questions be asked all over again. At first blush, this seems inefficient ("regenerate *all* the data??"); but it isn't. Remember, in a table that caches reusable cells, there are no cells of interest other than those actually showing in the table at this moment. Thus, having worked out the layout of the table through the section header and footer heights and row heights, the table has to regenerate only those cells that are actually visible.

You can cause the table data to be refreshed using any of several methods:

reloadData
> The table view will ask the Three Big Questions all over again, including heights of rows and section headers and footers, and the index, exactly as it does automatically when the table view first appears.

reloadRowsAtIndexPaths:withRowAnimation:
> The table view will ask the Three Big Questions all over again, including heights, but not index entries. Cells are requested only for visible cells among those you specify. The first parameter is an array of index paths; to form an index path, use the NSIndexPath class method indexPathForRow:inSection:.

reloadSections:withRowAnimation:
> The table view will ask the Three Big Questions all over again, including heights of rows and section headers and footers, and the index. Cells, headers, and footers are requested only for visible elements of the sections you specify. The first parameter is an NSIndexSet.

The second two methods can perform animations that cue the user as to what's changing. For the rowAnimation: argument, you'll pass one of the following:

UITableViewRowAnimationFade
> The old fades into the new.

UITableViewRowAnimationRight, UITableViewRowAnimationLeft
UITableViewRowAnimationTop, UITableViewRowAnimationBottom
> The old slides out in the stated direction, and is replaced from the opposite direction.

UITableViewRowAnimationNone
> No animation.

UITableViewRowAnimationMiddle
> Hard to describe; it's a sort of venetian blind effect on each cell individually.

UITableViewRowAnimationAutomatic
> The table view just "does the right thing". This is especially useful for grouped style tables, because if you pick the wrong animation, the display can look very funny as it proceeds.

If all you need to do is to refresh the index, call reloadSectionIndexTitles; this calls the data source's sectionIndexTitlesForTableView:.

If you want the table view to be laid out freshly without reloading *any* cells, send it begin-Updates immediately followed by endUpdates. The section and row structure of the table will be asked for, along with calculation of all heights, but no cells and no headers or footers are requested. This is useful as a way of alerting the table that its measurements have changed. It might be considered a misuse of an updates block (the real use of such a block is discussed later in this chapter); but Apple takes advantage of this trick in the Table View Animations and Gestures example, in which a pinch gesture is used to change a table's row height in real time, so it must be legal.

It is also possible to access and alter a table's individual cells directly. This can be a lightweight approach to refreshing the table, plus you can supply your own animation within the cell as it alters its appearance. It is important to bear in mind, however, that the cells are not the data (view is not model). If you change the content of a cell manually, make sure that you have also changed the model corresponding to it, so that the row will appear correctly if its data is reloaded later.

To do this, you need direct access to the cell you want to change. You'll probably want to make sure the cell is visible within the table view's bounds; nonvisible cells don't really exist (except as potential cells waiting in the reuse cache), and there's no point changing them manually, as they'll be changed when they are scrolled into view, through the usual call to `tableView:cellForRowAtIndexPath:`.

Here are some UITableView methods that mediate between cells, rows, and visibility:

`visibleCells`
: An array of the cells actually showing within the table's bounds.

`indexPathsForVisibleRows`
: An array of the rows actually showing within the table's bounds.

`cellForRowAtIndexPath:`
: Returns a UITableViewCell if the table is maintaining a cell for the given row (typically because this is a visible row); otherwise, returns nil.

`indexPathForCell:`
: Given a cell obtained from the table view, returns the row into which it is slotted.

By the same token, you can get access to the views constituting headers and footers, by calling `headerViewForSection:` or `footerViewForSection:`. Thus you could modify a view directly. You should assume that if a section is returned by `indexPathsForVisibleRows`, its header or footer might be visible.

If you want to grant the user some interface for requesting that a table view be refreshed, you might like to use a UIRefreshControl. You aren't required to use this; it's just Apple's attempt to provide a standard interface. In iOS 7, it is located behind the top of the scrolling part of the table view, *behind the table view's `backgroundView`*. To request a refresh, the user scrolls the table view downward to reveal the refresh control and holds long enough to indicate that this scrolling is deliberate. The refresh control then acknowledges visually that it is refreshing, and remains visible until refreshing is complete.

To give a table view a refresh control, assign a UIRefreshControl to the table view controller's refreshControl property; it is a control (UIControl, Chapter 12), and you will want to hook its Value Changed event to an action method:

```
self.refreshControl = [UIRefreshControl new];
[self.refreshControl addTarget:self action:@selector(doRefresh:)
    forControlEvents:UIControlEventValueChanged];
```

You can also configure a table view controller's refresh control in the nib editor.

Once a refresh control's action message has fired, the control remains visible and indicates by animation (similar to an activity indicator) that it is refreshing, until you send it the endRefreshing message:

```
-(void)doRefresh:(UIRefreshControl*) sender {
    // ... refresh the table data ...
    [sender endRefreshing];
}
```

You can initiate a refresh animation in code with beginRefreshing, but this does not fire the action message or display the refresh control; to display it, scroll the table view:

```
[self.tableView setContentOffset:
    CGPointMake(0,-self.refreshControl.bounds.size.height)
        animated:YES];
[self.refreshControl beginRefreshing];
// ... now actually do refresh, and later send endRefreshing
```

A refresh control also has these properties:

refreshing *(read-only)*
    Whether the refresh control is refreshing.

tintColor
    The refresh control's color. It is *not* inherited from the view hierarchy (I regard this as a bug).

attributedTitle
    Styled text displayed below the refresh control's activity indicator. On attributed strings, see Chapter 10.

backgroundColor *(inherited from UIView)*
    If you give a table view controller's refreshControl a background color, that color completely covers the table view's own background color when the refresh control is revealed. For some reason, I find the drawing of the attributedTitle more reliable if the refresh control has a background color.

Variable Row Heights

Most tables have rows that are all the same height, as set by the table view's row-Height. However, the delegate's `tableView:heightForRowAtIndexPath:` can be used to make different rows different heights. You can see an example in the TidBITS News app (Figure 6-1).

Implementing variable row heights can be a tricky business. One problem is that as a cell is reused or instantiated from a nib, its height may be changed, which is likely to expose any weaknesses in your practice for laying out subviews. (Can you guess that I'm speaking from experience here?) A mistake in the `autoresizingMask` value of subviews can result in display errors that would not have arisen if all the rows were the same height. You may have to resort to manual layout (such as implementing `layoutSubviews` in a UITableViewCell subclass); alternatively, constraints can be a big help.

Another problem has to do with time consumed and the order of events. The runtime needs to know the heights of *everything* in your table immediately, before it starts asking for any cells. In effect, this means you have to gather *all* the data and lay out *all* the cells before you can start showing the data in any *single* row. If that takes a long time, your table view will remain blank during the calculation. Plus, there is now a danger of duplicating your own work, since you'll be laying out every cell *twice*, once when you're asked for all the heights and again when you're asked for the actual cell.

In iOS 7, this second problem is not as severe as it used to be, thanks to three new table view properties:

- `estimatedRowHeight`
- `estimatedSectionHeaderHeight`
- `estimatedSectionFooterHeight`

To accompany those, there are also three new table view delegate methods:

- `tableView:estimatedHeightForRowAtIndexPath:`
- `tableView:estimatedHeightForHeaderInSection:`
- `tableView:estimatedHeightForFooterInSection:`

The idea is that if you implement these, the runtime will use their values whenever it gathers the heights for the whole table at once. Then, when a cell or a header or footer is about to appear onscreen, the runtime will ask for its real height in the usual way. You can thus get the table to appear quickly and postpone the calculation of an actual height until it is needed (by which time you might have calculated all the real heights in a background thread).

To illustrate, I'll describe the strategy I use in the TidBITS News app. It predates the estimated heights, so I don't use them. The key is an NSMutableArray property, self.rowHeights, consisting of NSNumbers wrapping floats. (An array is all that's needed, because the table has just one section; the row number can thus serve directly as an index into the array.) Once that array is constructed, it can be used to supply a requested height *instantly*.

As I've already said, calculating a cell height requires me to lay out that cell. Each cell displays an attributed string. I have a utility method, attributedStringForIndex-Path:, which generates the attributed string for a given row of the table (by consulting the data model to obtain the title and description of the story represented by that row).

When the delegate's tableView:heightForRowAtIndexPath: is called, either we've already constructed self.rowHeights or we haven't. If we haven't, we construct it, by calling attributedStringForIndexPath: for *every* index path, laying out its cell rectangle, and storing the height of that rectangle. Now we have all the heights, so from now on we simply return the one we are asked for:

```
-(CGFloat)tableView:(UITableView *)tableView
      heightForRowAtIndexPath:(NSIndexPath *)indexPath {
    if (!self.rowHeights) {
        NSMutableArray* heights = [NSMutableArray array];
        for (int i = 0; i < self.parsedData.items.count; i++) {
            NSAttributedString* s =
                [self attributedStringForIndexPath:
                    [NSIndexPath indexPathForRow:i inSection:0]];
            CGFloat maxheight = // maximum permissible cell height
            CGRect r =
                [s boundingRectWithSize:CGSizeMake(320,maxheight)
                    options:
                        NSStringDrawingUsesLineFragmentOrigin |
                        NSStringDrawingTruncatesLastVisibleLine
                        context:nil];
            [heights addObject:@(r.size.height)];
        }
        self.rowHeights = heights;
    }
    CGFloat result = [self.rowHeights[indexPath.row] floatValue];
    return result;
}
```

In tableView:cellForRowAtIndexPath:, I call attributedStringForIndexPath: *again*. (I suppose I could have cached the attributed strings in an array as well, but this is not a time-consuming routine.) The wonderful thing is that, thanks to dequeue-ReusableCellWithIdentifier:forIndexPath:, the cell already has the correct height, and constraints have taken care of positioning its subviews correctly. So I just plop the attributed string into it, configure the rest of the cell, and hand back the cell:

```
- (UITableViewCell *)tableView:(UITableView *)tableView
      cellForRowAtIndexPath:(NSIndexPath *)indexPath {
    FPItem* item = self.parsedData.items[indexPath.row];
    Cell* cell =
        [tableView dequeueReusableCellWithIdentifier:@"Cell"
            forIndexPath:indexPath];
    cell.drawer.attributedText = [self attributedStringForIndexPath: indexPath];
    cell.speaker.hidden = !(item.enclosures && [item.enclosures count]);
    return cell;
}
```

Now I'll adapt my approach to use estimated heights. My table view has an estimated-RowHeight of 80; on average, this should set the scrolling content height to be roughly correct from the outset. All I really need to change now is my implementation of table-View:heightForRowAtIndexPath:, to take account of the fact that I can no longer predict when this method will be called for any given row. If we don't have any self.row-Heights array at all, I create it, and I fill it with [NSNull null] as a placeholder. If the self.rowHeights entry for the requested row is [NSNull null], I calculate the actual row height and set it as that entry. Finally, I return the self.rowHeights entry for the requested row:

```
-(CGFloat)tableView:(UITableView *)tableView
      heightForRowAtIndexPath:(NSIndexPath *)indexPath {
    if (!self.rowHeights) {
        NSMutableArray* heights = [NSMutableArray array];
        for (int i = 0; i < self.parsedData.items.count; i++)
            heights[i] = [NSNull null];
        self.rowHeights = heights;
    }
    int ix = indexPath.row;
    if (self.rowHeights[indexPath.row] == [NSNull null]) {
        NSAttributedString* s =
            [self attributedStringForIndexPath:
                [NSIndexPath indexPathForRow:ix inSection:0]];
        CGFloat maxheight = // maximum permissible cell height
        CGRect r =
            [s boundingRectWithSize:CGSizeMake(320,maxheight)
                options:
                    NSStringDrawingUsesLineFragmentOrigin |
                    NSStringDrawingTruncatesLastVisibleLine
                    context:nil];
        self.rowHeights[ix] = @(r.size.height);
    }
    CGFloat result = [self.rowHeights[ix] floatValue];
    return result;
}
```

This method is called four or five times at launch, for the cells that will initially appear onscreen, and after that only for individual cells as they are scrolled into view.

Table View Cell Selection

A table view cell has a normal state, a highlighted state (according to its `highlighted` property), and a selected state (according to its `selected` property). It is possible to change these states directly, possibly with animation, by calling `set-Highlighted:animated:` or `setSelected:animated:` on the cell. But you don't want to act behind the table's back, so you are more likely to manage selection through the table view, letting the table view manage and track the state of its cells.

These two states are closely related. In particular, when a cell is selected, it propagates the highlighted state down through its subviews by setting each subview's `highlighted` property if it has one. That is why a UILabel's `highlightedTextColor` applies when the cell is selected. Similarly, a UIImageView (such as the cell's `imageView`) can have a `highlightedImage` that is shown when the cell is selected, and a UIControl (such as a UIButton) takes on its `highlighted` state when the cell is selected.

One of the chief purposes of your table view is likely to be to let the user select a cell. This will be possible, provided you have not set the value of the table view's `allows-Selection` property to NO. The user taps a normal cell, and the cell switches to its selected state. By default, this will mean that the cell is redrawn with a gray background view, but you can change this at the individual cell level, as I've already explained: you can set a cell's `selectedBackgroundView` (or `multipleSelectionBackgroundView`), or change its `selectionStyle`. If the user taps an already selected cell, by default it stays selected.

Table views can permit the user to select multiple cells simultaneously. Set the table view's `allowsMultipleSelection` property to YES. If the user taps an already selected cell, by default it is deselected.

Managing Cell Selection

Your code can learn and manage the selection through these UITableView instance methods:

`indexPathForSelectedRow`
`indexPathsForSelectedRows`
> These methods report the currently selected row(s), or nil if there is no selection. Don't accidentally call the wrong one. For example, calling `indexPathForSelected-Row` when the table view allows multiple selection gives a result that will have you scratching your head in confusion. (As usual, I speak from experience.)

`selectRowAtIndexPath:animated:scrollPosition:`
> The animation involves fading in the selection, but the user may not see this unless the selected row is already visible. The last parameter dictates whether and how the table view should scroll to reveal the newly selected row:

- UITableViewScrollPositionTop

- UITableViewScrollPositionMiddle

- UITableViewScrollPositionBottom

- UITableViewScrollPositionNone

For the first three options, the table view scrolls (with animation, if the second parameter is YES) so that the selected row is at the specified position among the visible cells. For UITableViewScrollPositionNone, the table view does not scroll; if the selected row is not already visible, it does not become visible.

deselectRowAtIndexPath:animated:
Deselects the given row (if it is selected); the optional animation involves fading out the selection. No automatic scrolling takes place.

To deselect *all* currently selected rows, call selectRowAtIndexPath:animated:scroll-Position: with a nil index path. Reloading a cell's data also deselects that cell, and calling reloadData deselects all selected rows.

Responding to Cell Selection

Response to user selection is through the table view's delegate:

- tableView:shouldHighlightRowAtIndexPath:

- tableView:didHighlightRowAtIndexPath:

- tableView:didUnhighlightRowAtIndexPath:

- tableView:willSelectRowAtIndexPath:

- tableView:didSelectRowAtIndexPath:

- tableView:willDeselectRowAtIndexPath:

- tableView:didDeselectRowAtIndexPath:

Despite their names, the two "will" methods are actually "should" methods and expect a return value:

- Return nil to prevent the selection (or deselection) from taking place.

- Return the index path handed in as argument to permit the selection (or deselection), or a different index path to cause a different cell to be selected (or deselected).

The "highlight" methods are more sensibly named, and they arrive first, so you can return NO from tableView:shouldHighlightRowAtIndexPath: to prevent a cell from being selected.

Let's focus in more detail on the relationship between a cell's highlighted state and its selected state. They are, in fact, two different states. When the user touches a cell, the cell passes through a complete highlight cycle. Then, if the touch turns out to be the beginning of a scroll motion, the cell is unhighlighted immediately, and the cell is not selected. Otherwise, the cell is unhighlighted and selected.

But the user doesn't know the difference between these two states: whether the cell is highlighted or selected, the cell's subviews are highlighted, and the selectedBackground-View appears. Thus, if the user touches and scrolls, what the user sees is the flash of the selectedBackgroundView and the highlighted subviews, until the table begins to scroll and the cell returns to normal. If the user touches and lifts the finger, the selected-BackgroundView and highlighted subviews appear and remain; there is actually a moment in the sequence where the cell has been highlighted and then unhighlighted and not yet selected, but the user doesn't see any momentary unhighlighting of the cell, because no redraw moment occurs (see Chapter 4).

Here's a summary of the sequence:

1. The user's finger goes down. If shouldHighlight permits, the cell highlights, which propagates to its subviews. Then didHighlight arrives.

2. There is a redraw moment. Thus, the user will *see* the cell as highlighted (including the appearance of the selectedBackgroundView), regardless of what happens next.

3. The user either starts scrolling or lifts the finger. The cell unhighlights, which also propagates to its subviews, and didUnhighlight arrives.

   a. If the user starts scrolling, there is a redraw moment, so the user now sees the cell unhighlighted. The sequence ends.

   b. If the user merely lifts the finger, there is no redraw moment, so the cell keeps its highlighted appearance. The sequence continues.

4. If willSelect permits, the cell is selected, and didSelect arrives. The cell is *not* highlighted, but highlighting is propagated to its subviews.

5. There's another redraw moment. The user still sees the cell as highlighted (including the appearance of the selectedBackgroundView).

When tableView:willSelectRowAtIndexPath: is called because the user taps a cell, and if this table view permits only single cell selection, tableView:willDeselectRowAt-IndexPath: will be called subsequently for any previously selected cells.

Here's an example of implementing tableView:willSelectRowAtIndexPath:. The default behavior for allowsSelection (not multiple selection) is that the user can select by tapping, and the cell remains selected; if the user taps a selected row, the selection does not change. We can alter this so that tapping a selected row deselects it:

```
- (NSIndexPath*) tableView:(UITableView*)tv
        willSelectRowAtIndexPath:(NSIndexPath*)ip {
    if ([tv cellForRowAtIndexPath:ip].selected) {
        [tv deselectRowAtIndexPath:ip animated:NO];
        return nil;
    }
    return ip;
}
```

Navigation From a Table View

An extremely common response to user selection is navigation. A master–detail architecture is typical: the table view lists things the user can see in more detail, and a tap
displays the detailed view of the selected thing. On the iPhone, very often the table view
will be in a navigation interface, and you will respond to user selection by creating the
detail view and pushing it onto the navigation controller's stack.

For example, here's the code from my Albumen app that navigates from the list of albums
to the list of songs in the album that the user has tapped:

```
- (void) tableView:(UITableView *)tableView
        didSelectRowAtIndexPath:(NSIndexPath *)indexPath {
    TracksViewController *t =
        [[TracksViewController alloc]
            initWithMediaItemCollection:(self.albums)[indexPath.row]];
    [self.navigationController pushViewController:t animated:YES];
}
```

This interface is so common that Xcode's Master–Detail Application project template
implements it for you.

In a storyboard, when you draw a segue from a UITableViewCell, you are given a choice
of two segue triggers: Selection Segue and Accessory Action. If you create a Selection
Segue, the segue will be triggered when the user selects a cell. Thus you can readily push
or present another view controller in response to cell selection.

If you're using a UITableViewController, then by default, whenever the table view appears, the selection is cleared automatically in viewWillAppear:, and the scroll indicators are flashed in viewDidAppear:. You can prevent this automatic clearing of the
selection by setting the table view controller's clearsSelectionOnViewWillAppear to
NO. I sometimes do that, preferring to implement deselection in viewDidAppear:; the
effect is that when the user returns to the table, the row is still momentarily selected
before it deselects itself:

```
- (void) viewDidAppear:(BOOL)animated {
    // deselect selected row
    [tableView selectRowAtIndexPath:nil animated:NO
        scrollPosition:UITableViewScrollPositionNone];
    [super viewDidAppear:animated];
}
```

By convention, if selecting a table view cell causes navigation, the cell should be given an `accessoryType` of `UITableViewCellAccessoryDisclosureIndicator`. This is a plain gray right-pointing chevron at the right end of the cell. The chevron itself doesn't respond to user interaction; it's not a button, but is just a visual cue that the user can tap the cell to learn more.

Two additional `accessoryType` settings *are* buttons:

`UITableViewCellAccessoryDetailButton`
> New in iOS 7. It is drawn as a letter "i" in a circle.

`UITableViewCellAccessoryDetailDisclosureButton`
> In iOS 7, it is drawn like `UITableViewCellAccessoryDetailButton`, along with a disclosure indicator chevron to its right.

To respond to the tapping of an accessory button, implement the table view delegate's `tableView:accessoryButtonTappedForRowWithIndexPath:`. Or, in a storyboard, you can Control-drag a connection from a cell and choose the Accessory Action segue.

A common convention is that selecting the cell as a whole does one thing and tapping the detail button does something else. For example, in Apple's Phone app, tapping a contact's listing in the Recents table places a call to that contact, but tapping the detail button navigates to that contact's detail view.

Cell Choice and Static Tables

Another use of cell selection is to implement a choice among cells, where a section of a table effectively functions as an iOS alternative to OS X radio buttons. The table view usually has the grouped format. An `accessoryType` of `UITableViewCellAccessory-Checkmark` is typically used to indicate the current choice. Implementing radio button behavior is up to you.

As an example, I'll implement the interface shown in Figure 8-2. The table view has the grouped style, with two sections. The first section, with a "Size" header, has three mutually exclusive choices: "Easy," "Normal," and "Hard." The second section, with a "Style" header, has two choices: "Animals" or "Snacks."

This is a *static table*; its contents are known beforehand and won't change. In a case like this, if we're using a UITableViewController subclass instantiated from a storyboard, the nib editor lets us design the entire table, including the headers and the cells *and their content*, directly in the storyboard. Select the table and set its Content pop-up menu in the Attributes inspector to Static Cells to make the table editable in this way (Figure 8-6).

Even though each cell is designed initially in the storyboard, I can still implement `table-View:cellForRowAtIndexPath:` to call `super` and then add further functionality. That's how I'll add the checkmarks. The user defaults are storing the current choice in each of

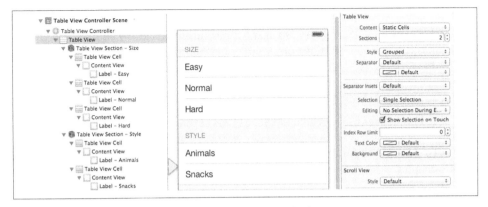

Figure 8-6. Designing a static table in the storyboard editor

the two categories; there's a `@"Size"` preference and a `@"Style"` preference, each consisting of a string denoting the title of the chosen cell:

```
- (UITableViewCell *)tableView:(UITableView *)tv
        cellForRowAtIndexPath:(NSIndexPath *)indexPath {
    UITableViewCell* cell =
        [super tableView:tv cellForRowAtIndexPath:indexPath];
    NSUserDefaults* ud = [NSUserDefaults standardUserDefaults];
    cell.accessoryType = UITableViewCellAccessoryNone;
    if ([[ud valueForKey:@"Style"] isEqualToString:cell.textLabel.text] ||
            [[ud valueForKey:@"Size"] isEqualToString:cell.textLabel.text])
        cell.accessoryType = UITableViewCellAccessoryCheckmark;
    return cell;
}
```

When the user taps a cell, the cell is selected. I want the user to see that selection momentarily, as feedback, but then I want to deselect, adjusting the checkmarks so that that cell is the only one checked in its section. In `tableView:didSelectRowAtIndexPath:`, I set the user defaults, and then I reload the table view's data. This removes the selection and causes `tableView:cellForRowAtIndexPath:` to be called to adjust the checkmarks:

```
- (void)tableView:(UITableView *)tv
        didSelectRowAtIndexPath:(NSIndexPath *)indexPath {
    NSUserDefaults* ud = [NSUserDefaults standardUserDefaults];
    NSString* setting = [tv cellForRowAtIndexPath:indexPath].textLabel.text;
    NSString* header =
        [self tableView:tv titleForHeaderInSection:indexPath.section];
    [ud setValue:setting forKey:header];
    [tv reloadData]; // deselect all cells, reassign checkmark as needed
}
```

Table View Scrolling and Layout

A UITableView is a UIScrollView, so everything you already know about scroll views is applicable (Chapter 7). In addition, a table view supplies two convenience scrolling methods:

- `scrollToRowAtIndexPath:atScrollPosition:animated:`
- `scrollToNearestSelectedRowAtScrollPosition:animated:`

The `scrollPosition` parameter is as for `selectRowAtIndexPath:...`, discussed earlier in this chapter.

The following UITableView methods mediate between the table's bounds coordinates on the one hand and table structure on the other:

- `indexPathForRowAtPoint:`
- `indexPathsForRowsInRect:`
- `rectForSection:`
- `rectForRowAtIndexPath:`
- `rectForFooterInSection:`
- `rectForHeaderInSection:`

The table's own header and footer are direct subviews of the table view, so their positions within the table's bounds are given by their frames.

Table View State Restoration

If a UITableView participates in state saving and restoration (Chapter 6), the restoration mechanism would like to restore the selection and the scroll position. In iOS 7, this behavior is automatic; the restoration mechanism knows both what cells should be visible and what cells should be selected, in terms of their index paths. If that's satisfactory, you've no further work to do.

In some apps, however, there is a possibility that when the app is relaunched, the underlying data may have been rearranged somehow. Perhaps what's meaningful in dictating what the user should see in such a case is not the previous index paths but the previous data. The state saving and restoration mechanism doesn't know anything about the relationship between the cells and the underlying data. If you'd like to tell it, adopt the UIDataSourceModelAssociation protocol and implement two methods:

`modelIdentifierForElementAtIndexPath:inView:`

Based on the index path, you return some string that you will *later* be able to use to identify uniquely this bit of model data.

`indexPathForElementWithModelIdentifier:inView:`

Based on the unique identifier you provided earlier, you return the index path at which this bit of model data is displayed in the table *now*.

Devising a system of unique identification and incorporating it into your data model is up to you. In the TidBITS News app, for example, where I was using this mechanism in iOS 6, it happens that my bits of data come from a parsed RSS feed and have a guid property that is a global unique identifier. So implementing the first method is easy:

```
- (NSString *) modelIdentifierForElementAtIndexPath:(NSIndexPath *)idx
                                             inView:(UIView *)view {
    FPItem* item = self.parsedData.items[idx.row];
    return item.guid;
}
```

Implementing the second method is a little more work; I walk the data model looking for the object whose guid matches the identifier in question, and construct its index path:

```
- (NSIndexPath*) indexPathForElementWithModelIdentifier:(NSString *)identifier
                                                 inView:(UIView *)view {
    __block NSIndexPath* path = nil;
    [self.parsedData.items
        enumerateObjectsUsingBlock:^(FPItem* item, NSUInteger idx, BOOL *stop)
    {
        if ([item.guid isEqualToString:identifier]) {
            path = [NSIndexPath indexPathForRow:idx inSection:0];
            *stop = YES;
        }
    }];
    return path;
}
```

It is crucial, when the app is relaunched, that the table should have data before that method is called, so I also call `reloadData` in my implementation of `decodeRestorableStateWithCoder:`.

In iOS 7, however, I no longer do any of that, since the automatic index path–based restoration of the table view's scroll position is sufficient.

Table View Searching

A table view is a common way to present the results of a search performed through a search field (a UISearchBar; see Chapter 12). This is such a standard interface, in fact, that a class is provided, UISearchDisplayController, to mediate between the search field where the user enters a search term and the table view listing the results of the search.

When the user initially taps in the search field, the UISearchDisplayController automatically constructs a new interface along with a nice animation. This indicates to the user that the search field is ready to receive input; when the user proceeds to enter characters into the search field, the UISearchDisplayController will display its own search results table view in this interface. The UISearchBar has a Cancel button that the user can tap to dismiss the interface created by the UISearchDisplayController.

The UISearchDisplayController needs the following things:

A search bar
A UISearchBar in the interface. This will be the UISearchDisplayController's `searchBar`.

A view controller
The view controller managing the view in the interface over which the search results are to appear. This will be the UISearchDisplayController's `searchContents-Controller`.

A results table view
The table view in which the search results will be presented. This will be the UISearchDisplayController's `searchResultsTableView`. It can already exist, or the UISearchDisplayController will create it.

A data source and delegate for the results table view
The UISearchDisplayController's `searchResultsDataSource` and `searchResults-Delegate`. They will control the data and structure of the search results table. They are commonly the same object, as for any table view; moreover, they are commonly the same as the view controller (the `searchContentsController`).

A delegate
An optional object adopting the UISearchDisplayDelegate protocol. It will be notified of events relating to the display of results. It, too, is commonly the view controller (the `searchContentsController`).

Moreover, the UISearchBar itself can also have a delegate, and this, too, is commonly the view controller (the `searchContentsController`).

A UISearchDisplayController's `searchContentsController` needn't be a UITableView-Controller, and the data that the user is searching needn't be the content of an existing table view. But they frequently are! That's because the mental connection between a table and a search is a natural one; when the search results are presented as a table view, the user feels that the search field is effectively filtering the contents of the original table view. A single object may thus be playing all of the following roles:

- The searchable table view's view controller
- The searchable table view's data source
- The searchable table view's delegate
- The view controller for the view over which the search results will appear
- The search results table view's data source
- The search results table view's delegate
- The UISearchDisplayController's delegate
- The UISearchBar's delegate

A common point of confusion among beginners, when using this architecture, is to suppose that the search bar is genuinely filtering the original table. It isn't! The search bar and the UISearchDisplayController know nothing of your table. What's being searched is just some data — whatever data you care to search. The fact that this may be the model data for your table is purely secondary.

Moreover, there are *two distinct tables*: yours (the original table view) and the UISearch-DisplayController's (the search results table view). You own the former, just as you would if no search were involved; you probably have a view controller that manages it, very likely a UITableViewController whose `tableView` is this table. But the search results table is a *completely different table*; you do *not* have a view controller managing it (the UISearchDisplayController does), and in particular it is *not* your UITableView-Controller's `tableView`. However, if you wish, you can make it *look* as if these are the same table, by configuring the two tables and their cells the same way — typically, with the same code.

To illustrate, we will implement a table view that is searchable through a UISearchBar and that displays the results of that search in a second table view managed by a UISearchDisplayController.

The first question is how to make the search field appear along with the table view.

One approach is to make the search field be the table view's header view. Indeed, this is such a common arrangement that, in the nib editor, if you drag a Search Bar and Search Display Controller object onto a UITableView, the search field *automatically* becomes the table's header view and a UISearchDisplayController is created for you with all properties hooked up appropriately through outlets, much as I just described.

It is more educational, however, to create the UISearchDisplayController and the UISearchBar in code. So let's do that. I'll adapt my earlier example displaying the names of states in a section-based table, so that it becomes searchable.

We already have a table managed by a UITableViewController. In `viewDidLoad`, we create the search bar and slot it in as the table's header view; we then load the data and scroll the header view out of sight. We also create the UISearchDisplayController and tie it to the search bar — and to ourselves (the UITableViewController) as the UISearchDisplayController's controller, delegate, search table data source, and search table delegate, as well as making ourselves the UISearchBar delegate. We also retain the UISearchDisplayController by assigning it to a property, so that it doesn't vanish in a puff of smoke before we can use it:

```
UISearchBar* b = [UISearchBar new];
[b sizeToFit];
b.autocapitalizationType = UITextAutocapitalizationTypeNone;
b.delegate = self;
[self.tableView setTableHeaderView:b];
[self.tableView reloadData];
[self.tableView
    scrollToRowAtIndexPath:[NSIndexPath indexPathForRow:0 inSection:0]
    atScrollPosition:UITableViewScrollPositionTop animated:NO];
UISearchDisplayController* c =
    [[UISearchDisplayController alloc] initWithSearchBar:b
                                      contentsController:self];
self.sdc = c; // retain the UISearchDisplayController
c.delegate = self;
c.searchResultsDataSource = self;
c.searchResultsDelegate = self;
```

 After the UISearchDisplayController is configured to use our view controller (self) as its contentsController, it is also pointed to by our view controller's built-in searchDisplayController read-only property. But that property does *not* retain it, as the documentation misleadingly implies; you still need to assign it to a strong property of your own.

Populating the search results table in response to what the user does in the UISearchBar is up to us. The amazing thing is that this is almost working already, because we have been fiendishly clever at the outset: the UITableViewController is both data source and delegate for the original table view, as well as data source and delegate for the search results table view, so by default the search results table will portray the same data as the original table!

It isn't quite working, however. We need to make a few tweaks.

As the UISearchDisplayController's table view comes into existence, we get a delegate message. This is the place to perform any initial configurations on the UISearchDisplayController's table view. For example, if my viewDidLoad is setting my table view's separator style to UITableViewCellSeparatorStyleNone, and if I want the two tables to look identical, this would be the place to set the UISearchDisplayController's table view's separator style to UITableViewCellSeparatorStyleNone as well. In this example,

I'll take advantage of this moment to suppress display of headers in the search results table:

```
-(void)searchDisplayController:(UISearchDisplayController *)controller
      didLoadSearchResultsTableView:(UITableView *)tableView {
    // configure search results table to look like our table
    tableView.sectionHeaderHeight = 0;
}
```

Next, let's talk about where the search results table is going to get its cells. At present, the original table gets its cells like this:

```
- (UITableViewCell *)tableView:(UITableView *)tableView
      cellForRowAtIndexPath:(NSIndexPath *)indexPath {
    UITableViewCell *cell =
        [tableView dequeueReusableCellWithIdentifier:@"Cell"
            forIndexPath:indexPath];
```

But when the search results table calls into this same delegate method, `tableView` will be the search results table. That's wrong. We don't want to use cells from the search results table; we want to use cells from the original table, so that they'll be structured like those of the original table. So we change `tableView` to `self.tableView`, referring explicitly to our original table as the source of cells:

```
- (UITableViewCell *)tableView:(UITableView *)tableView
      cellForRowAtIndexPath:(NSIndexPath *)indexPath {
    UITableViewCell *cell =
        [self.tableView dequeueReusableCellWithIdentifier:@"Cell"
            forIndexPath:indexPath];
```

Our search interface has now sprung to life! We can type in the search field, and a search results table appears. It looks just like our original table, except that it has no sections. The only problem is that the search bar itself is not doing anything. Instead of searching, we're displaying *all* the same data as the original table.

Clearly, we need to check whether the table view that's talking to us is the search results table view (this will be the UISearchDisplayController's `searchResultsTableView`). If it is, we want to limit our returned data with respect to the search bar's text. The strategy for doing this should be fairly obvious if we are maintaining our source data in a sensible model.

Recall that our original table is displaying the names of the 50 United States, which it is getting from a mutable array of mutable arrays of strings called `sectionData`. Let's restructure our responses to the Three Big Questions so that they refer to this array as `model`, like this:

```
- (NSInteger)numberOfSectionsInTableView:(UITableView *)tableView {
    return [self.sectionNames count];
}
- (NSInteger)tableView:(UITableView *)tableView
      numberOfRowsInSection:(NSInteger)section {
```

```
        NSArray* model = self.sectionData;
        return [model[section] count];
    }
    - (UITableViewCell *)tableView:(UITableView *)tableView
            cellForRowAtIndexPath:(NSIndexPath *)indexPath {
        UITableViewCell *cell =
            [self.tableView dequeueReusableCellWithIdentifier:@"Cell"
                forIndexPath:indexPath];
        NSArray* model = self.sectionData;
        NSString* s = model[indexPath.section][indexPath.row];
        cell.textLabel.text = s;
        return cell;
    }
```

To implement searching, each time we speak of the NSArray called model, we will decide
whether it should be self.sectionData, as now, or whether it should be a *different*
array that is filtered with respect to the current search — let's call it self.filtered-
SectionData. There are two occurrences of this line:

```
    NSArray* model = self.sectionData;
```

They are now to be replaced by this:

```
    NSArray* model =
        (tableView == self.sdc.searchResultsTableView) ?
            self.filteredSectionData : self.sectionData;
```

The remaining question is when and how this self.filteredSectionData array should
be calculated. An excellent approach, given our small and readily available data set, is
to generate a new set of search results every time the user types in the search field,
effectively implementing a "live" search (Figure 8-7). We are informed of the user typing
through a UISearchBar delegate method, searchBar:textDidChange:, so we implement this to generate self.filteredSectionData freshly. There is no need to reload
the search results table's data, as by default the UISearchDisplayController will do that
automatically:

```
    - (void)searchBar:(UISearchBar *)searchBar
            textDidChange:(NSString *)searchText {
        // this is the search criteria
        NSPredicate* p =
            [NSPredicate predicateWithBlock: ^BOOL(id obj, NSDictionary *d) {
                NSString* s = obj;
                return ([s rangeOfString:searchText
                    options:NSCaseInsensitiveSearch].location != NSNotFound);
            }];
        // generate filtered section data
        NSMutableArray* filteredData = [NSMutableArray new];
        // sectionData is an array of arrays; for every array...
        for (NSMutableArray* arr in self.sectionData) {
            // generate an array of strings passing the search criteria
```

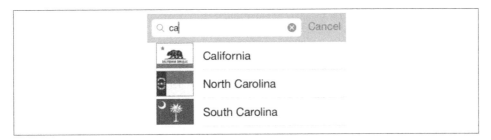

Figure 8-7. Filtering a table with a search bar

```
        [filteredData addObject: [arr filteredArrayUsingPredicate:p]];
    }
    self.filteredSectionData = filteredData;
}
```

Our search interface is now working! In the rest of this section, I'll discuss some additional optional tweaks.

A UISearchBar can display scope buttons, letting the user alter the meaning of the search. If you add these, then of course you must take them into account when filtering the model data. For example, let's have two scope buttons, "Starts With" and "Contains":

```
UISearchBar* b = [UISearchBar new];
[b sizeToFit];
b.scopeButtonTitles = @[@"Starts With", @"Contains"];
```

Our filtering routine must now take the state of the scope buttons into account. Moreover, the search results table view will reload when the user changes the scope; we can detect this in another UISearchBar delegate method, searchBar:selectedScopeButton-IndexDidChange:. If we're doing a live search, we must respond by filtering the data then as well. To prevent repetition, we'll abstract the filtering routine into a method of its own:

```
- (void) filterData: (UISearchBar*) sb {
    NSPredicate* p =
        [NSPredicate predicateWithBlock: ^BOOL(id obj, NSDictionary *d) {
            NSString* s = obj;
            NSStringCompareOptions options = NSCaseInsensitiveSearch;
            if (sb.selectedScopeButtonIndex == 0)
                options |= NSAnchoredSearch;
            return ([s rangeOfString:sb.text
                options:options].location != NSNotFound);
        }];
    NSMutableArray* filteredData = [NSMutableArray new];
    for (NSMutableArray* arr in self.sectionData) {
        [filteredData addObject: [arr filteredArrayUsingPredicate:p]];
    }
    self.filteredSectionData = filteredData;
```

```
    }
- (void)searchBar:(UISearchBar *)searchBar
        textDidChange:(NSString *)searchText {
    [self filterData: searchBar];
}
- (void)searchBar:(UISearchBar *)searchBar
        selectedScopeButtonIndexDidChange:(NSInteger)selectedScope {
    [self filterData: searchBar];
}
```

In our original table, the search bar is initially scrolled out of sight. Let's make it easier
for the user to discover its existence and summon it. In an indexed list — one with
sections and an index running down the right side — a "magnifying glass" search symbol
can be made to appear in the index by including UITableViewIndexSearch (usually as
the first item) in the string array returned from sectionIndexTitlesForTableView:.
The section names are already in an array called sectionNames:

```
- (NSArray *)sectionIndexTitlesForTableView:(UITableView *)tableView {
    if (tableView != self.tableView)
        return nil;
    return [@[UITableViewIndexSearch]
        arrayByAddingObjectsFromArray:self.sectionNames];
}
```

The magnifying glass appears in the section index, but now there's a bug: the correspondence between index entries and sections is off by one. To fix that, we need to
implement tableView:sectionForSectionIndexTitle:atIndex:. If the user taps on
or above the magnifying glass in the index, we scroll to reveal the search field (and we'll
also have to return a bogus section number, but there is no penalty for that):

```
- (NSInteger)tableView:(UITableView *)tableView
        sectionForSectionIndexTitle:(NSString *)title
                        atIndex:(NSInteger)index {
    if (index == 0)
        [tableView scrollRectToVisible:tableView.tableHeaderView.frame
                            animated:NO];
    return index-1;
}
```

Whenever the search results table becomes empty (because the search bar is nonempty
and self.filteredSectionData is nil), the words "No Results" appear in a label superimposed on it. I find this label incredibly obnoxious; yet, after all these years, Apple
still hasn't granted programmers an official way to remove or customize it. Here's an
unofficial way:

```
-(BOOL)searchDisplayController:(UISearchDisplayController *)controller
        shouldReloadTableForSearchString:(NSString *)searchString {
    dispatch_async(dispatch_get_main_queue(), ^{
        for (UIView* v in controller.searchResultsTableView.subviews) {
            if ([v isKindOfClass: [UILabel class]] &&
                    [[(UILabel*)v text] isEqualToString:@"No Results"]) {
```

```
                [(UILabel*)v setText: @""];
                break;
            }
        }
    });
    return YES;
}
```

New in iOS 7, if our view controller (the UISearchDisplayController's searchContents-Controller) is the child of a UINavigationController, we can make the search bar appear in the navigation bar. To do so, set the UISearchDisplayController's displaysSearch-BarInNavigationBar property to YES. If the UISearchDisplayController also has a navigationItem, it is used instead of our view controller's navigationItem to populate the navigation bar.

This doesn't mean that you can toggle displaysSearchBarInNavigationBar to make a search bar appear and disappear in your navigation bar. On the contrary, the UISearch-DisplayController must be created early, and the search bar then will always be present in the navigation bar for this view controller. However, you're in a navigation interface, so you can easily work around this limitation by navigating to and from the searchable view controller.

Also, a search bar in a navigation bar can't have scope buttons, and its Cancel button doesn't come and go automatically — either it is constantly present (because you set its showsCancelButton to YES) or it never appears.

This example code is from our view controller's viewDidLoad:

```
UISearchBar* b = [UISearchBar new];
b.delegate = self;
b.showsCancelButton = YES;
b.autocapitalizationType = UITextAutocapitalizationTypeNone;
UISearchDisplayController* c =
    [[UISearchDisplayController alloc] initWithSearchBar:b
        contentsController:self];
self.sdc = c; // retain the UISearchDisplayController
c.delegate = self;
c.searchResultsDataSource = self;
c.searchResultsDelegate = self;
c.displaysSearchBarInNavigationBar = YES;
```

The result is that our navigation bar's title view is the search bar. The back bar button item, if any, is shown, so the user can pop this view controller in the usual way. Any other buttons you want to have appear in the navigation bar must added to the UISearchDisplayController's navigationItem (not the view controller's navigation-Item, which is ignored).

A UISearchBar has many properties through which its appearance can be configured; I'll discuss them in Chapter 12. Both the UISearchBar and UISearchDisplayController send their delegate numerous messages that you can take advantage of to customize behavior; consult the documentation. A UISearchBar in a UIToolbar on the iPad can display its results in a popover; I'll talk about that in Chapter 9.

Table View Editing

A table view cell has a normal state and an editing state, according to its `editing` property. The editing state is typically indicated visually by one or more of the following:

Editing controls
> At least one editing control will usually appear, such as a Minus button (for deletion) at the left side.

Shrinkage
> The content of the cell will usually shrink to allow room for an editing control. If there is no editing control, you can prevent a cell shifting its left end rightward in editing mode with the table delegate's `tableView:shouldIndentWhileEditingRow-AtIndexPath:`. (There is also a cell property `shouldIndentWhileEditing`, but I find it unreliable.)

Changing accessory view
> The cell's accessory view will change automatically in accordance with its `editing-AccessoryType` or `editingAccessoryView`. If you assign neither, so that they are nil, the cell's existing accessory view will vanish when in editing mode.

As with selection, you could set a cell's `editing` property directly (or use `set-Editing:animated:` to get animation), but you are more likely to let the table view manage editability. Table view editability is controlled through the table view's `editing` property, usually by sending the table the `setEditing:animated:` message. The table is then responsible for putting its cells into edit mode.

A cell in edit mode can also be selected by the user if the table view's `allowsSelection-DuringEditing` or `allowsMultipleSelectionDuringEditing` is YES. But this would be unusual.

Putting the table into edit mode is usually left up to the user. A typical interface would be an Edit button that the user can tap. In a navigation interface, we might have our view controller supply the button as the navigation item's right button:

```
UIBarButtonItem* bbi =
    [[UIBarButtonItem alloc]
        initWithBarButtonSystemItem:UIBarButtonSystemItemEdit
        target:self action:@selector(doEdit:)];
self.navigationItem.rightBarButtonItem = bbi;
```

Our action handler will be responsible for putting the table into edit mode, so in its simplest form it might look like this:

```
- (void) doEdit: (id) sender {
    [self.tableView setEditing:YES animated:YES];
}
```

But that does not solve the problem of getting *out* of editing mode. The standard solution is to have the Edit button replace itself by a Done button:

```
- (void) doEdit: (id) sender {
    int which;
    if (![self.tableView isEditing]) {
        [self.tableView setEditing:YES animated:YES];
        which = UIBarButtonSystemItemDone;
    } else {
        [self.tableView setEditing:NO animated:YES];
        which = UIBarButtonSystemItemEdit;
    }
    UIBarButtonItem* bbi = [[UIBarButtonItem alloc]
        initWithBarButtonSystemItem:which
        target:self action:@selector(doEdit:)];
    self.navigationItem.rightBarButtonItem = bbi;
}
```

However, it turns out that all of that is completely unnecessary! If we want standard behavior, it's already implemented for us. A UIViewController supplies an editButton-Item that calls the UIViewController's setEditing:animated: when tapped, tracks whether we're in edit mode with the UIViewController's editing property, and changes its own title accordingly (Edit or Done). Moreover, a UITableViewController's implementation of setEditing:animated: is to call setEditing:animated: on its table view. Thus, if we're using a UITableViewController, we get all of that behavior for free, just by inserting the editButtonItem into our interface:

```
self.navigationItem.rightBarButtonItem = self.editButtonItem;
```

When the table view enters edit mode, it consults its data source and delegate about the editability of individual rows:

tableView:canEditRowAtIndexPath: *to the data source*
> The default is YES. The data source can return NO to prevent the given row from entering edit mode.

tableView:editingStyleForRowAtIndexPath: *to the delegate*
> Each standard editing style corresponds to a control that will appear in the cell. The choices are:

UITableViewCellEditingStyleDelete
> The cell shows a Minus button at its left end. The user can tap this to summon a Delete button, which the user can then tap to confirm the deletion. This is the default.

`UITableViewCellEditingStyleInsert`
> The cell shows a Plus button at its left end; this is usually taken to be an insert button.

`UITableViewCellEditingStyleNone`
> No editing control appears.

If the user taps an insert button (the Plus button) or a delete button (the Delete button that appears after the user taps the Minus button), the data source is sent the `table-View:commitEditingStyle:forRowAtIndexPath:` message and is responsible for obeying it. In your response, you will probably want to alter the structure of the table, and UITableView methods for doing this are provided:

- `insertRowsAtIndexPaths:withRowAnimation:`

- `deleteRowsAtIndexPaths:withRowAnimation:`

- `insertSections:withRowAnimation:`

- `deleteSections:withRowAnimation:`

- `moveSection:toSection:`

- `moveRowAtIndexPath:toIndexPath:`

The row animations here are effectively the same ones discussed earlier in connection with refreshing table data; "left" for an insertion means to slide in from the left, and for a deletion it means to slide out to the left, and so on. The two "move" methods provide animation with no provision for customizing it.

If you're issuing more than one of these commands, you can combine them by surrounding them with `beginUpdates` and `endUpdates`, forming an *updates block*. An updates block combines not just the animations but the requested changes themselves. This relieves you from having to worry about how a command is affected by earlier commands in the same updates block; indeed, order of commands within an updates block doesn't really matter.

For example, if you delete row 1 of a certain section and then (in a separate command) delete row 2 of the same section, you delete two successive rows, just as you would expect; the notion "2" does not change its meaning because you deleted an earlier row first, because you *didn't* delete an earlier row first — the updates block combines the commands for you, interpreting both index paths with respect to the state of the table before any changes are made. If you perform insertions and deletions together in one animation, the deletions are performed first, regardless of the order of your commands, and the insertion row and section numbers refer to the state of the table after the deletions.

An updates block can also include `reloadRows...` and `reloadSections...` commands (but not `reloadData`).

I need hardly emphasize once again (but I will anyway) that view is not model. It is one thing to rearrange the appearance of the table, another to alter the underlying data. It is up to you to make certain you do both together. Do not, even for a moment, permit the data and the view to get out of synch with each other. If you delete a row, remove from the model the datum that it represents. The runtime will try to help you with error messages if you forget to do this, but in the end the responsibility is yours. I'll give examples as we proceed.

Deleting Table Items

Deletion of table items is the default, so there's not much for us to do in order to implement it. If our view controller is a UITableViewController and we've displayed the Edit button as its navigation item's right button, everything happens automatically: the user taps the Edit button, the view controller's `setEditing:animated:` is called, the table view's `setEditing:animated:` is called, and the cells all show the Minus button at the left end. The user can then tap a Minus button; a Delete button is shown at the cell's right end. You can customize the Delete button's title with the table delegate method `tableView:titleForDeleteConfirmationButtonForRowAtIndexPath:`.

What is *not* automatic is the actual response to the Delete button. For that, we need to implement `tableView:commitEditingStyle:forRowAtIndexPath:`. Typically, you'll remove the corresponding entry from the underlying model data, and you'll call `delete-RowsAtIndexPaths:withRowAnimation:` or `deleteSections:withRowAnimation:` to update the appearance of the table. As I said a moment ago, you must delete the row or section in such a way as to keep the table display coordinated with the model's structure. Otherwise, the app may crash (with an extremely helpful error message).

To illustrate, let's suppose once again that the underlying model is a pair of parallel arrays, a mutable array of strings (`sectionNames`) and a mutable array of arrays (`section-Data`). Our approach will be in two stages:

1. Deal with the model data. We'll delete the requested row; if this empties the section array, we'll also delete that section array and the corresponding section name.

2. Deal with the table's appearance. If we deleted the section array, we'll call `delete-Sections:withRowAnimation:` (and reload the section index if there is one); otherwise, we'll call `deleteRowsAtIndexPaths:withRowAnimation::`

```
- (void)tableView:(UITableView *)tableView
      commitEditingStyle:(UITableViewCellEditingStyle)editingStyle
        forRowAtIndexPath:(NSIndexPath *)ip {
    [self.sectionData[ip.section] removeObjectAtIndex:ip.row];
    if ([self.sectionData[ip.section] count] == 0) {
```

```
        [self.sectionData removeObjectAtIndex: ip.section];
        [self.sectionNames removeObjectAtIndex: ip.section];
        [tableView deleteSections:[NSIndexSet indexSetWithIndex: ip.section]
                withRowAnimation:UITableViewRowAnimationAutomatic];
        [tableView reloadSectionIndexTitles];
    } else {
        [tableView deleteRowsAtIndexPaths:@[ip]
                    withRowAnimation:UITableViewRowAnimationAutomatic];
    }
}
```

The user can also delete a row by sliding it to the left to show its Delete button *without* having explicitly entered edit mode; no other row is editable, and no other editing controls are shown. (In iOS 7, the table cell is itself inside a little horizontal scroll view; the user is actually scrolling the cell to the left, revealing the Delete button behind it.) This feature is implemented "for free" by virtue of our having supplied an implementation of tableView:commitEditingStyle:forRowAtIndexPath:. If you're like me, your first response will be: "Thanks for the free functionality, Apple, and now how do I turn this off?" Because the Edit button is already using the UIViewController's editing property to track edit mode, we can take advantage of this and refuse to let any cells be edited unless the view controller *is* in edit mode:

```
- (UITableViewCellEditingStyle)tableView:(UITableView *)aTableView
        editingStyleForRowAtIndexPath:(NSIndexPath *)indexPath {
    return self.editing ?
        UITableViewCellEditingStyleDelete : UITableViewCellEditingStyleNone;
}
```

Editable Content in Table Items

A table item might have content that the user can edit directly, such as a UITextField (Chapter 10). Because the user is working in the view, you need a way to reflect the user's changes into the model. This will probably involve putting yourself in contact with the interface objects where the user does the editing.

To illustrate, I'll implement a table view cell with a text field that is editable when the cell is in editing mode. Imagine an app that maintains a list of names and phone numbers. A name and phone number are displayed as a grouped style table, and they become editable when the user taps the Edit button (Figure 8-8).

We don't need a button at the left end of the cell when it's being edited:

```
- (UITableViewCellEditingStyle)tableView:(UITableView *)tableView
        editingStyleForRowAtIndexPath:(NSIndexPath *)indexPath {
    return UITableViewCellEditingStyleNone;
}
```

A UITextField is editable if its enabled is YES. To tie this to the cell's editing state, it is probably simplest to implement a custom UITableViewCell class. I'll call it MyCell,

Figure 8-8. A simple phone directory app

and I'll design it in the nib, giving it a single UITextField that's pointed to through a property called `textField`. In the code for MyCell, we override `didTransitionTo-State:`, as follows:

```
- (void) didTransitionToState:(UITableViewCellStateMask)state {
    [super didTransitionToState:state];
    if (state == UITableViewCellStateEditingMask) {
        self.textField.enabled = YES;
    }
    if (state == UITableViewCellStateDefaultMask) {
        self.textField.enabled = NO;
    }
}
```

In the table's data source, we make ourselves the text field's delegate when we create and configure the cell:

```
- (UITableViewCell *)tableView:(UITableView *)tableView
        cellForRowAtIndexPath:(NSIndexPath *)indexPath {
    MyCell* cell =
        [tableView dequeueReusableCellWithIdentifier:@"Cell"
            forIndexPath:indexPath];
    if (indexPath.section == 0)
        cell.textField.text = self.name;
    if (indexPath.section == 1) {
        cell.textField.text = self.numbers[indexPath.row];
        cell.textField.keyboardType = UIKeyboardTypeNumbersAndPunctuation;
    }
    cell.textField.delegate = self;
    return cell;
}
```

We are the UITextField's delegate, so we are responsible for implementing the Return button in the keyboard to dismiss the keyboard (I'll talk more about this in Chapter 10):

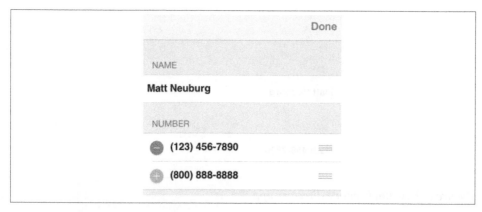

Figure 8-9. Phone directory app in editing mode

```
- (BOOL)textFieldShouldReturn:(UITextField *)tf {
    [tf endEditing:YES];
    return NO;
}
```

When a text field stops editing, we are its delegate, so we can hear about it in `textField-DidEndEditing:`. We work out which cell it belongs to, and update the model accordingly:

```
- (void)textFieldDidEndEditing:(UITextField *)tf {
    // some cell's text field has finished editing; which cell?
    UIView* v = tf;
    do {
        v = v.superview;
    } while (![v isKindOfClass: [UITableViewCell class]]);
    MyCell* cell = (MyCell*)v;
    // update data model to match
    NSIndexPath* ip = [self.tableView indexPathForCell:cell];
    if (ip.section == 1)
        self.numbers[ip.row] = cell.textField.text;
    else if (ip.section == 0)
        self.name = cell.textField.text;
}
```

Inserting Table Items

You are unlikely to attach a Plus (insert) button to every row. A more likely interface is that when a table is edited, every row has a Minus button except the last row, which has a Plus button; this shows the user that a new row can be appended at the end of the list.

Let's implement this for phone numbers in our name-and-phone-number app, allowing the user to give a person any quantity of phone numbers (Figure 8-9):

```
- (UITableViewCellEditingStyle)tableView:(UITableView *)tableView
        editingStyleForRowAtIndexPath:(NSIndexPath *)indexPath {
    if (indexPath.section == 1) {
        NSInteger ct =
            [self tableView:tableView numberOfRowsInSection:indexPath.section];
        if (ct-1 == indexPath.row)
            return UITableViewCellEditingStyleInsert;
        return UITableViewCellEditingStyleDelete;
    }
    return UITableViewCellEditingStyleNone;
}
```

The person's name has no editing control (a person must have exactly one name), so we prevent it from indenting in edit mode:

```
- (BOOL)tableView:(UITableView *)tableView
        shouldIndentWhileEditingRowAtIndexPath:(NSIndexPath *)indexPath {
    if (indexPath.section == 1)
        return YES;
    return NO;
}
```

When the user taps an editing control, we must respond. We immediately force our text fields to cease editing: the user have may tapped the editing control while editing, and we want our model to contain the very latest changes, so this is effectively a way of causing our `textFieldDidEndEditing:` to be called. The model for our phone numbers is a mutable array of strings (`self.numbers`). We already know what to do when the tapped control is a delete button; things are similar when it's an insert button, but we've a little more work to do. The new row will be empty, and it will be at the end of the table; so we append an empty string to the `self.numbers` model array, and then we insert a corresponding row at the end of the view. But now two successive rows have a Plus button; the way to fix that is to reload the first of those rows. Finally, we also show the keyboard for the new, empty phone number, so that the user can start editing it immediately; we do that outside the updates block:

```
- (void) tableView:(UITableView *)tableView
        commitEditingStyle:(UITableViewCellEditingStyle)editingStyle
        forRowAtIndexPath:(NSIndexPath *)indexPath {
    [tableView endEditing:YES];
    if (editingStyle == UITableViewCellEditingStyleInsert) {
        [self.numbers addObject: @""];
        NSInteger ct = [self.numbers count];
        [tableView beginUpdates];
        [tableView insertRowsAtIndexPaths:
         @[[NSIndexPath indexPathForRow: ct-1 inSection:1]]
                     withRowAnimation:UITableViewRowAnimationAutomatic];
        [self.tableView reloadRowsAtIndexPaths:
            @[[NSIndexPath indexPathForRow:ct-2 inSection:1]]
                     withRowAnimation:UITableViewRowAnimationAutomatic];
        [tableView endUpdates];
        // crucial that this next bit be *outside* the updates block
```

```
            UITableViewCell* cell =
                [self.tableView cellForRowAtIndexPath:
                        [NSIndexPath indexPathForRow:ct-1 inSection:1]];
            [((MyCell*)cell).textField becomeFirstResponder];
        }
        if (editingStyle == UITableViewCellEditingStyleDelete) {
            [self.numbers removeObjectAtIndex:indexPath.row];
            [tableView beginUpdates];
            [tableView deleteRowsAtIndexPaths:@[indexPath]
                        withRowAnimation:UITableViewRowAnimationAutomatic];
            [tableView reloadSections:[NSIndexSet indexSetWithIndex:1]
                    withRowAnimation:UITableViewRowAnimationAutomatic];
            [tableView endUpdates];
        }
    }
}
```

Rearranging Table Items

If the data source implements tableView:moveRowAtIndexPath:toIndexPath:, the table displays a reordering control at the right end of each row in editing mode (Figure 8-9), and the user can drag it to rearrange table items. The reordering control can be suppressed for individual table items by implementing tableView:canMoveRow-AtIndexPath:. The user is free to move rows that display a reordering control, but the delegate can limit where a row can be moved to by implementing tableView:target-IndexPathForMoveFromRowAtIndexPath:toProposedIndexPath:.

To illustrate, we'll add to our name-and-phone-number app the ability to rearrange phone numbers. There must be multiple phone numbers to rearrange:

```
- (BOOL)tableView:(UITableView *)tableView
      canMoveRowAtIndexPath:(NSIndexPath *)indexPath {
    if (indexPath.section == 1 && [self.numbers count] > 1)
        return YES;
    return NO;
}
```

A phone number must not be moved out of its section, so we implement the delegate method to prevent this. We also take this opportunity to dismiss the keyboard if it is showing.

```
- (NSIndexPath *)tableView:(UITableView *)tableView
      targetIndexPathForMoveFromRowAtIndexPath:(NSIndexPath*)sourceIndexPath
      toProposedIndexPath:(NSIndexPath*)proposedDestinationIndexPath {
    [tableView endEditing:YES];
    if (proposedDestinationIndexPath.section == 0)
        return [NSIndexPath indexPathForRow:0 inSection:1];
    return proposedDestinationIndexPath;
}
```

After the user moves an item, `tableView:moveRowAtIndexPath:toIndexPath:` is called, and we trivially update the model to match. We also reload the table, to fix the editing controls:

```
- (void)tableView:(UITableView *)tableView
        moveRowAtIndexPath:(NSIndexPath *)fromIndexPath
               toIndexPath:(NSIndexPath *)toIndexPath {
    NSString* s = self.numbers[fromIndexPath.row];
    [self.numbers removeObjectAtIndex: fromIndexPath.row];
    [self.numbers insertObject:s atIndex: toIndexPath.row];
    [tableView reloadData];
}
```

Dynamic Table Items

A table may be rearranged not just in response to the user working in edit mode, but for some other reason entirely. In this way, many interesting and original interfaces are possible.

In this example, we permit the user to double tap on a section header as a way of collapsing or expanding the section — that is, we'll suppress or permit the display of the rows of the section, with a nice animation as the change takes place. (This idea is shamelessly stolen from a WWDC 2010 video.)

One more time, our data model consists of the two arrays, `sectionNames` and `section-Data`. I've also got an NSMutableSet, `hiddenSections`, in which I'll list the sections that aren't displaying their rows. That list is all I'll need, since either a section is showing all its rows or it's showing none of them:

```
- (NSInteger)tableView:(UITableView *)tableView
        numberOfRowsInSection:(NSInteger)section {
    if ([self.hiddenSections containsObject:@(section)])
        return 0;
    return [self.sectionData[section] count];
}
```

We need a correspondence between a section header and the number of its section. It's odd that UITableView doesn't give us such a correspondence; it provides `indexPathFor-Cell:`, but there is no `sectionForHeaderFooterView:`. My solution is to subclass UITableViewHeaderFooterView and give my subclass a public property `section`, to which I assign the current section number whenever `tableView:viewForHeaderInSection:` is called:

```
- (UIView *)tableView:(UITableView *)tableView
        viewForHeaderInSection:(NSInteger)section {
    MyHeaderView* h =
        [tableView dequeueReusableHeaderFooterViewWithIdentifier:@"Header"];
```

```
    // ...
    h.section = section;
    return h;
}
```

The section headers are a UITableViewHeaderFooterView subclass with user-
InteractionEnabled set to YES and a UITapGestureRecognizer attached, so we can
detect a double tap. When the user double taps a section header, we learn from the
header what section this is; we also find out from the model how many rows this section
has, as we'll need to know that later, regardless of whether we're about to show or hide
rows. Then we look for the section number in our hiddenSections set. If it's there, we're
about to display the rows, so we remove that section number from hiddenSections;
now we work out the index paths of the rows we're about to insert, and we insert them.
If it's not there, we're about to hide the rows, so we insert that section number into
hiddenSections; again, we work out the index paths of the rows we're about to delete,
and we delete them:

```
- (void) tap: (UIGestureRecognizer*) g {
    UITableViewHeaderFooterView* v = (id)g.view;
    NSUInteger sec = v.section;
    NSUInteger ct = [(NSArray*)(self.sectionData)[sec] count];
    NSNumber* secnum = @(sec);
    if ([self.hiddenSections containsObject:secnum]) {
        [self.hiddenSections removeObject:secnum];
        [self.tableView beginUpdates];
        NSMutableArray* arr = [NSMutableArray array];
        for (int ix = 0; ix < ct; ix ++) {
            NSIndexPath* ip = [NSIndexPath indexPathForRow:ix inSection:sec];
            [arr addObject: ip];
        }
        [self.tableView insertRowsAtIndexPaths:arr
            withRowAnimation:UITableViewRowAnimationAutomatic];
        [self.tableView endUpdates];
        [self.tableView scrollToRowAtIndexPath:[arr lastObject]
                        atScrollPosition:UITableViewScrollPositionNone
                                animated:YES];
    } else {
        [self.hiddenSections addObject:secnum];
        [self.tableView beginUpdates];
        NSMutableArray* arr = [NSMutableArray array];
        for (int ix = 0; ix < ct; ix ++) {
            NSIndexPath* ip = [NSIndexPath indexPathForRow:ix inSection:sec];
            [arr addObject: ip];
        }
        [self.tableView deleteRowsAtIndexPaths:arr
            withRowAnimation:UITableViewRowAnimationAutomatic];
        [self.tableView endUpdates];
    }
}
```

Table View Menus

A menu, in iOS, is a sort of balloon containing tappable words such as Copy, Cut, and Paste. You can permit the user to display a menu from a table view cell by performing a long press on the cell. The long press followed by display of the menu gives the cell a selected appearance, but in iOS 7, the selected appearance goes away when the menu is dismissed.

To allow the user to display a menu from a table view's cells, you implement three delegate methods:

`tableView:shouldShowMenuForRowAtIndexPath:`
> Return YES if the user is to be permitted to summon a menu by performing a long press on this cell.

`tableView:canPerformAction:forRowAtIndexPath:withSender:`
> You'll be called repeatedly with selectors for various actions that the system knows about. Returning YES, regardless, causes the Copy, Cut, and Paste menu items to appear in the menu, corresponding to the `copy:`, `cut:`, and `paste:` actions; return NO to prevent the menu item for an action from appearing. The menu itself will then appear unless you return NO to all three actions. The sender is the shared UIMenuController, which I'll discuss more in Chapter 10 and Chapter 26.

`tableView:performAction:forRowAtIndexPath:withSender:`
> The user has tapped one of the menu items; your job is to respond to it somehow.

Here's an example where the user can summon a Copy menu from any cell (Figure 8-10):

```
- (BOOL)tableView:(UITableView *)tableView
        shouldShowMenuForRowAtIndexPath:(NSIndexPath *)indexPath {
    return YES;
}
- (BOOL)tableView:(UITableView *)tableView canPerformAction:(SEL)action
        forRowAtIndexPath:(NSIndexPath *)indexPath withSender:(id)sender {
    return (action == NSSelectorFromString(@"copy:"));
}
- (void)tableView:(UITableView *)tableView performAction:(SEL)action
        forRowAtIndexPath:(NSIndexPath *)indexPath withSender:(id)sender {
    NSString* s = self.sectionData[indexPath.section][indexPath.row];
    if (action == NSSelectorFromString(@"copy:")) {
        // ... do whatever copying consists of ...
    }
}
```

To add a custom menu item to the menu (other than `copy:`, `cut:`, and `paste:`) is a little more work. First, you must tell the shared UIMenuController to append the menu item to the global menu; the `tableView:shouldShowMenuForRowAtIndexPath:` delegate method is a good place to do this:

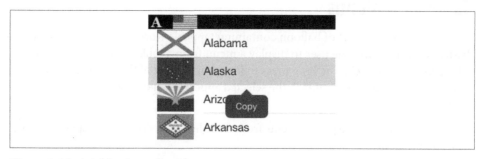

Figure 8-10. A table view cell with a menu

```
- (BOOL)tableView:(UITableView *)tableView
        shouldShowMenuForRowAtIndexPath:(NSIndexPath *)indexPath {
    // extra menu item
    UIMenuItem* mi =
        [[UIMenuItem alloc] initWithTitle:@"Abbrev"
        action:NSSelectorFromString(@"abbrev:")];
    [[UIMenuController sharedMenuController] setMenuItems:@[mi]];
    return YES;
}
```

We have now given the menu an additional menu item whose title is Abbrev, and whose
action when the menu item is tapped is `abbrev:`. (I am imagining here a table of the
names of U.S. states, where one can copy a state's two-letter abbreviation to the clip-
board.) If we want this menu item to appear in the menu, and if we want to respond to
it when the user taps it, we must add that selector to the two `performAction:` delegate
methods:

```
- (BOOL)tableView:(UITableView *)tableView canPerformAction:(SEL)action
        forRowAtIndexPath:(NSIndexPath *)indexPath withSender:(id)sender {
    return (action == NSSelectorFromString(@"copy:") ||
        action == NSSelectorFromString(@"abbrev:"));
}
- (void)tableView:(UITableView *)tableView performAction:(SEL)action
        forRowAtIndexPath:(NSIndexPath *)indexPath withSender:(id)sender {
    NSString* s = self.sectionData[indexPath.section][indexPath.row];
    if (action == NSSelectorFromString(@"copy:")) {
        // ... do whatever copying consists of ...
        NSLog(@"copying %@", s);
    }
    if (action == NSSelectorFromString(@"abbrev:")) {
        // ... do whatever abbreviating consists of ...
        NSLog(@"abbreviating %@", s);
    }
}
```

Now comes the tricky part: we must implement our custom selector, `abbrev:`, *in the cell.* We will therefore need our table to use a custom UITableViewCell subclass. Let's call it MyCell:

```
#import "MyCell.h"
@implementation MyCell
-(void)abbrev:(id)sender {
    // ...
}
@end
```

The Abbrev menu item now appears when the user long-presses a cell of our table, and the cell's `abbrev:` method is called when the user taps that menu item. We could respond directly to the tap in the cell, but it seems more consistent that our table view delegate should respond. So we work out what table view this cell belongs to and send its delegate the very message it is already expecting:

```
-(void)abbrev:(id)sender {
    // find my table view
    UIView* v = self;
    do {
        v = v.superview;
    } while (![v isKindOfClass:[UITableView class]]);
    UITableView* tv = (UITableView*) v;
    // ask it what index path we are
    NSIndexPath* ip = [tv indexPathForCell:self];
    // talk to its delegate
    if (tv.delegate && [tv.delegate respondsToSelector:
            @selector(tableView:performAction:forRowAtIndexPath:withSender:)])
        [tv.delegate tableView:tv performAction:_cmd
            forRowAtIndexPath:ip withSender:sender];
}
```

Collection Views

A collection view (UICollectionView) is a UIScrollView subclass that generalizes the notion of a UITableView. It has many similarities to a table view; indeed, knowing about table views, you know a great deal about collection views already:

- Like a UITableView, you might well manage your UICollectionView through a UIViewController subclass — a subclass of UICollectionViewController.

- Like a UITableView, a collection view has reusable cells. These are UICollection-ViewCell instances, and are extremely minimal.

- Like a UITableView, you'll make the cells reusable by registering a class or nib with the collection view, calling `registerClass:forCellWithReuseIdentifier:` or `registerNib:forCellWithReuseIdentifier:`. Alternatively, if you've started with a UICollectionViewController in a storyboard, just assign the reuse identifier in the storyboard.

- Like a UITableView, a collection view has a data source (UICollectionViewData-Source) and a delegate (UICollectionViewDelegate), and it's going to ask the data source Three Big Questions:

  — `numberOfSectionsInCollectionView:`

  — `collectionView:numberOfItemsInSection:`

  — `collectionView:cellForItemAtIndexPath:`

- Like a UITableView, to answer the third Big Question, your data source will supply a cell by calling `dequeueReusableCellWithReuseIdentifier:forIndexPath:`.

- Like a UITableView, a collection view can clump its data into sections, identified by section number. A section can have a header and footer, though the collection view itself does not call them that; instead, it generalizes its subview types into cells, on the one hand, and *supplementary views*, on the other. A supplementary view is just a UICollectionReusableView, which happens to be UICollectionViewCell's superclass. A supplementary view is associated with a *kind*, which is just an NSString identifying its type; thus you can have a header as one kind, a footer as another kind, and anything else you can imagine.

  As with a UITableView, you make supplementary views reusable by registering a class with the collection view, calling `registerClass:forSupplementaryViewOf-Kind:withReuseIdentifier:` (or by entering a reuse identifier in a storyboard). The data source method where you are asked for a supplementary view will be `collectionView:viewForSupplementaryElementOfKind:atIndexPath:`. In it, you'll call `dequeueReusableSupplementaryViewOfKind:withReuseIdentifier: forIndexPath:`. (The use of an `indexPath:` instead of a pure section number is surprising; you'll typically be interested only in the NSIndexPath's `section`.)

- Like a UITableView, a collection view allows the user to select a cell, or multiple cells. The delegate is notified of highlighting and selection just like a table view delegate. Your code can rearrange the cells, inserting, moving, and deleting cells or entire sections. If the delegate permits, the user can long-press a cell to produce a menu.

The big difference between a table view and a collection view is how the collection view lays out its elements (cells and supplementary views). A table view lays out its cells in just one way: a vertically scrolling column, where the cells are the width of the table view, the height dictated by the table view or the delegate, and touching one another. A collection view doesn't do that. In fact, a collection view doesn't lay out its elements at all! That job is left to another class, a subclass of UICollectionViewLayout.

A UICollectionViewLayout subclass instance is responsible for the overall layout of the collection view that owns it. It does this by answering some Big Questions of its own, posed by the collection view; the most important are these:

collectionViewContentSize
How big is the entire layout? The collection view needs to know this, because the collection view is a scroll view (Chapter 7), and this will be the content size of the scrollable material that it will display.

layoutAttributesForElementsInRect:
Where do all the elements go? The layout attributes, as I'll explain in more detail in a moment, are bundles of positional information.

To answer these questions, the collection view layout needs to ask the collection view some questions of its own, such as numberOfSections and numberOfItemsIn-Section:. (The collection view, in turn, gets the answers to those questions from its data source.)

The collection view layout can thus assign the elements any positions it likes, and the collection view will faithfully draw them in those positions within its content rectangle. The elements are actually of *three* kinds:

Cells
These, as I've already said, are parallel to table view cells. The collection view learns the position of each cell from its layout, and obtains the actual UICollectionView-Cell objects from its data source by calling collectionView:cellForItemAtIndex-Path:.

Supplementary views
These represent the generalized notion of a header or footer. It is up to the collection view layout to say what kinds of supplementary views it supports; it identifies each kind by a string. For example, if it wants each section to be able to have a header and a footer, it might call the kinds @"Header" and @"Footer". The collection view learns the position of each supplementary view from its layout, and obtains the actual UICollectionReusableView objects from its data source by calling collectionView:viewForSupplementaryElementOfKind:atIndexPath:.

Decoration views
These are not directly analogous to anything in a table view (they are closest, perhaps, to the section index). They don't represent data; the collection view won't ask the data source about them, and the collection view has no methods about them. They are purely up to the collection view layout; it defines any decoration view types, gives its decoration views actual view content, and states the positions its decoration views are to have. I've never written or used a collection view layout that implemented decoration views, and I'm not going to say any more about them.

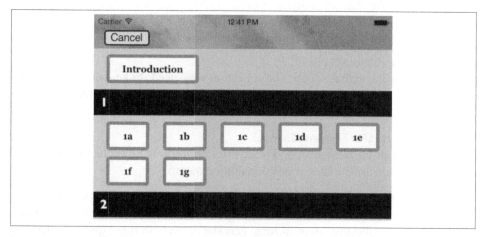

Figure 8-11. A collection view in my Latin flashcard app

The collection view layout can position its elements wherever it likes. That seems very open-ended, and indeed it is. To get you started, there's a built-in UICollectionView-Layout subclass — UICollectionViewFlowLayout.

UICollectionViewFlowLayout arranges its cells in something like a grid. The grid can be scrolled either horizontally or vertically, so this grid is a series of rows or columns. Through properties and a delegate protocol of its own (UICollectionViewDelegate-FlowLayout), the UICollectionViewFlowLayout instance lets you provide hints about how big the cells are and how they should be spaced out. It defines two supplementary view types, using them to let you give each section a header and a footer.

Figure 8-11 shows a collection view, laid out with a flow layout, from my Latin flashcard app. This interface simply lists the chapters and lessons into which the flashcards them-selves are divided, and allows the user to jump to a desired lesson by tapping it. Previ-ously, I was using a table view to present this list; when collection views were introduced (in iOS 6), I adopted one for this interface, and you can see why. Instead of a lesson item like "1a" occupying an entire row that stretches the whole width of a table, it's just a little rectangle; in landscape orientation, the flow layout fits five of these rectangles onto a line for me. So a collection view is a much more compact and appropriate way to present this interface than a table view.

If UICollectionViewFlowLayout doesn't quite meet your needs, you can subclass it, or you can subclass UICollectionViewLayout itself. I'll talk more about that later on.

Collection View Classes

Here are the main classes associated with UICollectionView. This is just a conceptual overview; I don't recite all the properties and methods of each class, which you can learn from the documentation:

UICollectionViewController

A UIViewController subclass. Like a table view controller, UICollectionViewController is convenient if a UICollectionView is to be a view controller's view, but is not required. It is the delegate and data source of its `collectionView` by default. The initializer, if you create one in code, requires you to supply a layout instance for the collection view's designated initializer:

```
RootViewController* rvc =
    [[RootViewController alloc]
        initWithCollectionViewLayout:[UICollectionViewFlowLayout new]];
```

Alternatively, there is a Collection View Controller nib object.

UICollectionView

A UIScrollView subclass. It has a `backgroundColor` (because it's a view) and optionally a `backgroundView` in front of that. Its designated initializer requires you to supply a layout instance, which will be its `collectionViewLayout`. Alternatively, there is a Collection View nib object, which comes with a Collection View Flow Layout by default; you can change the collection view layout class with the Layout pop-up menu in the Collection View's Attributes inspector.

A collection view's methods are very much parallel to those of a UITableView, only fewer and simpler:

- Where a table view speaks of rows, a collection view speaks of *items*. UICollectionView even adds a category to NSIndexPath so that you can refer to its `item` property instead of its `row` property.

- Where a table view speaks of a header or footer, a collection view speaks of a *supplementary view.*

- A UICollectionView doesn't do layout, so it is not where things like header and cell size are configured.

- A UICollectionView has no notion of editing.

- A UICollectionView has no section index.

- Where a table view batches updates with `beginUpdates` and `endUpdates`, a collection view uses `performBatchUpdates:completion:`, which takes blocks.

- A collection view performs animation when you insert, delete, or move sections or items, but you don't specify an animation type. (The layout can modify the animation.)

Having made those mental adjustments, you can guess correctly all the methods of a UICollectionView, except for a couple whose names begin with layout-Attributes.... To understand what they do, you need to know about UICollectionViewLayoutAttributes.

UICollectionViewLayoutAttributes

A UICollectionViewLayoutAttributes object is basically just a glorified struct, tying together an element's index path within the collection view (indexPath) and the specifications for how and where it should be drawn — specifications that are remarkably reminiscent of view or layer properties, with names like frame, center, size, transform, and so forth. Layout attributes objects function as the mediators between the layout and the collection view; they are what the layout passes to the collection view to tell it where all the elements of the view should go.

UICollectionViewCell

An extremely minimal view class. It has a highlighted property and a selected property. It has a contentView, a selectedBackgroundView, a backgroundView, and of course (since it's a view) a backgroundColor, layered in that order, just like a table view cell; everything else is up to you.

If you start with a collection view controller in a storyboard, you get prototype cells, just like a table view controller, which you obtain by dequeuing. Otherwise, you obtain cells through registration and dequeuing. This is all exactly parallel to UITableView.

UICollectionReusableView

The superclass of UICollectionViewCell — so it is even more minimal! This is the class of supplementary views such as headers and footers. You obtain reusable views through registration and dequeuing; if you're using a flow layout in a storyboard, you are given a header and footer prototype view.

UICollectionViewLayout

The layout workhorse class for a collection view. A collection view cannot exist without a layout instance! As I've already said, the layout knows how much room all the subviews occupy, and supplies the collectionViewContentSize that sets the contentSize of the collection view, *qua* scroll view. In addition, the layout must answer questions from the collection view, by supplying a UICollectionViewLayoutAttributes object, or an NSArray of such objects, saying where and how elements should be drawn. These questions come in two categories:

Static attributes

The collection view wants to know the layout attributes of an item, supplementary view, or decoration view, specified by index path, or of all elements within a given rect.

Dynamic attributes

The collection view is inserting or removing elements. It asks for the layout attributes that an element, specified by index path, should have before insertion or after removal. The collection view can thus animate between the element's static attributes and these dynamic attributes. For example, if an element's layout attributes alpha is 0 after removal, the element will appear to fade away as it is removed.

The collection view also notifies the layout of pending changes through some methods whose names start with prepare and finalize. This is another way for the layout to participate in animations, or to perform other kinds of preparation and cleanup.

UICollectionViewLayout is an abstract class; to use it, you must subclass it, or start with the built-in subclass, UICollectionViewFlowLayout.

UICollectionViewFlowLayout

A concrete subclass of UICollectionViewLayout; you can use it as is, or you can subclass it. It lays out items in a grid that can be scrolled either horizontally or vertically, and it defines two supplementary element types to serve as the header and footer of a section. A collection view in the nib editor has a Layout pop-up menu that lets you choose a Flow layout, and you can configure the flow layout in the Size inspector; in a storyboard, you can even add and design a header and a footer.

A flow layout has a scroll direction, a sectionInset (the margins for a section), an itemSize along with a minimumInteritemSpacing and minimumLineSpacing, and a headerReferenceSize and footerReferenceSize. That's all! At a minimum, if you want to see any section headers, you must assign the flow layout a header-ReferenceSize, because the default is {0,0}. Otherwise, you get initial defaults that will at least allow you to see something immediately, such as an itemSize of {50,50} and reasonable default spacing between items and lines.

UICollectionViewFlowLayout also defines a delegate protocol, UICollectionView-DelegateFlowLayout. The flow layout automatically treats the collection view's delegate as its own delegate. The section margins, item size, item spacing, line spacing, and header and footer size can be set individually through this delegate.

Using a Collection View

To show that using a collection view is easy, here's how the view shown in Figure 8-11 is created. I have a UICollectionViewController subclass, LessonListController. Every collection view must have a layout, so LessonListController's designated initializer initializes itself with a UICollectionViewFlowLayout:

```
- (id) initWithTerms: (NSArray*) data {
    UICollectionViewFlowLayout* layout = [UICollectionViewFlowLayout new];
    self = [super initWithCollectionViewLayout:layout];
    if (self) {
        // ... perform other self-initializations here ...
    }
    return self;
}
```

In viewDidLoad, we give the flow layout its hints about the sizes of the margins, cells, and headers, as well as registering for cell and header reusability:

```
- (void)viewDidLoad {
    [super viewDidLoad];
    UICollectionViewFlowLayout* layout =
        (id)self.collectionView.collectionViewLayout;
    layout.sectionInset = UIEdgeInsetsMake(10, 20, 10, 20);
    layout.headerReferenceSize = CGSizeMake(0,40); // only height matters
    layout.itemSize = CGSizeMake(70,45);
    [self.collectionView
        registerNib:[UINib nibWithNibName:@"LessonCell" bundle:nil]
        forCellWithReuseIdentifier:@"LessonCell"];
    [self.collectionView
        registerClass:[UICollectionReusableView class]
        forSupplementaryViewOfKind:UICollectionElementKindSectionHeader
        withReuseIdentifier:@"LessonHeader"];
    self.collectionView.backgroundColor = [UIColor myGolden];
    // ...
}
```

The first two of the Three Big Questions to the data source are boring and familiar:

```
-(NSInteger)numberOfSectionsInCollectionView:
        (UICollectionView *)collectionView {
    return [self.sectionNames count];
}
-(NSInteger)collectionView:(UICollectionView *)collectionView
        numberOfItemsInSection:(NSInteger)section {
    return [self.sectionData[section] count];
}
```

The third of the Three Big Questions to the data source creates and configures the cells. In a *.xib* file, I've designed the cell with a single subview, a UILabel with tag 1; if the text of that label is still @"Label", this is a sign that the cell has come freshly minted from the nib and needs further initial configuration. Among other things, I assign each new cell a `selectedBackgroundView` and give the label a `highlightedTextColor`, to get an automatic indication of selection:

```
- (UICollectionViewCell *)collectionView:(UICollectionView *)collectionView
        cellForItemAtIndexPath:(NSIndexPath *)indexPath {
    UICollectionViewCell* cell =
        [collectionView dequeueReusableCellWithReuseIdentifier:@"LessonCell"
                                            forIndexPath:indexPath];
    UILabel* lab = (UILabel*)[cell viewWithTag:1];
    if ([lab.text isEqualToString:@"Label"]) {
        lab.highlightedTextColor = [UIColor whiteColor];
        cell.backgroundColor = [UIColor myPaler];
        cell.layer.borderColor = [UIColor brownColor].CGColor;
        cell.layer.borderWidth = 5;
        cell.layer.cornerRadius = 5;
        UIView* v = [UIView new];
        v.backgroundColor =
            [[UIColor blueColor] colorWithAlphaComponent:0.8];
        cell.selectedBackgroundView = v;
    }
    Term* term = self.sectionData[indexPath.section][indexPath.item];
    lab.text = term.lesson;
    return cell;
}
```

The fourth data source method asks for the supplementary element views; in my case, these are the section headers. I haven't bothered to design the header in a nib; instead, I configure the entire thing in code. Again I distinguish between newly minted views and reused views; the latter will already have a single subview, a UILabel:

```
-(UICollectionReusableView *)collectionView:(UICollectionView *)collectionView
        viewForSupplementaryElementOfKind:(NSString *)kind
                        atIndexPath:(NSIndexPath *)indexPath {
    UICollectionReusableView* v =
        [collectionView
            dequeueReusableSupplementaryViewOfKind:
                UICollectionElementKindSectionHeader
            withReuseIdentifier:@"LessonHeader"
            forIndexPath:indexPath];
    if ([v.subviews count] == 0) { // no label? make one, configure
        UILabel* lab = [[UILabel alloc] initWithFrame:CGRectMake(10,0,100,40)];
        lab.font = [UIFont fontWithName:@"GillSans-Bold" size:20];
        lab.backgroundColor = [UIColor clearColor];
        [v addSubview:lab];
        v.backgroundColor = [UIColor blackColor];
        lab.textColor = [UIColor myPaler];
    }
    UILabel* lab = (UILabel*)v.subviews[0];
    lab.text = self.sectionNames[indexPath.section];
    return v;
}
```

As you can see from Figure 8-11, the first section is treated specially — it has no header, and its cell is wider. I take care of that with two UICollectionViewDelegateFlowLayout methods:

```
- (CGSize)collectionView:(UICollectionView *)collectionView
        layout:(UICollectionViewLayout*)collectionViewLayout
        sizeForItemAtIndexPath:(NSIndexPath *)indexPath {
    CGSize sz =
        ((UICollectionViewFlowLayout*)collectionViewLayout).itemSize;
    if (indexPath.section == 0)
        sz.width = 150;
    return sz;
}
- (CGSize)collectionView:(UICollectionView *)collectionView
        layout:(UICollectionViewLayout*)collectionViewLayout
        referenceSizeForHeaderInSection:(NSInteger)section {
    CGSize sz =
        [(UICollectionViewFlowLayout*)collectionViewLayout)
            headerReferenceSize];
    if (section == 0)
        sz.height = 0;
    return sz;
}
```

When the user taps a cell, I hear about it through the delegate method collection-View:didSelectItemAtIndexPath: and respond accordingly. That is the entire code for managing this collection view!

Here's an example of deleting cells in a collection view. Let's assume that the cells to be deleted have been selected, with multiple selection being possible. If there are selected cells, they are provided as an array of NSIndexPaths. My data model is once again the usual pair of parallel arrays, a mutable array of strings (sectionNames) and a mutable array of arrays (sectionData); each NSIndexPath gets me directly to the corresponding piece of data in sectionData, so I delete each piece of data in reverse order, keeping track of any arrays (sections) that end up empty. Finally, I delete the items from the collection view, and then do the same for the sections:

```
- (void) doDelete:(id)sender {
    // delete selected
    NSArray* arr = [self.collectionView indexPathsForSelectedItems];
    if (!arr || ![arr count])
        return;
    // sort, reverse, delete items from model, keep track of empty sections
    arr = [arr sortedArrayUsingSelector:@selector(compare:)];
    NSMutableIndexSet* empties = [NSMutableIndexSet indexSet];
    for (NSIndexPath* ip in [arr reverseObjectEnumerator]) {
        [self.sectionData[ip.section] removeObjectAtIndex:ip.item];
        if (![self.sectionData[ip.section] count])
            [empties addIndex:ip.section];
    }
```

```
    // delete items from view
    [self.collectionView performBatchUpdates:^{
        [self.collectionView deleteItemsAtIndexPaths:arr];
    } completion:^(BOOL finished) {
        // delete sections from model and then from view
        if ([empties count]) {
            [self.sectionNames removeObjectsAtIndexes:empties];
            [self.sectionData removeObjectsAtIndexes:empties];
            [self.collectionView deleteSections:empties];
        }
    }];
}
```

Menu handling is also completely parallel to a table view; if you want additional menu items beyond the standard Copy, Cut, and Paste, the corresponding custom selectors must be implemented in a UICollectionViewCell subclass.

Custom Collection View Layouts

To explore what's involved in writing your own layout class, let's introduce a simple modification of UICollectionViewFlowLayout.

By default, the flow layout wants to full-justify every row of cells horizontally, spacing the cells evenly between the left and right margins, except for the last row, which is left-aligned. Let's say that this isn't what you want — you'd rather that *every* row be left-aligned, with every cell as far to the left as possible given the size of the preceding cell and the minimum spacing between cells.

To achieve this, you'll need to subclass UICollectionViewFlowLayout and override two methods, `layoutAttributesForElementsInRect:` and `layoutAttributesForItemAtIndexPath:`. Fortunately, we're starting with a layout, UICollectionViewFlowLayout, whose answers to these questions are almost right. So we call `super` and make modifications as necessary.

The really important method here is `layoutAttributesForItemAtIndexPath:`, which returns a single UICollectionViewLayoutAttributes object.

If the index path's `item` is 0, we have a degenerate case: the answer we got from `super` is right. Alternatively, if this cell is at the start of a row — we can find this out by asking whether the left edge of its frame is close to the margin — we have another degenerate case: the answer we got from `super` is right.

Otherwise, where this cell goes depends on where the previous cell goes, so we obtain the frame of the previous cell recursively; we propose to position our left edge a minimal spacing amount from the right edge of the previous cell. We do that by changing the `frame` of the UICollectionViewLayoutAttributes object. Then we return that object:

```
- (UICollectionViewLayoutAttributes *)layoutAttributesForItemAtIndexPath:
        (NSIndexPath *)indexPath {
    UICollectionViewLayoutAttributes* atts =
        [super layoutAttributesForItemAtIndexPath:indexPath];
    if (indexPath.item == 0)
        return atts;
    if (atts.frame.origin.x - 1 <= self.sectionInset.left)
        return atts;
    NSIndexPath* ipPrev =
        [NSIndexPath indexPathForItem:indexPath.item-1
                            inSection:indexPath.section];
    CGRect fPrev =
        [self layoutAttributesForItemAtIndexPath:ipPrev].frame;
    CGFloat rightPrev =
        fPrev.origin.x + fPrev.size.width + self.minimumInteritemSpacing;
    CGRect f = atts.frame;
    f.origin.x = rightPrev;
    atts.frame = f;
    return atts;
}
```

The other method, layoutAttributesForElementsInRect:, returns an NSArray of UICollectionViewLayoutAttributes objects for all the cells and supplementary views in a rect. Again we call super and modify the resulting array so that if an element is a cell, its UICollectionViewLayoutAttributes is the result of our layoutAttributesForItem-AtIndexPath::

```
- (NSArray *)layoutAttributesForElementsInRect:(CGRect)rect {
    NSArray* arr = [super layoutAttributesForElementsInRect:rect];
    for (UICollectionViewLayoutAttributes* atts in arr) {
        if (nil == atts.representedElementKind) { // it's a cell
            NSIndexPath* ip = atts.indexPath;
            atts.frame =
                [self layoutAttributesForItemAtIndexPath:ip].frame;
        }
    }
    return arr;
}
```

Apple supplies some further interesting examples of subclassing UICollectionView-FlowLayout. For instance, the LineLayout example (accompanying the WWDC 2012 videos) implements a single row of horizontally scrolling cells, where a cell grows as it approaches the center of the screen and shrinks as it moves away. To do this, it first of all overrides a UICollectionViewLayout method I didn't mention earlier, should-InvalidateLayoutForBoundsChange:; this causes layout to happen repeatedly while the collection view is scrolled. It then overrides layoutAttributesForElementsIn-Rect: to do the same sort of thing I did a moment ago: it calls super and then modifies, as needed, the transform3D property of the UICollectionViewLayoutAttributes for the onscreen cells.

(It also overrides another UICollectionViewLayout method I didn't mention, `target-ContentOffsetForProposedContentOffset:withScrollingVelocity:`, which is like UIScrollViewDelegate's `scrollViewWillEndDragging:withVelocity:targetContent-Offset:`. This is just a nice touch so that when the user scrolls, a cell always ends up exactly centered on the screen.)

You can also subclass UICollectionViewLayout itself. The WWDC 2012 videos demonstrate a UICollectionViewLayout subclass that arranges its cells in a circle; the WWDC 2013 videos demonstrate a UICollectionViewLayout subclass that piles its cells into a single stack in the center of the collection view, like a deck of cards seen from above.

A collection view layout can be powerful and complex, but getting started writing one from scratch is not difficult. To illustrate, I'll write a collection view layout that ignores sections and presents all cells as a simple grid of squares.

In my UICollectionViewLayout subclass, called MyLayout, the really big questions I need to answer are `collectionViewContentSize` and `layoutAttributesForElements-InRect:`. To answer them, I'll calculate the entire layout of my grid beforehand. The `prepareLayout` method is the perfect place to do this; it is called every time something about the collection view or its data changes. I'll calculate the grid of cells and express their positions as an array of UICollectionViewLayoutAttributes objects; I'll store that array in an instance variable `_atts`, and I'll store the size of the grid in an instance variable `_sz`:

```
-(void)prepareLayout {
    // how many items are there in total?
    int total = 0;
    NSInteger sections = [self.collectionView numberOfSections];
    for (int i = 0; i < sections; i++)
        total += [self.collectionView numberOfItemsInSection:i];
    // work out cell size based on bounds width
    CGSize sz = self.collectionView.bounds.size;
    CGFloat width = sz.width;
    int shortside = floor(width/50.0);
    CGFloat cellside = width/(float)shortside;
    // generate attributes for all cells
    int x = 0;
    int y = 0;
    NSMutableArray* atts = [NSMutableArray new];
    for (int i = 0; i < sections; i++) {
        int jj = [self.collectionView numberOfItemsInSection:i];
        for (int j = 0; j < jj; j++) {
            UICollectionViewLayoutAttributes* att =
                [UICollectionViewLayoutAttributes
                 layoutAttributesForCellWithIndexPath:
                 [NSIndexPath indexPathForItem:j
                                     inSection:i]];
            att.frame =
                CGRectMake(x*cellside,y*cellside,cellside,cellside);
```

```
            [atts addObject:att];
            x++;
            if (x >= shortside) {
                x = 0;
                y++;
            }
        }
    }
    self->_atts = atts;
    // generate overall grid size
    int fluff = (x == 0) ? 0 : 1;
    self->_sz = CGSizeMake(width, (y+fluff) * cellside);
}
```

collectionViewContentSize and layoutAttributesForElementsInRect: are obvious: I'll just return the _sz or _atts instance variable, respectively. I'm ignoring the
rect: parameter in layoutAttributesForElementsInRect:, as there is no efficiency
to be gained by limiting myself to it; I have the entire array of UICollectionView-
LayoutAttributes objects ready, so it is simplest and quickest to provide a pointer to it:

```
- (CGSize)collectionViewContentSize {
    return self->_sz;
}
- (NSArray *)layoutAttributesForElementsInRect:(CGRect)rect {
    return self->_atts;
}
```

layoutAttributesForItemAtIndexPath: is implemented by looking up the corresponding value in my _atts array:

```
- (UICollectionViewLayoutAttributes*)layoutAttributesForItemAtIndexPath:
        (NSIndexPath *)indexPath {
    for (UICollectionViewLayoutAttributes* att in self->_atts) {
        if ([att.indexPath isEqual:indexPath])
            return att;
    }
    return nil; // shouldn't happen
}
```

Finally, I implement shouldInvalidateLayoutForBoundsChange: to return YES, so
that if the interface is rotated, my prepareLayout will be called again to recalculate the
grid. There's a potential source of inefficiency here: the user scrolling the collection view
counts as a bounds change as well. Therefore I return NO unless the bounds width has
changed:

```
-(BOOL)shouldInvalidateLayoutForBoundsChange:(CGRect)newBounds {
    return newBounds.size.width != self->_sz.width;
}
```

Switching Layouts

An astonishing and delightful feature of a collection view is that its layout object can be swapped out on the fly. You can substitute one layout for another, by calling `set-CollectionViewLayout:animated:completion:`. The data hasn't changed, and the collection view can identify each element uniquely and persistently, so it responds by moving every element from its position according to the old layout to its position according to the new layout — and, if the `animated:` argument is YES, it does this with animation! Thus the elements are seen to rearrange themselves, as if by magic.

New in iOS 7, this animated change of layout can be driven interactively (in response, for example, to a user gesture; compare Chapter 6 on interactive transitions). You call `startInteractiveTransitionToCollectionViewLayout:completion:` on the collection view, and a special layout object is returned — a UICollectionViewTransitionLayout instance (or a subclass thereof; to make it a subclass, you need to have implemented `collectionView:transitionLayoutForOldLayout:newLayout:` in your collection view delegate). This transition layout is temporarily made the collection view's layout, and your job is then to keep it apprised of the transition's progress (through its `transitionProgress` property) and ultimately to call `finishInteractive-Transition` or `cancelInteractiveTransition` on the collection view.

Furthermore, also new in iOS 7, when one collection view controller is pushed on top of another in a navigation interface, the runtime will do exactly the same thing for you, as a custom view controller transition (again, compare Chapter 6). To arrange this, the first collection view controller's `useLayoutToLayoutNavigationTransitions` property must be NO and the second collection view controller's `useLayoutToLayoutNavigation-Transitions` property must be YES. The result is that when the second collection view controller is pushed onto the navigation controller, *the collection view remains in place*, and the layout specified by the second collection view controller is substituted for the collection view's existing layout, with animation.

The effect, as the second collection view controller is pushed onto the navigation stack, is conceptually rather unsettling. Although there are two collection view controllers, and although the second view controller has a view (the collection view), and its `view-DidLoad` and `viewWillAppear:` (as well as the first view controller's `viewWill-Disappear:`) are called as you would expect, the same collection view is also still the *first* view controller's view, and the collection view's data source and delegate are still the *first* view controller. Later, after the transition is complete, the collection view's delegate becomes the *second* view controller, but its data source is *still* the *first* view controller. I find this profoundly weird.

Collection Views and UIKit Dynamics

The UICollectionViewLayoutAttributes class adopts the UIDynamicItem protocol (see Chapter 4). Thus, collection view elements can be animated under UIKit dynamics. The world of the animator here is not a superview but the layout itself; instead of `initWith-ReferenceView:`, you'll create the UIDynamicAnimator with `initWithCollection-ViewLayout:`. The layout's `collectionViewContentSize` determines the bounds of this world. Convenience methods are provided so that your code can access an animated collection view item's layout attributes directly from the animator.

You'll need a custom collection view layout subclass, because otherwise you won't be able to see any animation. On every frame of its animation, the UIDynamicAnimator is going to change the layout attributes of some items, but the collection view is still going to draw those items in accordance with the layout's `layoutAttributesFor-ElementsInRect:`. The simplest solution is to override `layoutAttributesForElements-InRect:` so as to obtain those layout attributes from the UIDynamicAnimator. This cooperation will be easiest if the layout itself owns and configures the animator.

In this example, we're in the layout subclass, setting up the animation. The layout subclass has a property to hold the animator, as well as a BOOL property to signal when an animation is in progress:

```
UIDynamicAnimator* anim =
    [[UIDynamicAnimator alloc] initWithCollectionViewLayout:self];
self.animator = anim;
self.animating = YES;
// ... configure rest of animation ...
```

Our implementation of `layoutAttributesForElementsInRect:`, if we are animating, substitutes the layout attributes that come from the animator for those we would normally return; the technique I use here relies on the fact that the animator convenience methods `layoutAttributesForCellAtIndexPath:` and so forth return nil if the specified item is not being animated. In this particular example, both cells and supplementary items (headers and footers) can be animated, so the two cases have to be distinguished:

```
- (NSArray *)layoutAttributesForElementsInRect:(CGRect)rect {
    NSArray* arr = [super layoutAttributesForElementsInRect:rect];
    if (self.animating) {
        NSMutableArray* marr = [NSMutableArray new];
        for (UICollectionViewLayoutAttributes* atts in arr) {
            NSIndexPath* path = atts.indexPath;
            UICollectionViewLayoutAttributes* atts2 = nil;
            switch (atts.representedElementCategory) {
                case UICollectionElementCategoryCell: {
                    atts2 =
                        [self.animator
                            layoutAttributesForCellAtIndexPath:path];
                    break;
```

```
            }
            case UICollectionElementCategorySupplementaryView: {
                NSString* kind = atts.representedElementKind;
                atts2 =
                    [self.animator
                        layoutAttributesForSupplementaryViewOfKind:kind
                        atIndexPath:path];
                break;
            }
            default:
                break;
        }
        [marr addObject: (atts2 ? atts2 : atts)];
    }
    return marr;
}
return arr;
}
```

CHAPTER 9

Popovers and Split Views

Popovers and split views are forms of interface that exist only on the iPad.

A *popover* (managed by a UIPopoverController) is a sort of secondary window or dialog: it displays a view layered on top of the main interface. It is usually associated, through a sort of arrow, with a view in the main interface — usually the button that the user tapped to summon the popover. In iOS 7, the popover dims out the rest of the screen, like a presented view whose presentation mode is UIModalPresentationPageSheet or UIModalPresentationFormSheet (see Chapter 6). It might be effectively modal, preventing the user from working in the rest of the interface; alternatively, it might vanish if the user taps outside it.

A popover, in effect, superimposes a roughly iPhone-sized screen on top of the iPad screen, and is useful in part precisely because it brings to the larger iPad the smaller, more lightweight flavor of the iPhone. For example, in my LinkSame app, both the settings view (where the user configures the game) and the help view (which describes how to play the game) are popovers (Figure 9-1). On the iPhone, both these views would occupy the entire screen; for each, we'd need a way to navigate to it, and then the user would have to return to the main interface afterward. But with the larger iPad screen, neither view is large enough, or important enough, to occupy the entire screen exclusively; the user can summon them without leaving the main interface. As popovers, they are characterized as smaller, secondary views which the user summons temporarily and then dismisses.

A *split view* (managed by a UISplitViewController) is a combination of two views, the first having the width of an iPhone screen in portrait orientation. When the iPad is in landscape orientation, the two views appear side by side. When the iPad is in portrait orientation, there are two possibilities:

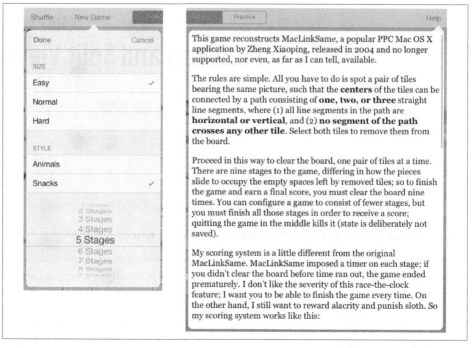

Figure 9-1. Two popovers

- Both views continue to appear side by side; the second view is narrower than it is in landscape orientation, because the screen is narrower. Apple's Settings app is an example.

- Only the second view appears, with an option to summon the first view by tapping a bar button item (or, optionally, by swiping to the right). When the first view is summoned in this way, it is a popover, although, since iOS 5.1, it hasn't looked like one — it has no arrow, its height is the full height of the screen, and it appears and disappears by sliding. Apple's Mail app is an example (Figure 9-2).

Like popovers, a split view may be regarded as an evolutionary link between the smaller iPhone interface and the larger iPad interface. On the iPhone, you might have a master–detail architecture in a navigation interface, where the master view is a table view, and the detail view is a completely different view pushed onto the navigation stack in place of the master view (Chapter 8). On the iPad, the large screen can accommodate the master view and the detail view *simultaneously*; the split view is a built-in way to do that. It is no coincidence that the Master–Detail Application template in Xcode generates a navigation interface for the iPhone and a split view for the iPad.

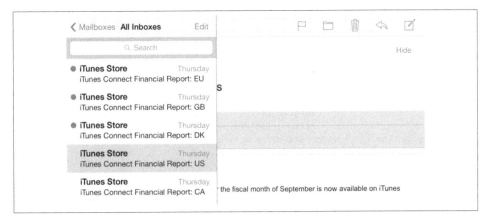

Figure 9-2. A familiar split view interface

Before iOS 5, UISplitViewController was the only legal way in which a single view controller could display the views of two child view controllers side by side. Nowadays, you are free to design your own custom parent view controllers (Chapter 6), so UISplit-ViewController is of diminished value. Nevertheless, it's built-in and easy to use.

Preparing a Popover

Before you can display a popover, you'll need a UIPopoverController, along with a view controller (UIViewController) whose view the popover will contain. UIPopover-Controller is *not* a UIViewController subclass! The view controller is the UIPopover-Controller's `contentViewController`. You'll set this property initially through UIPopoverController's designated initializer, `initWithContentViewController:`. Subsequently, if you like, you can swap out a popover controller's view controller (and hence its contained view) by calling `setContentViewController:animated:`.

Here's how the UIPopoverController for the first popover in Figure 9-1 gets its content. I have a UIViewController subclass, NewGameController. NewGameController's view contains a grouped table (whose code I showed you in Chapter 8) and a UIPickerView (see Chapter 12), and is itself the data source and delegate for both. I instantiate New-GameController and use this instance as the root view controller of a UINavigation-Controller, giving its `navigationItem` a Done `leftBarButtonItem` and a Cancel `right-BarButtonItem`. (I don't really intend to do any navigation, but the navigation controller's navigation bar is a convenient way of adding the two buttons to the interface.) The UINavigationController then becomes a UIPopoverController's view controller:

```
NewGameController* dlg = [NewGameController new];
UIBarButtonItem* b = [[UIBarButtonItem alloc]
    initWithBarButtonSystemItem: UIBarButtonSystemItemCancel
                        target: self
                        action: @selector(cancelNewGame:)];
dlg.navigationItem.rightBarButtonItem = b;
b = [[UIBarButtonItem alloc]
    initWithBarButtonSystemItem: UIBarButtonSystemItemDone
                        target: self
                        action: @selector(saveNewGame:)];
dlg.navigationItem.leftBarButtonItem = b;
UINavigationController* nav =
    [[UINavigationController alloc] initWithRootViewController:dlg];
UIPopoverController* pop =
    [[UIPopoverController alloc] initWithContentViewController:nav];
```

That code doesn't cause the popover to appear on the screen! I'll come to that in the next section. Observe also that I have done nothing as yet about *retaining* the UIPopoverController; if I fail to do that, it will vanish in a puff of smoke. I'll talk about that in the next section as well.

Popover Size

The popover controller also needs to know the size of the view it is to display, which will determine the size of the popover. You can provide the popover size in one of two ways:

UIPopoverController's `popoverContentSize` *property*
> This property can be set before the popover appears; it can also be changed while the popover is showing, with `setPopoverContentSize:animated:`.

UIViewController's `preferredContentSize` *property*
> The UIViewController in question is the UIPopoverController's `contentView-Controller` (or is contained by that view controller, as in a tab bar interface or navigation interface). This approach often makes more sense, because a UIView-Controller will generally know its own view's ideal size. If a view controller is to be instantiated from a nib, this value can be set in the Attributes inspector.

> (This property is new in iOS 7, and replaces the older `contentSizeForViewIn-Popover` property, which is now deprecated.)

The default popover size is {320,480} (the size of an original iPhone screen); the documentation suggests that a maximum width of 600 is permitted — the second popover in Figure 9-1 adopts this width — but in fact there doesn't seem to be any penalty for using a larger width. The popover's size is automatically restricted, however, based on the amount of screen space actually available, and your view may need to be prepared (through autoresizing or constraints) for the possibility that it won't be shown at the size you requested.

In the case of the first popover in Figure 9-1, the NewGameController sets its own `preferredContentSize` in `viewDidLoad`, based on the size of its main view as it comes from the nib:

```
self.preferredContentSize = self.view.bounds.size;
```

The popover itself, however, will need to be somewhat taller, because the NewGame-Controller is embedded in a UINavigationController, whose navigation bar occupies additional vertical space. Delightfully, the UINavigationController takes care of that automatically; its own `preferredContentSize` adds the necessary height.

If the UIPopoverController and the UIViewController have different settings for their respective content size properties at the time the popover is initially displayed, the UIPopoverController's setting wins. But once the popover is visible, if *either* property is changed (not merely set to the value it already has), the change is obeyed; if the UIViewController's `preferredContentSize` is changed, the UIPopoverController adopts that value as its `popoverContentSize` and the popover's size is adjusted accordingly (with animation).

If a popover's `contentViewController` is a UINavigationController, and a view controller is pushed onto or popped off of its stack, then if the new current view controller's `preferredContentSize` differs from that of the previously displayed view controller, my experiments suggest that the popover's *width* will change to match the new width, but the popover's *height* will change only if the new height is *taller*. This feels like a bug. A possible workaround is to implement the UINavigationController's delegate method `navigationController:didShowViewController:animated:`, so as to set the navigation controller's `preferredContentSize` explicitly:

```
- (void)navigationController:(UINavigationController *)navigationController
      didShowViewController:(UIViewController *)viewController
                  animated:(BOOL)animated {
    navigationController.preferredContentSize =
        viewController.preferredContentSize;
}
```

The result is still cosmetically disturbing, however, and it is probably better not to do that sort of thing in the first place.

Popover Appearance Customization

By default, a popover controller in iOS 7 takes charge of the background color of its view controller's view, including the navigation bar in a navigation interface. You can see this in Figure 9-1; the first popover, along with its navigation bar, has automatically adopted a somewhat transparent cream color that is apparently derived somehow from the color of what's behind it.

Figure 9-3. A very silly popover

If you don't want this automatic background color and transparency, you can set the popover controller's `backgroundColor` (new in iOS 7). You can change the navigation bar's color separately, and customize the position and appearance of the navigation bar's bar button items; see Chapter 12.

You can also customize the outside of the popover — that is, the "frame" surrounding the content, along with the arrow that points to the button that summoned it. To do so, you set the UIPopoverController's `popoverBackgroundViewClass` to your own subclass of UIPopoverBackgroundView (a UIView subclass) — at which point you can achieve just about anything you want, including the very silly popover shown in Figure 9-3.

Configuring your UIPopoverBackgroundView subclass is a bit tricky, because this single view is responsible for drawing both the arrow and the frame. Thus, in a complete and correct implementation, you'll have to draw differently depending on the arrow direction, which you can learn from the UIPopoverBackgroundView's `arrowDirection` property; it will be one of the following:

- `UIPopoverArrowDirectionUp`, `UIPopoverArrowDirectionDown`
- `UIPopoverArrowDirectionLeft`, `UIPopoverArrowDirectionRight`

I'll give a simplified example in which I cheat by assuming that (as in Figure 9-3) the arrow direction will be `UIPopoverArrowDirectionUp`. Drawing the frame is easy: here, I divide the view's overall rect into two areas, the arrow area on top (its height is a

#defined constant, `ARHEIGHT`) and the frame area on the bottom, and I draw the frame into the bottom area as a resizable image (Chapter 2):

```
UIImage* linOrig = [UIImage imageNamed: @"linen.png"];
CGFloat capw = linOrig.size.width / 2.0 - 1;
CGFloat caph = linOrig.size.height / 2.0 - 1;
UIImage* lin = [linOrig
    resizableImageWithCapInsets:UIEdgeInsetsMake(caph, capw, caph, capw)
                   resizingMode:UIImageResizingModeTile];
// ... draw arrow here ...
CGRect arrow;
CGRect body;
CGRectDivide(rect, &arrow, &body, ARHEIGHT, CGRectMinYEdge);
[lin drawInRect:body];
```

I omitted the drawing of the arrow; now let's insert it. The UIPopoverBackgroundView has `arrowHeight` and `arrowBase` class methods that you've overridden to describe the arrow dimensions to the runtime. (In my code, their values are provided by two #defined constants, `ARHEIGHT` and `ARBASE`; I've set them both to 20.) My arrow will consist simply of a texture-filled isosceles triangle, with an excess base consisting of a rectangle joining it to the frame. The UIPopoverBackgroundView also has an `arrow-Offset` property that the runtime has set to tell you where to draw the arrow: this offset measures the positive distance between the center of the view's edge and the center of the arrow. However, the runtime will have no hesitation in setting the `arrowOffset` all the way at the edge of the view, or even beyond its bounds (in which case it won't be drawn); to prevent this, I provide a maximum offset limit:

```
CGContextRef con = UIGraphicsGetCurrentContext();
CGContextSaveGState(con);
CGFloat proposedX = self.arrowOffset;
CGFloat limit = 22.0;
CGFloat maxX = rect.size.width/2.0 - limit;
if (proposedX > maxX)
    proposedX = maxX;
if (proposedX < limit)
    proposedX = limit;
CGContextTranslateCTM(con, rect.size.width/2.0 + proposedX - ARBASE/2.0, 0);
CGContextMoveToPoint(con, 0, ARHEIGHT);
CGContextAddLineToPoint(con, ARBASE / 2.0, 0);
CGContextAddLineToPoint(con, ARBASE, ARHEIGHT);
CGContextClosePath(con);
CGContextAddRect(con, CGRectMake(0,ARHEIGHT,ARBASE,15));
CGContextClip(con);
[lin drawAtPoint:CGPointMake(-40,-40)];
CGContextRestoreGState(con);
```

The thickness of the four sides of the frame is dictated by implementing the `content-ViewInsets` class method.

Summoning and Dismissing a Popover

A popover is made to appear onscreen by sending a UIPopoverController one of the following messages (and the UIPopoverController's `popoverVisible` property then becomes YES):

- `presentPopoverFromRect:inView:permittedArrowDirections:animated:`

- `presentPopoverFromBarButtonItem:permittedArrowDirections:animated:`

The difference between the two methods lies in how you specify the region to which the popover's arrow will point. With the first method, you can provide any CGRect with respect to any visible UIView's coordinate system; for example, to make the popover emanate from a UIButton, you could provide the UIButton's frame with respect to its superview, or (better) the UIButton's bounds with respect to itself. But you can't do that with a UIBarButtonItem, because a UIBarButtonItem isn't a UIView and doesn't have a frame or bounds; hence the second method is provided.

The permitted arrow directions restrict which sides of the popover the arrow can appear on. It's a bitmask, and your choices are:

- `UIPopoverArrowDirectionUp`, `UIPopoverArrowDirectionDown`

- `UIPopoverArrowDirectionLeft`, `UIPopoverArrowDirectionRight`

- `UIPopoverArrowDirectionAny`

Usually, you'd specify `UIPopoverArrowDirectionAny`, allowing the runtime to put the arrow on whatever side it feels is appropriate.

Even if you specify a particular arrow direction, you still have no precise control over a popover's location. However, you do get some veto power: set the UIPopoverController's `popoverLayoutMargins` beforehand to a UIEdgeInsets stating the margins, with respect to the root view bounds, within which the popover must appear. If the inset that you give is so large that the arrow can no longer touch the presenting rect, it may be ignored, or the arrow may become disconnected from its presenting rect; you probably shouldn't do that.

Popover Segues

If you're using a storyboard, you can draw (Control-drag) a segue from the button that is to summon the popover to the view controller that is to be the UIPopoverController's `contentViewController` and specify "popover" as the segue type. The result is a *popover segue*.

A popover segue, when it is triggered, will be an instance of UIStoryboardPopoverSegue. This is a subclass of UIStoryboardSegue, and it has a `popoverController` property. The segue, as it is triggered, creates the UIPopoverController for you, and initializes it with the `contentViewController` you specified by drawing the segue in the first place. You can then retrieve this UIPopoverController as the segue's `popoverController` in your implementation of `prepareForSegue:sender:`. The triggered segue also presents the popover for you, calling the version of `presentPopover...` appropriate to the type of object at the source of the segue (a normal button or a bar button item).

I must warn you that I do *not* recommend creation of a popover controller using this approach. If you prefer using a storyboard rather a *.xib* file, you can certainly configure the view controller in a storyboard, but then I recommend that you instantiate it as needed by calling `instantiateViewControllerWithIdentifier:`. In any case, I suggest that you create and configure the popover controller, and summon the popover itself, entirely in code, avoiding popover segues; they are simple, but they can easily become more trouble than they are worth, and for any serious use they won't represent any savings over popover creation in code.

Managing a Popover Controller

Unlike a presented view controller or a child view controller, a UIPopoverController instance that you create in code is not automatically retained for you by some presenting view controller or parent view controller just because you have displayed its popover. You must retain it yourself. If you fail to do so, then if the UIPopoverController goes out of existence while its popover is on the screen, your app will crash (with a helpful message: "-[UIPopoverController dealloc] reached while popover is still visible").

In any case, you might need the retained reference to the UIPopoverController later, when the time comes to dismiss the popover. Indeed, the entire question of how you want and expect this popover to be dismissed can require some careful planning, as I'll explain further in a moment. There are actually *two* ways in which a popover can be dismissed:

The user can tap outside the popover
> The user will have a natural expectation of being able to do this. As I'll explain, however, you can configure exactly *where* a tap outside the popover will have the effect of dismissing it.

You can explicitly dismiss the popover, in code
> In order to dismiss the popover explicitly, you send its UIPopoverController the `dismissPopoverAnimated:` message. (That's what I do with the first popover in Figure 9-1 when the user taps the Done button or the Cancel button.) Obviously, then, you need a reference to the UIPopoverController!

Even if a popover is *normally* dismissed automatically by the user tapping outside it, you *still* might want to dismiss it explicitly *sometimes* — so you still might need a reference to the popover controller.

A UIPopoverController that is created automatically by triggering a UIStoryboard-PopoverSegue, on the other hand, does not have to be retained by your code; the segue, which is itself retained by the runtime, retains the popover controller. Nevertheless, as I've just said, you still might need a reference to the popover controller, in order to dismiss it later.

The obvious solution is an instance variable or property with a strong (retain) policy. In the case where you create the popover controller explicitly, you should immediately assign it to such a property, so that it will persist as long as the popover is showing. In the case where the popover controller is created for you by a segue, you should implement `prepareForSegue:sender:` to grab a reference to the segue's `popoverController` and assign it to the property.

If, over the lifetime of the app, we're going to be displaying more than one popover, how many UIPopoverController properties do we need? In my view, one is enough. A well-behaved app, in accordance with Apple's interface guidelines, is never going to display more than one popover *simultaneously*. Thus, this one property can be handed a reference to the current popover controller each time we present a popover; using that reference, we will be able later to dismiss the current popover. In fact, I usually call this property something like `currentPop`.

Dismissing a Popover

In my earlier discussion of preparing a popover, I omitted one of the most important aspects of popover configuration — whether, and to what extent, the user is to be permitted to operate outside the popover without automatically dismissing it. Two properties are involved in determining this:

UIPopoverController's `passthroughViews` *property*
  This is an array of views in the interface behind the popover; the user can interact normally with these views while the popover is showing, and the popover will not be dismissed. What happens if the user taps a view that is *not* listed in the `passthroughViews` array depends on the `modalInPopover` property.

UIViewController's `modalInPopover` *property*
  If this is YES for the popover controller's view controller (or for its current child view controller, as in a tab bar interface or navigation interface), then if the user taps outside the popover on a view *not* listed in the popover controller's `passthroughViews`, nothing at all happens (the popover is *not* dismissed).

  If it is NO (the default), then if the user taps outside the popover on a view *not* listed in the popover controller's `passthroughViews`, the view tapped on is unaffected, and the popover *is* dismissed.

The claim made by the documentation (and by some earlier editions of this book), that modalInPopover prevents *all* user interaction outside a popover, is wrong. The user can still interact with a view listed in the passthroughViews, even if modalInPopover is YES.

You should give attention to your popover controller's passthroughViews, as the default behavior may be undesirable. In particular, if a popover is summoned by the user tapping a UIBarButton item in a toolbar using presentPopoverFromBarButtonItem:..., the *entire toolbar* is a passthrough view. This means that the user can tap any button in the toolbar — including the button that summoned the popover in the first place! The user can thus by default summon *another copy of the same popover* while this popover is already showing, which is certainly not what you want. I like to set the passthrough-Views to nil; at the very least, while the popover is showing, you should probably disable the UIBarButtonItem that summoned it.

Getting the timing right on setting a UIPopoverController's passthroughViews is not easy. It might not have any effect unless the UIPopoverController has *already* been sent presentPopover.... This is one of the reasons I dislike popover segues; you don't get an event after the segue presents the popover, so there's no good moment to set the passthroughViews to nil — and, although you can set the passthroughViews in the nib editor, you can't set them to nil there.

We are now ready for a rigorous specification of the two ways in which a popover can be dismissed:

- The popover controller's view controller's modalInPopover is NO, and the user taps outside the popover on a view not listed in the popover controller's passthrough-Views.

  The UIPopoverController's delegate (adopting the UIPopoverControllerDelegate protocol) is sent popoverControllerShouldDismissPopover:; if it doesn't return NO (which might be because it doesn't implement this method), the popover is dismissed, and the delegate is sent popoverControllerDidDismissPopover:.

- The UIPopoverController is sent dismissPopoverAnimated: by your code; the delegate methods are *not* sent in that case.

  If you're using a popover segue, an unwind segue (see Chapter 6) in the popover segue's destination view controller will, when triggered, send dismissPopover-Animated: to the popover controller for you.

Because a popover can be dismissed in two different ways, if you have a cleanup task to perform as the popover vanishes, you may have to see to it that the task is performed under two different circumstances. This can get tricky.

To illustrate, I'll describe what actually happens in my LinkSame app when the first popover in Figure 9-1 is dismissed. Within this popover, the user is interacting with several settings in the user defaults. But if the user taps Cancel, or if the user taps outside the popover (which I take to be equivalent to canceling), I want to revert those defaults to the way they were before the popover was summoned. Therefore, as I initially present the popover, I preserve the relevant current user defaults through a property:

```
// save defaults so we can restore them later if user cancels
self.oldDefs =
    [[NSUserDefaults standardUserDefaults]
        dictionaryWithValuesForKeys: @[@"Style", @"Size", @"Stages"]];
```

The user now works within the popover. Any settings that the user changes within the popover are immediately saved into the user defaults. So, if the user then taps Done, the user's settings within the popover have *already* been saved; I explicitly dismiss the popover and proceed to initiate the new game that the user has asked for:

```
- (void) saveNewGame: (id) sender { // done button in New Game popover
    [self.currentPop dismissPopoverAnimated:YES];
    self.currentPop = nil;
    // ... set up new game interface, initialize scores, etc. ...
}
```

On the other hand, if the user taps Cancel, I must revert the user defaults as I dismiss the popover:

```
- (void) cancelNewGame: (id) sender { // cancel button in New Game popover
    [self.currentPop dismissPopoverAnimated:YES];
    self.currentPop = nil;
    [[NSUserDefaults standardUserDefaults]
        setValuesForKeysWithDictionary:self.oldDefs];
}
```

So far, so good. But we have not yet covered every case. What if the user taps outside the popover to dismiss it? I take that to mean Cancel (the user did not tap Done, after all). Therefore I implement the delegate method to detect this, and I revert the user defaults here as well:

```
- (void)popoverControllerDidDismissPopover:(UIPopoverController *)pc {
    [[NSUserDefaults standardUserDefaults]
        setValuesForKeysWithDictionary:self.oldDefs];
    self.currentPop = nil;
}
```

But wait — there's more. My app has *another* popover (the second popover in Figure 9-1). This popover, too, can be dismissed by the user tapping outside it; in fact, that's the only way the user can dismiss it. The popover controllers for both popovers have the *same delegate*. Thus, when the second popover is dismissed, the same popover-ControllerDidDismissPopover: implementation will be called. But now we *don't* want to call `setValuesForKeysWithDictionary:`; it's the *wrong popover*, and we have no preserved defaults to revert.

Fortunately, the popover controller whose popover was dismissed is passed in as the parameter to `popoverControllerDidDismissPopover:`. Unfortunately, it's a bit hard to see what there is about different popover controllers that distinguishes them from one another! You can't assign a popover controller a name or other identifier (unless you subclass UIPopoverController). Luckily, my popover controllers have different types of content view controller, but this problem is by no means always so easy to solve:

```
- (void)popoverControllerDidDismissPopover:(UIPopoverController *)pc {
    if ([pc.contentViewController isKindOfClass:
            [UINavigationController class]])
        [[NSUserDefaults standardUserDefaults]
            setValuesForKeysWithDictionary:self.oldDefs];
    self.currentPop = nil;
}
```

Popovers During Rotation or Backgrounding

A question arises of what should happen to a displayed popover when the app is rotated, or goes into the background. If your app's popovers behave properly through rotation or backgrounding, there may be nothing to do. On the other hand, if a popover doesn't correctly recover automatically after rotation or backgrounding, it might be better to dismiss it, giving the user the option to summon it again. You can respond to rotation by implementing `willRotateToInterfaceOrientation:duration:` (see Chapter 6), and you can hear about backgrounding by registering for `UIApplicationDidEnter-BackgroundNotification` (see Appendix A).

Continuing from the preceding example, I'll dismiss my popovers on rotation and backgrounding. In the example, this kind of dismissal should count as canceling the user's actions within the popover, so I must perform the same tests as in `popover-ControllerDidDismissPopover:`, restoring the user defaults if this popover is the one for which the defaults were saved beforehand:

```
-(void)willRotateToInterfaceOrientation:(UIInterfaceOrientation)io
        duration:(NSTimeInterval)duration {
    UIPopoverController* pc = self.currentPop;
    if (pc) {
        if ([pc.contentViewController isKindOfClass:
                [UINavigationController class]])
            [[NSUserDefaults standardUserDefaults]
                setValuesForKeysWithDictionary:self.oldDefs];
        [pc dismissPopoverAnimated:NO];
        self.currentPop = nil;
    }
}
-(void)backgrounding:(NSNotification*)n {
```

```
        UIPopoverController* pc = self.currentPop;
        if (pc) {
            if ([pc.contentViewController isKindOfClass:
                    [UINavigationController class]])
                [[NSUserDefaults standardUserDefaults]
                    setValuesForKeysWithDictionary:self.oldDefs];
            [pc dismissPopoverAnimated:NO];
            self.currentPop = nil;
        }
    }
```

Another reason for dismissing a popover manually on rotation is that the rotation may result in the interface changing in such a way that the presence of the popover will no longer make sense. For example, the button that the user tapped to summon the popover may no longer be present after rotation.

If your popover was presented originally by calling `presentPopoverFromRect:in-View:...`, a new iOS 7 UIPopoverController delegate method allows you to respond to rotation by presenting the popover attached to a different view, or a different rectangle:

- `popoverController:willRepositionPopoverToRect:inView:`

In that method, the `rect:` is typed as a pointer to a CGRect, and the `view:` is typed as a pointer to a pointer to a UIView. Thus you can set either or both of them by indirection; in effect, you are being given the chance to do all over again what you did in `present-PopoverFromRect:inView:...`. For example:

```
-(void)popoverController:(UIPopoverController *)popoverController
        willRepositionPopoverToRect:(inout CGRect *)rect
        inView:(inout UIView *__autoreleasing *)view {
    if (*view == self.button1) {
        *rect = self.button2.bounds;
        *view = self.button2;
    }
}
```

Popovers and Presented Views

A popover can present a view controller internally; you'll specify a `modalPresentation-Style` of `UIModalPresentationCurrentContext`, because otherwise the presented view will be fullscreen by default (see Chapter 6). You'll also specify a transition style of `UIModalTransitionStyleCoverVertical` — with any other transition style, your app will crash with this message: "Application tried to present inside popover with transition style other than UIModalTransitionStyleCoverVertical."

The presented view controller's `modalInPopover` is automatically set to YES. (You can subvert this by setting the presented view controller's `modalInPopover` to NO *after* it is presented, but you probably shouldn't.)

If a presented view inside a popover proves troublesome — I've encountered some bugs connected with this arrangement — I suggest trying an alternative interface, such as replacing the popover controller's content view controller with a different view controller.

Automatic Popovers

In a few situations, the framework will automatically create and display a popover for you. One such situation is what happens when a search bar (a UISearchBar) tied to a search display controller (UISearchDisplayController) appears in a toolbar (UIToolbar) on the iPad.

Recall the search display controller example from Chapter 8, where we search a list of the 50 United States; I'll modify that example to demonstrate. Bear in mind that in *this* example there is no illusion of a searchable table; there's just a search bar which presents its *results* in a table (in a popover).

In the nib editor, start with a toolbar at the top of the root view, and drag into it the combined Search Bar and Search Display Controller object from the Object library. This causes a whole bunch of outlets to be configured automatically:

- The search bar's delegate is the nib owner. (The nib owner in a storyboard is the view controller for this scene; in a *.xib* file, it's the File's Owner proxy object.)
- The nib owner's `searchDisplayController` is the search display controller. When a UISearchDisplayController is instantiated from a nib, this property is an outlet that *retains the search display controller*, as well as providing access to it in code.
- The search display controller's search bar is the search bar.
- The search display controller's delegate, `searchContentsController`, `search-ResultsDataSource`, and `searchResultsDelegate` are the nib owner. Of these, only the latter two appear to be of importance in this example.

Now for the code. When our view controller loads its view, we also load the model (the list of states) into an NSArray property called `states`. We also have an NSArray property called `filteredStates`. Here is the code for dealing with the search bar and the search display controller's results table:

```
-(void)searchDisplayController:(UISearchDisplayController *)controller
        didLoadSearchResultsTableView:(UITableView *)tableView {
    [tableView registerClass:[UITableViewCell class]
        forCellReuseIdentifier:@"cell"];
}
- (NSInteger)numberOfSectionsInTableView:(UITableView *)tableView {
    return 1;
}
- (NSInteger)tableView:(UITableView *)tableView
```

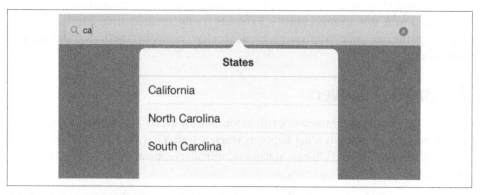

Figure 9-4. An automatically created search results popover

```
          numberOfRowsInSection:(NSInteger)section {
      return [self.filteredStates count];
}
- (UITableViewCell *)tableView:(UITableView *)tableView
        cellForRowAtIndexPath:(NSIndexPath *)indexPath {
      UITableViewCell *cell =
        [tableView dequeueReusableCellWithIdentifier:@"cell"
                                      forIndexPath:indexPath];
      cell.textLabel.text = self.filteredStates[indexPath.row];
      return cell;
}
- (void) filterData {
    NSString* target = self.searchDisplayController.searchBar.text;
    NSPredicate* p =
        [NSPredicate predicateWithBlock: ^(id obj, NSDictionary *d) {
            NSString* s = obj;
            NSStringCompareOptions options = NSCaseInsensitiveSearch;
            BOOL b =
                [s rangeOfString:target options:options].location
                    != NSNotFound;
            return b;
        }];
    self.filteredStates = [states filteredArrayUsingPredicate:p];
}
- (void)searchBar:(UISearchBar *)searchBar
        textDidChange:(NSString *)searchText {
    [self filterData];
}
```

That's all. There is no mention anywhere of a UIPopoverController; nevertheless, when the user enters text in the search bar, a popover appears, containing a table of search results (Figure 9-4)!

Although that's very easy, I am not fond of this automatic way of creating a popover, and I'm sure you can guess why: when things are so automatic, the programmer has great difficulty getting control of anything. For example, there's no reference to the popover controller, so how is your code supposed to dismiss the popover? The best way I've found, which is not very satisfactory, is to set the search display controller's `active` to NO:

```
-(void)tableView:(UITableView *)tableView
        didSelectRowAtIndexPath:(NSIndexPath *)indexPath {
    NSLog(@"You selected %@", self.filteredStates[indexPath.row]);
    [self.searchDisplayController setActive:NO animated:YES];
}
```

There is also a weird cosmetic bug where the search result's table content inset is automatically set incorrectly. I work around that by setting its `contentInset` (and `scroll-IndicatorInsets`) when the table is about to appear. I also take advantage of this moment to set the UISearchDisplayController's `searchResultsTitle` property, so that the popover doesn't say "Results" at the top; alternatively, it's possible to do that in the nib editor:

```
-(void)searchDisplayController:(UISearchDisplayController *)controller
        willShowSearchResultsTableView:(UITableView *)tableView {
    [tableView setContentInset:UIEdgeInsetsZero]; // work around weird bug
    [tableView setScrollIndicatorInsets:UIEdgeInsetsZero];
    controller.searchResultsTitle = @"States";
}
```

In general, I find the behavior of this automatic popover very peculiar and difficult to customize, and I suggest you avoid it. Another example of an automatic popover on the iPad is the alert sheet, discussed in Chapter 13.

Split Views

A split view (Figure 9-2) is implemented through a UISplitViewController (a UIViewController subclass) whose children are the two UIViewControllers whose views are to be displayed in the two regions of the split view. You provide the children through the UISplitViewController's `viewControllers` property (an NSArray); it can be configured in code or in a nib. A UIViewController that is a child, at any depth, of a UISplitViewController has a reference to the UISplitViewController through its `splitViewController` property.

Using a Split View

There is very little work for you to do with regard to a split view controller. You can hear about what the split view controller is doing through its delegate (adopting the UISplitViewControllerDelegate protocol), which receives these messages:

`splitViewController:willHideViewController:withBarButtonItem:forPopover-Controller:`

> The split view is rotating to portrait orientation, so it's hiding the first view. The split view controller creates a UIBarButtonItem and hands it to you as the third parameter. The split view controller has already set things up so that if the user taps this bar button item, a popover will be presented through the popover controller (fourth parameter) displaying the view of the first view controller (second parameter). Your mission, should you decide to accept it, is to put that bar button item into the interface. You are free to configure the bar button item's appearance as you do so.
>
> It's common practice to keep a reference to the popover controller, in case you need it in order to dismiss the popover later (but don't set its delegate).
>
> If an app with a split view interface launches into portrait orientation, this delegate method is called.

`splitViewController:popoverController:willPresentViewController:`

> The user has tapped the bar button item you were handed in the first delegate method, and the popover is about to appear. You probably won't need to implement this method.

`splitViewController:willShowViewController:invalidatingBarButtonItem:`

> This is the opposite of the first delegate method: the split view is rotating to landscape orientation, so the split view controller going to break the connection between the bar button item and the popover controller and is going to put the first view back into the interface. You should remove the bar button item from the interface.

How you get the bar button item into and out of your interface depends on the nature your interface. The current version of the iPad Master–Detail Application project template, which demonstrates a split view interface, uses a navigation interface in order to get the navigation bar. As a result, the DetailViewController instance, functioning as the UISplitViewController's delegate, gets the bar button item into and out of the interface by setting its own `navigationItem.leftBarButtonItem`:

```
- (void)splitViewController:(UISplitViewController *)splitController
      willHideViewController:(UIViewController *)viewController
           withBarButtonItem:(UIBarButtonItem *)barButtonItem
         forPopoverController:(UIPopoverController *)popoverController
{
    [self.navigationItem setLeftBarButtonItem:barButtonItem animated:YES];
    self.masterPopoverController = popoverController;
}
- (void)splitViewController:(UISplitViewController *)splitController
      willShowViewController:(UIViewController *)viewController
   invalidatingBarButtonItem:(UIBarButtonItem *)barButtonItem
```

```
{
    [self.navigationItem setLeftBarButtonItem:nil animated:YES];
    self.masterPopoverController = nil;
}
```

In addition, you might want to set the bar button item's `title` in `willHide...`; by default, it will be the first view controller's `title`.

Split Views in a Storyboard

In a storyboard, the split view controller is hooked to its child view controllers by relationships; those child view controllers are navigation controllers, and are themselves hooked to their root view controllers by relationships in the storyboard as well. Thus, five view controllers are instantiated together, automatically, as the split view interface loads.

Some things, however, can't be configured in the storyboard. For example, there needs to be a delegate relationship between the UISplitViewController and the DetailViewController; they are both in the storyboard together, but they're in different scenes, so no outlet can be drawn between them. To solve this, the Master–Detail Application template includes the following code in the app delegate's `application:didFinish-LaunchingWithOptions:`:

```
UISplitViewController *splitViewController =
    (UISplitViewController *)self.window.rootViewController;
UINavigationController *navigationController =
    [splitViewController.viewControllers lastObject];
splitViewController.delegate = (id)navigationController.topViewController;
```

By the time that code runs, the window's `rootViewController` has been set and all the view controllers are in place, in their various parent–child relationships; the code is thus able to work its way through the parent–child hierarchy to get references to the two desired view controllers and can make the one the delegate of the other.

Similarly, the first child view controller will probably need a reference to the second child view controller. In the Master–Detail Application template, the MasterViewController works out its reference to the DetailViewController in its `viewDidLoad`:

```
self.detailViewController =
    (DetailViewController*)
        [[self.splitViewController.viewControllers lastObject]
            topViewController];
```

The storyboard editor also lets you create a "replace" segue for use in connection with a split view. This allows either of the split view controller's child view controllers to be swapped out. A typical use is that the user taps something in the left (master) view controller to cause the right (detail) view controller to be replaced by a different view controller. To set that up, you'd create a replace segue leading from the tapped thing in the master view controller to the new view controller; then, in the segue's Attributes inspector, set the Destination pop-up menu to Detail Split.

Other Split View Configurations

If the UISplitViewController's `presentsWithGesture` is YES, the second view in portrait orientation will detect a rightward swipe and will respond by summoning the first view (the popover). Otherwise, the bar button item will be the only way to summon the popover in portrait orientation.

It is also possible for a split view interface *not* to hide the first view in portrait orientation. Instead, the left and right view both appear in both orientations; the left view's width is unchanged, while the right view is resized appropriately (as in Apple's Settings app). To get that behavior, implement this delegate method:

`splitViewController:shouldHideViewController:inOrientation:`
> Allows the left view controller to be hidden (return YES) or not (return NO) as the interface rotates to the given orientation. If you return NO, the other delegate methods won't be called in this orientation; there will be no bar button item and no popover.

New in iOS 7, a split view controller's delegate gets a say in how the app is permitted to rotate:

- `splitViewControllerSupportedInterfaceOrientations:`
- `splitViewControllerPreferredInterfaceOrientationForPresentation:`

Thus, as with a navigation controller or tab bar controller, it isn't necessary to subclass UISplitViewController just in order to control app rotation (see Chapter 6).

On the other hand, there are no parallel delegate messages for configuring the status bar, and a split view controller doesn't consult its children on the matter, so if you want your split view to affect the status bar (for example, by hiding it), you *will* need to subclass UISplitViewController.

Finally, there's a rather confusing issue when a non-fullscreen presented view controller (such as a `UIModalPresentationFormSheet` view controller) appearing in front of a split view is to be dismissed through an unwind segue. The symptom is that when the unwind method is called, the presented view isn't dismissed. The solution is, again, to subclass UISplitViewController and put the unwind method in the subclass.

CHAPTER 10

Text

Drawing text into your app's interface is one of the most complex and powerful things that iOS does for you. Fortunately, iOS also shields you from as much of that complexity as you like. All you need is some text to draw, and possibly an interface object to draw it for you.

Text to appear in your app's interface will be an NSString or an NSAttributedString. NSAttributedString adds text styling to an NSString, including runs of different character styles, along with paragraph-level features such as alignment, line spacing, and margins.

To make your NSString or NSAttributedString appear in the interface, you can draw it into a graphics context, or hand it to an interface object that knows how to draw it:

Self-drawing text
> Both NSString and NSAttributedString have methods (supplied by the NSString-Drawing category) for drawing themselves into any graphics context.

Text-drawing interface objects
> Interface objects that know how to draw an NSString or NSAttributedString are:

> *UILabel*
>> Displays text, possibly consisting of multiple lines; neither scrollable nor editable.

> *UITextField*
>> Displays a single line of user-editable text; may have a border, a background image, and overlay views at its right and left end.

> *UITextView*
>> Displays scrollable multiline text, possibly user-editable.

(Another way of drawing text is to use a UIWebView, a scrollable view displaying rendered HTML. UIWebView can also display various additional document types, such as PDF, RTF, and *.doc*. UIWebViews are a somewhat different technology, and are discussed in Chapter 11.)

Deep under the hood, all text drawing is performed through a low-level technology with a C API called Core Text. Before iOS 7, certain powerful and useful text-drawing features were available *only* by working with Core Text.

New in iOS 7, however, is Text Kit, a middle-level technology with an Objective-C API, lying on top of Core Text. UITextView in iOS 7 is largely just a lightweight drawing wrapper around Text Kit, and Text Kit can also draw directly into a graphics context. By working with Text Kit, you can readily do all sorts of useful text-drawing tricks that previously would have required you to sweat your way through Core Text.

Fonts

There are two ways of describing a font: as a UIFont (suitable for use in an NSString or a UIKit interface object) or as a CTFont (suitable for Core Text). Using CTFont, it is fairly easy to perform various convenient font transformations, such as deriving one font from another through the addition of a symbolic trait; for example, you could say, "Here's a font; please give me a bold version of it if there is one."

Before iOS 7, CTFont and UIFont were unfortunately *not* toll-free bridged to one another, and what you usually started with and wanted to end with was a UIFont; thus, in order to perform font transformations, it was necessary to convert a UIFont to a CTFont manually, work with the CTFont, and then convert back to a UIFont manually — which was by no means trivial.

In iOS 7, however, UIFont and CTFont *are* toll-free bridged to one another. Moreover, another important Core Text type, CTFontDescriptorRef, is toll-free bridged to a new iOS 7 class, UIFontDescriptor, which can be helpful for performing font transformations.

Fonts and Dynamic Type

A font (UIFont, toll-free bridged in iOS 7 to Core Text's CTFontRef) is an extremely simple object. You specify a font by its name and size by calling the UIFont class method `fontWithName:size:`, and you can also transform a font of one size to the same font in a different size. UIFont also provides some methods for learning a font's various measurements, such as its `lineHeight` and `capHeight`.

In order to ask for a font, you have to know the font's name. Every font variant (bold, italic, and so on) counts as a different font, and font variants are clumped into families. To learn, in the console, the name of every installed font, you would say:

```
for (NSString* s in [UIFont familyNames])
    NSLog(@"%@: %@", s, [UIFont fontNamesForFamilyName:s]);
```

You can specify a font by its family name or by its font name (technically, its PostScript name). For example, @"Avenir" is a family name; the plain font within that family is @"Avenir-Roman". Either is legal as the first argument of fontWithName:size:.

A few fonts can be obtained with reference to their functionality; for example, you can ask for systemFontOfSize: to get the font used by default in a UIButton. You should never use the name of such a font for anything, however, as the details are private and subject to change.

New in iOS 7 is a set of fonts that you specify by their intended usage rather than by name. These are the so-called Dynamic Type fonts. They are linked to the slider that the user can adjust in the Settings app, under General → Text Size. The idea is that if you have text for the user to read or edit (as opposed, say, to the static text of a button), you can use a Dynamic Type font; it will be sized and styled for you in accordance with the user's Text Size preference and the role that this text is to play in your layout.

To obtain a Dynamic Type font, call preferredFontForTextStyle:. Possible roles that you can supply as the argument are:

- UIFontTextStyleHeadline
- UIFontTextStyleSubheadline
- UIFontTextStyleBody
- UIFontTextStyleFootnote
- UIFontTextStyleCaption1
- UIFontTextStyleCaption2

You'll probably want to experiment with specifying various roles for your individual pieces of text, to see which looks appropriate in context. For example, in Figure 6-1, the headlines are UIFontTextStyleSubheadline and the blurbs are UIFontTextStyle-Caption1.

Dynamic Type fonts are not actually dynamic; preferredFontForTextStyle: will return a font whose size is proportional to the user's Text Size preference only at the moment when it is called. If the user changes that preference, you'll need to call preferredFontForTextStyle: again. To hear about such changes, register for UIContentSizeCategoryDidChangeNotification. When the notification arrives, you will need to set the fonts for your Dynamic Type–savvy text all over again. This, in turn, may have consequences for the physical features of your interface as a whole; autolayout can be a big help here (Chapter 1).

In this example, we have a label (`self.lab`) whose font uses Dynamic Type; we set its font both when the label first appears in the interface and subsequently whenever `UIContentSizeCategoryDidChangeNotification` arrives:

```
- (void)viewDidLoad {
    [super viewDidLoad];
    [self doDynamicType:nil];
    [[NSNotificationCenter defaultCenter] addObserver:self
        selector:@selector(doDynamicType:)
        name:UIContentSizeCategoryDidChangeNotification
        object:nil];
}
- (void) doDynamicType: (NSNotification*) n {
    self.lab.font = [UIFont preferredFontForTextStyle:UIFontTextStyleBody];
}
```

In the nib editor, wherever the Attributes inspector lets you supply a font for an interface object, the Dynamic Type roles are available in a pop-up menu. But you will *still* have to set the font of every such interface object again, in code, when `UIContentSizeCategoryDidChangeNotification` arrives.

You are not limited to fonts installed by default as part of iOS 7. There are two other ways to obtain additional fonts:

Include a font in your app bundle
A font included at the top level of your app bundle will be loaded at launch time if your *Info.plist* lists it under the "Fonts provided by application" key (`UIAppFonts`).

Download a font in real time
All OS X fonts are available for download from Apple's servers; you can obtain and install one while your app is running.

To download a font in real time, you'll have specify the font as a font descriptor (discussed in the next section) and drop down to the level of Core Text (`@import Core-Text`) to call `CTFontDescriptorMatchFontDescriptorsWithProgressHandler`. This function takes a block which is called repeatedly at every stage of the download process; the block is called on a background thread, so if you want to use the downloaded font immediately in the interface, you must step out to the main thread (see Chapter 25).

In this example, I'll attempt to use Lucida Grande as my UILabel's font; if it isn't installed, I'll attempt to download it and *then* use it as my UILabel's font. I've inserted a lot of unnecessary logging to mark the stages of the download process:

```
NSString* name = @"LucidaGrande";
CGFloat size = 12;
UIFont* f = [UIFont fontWithName:name size:size];
if (f) {
    self.lab.font = f;
    NSLog(@"%@", @"already installed");
    return;
```

```
    }
    NSLog(@"%@", @"attempting to download font");
    UIFontDescriptor* desc =
        [UIFontDescriptor fontDescriptorWithName:name size:size];
    CTFontDescriptorMatchFontDescriptorsWithProgressHandler(
        (__bridge CFArrayRef)@[desc], nil,
        ^(CTFontDescriptorMatchingState state, CFDictionaryRef prog) {
        if (state == kCTFontDescriptorMatchingDidBegin) {
            NSLog(@"%@", @"matching did begin");
        }
        else if (state == kCTFontDescriptorMatchingWillBeginDownloading) {
            NSLog(@"%@", @"downloading will begin");
        }
        else if (state == kCTFontDescriptorMatchingDownloading) {
            NSDictionary* d = (__bridge NSDictionary*)prog;
            NSLog(@"progress: %@%%",
                d[(__bridge NSString*)kCTFontDescriptorMatchingPercentage]);
        }
        else if (state == kCTFontDescriptorMatchingDidFinishDownloading) {
            NSLog(@"%@", @"downloading did finish");
        }
        else if (state == kCTFontDescriptorMatchingDidFailWithError) {
            NSLog(@"%@", @"downloading failed");
        }
        else if (state == kCTFontDescriptorMatchingDidFinish) {
            NSLog(@"%@", @"matching did finish");
            dispatch_async(dispatch_get_main_queue(), ^{
                UIFont* f = [UIFont fontWithName:name size:size];
                if (f) {
                    NSLog(@"%@", @"got the font!");
                    self.lab.font = f;
                }
            });
        }
        return (bool)YES;
    });
```

Font Descriptors

A font descriptor (UIFontDescriptor, new in iOS 7, toll-free bridged to Core Text's CTFontDescriptorRef) is a way of describing a font, or converting between one font description and another, in terms of its features. For example, given a font descriptor, you can ask for a corresponding italic font descriptor like this:

```
desc = [desc fontDescriptorWithSymbolicTraits:UIFontDescriptorTraitItalic];
```

If desc was originally a descriptor for Avenir 15, it is now a descriptor for Avenir-Oblique 15. However, it is not the *font* Avenir-Oblique 15; a font descriptor is not a font.

To convert from a font to a font descriptor, take its fontDescriptor property; to convert from a font descriptor to a font, call the UIFont class method fontWith-

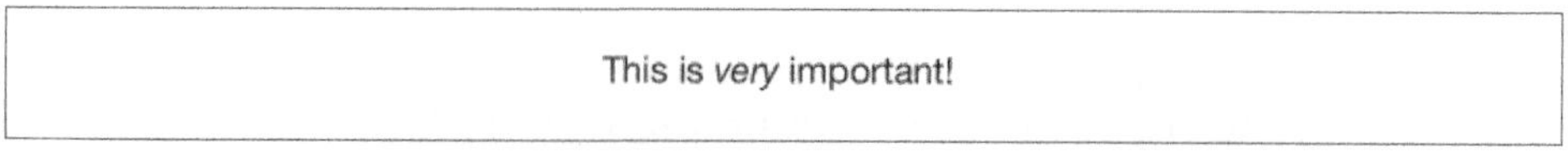

Figure 10-1. A Dynamic Type font with an italic variant

`Descriptor:size:`, typically supplying a size of 0 to signify that the size should not change. Thus, this will be a typical pattern in your code, as you convert from font to font descriptor to perform some transformation, and then back to font:

```
UIFont* font = // ...
UIFontDescriptor* desc = [font fontDescriptor];
desc = // font descriptor derived from desc
font = [UIFont fontWithDescriptor:desc size:0];
```

This same technique is useful also for obtaining styled variants of the Dynamic Type fonts. A UIFontDescriptor class method, `preferredFontDescriptorWithTextStyle:`, saves you from having to start with a UIFont. In this example, I form an NSAttributedString whose font is mostly `UIFontTextStyleBody`, but with one italicized word (Figure 10-1):

```
UIFontDescriptor* body =
    [UIFontDescriptor preferredFontDescriptorWithTextStyle:
        UIFontTextStyleBody];
UIFontDescriptor* emphasis =
    [body fontDescriptorWithSymbolicTraits:UIFontDescriptorTraitItalic];
UIFont* fbody = [UIFont fontWithDescriptor:body size:0];
UIFont* femphasis = [UIFont fontWithDescriptor:emphasis size:0];
NSString* s = @"This is very important!";
NSMutableAttributedString* mas =
    [[NSMutableAttributedString alloc] initWithString:s
     attributes:@{NSFontAttributeName:fbody}];
[mas addAttribute:NSFontAttributeName value:femphasis
    range:[s rangeOfString:@"very"]];
```

Unfortunately, converting between fonts by calling `fontDescriptorWithSymbolic-Traits:` doesn't work for every font family. (I regard this as a bug.) You might have to drop down to the level of Core Text. Fortunately, in iOS 7, CTFontRef and UIFont are toll-free bridged, so that's not such a daunting prospect. You'll have to `@import Core-Text` first:

```
UIFont* f = [UIFont fontWithName:@"GillSans" size:15];
CTFontRef font2 =
    CTFontCreateCopyWithSymbolicTraits (
        (__bridge CTFontRef)f, 0, nil,
         kCTFontItalicTrait, kCTFontItalicTrait);
UIFont* f2 = CFBridgingRelease(font2);
```

`CTFontCreateCopyWithSymbolicTraits` takes two bitmasks: the first lists the traits you care about, and the second says which traits those are. For example, suppose I'm starting

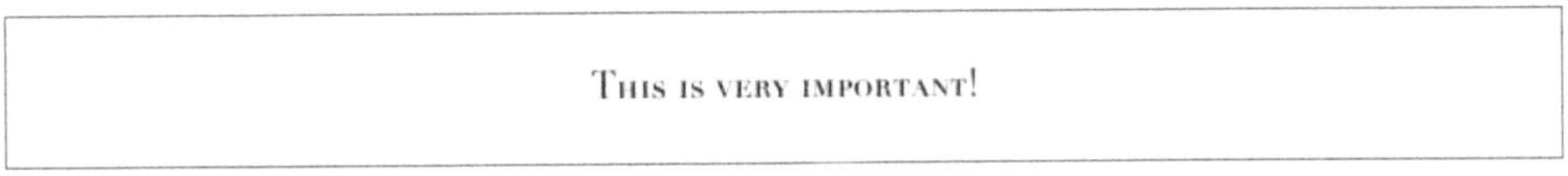

Figure 10-2. A small caps font variant

with a font that might or might not be bold, and I want to obtain its italic variant —
meaning that if it *is* bold, I want a bold italic font. It isn't enough to supply a bitmask
whose value is kCTFontItalicTrait, because this appears to switch italics on and everything else off. Thus, the second bitmask says, "Only this one bit is important to me."
By the same token, to get a nonitalic variant of a font that might be italic, you'd supply
0 as the fourth argument and kCTFontItalicTrait as the fifth argument.

Another use of font descriptors is to access hidden built-in typographical features of
individual fonts. In this example, I'll obtain a variant of the Didot font that draws its
minuscules as small caps (Figure 10-2). Before iOS 7, you could obtain the small caps
Didot font at the level of Core Text, but you couldn't use it in a UIKit interface object,
because it wasn't a UIFont. In iOS 7, everything happens at the UIKit level (though you
will need to @import CoreText to get the symbolic feature names kLetterCaseType
and kSmallCapsSelector; alternatively, use @3 for each):

```
UIFontDescriptor* desc =
    [UIFontDescriptor fontDescriptorWithName:@"Didot" size:18];
NSArray* arr =
    @[@{UIFontFeatureTypeIdentifierKey:@(kLetterCaseType),
        UIFontFeatureSelectorIdentifierKey:@(kSmallCapsSelector)}]];
desc =
    [desc fontDescriptorByAddingAttributes:
        @{UIFontDescriptorFeatureSettingsAttribute:arr}];
UIFont* f = [UIFont fontWithDescriptor:desc size:0];
```

Attributed Strings

The basis of styled text — that is, text consisting of multiple style runs, with different
font, size, color, and other text features in different parts of the text — is the *attributed
string*. Attributed strings (NSAttributedString and its mutable subclass, NSMutableAttributedString) have been around in iOS for a long time, but before iOS 6 they were
difficult to use — you had to drop down to the level of Core Text — and they couldn't
be used at all in connection with UIKit interface classes such as UILabel and UITextView.
Thus, such interface classes couldn't display styled text. In iOS 6, NSAttributedString
became a first-class citizen; it can now be used to draw styled text directly, and can be
drawn by built-in interface classes.

In general, interface object methods and properties that accept attributed strings stand side by side with their pre-iOS 6 equivalents; the new ones tend to have "attributed" in their name. Thus, you don't *have* to use attributed strings. If a UILabel, for example, is to display text in a single font, size, color, and alignment, it might be easiest to use the pre-iOS 6 plain-old-NSString features of UILabel. If you do use an attributed string with an interface object, it is best not to mix in any of the pre-iOS 6 settings: let the attributed string do *all* the work of dictating text style features.

An NSAttributedString consists of an NSString (its `string`) plus the attributes, applied in ranges. For example, if the string "one red word" is blue except for the word "red" which is red, and if these are the only changes over the course of the string, then there are three distinct style runs — everything before the word "red," the word "red" itself, and everything after the word "red." However, we can apply the attributes in two steps, first making the whole string blue, and then making the word "red" red, just as you would expect.

Attributed String Attributes

The attributes applied to a range of an attributed string are described in dictionaries. Each possible attribute has a predefined name, used as a key in these dictionaries; here are some of the most important attributes (for the full list, see Apple's *NSAttributedString UIKit Additions Reference*):

NSFontAttributeName
: A UIFont.

NSForegroundColorAttributeName
: The text color, a UIColor.

NSBackgroundColorAttributeName
: The color *behind* the text, a UIColor. You could use this to highlight a word, for example.

NSLigatureAttributeName
: An NSNumber wrapping 0 or 1, expressing whether or not you want ligatures used.

NSKernAttributeName
: An NSNumber wrapping the floating-point amount of kerning. A negative value brings a glyph closer to the following glyph; a positive value adds space between them. (In iOS 6, the special value [`NSNull null`] turns on inherent autokerning if the font supports it; in iOS 7, autokerning is the default.)

`NSStrikethroughStyleAttributeName`
`NSUnderlineStyleAttributeName`
>   Prior to iOS 7, could be only an NSNumber wrapping 0 or 1. Now, an NSNumber wrapping one of these values describing the line weight (despite `Underline` in their names, they apply equally to strikethrough):

- `NSUnderlineStyleNone`

- `NSUnderlineStyleSingle`

- `NSUnderlineStyleDouble`

- `NSUnderlineStyleThick`

>   Optionally, you may append (using logical-or) a specification of the line pattern, with names like `NSUnderlinePatternDot`, `NSUnderlinePatternDash`, and so on.

>   Optionally, you may append (using logical-or) `NSUnderlineByWord`; if you do not, then if the underline or strikethrough range involves multiple words, the whitespace between the words will be underlined or struck through.

`NSStrikethroughColorAttributeName`
`NSUnderlineColorAttributeName`
>   A UIColor. New in iOS 7. If not defined, the foreground color is used.

`NSStrokeWidthAttributeName`
>   An NSNumber wrapping a float. The stroke width is peculiarly coded. If it isn't zero, it's either a positive or negative float (wrapped in an NSNumber). If it's positive, then the text glyphs are stroked but not filled, giving an outline effect, and the foreground color is used unless a separate stroke color is defined. If it's negative, then its absolute value is the width of the stroke, and the glyphs are both filled (with the foreground color) and stroked (with the stroke color).

`NSStrokeColorAttributeName`
>   The stroke color, a UIColor.

`NSShadowAttributeName`
>   An NSShadow object. An NSShadow is just a glorified struct (what Apple calls a "value object"), combining a `shadowOffset`, `shadowColor`, and `shadowBlurRadius`.

`NSTextEffectAttributeName`
>   If defined, the only possible value is `NSTextEffectLetterpressStyle`. New in iOS 7.

`NSAttachmentAttributeName`
>   An NSTextAttachment object. New in iOS 7. A text attachment is basically an inline image. I'll discuss text attachments later on.

`NSLinkAttributeName`

An NSURL. New in IOS 7. In a noneditable, selectable UITextView, the link is tappable to go to the URL (depending on your implementation of the UITextView-Delegate method `textView:shouldInteractWithURL:inRange:`). By default, appears as blue without an underline in a UITextView. Appears as blue with an underline in a UILabel, but is not a tappable link there.

`NSBaselineOffsetAttributeName`
`NSObliquenessAttributeName`
`NSExpansionAttributeName`

An NSNumber wrapping a float. New in iOS 7.

`NSParagraphStyleAttributeName`

An NSParagraphStyle object. This is basically just a glorified struct, assembling text features that apply properly to paragraphs as a whole, not merely to characters, even if your string consists only of a single paragraph. Here are its most important properties:

- `alignment`
  - `NSTextAlignmentLeft`
  - `NSTextAlignmentCenter`
  - `NSTextAlignmentRight`
  - `NSTextAlignmentJustified`
  - `NSTextAlignmentNatural` (left-aligned or right-aligned depending on the writing direction)
- `lineBreakMode`
  - `NSLineBreakByWordWrapping`
  - `NSLineBreakByCharWrapping`
  - `NSLineBreakByClipping`
  - `NSLineBreakByTruncatingHead`
  - `NSLineBreakByTruncatingTail`
  - `NSLineBreakByTruncatingMiddle`
- `firstLineHeadIndent`, `headIndent` (left margin), `tailIndent` (right margin)
- `lineHeightMultiple`, `maximumLineHeight`, `minimumLineHeight`
- `lineSpacing`
- `paragraphSpacing`, `paragraphSpacingBefore`

- hyphenationFactor (0 or 1)
- defaultTabInterval, tabStops (new in iOS 7; the tab stops are an array of NSTextTab objects)

To construct an NSAttributedString, you can call initWithString:attributes: if the entire string has the same attributes; otherwise, you'll use its mutable subclass NSMutableAttributedString, which lets you set attributes over a range.

To construct an NSParagraphStyle, you'll use its mutable subclass NSMutableParagraphStyle. (The properties of NSParagraphStyle itself are all read-only, for historical reasons.) It is sufficient to apply a paragraph style to the first character of a paragraph; to put it another way, the paragraph style of the first character of a paragraph dictates how the whole paragraph is rendered.

Both NSAttributedString and NSParagraphStyle come with default values for all attributes, so you only have to set the attributes you care about.

Making an Attributed String

We now know enough for an example! I'll draw my attributed strings in a disabled (noninteractive) UITextView; its background is white, but its superview's background is gray, so you can see the text view's bounds relative to the text. (Ignore the text's vertical positioning, which is configured by applying a top contentInset.)

First, two words of my attributed string are made extra-bold by stroking in a different color. I start by dictating the entire string and the overall style of the text; then I apply the special style to the two stroked words (Figure 10-3):

```
NSString* s1 = @"The Gettysburg Address, as delivered on a certain occasion "
    @"(namely Thursday, November 19, 1863) by A. Lincoln";
NSMutableAttributedString* content =
    [[NSMutableAttributedString alloc]
     initWithString:s1
     attributes:
        @{
          NSFontAttributeName:
              [UIFont fontWithName:@"Arial-BoldMT" size:15],
          NSForegroundColorAttributeName:
              [UIColor colorWithRed:0.251 green:0.000 blue:0.502 alpha:1]
        }];
NSRange r = [s1 rangeOfString:@"Gettysburg Address"];
[content addAttributes:
    @{
      NSStrokeColorAttributeName:[UIColor redColor],
      NSStrokeWidthAttributeName: @-2.0
    } range:r];
self.tv.attributedText = content;
```

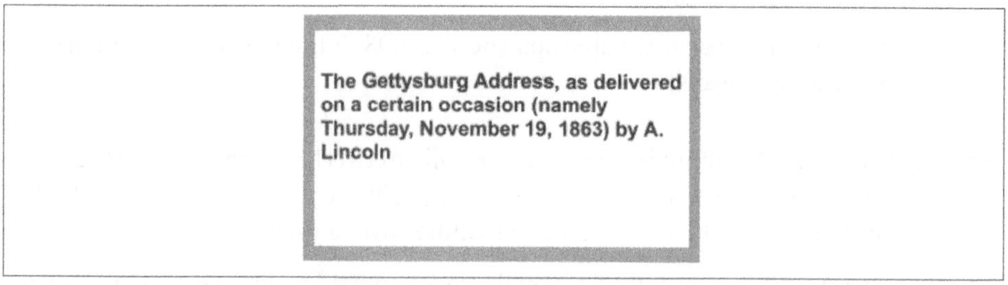

Figure 10-3. An attributed string

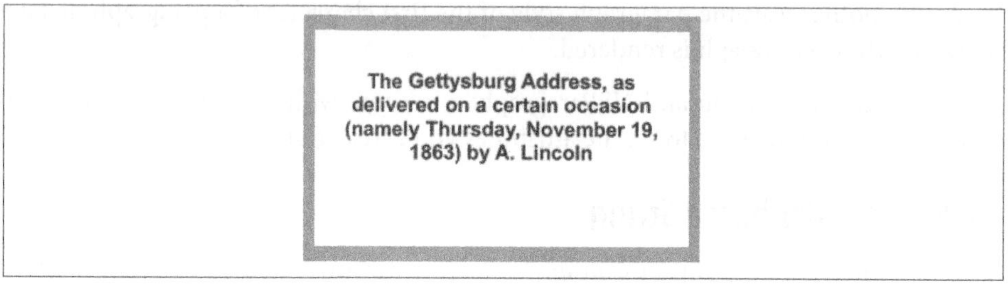

Figure 10-4. An attributed string with a paragraph style

Carrying on from the previous example, I'll also make the whole paragraph centered and indented from the edges of the text view. To do so, I create the paragraph style and apply it to the first character. Note how the margins are dictated: the `tailIndent` is negative, to bring the right margin leftward, and the `firstLineHeadIndent` must be set separately, as the `headIndent` does not automatically apply to the first line (Figure 10-4):

```
NSMutableParagraphStyle* para = [NSMutableParagraphStyle new];
para.headIndent = 10;
para.firstLineHeadIndent = 10;
para.tailIndent = -10;
para.lineBreakMode = NSLineBreakByWordWrapping;
para.alignment = NSTextAlignmentCenter;
para.paragraphSpacing = 15;
[content addAttribute:NSParagraphStyleAttributeName
             value:para range:NSMakeRange(0,1)];
self.tv.attributedText = content;
```

In this next example, I'll enlarge the first character of a paragraph. I assign the first character a larger font size, I expand its width slightly (a new iOS 7 feature), and I reduce its kerning (Figure 10-5):

```
NSString* s2 = @"Fourscore and seven years ago, our fathers brought forth "
@"upon this continent a new nation, conceived in liberty and dedicated "
@"to the proposition that all men are created equal.";
NSMutableAttributedString* content2 =
```

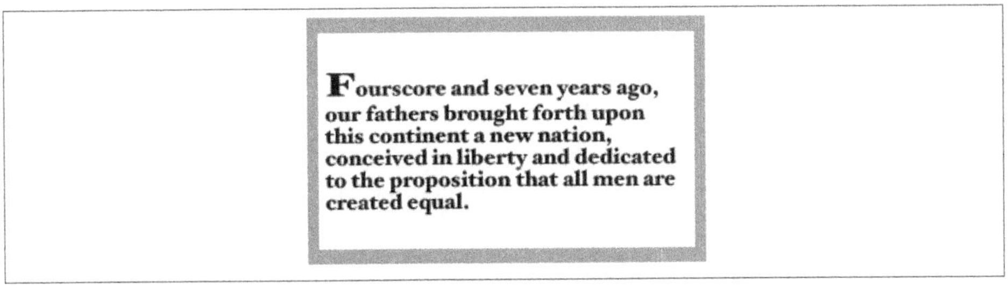

Fourscore and seven years ago, our fathers brought forth upon this continent a new nation, conceived in liberty and dedicated to the proposition that all men are created equal.

Figure 10-5. An attributed string with an expanded first character

```
[[NSMutableAttributedString alloc]
 initWithString:s2
 attributes:
 @{
    NSFontAttributeName:
        [UIFont fontWithName:@"HoeflerText-Black" size:16]
    }];
[content2 addAttributes:
 @{
    NSFontAttributeName:[UIFont fontWithName:@"HoeflerText-Black" size:24],
    NSExpansionAttributeName:@0.3,
    NSKernAttributeName:@-4
    } range:NSMakeRange(0,1)];
self.tv.attributedText = content2;
```

(I don't know why I can't get the "o" to come any closer to the "F" in Figure 10-5.)

Carrying on from the previous example, I'll once again construct a paragraph style and add it to the first character. My paragraph style illustrates full justification and automatic hyphenation (Figure 10-6):

```
NSMutableParagraphStyle* para2 = [NSMutableParagraphStyle new];
para2.headIndent = 10;
para2.firstLineHeadIndent = 10;
para2.tailIndent = -10;
para2.lineBreakMode = NSLineBreakByWordWrapping;
para2.alignment = NSTextAlignmentJustified;
para2.lineHeightMultiple = 1.2;
para2.hyphenationFactor = 1.0;
[content2 addAttribute:NSParagraphStyleAttributeName
                value:para2 range:NSMakeRange(0,1)];
self.tv.attributedText = content2;
```

Now we come to the Really Amazing Part. I can make a *single* attributed string consisting of *both* paragraphs, and a single text view can portray it (Figure 10-7):

```
int end = content.length;
[content replaceCharactersInRange:NSMakeRange(end, 0) withString:@"\n"];
[content appendAttributedString:content2];
self.tv.attributedText = content;
```

Fourscore and seven years ago,
our fathers brought forth upon
this continent a new nation,
conceived in liberty and dedicated to the proposition that all
men are created equal.

Figure 10-6. An attributed string with justification and autohyphenation

The Gettysburg Address, as
delivered on a certain occasion
(namely Thursday, November 19,
1863) by A. Lincoln

Fourscore and seven years ago,
our fathers brought forth upon
this continent a new nation,
conceived in liberty and dedicated to the proposition that all
men are created equal.

Figure 10-7. A single attributed string comprising differently styled paragraphs

The nib editor includes an ingenious interface for letting you construct attributed strings wherever built-in interface objects (such as
UILabel or UITextView) accept them as a property; it's not perfect, however, and isn't suitable for lengthy or complex text.

Tab stops

Tab stops are new in iOS 7. A tab stop is an NSTextTab, the initializer of which lets you
set its location (points from the left edge) and alignment. An options dictionary lets
you set the tab stop's column terminator characters; a common use is to create a decimal
tab stop, for aligning currency values at their decimal point. The key, in that case, is
NSTabColumnTerminatorsAttributeName; you can obtain a value appropriate to a given
NSLocale by calling NSTextTab's class method columnTerminatorsForLocale:.

Here's an example (Figure 10-8); I have deliberately omitted the "0" from the end of the
second currency value, to prove that the tab stop really is aligning the numbers at their
decimal points:

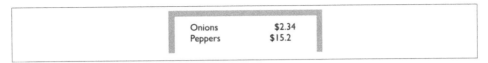

Figure 10-8. Tab stops in an attributed string

```
NSString* s = @"Onions\t$2.34\nPeppers\t$15.2\n";
NSMutableParagraphStyle* p = [NSMutableParagraphStyle new];
NSMutableArray* tabs = [NSMutableArray new];
NSCharacterSet* terms =
    [NSTextTab columnTerminatorsForLocale:[NSLocale currentLocale]];
NSTextTab* tab =
    [[NSTextTab alloc] initWithTextAlignment:NSTextAlignmentRight
        location:170 options:@{NSTabColumnTerminatorsAttributeName:terms}];
[tabs addObject:tab];
p.tabStops = tabs;
p.firstLineHeadIndent = 20;
NSMutableAttributedString* mas =
    [[NSMutableAttributedString alloc] initWithString:s
    attributes:@{
        NSFontAttributeName:[UIFont fontWithName:@"GillSans" size:15],
        NSParagraphStyleAttributeName:p
    }];
self.tv.attributedText = mas;
```

Text attachments

Text attachments are also new in iOS 7. A text attachment is basically an inline image. To make one, you need an instance of NSTextAttachment initialized with image data; the easiest way to do this in iOS 7 is to start with a UIImage and assign directly to the NSTextAttachment's image property. You must also give the NSTextAttachment a non-zero bounds; the image will be scaled to the size of the bounds you provide, and a zero origin places the image on the text baseline.

A text attachment is attached to an NSAttributedString using the NSAttachment-AttributeName key; the text attachment itself is the value. The range of the string that has this attribute must be a special nonprinting character, NSAttachmentCharacter (0xFFFC). The simplest way to arrange that is to call the NSAttributedString class method attributedStringWithAttachment:; you hand it an NSTextAttachment and it hands you an attributed string consisting of the NSAttachmentCharacter with the NSAttachmentAttributeName attribute set to that text attachment. You can then insert this attributed string into your own attributed string at the point where you want the image to appear.

Figure 10-9. Text attachments in an attributed string

To illustrate, I'll add an image of onions and an image of peppers just after the words "Onions" and "Peppers" in the attributed string (mas) that I created in the previous example (Figure 10-9):

```
UIImage* onions = // ...
UIImage* peppers = // ...
NSTextAttachment* onionatt = [NSTextAttachment new];
onionatt.image = onions;
onionatt.bounds =
    CGRectMake(0,-5,onions.size.width,onions.size.height);
NSAttributedString* onionattchar =
    [NSAttributedString attributedStringWithAttachment:onionatt];
NSTextAttachment* pepperatt = [NSTextAttachment new];
pepperatt.image = peppers;
pepperatt.bounds =
    CGRectMake(0,-1,peppers.size.width,peppers.size.height);
NSAttributedString* pepperattchar =
    [NSAttributedString attributedStringWithAttachment:pepperatt];
NSRange r = [[mas string] rangeOfString:@"Onions"];
[mas insertAttributedString:onionattchar atIndex:(r.location + r.length)];
r = [[mas string] rangeOfString:@"Peppers"];
[mas insertAttributedString:pepperattchar atIndex:(r.location + r.length)];
self.tv.attributedText = mas;
```

Modifying and Querying an Attributed String

Although attributes are *applied* to ranges, they actually *belong* to each individual character. Thus we can coherently modify just the string part of a mutable attributed string. The key method here is replaceCharactersInRange:withString:, which can be used to replace characters with a plain string or, using a zero range length, to insert a plain string at the start, middle, or end of an attributed string (as demonstrated in the preceding code). The rule is:

- If we *replace* characters, the inserted string takes on the attributes of the *first replaced* character.

- If we *insert* characters, the inserted string takes on the attributes of the character *preceding* the insertion — except that, if we insert at the *start*, there is no preceding character, so the inserted string takes on the attributes of the character *following* the insertion.

You can query an attributed string about its attributes one character at a time — asking either about all attributes at once (`attributesAtIndex:effectiveRange:`) or about a particular attribute by name (`attribute:atIndex:effectiveRange:`). In those methods, the `effectiveRange` parameter is a pointer to an NSRange variable, which will be set by indirection to the range over which this same attribute value, or set of attribute values, applies:

```
NSRange range;
NSDictionary* d =
    [content attributesAtIndex:content.length-1 effectiveRange:&range];
```

Because style runs are something of an artifice, however, you might not end up with what you would think of as the *entire* style run. The methods with `longestEffective-Range:` in their names, on the other hand, do (at the cost of some efficiency) work out the entire style run for you. In practice, you typically don't need the entire style run range, because you're cycling through ranges; you want to do that as fast as possible, and speed matters more than getting the longest effective range every time.

In this example, I start with the combined two-paragraph attributed string constructed in the previous examples, and change all the size 15 material to Arial Bold 20. I don't care whether I'm handed longest effective ranges (and my code explicitly says so); I just want to cycle efficiently:

```
[content enumerateAttribute:NSFontAttributeName
    inRange:NSMakeRange(0,content.length)
    options:NSAttributedStringEnumerationLongestEffectiveRangeNotRequired
    usingBlock:^(id value, NSRange range, BOOL *stop)
{
    UIFont* font = value;
    if (font.pointSize == 15)
        [content addAttribute:NSFontAttributeName
                        value:[UIFont fontWithName: @"Arial-BoldMT" size:20]
                        range:range];
}];
```

Measuring and Drawing an Attributed String

You can draw an attributed string directly, without hosting it in a built-in interface object, and sometimes this will prove to be the most reliable approach. Just as an NSString can be drawn into a rect with `drawInRect:withFont:` and related methods, an NSAttributedString can be drawn with `drawAtPoint:`, `drawInRect:`, and `drawWith-Rect:options:context:`.

Here, I draw an attributed string into an image (which might then be displayed by an image view):

```
UIGraphicsBeginImageContextWithOptions(rect.size, YES, 0);
[[UIColor whiteColor] setFill];
CGContextFillRect(UIGraphicsGetCurrentContext(), rect);
[content drawInRect:rect]; // draw attributed string
UIImage* im = UIGraphicsGetImageFromCurrentImageContext();
UIGraphicsEndImageContext();
```

Similarly, you can draw an attributed string directly in a UIView's `drawRect:`. That, in fact, is how the TidBITS News app works (Figure 6-1): each table view cell portrays a single attributed string consisting of the article title and the article summary.

I'll describe how the attributed string is drawn in the TidBITS News app. The cell's `contentView` is completely occupied by a custom UIView class that I call StringDrawer; it has a public `attributedText` property. In `tableView:cellForRowAtIndexPath:`, I set that property by calling a utility method that generates this cell's attributed string by consulting my data model:

```
cell.drawer.attributedText = [self attributedStringForIndexPath: indexPath];
```

StringDrawer's `drawRect:` draws its `attributedText`:

```
- (void)drawRect:(CGRect)rect {
    CGRect r = CGRectOffset(rect, 0, 2); // shoved down a little from top
    [self.attributedText drawWithRect:r
        options:NSStringDrawingTruncatesLastVisibleLine |
                NSStringDrawingUsesLineFragmentOrigin
        context:nil];
}
```

Note the `options:` argument in that code. I want an ellipsis at the end of the second paragraph if the whole thing doesn't fit in the given rect. This can't be achieved using `NSLineBreakByTruncatingTail`, which truncates the *first line* of the paragraph to which it is applied. Therefore, I'm using `drawWithRect:options:context:`, instead of simple `drawInRect:`, because it allows me to specify the option `NSStringDrawingTruncates-LastVisibleLine`. However, I must then also specify `NSStringDrawingUsesLine-FragmentOrigin`; otherwise, the string is drawn with its *baseline* at the rect origin (so that it appears *above* that rect) and it doesn't wrap. The rule is that `NSStringDrawing-UsesLineFragmentOrigin` is the implicit default for simple `drawInRect:`, but with `draw-WithRect:options:context:` you must specify it explicitly.

To derive the height of the cell, I also *measure* the attributed string beforehand, in `table-View:heightForRowAtIndexPath:`. Again, the option `NSStringDrawingUsesLine-FragmentOrigin` is crucial; without it, the measured text doesn't wrap and the returned height will be very small. New in iOS 7, the documentation warns that the returned height can be fractional and that you should round up with the `ceil` function if the height of a view is going to depend on this result:

```
CGRect r =
    [s boundingRectWithSize:CGSizeMake(320,10000)
        options:NSStringDrawingUsesLineFragmentOrigin context:nil];
CGFloat result = ceil(r.size.height);
```

The context: parameter of drawWithRect:options:context: and boundingRectWith-Size:options:context: lets you attach an instance of NSStringDrawingContext. This simple class tells you where you just drew. With a plain NSString, you derive this information from the return value of the drawing command; for example, drawIn-Rect:withFont: returns a CGSize telling you the size of the drawn string. But drawWith-Rect:options:context: has no return value. Instead, if you attach an NSString-DrawingContext, its totalBounds property tells you, after you draw, the bounds of the drawn string.

 Other features of NSStringDrawingContext, such as minimumScale-Factor, appear to be nonfunctional in iOS 7.

Labels

A label (UILabel) is a simple built-in interface object for displaying strings. I listed some of its chief properties in Chapter 8 (in "Built-In Cell Styles" on page 393).

If you're displaying a plain NSString in a label, by way of the label's text property, then you are likely also to set its font, textColor, and textAlignment properties, and possibly its shadowColor and shadowOffset properties. The label's text can have an alternate highlightedTextColor, to be used when its highlighted property is YES — as happens, for example, when the label is in a selected cell of a table view.

On the other hand, if you're using an NSAttributedString, then you'll set just the label's attributedText property and let the attributes dictate things like color, alignment, and shadow. Those other UILabel properties do mostly still work, but they're going to change the attributes of your *entire* attributed string, in ways that you might not intend. Setting the text of a UILabel that has attributedText will basically eliminate the attributes. The highlightedTextColor property does *not* work on the attributedText.

Number of Lines

A UILabel's numberOfLines property is extremely important. Together with the label's line breaking behavior and resizing behavior, it determines how much of the text will appear. The default is 1 — a single line. To make a label display more than one line of text, set its numberOfLines to a value greater than 1, or to 0 to indicate that there is to be no maximum.

Line break characters in a label's text are honored. Thus, for example, in a single-line label, you won't see whatever follows the first line break character. (This is new behavior in iOS 7; in iOS 6 and before, if a single-line UILabel's `text` contained a line break, it was treated as a space.)

Wrapping and Truncation

UILabel line breaking (wrapping) and truncation behavior, which applies to both single-line and multiline labels, is determined by the `lineBreakMode` (of the label or the attributed string). Your options are:

`NSLineBreakByWordWrapping`
Lines break at word-end, but if this is a single-line label, indistinguishable from `NSLineBreakByClipping`.

`NSLineBreakByClipping`
Lines break at word-end, but the last line can continue past its boundary, even if this leaves a character showing only partially.

`NSLineBreakByCharWrapping`
Identical to `NSLineBreakByWordWrapping`. (This is new behavior in iOS 7; in iOS 6 and before, this mode meant that lines could break in mid-word in order to maximize the number of characters in each line. This may be a bug.)

`NSLineBreakByTruncatingHead`
`NSLineBreakByTruncatingMiddle`
`NSLineBreakByTruncatingTail`
Lines break at word-end; if the text is too long for the label, then the last line displays an ellipsis at the start, middle, or end of the line respectively, and text is omitted at the point of the ellipsis.

The default line break mode for a new label is `NSLineBreakByTruncatingTail`. But the default line break mode for an attributed string's NSParagraphStyle is `NSLineBreakByWordWrapping`.

 UILabel line break behavior is *not the same* as NSParagraphStyle line break behavior. For example, an attributed string paragraph whose line break mode has `Truncating` in its name *doesn't wrap* when drawn directly or in a UITextView — though it may wrap when drawn in a label. And an attributed string paragraph whose line break mode is `NSLineBreakByCharWrapping` does break lines in mid-word, as expected, *even* in a label.

Label Resizing

If a label is too small for its text, the entire text won't show. If a label is too big for its text, the text is vertically centered in the label, with white space above and below, which may be undesirable. You might like to shrink or grow a label to fit its text.

If you're not using autolayout, in most simple cases `sizeToFit` will do exactly the right thing; I believe that behind the scenes it is calling `boundingRectWithSize:options:context:`.

 There are cases where UILabel's `sizeToFit` will misbehave. The problem arises particularly with paragraph styles involving margins (`headIndent` and `tailIndent`) — presumably because `boundingRectWithSize:options:context:` ignores the margins.

If you're using autolayout, a label will correctly configure its own `intrinsicContentSize` automatically, based on its contents — and therefore, all other things being equal, will size itself to fit its contents *with no code at all*. Every time you reconfigure the label in a way that affects its contents (setting its text, changing its font, setting its attributed text, and so forth), the label automatically invalidates and recalculates its intrinsic content size.

In the case of a short single-line label, you might give the label no width or height constraints; you'll constrain its position, but you'll let the label's `intrinsicContentSize` provide both the label's width and its height.

For a multiline label, it is more likely that you'll want to dictate the label's width, while letting the label's height change automatically to accommodate its contents. There are two ways to do this:

Set the label's width constraint
> This is appropriate particularly when the label's width is to remain fixed ever after.

Set the label's `preferredMaxLayoutWidth`
> This property is a hint to help the label's calculation of its `intrinsicContentSize`. It is the width at which the label, as its contents increase, will stop growing horizontally to accommodate those contents, and start growing vertically instead.

If a label's width is to be permitted to vary because of constraints, you can tell it recalculate its height to fit its contents by setting its `preferredMaxLayoutWidth` to its actual width. For example, consider a label whose left and right edges are both pinned to the superview. And imagine that the superview's width can change, thus changing the width of the label. (For example, perhaps the superview is the app's main view, and the app's interface is permitted to rotate, thus changing the main view's width to match the new orientation of the screen.) Here is the code for a UILabel subclass that will respond to that situation by resizing its own height automatically to fit its contents:

```
@implementation MySelfAdjustingLabel
-(void)layoutSubviews {
    [super layoutSubviews];
    self.preferredMaxLayoutWidth = self.bounds.size.width;
}
@end
```

Alternatively, you can change a label's `preferredMaxLayoutWidth` in the view controller's `viewDidLayoutSubviews`, but then you may need to use delayed performance to wait until the label's width has finished adjusting itself:

```
- (void)viewDidLayoutSubviews {
    // wait until *after* constraint-based layout has finished
    // that way, the label's width is correct when this code executes
    dispatch_async(dispatch_get_main_queue(), ^{
        self.theLabel.preferredMaxLayoutWidth =
            self.theLabel.bounds.size.width;
    });
}
```

Instead of letting a label grow, you can elect to permit its text font size to shrink if this would allow more of the text to fit. How the text is repositioned when the font size shrinks is determined by the label's `baselineAdjustment` property. The conditions under which this feature operates are:

- The label's `adjustsFontSizeToFitWidth` property must be YES.
- The label's `minimumScaleFactor` must be less than `1.0`.
- The label's size must be limited.
- *Either* this must be a single-line label (`numberOfLines` is 1) *or* the line break mode (of the label or the attributed string) must not have `Wrapping` in its name. (This is new behavior in iOS 7; in iOS 6 and before, *both* those conditions had to be met.)

Customized Label Drawing

Methods that you can override in a subclass to modify a label's drawing are `drawText-InRect:` and `textRectForBounds:limitedToNumberOfLines:`.

For example, this is the code from a UILabel subclass that outlines the label with a black rectangle and puts a five-point margin around the label's contents:

```
- (void)drawTextInRect:(CGRect)rect {
    CGContextRef context = UIGraphicsGetCurrentContext();
    CGContextStrokeRect(context, CGRectInset(self.bounds, 1.0, 1.0));
    [super drawTextInRect:CGRectInset(rect, 5.0, 5.0)];
}
```

 A CATextLayer (Chapter 3) is like a lightweight, layer-level version of a UILabel. If the width of the layer is insufficient to display the entire string, we can get truncation behavior with the truncationMode property. If the wrapped property is set to YES, the string will wrap. We can also set the alignment with the alignmentMode property. And its string property can be an NSAttributedString.

Text Fields

A text field (UITextField) portrays just a single line of text; any line break characters in its text are treated as spaces. It has many of the same properties as a label. You can can provide it with a plain NSString, setting its text, font, textColor, and text-Alignment, or provide it with an attributed string, setting its attributedText. New in iOS 7, you can learn a text field's overall text attributes as an attributes dictionary through its defaultTextAttributes property. (Under the hood, the text is *always* attributed text, so the displayed text can end up as a combination of, say, the attributedText and the textColor.)

Under autolayout, a text field's intrinsicContentSize will attempt to set its width to fit its contents; if its width is fixed, you can set its adjustsFontSizeToFitWidth and minimumFontSize properties to allow the text size to shrink somewhat.

Text that is too long for the text field is displayed with an ellipsis at the end. A text field has no lineBreakMode, but you can change the position of the ellipsis by assigning the text field an attributed string with different truncation behavior, such as NSLineBreak-ByTruncatingHead. When long text is being edited, the ellipsis (if any) is removed, and the text shifts horizontally to show the insertion point.

Regardless of whether you originally supplied a plain string or an attributed string, if the text field's allowsEditingTextAttributes property is YES, the user, when editing in the text field, can summon a menu toggling the selected text's bold, italics, or underline features. (Oddly, there's no way to set this property in a nib.)

A text field has a placeholder property, which is the text that appears faded within the text field when it has no text (its text or attributedText has been set to nil, or the user has removed all the text); the idea is that you can use this to suggest to the user what the text field is for. It has a styled text alternative, attributedPlaceholder; the runtime will apply an overall light gray color to your attributed string.

If a text field's `clearsOnBeginEditing` property is YES, it automatically deletes its existing text (and displays the placeholder) when editing begins within it. If a text field's `clearsOnInsertion` property is YES, then when editing begins within it, the text remains, but is invisibly selected, and will be replaced by the user's typing.

A text field's border drawing is determined by its `borderStyle` property. Your options are:

`UITextBorderStyleNone`
> No border.

`UITextBorderStyleLine`
> A plain black rectangle.

`UITextBorderStyleBezel`
> A gray rectangle, where the top and left sides have a very slight, thin shadow.

`UITextBorderStyleRoundedRect`
> In iOS 7, a larger rectangle with slightly rounded corners and a flat, faded gray color. (In iOS 6 and before, the corners are more rounded, and the top and left sides have a strong shadow, so that the text appears markedly recessed behind the border.)

You can supply a background image (`background`); if you combine this with `UITextBorderStyleNone`, or if the image has no transparency, you thus get to supply your own border — unless the `borderStyle` is `UITextBorderStyleRoundedRect`, in which case the background is ignored. The image is automatically resized as needed (and you will probably supply a resizable image). A second image (`disabledBackground`) can be displayed when the text field's `enabled` property, inherited from UIControl, is NO. The user can't interact with a disabled text field, but without a `disabledBackground` image, the user may lack any visual clue to this fact. You can't set the `disabledBackground` unless you have also set the `background`.

A text field may contain one or two ancillary overlay views, its `leftView` and `rightView`, and possibly a Clear button (a gray circle with a white X). The automatic visibility of each of these is determined by the `leftViewMode`, `rightViewMode`, and `clearViewMode`, respectively. The view mode values are:

`UITextFieldViewModeNever`
> The view never appears.

`UITextFieldViewModeWhileEditing`
> A Clear button appears if there is text in the field and the user is editing. A left or right view appears if there is *no* text in the field and the user is editing.

UITextFieldViewModeUnlessEditing
> A Clear button appears if there is text in the field and the user is not editing. A left or right view appears if the user is not editing, or if the user is editing but there is no text in the field.

UITextFieldViewModeAlways
> A Clear button appears if there is text in the field. A left or right view always appears.

Depending on what sort of view you use, your leftView and rightView may have to be sized manually so as not to overwhelm the text view contents. If a right view and a Clear button appear at the same time, the right view may cover the Clear button unless you reposition it.

The positions and sizes of *any* of the components of the text field can be set in relation to the text field's bounds by overriding the appropriate method in a subclass:

- clearButtonRectForBounds:
- leftViewRectForBounds:
- rightViewRectForBounds:
- borderRectForBounds:
- textRectForBounds:
- placeholderRectForBounds:
- editingRectForBounds:

 You should make no assumptions about when or how frequently these methods will be called; the same method might be called several times in quick succession. Also, these methods should all be called with a parameter that is the bounds of the text field, but some are sometimes called with a 100×100 bounds; this feels like a bug.

You can also override in a subclass the methods drawTextInRect: and draw-PlaceholderInRect:. You should either draw the specified text or call super to draw it; if you do neither, the text won't appear. Both these methods are called with a parameter whose size is the dimensions of the text field's text area, but whose origin is {0,0}. In effect what you've got is a graphics context for just the text area; any drawing you do outside the given rectangle will be clipped.

Summoning and Dismissing the Keyboard

Making the onscreen simulated keyboard appear when the user taps in a text field is no work at all — it's automatic, as you've probably observed already. Making the keyboard vanish again, on the other hand, can be a bit tricky. (Another problem is that the keyboard can cover the text field that the user just tapped in; I'll talk about that in a moment.)

The presence or absence of the keyboard, and a text field's editing state, are intimately tied to one another, and to the text field's status as the *first responder*:

- When a text field is first responder, it is being edited and the keyboard is present.
- When a text field is no longer first responder, it is no longer being edited, and if no other text field (or text view) becomes first responder, the keyboard is not present. The keyboard is not dismissed if one text field takes over first responder status from another.

Thus, you can programmatically control the presence or absence of the keyboard, together with a text field's editing state, by way of the text field's first responder status:

Becoming first responder

To make the insertion point appear within a text field and to cause the keyboard to appear, you send `becomeFirstResponder` to that text field.

You won't often have to do that; more often, the user will tap in a text field and it will become first responder automatically. Still, sometimes it's useful to make a text field the first responder programmatically; an example appeared in Chapter 8 ("Inserting Table Items" on page 448).

Resigning first responder

To make a text field stop being edited and to cause the keyboard to disappear, you send `resignFirstResponder` to that text field. (Actually, `resignFirstResponder` returns a BOOL, because a responder might return NO to indicate that for some reason it refuses to obey this command.)

Alternatively, send the UIView `endEditing:` method to the first responder *or any superview* (including the window) to ask or compel the first responder to resign first responder status.

In a view presented in the `UIModalPresentationFormSheet` style on the iPad (Chapter 6), the keyboard, by default, does *not* disappear when a text field resigns first responder status. This is presumably because a form sheet is intended primarily for text input, so the keyboard is felt as accompanying the form as a whole, not individual text fields. Optionally, you can prevent this exceptional behavior: in your UIViewController subclass, override `disablesAutomaticKeyboardDismissal` to return NO.

There is no simple way to learn what view is first responder! This is very odd, because a window surely knows what its first responder is — but it won't tell you. There's a method `isFirstResponder`, but you'd have to send it to every view in a window until you find the first responder. One workaround is to store a reference to the first responder yourself, typically in your implementation of the text field delegate's `textFieldDid-BeginEditing:`.

 Do not name such a reference `firstResponder`! This name is apparently already in use by Cocoa, and a name collision can cause your app to misbehave. (Can you guess how I know that?)

Once the user has tapped in a text field and the keyboard has automatically appeared, how is the user supposed to get rid of it? On the iPad, the keyboard typically contains a special button that dismisses the keyboard. But on the iPhone, this is an oddly tricky issue. You would think that the "return" button in the keyboard would dismiss the keyboard; but, of itself, it doesn't.

One solution is to be the text field's delegate and to implement a text field delegate method, `textFieldShouldReturn:`. When the user taps the Return key in the keyboard, we hear about it through this method, and we tell the text field to resign its first responder status, which dismisses the keyboard:

```
- (BOOL)textFieldShouldReturn: (UITextField*) tf {
    [tf resignFirstResponder];
    return YES;
}
```

I'll provide a more automatic solution later in this chapter.

Keyboard Covers Text Field

The keyboard has a position "docked" at the bottom of the screen. This may cover the text field in which the user wants to type, even if it is first responder. On the iPad, this may not be an issue, because the user can "undock" the keyboard (possibly also splitting and shrinking it) and slide it up and down the screen freely. On the iPhone, you'll typically want to do something to reveal the text field.

To help with this, you can register for keyboard-related notifications:

- `UIKeyboardWillShowNotification`
- `UIKeyboardDidShowNotification`
- `UIKeyboardWillHideNotification`
- `UIKeyboardDidHideNotification`

Those notifications all have to do with the *docked* position of the keyboard. On the iPhone, keyboard docking and keyboard visibility are equivalent: the keyboard is visible if and only if it is docked. On the iPad, the keyboard is said to "show" if it is being docked, whether that's because it is appearing from offscreen or because the user is docking it;

and it is said to "hide" if it is undocked, whether that's because it is moving offscreen or because the user is undocking it.

Two additional notifications are sent *both* when the keyboard enters and leaves the screen *and* (on the iPad) when the user drags it, splits or unsplits it, and docks or undocks it:

- `UIKeyboardWillChangeFrameNotification`
- `UIKeyboardDidChangeFrameNotification`

The notification's `userInfo` dictionary contains information about the keyboard describing what it will do or has done, under these keys:

- `UIKeyboardFrameBeginUserInfoKey`
- `UIKeyboardFrameEndUserInfoKey`
- `UIKeyboardAnimationDurationUserInfoKey`
- `UIKeyboardAnimationCurveUserInfoKey`

Thus, to a large extent, you can coordinate your actions with those of the keyboard. In particular, by looking at the `UIKeyboardFrameEndUserInfoKey`, you know what position the keyboard is moving to; you can compare this with the screen bounds to learn whether the keyboard will now be on or off the screen and, if it will now be on the screen, you can see whether it will cover a text field.

Finding a strategy for dealing with the keyboard's presence depends on the needs of your particular app. I'll concentrate on the most universal case, where the keyboard moves into and out of docked position and we detect this with `UIKeyboardWillShow-Notification` and `UIKeyboardWillHideNotification`. What should we do if, when the keyboard appears, it covers the text field being edited?

Sliding the interface

One natural-looking approach is to slide the entire interface upward as the keyboard appears. To make this easy, you might start with a view hierarchy like this: the root view contains a transparent view that's the same size as the root view; everything else is contained in that transparent view. The transparent view's purpose is to host the rest of the interface; if we slide it upward, the whole interface will slide upward.

Here's an implementation involving constraints. The transparent view, which I'll called the *sliding view*, is pinned by constraints at the top and bottom to its superview with a `constant` of 0, and we have outlets to those constraints. We also have an outlet to the sliding view itself, and we've got a property prepared to hold the first responder:

```
@interface ViewController ()
@property (weak, nonatomic) IBOutlet NSLayoutConstraint* topConstraint;
@property (weak, nonatomic) IBOutlet NSLayoutConstraint* bottomConstraint;
@property (weak, nonatomic) IBOutlet UIView *slidingView;
@property (nonatomic, weak) UIView* fr;
@end
```

In our view controller's `viewDidLoad`, we register for the keyboard notifications:

```
[super viewDidLoad];
[[NSNotificationCenter defaultCenter] addObserver:self
    selector:@selector(keyboardShow:)
    name:UIKeyboardWillShowNotification object:nil];
[[NSNotificationCenter defaultCenter] addObserver:self
    selector:@selector(keyboardHide:)
    name:UIKeyboardWillHideNotification object:nil];
```

We are the delegate of the various text fields in our interface. When one of them starts editing, we keep a reference to it as first responder:

```
- (void)textFieldDidBeginEditing:(UITextField *)tf {
    self.fr = tf; // keep track of first responder
}
```

As I suggested in the previous section, we also dismiss the keyboard by resigning first responder when the user taps the Return button in the keyboard:

```
- (BOOL)textFieldShouldReturn: (UITextField*) tf {
    [tf resignFirstResponder];
    self.fr = nil;
    return YES;
}
```

As the keyboard threatens to appear, we examine where its top will be. If the keyboard will cover the text field that's about to be edited, we animate the sliding view upward to compensate, by changing the `constant` value of the constraints that pin its top and bottom, gearing our animation to that of the keyboard. The keyboard's frame comes to us in window/screen coordinates, so it is necessary to convert it to our sliding view's coordinates in order to make sense of it:

```
- (void) keyboardShow: (NSNotification*) n {
    NSDictionary* d = [n userInfo];
    CGRect r = [d[UIKeyboardFrameEndUserInfoKey] CGRectValue];
    r = [self.slidingView convertRect:r fromView:nil];
    CGRect f = self.fr.frame;
    CGFloat y =
        CGRectGetMaxY(f) + r.size.height -
        self.slidingView.bounds.size.height + 5;
    NSNumber* duration = d[UIKeyboardAnimationDurationUserInfoKey];
    NSNumber* curve = d[UIKeyboardAnimationCurveUserInfoKey];
    if (r.origin.y < CGRectGetMaxY(f)) {
        [UIView animateWithDuration:duration.floatValue
                             delay:0
```

```
                options:curve.integerValue << 16
             animations:^{
        self.topConstraint.constant = -y;
        self.bottomConstraint.constant = y;
        [self.view layoutIfNeeded];
    } completion:nil];
    }
}
```

When the keyboard disappears, we reverse the procedure:

```
- (void) keyboardHide: (NSNotification*) n {
    NSNumber* duration = n.userInfo[UIKeyboardAnimationDurationUserInfoKey];
    NSNumber* curve = n.userInfo[UIKeyboardAnimationCurveUserInfoKey];
    [UIView animateWithDuration:duration.floatValue
                          delay:0
                        options:curve.integerValue << 16
                     animations:^{
        self.topConstraint.constant = 0;
        self.bottomConstraint.constant = 0;
        [self.view layoutIfNeeded];
    } completion:nil];
}
```

Text field in a scroll view

Instead of moving the sliding view itself, we could instead shift its bounds origin. If we're going to do that, we might as well make the sliding view a scroll view — a view that already knows all about shifting its bounds origin! This approach has two notable advantages over the preceding approach:

- We can permit the user to scroll the view within the area not covered by the keyboard. This is a job for contentInset, whose purpose, you will recall (Chapter 7), is precisely to make it possible for the user to view all of the scroll view's content even though part of the scroll view is being covered by something.

  (This behavior is in fact implemented automatically by a UITableViewController. When a text field inside a table cell is first responder, the table view controller adjusts the table view's contentInset and scrollIndicatorInsets to compensate for the keyboard. The result is that the entire table view is available within the space between the top of the keyboard and the top of the screen.)

- A scroll view has some built-in behavior that will help us: it scrolls automatically to reveal the first responder. Furthermore, new in iOS 7, a UIScrollView has a keyboardDismissMode, governing what will happen to the keyboard when the user scrolls.

Let's imitate UITableViewController's behavior with a scroll view containing text fields. In viewDidLoad, we register for keyboard notifications, and we are the delegate of any text fields, exactly as in the previous example. When the keyboard appears, we store the current content offset, content inset, and scroll indicator insets; then we alter them. I set the scroll view's bounds directly, rather than calling setContentOffset: animated:, because I want to match the keyboard animation:

```
- (void) keyboardShow: (NSNotification*) n {
    self->_oldContentInset = self.scrollView.contentInset;
    self->_oldIndicatorInset = self.scrollView.scrollIndicatorInsets;
    self->_oldOffset = self.scrollView.contentOffset;
    NSDictionary* d = [n userInfo];
    CGRect r = [[d objectForKey:UIKeyboardFrameEndUserInfoKey] CGRectValue];
    r = [self.scrollView convertRect:r fromView:nil];
    CGRect f = self.fr.frame;
    CGFloat y =
        CGRectGetMaxY(f) + r.size.height -
        self.scrollView.bounds.size.height + 5;
    if (r.origin.y < CGRectGetMaxY(f)) {
        NSNumber* duration = d[UIKeyboardAnimationDurationUserInfoKey];
        NSNumber* curve = d[UIKeyboardAnimationCurveUserInfoKey];
        [UIView animateWithDuration:duration.floatValue
                              delay:0
                            options:curve.integerValue << 16
                         animations:^{
                            CGRect b = self.scrollView.bounds;
                            b.origin = CGPointMake(0, y);
                            self.scrollView.bounds = b;
                        } completion: nil];
    }
    UIEdgeInsets insets = self.scrollView.contentInset;
    insets.bottom = r.size.height;
    self.scrollView.contentInset = insets;
    insets = self.scrollView.scrollIndicatorInsets;
    insets.bottom = r.size.height;
    self.scrollView.scrollIndicatorInsets = insets;
}
```

When the keyboard disappears, we restore the saved values:

```
- (void) keyboardHide: (NSNotification*) n {
    NSNumber* duration = n.userInfo[UIKeyboardAnimationDurationUserInfoKey];
    NSNumber* curve = n.userInfo[UIKeyboardAnimationCurveUserInfoKey];
    [UIView animateWithDuration:duration.floatValue
                          delay:0
                        options:curve.integerValue << 16
                     animations:^{
                        CGRect b = self.scrollView.bounds;
                        b.origin = self->_oldOffset;
                        self.scrollView.bounds = b;
                        self.scrollView.scrollIndicatorInsets =
                            self->_oldIndicatorInset;
```

```
                    self.scrollView.contentInset =
                        self->_oldContentInset;
            } completion:nil];
    }
```

New in iOS 7, UIScrollView's `keyboardDismissMode` provides some new ways letting the user dismiss the keyboard. The options are:

`UIScrollViewKeyboardDismissModeNone`
: The default. The same as the old behavior; we must use code to dismiss the keyboard.

`UIScrollViewKeyboardDismissModeInteractive`
: The user can dismiss the keyboard by dragging it down, a completely new iOS 7 behavior.

`UIScrollViewKeyboardDismissModeOnDrag`
: The keyboard dismisses itself if the user scrolls the scroll view.

Configuring the Keyboard

A UITextField implements the UITextInputTraits protocol, which defines properties on the UITextField that you can set to determine how the keyboard will look and how typing in the text field will behave. (These properties can also be set in the nib.) For example, you can set the `keyboardType` to `UIKeyboardTypePhonePad` to make the keyboard for this text field consist of digits only. You can set the `returnKeyType` to determine the text of the Return key (if the keyboard is of a type that has one). New in iOS 7, you can give the keyboard a dark or light shade (`keyboardAppearance`). You can turn off autocapitalization (`autocapitalizationType`) or autocorrection (`autocorrectionType`), make the Return key disable itself if the text field has no content (`enablesReturnKeyAutomatically`), and make the text field a password field (`secureTextEntry`). You can even supply your own keyboard or other input mechanism by setting the text field's `inputView`.

You can attach an accessory view to the top of the keyboard by setting the text field's `inputAccessoryView`. In this example, the accessory view has been loaded from a nib and is available through a property, `accessoryView`. When editing starts, we configure the keyboard as we store our reference to the text field:

```
- (void)textFieldDidBeginEditing:(UITextField *)tf {
    self.fr = tf; // keep track of first responder
    tf.inputAccessoryView = self.accessoryView;
}
```

We have an NSArray property populated with references to all our text fields (this might be an appropriate use of an outlet collection). The accessory view contains a Next button, whose action method is `doNextField:`. When the user taps the button, we move editing to the next text field:

```
- (void) doNextButton: (id) sender {
    NSUInteger ix = [self.textFields indexOfObject:self.fr];
    if (ix == NSNotFound)
        return; // shouldn't happen
    ix++;
    if (ix >= [self.textFields count])
        ix = 0;
    UIView* v = self.textFields[ix];
    [v becomeFirstResponder];
}
```

The user can control the localization of the keyboard character set in the Settings app, either through a choice of the system's base language or by enabling additional "international keyboards." In the latter case, the user can switch among keyboard character sets while the keyboard is showing. But, as far as I can tell, your code can't make this choice; you cannot, for example, force a certain text field to display the Cyrillic keyboard. You can ask the user to switch keyboards manually, but if you really want a particular keyboard to appear regardless of the user's settings and behavior, you'll have to create it yourself and provide it as the `inputView`.

Text Field Delegate and Control Event Messages

As editing begins and proceeds in a text field, a sequence of messages is sent to the text field's delegate, adopting the UITextFieldDelegate protocol. (Some of these messages are also available as notifications.) Using them, you can customize the text field's behavior during editing:

`textFieldShouldBeginEditing:`
> Return NO to prevent the text field from becoming first responder.

`textFieldDidBeginEditing:`
`UITextFieldTextDidBeginEditingNotification`
> The text field has become first responder.

`textFieldShouldClear:`
> Return NO to prevent the operation of the Clear button or of automatic clearing on entry (`clearsOnBeginEditing`). This event is *not* sent when the text is cleared because `clearsOnInsertion` is YES, because the user is not clearing the text but rather changing it.

`textFieldShouldReturn:`
> The user has tapped the Return button in the keyboard. We have already seen that this can be used as a signal to dismiss the keyboard.

`textField:shouldChangeCharactersInRange:replacementString:`
> Sent when the user changes the text in the field by typing or pasting, or by backspacing or cutting (in which case the replacement string will have zero length).

Return NO to prevent the proposed change; you can substitute text by changing the text field's `text` directly (there is no circularity, as this delegate method is not called when you do that).

In this example, the user can enter only lowercase characters:

```
-(BOOL)textField:(UITextField *)textField
      shouldChangeCharactersInRange:(NSRange)range
      replacementString:(NSString *)string {
    NSString* lc = [string lowercaseString];
    textField.text =
        [textField.text stringByReplacingCharactersInRange:range
                                                withString:lc];
    return NO;
}
```

Another use of `textField:shouldChangeCharactersInRange:replacement-String:` is to take advantage of the `typingAttributes` property to set the attributes of the text the user is about to enter. In this example, I'll set the user's text to be red underlined (in iOS 6, due to a bug, this code didn't work):

```
NSDictionary* d = textField.typingAttributes;
NSMutableDictionary* md = [d mutableCopy];
[md addEntriesFromDictionary:
    @{NSForegroundColorAttributeName:[UIColor redColor],
      NSUnderlineStyleAttributeName:@(NSUnderlineStyleSingle)}];
textField.typingAttributes = md;
```

It is common practice to implement `textField:shouldChangeCharactersIn-Range:replacementString:` as a way of learning that the text has been changed, even if you then always return YES. This method is *not* called when the user changes text styling through the Bold, Italics, or Underline menu items.

`UITextFieldTextDidChangeNotification` corresponds loosely.

`textFieldShouldEndEditing:`
Return NO to prevent the text field from resigning first responder (even if you just sent `resignFirstResponder` to it). You might do this, for example, because the text is invalid or unacceptable in some way. The user will not know why the text field is refusing to end editing, so the usual thing is to put up an alert (Chapter 13) explaining the problem.

`textFieldDidEndEditing:`
`UITextFieldTextDidEndEditingNotification`
The text field has resigned first responder. See Chapter 8 ("Editable Content in Table Items" on page 446) for an example of using `textFieldDidEndEditing:` to fetch the text field's current text and store it in the model.

A text field is also a control (UIControl; see also Chapter 12). This means you can attach a target–action pair to any of the events that it reports in order to receive a message when that event occurs:

- The user can touch and drag, triggering Touch Down and the various Touch Drag events.
- If the user touches in such a way that the text field enters editing mode (and the keyboard appears), Editing Did Begin and Touch Cancel are triggered; if the user causes the text field to enter editing mode in some other way (such as by tabbing into it), Editing Did Begin is triggered without any Touch events.
- As the user edits (including changing attributes), Editing Changed is triggered.
- If the user taps while in editing mode, Touch Down (and possibly Touch Down Repeat) and Touch Cancel are triggered.
- When editing ends, Editing Did End is triggered; if the user stops editing by tapping Return in the keyboard, Did End on Exit is triggered first.

In general, you're more likely to treat a text field as a text field (through its delegate messages) than as a control (through its control events). However, the Did End on Exit event message has an interesting property: it provides an alternative way to dismiss the keyboard when the user taps a text field keyboard's Return button. If there is a Did End on Exit target–action pair for this text field, then if the text field's delegate does not return NO from textFieldShouldReturn:, the keyboard will be dismissed *automatically* when the user taps the Return key. (The action handler for Did End on Exit doesn't actually have to *do* anything.)

This suggests the following trick for getting automatic keyboard dismissal *with no code at all*. In the nib, edit the First Responder proxy object in the Attributes inspector, adding a new First Responder Action; let's call it dummy:. Now hook the Did End on Exit event of the text field to the dummy: action of the First Responder proxy object. That's it! Because the text field's Did End on Exit event now has a target–action pair, the text field automatically dismisses its keyboard when the user taps Return; there is no penalty for not finding a handler for a message sent up the responder chain, so the app doesn't crash even though there is no implementation of dummy: anywhere.

Alternatively, you can implement the same trick in code:

```
[textField addTarget:nil action:@selector(dummy:)
    forControlEvents:UIControlEventEditingDidEndOnExit];
```

A disabled text field emits no delegate messages or control events.

Text Field Menu

When the user double-taps or long-presses in a text field, the menu appears. It contains menu items such as Select, Select All, Paste, Copy, Cut, and Replace; which menu items appear depends on the circumstances. The menu can be customized; the key facts you need to know are these:

- You can add potential menu items to the menu through the singleton global shared UIMenuController object. Its menuItems property is an array of *custom* menu items — that is, menu items that *may* appear *in addition* to those that the system puts there. A menu item is a UIMenuItem, which is simply a title (which appears in the menu) plus an action selector. The action will be called, nil-targeted, thus sending it up the responder chain, when the user taps the menu item.

- The actions for the standard menu items are nil-targeted, so they percolate up the responder chain, and you can interfere with their behavior by implementing their actions. Many of the selectors are listed in the UIResponderStandardEditActions informal protocol. Commonly used standard actions are:

  — cut:

  — copy:

  — select:

  — selectAll:

  — paste:

  — delete:

  — _promptForReplace:

  — _define:

  — _showTextStyleOptions:

  — toggleBoldface:

  — toggleItalics:

  — toggleUnderline:

- You govern the presence or absence of *any* menu item by implementing the UIResponder method canPerformAction:withSender: in the responder chain.

As an example, we'll devise a text field whose menu includes our own menu item, Expand. I'm imagining here, for instance, a text field where the user can select a U.S. state two-letter abbreviation (such as "CA") and can then summon the menu and tap Expand to replace it with the state's full name (such as "California").

At some point before the user can tap in an instance of our UITextField subclass, we modify the global menu:

```
UIMenuItem *mi = [[UIMenuItem alloc] initWithTitle:@"Expand"
                                   action:@selector(expand:)];
UIMenuController *mc = [UIMenuController sharedMenuController];
mc.menuItems = @[mi];
```

In a UITextField subclass, we implement canPerformAction:withSender: to govern the contents of the menu. The reason for putting this code in a subclass is to guarantee that this implementation of canPerformAction:withSender: will be called when an instance of this subclass is first responder, but at no other time. Let's presume that we want our Expand menu item to be present only if the selection consists of a two-letter state abbreviation. UITextField itself provides no way to learn the selected text, but it conforms to the UITextInput protocol, which does:

```
- (BOOL) canPerformAction:(SEL)action withSender: (id) sender {
    if (action == @selector(expand:)) {
        NSString* s = [self textInRange:self.selectedTextRange];
        return (s.length == 2 && [self.class stateForAbbrev: s]);
    }
    return [super canPerformAction:action withSender:sender];
}
```

When the user chooses the Expand menu item, the expand: message is sent up the responder chain. We catch it in our UITextField subclass and obey it by replacing the selected text with the corresponding state name:

```
- (void) expand: (id) sender {
    NSString* s = [self textInRange:self.selectedTextRange];
    s = [self stateForAbbrev:s]; // left as an exercise for the reader
    [self replaceRange:self.selectedTextRange withText:s];
}
```

We can also implement the selector for, and thus modify the behavior of, any of the standard menu items. For example, I'll implement copy: and modify its behavior. First we call super to get standard copying behavior; then we modify what's now on the pasteboard:

```
- (void) copy: (id) sender {
    [super copy: sender];
    UIPasteboard* pb = [UIPasteboard generalPasteboard];
    NSString* s = pb.string;
    // ... alter s here ....
    pb.string = s;
}
```

(Implementing the selectors for toggleBoldface:, toggleItalics:, and toggle-Underline: is probably the best way to get an event when the user changes these attributes.)

Text Views

A text view (UITextView) is a scroll view subclass (UIScrollView); it is *not* a control. Many of its properties are similar to those of a text field:

- A text view has `text`, `font`, `textColor`, and `textAlignment` properties; it can be user-editable or not, according to its `editable` property.
- A text view has `attributedText`, `allowsEditingTextAttributes`, and `typing-Attributes` properties, as well as `clearsOnInsertion`.
- An editable text view governs its keyboard just as a text field does: when it is first responder, it is being edited and shows the keyboard, and it implements the UIText-Input protocol and has `inputView` and `inputAccessoryView` properties.
- A text view's menu works the same way as a text field's.

A text view provides (official) information about, and control of, its selection: it has a `selectedRange` property which you can get and set, along with a `scrollRangeTo-Visible:` method so that you can scroll in terms of a range of its text.

A text view's delegate messages (UITextViewDelegate protocol) and notifications, too, are similar to those of a text field. The following delegate methods (and notifications) should have a familiar ring:

- `textViewShouldBeginEditing:`
- `textViewDidBeginEditing:` (UITextViewTextDidBeginEditingNotification)
- `textViewShouldEndEditing:`
- `textViewDidEndEditing:` (UITextViewTextDidEndEditingNotification)
- `textView:shouldChangeTextInRange:replacementText:`

Some differences are:

`textViewDidChange:`
UITextViewTextDidChangeNotification
   Sent when the user changes text or attributes. A text field has no corresponding delegate method, though the Editing Changed control event and notification are similar.

`textViewDidChangeSelection:`
   In contrast, a text field is officially uninformative about the selection.

New in iOS 7, a text view's delegate can also decide how to respond when the user taps on a text attachment or a link. The text view must have its `selectable` property (new in iOS 7) set to YES, and its `editable` property set to NO:

`textView:shouldInteractWithTextAttachment:inRange:`
> The default behavior (you return YES) is an action sheet letting the user copy the image to the clipboard or the camera roll.

`textView:shouldInteractWithURL:inRange:`
> The default behavior (you return YES) is that the URL is opened in Safari.

By returning NO from either of those methods, you can substitute your own response, effectively treating the image or URL as a button.

A text view also has a `dataDetectorTypes` property; this, too, if the text view is selectable but not editable, allows text of certain types, specified as a bitmask (and presumably located using NSDataDetector), to be treated as tappable links; the types are:

`UIDataDetectorTypePhoneNumber`
> The default response to a tap is an alert view with an option to call the number; the default response to a long press is an action sheet with options Call, Send Message, Add to Contacts, and Copy.

`UIDataDetectorTypeLink`
> The default response to a tap is to go the URL in Mobile Safari; the default response to a long press is an action sheet with options Open, Add to Reading List, and Copy.

`UIDataDetectorTypeAddress`
> The default response to a tap is to search for the address in the Maps app; the default response to a long press is an action sheet with options Open in Maps, Add to Contacts, and Copy.

`UIDataDetectorTypeCalendarEvent`
> The default response is an action sheet with options Create Event, Show in Calendar, and Copy.

New in iOS 7, the delegate's implementation of `textView:shouldInteractWithURL:in-Range:` catches data detector taps as well, so you can prevent the default behavior and substitute your own. You can distinguish a phone number through the URL's `scheme` (it will be `@"tel"`), but an address or calendar event will be opaque (the scheme is `@"x-apple-data-detectors"`) and returning NO probably makes no sense. The delegate method doesn't distinguish a tap from a long press for you.

Text View as Scroll View

A text view is a scroll view, so everything you know about scroll views applies (see Chapter 7). It has, by default, no border, because a scroll view has no border. It can be user-scrollable or not.

A text view's `contentSize` is maintained for you, automatically, as the text changes, so as to contain the text exactly; thus, if the text view is scrollable, the user can see any of its text. You can track changes to the content size by tracking changes to the text (in the delegate's `textViewDidChange:`, for example). A common reason for doing so is to implement a *self-sizing* text view, that is, a text view that adjusts its height automatically to embrace the amount of text it contains. In this example, we have an outlet to the text view's internal height constraint:

```
- (void)textViewDidChange:(UITextView *)textView {
    self.heightConstraint.constant = textView.contentSize.height;
}
```

Text View and Keyboard

The fact that a text view is a scroll view comes in handy also when the keyboard partially covers a text view. The text view quite often dominates the screen, or a large portion of the screen, and you can respond to the keyboard partially covering it by adjusting the text view's `contentInset`, just as we did earlier in this chapter with a scroll view ("Text field in a scroll view" on page 522).

Here's a fairly straightforward implementation for dealing with what happens when the user taps in the text view to start editing and the keyboard partially covers the text view (`self.tv`):

```
-(void)viewDidLoad {
    [[NSNotificationCenter defaultCenter] addObserver:self
        selector:@selector(keyboardShow:)
        name:UIKeyboardWillShowNotification object:nil];
    [[NSNotificationCenter defaultCenter] addObserver:self
        selector:@selector(keyboardHide:)
        name:UIKeyboardWillHideNotification object:nil];
}
- (void) keyboardShow: (NSNotification*) n {
    NSDictionary* d = [n userInfo];
    CGRect r = [[d objectForKey:UIKeyboardFrameEndUserInfoKey] CGRectValue];
    r = [self.tv.superview convertRect:r fromView:nil];
    CGRect f = self.tv.frame;
    CGRect fs = self.tv.superview.bounds;
    CGFloat diff = fs.size.height - f.origin.y - f.size.height;
    CGFloat keyboardTop = r.size.height - diff;
    UIEdgeInsets insets = self.tv.contentInset;
    insets.bottom = keyboardTop;
    self.tv.contentInset = insets;
    insets = self.tv.scrollIndicatorInsets;
    insets.bottom = keyboardTop;
    self.tv.scrollIndicatorInsets = insets;
}
```

However, in iOS 7 there's a bug: if the keyboard now covers the spot in the text view where the user tapped, the selection remains hidden behind the keyboard — and calling `scrollRangeToVisible:` doesn't help. (In previous versions of iOS, the text view scrolled automatically to reveal the selection.) And there's another bug: as the user types, the text view doesn't automatically scroll up to keep newly entered characters above the top of the keyboard. (In previous versions of iOS, it did.)

A possible workaround involves taking advantage of the fact that UITextView implements the UITextInput protocol. For example:

```
-(void)textViewDidChange:(UITextView *)textView {
    // prevent typed characters from going behind keyboard
    // the keyboard should be doing this for us automatically!
    CGRect r =
        [textView caretRectForPosition:textView.selectedTextRange.end];
    [textView scrollRectToVisible:r animated:NO];
}
```

Now let's talk about what happens when the keyboard is dismissed. First of all, *how* is the keyboard to be dismissed? On the iPad, the virtual keyboard usually contains a button that dismisses the keyboard. But what about the iPhone? The Return key is meaningful for character entry; you aren't likely to want to misuse it as a way of dismissing the keyboard.

On the iPhone, the interface might well consist of a text view and the keyboard, which is *always* showing: instead of dismissing the keyboard, the user dismisses the entire interface. For example, in Apple's Mail app on the iPhone, when the user is composing a message, in what is presumably a presented view controller, the keyboard is present the whole time; the keyboard is dismissed because the user sends or cancels the message and the presented view controller is dismissed.

Alternatively, you can provide interface for dismissing the keyboard explicitly. For example, in Apple's Notes app, a note alternates between being read fullscreen and being edited with the keyboard present; in the latter case, a Done button appears, and the user taps it to dismiss the keyboard. If there's no good place to put a Done button in the interface, you could attach an accessory view to the keyboard itself.

Here's a possible implementation of a Done button's action method, with resulting dismissal of the keyboard:

```
- (IBAction)doDone:(id)sender {
    [self.view endEditing:NO];
}
- (void) keyboardHide: (NSNotification*) n {
    NSDictionary* d = [n userInfo];
    NSNumber* curve = d[UIKeyboardAnimationCurveUserInfoKey];
    NSNumber* duration = d[UIKeyboardAnimationDurationUserInfoKey];
    [UIView animateWithDuration:duration.floatValue delay:0
                        options:curve.integerValue << 16
                     animations:
     ^{
         [self.tv setContentOffset:CGPointZero];
     } completion:^(BOOL finished) {
```

```
            self.tv.contentInset = UIEdgeInsetsZero;
            self.tv.scrollIndicatorInsets = UIEdgeInsetsZero;
        }];
    }
```

Text Kit

New in iOS 7, Text Kit has been introduced — actually, imported from OS X, where you may already be more familiar with its use than you realize. For example, much of the text-editing "magic" of Xcode is due to Text Kit.

Text Kit is a group of Objective-C classes that are responsible for drawing text; simply put, they turn an NSAttributedString into graphics. You can take advantage of Text Kit to modify text drawing in ways that were possible in previous systems only by dipping down to the low-level C-based world of Core Text (if at all).

A UITextView in iOS 7 provides direct access to the underlying Text Kit engine. It has the following Text Kit–related properties:

textContainer
> The text view's text container (an NSTextContainer instance). The designated initializer is now initWithFrame:textContainer:.

textContainerInset
> The margins of the text container, designating the area within the contentSize rectangle in which the text as a whole is drawn. Changing this value changes the margins immediately, causing the text to be freshly laid out (try it!).

layoutManager
> The text view's layout manager (an NSLayoutManager instance).

textStorage
> The text view's text storage (an NSTextStorage instance).

When you initialize a text view with a text container, you hand it the entire "stack" of Text Kit instances: a text container, a layout manager, and a text storage. In the simplest and most common case, a text storage has a layout manager, and a layout manager has a text container, thus forming the "stack". If the text container is a UITextView's text container, the stack is retained, and the text view is operative. Thus, the simplest case might look like this (and we may suppose that this is in fact what the runtime does when you call UITextView's initWithFrame:):

```
CGRect r = // ... frame for the new text view
NSLayoutManager* lm = [NSLayoutManager new];
NSTextStorage* ts = [NSTextStorage new];
[ts addLayoutManager:lm];
NSTextContainer* tc =
```

```
    [[NSTextContainer alloc]
        initWithSize:CGSizeMake(r.size.width, CGFLOAT_MAX)];
[lm addTextContainer:tc];
UITextView* tv = [[UITextView alloc] initWithFrame:r textContainer:tc];
```

Here's what the three chief Text Kit classes do:

NSTextStorage
> A subclass of NSMutableAttributedString. It is, or holds, the underlying text. It has one or more layout managers, and notifies them when the text changes. By subclassing and delegation (NSTextStorageDelegate), its behavior can be modified so that it applies attributes in a custom fashion.

NSTextContainer
> It is owned by a layout manager, and helps that layout manager by defining the region in which the text is to be laid out. It does this in three primary ways:
>
> - It has a size. The text container's top left is the origin for the text layout coordinate system, and the text will be laid out within the text container's rectangle.
>
> - It can specify *exclusion paths* (exclusionPaths property). These are UIBezierPath objects within which no text is to be drawn.
>
> - It can be subclassed to override lineFragmentRectForProposedRect:atIndex:writingDirection:remainingRect:, thus placing the next chunk of text drawing anywhere at all (except inside an exclusion path).

NSLayoutManager
> This is the master text drawing class! It has one or more text containers, and is owned by a text storage — thus forming the Text Kit stack. It draws the text storage's text into the boundaries defined by the text container(s).
>
> A layout manager can have a delegate (NSLayoutManagerDelegate), and can be subclassed. This, as you may well imagine, is a powerful and sophisticated class.

Text Container

An NSTextContainer has a size, within which the text will be drawn. By default, as in the preceding code, a text view's text container's width is the width of the text view, while its height is effectively infinite, allowing the drawing of the text to grow vertically but not horizontally beyond the bounds of the text view, and making it possible to scroll the text vertically.

It also has heightTracksTextView and widthTracksTextView properties, causing the text container to be resized to match changes in the size of the text view — for example, if the text view is resized because of interface rotation. By default, as you might expect, widthTracksTextView is YES (the documentation is wrong about this), while heightTracksTextView is NO: the text fills the width of the text view, and is laid out freshly if

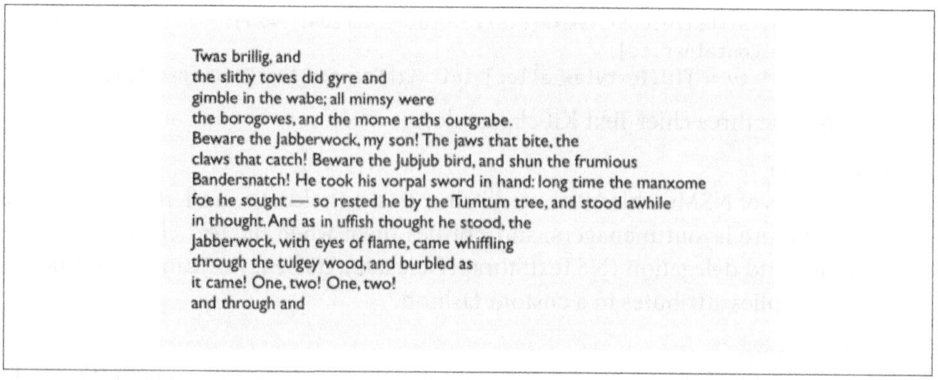

```
Twas brillig, and
the slithy toves did gyre and
gimble in the wabe; all mimsy were
the borogoves, and the mome raths outgrabe.
Beware the Jabberwock, my son! The jaws that bite, the
claws that catch! Beware the Jubjub bird, and shun the frumious
Bandersnatch! He took his vorpal sword in hand: long time the manxome
foe he sought — so rested he by the Tumtum tree, and stood awhile
in thought. And as in uffish thought he stood, the
Jabberwock, with eyes of flame, came whiffling
through the tulgey wood, and burbled as
it came! One, two! One, two!
and through and
```

Figure 10-10. A text view with an exclusion path

the text view's width changes, but its height remains effectively infinite. The text view itself, of course, configures its own contentSize so that the user can scroll just to the bottom of the existing text.

When you change a text view's textContainerInset, it modifies its text container's size to match, as necessary. In the default configuration, this means that it modifies the text container's width; the top and bottom insets are implemented through the text container's position within the content rect. Within the text container, additional side margins correspond to the text container's lineFragmentPadding; the default is 5, but you can change it.

If the text view's scrollEnabled is NO, then by default its text container's heightTracksTextView and widthTracksTextView are both YES, and the text container size is adjusted so that the text fills the text view. In that case, you can also set the text container's lineBreakMode. This works like the line break mode of a UILabel. For example, if the line break mode is NSLineBreakByTruncatingTail, then the last line has an ellipsis at the end (if the text is too long for the text view). You can also set the text container's maximumNumberOfLines, which is like a UILabel's numberOfLines. In effect, you've turned the text view into a label!

But, of course, a nonscrolling text view isn't *just* a label, because you've got access to the Text Kit stack that backs it. For example, you can apply exclusion paths to the text container. Figure 10-10 shows a case in point. The text wraps in longer and longer lines, and then in shorter and shorter lines, because there's an exclusion path on the right side of the text container that's a rectangle with a large V-shaped indentation.

In Figure 10-10, the text view (self.tv) is initially configured in the view controller's viewDidLoad:

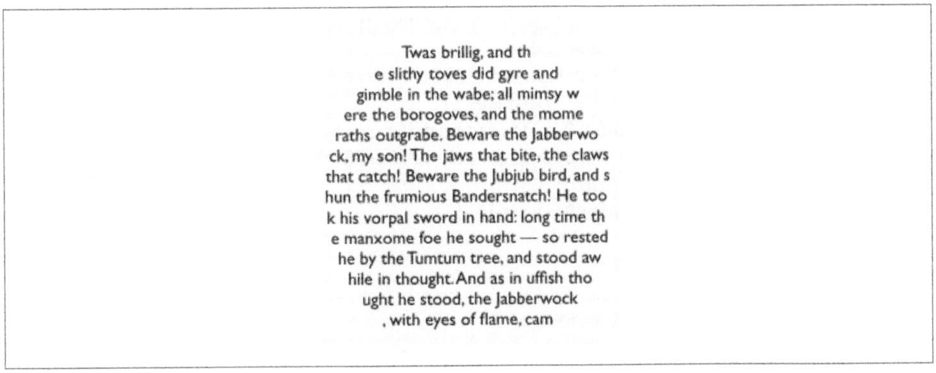

```
                    Twas brillig, and th
              e slithy toves did gyre and
            gimble in the wabe; all mimsy w
            ere the borogoves, and the mome
           raths outgrabe. Beware the Jabberwo
          ck, my son! The jaws that bite, the claws
         that catch! Beware the Jubjub bird, and s
         hun the frumious Bandersnatch! He too
          k his vorpal sword in hand: long time th
           e manxome foe he sought — so rested
            he by the Tumtum tree, and stood aw
             hile in thought. And as in uffish tho
              ught he stood, the Jabberwock
                 , with eyes of flame, cam
```

Figure 10-11. A text view with a subclassed text container

```
self.tv.attributedText = // ...
self.tv.textContainerInset = UIEdgeInsetsMake(20, 20, 20, 0);
self.tv.scrollEnabled = NO;
```

The exclusion path is then drawn and applied in `viewDidLayoutSubviews`:

```
-(void)viewDidLayoutSubviews {
    CGSize sz = self.tv.textContainer.size;
    UIBezierPath* p = [UIBezierPath new];
    [p moveToPoint:CGPointMake(sz.width/4.0,0)];
    [p addLineToPoint:CGPointMake(sz.width,0)];
    [p addLineToPoint:CGPointMake(sz.width,sz.height)];
    [p addLineToPoint:CGPointMake(sz.width/4.0,sz.height)];
    [p addLineToPoint:CGPointMake(sz.width,sz.height/2.0)];
    [p closePath];
    self.tv.textContainer.exclusionPaths = @[p];
}
```

Instead of (or in addition to) an exclusion path, you can subclass NSTextContainer to modify the rectangle in which the layout manager wants to position a piece of text. (Each piece of text is actually a line fragment; I'll explain in the next section what a line fragment is.) In Figure 10-11, the text is inside a circle.

To achieve the layout shown in Figure 10-11, I set the attributed string's line break mode to `NSLineBreakByCharWrapping` (to bring the right edge of each line as close as possible to the circular shape), and constructed the TextKit stack by hand to include an instance of my NSTextContainer subclass. That subclass contains this code, in which I simple-mindedly increase each line fragment's horizontal origin and decrease its width until its top edge fits entirely within a circle:

```
-(CGRect)lineFragmentRectForProposedRect:(CGRect)proposedRect
        atIndex:(NSUInteger)characterIndex
        writingDirection:(NSWritingDirection)baseWritingDirection
        remainingRect:(CGRect *)remainingRect {
```

```
CGRect result =
    [super lineFragmentRectForProposedRect:proposedRect
        atIndex:characterIndex
        writingDirection:baseWritingDirection
        remainingRect:remainingRect];
CGRect r = CGRectMake(0,0,self.size.width,self.size.height);
UIBezierPath* circle = [UIBezierPath bezierPathWithOvalInRect:r];
CGPoint p = result.origin;
while (![circle containsPoint:p]) {
    p.x += .1;
    result.origin = p;
}
CGFloat w = result.size.width;
p = result.origin;
p.x += w;
while (![circle containsPoint:p]) {
    w -= .1;
    result.size.width = w;
    p = result.origin;
    p.x += w;
}
return result;
}
```

Alternative Text Kit Stack Architectures

The default Text Kit stack is one text storage, which has one layout manager, which has one text container. But a text storage can have multiple layout managers, and a layout manager can have multiple text containers. What's that all about?

If a layout manager has multiple text containers, the overflow from each text container is drawn in the next one. For example, in Figure 10-12, there are two text views; the text has filled the first text view, and has then continued by flowing into and filling the second text view. As far as I can tell, the text views can't be made editable in this configuration. But clearly this is a way to achieve a multicolumn or multipage layout, or you could use text views of different sizes for a magazine-style layout.

It is possible to achieve that arrangement by disconnecting the layout managers of existing text views from their text containers and rebuilding the stack from below. However, I think it's probably safer to build the entire stack by hand:

```
CGRect r = //
CGRect r2 = //
NSAttributedString* mas = //
NSTextStorage* ts1 = [[NSTextStorage alloc] initWithAttributedString:mas];
NSLayoutManager* lm1 = [NSLayoutManager new];
[ts1 addLayoutManager:lm1];
NSTextContainer* tc1 = [[NSTextContainer alloc] initWithSize:r.size];
[lm1 addTextContainer:tc1];
UITextView* tv = [[UITextView alloc] initWithFrame:r textContainer:tc1];
```

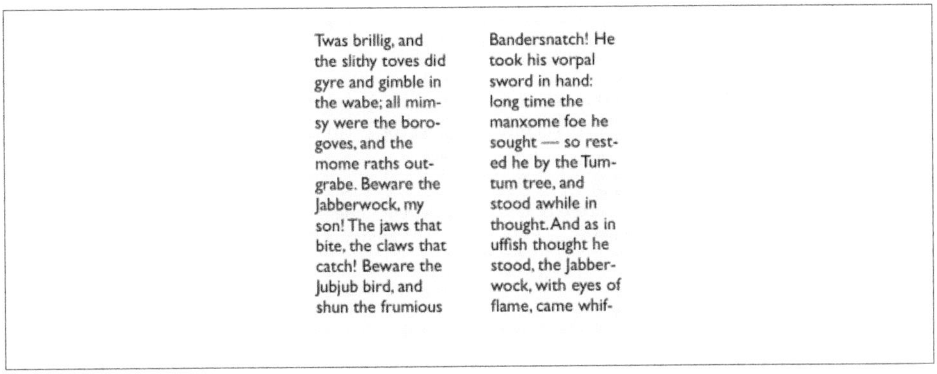

Figure 10-12. A layout manager with two text containers

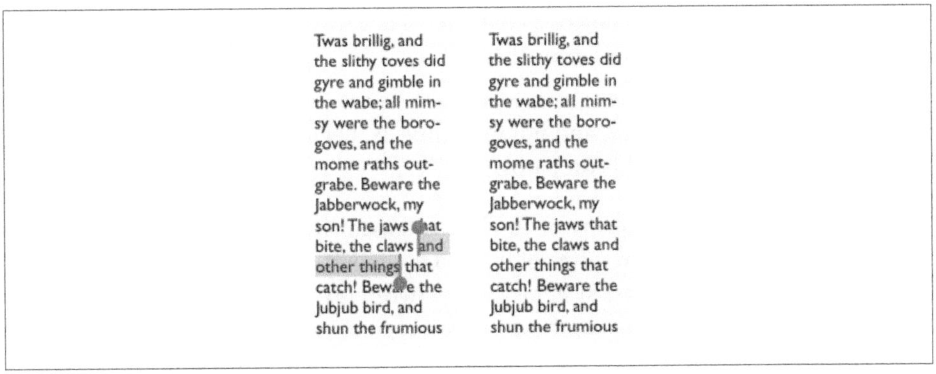

Figure 10-13. A text storage with two layout managers

```
tv.scrollEnabled = NO;
NSTextContainer* tc2 = [[NSTextContainer alloc] initWithSize:r2.size];
[lm1 addTextContainer:tc2];
UITextView* tv2 = [[UITextView alloc] initWithFrame:r2 textContainer:tc2];
tv2.scrollEnabled = NO;
```

If a text storage has multiple layout managers, then each layout manager is laying out the same text. For example, in Figure 10-13, there are two text views displaying the same text. The remarkable thing is that if you edit one text view, the other changes to match. (That's how Xcode lets you edit the same code file in different windows, tabs, or panes.)

Again, this arrangement is probably best achieved by building the entire text stack by hand:

```
CGRect r = //
CGRect r2 = //
NSAttributedString* mas = //
NSTextStorage* ts1 = [[NSTextStorage alloc] initWithAttributedString:mas];
```

```
NSLayoutManager* lm1 = [NSLayoutManager new];
[ts1 addLayoutManager:lm1];
NSLayoutManager* lm2 = [NSLayoutManager new];
[ts1 addLayoutManager:lm2];
NSTextContainer* tc1 = [[NSTextContainer alloc] initWithSize:r.size];
NSTextContainer* tc2 = [[NSTextContainer alloc] initWithSize:r2.size];
[lm1 addTextContainer:tc1];
[lm2 addTextContainer:tc2];
UITextView* tv = [[UITextView alloc] initWithFrame:r textContainer:tc1];
UITextView* tv2 = [[UITextView alloc] initWithFrame:r2 textContainer:tc2];
```

Layout Manager

The first thing to know about a layout manager is the geometry in which it thinks. To envision a layout manager's geometrical world, think in terms of glyphs and line fragments:

- A *glyph* is the drawn analog of a character. The layout manager's primary job is to get glyphs from a font and draw them.

- A *line fragment* is a rectangle in which glyphs are drawn, one after another. (The reason it's a line *fragment*, and not just a line, is that a line might be interrupted by the text container's exclusion paths.)

A glyph has a location in terms of the line fragment into which it is drawn. A line fragment's coordinates are in terms of the text container. The layout manager can convert between these coordinate systems, and between text and glyphs. Given a range of text in the text storage, it knows where the corresponding glyphs are drawn in the text container. Conversely, given a location in the text container, it knows what glyph is drawn there and what range of text in the text storage that glyph represents.

What's missing from that geometry is what, if anything, the text container corresponds to in the real world. A text container is not, itself, a real rectangle in the real world; it's just a class that tells the layout manager a size to draw into. Making that rectangle meaningful for drawing purposes is up to some other class outside the Text Kit stack. A UITextView, for example, has a text container, which it shares with a layout manager. The text view knows how its own content is scrolled and how the rectangle represented by its text container is inset within that scrolling content. The layout manager, however, doesn't know anything about that; it sees the text container as a purely theoretical rectangular boundary. (Only when the layout manager actually draws does it make contact with the real world of some graphics context — and it must be told, on those occasions, how the text container's rectangle is offset within that graphics context.)

To illustrate, I'll use a TextKit method to learn the index of the first character visible at the top left of a text view (self.tv); I'll then use NSLinguisticTagger to derive the first *word* visible at the top left of the text view. I can ask the layout manager what character or glyph corresponds to a certain point in the text container, but what point should I ask about? Translating from the real world to text container coordinates is up to me; I must take into account both the scroll position of the text view's content and the inset of the text container within that content:

```
CGPoint off = self.tv.contentOffset;
CGFloat top = self.tv.textContainerInset.top;
CGPoint tctopleft = CGPointMake(0, off.y - top);
```

Now I'm speaking in terms of text container coordinates, which are layout manager coordinates. One possibility is then to ask directly for the index (in the text storage's string) of the corresponding character:

```
NSUInteger ix =
    [self.tv.layoutManager characterIndexForPoint:tctopleft
        inTextContainer:self.tv.textContainer
        fractionOfDistanceBetweenInsertionPoints:nil];
```

That, however, does not give quite the results one might intuitively expect. If *any* of a word is poking down from above into the visible area of the text view, that is the word whose first character is returned. I think we intuitively expect, if a word isn't fully visible, that the answer should be the word that starts the *next* line, which *is* fully visible. So I'll modify that code in a simpleminded way. I'll obtain the index of the *glyph* at my initial point; from this, I can derive the rect of the line fragment containing it. If that line fragment is not at least three-quarters visible, I'll add one line fragment height to the starting point and derive the glyph index again. Then I'll convert the glyph index to a character index:

```
NSUInteger ix =
    [self.tv.layoutManager glyphIndexForPoint:tctopleft
        inTextContainer:self.tv.textContainer
        fractionOfDistanceThroughGlyph:nil];
CGRect frag =
    [self.tv.layoutManager lineFragmentRectForGlyphAtIndex:ix
                                    effectiveRange:nil];
if (tctopleft.y > frag.origin.y + .5*frag.size.height) {
    tctopleft.y += frag.size.height;
    ix = [self.tv.layoutManager glyphIndexForPoint:tctopleft
            inTextContainer:self.tv.textContainer
            fractionOfDistanceThroughGlyph:nil];
}
NSRange charRange =
    [self.tv.layoutManager characterRangeForGlyphRange:NSMakeRange(ix,0)
                                    actualGlyphRange:nil];
ix = charRange.location;
```

Finally, I'll use NSLinguisticTagger to get the range of the entire word to which this character belongs:

```
NSLinguisticTagger* t =
    [[NSLinguisticTagger alloc]
     initWithTagSchemes:@[NSLinguisticTagSchemeTokenType] options:0];
t.string = self.tv.text;
NSRange r;
NSString* tag =
    [t tagAtIndex:ix scheme:NSLinguisticTagSchemeTokenType
        tokenRange:&r sentenceRange:nil];
if ([tag isEqualToString: NSLinguisticTagWord])
    NSLog(@"%@", [self.tv.text substringWithRange:r]);
```

Clearly, the same sort of technique could be used to formulate a custom response to a tap ("what word did the user just tap on?").

By subclassing NSLayoutManager (and by implementing its delegate), many powerful effects can be achieved. As a simple example, I'll carry on from the preceding code by drawing a rectangular outline around the word we just located. To make this possible, I have an NSLayoutManager subclass, MyLayoutManager, an instance of which is built into the Text Kit stack for this text view. MyLayoutManager has a public NSRange property, wordRange. Having worked out what word I want to outline, I set the layout manager's wordRange and invalidate its drawing of that word, to force a redraw:

```
MyLayoutManager* lm = (MyLayoutManager*)self.tv.layoutManager;
lm.wordRange = r;
[lm invalidateDisplayForCharacterRange:r];
```

In MyLayoutManager, I've overridden the method that draws the background behind glyphs. At the moment this method is called, there is already a graphics context.

First, I call super. Then, if the range of glyphs to be drawn includes the glyphs for the range of characters in self.wordRange, I ask for the rect of the bounding box of those glyphs, and stroke it to form the rectangle. As I mentioned earlier, the bounding box is in text container coordinates, but now we're drawing in the real world, so I have to compensate by offsetting the drawn rectangle by the same amount that the text container is supposed to be offset in the real world; fortunately, the text view tells us (origin) what that offset is:

```
-(void)drawBackgroundForGlyphRange:(NSRange)glyphsToShow
        atPoint:(CGPoint)origin {
    [super drawBackgroundForGlyphRange:glyphsToShow atPoint:origin];
    if (!self.wordRange.length)
        return;
    NSRange range =
        [self glyphRangeForCharacterRange:self.wordRange
            actualCharacterRange:nil];
    range = NSIntersectionRange(glyphsToShow, range);
    if (!range.length)
        return;
    NSTextContainer* tc =
        [self textContainerForGlyphAtIndex:range.location
```

```
        effectiveRange:nil];
    CGRect r = [self boundingRectForGlyphRange:range inTextContainer:tc];
    r.origin.x += origin.x;
    r.origin.y += origin.y;
    CGContextRef c = UIGraphicsGetCurrentContext();
    CGContextSaveGState(c);
    CGContextSetStrokeColorWithColor(c, [UIColor blackColor].CGColor);
    CGContextSetLineWidth(c, 1.0);
    CGContextStrokeRect(c, r);
    CGContextRestoreGState(c);
}
```

Text Kit Without a Text View

UITextView is the only built-in iOS class that has a Text Kit stack to which you are given
programmatic access. But that doesn't mean it's the only place where you can draw with
Text Kit! You can draw with Text Kit *anywhere you can draw* — that is, in any graphics
context (Chapter 2). When you do so, you should always call both drawBackgroundFor-
GlyphRange:atPoint: (the method I overrode in the previous example) and draw-
GlyphsForGlyphRange:atPoint:, in that order. The point: argument is where you
consider the text container's origin to be within the current graphics context.

To illustrate, I'll change the implementation of the StringDrawer class that I described
earlier in this chapter. Previously, StringDrawer's drawRect: implementation told the
attributed string (self.attributedText) to draw itself:

```
- (void)drawRect:(CGRect)rect {
    CGRect r = CGRectOffset(rect, 0, 2); // shoved down a little from top
    [self.attributedText drawWithRect:r
        options:NSStringDrawingTruncatesLastVisibleLine |
                NSStringDrawingUsesLineFragmentOrigin
        context:nil];
}
```

Instead, I'll construct the Text Kit stack and tell its layout manager to draw the text:

```
- (void)drawRect:(CGRect)rect {
    NSLayoutManager* lm = [NSLayoutManager new];
    NSTextStorage* ts =
        [[NSTextStorage alloc] initWithAttributedString:self.attributedText];
    [ts addLayoutManager:lm];
    NSTextContainer* tc =
        [[NSTextContainer alloc] initWithSize:rect.size];
    [lm addTextContainer:tc];
    tc.lineBreakMode = NSLineBreakByTruncatingTail;
    tc.lineFragmentPadding = 0;
    NSRange r = [lm glyphRangeForTextContainer:tc];
    [lm drawBackgroundForGlyphRange:r atPoint:CGPointMake(0,2)];
    [lm drawGlyphsForGlyphRange:r atPoint:CGPointMake(0,2)];
}
```

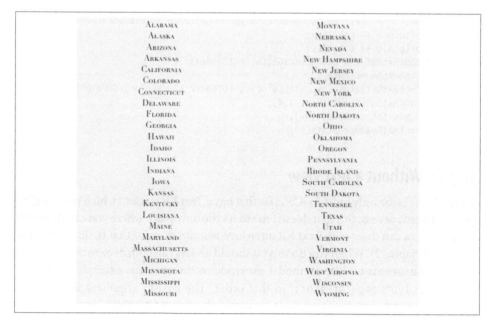

ALABAMA	MONTANA
ALASKA	NEBRASKA
ARIZONA	NEVADA
ARKANSAS	NEW HAMPSHIRE
CALIFORNIA	NEW JERSEY
COLORADO	NEW MEXICO
CONNECTICUT	NEW YORK
DELAWARE	NORTH CAROLINA
FLORIDA	NORTH DAKOTA
GEORGIA	OHIO
HAWAII	OKLAHOMA
IDAHO	OREGON
ILLINOIS	PENNSYLVANIA
INDIANA	RHODE ISLAND
IOWA	SOUTH CAROLINA
KANSAS	SOUTH DAKOTA
KENTUCKY	TENNESSEE
LOUISIANA	TEXAS
MAINE	UTAH
MARYLAND	VERMONT
MASSACHUSETTS	VIRGINIA
MICHIGAN	WASHINGTON
MINNESOTA	WEST VIRGINIA
MISSISSIPPI	WISCONSIN
MISSOURI	WYOMING

Figure 10-14. Two-column text in small caps

Building the entire Text Kit stack by hand may seem like overkill for that simple example, but imagine what *else* I could do now that I have access to the entire Text Kit stack! I can use properties, subclassing and delegation, and alternative stack architectures to achieve customizations and effects that, before iOS 7, were difficult or impossible to achieve without dipping down to the level of Core Text.

For example, the two-column display of U.S. state names on the iPad shown in Figure 10-14 was a Core Text example in previous editions of this book, requiring 50 or 60 lines of elaborate C code, complicated by the necessity of flipping the context to prevent the text from being drawn upside-down. But in iOS 7 it can be achieved easily through Objective-C and Text Kit — effectively just by reusing code from earlier examples in this chapter.

Furthermore, the example from previous editions went on to describe how to make the display of state names interactive, with the name of the tapped state briefly outlined with a rectangle (Figure 10-15). With Core Text, this was almost insanely difficult, not least because we had to keep track of all the line fragment rectangles ourselves. But it's easy with Text Kit, because the layout manager knows all the answers.

We have a UIView subclass, StyledText. In its `layoutSubviews`, it creates the Text Kit stack — a layout manager with two text containers, to achieve the two-column layout — and stores the whole stack, along with the rects at which the two text containers are to be drawn, in properties:

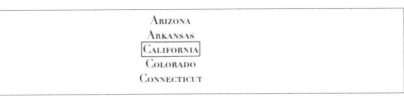

Figure 10-15. The user has tapped on California

```
-(void)layoutSubviews {
    [super layoutSubviews];
    CGRect r1 = self.bounds;
    r1.origin.y += 2; // a little top space
    r1.size.width /= 2.0; // column 1
    CGRect r2 = r1;
    r2.origin.x += r2.size.width; // column 2
    NSLayoutManager* lm = [MyLayoutManager new];
    NSTextStorage* ts =
        [[NSTextStorage alloc] initWithAttributedString:self.text];
    [ts addLayoutManager:lm];
    NSTextContainer* tc = [[NSTextContainer alloc] initWithSize:r1.size];
    [lm addTextContainer:tc];
    NSTextContainer* tc2 = [[NSTextContainer alloc] initWithSize:r2.size];
    [lm addTextContainer:tc2];
    self.lm = lm;
    self.ts = ts;
    self.tc = tc;
    self.tc2 = tc2;
    self.r1 = r1;
    self.r2 = r2;
}
```

Our `drawRect:` is just like the previous example, except that we have two text containers to draw:

```
- (void) drawRect:(CGRect)rect {
    NSRange range1 = [self.lm glyphRangeForTextContainer:self.tc];
    [self.lm drawBackgroundForGlyphRange:range1 atPoint:self.r1.origin];
    [self.lm drawGlyphsForGlyphRange:range1 atPoint:self.r1.origin];
    NSRange range2 = [self.lm glyphRangeForTextContainer:self.tc2];
    [self.lm drawBackgroundForGlyphRange:range2 atPoint:self.r2.origin];
    [self.lm drawGlyphsForGlyphRange:range2 atPoint:self.r2.origin];
}
```

So much for drawing the text! Now, when the user taps on our view, a tap gesture recognizer's action handler is called. We are using the same layout manager subclass developed earlier in this chapter; it draws a rectangle around the glyphs corresponding to the characters of its `wordRange` property. Thus, all we have to do in order to make the flashing rectangle around the tapped word is work out what that range is, set the layout manager's `wordRange` and redraw ourselves, and then set the layout manager's word-Range back to a zero range and redraw ourselves again to remove the rectangle.

We start by working out which column the user tapped in; this tells us which text container it is, and what the tapped point is in text container coordinates:

```
CGPoint p = [g locationInView:self]; // g is the tap gesture recognizer
NSTextContainer* tc = self.tc;
if (!CGRectContainsPoint(self.r1, p)) {
    tc = self.tc2;
    p.x -= self.r1.size.width;
}
```

Now we can ask the layout manager what glyph the user tapped on, and hence the whole range of glyphs within the line fragment the user tapped in. If the user tapped to the left of the first glyph or to the right of the last glyph, no word was tapped, and we return:

```
CGFloat f;
NSUInteger ix =
    [self.lm glyphIndexForPoint:p inTextContainer:tc
        fractionOfDistanceThroughGlyph:&f];
NSRange glyphRange;
[self.lm lineFragmentRectForGlyphAtIndex:ix effectiveRange:&glyphRange];
if (ix == glyphRange.location && f == 0.0)
    return;
if (ix == glyphRange.location + glyphRange.length - 1 && f == 1.0)
    return;
```

If the last glyph of the line fragment is a whitespace glyph, we don't want to include it in our rectangle, so we subtract it from the end of our range. Now we're ready to convert to a character range, and thus we can learn the name of the state that the user tapped on:

```
while (NSGlyphPropertyControlCharacter &
    [self.lm propertyForGlyphAtIndex:
        glyphRange.location + glyphRange.length - 1])
    glyphRange.length -= 1;
NSRange characterRange =
    [self.lm characterRangeForGlyphRange:glyphRange actualGlyphRange:nil];
NSString* s = [self.text.string substringWithRange:characterRange];
NSLog(@"you tapped %@", s);
```

Finally, we flash the rectangle around the state name by setting and resetting the word-Range property of the subclassed layout manager:

```
MyLayoutManager* lm = (MyLayoutManager*)self.lm;
lm.wordRange = characterRange;
[self setNeedsDisplay];
dispatch_time_t popTime =
    dispatch_time(DISPATCH_TIME_NOW, (int64_t)(0.3 * NSEC_PER_SEC));
```

```
dispatch_after(popTime, dispatch_get_main_queue(), ^{
    lm.wordRange = NSMakeRange(0, 0);
    [self setNeedsDisplay];
});
```

CHAPTER 11

Web Views

A web view (UIWebView) is a UIView subclass that acts as a versatile renderer of text in various formats, including:

- HTML
- PDF
- RTF, including *.rtfd* (which must be supplied in a zipped format, *.rtfd.zip*)
- Microsoft Word (*.doc*), Excel (*.xls*), and PowerPoint (*.ppt*)
- Pages, Numbers, and Keynote; before iWork 2009, these must be zipped (e.g., *.key.zip*), but starting with iWork 2009 they must *not* be zipped.

In addition to displaying rendered text, a web view is a web browser. If you ask a web view to display HTML that refers to a resource available on disk or over the Internet, such as an image to be shown as the source of an <img> tag, the web view will attempt to fetch it and display it. Similarly, if the user taps, within the web view, on a link that leads to content on disk or over the Internet that the web view can render, the web view by default will attempt to fetch that content and display it. Indeed, a web view is, in effect, a front end for WebKit, the same rendering engine used by Mobile Safari (and by Safari on OS X). A web view can display non-HTML file formats such as PDF, RTF, and so on, precisely because WebKit can display them.

As the user taps links and displays web pages, the web view keeps a Back list and a Forward list, just like a web browser. Two properties, canGoBack and canGoForward, and two methods, goBack and goForward, let you interact with this list. Your interface could thus contain Back and Forward buttons, like a miniature web browser.

A web view is scrollable, but UIWebView is *not* a UIScrollView subclass (Chapter 7); it *has* a scroll view, rather than *being* a scroll view. You can access a web view's scroll view as its scrollView property. You can use the scroll view to learn and set how far the content is scrolled and zoomed, and you can install a gesture recognizer on it, to detect gestures not intended for the web view itself.

A web view is zoomable if its `scalesToFit` property is YES; in that case, it initially scales its content to fit, and the user can zoom the content (this includes use of the gesture, familiar from Mobile Safari, whereby double-tapping part of a web page zooms to that region of the page). Like a text view (Chapter 10), its `dataDetectorTypes` property lets you set certain types of data to be automatically converted to tappable links.

It is possible to design an entire app that is effectively nothing but a UIWebView — especially if you have control of the server with which the user is interacting. Indeed, before the advent of iOS, an iPhone app *was* a web application. There are still iPhone apps that work this way, but such an approach to app design is outside the scope of this book.

A web view's most important task is to render HTML content; like any browser, a web view understands HTML, CSS, and JavaScript. In order to construct content for a web view, *you* must know HTML, CSS, and JavaScript. Discussion of those languages is beyond the scope of this book; each would require a book (at least) of its own. The thing to bear in mind is that you can use a web view to display content that isn't fetched from the Internet or that isn't obviously (to the user) a web page. WebKit is a powerful layout (and animation) engine; HTML and CSS (and JavaScript) are how you tell it what to do. In my TidBITS News app, a UIWebView is the obvious way to present each individual article, because an article arrives through the RSS feed as HTML; but in other apps, such as my Latin flashcard app or my Zotz! game, I present the Help documentation in a UIWebView just because it's so convenient for laying out styled text with pictures.

Web View Content

To obtain content for a web view initially, you're going to need one of three things:

An NSURLRequest
> Construct an NSURLRequest and call `loadRequest:`. An NSURLRequest might involve a file URL referring to a file on disk (within your app's bundle, for instance); the web view will deduce the file's type from its extension. But it might also involve the URL of a resource to be fetched across the Internet, in which case you can configure various additional aspects of the request (for example, you can form a POST request). This is the only form of loading that works with `goBack`, because in the other two forms, there is no URL to go back to.

An HTML string
> Construct an NSString consisting of valid HTML and call `loadHTMLString:base-URL:`. The `baseURL:` will be used to fetch any resources referred to by a partial (relative) URL in the string. For example, you could cause partial URLs to refer to resources inside your app's bundle.

Data and a MIME type

Obtain an NSData object and call `loadData:MIMEType:textEncodingName:base-` `URL:`. Obviously, this requires that you know the appropriate MIME type, and that you obtain the content as NSData (or convert it to NSData). Typically, this will be because the content was itself obtained by fetching it from the Internet (more about that in Chapter 24).

There is often more than one way to load a given piece of content. For instance, one of Apple's own examples suggests that you display a PDF file in your app's bundle by loading it as data, along these lines:

```
NSString *thePath =
    [[NSBundle mainBundle] pathForResource:@"MyPDF" ofType:@"pdf"];
NSData *pdfData = [NSData dataWithContentsOfFile:thePath];
[self.wv loadData:pdfData MIMEType:@"application/pdf"
                textEncodingName:@"utf-8" baseURL:nil];
```

But the same thing can be done with a file URL and `loadRequest:`, like this:

```
NSURL* url =
    [[NSBundle mainBundle] URLForResource:@"MyPDF" withExtension:@"pdf"];
NSURLRequest* req = [[NSURLRequest alloc] initWithURL:url];
[self.wv loadRequest:req];
```

Similarly, in one of my apps, where the Help screen is a web view (Figure 11-1), the content is an HTML file along with some referenced image files. I used to load it like this:

```
NSString* path =
    [[NSBundle mainBundle] pathForResource:@"help" ofType:@"html"];
NSURL* url = [NSURL fileURLWithPath:path];
NSError* err = nil;
NSString* s = [NSString stringWithContentsOfURL:url
                encoding:NSUTF8StringEncoding error:&err];
// error-checking omitted
[self.wv loadHTMLString:s baseURL:url];
```

Observe that I obtain both the string contents of the HTML file and the URL reference to the same file, the latter to act as a base URL so that the relative references to the images will work properly.

At the time I wrote that code, the NSBundle method `URLForResource:with-Extension:` didn't yet exist. Now it does, and I load the web view simply by calling `load-Request:` with the file URL:

```
NSString* path =
    [[NSBundle mainBundle] pathForResource:@"help" ofType:@"html"];
NSURL* url = [NSURL fileURLWithPath:path];
NSURLRequest* req = [[NSURLRequest alloc] initWithURL:url];
[self.wv loadRequest: req];
```

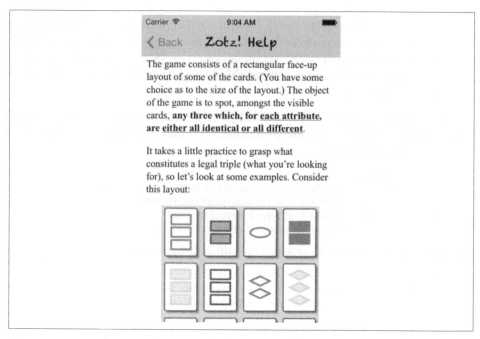

The game consists of a rectangular face-up layout of some of the cards. (You have some choice as to the size of the layout.) The object of the game is to spot, amongst the visible cards, **any three which, for <u>each attribute,</u> are <u>either all identical or all different</u>**.

It takes a little practice to grasp what constitutes a legal triple (what you're looking for), so let's look at some examples. Consider this layout:

Figure 11-1. A Help screen that's a web view

You can use loadHTMLString:baseURL: to form your own web view content dynamically as an NSString. For example, in the TidBITS News app, the content of an article is displayed in a web view that is loaded using loadHTMLString:baseURL:. The body of the article comes from an RSS feed, but it is wrapped in programmatically supplied material. Thus, in Figure 11-2, the right-aligned author byline and publication date, along with the overall formatting of the text (including the font size), are imposed as the web view appears.

There are many possible strategies for doing this. In the case of the TidBITS News app, I start with a template loaded from disk:

```
<!DOCTYPE HTML PUBLIC "-//W3C//DTD HTML 4.01 Transitional//EN"
"http://www.w3.org/TR/html4/loose.dtd">
<html>
<head>
  <meta http-equiv="content-type" content="text/html; charset=utf-8">
  <meta name="viewport" content="initial-scale=1.0, user-scalable=no">
    <style type="text/css">
      p.inflow_image {
        text-align:center;
      }
      div.indented_image {
        text-align:center;
```

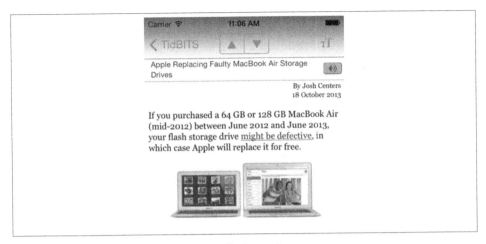

Figure 11-2. A web view with dynamically formed content

```
      margin-left:0;
    }
    img {
      max-width:<maximagewidth>;
      height:auto;
    }
  </style>
  <title>no title</title>
</head>
<body style="font-size:<fontsize>px; font-family:Georgia;
margin:1px <margin>px">
  <!-- author and date -->
  <div style="width:100%">
    <span style="float:right; margin-bottom: 15px; display:block;
    text-align:right; font-size:80%;">
      By <author><br><date>
    </span>
  </div>
  <!-- body, from feed -->
  <div style="clear:both; margin:30px 0px;">
    <content>
  </div>
</body>
</html>
```

The template defines the structure of an HTML document — the opening and closing tags, the head area (including some CSS styling), and a body consisting of <div>s laying out the parts of the page. But it also includes some pseudotags that are not HTML — <maximagewidth>, <fontsize>, and so on. When the web view is to be loaded, the template will be read from disk and real values will be substituted for those pseudotags:

```
NSString* template =
    [NSString stringWithContentsOfFile:
        [[NSBundle mainBundle] pathForResource:@"template" ofType:@"txt"]
            encoding: NSUTF8StringEncoding error:nil];
NSString* s = template;
s = [s stringByReplacingOccurrencesOfString:@"<maximagewidth>"
                                 withString:maxImageWidth];
s = [s stringByReplacingOccurrencesOfString:@"<fontsize>"
                                 withString:fontsize.stringValue];
s = [s stringByReplacingOccurrencesOfString:@"<margin>"
                                 withString:margin];
s = [s stringByReplacingOccurrencesOfString:@"<author>"
                                 withString:anitem.authorOfItem];
s = [s stringByReplacingOccurrencesOfString:@"<date>"
                                 withString:date];
s = [s stringByReplacingOccurrencesOfString:@"<content>"
                                 withString:anitem.content];
```

Some of these arguments, such as `anitem.authorOfItem` and `anitem.content`, slot values more or less directly from the app's model into the web view. Others are derived from the current circumstances. For example, the local variable `margin` has been set depending on whether the app is running on the iPhone or on the iPad; `fontsize` comes from the user defaults, because the user is allowed to determine how large the text should be. The result is an HTML string ready for `loadHTMLString:baseURL:`.

Loading Web View Content

Web view content is loaded *asynchronously* (gradually, in a thread of its own), and it might not be loaded at all (because the user might not be connected to the Internet, the server might not respond properly, and so on). If you're loading a resource directly from disk, loading is quick and nothing is going to go wrong; nevertheless, rendering the content can take time, and even a resource loaded from disk, or content formed directly as an HTML string, might refer to material out on the Internet that takes time to fetch.

Your app's interface is not blocked or frozen while the content is loading. On the contrary, it remains accessible and operative; that's what "asynchronous" means. The web view, in fetching a web page and its linked components, is doing something quite complex, involving both threading and network interaction — I'll have a lot more to say about this in Chapter 24 and Chapter 25 — but it shields you from this complexity. Your own interaction with the web view stays on the main thread and is straightforward. You ask the web view to load some content; then you sit back and let it worry about the details.

Indeed, there's very little you *can* do once you've asked a web view to load content. Your main concerns will probably be to know when loading really starts, when it has finished, and whether it succeeded. To help you with this, a UIWebView's delegate (adopting the UIWebViewDelegate protocol) gets three messages:

- `webViewDidStartLoad:`
- `webViewDidFinishLoad:`
- `webView:didFailLoadWithError:`

In this example from the TidBITS News app, I mask the delay while the content loads by displaying in the center of the interface an activity indicator (a UIActivityIndicator-View, Chapter 12), referred to by a property, `activity`:

```
- (void)webViewDidStartLoad:(UIWebView *)wv {
    [self.view addSubview:self.activity];
    self.activity.center = CGPointMake(CGRectGetMidX(self.view.bounds),
                                       CGRectGetMidY(self.view.bounds));
    [self.activity startAnimating];
    [[UIApplication sharedApplication] beginIgnoringInteractionEvents];
}
- (void)webViewDidFinishLoad:(UIWebView *)webView {
    [self.activity stopAnimating];
    [self.activity removeFromSuperview];
    [[UIApplication sharedApplication] endIgnoringInteractionEvents];
}
- (void)webView:(UIWebView *)webView didFailLoadWithError:(NSError *)error {
    [self.activity stopAnimating];
    [self.activity removeFromSuperview];
    [[UIApplication sharedApplication] endIgnoringInteractionEvents];
}
```

Exceptions triggered by UIWebViewDelegate code are caught by Web-Kit. This means that you can make a serious programming error without the exception percolating up to crash your app; you'll get a message in the console ("WebKit discarded an uncaught exception"), but you might not notice that. The solution is an exception breakpoint. (Thanks to reader Jonathan Lundell for bringing this phenomenon to my attention.)

A web view's `loading` property tells you whether it is in the process of loading a request. If, at the time a web view is to be destroyed, its `loading` is YES, it is up to you to cancel the request by sending it the `stopLoading` message first; actually, it does no harm to send the web view `stopLoading` in any case. In addition, UIWebView is one of those weird classes whose memory management behavior is odd: Apple's documentation warns that if you assign a UIWebView a delegate, you must nilify its `delegate` property before releasing the web view. Thus, in a controller class whose view contains a web view, I do an extra little dance in `dealloc`:

```
- (void) dealloc {
    [self.wv stopLoading];
    self.wv.delegate = nil;
}
```

A related problem is that a web view will sometimes leak memory. I've never understood what causes this, but the workaround appears to be to load the empty string into the web view. The TidBITS News app does this in the view controller whose view contains the web view:

```
- (void) viewWillDisappear:(BOOL)animated {
    if (self.isMovingFromParentViewController) {
        [self.wv loadHTMLString: @"" baseURL: nil];
    }
}
```

The suppressesIncrementalRendering property changes nothing about the request-loading process, but it does change what the user *sees*. The default is NO: the web view assembles its display of a resource incrementally, as it arrives. If this property is YES, the web view does nothing outwardly until the resource has completely arrived and the web view is ready to render the whole thing.

Designing Web View Content

Before designing the HTML to be displayed in a web view, you might want to read up on the brand of HTML native to the mobile WebKit engine. There are certain limitations; for example, mobile WebKit notoriously doesn't use plug-ins, such as Flash, and it imposes limits on the size of resources (such as images) that it can display. On the plus side, WebKit is in the forefront of the march toward HTML 5 and CSS 3, and has many special capabilities suited for display on a mobile device.

A good place to start is Apple's *Safari Web Content Guide*. It contains links to all the other relevant documentation, such as the *Safari CSS Visual Effects Guide*, which describes some things you can do with WebKit's implementation of CSS3 (like animations), and the *Safari HTML5 Audio and Video Guide*, which describes WebKit's audio and video player support.

If nothing else, you'll definitely want to be aware of one important aspect of web page content — the *viewport*. You'll notice that the TidBITS News HTML template I showed a moment ago contains this line within its <head> area:

```
<meta name="viewport" content="initial-scale=1.0, user-scalable=no">
```

Without that line, the HTML string is laid out incorrectly when it is rendered. This is noticeable especially with the iPad version of TidBITS News, where the web view can be rotated when the device is rotated, causing its width to change: in one orientation or the other, the text will be too wide for the web view, and the user has to scroll horizontally to read it. The *Safari Web Content Guide* explains why: if no viewport is specified, the

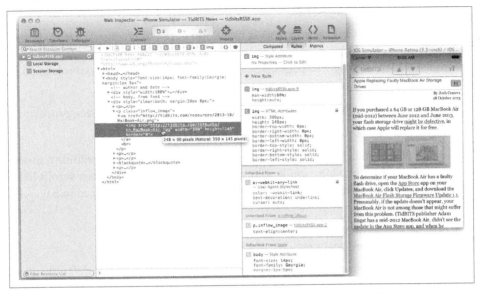

Figure 11-3. The Web Inspector inspects an app running in the Simulator

viewport can change when the app rotates. Setting the initial-scale causes the viewport size to adopt correct values in both orientations.

Another important section of the *Safari Web Content Guide* describes how you can use a media attribute in the <link> tag that loads your CSS to load *different* CSS depending on what kind of device your app is running on. For example, you might have one CSS file that lays out your web view's content on an iPhone, and another that lays it out on an iPad.

Inspecting, debugging, and experimenting with UIWebView content is greatly eased by the Web Inspector, built into Safari 6.1 and later. It can see a web view in your app running in the Simulator, and lets you analyze every aspect of how it works. For example, in Figure 11-3, I'm examining an image to see how it is sized and scaled.

Moreover, the Web Inspector lets you change your web view's content in real time, with many helpful features such as CSS autocompletion; this can be a better way to discover WebKit CSS features than the documentation, which isn't always kept up to date. For example, your web view can display Dynamic Type fonts, as discussed in Chapter 10, by setting the font CSS property to -apple-system-body and so forth; but, as of this writing, the only way to discover that is apparently through the Web Inspector's autocompletion.

Paginated Web Views

New in iOS 7, a web view can break its content into pages, allowing the user to browse that content in chunks by scrolling horizontally or vertically. This may seem an unaccustomed way of viewing web pages, but as I mentioned earlier, a web view is good for content that is not obviously a web page.

Configuration can be as simple as setting the web view's `paginationMode` property:

```
self.wv.paginationMode = UIWebPaginationModeLeftToRight;
```

The result of that code is that the web view's content is rendered into columns; instead of scrolling down in one long single column to read the content, the user scrolls left or right to see one screenful at a time. Scrolling does not automatically snap to pages, but you can enable that through the web view's `scrollView`:

```
self.wv.paginationMode = UIWebPaginationModeLeftToRight;
self.wv.scrollView.pagingEnabled = YES;
```

You can set the page size (`pageLength`, the same as the viewport size by default) and the gap between pages (`gapBetweenPages`, 0 by default).

Web View State Restoration

If you provided an HTML string to your web view, then restoring its state when the app is relaunched is up to you; you can use the built-in state saving and restoration to help you, but you'll have to do all the work yourself. The web view has a `scrollView` which has a `contentOffset`, so it's easy to save the scroll position (as an NSValue wrapping a CGPoint) in `encodeRestorableStateWithCoder:`, and restore it in `decodeRestorableStateWithCoder:`.

What the TidBITS News app does is to restore the scroll position initially into an instance variable:

```
-(void)decodeRestorableStateWithCoder:(NSCoder *)coder {
    // scroll position is a CGPoint wrapped in an NSValue
    self.lastOffset = [coder decodeObjectForKey:@"lastOffset"];
    // ... other stuff ...
    [super decodeRestorableStateWithCoder:coder];
}
```

Then we reload the web view content (manually); when the web view has loaded, we set its scroll position:

```
- (void)webViewDidFinishLoad:(UIWebView *)webView {
    if (self.lastOffset)
        webView.scrollView.contentOffset = self.lastOffset.CGPointValue;
    // ...
}
```

If, however, the web view had a URL request (not an HTML string) when the user left the app, then the state restoration mechanism will restore that request, in the web view's `request` property, along with its Back and Forward lists. To restore the web view's actual content, send it the `reload` message. The web view will then restore its contents and its scroll position. A good place to do this is `applicationFinishedRestoringState`:

```
-(void)applicationFinishedRestoringState {
    UIWebView* wv = (id)self.view;
    if (wv.request)
        [wv reload];
}
```

If we'd like to load a default page in `viewDidAppear:` when state restoration has *not* taken place, we can use our web view's `request` property as a flag:

```
UIWebView* wv = (id)self.view;
if (wv.request) { // state has been restored already
    return;
}
NSURL* url = // default URL
[wv loadRequest:[NSURLRequest requestWithURL:url]];
```

Communicating with a Web View

Having loaded a web view with content, you don't so much configure or command the web view as communicate with it. There are two modes of communication with a web view and its content:

JavaScript execution
> You can speak JavaScript to a web view's content by sending it the `stringBy-EvaluatingJavaScriptFromString:` message. Thus you can enquire as to the nature and details of that content, and you can alter the content dynamically.

Load requests
> When a web view is asked to load content, possibly because the user has tapped a link within it, its delegate is sent the message `webView:shouldStartLoadWith-Request:navigationType:`. This is your opportunity to interfere with the web view's loading behavior; if you return NO, the content won't load.

The second parameter is an NSURLRequest, whose `URL` property you can easily analyze. The third parameter is a constant describing the type of navigation involved, whose value will be one of the following:

- `UIWebViewNavigationTypeLinkClicked`
- `UIWebViewNavigationTypeFormSubmitted`
- `UIWebViewNavigationTypeBackForward`
- `UIWebViewNavigationTypeReload`

- UIWebViewNavigationTypeFormResubmitted

- UIWebViewNavigationTypeOther (includes loading the web view with content initially)

In the TidBITS News app, I don't want my web view to function as a web browser; if the user taps a link, I want to open it in Mobile Safari. So I implement webView:should-StartLoadWithRequest:navigationType: to pass any link-tap requests on to the system, and return NO:

```
- (BOOL)webView:(UIWebView *)webView
      shouldStartLoadWithRequest:(NSURLRequest *)r
      navigationType:(UIWebViewNavigationType)nt {
    if (nt == UIWebViewNavigationTypeLinkClicked) {
        [[UIApplication sharedApplication] openURL:[r URL]];
        return NO;
    }
    return YES;
}
```

Note that in the general case I still return YES, because otherwise the web view won't load my initial HTML content!

Another use of webView:shouldStartLoadWithRequest:navigationType: is to respond to link taps by doing something that has nothing to do with the web view itself. For example, in TidBITS News, the Listen button, which the user taps to hear the podcast recording of an article, used to be an image in the web view itself. When the user taps that image, I want to navigate to a different view controller entirely. To implement this, I wrapped the image in an <a> tag whose onclick script executes this JavaScript code:

```
document.location='play:me'
```

When the user taps the button, the web view delegate's webView:shouldStartLoadWith-Request:navigationType: gets an NSURLRequest play:me. That, of course, is a totally bogus URL; it's just an internal signal, telling me that the user has tapped the Listen image:

```
- (BOOL)webView:(UIWebView *)webView
      shouldStartLoadWithRequest:(NSURLRequest *)r
      navigationType:(UIWebViewNavigationType)nt {
    if ([r.URL.scheme isEqualToString: @"play"]) {
        [self doPlay:nil];
        return NO;
    }
    // ...
}
```

JavaScript and the document object model (*DOM*) are quite powerful. Event listeners even allow JavaScript code to respond directly to touch and gesture events, so that the user can interact with elements of a web page much as if they were touchable views; it can also take advantage of Core Location and Core Motion facilities to respond to where the user is on earth and how the device is positioned (Chapter 22). Additional helpful documentation includes Apple's *WebKit DOM Programming Topics* and *Safari DOM Additions Reference*.

 New in iOS 7, your Objective-C code can load a JavaScript virtual machine and communicate back and forth between JavaScript and Objective-C. See Apple's *JavaScriptCore Framework Reference* (currently documented only for OS X, not iOS). I don't think this has anything to do with UIWebView *per se*, but it's so cool that I couldn't resist mentioning it.

CHAPTER 12

Controls and Other Views

This chapter discusses all UIView subclasses provided by UIKit that haven't been discussed already (except for the two modal dialog classes, which are described in the next chapter). It's remarkable how few of them there are; UIKit exhibits a noteworthy economy of means in this regard.

Additional UIView subclasses, as well as UIViewController subclasses that create interface, are provided by other frameworks. There will be lots of examples in Part III. For example, the Map Kit framework provides the MKMapView (Chapter 21); and the MessageUI framework provides MFMailComposeViewController, which supplies a user interface for composing and sending a mail message (Chapter 20).

UIActivityIndicatorView

An activity indicator (UIActivityIndicatorView) appears as the spokes of a small wheel. You set the spokes spinning with `startAnimating`, giving the user a sense that some time-consuming process is taking place. You stop the spinning with `stopAnimating`. If the activity indicator's `hidesWhenStopped` is YES (the default), it is visible only while spinning.

An activity indicator comes in a style, its `activityIndicatorViewStyle`; if it is created in code, you'll set its style with `initWithActivityIndicatorStyle:`. Your choices are:

- `UIActivityIndicatorViewStyleWhiteLarge`
- `UIActivityIndicatorViewStyleWhite`
- `UIActivityIndicatorViewStyleGray`

An activity indicator has a standard size, which depends on its style. Changing its size in code changes the size of the view, but not the size of the spokes. For bigger spokes, you can resort to a scale transform.

Figure 12-1. A large activity indicator

You can assign an activity indicator a `color`; this overrides the color assigned through the style. An activity indicator is a UIView, so you can set its `backgroundColor`; a nice effect is to give an activity indicator a contrasting background color and to round its corners by way of the view's layer (Figure 12-1).

Here's some code from a UITableViewCell subclass in one of my apps. In this app, it takes some time, after the user taps a cell to select it, for me to construct the next view and navigate to it; to cover the delay, I show a spinning activity indicator in the center of the cell while it's selected:

```
- (void)setSelected:(BOOL)selected animated:(BOOL)animated {
    [super setSelected:selected animated:animated];
    if (selected) {
        UIActivityIndicatorView* v =
            [[UIActivityIndicatorView alloc]
                initWithActivityIndicatorStyle:
                    UIActivityIndicatorViewStyleWhiteLarge];
        v.color = [UIColor yellowColor];
        dispatch_async(dispatch_get_main_queue(), ^{
            // cell tries to change background color match selection color
            v.backgroundColor = [UIColor colorWithWhite:0.2 alpha:0.6];
        });
        v.layer.cornerRadius = 10;
        CGRect f = v.frame;
        f = CGRectInset(f, -10, -10);
        v.frame = f;
        CGRect cf = self.frame;
        cf = [self.contentView convertRect:cf fromView:self];
        v.center = CGPointMake(CGRectGetMidX(cf), CGRectGetMidY(cf));
        v.tag = 1001;
        [self.contentView addSubview:v];
        [v startAnimating];
    } else {
        UIView* v = [self viewWithTag:1001];
        if (v) {
            [v removeFromSuperview];
        }
    }
}
```

If activity involves the network, you might want to set UIApplication's `networkActivity-IndicatorVisible` to YES. This displays a small spinning activity indicator in the status

Figure 12-2. A progress view

bar. The indicator is not reflecting actual network activity; if it's visible, it's spinning. Be sure to set it back to NO when the activity is over.

An activity indicator is simple and standard, but you can't change the way it's drawn. One obvious alternative would be a UIImageView with an animated image, as described in Chapter 4.

UIProgressView

A progress view (UIProgressView) is a "thermometer," graphically displaying a percentage. It is often used to represent a time-consuming process whose percentage of completion is known (if the percentage of completion is unknown, you're more likely to use an activity indicator). But it's good for static percentages too. In one of my apps, I use a progress view to show the current position within the song being played by the built-in music player; in another app, which is a card game, I use a progress view to show how many cards are left in the deck.

A progress view comes in a style, its `progressViewStyle`; if the progress view is created in code, you'll set its style with `initWithProgressViewStyle:`. Your choices are:

- `UIProgressViewStyleDefault`
- `UIProgressViewStyleBar`

`UIProgressViewStyleBar` is intended for use in a UIBarButtonItem, as the title view of a navigation item, and so on. In iOS 7, both styles by default draw the thermometer extremely thin — just 2 pixels and 3 pixels, respectively. (Figure 12-2 shows a `UIProgressViewStyleDefault` progress view.) Changing a progress view's frame height directly has no visible effect on how the thermometer is drawn. Under autolayout, to make a thicker thermometer, supply a height constraint with a larger value (thus overriding the intrinsic content height).

The fullness of the thermometer is the progress view's `progress` property. This is a value between 0 and 1, inclusive; you'll usually need to do some elementary arithmetic in order to convert from the actual value you're reflecting to a value within that range. For example, to reflect the number of cards remaining in a deck of 52 cards:

```
prog.progress = [[deck cards] count] / 52.0;
```

A change in `progress` value can be animated by calling `setProgress:animated:`.

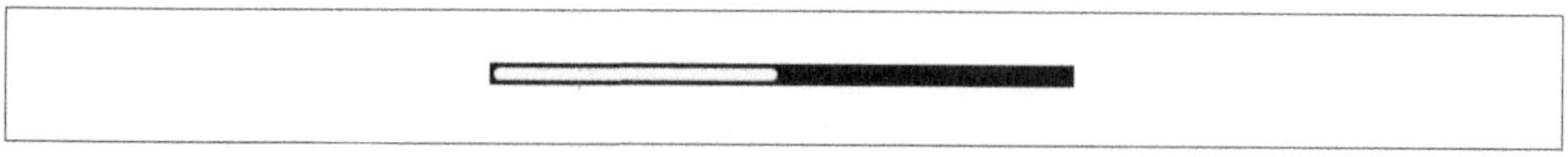

Figure 12-3. A thicker progress view using a custom progress image

In iOS 7, the default color of the filled portion of a progress view is the `tintColor` (which may be inherited from higher up the view hierarchy). The default color for the unfilled portion is gray for a `UIProgressViewStyleDefault` progress view and transparent for a `UIProgressViewStyleBar` progress view. You can customize the colors; set the progress view's `progressTintColor` and `trackTintColor`, respectively. This can also be done in the nib.

Alternatively, you can customize the image used to draw the filled portion of the progress view, the progress view's `progressImage`. If you do that, you can optionally customize also the image used to draw the unfilled portion, the `trackImage`. This can also be done in the nib. Each image must be stretched to the length of the filled or unfilled area, so you'll want to use a resizable image.

Here's a simple example from one of my apps (Figure 12-3):

```
self.prog.backgroundColor = [UIColor blackColor];
self.prog.trackTintColor = [UIColor blackColor];
UIGraphicsBeginImageContextWithOptions(CGSizeMake(10,10), YES, 0);
CGContextRef con = UIGraphicsGetCurrentContext();
CGContextSetFillColorWithColor(con, [UIColor yellowColor].CGColor);
CGContextFillRect(con, CGRectMake(0, 0, 10, 10));
CGRect r = CGRectInset(CGContextGetClipBoundingBox(con),1,1);
CGContextSetLineWidth(con, 2);
CGContextSetStrokeColorWithColor(con, [UIColor blackColor].CGColor);
CGContextStrokeRect(con, r);
CGContextStrokeEllipseInRect(con, r);
self.prog.progressImage =
    [UIGraphicsGetImageFromCurrentImageContext()
        resizableImageWithCapInsets:UIEdgeInsetsMake(0, 4, 0, 4)];
UIGraphicsEndImageContext();
```

For maximum flexibility, you can design your own UIView subclass that draws something similar to a thermometer. Figure 12-4 shows a simple custom thermometer view; it has a `value` property, and you set this to something between 0 and 1 and call `setNeeds-Display` to make the view redraw itself. Here's its `drawRect:` code:

```
- (void)drawRect:(CGRect)rect {
    CGContextRef c = UIGraphicsGetCurrentContext();
    [[UIColor whiteColor] set];
    CGFloat ins = 2.0;
    CGRect r = CGRectInset(self.bounds, ins, ins);
    CGFloat radius = r.size.height / 2.0;
    CGMutablePathRef path = CGPathCreateMutable();
```

Figure 12-4. A custom progress view

```
    CGPathMoveToPoint(path, nil, CGRectGetMaxX(r)-radius, ins);
    CGPathAddArc(path, nil,
        radius+ins, radius+ins, radius, -M_PI/2.0, M_PI/2.0, true);
    CGPathAddArc(path, nil,
        CGRectGetMaxX(r)-radius, radius+ins, radius,
        M_PI/2.0, -M_PI/2.0, true);
    CGPathCloseSubpath(path);
    CGContextAddPath(c, path);
    CGContextSetLineWidth(c, 2);
    CGContextStrokePath(c);
    CGContextAddPath(c, path);
    CGContextClip(c);
    CGContextFillRect(c, CGRectMake(
        r.origin.x, r.origin.y, r.size.width * self.value, r.size.height));
}
```

UIPickerView

A picker view (UIPickerView) displays selectable choices using a rotating drum meta-phor. It has a standard legal range of possible heights, which is undocumented but seems to be between 162 and 180; its width is largely up to you. Each drum, or column, is called a *component*.

Your code configures the UIPickerView's content through its data source (UIPicker-ViewDataSource) and delegate (UIPickerViewDelegate), which are usually the same object. Your data source and delegate must answer questions similar to those posed by a UITableView (Chapter 8):

numberOfComponentsInPickerView: *(data source)*
> How many components (drums) does this picker view have?

pickerView:numberOfRowsInComponent: *(data source)*
> How many rows does this component have? The first component is numbered 0.

pickerView:titleForRow:forComponent:
pickerView:attributedTitleForRow:forComponent:
pickerView:viewForRow:forComponent:reusingView: *(delegate)*
> What should this row of this component display? The first row is numbered 0. You can supply a simple string, an attributed string (Chapter 10), or an entire view such as a UILabel; but you should supply every row of every component the same way. The reusingView parameter, if not nil, is a view that you supplied for a row now

Figure 12-5. A picker view

no longer visible, giving you a chance to reuse it, much as cells are reused in a table view.

Here's the code for a UIPickerView (Figure 12-5) that displays the names of the 50 U.S. states, stored in an array. We implement `pickerView:viewForRow:for-Component:reusingView:` just because it's the most interesting case; as our views, we supply UILabel instances. The state names appear centered because the labels are centered within the picker view:

```
- (NSInteger)numberOfComponentsInPickerView:(UIPickerView *)pickerView {
    return 1;
}
- (NSInteger)pickerView:(UIPickerView *)pickerView
        numberOfRowsInComponent:(NSInteger)component {
    return 50;
}
- (UIView *)pickerView:(UIPickerView *)pickerView viewForRow:(NSInteger)row
        forComponent:(NSInteger)component reusingView:(UIView *)view {
    UILabel* lab;
    if (view)
        lab = (UILabel*)view; // reuse it
    else
        lab = [UILabel new];
    lab.text = self.states[row];
    lab.backgroundColor = [UIColor clearColor];
    [lab sizeToFit];
    return lab;
}
```

The delegate may further configure the UIPickerView's physical appearance by means of these methods:

- `pickerView:rowHeightForComponent:`

- `pickerView:widthForComponent:`

Figure 12-6. A search bar with a search results button

The delegate may implement `pickerView:didSelectRow:inComponent:` to be notified each time the user spins a drum to a new position. You can also query the picker view directly by sending it `selectedRowInComponent:`.

You can set the value to which any drum is turned using `selectRow:inComponent:animated:`. Other handy picker view methods allow you to request that the data be reloaded, and there are properties and methods to query the picker view's contents (though of course they do not relieve you of responsibility for knowing the data model from which the picker view's contents are supplied):

- `reloadComponent:`
- `reloadAllComponents`
- `numberOfComponents`
- `numberOfRowsInComponent:`
- `viewForRow:forComponent:`

By implementing `pickerView:didSelectRow:inComponent:` and using `reloadComponent:`, you can make a picker view where the values displayed by one drum depend dynamically on what is selected in another. For example, one can imagine expanding our U.S. states example to include a second drum listing major cities in each state; when the user switches to a different state in the first drum, a different set of major cities appears in the second drum.

UISearchBar

A search bar (UISearchBar) is essentially a wrapper for a text field; it has a text field as one of its subviews, though there is no official access to it. It is displayed by default as a rounded rectangle containing a magnifying glass icon, where the user can enter text (Figure 12-6). It does not, of itself, do any searching or display the results of a search; a common interface involves displaying the results of a search as a table, and the UISearchDisplayController class makes this easy to do (see Chapter 8).

A search bar's current text is its `text` property. It can have a `placeholder`, which appears when there is no text. A `prompt` can be displayed above the search bar to explain its purpose. Delegate methods (UISearchBarDelegate) notify you of editing events; for their use, compare the text field and text view delegate methods discussed in Chapter 10:

- `searchBarShouldBeginEditing:`
- `searchBarTextDidBeginEditing:`
- `searchBar:textDidChange:`
- `searchBar:shouldChangeTextInRange:replacementText:`
- `searchBarShouldEndEditing:`
- `searchBarTextDidEndEditing:`

A search bar has a `barStyle`, for which your choices and their default appearances are:

- `UIBarStyleDefault`, a flat light gray background and a white search field
- `UIBarStyleBlack`, a black background and a black search field

In iOS 7, both styles are translucent. In addition, iOS 7 introduces a `searchBarStyle` property:

- `UISearchBarStyleDefault`, as already described
- `UISearchBarStyleProminent`, identical to `UISearchBarStyleDefault`
- `UISearchBarStyleMinimal`, transparent background and dark transparent search field

Alternatively, you can set a `UISearchBarStyleDefault` search bar's `barTintColor` to change its background color; if the bar style is `UIBarStyleBlack`, the `barTintColor` will also tint the search field itself. An opaque `barTintColor` is a way to make a search bar opaque. This property is new in iOS 7; the old `tintColor` property, whose value may be inherited from higher up the view hierarchy, now governs the color of search bar components such as the Cancel button title and the flashing insertion cursor.

A search bar can also have a custom `backgroundImage`; this will be treated as a resizable image. The full setter method in iOS 7 is `setBackgroundImage:forBarPosition:bar-Metrics:`; I'll talk later about what bar position and bar metrics are. The background-Image overrides all other ways of determining the background, and the search bar's `backgroundColor`, if any, appears behind it — though under some circumstances, if the search bar's `translucent` is NO, the `barTintColor` may appear behind it instead.

The search field area where the user enters text can be offset with respect to its background, using the `searchFieldBackgroundPositionAdjustment` property; you might do this, for example, if you had enlarged the search bar's height and wanted to position the search field within that height. The text can be offset within the search field with the `searchTextPositionAdjustment` property.

You can also replace the image of the search field itself; this is the image that is normally a rounded rectangle. To do so, call `setSearchFieldBackgroundImage:forState:`. According to the documentation, the possible `state:` values are `UIControlStateNormal` and `UIControlStateDisabled`; but the API provides no way to disable a search field, so what does Apple have in mind here? The only way I've found is to cycle through the search bar's subviews, find the search field, and disable it:

```
for (UIView* v in [self.searchbar.subviews[0] subviews]) {
    if ([v isKindOfClass: [UITextField class]]) {
        UITextField* tf = (UITextField*)v;
        tf.enabled = NO;
        break;
    }
}
```

The search field image will be drawn in front of the background and behind the contents of the search field (such as the text); its width will be adjusted for you, but its height will not be — instead, the image is placed vertically centered where the search field needs to go. It's up to you choose an appropriate height, and to ensure an appropriate color in the middle so the user can read the text.

A search bar displays an internal cancel button automatically (normally an X in a circle) if there is text in the search field. Internally, at its right end, a search bar may display a search results button (`showsSearchResultsButton`), which may be selected or not (`searchResultsButtonSelected`), or a bookmark button (`showsBookmarkButton`); if you ask to display both, you'll get the search results button. These buttons vanish if text is entered in the search bar so that the cancel button can be displayed. There is also an option to display a Cancel button externally (`showsCancelButton`, or call `setShowsCancelButton:animated:`). The internal cancel button works automatically to remove whatever text is in the field; the other buttons do nothing, but delegate methods notify you when they are tapped:

- `searchBarResultsListButtonClicked:`
- `searchBarBookmarkButtonClicked:`
- `searchBarCancelButtonClicked:`

You can customize the images used for the search icon (a magnifying glass, by default) and any of the internal right icons (the internal cancel button, the search results button, and the bookmark button) with `setImage:forSearchBarIcon:state:`. The images will be resized for you, except for the internal cancel button, for which about 20×20 seems to be a good size. The icons are specified with constants:

- `UISearchBarIconSearch`

- `UISearchBarIconClear` (the internal cancel button)

- `UISearchBarIconBookmark`

- `UISearchBarIconResultsList`

The documentation says that the possible `state:` values are `UIControlStateNormal` and `UIControlStateDisabled`, but this is wrong; the choices are `UIControlState-Normal` and `UIControlStateHighlighted`. The highlighted image appears while the user taps on the icon (except for the search icon, which isn't a button). If you don't supply a normal image, the default image is used; if you supply a normal image but no highlighted image, the normal image is used for both. Setting `searchResultsButton-Selected` to YES reverses this button's behavior: it displays the highlighted image, but when the user taps it, it displays the normal image.

The position of an icon can be adjusted with `setPositionAdjustment:forSearchBar-Icon:`.

A search bar may also display scope buttons (see the example in Chapter 8). These are intended to let the user alter the meaning of the search; precisely how you use them is up to you. To make the scope buttons appear, use the `showsScopeBar` property; the button titles are the `scopeButtonTitles` property, and the currently selected scope button is the `selectedScopeButtonIndex` property. The delegate is notified when the user taps a different scope button:

- `searchBar:selectedScopeButtonIndexDidChange:`

 A background image applied with `setBackgroundImage:forBar-Position:barMetrics:` using `UIBarMetricsDefault` will not appear when the scope bar is showing. In iOS 7, when the scope bar is showing, the bar metrics value becomes `UIBarMetricsDefaultPrompt` (or `UIBarMetricsLandscapePhonePrompt`).

The overall look of the scope bar can be heavily customized. Its background is the `scope-BarBackgroundImage`, which will be stretched or tiled as needed. To set the background of the smaller area constituting the actual buttons, call `setScopeBarButtonBackground-Image:forState:`; the states are `UIControlStateNormal` and `UIControlState-Selected`. If you don't supply a separate selected image, a darkened version of the normal image is used. If you don't supply a resizable image, the image will be made resizable for you; the runtime decides what region of the image will be stretched behind each button.

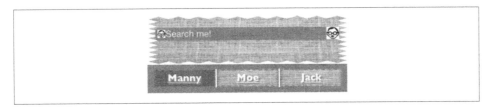

Figure 12-7. A horrible search bar

The dividers between the buttons are normally vertical lines, but you can customize them as well: call `setScopeBarButtonDividerImage:forLeftSegmentState:right-SegmentState:`. A full complement of dividers consists of three images, one when the buttons on both sides of the divider are normal (unselected) and one each when a button on one side or the other is selected; if you supply an image for just one state combination, it is used for the other two state combinations. The height of the divider image is adjusted for you, but the width is not; you'll normally use an image just a few pixels wide.

The font attributes of the titles of the scope buttons can customized by calling `setScope-BarButtonTitleTextAttributes:forState:`. In iOS 7, the `attributes:` argument is an NSAttributedString attributes dictionary; in earlier systems, you could set only the font, text color, and text shadow, but in iOS 7 it is legal to provide other attributes, such as an underline.

 It may appear that there is no way to customize the external Cancel button, but in fact, although you've no official direct access to it through the search bar, the Cancel button is a UIBarButtonItem and you can customize it using the UIBarButtonItem appearance proxy, discussed later in this chapter.

By combining the various customization possibilities, a completely unrecognizable search bar of inconceivable ugliness can easily be achieved (Figure 12-7). Let's be careful out there.

The problem of allowing the keyboard to appear without hiding the search bar is exactly as for a text field (Chapter 10). Text input properties of the search bar configure its keyboard and typing behavior like a text field as well:

- `keyboardType`
- `autocapitalizationType`
- `autocorrectionType`

- spellCheckingType
- inputAccessoryView

When the user taps the Search key in the keyboard, the delegate is notified, and it is then up to you to dismiss the keyboard (resignFirstResponder) and perform the search:

- searchBarSearchButtonClicked:

A common interface is a search bar at the top of the screen. On the iPad, a search bar can be embedded as a bar button item's view in a toolbar at the top of the screen. On the iPhone, a search bar can be a navigation item's titleView. In Chapter 8, I discussed UISearchDisplayController's displaysSearchBarInNavigationBar property. A search bar used in this way, however, has some limitations: for example, there may be no room for a prompt, scope buttons, or an external Cancel button, and you might not be able to assign it a background image or change its barTintColor.

On the other hand, in iOS 7, a UISearchBar can itself function as a top bar, *like* a navigation bar without being *in* a navigation bar. If you use a search bar in this way, you'll want its height to be extended automatically under the status bar; I'll explain later in this chapter how to arrange that.

UIControl

UIControl is a subclass of UIView whose chief purpose is to be the superclass of several further built-in classes and to endow them with common behavior. These are classes representing views with which the user can interact (controls).

The most important thing that controls have in common is that they automatically track and analyze touch events (Chapter 5) and report them to your code as significant control events by way of action messages. Each control implements some subset of the possible control events. The full set of control events is listed under UIControlEvents in the Constants section of the UIControl class documentation:

- UIControlEventTouchDown
- UIControlEventTouchDownRepeat
- UIControlEventTouchDragInside
- UIControlEventTouchDragOutside
- UIControlEventTouchDragEnter
- UIControlEventTouchDragExit
- UIControlEventTouchUpInside

- `UIControlEventTouchUpOutside`
- `UIControlEventTouchCancel`
- `UIControlEventValueChanged`
- `UIControlEventEditingDidBegin`
- `UIControlEventEditingChanged`
- `UIControlEventEditingDidEnd`
- `UIControlEventEditingDidEndOnExit`
- `UIControlEventAllTouchEvents`
- `UIControlEventAllEditingEvents`
- `UIControlEventAllEvents`

The control events also have informal names that are visible in the Connections inspector when you're editing a nib. I'll mostly use the informal names in the next couple of paragraphs.

Control events fall roughly into three groups: the user has touched the screen (Touch Down, Touch Drag Inside, Touch Up Inside, etc.), edited text (Editing Did Begin, Editing Changed, etc.), or changed the control's value (Value Changed).

Apple's documentation is rather coy about which controls normally emit actions for which control events, so here's a list obtained through experimentation (but keep in mind that Apple's silence on this matter may mean that the details are subject to change):

UIButton
　　All "Touch" events.

UIDatePicker
　　Value Changed.

UIPageControl
　　All "Touch" events, Value Changed.

UIRefreshControl
　　Value Changed.

UISegmentedControl
　　Value Changed.

UISlider
　　All "Touch" events, Value Changed.

UISwitch
　　All "Touch" events, Value Changed.

Touch Inside and Touch Outside

There is no explicit "Touch Down Inside" event, because *any* sequence of "Touch" events begins with "Touch Down," which *must* be inside the control. (If it weren't, this sequence of touches would not "belong" to the control, and there would be no control events at all.)

When the user taps within a control and starts dragging, the "Inside" events are triggered even after the drag moves outside the control's bounds. But after a certain distance from the control is exceeded, an invisible boundary is crossed, Touch Drag Exit is triggered, and now "Outside" events are reported until the drag crosses back within the invisible boundary, at which point Touch Drag Enter is triggered and the "Inside" events are reported again. In the case of a UIButton, the crossing of this invisible boundary is exactly when the button automatically unhighlights (as the drag exits). Thus, to catch a legitimate button press, you probably want to consider only Touch Up Inside.

For other controls, there may be some slight complications. For example, a UISwitch will unhighlight when a drag reaches a certain distance from it, but the touch is still considered legitimate and can still change the UISwitch's value; therefore, when the user's finger leaves the screen, the UISwitch reports a Touch Up Inside event, even while reporting Touch Drag Outside events.

UIStepper
> All "Touch" events, Value Changed.

UITextField
> All "Touch" events except the "Up" events, and all "Editing" events (see Chapter 10 for details).

UIControl (generic)
> All "Touch" events.

For each control event that you want to hear about automatically, you attach to the control one or more target–action pairs. You can do this in the nib or in code.

For any given control, each control event and its target–action pairs form a dispatch table. The following methods permit you to manipulate and query the dispatch table:

- `addTarget:action:forControlEvents:`
- `removeTarget:action:forControlEvents:`
- `actionsForTarget:forControlEvent:`

- `allTargets`
- `allControlEvents` (a bitmask of control events to which a target–action pair is attached)

An action method (the method that will be called on the target when the control event occurs) may adopt any of three signatures, whose parameters are:

- The control and the UIEvent
- The control only
- No parameters

The second signature is by far the most common. It's unlikely that you'd want to dispense altogether with the parameter telling you which control sent the control event. On the other hand, it's equally unlikely that you'd want to examine the original UIEvent that triggered this control event, since control events deliberately shield you from dealing with the nitty-gritty of touches — though you might have some reason to examine the UIEvent's `timestamp`.

When a control event occurs, the control consults its dispatch table, finds all the target–action pairs associated with that control event, and reports the control event by sending each action message to the corresponding target.

> The action messaging mechanism is actually more complex than I've just stated. The UIControl does not really send the action message directly; rather, it tells the shared application to send it. When a control wants to send an action message reporting a control event, it calls its own `sendAction:to:forEvent:` method. This in turn calls the shared application instance's `sendAction:to:from:forEvent:`, which actually sends the specified action message to the specified target. In theory, you could call or override either of these methods to customize this aspect of the message-sending architecture, but it is extremely unlikely that you would do so.

To make a control emit its action message(s) corresponding to a particular control event right now, in code, call its `sendActionsForControlEvents:` method (which is never called automatically by the framework). For example, suppose you tell a UISwitch programmatically to change its setting from Off to On. This doesn't cause the switch to report a control event, as it would if the *user* had slid the switch from Off to On; if you wanted it to do so, you could use `sendActionsForControlEvents:`, like this:

```
[self.sw setOn: YES animated: YES];
[self.sw sendActionsForControlEvents:UIControlEventValueChanged];
```

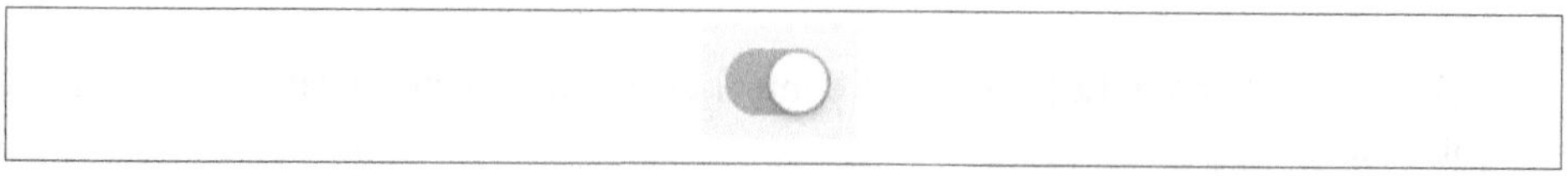

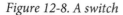

Figure 12-8. A switch

You might also use `sendActionsForControlEvents:` in a subclass to customize the circumstances under which a control reports control events.

A control has `enabled`, `selected`, and `highlighted` properties; any of these can be YES or NO independently of the others. Together, they correspond to the control's `state`, which is reported as a bitmask of three possible values:

- `UIControlStateHighlighted`
- `UIControlStateDisabled`
- `UIControlStateSelected`

A fourth state, `UIControlStateNormal`, corresponds to a zero `state` bitmask, and means that `enabled`, `selected`, and `highlighted` are all NO.

A control that is not enabled does not respond to user interaction. Whether the control also portrays itself differently, to cue the user to this fact, depends upon the control. For example, a disabled UISwitch is faded; but a rounded rect text field gives the user no cue that it is disabled. The visual nature of control selection and highlighting, too, depends on the control. Neither highlighting nor selection make any difference to the appearance of a UISwitch, but a highlighted UIButton usually looks quite different from a nonhighlighted UIButton.

A control has `contentHorizontalAlignment` and `contentVerticalAlignment` properties. These matter only if the control has content that can be aligned. You are most likely to use them in connection with a UIButton to position its title and internal image.

A text field (UITextField) is a control; see Chapter 10. A refresh control (UIRefreshControl) is a control; see Chapter 8. The remaining controls are covered here, and then I'll give a simple example of writing your own custom control.

UISwitch

A switch (UISwitch, Figure 12-8) portrays a BOOL value: it looks like a sliding switch, and its on property is either YES or NO. The user can slide or tap to toggle the switch's position. When the user changes the switch's position, the switch reports a Value Changed control event. To change the on property's value with accompanying animation, call `setOn:animated:`.

Figure 12-9. A stepper

A switch has only one size (radically changed in iOS 7 to 51×31); any attempt to set its size will be ignored.

You can customize a switch's appearance by setting these properties:

onTintColor
  The color of the track when the switch is in the On position.

thumbTintColor
  The color of the slidable button.

tintColor
  In iOS 7, the color of the outline when the switch is in the Off position.

In iOS 7, a switch's track when the switch is in the Off position is transparent, and can't be customized. I regard this as a bug. (Changing the switch's backgroundColor is not a successful workaround, because the background color shows outside the switch's outline.)

The UISwitch properties onImage and offImage, added in iOS 6 after much clamoring (and hacking) by developers, are withdrawn in iOS 7.

 Don't name a UISwitch instance variable or property switch, as this is a reserved word in C.

UIStepper

A stepper (UIStepper, Figure 12-9) lets the user increase or decrease a numeric value: it looks like two buttons side by side, one labeled (by default) with a minus sign, the other with a plus sign. The user can tap or hold a button, and can slide a finger from one button to the other as part of the same interaction with the stepper. It has only one size (apparently 94×29). It maintains a numeric value, which is its value. Each time the user increments or decrements the value, it changes by the stepper's stepValue. If the minimumValue or maximumValue is reached, the user can go no further in that direction, and to show this, the corresponding button is disabled — unless the stepper's wraps property is YES, in which case the value goes beyond the maximum by starting again at the minimum, and *vice versa*.

As the user changes the stepper's `value`, a Value Changed control event is reported. Portraying the numeric value itself is up to you; you might, for example, use a label or (as here) a progress view:

```
- (IBAction)doStep:(UIStepper*)step {
    self.prog.progress = step.value / (step.maximumValue - step.minimumValue);
}
```

If a stepper's `continuous` is YES (the default), a long touch on one of the buttons will update the value repeatedly; the updates start slowly and get faster. If the stepper's `autorepeat` is NO, the updated value is not reported as a Value Changed control event until the entire interaction with the stepper ends; the default is YES.

The appearance of a stepper can be customized. In iOS 7, the color of the outline and the button captions is the stepper's `tintColor`, which may be inherited from further up the view hierarchy. You can also dictate the images that constitute the stepper's structure with these methods:

- `setDecrementImageForState:`
- `setIncrementImageForState:`
- `setDividerImage:forLeftSegmentState:rightSegmentState:`
- `setBackgroundImage:forState:`

The images work similarly to a search bar's scope bar (described earlier in this chapter). The background images should probably be resizable. They are stretched behind both buttons, half the image being seen as the background of each button. If the button is disabled (because we've reached the value's limit in that direction), it displays the `UIControlStateDisabled` background image; otherwise, it displays the `UIControlStateNormal` background image, except that it displays the `UIControlStateHighlighted` background image while the user is tapping it. You'll probably want to provide all three background images if you're going to provide any; the default is used if a state's background image is nil. You'll probably want to provide three divider images as well, to cover the three combinations normal left and normal right, highlighted left and normal right, and normal left and highlighted right. The increment and decrement images are composited on top of the background image; in iOS 7, they are treated as template images, colored by the `tintColor`, unless you explicitly provide a `UIImageRenderingModeAlwaysOriginal` image. At a minimum, you'll provide a `UIControlStateNormal` image, which will be adjusted automatically for the other two states, though of course you can provide all three images for each button. Figure 12-9 shows a customized stepper.

Figure 12-10. A customized stepper

UIPageControl

A page control (UIPageControl) is a row of dots; each dot is called a *page*, because it is intended to be used in conjunction with some other interface that portrays something analogous to pages, such as a UIScrollView with its `pagingEnabled` set to YES. Coordinating the page control with this other interface is usually up to you; see Chapter 7 for an example. A UIPageViewController in scroll style can optionally display a page control that's automatically coordinated with its content (Chapter 6).

The number of dots is the page control's `numberOfPages`. To learn the minimum size required for a given number of pages, call `sizeForNumberOfPages:`. You can make the page control wider than the dots to increase the target region on which the user can tap. The user can tap to one side or the other of the current page's dot to increment or decrement the current page; the page control then reports a Value Changed control event. It is possible to set a page control's `backgroundColor` to show the user the tappable area, but that isn't commonly done: the background is usually transparent.

The dot colors differentiate the current page, the page control's `currentPage`, from the others; by default, the current page is portrayed as a solid dot, while the others are slightly transparent. You can customize a page control's `pageIndicatorTintColor` (the color of the dots in general) and `currentPageIndicatorTintColor` (the color of the current page's dot).

If a page control's `hidesForSinglePage` is YES, the page control becomes invisible when its `numberOfPages` changes to 1.

If a page control's `defersCurrentPageDisplay` is YES, then when the user taps to increment or decrement the page control's value, the display of the current page is not changed. A Value Changed control event is reported, but it is up to your code to handle this action and call `updateCurrentPageDisplay`. A case in point might be if the user's changing the current page triggers an animation, but you don't want the current page dot to change until the animation ends.

UIDatePicker

A date picker (UIDatePicker) looks like a UIPickerView (discussed earlier in this chapter), but it is not a UIPickerView subclass; it uses a UIPickerView to draw itself, but it provides no official access to that picker view. Its purpose is to express the notion of a date and time, taking care of the calendrical and numerical complexities so that you don't have to. When the user changes its setting, the date picker reports a Value Changed control event.

A UIDatePicker has one of four modes (`datePickerMode`), determining how it is drawn:

UIDatePickerModeTime

> The date picker displays a time; for example, it has an hour component and a minutes component.

UIDatePickerModeDate

> The date picker displays a date; for example, it has a month component, a day component, and a year component.

UIDatePickerModeDateAndTime

> The date picker displays a date and time; for example, it has a component showing day of the week, month, and day, plus an hour component and a minutes component.

UIDatePickerModeCountDownTimer

> The date picker displays a number of hours and minutes; for example, it has an hours component and a minutes component.

Exactly what components a date picker displays, and what values they contain, depends by default upon the user's preferences in the Settings app (General → International → Region Format). For example, a U.S. time displays an hour numbered 1 through 12 plus minutes and AM or PM, but a British time displays an hour numbered 1 through 24 plus minutes. If the user changes the region format in the Settings app, the date picker's display will change immediately.

A date picker has `calendar` and `timeZone` properties, respectively an NSCalendar and an NSTimeZone; these are nil by default, meaning that the date picker responds to the user's system-level settings. You can also change these values manually; for example, if you live in California and you set a date picker's `timeZone` to GMT, the displayed time is shifted forward by 8 hours, so that 11 AM is displayed as 7 PM (if it is winter).

 Don't change the `timeZone` of a UIDatePickerModeCountDownTimer date picker; if you do, the displayed value will be shifted, and you will confuse the heck out of yourself and your users.

The minutes component, if there is one, defaults to showing every minute, but you can change this with the `minuteInterval` property. The maximum value is 30, in which case the minutes component values are 0 and 30. An attempt to set a value that doesn't divide evenly into 60 will be silently ignored.

The date represented by a date picker (unless its mode is UIDatePickerModeCountDownTimer) is its `date` property, an NSDate. The default date is now, at the time the date picker is instantiated. For a `UIDatePickerModeDate` date picker, the time by default is 12 AM (midnight), local time; for a `UIDatePickerModeTime` date picker, the date by default is today. The internal value is reckoned in the local time zone, so it may be different from the displayed value, if you have changed the date picker's `timeZone`.

The maximum and minimum values enabled in the date picker are determined by its `maximumDate` and `minimumDate` properties. Values outside this range may appear disabled. There isn't really any practical limit on the range that a date picker can display, because the "drums" representing its components are not physical, and values are added dynamically as the user spins them. In this example, we set the initial minimum and maximum dates of a date picker (`self.picker`) to the beginning and end of 1954. We also set the actual `date`, so that the date picker will be set initially to a value within the minimum–maximum range:

```
self.picker.datePickerMode = UIDatePickerModeDate;
NSDateComponents* dc = [NSDateComponents new];
[dc setYear:1954];
[dc setMonth:1];
[dc setDay:1];
NSCalendar* c =
    [[NSCalendar alloc] initWithCalendarIdentifier:NSGregorianCalendar];
NSDate* d = [c dateFromComponents:dc];
self.picker.minimumDate = d;
[dc setYear:1955];
d = [c dateFromComponents:dc];
self.picker.maximumDate = d;
self.picker.date = self.picker.minimumDate;
```

 Don't set the `maximumDate` and `minimumDate` properties values for a `UIDatePickerModeCountDownTimer` date picker; if you do, you might cause a crash with an out-of-range exception.

To convert between an NSDate and a string, you'll need an NSDateFormatter (see Apple's *Date and Time Programming Guide*):

```
NSDate* d = self.picker.date;
NSDateFormatter* df = [NSDateFormatter new];
[df setTimeStyle:kCFDateFormatterFullStyle];
[df setDateStyle:kCFDateFormatterFullStyle];
NSLog(@"%@", [df stringFromDate:d]);
// "Tuesday, August 10, 1954, 3:16:25 AM GMT-07:00"
```

The value displayed in a `UIDatePickerModeCountDownTimer` date picker is its `count-DownDuration`; this is an NSTimeInterval, which is a double representing a number of seconds, even though the minimum interval displayed is a minute. A `UIDatePicker-ModeCountDownTimer` date picker does not actually do any counting down! You are expected to use some other interface to display the countdown. The Timer tab of Apple's

Clock app shows a typical interface; the user configures the date picker to set the count-DownDuration initially, but once the counting starts, the date picker is hidden and a label displays the remaining time.

Converting the countDownDuration from an NSTimeInterval to hours and minutes is up to you; you could use the built-in calendrical classes:

```
NSTimeInterval t = self.picker.countDownDuration;
NSDate* d = [NSDate dateWithTimeIntervalSinceReferenceDate:t];
NSCalendar* c =
    [[NSCalendar alloc] initWithCalendarIdentifier:NSGregorianCalendar];
[c setTimeZone: [NSTimeZone timeZoneForSecondsFromGMT:0]]; // normalize
NSUInteger units = NSHourCalendarUnit | NSMinuteCalendarUnit;
NSDateComponents* dc = [c components:units fromDate:d];
NSLog(@"%d hr, %d min", [dc hour], [dc minute]);
```

 A nasty iOS 7 bug makes the Value Changed event from a UIDate-PickerModeCountDownTimer date picker unreliable (especially just after the app launches, and whenever the user has tried to set the timer to zero). The workaround is not to rely on the Value Changed event; for example, provide a button in the interface that the user can tap to make your code read the date picker's countDownDuration.

UISlider

A slider (UISlider) is an expression of a continuously settable value (its value) between some minimum and maximum (its minimumValue and maximumValue; they are 0 and 1 by default). It is portrayed as an object, the *thumb*, positioned along a *track*. As the user changes the thumb's position, the slider reports a Value Changed control event; it may do this continuously as the user presses and drags the thumb (if the slider's continuous is YES, the default) or only when the user releases the thumb (if its continuous is NO). While the user is pressing on the thumb, the slider is in the highlighted state. To change the slider's value with animation, call setValue:animated:. (But in iOS 7, there's no animation; that's presumably a bug.)

A commonly expressed desire is to modify a slider's behavior so that if the user taps on its track, the slider moves to the spot where the user tapped. Unfortunately, a slider does not, of itself, respond to taps on its track; such a tap doesn't even cause it to report a Touch Up Inside control event. However, with a gesture recognizer, most things are possible; here's the action handler for a UITapGestureRecognizer attached to a UISlider:

```
- (void) tapped: (UIGestureRecognizer*) g {
    UISlider* s = (UISlider*)g.view;
    if (s.highlighted)
        return; // tap on thumb, let slider deal with it
    CGPoint pt = [g locationInView: s];
    CGRect track = [s trackRectForBounds:s.bounds];
```

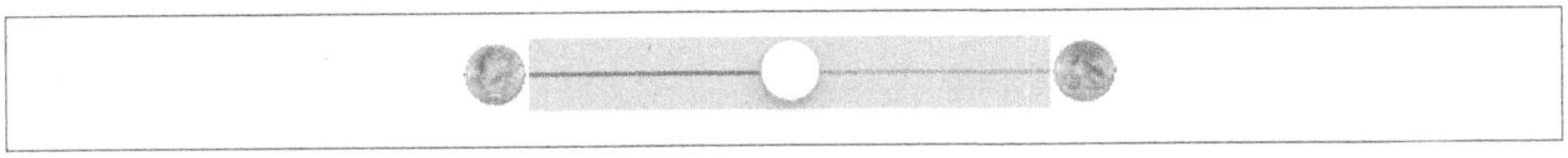

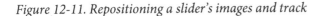

Figure 12-11. Repositioning a slider's images and track

```
    if (!CGRectContainsPoint(CGRectInset(track, 0, -10), pt))
        return; // not on track, forget it
    CGFloat percentage = pt.x / s.bounds.size.width;
    CGFloat delta = percentage * (s.maximumValue - s.minimumValue);
    CGFloat value = s.minimumValue + delta;
    [s setValue:value animated:YES];
}
```

In iOS 7, a slider's `tintColor` (which may be inherited from further up the view hierarchy) determines the color of the track to the left of the thumb. You can change the color of the two parts of the track with the `minimumTrackTintColor` and `maximumTrackTintColor` properties. (The `thumbTintColor` property does not affect the thumb color in iOS 7.)

To go further, you can provide your own thumb image and your own track image, along with images to appear at each end of the track, and you can override in a subclass the methods that position these.

The images at the ends of the track are the slider's `minimumValueImage` and `maximumValueImage`, and they are nil by default. If you set them to actual images (which can also be done in the nib), the slider will attempt to position them within its own bounds, shrinking the drawing of the track to compensate.

You can change that behavior by overriding `minimumValueImageRectForBounds:`, `maximumValueImageRectForBounds:`, and `trackRectForBounds:` in a subclass. The bounds passed in are the slider's bounds. In this example (Figure 12-11), we expand the track width to the full width of the slider, and draw the images outside the slider's bounds. The images are still visible, because the slider does not clip its subviews to its bounds. In the figure, I've given the slider a green background color so you can see how the track and images are related to its bounds:

```
- (CGRect)maximumValueImageRectForBounds:(CGRect)bounds {
    CGRect result = [super maximumValueImageRectForBounds:bounds];
    result = CGRectOffset(result, 31, 0);
    return result;
}
- (CGRect)minimumValueImageRectForBounds:(CGRect)bounds {
    CGRect result = [super minimumValueImageRectForBounds:bounds];
    result = CGRectOffset(result, -31, 0);
    return result;
}
- (CGRect)trackRectForBounds:(CGRect)bounds {
```

Figure 12-12. Replacing a slider's thumb

```
        CGRect result = [super trackRectForBounds:bounds];
        result.origin.x = 0;
        result.size.width = bounds.size.width;
        return result;
    }
```

The thumb is also an image, and you set it with `setThumbImage:forState:`. There are two chiefly relevant states, `UIControlStateNormal` and `UIControlStateHighlighted`. If you supply images for both, the thumb will change automatically while the user is dragging it. By default, the image will be centered in the track at the point represented by the slider's current value; you can shift this position by overriding `thumbRectFor-Bounds:trackRect:value:` in a subclass. In this example, the image is repositioned upward slightly (Figure 12-12):

```
    - (CGRect)thumbRectForBounds:(CGRect)bounds
                    trackRect:(CGRect)rect value:(float)value {
        CGRect result =
            [super thumbRectForBounds:bounds trackRect:rect value:value];
        result = CGRectOffset(result, 0, -7);
        return result;
    }
```

Enlarging or offsetting a slider's thumb can mislead the user as to the area on which it can be touched to drag it. The slider, not the thumb, is the touchable UIControl; only the part of the thumb that intersects the slider's bounds will be draggable. The user may try to drag the part of the thumb that is drawn outside the slider's bounds, and will fail (and be confused). A solution is to increase the slider's height; if you're using autolayout, you can add an explicit height constraint in the nib, or override `intrinsicContent-Size` in code (Chapter 1).

The track is two images, one appearing to the left of the thumb, the other to its right. They are set with `setMinimumTrackImage:forState:` and `setMaximumTrackImage:for-State:`. If you supply images both for normal state and for highlighted state, the images will change while the user is dragging the thumb.

The images should be resizable, because that's how the slider cleverly makes it look like the user is dragging the thumb along a single static track. In reality, there are two images; as the user drags the thumb, one image grows horizontally and the other shrinks horizontally. For the left track image, the right end cap inset will be partially or entirely hidden under the thumb; for the right track image, the left end cap inset will be partially

Figure 12-13. Replacing a slider's track

Figure 12-14. A segmented control

or entirely hidden under the thumb. Figure 12-13 shows a track derived from a single 15×15 image of a circular object (a coin):

```
UIImage* coin = [UIImage imageNamed: @"coin.png"];
UIImage* coinEnd = [coin resizableImageWithCapInsets:UIEdgeInsetsMake(0,7,0,7)
                                  resizingMode:UIImageResizingModeStretch];
[slider setMinimumTrackImage:coinEnd forState:UIControlStateNormal];
[slider setMaximumTrackImage:coinEnd forState:UIControlStateNormal];
```

UISegmentedControl

A segmented control (UISegmentedControl, Figure 12-14) is a row of tappable segments; a segment is rather like a button. The user is thus choosing among options. By default (momentary is NO), the most recently tapped segment remains selected. Alternatively (momentary is YES), the tapped segment is shown as highlighted momentarily (by default, highlighted is indistinguishable from selected, but you can change that); afterward, no segment selection is displayed, though internally the tapped segment remains the selected segment.

The selected segment can be set and retrieved with the selectedSegmentIndex property; when you set it in code, the selected segment remains visibly selected, even for a momentary segmented control. A selectedSegmentIndex value of UISegmented-ControlNoSegment means no segment is selected. When the user taps a segment that isn't already visibly selected, the segmented control reports a Value Changed event.

A segment can be separately enabled or disabled with setEnabled:forSegmentAt-Index:, and its enabled state can be retrieved with isEnabledForSegmentAtIndex:. A disabled segment, by default, is drawn faded; the user can't tap it, but it can still be selected in code.

A segment has either a title or an image; when one is set, the other becomes nil. In iOS 7, an image is treated as a template image, colored by the tintColor, unless you explicitly provide a UIImageRenderingModeAlwaysOriginal image. The methods for setting and fetching the title and image for existing segments are:

- `setTitle:forSegmentAtIndex:`, `titleForSegmentAtIndex:`
- `setImage:forSegmentAtIndex:`, `imageForSegmentAtIndex:`

You will also want to set the title or image when creating the segment. You can do this in code if you're creating the segmented control from scratch, with `initWithItems:`, which takes an array each item of which is either a string or an image.

Methods for managing segments dynamically are:

- `insertSegmentWithTitle:atIndex:animated:`
- `insertSegmentWithImage:atIndex:animated:`
- `removeSegmentAtIndex:animated:`
- `removeAllSegments`

The number of segments can be retrieved with the read-only `numberOfSegments` property.

A segmented control has a standard height; if you're using autolayout, you can change the height through constraints or by overriding `intrinsicContentSize` — or by setting its background image, as I'll describe in a moment.

If you're using autolayout, the width of all segments and the `intrinsicContentSize` width of the entire segmented control are adjusted automatically whenever you set a segment's title or image. If the segmented control's `apportionsSegmentWidthsBy-Content` property is NO, segment sizes will be made equal to one another; if it is YES, each segment will be sized individually to fit its content. Alternatively, you can set a segment's width explicitly with `setWidth:forSegmentAtIndex:` (and retrieve it with `widthForSegmentAtIndex:`); setting a width of 0 means that this segment is to be sized automatically.

To change the position of the content (title or image) within a segment, call `setContent-Offset:forSegmentAtIndex:` (and retrieve it with `contentOffsetForSegmentAt-Index:`).

In iOS 7, the color of a segmented control's outline, title text, and selection are dictated by its `tintColor`, which may be inherited from further up the view hierarchy. (The `segmentedControlStyle` property is deprecated in iOS 7.)

Further methods for customizing a segmented control's appearance are parallel to those for setting the look of a stepper or the scope bar portion of a search bar, both described earlier in this chapter. You can set the overall background, the divider image, the text attributes for the segment titles, and the position of segment contents:

- `setBackgroundImage:forState:barMetrics:`

Figure 12-15. A segmented control, customized

- `setDividerImage:forLeftSegmentState:rightSegmentState:barMetrics:`
- `setTitleTextAttributes:forState:`
- `setContentPositionAdjustment:forSegmentType:barMetrics:`

You don't have to customize for every state, as the segmented control will use the normal state setting for the states you don't specify. As I mentioned a moment ago, setting a background image changes the segmented control's height.

Here's the code that achieved Figure 12-15; selecting a segment automatically darkens the background image for us (similar to a button's `adjustsImageWhenHighlighted`, described in the next section), so there's no need to specify a separate selected image:

```
// background, set desired height but make width resizable
// sufficient to set for Normal only
UIImage* image = [UIImage imageNamed: @"linen.png"];
CGFloat w = 100;
CGFloat h = 60;
UIGraphicsBeginImageContextWithOptions(CGSizeMake(w,h), NO, 0);
[image drawInRect:CGRectMake(0,0,w,h)];
UIImage* image2 = UIGraphicsGetImageFromCurrentImageContext();
UIGraphicsEndImageContext();
UIImage* image3 =
    [image2 resizableImageWithCapInsets:UIEdgeInsetsMake(0,10,0,10)
                        resizingMode:UIImageResizingModeStretch];
[self.seg setBackgroundImage:image3 forState:UIControlStateNormal
                barMetrics:UIBarMetricsDefault];
// segment images, redraw at final size
NSArray* pep = @[@"manny.jpg", @"moe.jpg", @"jack.jpg"];
for (int i = 0; i < 3; i++) {
    UIImage* image = [UIImage imageNamed: pep[i]];
    UIGraphicsBeginImageContextWithOptions(CGSizeMake(30,30), NO, 0);
    [image drawInRect:CGRectMake(0,0,30,30)];
    UIImage* image2 = UIGraphicsGetImageFromCurrentImageContext();
    UIGraphicsEndImageContext();
    image2 =
        [image2 imageWithRenderingMode:UIImageRenderingModeAlwaysOriginal];
    [self.seg setImage:image2 forSegmentAtIndex:i];
    [self.seg setWidth:80 forSegmentAtIndex:i];
}
// divider, set at desired width, sufficient to set for Normal only
UIGraphicsBeginImageContextWithOptions(CGSizeMake(1,10), NO, 0);
[[UIColor whiteColor] set];
```

```
CGContextFillRect(UIGraphicsGetCurrentContext(), CGRectMake(0,0,1,10));
UIImage* div = UIGraphicsGetImageFromCurrentImageContext();
UIGraphicsEndImageContext();
[self.seg setDividerImage:div
        forLeftSegmentState:UIControlStateNormal
          rightSegmentState:UIControlStateNormal
                  barMetrics:UIBarMetricsDefault];
```

The segmentType: parameter in setContentPositionAdjustment:forSegmentType: barMetrics: is needed because, by default, the segments at the two extremes have rounded ends (and, if a segment is the lone segment, both its ends are rounded). The argument allows you distinguish between the various possibilities:

- UISegmentedControlSegmentAny

- UISegmentedControlSegmentLeft

- UISegmentedControlSegmentCenter

- UISegmentedControlSegmentRight

- UISegmentedControlSegmentAlone

The barMetrics: parameter will be ignored in iOS 7 unless its value is UIBarMetrics-Default.

UIButton

A button (UIButton) is a fundamental tappable control, which may contain a title, an image, and a background image (and may have a backgroundColor). A button has a type, and the code creation method is a class method, buttonWithType:. The types are:

UIButtonTypeSystem
> New in iOS 7. The title text appears in the button's tintColor, which may be inherited from further up the view hierarchy; when the button is tapped, the title text color momentarily changes to a color derived from what's behind it (which might be the button's backgroundColor). The image is treated as a template image, colored by the tintColor, unless you explicitly provide a UIImageRenderingModeAlways-Original image; when the button is tapped, the image (even if it isn't a template image) is momentarily tinted to a color derived from what's behind it.

UIButtonTypeDetailDisclosure
UIButtonTypeInfoLight
UIButtonTypeInfoDark
UIButtonTypeContactAdd
> Basically, these are all UIButtonTypeSystem buttons whose image is set automatically to standard button images. In iOS 7, the first three are an "i" in a circle, and the last is a Plus in a circle; the two Info types are identical, and they differ from

the `DetailDisclosure` type only in that their `showsTouchWhenHighlighted` is YES by default.

`UIButtonTypeCustom`

> In iOS 7, identical to `UIButtonTypeSystem`, except that there's no automatic coloring of the title or image by the `tintColor` or the color of what's behind the button, and the image is a normal image by default.

`UIButtonTypeSystem` replaces the old `UIButtonTypeRoundedRect`, which equates to it numerically. There is no built-in iOS 7 button type with an outline (border). You can add an outline — by adding a background image, for example, or by manipulating the button's layer — but the default look of an iOS 7 button is the text or image alone. In one of my apps, I make a button stand out a bit more, like a pre-iOS 7 button, entirely through settings made in the nib:

- In the Attributes inspector, I give the button a background color.
- In the Identity inspector, I use the User Defined Runtime Attributes to set the button's `layer.borderWidth` to 2 and its `layer.cornerRadius` to 5.

A button has a title, a title color, and a title shadow color — or you can supply an attributed title, thus dictating these features and more in a single value through an NSAttributedString (Chapter 10).

Distinguish a button's internal image from its background image. The background image, if any, is stretched, if necessary, to fill the button's bounds (technically, its `backgroundRectForBounds:`). The image, on the other hand, if smaller than the button, is not resized, and is thus shown internally within the button. The button can have both a title and an image, if the image is small enough; in that case, the image is shown to the left of the title by default.

These six features (title, title color, title shadow color, attributed title, image, and background image) can all be made to vary depending on the button's current state: `UIControlStateHighlighted`, `UIControlStateSelected`, `UIControlStateDisabled`, and `UIControlStateNormal`. The button can be in more than one state at once, except for `UIControlStateNormal` which means "none of the other states". A state change, whether automatic (the button is highlighted while the user is tapping it) or programmatically imposed, will thus in and of itself alter a button's appearance. The methods for setting these button features, therefore, all involve specifying a corresponding state — or multiple states, using a bitmask:

- `setTitle:forState:`
- `setTitleColor:forState:`
- `setTitleShadowColor:forState:`

- setAttributedTitle:forState:

- setImage:forState:

- setBackgroundImage:forState:

Similarly, when getting these button features, you must either specify a single state you're interested in or ask about the feature as currently displayed:

- titleForState:, currentTitle

- titleColorForState:, currentTitleColor

- titleShadowColorForState:, currentTitleShadowColor

- attributedTitleForState:, currentAttributedTitle

- imageForState:, currentImage

- backgroundImageForState:, currentBackgroundImage

If you don't specify a feature for a particular state, or if the button adopts more than one state at once, an internal heuristic is used to determine what to display. I can't describe all possible combinations, but here are some general observations:

- If you specify a feature for a particular state (highlighted, selected, or disabled), and the button is in *only* that state, that feature will be used.

- If you *don't* specify a feature for a particular state (highlighted, selected, or disabled), and the button is in *only* that state, the normal version of that feature will be used as fallback. (That's why many examples earlier in this book have assigned a title for UIControlStateNormal only; this is sufficient to give the button a title in every state.)

- Combinations of states often cause the button to fall back on the feature for normal state. For example, if a button is both highlighted and selected, the button will display its normal title, even if it has a highlighted title, a selected title, or both.

A UIButtonTypeSystem button with an attributed normal title will tint the title to the tintColor if you don't give the attributed string a color, and will tint the title while highlighted to the color derived from what's behind the button if you haven't supplied a highlighted title with its own color. But a UIButtonTypeCustom button will not do any of that; it leaves control of the title color for each state completely up to you.

In addition, a UIButton has some properties determining how it draws itself in various states, which can save you the trouble of specifying different images for different states:

showsTouchWhenHighlighted
    If YES, then the button projects a circular white glow when highlighted. If the button has an internal image, the glow is centered behind it; thus, this feature is suitable

particularly if the button image is small and circular; for example, it's the default behavior for a `UIButtonTypeInfoLight` or `UIButtonTypeInfoDark` button. If the button has no internal image, the glow is centered at the button's center. The glow is drawn on top of the background image or color, if any.

`adjustsImageWhenHighlighted`

In a `UIButtonTypeCustom` button, if this property is YES (the default), then if there is no separate highlighted image (and if `showsTouchWhenHighlighted` is NO), the normal image is darkened when the button is highlighted. This applies equally to the internal image and the background image. (A `UIButtonTypeSystem` button is already tinting its highlighted image, so this property doesn't apply.)

`adjustsImageWhenDisabled`

If YES, then if there is no separate disabled image, the normal image is shaded when the button is disabled. This applies equally to the internal image and the background image. The default is YES for a `UIButtonTypeCustom` button and NO for a `UIButton-TypeSystem` button.

A button has a natural size in relation to its contents. If you're using autolayout, the button can adopt that size automatically as its `intrinsicContentSize`, and you can modify the way it does this by overriding `intrinsicContentSize` in a subclass or by applying explicit constraints. If you're not using autolayout and you create a button in code, send it `sizeToFit` or give it an explicit size — otherwise, the button will have a zero size and you'll be left wondering why your button hasn't appeared in the interface.

The title is a UILabel (Chapter 10), and the label features of the title can be accessed through the button's `titleLabel`. Its properties may be set, provided they do not conflict with existing UIButton features. For example, you can set the title's `font` and `shadow-Offset` by way of the label, but the title's text, color, and shadow color should be set using the appropriate button methods. If the title is given a shadow in this way, then the button's `reversesTitleShadowWhenHighlighted` property also applies: if YES, the `shadowOffset` values are replaced with their additive inverses when the button is highlighted. Similarly, you can manipulate the label's wrapping behavior to make the button's title consist of multiple lines. The modern way, however, is to manipulate all these features using attributed strings.

The internal image is drawn by a UIImageView (Chapter 2), whose features can be accessed through the button's `imageView`. Thus, for example, you can change the internal image view's `alpha` to make the image more transparent.

The internal position of the image and title as a whole are governed by the button's `contentVerticalAlignment` and `contentHorizontalAlignment` (inherited from UI-Control). You can also tweak the position of the image and title, together or separately, by setting the button's `contentEdgeInsets`, `titleEdgeInsets`, or `imageEdgeInsets`.

Increasing an inset component increases that margin; thus, for example, a positive top component makes the distance between that object and the top of the button larger than normal (where "normal" is where the object would be according to the alignment settings). The `titleEdgeInsets` or `imageEdgeInsets` values are added to the overall `contentEdgeInsets` values. So, for example, if you really wanted to, you could make the internal image appear to the right of the title by decreasing the left `titleEdgeInsets` and increasing the left `imageEdgeInsets`.

Four methods also provide access to the button's positioning of its elements:

- `titleRectForContentRect:`
- `imageRectForContentRect:`
- `contentRectForBounds:`
- `backgroundRectForBounds:`

These methods are called whenever the button is redrawn, including every time it changes state. The content rect is the area in which the title and image are placed. By default, `contentRectForBounds:` and `backgroundRectForBounds:` yield the same result. You can override these methods in a subclass to change the way the button's elements are positioned.

Here's an example of a customized button. In a UIButton subclass, we increase the button's `intrinsicContentSize` to give it larger margins around its content, and we override `backgroundRectForBounds` to shrink the button slightly when highlighted as a way of providing feedback:

```
- (CGRect)backgroundRectForBounds:(CGRect)bounds {
    CGRect result = [super backgroundRectForBounds:bounds];
    if (self.highlighted)
        result = CGRectInset(result, 3, 3);
    return result;
}
-(CGSize)intrinsicContentSize {
    CGSize sz = [super intrinsicContentSize];
    sz.height += 16;
    sz.width += 20;
    return sz;
}
```

The button, which is a UIButtonTypeCustom button, is assigned an internal image and a background image from the same image, along with an attributed title. When highlighted, its title color changes, thanks to a second attributed string, and its image glows, thanks to adjustsImageWhenHighlighted (Figure 12-16):

Figure 12-16. A custom button

```
UIImage* im = [UIImage imageNamed: @"coin2.png"];
CGSize sz = [im size];
UIImage* im2 =
    [im resizableImageWithCapInsets:
        UIEdgeInsetsMake(sz.height/2.0, sz.width/2.0,
                         sz.height/2.0, sz.width/2.0)
        resizingMode: UIImageResizingModeStretch];
[self.button setBackgroundImage: im2 forState: UIControlStateNormal];
self.button.backgroundColor = [UIColor clearColor];
[self.button setImage: im2 forState: UIControlStateNormal];
NSMutableAttributedString* mas =
    [[NSMutableAttributedString alloc]
        initWithString: @"Pay Tribute"
        attributes: @{
            NSFontAttributeName:
                [UIFont fontWithName:@"GillSans-Bold" size:16],
            NSForegroundColorAttributeName:
                [UIColor purpleColor] }];
[mas addAttributes: @{
    NSStrokeColorAttributeName:[UIColor redColor],
    NSStrokeWidthAttributeName:@(-2.0),
    NSUnderlineStyleAttributeName:@1}
            range: NSMakeRange(4,mas.length-4)];
[self.button setAttributedTitle: mas forState: UIControlStateNormal];
mas = [mas mutableCopy];
[mas addAttributes: @{
    NSForegroundColorAttributeName:[UIColor whiteColor]}
            range: NSMakeRange(0,mas.length)];
[self.button setAttributedTitle: mas forState: UIControlStateHighlighted];
self.button.adjustsImageWhenHighlighted = YES;
```

Custom Controls

The UIControl class implements several touch-tracking methods that you might override in order to customize a built-in UIControl type or to create your own UIControl subclass, along with properties that tell you whether touch tracking is going on:

- beginTrackingWithTouch:withEvent:

- continueTrackingWithTouch:withEvent:

- endTrackingWithTouch:withEvent:

Figure 12-17. A custom control

- `cancelTrackingWithEvent:`
- `tracking` (property)
- `touchInside` (property)

With the advent of gesture recognizers (Chapter 5), such direct involvement with touch tracking is probably less needed than it used to be, especially if your purpose is to modify the behavior of a built-in UIControl subclass. So, to illustrate their use, I'll give a simple example of creating a custom control. The main reason for doing this (rather than using, say, a UIView and gesture recognizers) would probably be to obtain the convenience of control events. Also, the touch-tracking methods, though not as high-level as gesture recognizers, are at least a level up from the UIResponder `touches...` methods (Chapter 5): they track a single touch, and both `beginTracking...` and `continue-Tracking...` return a BOOL, giving you a chance to stop tracking the current touch.

We'll build a simplified knob control (Figure 12-17). The control starts life at its minimum position, with an internal angle value of 0; it can be rotated clockwise with a single finger as far as its maximum position, with an internal angle value of 5 (radians). To keep things simple, the words "Min" and "Max" appearing in the interface are actually labels; the control just draws the knob, and to rotate it we'll apply a rotation transform.

Our control is a UIControl subclass, MyKnob. It has a public CGFloat `angle` property, and a CGFloat instance variable `_initialAngle` that we'll use internally during rotation. Because a UIControl is a UIView, it can draw itself, which it does with an image file included in our app bundle:

```
- (void) drawRect:(CGRect)rect {
    UIImage* knob = [UIImage imageNamed:@"knob.png"];
    [knob drawInRect:rect];
}
```

We'll need a utility function for transforming a touch's Cartesian coordinates into polar coordinates, giving us the angle to be applied as a rotation to the view:

```
static inline CGFloat pToA (UITouch* touch, UIView* self) {
    CGPoint loc = [touch locationInView: self];
    CGPoint c = CGPointMake(CGRectGetMidX(self.bounds),
                            CGRectGetMidY(self.bounds));
    return atan2(loc.y - c.y, loc.x - c.x);
}
```

Now we're ready to override the tracking methods. `beginTrackingWithTouch:with-Event:` simply notes down the angle of the initial touch location. `continueTracking-WithTouch:withEvent:` uses the difference between the current touch location's angle and the initial touch location's angle to apply a transform to the view, and updates the `angle` property. `endTrackingWithTouch:withEvent:` triggers the Value Changed control event. So our first draft looks like this:

```
- (BOOL) beginTrackingWithTouch:(UITouch*)touch withEvent:(UIEvent*)event {
    self->_initialAngle = pToA(touch, self);
    return YES;
}
- (BOOL) continueTrackingWithTouch:(UITouch*)touch withEvent:(UIEvent*)event {
    CGFloat ang = pToA(touch, self);
    ang -= self->_initialAngle;
    CGFloat absoluteAngle = self->_angle + ang;
    self.transform = CGAffineTransformRotate(self.transform, ang);
    self->_angle = absoluteAngle;
    return YES;
}
- (void) endTrackingWithTouch:(UITouch *)touch withEvent:(UIEvent *)event {
    [self sendActionsForControlEvents:UIControlEventValueChanged];
}
```

This works: we can put a MyKnob into the interface and hook up its Value Changed control event (this can be done in the nib editor), and sure enough, when we run the app, we can rotate the knob and, when our finger lifts from the knob, the Value Changed action handler is called. However, `continueTrackingWithTouch:withEvent:` needs modification.

First, we need to peg the minimum and maximum rotation at 0 and 5, respectively. For simplicity, we'll just stop tracking, by returning NO, if the rotation goes below 0 or above 5, fixing the angle at the exceeded limit. However, because we're no longer tracking, `end-Tracking...` will never be called, so we also need to trigger the Value Changed control event. (Doubtless you can come up with a more sophisticated way of pegging the knob at its minimum and maximum, but remember, this is only a simple example.) Second, it might be nice to give the programmer the option to have the Value Changed control event reported continuously as `continueTracking...` is called repeatedly. So we'll add a public `continuous` BOOL property and obey it.

Here, then, is our revised `continueTracking...` implementation:

```
- (BOOL) continueTrackingWithTouch:(UITouch*)touch withEvent:(UIEvent*)event {
    CGFloat ang = pToA(touch, self);
    ang -= self->_initialAngle;
    CGFloat absoluteAngle = self->_angle + ang;
    if (absoluteAngle < 0) {
        self.transform = CGAffineTransformIdentity;
        self->_angle = 0;
        [self sendActionsForControlEvents:UIControlEventValueChanged];
        return NO;
    }
    if (absoluteAngle > 5) {
        self.transform = CGAffineTransformMakeRotation(5);
        self->_angle = 5;
        [self sendActionsForControlEvents:UIControlEventValueChanged];
        return NO;
    }
    self.transform = CGAffineTransformRotate(self.transform, ang);
    self->_angle = absoluteAngle;
    if (self->continuous)
        [self sendActionsForControlEvents:UIControlEventValueChanged];
    return YES;
}
```

Finally, we'll probably want a method that sets the angle programmatically as a way of rotating the knob:

```
- (void) setAngle: (CGFloat) ang {
    if (ang < 0)
        ang = 0;
    if (ang > 5)
        ang = 5;
    self.transform = CGAffineTransformMakeRotation(ang);
    self->_angle = ang;
}
```

Bars

There are three bar types: navigation bar (UINavigationBar), toolbar (UIToolbar), and tab bar (UITabBar). They are often used in conjunction with a built-in view controller (Chapter 6):

- A UINavigationController has a UINavigationBar.
- A UINavigationController has a UIToolbar.
- A UITabBarController has a UITabBar.

You can also use these bar types independently. You are most likely to do that with a UIToolbar, which is often used as an independent bottom bar. On the iPad, it can also be used as a top bar, adopting a role analogous to a menu bar on the desktop. That's such a common interface, in fact, that certain special automatic behaviors are associated with it; for example, a UISearchBar in a UIToolbar and managed by a UISearchDisplay-Controller will automatically display its search results table in a popover (Chapter 9).

This section summarizes the facts about the three bar types (along with UISearchBar, which can act as a top bar), and about the items that populate them.

Bar Position and Bar Metrics

If a navigation bar or toolbar — or a search bar (discussed earlier in this chapter) — is to occupy the top of the screen, the iOS 7 convention is that its height should be increased to underlap the transparent status bar. To make this possible, iOS 7 introduces the notion of a *bar position*. The UIBarPositioning protocol, adopted by UINavigationBar, UI-Toolbar, and UISearchbar, defines one property, `barPosition`, whose possible values are:

- `UIBarPositionAny`
- `UIBarPositionBottom`
- `UIBarPositionTop`
- `UIBarPositionTopAttached`

But `barPosition` is read-only, so how are you supposed to set it? The UIBarPosition-Delegate protocol defines one method, `positionForBar:`. This provides a way for a bar's delegate to dictate the bar's `barPosition`. The delegate protocols UINavigation-BarDelegate, UIToolbarDelegate, and UISearchBarDelegate all conform to UIBarPositionDelegate.

Thus, if you use one of these bar types alone (not in conjunction with a view controller), you can give it a delegate and, in that delegate, implement `positionForBar:` to return the bar's desired `barPosition` value.

The rule is then that the bar's height will be extended upward, so that its top can go behind the status bar, if the bar's delegate returns `UIBarPositionTopAttached` from its implementation of `positionForBar:`. To get the final position right, the bar's top should also have a zero-length constraint to the view controller's top layout guide — or, if you're not using autolayout, then the bar's top should have a y value of 20. Unfortunately, a toolbar in the nib editor has no `delegate` outlet — I regard that as a bug — so you'll have to form an outlet to the toolbar and assign the toolbar a delegate in code. Here's an example for a toolbar:

```
- (UIBarPosition)positionForBar: (id<UIBarPositioning>) bar {
    return UIBarPositionTopAttached;
}
- (void)viewDidLoad {
    [super viewDidLoad];
    self.toolbar.delegate = self;
}
```

A bar's height is reflected also by its *bar metrics*. If a navigation bar or toolbar belongs to a UINavigationController on the iPhone (not on the iPad), then if the interface rotates, the UINavigationController changes the height of the bar. The standard heights are 44 (portrait) and 32 (landscape) — plus 20 if the bar also underlaps the status bar. Possible bar metrics values are:

- UIBarMetricsDefault
- UIBarMetricsLandscapePhone
- UIBarMetricsDefaultPrompt
- UIBarMetricsLandscapePhonePrompt

(The two Prompt values, new in iOS 7, apply to a bar whose height is extended downward to accommodate prompt text.)

When you're customizing a feature of a bar, you may find yourself calling a method that takes a bar metrics parameter, and possibly a bar position parameter as well. The idea is that you can customize that feature differently depending on the bar metrics and the bar position. You don't have to set that value for *every* possible combination of bar position and bar metrics! In general (though, unfortunately, the details are a little inconsistent from class to class), UIBarPositionAny and UIBarMetricsDefault are treated as defaults that encompass any positions and metrics you don't specify.

The interface object classes and their features that participate in this system are:

UISearchBar

> A search bar can function as a top bar and can have a prompt. You can set its background image.

UINavigationBar

> A navigation bar can function as a top bar, it can have a prompt, and its height in a navigation interface is changed automatically on the iPhone depending on the app's orientation. You can set its background image. In addition, the vertical offset of its title can depend on the bar metrics.

UIToolbar

> A toolbar can function as a top bar or a bottom bar, and its height in a navigation interface is changed automatically on the iPhone depending on the app's orienta-

tion. You can set its background image. In addition, its shadow can depend on its bar position.

UIBarButtonItem

You can set a bar button item's image, image inset, background image, title offset, and background offset, so as to depend upon the bar metrics of the containing bar, either a UINavigationBar or a UIToolbar (and the bar position is irrelevant).

Bar Appearance

In iOS 7, the overall look of the three bar types is identical by default, and the ways of customizing that overall look are unified. A bar can be styled at three levels:

`barStyle`, `translucent`

The `barStyle` options are:

- `UIBarStyleDefault`
- `UIBarStyleBlack`

In iOS 7 the bar styles are flat white and flat black respectively. The `translucent` property turns on or off the blurry translucency that is so characteristic of iOS 7.

`barTintColor`

This property tints the bar with a solid color, replacing the earlier `tintColor` property which is used for something else in iOS 7 (namely, it is inherited by bar button items to be the default color of their titles and template images). If you set the `barTintColor` and you want translucency, then supplying a color with a low `alpha` component is up to you. However, if you set the bar's `translucent` to NO, then the `barTintColor` is treated as opaque.

`backgroundImage`

This, as I've just explained, can vary depending on the bar position and bar metrics (`setBackgroundImage:forBarPosition:barMetrics:`). The transparency of the image is obeyed, but if you set the bar's `translucent` to NO, then the `barTintColor` will appear opaque behind the image. If the image is too large, it is sized down to fit in iOS 7; if it is too small, it is tiled by default, but you can change that by supplying a resizable image.

If you assign a bar a background image, you can also customize its shadow, which is cast from the bottom of the bar (if the bar is at the top) or the top of the bar (if the bar is at the bottom) on whatever is behind it. The setter is usually the `shadowImage` property, but a toolbar can be either at the top or the bottom, so its setter is `setShadowImage:forToolbarPosition:`, and the `barPosition` is used to decide whether the shadow should appear at the top or the bottom of the toolbar.

You'll want a shadow image to be very small and very transparent; the image will be tiled horizontally. Here's an example for a navigation bar:

```
UIGraphicsBeginImageContextWithOptions(CGSizeMake(4,4), NO, 0);
[[[UIColor grayColor] colorWithAlphaComponent:0.3] setFill];
CGContextFillRect(UIGraphicsGetCurrentContext(), CGRectMake(0,0,4,2));
[[[UIColor grayColor] colorWithAlphaComponent:0.15] setFill];
CGContextFillRect(UIGraphicsGetCurrentContext(), CGRectMake(0,2,4,2));
im = UIGraphicsGetImageFromCurrentImageContext();
UIGraphicsEndImageContext();
self.navbar.shadowImage = im;
```

UIBarButtonItem

The only things that can appear inside a navigation bar or a toolbar — aside from a navigation bar's title and prompt — are bar button items (UIBarButtonItem, a subclass of UIBarItem). This is not much of a limitation, however, because a bar button item can contain a custom view, which can be any type of UIView at all. A bar button item itself, however, is not a UIView subclass.

A bar button item may be instantiated with any of five methods:

- `initWithBarButtonSystemItem:target:action:`
- `initWithTitle:style:target:action:`
- `initWithImage:style:target:action:`
- `initWithImage:landscapeImagePhone:style:target:action:`
- `initWithCustomView:`

In iOS 7, a bar button item's image is treated by default as a template image, unless you explicitly provide a `UIImageRenderingModeAlwaysOriginal` image.

The `style:` options are:

- `UIBarButtonItemStylePlain`
- `UIBarButtonItemStyleDone` (in iOS 7, the title text is bold)

As I mentioned a moment ago, many aspects of a bar button item can be made dependent upon the bar metrics of the containing bar. Thus, you can initialize a bar button item with both an `image` and a `landscapeImagePhone`, the latter to be used when the bar metrics has `landscape` in its name. A bar button item inherits from UIBarItem the ability to adjust the image position with `imageInsets` (and `landscapeImagePhone-Insets`), plus the `enabled` and `tag` properties. Recall from Chapter 6 that you can also set a bar button item's `possibleTitles` and `width` properties, to determine its width.

A bar button item's `tintColor` property, in iOS 7, tints the title text or template image of the button; it is inherited from the `tintColor` of the bar, or you can override it for an individual bar button item.

You can apply a text attributes dictionary to a bar button item's title, and you can give it a background image:

- `setTitleTextAttributes:forState:` (inherited from UIBarItem)
- `setTitlePositionAdjustment:forBarMetrics:`
- `setBackgroundImage:forState:barMetrics:`
- `setBackgroundImage:forState:style:barMetrics:`
- `setBackgroundVerticalPositionAdjustment:forBarMetrics:`

In addition, these methods apply only if the bar button item is being used as a back button item in a navigation bar (as I'll describe in the next section):

- `setBackButtonTitlePositionAdjustment:forBarMetrics:`
- `setBackButtonBackgroundImage:forState:barMetrics:`
- `setBackButtonBackgroundVerticalPositionAdjustment:forBarMetrics:`

 In a bar button item with a custom view, the background vertical position adjustment doesn't apply (because the custom view is the button's content, not its background). To shift the apparent position of a custom view, construct the custom view as a subview within a superview, and shift the position of the subview. This technique can cause the subview to appear outside the containing bar, so be careful.

In iOS 7, no bar button item style supplies an outline (border); the default look of a button is just the text or image. (The old bar button item style `UIBarButtonItemStyle-Bordered`, in iOS 7, is identical to `UIBarButtonItemStylePlain`.) If you want an outline, you have to supply it yourself by way of the background image. Here's how I create the outlined left bar button item in the settings view of my Zotz! app (Figure 12-18):

```
UIBarButtonItem* bb =
    [[UIBarButtonItem alloc] initWithTitle:@"New Game"
        style:UIBarButtonItemStylePlain
        target:self
        action:@selector(doNewGame:)];
[bb setTitleTextAttributes:
    @{NSFontAttributeName:[UIFont fontWithName:@"Avenir-Medium" size:11]}
                forState:UIControlStateNormal];
CAGradientLayer* grad = [CAGradientLayer new];
```

Figure 12-18. A bar button item with a border

```
grad.frame = CGRectMake(0,0,15,15);
grad.colors =
    @[(id)[UIColor colorWithRed:1 green:1 blue:0 alpha:0.8].CGColor,
      (id)[UIColor colorWithRed:.7 green:.7 blue:.3 alpha:0.8].CGColor];
UIGraphicsBeginImageContextWithOptions(CGSizeMake(15,15), NO, 0);
UIBezierPath* p =
    [UIBezierPath bezierPathWithRoundedRect:CGRectMake(0,0,15,15)
                            cornerRadius:8];
[p addClip];
[grad renderInContext:UIGraphicsGetCurrentContext()];
[[UIColor blackColor] setStroke];
p.lineWidth = 2;
[p stroke];
UIImage* im = UIGraphicsGetImageFromCurrentImageContext();
UIGraphicsEndImageContext();
im = [im resizableImageWithCapInsets:UIEdgeInsetsMake(7,7,7,7)
                        resizingMode:UIImageResizingModeStretch];
[bb setBackgroundImage:im forState:UIControlStateNormal
            barMetrics:UIBarMetricsDefault];
```

UINavigationBar

A navigation bar (UINavigationBar) is populated by navigation items (UINavigation-
Item). The UINavigationBar maintains a stack; UINavigationItems are pushed onto and
popped off of this stack. Whatever UINavigationItem is currently topmost in the stack
(the UINavigationBar's topItem), in combination with the UINavigationItem just beneath it in the stack (the UINavigationBar's backItem), determines what appears in the
navigation bar:

title, titleView

> The title (string) or titleView (UIView) of the topItem appears in the center of
> the navigation bar.

prompt

> The prompt (string) of the topItem appears at the top of the navigation bar, whose
> height increases to accommodate it.

rightBarButtonItem, leftBarButtonItem

> The rightBarButtonItem and leftBarButtonItem appear at the right and left ends
> of the navigation bar. A UINavigationItem can have multiple right bar button items
> and multiple left bar button items; its rightBarButtonItems and leftBarButton-

Figure 12-19. A back button animating to the left

`Items` properties are arrays (of bar button items). The bar button items are displayed from the outside in: that is, the first item in the `leftBarButtonItems` is leftmost, while the first item in the `rightBarButtonItems` is rightmost. If there are multiple buttons on a side, the `rightBarButtonItem` is the first item of the `rightBarButton-Items` array, and the `leftBarButtonItem` is the first item of the `leftBarButton-Items` array.

`backBarButtonItem`

The `backBarButtonItem` *of the backItem* appears at the left end of the navigation bar. It is automatically configured so that, when tapped, the `topItem` is popped off the stack. If the `backItem` has *no* `backBarButtonItem`, then there is *still* a back button at the left end of the navigation bar, taking its title from the `title` of the `backItem`. However, if the `topItem` has its `hidesBackButton` set to YES, the back button is suppressed. Also, unless the `topItem` has its `leftItemsSupplementBack-Button` set to YES, the back button is suppressed if the `topItem` has a `leftBarButton-Item`.

In iOS 7, the indication that the back button *is* a back button is supplied by the navigation bar's `backIndicatorImage`, which by default is a left-pointing chevron appearing to the left of the back button. You can customize this image; the image that you supply is treated as a template image by default. If you set the `backIndicatorImage`, you must also supply a `backIndicatorTransitionMaskImage`. The purpose of the mask image is to indicate the region where the back button should disappear as it slides out to the left when a new navigation item is pushed onto the stack. For example, in Figure 12-19, the back button title is visible to the right of the chevron but not to the left of the chevron; that's because on the left side of the chevron it is masked out (the mask is transparent).

In this example, I replace the chevron with a vertical bar. The vertical bar is not the entire image; the image is actually a wider rectangle, with the vertical bar at its right side. The mask is the entire wider rectangle, and is completely transparent; thus, the back button disappears as it passes behind the bar and stays invisible as it continues on to the left:

```
UIGraphicsBeginImageContextWithOptions(CGSizeMake(10,20), NO, 0);
CGContextFillRect(UIGraphicsGetCurrentContext(), CGRectMake(6,0,4,20));
UIImage* im = UIGraphicsGetImageFromCurrentImageContext();
UIGraphicsEndImageContext();
self.navbar.backIndicatorImage = im;
```

```
UIGraphicsBeginImageContextWithOptions(CGSizeMake(10,20), NO, 0);
UIImage* im2 = UIGraphicsGetImageFromCurrentImageContext();
UIGraphicsEndImageContext();
self.navbar.backIndicatorTransitionMaskImage = im2;
```

Changes to the navigation bar's buttons can be animated by sending its topItem any of these messages:

- setRightBarButtonItem:animated:

- setLeftBarButtonItem:animated:

- setRightBarButtonItems:animated:

- setLeftBarButtonItems:animated:

- setHidesBackButton:animated:

UINavigationItems are pushed and popped with pushNavigationItem:animated: and popNavigationItemAnimated:, or you can set all items on the stack at once with setItems:animated:.

You can set the title's attributes dictionary (titleTextAttributes), and you can shift the title's vertical position by calling setTitleVerticalPositionAdjustment:forBarMetrics:.

When you use a UINavigationBar implicitly as part of a UINavigationController interface, the navigation controller is the navigation bar's delegate. If you were to use a UINavigationBar on its own, you might want to supply your own delegate. The delegate methods are:

- navigationBar:shouldPushItem:

- navigationBar:didPushItem:

- navigationBar:shouldPopItem:

- navigationBar:didPopItem:

This simple (and silly) example of a standalone UINavigationBar implements the legendary baseball combination trio of Tinker to Evers to Chance; see the relevant Wikipedia article if you don't know about them (Figure 12-20, which also shows the custom back indicator and shadow I described earlier):

```
- (void)viewDidLoad {
    [super viewDidLoad];
    UINavigationItem* ni =
        [[UINavigationItem alloc] initWithTitle:@"Tinker"];
    UIBarButtonItem* b =
        [[UIBarButtonItem alloc] initWithTitle:@"Evers"
            style:UIBarButtonItemStylePlain
```

Figure 12-20. A navigation bar

Figure 12-21. A toolbar

```
            target:self action:@selector(pushNext:)];
    ni.rightBarButtonItem = b;
    self.navbar.items = @[ni];
}
- (void) pushNext: (id) sender {
    UIBarButtonItem* oldb = sender;
    NSString* s = oldb.title;
    UINavigationItem* ni = [[UINavigationItem alloc] initWithTitle:s];
    if ([s isEqualToString: @"Evers"]) {
        UIBarButtonItem* b =
            [[UIBarButtonItem alloc] initWithTitle:@"Chance"
                style:UIBarButtonItemStylePlain
                target:self action:@selector(pushNext:)];
        ni.rightBarButtonItem = b;
    }
    [self.navbar pushNavigationItem:ni animated:YES];
}
```

UIToolbar

A toolbar (UIToolbar, Figure 12-21) is intended to appear at the bottom of the screen; on the iPad, it may appear at the top of the screen. It displays a row of UIBarButtonItems, which are its `items`. The items are displayed from left to right in the order in which they appear in the `items` array. You can set the items with animation by calling `setItems:animated:`. The items within the toolbar are positioned automatically; you can intervene in this positioning by using the system bar button items `UIBarButtonSystemItemFlexibleSpace` and `UIBarButtonSystemItemFixedSpace`, along with the UIBarButtonItem `width` property.

UITabBar

A tab bar (UITabBar) displays tab bar items (UITabBarItem), its `items`, each consisting of an image and a name. To change the items in an animated fashion, call `setItems:animated:`. The tab bar maintains a current selection among its items, its `selectedItem`, which is a UITabBarItem, not an index number. If no item is selected initially, you can set the initial selection in code:

```
self.tabbar.selectedItem = self.tabbar.items[0];
```

To hear about the user changing the selection, implement `tabBar:didSelectItem:` in the delegate (UITabBarDelegate).

New in iOS 7, you get some control over how the tab bar items are laid out:

`itemPositioning`
There are three possible values:

`UITabBarItemPositioningCentered`
The items are crowded together at the center.

`UITabBarItemPositioningFill`
The items are spaced out evenly.

`UITabBarItemPositioningAutomatic`
On the iPad, the same as `Centered`; on the iPhone, the same as `Fill`.

`itemSpacing`
The space between items, if the positioning is `Centered`. For the default space, specify 0.

`itemWidth`
The width of items, if the positioning is `Centered`. For the default width, specify 0.

You can set the image drawn behind the selected tab bar item to indicate that it's selected, the `selectionIndicatorImage`.

A UITabBarItem is created with one of these two methods:

* `initWithTabBarSystemItem:tag:`
* `initWithTitle:image:tag:`

UITabBarItem is a subclass of UIBarItem, so in addition to its `title` and `image` it inherits the ability to adjust the image position with `imageInsets`, plus the `enabled` and `tag` properties.

In iOS 7, a bar item title text and template image are tinted, by default, with the tab bar's `tintColor` *when selected* (this is a change from iOS 6 behavior); the tab bar's `selectedImageTintColor` is ignored, and there's no way to set the deselected tint color (I regard this as a bug).

In iOS 7, a tab bar item's image is treated as a template image, but you can override that by supplying a `UIImageRenderingModeAlwaysOriginal` image. For this reason, the method introduced in iOS 6 for specifying a nontemplate image (`setFinishedSelected-`

Figure 12-22. A tab bar

Image:withFinishedUnselectedImage:) is unnecessary and has been deprecated. Similarly, you can customize a tab bar item's title (including its color) with an attributes dictionary (setTitleTextAttributes:forState:, inherited from UIBarItem), and you can adjust the title's position with the titlePositionAdjustment property.

Figure 12-22 (from the first screen shown in Figure 6-9) is an example of a customized tab bar; I've set the selection indicator image (the checkmark), the tint color, and the text attributes (including the color, when selected) of the tab bar items.

The user can be permitted to alter the contents of the tab bar, setting its tab bar items from among a larger repertory of tab bar items. To summon the interface that lets the user do this, call beginCustomizingItems:, passing an array of UITabBarItems that may or may not appear in the tab bar. (To prevent the user from removing an item from the tab bar, include it in the tab bar's items and *don't* include it in the argument passed to beginCustomizingItems:.) A presented view with a Done button appears, behind the tab bar but in front of everything else, displaying the customizable items. The user can then drag an item into the tab bar, replacing an item that's already there. To hear about the customizing view appearing and disappearing, implement delegate methods:

- tabBar:willBeginCustomizingItems:
- tabBar:didBeginCustomizingItems:
- tabBar:willEndCustomizingItems:changed:
- tabBar:didEndCustomizingItems:changed:

A UITabBar on its own (outside a UITabBarController) does not provide any automatic access to the user customization interface; it's up to you. In this (silly) example, we populate a UITabBar with four system tab bar items and a More item; we also populate an instance variable array with those same four system tab bar items, plus four more. When the user taps the More item, we show the user customization interface with all eight tab bar items:

```
- (void)viewDidLoad {
    [super viewDidLoad];
    NSMutableArray* arr = [NSMutableArray new];
    for (int ix = 1; ix < 8; ix++) {
        UITabBarItem* tbi =
            [[UITabBarItem alloc] initWithTabBarSystemItem:ix tag:ix];
        [arr addObject: tbi];
```

Figure 12-23. Automatically generated More list

```
    }
    self.items = arr; // copy policy
    [arr removeAllObjects];
    [arr addObjectsFromArray:
        [self.items subarrayWithRange:NSMakeRange(0,4)]];
    UITabBarItem* tbi =
        [[UITabBarItem alloc] initWithTabBarSystemItem:0 tag:0];
    [arr addObject: tbi]; // More button
    self.tabbar.items = arr;
    self.tabbar.selectedItem = self.tabbar.items[0];
}
- (void)tabBar:(UITabBar *)tabBar didSelectItem:(UITabBarItem *)item {
    NSLog(@"did select item with tag %d", item.tag);
    if (item.tag == 0) {
        // More button
        tabBar.selectedItem = nil;
        [tabBar beginCustomizingItems:self.items];
    }
}
-(void)tabBar:(UITabBar *)tabBar didEndCustomizingItems:(NSArray *)items
        changed:(BOOL)changed {
    self.tabbar.selectedItem = self.tabbar.items[0];
}
```

When used in conjunction with a UITabBarController, the customization interface is provided automatically, in an elaborate way. If there are a lot of items, a More item is automatically present, and can be used to access the remaining items in a table view. Here, the user can select any of the excess items, navigating to the corresponding view. Or, the user can switch to the customization interface by tapping the Edit button. (See the iPhone Music app for a familiar example.) Figure 12-23 shows how a More list looks by default.

The way this works is that the automatically provided More item corresponds to a UINavigationController with a root view controller (UIViewController) whose view is a UITableView. Thus, a navigation interface containing this UITableView appears through the tabbed interface when the user taps the More button. When the user selects an item in the table, the corresponding UIViewController is pushed onto the UINavigationController's stack.

You can access this UINavigationController: it is the UITabBarController's more-NavigationController. Through it, you can access the root view controller: it is the first item in the UINavigationController's viewControllers array. And through that, you can access the table view: it is the root view controller's view. This means you can customize what appears when the user taps the More button! For example, let's make the navigation bar black with white button titles, and let's remove the word More from its title:

```
UINavigationController* more =
    self.tabBarController.moreNavigationController;
UIViewController* list = more.viewControllers[0];
list.title = @"";
UIBarButtonItem* b = [UIBarButtonItem new];
b.title = @"Back";
list.navigationItem.backBarButtonItem = b; // so user can navigate back
more.navigationBar.barStyle = UIBarStyleBlack;
more.navigationBar.tintColor = [UIColor whiteColor];
```

We can go even further by supplementing the table view's data source with a data source of our own, thus proceeding to customize the table itself. This is tricky because we have no internal access to the actual data source, and we mustn't accidentally disable it from populating the table. Still, it can be done. I'll start by replacing the table view's data source with an instance of my own MyDataSource. It has a public instance variable called originalDataSource; in it, I'll store a reference to the *original* data source object:

```
UITableView* tv = (UITableView*)list.view;
MyDataSource* mds = [MyDataSource new];
self.myDataSource = mds; // retain policy
self.myDataSource.originalDataSource = tv.dataSource;
tv.dataSource = self.myDataSource;
```

In MyDataSource, I'll use Objective-C's automatic message forwarding mechanism (see Apple's *Objective-C Runtime Programming Guide*) so that MyDataSource acts as a front end for originalDataSource. MyDataSource will magically appear to respond to any message that originalDataSource responds to, and any message that arrives that My-DataSource can't handle will be magically forwarded to originalDataSource. This way, the insertion of the MyDataSource instance as data source doesn't break whatever the original data source does:

```
- (id)forwardingTargetForSelector:(SEL)aSelector {
    if ([self.originalDataSource respondsToSelector: aSelector])
        return self.originalDataSource;
    return [super forwardingTargetForSelector:aSelector];
}
```

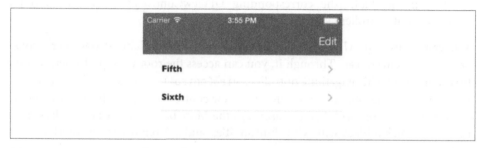

Figure 12-24. Customized More list

Finally, we'll implement the two Big Questions required by the UITableViewDataSource protocol, to quiet the compiler. In both cases, we first pass the message along to original-DataSource (somewhat analogous to calling super); then we add our own customizations as desired. Here, just as a proof of concept, I'll change each cell's text font (Figure 12-24):

```
- (NSInteger)tableView:(UITableView *)tv numberOfRowsInSection:(NSInteger)sec {
    // this is just to quiet the compiler
    return [self.originalDataSource tableView:tv numberOfRowsInSection:sec];
}
- (UITableViewCell *)tableView:(UITableView *)tv
        cellForRowAtIndexPath:(NSIndexPath *)ip {
    UITableViewCell* cell =
        [self.originalDataSource tableView:tv cellForRowAtIndexPath:ip];
    cell.textLabel.font = [UIFont fontWithName:@"GillSans-Bold" size:14];
    return cell;
}
```

Tint Color

New in iOS 7, tintColor is a UIView property, and it has a remarkable built-in feature: its value, if not set explicitly (or if set to nil), is inherited from its superview. The idea is to simplify the task of giving your app a consistent overall appearance.

This works exactly the way you would expect. You can set the tintColor of your UI-Window instance, and its value will be inherited by every view that ever appears. Any built-in view (or view-like interface object, such as a UIBarItem) whose details are colored by the tintColor will display this same color. For example, if you set your window's tintColor to red, then every UIButtonTypeSystem button that appears anywhere in your interface will have red title text by default.

Moreover, the inherited tintColor can be overridden by setting a view's tintColor explicitly. In other words, you can set the tintColor of a view partway down the view hierarchy so that it and all its subviews have a *different* tintColor from the rest of the interface. In this way, you might subtly suggest that the user has entered a different world.

If you change the `tintColor` of a view, the change immediately propagates down the hierarchy of its subviews — except, of course, that a view whose `tintColor` has been explicitly set to a color of its own is unaffected, along with its subviews.

When you ask a view for its `tintColor`, what you get is the `tintColor` of the view itself, if its own `tintColor` has been explicitly set to a color, or else the `tintColor` inherited from up the view hierarchy. In this way, you can always learn what the *effective* tint color of a view is.

Whenever a view's `tintColor` changes, including when its `tintColor` is initially set at launch time, *it and all its affected subviews* are sent the `tintColorDidChange` message. A subview whose `tintColor` has previously been explicitly set to a color of its own isn't affected, so it is *not* sent the `tintColorDidChange` message merely because its superview's `tintColor` changes — the subview's own `tintColor` *didn't* change.

A UIView also has a `tintAdjustmentMode`. Under certain circumstances, such as the summoning of a UIAlertView (Chapter 13) or a popover (Chapter 9), the system will set the `tintAdjustmentMode` of the view at the top of the view hierarchy to `UIViewTint-AdjustmentModeDimmed`. This causes the `tintColor` to change to a variety of gray. The idea is that the tinting of the background should become monochrome, thus emphasizing the primacy of the view that occupies the foreground (the alert view or popover). This change in the `tintAdjustmentMode` propagates all the way down the view hierarchy, changing *all* `tintAdjustmentMode` values and *all* `tintColor` values — and sending *all* subviews the `tintColorDidChange` message. When the foreground view goes away, the system will set the topmost view's `tintAdjustmentMode` to `UIViewTintAdjustmentMode-Normal`, and that change will propagate down the hierarchy.

The default `tintAdjustmentMode` value is `UIViewTintAdjustmentModeAutomatic`, meaning that you want this view's `tintAdjustmentMode` to adopt its superview's `tint-AdjustmentMode` automatically. When you ask for such a view's `tintAdjustmentMode`, what you get is just like what you get for `tintColor` — you're told the *effective* tint adjustment mode (`UIViewTintAdjustmentModeNormal` or `UIViewTintAdjustmentMode-Dimmed`) inherited from up the view hierarchy.

If, on the other hand, you set a view's `tintAdjustmentMode` *explicitly* to `UIViewTint-AdjustmentModeNormal` or `UIViewTintAdjustmentModeDimmed`, this tells the system that you want to be left in charge of the `tintAdjustmentMode` for this part of the hierarchy; the automatic propagation of the `tintAdjustmentMode` down the view hierarchy is prevented. To turn automatic propagation back on, set the `tintAdjustmentMode` back to `UIViewTintAdjustmentModeAutomatic`. (See "Custom Presented View Controller

Transition" on page 301 for an example of setting the interface's `tintAdjustmentMode` to `UIViewTintAdjustmentModeDimmed` in imitation of an alert view.)

You can take advantage of `tintColorDidChange` to make your custom UIView subclass behave like a built-in UIView subclass. For example, if you subclass UIButton, your subclass might not automatically dim the title text color; your button's `tintColor` is being dimmed, but that color isn't being applied to the visible interface. You might be able to correct that problem just by calling `super`:

```
-(void)tintColorDidChange {
    [super tintColorDidChange];
}
```

In a more elaborate case, you might have to apply the `tintColor` explicitly to some aspect of your view subclass's interface. In this example, I apply the `tintColor` to my button subclass's attributed string title:

```
-(void)tintColorDidChange {
    NSMutableAttributedString* mas =
        [[self attributedTitleForState:UIControlStateNormal] mutableCopy];
    [mas addAttribute:NSForegroundColorAttributeName
        value:self.tintColor range:NSMakeRange(0,mas.length)];
    [self setAttributedTitle:mas forState:UIControlStateNormal];
}
```

 Don't set the `tintColor` from within `tintColorDidChange` without taking precautions against an infinite recursion.

Appearance Proxy

Instead of sending messages that customize the look of an interface object to the object itself, you can send them to an *appearance proxy* for that object's class. The appearance proxy then passes that same message along to the actual *future* instances of that class. You'll usually configure your appearance proxies very early in the lifetime of the app, and never again. The app delegate's `application:didFinishLaunchingWithOptions:`, before the app's window has been displayed, is the most obvious and common location.

Thus, for example, instead of sending `setTitleTextAttributes:forState:` to a particular UIBarButtonItem, you could send it to a UIBarButtonItem appearance proxy. *All* actual UIBarButtonItems *from then on* would have the text attributes you specified.

Like the `tintColor` that I discussed in the previous section, this architecture helps you give your app a consistent appearance, as well as saving you from having to write a lot of code; instead of having to send `setTitleTextAttributes:forState:` to *every* UIBarButtonItem your app *ever* instantiates, you send it *once* to the appearance proxy, and it is sent to all future UIBarButtonItems for you.

Also, the appearance proxy sometimes provides access to interface objects that might otherwise be difficult to refer to. For example, you don't get direct access to a search bar's external Cancel button, but it is a UIBarButtonItem and you can customize it through the UIBarButtonItem appearance proxy.

There are two class methods for obtaining an appearance proxy:

appearance
> Returns a general appearance proxy for the receiver class.

appearanceWhenContainedIn:
> The argument is a nil-terminated list (not an array!) of classes, arranged in order of containment from inner to outer. The method you send to the appearance proxy returned from this call will be passed on only to instances of the receiver class that are actually contained in the way you describe. The notion of what "contained" means is deliberately left vague; basically, it works the way you intuitively expect it to work.

When configuring appearance proxy objects, *specificity trumps generality*. Thus, you could call appearance to say what should happen for *most* instances of some class, and call appearanceWhenContainedIn: to say what should happen *instead* for *certain* instances of that class. Similarly, longer appearanceWhenContainedIn: chains are more specific than shorter ones.

For example, here's some code from my Latin flashcard app (myGolden and myPaler are methods defined by a category on UIColor):

```
[[UIBarButtonItem appearance]
    setTintColor: [UIColor myGolden]]; ❶
[[UIBarButtonItem appearanceWhenContainedIn:
    [UIToolbar class], nil]
        setTintColor: [UIColor myPaler]]; ❷
[[UIBarButtonItem appearanceWhenContainedIn:
    [UIToolbar class], [DrillViewController class], nil]
        setTintColor: [UIColor myGolden]]; ❸
```

That means:

❶ In general, bar button items should be tinted golden.

❷ But bar button items in a toolbar are an exception: they should be tinted paler.

❸ But bar button items in a toolbar in DrillViewController's view are an exception to the exception: they should be tinted golden.

(If you're looking at this book's figures in color, you can see this difference made manifest in Figure 6-3 and Figure 6-5.)

Sometimes, in order to express sufficient specificity, I find myself defining subclasses for no other purpose than to refer to them when obtaining an appearance proxy. For example, here's some more code from my Latin flashcard app:

```
[[UINavigationBar appearance] setBackgroundImage:marble2
                              forBarMetrics:UIBarMetricsDefault];
// counteract the above for the black navigation bar
[[BlackNavigationBar appearance] setBackgroundImage:nil
                              forBarMetrics:UIBarMetricsDefault];
```

In that code, BlackNavigationBar is a UINavigationBar subclass that does nothing whatever. Its sole purpose is to tag one navigation bar in my interface so that I can refer to it in that code! Thus, I'm able to say, in effect, "All navigation bars in this app should have marble2 as their background image, unless they are instances of BlackNavigation-Bar."

The ultimate in specificity is, of course, to customize the look of an instance directly. Thus, for example, if you set one particular UIBarButtonItem's tintColor property, then setTintColor: sent to a UIBarButtonItem appearance proxy will have no effect on that particular bar button item.

The appearance proxy object returned by appearance or appearanceWhenContained-In is, in reality, an instance of some hidden class that performs some deep trickery called *method swizzling*. The API has to cover this fact somehow, so this object was typed as an id in earlier systems. In iOS 7, however, it's an instancetype. This means that, regardless of its real class, the compiler sees it as equivalent to an instance of the class to which the message was sent. This is extremely convenient, for several reasons:

- The compiler won't let you send the appearance proxy a message that you can't send to an instance of that class. This won't compile:

  ```
  [[UINavigationBar appearance] setWidth: 7];
  ```

- You can use dot-notation with properties. Previously, you had to say this:

  ```
  [[UINavigationBar appearance] setBarTintColor:[UIColor redColor]];
  ```

  But in iOS 7, you can say this:

  ```
  [UINavigationBar appearance].barTintColor = [UIColor redColor];
  ```

- Code completion works.

However, just because your code will compile doesn't mean it's legal. Not every message that can be sent to an instance of a class can be sent to that class's appearance proxy. For example:

```
[UINavigationBar appearance].translucent = NO;
```

That code is legal in the sense that it compiles, but we crash when it is encountered ("Illegal type for appearance setter").

So how are you supposed to know which messages *can* be sent to the appearance proxies for which classes? One way is to try it and see whether you crash! Another way is to look in the header for that class (or a superclass); an appropriate property or method should be tagged UI_APPEARANCE_SELECTOR. For example, here's how the barTint-Color property is declared in *UINavigationBar.h*:

```
@property(nonatomic,retain) UIColor *barTintColor NS_AVAILABLE_IOS(7_0)
                                          UI_APPEARANCE_SELECTOR;
```

Finally, you can look in the class documentation; there should be a subsection of the Tasks section that lists the properties and methods applicable to the appearance proxy for this class. For example, the UINavigationBar class documentation has a section called "Customizing the Bar Appearance", the UIBarButtonItem class documentation has a section called "Customizing Appearance", and so forth.

 In iOS 7, tintColor *is* a legal appearance proxy message. I stress this because the headers do not make this fact clear (it is not tagged with UI_APPEARANCE_SELECTOR). Moreover, early in the iOS 7 beta process it *wasn't* a legal appearance proxy message, and you may encounter claims, on the Internet and even in the documentation, to that effect. Ignore them.

CHAPTER 13

Modal Dialogs

A modal dialog demands attention; while it is present, the user can do nothing other than work within it or dismiss it. You might need to put up a simple modal dialog in order to give the user some information or to ask the user how to proceed. Two UIView subclasses, UIAlertView and UIActionSheet, construct and present rudimentary modal dialogs.

One sees occasionally a misuse of the built-in dialogs to include additional interface. For example, a UIActionSheet is a UIView, so in theory you can add a subview to it. I cannot recommend such behavior; it clearly isn't intended, and there's no need for it. If what you want isn't what a built-in dialog normally does, don't use a built-in dialog. I'll suggest some alternatives later.

A local notification is an alert that the system presents at a predetermined time on your app's behalf when your app isn't frontmost. This alert can generate a UIAlertView, so I discuss it in this chapter as well.

An activity view is a modal dialog displaying icons representing possible courses of action, and intended in certain circumstances to replace the action sheet. For example, Mobile Safari presents an activity view from its Action button; the icons represent external modes of sharing a URL such as Mail, Message, and Twitter, as well as internal actions such as Bookmark and Add to Reading List.

In iOS 7, an alert view, an action sheet, and an activity view all interpose a "through a glass darkly" shadow view between themselves and the interface in front of which they appear, as well as setting that interface's `tintAdjustmentMode` to `UIViewTintAdjustmentModeDimmed` (see Chapter 12).

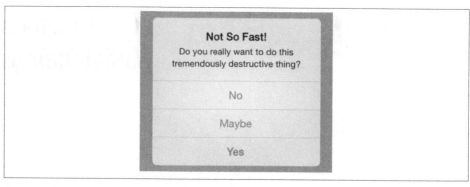

Figure 13-1. An alert view

Alert View

An alert view (UIAlertView) pops up unexpectedly with an elaborate animation and may be thought of as an attention-getting interruption. An alert is displayed in the center of the screen; it contains a title, a message, and some number of buttons, one of which may be the cancel button, meaning that it does nothing but dismiss the alert. In addition, an alert view may contain a text field, a password field, or both.

Alert views are minimal, but intentionally so; they are intended for simple, quick interaction or display of information. Often there is only a cancel button, the primary purpose of the alert being to show the user the message ("You won the game"); additional buttons may be used to give the user a choice of how to proceed ("You won the game; would you like to play another?" "Yes," "No," "Replay"). The text field and password field might allow the user to supply login credentials.

The basic method for constructing an alert view is:

- `initWithTitle:message:delegate:cancelButtonTitle:otherButtonTitles:`

The method for making a constructed alert view appear onscreen is show. The alert is automatically dismissed as soon as the user taps any button. Here's an example (Figure 13-1):

```
UIAlertView* alert = [[UIAlertView alloc] initWithTitle:@"Not So Fast!"
    message:@"Do you really want to do this tremendously destructive thing?"
    delegate:self cancelButtonTitle:@"Yes"
    otherButtonTitles:@"No", @"Maybe", nil];
[alert show];
```

The otherButtonTitles parameter is of indefinite length, so it must be either nil or a nil-terminated list (not an array!) of strings. The cancel button needn't be titled "Cancel"; its text is bolder than the other buttons and it comes last in a column of buttons, as you can see from Figure 13-1. If there are more than two `otherButtonTitles` and a nil `cancelButtonTitle`, the last of the `otherButtonTitles` is drawn as if it were a cancel button; this code, too, produces Figure 13-1:

```
UIAlertView* alert = [[UIAlertView alloc] initWithTitle:@"Not So Fast!"
    message:@"Do you really want to do this tremendously destructive thing?"
    delegate:self cancelButtonTitle:nil
    otherButtonTitles:@"No", @"Maybe", @"Yes", nil];
```

If an alert view is to contain a text field, it probably should have at most one or two buttons, with short titles such as "OK" and "Cancel". Otherwise, there might not be room on the screen for the alert view and the keyboard (and the problem is even more severe in landscape orientation). To add a text field to the alert view, modify its `alert-ViewStyle` before calling show. Your choices are:

- `UIAlertViewStyleDefault`, the default (no text fields)
- `UIAlertViewStylePlainTextInput`, one normal text field
- `UIAlertViewStyleSecureTextInput`, one `secureTextEntry` text field
- `UIAlertViewStyleLoginAndPasswordInput`, one normal text field and one `secure-TextEntry` text field

You can retrieve the text fields with `textFieldAtIndex:`; possible arguments are 0 and 1 (where 1 is the password field when the style is `UIAlertViewStyleLoginAndPassword-Input`). You can treat the text fields as you would any text field (see Chapter 10); for example, you can set the text field's delegate, arrange to receive control events from the text field, determine the text field's keyboard type, and so on:

```
UIAlertView* alert = [[UIAlertView alloc] initWithTitle:@"Enter a number:"
    message:nil delegate:self cancelButtonTitle:@"Cancel"
    otherButtonTitles:@"OK", nil];
alert.alertViewStyle = UIAlertViewStylePlainTextInput;
UITextField* tf = [alert textFieldAtIndex:0];
tf.keyboardType = UIKeyboardTypeNumberPad;
[tf addTarget:self action:@selector(textChanged:)
        forControlEvents:UIControlEventEditingChanged];
[alert show];
```

The alert dialog is modal, but the code that presents it is not: after the alert is shown, your code continues to run. If an alert consists of a single button (the cancel button), you might show it and forget about it, secure in the knowledge that the user must dismiss it sooner or later and that nothing can happen until then. But if you want to respond at the time the user dismisses the alert, or if there are several buttons and you want to know which one the user tapped to dismiss the alert, you'll need to implement at least one of these delegate methods (UIAlertViewDelegate):

- `alertView:clickedButtonAtIndex:`

- `alertView:willDismissWithButtonIndex:`
- `alertView:didDismissWithButtonIndex:`

The cancel button index is usually 0, with the remaining button indexes increasing in the order in which they were defined. If you're in any doubt, or if you need the button title for any other reason, you can call `buttonTitleAtIndex:`. Properties allow you to work out the correspondence between indexes and buttons without making any assumptions:

- `cancelButtonIndex` (-1 if none)
- `firstOtherButtonIndex` (-1 if none)
- `numberOfButtons` (including the cancel button)

You can also dismiss an alert view programmatically, by calling `dismissWithClicked-ButtonIndex:animated:`. The delegate method `alertView:clickedButtonAtIndex:` is then *not* called, because no button was actually clicked by the user. But the button index you specify is still passed along to the two `dismiss` delegate methods. The button index you specify needn't correspond to any existing button; thus, you could use it as a way of telling your delegate method that your code, and not the user, dismissed the alert.

Two additional delegate methods notify you when the alert is initially shown:

- `willPresentAlertView:`
- `didPresentAlertView:`

A further delegate method asks whether the first "other button" should be enabled:

- `alertViewShouldEnableFirstOtherButton:`

The delegate receives that message each time the state of things changes in the alert — in particular, when the alert appears and when the text in a text field changes. In this example, there's a text field, my cancel button says Cancel, and my other button says OK; I enable the OK button only if there is text in the text field:

```
- (BOOL)alertViewShouldEnableFirstOtherButton:(UIAlertView *)alertView {
    UITextField* tf = [alertView textFieldAtIndex:0];
    return [tf.text length] > 0;
}
```

Action Sheet

An action sheet (UIActionSheet) may be considered the iOS equivalent of a menu. On the iPhone, it slides up from the bottom of the screen; on the iPad, it appears in the middle of the screen like an alert view, or may be displayed as (or in) a popover. It consists of some number of buttons (and an optional title); one may be the cancel button, which appears last, and one may be a "destructive" button, which appears first in red, emphasizing the severity of that option.

Where a UIAlertView is an interruption, a UIActionSheet is a logical branching of what the user is already doing: it typically divides a single piece of interface into multiple possible courses of action. For example, in Apple's Mail app, a single Action button summons an action sheet that lets the user reply to the current message, forward it, or print it (or cancel and do nothing).

The basic method for constructing an action sheet is:

- `initWithTitle:delegate:cancelButtonTitle:destructiveButton-Title:otherButtonTitles:`

There are various methods for summoning the actual sheet, depending on what part of the interface you want the sheet to arise from. The following are appropriate on the iPhone, where the sheet typically rises from the bottom of the screen:

`showInView:`
> On the iPhone, far and away the most commonly used method. You will usually specify the root view controller's view. Don't specify a view whose view controller is contained by a view controller that hides the bottom of the interface, such as a tab bar controller or a navigation controller with a toolbar; if you do, some of the buttons may not function (and you get a helpful warning in the console: "Presenting action sheet clipped by its superview"). Instead, specify the tab bar controller's view itself, or the navigation controller's view itself, or use one of the other methods. For example, in my Zotz! app, which has a tab bar interface, the settings view controller summons an action sheet like this (Figure 13-2):
>
> ```
> [sheet showInView: self.tabBarController.view];
> ```

`showFromTabBar:`
`showFromToolbar:`
> On the iPhone, these cause the sheet to rise from the bottom of the screen, just like `showInView:`, because the tab bar or toolbar is at the bottom of the screen; however, they avoid the clipping problem with `showInView:` described earlier.

On the iPad, the same methods are available, and cause the action sheet to appear floating in the middle of the screen like an alert view. Alternatively, you can use one of the following methods, which resemble the methods for presenting a popover (Chapter 9); they do in fact present the action sheet as a popover, with its arrow pointing to the specified part of the interface (Figure 13-3):

- `showFromRect:inView:animated:`

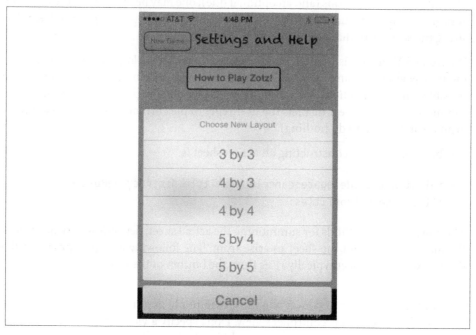

Figure 13-2: An action sheet on the iPhone

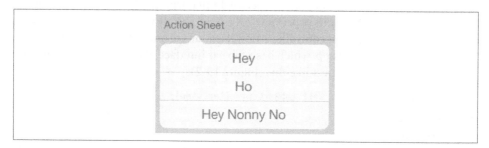

Figure 13-3. An action sheet presented as a popover

- `showFromBarButtonItem:animated:`

On the iPad, the `cancelButtonTitle:` argument is ignored; there is no cancel button. Regardless of whether the action sheet appears floating in the middle of the screen or as a popover, it is configured to be dismissed when the user taps outside it, which is the same as canceling it.

Alternatively, it is possible on the iPad to show an alert sheet *in an existing popover*. In this scenario, we are already presenting the popover, and then we summon an action sheet within the popover's view. The action sheet then behaves just as if the popover

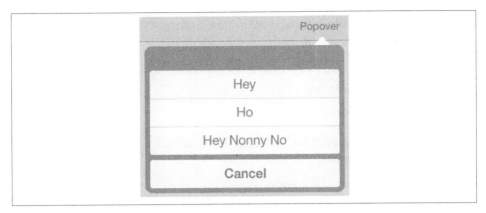

Figure 13-4. An action sheet presented inside a popover

were an iPhone: you summon the action sheet with `showInView:`, it slides up from the bottom of the popover, and the cancel button, if specified, does appear (Figure 13-4). The action sheet behaves like a presented view inside a popover, where `modalIn-Popover` is YES.

In other respects an action sheet is managed in a manner largely parallel to an alert view. When one of its buttons is tapped, the sheet is dismissed automatically, but you'll probably want to implement a delegate method (UIActionSheetDelegate) in order to learn which button it was:

- `actionSheet:clickedButtonAtIndex:`
- `actionSheet:willDismissWithButtonIndex:`
- `actionSheet:didDismissWithButtonIndex:`

To respond appropriately to the delegate methods without making assumptions about how the indexes correspond to the buttons, you can use the `buttonTitleAtIndex:` method, and these properties:

- `cancelButtonIndex`
- `destructiveButtonIndex`
- `firstOtherButtonIndex`
- `numberOfButtons`

In iOS 7, the action sheet can be dismissed by the user tapping outside it; in that case, the button index parameter to your delegate methods will be `actionSheet.cancelButtonIndex` — even if (as on the iPad) there is no Cancel button.

You can dismiss an action sheet programmatically with dismissWithClickedButton-Index:animated:, in which case actionSheet:clickedButtonAtIndex: is not called, but the two dismiss delegate methods are. Two additional delegate methods notify you when the sheet is initially shown:

- willPresentActionSheet:

- didPresentActionSheet:

Here's the code that presents the action sheet shown in Figure 13-2, along with the code that responds to its dismissal:

```
- (void) chooseLayout: (id) sender {
    UIActionSheet* sheet = [[UIActionSheet alloc]
        initWithTitle:@"Choose New Layout"
        delegate:self
        cancelButtonTitle:@"Cancel" destructiveButtonTitle:nil
        otherButtonTitles:@"3 by 3", @"4 by 3", @"4 by 4",
                          @"5 by 4", @"5 by 5", nil];
    [sheet showInView: self.tabBarController.view];
}
- (void)actionSheet:(UIActionSheet*)as clickedButtonAtIndex:(NSInteger)ix {
    if (ix == as.cancelButtonIndex)
        return;
    NSString* s = [as buttonTitleAtIndex:ix];
    // ...
}
```

 The UIActionSheet actionSheetStyle property appears to have no effect in iOS 7.

An action sheet shown as a popover or inside an existing popover on an iPad introduces all the same issues with regard to the popover's passthroughViews that I enumerated in Chapter 9. When an action sheet is shown as a popover from a bar button item in a toolbar, the toolbar becomes a passthrough view for the popover, and the user can now tap a bar button item without causing the action sheet's popover to be dismissed, possibly even summoning simultaneously another popover — perhaps even another instance of the *same action sheet*. You can't solve this problem by adjusting the popover controller's passthroughViews, because you've no access to the popover controller! One work-around is to implement the delegate methods to toggle user interaction with the toolbar:

```
- (IBAction)doButton:(id)sender { // sender is a bar button item
    UIActionSheet* act = [[UIActionSheet alloc]
        initWithTitle:nil delegate:self cancelButtonTitle:nil
        destructiveButtonTitle:nil
        otherButtonTitles:@"Hey", @"Ho", @"Hey Nonny No", nil];
```

Figure 13-5. A presented view behaving like an alert view

```
    [act showFromBarButtonItem:sender animated:YES];
}
- (void)didPresentActionSheet:(UIActionSheet *)actionSheet {
    [self.toolbar setUserInteractionEnabled:NO];
}
- (void)actionSheet:(UIActionSheet *)actionSheet
        didDismissWithButtonIndex:(NSInteger)buttonIndex {
    [self.toolbar setUserInteractionEnabled:YES];
}
```

Similarly, an action sheet shown inside a popover causes the popover to behave as if modalInPopover is YES; thus, while the action sheet is showing, the user can't dismiss the popover by tapping anywhere that isn't listed in the popover's passthroughViews. So far, so good. But you must take care that the popover's passthroughViews make sense for this situation; setting the passthroughViews property to nil while the action sheet is present (if it isn't nil already) might be a good idea. But the view controller that presents the action sheet might not have ready access to the popover controller in order to set its passthroughViews! This entire situation is just another maddening consequence of iOS's poor built-in popover management.

Dialog Alternatives

Alert views and action sheets are limited, inflexible, and inappropriate to any but the simplest cases. Some developers have hacked into their alert views or action sheets in an attempt to force them to be more customizable. But there is really no need for such extremes, especially in iOS 7, where, as I have already shown ("Custom Presented View Controller Transition" on page 301), it is now perfectly possible to create a smaller presented view that looks and behaves quite like an alert view or action sheet, floating in front of the main interface and darkening everything behind it — the difference being that this is an ordinary view controller's view, belonging entirely to you, and capable of being populated with any interface you like (Figure 13-5).

More generally, on the iPhone, it is always possible to navigate to a new screenful of interface, whether by way of a navigation interface or by using a presented view (Chap-

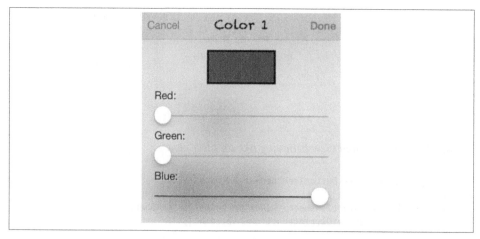

Figure 13-6. A presented view functioning as a modal dialog

ter 6). The color picker in my Zotz! app (Figure 13-6) has the same lightweight, temporary quality that an alert view offers, and on the desktop would probably be presented as part of a secondary Preferences window acting as a dialog; it happens that, on the iPhone, it occupies the entire screen, but it is still effectively a modal dialog (and, in iOS 7, it even appears to be covering the previous interface; see "Custom Presented View Controller Transition" on page 301 for an explanation of how this effect is achieved).

On the iPad, a popover is virtually a secondary window, and can be truly modal. The popovers in Figure 9-1, for example, are effectively modal dialogs. A popover can internally display a secondary presented view or even an action sheet, as we've already seen. Also on the iPad, a presented view can use the UIModalPresentationFormSheet presentation style, which is effectively a dialog window smaller than the screen; and iOS 7 lets you make a presented view any size you like — the presented view shown in Figure 13-5 works just as well on the iPad as on the iPhone.

Local Notifications

A *local notification* is an alert to the user that can appear even if your app is not running. It may appear, according to the user's preferences under Notification Center in the Settings app, as an alert view interrupting whatever the user is doing at that moment (optionally popping up even in the lock screen), or as a momentary banner at the top of the screen. It can be accompanied by a sound. It can be listed in the Notification Center. The user, however, can veto any of these options — no alert or banner, no sound, no listing in the Notification Center — effectively suppressing your local notifications completely.

This use of the term *notification* has nothing to do with NSNotification. The ambiguity is unfortunate.

Your app does not present a local notification alert; the system does. You hand the system instructions for when the local notification is to *fire*, and then you just stand back and let the system deal with it. That's why the local notification can appear even if your app isn't frontmost or isn't even running. Indeed, if your app is frontmost, the local notification's alert view or banner does *not* automatically appear when it fires; instead, your app is notified, and you can notify the user if you like. The only local notification alert view that can appear when your app is frontmost is some *other* app's local notification (and in that case, your app will become inactive; see Appendix A).

The interface whereby a notification presents itself provides a way for the user to summon your app in response, bringing it to the front if it is backgrounded, and launching it if it isn't running. If the notification is a banner or a listing in the Notification Center, the user can tap it. If the notification appears in the lock screen, the user can slide it. If the notification is an alert, the user can tap its action button. Your app will know that it was summoned by way of the user's action, as I'll explain in a moment.

To create a local notification, you configure a UILocalNotification object and hand it to the shared UIApplication instance by calling scheduleLocalNotification:. The UILocalNotification object has properties as follows:

alertBody
   The message displayed in the notification.

alertAction
   This matters only if your notification is displayed as an alert; in that case, this is the text of the action button. If you don't set alertAction, the text of the action button will be "Launch" (in the user's chosen system language).

   (According to the documentation, you should be able to set hasAction to NO to suppress the action button altogether, but in my testing, doing so has no effect.)

soundName
   The name of a sound file at the top level of your app bundle, to be played when the alert appears. This should be an uncompressed sound (AIFF or WAV). Alternatively, you can specify the default sound, UILocalNotificationDefaultSound-Name. If you don't set this property, there won't be a sound.

   (Regardless of the value you supply here, the user can prevent your app's notifications from emitting a sound.)

`userInfo`

An optional NSDictionary whose contents are up to you. Your app can retrieve this dictionary later on, if it receives the notification after the notification fires.

`fireDate, timeZone`

When you want the local notification to fire. The `fireDate` is an NSDate. If you don't include a `timeZone`, the date is measured against universal time; if you do include a `timeZone`, the date is measured against the user's local time zone, and thus it keeps working correctly if that time zone changes (because the user travels, for instance).

`repeatInterval, repeatCalendar`

If set, the local notification will recur. Setting the `repeatInterval` to NSSecond-CalendarUnit will result in a value of NSMinuteCalendarUnit. Recurrence survives a restart of the device.

Additional UIApplication methods let you manipulate the list of local notifications you've already scheduled. You can cancel one or all scheduled local notifications (`cancel-LocalNotification:`, `cancelAllLocalNotifications:`); you can also manipulate the list directly by setting UIApplication's `scheduledLocalNotifications`, an NSArray property.

 Canceling a recurring local notification is up to your code; if you don't provide a way of doing that, and if the user wants to prevent the notification from recurring, the user's only recourse will be to delete your app.

Figure 13-7 shows an alert generated by the firing of a local notification, in its banner form and in its alert view form. Here's a simple example of creating and scheduling the local notification that resulted in that alert:

```
UILocalNotification* ln = [UILocalNotification new];
ln.alertBody = @"Time for another cup of coffee!";
ln.fireDate = [NSDate dateWithTimeIntervalSinceNow:15];
ln.soundName = UILocalNotificationDefaultSoundName;
[[UIApplication sharedApplication] scheduleLocalNotification:ln];
```

Now let's talk about what happens when one of your scheduled local notifications fires. There are three possibilities, depending on the state of your app at that moment:

Your app is frontmost

The user won't be informed by the system that the notification has fired; if there is an attached sound, it won't be played.

Figure 13-7. Things the system can display when a local notification fires

Your app delegate will receive `application:didReceiveLocalNotification:`, where the second parameter is the UILocalNotification, and your application's `applicationState` will be `UIApplicationStateActive`.

Your app is suspended in the background
If the user summons your app from a notification, your app is brought to the front.

Your app delegate will then receive `application:didReceiveLocal-Notification:`, where the second parameter is the UILocalNotification, and your application's `applicationState` will be `UIApplicationStateInactive`.

Your app isn't running
If the user summons your app from a notification, your app is launched.

Your app delegate will then receive `application:didFinishLaunchingWith-Options:`, with an NSDictionary parameter that includes the `UIApplication-LaunchOptionsLocalNotificationKey`, whose value is the UILocalNotification.

Thus, to cover all possible cases, you should implement `application:didReceiveLocal-Notification:` to check the UIApplication's `applicationState`, and you should implement `application:didFinishLaunchingWithOptions:` to check its second parameter to see whether we are launching in response to a local notification.

If your app wasn't frontmost and the user summons it from a notification, you may want to show the user, immediately, some interface appropriate to this local notification. However, as your app appears, the user will first see either your default launch image (if the app is launched from scratch) or the screenshot image taken by the system when your app was suspended (if the app is activated from the background). To prevent a mismatch between that image and what the user will see when your app's interface actually appears, you can include in the original UILocalNotification an `alertLaunch-Image` that more closely matches your app's interface.

Figure 13-8. An activity view

Under some special circumstances (addressed, for example, in Chapter 14 and Chapter 22), your app might be running, *not* suspended, in the background. In this case, the situation is similar to what happens when your app *is* suspended: the user may be notified, and can summon your app to the front. Your running-in-the-background app can even schedule a notification to fire immediately with the convenience method `presentLocalNotificationNow:`.

Activity View

An activity view is the view belonging to a UIActivityViewController. You start with one or more pieces of data, such as an NSString, that you want the user to have the option of sharing or working with in your app. The activity view contains an icon for every activity (UIActivity) that can work with this type of data. There are 14 built-in activities in iOS 7 (up from 9 in iOS 6), and your app can provide more. The user may tap an icon in the activity view, and is then perhaps shown additional interface, belonging to the provider of the chosen activity. For example, as I mentioned earlier, the Action button in Mobile Safari presents an activity view (Figure 13-8).

> Don't confuse UIActivityViewController, UIActivity, UIActivity-ItemProvider, and UIActivityItemSource, on the one hand, with UIActivityIndicatorView (Chapter 12) on the other. The similarity of the names is unfortunate.

Presenting an activity view is easy. You instantiate UIActivityViewController by calling `initWithActivityItems:applicationActivities:`, where the first argument is an NSArray of objects — the activity items — to be shared or operated on, such as NSString or UIImage objects. Presumably these are objects associated somehow with the interface the user is looking at right now. You set the controller's `completionHandler` to a block that will be called when the user's interaction with the activity interface ends. Then you present the controller, as a presented controller on the iPhone or as a popover on the iPad. The presented view or popover will be dismissed automatically when the user cancels or chooses an activity. So, for example, on the iPhone:

```
UIActivityViewController* avc =
    [[UIActivityViewController alloc] initWithActivityItems:@[myCoolString]
                                applicationActivities:nil];
avc.completionHandler = ^(NSString *activityType, BOOL completed) {
    // ...
};
[self presentViewController:avc animated:YES completion:nil];
```

And on the iPad:

```
UIActivityViewController* avc =
    [[UIActivityViewController alloc] initWithActivityItems:@[myCoolString]
                                applicationActivities:nil];
avc.completionHandler = ^(NSString *activityType, BOOL completed) {
    // ...
};
UIPopoverController* pop =
    [[UIPopoverController alloc] initWithContentViewController:avc];
self.currentPop = pop;
[pop presentPopoverFromBarButtonItem:sender
    permittedArrowDirections:UIPopoverArrowDirectionAny animated:YES];
pop.passthroughViews = nil;
```

There is no Cancel button in the popover presentation of the activity view; the user cancels by tapping outside the popover. In iOS 7, the user can cancel by tapping outside the activity view even on the iPhone.

The activity view is populated automatically with known system-wide activities that can handle any of the types of data you provided as activity items. These activities represent UIActivity types, and are designated by NSString constants:

- UIActivityTypePostToFacebook
- UIActivityTypePostToTwitter
- UIActivityTypePostToWeibo
- UIActivityTypeMessage
- UIActivityTypeMail
- UIActivityTypePrint
- UIActivityTypeCopyToPasteboard
- UIActivityTypeAssignToContact

- UIActivityTypeSaveToCameraRoll

- UIActivityTypeAddToReadingList

- UIActivityTypePostToFlickr

- UIActivityTypePostToVimeo

- UIActivityTypePostToTencentWeibo

- UIActivityTypeAirDrop

Consult the UIActivity class documentation to learn what types of activity item each of these activities can handle. For example, the UIActivityTypeMail activity will accept an NSString, a UIImage, or a file on disk (such as an image file) designated by an NSURL; it will present a mail composition interface with the activity item in the body of the email.

Since the default is to include all the system-wide activities that can handle the provided data, if you *don't* want a certain system-wide activity included in the activity view, you must exclude it explicitly. You do this by setting the UIActivityViewController's excludedActivityTypes property to an NSArray of activity type constants.

The UIActivityItemSource protocol and the UIActivityItemProvider class give you a way to supply an activity item whose real value differs from its surface value, or whose real data takes time to obtain. I'm not going to go into detail about them.

 A commonly asked question is how to use the Mail activity and populate the mail composition form with a recipient and a subject. In iOS 7, there's now an official and easy way to provide a subject: supply as one of the activity items an object (which might be self) that adopts the UIActivityItemSource protocol and that implements activityView-Controller:subjectForActivityType:. But there is still no official way to provide a recipient!

The purpose of the applicationActivities: parameter of initWithActivity-Items:applicationActivities: is for you to list any additional activities implemented by your own app, so that their icons will appear as choices in the activity view as well. Each activity will be an instance of one of your own UIActivity subclasses.

To illustrate, I'll create a minimal (and nonsensical) activity called Be Cool that accepts NSString activity items. It is a UIActivity subclass called MyCoolActivity. So, to include Be Cool among the choices presented to the user by a UIActivityViewController, I'd say:

```
UIActivityViewController* avc =
    [[UIActivityViewController alloc]
        initWithActivityItems:@[myCoolString]
        applicationActivities:@[[MyCoolActivity new]]];
```

Now let's implement MyCoolActivity. It has an NSArray property called `items`, for reasons that will be apparent in a moment. We need to arm ourselves with an image to represent this activity in the activity view; this will be treated as a template image. In iOS 7, it should be no larger than 60×60 (76×76 on iPad); it can be smaller, and looks better if it is, because the system will draw a rounded rectangle around it, and the image should be somewhat inset from this. It needn't be square, as it will be centered in the rounded rectangle automatically.

Here's the preparatory part of the implementation of MyCoolActivity:

```
+ (UIActivityCategory)activityCategory {
    return UIActivityCategoryAction;
}
-(NSString *)activityType {
    return @"com.neuburg.matt.coolActivity"; // make up your own unique string
}
-(NSString *)activityTitle {
    return @"Be Cool";
}
-(UIImage *)activityImage {
    return self.image; // prepared beforehand
}
-(BOOL)canPerformWithActivityItems:(NSArray *)activityItems {
    for (id obj in activityItems) {
        if ([obj isKindOfClass: [NSString class]])
            return YES;
    }
    return NO;
}
-(void)prepareWithActivityItems:(NSArray *)activityItems {
    self.items = activityItems;
}
```

If we return YES from `canPerformWithActivityItems:`, then an icon for this activity, labeled Be Cool and displaying our `activityImage`, will appear in the activity view. If the user taps our icon, `prepareWithActivityItems:` will be called. We retain the `activityItems` into a property, because they won't be arriving again when we are actually told to perform the activity.

To perform the activity, we implement one of two methods:

`performActivity`

We simply perform the activity directly, using the activity items we've already retained. If the activity is time-consuming, the activity should be performed on a background thread (Chapter 25) so that we can return immediately; the activity view interface will be taken down and the user will be able to go on interacting with the app.

`activityViewController`

We have further interface that we'd like to show the user as part of the activity, so we return a UIViewController subclass. The activity view mechanism will present this UIViewController as a presented view controller; it is not our job to present or dismiss it. (We may, however, present or dismiss dependent interface. For example, if our UIViewController is a navigation controller with a custom root view controller, we might push another view controller onto its stack while the user is working on the activity.)

No matter which of these two methods we implement, we *must* eventually call this activity instance's `activityDidFinish:`. This is the signal to the activity view mechanism that the activity is over. If the activity view mechanism is still presenting any interface, it will be taken down, and the argument we supply here, a BOOL signifying whether the activity completed successfully, will be passed into the block we supplied earlier as the activity view controller's `completionHandler`. So, for example:

```
-(void)performActivity {
    // ... do something with self.items here ...
    [self activityDidFinish:YES];
}
```

If your UIActivity is returning a view controller from `activityViewController`, it will want to hand that view controller a reference to `self` before returning it, so that the view controller can call its `activityDidFinish:` when the time comes.

For example, suppose our activity involves letting the user draw a mustache on a photo of someone. Our view controller will provide interface for doing that, including some way of letting the user signal completion, such as a Cancel button and a Done button. When the user taps either of those, we'll do whatever else is necessary (such as saving the altered photo somewhere if the user tapped Done) and then call `activityDid-Finish:`. Thus, we could implement `activityViewController` like this:

```
-(UIViewController *)activityViewController {
    MustacheViewController* mvc = [MustacheViewController new];
    mvc.activity = self; // weak
    mvc.items = self.items; // copy
    return mvc;
}
```

And then MustacheViewController would have code like this:

```
- (IBAction)doCancel:(id)sender {
    [self.activity activityDidFinish:NO];
}
- (IBAction)doDone:(id)sender {
    [self.activity activityDidFinish:YES];
}
```

PART III

Some Frameworks

Cocoa supplies numerous specialized optional frameworks. This part of the book explains the basics of some of these frameworks, showing you how to get started, and training you to understand and explore these and related frameworks independently if your app requires a further level of depth and detail.

- Chapter 14 introduces the various iOS means for playing sound files, including audio sessions and playing sounds in the background.
- Chapter 15 describes some basic ways of playing video (movies), along with an introduction to the powerful AV Foundation framework.
- Chapter 16 is about how an app can access the user's music library.
- Chapter 17 is about how an app can access the user's photo library, along with the ability to take photos and capture movies.
- Chapter 18 discusses how an app can access the user's address book.
- Chapter 19 talks about how an app can access the user's calendar data.
- Chapter 20 describes how an app can allow the user to compose and send email and SMS messages and social media posts.
- Chapter 21 explains how an app can display a map, along with custom annotations and overlays. It also talks about how a map can display the user's current location and how to convert between a location and an address.
- Chapter 22 is about how an app can learn where the device is located, how it is moving, and how it is oriented.

CHAPTER 14

Audio

iOS provides various means and technologies for allowing your app to produce and input sound. The topic is a large one, so this chapter can only introduce it; I'll concentrate on basic sound production. You'll want to read Apple's *Multimedia Programming Guide* and *Core Audio Overview*.

None of the classes discussed in this chapter provides any user interface within your application for allowing the user to stop and start playback of sound. You can create your own such interface, and I'll discuss how you can associate the "remote control" buttons with your application. Also, a web view (Chapter 11) supports the HTML 5 <audio> tag; this can be a simple, lightweight way to play audio and to allow the user to control playback. (By default, a web view even allows use of AirPlay.) Alternatively, you could treat the sound as a movie and use the MPMoviePlayerController class discussed in Chapter 15; this can also be a good way to play a sound file located remotely over the Internet.

System Sounds

The simplest form of sound is *system sound*, which is the iOS equivalent of the basic computer "beep." This is implemented through System Sound Services, part of the Audio Toolbox framework; you'll need to @import AudioToolbox. You'll be calling one of two C functions, which behave very similarly to one another:

AudioServicesPlayAlertSound
> On an iPhone, may also vibrate the device, depending on the user's settings.

AudioServicesPlaySystemSound
> On an iPhone, there won't be an accompanying vibration, but you can specifically elect to have this "sound" *be* a device vibration (by passing kSystemSound-ID_Vibrate as the name of the "sound").

The sound file to be played needs to be an uncompressed AIFF or WAV file (or an Apple CAF file wrapping one of these). To hand the sound to these functions, you'll need a SystemSoundID, which you obtain by calling AudioServicesCreateSystemSoundID with a CFURLRef (or NSURL) that points to a sound file. In this example, the sound file is in our app bundle:

```
NSURL* sndurl =
    [[NSBundle mainBundle] URLForResource:@"test" withExtension:@"aif"];
SystemSoundID snd;
AudioServicesCreateSystemSoundID ((__bridge CFURLRef)sndurl, &snd);
AudioServicesPlaySystemSound(snd);
```

However, there's a problem with that code: we have failed to exercise proper memory management. We need to call AudioServicesDisposeSystemSoundID to release our SystemSoundID. But when shall we do this? AudioServicesPlaySystemSound executes asynchronously. So the solution can't be to call AudioServicesDisposeSystemSound-ID in the next line of the same snippet, because this would release our sound just as it is about to start playing, resulting in silence. The solution is to implement a sound completion handler, a function that is called when the sound has finished playing. So, our sound-playing snippet now looks like this:

```
NSURL* sndurl =
    [[NSBundle mainBundle] URLForResource:@"test" withExtension:@"aif"];
SystemSoundID snd;
AudioServicesCreateSystemSoundID((__bridge CFURLRef)sndurl, &snd);
AudioServicesAddSystemSoundCompletion(snd, nil, nil, SoundFinished, nil);
AudioServicesPlaySystemSound(snd);
```

And here is our sound completion handler, the SoundFinished function referred to in the previous snippet:

```
void SoundFinished (SystemSoundID snd, void* context) {
    AudioServicesRemoveSystemSoundCompletion(snd);
    AudioServicesDisposeSystemSoundID(snd);
}
```

Note that because we are about to release the sound, we first release the sound completion handler information applied to it. The last argument passed to AudioServicesAdd-SystemSoundCompletion is a pointer-to-void that comes back as the second parameter of our sound completion handler function; you can use this parameter in any way you like, such as to help identify the sound.

Audio Session

If your app is going to use a more sophisticated way of producing sound, such as an audio player (discussed in the next section), it must specify a *policy* regarding that sound. This policy will answer such questions as:

- Should sound stop when the screen is locked?
- Should sound interrupt existing sound (being played, for example, by the Music app) or should it be layered on top of it?

Your policy is declared in an *audio session*, which is a singleton AVAudioSession instance created automatically as your app launches. This is part of the AV Foundation framework; you'll need to @import AVFoundation. You'll refer to your app's AVAudioSession by way of the class method sharedInstance. This shared audio session instance is actually your pipeline to the part of the system that mediates *all* audio belonging to *all* apps and processes, the *media services daemon*; this daemon must juggle many demands, which is why your app's audio can be affected and even overruled by other apps and external factors.

To declare your audio session's policy, you'll set its *category*, by calling setCategory:withOptions:error:. The basic policies for audio playback are:

*Ambient (*AVAudioSessionCategoryAmbient*)*
> Your app's audio plays even while Music app music or other background audio is playing, and is silenced by the phone's Silent switch and screen locking.

*Solo Ambient (*AVAudioSessionCategorySoloAmbient*, the default)*
> Your app stops Music app music or other background audio from playing, and is silenced by the phone's Silent switch and screen locking.

*Playback (*AVAudioSessionCategoryPlayback*)*
> Your app stops Music app music or other background audio from playing, and is *not* silenced by the Silent switch. It is silenced by screen locking, unless it is also configured to play in the background (as explained later in this chapter).

Your audio session's otherAudioPlaying property can tell you whether audio is already playing in some other app, such as the Music app. Apple suggests that you might want your choice of audio session policy, and perhaps what kinds of sound your app plays, to take into account the answer to that question.

Audio session category options (the withOptions: parameter of setCategory:withOptions:error:) allow you to modify the playback policies to some extent:

Mixable audio
> You can override the Playback policy so as to allow Music app music or other background audio to play (AVAudioSessionCategoryOptionMixWithOthers). Your sound is then said to be *mixable*. If you don't make your sound mixable, then mixable background audio will still be able to play, but non-mixable background audio won't be able to play.

Ducking audio

You can override a policy that allows Music app music or other background audio to play, so as to *duck* (diminish the volume of) that background audio (AVAudio-SessionCategoryOptionDuckOthers). Ducking does *not* depend automatically on whether your app is actively producing any sound; rather, it starts as soon as you turn this override on and remains in place until your audio session is deactivated.

It is common practice to declare your app's initial audio session policy very early in the life of the app, possibly as early as application:didFinishLaunchingWithOptions:. You can later, if necessary, change your audio session policy as your app runs.

Your audio session policy is not in effect, however, unless your audio session is also *active*. By default, it isn't. Thus, asserting your audio session policy is done by a combination of configuring the audio session and activating the audio session. To activate (or deactivate) your audio session, you call setActive:withOptions:error:.

The question then is *when* to call setActive:withOptions:error:. This is a little tricky because of multitasking. Your audio session can be deactivated automatically if your app is no longer active. So if you want your policy to be obeyed under all circumstances, you must explicitly activate your audio session each time your app becomes active. The best place to do this is in applicationDidBecomeActive:, as this is the only method guaranteed to be called every time your app is reactivated under circumstances where your audio session might have been deactivated in the background (see Appendix A).

 Apple also suggests that you might want to register for AVAudioSession-MediaServicesWereResetNotification and activate your audio session in response, as well as resetting and recreating various audio-related objects. See Apple's *Technical Q&A QA1749*.

The first parameter to setActive:withOptions:error: is a BOOL saying whether we want to activate or deactivate our audio session. There are various reasons why you might deactivate (and perhaps reactivate) your audio session over the lifetime of your app.

One such reason is that you no longer need to hog the device's audio, and you want to yield to other apps to play music in the background. The second parameter to setActive:withOptions:error: lets you supply a single option, AVAudioSessionSet-ActiveOptionNotifyOthersOnDeactivation (only when the first parameter is NO). By doing this, you tell the system to allow any audio suspended by the activation of your audio session to resume. After all, enforcing a Playback audio session policy that silences music that was playing in the background is not very nice if your app isn't actively producing any sound *at the moment*; better to activate your Playback audio session only when your app is actively producing sound, and deactivate it when your sound finishes.

When you do that along with this option, the effect is one of pausing background audio, playing your audio, and then resuming background audio (if the app providing the background audio responds correctly to this option). I'll give an example later in this chapter.

Another reason for deactivating (and reactivating) your audio session is to bring a change of audio policy into effect. A good example is *ducking*. Let's say that, in general, we don't play any sounds, and we want background sound, such as Music app sound, to continue playing while our app runs. So we configure our audio session to use the Ambient policy in `application:didFinishLaunchingWithOptions:`, as follows:

```
[[AVAudioSession sharedInstance] setCategory: AVAudioSessionCategoryAmbient
                                  withOptions: 0 error: nil];
```

We aren't interrupting any other audio with our Ambient policy, so it does no harm to activate our audio session every time our app becomes active, no matter how, in `applicationDidBecomeActive:`, like this:

```
[[AVAudioSession sharedInstance] setActive: YES withOptions: 0 error: nil];
```

That's all it takes to set and enforce your app's overall audio session policy. Now let's say we do *sometimes* play a sound, but it's brief and doesn't require background sound to stop entirely; it suffices for background audio to be quieter momentarily while we're playing our sound. That's ducking! So, just before we play our sound, we duck any background sound by changing the options on our Ambient category:

```
[[AVAudioSession sharedInstance]
    setCategory: AVAudioSessionCategoryAmbient
    withOptions: AVAudioSessionCategoryOptionDuckOthers
          error: nil];
```

When we finish playing our sound, we turn off ducking. This is the tricky part. Not only must we remove the ducking property from our audio session policy, but we must also *deactivate our audio session* to make the change take effect immediately and bring the background sound back to its original level; there is then no harm in reactivating our audio session:

```
[[AVAudioSession sharedInstance] setActive:NO withOptions:0 error:nil];
[[AVAudioSession sharedInstance] setCategory: AVAudioSessionCategoryAmbient
                                  withOptions: 0
                                        error: nil];
[[AVAudioSession sharedInstance] setActive:YES withOptions: 0 error:nil];
```

Interruptions

Your audio session can be *interrupted*. This could mean that some other app deactivates it: for example, on an iPhone a phone call can arrive or an alarm can go off. In the multitasking world, it could mean that another app asserts its audio session over yours.

To learn of interruptions, register for this notification:

- `AVAudioSessionInterruptionNotification`

To learn whether the interruption began or ended, examine the `AVAudioSession-InterruptionTypeKey` entry in the notification's `userInfo` dictionary; this will be one of the following:

- `AVAudioSessionInterruptionTypeBegan`
- `AVAudioSessionInterruptionTypeEnded`

In the latter case, the `AVAudioSessionInterruptionOptionKey` entry may be present, containing an NSNumber wrapping `AVAudioSessionInterruptionOptionShould-Resume`; this is the flip side of `AVAudioSessionSetActiveOptionNotifyOthersOn-Deactivation`, which I mentioned earlier: some other app that interrupted you has now deactivated its audio session, and is telling you to feel free to resume your audio.

Interruptions are not as intrusive as you might suppose. When your audio session is interrupted, your audio has already stopped and your audio session has been deactivated; you might respond by altering something about your app's user interface to reflect the fact that your audio isn't playing, but apart from this there's no particular work for you to do. When the interruption ends, on the other hand, activating your audio session and possibly resuming playback of your audio might be up to you.

In the multitasking world, when your app switches to the background, your audio is paused (unless your app plays audio in the background, as discussed later in this chapter). Various things can happen when your app comes back to the front:

- If you were playing audio with an audio player (AVAudioPlayer, discussed in the next section), it's possible that the AVAudioPlayer will handle the entire situation: it will automatically reactivate your audio session and resume playing, and *you won't get any interruption notifications.*

- If you're *not* using an AVAudioPlayer, it is likely that being moved into the background will count as an interruption of your audio session. You don't get any notifications while you're suspended in the background, so everything happens at once when your app comes back to the front: at that time, you'll be notified that the interruption began, then notified that it ended, and then your `applicationDid-BecomeActive:` will be called, all in quick succession (and in that order). Make sure that your responses to these events, arriving in a sudden cluster, don't step on each other's toes somehow.

When your app is frontmost and the user brings up the Control Center and uses the Play button to resume the current Music app song, you get a notification that an interruption began; when the user dismisses the Control Center, you get `applicationDidBecomeActive:`, but you do *not* get any notification that the interruption has ended (and an AVAudioPlayer does not automatically resume playing). This seems incoherent.

Routing Changes

Your audio is routed through a particular output (and input). The user can make changes in this routing — for example, by plugging headphones into the device, which causes sound to stop coming out of the speaker and to come out of the headphones instead. By default, your audio continues uninterrupted if any is playing, but your code might like to be notified when routing is changed. You can register for AVAudioSessionRoute-ChangeNotification to hear about routing changes.

The notification's `userInfo` dictionary is chock full of useful information about what just happened. Here's NSLog's display of the dictionary that results when I detach headphones from the device:

```
AVAudioSessionRouteChangePreviousRouteKey =
    "<AVAudioSessionRouteDescription: 0x1f028840,
        inputs = (null);
        outputs = (
            "<AVAudioSessionPortDescription: 0x1f02af30,
                type = Headphones;
                name = Headphones;
                UID = Wired Headphones;
                selectedDataSource = (null)
            >"
        )>";
AVAudioSessionRouteChangeReasonKey = 2;
```

Upon receipt of this notification, I can find out what the audio route is now, by calling AVAudioSession's `currentRoute` method:

```
<AVAudioSessionRouteDescription: 0x14e34c10,
    inputs = (null);
    outputs = (
        "<AVAudioSessionPortDescription: 0x14e59bc0,
            type = Speaker;
            name = Speaker;
            UID = Built-In Speaker;
            selectedDataSource = (null)
        >"
    )>
```

The classes mentioned here — AVAudioSessionRouteDescription and AVAudioSessionPortDescription — are value classes (glorified structs). For the meaning of the AVAudioSessionRouteChangeReasonKey, see the AVAudioSession class reference; the value here, 2, is `AVAudioSessionRouteChangeReasonOldDeviceUnavailable` — we stopped using the headphones because there are no headphones any longer.

A routing change may not of itself interrupt your sound, but Apple suggests that in this particular situation you might like to respond by stopping your audio deliberately, because otherwise sound may now suddenly be coming out of the speaker in a public place.

Audio Player

An *audio player* (AVAudioPlayer) is the easiest way to play sounds with any degree of sophistication. A wide range of sound types is acceptable, including MP3, AAC, and ALAC, as well as AIFF and WAV. You can set a sound's volume and stereo pan features, loop a sound, synchronize the playing of multiple sounds simultaneously, change the playing rate, and set playback to begin somewhere in the middle of a sound.

AVAudioPlayer is part of the AV Foundation framework; you'll need to `@import AVFoundation`. An audio player should always be used in conjunction with an audio session; see the previous section.

Not every device type can play a compressed sound format in every degree of compression, and the limits can be difficult or impossible to learn except by experimentation. I encountered this issue when an app of mine worked correctly on an iPod touch 32GB but failed to play its sounds on an iPod touch 8GB (even though the latter was newer). Even more frustrating, the files played just fine in the Music app on *both* devices. The problem appears to be that the compression bit rate of my sound files was too low for AVAudioPlayer on the 8GB device, but not on the 32GB device. But there is no documentation of the limits involved.

An audio player can possess and play only one sound, but it can play that sound repeatedly, and you can have multiple audio players, possibly playing simultaneously. An audio player is initialized with its sound, using a local file URL or NSData. (New in iOS 7, the initializer can also state the expected sound file format.) To play the sound, first tell the audio player to `prepareToPlay`, causing it to load buffers and initialize hardware; then tell it to `play`. The audio player's delegate (AVAudioPlayerDelegate) is notified when the sound finishes playing (`audioPlayerDidFinishPlaying:successfully:`); do *not* repeatedly check the audio player's `playing` property to learn its state. Other useful methods include `pause` and `stop`; the chief difference between them is that `pause` doesn't release the buffers and hardware set up by `prepareToPlay`, but `stop` does (so you'd want to call `prepareToPlay` again before resuming play). Neither `pause` nor `stop` changes the playhead position (the point in the sound where playback will start if `play` is sent again); for that, use the `currentTime` property.

 In a WWDC 2011 video, Apple points out that simultaneously playing multiple sounds that have different sample rates is computationally expensive, and suggests that you prepare your sounds beforehand by converting them to a single sample rate. Also, decoding AAC is faster and less expensive than decoding MP3.

Devising a strategy for instantiating, retaining, and releasing your audio players is up to you. In one of my apps, I use a class called Player, which implements a `play:` method expecting a string path to a sound file in the app bundle. This method creates a new AVAudioPlayer, stores it as an instance variable, and tells it to play the sound file; it also sets itself up as that audio player's delegate, and emits a notification when the sound finishes playing. In this way, by maintaining a single Player instance, I can play different sounds in succession:

```
- (void) play: (NSString*) path {
    NSURL *fileURL = [[NSURL alloc] initFileURLWithPath:path];
    NSError* err = nil;
    AVAudioPlayer *newPlayer =
        [[AVAudioPlayer alloc] initWithContentsOfURL:fileURL error:&err];
    // error-checking omitted
    self.player = newPlayer; // retain policy
    [self.player prepareToPlay];
    [self.player setDelegate: self];
    [self.player play];
}
- (void)audioPlayerDidFinishPlaying:(AVAudioPlayer *)player
                  successfully:(BOOL)flag {
    [[NSNotificationCenter defaultCenter]
        postNotificationName:@"soundFinished" object:nil];
}
```

Here are some useful audio player properties:

`pan`, `volume`
Stereo positioning and loudness, respectively.

`numberOfLoops`
How many times the sound should repeat after it finishes playing; 0 (the default) means it doesn't repeat. A negative value causes the sound to repeat indefinitely (until told to `stop`).

`duration`
The length of the sound (read-only).

currentTime

The playhead position within the sound. If the sound is paused or stopped, play will start at the currentTime. You can set this in order to "seek" to a playback position within the sound.

enableRate, rate

These properties allow the sound to be played at anywhere from half speed (0.5) to double speed (2.0). Set enableRate to YES *before* calling prepareToPlay; you are then free to set the rate.

meteringEnabled

If YES (the default is NO), you can call updateMeters followed by averagePower-ForChannel: and/or peakPowerForChannel:, periodically, to track how loud the sound is. Presumably this would be so you could provide some sort of graphical representation of this value in your interface.

settings

A read-only dictionary describing features of the sound, such as its bit rate (AVEncoderBitRateKey), its sample rate (AVSampleRateKey), and its data format (AVFormatIDKey).

The playAtTime: method allows playing to be scheduled to start at a certain time. The time should be described in terms of the audio player's deviceCurrentTime property.

As I mentioned in the previous section, an audio player resumes playing when your app comes to the front if it was playing and was forced to stop playing when your app was moved to the background. There are delegate methods audioPlayerBegin-Interruption: and audioPlayerEndInterruption:withOptions:, but my experience is that the audio player will normally resume playing automatically and the delegate won't be sent these messages at all. In fact, I have yet to discover a situation in which audioPlayerEndInterruption:withOptions: is *ever* called when your app is in the foreground (active); it may, however, be called when your app is capable of playing sound in the background, as I'll explain later in this chapter.

Remote Control of Your Sound

Various sorts of signal constitute *remote control.* There is hardware remote control; the user might be using earbuds with buttons, for example. There is also software remote control — for example, the playback controls that you see in the Control Center (Figure 14-1). Similarly, the buttons that appear when the screen is locked and sound is playing are a form of software remote control (Figure 14-2).

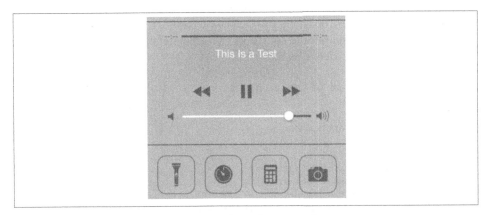

Figure 14-1. The software remote controls in the Control Center

Figure 14-2. The software remote controls on the locked screen

Your app can arrange to be targeted by *remote control events* reporting that the user has tapped a remote control. Your sound-playing app can respond to the remote play/pause button, for example, by playing or pausing its sound.

Remote control events are a form of UIEvent, and they are sent initially to the first responder. To arrange to be a recipient of remote control events:

- Your app must contain a UIResponder in its responder chain that returns YES from `canBecomeFirstResponder`, and that responder must actually be first responder.
- Some UIResponder in the responder chain, at or above the first responder, must implement `remoteControlReceivedWithEvent:`.
- Your app must call the UIApplication instance method `beginReceivingRemote-ControlEvents`.
- Your app's audio session policy must be Playback.

- Your app must emit some sound. The rule is that the running app that is capable of receiving remote control events and that last actually produced sound is the target of remote events. The remote control event target defaults to the Music app if no other app takes precedence by this rule.

A typical place to put all of this is in your view controller, which is, after all, a UIResponder:

```
- (BOOL)canBecomeFirstResponder {
    return YES;
}
- (void) viewDidAppear:(BOOL)animated {
    [super viewDidAppear: animated];
    [self becomeFirstResponder];
    [[UIApplication sharedApplication] beginReceivingRemoteControlEvents];
}
- (void)remoteControlReceivedWithEvent:(UIEvent *)event {
    // ...
}
```

The question is then how to implement `remoteControlReceivedWithEvent:`. Your implementation will examine the `subtype` of the incoming UIEvent to decide what to do. There are many possible `subtype` values, listed under UIEventSubtype in the UIEvent class documentation.

Earbuds with a central button will probably send `UIEventSubtypeRemoteControl-TogglePlayPause`. The software remote control play/pause button *used* to send `UIEvent-SubtypeRemoteControlTogglePlayPause` as well, but, new in iOS 7, it sends `UIEvent-SubtypeRemoteControlPlay` or `UIEventSubtypeRemoteControlPause`. So your code needs to cover all three possibilities.

 This is a *major* change in iOS 7. It breaks the ability of existing apps to respond to the software remote control play/pause button, even if they are linked against iOS 6 or earlier.

Here's an example in an app where sound is produced by an AVAudioPlayer:

```
- (void)remoteControlReceivedWithEvent:(UIEvent *)event {
    UIEventSubtype rc = event.subtype;
    if (rc == UIEventSubtypeRemoteControlTogglePlayPause) {
        if ([self.player isPlaying])
            [self.player stop];
        else
            [self.player play];
    } else if (rc == UIEventSubtypeRemoteControlPlay) {
        [self.player play];
```

```
        } else if (rc == UIEventSubtypeRemoteControlPause) {
            [self.player stop];
        }
    }
```

You can also influence what information the user will see, in the remote control interface, about what's being played. For that, you'll use MPNowPlayingInfoCenter, from the Media Player framework; you'll need to @import MediaPlayer. Call the class method defaultCenter and set the resulting instance's nowPlayingInfo property to a dictionary. The relevant keys are listed in the class documentation; they will make more sense after you've read Chapter 16, which discusses the Media Player framework. Here's some example code from my TidBITS News app:

```
MPNowPlayingInfoCenter* mpic = [MPNowPlayingInfoCenter defaultCenter];
mpic.nowPlayingInfo = @{
    MPMediaItemPropertyTitle: self.titleLabel.text,
    MPMediaItemPropertyArtist: self.authorLabel.text
};
```

Playing Sound in the Background

In the multitasking world, when the user switches away from your app to another app, by default, your app is suspended and stops producing sound. But if the business of your app is to play sound, you might like your app to continue playing sound in the background. In earlier sections of this chapter, I've spoken about how your app, in the foreground, relates its sound production to background sound such as the Music app. Now we're talking about how your app can *be* that background sound, possibly playing sound while some other app is in the foreground.

To play sound in the background, your app must do these things:

- In your *Info.plist*, you must include the "Required background modes" key (UIBackgroundModes) with a value that includes "App plays audio" (audio). This is simpler to arrange in Xcode 5 than in previous versions of Xcode; there's a checkbox in the Capabilities tab of the target editor (Figure 14-3).
- Your audio session's policy must be active and must be Playback.

If those things are true, then the sound that your app is playing when the user clicks the Home button and dismisses your application, or switches to another app, will go right on playing.

 When the screen is locked, your app can continue to play sound only if it is capable of playing sound in the background.

Figure 14-3. Using Capabilities to enable background audio

Moreover, your app may be able to start playing in the background even if it was *not* playing previously — namely, if it is mixable (`AVAudioSessionCategoryOptionMixWith-Others`, see earlier in this chapter), or if it is capable of being the remote control target. Indeed, an extremely cool feature of playing sound in the background is that remote control events continue to work. Even if your app was not actively playing at the time it was put into the background, it may be the remote control target (because it *was* playing sound earlier, as explained in the preceding section). In that case, if the user causes a remote control event to be sent, your app, if suspended in the background, will be woken up (still in the background) in order to receive the remote control event and can begin playing sound. However, the rules for interruptions still apply; another app can interrupt your app's audio session while your app is in the background, and if that app receives remote control events, then your app is no longer the remote control target.

If your app is the remote control target in the background, then another app can interrupt your app's audio, play some audio of its own, and then deactivate its own audio session with the option telling your app to resume playing. I'll give a minimal example of how this works with an AVAudioPlayer.

Let's call the two apps BackgroundPlayer and Interrupter. Suppose Interrupter has an audio session policy of Ambient. This means that when it comes to the front, background audio doesn't stop. But now Interrupter wants to play a sound of its own, temporarily stopping background audio. To pause the background audio, it sets its own audio session policy to Playback:

```
[[AVAudioSession sharedInstance] setCategory:AVAudioSessionCategoryPlayback
                                 withOptions:0 error:nil];
[[AVAudioSession sharedInstance] setActive:YES withOptions:0 error:nil];
[self.player setDelegate: self];
[self.player prepareToPlay];
[self.player play];
```

When Interrupter's sound finishes playing, its AVAudioPlayer's delegate is notified. In response, Interrupter deactivates its audio session with the AVAudioSessionSetActive-OptionNotifyOthersOnDeactivation option; then it's fine for it to switch its audio session policy back to Ambient and activate it once again:

```
[[AVAudioSession sharedInstance] setActive:NO
    withOptions:AVAudioSessionSetActiveOptionNotifyOthersOnDeactivation
    error:nil];
[[AVAudioSession sharedInstance] setCategory:AVAudioSessionCategoryAmbient
                                 withOptions:0 error:nil];
[[AVAudioSession sharedInstance] setActive: YES withOptions:0 error:nil];
```

So much for Interrupter. Now let's turn to BackgroundPlayer, which was playing in the background when Interrupter came along and changed its own audio session policy to Playback. At that moment, here's what happens to BackgroundPlayer:

- It is sent AVAudioSessionInterruptionNotification (if registered for it) with AVAudioSessionInterruptionTypeKey set to 1 (meaning that the interruption began).
- Its AVAudioPlayer stops playing.
- Its AVAudioPlayer's delegate is sent audioPlayerBeginInterruption:.

When Interrupter deactivates its audio session, here's what happens to Background-Player:

- It is sent AVAudioSessionInterruptionNotification (if registered for it) with AVAudioSessionInterruptionTypeKey set to 0 (meaning that the interruption ended) and AVAudioSessionInterruptionOptionKey set to 1 (meaning that playing should resume).
- Its AVAudioPlayer delegate is sent audioPlayerEndInterruption:withOptions:.

So now, BackgroundPlayer's AVAudioPlayer delegate can test for the resume option and, if it is set, can start playing again:

```
-(void)audioPlayerEndInterruption:(AVAudioPlayer *)p
        withOptions:(NSUInteger)opts {
    if (opts & AVAudioSessionInterruptionOptionShouldResume) {
        [p prepareToPlay];
        [p play];
    }
}
```

An interesting byproduct of your app being capable of playing sound in the background is that while it *is* playing sound, a timer can fire. The timer must have been created and scheduled in the foreground, but after that, it will fire even while your app is in the background, unless your app is currently not playing any sound. This is remarkable, because many other sorts of activity are forbidden when your app is running in the background.

Another byproduct of your app playing sound in the background has to do with app delegate events (see Appendix A). Typically, your app delegate will probably never receive the `applicationWillTerminate:` message, because by the time the app terminates, it will already have been suspended and incapable of receiving any events. However, an app that is playing sound in the background is *not* suspended, even though it is in the background. If it is terminated while playing sound in the background, it will receive `applicationDidEnterBackground:`, even though it has *already* received this event previously when it was moved into the background, and then it *will* receive `applicationWillTerminate:`. This is one of the few situations in which `application-WillTerminate:` is sent to an app in the modern multitasking world.

Further Topics in Sound

iOS is a powerful milieu for production and processing of sound; its sound-related technologies are extensive. This is a big topic, and an entire book could be written about it (in fact, such books do exist). I'll talk in Chapter 16 about accessing sound files in the user's music library. But here are some further topics that there is no room to discuss here:

Other audio session policies
> If your app accepts sound input or does audio processing, you'll want to look into additional audio session policies I didn't talk about earlier — Record, Play and Record, and Audio Processing. In addition, if you're using Record or Play and Record, there are modes — voice chat, video recording, and measurement (of the sound being input) — that optimize how sound is routed (for example, what microphone is used) and how it is modified.

New in iOS 7, your app must obtain the user's permission to use the microphone. This permission will be requested on your behalf when you adopt a Record audio session policy. You can modify the body of the system alert by setting the "Privacy — Microphone Usage Description" key (NSMicrophoneUsageDescription) in your app's *Info.plist*. You can learn whether permission has been granted by calling the AVAudioSession method requestRecordPermission:.

Recording sound

To record sound simply, use AVAudioRecorder. Your audio session policy will need to adopt a Record policy before recording begins.

Audio queues

Audio queues implement sound playing and recording through a C API with more granularity than the Objective-C AVAudioPlayer and AVAudioRecorder (though it is still regarded as a high-level API), giving you access to the buffers used to move chunks of sound data between a storage format (a sound file) and sound hardware.

Extended Audio File Services

A C API for reading and writing sound files in chunks. It is useful in connection with technologies such as audio queues.

Audio Converter Services

A C API for converting sound files between formats.

Streaming audio

Audio streamed in real time over the network, such as an Internet radio station, can be played with Audio File Stream Services, in connection with audio queues.

OpenAL

An advanced technology for playing sound with fine control over its stereo stage and directionality.

Audio units

Plug-ins that filter and modify the nature and quality of a sound as it passes through them. See the *Audio Unit Hosting Guide for iOS*.

MIDI

The CoreMIDI framework allows interaction with MIDI devices. The Audio Toolbox framework allows you to play a MIDI file, possibly passing it through an AUGraph that uses the AUSampler audio unit to produce synthesized sound.

Sound sharing

New in iOS 7, sound generated or processed by one app can be streamed to and recorded by another app. An astounding WWDC 2013 video demonstrates some of the possibilities.

Speech synthesis

New in iOS 7, text can be transformed into synthesized speech. This can be extremely easy to do, using the AVSpeechUtterance and AVSpeechSynthesizer classes. In this example, I also use the AVSpeechSynthesisVoice class to make sure the device speaks the text in English, regardless of the user's language settings:

```
NSString* s = @"Polly, want a cracker?";
AVSpeechUtterance* utter =
    [[AVSpeechUtterance alloc] initWithString:s];
AVSpeechSynthesisVoice* v =
    [AVSpeechSynthesisVoice voiceWithLanguage:@"en-US"];
utter.voice = v;
CGFloat rate =
    AVSpeechUtteranceMaximumSpeechRate -
        AVSpeechUtteranceMinimumSpeechRate;
rate = rate * 0.3 + AVSpeechUtteranceMinimumSpeechRate;
utter.rate = rate;
if (!self.talker)
    self.talker = [AVSpeechSynthesizer new];
self.talker.delegate = self;
[self.talker speakUtterance:utter];
```

The delegate (AVSpeechSynthesizerDelegate) is told when the speech starts, when it comes to a new range of text (usually a word), and when it finishes.

CHAPTER 15

Video

Simple video playback is performed in a view provided by the Media Player framework. You'll need to @import MediaPlayer. There are two relevant classes:

MPMoviePlayerController
Vends a view that plays a movie, along with controls letting the user regulate playback.

MPMoviePlayerViewController
A UIViewController subclass that owns an MPMoviePlayerController and displays its view.

A simple interface for letting the user trim video (UIVideoEditorController) is also supplied.

Sophisticated video playing and editing can be performed through the AV Foundation framework. I'll introduce AV Foundation, describing AVPlayer, an alternative class for playing a movie or a sound, and demonstrating AV Foundation's video- and audio-editing capabilities.

If an MPMoviePlayerController or an AVPlayer produces sound, you may need to concern yourself with your application's audio session; see Chapter 14. Both classes deal gracefully with the app being sent into the background; they will pause when your app is backgrounded and resume when your app returns to the foreground.

A movie file can be in a standard movie format, such as *.mov* or *.mp4*, but it can also be a sound file. An MPMoviePlayerController or MPMoviePlayerViewController is thus an easy way to play a sound file, including a sound file obtained in real time over the Internet, along with standard controls for pausing the sound and moving the playhead — unlike AVAudioPlayer, which, as I pointed out in Chapter 14, lacks a user interface.

A mobile device does not have unlimited power for decoding and presenting video in real time. A video that plays on your computer might not play at all on an iOS device.

See the "Media Layer" chapter of Apple's *iOS Technology Overview* for a list of specifications and limits within which video is eligible for playing.

A web view (Chapter 11) supports the HTML 5 <video> tag. This can be a simple lightweight way to present video and to allow the user to control playback. Both web view video and MPMoviePlayerController support AirPlay.

MPMoviePlayerController

An MPMoviePlayerController vends and controls a view, its view property; you assign it a movie described by a URL, its contentURL, which it will present in that view. You are responsible for instantiating and retaining the MPMoviePlayerController, and you'll provide the contentURL in its initializer, initWithContentURL:. The movie URL can be a local file URL, so that the player can show, for example, a movie stored as a file in the app's bundle, or obtained from the user's photo library (see Chapter 17); or it can be a resource (possibly streamed) to be fetched over the Internet, in which case the MPMoviePlayerController initiates the download automatically as soon as it has the contentURL.

You are also responsible for placing the MPMoviePlayerController's view into your interface. MPMoviePlayerController is not a UIViewController, so you can put its view *directly* into your interface. No law says you *have* to put the MPMoviePlayerController's view into your interface, but if you don't, the user won't be able to see the movie or the controls. An MPMoviePlayerController's view is a real view; you can set its frame, its autoresizingMask, and so forth, and you can give it subviews. An MPMoviePlayerController also has a backgroundView which automatically appears behind its view; you can give the backgroundView subviews as well.

Before you can display a movie in your interface with an MPMoviePlayerController, you must call prepareToPlay, which is part of the MPMediaPlayer protocol, adopted by MPMoviePlayerController.

Things happen slowly with a movie. Even when a movie is a local file, a certain amount of it has to load before the MPMoviePlayerController knows enough about the movie to report its specifications, to display its first frame, or to begin playing it. The delay can be perceptible. In the case of a remote resource, this loading process will take even longer. I'll talk in a moment about how you can know when the movie is ready to play.

If an MPMoviePlayerController fails to load its movie into its view when you're testing your app in the Simulator, this may be due to an All Exceptions breakpoint. If you have such a breakpoint, try disabling it. Alternatively, test on a device.

If the MPMoviePlayerController's shouldAutoplay property is YES (the default), play will begin as soon as possible, with no further action from you or the user; indeed, play will begin even if you don't put the MPMoviePlayerController's view into your interface! If the movie has sound, the user will then hear it without being able to see it, which could be confusing. To prevent this, put the view into your interface, or set should-Autoplay to NO (or both).

In this example, we create an MPMoviePlayerController, give it a reference to a movie from our app bundle, retain it through a property, and put its view into our interface:

```
NSURL* m = [[NSBundle mainBundle] URLForResource:@"ElMirage"
                                   withExtension:@"mp4"];
MPMoviePlayerController* mp =
    [[MPMoviePlayerController alloc] initWithContentURL:m];
self.mpc = mp; // retain policy
self.mpc.shouldAutoplay = NO;
[self.mpc prepareToPlay];
self.mpc.view.frame = CGRectMake(10, 10, 300, 250);
self.mpc.backgroundView.backgroundColor = [UIColor redColor];
[self.view addSubview:self.mpc.view];
```

However, as I mentioned a moment ago, it takes time before the movie is ready even for initial display. It is probably better to wait until the movie is ready before putting the MPMoviePlayerController's view into the interface. How can we know when it is ready? An MPMoviePlayerController doesn't have a delegate. Instead, to learn of events as they happen, you must register for notifications. In this case, we'll wait for MPMoviePlayer-ReadyForDisplayDidChangeNotification:

```
// ... prepare self.mpc as before ...
// but don't add its view to the interface just yet
// [self.view addSubview:self.mpc.view];
__block id observer =
    [[NSNotificationCenter defaultCenter]
     addObserverForName:MPMoviePlayerReadyForDisplayDidChangeNotification
     object:nil queue:nil usingBlock:^(NSNotification *note)
    {
        if (self.mpc.readyForDisplay) {
            [[NSNotificationCenter defaultCenter] removeObserver:observer];
            [self.view addSubview:self.mpc.view];
        }
    }];
```

The controls (controlStyle is MPMovieControlStyleEmbedded) include a play/pause button, a slider for changing the current frame of the movie (which may be omitted if the runtime feels the view isn't wide enough to display it), and a fullscreen button (Figure 15-1); there may also be an AirPlay route button, if an appropriate device is found on the network. The controls appear at the bottom of the view. The user can tap the view to show or hide the controls; the controls may also disappear automatically after play begins.

Figure 15-1. A movie player with controls

Figure 15-2. A movie player whose view fits its movie

The movie itself is centered and scaled to fill the size of the view in accordance with the MPMoviePlayerController's scalingMode; the default is MPMovieScalingModeAspect-Fit, which scales to fit, keeping the correct aspect ratio, and fills the unfilled dimension with the color of the MPMoviePlayerController's backgroundView.

That explains why Figure 15-1 doesn't look very good. Our code is not sophisticated about the dimensions of the movie; it just tells the movie's view to adopt a certain size. It would be better to set the size of the view in relation to the dimensions of the movie. You can learn the actual size and aspect ratio of the movie, so as to eliminate the excess unfilled dimension, by getting the MPMoviePlayerController's naturalSize; but, as I mentioned earlier, it takes time (after the content URL is set and you call prepareTo-Play) before this value can be determined. In this example, I'll wait for MPMovieNatural-SizeAvailableNotification; then I'll embed the movie view into the interface, at the correct aspect ratio (Figure 15-2):

```
- (void) setUpMPC {
    NSURL* m = [[NSBundle mainBundle] URLForResource:@"ElMirage"
                                       withExtension:@"mp4"];
    // ... the rest as before; do NOT add to view yet ...
    __block id observer =
```

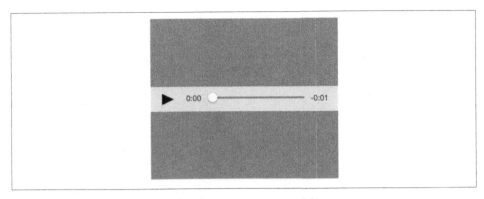

Figure 15-3. A movie player when the movie is a sound file

```
[[NSNotificationCenter defaultCenter]
    addObserverForName:MPMovieNaturalSizeAvailableNotification
    object:nil queue:nil usingBlock:^(NSNotification *note)
{
    [[NSNotificationCenter defaultCenter] removeObserver:observer];
    [self finishSetup];
}];
}
- (void) finishSetup {
    CGRect f = self.mpc.view.bounds;
    f.size = self.mpc.naturalSize; // safe to ask for this now
    // make width 300, keep ratio
    CGFloat ratio = 300.0/f.size.width;
    f.size.width *= ratio;
    f.size.height *= ratio;
    self.mpc.view.bounds = f;
    [self.view addSubview:self.mpc.view];
}
```

If the "movie" is actually a sound file, the controls are drawn differently: there is a start/pause button, a slider, and possibly an AirPlay route button, and that's all. The controls are centered in the view (Figure 15-3).

If the user taps the fullscreen button (or pinches outward) to enter fullscreen mode, the controls (controlStyle is MPMovieControlStyleFullscreen) at the top include a Done button, a slider, and an increased fullscreen button, and a second set of controls appears at the bottom with a play/pause button and rewind and fast-forward buttons, plus possibly a volume slider and an AirPlay route button. The user can tap to dismiss or summon the controls, double-tap to toggle increased fullscreen mode, and tap Done to stop play and leave fullscreen mode (Figure 15-4). The user can also pinch inward to leave fullscreen mode without stopping play.

Figure 15-4. A movie player in fullscreen mode, with controls

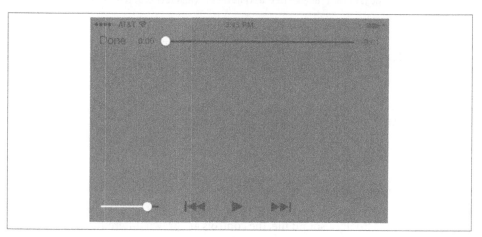

Figure 15-5. A fullscreen movie player when the movie is a sound file

If the "movie" is a sound file, the controller lacks a fullscreen button, but the user can pinch outward to enter fullscreen mode anyway (Figure 15-5).

You can set the style of the controls (`controlStyle`) manually; for example, you might want to make it impossible for the user to summon the controls (`MPMovieControlStyle-None`). You can programmatically toggle between fullscreen and not, with `set-Fullscreen:animated:`.

The fullscreen rendering will rotate to compensate for a change in device orientation even if the view controller in whose interface the MPMoviePlayerController's view is embedded would not. I regard this as a bug.

The movie can be made to repeat automatically (repeatMode) when it reaches its end. You can get the movie's duration. You can change its initialPlaybackTime and endPlaybackTime, effectively trimming the start and end off the movie.

Further programmatic control over the actual playing of the movie is obtained through the MPMediaPlayback protocol, which (as I mentioned a moment ago) MPMoviePlayerController adopts. This gives you the expected play, pause, and stop methods, as well as commands for seeking quickly forward and backward, and you can get and set the currentPlaybackTime to position the playhead. You can also set the currentPlaybackRate, making the movie play slower or faster than normal, and even backward.

Additional notifications tell such things as when fullscreen mode is entered and exited, and when the movie finishes playing. One of the most important notifications is MPMoviePlayerPlaybackStateDidChangeNotification; to learn the actual playback state, query the MPMoviePlayerController's playbackState, which will be one of these:

- MPMoviePlaybackStateStopped
- MPMoviePlaybackStatePlaying
- MPMoviePlaybackStatePaused
- MPMoviePlaybackStateInterrupted
- MPMoviePlaybackStateSeekingForward
- MPMoviePlaybackStateSeekingBackward

If the content comes from the Internet, there is of course many a slip possible. Things take time; the Internet might slow down, or go away completely; the resource to be fetched might not exist. You'll want to register for notifications that tell you when things happen — especially when things go wrong. In the TidBITS News app, where an MPMoviePlayerController is used to play a sound file located remotely across the Internet, I register for MPMoviePlayerLoadStateDidChangeNotification. When the notification arrives, I check the MPMoviePlayerController's loadState; it's a bitmask, and I look to see whether the MPMovieLoadStatePlaythroughOK bit is set:

```
if (self.mpc.loadState & MPMovieLoadStatePlaythroughOK) { // ...
```

If, on the other hand, the MPMovieLoadStateStalled bit is set, we can assume that the network is in trouble. Play will not stop automatically; the MPMoviePlayerController will keep trying to obtain data. If we want to prevent that, we have to stop it manually (at which point I'd put up an alert informing the user that there's a problem).

Another way to detect a problem is by registering for MPMoviePlayerPlaybackDidFinishNotification. If there's an error, the userInfo dictionary's MPMoviePlayerPlaybackDidFinishReasonUserInfoKey will be an NSNumber wrapping MPMovieFinishReasonPlaybackError, and the dictionary may also have a key called @"error", which will be an NSError; the localizedDescription of this NSError could be suitable for presentation to the user as a statement of the difficulty.

For extended information about the playback of a movie streamed across the Internet, look into MPMoviePlayerController's accessLog and errorLog properties.

MPMoviePlayerViewController

An MPMoviePlayerViewController is, as its name implies, a view controller (a UIViewController subclass, Chapter 6). It manages an MPMoviePlayerController (its moviePlayer) and automatically provides a fullscreen presentation of the MPMoviePlayerController's view. Thus, an MPMoviePlayerViewController has some strong advantages of simplicity.

(On the other hand, that very simplicity means that a number of choices are made for you, and you may find yourself struggling against them. For example, when an MPMoviePlayerViewController's view is showing, it becomes a recipient of remote control events — see Chapter 14. That's convenient, but if it's not what you want, it is not easily overcome; there is no property for turning it off.)

The documentation says that you can use an MPMoviePlayerViewController wherever you would use a UIViewController, such as a child view controller in a tab bar interface or navigation interface, but the MPMoviePlayerViewController's own interface seems to make the most sense when it is a presented view controller. A category on UIViewController even provides a special method for presenting it, presentMoviePlayerViewControllerAnimated:, which uses a special style of animation, whereby the current view slides out to reveal the movie view. To remove the view in code, you could then call `dismissMoviePlayerViewControllerAnimated`. Here's a simple example:

```
NSURL* m = [[NSBundle mainBundle] URLForResource:@"ElMirage"
                                   withExtension:@"mp4"];
MPMoviePlayerViewController* mpvc =
    [[MPMoviePlayerViewController alloc] initWithContentURL: m];
mpvc.moviePlayer.shouldAutoplay = NO; // optional
[self presentMoviePlayerViewControllerAnimated:mpvc];
```

In that code, I've set the MPMoviePlayerViewController's `moviePlayer`'s `should-Autoplay` property just to show that it can be done; the `moviePlayer` is an MPMoviePlayerController, and can be sent the same messages you'd send it if you were using it on its own. For example, you can register for its notifications. You will not, however, need to send it `prepareToPlay`.

You can detect the user pressing the Done button by registering for the `MPMoviePlayer-PlaybackDidFinishNotification`. If the user tapped Done, the `MPMoviePlayer-PlaybackDidFinishReasonUserInfoKey` in the notification's `userInfo` dictionary will be an NSNumber wrapping `MPMovieFinishReasonUserExited`. If the MPMoviePlayerViewController is a presented view controller, it is dismissed automatically when the user taps the Done button or when the movie plays to its end (in which case the `MPMovie-PlayerPlaybackDidFinishReasonUserInfoKey` is `MPMovieFinishReasonPlayback-Ended`). If you use the MPMoviePlayerViewController in some other way, the Done button stops play but that's all, and dealing with the interface is up to you.

MPMoviePlayerViewController is a view controller, so if it is used as a presented view controller, it takes charge of whether to rotate in response to a change in the device orientation. By default, it does nothing, meaning that it will rotate to any orientation permitted by the app and the app delegate. You can subclass MPMoviePlayerViewController to override `supportedInterfaceOrientations` if that isn't what you want.

After an MPMoviePlayerViewController's view is dismissed, if your app's revealed interface contains an MPMoviePlayerController's view, that view may be unable to play its movie — see "There Can Be Only One" on page 664. The MPMoviePlayerViewController's view was the One, so now the MPMoviePlayerController's view is broken. To fix it, send `prepareToPlay` to the MPMoviePlayerController.

UIVideoEditorController

UIVideoEditorController is a view controller that presents an interface where the user can trim video. Its view and internal behavior are outside your control, and you're not supposed to subclass it. You are expected to show the view controller's view as a presented view on the iPhone or in a popover on the iPad, and respond by way of its delegate.

Before summoning a UIVideoEditorController, be sure to call its class method `canEdit-VideoAtPath:`. (This call can take some noticeable time to return.) If this call returns NO, don't instantiate UIVideoEditorController to edit the given file. Not every video format is editable, and not every device supports video editing. You must also set the UIVideoEditorController instance's `delegate` and `videoPath` before presenting it; the delegate should adopt both UINavigationControllerDelegate and UIVideoEditorController-Delegate:

```
NSURL* m = [[NSBundle mainBundle] URLForResource:@"ElMirage"
                                    withExtension:@"mp4"];
BOOL can = [UIVideoEditorController canEditVideoAtPath:path];
if (!can) {
    NSLog(@"can't edit this video");
    return;
}
UIVideoEditorController* vc = [UIVideoEditorController new];
vc.delegate = self;
vc.videoPath = path;
if ([[UIDevice currentDevice] userInterfaceIdiom]
        == UIUserInterfaceIdiomPad) {
    UIPopoverController* pop =
        [[UIPopoverController alloc] initWithContentViewController:vc];
    pop.delegate = self;
    self.currentPop = pop;
    [pop presentPopoverFromRect:[sender bounds]
        inView:sender permittedArrowDirections:UIPopoverArrowDirectionAny
                                        animated:NO];
}
else {
    [self presentViewController:vc animated:YES completion:nil];
}
```

 In actual fact I have *never* been able to get a UIVideoEditor-Controller to work properly on the iPad! I can summon the interface in a popover, but it is not the correct interface — its title is Choose Video, the right button says Use, and the Cancel button does nothing — and trying to summon the interface as a presented view controller causes a crash. This is a *very* long-standing bug, and I am astounded that Apple has done nothing about it.

The view's interface (on the iPhone) contains Cancel and Save buttons, a trimming box displaying thumbnails from the movie, a Play/Pause button, and the movie itself. The user slides the ends of the trimming box to set the beginning and end of the saved movie. The Cancel and Save buttons do *not* dismiss the presented view; you must do that in your implementation of the delegate methods. There are three of them, and you should implement all three and dismiss the presented view in all of them:

- `videoEditorController:didSaveEditedVideoToPath:`
- `videoEditorControllerDidCancel:`
- `videoEditorController:didFailWithError:`

Implementing the second two delegate methods is straightforward:

```
-(void)videoEditorControllerDidCancel:(UIVideoEditorController *)editor {
    [self dismissViewControllerAnimated:YES completion:nil];
}
-(void)videoEditorController:(UIVideoEditorController *)editor
        didFailWithError:(NSError *)error {
    NSString* s = [error localizedDescription];
    NSLog(@"error: %@", s); // should do something with this information
    [self dismissViewControllerAnimated:YES completion:nil];
}
```

Saving the trimmed video is more involved. Like everything else about a movie, it takes time. When the user taps Save, there's a progress view while the video is trimmed and compressed. By the time the delegate method `videoEditorController:didSaveEdited-VideoToPath:` is called, the trimmed video has *already* been saved to a file in your app's temporary directory (the same directory returned from a call to `NSTemporary-Directory`).

Doing something useful with the saved file at this point is up to you; if you merely leave it in the temporary directory, you can't rely on it to persist. In this example, I copy the edited movie into the user's Camera Roll photo album (called Saved Photos if the device has no camera). That takes time too, so when I call `UISaveVideoAtPathToSavedPhotos-Album`, I use the second and third arguments to call a method that dismisses the editor *after* the saving is over:

```
- (void) videoEditorController: (UIVideoEditorController*) editor
        didSaveEditedVideoToPath: (NSString*) editedVideoPath {
    if (UIVideoAtPathIsCompatibleWithSavedPhotosAlbum(editedVideoPath))
        UISaveVideoAtPathToSavedPhotosAlbum(editedVideoPath, self,
            @selector(video:savedWithError:ci:), nil);
    else
        // need to think of something else to do with it
}
```

In our secondary method (here, `video:savedWithError:ci:`), it's important to check for errors, because things can still go wrong. In particular, the user could deny us access to the photo library (see Chapter 17 for more about that). If that's the case, we'll get an NSError whose `domain` is `ALAssetsLibraryErrorDomain`:

```
-(void)video:(NSString*)path savedWithError:(NSError*)err ci:(void*)ci {
    if (err)
        NSLog(@"error in saving: %@", err);
    [self dismissViewControllerAnimated:YES completion:nil];
}
```

Introduction to AV Foundation

The AV Foundation framework provides an extensive suite of tools for working directly with video — and audio, since video files can have audio tracks. (Recall that AVAudio-Player, the simple audio player class described in Chapter 14, comes from AV Foundation.) You will need to `@import AVFoundation`. The AV Foundation framework has an object-oriented Objective-C API, but a few fundamental types and C functions for working with them live in the Core Media framework, so you will probably need to `@import CoreMedia` as well.

In working with AV Foundation, there are two main facts to be aware of:

There are a lot of classes
> The *AV Foundation Framework Reference* lists about 90 classes and 16 protocols. This may seem daunting, but there's a good reason for it: video has a lot of structure and can be manipulated in many ways, and AV Foundation very carefully and correctly draws all the distinctions needed for good object-oriented encapsulation.

Things take time
> Working with with video is time-consuming, from reading a video a file to learn its metadata to transcoding and saving a video file. The user interface must not freeze while a video task is in progress, so AV Foundation relies heavily on threading (Chapter 25). You'll frequently use key–value observing and blocks to run your code at the right moment.

AV Foundation is a very big topic; the rest of this chapter will barely scratch the surface, just to orient you initially and give you a sense of what it's like to use AV Foundation. Further AV Foundation examples will appear in Chapter 16 and Chapter 17. But eventually you'll want to read Apple's *AV Foundation Programming Guide* for a full overview.

Some AV Foundation Building Blocks

A full unit of media, such as a media file, is expressed as an AVAsset; this provides access to metadata and tracks (AVAssetTrack). Actual playing of media is performed by an AVPlayer. The media that it will play is its AVPlayerItem, whose tracks, as seen from the player's point of view, are AVPlayerItemTrack objects, which can be individually enabled or disabled. (That's an example of what I said a moment ago about how AV Foundation draws object distinctions correctly: an AVAssetTrack is a fact about an AVAsset, but an AVPlayerItemTrack lets a track be manipulated for purposes of playback.)

An AVPlayer can be an AVQueuePlayer, a subclass that allows multiple AVPlayerItems to be loaded up and then played in sequence; I'll give an example in Chapter 16 of using an AVQueuePlayer to play a series of songs. AVQueuePlayer also has an `advanceToNext-Item` method, and its list of items can be changed dynamically, so you could use it to give the user access to a set of "chapters."

An AVPlayer is not an interface object. The corresponding interface object — an AV-Player made visible, as it were — is an AVPlayerLayer (a CALayer subclass). It has no controls for letting the user play and pause a movie and visualize its progress; it just shows the movie, acting as a bridge between the AV Foundation world of media and the CALayer world of things the user can see.

Time is measured in its own way in the media world. This is necessary because calculations using an ordinary built-in numeric class such as CGFloat will always have slight rounding errors that quickly begin to matter when you're trying to specify a time within a large piece of media. That's why the Core Media framework provides the CMTime class, which under the hood is a pair of integers; they are called the `value` and the `timescale`, but they are simply the numerator and denominator of a rational number.

Displaying a Movie

As an example, let's configure an AVPlayerLayer in our interface and show a movie. There are two ways to do this — the easy way and the real way. The easy way comes from an AVPlayer convenience initializer, `playerWithURL:`, which bypasses direct contact with the underlying AVAsset:

```
NSURL* m = [[NSBundle mainBundle] URLForResource:@"ElMirage"
                                   withExtension:@"mp4"];
AVPlayer* p = [AVPlayer playerWithURL:m];
self.player = p; // we'll need a reference later
AVPlayerLayer* lay = [AVPlayerLayer playerLayerWithPlayer:p];
lay.frame = CGRectMake(10,10,300,200);
[self.view.layer addSublayer:lay];
```

The real way to configure an AVPlayerLayer is to start with an AVAsset and work upward. Instead of saying this:

```
AVPlayer* p = [AVPlayer playerWithURL:m];
```

We say this:

```
AVURLAsset* asset = [AVURLAsset URLAssetWithURL:m options:nil];
AVPlayerItem* item = [AVPlayerItem playerItemWithAsset:asset];
AVPlayer* p = [AVPlayer playerWithPlayerItem:item];
```

As with the earlier MPMoviePlayerController example, we might like to postpone putting the AVPlayerLayer into the interface until the movie is ready for display. We can check for this by way of AVPlayerLayer's `readyForDisplay` property. We must not poll this property repeatedly, and there's no notification; instead, we construct our own notification through key–value observing. I don't want to make any assumptions about whether key-value observing will call me back on the main thread, so I deliberately jump out to the main thread before proceeding (Chapter 25). Here's the complete code for getting our movie into the interface, starting in viewDidLoad:

```
- (void) viewDidLoad {
    [super viewDidLoad];
    NSURL* m = [[NSBundle mainBundle] URLForResource:@"ElMirage"
                                       withExtension:@"mp4"];
    AVURLAsset* asset = [AVURLAsset URLAssetWithURL:m options:nil];
    AVPlayerItem* item = [AVPlayerItem playerItemWithAsset:asset];
    AVPlayer* p = [AVPlayer playerWithPlayerItem:item];
    self.player = p; // we'll need a reference later
    AVPlayerLayer* lay = [AVPlayerLayer playerLayerWithPlayer:p];
    lay.frame = CGRectMake(10,10,300,200);
    self.playerLayer = lay; // we'll need a reference later
    [lay addObserver:self forKeyPath:@"readyForDisplay"
            options:0 context:nil];
}
-(void)observeValueForKeyPath:(NSString *)keyPath ofObject:(id)object
        change:(NSDictionary *)change context:(void *)context {
    if ([keyPath isEqualToString: @"readyForDisplay"]) {
        dispatch_async(dispatch_get_main_queue(), ^{
            [self finishConstructingInterface];
        });
    }
}
-(void) finishConstructingInterface {
    if (!self.playerLayer.readyForDisplay)
        return;
    [self.playerLayer removeObserver:self forKeyPath:@"readyForDisplay"];
    [self.view.layer addSublayer:self.playerLayer];
}
```

The movie is now visible in the interface, but it isn't doing anything. We haven't told our AVPlayer to play, and we haven't given the user a way to do so either. To let the user start playing the movie, let's provide a Play button. Here, the button toggles the playing status of the movie by changing its rate:

```
- (IBAction) doButton: (id) sender {
    CGFloat rate = self.player.rate;
    if (rate < 0.01)
        self.player.rate = 1;
    else
        self.player.rate = 0;
}
```

It might be nice for the user to have a way to jump the playhead back to the start of the movie. The playhead position is a feature, not of an AVPlayer, but of an AVPlayerItem:

```
- (IBAction) restart: (id) sender {
    AVPlayerItem* item = [self.player currentItem];
    [item seekToTime:CMTimeMake(0, 1)];
}
```

Synchronizing Video With Animation

Just as an AVPlayerLayer crosses the bridge between the world of video and the visible interface, an AVSynchronizedLayer crosses the bridge between video time (the CMTime within the progress of a movie) and Core Animation time (the time within the progress of an animation). This means that you can coordinate animation in your interface (Chapter 4) with the playing of the movie. You attach an animation to a layer in more or less the usual way, but the animation takes place in movie playback time: if the movie is stopped, the animation is stopped, and if the movie is run at double rate, the animation runs at double rate.

To demonstrate, I'll extend the previous example; after we insert our AVPlayerLayer into the interface, we also create and insert an AVSynchronizedLayer:

```
// create synch layer, put it in the interface
AVPlayerItem* item = self.player.currentItem;
AVSynchronizedLayer* syncLayer =
[AVSynchronizedLayer synchronizedLayerWithPlayerItem:item];
syncLayer.frame = CGRectMake(10,220,300,10);
syncLayer.backgroundColor = [[UIColor lightGrayColor] CGColor];
[self.view.layer addSublayer:syncLayer];
// give synch layer a sublayer
CALayer* subLayer = [CALayer layer];
subLayer.backgroundColor = [[UIColor blackColor] CGColor];
subLayer.frame = CGRectMake(0,0,10,10);
[syncLayer addSublayer:subLayer];
// animate the sublayer
CABasicAnimation* anim = [CABasicAnimation animationWithKeyPath:@"position"];
anim.fromValue = [NSValue valueWithCGPoint: subLayer.position];
anim.toValue = [NSValue valueWithCGPoint: CGPointMake(295,5)];
anim.removedOnCompletion = NO;
anim.beginTime = AVCoreAnimationBeginTimeAtZero; // important trick
anim.duration = CMTimeGetSeconds(item.asset.duration);
[subLayer addAnimation:anim forKey:nil];
```

The result is shown in Figure 15-6. The gray rectangle is the AVSynchronizedLayer, tied to our movie. The little black square inside it is its sublayer; when we animate the black square, that animation will be synchronized to the movie, changing its position from the left end of the gray rectangle to the right end, starting at the beginning of the movie and with the same duration as the movie. Thus, although we attach this animation to the black square layer in the usual way, the black square *doesn't move* until we tap the button to call doButton: and start the movie playing. Moreover, if we tap the button again to pause the movie, the black square stops. The black square is thus *automatically* representing the current play position within the movie!

Figure 15-6. The black square's position is synchronized to the movie

Building Media

AV Foundation allows you to construct your own media asset in code (AVComposition, an AVAsset subclass, along with *its* subclass, AVMutableComposition). In this example, I start with an AVAsset (a video file) and assemble its first 5 seconds and its last 5 seconds of video into a new AVAsset:

```
AVAsset* oldAsset = // whatever
NSString* type = AVMediaTypeVideo;
NSArray* arr = [oldAsset tracksWithMediaType:type];
AVAssetTrack* track = [arr lastObject];
CMTime duration = track.timeRange.duration;
CGFloat dur = CMTimeGetSeconds(duration);
AVMutableComposition* comp = [AVMutableComposition composition];
AVMutableCompositionTrack* comptrack =
    [comp addMutableTrackWithMediaType:type
        preferredTrackID:kCMPersistentTrackID_Invalid];
[comptrack insertTimeRange:
    CMTimeRangeMake(CMTimeMakeWithSeconds(0,1),
                    CMTimeMakeWithSeconds(5,1))
        ofTrack:track atTime:CMTimeMakeWithSeconds(0,1) error:nil];
[comptrack insertTimeRange:
    CMTimeRangeMake(CMTimeMakeWithSeconds(dur-5,1),
                    CMTimeMakeWithSeconds(5,1))
        ofTrack:track atTime:CMTimeMakeWithSeconds(5,1) error:nil];
```

An AVMutableComposition is an AVAsset, so we can now, for instance, display it in an AVPlayerLayer.

We are not very good video editors, however, as we have forgotten the corresponding soundtrack. Let's go back and get it and add it to our AVMutableComposition (comp):

```
type = AVMediaTypeAudio;
arr = [oldAsset tracksWithMediaType:type];
track = [arr lastObject];
comptrack =
    [comp addMutableTrackWithMediaType:type
```

```
                 preferredTrackID:kCMPersistentTrackID_Invalid];
[comptrack insertTimeRange:
    CMTimeRangeMake(CMTimeMakeWithSeconds(0,1),
                    CMTimeMakeWithSeconds(5,1))
        ofTrack:track atTime:CMTimeMakeWithSeconds(0,1) error:nil];
[comptrack insertTimeRange:
    CMTimeRangeMake(CMTimeMakeWithSeconds(dur-5,1),
                    CMTimeMakeWithSeconds(5,1))
        ofTrack:track atTime:CMTimeMakeWithSeconds(5,1) error:nil];
```

But wait! Now let's overlay *another* audio track; this might be, for example, some additional narration:

```
type = AVMediaTypeAudio;
NSURL* s = [[NSBundle mainBundle] URLForResource:@"aboutTiagol"
                                   withExtension:@"m4a"];
AVAsset* asset = [AVURLAsset URLAssetWithURL:s options:nil];
arr = [asset tracksWithMediaType:type];
track = [arr lastObject];
comptrack =
    [comp addMutableTrackWithMediaType:type
        preferredTrackID:kCMPersistentTrackID_Invalid];
[comptrack insertTimeRange:
    CMTimeRangeMake(CMTimeMakeWithSeconds(0,1),
                    CMTimeMakeWithSeconds(10,1))
        ofTrack:track atTime:CMTimeMakeWithSeconds(0,1) error:nil];
```

You can also apply audio volume changes and video opacity and transform changes to the playback of individual tracks. I'll continue from the previous example, applying a fadeout to the last three seconds of the narration track (comptrack) by creating an AVAudioMix. The audio mix must be applied to a playback milieu, such as an AVPlayerItem, so I'll make one out of our existing AVAsset (comp):

```
AVMutableAudioMixInputParameters* params =
    [AVMutableAudioMixInputParameters
        audioMixInputParametersWithTrack:comptrack];
[params setVolume:1 atTime:CMTimeMakeWithSeconds(0,1)];
[params setVolumeRampFromStartVolume:1 toEndVolume:0
    timeRange:CMTimeRangeMake(CMTimeMakeWithSeconds(6,1),
                              CMTimeMakeWithSeconds(2,1))];
AVMutableAudioMix* mix = [AVMutableAudioMix new];
mix.inputParameters = @[params];
AVPlayerItem* item = [AVPlayerItem playerItemWithAsset:comp];
item.audioMix = mix;
```

Further Exploration of AV Foundation

Here are some other things you can do with AV Foundation:

- Extract single images ("thumbnails") from a movie (AVAssetImageGenerator).

- Export a movie in a different format (AVAssetExportSession), or read/write raw uncompressed data through a buffer to or from a track (AVAssetReader, AVAsset-ReaderOutput, AVAssetWriter, AVAssetWriterInput, and so on). New in iOS 7 is AVOutputSettingsAssistant, a class that embodies presets likely to be useful with AVAssetWriter.

- Capture audio, video, and stills (AVCaptureSession and so on). I'll say more about this in Chapter 17.

- Tap into video and audio being captured or played, including capturing video frames as still images (AVPlayerItemVideoOutput, AVCaptureVideoDataOutput, and so on; and see Apple's *Technical Q&A QA1702*).

CHAPTER 16

Music Library

An iOS device can be used for the same purpose as the original iPod — to hold and play music, podcasts, and audiobooks. These items constitute the device's *iPod library*, or *music library*. iOS provides the programmer with various forms of access to the device's music library; you can:

- Explore the music library.
- Play an item from the music library.
- Learn and control what the Music app's music player is doing.
- Present a standard interface for allowing the user to select a music library item.

These abilities are provided by the Media Player framework. You'll need to @import MediaPlayer.

Exploring the Music Library

Everything in the music library, as seen by your code, is an MPMediaEntity. This is an abstract class that endows its subclasses with the ability to describe themselves through key–value pairs called *properties*. (This use of the word "properties" has nothing to do with Objective-C language properties; these properties are more like entries in an NSDictionary.)

MPMediaEntity has two concrete subclasses, MPMediaItem and MPMediaCollection. An MPMediaItem is a single item (a "song"). An MPMediaCollection is an ordered list of MPMediaItems, rather like an array; it has a count, and its items property *is* an array.

An MPMediaItem has a type, according to the value of its MPMediaItemPropertyMediaType property: it might, for example, be music, a podcast, an audiobook, or a video. A media item's properties will be intuitively familiar from your use of iTunes: it has a title, an album title, a track number, an artist, a composer, and so on. Different types of item have slightly different properties; for example, a podcast, in addition to its normal title, has a podcast title.

A playlist is an MPMediaPlaylist, a subclass of MPMediaCollection. Its properties include a title, a flag indicating whether it is a "smart" playlist, and so on.

The property keys have names like `MPMediaItemPropertyTitle`. To fetch a property's value, call `valueForProperty:` with its key. You can fetch multiple properties with `enumerateValuesForProperties:usingBlock:`.

An item's artwork image is an instance of the MPMediaItemArtwork class, from which you are supposed to be able to get the image itself scaled to a specified size by calling `imageWithSize:`; my experience is that in reality you'll receive an image of any old size the system cares to give you, so you may have to scale it further yourself. This, for example, is what my Albumen app does:

```
MPMediaItemArtwork* art = //...
UIImage* im = [art imageWithSize:CGSizeMake(36,36)];
// but it probably *isn't* 36 by 36; scale it so that it is
if (im) {
    CGFloat scalew = 36.0/im.size.width;
    CGFloat scaleh = 36.0/im.size.height;
    CGFloat scale = (scalew < scaleh) ? scalew : scaleh;
    CGSize sz = CGSizeMake(im.size.width*scale, im.size.height*scale);
    UIGraphicsBeginImageContextWithOptions(sz, NO, 0);
    [im drawInRect:CGRectMake(0,0,sz.width,sz.height)];
    im = UIGraphicsGetImageFromCurrentImageContext();
    UIGraphicsEndImageContext();
}
```

Querying the Music Library

Obtaining actual information from the music library requires a *query*, an MPMedia-Query. First, you *form* the query. There are two main ways to do this:

With a convenience constructor
MPMediaQuery provides several class methods that form a query ready to ask the music library for all of its songs, or all of its podcasts, and so on. Here's the complete list:

- songsQuery
- podcastsQuery
- audiobooksQuery
- playlistsQuery
- albumsQuery

- artistsQuery
- composersQuery
- genresQuery
- compilationsQuery

With filter predicates

You can attach to the query one or more MPMediaPropertyPredicate instances, forming a set (NSSet) of predicates. These predicates filter the music library according to criteria you specify; to be included in the result, a media item must successfully pass through all the filters (in other words, the predicates are combined using logical-and). A predicate is a simple comparison. It has three aspects:

A property

The key to the property you want to compare against. Not every property can be used in a filter predicate; the documentation makes the distinction clear (and you can get additional help from an MPMediaEntity class method, canFilterByProperty:).

A value

The value that the property must have in order to pass through the filter.

A comparison type (optional)

In order to pass through the filter, a media item's property value can either *match* the value you provide (MPMediaPredicateComparisonEqualTo, the default) or *contain* the value you provide (MPMediaPredicateComparisonContains).

These two ways of forming a query are actually the same; a convenience constructor is just a quick way of obtaining a query already endowed with a filter predicate.

A query also *groups* its results, according to its groupingType. Your choices are:

- MPMediaGroupingTitle
- MPMediaGroupingAlbum
- MPMediaGroupingArtist
- MPMediaGroupingAlbumArtist
- MPMediaGroupingComposer
- MPMediaGroupingGenre
- MPMediaGroupingPlaylist
- MPMediaGroupingPodcastTitle

The query convenience constructors all supply a groupingType in addition to a filter predicate. Indeed, the grouping is often the salient aspect of the query. For example, an albumsQuery is in fact merely a songsQuery with the added feature that its results are grouped by album.

The groups resulting from a query are *collections*; that is, each is an MPMediaItem-Collection. This class, you will recall, is an MPMediaEntity subclass, so a collection has properties. In addition, it has items and a count. It also has a representativeItem property, which gives you just one item from the collection. The reason you need this is that properties of a collection are often embodied in its items rather than in the collection itself. For example, an album has no title; rather, its items have album titles that are all the same. So to learn the title of an album, you ask for the album title of a representative item.

After you form the query, you *perform* the query. You do this simply by asking for the query's results. You can ask either for its collections (if you care about the groups returned from the query) or for its items. Here, I'll discover the titles of all the albums:

```
MPMediaQuery* query = [MPMediaQuery albumsQuery];
NSArray* result = [query collections];
// prove we've performed the query, by logging the album titles
for (MPMediaItemCollection* album in result)
    NSLog(@"%@", [album.representativeItem
        valueForProperty:MPMediaItemPropertyAlbumTitle]);
/*
Output starts like this on my device:
Beethoven Canons
Beethoven Dances
Beethoven Piano Duet
Beethoven Piano Other
Brahms Lieder
...
*/
```

Now let's make our query more elaborate; we'll get the titles of all the albums whose name contains "Beethoven". Observe that what we really do is to ask for all songs whose album title contains "Beethoven", grouped by album; then we learn the album title of a representative item from each resulting collection:

```
MPMediaQuery* query = [MPMediaQuery albumsQuery];
MPMediaPropertyPredicate* hasBeethoven =
    [MPMediaPropertyPredicate predicateWithValue:@"Beethoven"
        forProperty:MPMediaItemPropertyAlbumTitle
        comparisonType:MPMediaPredicateComparisonContains];
[query addFilterPredicate:hasBeethoven];
NSArray* result = [query collections];
for (MPMediaItemCollection* album in result)
    NSLog(@"%@", [album.representativeItem
        valueForProperty:MPMediaItemPropertyAlbumTitle]);
/*
```

```
Output on my device:
Beethoven Canons
Beethoven Dances
Beethoven Piano Duet
Beethoven Piano Other
*/
```

Similarly, we can get the titles of all the albums containing any songs whose name contains "Sonata". To do so, we ask for all songs whose title contains "Sonata", grouped by album; then, as before, we learn the album title of a representative item from each resulting collection:

```
MPMediaQuery* query = [MPMediaQuery albumsQuery];
MPMediaPropertyPredicate* hasSonata =
    [MPMediaPropertyPredicate predicateWithValue:@"Sonata"
        forProperty:MPMediaItemPropertyTitle
     comparisonType:MPMediaPredicateComparisonContains];
[query addFilterPredicate:hasSonata];
NSArray* result = [query collections];
for (MPMediaItemCollection* album in result)
    NSLog(@"%@", [album.representativeItem
        valueForProperty:MPMediaItemPropertyAlbumTitle]);
/*
Output on my device:
Beethoven Piano Duet
Beethoven Piano Other
Scarlatti Complete Sonatas, Vol. I
*/
```

An interesting complication is that the Scarlatti album listed in the results of that example is not actually present on my device. The user's music library can include purchases and iTunes Match songs that are actually off in "the cloud". The user can prevent such songs from appearing in the Music app (in the Settings app, Music → Show All Music → Off), but they are still present in the library, and therefore in the results of our queries.

I'll modify the previous example to list only albums containing "Sonata" songs that are present on the device. The concept "present on the device" is embodied by the MPMedia-ItemPropertyIsCloudItem property. All we have to do is add a second predicate:

```
MPMediaQuery* query = [MPMediaQuery albumsQuery];
MPMediaPropertyPredicate* hasSonata =
    [MPMediaPropertyPredicate predicateWithValue:@"Sonata"
        forProperty:MPMediaItemPropertyTitle
     comparisonType:MPMediaPredicateComparisonContains];
[query addFilterPredicate:hasSonata];
MPMediaPropertyPredicate* isPresent =
    [MPMediaPropertyPredicate predicateWithValue:@NO
        forProperty:MPMediaItemPropertyIsCloudItem
     comparisonType:MPMediaPredicateComparisonEqualTo];
[query addFilterPredicate:isPresent];
```

```
NSArray* result = [query collections];
for (MPMediaItemCollection* album in result)
    NSLog(@"%@", [album.representativeItem
        valueForProperty:MPMediaItemPropertyAlbumTitle]);
/*
Output on my device:
Beethoven Piano Duet
Beethoven Piano Other
*/
```

The results of an albumsQuery are actually songs (MPMediaItems). That means we can
immediately access any song in any of those albums. Let's modify the output from our
previous query to print the titles of all the matching songs in the first album returned,
which happens to be the Beethoven Piano Duet album. We don't have to change our
query, so I'll start at the point where we perform it; result is the array of collections
returned from our query:

```
// ... same as before ...
MPMediaItemCollection* album = result[0];
for (MPMediaItem* song in album.items)
    NSLog(@"%@", [song valueForProperty:MPMediaItemPropertyTitle]);
/*
Output on my device:
Sonata for piano 4-hands in D major Op. 6 - 1. Allegro molto
Sonata for piano 4-hands in D major Op. 6 - 2. Rondo
*/
```

Persistence and Change in the Music Library

One of the properties of an MPMediaEntity is its *persistent ID*, which uniquely identifies
this song (MPMediaItemPropertyPersistentID) or playlist (MPMediaPlaylist-
PropertyPersistentID). No other means of identification is guaranteed unique; two
songs or two playlists can have the same title, for example. Using the persistent ID, you
can retrieve again at a later time the same song or playlist you retrieved earlier, even
across launches of your app. All sorts of things have persistent IDs — entities in general
(MPMediaEntityPropertyPersistentID), albums, artists, composers, and more.

While you are maintaining the results of a search, the contents of the music library may
themselves change. For example, the user might connect the device to a computer and
add or delete music with iTunes. This can put your results out of date. For this reason,
the library's own modified date is available through the MPMediaLibrary class. Call the
class method defaultMediaLibrary to get the actual library instance; now you can ask
it for its lastModifiedDate. You can also register to receive a notification, MPMedia-
LibraryDidChangeNotification, when the music library is modified. This notification
is not emitted unless you first send the library beginGeneratingLibraryChange-
Notifications; you should eventually balance this with endGeneratingLibrary-
ChangeNotifications.

The user can play a song that lives in the cloud without explicitly downloading it. In iOS 7, this can cause `MPMediaLibraryDidChangeNotification` to be triggered even though there is no change in the library — the library still consists of the same songs, and this song is still in the cloud (its `MPMediaItemPropertyIsCloudItem` is still `@YES`). Alternatively, the user can explicitly download the song; this causes the song to be no longer a cloud item, which is correct, but it can also cause `MPMediaLibraryDidChange-Notification` to be triggered *twice* in quick succession. Finally, if the user deletes the song from the device (so that it returns to being a cloud item), `MPMediaLibraryDid-ChangeNotification` is *not* triggered. Also, if the user so much as *looks* at the Radio tab in the Music app, `MPMediaLibraryDidChangeNotification` may be triggered many times in quick succession. I regard all of this as a bug.

Music Player

The Media Player framework class for playing an MPMediaItem is MPMusicPlayer-Controller. It comes in two flavors, depending on which class method you use to get an instance:

iPodMusicPlayer

> The global music player — the very same player used by the Music app. This might already be playing an item, or might be paused with a current item, at any time while your app runs; you can learn or change what item this is. The global music player continues playing independently of the state of your app, and the user, by way of the Music app, can at any time alter what it is doing.

applicationMusicPlayer

> Plays an MPMediaItem from the music library within your application. The song being played by the `applicationMusicPlayer` can be different from the Music app's current song. This player stops when your app is not in the foreground.

> An `applicationMusicPlayer` MPMusicPlayerController is not really inside your app. It is actually the global music player behaving differently. It has its own audio session. You cannot play its audio when your app is in the background. You cannot make it the target of remote control events. If these limitations prove troublesome, use the `iPodMusicPlayer` (or some other means of playing the song, as discussed later in this chapter).

A music player doesn't merely play an item; it plays from a *queue* of items. This behavior is familiar from iTunes and the Music app. For example, in iTunes, when you switch to a playlist and double-click the first song to start playing, when iTunes comes to the end of that song, it proceeds by default to the next song in the playlist. So at that moment, its queue is the totality of songs in the playlist. The music player behaves the same way; when it reaches the end of a song, it proceeds to the next song in its queue.

Your methods for controlling playback also reflect this queue-based orientation. In addition to the expected play, pause, and stop commands, there's a skipToNextItem and skipToPreviousItem command. Anyone who has ever used iTunes or the Music app (or, for that matter, an old-fashioned iPod) will have an intuitive grasp of this and everything else a music player does. For example, you can also set a music player's repeatMode and shuffleMode, just as in iTunes.

You provide a music player with its queue in one of two ways:

With a query

You hand the music player an MPMediaQuery. The query's items are the items of the queue.

With a collection

You hand the music player an MPMediaItemCollection. This might be obtained from a query you performed, but you can also assemble your own collection of MPMediaItems in any way you like, putting them into an array and calling collectionWithItems: or initWithItems:.

In this example, we collect all songs actually present in the library shorter than 30 seconds into a queue and set the queue playing in random order using the application-internal music player:

```
MPMediaQuery* query = [MPMediaQuery songsQuery];
MPMediaPropertyPredicate* isPresent =
    [MPMediaPropertyPredicate predicateWithValue:@NO
        forProperty:MPMediaItemPropertyIsCloudItem
        comparisonType:MPMediaPredicateComparisonEqualTo];
[query addFilterPredicate:isPresent];
NSMutableArray* marr = [NSMutableArray array];
MPMediaItemCollection* queue = nil;
for (MPMediaItem* song in query.items) {
    NSNumber* dur =
        [song valueForProperty:MPMediaItemPropertyPlaybackDuration];
    if ([dur floatValue] < 30)
        [marr addObject: song];
}
if ([marr count] == 0)
    NSLog(@"No songs that short!");
else
    queue = [MPMediaItemCollection collectionWithItems:marr];
if (queue) {
    MPMusicPlayerController* player =
        [MPMusicPlayerController applicationMusicPlayer];
    [player setQueueWithItemCollection:queue];
    player.shuffleMode = MPMusicShuffleModeSongs;
    [player play];
}
```

If a music player is currently playing, setting its queue will stop it; restarting play is up to you.

You can ask a music player for its nowPlayingItem, and since this is an MPMediaItem, you can learn all about it through its properties. Unfortunately, you can't query a music player as to its queue, but you can keep your own pointer to the MPMediaItemCollection constituting the queue when you hand it to the music player, and you can ask the music player for which song within the queue is currently playing (indexOfNowPlaying-Item). The user can completely change the queue of an iPodMusicPlayer, so if control over the queue is important to you, use the applicationMusicPlayer.

A music player has a playbackState that you can query to learn what it's doing (whether it is playing, paused, stopped, or seeking). It also emits notifications so you can hear about changes in its state:

- MPMusicPlayerControllerPlaybackStateDidChangeNotification
- MPMusicPlayerControllerNowPlayingItemDidChangeNotification
- MPMusicPlayerControllerVolumeDidChangeNotification

These notifications are not emitted until you tell the music player to beginGenerating-PlaybackNotifications. This is an instance method, so you can arrange to receive notifications from just one of the two possible music players. If you do receive notifications from both, you can distinguish them by examining the NSNotification's object and comparing it to each player. You should eventually balance this call with end-GeneratingPlaybackNotifications.

To illustrate, I'll extend the previous example to set a UILabel in our interface every time a different song starts playing. Before we start the player playing, we insert these lines to generate the notifications:

```
[player beginGeneratingPlaybackNotifications];
[[NSNotificationCenter defaultCenter] addObserver:self
    selector:@selector(changed:)
    name:MPMusicPlayerControllerNowPlayingItemDidChangeNotification
    object:player];
self.q = queue; // retain a pointer to the queue
```

And here's how we respond to those notifications:

```
- (void) changed: (NSNotification*) n {
    MPMusicPlayerController* player =
        [MPMusicPlayerController applicationMusicPlayer];
    if ([n object] == player) { // just playing safe
        NSString* title =
            [player.nowPlayingItem
                valueForProperty:MPMediaItemPropertyTitle];
        NSUInteger ix = player.indexOfNowPlayingItem;
```

```
        if (NSNotFound == ix)
            self.label.text = @"";
        else
            self.label.text = [NSString stringWithFormat:@"%i of %i: %@",
                               ix+1, [self.q count], title];
    }
}
```

There's no periodic notification as a song plays and the current playhead position advances. To get this information, you'll have to resort to polling. This is not objectionable as long as your polling interval is reasonably sparse; your display may occasionally fall a little behind reality, but this won't usually matter. To illustrate, let's add to our existing example a UIProgressView (`self.prog`) showing the current percentage of the current song played by the global player. I'll use an NSTimer to poll the state of the player every second:

```
self.timer = [NSTimer scheduledTimerWithTimeInterval:1
                      target:self selector:@selector(timerFired:)
                      userInfo:nil repeats:YES];
self.timer.tolerance = 0.1;
```

When the timer fires, the progress view displays the state of the currently playing item:

```
- (void) timerFired: (id) dummy {
    MPMusicPlayerController* mp =
        [MPMusicPlayerController applicationMusicPlayer];
    MPMediaItem* item = mp.nowPlayingItem;
    if (!item || mp.playbackState == MPMusicPlaybackStateStopped) {
        self.prog.hidden = YES;
        return;
    }
    self.prog.hidden = NO;
    NSTimeInterval current = mp.currentPlaybackTime;
    NSTimeInterval total =
        [[item valueForProperty:MPMediaItemPropertyPlaybackDuration]
            doubleValue];
    self.prog.progress = current / total;
}
```

The `applicationMusicPlayer` has no user interface, unless you count the remote playback controls (Figure 14-1); if you want the user to have controls for playing and stopping a song, you'll have to create them yourself. The `iPodMusicPlayer` has its own natural interface — the Music app.

MPVolumeView

The Media Player framework offers a slider for letting the user set the system output volume, along with an AirPlay route button if appropriate; this is an MPVolumeView. An MPVolumeView works only on a device — not in the Simulator. It is customizable similarly to a UISlider; you can set the images for the two halves of the track, the thumb, and even the AirPlay route button, for both the normal and the highlighted state (while the user is touching the thumb). New in iOS 7, you can also customize the image (volume-WarningSliderImage) that flashes in the right half of the track when the user tries to exceed the volume limit (set in the Settings app, Music → Volume Limit). In this example, we make the left half of the track black and the right half red, with flashing orange if the volume limit is exceeded, and we provide a custom thumb image:

```
CGSize sz = CGSizeMake(20,20);
UIGraphicsBeginImageContextWithOptions(
    CGSizeMake(sz.height,sz.height), NO, 0);
[[UIColor blackColor] setFill];
[[UIBezierPath bezierPathWithOvalInRect:
    CGRectMake(0,0,sz.height,sz.height)] fill];
UIImage* im1 = UIGraphicsGetImageFromCurrentImageContext();
[[UIColor redColor] setFill];
[[UIBezierPath bezierPathWithOvalInRect:
    CGRectMake(0,0,sz.height,sz.height)] fill];
UIImage* im2 = UIGraphicsGetImageFromCurrentImageContext();
[[UIColor orangeColor] setFill];
[[UIBezierPath bezierPathWithOvalInRect:
    CGRectMake(0,0,sz.height,sz.height)] fill];
UIImage* im3 = UIGraphicsGetImageFromCurrentImageContext();
UIGraphicsEndImageContext();
[self.vv setMinimumVolumeSliderImage:
 [im1 resizableImageWithCapInsets:UIEdgeInsetsMake(9,9,9,9)
                    resizingMode:UIImageResizingModeStretch]
                      forState:UIControlStateNormal];
[self.vv setMaximumVolumeSliderImage:
 [im2 resizableImageWithCapInsets:UIEdgeInsetsMake(9,9,9,9)
                    resizingMode:UIImageResizingModeStretch]
                      forState:UIControlStateNormal];
[self.vv setVolumeWarningSliderImage:
 [im3 resizableImageWithCapInsets:UIEdgeInsetsMake(9,9,9,9)
                    resizingMode:UIImageResizingModeStretch]];
UIImage* thumb = [UIImage imageNamed:@"SmileyRound.png"];
sz = CGSizeMake(40,40);
UIGraphicsBeginImageContextWithOptions(sz, NO, 0);
[thumb drawInRect:CGRectMake(0,0,sz.width,sz.height)];
thumb = UIGraphicsGetImageFromCurrentImageContext();
UIGraphicsEndImageContext();
[self.vv setVolumeThumbImage:thumb forState:UIControlStateNormal];
```

In my testing, the orange warning flash never appeared unless the EU Volume Limit setting was also switched to On (Developer → EU Volume Limit in the Settings app). Presumably this feature works on devices destined for the European Union market, but on my device, the MPVolumeView ignores the Volume Limit from the Settings app.

For further customization, you can subclass MPVolumeView and override volume-SliderRectForBounds:. (An additional overridable method is documented, volume-ThumbRectForBounds:volumeSliderRect:value:, but in my testing it is never called; I regard this as a bug.)

New in iOS 7, you can register for notifications when a wireless route (Bluetooth or AirPlay) appears or disappears (MPVolumeViewWirelessRoutesAvailableDidChange-Notification) and when a wireless route becomes active or inactive (MPVolumeView-WirelessRouteActiveDidChangeNotification).

Playing Songs With AV Foundation

MPMusicPlayerController is convenient and simple, but it's also simpleminded. Its audio session isn't your audio session; the music player doesn't really belong to you. An MPMediaItem, however, has an MPMediaItemPropertyAssetURL key whose value is a URL. Now everything from Chapter 14 and Chapter 15 comes into play.

So, for example, having obtained an MPMediaItem's MPMediaItemPropertyAssetURL, you could use that URL in any of the following ways:

- Initialize an AVAudioPlayer (initWithContentsOfURL:error: or initWith-ContentsOfURL:fileTypeHint:error:).
- Set the contentURL of an MPMoviePlayerController.
- Initialize an AVPlayer (initWithURL: or playerWithURL:).
- Form an AVAsset (assetWithURL:).

Each of these ways of playing an MPMediaItem has its advantages. For example, AVAudioPlayer is easy to use, and lets you loop a sound, poll the power value of its channels, and so forth. MPMoviePlayerController gives you a built-in play/pause button and playhead slider. AVAsset gives you the full power of the AV Foundation framework, letting you edit the sound, assemble multiple sounds, perform a fadeout effect, and even attach the sound to a video (and then play it with an AVPlayer).

To demonstrate the use of AVAsset and AVPlayer, I'll use AVQueuePlayer (an AVPlayer subclass) to play a sequence of MPMediaItems, just as MPMusicPlayerController does:

```
NSArray* arr = // array of MPMediaItem
NSMutableArray* assets = [NSMutableArray array];
for (MPMediaItem* item in arr) {
    AVPlayerItem* pi = [[AVPlayerItem alloc] initWithURL:
        [item valueForProperty:MPMediaItemPropertyAssetURL]];
    [assets addObject:pi];
}
self.qp = [AVQueuePlayer queuePlayerWithItems:assets];
[self.qp play];
```

That works, but I have the impression, based on something said in one of the WWDC 2011 videos, that instead of adding a whole batch of AVPlayerItems to an AVQueue-Player all at once, you're supposed to add just a few AVPlayerItems to start with and then add each additional AVPlayerItem when an item finishes playing. So I'll start out by adding just three AVPlayerItems, and use key–value observing to watch for changes in the AVQueuePlayer's currentItem:

```
NSArray* arr = // array of MPMediaItem
self.assets = [NSMutableArray array];
for (MPMediaItem* item in arr) {
    AVPlayerItem* pi = [[AVPlayerItem alloc] initWithURL:
        [item valueForProperty:MPMediaItemPropertyAssetURL]];
    [self.assets addObject:pi];
}
self->_curnum = 0; // we'll need this later
self->_total = [self.assets count]; // ditto
self.qp = [AVQueuePlayer queuePlayerWithItems:
    [self.assets objectsAtIndexes:
        [NSIndexSet indexSetWithIndexesInRange:NSMakeRange(0,3)]]];
[self.assets removeObjectsAtIndexes:
    [NSIndexSet indexSetWithIndexesInRange:NSMakeRange(0,3)]];
[self.qp addObserver:self
    forKeyPath:@"currentItem" options:0 context:nil];
[self.qp play];
```

The implementation of observeValueForKeyPath:... looks like this:

```
AVPlayerItem* item = self.qp.currentItem;
NSArray* arr = item.asset.commonMetadata;
arr = [AVMetadataItem metadataItemsFromArray:arr
            withKey:AVMetadataCommonKeyTitle
            keySpace:AVMetadataKeySpaceCommon];
AVMetadataItem* met = arr[0];
[met loadValuesAsynchronouslyForKeys:@[@"value"]
                completionHandler:^{
    dispatch_async(dispatch_get_main_queue(), ^{
        self.label.text =
            [NSString stringWithFormat:@"%d of %d: %@",
                ++self->_curnum, self->_total, met.value];
    });
}];
if (![self.assets count])
    return;
AVPlayerItem* newItem = self.assets[0];
[self.qp insertItem:newItem afterItem:[self.qp.items lastObject]];
[self.assets removeObjectAtIndex:0];
```

That code illustrates how to extract metadata from an AVAsset by way of an AVMetadataItem; in this case, we fetch the AVMetadataCommonKeyTitle and get its value property, as the equivalent of fetching an MPMediaItem's MPMediaItemProperty-Title property in our earlier code. As with everything else in the AV Foundation world, it can take time for the `value` property to become available, so we call `loadValues-AsynchronouslyForKeys:completionHandler:` to run our completion handler when it *is* available. There are no guarantees about what thread the completion handler will be called on, so to set the label's text, I step out to the main thread (Chapter 25).

In the last three lines, we pull an AVPlayerItem off the front of our `assets` mutable array and add it to the end of the AVQueuePlayer's queue. The AVQueuePlayer itself deletes an item from the start of its queue after playing it, so this way the queue never exceeds three items in length.

Just as in the previous example, where we updated a progress view in response to the firing of a timer to reflect an MPMusicPlayerController's current item's time and duration, we can do the same thing with the currently playing AVPlayerItem. Again, we can't be certain when the `duration` property will become available, so we call `loadValues-AsynchronouslyForKeys:completionHandler:`, and again, to update the progress view, we step out to the main thread:

```
if (!self.qp.currentItem) { // finished!
    self.prog.hidden = YES;
    [self.timer invalidate];
} else {
    AVPlayerItem* item = self.qp.currentItem;
    AVAsset* asset = item.asset;
    [asset loadValuesAsynchronouslyForKeys:@[@"duration"]
                        completionHandler:^{
        dispatch_async(dispatch_get_main_queue(), ^{
            CMTime cur = self.qp.currentTime;
            CMTime dur = asset.duration;
            self.prog.progress =
                CMTimeGetSeconds(cur)/CMTimeGetSeconds(dur);
            self.prog.hidden = NO;
        });
    }];
}
```

Music Picker

The music picker (MPMediaPickerController), supplied by the Media Player framework, is a view controller (UIViewController) whose view is a self-contained navigation interface in which the user can select a media item. This interface looks very much like the iPhone Music app. You have no access to the actual view; you are expected to present the view controller (`presentViewController:animated:completion:`).

You can limit the type of media items displayed by creating the controller using `init-WithMediaTypes:`. You can make a prompt appear at the top of the navigation bar (`prompt`). And you can govern whether the user can choose multiple media items or just one, with the `allowsPickingMultipleItems` property. You can filter out items stored in the cloud by setting `showsCloudItems` to NO.

While the view is showing, you learn what the user is doing through two delegate methods (MPMediaPickerControllerDelegate); the presented view controller is not automatically dismissed, so it is up to you dismiss it in these delegate methods:

- `mediaPicker:didPickMediaItems:`
- `mediaPickerDidCancel:`

The behavior of the delegate methods depends on the value of the controller's `allows-PickingMultipleItems`:

The controller's `allowsPickingMultipleItems` *is NO (the default)*
> There's a Cancel button. Every time the user taps a media item, your `media-Picker:didPickMediaItems:` is called, handing you an MPMediaItemCollection consisting of that item; you are likely to dismiss the presented view controller at this point. When the user taps Cancel, your `mediaPickerDidCancel:` is called.

The controller's `allowsPickingMultipleItems` *is YES*
> There's a Done button. Every time the user taps a media item, it is disabled to indicate that it has been selected. When the user taps Done, `mediaPicker:didPick-MediaItems:` is called, handing you an MPMediaItemCollection consisting of all items the user tapped. Your `mediaPickerDidCancel:` is *never* called.

In this example, we put up the music picker; we then play the user's chosen media item with the application's music player. The example works equally well whether `allows-PickingMultipleItems` is YES or NO:

```
- (void) presentPicker {
    MPMediaPickerController* picker = [MPMediaPickerController new];
    picker.delegate = self;
    // picker.allowsPickingMultipleItems = YES;
    [self presentViewController:picker animated:YES completion:nil];
}
- (void) mediaPicker: (MPMediaPickerController*) mediaPicker
        didPickMediaItems: (MPMediaItemCollection*) mediaItemCollection {
    MPMusicPlayerController* player =
        [MPMusicPlayerController applicationMusicPlayer];
    [player setQueueWithItemCollection:mediaItemCollection];
    [player play];
    [self dismissViewControllerAnimated:YES completion:nil];
}
- (void) mediaPickerDidCancel: (MPMediaPickerController*) mediaPicker {
    [self dismissViewControllerAnimated:YES completion:nil];
}
```

On the iPad, the music picker can be displayed as a presented view, and I think it looks best that way. But it also works reasonably well in a popover, especially if we increase its popoverContentSize; so I'll use this opportunity to provide a complete example (Example 16-1) of managing a single view controller as either a presented view on the iPhone or a popover on the iPad.

The presentPicker method is now a button's control event action handler, so that we can point the popover's arrow to the button. How we summon the picker depends on the device; we use UI_USER_INTERFACE_IDIOM to distinguish the two cases. If it's an iPad, we create a popover and set an instance variable to retain it (as discussed in Chapter 9). Two methods dismiss the picker, so that operation is factored out into a utility method (dismissPicker:) that does one thing if there's a popover and another if there's a presented view controller.

Example 16-1. A presented view on the iPhone, a popover on the iPad

```
- (void) presentPicker: (id) sender {
    MPMediaPickerController* picker = [MPMediaPickerController new];
    picker.delegate = self;
    // picker.allowsPickingMultipleItems = YES;
    if (UI_USER_INTERFACE_IDIOM() == UIUserInterfaceIdiomPhone)
        [self presentViewController:picker animated:YES completion:nil];
    else {
        UIPopoverController* pop =
            [[UIPopoverController alloc] initWithContentViewController:picker];
        self.currentPop = pop;
        pop.popoverContentSize = CGSizeMake(500,600);
        [pop presentPopoverFromRect:[sender bounds] inView:sender
            permittedArrowDirections:UIPopoverArrowDirectionAny animated:YES];
        pop.passthroughViews = nil;
    }
}
- (void) dismissPicker: (MPMediaPickerController*) mediaPicker {
    if (self.currentPop && self.currentPop.popoverVisible) {
        [self.currentPop dismissPopoverAnimated:YES];
        self.currentPop = nil;
    } else {
        [self dismissViewControllerAnimated:YES completion:nil];
    }
}
- (void)mediaPicker: (MPMediaPickerController *)mediaPicker
        didPickMediaItems:(MPMediaItemCollection *)mediaItemCollection {
    MPMusicPlayerController* player =
        [MPMusicPlayerController applicationMusicPlayer];
    [player setQueueWithItemCollection:mediaItemCollection];
    [player play];
    [self dismissPicker: mediaPicker];
}
- (void)mediaPickerDidCancel:(MPMediaPickerController *)mediaPicker {
    [self dismissPicker: mediaPicker];
```

```
}
- (void)popoverControllerDidDismissPopover:(UIPopoverController*)popoverController {
    self.currentPop = nil;
}
```

CHAPTER 17

Photo Library and Image Capture

The still photos and movies accessed by the user through the Photos app constitute the *photo library*. Your app can give the user an interface for exploring this library through the UIImagePickerController class.

In addition, the Assets Library framework lets you access the photo library and its contents programmatically. You'll need to @import AssetsLibrary.

The UIImagePickerController class can also be used to give the user an interface similar to the Camera app, letting the user take photos and videos on devices with the necessary hardware.

At a deeper level, the AV Foundation framework (Chapter 15) provides direct control over the camera hardware. You'll need to @import AVFoundation (and probably Core-Media).

Constants such as kUTTypeImage, referred to in this chapter, are provided by the Mobile Core Services framework; you'll need to @import MobileCoreServices.

Choosing From the Photo Library

UIImagePickerController is a view controller (UINavigationController) providing a navigation interface in which the user can choose an item from the photo library. There are two ways to show this interface:

As a presented view controller

This is the expected approach on the iPhone; it does also work on the iPad. (In earlier versions of iOS, trying to present a UIImagePickerController as a presented view controller on the iPad caused a runtime error; the documentation claims that this is still the case, but it isn't.) This presented view controller will appear in portrait orientation, regardless of your app's rotation settings.

As a popover

This is the expected approach on the iPad, according to the documentation.

To let the user choose an item from the photo library, instantiate UIImagePicker-Controller and assign its sourceType one of these values:

`UIImagePickerControllerSourceTypeSavedPhotosAlbum`
The user is confined to the contents of the Camera Roll / Saved Photos album.

`UIImagePickerControllerSourceTypePhotoLibrary`
The user is shown a table of all albums, and can navigate into any of them.

You should call the class method isSourceTypeAvailable: beforehand; if it doesn't return YES, don't present the controller with that source type.

You'll probably want to specify an array of mediaTypes you're interested in. This array will usually contain kUTTypeImage, kUTTypeMovie, or both; or you can specify all available types by calling the class method availableMediaTypesForSourceType:.

After doing all of that, and having supplied a delegate (adopting UIImagePicker-ControllerDelegate and UINavigationControllerDelegate), present the view controller. Here's a complete example for the iPhone:

```
UIImagePickerControllerSourceType type =
    UIImagePickerControllerSourceTypePhotoLibrary;
BOOL ok = [UIImagePickerController isSourceTypeAvailable:type];
if (!ok) {
    NSLog(@"alas");
    return;
}
UIImagePickerController* picker = [UIImagePickerController new];
picker.sourceType = type;
picker.mediaTypes =
    [UIImagePickerController availableMediaTypesForSourceType:type];
picker.delegate = self;
[self presentViewController:picker animated:YES completion:nil]; // iPhone
```

Your app is now attempting to access the photo library. The very first time your app does that, a system alert will appear, prompting the user to grant your app permission (Figure 17-1). You can modify the body of this alert by setting the "Privacy — Photo Library Usage Description" key (NSPhotoLibraryUsageDescription) in your app's *Info.plist* to tell the user *why* you want to access the photo library. This is a kind of "elevator pitch"; you need to persuade the user in very few words.

If the user denies your app access, you'll still be able to present the UIImagePicker-Controller, but it will be empty (with a reminder that the user has denied your app access to the photo library) and the user won't be able to do anything but cancel (Figure 17-2). Thus, your code is unaffected. You *can* check beforehand to learn whether your app has access to the photo library — I'll explain how later in this chapter — and opt to do

Figure 17-1. The system prompts for photo library access

Figure 17-2. The image picker, when the user has denied access

something other than present the UIImagePickerController if access has been denied; but you don't *have* to, because the user will see a coherent interface and will cancel, and your app will proceed normally from there.

 To retest the system alert and other access-related behaviors, go to the Settings app and choose General → Reset → Reset Location & Privacy. This, unfortunately, causes the system to revert to its default settings for *everything* in the Privacy section of Settings: Location Services and all System Services will be On, and all permissions lists will be empty.

 If the user does what Figure 17-2 suggests, switching to the Settings app and enabling access for your app under Privacy → Photos, your app will be terminated in the background! This is unfortunate, but is probably not a bug; Apple presumably feels that in this situation your app cannot continue coherently and should start over from scratch.

On the iPhone, the delegate will receive one of these messages:

- `imagePickerController:didFinishPickingMediaWithInfo:`
- `imagePickerControllerDidCancel:`

On the iPad, if you're using a popover, there's no Cancel button, so there's no `image-PickerControllerDidCancel:`; you can detect the dismissal of the popover through the popover delegate. With a presented view controller, if a UIImagePickerController-Delegate method is not implemented, the view controller is dismissed automatically at the point where that method would be called; but rather than relying on this, you should probably implement both delegate methods and dismiss the view controller yourself in each.

The `didFinish...` method is handed a dictionary of information about the chosen item. The keys in this dictionary depend on the media type:

An image
> The keys are:

> `UIImagePickerControllerMediaType`
>> A UTI; probably `@"public.image"`, which is the same as `kUTTypeImage`.

> `UIImagePickerControllerReferenceURL`
>> An ALAsset URL pointing to the *original* image file in the library.

> `UIImagePickerControllerOriginalImage`
>> A UIImage. This is the output you are expected to use. For example, you might display it in a UIImageView.

A movie
> The keys are:

> `UIImagePickerControllerMediaType`
>> A UTI; probably `@"public.movie"`, which is the same as `kUTTypeMovie`.

> `UIImagePickerControllerReferenceURL`
>> An ALAsset URL pointing to the *original* movie file in the library.

> `UIImagePickerControllerMediaURL`
>> A file URL to a copy of the movie saved into a temporary directory. This is the output you are expected to use. For example, you might display it in an MPMoviePlayerController or an AVPlayerLayer (Chapter 15).

Optionally, you can set the view controller's `allowsEditing` to YES. In the case of an image, the interface then allows the user to scale the image up and to move it so as to be cropped by a preset rectangle; the dictionary will include two additional keys:

`UIImagePickerControllerCropRect`
An NSValue wrapping a CGRect.

`UIImagePickerControllerEditedImage`
A UIImage. This becomes the image you are expected to use.

In the case of a movie, if the view controller's `allowsEditing` is YES, the user can trim the movie just as with a UIVideoEditorController (Chapter 15). The dictionary keys are the same as before.

Here's an example implementation of `imagePickerController:didFinishPicking-MediaWithInfo:` that covers the fundamental cases:

```
-(void)imagePickerController:(UIImagePickerController *)picker
        didFinishPickingMediaWithInfo:(NSDictionary *)info {
    NSURL* url = info[UIImagePickerControllerMediaURL];
    UIImage* im = info[UIImagePickerControllerOriginalImage];
    UIImage* edim = info[UIImagePickerControllerEditedImage];
    if (edim)
        im = edim;
    if (!self.currentPop) { // presented view
        [self dismissViewControllerAnimated:YES completion:nil];
    }
    else { // popover
        [self.currentPop dismissPopoverAnimated:YES];
        self.currentPop = nil;
    }
    NSString* type = info[UIImagePickerControllerMediaType];
    if ([type isEqualToString: (NSString*)kUTTypeImage] && im)
        [self showImage:im];
    else if ([type isEqualToString: (NSString*)kUTTypeMovie] && url)
        [self showMovie:url];
}
```

Assets Library Framework

The Assets Library framework does for the photo library roughly what the Media Player framework does for the music library (Chapter 16), letting your code explore the library's contents. One obvious use of the Assets Library framework might be to implement your own interface for letting the user choose an image, in a way that transcends the limitations of UIImagePickerController. But you can go further with the photo library than you can with the media library: you can save media into the Camera Roll / Saved Photos album, and you can even create a new album and save media into it.

A photo or video in the photo library is an ALAsset. Like a media entity, an ALAsset can describe itself through key–value pairs called *properties*. (This use of the word "properties" has nothing to do with Objective-C language properties.) For example, it can report its type (photo or video), its creation date, its orientation if it is a photo whose metadata contains this information, and its duration if it is a video. You fetch a property value with `valueForProperty:`. The properties have names like `ALAssetPropertyType`.

A photo can provide multiple *representations* (roughly, image file formats). A given photo ALAsset lists these representations as one of its properties, `ALAssetProperty-Representations`, an array of strings giving the UTIs identifying the file formats; a typical UTI might be `@"public.jpeg"` (`kUTTypeJPEG`). A representation is an ALAsset-Representation. You can get a photo's `defaultRepresentation`, or ask for a particular representation by submitting a file format's UTI to `representationForUTI:`.

Once you have an ALAssetRepresentation, you can interrogate it to get the actual image, either as raw data or as a CGImage (see Chapter 2). The simplest way is to ask for its `fullResolutionImage` or its `fullScreenImage` (the latter is more suitable for display in your interface, and is identical to what the Photos app displays); you may then want to derive a UIImage from this using `imageWithCGImage:scale:orientation:`. The original scale and orientation of the image are available as the ALAssetRepresentation's `scale` and `orientation`. Alternatively, if all you need is a small version of the image to display in your interface, you can ask the ALAsset itself for its `aspectRatio-Thumbnail`. An ALAssetRepresentation also has a `url`, which is the unique identifier for the ALAsset.

The photo library itself is an ALAssetsLibrary instance. It is divided into groups (ALAssetsGroup), which have types. For example, the user might have multiple albums; each of these is a group of type `ALAssetsGroupAlbum`. You also have access to the Photo-Stream album. An ALAssetsGroup has properties, such as a name, which you can fetch with `valueForProperty:`; one such property, the group's URL (`ALAssetsGroup-PropertyURL`), is its unique identifier. To fetch assets from the library, you either fetch one specific asset by providing its URL, or you can start with a group, in which case you can then enumerate the group's assets. To obtain a group, you can enumerate the library's groups of a certain type, in which case you are handed each group as an ALAssetsGroup, or you can provide a particular group's URL. Before enumerating a group's assets, you may optionally filter the group using a simple ALAssetsFilter; this limits any subsequent enumeration to photos only, videos only, or both.

The Assets Library framework uses Objective-C blocks for fetching and enumerating assets and groups. These blocks behave in a special way: at the end of the enumeration, they are called *one extra time with a nil first parameter*. Thus, you must code your block carefully to avoid treating the first parameter as real on that final call. I was initially mystified by this curious block enumeration behavior, but one day the reason for it came to me in a flash: these blocks are all called *asynchronously* (on the main thread), meaning that the rest of your code has already finished running, so you're given an extra pass through the block as your first opportunity to *do* something with all the data you've presumably gathered in the previous passes.

As I mentioned in the previous section, the system will ask the user for permission the first time your app tries to access the photo library, and the user can refuse. You can learn directly beforehand whether access has been refused:

```
ALAuthorizationStatus stat = [ALAssetsLibrary authorizationStatus];
if (stat == ALAuthorizationStatusDenied ||
        stat == ALAuthorizationStatusRestricted) {
    NSLog(@"%@", @"No access");
    return;
}
```

There is, however, no need to do this, because all the block-based methods for accessing the library allow you to supply a failure block; thus, your code will be able to retreat in good order when it discovers that it can't access the library.

We now know enough for an example! Given an album title, I'll find that album, pull out the first photo, and display that photo in the interface. The first step is to find the album; I do that by cycling through all albums, stopping when I find the one whose title matches the target title. The block will then be called one last time; at that point, I call another method to pull the first photo out of that album:

```
- (void) findAlbumWithTitle: (NSString*) albumTitle {
    __block ALAssetsGroup* album = nil;
    ALAssetsLibrary* library = [ALAssetsLibrary new];
    [library enumerateGroupsWithTypes: ALAssetsGroupAlbum
        usingBlock: ^ (ALAssetsGroup *group, BOOL *stop) {
            if (group) {
                NSString* title =
                [group valueForProperty: ALAssetsGroupPropertyName];
                if ([title isEqualToString: albumTitle]) {
                    album = group;
                    *stop = YES;
                }
            } else { // afterward
                if (!album) {
                    NSLog(@"%@", @"failed to find album");
                    return;
                }
                [self showFirstPhotoOfGroup:album];
            }
        }
        failureBlock: ^ (NSError *error) {
            NSLog(@"oops! %@", [error localizedDescription]);
            // e.g. "Global denied access"
        }
    ];
}
```

And here's the second method; it starts to enumerate the items of the album, stopping immediately after the first photo and showing that photo in the interface. I don't need a very big version of the photo, so I use the asset's aspectRatioThumbnail:

```
- (void) showFirstPhotoOfGroup: (ALAssetsGroup*) group {
    __block ALAsset* photo;
    [group enumerateAssetsUsingBlock:
     ^(ALAsset *result, NSUInteger index, BOOL *stop) {
         if (result) {
             NSString* type = [result valueForProperty:ALAssetPropertyType];
             if ([type isEqualToString: ALAssetTypePhoto]) {
                 photo = result;
                 *stop = YES;
             }
         } else { // afterward
             if (!photo)
                 return;
             CGImageRef im = photo.aspectRatioThumbnail;
             UIImage* im2 = [UIImage imageWithCGImage:im scale:0
                                         orientation:UIImageOrientationUp];
             self.iv.image = im2; // put image into our UIImageView
         }
     }];
}
```

You can write files into the Camera Roll / Saved Photos album. The basic function for writing an image file to this location is `UIImageWriteToSavedPhotosAlbum`. Some kinds of video file can also be saved here; in an example in Chapter 15, I checked whether this was true of a certain video file by calling `UIVideoAtPathIsCompatibleWithSaved-PhotosAlbum`, and I saved the file by calling `UISaveVideoAtPathToSavedPhotosAlbum`.

The ALAssetsLibrary class extends these abilities by providing five additional methods:

`writeImageToSavedPhotosAlbum:orientation:completionBlock:`
Takes a CGImageRef and orientation.

`writeImageToSavedPhotosAlbum:metadata:completionBlock:`
Takes a CGImageRef and optional metadata dictionary (such as might arrive through the `UIImagePickerControllerMediaMetadata` key when the user takes a picture using UIImagePickerController).

`writeImageDataToSavedPhotosAlbum:metadata:completionBlock:`
Takes raw image data (NSData) and optional metadata.

`videoAtPathIsCompatibleWithSavedPhotosAlbum:`
Takes a file path string. Returns a boolean.

`writeVideoAtPathToSavedPhotosAlbum:completionBlock:`
Takes a file path string.

Saving takes time, so a completion block allows you to be notified when it's over. The completion block supplies two parameters: an NSURL and an NSError. If the first parameter is not nil, the write succeeded, and this is the URL of the resulting ALAsset. If the first parameter *is* nil, the write failed, and the second parameter describes the error.

You can create in the Camera Roll / Saved Photos album an image or video that is considered to be a modified version of an existing image or video, by calling an instance method on the original asset:

- `writeModifiedImageDataToSavedPhotosAlbum:metadata:completionBlock:`
- `writeModifiedVideoAtPathToSavedPhotosAlbum:completionBlock:`

Afterward, you can get from the modified asset to the original asset through the former's `originalAsset` property.

You are also allowed to "edit" an asset — that is, you can replace an image or video in the library with a different image or video — but only if your application created the asset. Check the asset's `editable` property; if it is YES, you can call either of these methods:

- `setImageData:metadata:completionBlock:`
- `setVideoAtPath:completionBlock:`

Finally, you are allowed to create an album:

- `addAssetsGroupAlbumWithName:resultBlock:failureBlock:`

If an album is `editable`, which would be because you created it, you can add an existing asset to it by calling `addAsset:`. This is not the same thing as saving a new asset to an album other than the Camera Roll / Saved Photos album; you can't do that, but once an asset exists, it can belong to more than one album.

Using the Camera

The simplest way to prompt the user to take a photo or video is to use our old friend UIImagePickerController, which provides an interface similar to the Camera app.

To use UIImagePickerController in this way, first check `isSourceTypeAvailable:` for `UIImagePickerControllerSourceTypeCamera`; it will be NO if the user's device has no camera or the camera is unavailable. If it is YES, call `availableMediaTypesForSourceType:` to learn whether the user can take a still photo (`kUTTypeImage`), a video (`kUTType-Movie`), or both. Now instantiate UIImagePickerController, set its source type to `UIImagePickerControllerSourceTypeCamera`, and set its `mediaTypes` in accordance with which types you just learned are available. Finally, set a delegate (adopting UINavigationControllerDelegate and UIImagePickerControllerDelegate), and present the view controller. In this situation, it is legal (and preferable) to use a presented view controller even on the iPad.

So, for example:

```
BOOL ok = [UIImagePickerController isSourceTypeAvailable:
        UIImagePickerControllerSourceTypeCamera];
if (!ok) {
    NSLog(@"no camera");
    return;
}
NSArray* arr = [UIImagePickerController availableMediaTypesForSourceType:
            UIImagePickerControllerSourceTypeCamera];
if ([arr indexOfObject:(NSString*)kUTTypeImage] == NSNotFound) {
    NSLog(@"no stills");
    return;
}
UIImagePickerController* picker = [UIImagePickerController new];
picker.sourceType = UIImagePickerControllerSourceTypeCamera;
picker.mediaTypes = @[(NSString*)kUTTypeImage];
picker.delegate = self;
[self presentViewController:picker animated:YES completion:nil];
```

For video, you can also specify the videoQuality and videoMaximumDuration. More-over, these additional properties and class methods allow you to discover the camera capabilities:

isCameraDeviceAvailable:
Checks to see whether the front or rear camera is available, using one of these values as argument:

- UIImagePickerControllerCameraDeviceFront
- UIImagePickerControllerCameraDeviceRear

cameraDevice
Lets you learn and set which camera is being used.

availableCaptureModesForCameraDevice:
Checks whether the given camera can capture still images, video, or both. You specify the front or rear camera; returns an NSArray of NSNumbers, from which you can extract the integer value. Possible modes are:

- UIImagePickerControllerCameraCaptureModePhoto
- UIImagePickerControllerCameraCaptureModeVideo

cameraCaptureMode
Lets you learn and set the capture mode (still or video).

isFlashAvailableForCameraDevice:
Checks whether flash is available.

cameraFlashMode
Lets you learn and set the flash mode (or, for a movie, toggles the LED "torch"). Your choices are:

- `UIImagePickerControllerCameraFlashModeOff`

- `UIImagePickerControllerCameraFlashModeAuto`

- `UIImagePickerControllerCameraFlashModeOn`

 Setting camera-related properties such as `cameraDevice` when there is no camera or when the UIImagePickerController is not set to camera mode can crash your app.

When the view controller's view appears, the user will see the interface for taking a picture, familiar from the Camera app, possibly including flash options, camera selection button, digital zoom (if the hardware supports it), photo/video option (if your `mediaTypes` setting allows both), and Cancel and Shutter buttons. If the user takes a picture, the presented view offers an opportunity to use the picture or to retake it.

New in iOS 7, the first time your app tries to let the user capture video, a system dialog will appear requesting access to the microphone. You can modify the body of this alert by setting the "Privacy — Microphone Usage Description" key (`NSMicrophoneUsage-Description`) in your app's *Info.plist*. See the discussion of privacy settings earlier in this chapter. You can learn whether microphone permission has been granted by calling the AVAudioSession method `requestRecordPermission:` (Chapter 14).

Allowing the user to edit the captured image or movie (`allowsEditing`), and handling the outcome with the delegate messages, is the same as I described earlier. There won't be any `UIImagePickerControllerReferenceURL` key in the dictionary delivered to the delegate, because the image isn't in the photo library. A still image might report a `UIImage-PickerControllerMediaMetadata` key containing the metadata for the photo. The photo library was not involved in the process of media capture, so no user permission to access the photo library is needed; of course, if you *now* propose to save the media into the photo library (as I described in the previous section), you *will* need permission.

 New in iOS 7, devices destined for some markets may request permission to access the camera itself. But I have not been able to test this feature.

Customizing the Image Capture Interface

You can customize the UIImagePickerController interface. If you need to do that, you should probably consider dispensing with UIImagePickerController altogether and designing your own image capture interface from scratch, based around AV Foundation and AVCaptureSession, which I'll introduce in the next section. Still, it may be that a modified UIImagePickerController is all you need.

In the image capture interface, you can hide the standard controls by setting shows-CameraControls to NO, replacing them with your own overlay view, which you supply as the value of the cameraOverlayView. In this case, you're probably going to want some means in your overlay view to allow the user to take a picture! You can do that through these methods:

- takePicture
- startVideoCapture
- stopVideoCapture

The key to customizing the look and behavior of the image capture interface is that a UIImagePickerController is a UINavigationController; the controls shown at the bottom of the default interface are the navigation controller's toolbar. In this example, I'll remove all the default controls and use a gesture recognizer on the cameraOverlay-View to permit the user to double-tap the image in order to take a picture:

```
// ... starts out as before ...
picker.delegate = self;
picker.showsCameraControls = NO;
CGRect f = self.view.window.bounds;
UIView* v = [[UIView alloc] initWithFrame:f];
UITapGestureRecognizer* t =
    [[UITapGestureRecognizer alloc] initWithTarget:self
                                        action:@selector(tap:)];
t.numberOfTapsRequired = 2;
[v addGestureRecognizer:t];
picker.cameraOverlayView = v;
[self presentViewController:picker animated:YES completion:nil];
self.picker = picker;
```

Our tap: gesture recognizer action handler simply calls takePicture:

```
- (void) tap: (id) g {
    [self.picker takePicture];
}
```

It would be nice, however, to *tell* the user to double-tap to take a picture; we also need to give the user a way to dismiss the image capture interface. We could put a button and a label into the cameraOverlayView, but here, I'll take advantage of the UINavigation-Controller's toolbar. We are the UIImagePickerController's delegate, meaning that we are not only its UIImagePickerControllerDelegate but also its UINavigationController-Delegate; I'll use a delegate method to populate the toolbar:

```
- (void)navigationController:(UINavigationController *)nc
        didShowViewController:(UIViewController *)vc
                    animated:(BOOL)animated {
    [nc setToolbarHidden:NO];
    UIGraphicsBeginImageContextWithOptions(CGSizeMake(10,10), NO, 0);
    [[[UIColor blackColor] colorWithAlphaComponent:0.1] setFill];
    CGContextFillRect(UIGraphicsGetCurrentContext(), CGRectMake(0,0,10,10));
    UIImage* im = UIGraphicsGetImageFromCurrentImageContext();
    UIGraphicsEndImageContext();
    [nc.toolbar setBackgroundImage:im forToolbarPosition:UIBarPositionAny
                        barMetrics:UIBarMetricsDefault];
    nc.toolbar.translucent = YES;
    UIBarButtonItem* b =
        [[UIBarButtonItem alloc] initWithTitle:@"Cancel"
            style:UIBarButtonItemStylePlain
            target:self
            action:@selector(doCancel:)];
    UILabel* lab = [UILabel new];
    lab.text = @"Double tap to take a picture";
    lab.textColor = [UIColor whiteColor];
    lab.backgroundColor = [UIColor clearColor];
    [lab sizeToFit];
    UIBarButtonItem* b2 = [[UIBarButtonItem alloc] initWithCustomView:lab];
    [nc.topViewController setToolbarItems:@[b, b2]];
}
```

When the user double-taps to take a picture, our `didFinishPickingMediaWithInfo` delegate method is called, just as before. We don't automatically get the secondary interface where the user is shown the resulting image and offered an opportunity to use it or retake the image. But we can provide such an interface ourselves, by pushing another view controller onto the navigation controller:

```
- (void)imagePickerController:(UIImagePickerController *)picker
        didFinishPickingMediaWithInfo:(NSDictionary *)info {
    UIImage* im = info[UIImagePickerControllerOriginalImage];
    if (!im)
        return;
    SecondViewController* svc =
        [[SecondViewController alloc] initWithNibName:nil
            bundle:nil image:im];
    [picker pushViewController:svc animated:YES];
}
```

(Designing the SecondViewController class is left as an exercise for the reader.)

Image Capture With AV Foundation

Instead of using UIImagePickerController, you can control the camera and capture images using the AV Foundation framework (Chapter 15). You get no help with interface (except for displaying in your interface what the camera "sees"), but you get vastly more detailed control than UIImagePickerController can give you; for example, for stills, you can control focus and exposure directly and independently, and for video, you can determine the quality, size, and frame rate of the resulting movie. You can also capture audio, of course.

The heart of all AV Foundation capture operations is an AVCaptureSession object. You configure this and provide it as desired with inputs (such as a camera) and outputs (such as a file); then you call startRunning to begin the actual capture. You can reconfigure an AVCaptureSession, possibly adding or removing an input or output, while it is running — indeed, doing so is far more efficient than stopping the session and starting it again — but you should wrap your configuration changes in beginConfiguration and commitConfiguration.

As a rock-bottom example, let's start by displaying in our interface, in real time, what the camera sees. This requires an AVCaptureVideoPreviewLayer, a CALayer subclass. This layer is not an AVCaptureSession output; rather, the layer receives its imagery by *owning* the AVCaptureSession. Our AVCaptureSession's input is the default video camera. We have no intention of doing anything with the captured video other than displaying it in the interface, so our AVCaptureSession doesn't need an output:

```
self.sess = [AVCaptureSession new];
// add input
AVCaptureDevice* cam =
    [AVCaptureDevice defaultDeviceWithMediaType:AVMediaTypeVideo];
AVCaptureDeviceInput* input =
    [AVCaptureDeviceInput deviceInputWithDevice:cam error:nil];
[self.sess addInput:input];
// create preview layer
AVCaptureVideoPreviewLayer* lay =
    [[AVCaptureVideoPreviewLayer alloc] initWithSession:self.sess];
lay.frame = // whatever
[self.view.layer addSublayer:lay];
self.previewLayer = lay; // keep a reference so we can remove it later
// go!
[self.sess startRunning];
```

Presto! Our interface now contains a window on the world, so to speak.

Expanding on that example, let's permit the user to snap a still photo, which our interface will display. Now we *do* need an output for our AVCaptureSession; since all we want is a still image, this will be an AVCaptureStillImageOutput, and we'll set its output-Settings to specify the quality of the JPEG image we're after. We also need to configure the quality of image that the camera is to capture; the simplest and most common way to set that is to apply a sessionPreset to the AVCaptureSession. In this case, since this image is to go directly into our interface, we won't need the full eight megapixel size of which the iPhone 4 and 5 cameras are capable; so we'll configure our AVCaptureSession's sessionPreset to ask for a much smaller image:

```
self.sess = [AVCaptureSession new];
self.sess.sessionPreset = AVCaptureSessionPreset640x480;
self.snapper = [AVCaptureStillImageOutput new];
self.snapper.outputSettings =
    @{AVVideoCodecKey: AVVideoCodecJPEG, AVVideoQualityKey:@0.6};
[self.sess addOutput:self.snapper];
// ... and the rest is as before ...
```

When the user asks to snap a picture, we send captureStillImageAsynchronouslyFrom-
Connection:completionHandler: to our AVCaptureStillImageOutput object. The first
argument is an AVCaptureConnection; to find it, we ask the output for its connection
that is currently inputting video. The second argument is the block that will be called,
possibly on a background thread, when the image data is ready; in the block, we capture
the data into a UIImage and, stepping out to the main thread (Chapter 25), we construct
in the interface a UIImageView containing that image, in place of the AVCapture-
VideoPreviewLayer we were displaying previously:

```
if (!self.sess || !self.sess.isRunning)
    return;
AVCaptureConnection *vc =
    [self.snapper connectionWithMediaType:AVMediaTypeVideo];
[self.snapper captureStillImageAsynchronouslyFromConnection:vc
                                          completionHandler:
 ^(CMSampleBufferRef buf, NSError *err) {
     NSData* data =
         [AVCaptureStillImageOutput jpegStillImageNSDataRepresentation:buf];
     UIImage* im = [UIImage imageWithData:data];
     dispatch_async(dispatch_get_main_queue(), ^{
         UIImageView* iv =
             [[UIImageView alloc] initWithFrame:self.previewLayer.frame];
         iv.contentMode = UIViewContentModeScaleAspectFit;
         iv.image = im;
         [self.view addSubview: iv];
         [self.iv removeFromSuperview];
         self.iv = iv;
         [self.previewLayer removeFromSuperlayer];
         self.previewLayer = nil;
         [self.sess stopRunning];
     });
 }];
```

My favorite part of that example is that capturing the image emits, automatically, the
built-in "shutter" sound!

Our code has not illustrated setting the focus, changing the flash settings, and so forth;
doing so is not difficult (see the class documentation on AVCaptureDevice), but note
that you should wrap such changes in calls to lockForConfiguration: and unlockFor-
Configuration. Also, always call the corresponding is...Supported: method before
setting any feature of an AVCaptureDevice; for example, before setting the flashMode,
call isFlashModeSupported: for that mode. You can turn on the LED "torch" by setting

the back camera's `torchMode` to `AVCaptureTorchModeOn`, even if no AVCaptureSession is running.

You can stop the flow of video data by setting the AVCaptureConnection's `enabled` to NO, and there are some other interesting AVCaptureConnection features, mostly involving stabilization of the video image (not relevant to the example, because a preview layer's video isn't stabilized). Plus, AVCaptureVideoPreviewLayer provides methods for converting between layer coordinates and capture device coordinates; without such methods, this can be a very difficult problem to solve. New in iOS 7, you can scan bar codes, shoot video at 60 frames per second (on some devices), and more.

AV Foundation's control over the camera, and its ability to process incoming data — especially video data — goes far deeper than there is room to discuss here, so consult the documentation; in particular, see the "Media Capture" chapter of the *AV Foundation Programming Guide*. There are also excellent WWDC videos on AV Foundation, and some fine sample code; I found Apple's AVCam example very helpful while preparing this discussion.

CHAPTER 18

Address Book

The user's address book, which the user sees through the Contacts app, is effectively a database that can be accessed directly through the Address Book framework. You'll need to @import AddressBook. This is, unfortunately, a C API, which means that you're going to be doing a lot of manual memory management.

A user interface for interacting with the address book is also provided, through Objective-C classes, by the Address Book UI framework. You'll need to @import AddressBookUI.

Address Book Database

The address book is an ABAddressBookRef obtained by calling ABAddressBookCreateWithOptions. There are in fact no options to pass, so the first parameter is always nil. The important thing is the second parameter, a pointer to a CFErrorRef; if the result is nil, the CFErrorRef describes the error. The reason there can be an error is that the user can deny your app access to the address book:

```
CFErrorRef err = nil;
ABAddressBookRef adbk = ABAddressBookCreateWithOptions(nil, &err);
if (nil == adbk) {
    NSLog(@"error: %@", err);
    return;
}
```

If access has neither been denied nor granted, however, the result will *not* be nil, and there will be *no* CFErrorRef. This can be a disaster, because you are now working with an ABAddressBookRef that is non-nil but is nevertheless invalid and useless, and whatever further actions you perform involving the address book will fail. To prevent this, you should call ABAddressBookGetAuthorizationStatus to learn the current status. If it is kABAuthorizationStatusNotDetermined, you should request authorization from the user before attempting to use the address book.

To request authorization when the authorization status is kABAuthorizationStatusNot-Determined, call ABAddressBookRequestAccessWithCompletion; it takes a completion handler that is called asynchronously, so you'll want to request authorization in a method that runs *before* you do anything involving the address book. Calling ABAddressBook-RequestAccessWithCompletion if access has already been granted does *not* summon the authorization request.

Calling ABAddressBookRequestAccessWithCompletion requires an ABAddressBook-Ref. If the authorization status was kABAuthorizationStatusNotDetermined and you call ABAddressBookRequestAccessWithCompletion with that ABAddressBookRef and access is granted, that ABAddressBookRef springs to life and becomes useful.

All of that suggests the following approach. I ascertain authorization status in my view controller's viewDidAppear:. I have an instance variable _authDone, so that viewDid-Appear: doesn't run this routine more than once, and an id property adbk, where I'll store a reference to the ABAddressBookRef — but only if access is granted. Thus, adbk serves both as an ABAddressBookRef usable by any subsequent methods for database access and as a flag telling those methods whether access has been granted; moreover, because it has been wrapped in an id property, this ABAddressBookRef is automatically memory-managed by ARC:

```
- (void) viewDidAppear:(BOOL)animated {
    [super viewDidAppear:animated];
    if (!self->_authDone) {
        self->_authDone = YES;
        ABAuthorizationStatus stat = ABAddressBookGetAuthorizationStatus();
        switch (stat) {
            case kABAuthorizationStatusDenied:
            case kABAuthorizationStatusRestricted: {
                NSLog(@"%@", @"no access");
                break;
            }
            case kABAuthorizationStatusAuthorized:
            case kABAuthorizationStatusNotDetermined: {
                CFErrorRef err = nil;
                ABAddressBookRef adbk =
                    ABAddressBookCreateWithOptions(nil, &err);
                if (nil == adbk) {
                    NSLog(@"error: %@", err);
                    return;
                }
                ABAddressBookRequestAccessWithCompletion
                    (adbk, ^(bool granted, CFErrorRef error) {
                        if (granted)
                            self.adbk = CFBridgingRelease(adbk);
                        else
```

```
                            NSLog(@"error: %@", error);
                });
        }
    }
 }
}
```

You can modify the body of the system alert prompting the user to grant your app permission to access the user's Contacts, by setting the "Privacy — Contacts Usage Description" key (NSContactsUsageDescription) in your app's *Info.plist* to tell the user *why* you want to access the address book. This is a kind of "elevator pitch"; you need to persuade the user in very few words.

If the user has denied your app access, you can't make the system alert appear again. You can, of course, use some other interface to request that the user grant access in the Settings app, under Privacy → Contacts. (If the authorization status is kABAuthorizationStatusRestricted, however, there's no point doing that, as the user is incapable of granting access.)

 To retest the system alert and other access-related behaviors, go to the Settings app and choose General → Reset → Reset Location & Privacy. This, unfortunately, causes the system to revert to its default settings for *everything* in the Privacy section of Settings: Location Services and all System Services will be On, and all permissions lists will be empty.

 If the user does in fact switch to the Settings app and enables access for your app under Privacy → Contacts, your app will be terminated in the background! This is unfortunate, but is probably not a bug; Apple presumably feels that in this situation your app cannot continue coherently and should start over from scratch.

Assuming that access has been granted, ABAddressBookCreateWithOptions returns a usable ABAddressBookRef object. This method's name contains "Create," so you must CFRelease the ABAddressBookRef when you're finished with it. (But don't release it until you *are* finished with it!) The address book's data starts out exactly the same as the user's Contacts data. If you make any changes to the data, they are not written through to the user's real address book until you call ABAddressBookSave.

The address book can change while your app is running (the user might edit with the Calendar app, or changes might percolate in from the network), which can put your information out of date. You can call ABAddressBookRegisterExternalChange-Callback, passing it the address of a function to be called when there's a change; this function must take three parameters: an ABAddressBookRef, a CFDictionaryRef, and a pointer-to-void. Apple recommends that, if you don't have (or can afford to lose) any unsaved changes, you should simply call `ABAddressBookRevert`, causing your reference to the address book to be updated.

The primary constituent record of the address book database is the ABPerson. You'll typically extract persons from the address book by using these functions:

- `ABAddressBookGetPersonCount`
- `ABAddressBookGetPersonWithRecordID`
- `ABAddressBookCopyPeopleWithName`
- `ABAddressBookCopyArrayOfAllPeople`

The result of the latter two is a CFArrayRef. Their names contain "Copy," so you must `CFRelease` the array when you're finished with it. (I'm going to stop reminding you about memory management from here on.)

An ABPerson doesn't formally exist as a type; it is actually an ABRecord (ABRecordRef), and by virtue of this has an ID, a type, and properties with values. To fetch the value of a property, you'll call `ABRecordCopyValue`, supplying a property identifier to specify the property that interests you. ABPerson properties, as you might expect, include things like first name, last name, and email.

Working with a property value is a little tricky, because the way you treat it depends on what type of value it is. You can learn a property value's type dynamically by calling `ABPersonGetTypeOfProperty`, but usually you'll know in advance. Some values are simple, but some are not. For example, a last name is a string, which is straightforward. But a person can have more than one email, so an email value is a "multistring." To work with it, you'll treat it as an ABMultiValue (ABMultiValueRef). This is like an array of values where each value also has a label and an identifier. The label categorizes (for example, a Home email as opposed to a Work email) but is not a unique specifier (because a person might have, say, two or more Work emails); the identifier is the unique specifier.

A person's address is even more involved because not only is it an ABMultiValue (a person can have more than one address), but also a particular address is itself a dictionary (a CFDictionary). Each dictionary may have a key for street, city, state, country, and so on. There is a lot more to parsing address book information, but that's enough to get you started.

We are now ready for an example! Assume we've already run the `viewDidAppear:` method I showed earlier. I'll fetch my own record out of the address book database on my device and detect that I've got two email addresses:

```
ABAddressBookRef adbk = (__bridge ABAddressBookRef)self.adbk;
if (!adbk)
    return;
ABRecordRef moi = nil;
CFArrayRef matts =
    ABAddressBookCopyPeopleWithName(adbk, (CFStringRef)@"Matt");
// might be multiple matts; let's find the one with last name Neuburg
for (CFIndex ix = 0; ix < CFArrayGetCount(matts); ix++) {
    ABRecordRef matt = CFArrayGetValueAtIndex(matts, ix);
    CFStringRef last = ABRecordCopyValue(matt, kABPersonLastNameProperty);
    if (last && CFStringCompare(last, (CFStringRef)@"Neuburg", 0) == 0)
        moi = matt;
    if (last) CFRelease(last);
}
if (nil == moi) {
    NSLog(@"Couldn't find myself");
    if (matts) CFRelease(matts);
    return;
}
// parse my emails
ABMultiValueRef emails = ABRecordCopyValue(moi, kABPersonEmailProperty);
for (CFIndex ix = 0; ix < ABMultiValueGetCount(emails); ix++) {
    CFStringRef label = ABMultiValueCopyLabelAtIndex(emails, ix);
    CFStringRef value = ABMultiValueCopyValueAtIndex(emails, ix);
    NSLog(@"I have a %@ address: %@", label, value);
    if (label) CFRelease(label);
    if (value) CFRelease(value);
}
if (emails) CFRelease(emails);
if (matts) CFRelease(matts);
/*
output:
I have a _$!<Home>!$_ address: matt@tidbits.com
I have a _$!<Work>!$_ address: matt@tidbits.com
*/
```

You can also modify an existing record, add a new record (ABAddressBookAddRecord), and delete a record (ABAddressBookRemoveRecord). In this example, I'll create a person called Snidely Whiplash with a Home email snidely@villains.com, add him to the database, and save the database:

```
// ... obtain adbk as before ...
ABRecordRef snidely = ABPersonCreate();
ABRecordSetValue(snidely, kABPersonFirstNameProperty, @"Snidely", nil);
ABRecordSetValue(snidely, kABPersonLastNameProperty, @"Whiplash", nil);
ABMutableMultiValueRef addr =
    ABMultiValueCreateMutable(kABStringPropertyType);
ABMultiValueAddValueAndLabel(addr,
    @"snidely@villains.com", kABHomeLabel, nil);
ABRecordSetValue(snidely, kABPersonEmailProperty, addr, nil);
```

Figure 18-1. A contact created programmatically

```
ABAddressBookAddRecord(adbk, snidely, nil);
ABAddressBookSave(adbk, nil);
if (addr) CFRelease(addr);
if (snidely) CFRelease(snidely);
```

Sure enough, if we then check the state of the database through the Contacts app, the new person exists (Figure 18-1).

There are also groups (ABGroup); a group, like a person, is a record (ABRecord), so you can add a new group, delete an existing group, add a person to a group, and remove a person from a group (which is more than the Contacts app allows the user to do!). A group doesn't own a person, nor a person a group; they are independent, and a person can be associated with multiple groups just as a group is associated with multiple persons. At an even higher level, there are sources (yet another kind of ABRecord): a person or group might be on the device or might come from an Exchange server or a CardDAV server. The source really does, in a sense, own the group or person; a person can't belong to two sources. A complicating factor, however, is that the same *real* person might appear in two different sources as two different ABPersons; to deal with this, it is possible for multiple persons to be linked, indicating that they are the same person. For a practical introduction to groups and sources, see Apple's ABUIGroups sample code.

Address Book Interface

The Address Book UI framework puts a user interface, similar to the Contacts app, in front of common tasks involving the address book database. This is a great help, because designing your own interface to do the same thing would be tedious and involved. The framework provides four UIViewController subclasses:

ABPeoplePickerNavigationController
> Presents a navigation interface, effectively the same as the Contacts app but without an Edit button: it lists the people in the database and allows the user to pick one and view the details.

ABPersonViewController
> Presents an interface showing the properties of a specific person in the database, possibly editable.

ABNewPersonViewController
> Presents an interface showing the editable properties of a new person.

ABUnknownPersonViewController
> Presents an interface showing a proposed person with a partial set of noneditable properties.

These view controllers operate coherently with respect to the question of whether your app has access to the address book. For example, if the user has never granted or denied your app access to the address book, attempting to use ABPeoplePickerNavigation-Controller will cause the system alert to appear, requesting access. If the user has denied your app access to the address book, the ABPeoplePickerNavigationController's view will appear, but it will be empty (like Figure 17-2). ABNewPersonViewController, similarly, will lack interface for saving into the database if your app has been denied access, and the user's only option will be to back out of the view controller. On the other hand, you can't even get started usefully with ABPersonViewController if you don't already have access, so if you lack access, you'll discover that fact beforehand.

ABPeoplePickerNavigationController

An ABPeoplePickerNavigationController is a UINavigationController. With it, the user can survey groups, along with the names of all persons in each group. Presenting it can be as simple as instantiating it, assigning it a delegate, and showing it as a presented view controller. On the iPad, you'll probably use a popover; presenting the view controller does work, but a popover looks better. (For the structure of a universal app, see Example 16-1.) Here's the code for an iPhone:

```
ABPeoplePickerNavigationController* picker =
    [ABPeoplePickerNavigationController new];
picker.peoplePickerDelegate = self; // note: not merely "delegate"
[self presentViewController:picker animated:YES completion:nil];
```

You should certainly provide a delegate, because without it the presented view will never be dismissed. This delegate is *not* the controller's `delegate` property! It is the controller's `peoplePickerDelegate` property. You should implement all three delegate methods:

`peoplePickerNavigationController:shouldContinueAfterSelectingPerson:`
> The user has tapped a person in the contacts list, provided to you as an ABRecord-Ref. You have two options:

> *Return NO*
> > The user has chosen a person and that's all you wanted done. The selected person remains selected unless the user chooses another person. You are likely to dismiss the picker at this point.

> *Return YES (and don't dismiss the picker)*
> > The view will navigate to a view of the person's properties. You can limit the set of properties the user will see at this point by setting the ABPeoplePicker-NavigationController's `displayedItems`. This is an array of NSNumbers wrapping the property identifiers such as `kABPersonEmailProperty`.

`peoplePickerNavigationController:shouldContinueAfterSelecting-`
`Person:property:identifier:`
> The user is viewing a person's properties and has tapped a property. Note that you are not handed the value of this property! You can fetch that yourself if desired, because you have the person and the property; plus, if the property has multiple values, you are handed an identifier so you can pick the correct one out of the array of values by calling `ABMultiValueGetIndexForIdentifier` and fetching the value at that index. You have two options:

> *Return NO*
> > The view is now still sitting there, displaying the person's properties. You are likely to dismiss the picker at this point.

> *Return YES*
> > This means that if the property is one that can be displayed in some other app, we will switch to that app. For example, if the user taps an address, it will be displayed in the Maps app; if the user taps an email, we will switch to the Mail app and compose a message addressed to that email.

`peoplePickerNavigationControllerDidCancel:`
> The user has cancelled; you should dismiss the picker.

In this example, we want the user to pick an email. We have limited the display of properties to emails only:

```
picker.displayedProperties = @[@(kABPersonEmailProperty)];
```

We return YES from the first delegate method. The second delegate method fetches the value of the tapped email and dismisses the picker:

```
- (BOOL)peoplePickerNavigationController:
        (ABPeoplePickerNavigationController *)peoplePicker
        shouldContinueAfterSelectingPerson:(ABRecordRef)person
        property:(ABPropertyID)property
        identifier:(ABMultiValueIdentifier)identifier {
    ABMultiValueRef emails = ABRecordCopyValue(person, property);
    CFIndex ix = ABMultiValueGetIndexForIdentifier(emails, identifier);
    CFStringRef email = ABMultiValueCopyValueAtIndex(emails, ix);
    NSLog(@"%@", email); // do something with the email here
    if (email) CFRelease(email);
    if (emails) CFRelease(emails);
    [self dismissViewControllerAnimated:YES completion:nil];
    return NO;
}
```

ABPersonViewController

An ABPersonViewController is a UIViewController. To use it, instantiate it, set its
displayedPerson and personViewDelegate (*not* delegate); in iOS 7 you must also
explicitly pass a reference to the address book to the ABPersonViewController, as its
addressBook property. Then push the ABPersonViewController onto an existing navigation controller's stack. The user's only way out of the resulting interface will be
through the back button. For example:

```
// ... obtain adbk as before ...
CFArrayRef snides =
    ABAddressBookCopyPeopleWithName(adbk, (CFStringRef)@"Snidely Whiplash");
if (CFArrayGetCount(snides) < 1) {
    NSLog(@"%@", @"No Snidely!");
    if (snides) CFRelease(snides);
    return;
}
ABRecordRef snidely = CFArrayGetValueAtIndex(snides, 0);
ABPersonViewController* pvc = [ABPersonViewController new];
pvc.addressBook = adbk;
pvc.displayedPerson = snidely;
pvc.personViewDelegate = self;
[self.navigationController pushViewController:pvc animated:YES];
if (snides) CFRelease(snides);
```

On the iPad, the same interface works, or alternatively you can use a popover. In the
latter case you'll probably make the ABPersonViewController the root view of a
UINavigationController created on the fly, especially if you intend to set allows-
Editing to YES, since without the navigation interface the Edit button won't appear.
No back button is present or needed, because the user can dismiss the popover by
tapping outside it.

You can limit the properties to be displayed, as with ABPeoplePickerNavigation-Controller, by setting the displayedProperties. You can highlight a property with set-HighlightedItemForProperty:withIdentifier:.

The delegate is notified when the user taps a property. As with ABPeoplePicker-NavigationController's second delegate method, you'll return YES to allow some other app, such as Maps or Mail, to open the tapped value; return NO to prevent this.

If ABPersonViewController's allowsActions is YES (the default), then buttons such as Send Message, FaceTime, Share Contact, and Add to Favorites appear in the interface. (Exactly what buttons appear depends on what categories of information are displayed.)

If ABPersonViewController's allowsEditing is YES (the default), the right bar button is an Edit button. If the user taps this, the interface is transformed into the same sort of editing interface as ABNewPersonViewController. The user can tap Done or Cancel; if Done, the edits are automatically saved into the database. Either way, the user returns to the original display of the person's properties.

Your code is not notified that the user has edited the person, or that the user has returned from the person view controller to the main interface. If that's the kind of thing you need to know, consider one of the next two view controllers.

ABNewPersonViewController

An ABNewPersonController is a UIViewController. To use it, instantiate it, set its new-PersonViewDelegate (*not* delegate), instantiate a UINavigationController with the ABNewPersonController as its root view, and present the navigation controller:

```
ABNewPersonViewController* npvc = [ABNewPersonViewController new];
npvc.newPersonViewDelegate = self;
UINavigationController* nc =
    [[UINavigationController alloc] initWithRootViewController:npvc];
[self presentViewController:nc animated:YES completion:nil];
```

The presented view controller works on the iPad as well. Alternatively, you can display the UINavigationController in a popover; the resulting popover is effectively modal.

The interface allows the user to fill in all properties of a new contact. You cannot limit the properties displayed. You can provide properties with default values by creating a fresh ABRecordRef representing an ABPerson with ABPersonCreate, giving it any property values you like, and assigning it to the displayedPerson property.

The delegate has one method, newPersonViewController:didCompleteWithNew-Person:, which is responsible for dismissing the presented view or popover. If the new person is nil, the user tapped Cancel. Otherwise, the user tapped Done; the new person is an ABRecordRef *and has already been saved into the database.*

But what if you don't want the new person saved into the database? What if you were presenting this interface merely because it's such a convenient way of letting the user fill in the property values of an ABPerson? Then simply remove the newly created person from the database, like this:

```
- (void)newPersonViewController:
        (ABNewPersonViewController*)newPersonViewController
        didCompleteWithNewPerson:(ABRecordRef)person {
    if (nil != person) {
        // if we didn't have access, we wouldn't be here!
        ABAddressBookRef adbk = (__bridge ABAddressBookRef)self.adbk;
        ABAddressBookRemoveRecord(adbk, person, nil);
        ABAddressBookSave(adbk, nil);
        CFStringRef name = ABRecordCopyCompositeName(person);
        NSLog(@"I have a person named %@", name);
        // do something with new person
        if (name) CFRelease(name);
    }
    [self dismissViewControllerAnimated:YES completion:nil];
}
```

ABUnknownPersonViewController

An ABUnknownPersonViewController is a UIViewController. It presents, as it were, a proposed partial person. You can set the name displayed as the controller's alternate-Name property, and the text below this as the controller's message property. You can add actual person property values just as for an ABNewPersonViewController, namely, by creating a fresh ABRecordRef representing an ABPerson with ABPersonCreate, giving it some property values, and assigning it to the displayedPerson property.

To use ABUnknownPersonViewController, instantiate it, set the properties listed in the foregoing paragraph, set its unknownPersonViewDelegate (*not* delegate), and push it onto the stack of an existing navigation controller. The user's only way out of the resulting interface will be through the back button. For example:

```
ABUnknownPersonViewController* unk =
    [ABUnknownPersonViewController new];
unk.message = @"Person who really knows trees";
unk.allowsAddingToAddressBook = YES;
ABRecordRef person = ABPersonCreate();
ABRecordSetValue(person, kABPersonFirstNameProperty, @"Johnny", nil);
ABRecordSetValue(person, kABPersonLastNameProperty, @"Appleseed", nil);
ABMutableMultiValueRef addr =
    ABMultiValueCreateMutable(kABStringPropertyType);
ABMultiValueAddValueAndLabel(addr, @"johnny@seeds.com",
                             kABHomeLabel, nil);
ABRecordSetValue(person, kABPersonEmailProperty, addr, nil);
unk.displayedPerson = person;
```

```
unk.unknownPersonViewDelegate = self;
[self.navigationController pushViewController:unk animated:YES];
if (person) CFRelease(person);
if (addr) CFRelease(addr);
```

On the iPad, make the ABUnknownPersonViewController the root view of a UINavigationController and present the navigation controller as a popover. No back button is present or needed, because the user can dismiss the popover by tapping outside it.

What the user can do here depends on two other properties:

`allowsAddingToAddressBook`
>   If YES (the default), and if your app has access to the address book, a Create New Contact button and an Add to Existing Contact button appear:
>
>   *The user taps Create New Contact*
>>   The editing interface appears (as in ABNewPersonViewController and an editable ABPersonViewController). It is filled in with the property values of the `displayedPerson`. If the user taps Done, the person is saved into the database.
>
>   *The user taps Add to Existing Contact*
>>   A list of all contacts appears (as in the first screen of ABPersonViewController). The user can Cancel or tap a person. If the user taps a person, the properties from the `displayedPerson` are merged into that person's record.

`allowsActions`
>   If YES (the default), buttons such as Send Message, FaceTime, and Share Contact appear. (Exactly what buttons appear depends on what categories of information are displayed.)

The delegate has two methods, the first of which is required:

`unknownPersonViewController:didResolveToPerson:`
>   Called if `allowsAddingToAddressBook` is YES and the user finishes working in a presented editing view. The editing view has already been dismissed and the user has either cancelled (the second parameter is nil) or has tapped Done (the second parameter is the ABPerson already saved into the database).

`unknownPersonViewController:shouldPerformDefaultActionForPerson:property:identifier:`
>   Return NO, as with ABPeoplePickerNavigationController, to prevent a tap on a property value from navigating to another app.

CHAPTER 19

Calendar

The user's calendar information, which the user sees through the Calendar app, is effectively a database of calendar events. Since iOS 6, the calendar database has also included reminders, which the user sees through the Reminders app. This database can be accessed directly through the Event Kit framework. You'll need to `@import Event-Kit`.

A user interface for interacting with the calendar is also provided, through the Event Kit UI framework. You'll need to `@import EventKitUI`.

Calendar Database

The calendar database is accessed as an instance of the EKEventStore class. This instance is expensive to obtain but lightweight to maintain, so your usual strategy will be to instantiate EKEventStore early on, maintaining that instance in an instance variable until you no longer need it (similar to what I did with the address book database in Chapter 18). In the examples in this chapter, my EKEventStore instance is called `self.database` throughout.

An attempt to work with the calendar database will fail unless the user has granted your app access to it. You should start by calling the class method `authorizationStatusFor-EntityType:` with either `EKEntityTypeEvent` (to work with calendar events) or `EKEntityTypeReminder` (to work with reminders). If the returned EKAuthorization-Status is `EKAuthorizationStatusNotDetermined`, you can call `requestAccessTo-EntityType:completion:`, with a non-nil completion block taking a BOOL and an NSError; this causes a system alert to appear, prompting the user to grant your app permission to access the user's Calendar or Reminders.

You can modify the body of this alert by setting the "Privacy — Calendars Usage Description" key (`NSCalendarsUsageDescription`) or the "Privacy — Reminders Usage

Description" key (`NSRemindersUsageDescription`) in your app's *Info.plist* to tell the user *why* you want to access the database. This is a kind of "elevator pitch"; you need to persuade the user in very few words.

I'll use my view controller's `viewDidAppear:` to check the authorization status, to ask the user for authorization if authorization has never been granted or denied, and to set `self.database` if authorization is granted; the code is exactly parallel to the first example in Chapter 18:

```
- (void)viewDidAppear:(BOOL)animated {
    [super viewDidAppear:animated];
    EKEntityType type = EKEntityTypeEvent;
    if (!self->_authDone) {
        self->_authDone = YES;
        EKAuthorizationStatus stat =
            [EKEventStore authorizationStatusForEntityType:type];
        switch (stat) {
            case EKAuthorizationStatusDenied:
            case EKAuthorizationStatusRestricted: {
                NSLog(@"%@", @"no access");
                break;
            }
            case EKAuthorizationStatusAuthorized:
            case EKAuthorizationStatusNotDetermined: {
                EKEventStore* database = [EKEventStore new];
                [database requestAccessToEntityType:type completion:
                 ^(BOOL granted, NSError *error) {
                     if (granted)
                         self.database = database;
                     else
                         NSLog(@"error: %@", error);
                 }];
            }
        }
    }
}
```

If the user has denied your app access, you can't make the system alert appear again. You can, of course, use some other interface to request that the user grant access in the Settings app, under Privacy → Calendars or Privacy → Reminders. (If the authorization status is `EKAuthorizationStatusRestricted`, however, there's no point doing that, as the user is incapable of granting access.)

To retest the system alert and other access-related behaviors, go to the Settings app and choose General → Reset → Reset Location & Privacy. This, unfortunately, causes the system to revert to its default settings for *everything* in the Privacy section of Settings: Location Services and all System Services will be On, and all permissions lists will be empty.

 If the user does in fact switch to the Settings app and enables access for your app under Privacy → Calendars or Privacy → Reminders, your app will be terminated in the background! This is unfortunate, but is probably not a bug; Apple presumably feels that in this situation your app cannot continue coherently and should start over from scratch.

Starting with an EKEventStore instance, you can obtain two kinds of object:

A calendar

A calendar represents a named (`title`) collection of calendar items, meaning events or reminders. It is an instance of EKCalendar. Curiously, however, an EKCalendar instance doesn't contain or link to its calendar items; to obtain and create calendar items, you work directly with the EKEventStore itself. A calendar's `allowedEntity-Types`, despite the plural, will probably return just one entity type; you can't create a calendar that allows both.

Calendars have various types (`type`), reflecting the nature of their origin: a calendar can be created and maintained by the user locally (`EKCalendarTypeLocal`), but it might also live remotely on the network (`EKCalendarTypeCalDAV`, `EKCalendarType-Exchange`), possibly being updated by subscription (`EKCalendarType-Subscription`); the Birthday calendar (`EKCalendarTypeBirthday`) is generated automatically from information in the address book.

The `type` is supplemented and embraced by the calendar's `source`, an EKSource whose `sourceType` can be `EKSourceTypeLocal`, `EKSourceTypeExchange`, `EKSource-TypeCalDAV` (which includes iCloud), and so forth; a source can also have a `title`, and it has a unique identifier (`sourceIdentifier`). You can get an array of all `sources` known to the EKEventStore, or specify a source by its identifier. You'll probably use the `source` exclusively and ignore the calendar's `type` property.

There are three ways of requesting a calendar:

All calendars

Fetch all calendars permitting a particular calendar item type (`EKEntityType-Event` or `EKEntityTypeReminder`) by calling `calendarsForEntityType:`. You can send this message either to the EKEventStore or to an EKSource.

Particular calendar

Fetch an individual calendar by means of a previously obtained `calendar-Identifier` by calling `calendarWithIdentifier:`.

Default calendar

Fetch the default calendar for a particular calendar item type through the `defaultCalendarForNewEvents` property or the `defaultCalendarForNew-Reminders` property; this is appropriate particularly if your intention is to create a new calendar item.

You can also create a calendar, by calling `calendarForEntityType:eventStore:`. At that point, you can specify the source to which the calendar belongs.

Depending on the source, a calendar will be modifiable in various ways. The calendar might be subscribed. If the calendar is `immutable`, you can't delete the calendar or change its attributes; but its `allowsContentModifications` might still be YES, in which case you can add, remove, and alter its events. You can update your copy of the calendar from any remote sources by calling `refreshSourcesIf-Necessary`.

A calendar item

A calendar item (EKCalendarItem) is either a calendar event (EKEvent) or a reminder (EKReminder). Think of it as a memorandum describing when something happens. As I mentioned a moment ago, you don't get calendar items from a calendar; rather, a calendar item has a `calendar`, but you get it from the EKEventStore as a whole. There are two chief ways of doing so:

By predicate

Fetch all events or reminders according to a predicate:

- `eventsMatchingPredicate:`
- `enumerateEventsMatchingPredicate:`
- `fetchRemindersMatchingPredicate:completion:`

Methods starting with `predicate...` allow you to form the predicate. The predicate specifies things like the calendar(s) the item is to come from and the item's date range. By identifier:: Fetch an individual calendar item by means of a previously obtained `calendarItemIdentifier` by calling `calendarItemWith-Identifier:`.

Changes to the database can be atomic. There are two prongs to the implementation of this feature:

- The methods for saving and removing calendar items and calendars have a `commit:` parameter. If you pass NO as the argument, the changes that you're ordering are batched; later, you can call `commit:` (or `reset` if you change your mind). If you pass NO and fail to call `commit:` later, your changes will never happen.

- An abstract class, EKObject, functions as the superclass for all the other persistent object types, such as EKCalendar, EKCalendarItem, EKSource, and so on. It endows those classes with methods `isNew` and `hasChanges`, along with `refresh`, `rollback`, and `reset`.

The calendar database is an odd sort of database, because calendars can be maintained in so many ways and places. A calendar can change while your app is running (the user might sync, or the user might edit with the Calendar app), which can put your information out of date. You can register for a single EKEventStore notification, `EKEventStoreChangedNotification`; if you receive it, you should assume that any calendar-related instances you're holding are invalid. This situation is made relatively painless, though, by the fact that every calendar-related instance can be refreshed with `refresh`. Keep in mind that `refresh` returns a Boolean; if it returns NO, this object is *really* invalid and you should stop working with it entirely (it may have been deleted from the database).

Creating Calendars and Events

Let's start by creating an events calendar. We need to assign a source; we'll choose `EKSourceTypeLocal`, meaning that the calendar will be created on the device itself.

 If an iPhone's calendar is subscribed to a remote source (such as iCloud), `EKCalendarTypeLocal` calendars are inaccessible. The examples in this chapter use a local calendar (because I don't want to risk damaging your online calendars); to test them, you'll have to unsubscribe from iCloud. The iPad can access both local and online calendars, so I regard the iPhone limitation as a bug.

Assume that the `viewWillAppear:` code from earlier in this chapter has already run. We can't ask the database for the local source directly, so we have to cycle through all sources looking for it. When we find it, we make a new calendar called "CoolCal":

```
if (!self.database)
    return;
EKSource* src = nil;
for (src in self.database.sources)
    if (src.sourceType == EKSourceTypeLocal)
        break;
if (!src) {
    NSLog(@"%@", @"failed to find local source");
    return;
}
```

```
EKCalendar* cal = [EKCalendar calendarForEntityType:EKEntityTypeEvent
                                        eventStore:self.database];
cal.source = src;
cal.title = @"CoolCal";
NSError* err;
BOOL ok = [self.database saveCalendar:cal commit:YES error:&err];
if (!ok) {
    NSLog(@"save calendar %@", err.localizedDescription);
    return;
}
NSLog(@"%@", @"no errors");
```

EKEvent is a subclass of EKCalendarItem, from which it inherits some of its important properties. If you've ever used the Calendar app in iOS or OS X, you already have a sense for how an EKEvent can be configured. It has a `title` and optional notes. It is associated with a `calendar`, as I've already said. It can have one or more alarms and one or more recurrence rules; I'll talk about both of those in a moment. All of that is inherited from EKCalendarItem. EKEvent itself adds the all-important `startDate` and `endDate` properties; these are NSDates and involve both date and time. If the event's `allDay` property is YES, the time aspect of its dates is ignored; the event is associated with a day or a stretch of days as a whole. If the event's `allDay` property is NO, the time aspect of its dates matters; a typical event will then usually be bounded by two times on the same day.

Making an event is simple, if tedious. You *must* provide a `startDate` and an `endDate`! The simplest way to construct dates is with NSDateComponents. I'll create an event and add it to our new calendar, which I'll locate by its title. We really should be using the `calendarIdentifier` to obtain our calendar; the title isn't reliable, since the user might change it, and since multiple calendars can have the same title. However, it's only an example:

```
if (!self.database)
    return;
// obtain calendar
EKCalendar* cal = nil;
NSArray* calendars =
    [self.database calendarsForEntityType:EKEntityTypeEvent];
for (cal in calendars) // (should be using identifier)
    if ([cal.title isEqualToString: @"CoolCal"])
        break;
if (!cal) {
    NSLog(@"%@", @"failed to find calendar");
    return;
}
// construct start and end dates
NSCalendar* greg =
    [[NSCalendar alloc] initWithCalendarIdentifier:NSGregorianCalendar];
NSDateComponents* comp = [NSDateComponents new];
comp.year = 2014;
```

```
comp.month = 8;
comp.day = 10;
comp.hour = 15;
NSDate* d1 = [greg dateFromComponents:comp];
comp.hour = comp.hour + 1;
NSDate* d2 = [greg dateFromComponents:comp];
// construct event
EKEvent* ev = [EKEvent eventWithEventStore:self.database];
ev.title = @"Take a nap";
ev.notes = @"You deserve it!";
ev.calendar = cal;
ev.startDate = d1;
ev.endDate = d2;
// save event
NSError* err;
BOOL ok =
    [self.database saveEvent:ev span:EKSpanThisEvent commit:YES error:&err];
if (!ok) {
    NSLog(@"save simple event %@", err.localizedDescription);
    return;
}
NSLog(@"%@", @"no errors");
```

An alarm is an EKAlarm, a very simple class; it can be set to fire either at an absolute date or at a relative offset from the event time. On an iOS device, an alarm fires through a local notification (Chapter 13). We could easily have added an alarm to our event as we were configuring it:

```
EKAlarm* alarm = [EKAlarm alarmWithRelativeOffset:-3600]; // one hour before
[ev addAlarm:alarm];
```

Recurrence

Recurrence is embodied in a recurrence rule (EKRecurrenceRule); a calendar item can have multiple recurrence rules, which you manipulate through its recurrenceRules property, along with methods addRecurrenceRule: and removeRecurrenceRule:. A simple EKRecurrenceRule is described by three properties:

Frequency
> By day, by week, by month, or by year.

Interval
> Fine-tunes the notion "by" in the frequency. A value of 1 means "every." A value of 2 means "every other." And so on.

End
> Optional, because the event might recur forever. It is an EKRecurrenceEnd instance, describing the limit of the event's recurrence either as an end date or as a maximum number of occurrences.

The options for describing a more complex EKRecurrenceRule are best summarized by its initializer:

```
- (id)initRecurrenceWithFrequency:(EKRecurrenceFrequency)type
                         interval:(NSInteger)interval
                   daysOfTheWeek:(NSArray *)days
                  daysOfTheMonth:(NSArray *)monthDays
                 monthsOfTheYear:(NSArray *)months
                 weeksOfTheYear:(NSArray *)weeksOfTheYear
                  daysOfTheYear:(NSArray *)daysOfTheYear
                   setPositions:(NSArray *)setPositions
                            end:(EKRecurrenceEnd *)end
```

The meanings of all these parameters are mostly obvious from their names. The arrays are of NSNumber, except for daysOfTheWeek, which is an array of EKRecurrenceDayOfWeek, a class that allows specification of a week number as well as a day number so that you can say things like "the fourth Thursday of the month." Many of these values can be negative to indicate counting backward from the last one. Numbers are all 1-based, not 0-based. The setPositions parameter is an array of numbers filtering the occurrences defined by the rest of the specification against the interval; for example, if daysOfTheWeek is Sunday, -1 means the final Sunday. You can use any valid combination of parameters; the penalty for an invalid combination is a return value of nil.

An EKRecurrenceRule is intended to embody the RRULE event component in the iCalendar standard specification (originally published as RFC 2445 and recently superseded by RFC 5545, *http://datatracker.ietf.org/doc/rfc5545*); in fact, the documentation tells you how each EKRecurrenceRule property corresponds to an RRULE attribute, and if you log an EKRecurrenceRule with NSLog, what you're shown *is* the underlying RRULE. RRULE can describe some amazingly sophisticated recurrence rules, such as this one:

```
RRULE:FREQ=YEARLY;INTERVAL=2;BYMONTH=1;BYDAY=SU
```

That means "every Sunday in January, every other year." Let's form this rule. Observe that we should attach it to an event whose startDate and endDate make sense as an example of the rule — that is, on a Sunday in January. Fortunately, NSDateComponents makes that easy:

```
// ... make sure we have authorization ...
// ... obtain our calendar (cal) ...
// form the rule
EKRecurrenceDayOfWeek* everySunday = [EKRecurrenceDayOfWeek dayOfWeek:1];
NSNumber* january = @1;
EKRecurrenceRule* recur =
    [[EKRecurrenceRule alloc]
     initRecurrenceWithFrequency:EKRecurrenceFrequencyYearly // every year
     interval:2 // no, every *two* years!
     daysOfTheWeek:@[everySunday]
     daysOfTheMonth:nil
```

```
        monthsOfTheYear:@[january]
        weeksOfTheYear:nil
        daysOfTheYear:nil
        setPositions: nil
        end:nil];
// create event with this rule
EKEvent* ev = [EKEvent eventWithEventStore:self.database];
ev.title = @"Mysterious biennial Sunday-in-January morning ritual";
[ev addRecurrenceRule: recur];
ev.calendar = cal;
// need a start date and end date
NSCalendar* greg =
    [[NSCalendar alloc] initWithCalendarIdentifier:NSGregorianCalendar];
NSDateComponents* comp = [NSDateComponents new];
comp.year = 2014;
comp.month = 1;
comp.weekday = 1; // Sunday
comp.weekdayOrdinal = 1; // *first* Sunday
comp.hour = 10;
ev.startDate = [greg dateFromComponents:comp];
comp.hour = 11;
ev.endDate = [greg dateFromComponents:comp];
// save the event
NSError* err;
BOOL ok = [self.database saveEvent:ev span:EKSpanFutureEvents
                            commit:YES error:&err];
if (!ok) {
    NSLog(@"save recurring event %@", err.localizedDescription);
    return;
}
NSLog(@"%@", @"no errors");
```

In that code, the event we save into the database is a recurring event. When we save or delete a recurring event, we must specify a span: argument. This is either EKSpanThis-Event or EKSpanFutureEvents, and corresponds exactly to the two buttons the user sees in the Calendar interface when saving or deleting a recurring event (Figure 19-1). The buttons and the span types reflect their meaning exactly: the change affects either this event alone, or this event plus all *future* (not past) recurrences. This choice determines not only how this and future recurrences of the event are affected now, but also how they relate to one another from now on.

Fetching Events

Now let's talk about how to extract an event from the database. One way, as I mentioned earlier, is by its unique identifier (calendarItemIdentifier). Not only is this identifier a fast and unique way to obtain an event, but also it's just a string, which means that it persists even if the EKEventStore subsequently goes out of existence. Remember to obtain it, though, while the EKEventStore *is* still in existence; an EKEvent drawn from the database loses its meaning and its usability if the EKEventStore instance is destroyed.

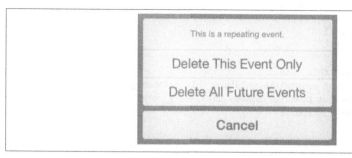

Figure 19-1. The user specifies a span

(Even this unique identifier *might* not survive changes in a calendar between launches of your app.)

You can also extract events from the database by matching a predicate (NSPredicate). To form this predicate, you specify a start and end date and an array of eligible calendars, and call the EKEventStore method `predicateForEventsWithStartDate:end-Date:calendars:`. That's the only kind of predicate you can use, so any further filtering of events is then up to you. In this example, I'll gather all events from our "CoolCal" calendar; because I have to specify a date range, I ask for events occurring over the next year. Because `enumerateEventsMatchingPredicate:` can be time-consuming, it's best to run it on a background thread (Chapter 25):

```
// ... make sure we have authorization ...
// ... obtain our calendar (cal) ...
NSDate* d1 = [NSDate date]; // today
// how to do calendrical arithmetic
NSCalendar* greg =
    [[NSCalendar alloc] initWithCalendarIdentifier:NSGregorianCalendar];
NSDateComponents* comp = [NSDateComponents new];
comp.year = 1; // we're going to add 1 to the year
NSDate* d2 = [greg dateByAddingComponents:comp toDate:d1 options:0];
NSPredicate* pred =
    [self.database predicateForEventsWithStartDate:d1 endDate:d2
                                        calendars:@[cal]];
NSMutableArray* marr = [NSMutableArray array];
dispatch_async(dispatch_get_global_queue(0, 0), ^{
    [self.database enumerateEventsMatchingPredicate:pred usingBlock:
     ^(EKEvent *event, BOOL *stop) {
        [marr addObject: event];
        if ([event.title rangeOfString:@"nap"].location != NSNotFound)
            self.napid = event.calendarItemIdentifier;
    }];
    [marr sortUsingSelector:@selector(compareStartDateWithEvent:)];
    NSLog(@"%@", marr);
});
```

That example shows you what I mean about further filtering of events. I obtain the "nap" event and the "mysterious biennial Sunday-in-January morning ritual" events, but the "nap" event is the one I really want, so I filter further to find it in the block. (In real life, if I weren't also testing this call by collecting all returned events into an array, I would then set *stop to YES to end the enumeration.) The events are enumerated in no particular order; the convenience method compareStartDateWithEvent: is provided as a sort selector to put them in order by start date.

When you extract events from the database, event recurrences are treated as separate events (as happened in the preceding example). Recurrences of the same event will have different start and end dates but the same identifier. When you fetch an event by identifier, you get the *earliest* event with that identifier. This makes sense, because if you're going to make a change affecting this and future recurrences of the event, you need the option to start with the earliest possible recurrence (so that "future" means "all").

Reminders

A reminder (EKReminder) is very parallel to an event (EKEvent); they both inherit from EKCalendarItem, so a reminder has a calendar (which the Reminders app refers to as a "list"), a title, notes, alarms, recurrence rules, and attendees. Instead of a start date and an end date, it has a start date, a due date, a completion date, and a completed property. The start date and due date are expressed directly as NSDateComponents, so you can supply as much detail as you wish: if you don't include any time components, it's an all-day reminder.

To illustrate, I'll make an all-day reminder for today:

```
// specify calendar
EKCalendar* cal = [self.database defaultCalendarForNewReminders];
if (!cal) {
    NSLog(@"%@", @"failed to find calendar");
    return;
}
// create and configure the reminder
EKReminder* rem = [EKReminder reminderWithEventStore:self.database];
rem.title = @"Get bread";
rem.calendar = cal;
NSDate* today = [NSDate date];
NSCalendar* greg =
    [[NSCalendar alloc] initWithCalendarIdentifier:NSGregorianCalendar];
unsigned comps =
    NSYearCalendarUnit | NSMonthCalendarUnit | NSDayCalendarUnit;
rem.dueDateComponents = [greg components:comps fromDate:today];
// save the reminder
NSError* err = nil;
BOOL ok = [self.database saveReminder:rem commit:YES error:&err];
if (!ok) {
```

```
        NSLog(@"save calendar %@", err.localizedDescription);
        return;
    }
    NSLog(@"%@", @"no error");
```

When you call `fetchRemindersMatchingPredicate:completion:`, the possible predicates let you fetch all reminders in given calendars, incomplete reminders, or completed reminders.

Proximity Alarms

A *proximity* alarm is triggered by the user's approaching or leaving a certain location (also known as *geofencing*). This is appropriate particularly for reminders: one might wish to be reminded of something when approaching the place where that thing can be accomplished. To form the location, you'll need to use the CLLocation class (see Chapter 22). Here, I'll attach a proximity alarm to a reminder (`rem`); the alarm will fire when I'm near my local Trader Joe's:

```
EKAlarm* alarm = [EKAlarm new];
EKStructuredLocation *loc =
    [EKStructuredLocation locationWithTitle:@"Trader Joe's"];
loc.geoLocation =
    [[CLLocation alloc] initWithLatitude:34.271848 longitude:-119.247714];
loc.radius = 10*1000; // meters
alarm.structuredLocation = loc;
alarm.proximity = EKAlarmProximityEnter; // "geofence": alarm when *arriving*
[rem addAlarm:alarm];
```

If Reminders doesn't have location access, it might ask for it when you save a reminder with a proximity alarm into the database. New in iOS 7, background use of geofencing can be disabled by the user (in the Settings app, under General → Background App Refresh). If you add a proximity alarm to the event database and the Reminders app can't perform background geofencing, the alarm will not fire (unless the Reminders app is frontmost).

Calendar Interface

The Event Kit UI framework provides three classes that manage views for letting the user work with events and calendars:

EKEventViewController
> Shows the description of a single event, possibly editable.

EKEventEditViewController
> Allows the user to create or edit an event.

EKCalendarChooser
> Allows the user to pick a calendar.

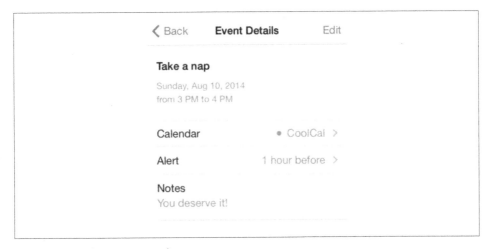

Figure 19-2. The event interface

These view controllers automatically listen for changes in the database and, if needed, will automatically call refresh on the information being edited, updating their display to match. If a view controller is displaying an event in the database and the database is deleted while the user is viewing it, the delegate will get the same notification as if the user had deleted it.

EKEventViewController

EKEventViewController shows the event display listing the event's title, date and time, calendar, alert, and notes, familiar from the Calendar app (Figure 19-2). To use EKEventViewController, instantiate it, give it an event in the database, and push it onto the stack of an existing UINavigationController. The user's only way out will be the back button.

> Do *not* use EKEventViewController for an event that isn't in the database, or at a time when the database isn't open! It won't function correctly if you do.

So, for example:

```
EKEventViewController* evc = [EKEventViewController new];
evc.event = ev; // must be an event in the database...
// ...and the database must be open (like our retained self.database)
evc.delegate = self;
evc.allowsEditing = YES;
[self.navigationController pushViewController:evc animated:YES];
```

If allowsEditing is YES (the default), an Edit button appears in the navigation bar, and by tapping this, the user can edit the various aspects of an event in the same interface as the Calendar app, including the Delete button at the bottom. If the user ultimately deletes the event, or edits it and taps Done, the change is saved into the database.

 Even if allowsEditing is NO, the user can change what calendar this event belongs to, and can change an alert's firing time if there is one. I regard this as a bug.

You can assign the EKEventViewController a delegate (EKEventViewDelegate) in order to hear about what the user did. However, the delegate method, eventView-Controller:didCompleteWithAction:, is called only if the user deletes an event or accepts an invitation. There is no EKEventViewController delegate method informing you that the user has left the interface (though of course you can learn this in some other way); if you want to know *what* editing the user may have performed on your event, you'll have to examine the event in the database.

On the iPad, you use the EKEventViewController as the root view of a navigation controller created on the fly, and set the navigation controller as a popover's view controller. A Done button appears as the right bar button; the delegate method eventView-Controller:didCompleteWithAction: is called if the user taps the Done button, and you'll need to dismiss the popover there. If allowsEditing is YES, the left bar button is the Edit button. Here's a complete example that works both on the iPhone and on the iPad:

```
- (IBAction) showEventUI:(id)sender {
    if (!self.database || !self.napid)
        return;
    // get event
    EKEvent* ev =
        (EKEvent*)[self.database calendarItemWithIdentifier:self.napid];
    if (!ev) {
        NSLog(@"failed to retrieve event");
        return;
    }
    // create and configure the controller
    EKEventViewController* evc = [EKEventViewController new];
    evc.event = ev;
    evc.delegate = self;
    evc.allowsEditing = YES;
    // on iPhone, push onto existing navigation interface
    if (UI_USER_INTERFACE_IDIOM() == UIUserInterfaceIdiomPhone)
        [self.navigationController pushViewController:evc animated:YES];
    // on iPad, create navigation interface in popover
    else {
        UINavigationController* nc =
            [[UINavigationController alloc] initWithRootViewController:evc];
```

```
            UIPopoverController* pop =
                [[UIPopoverController alloc] initWithContentViewController:nc];
            self.currentPop = pop;
            [pop presentPopoverFromRect:[sender bounds] inView:sender
                permittedArrowDirections:UIPopoverArrowDirectionAny animated:YES];
        }
    }
    -(void)eventViewController:(EKEventViewController *)controller
            didCompleteWithAction:(EKEventViewAction)action {
        if (self.currentPop && self.currentPop.popoverVisible) {
            [self.currentPop dismissPopoverAnimated:YES];
            self.currentPop = nil;
        }
    }
```

EKEventEditViewController

EKEventEditViewController (a UINavigationController) presents the interface for editing an event. To use it, set its `eventStore` and `editViewDelegate` (EKEventEditViewDelegate, *not* `delegate`), and optionally its `event`, and present it as a presented view controller (or, on the iPad, in a popover). The event can be nil for a completely empty new event; it can be an event you've just created (and possibly partially configured) and not stored in the database, or it can be an existing event from the database. If access to the database has been denied, the interface will be empty (like Figure 17-2) and the user will simply cancel.

The delegate method `eventEditViewControllerDefaultCalendarForNewEvents:` may be implemented to specify what calendar a completely new event should be assigned to. If you're partially constructing a new event, you can assign it a calendar then, and of course an event from the database already has a calendar.

You must implement the delegate method `eventEditViewController:didCompleteWithAction:` so that you can dismiss the presented view. Possible actions are that the user cancelled, saved the edited event into the database, or deleted an already existing event from the database. You can get a reference to the edited event as the EKEventEditViewController's `event`.

On the iPad, the presented view works, or you can present the EKEventEditViewController as a popover. You'll use `eventEditViewController:didCompleteWithAction:` to dismiss the popover; the user can also dismiss it by tapping outside it (in which case the user's changes are not saved to the database). Here's a complete example that works on both platforms to let the user create an event from scratch:

```
    - (IBAction)editEvent:(id)sender {
        EKEventEditViewController* evc = [EKEventEditViewController new];
        evc.eventStore = self.database;
        evc.editViewDelegate = self;
        if (UI_USER_INTERFACE_IDIOM() == UIUserInterfaceIdiomPhone)
```

```
            [self presentViewController:evc animated:YES completion:nil];
        else {
            UIPopoverController* pop =
                [[UIPopoverController alloc] initWithContentViewController:evc];
            self.currentPop = pop;
            [pop presentPopoverFromRect:[sender bounds] inView:sender
                permittedArrowDirections:UIPopoverArrowDirectionAny animated:YES];
        }
    }
    -(void)eventEditViewController:(EKEventEditViewController *)controller
            didCompleteWithAction:(EKEventEditViewAction)action {
        NSLog(@"%@", controller.event); // could do something with event here
        if (self.currentPop && self.currentPop.popoverVisible) {
            [self.currentPop dismissPopoverAnimated:YES];
            self.currentPop = nil;
        } else if (self.presentedViewController)
            [self dismissViewControllerAnimated:YES completion:nil];
    }
```

EKCalendarChooser

EKCalendarChooser displays a list of calendars. To use it, call `initWithSelection-`
`Style:displayStyle:entityType:eventStore:`, set a `delegate` (EKCalendar-
ChooserDelegate), create a UINavigationController with the EKCalendarChooser as its
root view controller, and show the navigation controller as a presented view controller
(iPhone) or a popover (iPad). The `selectionStyle` dictates whether the user can pick
one or multiple calendars; the `displayStyle` states whether all calendars or only writable calendars will be displayed. If access to the database has been denied, the interface
will be empty (like Figure 17-2) and the user will simply cancel.

Two properties, `showsCancelButton` and `showsDoneButton`, determine whether these
buttons will appear in the navigation bar. In a presented view controller, you'll certainly
show at least one and probably both, because otherwise the user has no way to dismiss
the presented view. In a popover, though, the user can dismiss the popover by tapping
elsewhere, and your delegate will hear about what the user does in the view, so depending
on the circumstances you might not need either button; for example, if your purpose is
to let the user change what calendar an existing event belongs to, this might be considered a reversible, nondestructive action, so it wouldn't need the overhead of Cancel and
Done buttons.

There are three delegate methods, all of them required:

- `calendarChooserSelectionDidChange:`
- `calendarChooserDidFinish:`
- `calendarChooserDidCancel:`

("Finish" means the user tapped the Done button.) In the Finish and Cancel methods, you'll certainly dismiss the presented view controller or popover. What else you do will depend on the circumstances.

In this example, we implement a potentially destructive action: we offer to delete the selected calendar. Because this is potentially destructive, we pass through a UIAction-Sheet for confirmation. There is no way to pass context information into a UIAction-Sheet, so we store the chosen calendar's identifier in an instance variable:

```
- (IBAction)deleteCalendar:(id)sender {
    EKCalendarChooser* choo =
    [[EKCalendarChooser alloc]
     initWithSelectionStyle:EKCalendarChooserSelectionStyleSingle
     displayStyle:EKCalendarChooserDisplayAllCalendars
     entityType:EKEntityTypeEvent
     eventStore:self.database];
    choo.showsDoneButton = YES;
    choo.showsCancelButton = YES;
    choo.delegate = self;
    UINavigationController* nav =
        [[UINavigationController alloc] initWithRootViewController:choo];
    if (UI_USER_INTERFACE_IDIOM() == UIUserInterfaceIdiomPhone)
        [self presentViewController:nav animated:YES completion:nil];
    // on iPad, create navigation interface in popover
    else {
        UIPopoverController* pop =
        [[UIPopoverController alloc] initWithContentViewController:nav];
        self.currentPop = pop;
        [pop presentPopoverFromRect:[sender bounds] inView:sender
            permittedArrowDirections:UIPopoverArrowDirectionAny animated:YES];
    }
}
-(void)calendarChooserDidCancel:(EKCalendarChooser *)calendarChooser {
    NSLog(@"chooser cancel");
    if (self.currentPop && self.currentPop.popoverVisible) {
        [self.currentPop dismissPopoverAnimated:YES];
        self.currentPop = nil;
    } else if (self.presentedViewController)
        [self dismissViewControllerAnimated:YES completion:nil];
}
-(void)calendarChooserDidFinish:(EKCalendarChooser *)calendarChooser {
    NSLog(@"chooser finish");
    NSSet* cals = calendarChooser.selectedCalendars;
    if (cals && cals.count) {
        self.calsToDelete = [cals valueForKey:@"calendarIdentifier"];
        UIActionSheet* act =
            [[UIActionSheet alloc] initWithTitle:@"Delete selected calendar?"
                delegate:self cancelButtonTitle:@"Cancel"
                destructiveButtonTitle:@"Delete" otherButtonTitles: nil];
        [act showInView:calendarChooser.view];
        return;
    }
```

```
    if (self.currentPop && self.currentPop.popoverVisible) {
        [self.currentPop dismissPopoverAnimated:YES];
        self.currentPop = nil;
    } else if (self.presentedViewController)
        [self dismissViewControllerAnimated:YES completion:nil];
}
-(void)calendarChooserSelectionDidChange:(EKCalendarChooser*)calendarChooser {
    NSLog(@"chooser change");
}
-(void)actionSheet:(UIActionSheet *)actionSheet
        didDismissWithButtonIndex:(NSInteger)buttonIndex {
    NSString* title = [actionSheet buttonTitleAtIndex:buttonIndex];
    if ([title isEqualToString:@"Delete"]) {
        for (id ident in self.calsToDelete) {
            EKCalendar* cal = [self.database calendarWithIdentifier:ident];
            if (cal)
                [self.database removeCalendar:cal commit:YES error:nil];
        }
        self.calsToDelete = nil;
    }
    if (self.currentPop && self.currentPop.popoverVisible) {
        [self.currentPop dismissPopoverAnimated:YES];
        self.currentPop = nil;
    } else if (self.presentedViewController)
        [self dismissViewControllerAnimated:YES completion:nil];
}
```

CHAPTER 20

Mail and Messages

Your app can present an interface allowing the user to edit and send a mail message or an SMS message. Two view controller classes are provided by the Message UI framework; you'll need to @import MessageUI. In addition, the Social framework lets you post to Twitter or Facebook on the user's behalf. You'll need to @import Social. The classes are:

MFMailComposeViewController
> Allows composition and sending of a mail message.

MFMessageComposeViewController
> Allows composition and sending of an SMS message.

SLComposeViewController
> Allows composition and sending of a Twitter or Facebook post. Alternatively, you can prepare and post a message directly using SLRequest.

UIActivityViewController (Chapter 13) also provides a unified interface for permitting the user to choose any of the built-in messaging milieus and to send a message through it. However, the Message UI framework and the Social framework remain important, because the user can be presented with a message form without having to pass through an activity view, and because you can fill in fields, such as the To field in a mail composition form, that UIActivityViewController doesn't let you fill in.

Mail Message

The MFMailComposeViewController class, a UINavigationController, allows the user to edit a mail message. The user can attempt to send the message there and then, or can cancel but save a draft, or can cancel completely. Before using this class to present a view, call canSendMail; if the result is NO, go no further, as a negative result means that the device is not configured for sending mail. A positive result does not mean that the device is connected to the network and can send mail right now, only that sending mail is generally possible with this device; actually sending the mail (or storing it as a draft) will be up to the device's internal processes.

To use MFMailComposeViewController, instantiate it, provide a `mailCompose-Delegate` (*not* `delegate`), and configure the message to any desired extent. Configuration methods are:

- `setSubject:`
- `setToRecipients:`
- `setCcRecipients:`
- `setBccRecipients:`
- `setMessageBody:isHTML:`
- `addAttachmentData:mimeType:fileName:`

Typically, you'll show the MFMailComposeViewController as a presented view controller. This approach works equally well on the iPad; use `UIModalPresentationForm-Sheet` if a fullscreen presentation feels too overwhelming. The user can later alter your preset configurations, at which time the message details will be out of your hands.

The delegate (MFMailComposeViewControllerDelegate) will receive the message `mail-ComposeController:didFinishWithResult:error:` describing the user's final action, which might be any of these:

- `MFMailComposeResultCancelled`
- `MFMailComposeResultSaved`
- `MFMailComposeResultSent`
- `MFMailComposeResultFailed`

Dismissing the presented view is up to you, in the delegate method. Here's a minimal example:

```
- (IBAction)doMail:(id)sender {
    BOOL ok = [MFMailComposeViewController canSendMail];
    if (!ok) return;
    MFMailComposeViewController* vc = [MFMailComposeViewController new];
    vc.mailComposeDelegate = self;
    [self presentViewController:vc animated:YES completion:nil];
}
-(void)mailComposeController:(MFMailComposeViewController *)controller
        didFinishWithResult:(MFMailComposeResult)result
```

```
        error:(NSError *)error {
    // could do something with result/error
    [self dismissViewControllerAnimated:YES completion:nil];
}
```

Text Message

The MFMessageComposeViewController class is a UINavigationController subclass. Before using this class to present a view, call `canSendText`; if the result is NO, go no further. The user has no option to save an SMS message as a draft, so even if this device sometimes *can* send text, there's no point proceeding if the device can't send text *now*. However, you can register for the `MFMessageComposeViewControllerTextMessage-AvailabilityDidChangeNotification` in the hope that the device might later be able to send text; if the notification arrives, examine its `MFMessageComposeViewController-TextMessageAvailabilityKey`.

To use MFMessageComposeViewController, instantiate the class, give it a `message-ComposeDelegate` (*not* `delegate`), and configure it as desired through the `recipients` (phone number strings) and body properties. New in iOS 7, you can also configure the message subject and provide attachments. For the subject, call the class method `canSend-Subject`, and if it returns YES, you can set the `subject`. For attachments, call the class method `canSendAttachments`, and if it returns YES, you may want to call `isSupported-AttachmentUTI:` to see if a particular file type can be sent as an attachment; finally, call `addAttachmentURL:withAlternateFilename:` (if you have a file URL) or `add-AttachmentData:typeIdentifier:filename:`.

When you've finished configuring the MFMessageComposeViewController, show it as a presented view controller. The user can later alter your preset configurations, at which time the message details will be out of your hands.

The delegate (MFMessageComposeViewControllerDelegate) will receive the message `messageComposeViewController:didFinishWithResult:` with a description of the user's final action, which might be any of these:

- `MessageComposeResultCancelled`

- `MessageComposeResultSent`

- `MessageComposeResultFailed`

Dismissing the presented view is up to you, in the delegate method. Here's a minimal example:

```
- (IBAction)doMessage:(id)sender {
    BOOL ok = [MFMessageComposeViewController canSendText];
    if (!ok) return;
    MFMessageComposeViewController* vc = [MFMessageComposeViewController new];
```

```
        vc.messageComposeDelegate = self;
        [self presentViewController:vc animated:YES completion:nil];
    }
    -(void)messageComposeViewController:(MFMessageComposeViewController*)controller
            didFinishWithResult:(MessageComposeResult)result {
        // could do something with result
        [self dismissViewControllerAnimated:YES completion:nil];
    }
```

Twitter Post

The interface for letting the user construct a Twitter post is SLComposeViewController, part of the Social framework. Twitter, together with Facebook (and Weibo), are represented by constant strings. You'll use the class method `isAvailableForServiceType:` to learn whether the desired service is available; if it is, you can instantiate SLComposeViewController for that service and present it as a presented view controller. Instead of a delegate, SLComposeViewController has a `completionHandler`. Set it to a block taking one parameter, an SLComposeViewControllerResult. In the block, dismiss the view controller. The result will be one of these:

- `SLComposeViewControllerResultCancelled`
- `SLComposeViewControllerResultDone`

Here's a minimal example:

```
BOOL ok =
    [SLComposeViewController
        isAvailableForServiceType:SLServiceTypeTwitter];
if (!ok) return;
SLComposeViewController* vc =
    [SLComposeViewController
        composeViewControllerForServiceType:SLServiceTypeTwitter];
if (!vc) return;
vc.completionHandler = ^(SLComposeViewControllerResult result) {
    // could do something with result
    [self dismissViewControllerAnimated:YES completion:nil];
};
[self presentViewController:vc animated:YES completion:nil];
```

You can also, with the user's permission, gain secure access to the user's account information through the ACAccountStore class (part of the Accounts framework). Using this, along with the SLRequest class, your app can construct and post a message *directly*, without passing through the message composition interface. The ACAccountStore class can manipulate accounts in other ways as well.

CHAPTER 21

Maps

Your app can imitate the Maps app, displaying a map interface and placing annotations and overlays on the map. The relevant classes are provided by the Map Kit framework. You'll need to `@import MapKit`. The classes used to describe locations in terms of latitude and longitude, whose names start with "CL", come from the Core Location framework, but you won't need to import it explicitly.

Displaying a Map

A map is displayed through a UIView subclass, an MKMapView. An MKMapView instance can be created in code or through the nib editor.

 To instantiate an MKMapView from the nib, you'll need to link your target explicitly to the MapKit framework (under Linked Frameworks and Libraries in the General tab when you edit the target); otherwise, your app will crash when the nib tries to load.

A map has a `type`, which is one of the following:

- `MKMapTypeStandard`
- `MKMapTypeSatellite`
- `MKMapTypeHybrid`

The area displayed on the map is its `region`, an MKCoordinateRegion. This is a struct comprising a location (a CLLocationCoordinate2D), describing the latitude and longitude of the point at the center of the region (the map's `centerCoordinate`), along with a span (an MKCoordinateSpan), describing the quantity of latitude and longitude

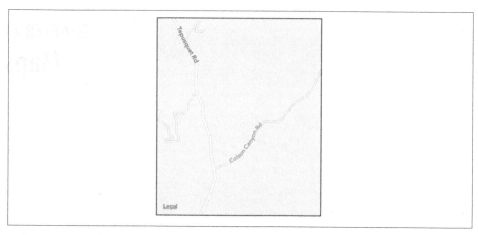

Figure 21-1. A map view showing a happy place

embraced by the region and hence the scale of the map. Convenience functions help you construct an MKCoordinateRegion.

In this example, I'll initialize the display of an MKMapView (`self.map`) to show a place where I like to go dirt biking (Figure 21-1):

```
CLLocationCoordinate2D loc =
    CLLocationCoordinate2DMake(34.927752,-120.217608);
MKCoordinateSpan span = MKCoordinateSpanMake(.015, .015);
MKCoordinateRegion reg = MKCoordinateRegionMake(loc, span);
self.map.region = reg;
```

Data types such as MKCoordinateSpan are documented in the *Map Kit Data Types Reference*, but convenience functions such as `MKCoordinateSpanMake` are documented in the *Map Kit Functions Reference* — and there are some useful constants in the *Map Kit Constants Reference*. For a better overview, refer to the *MKGeometry.h* header.

An MKCoordinateSpan is described in degrees of latitude and longitude. It may be, however, that what you know is the region's proposed dimensions in meters. To convert, call `MKCoordinateRegionMakeWithDistance`. The ability to perform this conversion is important, because an MKMapView shows the world through a Mercator projection, where longitude lines are parallel and equidistant, and scale increases at higher latitudes.

I happen to know that the area I want to display is about 1200 meters on a side. Hence, this is another way of displaying roughly the same region:

```
CLLocationCoordinate2D loc =
    CLLocationCoordinate2DMake(34.927752,-120.217608);
MKCoordinateRegion reg = MKCoordinateRegionMakeWithDistance(loc, 1200, 1200);
self.map.region = reg;
```

Another way of describing a map region is with an MKMapRect, a struct built up from MKMapPoint and MKMapSize. The earth has already been projected onto the map for us, and now we are describing a rectangle of that map, in terms of the units in which the map is drawn. The exact relationship between an MKMapPoint and the corresponding latitude/longitude coordinates is arbitrary and of no interest; what matters is that you can ask for the conversion, along with the ratio of points to meters (which will vary with latitude):

- MKMapPointForCoordinate
- MKCoordinateForMapPoint
- MKMetersPerMapPointAtLatitude
- MKMapPointsPerMeterAtLatitude
- MKMetersBetweenMapPoints

To determine what the map view is showing in MKMapRect terms, use its visibleMap-Rect property. Thus, this is yet another way of displaying approximately the same region:

```
CLLocationCoordinate2D loc =
    CLLocationCoordinate2DMake(34.927752,-120.217608);
MKMapPoint pt = MKMapPointForCoordinate(loc);
double w = MKMapPointsPerMeterAtLatitude(loc.latitude) * 1200;
self.map.visibleMapRect = MKMapRectMake(pt.x - w/2.0, pt.y - w/2.0, w, w);
```

 A map of the entire world displays MKMapRectWorld. New in iOS 7, such a map may be scrolled continuously left or right (east or west); in previous versions of iOS, it stopped at the 180th meridian, just as it stops at zero latitude north and south.

In none of those examples did I bother with the question of the actual dimensions of the map view itself. I simply threw a proposed region at the map view, and it decided how best to portray the corresponding area. Values you assign to the map's region and visibleMapRect are unlikely to be the exact values the map adopts in any case; that's because the map view will optimize for display without distorting the map's scale. You can perform this same optimization in code by calling these methods:

- regionThatFits:
- mapRectThatFits:

- `mapRectThatFits:edgePadding:`

By default, the user can zoom and scroll the map with the usual gestures; you can turn this off by setting the map view's `zoomEnabled` and `scrollEnabled` to NO. Usually you will set them both to YES or both to NO. For further customization of an MKMapView's response to touches, use a UIGestureRecognizer (Chapter 5).

You can change programmatically the region displayed, optionally with animation, by calling these methods:

- `setRegion:animated:`
- `setCenterCoordinate:animated:`
- `setVisibleMapRect:animated:`
- `setVisibleMapRect:edgePadding:animated:`

The map view's delegate (MKMapViewDelegate) is notified as the map loads and as the region changes (including changes triggered programmatically):

- `mapViewWillStartLoadingMap:`
- `mapViewDidFinishLoadingMap:`
- `mapViewDidFailLoadingMap:withError:`
- `mapView:regionWillChangeAnimated:`
- `mapView:regionDidChangeAnimated:`

New in iOS 7, you can enable 3D viewing of the map (`pitchEnabled`), and there's a large and powerful API putting control of 3D viewing in your hands. Discussion of 3D map viewing is beyond the scope of this chapter; an excellent WWDC 2013 video surveys the topic.

Annotations

An annotation is a marker associated with a location on a map. To make an annotation appear on a map, two objects are needed:

The object attached to the MKMapView
> The annotation itself is attached to the MKMapView. It consists of any instance whose class adopts the MKAnnotation protocol, which specifies a `coordinate`, a `title`, and a `subtitle` for the annotation. You might have reason to define your own class to handle this task, or you can use the simple built-in MKPointAnnotation class. The annotation's coordinate is crucial; it says where on earth the annotation should be drawn. The title and subtitle are optional, to be displayed in a callout.

The object that draws the annotation

An annotation is drawn by an MKAnnotationView, a UIView subclass. This can be extremely simple. In fact, even a nil MKAnnotationView might be perfectly satisfactory: it draws a red pin. If red is not your favorite color, a built-in MKAnnotation-View subclass, MKPinAnnotationView, displays a pin in red, green, or purple; by convention you are supposed to use these colors for different purposes (destination points, starting points, and user-specified points, respectively). For more flexibility, you can provide your own UIImage as the MKAnnotationView's `image` property. And for even *more* flexibility, you can take over the drawing of an MKAnnotation-View by overriding `drawRect:` in a subclass.

Not only does an annotation require two separate objects, but in fact those objects do not initially exist together. An annotation object has no pointer to the annotation view object that will draw it. Rather, it is up to you to supply the annotation view object in real time, on demand, in the MKMapView's delegate. This architecture may sound confusing, but in fact it's a very clever way of reducing the amount of resources needed at any given moment. An annotation itself is merely a lightweight object that a map can always possess; the corresponding annotation view is a heavyweight object that is needed only so long as that annotation's coordinates are within the visible portion of the map.

Let's add the simplest possible annotation to our map. The point where the annotation is to go has been stored in an instance variable:

```
self.annloc = CLLocationCoordinate2DMake(34.923964,-120.219558);
```

We create the annotation, configure its properties, and add it to the MKMapView:

```
MKPointAnnotation* ann = [MKPointAnnotation new];
ann.coordinate = self.annloc;
ann.title = @"Park here";
ann.subtitle = @"Fun awaits down the road!";
[self.map addAnnotation:ann];
```

That code is sufficient to produce Figure 21-2. I didn't implement any MKMapView delegate methods, so the MKAnnotationView is nil. But a nil MKAnnotationView, as I've already said, produces a red pin. I've also tapped the annotation, to display its callout, containing the annotation's title and subtitle.

Custom Annotation View

The location marked by our annotation is the starting point of a suggested dirt bike ride, so by convention the pin should be green. We can easily create a green pin using MKPinAnnotationView, which has a `pinColor` property. To supply the annotation view, we must give the map view a delegate (MKMapViewDelegate) and implement `mapView:viewForAnnotation:`.

Figure 21-2. A simple annotation

The structure of `mapView:viewForAnnotation:` is rather similar to the structure of `tableView:cellForRowAtIndexPath:` (Chapter 8), which is not surprising, considering that they both do the same sort of thing. Recall that the goal of `tableView:cellForRowAtIndexPath:` is to allow the table view to reuse cells, so that at any given moment only as many cells are needed as are *visible* in the table view, regardless of how many rows the table as a whole may consist of. The same thing holds for a map and its annotation views. The map may have a huge number of annotations, but it needs to display annotation views for only those annotations that are within its current `region`. Any extra annotation views that have been scrolled out of view can thus be reused and are held for us by the map view in a cache for exactly this purpose.

So, in `mapView:viewForAnnotation:`, we start by calling `dequeueReusableAnnotationViewWithIdentifier:` to see whether there's an already existing annotation view that's not currently being displayed and that we might be able to reuse. If there isn't, we create one, attaching to it an appropriate reuse identifier.

Here's our implementation of `mapView:viewForAnnotation:`. Observe that in creating our green pin, we explicitly set its `canShowCallout` to YES, as this is not the default:

```
- (MKAnnotationView *)mapView:(MKMapView *)mapView
            viewForAnnotation:(id <MKAnnotation>)annotation {
    MKAnnotationView* v = nil;
    if ([annotation.title isEqualToString:@"Park here"]) { ❶
        static NSString* ident = @"greenPin"; ❷
        v = [mapView dequeueReusableAnnotationViewWithIdentifier:ident];
        if (v == nil) {
            v = [[MKPinAnnotationView alloc] initWithAnnotation:annotation
                                             reuseIdentifier:ident];
            ((MKPinAnnotationView*)v).pinColor = MKPinAnnotationColorGreen;
            v.canShowCallout = YES;
        }
```

```
        v.annotation = annotation; ❸
    }
    return v;
}
```

The structure of this implementation of `mapView:viewForAnnotation:` is typical (though it seems pointlessly elaborate when we have only one annotation in our map):

❶   We might have more than one reusable type of annotation view, so we must somehow distinguish the possible cases, based on *something about the incoming annotation*. Here, I use the annotation's title as a distinguishing mark; later in this chapter, I'll suggest a much better approach.

❷   For each reusable type, we proceed much as with table view cells. We have an identifier that categorizes this sort of reusable view. We try to dequeue an unused annotation view of the appropriate type, and if we can't, we create one and configure it.

❸   Even if we *can* dequeue an unused annotation view, and even if we have no other configuration to perform, we must associate the annotation view with the incoming annotation by assigning the annotation to this annotation view's `annotation` property.

MKAnnotationView has one more option of which we might avail ourselves: when it draws the annotation view (the pin), it can animate it into place, dropping it in the manner familiar from the Maps app. All we have to do is add one line of code:

```
((MKPinAnnotationView*)v).animatesDrop = YES;
```

Now let's go further. Instead of a green pin, we'll substitute our own artwork. I'll revise the code at the heart of my `mapView:viewForAnnotation:` implementation, such that instead of creating an MKPinAnnotationView, I create an instance of its superclass, MKAnnotationView, and give it a custom image showing a dirt bike. The image is too large, so I shrink the view's bounds before returning it; I also move the view up a bit, so that the bottom of the image is at the coordinates on the map (Figure 21-3):

```
- (MKAnnotationView *)mapView:(MKMapView *)mapView
        viewForAnnotation:(id <MKAnnotation>)annotation {
    MKAnnotationView* v = nil;
    if ([annotation.title isEqualToString:@"Park here"]) {
        static NSString* ident = @"greenPin";
        v = [mapView dequeueReusableAnnotationViewWithIdentifier:ident];
        if (v == nil) {
            v = [[MKAnnotationView alloc] initWithAnnotation:annotation
                                          reuseIdentifier:ident];
            v.image = [UIImage imageNamed:@"clipartdirtbike.gif"];
            CGRect f = v.bounds;
            f.size.height /= 3.0;
            f.size.width /= 3.0;
            v.bounds = f;
```

Figure 21-3. A custom annotation image

```
            v.centerOffset = CGPointMake(0,-20);
            v.canShowCallout = YES;
        }
        v.annotation = annotation;
    }
    return v;
}
```

For more flexibility, we can create our own MKAnnotationView subclass and endow it with the ability to draw itself. At a minimum, such a subclass should override the initializer and assign itself a frame, and should implement drawRect:. Here's the implementation for a class MyAnnotationView that draws a dirt bike:

```
- (id)initWithAnnotation:(id <MKAnnotation>)annotation
        reuseIdentifier:(NSString *)reuseIdentifier {
    self = [super initWithAnnotation:annotation
                    reuseIdentifier:reuseIdentifier];
    if (self) {
        UIImage* im = [UIImage imageNamed:@"clipartdirtbike.gif"];
        self.frame =
            CGRectMake(0, 0, im.size.width/3.0 + 5, im.size.height/3.0 + 5);
        self.centerOffset = CGPointMake(0,-20);
        self.opaque = NO;
    }
    return self;
}
- (void) drawRect: (CGRect) rect {
    UIImage* im = [UIImage imageNamed:@"clipartdirtbike.gif"];
    [im drawInRect:CGRectInset(self.bounds, 5, 5)];
}
```

The corresponding implementation of mapView:viewForAnnotation: now has much less work to do:

```
- (MKAnnotationView *)mapView:(MKMapView *)mapView
        viewForAnnotation:(id <MKAnnotation>)annotation {
    MKAnnotationView* v = nil;
    if ([annotation.title isEqualToString:@"Park here"]) {
        static NSString* ident = @"bike";
        v = [mapView dequeueReusableAnnotationViewWithIdentifier:ident];
        if (v == nil) {
            v = [[MyAnnotationView alloc] initWithAnnotation:annotation
                                        reuseIdentifier:ident];
            v.canShowCallout = YES;
        }
        v.annotation = annotation;
    }
    return v;
}
```

Custom Annotation Class

For ultimate flexibility, we can provide our own annotation class as well! A minimal annotation class will look like this:

```
@interface MyAnnotation : NSObject <MKAnnotation>
@property (nonatomic) CLLocationCoordinate2D coordinate;
@property (nonatomic, copy) NSString *title, *subtitle;
- (id)initWithLocation:(CLLocationCoordinate2D)coord;
@end
@implementation MyAnnotation
- (id)initWithLocation: (CLLocationCoordinate2D) coord {
    self = [super init];
    if (self) {
        self->_coordinate = coord;
    }
    return self;
}
@end
```

Now when we create our annotation and add it to our map, our code looks like this:

```
MyAnnotation* ann = [[MyAnnotation alloc] initWithLocation:self.annloc];
ann.title = @"Park here";
ann.subtitle = @"Fun awaits down the road!";
[self.map addAnnotation:ann];
```

A major advantage of this change appears in our implementation of mapView:viewFor-Annotation:, where we test for the annotation type. Formerly, it wasn't easy to distinguish those annotations that needed to be drawn as a dirt bike; we were rather artificially examining the title:

```
if ([annotation.title isEqualToString:@"Park here"]) {
```

Now, however, we can just look at the class:

```
if ([annotation isKindOfClass:[MyAnnotation class]]) {
```

A further advantage of supplying our own annotation class is that this approach gives our implementation room to grow. For example, at the moment, every MyAnnotation is drawn as a bike, but we could now add another property to MyAnnotation that tells us what drawing to use. We could also give MyAnnotation further properties saying such things as which way the bike should face, what angle it should be drawn at, and so on. Each instance of MyAnnotationView will end up with a reference to the corresponding MyAnnotation instance (as its annotation property), so it would be able to read those MyAnnotation properties and draw itself appropriately.

Other Annotation Features

To add our own animation to an annotation view as it appears on the map, analogous to the built-in MKPinAnnotationView pin-drop animation, we implement the map view delegate method mapView:didAddAnnotationViews:. The key fact here is that at the moment this method is called, the annotation view has been added but the redraw moment has not yet arrived (Chapter 4). So if we animate the view, that animation will be performed at the moment the view appears onscreen. Here, I'll animate the opacity of the view so that it fades in, while growing the view from a point to its full size; I identify the view type through its reuseIdentifier:

```
- (void)mapView:(MKMapView *)mapView didAddAnnotationViews:(NSArray *)views {
    for (MKAnnotationView* aView in views) {
        if ([aView.reuseIdentifier isEqualToString:@"bike"]) {
            aView.transform = CGAffineTransformMakeScale(0, 0);
            aView.alpha = 0;
            [UIView animateWithDuration:0.8 animations:^{
                aView.alpha = 1;
                aView.transform = CGAffineTransformIdentity;
            }];
        }
    }
}
```

The callout is visible in Figure 21-2 and Figure 21-3 because before taking the screenshot, I tapped on the annotation, thus *selecting* it. MKMapView has methods allowing annotations to be selected or deselected programmatically, thus (by default) causing their callouts to appear or disappear. The delegate has methods notifying you when the user selects or deselects an annotation, and you are free to override your custom MKAnnotationView's setSelected:animated: if you want to change what happens when the user taps an annotation. For example, you could show and hide a custom view instead of, or in addition to, the built-in callout.

A callout can contain left and right accessory views; these are the MKAnnotationView's leftCalloutAccessoryView and rightCalloutAccessoryView. They are UIViews, and should be small (less than 32 pixels in height). In iOS 7, the map view's tint-Color (see Chapter 12) affects such accessory view elements as template images and button titles. You can respond to taps on these views as you would any view or control; as a convenience, a delegate method `mapView:annotationView:calloutAccessory-ControlTapped:` is called when the user taps an accessory view, provided it is a UI-Control.

An MKAnnotationView can optionally be draggable by the user; set its `draggable` property to YES and implement the map view delegate's `mapView:annotationView:did-ChangeDragState:fromOldState:`. You can also customize changes to the appearance of the view as it is dragged, by implementing your annotation view class's `setDrag-State:animated:` method. If you're using a custom annotation class, you'll also need to implement its `setCoordinate:` method; in our custom annotation class, My-Annotation, that's done automatically, as the `coordinate` property is synthesized and is not `readonly`.

Certain annotation properties and annotation view properties are automatically animatable through view animation, provided you've implemented them in a KVO compliant way. For example, in MyAnnotation, the `coordinate` property is synthesized, so it is KVO compliant; therefore, we are able to animate the shifting of the annotation's position:

```
[UIView animateWithDuration:0.25 animations:^{
    CLLocationCoordinate2D loc = ann.coordinate;
    loc.latitude = loc.latitude + 0.0005;
    loc.longitude = loc.longitude + 0.001;
    ann.coordinate = loc;
}];
```

MKMapView has extensive support for adding and removing annotations. New in iOS 7, given a bunch of annotations, you can ask your MKMapView to zoom in such a way that all of them are showing (`showAnnotations:animated:`).

Annotation views don't change size as the map is zoomed in and out, so if there are several annotations and they are brought close together by the user zooming out, the display can become crowded. Moreover, if too many annotations are being drawn simultaneously in a map view, scroll and zoom performance can degrade. The only way to prevent this is to respond to changes in the map's visible region (for example, in the delegate method `mapView:regionDidChangeAnimated:`) by removing and adding annotations dynamically. This is a tricky problem; new in iOS 7, MKMapView's `annotationsInMapRect:` efficiently lists the annotations within a given MKMapRect, but deciding which ones to eliminate or restore, and when, is still up to you.

Overlays

An overlay differs from an annotation in being drawn entirely with respect to points on the surface of the earth. Thus, whereas an annotation's size is always the same, an overlay's size is tied to the zoom of the map view.

Overlays are implemented much like annotations. You provide an object that adopts the MKOverlay protocol (which itself conforms to the MKAnnotation protocol) and add it to the map view. When the map view delegate method `mapView:viewFor-Overlay:` is called, you provide an MKOverlayRenderer and hand it the overlay object; the overlay renderer then draws the overlay on demand. As with annotations, this architecture means that the overlay itself is a lightweight object, and the overlay is drawn only if the part of the earth that the overlay covers is actually being displayed in the map view. An MKOverlayRenderer has no reuse identifier.

MKOverlayRenderer and related overlay classes are new in iOS 7, replacing MKOverlayView and its companions. This change is intended to improve performance; a separate UIView for each overlay was too heavy-handed, since all the overlay really needs to know is how to draw itself directly into the MKMapView's sublayer hierarchy. Fortunately, the behavior of the new classes is just the same as that of the old classes; if you have existing code from iOS 6 or before, globally replace "view" with "renderer" in the names of all classes and methods, and your code will continue to work. (I actually performed such a substitution, which is why the overlay renderer variables in my code have names like v — they used to be views!)

Some built-in MKShape subclasses adopt the MKOverlay protocol: MKCircle, MKPolygon, and MKPolyline. In parallel to those, MKOverlayRenderer has built-in subclasses MKCircleRenderer, MKPolygonRenderer, and MKPolylineRenderer, ready to draw the corresponding shapes. Thus, as with annotations, you can base your overlay entirely on the power of existing classes.

In this example, I'll use MKPolygonRenderer to draw an overlay triangle pointing up the road from the parking place annotated in our earlier examples (Figure 21-4). We add the MKPolygon as an overlay to our map view, and derive the MKPolygonRenderer from it in our implementation of `mapView:viewForOverlay:`. First, the MKPolygon overlay:

```
CGFloat lat = self.annloc.latitude;
CLLocationDistance metersPerPoint = MKMetersPerMapPointAtLatitude(lat);
MKMapPoint c = MKMapPointForCoordinate(self.annloc);
c.x += 150/metersPerPoint;
c.y -= 50/metersPerPoint;
MKMapPoint p1 = MKMapPointMake(c.x, c.y);
p1.y -= 100/metersPerPoint;
MKMapPoint p2 = MKMapPointMake(c.x, c.y);
p2.x += 100/metersPerPoint;
MKMapPoint p3 = MKMapPointMake(c.x, c.y);
```

Figure 21-4. An overlay

```
p3.x += 300/metersPerPoint;
p3.y -= 400/metersPerPoint;
MKMapPoint pts[3] = {
    p1, p2, p3
};
MKPolygon* tri = [MKPolygon polygonWithPoints:pts count:3];
[self.map addOverlay:tri];
```

Second, the delegate method, where we provide the MKPolygonRenderer:

```
- (MKOverlayRenderer *)mapView:(MKMapView *)mapView
            rendererForOverlay:(id <MKOverlay>)overlay {
    MKPolygonRenderer* v = nil;
    if ([overlay isKindOfClass:[MKPolygon class]]) {
        v = [[MKPolygonRenderer alloc] initWithPolygon:(MKPolygon*)overlay];
        v.fillColor = [[UIColor redColor] colorWithAlphaComponent:0.1];
        v.strokeColor = [[UIColor redColor] colorWithAlphaComponent:0.8];
        v.lineWidth = 2;
    }
    return v;
}
```

Custom Overlay Class

The triangle in Figure 21-4 is rather crude; I could draw a better arrow shape using a CGPath (Chapter 2). The built-in MKOverlayRenderer subclass that lets me do that is MKOverlayPathRenderer. To structure my use of MKOverlayRenderer similarly to the preceding example, I'll supply the CGPath when I add the overlay instance to the map view. No built-in class lets me do that, so I'll use a custom class, MyOverlay, that implements the MKOverlay protocol.

A minimal overlay class looks like this:

```
@interface MyOverlay : NSObject <MKOverlay>
@property (nonatomic, readonly) CLLocationCoordinate2D coordinate;
@property (nonatomic, readonly) MKMapRect boundingMapRect;
- (id) initWithRect: (MKMapRect) rect;
```

```
@end
@implementation MyOverlay
- (id) initWithRect: (MKMapRect) rect {
    self = [super init];
    if (self) {
        self->_boundingMapRect = rect;
    }
    return self;
}
- (CLLocationCoordinate2D) coordinate {
    MKMapPoint pt = MKMapPointMake(
        MKMapRectGetMidX(self.boundingMapRect),
        MKMapRectGetMidY(self.boundingMapRect));
    return MKCoordinateForMapPoint(pt);
}
@end
```

Our actual MyOverlay class will also have a `path` property; this will be a UIBezierPath that holds our CGPath and supplies it to the MKOverlayRenderer.

Just as the `coordinate` property of an annotation tells the map view where on earth the annotation is to be drawn, the `boundingMapRect` property of an overlay tells the map view where on earth the overlay is to be drawn. Whenever any part of the `boundingMap-Rect` is displayed within the map view's bounds, the map view will have to concern itself with drawing the overlay. With MKPolygon, we supplied the points of the polygon in earth coordinates and the `boundingMapRect` was calculated for us. With our custom overlay class, we must supply or calculate it ourselves.

At first it may appear that there is a typological impedance mismatch: the `boundingMap-Rect` is an MKMapRect, whereas a CGPath is defined by CGPoints. However, it turns out that these units are interchangeable: the CGPoints of our CGPath will be translated for us directly into MKMapPoints on the same scale — that is, the *distance* between any two CGPoints will be the distance between the two corresponding MKMapPoints. However, the *origins* are different: the CGPath must be described relative to the top-left corner of the `boundingMapRect` — that is, the `boundingMapRect` is described in earth coordinates, but the top-left corner of the `boundingMapRect` is {0,0} as far as the CGPath is concerned. (You might think of this difference as analogous to the difference between a UIView's frame and its bounds.)

To make life simple, I'll think in meters; actually, I'll think in chunks of 75 meters, because this turns out to be a good unit for positioning and laying out the arrow. In other words, a line one `unit` long would in fact be 75 meters long if I were to arrive at this actual spot on the earth and discover the overlay literally drawn on the ground. Having derived this chunk (`unit`), I use it to lay out the `boundingMapRect`, four units on a side and positioned slightly east and north of the annotation point (because that's where the road is). Then I simply construct the arrow shape within the 4×4-unit square, rotating it so that it points in roughly the same direction as the road:

```
// start with our position and derive a nice unit for drawing
CGFloat lat = self.annloc.latitude;
CLLocationDistance metersPerPoint = MKMetersPerMapPointAtLatitude(lat);
MKMapPoint c = MKMapPointForCoordinate(self.annloc);
CGFloat unit = 75.0/metersPerPoint;
// size and position the overlay bounds on the earth
CGSize sz = CGSizeMake(4*unit, 4*unit);
MKMapRect mr =
    MKMapRectMake(c.x + 2*unit, c.y - 4.5*unit, sz.width, sz.height);
// describe the arrow as a CGPath
CGMutablePathRef p = CGPathCreateMutable();
CGPoint start = CGPointMake(0, unit*1.5);
CGPoint p1 = CGPointMake(start.x+2*unit, start.y);
CGPoint p2 = CGPointMake(p1.x, p1.y-unit);
CGPoint p3 = CGPointMake(p2.x+unit*2, p2.y+unit*1.5);
CGPoint p4 = CGPointMake(p2.x, p2.y+unit*3);
CGPoint p5 = CGPointMake(p4.x, p4.y-unit);
CGPoint p6 = CGPointMake(p5.x-2*unit, p5.y);
CGPoint points[] = {
    start, p1, p2, p3, p4, p5, p6
};
// rotate the arrow around its center
CGAffineTransform t1 = CGAffineTransformMakeTranslation(unit*2, unit*2);
CGAffineTransform t2 = CGAffineTransformRotate(t1, -M_PI/3.5);
CGAffineTransform t3 = CGAffineTransformTranslate(t2, -unit*2, -unit*2);
CGPathAddLines(p, &t3, points, 7);
CGPathCloseSubpath(p);
// create the overlay and give it the path
MyOverlay* over = [[MyOverlay alloc] initWithRect:mr];
over.path = [UIBezierPath bezierPathWithCGPath:p];
CGPathRelease(p);
// add the overlay to the map
[self.map addOverlay:over];
```

The delegate method, where we provide the MKOverlayPathRenderer, is simple. We pull the CGPath out of the MyOverlay instance and hand it to the MKOverlayPathRenderer, also telling the MKOverlayPathRenderer how to stroke and fill that path:

```
- (MKOverlayRenderer*)mapView:(MKMapView*)mapView
        rendererForOverlay:(id <MKOverlay>)overlay {
    MKOverlayRenderer* v = nil;
    if ([overlay isKindOfClass: [MyOverlay class]]) {
        v = [[MKOverlayPathRenderer alloc] initWithOverlay:overlay];
        MKOverlayPathRenderer* vv = (MKOverlayPathRenderer*)v;
        vv.path = ((MyOverlay*)overlay).path.CGPath;
        vv.strokeColor = [UIColor blackColor];
        vv.fillColor = [[UIColor redColor] colorWithAlphaComponent:0.2];
        vv.lineWidth = 2;
    }
    return v;
}
```

Figure 21-5. A nicer overlay

The result is a much nicer arrow (Figure 21-5), and of course this technique can be generalized to draw an overlay from any CGPath we like.

Custom Overlay Renderer

For full generality, you could define your own MKOverlayRenderer subclass; your subclass must override and implement drawMapRect:zoomScale:inContext:. The incoming mapRect: parameter describes a tile of the visible map (not the size and position of the overlay). The overlay itself is available through the inherited overlay property, and conversion methods such as rectForMapRect: are provided for converting between the map's mapRect: coordinates and the overlay renderer's graphics context coordinates.

In our example, we can move the entire functionality for drawing the arrow into an MKOverlayRenderer subclass, which I'll call MyOverlayRenderer. Its initializer takes an angle: parameter, with which I'll set its angle property; now our arrow can point in any direction. Another nice benefit of this architectural change is that we can use the zoomScale: parameter to determine the stroke width. For simplicity, our implementation of drawMapRect:zoomScale:inContext: ignores the incoming mapRect value and just draws the entire arrow every time it is called:

```
- (id) initWithOverlay:(id <MKOverlay>)overlay angle: (CGFloat) ang {
    self = [super initWithOverlay:overlay];
    if (self) {
        self->_angle = ang;
    }
    return self;
}
- (void)drawMapRect:(MKMapRect)mapRect zoomScale:(MKZoomScale)zoomScale
        inContext:(CGContextRef)context {
    NSLog(@"draw this: %@", MKStringFromMapRect(mapRect));
    CGContextSetStrokeColorWithColor(context, [UIColor blackColor].CGColor);
    CGContextSetFillColorWithColor(context,
        [[UIColor redColor] colorWithAlphaComponent:0.2].CGColor);
    CGContextSetLineWidth(context, 1.2/zoomScale);
```

```
    CGFloat unit = MKMapRectGetWidth([self.overlay boundingMapRect])/4.0;
    CGMutablePathRef p = CGPathCreateMutable();
    CGPoint start = CGPointMake(0, unit*1.5);
    CGPoint p1 = CGPointMake(start.x+2*unit, start.y);
    CGPoint p2 = CGPointMake(p1.x, p1.y-unit);
    CGPoint p3 = CGPointMake(p2.x+unit*2, p2.y+unit*1.5);
    CGPoint p4 = CGPointMake(p2.x, p2.y+unit*3);
    CGPoint p5 = CGPointMake(p4.x, p4.y-unit);
    CGPoint p6 = CGPointMake(p5.x-2*unit, p5.y);
    CGPoint points[] = {
        start, p1, p2, p3, p4, p5, p6
    };
    // rotate the arrow around its center
    CGAffineTransform t1 = CGAffineTransformMakeTranslation(unit*2, unit*2);
    CGAffineTransform t2 = CGAffineTransformRotate(t1, self.angle);
    CGAffineTransform t3 = CGAffineTransformTranslate(t2, -unit*2, -unit*2);
    CGPathAddLines(p, &t3, points, 7);
    CGPathCloseSubpath(p);
    CGContextAddPath(context, p);
    CGContextDrawPath(context, kCGPathFillStroke);
    CGPathRelease(p);
}
```

To add the overlay to our map, we still must determine its MKMapRect:

```
CGFloat lat = self.annloc.latitude;
CLLocationDistance metersPerPoint = MKMetersPerMapPointAtLatitude(lat);
MKMapPoint c = MKMapPointForCoordinate(self.annloc);
CGFloat unit = 75.0/metersPerPoint;
// size and position the overlay bounds on the earth
CGSize sz = CGSizeMake(4*unit, 4*unit);
MKMapRect mr =
    MKMapRectMake(c.x + 2*unit, c.y - 4.5*unit, sz.width, sz.height);
MyOverlay* over = [[MyOverlay alloc] initWithRect:mr];
[self.map addOverlay:over];
```

The delegate, providing the overlay renderer, now has very little work to do; in our implementation, it must supply an angle for the arrow:

```
- (MKOverlayRenderer *)mapView:(MKMapView *)mapView
         rendererForOverlay:(id <MKOverlay>)overlay {
    MKOverlayRenderer* v = nil;
    if ([overlay isKindOfClass: [MyOverlay class]]) {
        v = [[MyOverlayRenderer alloc] initWithOverlay: overlay
                                                 angle: -M_PI/3.5];
    }
    return v;
}
```

Other Overlay Features

Our MyOverlay class, adopting the MKOverlay protocol, also implements the `coordinate` getter method to return the center of the `boundingMapRect`. This is crude, but it's a good minimal implementation. The purpose of the MKOverlay `coordinate` property is to specify the position where you would add an annotation describing the overlay. For example:

```
// ... create overlay and assign it a path as before ...
[self.map addOverlay:over];
MKPointAnnotation* annot = [MKPointAnnotation new];
annot.coordinate = over.coordinate;
annot.title = @"This way!";
[self.map addAnnotation:annot];
```

The MKOverlay protocol also lets you provide an implementation of `intersectsMapRect:` to refine your overlay's definition of what constitutes an intersection with itself; the default is to use the `boundingMapRect`, but if your overlay is drawn in some non-rectangular shape, you might want to use its actual shape as the basis for determining intersection.

Overlays are maintained by the map view as an array and are drawn from back to front starting at the beginning of the array. MKMapView has extensive support for adding and removing overlays, and for managing their layering order. New in iOS 7, when you add the overlay to the map, you can say where you want it drawn among the map view's sublayers; methods for adding and inserting overlays have a `level:` parameter (for example, `addOverlay:level:`). The levels are:

- `MKOverlayLevelAboveRoads` (and below labels)
- `MKOverlayLevelAboveLabels`

Figure 21-6 shows our overlay drawn with `MKOverlayLevelAboveRoads`; the road name is drawn on top of the overlay, and stands out a little more clearly.

New in iOS 7 is the MKOverlayTile class, adopting the MKOverlay protocol. It lets you superimpose, or even substitute (`canReplaceMapContent`), a map view's drawing of the map itself. It works much like CATiledLayer (Chapter 7): you provide a set of tiles at multiple sizes to match multiple zoom levels, and the map view fetches and draws the tiles needed for the current `region` and degree of zoom. In this way, for example, you could integrate your own topo map into an MKMapView's display. It takes a lot of tiles to draw an area of any size, so MKOverlayTile starts with a URL, which can be a remote URL for tiles to be fetched across the Internet.

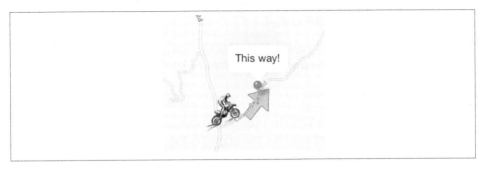

Figure 21-6. An overlay drawn behind a road label

Map Kit and Current Location

A device may have sensors that can determine its current location (Chapter 22). Map Kit provides simple integration with these facilities. Keep in mind that the user can turn off these sensors or can refuse your app access to them (in the Settings app, under Privacy → Location Services), so trying to use these features may fail. Also, determining the device's location can take time.

You can ask an MKMapView in your app to display the device's location just by setting its showsUserLocation property to YES. If your app has not been granted or denied access to Location Services, the system alert requesting authorization will appear. If access is granted, the map automatically puts an annotation at that location.

The userLocation property of the map view is an MKUserLocation, adopting the MKAnnotation protocol. It has a location property, a CLLocation, whose coordinate is a CLLocationCoordinate2D; if the map view's showsUserLocation is YES and the map view has actually worked out the user's location, the coordinate describes that location. It also has title and subtitle properties, plus you can check whether it is currently updating. In iOS 7, the default annotation appearance comes from the map view's tintColor. You are free to supply your own annotation view to be displayed for this annotation, just as for any annotation.

Displaying the appropriate region of the map — that is, actually *showing* the part of the world where the user is located — is the responsibility of the map view delegate's map-View:didUpdateUserLocation: method. Here's an example:

```
- (void)mapView:(MKMapView *)mapView
        didUpdateUserLocation:(MKUserLocation *)userLocation {
    CLLocationCoordinate2D coordinate = userLocation.location.coordinate;
    MKCoordinateRegion reg =
        MKCoordinateRegionMakeWithDistance(coordinate, 600, 600);
    mapView.region = reg;
}
```

You can ask the map view whether the user's location, if known, is in the visible region of the map (`isUserLocationVisible`).

MKMapView also has a `userTrackingMode` that you can set to determine how the user's real-world location should be tracked *automatically* by the map display; your options are:

`MKUserTrackingModeNone`

> If `showsUserLocation` is YES, the map gets an annotation at the user's location, but that's all. Deciding whether to set the map's `region` in `mapView:didUpdateUser-Location:`, as I've just shown, is up to you.

`MKUserTrackingModeFollow`

> Setting this mode sets `showsUserLocation` to YES. The map automatically centers the user's location and scales appropriately. You should *not* set the map's `region` in `mapView:didUpdateUserLocation:`, as you'll be struggling against the tracking mode's attempts to do the same thing.

`MKUserTrackingModeFollowWithHeading`

> Like `MKUserTrackingModeFollow`, but the map is also rotated so that the direction the user is facing is up. In this case, the `userLocation` annotation also has a `heading` property, a CLHeading; I'll talk more about headings in Chapter 22.

When the `userTrackingMode` is one of the `follow` modes, if the user is left free to zoom and scroll the map, and if the user scrolls in such a way that the user location annotation is no longer visible, the `userTrackingMode` may be automatically changed back to `MKUserTrackingModeNone` (and the user location annotation may be removed). You'll probably want to provide a way to let the user turn tracking back on again, or to toggle among the three tracking modes.

One way to do that is with an MKUserTrackingBarButtonItem, a UIBarButtonItem subclass. You initialize MKUserTrackingBarButtonItem with a map view, and its behavior is automatic from then on: when the user taps it, it switches the map view to the next tracking mode, and its icon reflects the current tracking mode. This is the same bar button item that appears at the far left in the toolbar of the Maps app.

Alternatively, you can ask the Maps app to display the device's current location, as I'll describe in the next section.

Communicating With the Maps App

Your app can communicate with the Maps app. For example, instead of displaying a point of interest in a map view in our own app, we can ask the Maps app to display it. The user could then bookmark or share the location. The channel of communication between your app and the Maps app is the MKMapItem class.

Figure 21-7. The Maps app displays our point of interest

Here, I'll ask the Maps app to display the same point marked by the annotation in our earlier examples, on a hybrid map portraying the same region of the earth (Figure 21-7):

```
MKPlacemark* p =
    [[MKPlacemark alloc] initWithCoordinate:self.annloc
                         addressDictionary:nil];
MKMapItem* mi = [[MKMapItem alloc] initWithPlacemark: p];
mi.name = @"A Great Place to Dirt Bike"; // label to appear in Maps app
NSValue* span = [NSValue valueWithMKCoordinateSpan:self.map.region.span];
[mi openInMapsWithLaunchOptions:
    @{MKLaunchOptionsMapTypeKey: @(MKMapTypeHybrid),
      MKLaunchOptionsMapSpanKey: span
    }
];
```

If you start with an MKMapItem returned by the class method `mapItemForCurrent-Location`, you're asking the Maps app to display the device's current location. This call doesn't attempt to determine the device's location, nor does it contain any location information; it merely generates an MKMapItem which, when sent to the Maps app, will cause *it* to attempt to determine (and display) the device's location:

```
MKMapItem* mi = [MKMapItem mapItemForCurrentLocation];
[mi openInMapsWithLaunchOptions:
    @{MKLaunchOptionsMapTypeKey:@(MKMapTypeStandard)}];
```

Geocoding, Searching, and Directions

Map Kit provides your app with three services that involve performing queries over the network. These services take time and might not succeed at all, as they depend upon network and server availability; moreover, results may be more or less uncertain. Therefore, they involve a completion handler that is called back asynchronously on the main thread. The three services are:

Geocoding
> Translation of a street address to a coordinate and *vice versa*. For example, what address am I at right now? Or conversely, what are the coordinates of my home address?

Searching
> Lookup of possible matches for a natural language search. For example, what are some Thai restaurants near me?

Directions
> Lookup of turn-by-turn instructions and route mapping from a source location to a destination location.

The completion handler is called, in every case, with a single response object plus an NSError. If the response object is nil, the NSError tells you what the problem was.

Geocoding

Geocoding functionality is encapsulated in the CLGeocoder class. The response, if things went well, is an NSArray of CLPlacemark objects, a series of guesses from best to worst; if things went *really* well, the array will contain exactly one CLPlacemark.

A CLPlacemark can be used to initialize an MKPlacemark, a CLPlacemark subclass that adopts the MKAnnotation protocol, and is therefore suitable to be handed directly over to an MKMapView for display.

Here is an (unbelievably simpleminded) example that allows the user to enter an address in a UISearchBar (Chapter 12) to be displayed in an MKMapView:

```
-(void)searchBarSearchButtonClicked:(UISearchBar *)searchBar {
    NSString* s = searchBar.text;
    [searchBar resignFirstResponder];
    CLGeocoder* geo = [CLGeocoder new];
    [geo geocodeAddressString:s
            completionHandler:^(NSArray *placemarks, NSError *error) {
        if (nil == placemarks) {
            NSLog(@"%@", error.localizedDescription);
            return;
        }
        CLPlacemark* p = [placemarks objectAtIndex:0];
        MKPlacemark* mp = [[MKPlacemark alloc] initWithPlacemark:p];
```

```
        [self.map removeAnnotations:self.map.annotations];
        [self.map addAnnotation:mp];
        [self.map setRegion:
            MKCoordinateRegionMakeWithDistance(mp.coordinate, 1000, 1000)
                    animated: YES];
    }];
}
```

By default, the resulting annotation's callout `title` contains a nicely formatted string describing the address.

That example illustrates *forward geocoding*, the conversion of an address to a coordinate. Instead of a string, you can provide a dictionary. By an amazing coincidence, the keys of this dictionary are exactly the keys you would get by extracting an address from the user's address book (Chapter 18); thus, you can go quite directly from an address book contact to a coordinate.

The converse operation is *reverse geocoding*: you start with a coordinate — actually a CLLocation, which you'll obtain from elsewhere, or construct from a coordinate using `initWithLatitude:longitude:` — and call `reverseGeocodeLocation:completionHandler:` in order to obtain an address. The address is expressed through the CLPlacemark `addressDictionary` property, which is an address in address book format; you can translate it to a string with `ABCreateStringWithAddressDictionary`. Alternatively, you can consult directly various CLPlacemark properties, such as `subthoroughfare` (such as a house number), `thoroughfare` (a street name), `locality` (a town), and `administrativeArea` (a state).

 Those properties are present in a placemark resulting from forward geocoding as well; thus, one nice byproduct of forward geocoding is that it can format and complete an address, including adding a zip code (`postalCode`) to the address.

In this example of reverse geocoding, we have an MKMapView that is already tracking the user, and so we have the user's location as the map's `userLocation`; we ask for the corresponding address:

```
CLGeocoder* geo = [CLGeocoder new];
CLLocation* loc = self.map.userLocation.location;
[geo reverseGeocodeLocation:loc
        completionHandler:^(NSArray *placemarks, NSError *error)
    {
        if (placemarks) {
            CLPlacemark* p = [placemarks objectAtIndex:0];
            NSLog(@"%@", p.addressDictionary); // do something with address
        }
    }];
```

Searching

The MKLocalSearch class, along with MKLocalSearchRequest and MKLocalSearchResponse, lets you ask the server to perform a natural language search for you. This is less formal than forward geocoding, described in the previous section; instead of searching for an address, you can search for a point of interest by name or description. It can be useful, for some types of search, to constrain the area of interest by setting the MKLocalSearchRequest's region. In this example, I'll do a natural language search for a Thai restaurant near the area currently displayed in the map, and I'll display it with an annotation in our map view:

```
- (IBAction) thaiFoodNearMapLocation: (id) sender {
    MKLocalSearchRequest* req = [MKLocalSearchRequest new];
    req.naturalLanguageQuery = @"Thai restaurant";
    req.region = self.map.region;
    MKLocalSearch* search = [[MKLocalSearch alloc] initWithRequest:req];
    [search startWithCompletionHandler:
     ^(MKLocalSearchResponse *response, NSError *error) {
        if (!response) {
            NSLog(@"%@", error);
            return;
        }
        self.map.showsUserLocation = NO;
        MKMapItem* where = response.mapItems[0]; // I'm feeling lucky
        MKPlacemark* place = where.placemark;
        CLLocationCoordinate2D loc = place.location.coordinate;
        MKCoordinateRegion reg =
        MKCoordinateRegionMakeWithDistance(loc, 1200, 1200);
        [self.map setRegion:reg animated:YES];
        MKPointAnnotation* ann = [MKPointAnnotation new];
        ann.title = where.name;
        ann.subtitle = where.phoneNumber;
        ann.coordinate = loc;
        [self.map addAnnotation:ann];
    }];
}
```

Directions

The MKDirections class (new in iOS 7), along with MKDirectionsRequest and MKDirectionsResponse, looks up walking or driving directions between two locations expressed as MKMapItem objects. The resulting MKDirectionsResponse includes an array of MKRoute objects; each MKRoute includes an MKPolyline suitable for display as an overlay in your map, as well as an array of MKRouteStep objects, each of which provides its own MKPolyline plus instructions and distances. The MKDirectionsResponse also has its own source and destination MKMapItems, which may be different from what we started with.

To illustrate, I'll continue from the Thai food example in the previous section. Presume that the map is displaying my location, and that we have performed the search from the previous section, so that the MKMapItem `where` corresponds to the restaurant location:

```
MKDirectionsRequest* req = [MKDirectionsRequest new];
req.source = [MKMapItem mapItemForCurrentLocation];
req.destination = where;
MKDirections* dir = [[MKDirections alloc] initWithRequest:req];
[dir calculateDirectionsWithCompletionHandler:
 ^(MKDirectionsResponse *response, NSError *error) {
    if (!response) {
        NSLog(@"%@", error);
        return;
    }
    MKRoute* route = response.routes[0]; // just get me there!
    MKPolyline* poly = route.polyline;
    [self.map addOverlay:poly];
    for (MKRouteStep* step in route.steps) {
        NSLog(@"In %d meters: %@", (int)step.distance, step.instructions);
    }
}];
```

The step-by-step instructions appear in the console; in real life, of course, we would presumably display these in our app's interface. The route is drawn in our map view, provided we have an appropriate implementation of `mapView:rendererForOverlay:`, such as this:

```
- (MKOverlayRenderer *)mapView:(MKMapView *)mapView
            rendererForOverlay:(id <MKOverlay>)overlay {
    MKPolylineRenderer* v = nil;
    if ([overlay isKindOfClass:[MKPolyline class]]) {
        v = [[MKPolylineRenderer alloc]
            initWithPolyline:(MKPolyline*)overlay];
        v.strokeColor = [[UIColor blueColor] colorWithAlphaComponent:0.8];
        v.lineWidth = 2;
    }
    return v;
}
```

CHAPTER 22

Sensors

A device may contain hardware for sensing the world around itself — where it is located, how it is oriented, how it is moving.

Information about the device's current location and how that location is changing over time, using its Wi-Fi, cellular networking, and GPS capabilities, along with information about the device's orientation relative to north, using its magnetometer, is provided through the Core Location framework. You'll need to `@import CoreLocation`.

Information about the device's change in speed and attitude using its accelerometer is provided through the UIEvent class (for device shake) and the Core Motion framework, which provides increased accuracy by incorporating the device's gyroscope, if it has one, as well as the magnetometer; you'll need to `@import CoreMotion`.

One of the major challenges associated with writing code that takes advantage of the sensors is that not all devices have all of this hardware. If you don't want to impose stringent restrictions on what devices your app will run on in the first place (`UIRequired-DeviceCapabilities` in *Info.plist*), your code must be prepared to fail gracefully and possibly provide a subset of its full capabilities when it discovers that the current device lacks certain features.

Moreover, certain sensors may experience momentary inadequacy; for example, Core Location might not be able to get a fix on the device's position because it can't see cell towers, GPS satellites, or both. And some sensors take time to "warm up," so that the values you'll get from them initially will be invalid. You'll want to respond to such changes in the external circumstances, in order to give the user a decent experience of your application regardless.

Core Location

The Core Location framework provides facilities for the device to determine and report its location (*location services*). It takes advantage of three sensors:

Wi-Fi
> The device, if Wi-Fi is turned on, may scan for nearby Wi-Fi devices and compare these against an online database.

Cell
> The device, if it has cell capabilities and they are not turned off, may compare nearby telephone cell towers against an online database.

GPS
> The device's GPS, if it has one, may be able to obtain a position fix from GPS satellites.

Core Location will automatically use whatever facilities the device has available; all *you* have to do is ask for the device's location. Core Location allows you to specify how accurate a position fix you want; more accurate fixes may require more time.

The notion of a location is encapsulated by the CLLocation class and its properties, which include:

`coordinate`
> A CLLocationCoordinate2D, a struct consisting of two doubles representing latitude and longitude.

`altitude`
> A CLLocationDistance, which is a double representing a number of meters.

`speed`
> A CLLocationSpeed, which is a double representing meters per second.

`course`
> A CLLocationDirection, which is a double representing degrees (*not* radians) clockwise from north.

`horizontalAccuracy`
> A CLLocationAccuracy, which is a double representing meters.

`timestamp`
> An NSDate.

In addition to the sensor-related considerations I mentioned a moment ago, use of Core Location poses the following challenges:

- Accuracy of a reported location may vary depending on a number of factors. The GPS is the most accurate location sensor, but it takes the longest to get a fix.

- Battery usage due to running the sensors is a serious concern. The GPS in particular is probably the most battery-intensive of all the onboard sensors.

- Behavior of your app may depend on the device's physical location. To help you test, Xcode lets you pretend that the device is at a particular location on earth. The Simulator's Debug → Location menu lets you enter a location; the Scheme editor lets you set a default location (under Options); and the Debug → Simulate Location menu lets you switch among locations. You can set a built-in location or supply a standard GPX file containing a waypoint. You can also set the location to None; it's important to test for what happens when no location information is available.

Basic Location Determination

To use Core Location and location services directly, you need a location manager — a CLLocationManager instance. Use of a location manager typically operates along the following lines:

1. You'll confirm that the desired services are available. CLLocationManager class methods let you find out whether the user has switched on the device's location services as a whole (`locationServicesEnabled`), whether the user has authorized *this* app to use location services (`authorizedStatus`), and whether a particular service is available.

   If location services are switched off, you can start using a location manager anyway, as a way of getting the runtime to present the dialog asking the user to switch them on. Be prepared, though, for the possibility that the user won't do so. You can modify the body of this alert by setting the "Privacy — Location Usage Description" key (`NSLocationUsageDescription`) in your app's *Info.plist* to tell the user *why* you want to use location services. This is a kind of "elevator pitch"; you need to persuade the user in very few words.

2. You'll instantiate CLLocationManager and retain the instance somewhere, usually an instance variable.

3. You'll set yourself as the location manager's delegate (CLLocationManager-Delegate).

4. You'll configure the location manager. I'll talk more about this in a moment.

5. You'll tell the location manager to begin generating information; for example, you'll call `startUpdatingLocation`. The location manager, in turn, will begin calling the appropriate delegate method repeatedly; in the case of `startUpdatingLocation`, it's `locationManager:didUpdateLocations:`. Your delegate will also always implement `locationManager:didFailWithError:`, to receive error messages. You'll

deal with each delegate method call in turn. Remember to call the corresponding stop... method when you no longer need location services.

Here are some location manager configuration properties that are useful to set:

desiredAccuracy
Your choices are:

- kCLLocationAccuracyBestForNavigation
- kCLLocationAccuracyBest
- kCLLocationAccuracyNearestTenMeters
- kCLLocationAccuracyHundredMeters
- kCLLocationAccuracyKilometer
- kCLLocationAccuracyThreeKilometers

It might be sufficient for your purposes to know very quickly but very roughly the device's location, and recall that highest accuracy may also cause the highest battery drain; indeed, kCLLocationAccuracyBestForNavigation is supposed to be used only when the device is connected to external power. The accuracy setting is not a filter: the location manager will send you whatever location information it has, even if it isn't as accurate as you asked for, and checking a location's horizontalAccuracy is then up to you.

distanceFilter
Perhaps you don't need a location report unless the device has moved a certain distance since the previous report. This property can help keep you from being bombarded with events you don't need.

activityType
Your choices are:

- CLActivityTypeOther
- CLActivityTypeAutomotiveNavigation
- CLActivityTypeFitness
- CLActivityTypeOtherNavigation

This affects how persistently and frequently updates will be sent, based on the movement of the device. With CLActivityTypeAutomotiveNavigation, updates can cease temporarily if the device is not moving significantly. With CLActivityTypeFitness, on the other hand, the user is assumed to be on foot, so updates will arrive even if the device is stationary.

New in iOS 7, you may be able to use the Core Motion framework's CMMotionActivityManager to learn what the user seems to be doing, along with a record of what the user has been doing earlier (e.g. walking or in a moving vehicle). This feature requires a special app entitlement and permission from the user, as well as appropriate hardware — presumably an iPhone 5S with the separate M7 chip. See also the new CMStepCounter, which accesses the record of the user's steps.

As a simple example, we'll turn on location services manually, just long enough to see if we can determine our position. We begin by ascertaining that location services are in fact available and that we have or can get authorization. If all is well, we instantiate CLLocationManager and retain it in an instance variable (`self.locman`), set ourselves as the delegate, configure the location manager, set some instance variables so we can track what's happening, and call `startUpdatingLocation` to turn on location services:

```
BOOL ok = [CLLocationManager locationServicesEnabled];
if (!ok) {
    NSLog(@"%@", @"Alas");
    return;
}
CLAuthorizationStatus stat = [CLLocationManager authorizationStatus];
if (stat == kCLAuthorizationStatusRestricted ||
    stat == kCLAuthorizationStatusDenied) {
    NSLog(@"%@", @"Oh well");
    return;
}
if (self.trying)
    return;
self.trying = YES;
CLLocationManager* locman = [CLLocationManager new];
self.locman = locman;
locman.delegate = self;
locman.desiredAccuracy = kCLLocationAccuracyBest;
locman.activityType = CLActivityTypeFitness;
self.startTime = nil;
[self.locman startUpdatingLocation];
```

We have a utility method for turning off updates and resetting our instance variables:

```
-(void) stopTrying {
    [self.locman stopUpdatingLocation];
    self.startTime = nil;
    self.trying = NO;
}
```

If something goes wrong, such as the user refusing to authorize this app, we'll just turn location services back off:

```
-(void)locationManager:(CLLocationManager *)manager
        didFailWithError:(NSError *)error {
    NSLog(@"%@", error);
    [self stopTrying];
}
```

If things *don't* go wrong, we'll be handed our location as soon as it is determined, in
`locationManager:didUpdateLocations:`. For purposes of this example, I'm going to
insist on a fairly high level of accuracy; if I don't get it, I wait for the next update. But I
don't want to wait too long, either, so on the very first pass I record the current time, so
that I can compare the location's `timestamp` on subsequent calls. (I also return immediately from the first update, as I find this seems to contain spurious information.) If I
get the desired accuracy within the desired time, I turn off updates and am ready to use
the location information:

```
#define REQ_ACC 10
#define REQ_TIME 10
-(void)locationManager:(CLLocationManager *)manager
        didUpdateLocations:(NSArray *)locations {
    CLLocation* loc = locations.lastObject;
    CLLocationAccuracy acc = loc.horizontalAccuracy;
    NSDate* time = loc.timestamp;
    CLLocationCoordinate2D coord = loc.coordinate;
    if (!self.startTime) {
        self.startTime = [NSDate date];
        return; // ignore first attempt
    }
    NSLog(@"%f", acc);
    NSTimeInterval elapsed = [time timeIntervalSinceDate:self.startTime];
    if (elapsed > REQ_TIME) {
        NSLog(@"%@", @"This is taking too long");
        [self stopTrying];
        return;
    }
    if (acc < 0 || acc > REQ_ACC) {
        return; // wait for the next one
    }
    // got it
    NSLog(@"You are at: %f %f", coord.latitude, coord.longitude);
    [self stopTrying];
}
```

Feel free to experiment with different values for the required accuracy and the required
time. On my device, it was clearly worth waiting a few seconds to get better accuracy:

```
2013-11-09 08:36:24.149 ch35p1032location[561:60b] 936.537122
2013-11-09 08:36:24.160 ch35p1032location[561:60b] 936.537159
2013-11-09 08:36:24.178 ch35p1032location[561:60b] 936.537511
2013-11-09 08:36:24.262 ch35p1032location[561:60b] 65.000000
2013-11-09 08:36:24.698 ch35p1032location[561:60b] 65.000000
2013-11-09 08:36:28.161 ch35p1032location[561:60b] 50.000000
```

```
2013-11-09 08:36:29.157 ch35p1032location[561:60b] 30.000000
2013-11-09 08:36:29.940 ch35p1032location[561:60b] 30.000000
2013-11-09 08:36:30.943 ch35p1032location[561:60b] 10.000000
2013-11-09 08:36:30.944 ch35p1032location[561:60b] You are at: ...
```

Heading

For appropriately equipped devices, Core Location supports use of the magnetometer to determine which way the device is facing (its *heading*). Although this information is accessed through a location manager, you do *not* need location services to be turned on, nor your app to be authorized, merely to use the magnetometer to report the device's orientation with respect to *magnetic* north; but you do need those things in order to report *true* north, as this depends on the device's location.

As with location, you'll first check that the desired feature is available (heading-Available); then you'll instantiate and configure the location manager, and call start-UpdatingHeading. The delegate will be sent locationManager:didUpdateHeading: (or locationManager:didFailWithError:). A heading object is a CLHeading instance; its magneticHeading and trueHeading properties are CLLocationDirection values, which report degrees (*not* radians) clockwise from the reference direction (magnetic or true north, respectively).

In this example, I'll use the device as a compass. The headingFilter setting is to prevent us from being bombarded constantly with readings. For best results, the device should probably be held level (like a tabletop, or a compass); we are setting the heading-Orientation so that the reported heading will be the direction in which the top of the device (the end away from the Home button) is pointing:

```
BOOL ok = [CLLocationManager headingAvailable];
if (!ok) {
    NSLog(@"drat");
    return;
}
CLLocationManager* lm = [CLLocationManager new];
self.locman = lm;
self.locman.delegate = self;
self.locman.headingFilter = 5;
self.locman.headingOrientation = CLDeviceOrientationPortrait;
[self.locman startUpdatingHeading];
```

In the delegate, I'll display our magnetic heading as a rough cardinal direction in a label in the interface (self.lab):

```
-(void)locationManager:(CLLocationManager *)manager
    didUpdateHeading:(CLHeading *)newHeading {
    CGFloat h = newHeading.magneticHeading;
    CGFloat h2 = newHeading.trueHeading; // will be -1
    __block NSString* dir = @"N";
    NSArray* cards = @[@"N", @"NE", @"E", @"SE",
```

```
                    @"S", @"SW", @"W", @"NW"];
    [cards enumerateObjectsUsingBlock:
     ^(id obj, NSUInteger idx, BOOL *stop) {
         if (h < 45.0/2.0 + 45*idx) {
             dir = obj;
             *stop = YES;
         }
     }];
    if (![self.lab.text isEqualToString:dir])
        self.lab.text = dir;
}
```

In that code, I asked only for the heading's `magneticHeading`. I can ask for its `true-Heading`, but the resulting value will be invalid (a negative number) unless we are *also* receiving location updates.

 If the user has switched off Compass Calibration in the Settings app (under Privacy → Location Services → System Services), the value of the heading's `trueHeading` will *always* be a negative number.

Background Location

You can use Core Location when your app is not in the foreground. There are two quite different ways to do this:

Continuous background location
> This is an extension of what we did earlier. You tell the location manager to `start-UpdatingLocation`, and updates are permitted to continue even if the app goes into the background. Your app runs in the background in order to receive these updates (except during periods when you elect to receive deferred updates, if the hardware supports it).

Significant event monitoring
> The system monitors location for you. Your app does not run in the background. If a significant location event occurs, your app is awakened in the background (or launched in the background, if it is not running) and notified. For example, a reminder alarm uses region monitoring to notify the user when approaching or leaving a specific place (*geofencing*), as shown in Chapter 19.

New in iOS 7, the user can deny your app any background use of Core Location. The user does this in the Settings app, under General → Background App Refresh; the user may switch off either Background App Refresh as a whole or the ability of your app in particular to use Core Location in the background. You can determine the situation through the shared UIApplication instance's `backgroundRefreshStatus` property; the possibilities are:

- `UIBackgroundRefreshStatusRestricted`
- `UIBackgroundRefreshStatusDenied`
- `UIBackgroundRefreshStatusAvailable`

If the status is not `UIBackgroundRefreshStatusAvailable` and your app goes into the background, your app won't receive any delegate update messages until it is frontmost once again. If your app was receiving delegate update messages in the background and the user kills your app (from the app switcher interface), the system won't relaunch it to receive delegate update messages.

Continuous background location

Use of Core Location to perform continuous background updates is similar to production and recording of sound in the background (Chapter 14): you set the `UIBackground-Modes` key of your app's *Info.plist*, giving it a value of `location` (in Xcode 5, check Location Updates under Background Modes in the Capabilities tab when editing the target). This tells the system that if you have a location manager to which you have sent `startUpdatingLocation` and the user sends your app into the background, your app should not be suspended, the use of location services should continue, and your delegate should keep receiving Core Location events.

Background use of location services can cause a power drain, but if you want your app to function as a positional data logger, for instance, it may be the only way; you can also help conserve power by making judicious choices, such as setting a coarse `distance-Filter` value, by not requiring overly high accuracy, and by being correct about the `activityType`.

Core Location may be able to operate in deferred mode (`allowDeferredLocation-UpdatesUntilTraveled:timeout:`) so that your background app doesn't receive updates until the user has moved a specified amount or until a fixed time interval has elapsed; this, too, can help conserve power, especially if the user locks the screen, as the device may be able to power down some of its sensors temporarily, and your app can be allowed to stop running in the background. This feature is dependent on hardware capabilities; use it only if the class method `deferredLocationUpdatesAvailable` returns YES. For this feature to work, the location manager's `desiredAccuracy` must be `kCLLocationAccuracyBest` or `kCLLocationAccuracyBestForNavigation`, and its `distanceFilter` must be `kCLDistanceFilterNone` (the default).

When you're using deferred updates, updates are accumulated and then delivered all at once after the specified distance or time: the delegate is sent these messages:

- `locationManager:didFinishDeferredUpdatesWithError:`

- `locationManager:didUpdateLocations:`

The second parameter of the second delegate method is an NSArray of all the accumulated updates. At this point, deferred updating has ceased; asking for the next set of updates to be deferred is up to you, by calling `allowDeferred...` again. If the user brings your app to the foreground, any undelivered accumulated updates are delivered then and there, so that your interface can present the most recent information.

Significant event monitoring

Using Core Location to perform significant event monitoring without being in the foreground doesn't require your app to run in the background, and you do *not* have to set the `UIBackgroundModes` of your *Info.plist*. There are two types of significant event monitoring:

Significant location monitoring
> If the class method `significantLocationChangeMonitoringAvailable` returns YES, you can call `startMonitoringSignificantLocationChanges`. The delegate's `locationManager:didUpdateLocations:` will be called when the device's location has changed significantly.

Region monitoring
> New in iOS 7, region monitoring has been divided into two types, which I'll call old-fashioned region monitoring and iBeacon monitoring. (iBeacon monitoring is so new that it's virtually experimental, and isn't discussed in this book.) To distinguish the two types, the old CLRegion class has been made abstract and broken into two subclasses, CLBeaconRegion and CLCircularRegion.
>
> Thus, to perform old-fashioned region monitoring in iOS 7, the procedure now is: first check the class method `isMonitoringAvailableForClass:` with an argument of [CLCircularRegion class]. If it returns YES, then you can call `startMonitoringForRegion:` for each region in which you are interested. Regions are collected as an NSSet, which is the location manager's `monitoredRegions`.

A region in iOS 7 is a CLCircularRegion, initialized with `initWithCenter:radius:identifier:`; the `identifier` serves as a unique key, so that if you start monitoring for a region whose identifier matches that of a region already in the `monitoredRegions` set, the latter will be ejected from the set. You should also set the region's `notifyOnEntry` or `notifyOnExit` to NO if you're interested in just one type of event.

The following delegate methods may be called:

- `locationManager:didEnterRegion:`
- `locationManager:didExitRegion:`
- `locationManager:monitoringDidFailForRegion:withError:`

Both significant location monitoring and region monitoring use cell tower position to estimate the device's location. Since the cell is probably working anyway — for example, the device is a phone, so the cell is always on and is always concerned with what cell towers are available — little or no additional power is required. Apple says that the system will also take advantage of other clues (requiring no extra battery drain) to decide that there may have been a change in location: for example, the device may observe a change in the available Wi-Fi networks, strongly suggesting that the device has moved.

Notifications for location monitoring and region monitoring can arrive even if your app isn't in the foreground. In that case, there are two possible states in which your app might find itself when an event arrives:

Your app is suspended in the background
Your app is woken up (remaining in the background) long enough to receive the normal delegate event and do something with it.

Your app is not running at all
Your app is relaunched (remaining in the background), and your app delegate will be sent `application:didFinishLaunchingWithOptions:` with an NSDictionary containing `UIApplicationLaunchOptionsLocationKey`, thus allowing it to discern the special nature of the situation. At this point you probably have no location manager — your app has just launched from scratch. So you should get yourself a location manager and start up location services for long enough to receive the normal delegate event.

Acceleration and Attitude

Acceleration results from the application of a force to the device, and is detected through the device's accelerometer, supplemented by the gyroscope if it has one. Gravity is a force, so the accelerometer always has something to measure, even if the user isn't consciously applying a force to the device; thus the device can report its attitude relative to the vertical.

Acceleration information can arrive in two ways:

As a prepackaged UIEvent
You can receive a UIEvent notifying you of a predefined gesture performed by accelerating the device. At present, the only such gesture is the user shaking the device.

With the Core Motion framework

You instantiate CMMotionManager and then obtain information of a desired type. You can ask for accelerometer information, gyroscope information, or device motion information (and you can also use Core Motion to get magnetometer information); device motion combines the gyroscope data with data from the other sensors to give you the best possible description of the device's attitude in space.

Shake Events

A shake event is a UIEvent (Chapter 5). Receiving shake events is rather like receiving remote events (Chapter 14), involving the notion of the first responder. To receive shake events, your app must contain a UIResponder which:

- Returns YES from `canBecomeFirstResponder`
- Is in fact first responder

This responder, or a UIResponder further up the responder chain, should implement some or all of these methods:

`motionBegan:withEvent:`
Something has started to happen that might or might not turn out to be a shake.

`motionEnded:withEvent:`
The motion reported in `motionBegan:withEvent:` is over and has turned out to be a shake.

`motionCancelled:withEvent:`
The motion reported in `motionBegan:withEvent:` wasn't a shake after all.

It might be sufficient to implement `motionEnded:withEvent:`, because this arrives if and only if the user performs a shake gesture. The first parameter will be the event subtype, but at present this is guaranteed to be `UIEventSubtypeMotionShake`, so testing it is pointless.

The view controller in charge of the current view is a good candidate to receive shake events. Thus, a minimal implementation might look like this:

```
- (BOOL) canBecomeFirstResponder {
    return YES;
}
- (void) viewDidAppear: (BOOL) animated {
    [super viewDidAppear: animated];
    [self becomeFirstResponder];
}
- (void)motionEnded:(UIEventSubtype)motion withEvent:(UIEvent *)event {
    NSLog(@"hey, you shook me!");
}
```

By default, if some other object is first responder, and is of a type that supports undo (such as a UITextField), and if motionBegan:withEvent: is sent up the responder chain, and if you have not set the shared UIApplication's applicationSupportsShakeToEdit property to NO, a shake will be handled through an Undo or Redo alert. Your view controller might not want to rob any responders in its view of this capability. A simple way to prevent this is to test whether the view controller is itself the first responder; if it isn't, we call super to pass the event on up the responder chain:

```
- (void)motionEnded:(UIEventSubtype)motion withEvent:(UIEvent *)event {
    if ([self isFirstResponder])
        NSLog(@"hey, you shook me!");
    else
        [super motionEnded:motion withEvent:event];
}
```

Raw Acceleration

If the device has an accelerometer but no gyroscope, you can learn about the forces being applied to it, but some compromises will be necessary. The chief problem is that, even if the device is completely motionless, its acceleration values will constitute a normalized vector pointing toward the center of the earth, popularly known as *gravity*. The accelerometer is thus constantly reporting a combination of gravity and user-induced acceleration. This is good and bad. It's good because it means that, with certain restrictions, you can use the accelerometer to detect the device's attitude in space. It's bad because gravity values and user-induced acceleration values are mixed together. Fortunately, there are ways to separate these values mathematically:

With a low-pass filter
    A low-pass filter will damp out user acceleration so as to report gravity only.

With a high-pass filter
    A high-pass filter will damp out the effect of gravity so as to detect user acceleration only, reporting a motionless device as having zero acceleration.

In some situations, it is desirable to apply both a low-pass filter and a high-pass filter, so as to learn both the gravity values and the user acceleration values. A common additional technique is to run the output of the high-pass filter itself through a low-pass filter to reduce noise and small twitches. Apple provides some nice sample code for implementing a low-pass or a high-pass filter; see especially the AccelerometerGraph example, which is also very helpful for exploring how the accelerometer behaves.

The technique of applying filters to the accelerometer output has some serious downsides, which are inevitable in a device that lacks a gyroscope:

- It's up to you to apply the filters; you have to implement boilerplate code and hope that you don't make a mistake.

- Filters mean *latency*. Your response to the accelerometer values will lag behind what the device is actually doing; this lag may be noticeable.

Reading raw accelerometer values with Core Motion is really a subset of how you read *any* values with Core Motion; in some ways it is similar to how you use Core Location:

1. You start by instantiating CMMotionManager; retain the instance somewhere, typically as an instance variable.

2. Confirm, using instance properties, that the desired hardware is available.

3. Set the interval at which you wish the motion manager to update itself with new sensor readings.

4. Call the appropriate `start` method.

5. Poll the motion manager whenever you want data, asking for the appropriate `data` property. This step is surprising; you probably expected that the motion manager would call into a delegate, but in fact a motion manager has no delegate. The polling interval doesn't have to be the same as the motion manager's update interval; when you poll, you'll obtain the motion manager's *current* data — that is, the data generated by its most recent update, whenever that was.

   If your app's purpose is to collect all the data, then instead of calling a `start` method, you can call a `start...UpdatesToQueue:withHandler:` method and receive callbacks in a block, possibly on a background thread, managed by an NSOperation-Queue (Chapter 25); but this is an advanced technique and you aren't likely to need it, so I'm not going to talk about it.

6. Don't forget to call the corresponding `stop` method when you no longer need data.

In this example, I will simply report whether the device is lying flat on its back. I start by creating and configuring my motion manager, and I launch a repeating timer to trigger polling:

```
self.motman = [CMMotionManager new];
if (!self.motman.accelerometerAvailable) {
    NSLog(@"oh well");
    return;
}
self.motman.accelerometerUpdateInterval = 1.0 / 30.0;
[self.motman startAccelerometerUpdates];
self.timer =
    [NSTimer
        scheduledTimerWithTimeInterval:
            self.motman.accelerometerUpdateInterval
        target:self selector:@selector(pollAccel:)
        userInfo:nil repeats:YES];
```

My `pollAccel:` method is now being called repeatedly. In `pollAccel:`, I ask the motion manager for its accelerometer data. This arrives as a CMAccelerometerData object, which is a timestamp plus a CMAcceleration; a CMAcceleration is simply a struct of three values, one for each axis of the device, measured in Gs. The positive x-axis points to the right of the device. The positive y-axis points toward the top of the device, away from the Home button. The positive z-axis points out the front of the screen.

The two axes orthogonal to gravity, which are the x- and y-axes when the device is lying more or less on its back, are much more accurate and sensitive to small variation than the axis pointing toward or away from gravity. So our approach is to ask first whether the x and y values are close to zero; only then do we use the z value to learn whether the device is on its back or on its face. To keep from updating our interface constantly, we implement a crude state machine; the state (an instance variable) starts out at -1, and then switches between 0 (device on its back) and 1 (device not on its back), and we update the interface only when there is a state change:

```
CMAccelerometerData* dat = self.motman.accelerometerData;
CMAcceleration acc = dat.acceleration;
CGFloat x = acc.x;
CGFloat y = acc.y;
CGFloat z = acc.z;
CGFloat accu = 0.08;
if (fabs(x) < accu && fabs(y) < accu && z < -0.5) {
    if (self->_state == -1 || self->_state == 1) {
        self->_state = 0;
        self.label.text = @"I'm lying on my back... ahhh...";
    }
} else {
    if (self->_state == -1 || self->_state == 0) {
        self->_state = 1;
        self.label.text = @"Hey, put me back down on the table!";
    }
}
```

This works, but it's sensitive to small motions of the device on the table. To damp this sensitivity, we can run our input through a low-pass filter. The low-pass filter code comes straight from Apple's own examples, and involves maintaining the previously filtered reading as a set of instance variables:

```
-(void)addAcceleration:(CMAcceleration)accel {
    double alpha = 0.1;
    self->_oldX = accel.x * alpha + self->_oldX * (1.0 - alpha);
    self->_oldY = accel.y * alpha + self->_oldY * (1.0 - alpha);
    self->_oldZ = accel.z * alpha + self->_oldZ * (1.0 - alpha);
}
```

Our polling code now starts out by passing the data through the filter:

```
CMAccelerometerData* dat = self.motman.accelerometerData;
CMAcceleration acc = dat.acceleration;
[self addAcceleration: acc];
CGFloat x = self->_oldX;
CGFloat y = self->_oldY;
CGFloat z = self->_oldZ;
// ... and the rest is as before ...
```

In this next example, the user is allowed to slap the side of the device into an open hand — perhaps as a way of telling it to go to the next or previous image or whatever it is we're displaying. We pass the acceleration input through a high-pass filter to eliminate gravity (again, the filter code comes straight from Apple's examples):

```
-(void)addAcceleration:(CMAcceleration)accel {
    double alpha = 0.1;
    self->_oldX =
        accel.x - ((accel.x * alpha) + (self->_oldX * (1.0 - alpha)));
    self->_oldY =
        accel.y - ((accel.y * alpha) + (self->_oldY * (1.0 - alpha)));
    self->_oldZ =
        accel.z - ((accel.z * alpha) + (self->_oldZ * (1.0 - alpha)));
}
```

What we're looking for, in our polling routine, is a high positive or negative x value. A single slap is likely to consist of several consecutive readings above our threshold, but we want to report each slap only once, so we take advantage of the timestamp attached to a CMAccelerometerData, maintaining the timestamp of our previous high reading as an instance variable and ignoring readings that are too close to one another in time. Another problem is that a sudden jerk involves both an acceleration (as the user starts the device moving) and a deceleration (as the device stops moving); thus a left slap might be preceded by a high value in the opposite direction, which we might interpret wrongly as a right slap. We can compensate crudely, at the expense of some latency, with delayed performance (the report: method simply logs to the console):

```
CMAccelerometerData* dat = self.motman.accelerometerData;
CMAcceleration acc = dat.acceleration;
[self addAcceleration: acc];
CGFloat x = self->_oldX;
CGFloat thresh = 1.0;
if ((x < -thresh) || (x > thresh))
    NSLog(@"%f", x);
if (x < -thresh) {
    if (dat.timestamp - self->_oldTime > 0.5 || self->_lastSlap == 1) {
        self->_oldTime = dat.timestamp;
        self->_lastSlap = -1;
        [NSObject cancelPreviousPerformRequestsWithTarget:self];
        [self performSelector:@selector(report:)
            withObject:@"left" afterDelay:0.5];
    }
}
if (x > thresh) {
```

```
    if (dat.timestamp - self->_oldTime > 0.5 || self->_lastSlap == -1) {
        self->_oldTime = dat.timestamp;
        self->_lastSlap = 1;
        [NSObject cancelPreviousPerformRequestsWithTarget:self];
        [self performSelector:@selector(report:)
            withObject:@"right" afterDelay:0.5];
    }
}
```

The gesture we're detecting is a little tricky to make: the user must slap the device into an open hand *and hold it there*; if the device jumps out of the open hand, that movement may be detected as the last in the series, resulting in the wrong report (left instead of right, or *vice versa*). And the latency of our gesture detection is very high; here's a typical successful detection of a leftward slap:

```
2013-11-09 18:19:56.055 ch35p1041smackMe[954:60b] -1.175150
2013-11-09 18:19:56.122 ch35p1041smackMe[954:60b] 1.086159
2013-11-09 18:19:56.189 ch35p1041smackMe[954:60b] 1.077831
2013-11-09 18:19:56.222 ch35p1041smackMe[954:60b] -2.716380
2013-11-09 18:19:56.289 ch35p1041smackMe[954:60b] -1.086869
2013-11-09 18:19:56.725 ch35p1041smackMe[954:60b] left
```

The gesture started with an involuntary shake; then the rapid acceleration to the left was detected as a positive value; finally, the rapid deceleration was detected as a negative value, and it took several tenths of a second for our delayed performance to decide that this was the end of the gesture and report a leftward slap. Of course we might try tweaking some of the magic numbers in this code to improve accuracy and performance, but a more sophisticated analysis would probably involve storing a stream of all the most recent CMAccelerometerData objects and studying the entire stream to work out the overall trend.

Gyroscope

The inclusion of an electronic gyroscope in the panoply of onboard hardware in some devices has made a huge difference in the accuracy and speed of gravity and attitude reporting. A gyroscope has the property that its attitude in space remains constant; thus it can detect any change in the attitude of the containing device. This has two important consequences for accelerometer measurements:

- The accelerometer can be supplemented by the gyroscope to detect quickly the difference between gravity and user-induced acceleration.
- The gyroscope can observe pure rotation, where little or no acceleration is involved and so the accelerometer would not have been helpful. The extreme case is constant attitudinal rotation around the gravity axis, which the accelerometer alone would be completely unable to detect (because there is no user-induced force, and gravity remains constant).

It is possible to track the raw gyroscope data: make sure the device has a gyroscope (gyroAvailable), and then call startGyroUpdates. What we get from the motion manager is a CMGyroData object, which combines a timestamp with a CMRotationRate that reports the *rate of rotation* around each axis, measured in radians per second, where a positive value is *counterclockwise* as seen by someone whose eye is pointed to by the positive axis. (This is the opposite of the direction graphed in Figure 3-9.) The problem, however, is that the gyroscope values are *scaled* and *biased*. This means that the values are based on an arbitrary scale and are increasing (or decreasing) at a roughly constant rate. Thus there is very little merit in the exercise of dealing with the raw gyroscope data.

What you are likely to be interested in is a combination of at least the gyroscope and the accelerometer. The mathematics required to combine the data from these sensors can be daunting. Fortunately, there's no need to know anything about that. Core Motion will happily package up the calculated combination of data as a CMDeviceMotion instance, with the effects of the sensors' internal bias and scaling already factored out. CMDeviceMotion consists of the following properties, all of which provide a triple of values corresponding to the device's natural 3D frame (x increasing to the right, y increasing to the top, z increasing out the front):

gravity
  A CMAcceleration expressing a vector with value 1 pointing to the center of the earth, measured in Gs.

userAcceleration
  A CMAcceleration describing user-induced acceleration, with no gravity component, measured in Gs.

rotationRate
  A CMRotationRate describing how the device is rotating around its own center. This is essentially the CMGyroData rotationRate with scale and bias accounted for.

magneticField
  A CMCalibratedMagneticField describing (in its field, a CMMagneticField) the magnetic forces acting on the device, measured in microteslas. The sensor's internal bias has already been factored out. The accuracy is one of the following:

  • CMMagneticFieldCalibrationAccuracyUncalibrated

  • CMMagneticFieldCalibrationAccuracyLow

  • CMMagneticFieldCalibrationAccuracyMedium

  • CMMagneticFieldCalibrationAccuracyHigh

attitude

A CMAttitude, descriptive of the device's instantaneous attitude in space. When you ask the motion manager to start generating updates, you can ask for any of four reference systems for the `attitude` (having first called the class method `available-AttitudeReferenceFrames` to ascertain that the desired reference frame is available on this device). In every case, the negative z-axis points at the center of the earth:

`CMAttitudeReferenceFrameXArbitraryZVertical`

The x-axis and y-axis, though orthogonal to the other axes, could be pointing anywhere.

`CMAttitudeReferenceFrameXArbitraryCorrectedZVertical`

The same as in the previous option, but the magnetometer is used to maintain accuracy (preventing drift of the reference frame over time).

`CMAttitudeReferenceFrameXMagneticNorthZVertical`

The x-axis points toward magnetic north.

`CMAttitudeReferenceFrameXTrueNorthZVertical`

The x-axis points toward true north. This value will be inaccurate unless you are also using Core Location to obtain the device's location.

The `attitude` value's numbers can be accessed through various CMAttitude properties corresponding to three different systems, each being convenient for a different purpose:

pitch, roll, yaw

The device's angle of offset from the reference frame, in radians, around the device's natural x-axis, y-axis, and z-axis respectively.

rotationMatrix

A CMRotationMatrix struct embodying a 3×3 matrix expressing a rotation in the reference frame.

quaternion

A CMQuaternion describing an attitude. (Quaternions are commonly used in OpenGL.)

In this example, we turn the device into a simple compass/clinometer, merely by asking for its `attitude` with reference to magnetic north and taking its `pitch`, `roll`, and `yaw`. We begin by making the usual preparations; notice the use of the `showsDeviceMovement-Display` property, intended to allow the runtime to prompt the user if the magnetometer needs calibration:

```
self.motman = [CMMotionManager new];
if (!self.motman.deviceMotionAvailable) {
    NSLog(@"oh well");
    return;
```

```
    }
    CMAttitudeReferenceFrame f =
        CMAttitudeReferenceFrameXMagneticNorthZVertical;
    if ((([CMMotionManager availableAttitudeReferenceFrames] & f) == 0) {
        NSLog(@"darn");
        return;
    }
    self.motman.showsDeviceMovementDisplay = YES;
    self.motman.deviceMotionUpdateInterval = 1.0 / 30.0;
    [self.motman startDeviceMotionUpdatesUsingReferenceFrame:f];
    NSTimeInterval t = self.motman.deviceMotionUpdateInterval * 10;
    self.timer =
        [NSTimer scheduledTimerWithTimeInterval:t target:self
            selector:@selector(pollAttitude:) userInfo:nil repeats:YES];
```

In pollAttitude:, we wait until the magnetometer is ready, and then we start taking attitude readings (converted to degrees):

```
    CMDeviceMotion* mot = self.motman.deviceMotion;
    if (mot.magneticField.accuracy <= CMMagneticFieldCalibrationAccuracyLow)
        return; // not ready yet
    CMAttitude* att = mot.attitude;
    CGFloat deg = 180.0 / M_PI; // I like degrees
    NSLog(@"%f %f %f", att.pitch*deg, att.roll*deg, att.yaw*deg);
```

The values are all close to zero when the device is level with its x-axis pointing to magnetic north, and each value increases as the device is rotated *counterclockwise* with respect to an eye that has the corresponding positive axis pointing at it. So, for example, a device held upright (top pointing at the sky) has a pitch approaching 90; a device lying on its right edge has a roll approaching 90; and a device lying on its back with its top pointing north has a yaw approaching -90.

There are some quirks in the way Euler angles operate mathematically:

- roll and yaw increase with counterclockwise rotation from 0 to π (180 degrees) and then jump to -π (-180 degrees) and continue to increase to 0 as the rotation completes a circle; but pitch increases to $\pi/2$ (90 degrees) and then decreases to 0, then decreases to -$\pi/2$ (-90 degrees) and increases to 0. This means that attitude alone, if we are exploring it through pitch, roll, and yaw, is insufficient to describe the device's attitude, since a pitch value of, say, $\pi/4$ (45 degrees) could mean two different things. To distinguish those two things, we can supplement attitude with the z-component of gravity:

```
    NSLog(@"%f %f %f", att.pitch*deg, att.roll*deg, att.yaw*deg);
    CMAcceleration g = mot.gravity;
    NSLog(@"pitch is tilted %@", g.z > 0 ? @"forward" : @"back");
```

- Values become inaccurate in certain orientations. In particular, when pitch is ±90 degrees (the device is upright or inverted), roll and yaw become erratic. (You may see this effect referred to as "the singularity" or as "gimbal lock.") I believe that, depending on what you are trying to accomplish, you can solve this by using a different expression of the attitude, such as the `rotationMatrix`, which does not suffer from this limitation.

This next (simple and very silly) example illustrates a use of CMAttitude's `rotation-Matrix` property. Our goal is to make a CALayer rotate in response to the current attitude of the device. We start as before, except that our reference frame is `CMAttitude-ReferenceFrameXArbitraryZVertical`; we are interested in how the device moves from its initial attitude, without reference to any particular fixed external direction such as magnetic north. In `pollAttitude`, our first step is to store the device's current attitude in a CMAttitude instance variable, `self.ref`:

```
CMDeviceMotion* mot = self.motman.deviceMotion;
CMAttitude* att = mot.attitude;
if (!self.ref) {
    self.ref = att;
    return;
}
```

That code works correctly because on the first few polls, as the attitude-detection hardware warms up, `att` is nil, so we don't get past the `return` call until we have a valid initial attitude. Our next step is highly characteristic of how CMAttitude is used: we call the CMAttitude instance method `multiplyByInverseOfAttitude:`, which transforms our attitude so that it is relative *to the stored initial attitude*:

```
[att multiplyByInverseOfAttitude:self.ref];
```

Finally, we apply the attitude's rotation matrix directly to a layer in our interface as a transform. Well, not quite directly: a rotation matrix is a 3×3 matrix, whereas a CATransform3D, which is what we need in order to set a layer's `transform`, is a 4×4 matrix. However, it happens that the top left nine entries in a CATransform3D's 4×4 matrix constitute its rotation component, so we start with an identity matrix and set those entries directly:

```
CMRotationMatrix r = att.rotationMatrix;
CATransform3D t = CATransform3DIdentity;
t.m11 = r.m11;
t.m12 = r.m12;
t.m13 = r.m13;
t.m21 = r.m21;
t.m22 = r.m22;
t.m23 = r.m23;
t.m31 = r.m31;
t.m32 = r.m32;
t.m33 = r.m33;
CALayer* lay = // whatever
[CATransaction setDisableActions:YES];
lay.transform = t;
```

The result is that the layer apparently tries to hold itself still as the device rotates. The example is rather crude because we aren't using OpenGL to draw a three-dimensional object, but it illustrates the principle well enough.

There is a quirk to be aware of in this case as well: over time, the transform has a tendency to drift. Thus, even if we leave the device stationary, the layer will gradually rotate. That is the sort of effect that CMAttitudeReferenceFrameXArbitraryCorrectedZVertical is designed to help mitigate, by bringing the magnetometer into play.

Here are some additional considerations to be aware of when using Core Motion:

- The documentation warns that your app should create only one CMMotionManager instance. This is not a terribly onerous restriction, but it's rather odd that, if this is important, the API doesn't provide a shared singleton instance accessed through a class method.

- Use of Core Motion is legal while your app is running in the background. To take advantage of this, your app would need to be running in the background for some *other* reason; there is no Core Motion UIBackgroundModes setting in an *Info.plist*. For example, you might run in the background because you're using Core Location, and take advantage of this to employ Core Motion as well.

- Core Motion requires that various sensors be turned on, such as the magnetometer and the gyroscope. This can result in some increased battery drain, so try not to use any sensors you don't have to, and remember to stop generating updates as soon as you no longer need them.

PART IV

Final Topics

This part of the book is a miscellany of topics.

- Chapter 23 is about files. It explains how your app can store data on disk to be retrieved the next time the app runs (including both standalone files and user defaults). It also discusses sharing files with the user through iTunes and with other apps, plus the document architecture and iCloud, and concludes with a survey of how iOS can work with some common file formats (XML, SQLite, Core Data, and image files).

- Chapter 24 introduces networking, with an emphasis on HTTP downloading of data. It also introduces in-app purchasing (a specialized form of networking) and Bonjour.

- Chapter 25 is about threads. Making your code multithreaded can introduce great complexity and is not a beginner topic, but you still might need to understand the basic concepts of multithreading, either in order to prevent a lengthy task from blocking user interaction with your app, or because some framework explicitly relies on it. Particular attention is paid to the advantages of NSOperation and (especially) Grand Central Dispatch.

- Chapter 26 describes how iOS supports Undo in your app.

CHAPTER 23

Persistent Storage

The device on which your app runs contains flash memory that functions as the equivalent of a hard disk, holding files that survive between runs of your app, even if the device is powered down. This chapter is about how and where files are saved and retrieved, and about some of the additional ways in which files can be manipulated: for example, apps can define document types in which they specialize and can hand such documents to one another, and can share documents into the cloud (iCloud), so that multiple copies of the same app can retrieve them on different devices. The chapter also explains how user preferences are maintained in NSUserDefaults, and describes some specialized file formats and ways of working with their data, such as XML, SQLite, Core Data, and images.

The Sandbox

The hard disk as a whole is not open to your app's view. A limited portion of the hard disk is dedicated to your app alone: this is your app's *sandbox*. The idea is that every app, seeing only its own sandbox, is hindered from spying or impinging on the files belonging to other apps, and in turn is protected from having its own files spied or impinged on by other apps. Your app's sandbox is thus a safe place for you to store your data. Your sandbox, and hence your data, will be deleted if the user deletes your app; otherwise, it should reliably persist. (Your app can also see some higher-level directories owned by the system as a whole, but cannot write to them.)

The sandbox contains some standard directories, and there are built-in methods for referring to them. For example, suppose you want a reference to the Documents directory. Here's one way to access it:

```
NSString* docs = [NSSearchPathForDirectoriesInDomains(
    NSDocumentDirectory, NSUserDomainMask, YES) lastObject];
```

That code returns a path string for the Documents directory. The preferred way to refer to a file or directory, however, is with a URL. You can obtain this from an NSFileManager instance:

```
NSFileManager* fm = [NSFileManager new];
NSError* err = nil;
NSURL* docsurl =
    [fm URLForDirectory:NSDocumentDirectory
              inDomain:NSUserDomainMask appropriateForURL:nil
                  create:YES error:&err];
// error-checking omitted
```

A question that will immediately occur to you is: *where* should I put files and folders that I want to save now and read later? The Documents directory can be a good place. But if your app supports file sharing (discussed later in this chapter), the user can see and modify your app's Documents directory through iTunes, so you might not want to put things there that the user isn't supposed to see and change.

Personally, I favor the Application Support directory for most purposes. In OS X, this directory is shared by multiple applications, each of which must confine itself to an individual subfolder, but on iOS each app has its own private Application Support directory in its own sandbox, so you can safely put files anywhere within it. This directory may not exist initially, so you can obtain it and create it at the same time:

```
NSURL* suppurl =
    [fm URLForDirectory:NSApplicationSupportDirectory
              inDomain:NSUserDomainMask appropriateForURL:nil
                  create:YES error:&err];
```

Temporary files, whose loss you are willing to accept (because their contents can be recreated), can be written into the Caches directory (NSCachesDirectory) or the Temporary directory (NSTemporaryDirectory). You can write temporary files into the Application Support folder, but by default this means they can be backed up by the user through iTunes or iCloud; to prevent that, exclude such a file from backup by way of its file URL:

```
BOOL ok = [myDocumentUrl setResourceValue:@YES
                            forKey:NSURLIsExcludedFromBackupKey
                            error:&err];
```

Although URLs are the favored way of referring to files and folders, they are a more recent innovation than path strings, and you may encounter file operations that still require a string. To derive a path string from an NSURL, send it the path message.

Basic File Operations

Let's say we intend to create a folder *MyFolder* inside the Documents directory. Assume that we have an NSFileManager instance fm and an NSURL docsurl pointing at the

Visually Inspecting the Sandbox

The Simulator's sandbox is a folder on your Mac that you can inspect visually. Applications appearing in the Simulator are actually located in a directory inside ~/*Library/ Application Support/iPhone Simulator*, followed by the system version of the SDK (for example, there might be a folder called *7.0.3*). Inside this folder you'll find an *Applications* folder; inside that are the sandbox folders for the apps you've run from Xcode on the Simulator. These sandbox folders have mysterious names, but you can identify a folder by opening it to reveal the name of the app.

You can also view the file structure of the sandbox on the device. When the device is connected and no app is being run from Xcode, look in the Applications section of the Organizer window. Choose your app; you'll see the entire hierarchy of its sandbox contents displayed at the bottom of the window. If you click Download, the whole sandbox is copied and arrives on your computer as an *.xcappdata* package; you can open it in the Finder with Show Package Contents.

Documents directory, as shown in the previous section. We can then generate a reference to *MyFolder*, from which we can ask our NSFileManager instance to create the folder if it doesn't exist already:

```
NSURL* myfolder = [docsurl URLByAppendingPathComponent:@"MyFolder"];
NSError* err = nil;
BOOL ok =
    [fm createDirectoryAtURL:myfolder
        withIntermediateDirectories:YES attributes:nil error:&err];
// ... error-checking omitted
```

To learn what files and folders exist within a directory, you can ask for an array of the directory's contents:

```
NSError* err = nil;
NSArray* arr =
    [fm contentsOfDirectoryAtURL:docsurl
        includingPropertiesForKeys:nil options:0 error:&err];
// ... error-checking omitted
NSLog(@"%@", [arr valueForKey:@"lastPathComponent"]);
/*
MyFolder
*/
```

The array resulting from contentsOfDirectoryAtURL:... lists full URLs of the directory's *immediate* contents; it is shallow. For a deep array, which might be very big, you can enumerate the directory, so that you are handed only one file reference at a time:

```
NSDirectoryEnumerator* dir =
    [fm enumeratorAtURL:docsurl
        includingPropertiesForKeys:nil options:0 errorHandler:nil];
for (NSURL* f in dir)
    if ([[f pathExtension] isEqualToString: @"txt"])
        NSLog(@"%@", [f lastPathComponent]);
/*
file1.txt
file2.txt
*/
```

A directory enumerator also permits you to decline to dive into a particular subdirectory (skipDescendants), so you can make your traversal even more efficient.

Consult the NSFileManager class documentation for more about what you can do with files, and see also Apple's *File System Programming Guide*.

Saving and Reading Files

To save or read a simple file, you are likely to use one of the convenience methods for the class appropriate to the file's contents. NSString, NSData, NSArray, and NSDictionary provide methods writeToURL... (for writing) and initWithContentsOfURL... (for reading).

NSString and NSData objects map directly between their own contents and the contents of the file. Here, I'll generate a text file from a string:

```
NSError* err = nil;
BOOL ok =
    [@"howdy" writeToURL:[myfolder URLByAppendingPathComponent:@"file1.txt"]
            atomically:YES encoding:NSUTF8StringEncoding error:&err];
// error-checking omitted
```

NSArray and NSDictionary files are actually property lists, and will work only if all the contents of the array or dictionary are property list types (NSString, NSData, NSDate, NSNumber, NSArray, and NSDictionary).

So how do you save to a file an object of some other class? Well, if an object's class adopts the NSCoding protocol, you can convert it to an NSData and back again using NSKeyed-Archiver and NSKeyedUnarchiver; an NSData can then be saved as a file or in a property list.

You can make your own class adopt the NSCoding protocol. This can become somewhat complicated because an object can refer (through an instance variable) to another object, which may also adopt the NSCoding protocol, and thus you can end up saving an entire graph of interconnected objects if you wish. However, I'll confine myself to illustrating a simple case (and you can read Apple's *Archives and Serializations Programming Guide* for more information).

Let's say, then, that we have a simple Person class with a firstName property and a last-Name property. We'll declare that it adopts the NSCoding protocol:

```
@interface Person : NSObject <NSCoding>
```

To make this class actually conform to NSCoding, we must implement encodeWith-Coder: (to archive the object) and initWithCoder: (to unarchive the object). In encode-WithCoder:, we must first call super if the superclass adopts NSCoding — in this case, it doesn't — and then call the appropriate encode... method for each instance variable we want preserved:

```
- (void)encodeWithCoder:(NSCoder *)encoder {
    //[super encodeWithCoder: encoder]; // not in this case
    [encoder encodeObject:self.lastName forKey:@"last"];
    [encoder encodeObject:self.firstName forKey:@"first"];
}
```

In initWithCoder, we must call super, using either initWithCoder: if the superclass adopts the NSCoding protocol or the designated initializer if not, and then call the appropriate decode... method for each instance variable stored earlier, finally returning self; memory management is up to us (but under ARC there will probably be no need to think about that):

```
- (id) initWithCoder:(NSCoder *)decoder {
    //self = [super initWithCoder: decoder]; // not in this case
    self = [super init];
    self->_lastName = [decoder decodeObjectForKey:@"last"];
    self->_firstName = [decoder decodeObjectForKey:@"first"];
    return self;
}
```

We can test our code by creating, configuring, and saving a Person instance as a file:

```
Person* moi = [Person new];
moi.firstName = @"Matt";
moi.lastName = @"Neuburg";
NSData* moidata = [NSKeyedArchiver archivedDataWithRootObject:moi];
NSURL* moifile = [docsurl URLByAppendingPathComponent:@"moi.txt"];
[moidata writeToURL:moifile atomically:NO];
```

We can retrieve the saved Person at a later time:

```
NSData* persondata = [[NSData alloc] initWithContentsOfURL:moifile];
Person* person = [NSKeyedUnarchiver unarchiveObjectWithData:persondata];
NSLog(@"%@ %@", person.firstName, person.lastName); // Matt Neuburg
```

If the NSData object is itself the entire content of the file, as here, then instead of using archivedDataWithRootObject: and unarchiveObjectWithData:, you can skip the intermediate NSData object and use archiveRootObject:toFile: and unarchiveObject-WithFile:.

Saving a single Person as an archive may seem like overkill; why didn't we just make a text file consisting of the first and last names? But imagine that a Person has a lot more properties, or that we have an array of hundreds of Persons, or an array of hundreds of dictionaries where one value in each dictionary is a Person; now the power of an archivable Person is evident. Even though Person now adopts the NSCoding protocol, an NSArray containing a Person object still cannot be written to disk using NSArray's writeToFile... or writeToURL..., because Person is still not a property list type. But the array can be archived and written to disk with NSKeyedArchiver.

User Defaults

User defaults (NSUserDefaults) are intended as the persistent storage of the user's preferences. They are little more, really, than a special case of an NSDictionary property list file. You talk to the NSUserDefaults standardUserDefaults object much as if it were a dictionary; it has keys and values. And the only legal values are property list values (see the preceding section); thus, for example, to store a Person in user defaults, you'd have to archive it first to an NSData object. Unlike NSDictionary, NSUserDefaults provides convenience methods for converting between a simple data type such as a float or a BOOL and the object that is stored in the defaults (setFloat:forKey:, floatForKey:, and so forth). But the defaults themselves are still a dictionary.

Meanwhile, somewhere on disk, this dictionary is being saved for you automatically as a property list file — though you don't concern yourself with that. You simply set or retrieve values from the dictionary by way of their keys, secure in the knowledge that the file is being read into memory or written to disk as needed. Your chief concern is to make sure that you've written everything needful into user defaults before your app terminates; in the multitasking world (Appendix A), this will usually mean when the app delegate receives applicationDidEnterBackground: at the latest. If you're worried that your app might crash, you can tell the standardUserDefaults object to synchronize as a way of forcing it to save right now, but this is rarely necessary.

To provide the value for a key before the user has had a chance to do so — the default default, as it were — use registerDefaults:. What you're supplying here is a dictionary whose key–value pairs will each be written into the user defaults, but only if there is no such key already. For example:

```
[[NSUserDefaults standardUserDefaults] registerDefaults:
    @{@"cardMatrixRows":@4, @"cardMatrixColumns":@3}];
```

The idea is that we call registerDefaults: extremely early as the app launches. Either the app has run at some time previously and the user has set these preferences, in which case this call has no effect and does no harm, or not, in which case we now have initial values for these preferences with which to get started. So, in the game app from which that code comes, we start out with a 4×3 game layout, but the user can change this at any time.

This leaves only the question of how the user is to interact with the defaults. One way is that your app provides some kind of interface.

For example, the game app from which the previous code comes has a tab bar interface; the second tab is where the user sets preferences (Figure 6-9). The app doesn't participate in the built-in state saving and restoration mechanism. So it uses (or misuses) the user defaults to store state information. It records the state of the game board and the card deck into user defaults every time these change, so that if the app is terminated and then launched again later, we can restore the game as it was when the user left off. One might argue that, while the current card layout may be state, the card deck itself is data — and so I am also misusing the user defaults to store data. However, while purists may grumble, it's a very small amount of data and I don't think the distinction is terribly significant in this case.

Alternatively, you can provide a *settings bundle*, consisting mostly of one or more property list files describing an interface and the corresponding user default keys and their initial values; the Settings app is then responsible for translating your instructions into an actual interface, and for presenting it to the user.

Using a settings bundle has some obvious disadvantages: the user may not think to look in the Settings app; the user has to leave your app to access preferences; and you don't get the kind of control over the interface that you have within your own app. Also, in a multitasking world, this means that the user can set preferences while your app is backgrounded; you'll need to register for NSUserDefaultsDidChangeNotification in order to hear about this.

In some situations, though, a settings bundle has some clear advantages. Keeping the preferences interface out of your app can make your app's own interface cleaner and simpler. You don't have to write any of the "glue" code that coordinates the preferences interface with the user default values. And it may be appropriate for the user to be able to set preferences for your app even when your app isn't running.

Writing a settings bundle is described in Apple's *Preferences and Settings Programming Guide*.

File Sharing

If your app supports file sharing, its Documents directory becomes available to the user through iTunes (Figure 23-1). The user can add files to your app's Documents directory, and can save files and folders from your app's Documents directory to the computer, as well as renaming and deleting files and folders. This could be appropriate, for example,

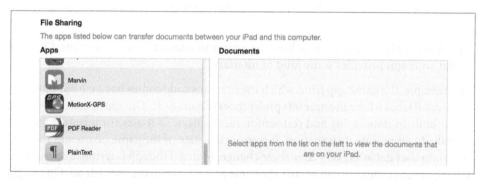

Figure 23-1. The iTunes file sharing interface

if your app works with common types of file that the user might obtain elsewhere, such as PDFs or JPEGs.

To support file sharing, set the *Info.plist* key "Application supports iTunes file sharing" (`UIFileSharingEnabled`).

Once your entire Documents directory is exposed to the user this way, you are unlikely to use the Documents directory to store private files. As I mentioned earlier, I like to use the Application Support directory instead.

Your app doesn't get any notification when the user has altered the contents of the Documents directory. Noticing that the situation has changed and responding appropriately is entirely up to you.

Document Types

Your app can declare itself willing to open documents of a certain type. In this way, if another app obtains a document of this type, it can propose to hand the document off to your app. For example, the user might download the document with Mobile Safari, or receive it in a mail message with the Mail app; now we need a way to get it from Safari or Mail to you.

To let the system know that your app is a candidate for opening a certain kind of document, you will configure the "Document types" (`CFBundleDocumentTypes`) key in your *Info.plist*. This is an array, where each entry will be a dictionary specifying a document type by using keys such as "Document Content Type UTIs" (`LSItemContentTypes`), "Document Type Name" (`CFBundleTypeName`), `CFBundleTypeIconFiles`, and `LSHandlerRank`. Far and away the simplest method for configuring the *Info.plist* is through the interface available in the Info tab when you edit the target.

For example, suppose I want to declare that my app opens PDFs. In my target's Info tab in Xcode 5, I would edit the Document Types section to look like Figure 23-2.

Figure 23-2. Creating a document type

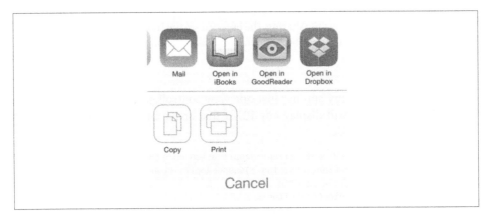

Figure 23-3. The Mail app offers to hand off a PDF

The result is that my *Info.plist* contains this entry:

```
<key>CFBundleDocumentTypes</key>
<array>
    <dict>
        <key>CFBundleTypeIconFiles</key>
        <array/>
        <key>CFBundleTypeName</key>
        <string>PDF</string>
        <key>LSItemContentTypes</key>
        <array>
            <string>com.adobe.pdf</string>
        </array>
    </dict>
</array>
```

Now suppose the user receives a PDF in an email message. The Mail app can display this PDF, but the user can also tap the Action button to bring up an activity view offering, among other things, to open the file in my app. The interface will resemble Figure 23-3, but with my app listed as one of the buttons.

Next, suppose the user actually *taps* the button that hands the PDF off to my app. For this to work, my app delegate must implement `application:openURL:source-Application:annotation:`. When that method is called, my app has been brought to the front, either by launching it from scratch or by reviving it from background suspension; its job is now to handle the opening of the document whose URL has arrived as the second parameter. To prevent me from peeking into another app's sandbox, the system has already copied the document into my sandbox, into the Inbox directory, which is created for exactly this purpose.

 The Inbox directory is created in your Documents folder. Thus, if your app implements file sharing, the user can see the Inbox folder; you may wish to delete the Inbox folder, therefore, as soon as you're done retrieving files from it.

In this simple example, my app has just one view controller, which has an outlet to a UIWebView where we will display any PDFs that arrive in this fashion. So my app delegate contains this code:

```
- (BOOL)application:(UIApplication *)application openURL:(NSURL *)url
        sourceApplication:(NSString *)sourceApplication
        annotation:(id)annotation {
    ViewController* viewController =
        (ViewController*)self.window.rootViewController;
    [viewController displayPDF:url];
    return YES;
}
```

And my view controller contains this code:

```
- (void) displayPDF: (NSURL*) url {
    NSURLRequest* req = [NSURLRequest requestWithURL:url];
    [self.wv loadRequest:req];
}
```

In real life, things might be more complicated. Our implementation of `application:openURL:...` might check to see whether this really *is* a PDF, and return NO if it isn't. Also, our app might be in the middle of something else, possibly displaying a completely different view controller's view; because `application:openURL:...` can arrive at any time, we may have to be prepared to drop whatever we were doing and display the incoming document instead.

If our app is launched from scratch by the arrival of this URL, `application:didFinish-LaunchingWithOptions:` will be sent to our app delegate as usual. The options dictionary (the second parameter) will contain the `UIApplicationLaunchOptionsURLKey`, and we can take into account, if we like, the fact that we are being launched specifically to open a document. We can also return NO to refuse to open the document. If we return

Figure 23-4. The document Open In activity view

YES as usual, `application:openURL:...` will arrive in good order after our interface has been set up.

The example I've been discussing assumes that the UTI for the document type is standard and well-known. It is also possible that your app will operate on a new document type, that is, a type of document that the app itself defines. In that case, you'll also want to add this UTI to your app's list of Exported UTIs in the *Info.plist*. I'll give an example later in this chapter.

Handing Off a Document

The converse of the situation discussed in the previous section is this: your app has somehow acquired a document and wants to let the user hand off a copy of it to whatever app can deal with it. This is done through the UIDocumentInteractionController class. This class operates asynchronously, so retaining an instance of it is up to you; typically, you'll store it in an instance variable with a retain setter policy.

For example, let's say our app has a PDF sitting in its Documents directory. Assuming we have an NSURL pointing to this document, presenting the interface for handing the document off to some other application (Figure 23-4) could be as simple as this (`sender` is a button that the user has just tapped):

```
self.dic =
    [UIDocumentInteractionController interactionControllerWithURL:url];
BOOL ok =
    [self.dic presentOpenInMenuFromRect:[sender bounds]
                            inView:sender animated:YES];
```

This interface is an activity view (Chapter 13). There are actually two activity views available:

`presentOpenInMenuFromRect:inView:animated:`

`presentOpenInMenuFromBarButtonItem:animated:`

> Presents an activity view listing apps in which the document can be opened (like Figure 23-4).

```
presentOptionsMenuFromRect:inView:animated:
presentOptionsMenuFromBarButtonItem:animated:
```
> Presents an activity view listing apps in which the document can be opened, along with other possible actions, such as Print, Copy, and Mail (like Figure 23-3).

These methods work on both iPhone and iPad interfaces; on the iPad, the buttons appear in a popover.

Your app can't learn *which* other applications are capable of accepting the document! Indeed, it can't even learn in advance whether *any* other applications are capable of accepting the document; your only clue is that the returned BOOL value afterward will be NO if UIDocumentInteractionController couldn't present the requested interface.

A UIDocumentInteractionController can also present a preview of the document, if the document is of a type for which preview is enabled, by calling presentPreview-Animated:. You must give the UIDocumentInteractionController a delegate (UIDocumentInteractionControllerDelegate), and the delegate must implement documentInteractionControllerViewControllerForPreview:, returning an existing view controller that will contain the preview's view controller. So, here we ask for the preview:

```
self.dic =
    [UIDocumentInteractionController interactionControllerWithURL:url];
self.dic.delegate = self;
[self.dic presentPreviewAnimated:YES];
```

In the delegate, we supply the view controller; it happens that, in my code, this delegate *is* a view controller — in fact, it's the very view controller that is presenting the UIDocumentInteractionController — so it simply returns self:

```
- (UIViewController *) documentInteractionControllerViewControllerForPreview:
        (UIDocumentInteractionController *) controller {
    return self;
}
```

If the view controller returned were a UINavigationController, the preview's view controller would be pushed onto it. In this case it isn't, so the preview's view controller is a presented view controller with a Done button. The preview interface also contains an Action button that lets the user summon the Options activity view. In fact, this preview interface is exactly the same interface already familiar from the Mail app.

Delegate methods allow you to track what's happening in the interface presented by the UIDocumentInteractionController. Probably most important are those that inform you that key stages of the interaction are ending:

- `documentInteractionControllerDidDismissOptionsMenu:`
- `documentInteractionControllerDidDismissOpenInMenu:`

- documentInteractionControllerDidEndPreview:
- documentInteractionController:didEndSendingToApplication:

Previews are actually provided through the Quick Look framework, and you can skip the UIDocumentInteractionController and present the preview yourself through a QLPreviewController; you'll need to @import QuickLook. It's a view controller, so to display the preview you show it as a presented view controller or push it onto a navigation controller's stack, just as UIDocumentInteractionController would have done. A nice feature of QLPreviewController is that you can give it more than one document to preview; the user can move between these, within the preview, using a table of contents summoned by a button at the bottom of the interface. Apart from this, the interface looks like the interface presented by the UIDocumentInteractionController.

In this example, I may have in my Documents directory, at some depth (like perhaps in the Inbox directory), one or more PDF documents. I acquire a list of their URLs and present a preview for them:

```
// obtain URLs of PDFs as an array
NSFileManager* fm = [NSFileManager new];
NSURL* docsurl =
    [fm URLForDirectory:NSDocumentDirectory inDomain:NSUserDomainMask
        appropriateForURL:nil create:NO error:nil];
NSDirectoryEnumerator* dir =
    [fm enumeratorAtURL:docsurl
        includingPropertiesForKeys:nil options:0 errorHandler:nil];
if (!dir)
    return; // proper error-checking omitted
NSMutableArray* marr = [NSMutableArray new];
for (NSURL* f in dir) {
    if ([[f pathExtension] isEqualToString: @"pdf"])
        [marr addObject: f];
}
self.pdfs = marr; // retain policy
if (![self.pdfs count])
    return;
// show preview interface
QLPreviewController* preview = [QLPreviewController new];
preview.dataSource = self;
[self presentViewController:preview animated:YES completion:nil];
```

You'll notice that I haven't told the QLPreviewController what documents to preview. That is the job of QLPreviewController's data source. In my code, this very same view controller is also the data source. It simply fetches the requested information from the list of URLs, which was previously saved into an instance variable:

```
- (NSInteger) numberOfPreviewItemsInPreviewController:
        (QLPreviewController *) controller {
    return [self.pdfs count];
}
```

```
- (id <QLPreviewItem>) previewController: (QLPreviewController *) controller
                    previewItemAtIndex: (NSInteger) index {
    return self.pdfs[index];
}
```

The second data source method requires us to return an object that adopts the QLPreviewItem protocol. By a wildly improbable coincidence, NSURL *does* adopt this protocol, so the example works.

Document Architecture

If your app opens and saves documents of a type peculiar to itself, you may want to take advantage of the *document architecture*. This architecture revolves around a class, UI-Document, that takes care of a number of pesky issues, such as the fact that loading or writing your data might take some time. Plus, UIDocument provides autosaving behavior, so that your data is written out automatically whenever it changes. Moreover, UIDocument is your gateway to allowing your documents to participate in iCloud; with iCloud, your app's documents on one of the user's devices will automatically be mirrored onto another of the user's devices.

Getting started with UIDocument is not difficult. You'll start with a UIDocument subclass, and you'll override two methods:

loadFromContents:ofType:error:
: Called when it's time to open a document from disk. You are expected to convert the contents value into a model object that your app can use, store that model object, and return YES. (If there was a problem, you'll set the error: by indirection and return NO.)

contentsForType:error:
: Called when it's time to save a document to disk. You are expected to convert the app's model object into an NSData instance (or, if your document is a package, an NSFileWrapper) and return it. (If there was a problem, you'll set the error: by indirection and return nil.)

Your UIDocument subclass will need a place to store and retrieve the data model object. Obviously, this can be an instance variable of the UIDocument subclass itself. At the same time, keep in mind that your UIDocument instance will probably be partnered in some way with a view controller instance, which will also need access to the same data.

To instantiate a UIDocument, call its designated initializer, initWithFileURL:. This sets the UIDocument's fileURL property, and associates the UIDocument with this file on disk, typically for the remainder of its lifetime.

In my description of the two key UIDocument methods that your subclass will override, I used the phrase, "when it's time" (to open or save the document). This raises the question of how your UIDocument instance will know when to open and save a document. There are three circumstances to distinguish:

Make a new document

The `fileURL:` points to a nonexistent file. Immediately after instantiating the UI-Document, you send it `saveToURL:forSaveOperation:completionHandler:`, where the second argument is `UIDocumentSaveForCreating`. (The first argument will be the UIDocument's own `fileURL`.) This in turn causes `contentsForType:error:` to be called, and the contents of an empty document are saved out to disk. This implies that your UIDocument subclass should know of some default value that represents the model data when there is no data.

Open an existing document

Send the UIDocument instance `openWithCompletionHandler:`. This in turn causes `loadFromContents:ofType:error:` to be called.

Save an existing document

There are two approaches to saving an existing document:

Autosave

Usually, you'll mark the document as "dirty" by calling `updateChangeCount:`. From time to time, the UIDocument will notice this situation and will save the document to disk, calling `contentsForType:error:` in the process.

Manual save

On certain occasions, waiting for autosave won't be appropriate. We've already seen an example of such an occasion — when the file itself needs to be created on the spot. Another is when the app is going into the background; we will want to preserve our document there and then, in case the app is terminated. You'll call `saveToURL:forSaveOperation:completionHandler:`; if the file is not being created for the first time, the second argument will be `UIDocumentSaveForOverwriting`. Alternatively, if you know you're finished with the document (perhaps the interface displaying the document is about to be torn down) you can call `closeWithCompletionHandler:`.

The `open...`, `close...`, and `saveTo...` methods have a `completionHandler:` argument. This is UIDocument's solution to the fact that reading and saving may take time. The file operations themselves take place on a background thread; the `completionHandler:` block is then called on the main thread.

We now know enough for an example! I'll reuse my Person class from earlier in this chapter. Imagine a document effectively consisting of multiple Person instances; I'll call each such document a *people group*. Our app, People Groups, will list all people groups in the user's Documents folder; it will also open any people group from disk and display its contents, allowing the user to edit any Person's `firstName` or `lastName` (Figure 23-5).

Figure 23-5. The People Groups interface

My first step is to define a custom UTI in my app's *Info.plist*, associating a file type
`com.neuburg.pplgrp` with a file extension `@"pplgrp"`. I then also define a document
type that uses this UTI, as shown earlier in this chapter (Figure 23-6).

A document consists of multiple Persons, so a natural model implementation is an
NSArray of Persons. Moreover, as I mentioned earlier, since Person implements NSCoding, an NSArray of Persons can be archived directly into an NSData. Thus, our UIDocument subclass (which I'll call PeopleDocument) has a public NSMutableArray `people`
property, and can be implemented very simply. We override `initWithFileURL:` to give
ourselves something to save if we are called upon to save a new empty document; then,
to mediate between our model and the data on disk, we use NSKeyedUnarchiver and
NSKeyedArchiver exactly as in our earlier examples:

```
-(id)initWithFileURL:(NSURL *)url {
    self = [super initWithFileURL:url];
    if (self) {
        self->_people = [NSMutableArray array];
    }
    return self;
}
- (BOOL)loadFromContents:(id)contents ofType:(NSString *)typeName
                   error:(NSError **)outError {
    NSArray* arr = [NSKeyedUnarchiver unarchiveObjectWithData:contents];
```

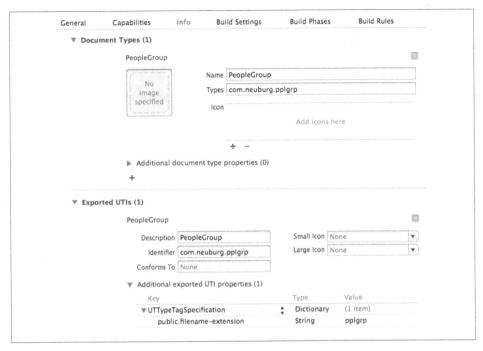

Figure 23-6. Defining a custom UTI

```
    self.people = [NSMutableArray arrayWithArray:arr];
    return YES;
}
- (id)contentsForType:(NSString *)typeName error:(NSError **)outError {
    NSData* data = [NSKeyedArchiver archivedDataWithRootObject:self.people];
    return data;
}
```

The remaining questions are architectural: when should a PeopleDocument be initialized, where should it be stored, and what should be the nature of communications with it?

The first view controller, DocumentLister, merely lists documents by name, and provides an interface for letting the user create a new group; only the second view controller, PeopleLister, the one that displays the first and last names of the people in the group, actually needs to work with PeopleDocument.

PeopleLister's designated initializer therefore requires that it be given a `fileURL:` argument, with which it sets its own `fileURL` property. In its `viewDidLoad` implementation, PeopleLister instantiates a PeopleDocument with that same `fileURL`, and retains it through a PeopleDocument property (`self.doc`). If the URL points to a nonexistent file, PeopleLister requests that it be created by calling `saveToURL:forSave-`

`Operation:completionHandler:`; otherwise, it requests that the document be read, by calling `openWithCompletionHandler:`. Either way, the completion handler points PeopleLister's own `people` property at the PeopleDocument's `people` property (so that they share the same data model object) and refreshes the interface:

```
NSFileManager* fm = [NSFileManager new];
self.doc = [[PeopleDocument alloc] initWithFileURL:self.fileURL];
void (^listPeople) (BOOL) = ^(BOOL success) {
    if (success) {
        self.people = self.doc.people;
        [self.tableView reloadData];
    }
};
if (![fm fileExistsAtPath:[self.fileURL path]])
    [self.doc saveToURL:doc.fileURL
        forSaveOperation:UIDocumentSaveForCreating
      completionHandler:listPeople];
else
    [self.doc openWithCompletionHandler:listPeople];
```

When the user performs a significant editing maneuver, such as creating or deleting a person or editing a person's first or last name, PeopleLister tells its PeopleDocument that the document is dirty, and allows autosaving to take it from there:

```
[self.doc updateChangeCount:UIDocumentChangeDone];
```

When the app is about to go into the background, or when PeopleLister's own view is disappearing, PeopleLister forces PeopleDocument to save immediately:

```
- (void) forceSave: (id) n {
    [self.tableView endEditing:YES];
    [self.doc saveToURL:doc.fileURL
        forSaveOperation:UIDocumentSaveForOverwriting
      completionHandler:nil];
}
```

That's all it takes; adding UIDocument support to your app is easy, because UIDocument is merely acting as a supplier and preserver of your app's data model object. UIDocument presents itself in the documentation as a large and complex class, but that's chiefly because it is so heavily customizable both at high and low levels; for the most part, you won't need any of that heavy customization, and use of UIDocument really will be as simple as what I've shown here. You might go further in order to give your UIDocument a more sophisticated understanding of what constitutes a significant change in your data by working with its undo manager; I'll talk about undo managers in Chapter 26. For further details, see Apple's *Document-based App Programming Guide for iOS*.

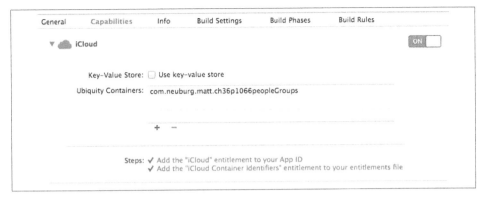

Figure 23-7. Turning on iCloud support

iCloud

Once your app is operating through UIDocument, iCloud compatibility effectively falls right into your lap. You have just two steps to perform:

Obtain iCloud entitlements
> In Xcode 5, all you have to do is edit the target and, in the Capabilities tab, set the iCloud switch to On. This causes a transaction to take place between Xcode and the Member Center; automatically, your app gets a Ubiquity Container, and an appropriately configured entitlements file is added to the project (Figure 23-7).

Obtain an iCloud-compatible directory
> Early in your app's lifetime, call NSFileManager's URLForUbiquityContainer-Identifier: (typically passing nil as the argument), on a background thread, to obtain the URL of a cloud-shared directory. It will probably be an app-specific directory in *file://localhost/private/var/mobile/Library/Mobile%20Documents/*; you are given sandbox access to this directory even though strictly speaking it isn't inside your sandbox area. Any documents your app puts here by way of a UIDocument subclass will be automatically shared into the cloud.

Thus, having switched on iCloud support, I was able to make my People Groups example app iCloud-compatible with just two code changes. In the app delegate, as my app launches, I step out to a background thread (Chapter 25), obtain the cloud-shared directory's URL, and then step back to the main thread and retain the URL through a property, self.ubiq:

```
dispatch_async(dispatch_get_global_queue(0, 0), ^{
    NSFileManager* fm = [NSFileManager new];
    NSURL* ubiq = [fm URLForUbiquityContainerIdentifier:nil];
    dispatch_async(dispatch_get_main_queue(), ^{
        self.ubiq = ubiq;
    });
});
```

(Actually, that code should probably be preceded by a call to NSFileManager's ubiquity-
IdentityToken. If the result is nil, iCloud isn't available, or this user hasn't registered
for iCloud, and we might as well omit any subsequent attempt to work with iCloud. If
it *isn't* nil, it identifies the user's iCloud account; this can be useful, for example, to detect
when the user has logged into a different account.)

Then, anywhere in my code where I was specifying the URL for the user's Documents
folder as the place to seek and save people groups, I now specify ubiq if it isn't nil:

```
NSURL* docsurl = [fm URLForDirectory:NSDocumentDirectory
                           inDomain:NSUserDomainMask
                 appropriateForURL:nil create:NO error:nil];
NSURL* ubiq =
    [(AppDelegate*)[[UIApplication sharedApplication] delegate] ubiq];
if (ubiq)
    docsurl = ubiq;
```

To test, I ran the app on a device (with iCloud → Documents & Data switched to On in
the Settings app) and created a people group with some people in it. I then switched to
a different device (also with iCloud → Documents & Data switched to On) and ran the
app there, and tapped the Refresh button, which looks through the docsurl directory
for pplgrp files:

```
NSDirectoryEnumerator* dir = [fm enumeratorAtURL:docsurl
                       includingPropertiesForKeys:nil options:0
                                     errorHandler:nil];
self.files = [NSMutableArray array];
for (NSURL* aFile in dir) {
    [dir skipDescendants];
    if ([[aFile pathExtension] isEqualToString:@"pplgrp"])
        [self.files addObject:aFile];
}
[self.tableView reloadData];
```

Presto, there was a people group with the same name containing the same people! It
was quite thrilling.

There are a few further refinements that my app probably needs in order to be a good
iCloud citizen. For example, my app is not automatically aware that a new document
has appeared in the cloud (that's why I had to tap Refresh to discover an existing people
group). To be notified of that, I'd want to run an NSMetadataQuery. The usual strategy
is: instantiate NSMetadataQuery, configure the search, register for notifications such as

`NSMetadataQueryDidFinishGatheringNotification` and `NSMetadataQueryDid-`
`UpdateNotification`, start the search, and retain the NSMetadataQuery instance with
the search continuing to run for the entire lifetime of the app.

Another concern is that my app should be notified when the currently open document
changes on disk because a new version of it was downloaded from the cloud (that is,
someone edited the document while I had it open). For that, register for `UIDocument-`
`StateChangedNotification`. To learn the document's state, consult its `document-`
`State` property. A big issue is likely to be what should happen if the document state is
`UIDocumentStateInConflict`. You'll want to resolve the conflict in coordination with
the NSFileVersion class; for details and example code, see the "Resolving Document
Version Conflicts" chapter of Apple's *Document-based App Programming Guide for iOS*.

Yet another issue is the question of what should happen if the availability of iCloud
changes in the course of our app's career. The problem here is that the data is stored in
two different places — the Documents directory or the cloud-shared directory. Suppose,
for example, that our app starts life without iCloud — because the user hasn't registered
for it, or has it turned off for our app — and then suddenly iCloud is available. We could
then call NSFileManager's `setUbiquitous:itemAtURL:destinationURL:error:` to
transfer the document to our ubiquity container directory. However, it is not so obvious
what to do if iCloud is switched from On to Off, as it is now too late to access the ubiquity
container directory to rescue the document; in effect, the cloud-based data is lost (until
the user logs back into that iCloud account).

Note also the "Use key–value store" checkbox in Figure 23-7. Instead of, or in addition
to, storing full-fledged documents in the cloud, your app might like to store some key-
value pairs, similar to a sort of online NSUserDefaults. To do so, check that checkbox,
and then use the NSUbiquitousKeyValueStore class; get the `defaultStore` shared object
and talk to it much as you would talk to NSUserDefaults. The `NSUbiquitousKeyValue-`
`StoreDidChangeExternallyNotification` tells you when data is changed in the cloud.
Material that you store in the cloud through NSUbiquitousKeyValueStore does *not*
count against the user's iCloud storage limit, but it needs to be kept short and simple.

Further iCloud details are outside the scope of this discussion; see Apple's *iCloud Design
Guide*. Getting started is easy; making your app a good iCloud citizen, capable of dealing
with the complexities that iCloud may entail, is not.

New in Xcode 5, iCloud apps can be tested in the Simulator. Also, the
Debug navigator adds an iCloud graph when your app is working with
iCloud, allowing you to track cloud storage and transfer (Figure 23-8);
in my testing, however, this worked only when running on a device.

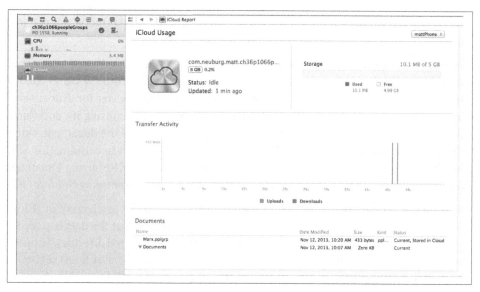

Figure 23-8. The iCloud graph in Xcode's Debug navigator

XML

XML is a highly flexible and widely used general-purpose text file format for storage and retrieval of structured data. You might use it yourself to store data that you'll need to retrieve later, or you could encounter it when obtaining information from elsewhere, such as the Internet.

OS X Cocoa provides a set of classes (NSXMLDocument and so forth) for reading, parsing, maintaining, searching, and modifying XML data in a completely general way, but iOS does *not* include these. I think the reason must be that their tree-based approach is too memory-intensive. Instead, iOS provides NSXMLParser, a much simpler class that walks through an XML document, sending delegate messages as it encounters elements. With this, you can parse an XML document once, but what you do with the pieces as they arrive is up to you. The general assumption here is that you know in advance the structure of the particular XML data you intend to read and that you have provided classes for storage of the same data in object form and for transforming the XML pieces into that storage.

To illustrate, let's return once more to our Person class with a firstName and a last-Name property. Imagine that as our app starts up, we would like to populate it with Person objects, and that we've stored the data describing these objects as an XML file in our app bundle, like this:

```
<?xml version="1.0" encoding="utf-8"?>
<people>
    <person>
        <firstName>Matt</firstName>
        <lastName>Neuburg</lastName>
    </person>
    <person>
        <firstName>Snidely</firstName>
        <lastName>Whiplash</lastName>
    </person>
    <person>
        <firstName>Dudley</firstName>
        <lastName>Doright</lastName>
    </person>
</people>
```

This data could be mapped to an array of Person objects, each with its `firstName` and `lastName` properties appropriately set. (This is a deliberately easy example, of course; not all XML is so readily expressed as objects.) Let's consider how we might do that.

Using NSXMLParser is not difficult in theory. You create the NSXMLParser, handing it the URL of a local XML file (or an NSData, perhaps downloaded from the Internet), set its delegate, and tell it to `parse`. The delegate starts receiving delegate messages. For simple XML like ours, there are only three delegate messages of interest:

`parser:didStartElement:namespaceURI:qualifiedName:attributes:`
> The parser has encountered an opening element tag. In our document, this would be `<people>`, `<person>`, `<firstName>`, or `<lastName>`.

`parser:didEndElement:namespaceURI:qualifiedName:`
> The parser has encountered the corresponding closing element tag. In our document this would be `</people>`, `</person>`, `</firstName>`, or `</lastName>`.

`parser:foundCharacters:`
> The parser has encountered some text between the starting and closing tags for the current element. In our document this would be, for example, `Matt` or `Neuburg` and so on.

In practice, responding to these delegate messages poses challenges of maintaining state. If there is just one delegate, it will have to bear in mind at every moment what element it is currently encountering; this could make for a lot of instance variables and a lot of if-statements in the implementation of the delegate methods. To aggravate the issue, `parser:foundCharacters:` can arrive multiple times for a single stretch of text; that is, the text may arrive in pieces, so we have to accumulate it into an instance variable.

An elegant way to meet these challenges is by resetting the NSXMLParser's delegate to different objects at different stages of the parsing process. We make each delegate responsible for parsing one element; when a child of that element is encountered, we make a new object and make *it* the delegate. The child element delegate is then responsible for making the parent the delegate once again when it finishes parsing its own element. This is slightly counterintuitive because it means `parser:didStartElement...` and `parser:didEndElement...` for the same element are arriving at two different objects. Imagine, for example, what the job of our `<people>` parser will be:

- When `parser:didStartElement...` arrives, the `<people>` parser looks to see if this is a `<person>`. If so, it creates an object that knows how to deal with a `<person>`, handing that object a reference to itself (the `<people>` parser), and makes it the delegate.

- Delegate messages now arrive at this newly created `<person>` parser. If any text is encountered, `parser:foundCharacters:` will be called, and the text must be accumulated into an instance variable.

- Eventually, `parser:didEndElement...` arrives. The `<person>` parser now uses its reference to make the `<people>` parser the delegate once again. Thus, the `<people>` parser is in charge once again, ready if another `<person>` element is encountered (and the old `<person>` parser might now go quietly out of existence).

With this in mind, we can design a simple all-purpose base class for parsing an element (simple especially because we are taking no account of namespaces, attributes, and other complications):

```
@interface MyXMLParserDelegate : NSObject <NSXMLParserDelegate>
@property (nonatomic, copy) NSString* name;
@property (nonatomic, strong) NSMutableString* text;
@property (nonatomic, weak) MyXMLParserDelegate* parent;
@property (nonatomic, strong) MyXMLParserDelegate* child;
- (void) start: (NSString*) elementName parent: (id) parent;
- (void) makeChild: (Class) class
        elementName: (NSString*) elementName
            parser: (NSXMLParser*) parser;
- (void) finishedChild: (NSString*) s;
@end
```

Here's how these properties and methods are intended to work:

name
> The name of the element we are parsing now.

text
> A place for any characters to accumulate as we parse our element.

parent
> The MyXMLParserDelegate who created us and whose child we are.

child

If we encounter a child element, we'll create a MyXMLParserDelegate and retain it here, making it the delegate.

start:parent:

When we create a child parser, we'll call this method on the child so that it knows who its parent is. The first parameter is the name of the element the child will be parsing; we know this because we, not the child, received `parser:didStart-Element....` (In a fuller implementation, this method would be more elaborate and we'd hand the child *all* the information we got with `parser:didStart-Element....`)

makeChild:elementName:parser:

If we encounter a child element, there's a standard dance to do: instantiate some subclass of MyXMLParserDelegate, make it our `child`, make it the parser's delegate, and send it `start:parent:`. This is a utility method that embodies that dance.

finishedChild:

When a child receives `parser:didEndElement...`, it sends this message to its parent before making its parent the delegate. The parameter is the `text`, but the parent can use this signal to obtain any information it expects from the child before the child goes out of existence.

Now we can sketch in the default implementation for MyXMLParserDelegate:

```
- (void) start: (NSString*) el parent: (id) p {
    self.name = el;
    self.parent = p;
    self.text = [NSMutableString string];
}
- (void) makeChild: (Class) class
        elementName: (NSString*) elementName
            parser: (NSXMLParser*) parser {
    MyXMLParserDelegate* del = [class new];
    self.child = del;
    parser.delegate = del;
    [del start: elementName parent: self];
}
- (void) finishedChild: (NSString*) s { // subclass implements as desired
}
- (void)parser:(NSXMLParser *)parser foundCharacters:(NSString *)string {
    [self.text appendString:string];
}
- (void)parser:(NSXMLParser *)parser didEndElement:(NSString *)elementName
        namespaceURI:(NSString *)namespaceURI qualifiedName:(NSString *)qName {
    if (self.parent) {
```

```
            [self.parent finishedChild: [self.text copy]];
            parser.delegate = self.parent;
        }
    }
```

Next, we create subclasses of MyXMLParserDelegate, one for each kind of element we
expect to parse. The chief responsibility of such a subclass, if it encounters a child element in `parser:didStartElement...`, is to create an instance of the appropriate My-
XMLParserDelegate subclass, send it `start:parent:`, and make it the delegate; we have
already embodied this in the utility method `makeChild:elementName:parser:`. The
reverse process is already built into the default implementation of `parser:didEnd-`
`Element...`: we call the parent's `finishedChild:` and make the parent the delegate.

We can now parse our sample XML into an array of Person objects very easily. We start
by obtaining the URL of the XML file, handing it to an NSXMLParser, creating our first
delegate parser and making it the delegate, and telling the NSXMLParser to start parsing:

```
NSURL* url =
    [[NSBundle mainBundle] URLForResource:@"folks" withExtension:@"xml"];
NSXMLParser* parser = [[NSXMLParser alloc] initWithContentsOfURL:url];
MyPeopleParser* people = [MyPeopleParser new];
[parser setDelegate: people];
[parser parse];
// ... do something with people.people ...
```

Here is MyPeopleParser. It is the top-level parser, so it has some extra work to do: when
it encounters the <people> element, which is the first thing that should happen, it creates
the people array that will hold the Person objects; this array will be the final result of
the entire parsing operation. If it encounters a <person> element, it does the standard
dance I described earlier, creating a <person> parser (MyPersonParser) as its child and
making it the delegate; when the <person> parser calls back to tell us it's finished, My-
PeopleParser expects the <person> parser to supply a Person through its person
property:

```
- (void)parser:(NSXMLParser *)parser didStartElement:(NSString *)elementName
        namespaceURI:(NSString *)namespaceURI
        qualifiedName:(NSString *)qualifiedName
        attributes:(NSDictionary *)attributeDict
{
    if ([elementName isEqualToString: @"people"])
        self.people = [NSMutableArray array];
    if ([elementName isEqualToString: @"person"])
        [self makeChild:[MyPersonParser class] elementName:elementName
                parser:parser];
}
- (void) finishedChild: (NSString*) s {
    [self.people addObject: [(MyPersonParser*)self.child person]];
}
```

MyPersonParser does the same child-making dance when it encounters a `<first-Name>` or a `<lastName>` element; it uses a plain vanilla MyXMLParserDelegate to parse these children, because the built-in ability to accumulate text and hand it back is all that's needed. In `finishedChild:`, it makes sure it has a Person object ready to hand back to its parent through its `person` property; key–value coding is elegantly used to match the name of the element with the name of the Person property to be set:

```
- (void)parser:(NSXMLParser *)parser didStartElement:(NSString *)elementName
        namespaceURI:(NSString *)namespaceURI
        qualifiedName:(NSString *)qualifiedName
        attributes:(NSDictionary *)attributeDict {
    [self makeChild:[MyXMLParserDelegate class] elementName:elementName
            parser:parser];
}
- (void) finishedChild:(NSString *)s {
    if (!self.person) {
        Person* p = [Person new];
        self.person = p; // retain policy
    }
    [self.person setValue: s forKey: self.child.name];
}
```

This may seem like a lot of work to parse such a simple bit of XML, but it is neatly object-oriented and requires very little new code once we've established the MyXMLParser-Delegate superclass, which is of course reusable in many other situations.

On the other hand, if you really want tree-based XML parsing along with XPath and so forth, you can have it, because the `libxml2` library is present in the SDK (and on the device). This is a C *dylib* (short for "dynamic library," extension *.dylib*), and Xcode doesn't automatically know during the build process where to find its headers (even though it's part of the SDK), so the instructions for accessing it in your project are a tiny bit more involved than linking to an Objective-C framework:

1. Add *libxml2.dylib* to the Link Binary With Libraries build phase for your app target, just as you would do with a framework.

2. Edit the target's build settings and set the Header Search Paths build setting to `$SDKROOT/usr/include/libxml2`. (When you close the dialog for adding a search path, this will transform itself into *iphoneos/usr/include/libxml2*.)

3. In your code, import `<libxml/tree.h>`.

You now have to talk to `libxml2` using C. This is no trivial task. Here's an example proving we can do it; we read our XML file, parse it into a tree, and traverse all its elements:

```
NSURL* url =
    [[NSBundle mainBundle] URLForResource:@"folks" withExtension:@"xml"];
NSString* path = [url absoluteString];
const char* filename = [path UTF8String];
xmlDocPtr doc = nil;
xmlNode *root_element = nil;
doc = xmlReadFile(filename, nil, 0);
root_element = xmlDocGetRootElement(doc);
traverse_elements(root_element); // must be previously defined
xmlFreeDoc(doc);
xmlCleanupParser();
```

Here's our definition for `traverse_elements`; it logs each person and the person's first and last name, just to prove we are traversing successfully:

```
void traverse_elements(xmlNode * a_node) {
    xmlNode *cur_node = nil;
    for (cur_node = a_node; cur_node; cur_node = cur_node->next) {
        if (cur_node->type == XML_ELEMENT_NODE) {
            if (strcmp(cur_node->name, "person") == 0)
                NSLog(@"found a person");
            if (strcmp(cur_node->name, "firstName") == 0)
                NSLog(@"First name: %s", cur_node->children->content);
            if (strcmp(cur_node->name, "lastName") == 0)
                NSLog(@"Last name: %s", cur_node->children->content);
        }
        traverse_elements(cur_node->children);
    }
}
```

If talking C to `libxml2` is too daunting, you can interpose an Objective-C front end by taking advantage of a third-party library. See, for example, *https://github.com/Touch Code/TouchXML*.

Keep in mind, however, that you're really not supposed to do what I just did. Even if you use `libxml2`, you're supposed to use stream-based parsing, not tree-based parsing. See Apple's XMLPerformance example code.

A foundation class for constructing and parsing JSON strings is also provided — NSJSONSerialization. It's a very simple class: all its methods are class methods, and eligible structures are required to be an array or dictionary (corresponding to what JSON calls an *object*) whose elements must be a string, number, array, dictionary, or null. NSData is used as the medium of exchange; you'll archive or unarchive as appropriate. JSON arises often as a lightweight way of communicating structured data across the network; for more information, see *http://www.json.org/*.

SQLite

SQLite (*http://www.sqlite.org/docs.html*) is a lightweight, full-featured relational database that you can talk to using SQL, the universal language of databases. This can be an appropriate storage format when your data comes in rows and columns (records and fields) and needs to be rapidly searchable. Also, the database as a whole is never loaded into memory; the data is accessed only as needed. This is valuable in an environment like an iOS device, where memory is at a premium.

To use SQLite, link to *libsqlite3.dylib* (and import `<sqlite3.h>`). As with `libxml2`, talking C to `sqlite3` may prove annoying. There are a number of lightweight Objective-C front ends. In this example, I use `fmdb` (*https://github.com/ccgus/fmdb*) to read the names of people out of a previously created database:

```
NSString* docsdir = [NSSearchPathForDirectoriesInDomains(
    NSDocumentDirectory, NSUserDomainMask, YES) lastObject];
NSString* dbpath = [docsdir stringByAppendingPathComponent:@"people.db"];
FMDatabase* db = [FMDatabase databaseWithPath:dbpath];
if (![db open]) {
    NSLog(@"Ooops");
    return;
}
FMResultSet *rs = [db executeQuery:@"select * from people"];
while ([rs next]) {
    NSLog(@"%@ %@", rs[@"firstname"], rs[@"lastname"]);
}
[db close];
/* output:
Matt Neuburg
Snidely Whiplash
Dudley Doright
*/
```

You can include a previously constructed SQLite file in your app bundle, but you can't write to it there; the solution is to copy it from your app bundle into another location, such as the Documents directory, before you start working with it.

Core Data

The Core Data framework provides a generalized way of expressing objects and properties that form a relational graph; moreover, it has built-in facilities for persisting those objects to disk — typically using SQLite as a storage format — and reading them from disk only when they are needed, thus making efficient use of memory. For example, a person might have not only multiple addresses but also multiple friends who are also persons; expressing persons and addresses as explicit object types, working out how to link them and how to translate between objects in memory and data in storage, and tracking the effects of changes, such as when a person is deleted from the data, can be tedious. Core Data can help.

It is important to stress, however, that Core Data is *not* a beginner-level technology. It is difficult to use and extremely difficult to debug. It expresses itself in a highly verbose, rigid, arcane way. It has its own elaborate way of doing things — everything you already know about how to create, access, alter, or delete an object within an object collection becomes completely irrelevant! — and trying to bend it to your particular needs can be tricky and can have unintended side effects. Nor should Core Data be seen as a substitute for a true relational database.

Therefore, I have no intention of explaining Core Data; that would require an entire book. Indeed, such books exist, and if Core Data interests you, you should read some of them. See also Apple's *Core Data Programming Guide* and the other resources referred to there. I will, however, illustrate what it's like to work with Core Data.

I will describe the People Groups example from earlier in this chapter as a Core Data app. We will no longer have multiple documents, each representing a single group of people; instead, we will now have a single document, maintained for us by Core Data, containing all of our groups and all of their people.

A Core Data project is linked to *CoreData.framework* and will import `<CoreData/Core-Data.h>`, usually in the precompiled header file. To construct a Core Data project from scratch, it is simplest to specify the Master–Detail Application template (or the Empty Application template) and check Use Core Data in the second screen. This gives you the necessary linkage to the Core Data framework, along with template code in the app delegate implementation file for constructing the Core Data *persistence stack*, a set of objects that work together to fetch and save your data; in most cases there will no reason to alter this template code, and I have not done so for this example.

The app delegate template code gives the app delegate three properties representing the important singleton objects constituting the persistence stack: `managedObject-Context`, `managedObjectModel`, and `persistentStoreCoordinator`. It also supplies "lazy" getters to give these properties their values when first needed. Of these, the `managedObjectContext` is the most important for other classes to have access to. The managed object context is the world in which your data objects live and move and have their being: to obtain an object, you fetch it from the managed object context; to create an object, you insert it into the managed object context; to save your data, you save the managed object context.

The Master–Detail Application template also gives the Master view controller a `managed-ObjectContext` property, and the app delegate sets its value. My Master view controller is called GroupLister, so the app delegate's `application:didFinishLaunchingWith-Options:` contains these lines:

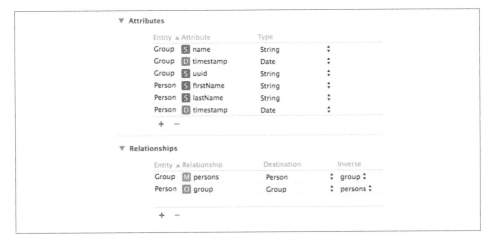

Figure 23-9. The Core Data model for the People Groups app

```
UINavigationController *navigationController =
    (UINavigationController *)self.window.rootViewController;
GroupLister *controller =
    (GroupLister *)navigationController.topViewController;
controller.managedObjectContext = self.managedObjectContext;
```

To describe the structure and relationships of the objects constituting your data model, you design an object graph in a data model document. Our object graph is very simple: a Group can have multiple Persons (Figure 23-9). The attributes, analogous to object properties, are all strings, except for the timestamps which are dates; the timestamps will be used for determining the sort order in which groups and people will be displayed in the interface — the display order is the order of creation.

Core Data attributes are not quite object properties. Group and Person are not classes; they are entity names. All Core Data model objects are instances of NSManagedObject, and therefore they do not, of themselves, have a name property, a firstName property, a lastName property, and so on. Instead, Core Data model objects make themselves dynamically KVC compliant for attribute names. For example, Core Data knows, thanks to our object graph, that a Person entity is to have a firstName attribute, so you can set a Person's firstName attribute using KVC (setValue:forKey:). I find this maddening, so, at the very least, I like to give NSManagedObject the necessary properties through a category:

```
// NSManagedObject+GroupAndPerson.h:
#import <CoreData/CoreData.h>
@interface NSManagedObject (GroupAndPerson)
@property (nonatomic) NSString *firstName, *lastName;
@property (nonatomic) NSString *name, *uuid;
@property (nonatomic) NSDate* timestamp;
```

```
@property (nonatomic) NSManagedObject* group;
@end

// NSManagedObject+GroupAndPerson.m:
#import "NSManagedObject+GroupAndPerson.h"
@implementation NSManagedObject (GroupAndPerson)
@dynamic firstName, lastName, name, uuid, timestamp, group;
@end
```

Now we'll be able to use `name` and `firstName` and the rest as properties, and CoreData will generate the corresponding accessors for us.

Now let's talk about the first view controller, GroupLister. Its job is to list groups and to allow the user to create a new group (Figure 23-5). The way you ask Core Data for a model object is with a fetch request. In iOS, where Core Data model objects are often the data source for a UITableView, fetch requests are conveniently managed through an NSFetchedResultsController. The template code gives us an NSFetchedResultsController property, along with a "lazy" getter method that generates an NSFetchedResultsController if the property is nil, and for GroupLister I've only had to change it a little bit: my entity name is Group and my cache name is Groups, and I've renamed the property itself, `frc`.

The result is that `self.frc` is the data model, analogous to an array of Group objects. The implementation of the table view's Three Big Questions to the data source, all pretty much straight from the template code, looks like this:

```
- (NSInteger)numberOfSectionsInTableView:(UITableView *)tableView {
    return [self.frc.sections count];
}
- (NSInteger)tableView:(UITableView *)tableView
        numberOfRowsInSection:(NSInteger)section {
    id<NSFetchedResultsSectionInfo> sectionInfo = self.frc.sections[section];
    return sectionInfo.numberOfObjects;
}
- (UITableViewCell *)tableView:(UITableView *)tableView
        cellForRowAtIndexPath:(NSIndexPath *)indexPath {
    UITableViewCell *cell =
        [tableView dequeueReusableCellWithIdentifier:@"Cell"
            forIndexPath:indexPath];
    cell.accessoryType = UITableViewCellAccessoryDisclosureIndicator;
    NSManagedObject *object = [self.frc objectAtIndexPath:indexPath];
    cell.textLabel.text = object.name;
    return cell;
}
```

Now let's talk about object creation. GroupLister's table is initially empty because our app starts out life with no data. When the user asks to create a group, I put up a UIAlert-View asking for the name of the new group. If the user provides a valid name, I create a new Group entity and save the managed object context. Again, this is almost boilerplate code, copied from the template's `insertNewObject:` method:

```
NSManagedObjectContext *context = self.frc.managedObjectContext;
NSEntityDescription *entity = self.frc.fetchRequest.entity;
NSManagedObject *mo =
    [NSEntityDescription insertNewObjectForEntityForName:entity.name
                                 inManagedObjectContext:context];
mo.name = name;
mo.uuid = [[NSUUID UUID] UUIDString];
mo.timestamp = [NSDate date];
// save context
NSError *error = nil;
BOOL ok = [context save:&error];
if (!ok) {
    NSLog(@"%@", error);
    return;
}
```

The second view controller class is PeopleLister (Figure 23-5). It lists all the people in a particular Group, so I don't want PeopleLister to be instantiated without a Group; therefore, its designated initializer is initWithNibName:bundle:groupManaged-Object:, and it looks like this:

```
- (id) initWithNibName:(NSString *)nibNameOrNil
            bundle:(NSBundle *)nibBundleOrNil
            groupManagedObject: (NSManagedObject*) object {
    self = [super initWithNibName:nibNameOrNil bundle:nibBundleOrNil];
    if (self) {
        self->_groupObject = object;
    }
    return self;
}
```

To navigate from the GroupLister view to the PeopleLister view, I instantiate People-Lister and push it onto the navigation controller's stack. For example, here's what happens when the user taps a Group name in the GroupLister table view:

```
- (void)tableView:(UITableView *)tableView
        didSelectRowAtIndexPath:(NSIndexPath *)indexPath {
    PeopleLister* pl =
        [[PeopleLister alloc] initWithNibName:@"PeopleLister" bundle:nil
            groupManagedObject:[self.frc objectAtIndexPath:indexPath]];
    [self.navigationController pushViewController:pl animated:YES];
}
```

PeopleLister, too, has an frc property, along with a getter that is almost identical to the template code for generating an NSFetchedResultsController — almost, but not quite. In the case of GroupLister, we wanted every group; but a PeopleLister instance should list only the People belonging to one particular group, which has been stored as the groupObject property. So PeopleLister's implementation of the frc getter method contains these lines:

```
NSPredicate* pred =
    [NSPredicate predicateWithFormat:@"group = %@", self.groupObject];
req.predicate = pred; // req is the NSFetchRequest we're configuring
```

As you can see from Figure 23-5, the PeopleLister interface consists of a table of text fields. Populating the table is easy enough:

```
- (UITableViewCell *)tableView:(UITableView *)tableView
        cellForRowAtIndexPath:(NSIndexPath *)indexPath {
    UITableViewCell *cell =
        [tableView dequeueReusableCellWithIdentifier:@"Person"
            forIndexPath:indexPath];
    NSManagedObject *object = [self.frc objectAtIndexPath:indexPath];
    UITextField* first = (UITextField*)[cell viewWithTag:1];
    UITextField* last = (UITextField*)[cell viewWithTag:2];
    first.text = object.firstName;
    last.text = object.lastName;
    first.delegate = last.delegate = self;
    return cell;
}
```

When the user edits a text field (the first or last name of a Person), I update the data model and save the managed object context; the first part of this code should be familiar from Chapter 8:

```
-(void)textFieldDidEndEditing:(UITextField *)textField {
    UIView* v = textField.superview;
    while (![v isKindOfClass: [UITableViewCell class]])
        v = v.superview;
    UITableViewCell* cell = (UITableViewCell*)v;
    NSIndexPath* ip = [self.tableView indexPathForCell:cell];
    NSManagedObject* object = [self.frc objectAtIndexPath:ip];
    [object setValue:textField.text
            forKey: ((textField.tag == 1) ? @"firstName" : @"lastName")];
    // save context
    NSError *error = nil;
    BOOL ok = [object.managedObjectContext save:&error];
    if (!ok) {
      NSLog(@"%@", error);
      return;
    }
}
```

The trickiest part is what happens when the user asks to make a new Person. It starts out analogously to making a new Group: I make a new Person entity, configure its attributes with an empty first name and last name, and save the context. But we must also make this empty Person appear in the table! To do so, we act as the NSFetchedResultsController's delegate (NSFetchedResultsControllerDelegate); the delegate methods are triggered by the change in the managed object context:

```
- (void) doAdd: (id) sender {
    [self.tableView endEditing:YES];
    NSManagedObjectContext *context = self.frc.managedObjectContext;
    NSEntityDescription *entity = self.frc.fetchRequest.entity;
    NSManagedObject *mo =
    [NSEntityDescription insertNewObjectForEntityForName:[entity name]
                                 inManagedObjectContext:context];
    mo.group = self.groupObject;
    mo.lastName = @"";
    mo.firstName = @"";
    mo.timestamp = [NSDate date];
    // save context
    NSError *error = nil;
    BOOL ok = [context save:&error];
    if (!ok) {
        NSLog(@"%@", error);
        return;
    }
}
// ================= delegate methods =====================
-(void)controllerWillChangeContent:(NSFetchedResultsController *)controller {
    [self.tableView beginUpdates];
}
-(void)controllerDidChangeContent:(NSFetchedResultsController *)controller {
    [self.tableView endUpdates];
}
-(void)controller:(NSFetchedResultsController *)controller
  didChangeObject:(id)anObject
      atIndexPath:(NSIndexPath *)indexPath
    forChangeType:(NSFetchedResultsChangeType)type
     newIndexPath:(NSIndexPath *)newIndexPath {
    if (type == NSFetchedResultsChangeInsert) {
        [self.tableView insertRowsAtIndexPaths:@[newIndexPath]
            withRowAnimation:UITableViewRowAnimationAutomatic];
        // wait for interface to settle...
        // ...then start editing first name of new person
        dispatch_async(dispatch_get_main_queue(), ^{
            UITableViewCell* cell =
                [self.tableView cellForRowAtIndexPath:newIndexPath];
            UITextField* tf = (UITextField*)[cell viewWithTag:1];
            [tf becomeFirstResponder];
        });
    }
}
```

Image File Formats

The Image I/O framework provides a simple, unified way to open image files (from disk
or downloaded from the network, as described in Chapter 24), to save image files, to
convert between image file formats, and to read metadata from standard image file

formats, including EXIF and GPS information from a digital camera. You'll need to @import ImageIO.

Obviously, such features were not entirely missing from iOS before the Image I/O framework was introduced (starting in iOS 4). UIImage can read the data from most standard image formats, and you can convert formats with functions such as UIImage-JPEGRepresentation and UIImagePNGRepresentation. But you could not, for example, save an image as a TIFF without the Image I/O framework.

The Image I/O framework introduces the notion of an *image source* (CGImageSource-Ref). This can be created from the URL of a file on disk or from an NSData object (actually CFDataRef, to which NSData is toll-free bridged). You can use this to obtain a CGImage of the source's image (or, if the source format contains multiple images, a particular image). But you can also obtain metadata from the source *without* transforming the source into a CGImage, thus conserving memory. For example:

```
NSURL* url =
    [[NSBundle mainBundle] URLForResource:@"colson"
                             withExtension:@"jpg"];
CGImageSourceRef src =
    CGImageSourceCreateWithURL((__bridge CFURLRef)url, nil);
CFDictionaryRef result1 = CGImageSourceCopyPropertiesAtIndex(src, 0, nil);
NSDictionary* result = CFBridgingRelease(result1);
// ... do something with result ...
CFRelease(src);
```

Without having opened the image file as an image, we now have a dictionary full of information about it, including its pixel dimensions (kCGImagePropertyPixelWidth and kCGImagePropertyPixelHeight), its resolution, its color model, its color depth, and its orientation — plus, because this picture originally comes from a digital camera, the EXIF data such as the aperture and exposure at which it was taken, plus the make and model of the camera.

We can obtain the image as a CGImage, with CGImageSourceCreateImageAtIndex. Alternatively, we can request a thumbnail version of the image. This is a very useful thing to do, and the name "thumbnail" doesn't really do it justice. If your purpose in opening this image is to display it in your interface, you don't care about the original image data; a thumbnail is *precisely* what you want, especially because you can specify any size for this "thumbnail" all the way up to the original size of the image! This is tremendously convenient, because to assign a small UIImageView a large image wastes all the memory reflected by the size difference.

To generate a thumbnail at a given size, you start with a dictionary specifying the size along with other instructions, and pass that, together with the image source, to CGImage-SourceCreateThumbnailAtIndex. The only pitfall is that, because we are working with a CGImage and specifying actual pixels, we must remember to take account of the scale of our device's screen. So, for example, let's say we want to scale our image so that its largest dimension is no larger than the width of the UIImageView (`self.iv`) into which we intend to place it:

```
NSURL* url =
    [[NSBundle mainBundle] URLForResource:@"colson"
                            withExtension:@"jpg"];
CGImageSourceRef src =
    CGImageSourceCreateWithURL((__bridge CFURLRef)url, nil);
CGFloat scale = [UIScreen mainScreen].scale;
CGFloat w = self.iv.bounds.size.width*scale;
NSDictionary* d =
    @{(id)kCGImageSourceShouldAllowFloat: (id)kCFBooleanTrue,
      (id)kCGImageSourceCreateThumbnailWithTransform: (id)kCFBooleanTrue,
      (id)kCGImageSourceCreateThumbnailFromImageAlways: (id)kCFBooleanTrue,
      (id)kCGImageSourceThumbnailMaxPixelSize: @((int)w)};
CGImageRef imref =
    CGImageSourceCreateThumbnailAtIndex(src, 0, (__bridge CFDictionaryRef)d);
UIImage* im =
    [UIImage imageWithCGImage:imref scale:scale
                  orientation:UIImageOrientationUp];
self.iv.image = im;
CFRelease(imref); CFRelease(src);
```

The Image I/O framework also introduces the notion of an *image destination*, used for saving an image into a specified file format. As a final example, I'll show how to save our image as a TIFF. We never open the image as an image! We save directly from the image source to the image destination:

```
NSURL* url =
    [[NSBundle mainBundle] URLForResource:@"colson"
                            withExtension:@"jpg"];
CGImageSourceRef src =
    CGImageSourceCreateWithURL((__bridge CFURLRef)url, nil);
NSFileManager* fm = [NSFileManager new];
NSURL* suppurl = [fm URLForDirectory:NSApplicationSupportDirectory
                            inDomain:NSUserDomainMask
                   appropriateForURL:nil
                              create:YES error:nil];
NSURL* tiff = [suppurl URLByAppendingPathComponent:@"mytiff.tiff"];
CGImageDestinationRef dest =
    CGImageDestinationCreateWithURL((__bridge CFURLRef)tiff,
                                    (CFStringRef)@"public.tiff", 1, nil);
CGImageDestinationAddImageFromSource(dest, src, 0, nil);
bool ok = CGImageDestinationFinalize(dest);
// error-checking omitted
CFRelease(src); CFRelease(dest);
```

CHAPTER 24

Basic Networking

Networking is difficult and complicated, chiefly because it's ultimately out of your control. My motto with regard to the network is, "There's many a slip 'twixt the cup and the lip." You can ask for a resource from across the network, but at that point anything can happen: the resource might not be found (the server is down, perhaps), it might take a while to arrive, it might never arrive, the network itself might vanish after the resource has partially arrived. iOS, however, makes at least the *basics* of networking very easy, so that's what this chapter will deal with.

To go further into networking than this chapter takes you, start with Apple's *URL Loading System Programming Guide*. To go even deeper under the hood, see the *CFNetwork Programming Guide*. Apple also provides a generous amount of sample code. See in particular SimpleURLConnections, AdvancedURLConnections, SimpleNetwork-Streams, SimpleFTPSample, and MVCNetworking.

Many earlier chapters have described interface and frameworks that network for you automatically. Put a UIWebView in your interface (Chapter 11) and poof, you're networking; the UIWebView does all the grunt work, and it does it a lot better than you'd be likely to do it from scratch. The same is true of MPMovieViewController (Chapter 15), MFMailComposeViewController (Chapter 20), and MKMapView (Chapter 24).

HTTP Requests

In iOS 7, an HTTP request is made through an NSURLSession object. An NSURLSession is a kind of grand overarching environment in which network-related tasks are to take place. You will often need only one NSURLSession object. For very simple, occasional use, this object might be the singleton sharedSession object. More generally, you'll create your own NSURLSession by calling sessionWithConfiguration: or sessionWithConfiguration:delegate:delegateQueue:, handing it an NSURLSessionConfiguration object describing the desired environment.

The NSURLSession class, together with its related classes, supersedes the NSURLConnection class from iOS 6 and before. NSURLConnection still exists and is not deprecated, but you won't need it unless you have backward-compatible code, so I'm not going to discuss it; the future, and the power, lies in NSURLSession.

To use the NSURLSession object to perform a request across the network, you ask it for a new NSURLSessionTask object. This is the object that actually performs (and represents) one upload or download process. NSURLSessionTask is an abstract class, embodying various properties, such as:

- A taskDescription and taskIdentifier; the former is up to you, while the latter is a unique identifier within the NSURLSession
- The originalRequest and currentRequest (the request can change because there might be a redirect)
- An initial response from the server
- Various countOfBytes... properties allowing you to track progress
- A state, which might be:
  — NSURLSessionTaskStateRunning
  — NSURLSessionTaskStateSuspended
  — NSURLSessionTaskStateCanceling
  — NSURLSessionTaskStateCompleted
- An error if the task failed

In addition, you can tell a task to resume, suspend, or cancel. A task is born suspended, and does not start until it is told to resume for the first time.

There are three kinds of actual session task:

NSURLSessionDataTask
An NSURLSessionTask subclass. With a data task, the data is provided incrementally to your app as it arrives across the network.

NSURLSessionDownloadTask
An NSURLSessionTask subclass. With a download task, the data is stored as a file, and the saved file URL is handed to you at the end of the process. The file is outside your sandbox and will be destroyed, so preserving it (or its contents) is up to you.

NSURLSessionUploadTask
> An NSURLSessionDataTask subclass. With an upload task, you can provide a file to be uploaded and stand back, though you can also hear about the upload progress if you wish.

Once you've obtained a new session task from the NSURLSession, you can keep a reference to it if you wish, but you don't have to; the NSURLSession retains it. The NSURL-Session will provide you with a list of its tasks in progress; call `getTasksWithCompletion-Handler:`. The completion handler is handed three arrays, one for each type of task. The NSURLSession releases a task after it is canceled or completed. Thus, if an NSURL-Session has no running or suspended tasks, the three arrays are empty.

There are two ways to ask your NSURLSession for a new NSURLSessionTask:

Call a convenience method
> The convenience methods all take a `completionHandler:` parameter. This completion handler is called when the task process ends.

Call a delegate-based method
> You give the NSURLSession a delegate when you create it, and the delegate is called back at various stages of a task's progress.

The two ways of asking for an NSURLSessionTask entail two different ways of working with it. I'll demonstrate both.

Simple HTTP Request

I'll start by illustrating the utmost in simplicity:

- We use the shared NSURLSession.
- We obtain a download task, handing it a URL and a completion handler.
- We call `resume` to start the data task.

Our code then finishes. Meanwhile, the download proceeds asynchronously on a background thread (so the interface is not blocked, and the user can tap buttons and so forth). When the download finishes, the completion handler is called. We must make no assumptions about when the completion handler will be called or what thread it will be called on; indeed, unless we take steps to the contrary, it will be a background thread. In this particular example, the URL is that of an image that I intend to display in my interface; therefore, I step out to the main thread (Chapter 25) in order to talk to the interface:

```
NSString* s = @"http://www.someserver.com/somefolder/someimage.jpg";
NSURL* url = [NSURL URLWithString:s];
NSURLSession* session = [NSURLSession sharedSession];
NSURLSessionDownloadTask* task =
```

```
    [session downloadTaskWithURL:url completionHandler:
        ^(NSURL *loc, NSURLResponse *response, NSError *error) {
            NSData* d = [NSData dataWithContentsOfURL:loc];
            UIImage* im = [UIImage imageWithData:d];
            dispatch_async(dispatch_get_main_queue(), ^{
                self.iv.image = im;
            });
    }];
[task resume];
```

There's many a slip, as I've already mentioned, so in real life I would probably hedge my
bets a little more by checking for errors along the way; but the skeleton of the structure
remains exactly the same:

```
NSString* s = @"http://www.someserver.com/somefolder/someimage.jpg";
NSURL* url = [NSURL URLWithString:s];
NSURLSession* session = [NSURLSession sharedSession];
NSURLSessionDownloadTask* task =
    [session downloadTaskWithURL:url completionHandler:
        ^(NSURL *loc, NSURLResponse *response, NSError *error) {
            NSLog(@"%@", @"here");
            if (error) {
                NSLog(@"%@", error);
                return;
            }
            NSInteger status = [(NSHTTPURLResponse*)response statusCode];
            NSLog(@"response status: %i", status);
            if (status != 200) {
                NSLog(@"%@", @"oh well");
                return;
            }
            NSData* d = [NSData dataWithContentsOfURL:loc];
            UIImage* im = [UIImage imageWithData:d];
            dispatch_async(dispatch_get_main_queue(), ^{
                self.iv.image = im;
                NSLog(@"%@", @"done");
            });
    }];
[task resume];
```

Formal HTTP Request

Now let's go to the other extreme and be very formal:

- We'll create and retain our own NSURLSession.

- We'll configure the NSURLSession with an NSURLSessionConfiguration object.

- We'll give the session a delegate.

- Instead of a mere URL, we'll start with an NSURLRequest.

The NSURLSession class method we'll call to create the session will be `sessionWith-Configuration:delegate:delegateQueue:`. This lets us supply an NSURLSession-Configuration object dictating various options to be applied to the session. Possible options include:

- Whether to permit cell data use, or to require Wi-Fi
- The maximum number of simultaneous connections to the remote server
- Timeout values:

    `timeoutIntervalForRequest`
    The maximum time you're willing to wait *between* pieces of data.

    `timeoutIntervalForResource`
    The maximum time for the *entire* download to arrive.

- Cookie, caching, and credential policies

We also specify a delegate, as well as stating the queue (roughly, the thread — see Chapter 25) on which the delegate methods are to be called. For each type of task, there's a delegate protocol, which is itself often a composite of multiple protocols.

For example, for a data task, we would want a data delegate — an object conforming to the NSURLSessionDataDelegate protocol, which itself conforms to the NSURLSessionTaskDelegate protocol, which in turn conforms to the NSURLSessionDelegate protocol, resulting in about a dozen delegate methods we could implement, though only a few are crucial:

`URLSession:dataTask:didReceiveData:`
Some data has arrived, as an NSData object. The data will arrive piecemeal, so this method may be called many times during the download process, supplying new data each time. Our job is to accumulate all those chunks of data; this involves maintaining state between calls.

`URLSession:task:didCompleteWithError:`
If there is an error, we'll find out about it here. If there's no error, this is our signal that the download is over; we can now do something with the accumulated data.

Similarly, for a download task, we need a download delegate, conforming to NSURLSessionDownloadDelegate, which conforms to NSURLSessionTaskDelegate, which conforms to NSURLSessionDelegate. We'll need to implement these methods:

`URLSession:downloadTask:didResumeAtOffset:expectedTotalBytes:`
This method is of interest only in the case of a resumable download that has in fact been paused and resumed, but we have to implement it in order to silence the compiler.

`URLSession:downloadTask:didWriteData:totalBytesWritten:totalBytes-ExpectedToWrite:`
> Called periodically, to keep us apprised of the download's progress.

`URLSession:downloadTask:didFinishDownloadingToURL:`
> Called at the end of the process; we must grab the downloaded file immediately, as it will be destroyed.

It's also a good idea to implement `URLSession:task:didCompleteWithError:`; it will be called in any case, but if there was a communication problem, the `error:` parameter will tell you about it.

Here, then, is my recasting of the same image file download as in the previous example. Since one NSURLSession can perform multiple tasks, there will typically be just one NSURLSession; so I'll start with a utility method that creates and configures it:

```
- (NSURLSession*) configureSession {
    NSURLSessionConfiguration* config =
        [NSURLSessionConfiguration ephemeralSessionConfiguration];
    config.allowsCellularAccess = NO;
    NSURLSession* session =
        [NSURLSession sessionWithConfiguration:config delegate:self
            delegateQueue:[NSOperationQueue mainQueue]];
    return session;
}
```

I've specified, for purposes of the example, that no caching is to take place and that data downloading via cell is forbidden; you could configure the NSURLSession much more heavily and meaningfully, of course. I have specified `self` as the delegate, and I have requested delegate callbacks on the main thread.

I'm going to keep a reference both to the NSURLSession (`self.session`) and to the current download task (`self.task`). In this particular example, I'll perform just one task at a time, so I can use the task instance variable as a flag to indicate that the task is in progress. I blank out the image view, to make the progress of the task more obvious for test purposes, and I create, retain, and start the download task:

```
if (self.task)
    return;
if (!self.session)
    self.session = [self configureSession];
NSString* s = @"http://www.someserver.com/somefolder/someimage.jpg";
NSURL* url = [NSURL URLWithString:s];
NSURLRequest* req = [NSURLRequest requestWithURL:url];
NSURLSessionDownloadTask* task =
    [self.session downloadTaskWithRequest:req];
self.task = task;
self.iv.image = nil;
[task resume];
```

In this particular example, there is very little merit in using an NSURLRequest instead of an NSURL to form our task. Still, an NSURLRequest can come in handy (as I'll demonstrate later in this chapter), and an upload task requires one.

 When using NSURLSession, do *not* use the NSURLRequest to configure properties of the request that are configurable through the session. For example, there is no point setting the NSURLRequest's timeoutInterval, as it is the NSURLSession's timeout properties that are significant.

Here are some delegate methods for responding to the download:

```
-(void)URLSession:(NSURLSession *)session
      downloadTask:(NSURLSessionDownloadTask *)downloadTask
      didWriteData:(int64_t)bytesWritten
      totalBytesWritten:(int64_t)totalBytesWritten
      totalBytesExpectedToWrite:(int64_t)totalBytesExpectedToWrite {
    NSLog(@"downloaded %d%%",
       (int)(100.0*totalBytesWritten/totalBytesExpectedToWrite));
}
-(void)URLSession:(NSURLSession *)session
      downloadTask:(NSURLSessionDownloadTask *)downloadTask
      didResumeAtOffset:(int64_t)fileOffset
      expectedTotalBytes:(int64_t)expectedTotalBytes {
    // unused in this example
}
-(void)URLSession:(NSURLSession *)session
      task:(NSURLSessionTask *)task
      didCompleteWithError:(NSError *)error {
    NSLog(@"completed; error: %@", error);
}
-(void)URLSession:(NSURLSession *)session
      downloadTask:(NSURLSessionDownloadTask *)downloadTask
      didFinishDownloadingToURL:(NSURL *)location {
    self.task = nil;
    NSHTTPURLResponse* response =
        (NSHTTPURLResponse*)downloadTask.response;
    NSInteger stat = response.statusCode;
    NSLog(@"status %i", stat);
    if (stat != 200)
        return;
    NSData* d = [NSData dataWithContentsOfURL:location];
    UIImage* im = [UIImage imageWithData:d];
    dispatch_async(dispatch_get_main_queue(), ^{
        self.iv.image = im;
    });
}
```

Some delegate methods provide a `completionHandler:` parameter. These are delegate methods that require a response from you. For example, in the case of a data task, `URLSession:dataTask:didReceiveResponse:completionHandler:` arrives when we first connect to the server. Here, we could check the status code of the initial NSHTTPURLResponse. We must also return a response saying whether or not to proceed (or whether to convert the data task to a download task, which could certainly come in handy). But because of the multithreaded nature of networking, we do this, not by returning a value directly, but by calling the `completionHandler:` that we're handed as a parameter and passing our response into it. Several of the delegate methods are constructed in this way.

So, for example:

```
-(void)URLSession:(NSURLSession *)session
        dataTask:(NSURLSessionDataTask *)dataTask
        didReceiveResponse:(NSURLResponse *)response
        completionHandler:(void (^)(NSURLSessionResponseDisposition))ch {
    NSInteger status = [(NSHTTPURLResponse*)response statusCode];
    NSLog(@"got response: %d", status);
    ch(NSURLSessionResponseAllow);
}
```

There is one final and extremely important consideration when using NSURLSession with a delegate — memory management. The NSURLSession *retains its delegate*. This is understandable, as it would be disastrous if the delegate could simply vanish out from the middle of an asynchronous time-consuming process; but it is also unusual, and requires special measures on our part. At the moment, we have a retain cycle! We have an NSURLSession instance variable `self.session`, but that NSURLSession is retaining `self` as its delegate.

Like an NSTimer, the solution is to invalidate the NSURLSession at some appropriate moment. There are two ways to do this:

`finishTasksAndInvalidate`
    Allows any existing tasks to run to completion. Afterward, the NSURLSession releases the delegate and cannot be used for anything further.

`invalidateAndCancel`
    Interrupts any existing tasks immediately. The NSURLSession releases the delegate and cannot be used for anything further.

Let's suppose that `self` is a view controller. Then `viewWillDisappear:` could be a good place to invalidate the NSURLSession. (We cannot use `dealloc`, because `dealloc` won't be called until *after* we have invalidated the NSURLSession; that's what it means to have a retain cycle.) We should also nilify our reference to the NSURLSession so that, in case the view controller instance does not also go out of existence, we won't accidentally try to use the invalid NSURLSession again:

```
-(void)viewWillDisappear:(BOOL)animated {
    [super viewWillDisappear:animated];
    [self.session finishTasksAndInvalidate];
    self.session = nil;
}
```

Multiple Tasks

The little memory-management dance at the end of the preceding section is rather unsatisfactory. Things would be better if we had an instance of some separate class whose job is to hold the NSURLSession in a property and to serve as its delegate. There would still be a retain cycle until the NSURLSession was invalidated, but at least the management of this object's memory would not be entangled with that of a view controller.

Imagine, for example, a class MyDownloader, which holds an NSURLSession and serves as its delegate, and which has a public method cancelAllTasks. Then our view controller could create and maintain an instance of MyDownloader early in its lifetime, and could invalidate it in dealloc:

```
- (void) viewWillAppear:(BOOL)animated {
    [super viewWillAppear:animated];
    if (!self.downloader) {
        MyDownloader* downloader = // ...
        self.downloader = downloader;
    }
    // ...
}
- (void) dealloc {
    if (self->_downloader)
        [self->_downloader cancelAllTasks];
}
```

In that code, I omitted the creation and initialization of MyDownloader. How should this work? The MyDownloader object will create its own NSURLSession, but I think the client should be allowed to configure the session; doing this is extremely convenient, because the NSURLSessionConfiguration is a separate object. So the missing initialization should look like this:

```
NSURLSessionConfiguration* config = // ... set up configuration
MyDownloader* downloader =
    [[MyDownloader alloc] initWithConfiguration:config];
```

Now let's decide how a client will get a MyDownloader object to perform a download. A client will hand a MyDownloader a URL string, and the MyDownloader will generate the NSURLSessionDownloadTask and tell it to resume. Acting as the NSURLSession's delegate, the MyDownloader will be told when the download is over. At that point, the MyDownloader has a file URL for the downloaded object, which it needs to hand back to the client immediately. How should this work?

MyDownloader might define a delegate protocol; the client would then be the delegate, and the MyDownloader could call the client back using a method defined by the protocol. But that's far too rigid and restrictive. One NSURLSession can have many simultaneous tasks; I want a MyDownloader to be able to serve as a central locus for lots of downloading activity. I'm imagining, for example, that a MyDownloader might have multiple clients, or that a single client might initiate multiple downloads from various different contexts. All that downloading takes place asynchronously, and perhaps simultaneously. When the MyDownloader hands a downloaded file's URL to a client, how is that client to know which download request this file URL corresponds to?

My solution, which I think is rather elegant, is that the client, when it orders the download at the outset, should also hand the MyDownloader a completion handler block. To return the file URL at the end of a download, the MyDownloader calls that block. From the client's point of view, the process looks something like this:

```
NSString* s = @"http://www.someserver.com/somefolder/someimage.jpg";
[self.downloader download:s completionHandler:^(NSURL* url){
    if (!url)
        return;
    NSData* d = [NSData dataWithContentsOfURL:url];
    UIImage* im = [UIImage imageWithData:d];
    dispatch_async(dispatch_get_main_queue(), ^{
        self.iv.image = im;
    });
}];
```

Now let's implement this architecture within MyDownloader. We have posited a method download:completionHandler:. When that method is called, MyDownloader asks for a new download task and sets it going:

```
- (void) download:(NSString*)s completionHandler:(void(^)(NSURL* url))ch {
    NSURL* url = [NSURL URLWithString:s];
    NSURLRequest* req = [NSURLRequest requestWithURL:url];
    NSURLSessionDownloadTask* task =
        [self.session downloadTaskWithRequest:req];
    // ... store the completion handler somehow ...
    [task resume];
}
```

When the download finishes, the MyDownloader hears about it (as session delegate) and calls the completion handler:

```
-(void)URLSession:(NSURLSession *)session
        downloadTask:(NSURLSessionDownloadTask *)downloadTask
        didFinishDownloadingToURL:(NSURL *)location {
    NSHTTPURLResponse* response = (NSHTTPURLResponse*)downloadTask.response;
    NSInteger stat = response.statusCode;
    NSLog(@"status %i", stat);
    NSURL* url = nil;
    if (stat == 200) {
        url = location;
```

```
        NSLog(@"downloaded %@", req.URL.lastPathComponent);
    }
    void(^ch)(NSURL* url) = // ... retrieve the completion handler somehow
    ch(url);
}
```

In the preceding two code snippets, I have twice thrown up my hands, using the word "somehow" in a comment to signify an unsolved problem. There are actually two problems here:

- The completion handler arrives in one method (`download:completionHandler:`) but is called in another (`URLSession:downloadTask:didFinishDownloadingTo-URL:`). The completion handler needs to be stored, in the first method, in such a way that it can be retrieved, in the second method.
- There can be multiple download tasks — and each one has a different completion handler associated with it. That's the entire point of this architecture! Thus we need a way to implement this association.

Clearly, we want to store each completion handler *together with* its download task. In fact, since we are guaranteed that the same download task instance makes its appearance in both methods, it would be truly ideal if we could store the completion handler *in* its download task!

At first glance, it appears that this is impossible, because we can't subclass NSURLSessionDownloadTask (and even if we could, we can't ask NSURLSession to generate an instance of our subclass). But there is, in fact, a way to do this. It turns out that we are allowed to attach an arbitrary property to an NSURLRequest, as long as we start with its mutable subclass, NSMutableURLRequest. The mechanism for doing this is a little weird — we actually call an NSURLProtocol class method — but that doesn't matter. The NSURLRequest is attached to the download task as its `originalRequest`, and we can retrieve it, and hence the arbitrary property, at the end of the download.

We are now ready to write MyDownloader for real. I'll make just one more change in its API: I'll have `download:completionHandler:` return the download task to the client. This is so that, if the client decides to cancel the download later, the client can send the cancel message directly to the task. Here is the whole of MyDownloader:

```
#import "MyDownloader.h"
@interface MyDownloader() <NSURLSessionDownloadDelegate>
@property (nonatomic, strong) NSURLSession* session;
@end
@implementation MyDownloader
// public method, initializer
- (id) initWithConfiguration: (NSURLSessionConfiguration*) config {
    self = [super init];
    if (self) {
        NSURLSession* session =
```

```
        [NSURLSession sessionWithConfiguration:config
                delegate:self delegateQueue:[NSOperationQueue mainQueue]];
        self->_session = session;
    }
    return self;
}
// public method, start one download
- (NSURLSessionTask*) download:(NSString*)s
        completionHandler:(void(^)(NSURL* url))ch {
    NSURL* url = [NSURL URLWithString:s];
    NSMutableURLRequest* req = [NSMutableURLRequest requestWithURL:url];
    [NSURLProtocol setProperty:ch forKey:@"ch" inRequest:req];
    NSURLSessionDownloadTask* task =
        [self.session downloadTaskWithRequest:req];
    [task resume];
    return task;
}
// delegate methods
-(void)URLSession:(NSURLSession *)session
        downloadTask:(NSURLSessionDownloadTask *)downloadTask
        didWriteData:(int64_t)bytesWritten
        totalBytesWritten:(int64_t)totalBytesWritten
        totalBytesExpectedToWrite:(int64_t)totalBytesExpectedToWrite {
    ;;;
}
-(void)URLSession:(NSURLSession *)session
        downloadTask:(NSURLSessionDownloadTask *)downloadTask
        didResumeAtOffset:(int64_t)fileOffset
        expectedTotalBytes:(int64_t)expectedTotalBytes {
    ;;;
}
-(void)URLSession:(NSURLSession *)session
        downloadTask:(NSURLSessionDownloadTask *)downloadTask
        didFinishDownloadingToURL:(NSURL *)location {
    NSURLRequest* req = downloadTask.originalRequest;
    void(^ch)(NSURL* url) =
        [NSURLProtocol propertyForKey:@"ch" inRequest:req];
    NSHTTPURLResponse* response = (NSHTTPURLResponse*)downloadTask.response;
    NSInteger stat = response.statusCode;
    NSURL* url = nil;
    if (stat == 200)
        url = location;
    ch(url);
}
// public method; client *must* call this for memory management
- (void) cancelAllTasks {
    [self.session invalidateAndCancel];
}
@end
```

To exercise MyDownloader, I'll show how to solve a pesky problem that arises quite
often in real life: we have a UITableView where each cell displays text and a picture, and

the picture needs to be downloaded in real time. The idea is to supply each picture lazily, on demand, downloading a picture only when its cell becomes visible.

The model, as we saw in Chapter 8, might be an array of dictionaries. So what I'm proposing is a model like this:

```
array
    dictionary (mutable)
        text: @"Manny"
        picurl: String URL for a downloadable image of Manny
    dictionary (mutable)
        text: @"Moe"
        picurl: String URL for a downloadable image of Moe
    dictionary (mutable)
        text: @"Jack"
        picurl: String URL for a downloadable image of Jack
    ....
```

When the table turns to the data source for a cell (`tableView:cellForRowAtIndex-Path:`), the data source will turn to the model and consult the dictionary corresponding to the requested row, asking for its @"im" entry, which is supposed to be its image. Initially, this will be missing. In that case, the data source will display no image in this cell — and will turn to the downloader and ask for the image to be downloaded from the @"picurl".

When the downloader succeeds in downloading an image, it calls the table's data source back through the completion block. Here we come to the *Insanely Cool Part* (pat. pend.). This completion block has captured the contextual environment from inside `table-View:cellForRowAtIndexPath:`, where it was defined. In effect, therefore, we are back in the very same call to `tableView:cellForRowAtIndexPath:`, accessing the very same mutable dictionary in the model! We can thus set that dictionary's @"im" entry, and tell the table to reload this row. The table thus calls `tableView:cellForRowAtIndexPath:` *again*, for the very same row, and the data source turns to the same dictionary and asks for its @"im" entry *again* — and finds it, and displays the image in the cell:

```
- (UITableViewCell *)tableView:(UITableView *)tableView
        cellForRowAtIndexPath:(NSIndexPath *)indexPath {
    UITableViewCell *cell =
        [tableView dequeueReusableCellWithIdentifier:@"Cell"
            forIndexPath:indexPath];
    NSMutableDictionary* d = (self.model)[indexPath.row];
    cell.textLabel.text = d[@"text"];
    // have we got a picture?
    if (d[@"im"]) {
        cell.imageView.image = d[@"im"];
    } else {
        cell.imageView.image = nil;
        NSURLSessionTask* task = [self.downloader download:d[@"picurl"]
                                      completionHandler:^(NSURL* url){
```

```
                    if (!url)
                        return;
                    NSData* data = [NSData dataWithContentsOfURL:url];
                    UIImage* im = [UIImage imageWithData:data];
                    d[@"im"] = im;
                    dispatch_async(dispatch_get_main_queue(), ^{
                        [self.tableView reloadRowsAtIndexPaths:@[indexPath]
                            withRowAnimation:UITableViewRowAnimationNone];
                    });
                }];
        }
        return cell;
}
```

A possible further refinement is this. Consider what happens when the user scrolls quickly through the entire table, possibly passing through hundreds of rows. The downloads for all of those rows, if they do not already have their pictures, will be initiated. This seems wasteful, as each row is scrolled out of sight before it has its picture, and therefore doesn't *need* its picture after all. To prevent such waste, we can implement tableView:didEndDisplayingCell:forRowAtIndexPath: to send cancel to the NSURLSessionTask we captured earlier, when calling the downloader's download: completionHandler:. I am proposing, for example, that we have stored our reference to the task in the model, in the mutable dictionary corresponding to this row:

```
-(void)tableView:(UITableView *)tableView
        didEndDisplayingCell:(UITableViewCell *)cell
        forRowAtIndexPath:(NSIndexPath *)indexPath {
    NSMutableDictionary* d = self.model[indexPath.row];
    NSURLSessionTask* task = d[@"task"];
    if (task && task.state == NSURLSessionTaskStateRunning) {
        [task cancel];
        [d removeObjectForKey: @"task"];
    }
}
```

The only missing piece of the puzzle is what should happen when a picture download fails. If the user scrolls the failed cell out of view and later scrolls it back into view, the table will ask the data source for that cell and the downloader will try again to download its image. But that won't happen for a failed cell that's never scrolled out of view. How you deal with this is up to you; it's a matter of providing the best user experience without having an undue impact upon performance, battery, and so forth. In this instance, because these images are fairly unimportant, I might arrange that when an NSTimer with a fairly large interval fires (every 60 seconds, say), we reload the visible rows; this will cause any visible row without an image to try again to download its image.

Background Downloads

If your app goes into the background while in the middle of a download, the download might be completed coherently, or it might not. To ensure that an NSURLSession-DownloadTask (or an NSURLSessionUploadTask) is carried out regardless, even if your app isn't frontmost — indeed, even if your app isn't running! — make your NSURL-SessionConfiguration a background configuration (call `backgroundSession-Configuration:` to create it).

This feature, new in iOS 7, hands the work of downloading over to the system. Your app is not actually involved. You still need an NSURLSession, but this serves primarily as a gateway for putting your app in touch with the download process; in particular, you need to operate as the NSURLSession's delegate.

The argument that you pass to `backgroundSessionConfiguration:` is a string identifier. This will distinguish your background session from all the other background sessions that other apps have requested from the system. Therefore, it should be unique to your app; a good approach is to use your app's bundle ID as its basis.

You may also want to set your configuration's `discretionary` to YES. This will permit the system to postpone network communications to some moment that will conserve bandwidth and battery — for example, when Wi-Fi is available, and the device is plugged into a power socket. Of course, that might be days from now! But this is part of the beauty of background downloads.

There are three possibilities for how a background download will conclude, depending on the state of your app at that moment:

Your app is frontmost

> If your app is frontmost during any part of a background download, the download is treated normally: your session delegate will get `URLSession:downloadTask:did-WriteData...` and `URLSession:downloadTask:didFinishDownloadingToURL:` messages, just as you expect.

Your app is suspended in the background

> Your app is awakened, still in the background, long enough to receive `URLSession:downloadTask:didFinishDownloadingToURL:` and deal with it.

Your app is not running

> Your app is launched in the background. You have no NSURLSession, because your app has just launched from scratch. You will need to create one, calling `background-SessionConfiguration:` with the same identifier as before; you will then be able to receive delegate messages, including `URLSession:downloadTask:didFinish-DownloadingToURL:`.

As with significant event monitoring (Chapter 22), your app does not formally run in the background, so you do *not* have to set the UIBackgroundModes of your *Info.plist*.

You do have to implement two extra methods, to be called if your app is not frontmost at the time the download is completed:

application:handleEventsForBackgroundURLSession:completionHandler:
> This message is sent *to the app delegate*. The session: parameter is the string identifier you handed earlier to the configuration object; you might use this to identify the session, or even as a prompt to create and configure the session if you haven't done so already. The app delegate must store the completionHandler: parameter as an instance variable, because it will be needed later.

URLSessionDidFinishEventsForBackgroundURLSession:
> This message is sent *to the session delegate*. The session delegate must call the previously stored completion handler. This is how the system knows that your app has finished updating its interface. The system will thereupon take a new snapshot of your app's interface, still in the background, to serve as your app's thumbnail in the app switcher interface — and your app will then be suspended.

All of this is much easier if the app delegate and the session delegate are one and the same object. In this example, the app delegate holds the NSURLSession property, as well as the completion handler property that will be needed if the download completes when we are not frontmost:

```
@interface AppDelegate () <NSURLSessionDownloadDelegate>
@property (nonatomic, strong) NSURLSession* session;
@property (nonatomic, strong) void (^ch)();
@end
```

To ensure that we always have an NSURLSession, we create the session at launch time. This is the app delegate, so it cannot leak; therefore, we have no memory management considerations connected with being the session delegate:

```
- (BOOL)application:(UIApplication *)application
        didFinishLaunchingWithOptions:(NSDictionary *)launchOptions {
    // Override point for customization after application launch.
    if (!self.session)
        self.session = [self configureSession];
    return YES;
}
- (NSURLSession*) configureSession {
    NSURLSessionConfiguration* config =
        [NSURLSessionConfiguration
            backgroundSessionConfiguration:MY_SESSION_ID];
    config.allowsCellularAccess = NO;
    // ... could set config.discretionary here ...
    NSURLSession* session =
```

```
        [NSURLSession sessionWithConfiguration:config delegate:self
            delegateQueue:[NSOperationQueue mainQueue]];
    return session;
}
```

The three NSURLSessionDownloadDelegate methods are exactly as before. Finally, we have the two extra methods that come into play only if the download completes when we are not frontmost:

```
-(void)application:(UIApplication *)application
      handleEventsForBackgroundURLSession:(NSString *)identifier
      completionHandler:(void (^)())completionHandler {
    self.ch = completionHandler;
}
-(void)URLSessionDidFinishEventsForBackgroundURLSession:
      (NSURLSession *)session {
    self.ch();
}
```

 If the user kills your app in the background by way of the app switcher interface, pending background downloads will *not* be completed. The system assumes that the user doesn't want your app coming magically back to life in the background.

Background App Refresh

Background app refresh, which is new in iOS 7, is the thing that the user can disable in the Settings app, under General → Background App Refresh, as I mentioned in Chapter 22. The idea is that if your app has a periodic network download to perform — because, for example, it is a news app — you can ask the system to wake or launch your app in the background from time to time so that it can perform that download in the background. That way, the next time the user brings your app to the front, it has already been refreshed with recent downloaded content.

This feature is a background mode; in the Capabilities tab for your app target, switch on Background Modes and check "Background fetch". Your code must also set the shared application's minimumBackgroundFetchInterval property; you can supply an actual number here, but in most cases you'll want to use UIApplicationBackgroundFetch-IntervalMinimum, which lets the system work out the best moments for your app to refresh its content, based on the user's behavior.

When it's time to perform a background fetch, the app delegate will be sent application:performFetchWithCompletionHandler:. At that moment, a clock starts counting down; your job is to do whatever needs doing, just as fast as possible, and then call the completionHandler: parameter to stop the clock, passing in one of these values:

- `UIBackgroundFetchResultNewData`
- `UIBackgroundFetchResultNoData`
- `UIBackgroundFetchResultFailed`

If you don't do that fast enough, the clock will time out and your app will be suspended; and the longer you take, the less willing the system will be to send you `application:performFetchWithCompletionHandler:` in the first place. If the value you return is `UIBackgroundFetchResultNewData`, a new snapshot will be taken, still with your app in the background, so that the thumbnail in the app switcher matches your updated app.

In-App Purchases

An in-app purchase is a specialized form of network communication: your app communicates with the App Store to permit the user to buy something there, or to confirm that something has already been bought there. For example, your app might be free, but the user could then be offered the opportunity to pay to unlock additional functionality. In-app purchases are made possible through the Store Kit framework; you'll need to `@import StoreKit`.

There are various kinds of in-app purchase; you'll want to read the relevant chapter in Apple's *iTunes Connect Developer Guide* and the *In-App Purchase Programming Guide*, along with the PDF *Getting Started* guide available at *https://developer.apple.com/in-app-purchase/In-App-Purchase-Guidelines.pdf*.

I'll describe the simplest possible in-app purchase: my app offers a single one-time purchase, which unlocks additional functionality, allowing the user to choose a photo from the photo library (Chapter 17). (This is what Apple calls a *non-consumable* purchase.) When the user taps the Choose button, if the in-app purchase has not been made, a pair of dialogs appear, offering and describing the purchase (Figure 24-1); if the in-app purchase *has* been made, a UIImagePickerController's view appears instead.

To configure an in-app purchase, you need first to use iTunes Connect to create, in connection with your app, something that the user can purchase; this is easiest to do if your app is already available through the App Store. For a simple non-consumable purchase like mine, you are associating your app's bundle ID with a name and arbitrary product ID representing your in-app purchase, along with a price. You'll also want to create a special Apple ID for testing purposes; you can't test your in-app purchase interface without such a test Apple ID. (If you accidentally perform the in-app purchase later when logged into the App Store with your real Apple ID, you'll be charged for the purchase and you won't be able to get your money back. Can you guess how I know that?)

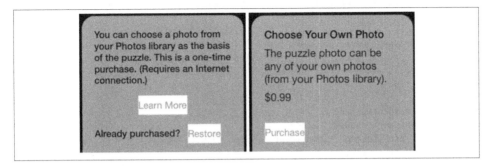

Figure 24-1. Interface for an in-app purchase

Let's skip merrily past all that and proceed to your app's interface and inner workings. For a non-consumable in-app purchase, your app must provide the following interface (all of which is visible in Figure 24-1):

- A place where the in-app purchase is described. I say "a place" rather than "a description" because you do not hard-code the description into your app; rather, it is downloaded in real time from the App Store, using the Display Name and Description (and price) that you entered at iTunes Connect.

- A button that launches the purchase process.

- A button that *restores* an existing purchase. The idea here is that the user has performed the purchase, but is now on a different device or has deleted and reinstalled your app, so that the NSUserDefaults entry stating that the purchase has been performed is missing. The user needs to be able to contact the App Store to get your app to recognize that the purchase has been performed and turn on the purchased functionality.

Both the purchase process and the restore process are performed through dialogs presented by the system. New in iOS 7, your iPhone app *must be in portrait orientation* when these dialogs appear, or there will not be room to display them (and the purchase will fail). To ensure this in my app, the interface shown in Figure 24-1 comes from two presented view controllers, StoreViewController and StoreViewController2, both of which support portrait orientation only:

```
-(NSUInteger)supportedInterfaceOrientations {
    return UIInterfaceOrientationMaskPortrait;
}
```

In my app, the purchase process proceeds in two stages. When the user taps the Learn More button (StoreViewController), I first confirm that the user has not been restricted from making purchases, and I then create an SKProductsRequest, which will attempt to download an SKProductsResponse object embodying the in-app purchase corresponding to my single product ID:

```
if (![SKPaymentQueue canMakePayments]) {
    UIAlertView* alert = // alert saying "Sorry, no purchases"
    [alert show];
    return;
}
SKProductsRequest* req =
    [[SKProductsRequest alloc]
        initWithProductIdentifiers:[NSSet setWithObject:@"MyProductID"]];
req.delegate = self;
[req start];
```

This kicks off some network activity, and eventually the delegate of this SKProductsRequest, namely `self` (conforming to SKProductsRequestDelegate), is called back with one of two delegate messages. If we get `request:didFailWithError:`, I put up an apologetic alert, and that's the end. But if we get `productsRequest:didReceiveResponse:`, the request has succeeded, and we can proceed to the second stage.

The response from the App Store arrives as an SKProductsResponse object containing an SKProduct representing the proposed purchase. I extract the descriptive information from this object, populate the second view controller, give it a reference to the SKProduct, and present it:

```
- (void) productsRequest:(SKProductsRequest *)request
        didReceiveResponse:(SKProductsResponse *)response {
    StoreViewController2* s = [StoreViewController2 new];
    SKProduct* p = response.products[0];
    // ... populate s, based on p.localizedTitle, p.localizedDescription, ...
    // ... and p.priceLocale and p.price ...
    s.product = p;
    [self presentViewController:s animated:YES completion:nil];;
}
```

We are now in my second view controller (StoreViewController2). If the user taps the Purchase button, I load the SKProduct into the default SKPaymentQueue and stand back:

```
SKPayment* p = [SKPayment paymentWithProduct:self.product];
SKPaymentQueue* q = [SKPaymentQueue defaultQueue];
[q addPayment:p];
```

The system is now in charge of presenting a sequence of dialogs, confirming the purchase, asking for the user's App Store password, and so forth. My app knows nothing about that; if the purchase fails, or if the user cancels, then we are still sitting there showing my second view controller's view, and it is up to the user to dismiss it. If the user performs the purchase, however, my app delegate will be sent `payment-Queue:updatedTransactions:`. I'll return in a moment to the implementation of this method.

Now let's talk about what happens when the user taps the Restore button (StoreView-Controller). It's very simple; I just tell the default SKPaymentQueue to restore any existing purchases:

```
[[SKPaymentQueue defaultQueue] restoreCompletedTransactions];
```

Again, what happens now in the interface is out of my hands; the system will present the necessary dialogs. If the purchase is restored, however, my app delegate will be sent paymentQueue:updatedTransactions:.

The rest of the action takes place in the app delegate. When my app launches, it must register to receive transactions from the payment queue:

```
- (BOOL)application:(UIApplication *)application
      didFinishLaunchingWithOptions:(NSDictionary *)launchOptions {
    // ...
    [[SKPaymentQueue defaultQueue] addTransactionObserver:self];
    return YES;
}
```

My app delegate adopts the SKPaymentTransactionObserver protocol. There is only one required method, and it is the only one my app delegate implements — payment-Queue:updatedTransactions:. This arrives with a reference to the payment queue and an array of SKPaymentTransaction objects. My job is to cycle through these transactions and, for each one, do whatever it requires, and then (*this is crucial*) send finish-Transaction: to the payment queue.

My implementation is extremely simple, because I have only one purchasable product, and because I'm not maintaining any separate record of receipts. For each transaction, I check its transactionState. If this is SKPaymentTransactionStatePurchased or SKPaymentTransactionStateRestored, I pull out its payment, confirm that the payment's productIdentifier is my product identifier (it had darned well better be, since I have only the one product), and, if so, I throw the NSUserDefaults switch that indicates to my app that the user has performed the purchase. Otherwise, I do nothing, but I *always* call finishTransaction:, no matter what:

```
- (void)paymentQueue:(SKPaymentQueue *)queue
      updatedTransactions:(NSArray *)transactions {
    for (SKPaymentTransaction* t in transactions) {
        if (t.transactionState == SKPaymentTransactionStatePurchased ||
              t.transactionState == SKPaymentTransactionStateRestored) {
            SKPayment* p = t.payment;
            if ([p.productIdentifier isEqualToString: @"MyProductID"]) {
                [[NSUserDefaults standardUserDefaults]
                    setBool:YES forKey:@"choose"];
                [queue finishTransaction:t];
                // ... put up interface alerting the user ...
            }
        }
    }
```

```
        else if (t.transactionState == SKPaymentTransactionStateFailed) {
            [queue finishTransaction:t];
        }
    }
}
```

Bonjour

Bonjour is the ingenious technology, originated at Apple and now becoming a universal standard, for allowing network devices to advertise services they provide and to discover dynamically other devices offering such services. Once an appropriate service is detected, a client device can resolve it to get a network address and can then begin communicating with the server device. Communicating itself is outside the scope of this book, but device discovery via Bonjour is easy.

In this example, we'll look to see whether any device, such as a Mac, is running iTunes with library sharing turned on. (This is not Home Sharing in the iTunes File menu; it's the "Share my library on my local network" checkbox in the iTunes Sharing preferences.) We can search for domains or for a particular service; here, we'll pass the empty string as the domain to signify "any domain," and concentrate on the service, which is @"_daap._tcp". We maintain two instance variables, the NSNetServiceBrowser that will look for devices, and a mutable array in which to store any services it discovers:

```
self.services = [NSMutableArray new];
NSNetServiceBrowser* browser = [NSNetServiceBrowser new];
self.nsb = browser;
self.nsb.delegate = self;
[self.nsb searchForServicesOfType:@"_daap._tcp" inDomain:@""];
```

The NSNetServiceBrowser is now searching for devices advertising iTunes sharing and will keep doing so until we destroy it or tell it to stop. It is common to leave the service browser running, because devices can come and go very readily. As they do, the service browser's delegate (NSNetServiceBrowserDelegate) will be informed. For purposes of this example, I'll simply maintain a list of services, and update the app's interface when the situation changes:

```
- (void)netServiceBrowser:(NSNetServiceBrowser *)netServiceBrowser
          didFindService:(NSNetService *)netService
              moreComing:(BOOL)moreServicesComing {
    [self.services addObject:netService];
    if (!moreServicesComing)
        [self updateInterface];
}
- (void)netServiceBrowser:(NSNetServiceBrowser *)netServiceBrowser
        didRemoveService:(NSNetService *)netService
              moreComing:(BOOL)moreServicesComing {
```

```
        [self.services removeObject:netService];
        if (!moreServicesComing)
            [self updateInterface];
}
```

The delegate messages very kindly tell me whether they have finished listing a series of changes, so I can wait to update the interface until after a full batch of changes has ended. In this example, I don't really have any interface to update; I'll just log the list of services, each of which is an NSNetService instance:

```
- (void) updateInterface {
    for (NSNetService* service in self.services) {
        if (service.port == -1) {
            NSLog(@"service %@ of type %@, not yet resolved",
                service.name, service.type);
        }
    }
}
```

To connect to a service, we would first need to *resolve* it, thus obtaining an address and other useful information. An unresolved service has port -1, as shown in the previous code. To resolve a service, you tell it to resolve (resolveWithTimeout:); you will probably also set a delegate on the service (NSNetServiceDelegate), so as to be notified when the resolution succeeds (or fails). Here, I'll have the delegate call my update-Interface method again if a resolution succeeds, and I'll extend updateInterface to show the port number for any resolved services:

```
- (void) updateInterface {
    for (NSNetService* service in self.services) {
        if (service.port == -1) {
            NSLog(@"service %@ of type %@, not yet resolved",
                service.name, service.type);
            [service setDelegate:self];
            [service resolveWithTimeout:10];
        } else {
            NSLog(@"service %@ of type %@, port %d, addresses %@",
                service.name, service.type, service.port, service.addresses);
        }
    }
}
- (void)netServiceDidResolveAddress:(NSNetService *)sender {
    [self updateInterface];
}
```

The addresses of a resolved service constitute an array of NSData. Logging an address like this is largely pointless, as it is not human-readable, but it's useful for handing to a CFSocket. In general you'll call the service's getInputStream:outputStream: to start talking over the connection; that's outside the scope of this discussion. See Apple's WiTap example for more.

CHAPTER 25

Threads

A *thread* is, simply put, a subprocess of your app that can execute even while other subprocesses are also executing. Such simultaneous execution is called *concurrency*. The iOS frameworks use threads all the time; if they didn't, your app would be less responsive to the user — perhaps even completely unresponsive. The genius of the frameworks, though, is that, for the most part, they use threads precisely so that you don't have to.

For example, suppose your app is downloading something from the network (Chapter 24). This download doesn't happen all by itself; somewhere, someone is running code that interacts with the network and obtains data. Similarly, how does Core Motion work (Chapter 22)? The data from the sensors is being gathered and processed constantly, with extra calculations to separate gravity from user-induced acceleration and to account for bias and scaling in the gyroscope. Yet none of that interferes with your code, or prevents the user from tapping and swiping things in your interface. That's concurrency in action.

It is a testament to the ingenuity of the iOS frameworks that this book has proceeded so far with so little mention of threads. Indeed, it would have been nice to dispense with the topic altogether. Threads are difficult and dangerous, and should be avoided if possible. But sometimes that *isn't* possible. So this chapter introduces threads, along with a warning: threads entail complications and subtle pitfalls, and can make your code hard to debug. There is much more to threading, and especially to making your threaded code safe, than this chapter can possibly touch on. For detailed information about the topics introduced in this chapter, read Apple's *Concurrency Programming Guide* and *Threading Programming Guide*.

Main Thread

You are always using *some* thread. All your code must run somewhere; "somewhere" means a thread. When code calls a method, that method normally runs on the same thread as the code that called it. Your code is called through events; those events normally call your code on the *main thread*. The main thread has certain special properties:

The main thread automatically has a run loop.

A *run loop* is a recipient of events. It is how your code is notified that something is happening; without a run loop, a thread can't receive events. Cocoa events normally arrive on the main thread's run loop; that's why your code, called by those events, executes on the main thread.

The main thread is the interface thread.

When the *user* interacts with the interface, those interactions are reported as events — on the main thread. When *your code* interacts with the interface, it too must do so on the main thread. Of course that will normally happen automatically, because your code normally runs on the main thread.

The main thread thus has a very great deal of work to do. Here's how life goes in your app:

1. An event arrives on the main thread; the user has tapped a button, for example, and this is reported to your app as a UIEvent and to the button through the touch delivery mechanism (Chapter 5) — on the main thread.

2. The control event causes your code (the action handler) to be called — on the main thread. Your code now runs — on the main thread. *While your code runs, nothing else can happen on the main thread.* Your code might command some changes in the interface; this is safe, because your code is running on the main thread.

3. Your code finishes. The main thread's run loop is now free to report more events, and the user is free to interact with the interface once again.

The bottleneck here is obviously step 2, the running of your code. Your code runs on the main thread. That means the main thread can't do anything else while your code is running. No events can arrive while your code is running. The user can't interact with the interface while your code is running. But this is usually no problem, because:

- Your code executes really fast. It's true that the user can't interact with the interface while your code runs, but this is such a tiny interval of time that the user will probably never even notice.

- Your code, as it runs, blocks the user from interacting with the interface. But that's not bad: it's good! Your code, in response to what the user does, might update the interface; it would be insane if the user could do something else in the interface while you're in the middle of updating it.

On the other hand, as I've already mentioned, the frameworks operate in secondary threads all the time. The reason this doesn't affect you is that they usually talk to *your* code on the *main* thread. You have seen many examples of this in the preceding chapters. For example:

- During an animation (Chapter 4), the interface remains responsive to the user, and it is possible for your code to run. The Core Animation framework is running the animation and updating the presentation layer on a background thread. But your delegate methods or completion blocks are called on the main thread.

- A UIWebView's fetching and loading of its content is asynchronous (Chapter 11); that means the work is done in a background thread. But your delegate methods are called on the main thread.

- Sounds are played asynchronously (Chapter 14 and Chapter 16). But your delegate methods are called on the main thread. Similarly, loading, preparation, and playing of movies happens asynchronously (Chapter 15). But your delegate methods are called on the main thread.

- Saving a movie file takes time (Chapter 15 and Chapter 17). So the saving takes place on a background thread. Similarly, UIDocument saves and reads on a background thread (Chapter 23). But your delegate methods or completion blocks are called on the main thread.

Thus, you can (and should) usually ignore threads and just keep plugging away on the main thread. However, there are two kinds of situation in which your code will need to be explicitly aware of threading issues:

Your code is called back, but not on the main thread.
Some frameworks explicitly inform you in their documentation that callbacks are not guaranteed to take place on the main thread. For example, the documentation on CATiledLayer (Chapter 7) warns that `drawLayer:inContext:` is called in a background thread. By implication, our `drawRect:` code, triggered by CATiled-Layer to update tiles, is running in a background thread. Fortunately, the UIKit drawing-related classes are thread-safe, and so is accessing the current context. Nevertheless, we cannot completely ignore the fact that this code is not running on the main thread.

Similarly, the documentation on AV Foundation (Chapter 15 and Chapter 17) warns that its blocks and notifications can arrive on a background thread. So if you intend to update the user interface, or use a value that might also be used by your main-thread code, you'll need to be thread-conscious.

Your code takes significant time.
If your code takes significant time to run, you might need to run that code on a background thread, rather than letting it block the main thread and prevent anything else from happening there. For example:

During startup

> You want your app to launch as quickly as possible. In Chapter 23, I called `URLForUbiquityContainerIdentifier:` during app launch. The documentation told me to call this method on a background thread, because it can take some time to return; we don't want to block the main thread waiting for it, because the app is trying to launch on the main thread, and the user won't see our interface until the launch process is over.

When the user can see or interact with the app

> In Chapter 19, I called `enumerateEventsMatchingPredicate:` on a background thread in order to prevent the user interface from freezing up in case the enumeration took a long time. If I hadn't done this, then when the user taps the button that triggers this call, the button will stay highlighted for a significant amount of time, during which the interface will be completely frozen.

Similarly, when your app is in the process of being suspended into the background, or resumed from the background, your app should not block the main thread for too long; it must act quickly and get out of the way. This isn't just a matter of aesthetics or politeness; the system "watchdog" will summarily kill your app if it discovers that the main thread is blocked for too long.

Why Threading Is Hard

The one certain thing about computer code is that it just clunks along the path of execution, one statement at a time. Lines of code, in effect, are performed in the order in which they appear. With threading, that certainty goes right out the window. If you have code that can be performed on a background thread, then you don't know when it will be performed in relation to the code being performed on any other thread. Any line of your background-thread code could be interleaved between any two lines of your main-thread code.

You also might not know *how many times* a piece of your background-thread code might be running simultaneously. Unless you take steps to prevent it, the same code could be spawned off as a thread even while it's already running in a thread. So any line of your background-thread code could be interleaved between any two lines of *itself*.

This situation is particularly threatening with regard to *shared data*. Suppose two threads were to get hold of the same object and change it. Who knows what horrors might result? Objects in general have state, adding up to the state of your app as a whole. If multiple threads are permitted to access your objects, they and your entire app can be put into an indeterminate or nonsensical state.

This problem cannot be solved by simple logic. For example, suppose you try to make data access safe with a condition, as in this pseudocode:

```
if (no other thread is touching this data)
    do something to the data...
```

Such logic cannot succeed. Suppose the condition succeeds; no other thread is touching this data. But between the time when that condition is evaluated and the time when the next line executes and you start to do something to the data, another thread can come along and start touching the data!

It is possible to request assistance at a deeper level to ensure that a section of code is not run by two threads simultaneously. For example, you can implement a *lock* around a section of code. But locks generate an entirely new level of potential pitfalls. In general, a lock is an invitation to forget to use the lock, or to forget to remove the lock after you've set it. And threads can end up contending for a lock in a way that permits neither thread to proceed.

Another problem is that the lifetime of a thread is independent of the lifetimes of other objects in your app. When an object is about to go out of existence and its `dealloc` has been called and executed, you are guaranteed that none of your code in that object will ever run again. But a thread might still be running, and might try to talk to your object, even after your object has gone out of existence. You cannot solve this problem by having the thread retain your object, because then there is the danger that the thread might be the *last* code retaining your object, so that when the thread releases your object, your object's `dealloc` is called on that thread rather than the main thread, which could be a disaster.

Not only is threaded code hard to get right; it's also hard to test and hard to debug. It introduces indeterminacy, so you can easily make a mistake that never appears in your testing, but that does appear for some user. The real danger is that the user's experience will consist only of distant consequences of your mistake, long after the point where you made it, making the true cause of the problem extraordinarily difficult to track down.

Perhaps you think I'm trying to scare you away from using threads. You're right! For an excellent (and suitably frightening) account of some of the dangers and considerations that threading involves, see Apple's *Technical Note TN2109*. If terms like *race condition* and *deadlock* don't strike fear into your veins, look them up on Wikipedia.

 Xcode's Debug navigator distinguishes threads. Moreover, when you call `NSLog` in your multithreaded code, the output in the console displays a number (in square brackets, after the colon) identifying the thread on which it was called. This is unbelievably helpful.

Three Ways of Threading

Without pretending to completeness or even safety, this section will illustrate three approaches to threading, progressing from worst to best. To give the examples a common base, we envision an app that draws the Mandelbrot set. (The actual code, not all of which is shown here, is adapted from a small open source project I downloaded from the Internet.) All it does is draw the basic Mandelbrot set in black and white, but that's enough crunching of numbers to introduce a significant delay. The idea is then to see how we can get that delay off the main thread.

The app contains a UIView subclass, MyMandelbrotView, which has one instance variable, a CGContextRef called _bitmapContext. Here's the structure of MyMandelbrotView's implementation:

```
// jumping-off point: draw the Mandelbrot set
- (void) drawThatPuppy {
    [self makeBitmapContext: self.bounds.size];
    CGPoint center =
        CGPointMake(CGRectGetMidX(self.bounds), CGRectGetMidY(self.bounds));
    [self drawAtCenter: center zoom: 1];
    [self setNeedsDisplay];
}
// create (and memory manage) instance variable
- (void) makeBitmapContext:(CGSize)size {
    if (self->_bitmapContext)
        CGContextRelease(self->_bitmapContext);
    // ... configure arguments ...
    CGContextRef context = CGBitmapContextCreate(nil, /* ... */);
    self->_bitmapContext = context;
}
// draw pixels of self->_bitmapContext
- (void) drawAtCenter:(CGPoint)center zoom:(CGFloat)zoom {
    // .... do stuff to self->_bitmapContext ...
}
// turn pixels of self->_bitmapContext into CGImage, draw into ourselves
- (void) drawRect:(CGRect)rect {
    CGContextRef context = UIGraphicsGetCurrentContext();
    CGImageRef im = CGBitmapContextCreateImage(self->_bitmapContext);
    CGContextDrawImage(context, self.bounds, im);
    CGImageRelease(im);
}
// final memory managment
- (void) dealloc {
    if (self->_bitmapContext)
        CGContextRelease(self->_bitmapContext);
}
```

The drawAtCenter:zoom: method, which calculates the pixels of the instance variable _bitmapContext, is time-consuming, and we can see this by running the app on a device. If the entire process is kicked off by tapping a button whose action handler calls draw-

ThatPuppy, there is a significant delay before the Mandelbrot graphic appears in the interface, during which time the button remains highlighted. That is a sure sign that we are blocking the main thread. We will consider three ways of moving this work off onto a background thread: with an old-fashioned manual thread, with NSOperation, and with Grand Central Dispatch.

Manual Threads

The simple way to create a thread manually is to call `performSelectorIn-Background:withObject:`, specifying a method to be performed on a background thread. Even with this simple approach, there is additional work to do:

Pack the arguments.
The method designated by the first argument to `performSelectorIn-Background:withObject:` can take only one parameter, whose value you supply as the second argument. So, if you want to pass more than one piece of information into the thread, or if the information you want to pass isn't an object, you'll need to pack it into a single object. Typically, this will be an NSDictionary.

Set up an autorelease pool.
Secondary threads don't participate in the global autorelease pool. So the first thing you must do in your threaded code is to wrap everything in an autorelease pool. Otherwise, you'll probably leak memory as autoreleased objects are created behind the scenes and are never released.

We'll rewrite MyMandelbrotView to use manual threading. Our `drawAtCenter:zoom:` method takes two parameters (and neither is an object), so we'll have to pack the argument that we pass into the thread, as a dictionary. Once inside the thread, we'll set up our autorelease pool and unpack the dictionary. This will all be made much easier if we interpose a trampoline method between `drawThatPuppy` and `drawAtCenter:zoom:`. So our implementation now looks like this (ignoring the parts that haven't changed):

```
- (void) drawThatPuppy {
    [self makeBitmapContext: self.bounds.size];
    CGPoint center =
        CGPointMake(CGRectGetMidX(self.bounds), CGRectGetMidY(self.bounds));
    NSDictionary* d =
        @{@"center": [NSValue valueWithCGPoint:center], @"zoom": @1};
    [self performSelectorInBackground:@selector(reallyDraw:) withObject:d];
    // [self setNeedsDisplay];
}
// trampoline, background thread entry point
- (void) reallyDraw: (NSDictionary*) d {
    @autoreleasepool {
```

```
        [self drawAtCenter: [d[@"center"] CGPointValue]
                       zoom: [d[@"zoom"] intValue]];
    }
}
```

So far so good, but we haven't yet figured out how to draw our view. We have commented out the call to setNeedsDisplay in drawThatPuppy, because it's too soon; the call to performSelectorInBackground:withObject: launches the thread and returns immediately, so our _bitmapContext instance variable isn't ready yet. Clearly, we need to call setNeedsDisplay *after* drawAtCenter:zoom: finishes generating the pixels of the graphics context. We can do this at the end of our trampoline method reallyDraw:, but we must remember that we're now in a background thread. Because setNeedsDisplay is a form of communication with the interface, we should call it on the main thread, with performSelectorOnMainThread:withObject:waitUntilDone:. For maximum flexibility, it will probably be best to implement a second trampoline method:

```
// trampoline, background thread entry point
- (void) reallyDraw: (NSDictionary*) d {
    @autoreleasepool {
        [self drawAtCenter: [[d objectForKey:@"center"] CGPointValue]
                       zoom: [[d objectForKey:@"zoom"] intValue]];
        [self performSelectorOnMainThread:@selector(allDone)
                               withObject:nil waitUntilDone:NO];
    }
}
// called on main thread! background thread exit point
- (void) allDone {
    [self setNeedsDisplay];
}
```

This code is specious; the seeds of nightmare are already sown. We now have a single object, MyMandelbrotView, some of whose methods are to be called on the main thread and some on a background thread; this invites us to become confused at some later time. Even worse, the main thread and the background thread are constantly sharing a piece of data, the instance variable _bitmapContext; what's to stop some other code from coming along and triggering drawRect: while drawAtCenter:zoom: is in the middle of filling _bitmapContext?

To solve these problems, we might need to use locks, and we would probably have to manage the thread more explicitly. For instance, we might use the NSThread class, which lets us retain our thread as an instance and query it from outside (with isExecuting and similar). Such code can become quite elaborate and difficult to understand, even with an extremely basic implementation. It will be easier and safer at this point to use NSOperation, the subject of the next threading approach.

NSOperation

The essence of NSOperation is that it encapsulates a task, not a thread. The operation described by an NSOperation object may be performed on a background thread, but you don't have to concern yourself with that directly. You describe the operation and add the NSOperation to an NSOperationQueue to set it going. You arrange to be notified when the operation ends, typically by the NSOperation posting a notification. You can query both the queue and its operations from outside with regard to their state.

We'll rewrite MyMandelbrotView to use NSOperation. We need a property, an NSOperationQueue; we'll call it queue. And we have a new class, MyMandelbrot-Operation, an NSOperation subclass. (It is possible to take advantage of a built-in NSOperation subclass such as NSInvocationOperation or NSBlockOperation, but I'm deliberately illustrating the more general case by subclassing NSOperation itself.)

Our implementation of drawThatPuppy makes sure that the queue exists; it then creates an instance of MyMandelbrotOperation, configures it, registers for its notification, and adds it to the queue:

```
- (void) drawThatPuppy {
    CGPoint center =
        CGPointMake(CGRectGetMidX(self.bounds), CGRectGetMidY(self.bounds));
    if (!self.queue) {
        NSOperationQueue* q = [NSOperationQueue new];
        self.queue = q; // retain policy
    }
    MyMandelbrotOperation* op =
        [[MyMandelbrotOperation alloc] initWithSize:self.bounds.size
                                            center:center zoom:1];
    [[NSNotificationCenter defaultCenter] addObserver:self
        selector:@selector(operationFinished:)
        name:@"MyMandelbrotOperationFinished"
        object:op];
    [self.queue addOperation:op];
}
```

Our time-consuming calculations are performed by MyMandelbrotOperation. An NSOperation subclass, such as MyMandelbrotOperation, will typically have at least two methods:

A designated initializer
The NSOperation may need some configuration data. Once the NSOperation is added to a queue, it's too late to talk to it, so you'll usually hand it this configuration data as you create it, in its designated initializer.

A main method
This method will be called (with no parameters) automatically by the NSOperation-Queue when it's time for the NSOperation to start.

MyMandelbrotOperation has three instance variables for configuration (_size, _center, and _zoom), to be set in its initializer; it must be told MyMandelbrotView's geometry explicitly because it is completely separate from MyMandelbrotView. MyMandelbrotOperation also has its own CGContextRef instance variable, _bitmapContext, along with a public accessor so that MyMandelbrotView can retrieve a reference to this graphics context when the operation has finished. Note that this is different from MyMandelbrotView's _bitmapContext; one of the benefits of using NSOperation is that we are no longer sharing data so promiscuously between threads.

Here's the implementation for MyMandelbrotOperation. All the calculation work has been transferred from MyMandelbrotView to MyMandelbrotOperation without change; the only difference is that _bitmapContext now means MyMandelbrotOperation's instance variable:

```
- (id) initWithSize: (CGSize) sz center: (CGPoint) c zoom: (CGFloat) z {
    self = [super init];
    if (self) {
        self->_size = sz;
        self->_center = c;
        self->_zoom = z;
    }
    return self;
}
- (void) dealloc {
    if (self->_bitmapContext)
        CGContextRelease(self->_bitmapContext);
}
- (CGContextRef) bitmapContext {
    return self->_bitmapContext;
}
- (void)makeBitmapContext:(CGSize)size {
    // ... same as before ...
}
- (void)drawAtCenter:(CGPoint)center zoom:(CGFloat)zoom {
    // ... same as before ...
}
- (void) main {
    if ([self isCancelled])
        return;
    [self makeBitmapContext: self->_size];
    [self drawAtCenter: self->_center zoom: self->_zoom];
    if (![self isCancelled])
        [[NSNotificationCenter defaultCenter]
            postNotificationName:@"MyMandelbrotOperationFinished"
            object:self];
}
```

The only method of interest is main. First, we call the NSOperation method isCancelled to make sure we haven't been cancelled while sitting in the queue; this is good practice.

Then, we do exactly what `drawThatPuppy` used to do, initializing our graphics context and drawing into its pixels.

When the operation is over, we need to notify MyMandelbrotView to come and fetch our data. There are two ways to do this; either `main` can post a notification through the NSNotificationCenter, or MyMandelbrotView can use key–value observing to be notified when our `isFinished` property changes. We've chosen the former approach; observe that we check one more time to make sure we haven't been cancelled.

Now we are back in MyMandelbrotView, hearing through the notification that My-MandelbrotOperation has finished. We must immediately pick up any required data, because the NSOperationQueue is about to release this NSOperation. However, we must be careful; the notification may have been posted on a background thread, in which case our method for responding to it will also be called on a background thread. We are about to set our own graphics context and tell ourselves to redraw; those are things we want to do on the main thread. So we immediately trampoline ourselves out to the main thread:

```
// warning! called on background thread
- (void) operationFinished: (NSNotification*) n {
    [self performSelectorOnMainThread:@selector(redrawWithOperation:)
                         withObject:[n object] waitUntilDone:NO];
}
```

As we set MyMandelbrotView's `_bitmapContext` by reading MyMandelbrotOperation's `_bitmapContext`, we must concern ourselves with the memory management of a CGContext obtained from an object that may be about to release that context:

```
// now we're back on the main thread
- (void) redrawWithOperation: (MyMandelbrotOperation*) op {
    [[NSNotificationCenter defaultCenter]
        removeObserver:self
        name:@"MyMandelbrotOperationFinished"
        object:op];
    CGContextRef context = [op bitmapContext];
    if (self->_bitmapContext)
        CGContextRelease(self->_bitmapContext);
    self->_bitmapContext = (CGContextRef) context;
    CGContextRetain(self->_bitmapContext);
    [self setNeedsDisplay];
}
```

Using NSOperation instead of manual threading may not seem like any reduction in work, but it is a tremendous reduction in headaches:

The operation is encapsulated.

Because MyMandelbrotOperation is an object, we've been able to move all the code having to do with drawing the pixels of the Mandelbrot set into it. No longer does MyMandelbrotView contain some code to be called on the main thread and some code to be called on a background thread. The *only* MyMandelbrotView method that can be called in the background is operationFinished:, and that's a method we'd never call explicitly ourselves, so we won't misuse it accidentally.

The data sharing is rationalized.

Because MyMandelbrotOperation is an object, it has its own _bitmapContext. The only moment of data sharing comes in redrawWithOperation:, when we must set MyMandelbrotView's _bitmapContext to MyMandelbrotOperation's _bitmap-Context. Even if multiple MyMandelbrotOperation objects are added to the queue, the moments when we set MyMandelbrotView's _bitmapContext all occur on the main thread, so they cannot conflict with one another.

If we are concerned with the possibility that more than one instance of MyMandelbrot-Operation might be added to the queue and executed concurrently, we have a further defense — we can set the NSOperationQueue's maximum concurrency level to 1:

```
NSOperationQueue* q = [NSOperationQueue new];
[q setMaxConcurrentOperationCount:1];
self.queue = q;
```

This turns the NSOperationQueue into a true serial queue; every operation on the queue must be completely executed before the next can begin. This might cause an operation added to the queue to take longer to execute, if it must wait for another operation to finish before it can even get started; however, this delay might not be important. What *is* important is that by executing the operations on this queue completely separately, we guarantee that only one operation at a time can do any data sharing. A serial queue is thus a form of data locking.

Because MyMandelbrotView can be destroyed (if, for example, its view controller is destroyed), there is still a risk that it will create an operation that will outlive it and will try to access it after it has been destroyed. We can reduce that risk by canceling all operations in our queue before releasing it:

```
- (void)dealloc {
    // release the bitmap context
    if (self->_bitmapContext)
        CGContextRelease(self->_bitmapContext);
    [self->_queue cancelAllOperations];
}
```

Operation queues are good to know about. A number of useful methods mentioned earlier in this book expect an NSOperationQueue argument; see Chapter 22 (start-DeviceMotionUpdatesToQueue:withHandler:, and similarly for the other sensors) and Chapter 24 (sessionWithConfiguration:delegate:delegateQueue:).

Grand Central Dispatch

Grand Central Dispatch, or *GCD*, is a sort of low-level analogue to NSOperation and NSOperationQueue (in fact, NSOperationQueue uses GCD under the hood). When I say GCD is low-level, I'm not kidding; it is effectively baked into the operating system kernel. Thus it can be used by any code whatsoever and is tremendously efficient.

Using GCD is like a mixture of the manual threading approach with the NSOperation-Queue approach. It's like the manual threading approach because code to be executed on one thread appears together with code to be executed on another; however, you have a much better chance of keeping the threads and data management straight, because GCD uses Objective-C blocks. It's like the NSOperationQueue approach because it uses queues; you express a task and add it to a queue, and the task is executed on a thread as needed. Moreover, by default these queues are serial queues, with each task on a queue finishing before the next is started, which, as I've already said, is a form of data locking.

We'll rewrite MyMandelbrotView to use GCD. The structure of its interface is very slightly changed from the original, nonthreaded version. Our `makeBitmapContext:` method now returns a graphics context rather than setting an instance variable directly; and our `drawAtCenter:zoom:` method now takes an additional parameter, the graphics context to draw into. Also, we have a new instance variable to hold our queue, which is a *dispatch queue*; a dispatch queue is a lightweight opaque pseudo-object consisting essentially of a list of blocks to be executed:

```
@implementation MyMandelbrotView {
    CGContextRef _bitmapContext;
    dispatch_queue_t _draw_queue;
}
```

In MyMandelbrotView's implementation, we create our dispatch queue as the view is created:

```
- (id)initWithCoder:(NSCoder *)aDecoder {
    self = [super initWithCoder: aDecoder];
    if (self) {
        self->_draw_queue =
            dispatch_queue_create("com.neuburg.mandeldraw", nil);
    }
    return self;
}
```

A call to `dispatch_queue_create` must be balanced by a call to `dispatch_release`. However, ARC understands GCD pseudo-objects and will take care of this for us (and in fact calling `dispatch_release` explicitly is forbidden).

Now for the implementation of `drawThatPuppy`. Here it is:

```
- (void) drawThatPuppy {
    CGPoint center = ❶
        CGPointMake(CGRectGetMidX(self.bounds), CGRectGetMidY(self.bounds));
    dispatch_async(self->_draw_queue, ^{ ❷
        CGContextRef bitmap = [self makeBitmapContext: self.bounds.size];
        [self drawAtCenter: center zoom: 1 context:bitmap];
        dispatch_async(dispatch_get_main_queue(), ^{ ❸
            if (self->_bitmapContext)
                CGContextRelease(self->_bitmapContext);
            self->_bitmapContext = bitmap;
            [self setNeedsDisplay];
        });
    });
}
```

That's all there is to it. No trampoline methods. No performSelector.... No packing arguments into a dictionary. No autorelease pools. No instance variables. No notifications. And effectively no sharing of data across threads. That's the beauty of blocks. Here's how drawThatPuppy works:

❶   We begin by calculating our center, as before. This value will be visible within the blocks, because blocks can see their surrounding context.

❷   Now comes our task to be performed in a background thread on our queue, _draw_queue. We specify this task with the dispatch_async function. GCD has a lot of functions, but this is the one you'll use 99 percent of the time; it's the most important thing you need to know about GCD. We specify a queue and we provide a block saying what we'd like to do. Thanks to the block, we don't need any trampoline methods. In the block, we begin by declaring bitmap as a variable *local to the block*. We then call makeBitmapContext: to create the graphics context bitmap, and drawAtCenter:zoom:context: to set its pixels; we make these calls *directly*, just as we would do if we weren't threading in the first place.

❸   Now we need to step back out to the main thread. How do we do that? With dispatch_async again! We specify the main queue (which is effectively the main thread) with a function provided for this purpose and describe what we want to do in *another* block. This second block is nested inside the first, so it isn't performed until the preceding commands in the first block have finished; moreover, because the first block is part of the second block's surrounding context, the second block can see our block-local bitmap variable! We set our _bitmapContext instance variable (with no need for further memory management, because makeBitmapContext has returned a retained graphics context), and call setNeedsDisplay.

The benefits and elegance of GCD as a form of concurrency management are stunning. The bitmap variable is not shared; it is local to each specific call to drawThatPuppy. The nested blocks are executed in succession, so any instance of `bitmap` must be completely filled with pixels before being used to set the `_bitmapContext` instance variable. Moreover, the *entire* operation is performed on a serial queue, and `_bitmapContext` is touched only from code running on the main thread; thus there is no data sharing and no possibility of conflict. Our code is also highly maintainable, because the entire task on all threads is expressed within the single `drawThatPuppy` method, thanks to the use of blocks; indeed, the code is only very slightly modified from the original, nonthreaded version.

You might object that we still have methods `makeBitmapContext:` and `drawAtCenter:zoom:context:` hanging around MyMandelbrotView, and that we must therefore still be careful not to call them on the main thread, or indeed from anywhere except from within `drawThatPuppy`. If that were true, we could at this point destroy `makeBitmapContext:` and `drawAtCenter:zoom:context:` and move their functionality completely into `drawThatPuppy`. But it *isn't* true, because these methods are now *thread-safe*: they are self-contained utilities that touch no instance variables or persistent objects, so it doesn't matter what thread they are called on. Still, I'll demonstrate in a moment how we can intercept an accidental attempt to call a method on the wrong thread.

The two most important GCD functions are:

`dispatch_async`
> Push a block onto the end of a queue for later execution, and proceed immediately with our own code. Thus, we can finish our own execution without waiting for the block to execute.
>
> Examples of using `dispatch_async` to execute code in a background thread (`dispatch_get_global_queue(0,0)`) appeared in Chapter 19 and Chapter 23. Examples of using `dispatch_async` as a way of stepping back onto the main thread (`dispatch_get_main_queue`) in order to talk to the interface from inside code that might be executed on a background thread appeared in Chapters 10, 15, 16, 17, and 24.
>
> Also, it can be useful to call `dispatch_async` to step out to the main thread even though you're *already* on the main thread, as a way of waiting for the run loop to complete and for the interface to settle down — a minimal form of delayed performance. I used that technique in Chapters 6, 8, 10, 12, and 23.

`dispatch_sync`
> Push a block onto the end of a queue for later execution, and wait until the block has executed before proceeding with our own code — because, for example, you intend to use a result that the block is to provide. The purpose of the queue would be, once again, as a lightweight, reliable version of a lock, mediating access to a shared resource. Here's a case in point, from Apple's own code:

```
- (AVAsset*)asset {
    __block AVAsset *theAsset = nil;
    dispatch_sync(assetQueue, ^{
        theAsset = [[self getAssetInternal] copy];
    });
    return theAsset;
}
```

Any thread might call the asset method; to avoid problems with shared data, we require that only blocks that are executed from a particular queue (assetQueue) may touch an AVAsset. But we need the result that this block returns; hence the call to dispatch_sync.

An interesting and useful exercise is to revise the MyDownloader class from Chapter 24 so that NSURLSession delegate messages are sent on a background thread, thus taking some strain off the main thread (and hence the user interface) while these messages are flying around behind the scenes. This looks like a reasonable and safe thing to do, because the NSURLSession and the delegate methods are all packaged inside the MyDownloader object, isolated from our view controller. To configure the NSURLSession in this way, we add an NSOperationQueue property, self.q, to MyDownloader:

```
- (id) initWithConfiguration: (NSURLSessionConfiguration*) config {
    self = [super init];
    if (self) {
        self->_q = [NSOperationQueue new];
        NSURLSession* session =
            [NSURLSession sessionWithConfiguration:config
                delegate:self delegateQueue:self->_q];
        self->_session = session;
    }
    return self;
}
```

We must now give some thought to what will happen in URLSession:downloadTask:did-FinishDownloadingToURL: when we call back into the client through the completion handler that we received in download:completionHandler:. It would not be very nice to involve the client in threading issues; our entire goal is to isolate such issues within MyDownloader itself. Therefore we must step out to the main thread as we call the completion handler. But there's a problem. We cannot simply say this:

```
dispatch_async(dispatch_get_main_queue(), ^{
    ch(url);
});
```

The problem is that the downloaded file is due to be destroyed as soon as we return from URLSession:downloadTask:didFinishDownloadingToURL: — and if we call dispatch_async, we will return *immediately*. Thus the downloaded file *will* be destroyed, and url will end up pointing at nothing by the time the client receives it. The solution is to use `dispatch_sync` instead; this is a good example of the kind of thing `dispatch_sync` is good for:

```
dispatch_sync(dispatch_get_main_queue(), ^{
    ch(url);
});
```

That code steps out to the main thread and also postpones returning from `URLSession:downloadTask:didFinishDownloadingToURL:` until the client has had an opportunity to do something with the file pointed to by `url`. We are blocking our background NSOperationQueue, but only very briefly; and, after all, if we were to read the file at `url` into a UIImage *inside* `URLSession:downloadTask:didFinishDownloading-ToURL:` ourselves, the effect would be exactly the same. Again, our real purpose in using `dispatch_sync` is to lock down some shared data — in this case, the downloaded file.

It is also good to know about the GCD function `dispatch_after`; examples in this book have made use of it (Chapters 2, 7, and 10) as an alternative to `performSelector:with-Object:afterDelay:`.

Another useful GCD function is `dispatch_once`, a thread-safe way of ensuring that a block is called only once; it's often used to vend a singleton.

Besides serial dispatch queues, there are also *concurrent* dispatch queues. A concurrent queue's blocks are started in the order in which they were submitted to the queue, but a block is allowed to start while another block is still executing. Obviously, you wouldn't want to submit to a concurrent queue a task that touches a shared resource — that would be throwing away the entire point of serial queues. The advantage of concurrent queues is a possible speed boost when you don't care about the order in which multiple tasks are finished — for example, when you want to do something with regard to every element of an array. The built-in global queues (available by calling `dispatch_get_global_queue`) are concurrent; you can also create a concurrent queue by passing `DISPATCH_QUEUE_CONCURRENT` as the second argument to `dispatch_queue_create`.

A frequent use of concurrent queues is with `dispatch_apply`. This function is like `dispatch_sync` (the caller pauses until the block has finished executing), but the block is called multiple times with an iterator argument. Thus, `dispatch_apply` on a concurrent queue is like a for loop whose iterations are multithreaded; on a device with multiple cores, this could result in a speed improvement. (Of course, this technique is applicable only if the iterations do not depend on one another.)

Arbitrary context data can be attached to a queue in the form of key–value pairs (`dispatch_queue_set_specific`) and retrieved by key. There are two ways to retrieve the context data:

`dispatch_queue_get_specific`

> Retrieves a key's value for a queue to which we already have a valid reference.

`dispatch_get_specific`

> Retrieves a key's value for the *current* queue, the one in whose thread we are actually running. In fact, `dispatch_get_specific` is the *only* valid way to identify the current queue. (`dispatch_get_current_queue`, a function formerly used for this purpose, has been shown to be potentially unsafe and is now deprecated.)

We can use this technique, for example, to make certain that a method is called only on the correct queue. Recall that in our Mandelbrot-drawing example, we may be concerned that a method such as `makeBitmapContext:` might be called on some other queue than the background queue that we created for this purpose. If this is really a worry, we can attach an identifying key–value pair to that queue when we create it. Both key and value should be pointers, so let's start by defining some static C strings:

```
static char* QKEY = "label";
static char* QVAL = "com.neuburg.mandeldraw";
```

We then create the queue like this:

```
self->_draw_queue = dispatch_queue_create(QVAL, nil);
dispatch_queue_set_specific(self->_draw_queue, QKEY, QVAL, nil);
```

Later, we can examine that identifying key–value pair for the queue on which a particular method is called:

```
- (CGContextRef) makeBitmapContext:(CGSize)size {
    NSAssert(dispatch_get_specific(QKEY) == QVAL, @"Wrong thread");
```

Note that we are comparing the values purely as pointers; the fact that either one of them is a C string is irrelevant. A common device, where threads generated by different instances of the same class need to be distinguished, is to attach to a queue a key–value pair whose value is the instance itself.

Threads and App Backgrounding

When your app is backgrounded and suspended, a problem arises if your code is running. The system doesn't want to stop your code while it's executing; on the other hand, some other app may need to be given the bulk of the device's resources now. So as your app goes into the background, the system waits a very short time for your app to finish doing whatever it may be doing, and it then suspends your app.

This shouldn't be a problem from your main thread's point of view, because your app shouldn't have any time-consuming code on the main thread in the first place; you now know that you can avoid this by using a background thread. On the other hand, it could be a problem for lengthy background operations, including asynchronous tasks performed by the frameworks. You can request extra time to complete a lengthy task (or at to least abort it yourself, coherently) in case your app is backgrounded, by wrapping it in calls to UIApplication's `beginBackgroundTaskWithExpirationHandler:` and `endBackgroundTask:`. Here's how you do it:

- You call `beginBackgroundTaskWithExpirationHandler:` to announce that a lengthy task is beginning; it returns an identification number. This tells the system that if your app is backgrounded, you'd like to be woken from suspension in the background now and then in order to complete the task.

- At the end of your lengthy task, you call `endBackgroundTask:`, passing in the same identification number that you got from your call to `beginBackgroundTaskWithExpirationHandler:`. This tells the system that your lengthy task is over and that there is no need to grant you any more background time.

The argument to `beginBackgroundTaskWithExpirationHandler:` is a block, but this block does *not* express the lengthy task. It expresses what you will do *if your extra time expires* before you finish your lengthy task. At the very least, your expiration handler must call `endBackgroundTask:`, just as your lengthy task would have done; otherwise, your app may be killed, as a punishment for trying to use too much background time. If your expiration handler block *is* called, you should make no assumptions about what thread it is running on.

Let's use MyMandelbrotView, from the preceding section, as an example. Let's say that if `drawThatPuppy` is started, we'd like it to be allowed to finish, even if the app is suspended in the middle of it, so that our `_bitmapContext` instance variable is updated as requested. To try to ensure this, we call `beginBackgroundTaskWithExpirationHandler:` beforehand and call `endBackgroundTask:` at the end of the innermost block:

```
- (void) drawThatPuppy {
    CGPoint center =
        CGPointMake(CGRectGetMidX(self.bounds), CGRectGetMidY(self.bounds));
    __block UIBackgroundTaskIdentifier bti =
        [[UIApplication sharedApplication]
            beginBackgroundTaskWithExpirationHandler: ^{
                [[UIApplication sharedApplication] endBackgroundTask:bti];
            }];
    if (bti == UIBackgroundTaskInvalid)
        return;
    dispatch_async(self->_draw_queue, ^{
        CGContextRef bitmap = [self makeBitmapContext: self.bounds.size];
        [self drawAtCenter: center zoom: 1 context:bitmap];
        dispatch_async(dispatch_get_main_queue(), ^{
            if (self->_bitmapContext)
                CGContextRelease(self->_bitmapContext);
            self->_bitmapContext = bitmap;
            [self setNeedsDisplay];
```

```
            [[UIApplication sharedApplication] endBackgroundTask:bti];
        });
    });
}
```

If our app is backgrounded while `drawThatPuppy` is in progress, it will (we hope) be given enough background time to run that it can eventually proceed all the way to the end. Thus, the instance variable `_bitmapContext` will be updated, and `setNeedsDisplay` will be called, while we are still in the background. Our `drawRect:` will not be called until our app is brought back to the front, but there's nothing wrong with that.

The `__block` qualifier on the declaration of `bti` allows us to see, inside the block, the value that `bti` *will* have when the call to `beginBackgroundTaskWithExpirationHandler:` returns. The check against `UIBackgroundTaskInvalid` can do no harm, and there may be situations or devices where our request to complete this task in the background will be denied.

It's good policy to use a similar technique when you're notified that your app is being backgrounded. You might respond to the app delegate message `applicationDidEnterBackground:` (or the corresponding `UIApplicationDidEnterBackgroundNotification`) by saving data and reducing memory usage, but this can take time, whereas you'd like to return from `applicationDidEnterBackground:` as quickly as possible. A reasonable solution is to implement `applicationDidEnterBackground:` very much like `drawThatPuppy` in the example I just gave: call `beginBackgroundTaskWithExpirationHandler:` and then call `dispatch_async` to get off the main thread, and do your saving and so forth in its block.

CHAPTER 26

Undo

The ability to undo the most recent action is familiar from OS X. The idea is that, provided the user realizes soon enough that a mistake has been made, that mistake can be reversed. Typically, a Mac application will maintain an internal stack of undoable actions; choosing Edit → Undo or pressing Command-Z will reverse the action at the top of the stack, and will also make that action available for Redo.

Some iOS apps, too, may benefit from at least a limited Undo facility, and this is not difficult to implement. Some built-in views — in particular, those that involve text entry, UITextField and UITextView (Chapter 10) — implement Undo already. And you can add it in other areas of your app.

Undo is provided through an instance of NSUndoManager, which basically just maintains a stack of undoable actions, along with a secondary stack of redoable actions. The goal in general is to work with the NSUndoManager so as to handle both Undo and Redo in the standard manner: when the user chooses to undo the most recent action, the action at the top of the Undo stack is popped off and reversed and is pushed onto the top of the Redo stack.

In this chapter, I'll illustrate a simple NSUndoManager for a simple app that has just one kind of undoable action. More complicated apps, obviously, will be more complicated! On the other hand, iOS apps, unlike OS X apps, do not generally need deep or pervasive Undo functionality. For more about the NSUndoManager class and how to use it, read Apple's *Undo Architecture* as well as the documentation for the class itself. See also Chapter 23; as I mentioned there, UIDocument has an undo manager (its undo-Manager property), and you can mark a file as dirty by using it.

Undo Manager

In our artificially simple app, the user can drag a small square around the screen. We'll start with an instance of a UIView subclass, MyView, to which has been attached a

UIPanGestureRecognizer to make it draggable, as described in Chapter 5. The gesture recognizer's action target is the MyView instance itself:

```
- (void) dragging: (UIPanGestureRecognizer*) p {
    if (p.state == UIGestureRecognizerStateBegan ||
            p.state == UIGestureRecognizerStateChanged) {
        CGPoint delta = [p translationInView: self.superview];
        CGPoint c = self.center;
        c.x += delta.x; c.y += delta.y;
        self.center = c;
        [p setTranslation: CGPointZero inView: self.superview];
    }
}
```

To make dragging of this view undoable, we need an NSUndoManager instance. Let's store this in an instance variable of MyView itself, accessible through a property, self.undoer.

Target–Action Undo

There are two ways to register an action as undoable. The one we'll use here involves the NSUndoManager method registerUndoWithTarget:selector:object:. This method uses a target–action architecture: you provide a target, a selector for a method that takes one parameter, and the object value to be passed as argument when the method is called. Then, later, if the NSUndoManager is sent the undo message, it simply sends that action to that target with that argument. The job of the action method is to undo whatever it is that needs undoing.

What we want to undo here is the setting of our center property. This can't expressed directly using a target–action architecture, because the parameter of setCenter: needs to be a CGPoint, which isn't an object. Therefore we're going to have to provide, as our action method, a secondary method that *does* take an object parameter. This is neither bad nor unusual; it is quite common for actions to have a special representation just for the purpose of making them undoable.

So, in our dragging: method, instead of setting self.center to c directly, we now call a secondary method (let's call it setCenterUndoably:):

```
CGPoint c = self.center;
c.x += delta.x; c.y += delta.y;
[self setCenterUndoably: [NSValue valueWithCGPoint:c]];
```

At a minimum, setCenterUndoably: should do the job that setting self.center used to do:

```
- (void) setCenterUndoably: (NSValue*) newCenter {
    self.center = [newCenter CGPointValue];
}
```

This works in the sense that the view is draggable exactly as before, but we have not yet made this action undoable. To do so, we must ask ourselves what message the NSUndoManager would need to send in order to undo the action we are about to perform. We would want the NSUndoManager to set `self.center` back to the value it has *now*, before we change it as we are about to do. And what method would NSUndoManager call in order to do that? It would call `setCenterUndoably:`, the very method we are implementing now! So:

```
- (void) setCenterUndoably: (NSValue*) newCenter {
    [self.undoer registerUndoWithTarget:self
        selector:@selector(setCenterUndoably:)
          object:[NSValue valueWithCGPoint:self.center]];
    self.center = [newCenter CGPointValue];
}
```

That code has a remarkable effect: it makes our action not only undoable but also redoable. The reason is that NSUndoManager has an internal state, and responds differently to `registerUndoWithTarget:selector:object:` depending on its state. If the NSUndoManager is sent `registerUndoWithTarget:selector:object:` *while it is undoing*, it puts the target–action information on the Redo stack instead of the Undo stack (because Redo *is* the Undo of an Undo, if you see what I mean).

Thus, here's how we Undo and then Redo an action:

1. We perform an action by way of `setCenterUndoably:`, which calls `registerUndoWithTarget:selector:object:` with the *old* value of `self.center`. The NSUndoManager adds this to its Undo stack.

2. Now suppose we want to undo that action. We send `undo` to the NSUndoManager.

3. The NSUndoManager calls `setCenterUndoably:` with the old value that we passed in earlier when we called `registerUndoWithTarget:selector:object:`. Thus, we are going to set the center back to that old value. But before we do that, we send `registerUndoWithTarget:selector:object:` to the NSUndoManager with the *current* value of `self.center`. The NSUndoManager knows that it is currently undoing, so it understands this registration as something to be added to its Redo stack.

4. Now suppose we want to redo that Undo. We send `redo` to the NSUndoManager, and sure enough, the NSUndoManager calls `setCenterUndoably:` with the value that we previously undid. (And, once again, we call `registerUndoWithTarget:selector:object:` with an action that goes onto the NSUndoManager's Undo stack.)

Undo Grouping

So far, so good. But our implementation of Undo is very annoying, because we are adding a single object to the Undo stack every time `dragging:` is called — and it is called many times during the course of a single drag. Thus, undoing merely undoes the tiny increment corresponding to one individual `dragging:` call. What we'd like, surely, is for undoing to undo an *entire* dragging gesture. We can implement this through *undo grouping*. As the gesture begins, we start a group; when the gesture ends, we end the group:

```
- (void) dragging: (UIPanGestureRecognizer*) p {
    if (p.state == UIGestureRecognizerStateBegan)
        [self.undoer beginUndoGrouping];
    if (p.state == UIGestureRecognizerStateBegan ||
            p.state == UIGestureRecognizerStateChanged) {
        CGPoint delta = [p translationInView: self.superview];
        CGPoint c = self.center;
        c.x += delta.x; c.y += delta.y;
        [self setCenterUndoably: [NSValue valueWithCGPoint:c]];
        [p setTranslation: CGPointZero inView: self.superview];
    }
    if (p.state == UIGestureRecognizerStateEnded ||
            p.state == UIGestureRecognizerStateCancelled)
        [self.undoer endUndoGrouping];
}
```

This works: each complete gesture of dragging MyView, from the time the user's finger contacts the view to the time it leaves, is now undoable (and then redoable) as a single unit.

A further refinement would be to animate the "drag" that the NSUndoManager performs when it undoes or redoes a user drag gesture. To do so, we take advantage of the fact that we, too, can examine the NSUndoManager's state by way of its `isUndoing` and `isRedoing` properties; we animate the `center` change when the NSUndoManager is "dragging," but not when the user is dragging:

```
- (void) setCenterUndoably: (NSValue*) newCenter {
    [self.undoer registerUndoWithTarget:self
        selector:@selector(setCenterUndoably:)
          object:[NSValue valueWithCGPoint:self.center]];
    if (self.undoer.isUndoing || self.undoer.isRedoing) { // animate
        UIViewAnimationOptions opt =
            UIViewAnimationOptionBeginFromCurrentState;
        [UIView animateWithDuration:0.4 delay:0.1 options:opt animations:^{
            self.center = [newCenter CGPointValue];
        } completion:nil];
    } else { // just do it
        self.center = [newCenter CGPointValue];
    }
}
```

Invocation Undo

Earlier I said that `registerUndoWithTarget:selector:object:` was one of two ways to register an action as undoable. The other is `prepareWithInvocationTarget:`. In general, the advantage of `prepareWithInvocationTarget:` is that it lets you specify a method with any number of parameters, and those parameters needn't be objects. You provide the target and, *in the same line of code*, send to the object returned from this call the message and arguments you want sent when the NSUndoManager is sent `undo` (or, if we are undoing now, `redo`). So, in our example, instead of this line:

```
[self.undoer registerUndoWithTarget:self
    selector:@selector(setCenterUndoably:)
        object:[NSValue valueWithCGPoint:self.center]];
```

You'd say this:

```
[[self.undoer prepareWithInvocationTarget:self]
    setCenterUndoably: [NSValue valueWithCGPoint:self.center]];
```

That code seems impossible: how can we send `setCenterUndoably:` without *calling* `setCenterUndoably:`? Either we are sending it to `self`, in which case it should actually be called at this moment, or we are sending it to some other object that doesn't implement `setCenterUndoably:`, in which case our app should crash. However, under the hood, the NSUndoManager is cleverly using Objective-C's dynamism (similarly to the message-forwarding example in Chapter 12) to capture this call as an NSInvocation object, which it can use later to send the same message with the same arguments to the specified target.

If we're going to use `prepareWithInvocationTarget:`, there's no need to wrap the CGPoint value representing the old and new `center` of our view as an NSNumber. So our complete implementation now looks like this:

```
- (void) setCenterUndoably: (CGPoint) newCenter {
    [[self.undoer prepareWithInvocationTarget:self]
        setCenterUndoably: self.center];
    if (self.undoer.isUndoing || self.undoer.isRedoing) { // animate
        UIViewAnimationOptions opt =
            UIViewAnimationOptionBeginFromCurrentState;
        [UIView animateWithDuration:0.4 delay:0.1 options:opt animations:^{
            self.center = newCenter;
        } completion:nil];
    } else { // just do it
        self.center = newCenter;
    }
}
- (void) dragging: (UIPanGestureRecognizer*) p {
    if (p.state == UIGestureRecognizerStateBegan)
        [self.undoer beginUndoGrouping];
    if (p.state == UIGestureRecognizerStateBegan ||
            p.state == UIGestureRecognizerStateChanged) {
```

```
            CGPoint delta = [p translationInView: self.superview];
            CGPoint c = self.center;
            c.x += delta.x; c.y += delta.y;
            [self setCenterUndoably: c];
            [p setTranslation: CGPointZero inView: self.superview];
        }
        if (p.state == UIGestureRecognizerStateEnded ||
                p.state == UIGestureRecognizerStateCancelled)
            [self.undoer endUndoGrouping];
    }
```

Undo Interface

We must also decide how to let the user *request* Undo and Redo. In developing the code from the preceding section, I used two buttons: an Undo button that sent undo to the NSUndoManager, and a Redo button that sent redo to the NSUndoManager. This can be a perfectly reasonable interface, but let's talk about some others.

Shake-To-Edit

By default, your app supports *shake-to-edit*. This means the user can shake the device to bring up an undo/redo interface. We discussed this briefly in Chapter 22. If you don't turn off this feature by setting the shared UIApplication's applicationSupportsShake-ToEdit property to NO, then when the user shakes the device, the runtime walks up the responder chain, starting with the first responder, looking for a responder whose inherited undoManager property returns an actual NSUndoManager instance. If it finds one, it puts up the undo/redo interface, allowing the user to communicate with that NSUndoManager.

You will recall what it takes for a UIResponder to be first responder in this sense: it must return YES from canBecomeFirstResponder, and it must actually be made first responder through a call to becomeFirstResponder. Let's make MyView satisfy these requirements. For example, we might call becomeFirstResponder at the end of dragging:, like this:

```
- (BOOL) canBecomeFirstResponder {
    return YES;
}
- (void) dragging: (UIPanGestureRecognizer*) p {
    // ... the rest as before ...
    if (p.state == UIGestureRecognizerStateEnded ||
            p.state == UIGestureRecognizerStateCancelled) {
        [self.undoer endUndoGrouping];
        [self becomeFirstResponder];
    }
}
```

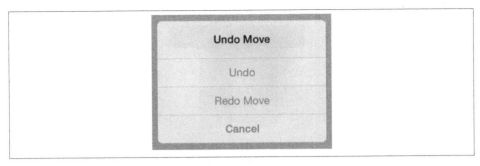

Figure 26-1. The shake-to-edit undo/redo interface

Then, to make shake-to-edit work, we have only to provide a getter for the undo-Manager property that returns our undo manager, self.undoer:

```
- (NSUndoManager*) undoManager {
    return self.undoer;
}
```

This works: shaking the device now brings up the undo/redo interface, and its buttons work correctly. However, I don't like the way the buttons are labeled; they just say Undo and Redo. To make this interface more expressive, we should provide a string describing each undoable action by calling setActionName:. We can appropriately and conveniently do this in setCenterUndoably:, as follows:

```
[[self.undoer prepareWithInvocationTarget:self]
    setCenterUndoably: self.center];
[self.undoer setActionName: @"Move"];
// ... and so on ...
```

Now the undo/redo interface has more informative labels, as shown in Figure 26-1.

Undo Menu

Another possible interface is through a menu (Figure 26-2). Personally, I prefer this approach, as I am not fond of shake-to-edit (it seems both violent and unreliable). This is the same menu used by a UITextField or UITextView for displaying the Copy and Paste menu items (Chapter 10). The requirements for summoning this menu are effectively the same as those for shake-to-edit: we need a responder chain with a first responder at the bottom of it. So the code we've just supplied for making MyView first responder remains applicable.

We can make a menu appear, for example, in response to a long press on our MyView instance. So let's attach another gesture recognizer to MyView. This will be a UILong-PressGestureRecognizer, whose action handler is called longPress:. Recall from Chapter 10 how to implement the menu: we get the singleton global UIMenuController object

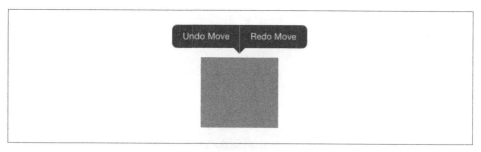

Figure 26-2. The shared menu as an undo/redo interface

and specify an array of custom UIMenuItems as its menuItems property. We can make the menu appear by sending the UIMenuController the setMenuVisible:animated: message. But a particular menu item will appear in the menu only if we also return YES from canPerformAction:withSender: for that menu item's action. Delightfully, the NSUndoManager's canUndo and canRedo methods tell us what value canPerformAction:withSender: should return. We can also get the titles for our custom menu items from the NSUndoManager itself, by calling undoMenuItemTitle:

```
- (void) longPress: (UIGestureRecognizer*) g {
    if (g.state == UIGestureRecognizerStateBegan) {
        UIMenuController *m = [UIMenuController sharedMenuController];
        [m setTargetRect:self.bounds inView:self];
        UIMenuItem *mi1 =
            [[UIMenuItem alloc] initWithTitle:[self.undoer undoMenuItemTitle]
                                       action:@selector(undo:)];
        UIMenuItem *mi2 =
            [[UIMenuItem alloc] initWithTitle:[self.undoer redoMenuItemTitle]
                                       action:@selector(redo:)];
        [m setMenuItems:@[mi1, mi2]];
        [m setMenuVisible:YES animated:YES];
    }
}
- (BOOL)canPerformAction:(SEL)action withSender:(id)sender {
    if (action == @selector(undo:))
        return [self.undoer canUndo];
    if (action == @selector(redo:))
        return [self.undoer canRedo];
    return [super canPerformAction:action withSender:sender];
}
- (void) undo: (id) dummy {
    [self.undoer undo];
}
- (void) redo: (id) dummy {
    [self.undoer redo];
}
```

Application Lifetime Events

Your app's one and only application object (a UIApplication instance, or on rare occasions a UIApplication subclass instance) is created for you as the shared application object by UIApplicationMain, along with its delegate; in the Xcode project templates, this is an instance of the AppDelegate class. The application reports lifetime events through method calls to its delegate; other instances can also register to receive most of these events as notifications.

What application lifetime events you can receive depends on whether or not your app participates in *multitasking*. It almost certainly will. In the old days, before iOS 4, there was no multitasking. If the user pressed the Home button while running your app, your app was terminated. The next time the user launched your app by tapping its icon, your app launched from scratch. Even under iOS 7, your app can opt out of multitasking and behave like a pre–iOS 4 app, if you set the "Application does not run in background" key (UIApplicationExitsOnSuspend) in your *Info.plist*. For some apps, such as certain games, this might be a reasonable thing to do.

In the multitasking world, however, the Home button doesn't terminate your app; it *backgrounds and suspends* it. This means that your app is essentially freeze-dried in the background; its process still exists, but it isn't actively running, and it isn't getting any events — though notifications can be stored by the system for later delivery if your app comes to the front once again. If your app is terminated, it's not because the user switches away from it, but because the system has killed it while it was suspended — for example, because it needed to reclaim the memory your suspended app was using, or because the user switched off the device.

(A backgrounded app can, however, continue to run certain specialized activities, such as playing music; and in iOS 7, a backgrounded app can be woken periodically in order to update its data via the network. See Chapters 14, 22, and 24. So a backgrounded app isn't always necessarily completely suspended. But in general, most backgrounded apps are suspended most of the time.)

The suite of basic application lifetime events in the multitasking world is quite limited; indeed, in my opinion, the information your app is given is unfortunately rather too coarse-grained. The events are as follows:

`application:didFinishLaunchingWithOptions:`
> The app has started up. You'll typically perform initializations here. If an app doesn't have a main storyboard, this code must also create the app's window and show it.

> In iOS 6 and iOS 7, another event, `application:willFinishLaunchingWith-Options:`, arrives even earlier. Its purpose is to allow your app to participate in the state saving and restoration mechanism discussed in Chapter 6.

`applicationDidBecomeActive:`
> Received after `application:didFinishLaunchingWithOptions:`. Also received after the end of the situation that caused the app delegate to receive `application-WillResignActive:`.

`applicationWillResignActive:`
> One possibility is that something has blocked the app's interface — for example, the screen has been locked. An alert dialog from outside your app, or an incoming phone call whose interface takes over the screen, could also cause this event. When this situation ends, the app delegate will receive `applicationDidBecomeActive:`. Alternatively, the app may be about to go into the background (and will then be suspended); in that case, the next event will be `applicationDidEnterBackground:`.

`applicationDidEnterBackground:`
> The application has been backgrounded (and is about to be suspended). Always preceded by `applicationWillResignActive:`.

`applicationWillEnterForeground:`
> The application was backgrounded (and suspended), and is now coming back to life. Always followed by `applicationDidBecomeActive:`.

An additional event, `applicationWillTerminate:`, was your last signal in the non-multitasking world to preserve state and perform other final cleanup tasks. In the multitasking world, however, you'll probably *never* get `applicationWillTerminate:`, because by the time your app is terminated by the system, it was already suspended and incapable of receiving events.

The application lifetime events are best understood through some typical scenarios:

The app launches freshly
> Your app delegate receives these messages:

> - `application:didFinishLaunchingWithOptions:`
> - `applicationDidBecomeActive:`

The user clicks the Home button

If your app is frontmost, it will be suspended; before that, your app delegate receives these messages:

- `applicationWillResignActive:`
- `applicationDidEnterBackground:`

The user summons your backgrounded app to the front

Your app delegate receives these messages:

- `applicationWillEnterForeground:`
- `applicationDidBecomeActive:`

If the user summons your backgrounded app to the front indirectly, another delegate message may be sent between these two calls. For example, if the user asks another app to hand a file off to your app (Chapter 23), your app receives `application:handleOpenURL:` between `applicationWillEnterForeground:` and `applicationDidBecomeActive:`.

The user double-clicks the Home button

The user can now work in the app switcher. If your app is frontmost, your app delegate receives this message:

- `applicationWillResignActive:`

The user, in the app switcher, chooses another app

If your app was frontmost, your app delegate receives this message:

- `applicationDidEnterBackground:`

The user, in the app switcher, chooses your app

If your app was the most recently frontmost app, then it was never backgrounded and suspended, so your app delegate receives this message:

- `applicationDidBecomeActive:`

The user summons the control center or notification center

If your app is frontmost, your app delegate receives this message:

- `applicationWillResignActive:`

The user dismisses the control center or notification center

If your app is frontmost, your app delegate receives this message:

- `applicationDidBecomeActive:`

A local notification alert from another app appears

If your app is frontmost, your app delegate receives this message:

- `applicationWillResignActive:`

From a local notification alert, the user launches the other app

Your app delegate receives these messages:

- `applicationDidBecomeActive:`
- `applicationWillResignActive:`
- `applicationDidEnterBackground:`

The screen is locked

If your app is frontmost, your app delegate receives these messages:

- `applicationWillResignActive:`
- `applicationDidEnterBackground:`

The screen is unlocked

If your app is frontmost, your app delegate receives these messages:

- `applicationWillEnterForeground:`
- `applicationDidBecomeActive:`

The user holds the screen-lock button down

The device offers to shut itself down. If your app is frontmost, your app delegate receives this message:

- `applicationWillResignActive:`

The user, as the device offers to shut itself down, cancels

If your app is frontmost, your app delegate receives this message:

- `applicationDidBecomeActive:`

The user, as the device offers to shut itself down, accepts

If your app is frontmost, the app delegate receives no further messages. (This is a major change from earlier systems.)

You can see what I mean when I say that this repertory of events is rather coarse-grained. `applicationWillResignActive:`, for example, could indicate (among other things) that the user is summoning the app switcher, or that another application's local notification alert has appeared in front of your app, or that the user is locking the screen, or that the user has single-clicked the Home button to leave your app altogether, or that a phone call has arrived while your app was frontmost, or that the user is about to shut down the device. But you can't distinguish *which* of these things is happening.

Perhaps the most significant lifetime issue for your app is when to save information that might be lost, but must not be, if your app were terminated. In the nonmultitasking world, the last moment to do that was `applicationWillTerminate:`. In the multitasking world, the last moment to do that used to be `applicationDidEnterBackground:`, but in iOS 7 you won't get that event if the user shuts down the device when your app is frontmost. This leaves only `applicationWillResignActive:`.

Index

A

ABNewPersonController, 718
ABPeoplePickerNavigationController, 715
ABPerson, 712
ABPersonViewController, 717
ABRecordRef, 712
ABUnknownPersonViewController, 719
accelerometer, 779
accessory views, 396, 430
action mechanism (implicit animation), 159
action message (control), 577
action search (implicit animation), 160
action selector signatures (control), 577
action sheet, 623
actions (animation), 160
actions (control), 576
activity indicator, 563
activity view, 632
address book, 709
Address Book framework, 709
Address Book UI framework, 709
address, converting to a coordinate, 764
address, natural language search, 766
alarms, 727
alarms, proximity, 732
ALAsset, 697
alert view, 620
animation, 121–184
    action mechanism, 159

action search, 160
animation controller, 291
animation "movie", 123
animations list, 157
autolayout vs. animation, 181
canceling, 132, 157
constraints, 182
delegate, 144
emitter layers, 166
gravity, 179
grouped animations, 151
hit-testing during animation, 213
image animation, 125
image view animation, 125
keyframe animation, 134, 149
layer animation, explicit, 143
layer animation, implicit, 139
layer, adding an animation to, 157
motion effects, 180
physics, 174
presented view, 267
preventing, 128, 140, 162
properties, animatable, 138
properties, custom animatable, 151
redrawing with animation, 136, 155
repeating, 130
slowing animation, 122
spring animation, 134, 179
stuttering animation, 116

We'd like to hear your suggestions for improving our indexes. Send email to index@oreilly.com.

K

keyboard, 517–525, 532–533
  customizing, 524
  dismissing, 519, 527, 533
  language, 525
  scrolling in response, 519
  table views, 522

L

labels, 511–514
  line breaking vs. attributed strings, 512
  number of lines, 511
  sizing to fit content, 513
  wrapping and truncation, 512
labels in built-in cell styles, 395
landscape orientation at startup, 258
layers, 91–184
  adding an animation to, 157
  animating a layer, 139, 143
  animations list, 157
  black background, 103
  borders, 115
  contents, 100
  contents, positioning, 104
  coordinates, 97
  depth, 97, 111
  drawing a layer, 100
  emitter layers, 166
  gradient layers, 107
  hierarchy, 94
  hit-testing layers, 210
  key–value coding, 118
  layer animation, explicit, 143
  layer animation, implicit, 139
  layer animation, preventing, 140, 162
  layout, 100
  mask, 115
  opaque, 103
  position, 98
  redisplaying, 101, 104
  resolution, 102
  shadows, 115
  shape layers, 107
  text layers, 107, 515
  transform, 108
  transparency, 87, 103
  transparent background, 103
  underlying layer, 92

layout bar, 40
layout events, 45
layout events and rotation, 255
layout of cells, 402
layout of layers, 100
layout of views, 22
layout, iOS 7 vs. iOS 6, 249
library, iPod, 675
library, music, 675
library, photo, 693
libsqlite3, 821
libxml2, 819
line breaking (see wrapping)
line fragment, 540
listing a folder's contents, 795
loading a view controller's view, 234
local notifications, 628
location manager, 771
location of device, 761, 770
location services, 770
location updates, deferred, 777
locked screen, controlling audio, 648
locking screen silences audio, 641
Lundell, Jonathan, 555

M

magnetometer, 775
mail, 739
main storyboard, xix, 5, 244
main thread, 856
main view of view controller, 224
main window, 4, 5
main window, background color of, 5
main window, coordinates, 17
main window, root view of, 4
main window, subclassing, 5
Map Kit framework, 743
map view, 743
map view, displaying user's location, 761
Maps app, 743
Maps app, displaying point of interest, 762
mask, 115
mask, orientation, 253
mask, transparency, 56
Master–Detail Application template, 290, 429, 490
master–detail interface, 389, 429
Media Player framework, 651, 657, 675
media timing functions, 141

NSXMLParser, 814

O

opaque graphics context, 88
opaque layers, 103
operation queues, 863
orientation mask, 253
orientation of device, 251
orientation of interface at startup, 258
overlay (on map), 754

P

page control, 581
page view controller, 310
parallax, 180
passthrough views (popovers), 482
password field, 524
pasteboard, 529
path, 75
path, compound, 77
patterns, 82
PDF files, 549
percent driver, 295
phases of a touch, 186
photo library, 693
photo, taking, 701
Photos app, 693
picker view, 567
pixels vs. points, 88
pixels, transparent, 212
points vs. pixels, 88
polar coordinates, 596
pool, autorelease, 861
popovers, 473–489, 623–627
    backgrounding of app, 485
    customizing, 477
    delegate, 483
    dismissing, 481, 482
    distinguishing, 485
    modal, 482
    passthrough views, 482
    preparing, 475
    presented view controller, 486
    reference to, 482, 489
    rotation, 485
    search results, 487
    size, 476
    storyboard, 480

summoning, 480
preferences, user (see NSUserDefaults)
presentation context, 269
presentation layer, 124, 213
presentation style, 268
presented view controllers and rotation, 271
presented view in popover, 486
presented view, animation of, 267
presented view, what view it replaces, 269
previewing a document, 804
progress view, 565
properties, animatable, 138
properties, custom animatable, 151
prototype cells, 407
proximity alarms, 732
purchase, in-app, 848

Q

QLPreviewController, 805
questions, three big, 409
queues (see threads)
Quick Look framework, 805

R

reading a file, 796
rectangle, rounded, 78, 115
redraw moment, 122, 141
redrawing with animation, 136
region monitoring, 778
Reminders app, 721
resizable image, 53
resolution, 50, 64, 103
resources in app bundle, 50
resources that differ on iPad, 50
responder chain, 218
restoration identifier, 340
restoration identifier path, 343
restoration of state, 337
Retina display (see screen, double resolution)
root view, 4
root view controller, 7, 224
rotating a drawing, 85
rotating interface, 251–260, 271
rotation, 258
    (see also orientation)
rotation 3D transform, 110
rotation and bar height, 600
rotation and navigation controllers, 281

About the Author

Matt Neuburg has a PhD in Classics and has taught at many universities and colleges. He has been programming computers since 1968. He has written applications for OS X and iOS, is a former editor of *MacTech Magazine*, and is a long-standing contributing editor for TidBITS. His previous O'Reilly books are *Frontier: The Definitive Guide*, *REALbasic: The Definitive Guide*, and *AppleScript: The Definitive Guide*. He makes a living writing books, articles, and software documentation, as well as by programming, consulting, and training.

Colophon

The animal on the cover of *Programming iOS 6* is a kingbird, one of the 13 species of North American songbirds making up the genus *Tyrannus*. A group of kingbirds is called a "coronation," a "court," or a "tyranny."

Kingbirds eat insects, which they often catch in flight, swooping from a perch to grab the insect midair. They may also supplement their diets with berries and fruits. They have long, pointed wings, and males perform elaborate aerial courtship displays.

Both the genus name (meaning "tyrant" or "despot") and the common name ("kingbird") refer to these birds' aggressive defense of their territories, breeding areas, and mates. They have been documented attacking red-tailed hawks (which are more than twenty times their size), knocking bluejays out of trees, and driving away crows and ravens. (For its habit of standing up to much larger birds, the gray kingbird has been adopted as a Puerto Rican nationalist symbol.)

"Kingbird" most often refers to the Eastern kingbird (*T. tyrannus*), an average-size kingbird (7.5–9 inches long, wingspan 13–15 inches) found all across North America. This common and widespread bird has a dark head and back, with a white throat, chest, and belly. Its red crown patch is rarely seen. Its high-pitched, buzzing, stuttering sounds have been described as resembling "sparks jumping between wires" or an electric fence.

The cover image is from *Cassell's Natural History*. The cover fonts are URW Typewriter and Guardian Sans. The text font is Adobe Minion Pro; the heading font is Adobe Myriad Condensed; and the code font is Dalton Maag's Ubuntu Mono.

Have it your way.

Get even more for your money.

Join the O'Reilly Community, and register the O'Reilly books you own. It's free, and you'll get:

- $4.99 ebook upgrade offer
- 40% upgrade offer on O'Reilly print books
- Membership discounts on books and events
- Free lifetime updates to ebooks and videos
- Multiple ebook formats, DRM FREE
- Participation in the O'Reilly community
- Newsletters
- Account management
- 100% Satisfaction Guarantee

Signing up is easy:

1. **Go to: oreilly.com/go/register**
2. **Create an O'Reilly login.**
3. **Provide your address.**
4. **Register your books.**

Note: English-language books only

To order books online:
oreilly.com/store

For questions about products or an order:
orders@oreilly.com

To sign up to get topic-specific email announcements and/or news about upcoming books, conferences, special offers, and new technologies:
elists@oreilly.com

For technical questions about book content:
booktech@oreilly.com

To submit new book proposals to our editors:
proposals@oreilly.com

O'Reilly books are available in multiple DRM-free ebook formats. For more information:
oreilly.com/ebooks

Spreading the knowledge of innovators   oreilly.com

CPSIA information can be obtained at www.ICGtesting.com
Printed in the USA
BVOW10s0520161213

339053BV00001B/1/P